THE AMERICAN NATION

The Great Seal of the United States, above, features the bald eagle, a symbol of power. When Congress adopted the Great Seal in 1782, it wanted to emphasize both the importance of the individual states and the unity of the nation as a whole. The eagle wears a shield with 13 vertical stripes—7 white and 6 red—that stand for the original 13 states. The blue bar above the stripes represents the government of the United States. In one talon, the eagle holds an olive branch, a symbol of peace. In the other, it holds 13 arrows, showing that it is prepared for war. In its mouth, the eagle holds a scroll with the Latin words E PLURIBUS UNUM (Out of Many, One).

Prentice Hall, A Division of Simon & Schuster
Englewood Cliffs, New Jersey 07632

THE AMERICAN NATION

James West Davidson
John E. Batchelor

James West Davidson

James West Davidson has authored books and papers on a wide range of American history topics including *After the Fact: The Art of Historical Detection* with Mark H. Lytle. With teaching experience at both the college and high school levels, Dr. Davidson consults on curriculum design for American history courses. While completing his Ph.D. at Yale University, he participated in the History Education Project sponsored by the National Endowment for the Humanities and the American Historical Association. Dr. Davidson is an avid canoer. *Great Heart: The History of a Labrador Adventure* is his story of a canoeing trip.

John E. Batchelor

John E. Batchelor teaches American history to junior high school students in the Guilford County, North Carolina, school system. Mr. Batchelor has also taught language arts and reading. Over the past 15 years, his students have won local, state, and national honors for their creative writing and history projects. Mr. Batchelor has written tests and teacher guide materials, conducted teacher workshops, and evaluated social studies curriculum for local and state boards of education. As a columnist for the Greensboro *News and Record*, Mr. Batchelor has written guest editorials and other articles.

REVISED SECOND EDITION

Supplementary Materials

Annotated Teacher's Edition
Teacher's Resource Book
Computer Test Bank
Student Study Guide

ISBN 0-13-028192-1   10 9 8 7 6 5 4 3 2

PRENTICE-HALL OF AUSTRALIA, PTY LTD., Sydney
PRENTICE-HALL CANADA INC., Toronto
PRENTICE-HALL HISPANOAMERICANA, S.A., Mexico
PRENTICE-HALL OF INDIA PRIVATE LTD., New Delhi
PRENTICE-HALL INTERNATIONAL (UK) LIMITED, London
PRENTICE-HALL OF JAPAN, INC., Tokyo
PRENTICE-HALL OF SOUTHEAST ASIA PTE. LTD., Singapore
EDITORA PRENTICE-HALL DO BRASIL LTDA., Rio de Janeiro

Cover Art: David Christensen
Front Matter Design: Taurins Associates, McNally Graphic Design
End Matter Design: Taurins Associates, McNally Graphic Design
Maps: Dick Sanderson and John Sanderson
Historical Atlas Maps: General Cartography, Inc.
Geographic Atlas Maps: R.R. Donnelley & Sons Company
Charts and Graphs: Geoffrey Hodgkinson, McNally Graphic Design
Photo Consultant: Michal Heron
Photo Researchers: Susan Marsden Kapsis, Barbara Scott

Illustration Credits

Frequently cited sources are abbreviated as follows: AMNH, American Museum of Natural History; LC, Library of Congress; MCNY, Museum of the City of New York; MFA, Museum of Fine Arts, Boston; MMA, Metropolitan Museum of Art, New York; NA, National Archives; NG, National Gallery of Art, Washington, D.C.; NMAA, National Museum of American Art; NYHS, courtesy of the New York Historical Society, New York; NYPL, New York Public Library; NYSHA, New York State Historical Association, Cooperstown; SI, Smithsonian Institution; UPI, United Press International; WW, Wide World, Yale, Yale University Art Gallery.

Key to position of illustrations:
b, bottom; *l*, left; *r*, right; *t*, top.

Page 1 LC; **5** *t* Arizona State Museum, University of Arizona, silkscreen print by Robert Spray for Margaret Schevill Link; *b* Harry T. Peters Collection, MCNY; **6** *t* Yale, *b* Mr. and Mrs. John Harney; **7** Brooklyn Museum, Gift of Miss Gwendolyn O.L. Conkling; **8** *t* NMAA, SI (detail); *b* The Granger Collection; **9** *t* US Navy, Combat Art Section; *b* Curtis Publishing Company; **14** *l to r* SI, Lee Boltin for American Heritage; Memphis Brooks Museum of Art; Texas Memorial Museum; The Rockwell Museum; National Portrait Gallery, SI; **15** NYHS.

UNIT 1 Pages 16–17 *l to r* MMA, Gift of H. L. Bach Foundation, 1969; US Naval Academy Museum; British Museum; Bettmann Archive; National Portrait Gallery, London; **19** NMAA, SI, lent by the US Department of the Interior, National Park Service; **20** Courtesy of the Library Services Department, AMNH; **22** US Geological Survey, photo by J.K. Hillers (detail); **23** *l* © David Muench 1984, *r* © David Muench; **25** © David Muench; **29** *l* © David Muench, *r* © David Muench; **33** Shostal Associates; **34** Chaco Center, National Park Service; **35** *t* Shostal Associates, *b* © David Muench; **37** Dept. of Ethnology, Royal Ontario Museum, Toronto, Canada; **39** Arizona State Museum, University of Arizona, silkscreen by Robert Spray for Margaret Schevill Link; **40** British Museum; **41** Courtesy of the Library Services Department, AMNH; **43** Peabody Museum, Harvard; **44** Giraudon/Art Resource, NY; **49** Bodleian Library Ms. Bodley 264, fol. 218

(continued on page 847)

Contents

UNIT 9　A Troubled Time　572

UNIT 10　Our Nation Today　648

Focus on Citizenship

Special Features

Americans Who Dared

Skill Lessons

History Writer's Handbook

Maps

Historical Atlas

Geographic Atlas

Charts, Graphs, and Time Lines

Historical Atlas

Exploring Our Living Constitution

Getting to Know Your Book

We as authors believe that history begins with a good story. *The American Nation* is the story of the many different people who settled this land. "Out of Many, One," the motto on the Great Seal of the United States, set a goal for the nation as it grew.

How the book is organized

The book is organized into 10 units and 32 chapters. The Table of Contents (pages 5–13) lists the titles of units and chapters. It also lists special features, skill lessons, maps, charts, graphs, and time lines in the text. At the back of the book is a reference section with useful maps, charts, and documents.

How each unit is organized

Unit Opener. Each unit opens with two pages that give an overview of the unit. Study the opener for Unit 5 below. The unit outline lists the chapters in the unit. The unit time line presents major dates and events. A star after a date shows that a new state entered the Union in that year. The time line also includes a President's band showing who was in office during the years covered in each unit. Pictures with captions illustrate events or developments during this period.

Unit Review. Each unit ends with two pages called the Unit Review. It has a summary of each chapter in the unit as well as multiple choice questions to help you review key information from the unit. Other questions and activities let you review main ideas and practice skills learned in the unit. A writer's handbook offers a lesson on writing a one-paragraph answer. Turn to pages 368–369 for the Unit 5 Review.

How each chapter is organized

Chapter Opener. Each chapter begins with a chapter outline that lists the numbered sections of the chapter. A chapter time line shows some of the main events that you will read about. The introduction, called **About This Chapter,** gives an overview of the chapter. A picture with caption illustrates an idea from the chapter. Look for these elements in the chapter opener on page 290.

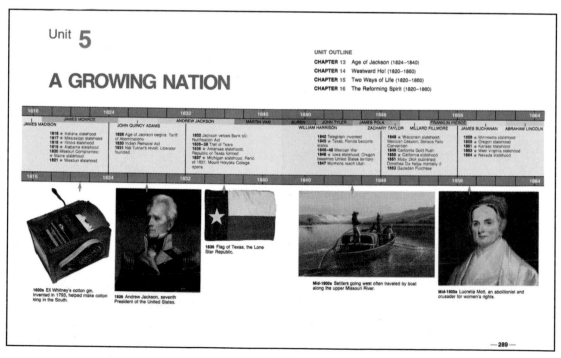

Individual Lessons. Each numbered section is a separate lesson. Each lesson begins with **Read to Learn** questions that let you focus on the main ideas of the section and study new vocabulary words. You can find these new words in the Glossary. **Section Review** questions at the end of each section let you locate places on maps, study vocabulary, and review the main ideas. Look at these parts of the lesson that starts on page 291, "The People's Choice."

Skill Lessons and Special Features. A skill lesson and two special features appear in every chapter. The skill lessons teach social studies skills such as reading maps and graphs and using time lines. Look at Skill Lesson 13 on page 298. Special features are stories about interesting people and events. They are presented under the titles Americans Who Dared, Spirit of America, Free Enterprise in Action, Geography in History, Arts in America, and Voices of Freedom. Find the lists of Special Features in the Table of Contents. Then pick one story that interests you and read it right now.

Maps, Graphs, Charts, and Pictures. There are more than 170 maps, graphs, and charts in this book and hundreds of pictures. Each tells a story. Captions help show how the visual is related to events in the chapter that you are studying. Look at the picture and caption at right.

Reading Aids. Reading aids are included to help you read and understand this book. Each new vocabulary word is printed in **dark slanted type.** A definition is given when the word first appears. Important events and ideas are printed in **dark slanted type,** too. A guide to pronunciation (pro NUN see ay shuhn) helps you read words and names that may be new to you. The Pronunciation Key is on page 785.

Chapter Review. Each chapter ends with two pages called the Chapter Review. The Chapter Review has a summary of the chapter as well as different kinds of questions and activities that let you test your understanding of the chapter. It also includes ideas for projects and research reports. Turn to Chapter 13 Review on pages 306–307.

This campaign banner shows William Henry Harrison's log cabin symbol. During the campaign, Whigs built log cabins in public places to get people to vote for Harrison.

Reference Section

The Reference Section can be found on pages 746–846. It includes:

- **Historical Atlas** with maps, graphs, and pictures to illustrate the growth of the United States.
- **Geographic Atlas** with five maps of the United States and one of the world.
- **The Fifty States** with useful information about each state.
- **Gazetteer of American History** with useful information about important places.
- **A Chronology of American History** with major events and developments.
- **Connections With American Literature** with ideas for readings from literature.
- **Presidents of the United States** with a portrait and information about every President.
- **Glossary** with definitions of all vocabulary words and other key terms.
- **The Declaration of Independence** with explanations.
- **Exploring Our Living Constitution** with a guide for understanding the Constitution.
- **The Constitution of the United States of America** with explanations.
- **Index** that tells you where to find a subject in the book.

As you study American history this year, you will use all the different parts of the book. We hope that they will help make history as exciting for you as students as it is for us as historians and teachers.

James West Davidson
John E. Batchelor

Unit 1

THE WORLD OF THE AMERICAS

Prehistory						1450				1500

10,000 YEARS AGO Last ice age ends
5,000 YEARS AGO Farming begins in America
3,000 YEARS AGO Mayas drain swamps for farmland

1001 Vikings reach North America
1095 Crusades begin
1300s Aztecs move into Valley of Mexico
1400s Inca empire expands
1418 Portuguese sailors begin to explore coast of Africa

1488 Dias rounds Cape of Good Hope
1492 Columbus reaches America
1498 Da Gama reaches India

Prehistory						1450				1500

Gold pendant made by Indians in South America.

1001 Leif Ericson reached Vinland in North America.

1498 The Portuguese explorer Vasco da Gama.

UNIT OUTLINE

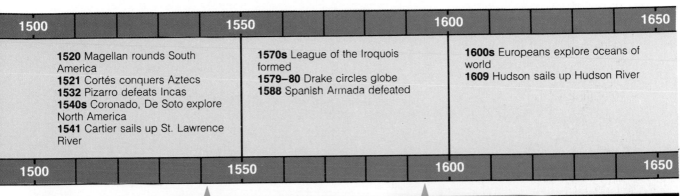

| 1500 | 1550 | 1600 | 1650 |

1520 Magellan rounds South America
1521 Cortés conquers Aztecs
1532 Pizarro defeats Incas
1540s Coronado, De Soto explore North America
1541 Cartier sails up St. Lawrence River

1570s League of the Iroquois formed
1579–80 Drake circles globe
1588 Spanish Armada defeated

1600s Europeans explore oceans of world
1609 Hudson sails up Hudson River

| 1500 | 1550 | 1600 | 1650 |

1540s Francisco Coronado searched for gold in the American Southwest.

Late 1500s Queen Elizabeth I of England.

1

The American Land (Prehistory—Present)

Chapter Outline

1 Discovering the Land
2 Different Climates

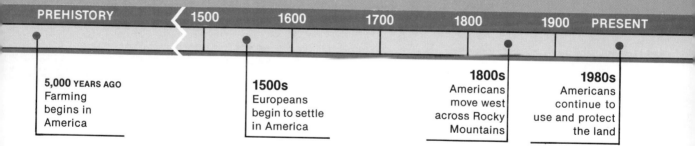

PREHISTORY	1500	1600	1700	1800	1900	PRESENT

5,000 YEARS AGO
Farming
begins in
America

1500s
Europeans
begin to settle
in America

1800s
Americans
move west
across Rocky
Mountains

1980s
Americans
continue to
use and protect
the land

About This Chapter

One hundred thousand years ago, you could have traveled from the northern tip of North America to the southern tip of South America without seeing another person. But you would have seen many kinds of plants and animals in many different landscapes and climates.

As you traveled across the Americas, you would have climbed up and down high mountains and walked into deep valleys. You would have crossed wide rivers and lakes and plodded through windswept deserts. You would have cut your way through steaming jungles and trekked through ice-covered regions.

Many different peoples settled in the Americas. They learned about the land in dif-ferent ways. The first Americans moved across the land, hunting game and gathering food. Later, they discovered ways to make the land produce crops, and they began to farm.

Thousands of years later, Europeans, Africans, and Asians crossed wide oceans to settle in the Americas. They, too, learned to adapt to the many lands and climates of North and South America.

America's history begins with the story of people learning to live in a new land. The physical features, climates, plants, animals, and resources of the land play an important role in this story.

Study the time line above. When did farming begin in America?

In the 1870s, artist Thomas Moran painted the grandeur of the West. This painting shows a canyon carved by the Yellowstone River.

1 Discovering the Land

Read to Learn

★ How did people first reach the Americas?
★ What are the major physical regions of North America?
★ What rivers flow through North America?
★ What do these words mean: geography, glacier, isthmus, mountain, elevation, hill, plain, plateau, tributary?

When the first Americans reached this land thousands of years ago, they spread out in many directions. They developed different ways of life. These differences were due in part to the geography of the Americas. *Geography* includes the physical features, climate, plants, animals, and resources of a region.

Geography influenced the way early Americans lived. Today, geography still affects where and how Americans live. Geography helps to explain history because it shows how people and the land are related.

The Last Ice Age

According to scientists, the first people to reach America came during the last ice age. The earth has gone through four ice ages. The last ice age occurred between 100,000 and 10,000 years ago. During that time, thick sheets of ice, called *glaciers,* spread out from the arctic regions. Almost one third of the earth was buried under these sheets of ice. In North America, glaciers stretched across Canada and reached as far south as Kentucky.

Glaciers changed the lands they covered. When a glacier moved south, it scooped up soil and huge boulders. When it retreated, or melted, it left behind great heaps of earth and rock. Long Island, New York, was created when a glacier retreated. So were Nantucket and Martha's Vineyard, islands off the coast of Massachusetts. Water from melting glaciers drained into channels, creating large rivers such as the Ohio and the Missouri.

The land bridge. Glaciers soaked up water from the oceans like giant sponges. This caused the levels of the oceans to drop. As a result, land appeared that had once been covered by water. Scientists think that during the last ice age a land bridge was exposed between Siberia in Asia and Alaska in North America. Today, this land is under the Bering Sea.

We do not know exactly when people first crossed the land bridge into North America. They may have reached this continent as early as 70,000 years ago. The first Americans were hunters who followed herds of wild animals such as woolly mammoths. Over thousands of years, they moved across North America into South America.

Temperatures got warmer. About 10,000 years ago, temperatures rose. Glaciers melted and flooded the land bridge between Siberia and Alaska. The warmer temperatures probably caused the woolly mammoths and mastodons to die out. But the peoples of America adapted to the new conditions. They hunted smaller game, gathered berries and grain, and caught fish.

About 5,000 years ago, some people learned to grow crops such as corn, beans, and squash. These farming people did not have to travel constantly in

Remains of woolly mammoths have been found in the Southwest. Woolly mammoths, or American elephants, grew to be 12 feet high. Armed only with spears and burning torches, early hunters killed these huge animals.

Maps are important tools used by historians and geographers. Maps have many uses. They show physical features such as lakes, rivers, and mountains. They show where people live, how people use the land, and where events took place.

A map shows part of the earth's surface. Almost all maps are flat, but the earth is not. Mapmakers have found ways to put the round earth on flat paper. But all maps, except globes, have some distortion.

To use a map, you need to be able to read its different parts. Most maps in this book have a title, key, scale, and directional arrow. Some also show relief. *Relief* is the difference in height of land that is shown by using special colors. (See the color bands on the map on page 762.)

1. **Look carefully at the map to see what it shows.** The *title* tells you the subject of the map. The *key* explains the meaning of the colors or symbols. (a) What is the title of the map at right? (b) What color shows the land bridge from Asia to North America?

2. **Practice reading distances on the map.** The *scale* helps you read distances on the map in miles or kilometers. On a small-scale map, one inch might equal 500 miles. On a large-scale map, one inch might equal only 5 miles. The map below is a small-scale map. (a) About how far in miles did glaciers stretch from north to south? (b) In kilometers?

3. **Study the map to read directions.** The *directional arrow* shows which way is north, south, east, and west. Generally, north is toward the top of a map, and south is toward the bottom. East is to the right, and west is to the left. (a) In what direction did early

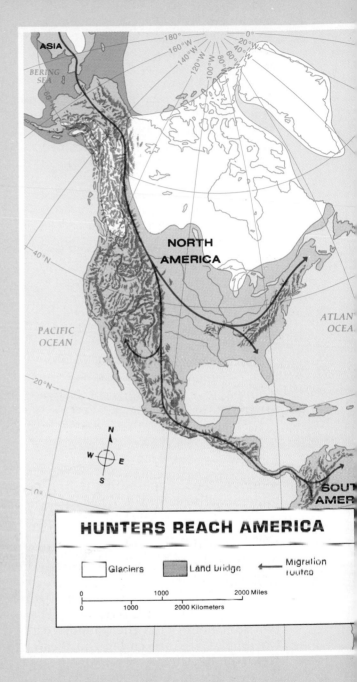

hunters travel to reach North America? (b) In what direction or directions did they move after they arrived here?

John Wesley Powell

In 1879, John Wesley Powell was named to head the United States Geological Survey. His job was to prepare accurate maps of the country. Powell had lost his right arm in the Civil War. Despite this handicap, he braved many dangers to study the land and make maps of the western United States. He also studied the cultures and languages of Native Americans in the West.

search of food. They built the first permanent villages in the Americas.

Different Landforms

What did the lands settled by the first Americans look like? North and South America are the world's third and fourth largest continents. These two continents plus the islands in the Caribbean Sea are called the *Western Hemisphere.*

As the map on pages 758–759 shows, the Atlantic Ocean washes the eastern shores of North and South America. The Pacific Ocean laps at their western shores. Far to the north lies the ice-choked Arctic Ocean. Far to the south is the Strait of Magellan (muh JEHL uhn), a water passage between the Atlantic and Pacific oceans. Joining the two continents is an *isthmus* (IHS muhs), or narrow strip of land. It is called the *Isthmus of Panama.*

North and South America have many different landscapes. There are high mountains, rolling hills, and long rivers. There are grassy plains, dense forests, and barren deserts. Within these landscapes, there are four basic landforms: mountains, hills, plains, and plateaus (pla TOHZ).

Mountains are high, rugged land. They rise to an *elevation,* or height, of at least 5,000 feet (1,500 m) above the surrounding land. Few people can live on the steep, rocky sides of high mountains. Yet, people often settle in valleys between mountains.

Hills are also raised parts of the earth's surface. But they are smaller, less steep, and more rounded than mountains. More people live in hilly areas than on mountains because farming is possible.

Plains are broad areas of fairly level land. Very few plains are totally flat. Most are gently rolling. Plains are usually not much above sea level. People often settle on plains because it is easy to build farms, roads, and cities on the level land.

Plateaus are areas of high, level land. Usually, plateaus rise to at least 2,000 feet (600 m) above sea level. Plateaus can be good for farming if they get enough rain. Some plateaus are surrounded by mountains. Such plateaus are called basins. Basins are often very dry because the mountains cut off rainfall.

Physical Regions of North America

The mountains, hills, plains, and plateaus of North America form seven major physical regions, as you can see on the map on page 24. These regions offer great contrasts. In some regions, the land is fertile. There, American farmers have been able to plant crops and reap rich harvests. Other regions have natural resources such as coal and oil. These resources have helped make America a strong nation.

Pacific Coast. The highest and most rugged part of North America is in the West. Tall mountain ranges stretch from Alaska to Mexico. In the United States, some of the western ranges hug the Pacific. The Cascades and *Sierra Nevada** stand a bit farther inland. The region containing these mountains is called the Pacific Coast. Some important cities of the Pacific Coast are Seattle, Portland, San Francisco, and Los Angeles.

Intermountain region. East of the coast ranges is an area known as the Intermountain region. It is a rugged region of mountain peaks, high plateaus, deep canyons, and deserts. The Grand Canyon, which is more than one mile deep, and the Great Salt Lake are two natural features of this region. Salt Lake City and Phoenix are among the few major cities of the Intermountain region.

Rocky Mountains. The third region, the Rocky Mountains, reaches from Alaska through Canada into the United States. Many peaks in the Rockies are over 14,000 feet (4,200 m) high.* The Rockies were a serious barrier to the settlement of the United States. When settlers moved west in the 1800s, crossing the Rockies posed great hardships. In Mexico, the Rocky Mountains are called the Sierra Madre (MAH dray), or mother range.

Interior Plains. Between the Rocky Mountains in the west and the Appalachian Mountains in the east is a large lowland area called the Interior Plains.

---

*Sierra (see EHR uh) is a Spanish word meaning mountain range. Nevada is Spanish for snowy. Spanish explorers were the first Europeans to see these snow-covered mountains.

*The highest peaks in North America are in Alaska. Mt. McKinley, Alaska, rises to 20,320 feet.

America is a land of great natural beauty and varied landscapes. In the photograph at left, waves sweep onto the Pacific coast of the United States. The photograph below shows the Grand Canyon through a limestone arch on the south rim. More than 9 million years ago, the Colorado River began carving this deep canyon in the Southwest.

The western part of the Interior Plains is called the *Great Plains.* The eastern part is called the *Central Plains.*

According to scientists, the Interior Plains were once covered by a great inland sea. Today, some parts are rich in coal and petroleum.* Chicago, St. Louis, and Dallas are in the Interior Plains. The *Badlands* are also found here. See page 25.

---

*The map on page 765 shows where natural resources are located in the United States.

Appalachian Mountains. The fifth region, the Appalachian Mountains, runs along the eastern part of North America. The Appalachians are called different names in different places. For example, the Green Mountains, Alleghenies, Blue Ridge, and Great Smokies are all part of the Appalachians.

The Appalachians are lower and less rugged than the Rockies. The highest Appalachian peak is Mt. Mitchell, which is only about 6,000 feet (1,850 m) high. Still, early settlers had a hard time crossing these mountains.

MAP SKILL The major physical regions of the United States are shown in different colors on this map. Find the four mountain ranges labeled on the map. Which range is in the eastern part of the United States?

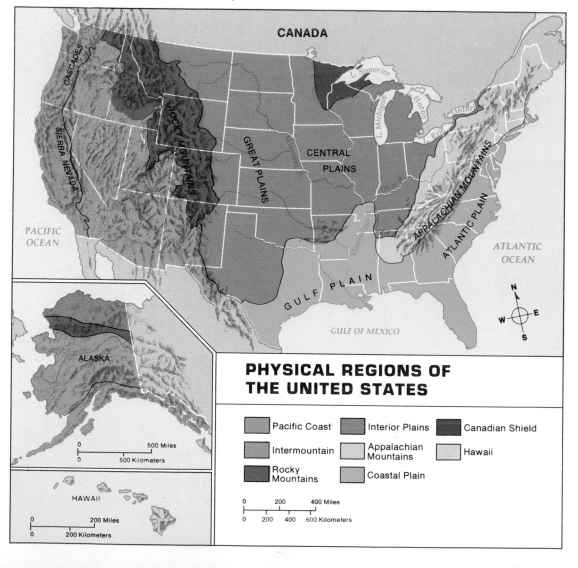

PHYSICAL REGIONS OF THE UNITED STATES

- Pacific Coast
- Intermountain
- Rocky Mountains
- Interior Plains
- Appalachian Mountains
- Coastal Plain
- Canadian Shield
- Hawaii

Strange and startling shapes rise up out of the Badlands of South Dakota. The Badlands got their name from the Dakota Indians. They called the area mako sica, or land that was bad, because it had little good water. Later, French and English settlers used words from their own languages to express the same idea.

Wind, weather, and rivers have carved strange shapes in the Badlands and have revealed traces of the ancient history of the Badlands. Rain and wind have exposed the bones of animals that roamed the land millions of years ago. Scientists have found the remains of ancient turtles, camels, and saber-toothed tigers. Today, bear, elk, moose, and deer live there.

People, too, have lived in the Badlands. For hundreds of years, Indians camped in the Badlands during buffalo hunts. In the early 1900s, white settlers built homes there. But lack of water forced many settlers to sell their land. In

1978, the Badlands were made a national park.

★ Why have few people settled in the Badlands?

Canadian Shield. The sixth region is the Canadian Shield. It is a lowland area. Most of it lies in eastern Canada. The southern part extends into the United States. The region was once an area of high mountains. The mountains were worn away to low hills and plains. The Canadian Shield lacks topsoil for farming. But it is rich in minerals.

Coastal Plains. The seventh region is a lowland area called the Coastal Plains. Part of this region, the *Atlantic Plain,* lies between the Atlantic Ocean and the foothills of the Appalachians. It was once under water and is now almost flat. The Atlantic Plain is narrow in the north, where Boston and New York City are located. It broadens in the south to include all of Florida.

Another part of the Coastal Plains is the *Gulf Plain,* which lies along the Gulf of Mexico. The Gulf Plain is rich in petroleum. New Orleans and Houston are major cities of the Gulf Plain.

Rivers and Lakes

Great river systems crisscross North America. They collect the runoff from rains and melting snows and carry it into the oceans. The longest and most important river system in the United States is made up of the Mississippi and Missouri rivers. This river system flows through the Interior Plains into the Gulf of Mexico. It has many *tributaries,* or branches. They include the Ohio, Tennessee, Arkansas, and Platte rivers.

The Mississippi River carries moisture across the Interior Plains. It also serves as a means of transportation. Today, barges carry freight up and down the river. Today, as in the past, people travel by boat along the river.

The Rio Grande and the St. Lawrence River form parts of the borders between the United States and its neighbors, Mexico and Canada.

Five large lakes, called the *Great Lakes,* also form part of the border between the United States and Canada. The Great Lakes are Superior, Michigan, Huron, Erie, and Ontario. Today, canals connect the Great Lakes, forming an important inland waterway.

The Niagara River connects Lake Erie to Lake Ontario. However, ships cannot use this fast-flowing river because at one point it plunges over broad cliffs, forming the spectacular Niagara Falls. Instead, ships travel through the Welland Canal, which connects these two Great Lakes.

Landscapes of South America

Like North America, South America has a variety of landscapes. The Andes are a rugged mountain chain. They stretch along the western part of South America. The tallest peaks of the Andes are much higher than those of the Rockies. The Andes plunge almost directly to the Pacific, leaving only a narrow coastal plain. Many people live in the high plateaus and valleys of the Andes.

To the east of the Andes is an interior plain. The plain is drained by three great river systems: the Orinoco, Amazon, and Parana–Paraguay. The Amazon is the world's second longest river. It flows 4,000 miles (6,500 km) from the Andes to the Atlantic.

━SECTION REVIEW━

1. **Locate:** Bering Sea, North America, South America, Atlantic Ocean, Pacific Ocean, Sierra Nevada, Rocky Mountains, Great Plains, Appalachian Mountains, Mississippi River.
2. **Define:** geography, glacier, isthmus, mountain, elevation, hill, plain, plateau, tributary.
3. (a) What are the seven physical regions of North America? (b) Describe one feature of each.
4. Where are the Great Lakes?
5. **What Do You Think?** Why do you think the Intermountain region has only a few cities?

2 Different Climates

Read to Learn
★ What are the major climates of the United States?
★ What climates does South America have?
★ What do these words mean: weather, climate, irrigate?

Geographic features such as mountains and rivers have affected the way Americans live. Another feature of geography that has affected Americans is climate. People have had to adapt to different climates in the Americas.

What Is Climate?

Climate is important to people's lives because it is always there. But just what is climate? How is it different from weather? *Weather* is the condition of the air at any given time and place. *Climate* is the average weather of a place over a period of 20 or 30 years.

Climates have changed over time. During the last ice age, climates grew very cold. The extreme cold affected plants, animals, and people around the world.

Several factors affect climate. One factor is how far north or south of the Equator a region is located. Lands close to the Equator generally have a tropical climate. They usually are hot and wet all year. Lands around the North and South poles have an arctic climate. They are cold all year. Alaska and northern Canada have a subarctic climate with long, cold winters and very short summers. Other lands have both warm and cold seasons.

Another factor that affects climate is altitude, or the height above sea level. In general, highland areas are cooler than lowland areas.

Ocean currents, wind currents, and mountains also influence climate. For example, when winds carrying moisture strike the side of a mountain, the air rises and cools rapidly. As the moisture cools, it falls as rain or snow. Plenty of moisture falls on one side of the mountain. The other side is usually quite dry because the winds have already dumped their moisture.

Climates of North America

Within North America, climates vary greatly. Many regions have mild temperatures and good rainfall. In such regions, Americans have been able to grow plentiful food crops.

The United States has ten major climates. Look at the map on page 28 and the chart at right. You have read about tropical, arctic, subarctic, and highland climates above. The other six climates are described below.

Marine. The strip of land from southern Alaska to northern California is sometimes called the Pacific Northwest. This region has a mild, moist marine climate. The Pacific Northwest has many forests that make it the center of the busy lumber industry.

Mediterranean. Most of California has a Mediterranean climate. Winters

Climates of the United States

Climate	Weather
Tropical	Hot, rainy, steamy
Humid subtropical	Humid summers; mild winters
Humid continental	Hot summers; cold winters; rainfall varies
Steppe	Very hot summers; very cold winters; little rainfall
Desert	Hot; very little rainfall
Mediterranean	Mild, wet winters; sunny, dry summers
Marine	Mild, rainy
Subarctic	Very short summers; long, cold winters
Arctic	Very cold winters; very short summers
Highlands	Seasons and rainfall vary with elevation

CHART SKILL Compare the ten climates on this chart to the climates on the map on page 28. The chart shows the weather found in each climate. Using the map and the chart, find the climate and weather for your state.

are mild and moist. Summers are hot and dry. In many areas, the soil is good, but plants need to be watered in the summer. So farmers and fruit growers *irrigate,* or bring water to, the land.

Desert. On the eastern side of the Cascades and Sierra Nevada, the land has a desert climate. This dry region stretches as far east as the Rockies. In the deserts of Nevada, Arizona, and southeastern California, there is almost no rainfall. In many areas, people irrigate the land so that they can grow crops.

Steppe. East of the Rockies are the Great Plains. They have a steppe climate with limited rainfall. The short grasses that grow on the Great Plains are excellent for grazing. Huge buffalo herds grazed there for hundreds of years. In the 1800s, settlers, brought cattle to graze on the plains.

Humid continental. The Central Plains and the northeastern United States have a humid continental climate. This climate has more rainfall than the steppe. Tall prairie grasses once covered the Central Plains. Today, American farmers raise much of the world's food in this area.

At one time, forests covered much of the northeastern United States. Early European settlers cleared forests to grow crops. But many forests remain, and the lumber industry thrives in some areas.

MAP SKILL The United States is a land of many climates. The mild climates of some areas have helped people. In other areas, people have struggled to survive under harsh climate conditions. Locate the state where you live on the map below. What climate or climates are found in your state?

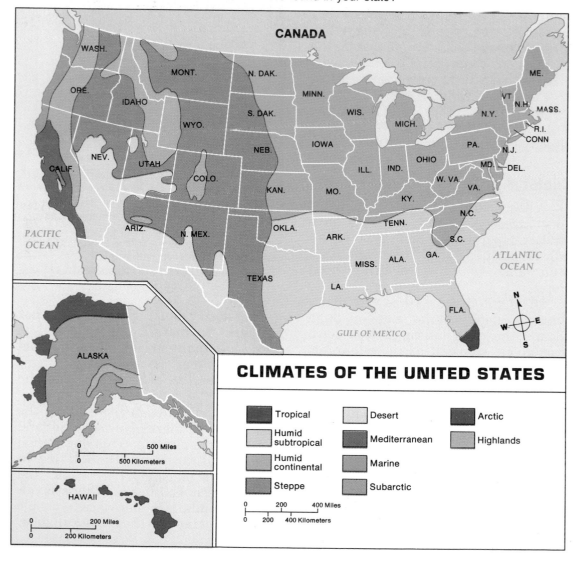

CLIMATES OF THE UNITED STATES

- Tropical
- Humid subtropical
- Humid continental
- Steppe
- Desert
- Mediterranean
- Marine
- Subarctic
- Arctic
- Highlands

American climates vary a lot, as these two photographs show. The one at left shows cactus in the desert climate of the Southwest. The one at right shows a cypress forest in the subtropical climate of the Southeast. What differences do you see in the plants of these climates?

Humid subtropical. The southeastern part of the country has a humid subtropical climate. Warm temperatures and regular rainfall make this region ideal for growing crops such as cotton, tobacco, and peanuts.

Climates of South America

South America has many climates. Thick tropical rain forests cover parts of southern Mexico, Central America,* and South America. The huge area drained by the Amazon River is largely rain forest.

The Andes Mountains are a barrier to moist winds. The mountains force the winds to dump rain on the eastern slopes of the Andes. But the western slopes are very dry. In fact, one of the world's driest deserts, the Atacama

Desert, stretches along the coast of Peru and northern Chile.

Large parts of Brazil have a savanna climate. These areas have a rainy season when huge amounts of moisture fall. The rainy season is followed by a dry season with no rainfall. Other countries in South America, such as Argentina, Uruguay, and Chile, have climates similar to those in the United States.

━━ **SECTION REVIEW** ━━━

1. **Define:** weather, climate, irrigate.
2. Name two factors that affect the climate of a region.
3. List the ten major climates of the United States.
4. Describe two climates found in South America.
5. **What Do You Think?** Why do you think climate is important to people's lives?

---

*Central America is the part of North America that lies between Mexico and South America.

Chapter 1 Review

★ Summary ★

During the last ice age, hunters moved across the frozen land bridge that connected Asia and North America. They became the first people to settle in the Americas. As these first Americans slowly moved across the two continents, they found many different lands and climates.

Geography is important to the study of American history because it shows how people and the land are related. North America has seven major physical regions and ten climates. For thousands of years, the different lands and climates have affected the way people live.

★ Reviewing the Facts   *2 pts. each* ★

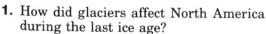

Key Terms. Match each term in Column 1 with the correct definition in Column 2.

Column 1	Column 2
1. geography	**a.** narrow strip of land
2. glacier	**b.** branch of a river
3. isthmus	**c.** broad area of gently rolling land
4. mountain	**d.** physical features of a region
5. hill	**e.** high, rugged land
6. plain	**f.** average weather over time
7. plateau	**g.** thick sheet of ice
8. tributary	**h.** condition of the air at a certain time and place
9. weather	**i.** raised, rounded part of the earth's surface
10. climate	**j.** high, level land

Key People, Events, and Ideas. Identify each of the following.

1. Western Hemisphere
2. Isthmus of Panama
3. Sierra Nevada
4. Great Plains
5. Central Plains
6. Great Lakes
7. Atlantic Plain
8. Gulf Plain
9. Badlands
10. John Wesley Powell

★ Chapter Checkup   *5 pts. each* ★

1. How did glaciers affect North America during the last ice age?
2. (a) How do scientists think the first Americans reached North America? (b) How did the lives of the first Americans change about 10,000 years ago?
3. Describe the major geographical features of South America.
4. (a) Name four major rivers of North America. (b) Why is the Mississippi River important?
5. Explain two ways that mountains influence climate.
6. Why do farmers in Nevada, Arizona, and southeastern California have to irrigate the land?

★ Thinking About History ★

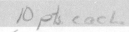

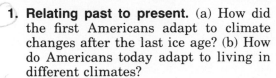

1. **Relating past to present.** (a) How did the first Americans adapt to climate changes after the last ice age? (b) How do Americans today adapt to living in different climates?

2. **Analyzing information.** (a) List two differences between the Great Plains and the Central Plains. (b) How does climate influence these differences?

3. **Understanding geography.** Review pages 26–29. (a) Which American climates are probably the easiest to live in? (b) Which climates are probably the hardest to live in? Why?

4. **Expressing an opinion.** Do you think that geography has as much influence on people today as it did in the past? Explain your answer.

★ Using Your Skills ★

1. **Map reading.** Review the map-reading steps in Skill Lesson 1 (page 21). Then study the map on page 24. (a) What is the title of the map? (b) What region is directly east of the Pacific Coast? (c) What region is directly west of the Atlantic Plain? (d) What is the approximate distance in miles east to west across the United States?

2. **Outlining.** Outlining is a way of presenting lots of information in an organized way. An outline helps you summarize and review facts. To outline a chapter, list its main topics and subtopics. Then give facts about each subtopic. To outline Chapter 1, write the first main topic—the numbered title on page 19. (See the sample below.) Below that, write the first subtopic—the subsection on page

19. Under each subtopic, write at least two facts. Complete the outline for Chapter 1.

I. Discovering the Land (main topic)
   A. The Last Ice Age (subtopic)
      1. formed land bridge between Siberia and Alaska
      2. people crossed land bridge to North America
   B. Different Landforms
      1.
      2.

3. **Comparing.** When you compare two or more things, you need to look for ways they are similar and ways they are different. Compare the Rocky Mountains and the Appalachians. (a) How are they similar? (b) How are they different?

★ More to Do ★

1. **Creating a travelogue.** As a group project, create a travelogue, describing the route taken by the first people who reached North America.

2. **Identifying place names.** Using a map of the United States, find place names that describe their geography—for example, Rocky Mountains.

3. **Creating a map.** On a blank map of the United States, draw in and label the rivers mentioned on pages 25 and 26.

Include the Great Lakes and the bodies of water around the United States. Use the map on pages 760–761 to find this information.

4. **Exploring local history.** Prepare a report on the land and climate of the area where you live. Describe the rivers, weather, plants, and animals of the area. Then list three ways that climate affects people in your area.

2

The First Americans (Prehistory–1600)

Chapter Outline

1 Studying the First Americans
2 Peoples of North America
3 Great Empires in the Americas

PREHISTORY	1200	1300	1400	1500	1600

3,000 YEARS AGO
Mayas drain swamps for farmland

1200s
Cahokia Mound completed

1300s
Aztecs move into Valley of Mexico

1400s
Inca empire expands

1492
Columbus reaches America

1570s
League of the Iroquois formed

About This Chapter

People have lived in the Americas for thousands of years. The first people to reach the Americas probably arrived about 70,000 years ago. Little is known about them. How did they live? Why did some stay in North America and others move thousands of miles into South America? Today, historians and scientists are trying to answer these and other questions about Native Americans, as the first Americans are called.

Recently, the cameras on a space satellite took pictures over the jungles of Guatemala in Central America. When the pictures were developed, scientists were puzzled by a series of straight lines that cut through the swampy jungle like a giant checkerboard. Two scientists went to Guatemala to learn about the lines. They paddled dugout canoes up streams and deep into the jungle. They found ditches crossing the jungle in the same checkerboard pattern that the satellite photos had shown.

The scientists realized that Native Americans dug these ditches. The people were the Mayas, who lived in the swampy jungle over 3,000 years ago. The Mayas dug the ditches to drain swamps and make fields for growing crops. Later, the Mayas built an empire in Central America. Discoveries such as this one have added greatly to our knowledge of the first Americans.

Study the time line above. Did the Mayas start farming before or after the Aztecs moved into Mexico?

In the 1500s, the Incas built the city of Machu Picchu (MA choo PEEK choo) high up in the Andes Mountains of Peru.

1 Studying the First Americans

Read to Learn

★ How do archaeologists learn about early people?

★ How did some people adapt to life in the desert?

★ What do these words mean: archaeologist, culture, adobe, pueblo, drought?

Like early people in other parts of the world, the first Americans left no written records. How, then, can we learn about the first Americans?

The Work of Archaeologists

People who did not write left behind other evidence of their lives. For example, when they roasted animals over fires, they left charred bones at their campsites. Some left clay cooking pots as well as weapons and tools made of bone and stone. Scientists who study the evidence left by early people are called *archaeologists* (ahr kee AHL uh jihsts). By studying the evidence, archaeologists have learned much about early people.

Archaeologists are interested in the *culture,* or the way of life, of early people. Culture includes the customs, ideas, and skills of a given people. It also includes their houses, clothes, and government.

The work of archaeologists is hard because much evidence about early people has been destroyed. Their first

Archaeologists have learned a lot about early Indian cultures. Here, an archaeologist measures the size of an ancient roasting pit before she makes a drawing of it.

task is to find evidence that has survived. Sometimes, archaeologists find evidence in unexpected places. A flood might wash away a river bank and uncover ancient bones. Or a bulldozer clearing land might dig up a buried campsite. When such finds occur, archaeologists learn as much as they can before the evidence is removed.

Archaeologists have to work carefully and keep detailed records of everything they find. They often use small picks and soft brushes to uncover an object without damaging it. Once they have dug out an object, they try to analyze, or explain, what it is. By looking closely at an object, archaeologists can learn a great deal about the people who made or used it. A sharp, finely shaped arrowhead suggests that the people were skilled at making weapons. Bits of pottery at a campsite suggest that the people knew how to shape clay into cookware.

The Mound Builders

Archaeologists have studied the evidence left behind by Native Americans. In recent years, they have learned much about groups of people called the *Mound Builders.* These people built thousands of mounds from eastern Oklahoma to the Atlantic Ocean. The mounds varied in size and shape. See the picture of the Great Serpent Mound at right.

The Mound Builders lived at various times from about 2,800 years ago until the 1700s. Among them were the Adenas, Hopewells, and Mississippians. Between about 900 and 1250, the Mississippians built the great Cahokia Mound in Illinois. It covers 116 acres and is so large it looks like a hill. Dozens of smaller mounds are clustered nearby.

The mounds served different purposes. Some were burial mounds. They were built over the graves of important people. Others were platform mounds. They were shaped like pyramids with flattened tops.

By studying these mounds, archaeologists have begun to learn about the lives of the Mound Builders. To build such large mounds, hundreds of people had to work together. So the Mound Builders must have had strong rulers who could organize large groups of workers. The mounds also show that religion and concern for the dead were important to the people.

Peoples of the Desert

Many peoples left their mark on the American Southwest. Among them were the *Hohokams* (HOH hoh kahmz) and *Anasazis* (ah NUH sah zeez). Each had their own customs, but they were alike in some ways.

Both peoples made excellent pottery and built their houses out of stone and sun-dried clay bricks, called *adobe.* Both were farmers who raised corn,

The Great Serpent Mound in Ohio was built more than 1,000 years ago. The serpent twists across the land for more than 1,200 feet (365 m). It is about 20 feet wide and 4 feet high. This mound may have been used for religious ceremonies.

beans, and squash. And both developed ways to irrigate the land. The Hohokams irrigated their crops by digging canals from the Salt and Gila rivers in Arizona. The Anasazis built dikes and dams to bring water from streams to their fields.

Some Anasazi villages still stand. They are known as *pueblos* (PWEHB lohz), the Spanish word for villages. In Pueblo Bonito, New Mexico, the houses are several stories high and have as many as 800 rooms. The rooms are tiny, but the Anasazis spent much of their time in the bright, warm plaza outside. The houses have no stairways or hallways. To reach rooms on the upper floors, people used ladders.

The Anasazis are known as Cliff Dwellers because some of them built their homes on cliff walls. They may have done this for protection from warlike neighbors. In the morning, men and women climbed to the top of the cliffs to take care of their crops. They climbed back down to their homes by using toeholds cut into the cliffs.

In the late 1200s, a *drought* (drowt), or long dry spell, hit these lands. The drought forced the people to leave their homes. The Anasazis never recovered from the disaster.

Cliff dwellings such as this one can be seen in the Mesa Verde National Park in Colorado. These cliff homes were built between 1100 and 1300. Archaeologists have found fine pottery, woven fabrics, and decorated walls inside.

1. **Define:** archaeologist, culture, adobe, pueblo, drought.
2. What kinds of evidence have early Native Americans left behind?
3. Why did the Mound Builders build huge earth mounds?
4. **What Do You Think?** Why do you think people today are interested in learning about the first Americans?

2 Peoples of North America

Read to Learn
★ What Native American cultures developed in North America?
★ How did different people adapt to their environment?
★ What do these words mean: igloo, potlatch, hogan, long house?

In 1492, when Christopher Columbus reached the Americas, he thought he had reached the East Indies. So he called the people he met Indians. This term is still used to refer to Native Americans. *Native Americans* are descended from the people who reached America thousands of years ago.

Millions of Native Americans lived in North America before 1492. They spoke hundreds of different languages and developed many cultures.* As the map on page 38 shows, Indians lived in all parts of North America.

Far North

The Far North is a land of bitterly cold winters and icy seas. The *Eskimos* were one of the peoples who adapted to this harsh land. They survived by making use of everything the land, sea, and sky had to offer. In the winter, they built *igloos,* or houses made of snow and ice. Lamps filled with seal oil kept the igloos warm even in the most bitter cold. In the summer, they made dwell-

*Some beliefs and customs described in this chapter are still practiced by Native Americans today.

ings out of animal skins. Eskimo women made warm clothing out of furs and sewed seal skins into waterproof boots.

In winter, several families traveled together in a hunting band. The Eskimos hunted wolves, foxes, and polar bears. When the seas were not frozen, they used kayaks (κī aks), or small skin boats, to hunt seals and walruses. Food was often scarce. Therefore, the Eskimos shared what they caught.

In their religion, the Eskimos showed concern for the animals they depended on for survival. The Eskimos believed that each animal had a spirit. So when an Eskimo hunter trapped a female fox, for example, he offered bone needles to the fox's spirit. This offering, he believed, ensured good hunting in the future.

The West

Indians in the West adapted to many different climates. Among the cultures of the West are the Northwest Coast and Intermountain.

Northwest Coast. Unlike the Eskimos, the peoples of the Northwest Coast did not face bitter winters or a scarce food supply. Instead, they enjoyed pleasant weather year round. Magnificent forests and nearby oceans and rivers were rich storehouses of deer, moose, bear, and salmon.

The people made good use of the forests. Men built houses and different

Geography in History

Shells as Money

In plentiful supply along the Pacific Coast, shellfish were a source of food for the peoples of the Northwest Coast. But one kind of shellfish—dentalia—served another purpose. Their tooth-shaped shells were used as money!

Dentalia usually lived in deep waters offshore, so they were hard to reach. Because dentalia were a difficult catch, the Native Americans prized the shells.

The Nootka of Vancouver Island were the main producers of dentalia shells. Off the island, dentalia lived in shallower waters. Using a long broomlike device, the Nootka were able to reach the dentalia, trap them in the wood splints of the broom, and then lift them out of the water.

Once on shore, the Nootka boiled out the flesh of the dentalia. Then they dried

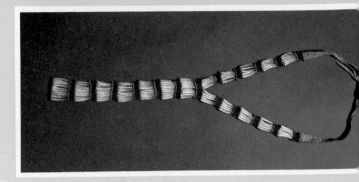

the shells and polished them with sand. As the final step, they grouped the shells by size and strung them together. The longer the string of shells, the greater was the value.

★ Why did Native Americans of the Northwest Coast value dentalia shells as money?

kinds of canoes out of wood. Some canoes were used for visiting. Others were for fishing or for war. The largest canoes were almost 70 feet (20 m) long and could carry up to 60 people. Women wove the soft inner bark of cedar trees into clothes and blankets.

In the 1800s, many groups of people lived in villages with their houses facing the sea. Each house was home to several families. In front of their house, people put up totem poles. A totem pole was a tall wooden post carved with animals or other figures.

Within each village, people were ranked according to how much they owned. A family held a *potlatch*, or ceremonial dinner, to show off its wealth. Sometimes, a family spent years preparing for a potlatch. Many guests were invited, and everyone received gifts. The more gifts a family gave to its guests, the greater fame the family

In the 1800s, Native Americans on the Northwest Coast carved totem poles showing animals such as beavers, bears, and eagles. A totem pole told visitors of the great deeds of a family.

NATIVE AMERICAN CULTURES

ARCTIC OCEAN

ESKIMO

KUTCHIN

ESKIMO

TLINGIT

FAR NORTH

NORTHWEST COAST

BEAVER

CREE

BELLA COOLA

PACIFIC OCEAN

CHIPPEWA

ALGONQUIN

HURON

IROQUOIS

BLACKFEET

NEZ PERCÉ

MANDAN

EASTERN WOODLANDS

COOS

CROW

DAKOTA

DELAWARE

CHEYENNE

MIAMI

POMO

CALIFORNIA-INTERMOUNTAIN

GREAT PLAINS

ATLANTIC OCEAN

SHOSHONE

SHAWNEE

ARAPAHO

OSAGE

CHEROKEE

NAVAJO

PUEBLO

COMANCHE

SOUTHEAST

HOPI

SOUTHWEST

NATCHEZ

APACHE

SEMINOLE

GULF OF MEXICO

MIDDLE AMERICA

MAYA

AZTEC

0   500   1000 Miles
0   500   1000 Kilometers

MAP SKILL By 1400, about 10 million Native Americans lived in North America north of Mexico. Native Americans spoke at least 500 different languages and had their own cultures. Scholars have divided North America into the culture regions shown here. Name two groups that lived in the Southwest.

won. At one potlatch, the gifts included 8 canoes, 54 elk skins, 2,000 silver bracelets, 7,000 brass bracelets, and 33,000 blankets.

Intermountain. In the dry Intermountain region, life was difficult. Without water, few plants or animals were able to live in the region. Native Americans like the Ute and Shoshone had a hard time finding food. They moved around in small groups. Often, a single family spent much of its time looking for food.

Southwest

In the Southwest, people like the Anasazis learned to farm in a dry, desert climate. Later groups like the *Pueblos* adopted many Anasazi customs. They built adobe houses and grew squash, beans, and corn.

The Pueblos believed that many spirits watched over the land. The spirits caused rain to fall and crops to grow. To keep the spirits happy so that they would give rain and good harvests, each Pueblo village set up a secret society. Members performed ceremonies and dances to please the spirits.

The Pueblos traced family lines through the woman's family. This custom gave women special importance. When a man married, he went to live with his wife's family. The wife owned most of the family property.

Another group in the Southwest were the *Navajos* (NAV uh hohz). At one time, they were hunters and food gatherers. But they learned to farm from the Pueblos. The Navajos lived in **hogans,** or houses built of mud plaster and supported by wooden poles.

The Navajos believed in two kinds of beings: Earth Surface People and Holy People. Earth Surface People included the Navajos and other humans. Holy People included gods. Like the Pueblos, the Navajos believed that they had to please the Holy People. They held special ceremonies to ensure good health and good harvests.

Great Plains

The peoples of the Great Plains were hunters and farmers. Many lived in villages on hills above rivers. They built their houses with great care. They dug pits for the foundations and used sod from the pits for the roofs. To make walls, they covered poles with grass. Each house had a hole in the roof to let out smoke from the cooking fire.

In the winter, the men hunted animals near the village. In the summer, they went on long trips in search of buffalo herds. Huge herds of buffalo stretched for miles across the plains.

In the spring when the snows melted, the river below the village often overflowed its banks for a few days. When the ground was soft and easy to work, the women used animal bones to break up the soil. They then planted corn, beans, and sunflowers.

Each village was ruled by a council made up of the best hunters. The chief was a council member respected by the others because he spoke well and judged wisely. Sometimes, a village had several chiefs. Each chief served on a different occasion, such as hunting, farming, or going to war.

Southeast

The Southeast had fertile land with more than 100 kinds of trees and plenty of rain. More Native Americans lived here than in any other area north of Mexico. Among the peoples of the Southeast were the *Natchez* (NACH ihz), who lived in Mississippi and Louisiana. The Natchez were descendants of the Mound Builders. They were farmers and hunters. Dividing the year into 13 months, they named each month after a food gathered or hunted during that time. The names of months included Deer, Strawberries, Little Corn, Mulberries, Turkey, Bison, and Bear.

Men and women shared the work of growing crops. During planting and

The Navajos drew sand paintings to use in healing the sick and in religious ceremonies. This Navajo sand painting shows Father Sky and Mother Earth, two of the most important Holy People.

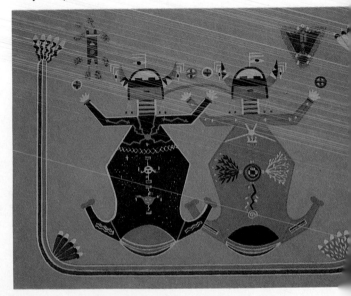

harvesting time, everyone in the village worked together. They moved from one field to the next. Men were also hunters. To hunt deer, they disguised themselves. Wearing a deerskin and antlers, a Natchez hunter could move quite close to a deer before shooting it with his bow and arrow.

The Natchez worshipped the sun as the source of all life. They kept a fire going day and night in a temple to the sun. The Natchez believed in an afterlife. The faithful would enjoy peace and plenty of food after they died. The unfaithful, however, would be forced to live in a swamp swarming with mosquitoes.

The Natchez were divided into social classes. At the top was the Great Sun, or chief. Below the Great Sun were other members of the chief's family, called Suns. Next came the Nobles and then the Honored People. The lowest class was the Stinkards.

Natchez laws required that the male children of a Sun, Noble, or Honored Person marry one class below them. As a result, the male descendants of a Great Sun eventually became Stinkards. The female children could hold on to their higher social class if their marriages were arranged carefully.

Eastern Woodlands

Many different groups of people lived in the Eastern Woodlands. In the forests and open lands, they hunted game such as deer, bear, and moose. They raised crops of squash, pumpkins, and corn—including popcorn.

The most powerful people in the Eastern Woodlands were the *Iroquois* (IHR uh kwoi), who lived in what is now New York State. The Iroquois lived in *long houses.* A typical long house was about 18 feet (5 m) wide and 60 feet (18 m) long. A hallway ran the length of the long house. On either side of the hallway were small rooms. Each room was a family's home. Families who lived across from each other shared a fire in the hallway.

Women played an important part in Iroquois life. Like a Pueblo man, an Iroquois man moved in with his wife's family when he married. Women owned all the property in the long house. They were in charge of planting and harvesting.

Iroquois women also had political power. The Iroquois were divided into five nations: the Mohawk, Seneca (SEHN ih kuh), Onondaga (ahn uhn DAH guh), Oneida (oh NĪ duh), and Cayuga (kay YOO gah). Each nation had its own

Many Indians of the Southeast lived along the coast and were skilled at fishing. Although fish was their main source of food, they also farmed. Notice the fire built on a pile of sand in the bottom of the boat. It kept the Indians warm while they fished.

This scene shows Indians of the Eastern Woodlands. Indians of this region hunted and farmed. The Indian near the center is grinding corn in a hollow log.

ruling council. Women chose the men who served as council members.

A major problem facing the councils was the constant fighting among the Iroquois nations. Sometime about 1570, the five nations formed a union, called the *League of the Iroquois*. A council of 50 leaders met at least once a year to settle disputes. Again, the women chose the leaders. At meetings, the leaders discussed problems and voted on ways to solve them. Each nation had one vote. The council could not act unless all five nations agreed.

SECTION REVIEW

1. **Define:** igloo, potlatch, hogan, long house.
2. List the seven major culture regions of North American Indians.
3. How did the Eskimos adapt to the arctic climate?
4. Why did the Pueblos believe the gods had to be pleased?
5. What power did Iroquois women have?
6. **What Do You Think?** Do you think the place where a group of people lived affected their way of life? Explain.

3 Great Empires in the Americas

Read to Learn

★ Where was the Maya empire?
★ How did the Aztecs build their capital city?
★ How did the Incas organize their large empire?
★ What does this word mean: pictograph?

Native Americans in Mexico and in Central and South America built large empires. Among them were the empires of the Mayas, Aztecs, and Incas. In each, the people learned to grow great amounts of food. The plentiful food supported a large population.

Mayas

The Maya empire stretched across large parts of Central America and Mexico. (See the map on page 45.) About 3,000 years ago, the Mayas began clearing the tropical rain forests of this region. The rain forests were difficult and dangerous places in which to live. They were hot and humid and were inhabited by wild animals. Fierce stinging ants, poisonous snakes, and mosquitoes brought disease and death to the people. The Mayas dug canals to drain the swampy land. They learned to grow beans, corn, and squash.

Most Mayas were farmers. They lived in houses with mud walls and thatch roofs. A family raised a few turkeys or deer to be killed for feasts. Maya farmers kept beehives for honey. The honey could be gathered easily because bees in the region did not sting.

Maya cities. From time to time, farmers who lived in small villages visited one of the great Maya cities, such as Tikal. In the city marketplace, farmers found woven baskets, blankets, bright feathers for headdresses, jade jewelry, pottery, and tools made of flint. What impressed visitors most, however, were the towering stone temples in the heart of the city. The main temple was shaped like a pyramid and rose up to ten stories high. Smaller temple pyramids stood nearby, each with steep steps leading to the top.

A city had tens of thousands of people. The people were divided into social classes. Priests were the highest class. Next came the nobles. Below them were the peasants, or farmers. At the bottom were the prisoners of war, who were slaves.

Important advances. Religion was central to Maya life. Every day, priests performed ceremonies in the temples to please the gods. Religion also led the Mayas to make important advances. Because time and the seasons were sacred, priests studied the movements of the sun and stars. With this information, they developed an accurate calendar.

The Mayas invented a method of writing. They drew *pictographs,* or pictures to represent objects. They carved these pictographs on stone tablets or painted them on paper made from tree bark.

Aztecs

In the 1300s, the Aztecs moved into the Valley of Mexico. The valley sits between two mountain ranges. The mountains kept rivers from draining into the sea. So the valley was very swampy.

The wonders of Tenochtitlan. The Aztecs built their capital city, *Tenochtitlan* (tay noch tee TLAHN), on an island in the middle of a swampy lake. They built canals to drain the lake. Aztec farmers learned to grow crops on the swampland. Using wooden stakes, they attached mats to the floor of the swamp. They then put layers of mud on the mats and planted their gardens. Farmers grew as many as seven crops a year on these floating gardens.

Tenochtitlan was the largest city in the Americas. By 1500, over 100,000 people lived there. People paddled canoes on the canals to bring food and other goods to the city. Three raised roads led into the city. They had drawbridges that could be lifted if an enemy attacked. Within the city, thousands of stone and mortar houses lined the streets. In the center, a great stone pyramid temple rose into the air. Scattered around the city were other temples.

The wealthiest and most powerful Aztec was the emperor. Below him were priests and nobles. Ordinary people included farmers and merchants.

When the emperor walked anywhere in the city, the nobles followed him. They threw cloth in his path so

Skill Lesson 2 A Painting as a Primary Source

Historians use primary sources to learn about the past. A *primary source* is firsthand information about people or events of the past.

Paintings are one kind of primary source. They show how the people of a certain time and place saw themselves. Often, they give useful evidence about aspects of daily life such as food, clothes, games, and homes.

The picture below was painted on the walls of a Maya temple. Use the following steps to learn how to use a painting as a primary source.

1. **Identify the subject of the painting.** Study the painting carefully. (a) List three things the people are doing. (b) What kinds of plants and animals are shown? (c) What title would you give to this painting? (d) Explain why you chose this title.

2. **Decide what the painting tells about the life of the people.** Study the painting and review what you have read about the life of the Mayas. (a) Where was the painting found? (b) Describe the houses of the people. (c) From this painting, what conclusions can you draw about the daily life of the Mayas?

3. **Decide if the painting is a reliable source.** A painting does not always tell the full story. An artist may have painted it for a special reason or may have left out some details. You need to decide whether it is a reliable source of information. (a) Do you think that the artist showed everything exactly as it was? Explain. (b) Does this painting give you a complete idea of the daily life of the Mayas? Explain.

Aztec Soldier

To keep their empire strong, the Aztecs needed many soldiers. Aztec soldiers filled the streets of Tenochtitlan, wearing colorful cloaks and headdresses. They often carried bouquets of flowers. In battle, soldiers carried shields and swords and wore quilted jackets as protection against arrows. Their swords were edged with sharp black glass.

The Aztecs believed that their gods required human sacrifices. When powerful Aztec armies conquered neighboring peoples, they took many prisoners and demanded heavy taxes. The Aztecs used prisoners of war as sacrifices. By the early 1500s, the sacrifice of so many prisoners and the burden of heavy taxes left the conquered peoples ready to revolt against Aztec rule.

Incas

The Incas built the largest empire in the Americas. In the 1400s, it stretched along the Pacific coast of South America for about 2,500 miles (4,000 km). The Inca capital was the city of Cuzco (KYOOS koh), located in the Andes Mountains of Peru. Find Cuzco on the map at right.

A well-organized empire. The Incas had a powerful, well-organized government. The Sapa Inca, or supreme ruler, lived in Cuzco. He had the power of life and death over his subjects. Priests and nobles helped the Sapa Inca rule.

The Incas built an excellent system of roads so that the army could move quickly to put down revolts. Inca engineers built log and stone bridges across rushing streams. In the steep mountain passes, they hung bridges made of ropes over deep gorges.

The Incas also set up a system for sending messages quickly across the empire. Every village had runners ready to carry news. A runner from Cuzco, for example, would carry a message to a village. From there, another runner would speed the news on its way.

Other achievements. In addition to building roads and bridges, Inca engineers made temples and forts out of huge stone blocks. Each block weighed hundreds of pounds. Workers moved the blocks up steep mountains without

that his feet would never touch the ground.

Religion. The Aztecs worshipped many gods. Their chief one was the sun god. Every day, they believed, the sun god fought its way across the heavens. They compared the sun's battles to their own wars.

Religion greatly affected daily life. Over 5,000 priests lived in Tenochtitlan. They directed religious ceremonies. Like the Maya priests, they studied the stars and planets and made accurate calendars.

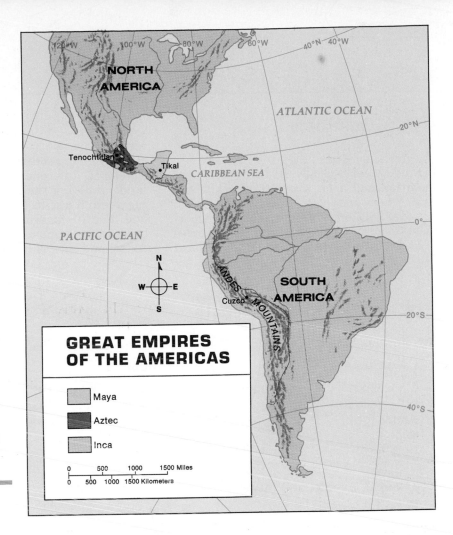

GREATEST EMPIRES OF THE AMERICAS

Maya

Aztec

Inca

| 0 | 500 | 1000 | 1500 Miles |
| 0 | 500 | 1000 | 1500 Kilometers |

MAP SKILL The Mayas, Aztecs, and Incas built empires in the Americas, as this map shows. Which of these three empires was the largest?

the help of animals or wheeled carts.* Each block was cut to fit in place exactly without cement. When earthquakes hit, the blocks slid apart gently but then slipped back together.

Inca farmers built terraces that looked like wide steps on the steep slopes. The terraces kept the rains from washing the soil and crops down the slopes of the Andes. The Incas made advances in medicine. They used quinine to treat malaria. They discovered

medicines that lessened pain and performed successful brain surgery.

In the 1520s, a civil war broke out in the Inca empire. The fighting weakened the Incas just when they were about to face a serious new threat—the arrival of explorers from Europe.

SECTION REVIEW

1. **Locate:** Central America, Mexico, Tikal, Tenochtitlan, Andes Mountains, Peru, Cuzco.

2. **Define:** pictograph.

3. What advances did the Mayas make?

4. Why did the Aztecs build floating gardens?

5. **What Do You Think?** Why do you think the Incas were able to control their huge empire?

---

*Horses once lived in the Americas, but they died out long before the first Americans arrived. Native Americans did not see horses until they were brought to the Americas by Europeans. Native Americans did put wheels on some toy carts but did not use wheels on full-sized carts.

Chapter 2 Review

★ Summary ★

Archaeologists study the evidence left behind by early people. By doing this, they have learned a lot about the lives of the first Americans.

Many different groups of Native Americans lived in North America. The peoples of each culture region adapted to the local climate and resources. Native Americans developed different ways of farming their lands, building their houses, and organizing their lives. In Mexico and in Central and South America, Native Americans built large empires, including the Maya, Aztec, and Inca empires.

★ Reviewing the Facts ★ *2 pts. each*

Key Terms. Match each term in Column 1 with the correct definition in Column 2.

Column 1
1. archaeologist
2. culture
3. pueblo
4. drought
5. pictograph

Column 2
a. way of life of a people
b. Spanish word for village
c. scientist who studies evidence of early people
d. picture that represents an object
e. long dry spell

Key People, Events, and Ideas. Identify each of the following.

1. Mound Builders
2. Anasazi
3. Native American
4. Eskimo
5. Pueblo
6. Navajo
7. Natchez
8. Iroquois
9. League of the Iroquois
10. Tenochtitlan

30

★ Chapter Checkup ★ *4 pts. each*

1. (a) Describe how archaeologists work to uncover the past. (b) What have archaeologists learned about the culture of the Mound Builders?
2. (a) Why are the Anasazis known as Cliff Dwellers? (b) Why did the Anasazis leave their homes in the late 1200s?
3. (a) List three Indian cultures of North America. (b) Describe how people in each of these cultures got their food.
4. Describe the kinds of work women did in different Indian groups.
5. How did each of the following peoples change the land on which they lived: (a) Mayas; (b) Aztecs; (c) Incas?
6. (a) Why did the Mayas develop an accurate calendar? (b) How did the Mayas record information?
7. (a) Describe three achievements of the Aztecs. (b) Why were many people unhappy with Aztec rule?
8. (a) How did the Incas send messages across their empire? (b) Why was the Inca empire weakened in the 1520s?

32

★ Thinking About History ★

10 pts. each

1. **Relating past to present.** How does the work of archaeologists help us learn more about the past?

2. **Understanding other cultures.** Reread "Shells as Money" on page 37. (a) Why could the Nootka harvest the shells? (b) What does this story tell you about the economy of the Northwest Coast?

3. **Understanding geography.** How did geography affect the ways of life of different Native American groups. Give at least three examples.

4. **Applying information.** What evidence shows that the Aztecs had an advanced empire?

★ Using Your Skills ★

extra credit

1. **Map reading.** Review the map-reading steps in Skill Lesson 1 (page 21). Then study the map on page 38. (a) What is the title of the map? (b) List three Native American groups that lived on the Great Plains. (c) Name one group that lived east of the Apaches. (d) Did the Chippewas live north or south of the Natchez?

2. **Making a generalization.** A *generalization* is a true statement based on facts. Before making a generalization, you need to gather facts. Review what you read about the way the peoples of the Northwest Coast lived. (a) List three facts about their way of life. (b) Make a generalization about their life based on the facts you listed.

3. **Comparing.** Compare the Mayas and the Incas. (a) How were they similar? (b) How were they different? (c) Why do you think these differences existed?

4. **Using a photograph as a primary source.** A photograph, as well as a painting, can be used as a primary source. Review Skill Lesson 2 (page 43). Study the photograph on page 33. (a) What does it show? (b) Why do you think the Incas built terraces on the side of the mountain?

★ More to Do ★

1. **Working with archaeologists.** As a group project, make a model of a campsite where early Native Americans lived. Then imagine that some archaeologists discover the site. How would the archaeologists describe and analyze what they find?

2. **Eyewitness reporting.** Imagine that you are a newspaper reporter visiting Tenochtitlan in 1450. Write an article describing life in the Aztec capital. Use information in this chapter as well as in encyclopedias and books.

3. **Researching a report.** Write a report on the everyday life of one of the Native American peoples you read about in this chapter. Include information about their homes, eating habits, customs, and government.

4. **Exploring local history.** List the names of parks, lakes, or streets in your local area that suggest a Native American influence. Then give a report about Native American peoples who lived or still live in your area.

CHAPTER

3

Europeans Explore America (1000–1650)

Chapter Outline

1 The Changing World of Europe
2 Search for New Routes to Asia
3 Exploring the New World
4 Early Claims to North America

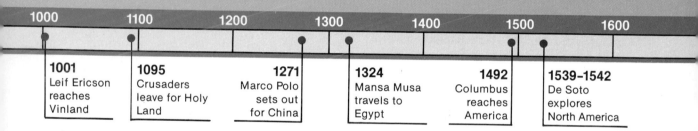

| 1000 | 1100 | 1200 | 1300 | 1400 | 1500 | 1600 |

1001
Leif Ericson reaches Vinland

1095
Crusaders leave for Holy Land

1271
Marco Polo sets out for China

1324
Mansa Musa travels to Egypt

1492
Columbus reaches America

1539–1542
De Soto explores North America

About This Chapter

In 1271, 17-year-old Marco Polo traveled east from Venice with his father and uncle. After a long and dangerous journey, the travelers finally reached Peking, China. Marco Polo spent 24 years in China. There, he became an official of the Chinese ruler, Kublai Khan.

When Marco Polo returned to Venice, he wrote a book about his travels. In it, he described the riches of China. He compared the splendid cities of China to the small cities of Europe. "I tell you truly," Polo wrote, "that more boats loaded with more . . . things and of greater value go and come" on one of China's rivers than on all the rivers of Europe. Most people who read Polo's book refused to

believe his stories. They called him the Prince of Liars. A few, however, were curious to know more about lands such as China.

At the time of Marco Polo's journey to China, Europe was changing. Eager to increase trade, merchants and rulers looked beyond Europe for new markets. In the 1400s and 1500s, European nations sent brave sailors out to explore every corner of the globe. During this age of exploration, Europeans came in contact with peoples of many different lands. And they soon claimed some of these lands as their own.

Study the time line above. Name two events that happened after Polo's visit to China.

When Marco Polo left Venice for China, his travels helped open new worlds to Europeans.

1 The Changing World of Europe

Read to Learn

★ What was life like in Europe during the Middle Ages?

★ Why did Europeans go on the Crusades?

★ What changes took place during the Renaissance?

★ What do these words mean: feudalism, manor, serf?

Until the late 1400s, Europeans knew nothing about the lands or peoples of the Americas. In fact, for hundreds of years most people in Europe lived and died without leaving their villages. Gradually, however, conditions changed. A new age dawned in which Europeans expanded their horizons and set off to explore new worlds.

Vikings Reach America

The first Europeans to reach North America were the Vikings. The *Vikings* were fierce, seagoing people from Scandinavia. They braved the stormy seas of the north to trade with and raid neighboring lands. Vikings settled Iceland. And from there, they explored farther west. See the map on page 51.

One Viking explorer was the red-haired, red-bearded Eric the Red. Eric explored a land west of Iceland, which he named Greenland. Actually, Greenland was a harsh land, much icier than Iceland. But Eric chose this pleasant-sounding name in order to attract farmers to settle there.

In 1001, Eric's son, Leif, decided to explore even farther to the west. He

The Vikings were great sailors. In small boats such as the ones shown here, they sailed the Atlantic as far as North America. Viking sailors used only the stars to steer their course at sea.

sailed into the sun until he reached a land where wheat and grapes grew wild. Large salmon swam up river. Leif Ericson named the place **Vinland,** or Wineland, because of the grapes. Vinland was in North America, but no one is sure where.*

For several years, Vikings sailed to Vinland. They brought sheep and cattle to their settlements. About 1013, the Vikings left Vinland. No one is sure why.

The Viking voyages to America remained unknown in the rest of Europe. What was happening in Eu-

*Archaeologists think Vinland was on the northernmost tip of Newfoundland. There, they have found the remains of Viking houses, tools, and weapons.

rope in the years after 1000? Why did no one hear about the Viking discovery? To answer these questions, you need to understand what life was like for most Europeans at the time.

Europe in the Middle Ages

The Viking voyages took place during the **Middle Ages,** the period from about 500 to 1350. During the early Middle Ages, Europe was divided into many small kingdoms. Life was hard, and most people worried only about surviving. Trade and travel was limited. Except for the Vikings, few people dared to sail far out into the oceans.

During the Middle Ages, kings divided up their lands among powerful nobles, called lords. Lords owed loyalty to their king. But they often acted on their own. The system of rule by lords who owe loyalty to their king is called **feudalism** (FYOOD′l ihz′m).

War was a way of life for many lords. They fought with each other for power and land. Thousands of peasants died in the constant fighting. Many starved when their crops and homes were destroyed.

Each lord had one or more manors. A **manor** included a village or several villages and the surrounding lands. Almost everyone lived on a manor. Most people were **serfs.** Serfs were peasants who had to stay on the manor where they were born.

A manor was self-sufficient. Serfs produced everything they needed. They planted and harvested crops. They raised sheep for wool, which was spun into cloth. And they made their own tools. From time to time, a peddler visited the manor, bringing goods and news from distant lands. In general, however, people knew little about life outside the manor.

Wider Horizons

By 1050, changes were taking place that made Europeans look beyond the narrow world of the manor. Peasants learned better ways of farming and grew more food. Warfare declined, and trade increased. Towns grew up along the trade routes. Unlike lords or peasants on manors, townspeople were very interested in trade and travel.

The Crusades. About this time, too, Christians set out on the Crusades. The *Crusades* were a series of wars aimed at conquering the Holy Land. The Holy Land referred to the places in the Middle East connected with the life of Jesus. For hundreds of years, the Holy Land was ruled by Arab Muslims. They allowed Christians to visit the Holy Land in peace. In the late 1000s, however, the Seljuk Turks conquered the Holy Land. Unlike the Arabs, the Seljuk Turks often attacked and killed Christian visitors to the Holy Land.

In the Middle Ages, all Christians in Western Europe belonged to the Catholic Church led by the Pope. They were not divided into many different churches as they are today. In 1095, the Pope called for a crusade to take the Holy Land from the Seljuk Turks. Thousands of Christians responded to the Pope's call. They sewed crosses to their clothes as badges of faith and set out for the Holy Land.

For 200 years, waves of Christian crusaders marched to the east. Many Christians and Muslims were slaughtered in the fighting.

Results of the Crusades. In the end, the Crusades failed to free the Holy Land from Muslim control. But they did help change Europe in several ways. First, shipbuilders of northern Italy and sailors learned a lot from

MAP SKILL In the late 1200s, Marco Polo traveled from Italy to China. He brought back stories of the riches of Asia. Later Europeans were eager to trade with Asia. They especially wanted spices from the East Indies. Where are the East Indies?

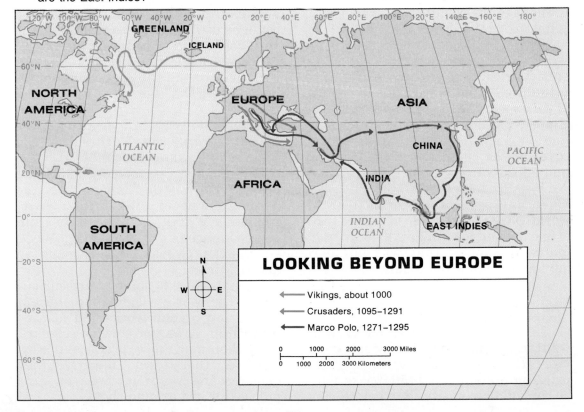

LOOKING BEYOND EUROPE

Vikings, about 1000
Crusaders, 1095–1291
Marco Polo, 1271–1295

In 1099, crusaders captured Jerusalem after fierce fighting. Christian knights killed all the defenders and massacred non-Christian families in the city. In this picture, knights fight their way into the city.

building and sailing the ships that took crusaders across the Mediterranean to the Holy Land.

Second, merchants increased their trade with the Middle East. Italian merchants controlled most of this trade. They bought the silks, spices, and cotton cloth that Arab traders brought to the Middle East from far-off Asia.

Third, crusaders returned home with tastes for foods of the Middle East such as rice, oranges, and dates. They introduced other Europeans to the use of spices such as ginger, cinnamon, and pepper. In the days before refrigerators, food spoiled easily. Spices helped cover up the bad flavor of spoiled meat and added variety to meals.

Finally, increased trade and travel made Europeans aware of more of the world. When Marco Polo of Venice traveled overland to China in the 1270s, he found an empire that was far more advanced than any in Europe.

The Renaissance

In the Middle Ages, books were written by hand, and few people could read. But with the invention of the printing press about 1450, books could be copied more easily than before. As a result, news and information spread more quickly.

The idea of a printing press grew slowly over hundreds of years. Building on earlier inventions, Johann Gutenberg (GOOT n berg) of Germany took the final step. He invented small pieces of metal engraved with letters of the alphabet. Because these pieces of type could be used and reused to form different words and sentences, they were called moveable type. In 1455, Gutenberg printed the Bible by using moveable type. The age of printing had begun.

The invention of the printing press helped spread the learning of the Renaissance (REHN uh sahns). *Renaissance* is a French word meaning rebirth. During the Renaissance, the period from about 1350 to 1600, Europeans made great advances. They uncovered much of the knowledge collected by the Greeks and Romans in ancient times.

Renaissance scholars were curious about the world. They read ancient Greek and Roman works and learned much from Arab and Jewish scholars. They then made new, practical discoveries of their own. Eagerly, they explored the world of ideas and the physical world around them.

Rise of Strong Nations

During the Renaissance, strong rulers gained control over feudal lords. They built the foundations of the nations we know today. In England and France, rulers increased their power when many feudal lords slaughtered each other in a long series of wars.

In Spain and Portugal, nation building was a long, slow process. During the Middle Ages, Arab Muslims conquered these lands. Christian knights fought for hundreds of years to drive out the Muslims. By 1249, Portugal had captured the last Muslim stronghold.

In Spain, knights slowly pushed the Muslims south. But the land remained divided among several rulers until the late 1400s. In 1469, Ferdinand, king of Aragon, and Isabella, queen of Castile, were married. Their marriage united much of Spain. The two rulers then joined forces against the Muslims.

European rulers were eager to increase their power through trade. Huge profits could be made trading silks from China and spices from the East Indies.* However, Arab and Italian merchants controlled the rich silk and spice trade because they controlled the trade routes across the Mediterranean. Other Europeans saw that they had only one choice—find another route to Asia.

---

*At the time, Europeans called the East Indies the Spice Islands, or simply the Indies.

■■ SECTION REVIEW ■■

1. **Locate:** Iceland, Greenland, Europe, Asia, China, East Indies.
2. **Define:** feudalism, manor, serf.
3. What lands did the Vikings explore?
4. Why was life difficult in the Middle Ages?
5. **What Do You Think?** Why do you think the Crusades have been called a "successful failure"?

2 Search for New Routes to Asia

Read to Learn

★ What new ways of sailing were developed?
★ How did the Portuguese reach India?
★ What did Columbus find on his voyages?
★ What do these words mean: navigation, caravel, magnetic compass, astrolabe, colony?

Portugal and Spain led the way in the search for a sea route to Asia. Both countries had similar goals. They wanted to find gold and increase trade. Each country, however, chose a different path. Portugal believed it could reach the East Indies by sailing south around the tip of Africa and then east to India. Spain hoped to reach the East Indies by sailing west across the Atlantic Ocean.

Portugal Leads the Way

Like other nations, Portugal was eager to expand its trade. But because its coast faced the Atlantic, it was cut off from the profitable Mediterranean trading routes. So in the early 1400s, the Portuguese began to explore the Atlantic coast of Africa.

Prince Henry. Prince Henry of Portugal knew the problems that faced sailors. He was determined to do what he could to improve *navigation,* or the practice of plotting a course at sea. Because of his efforts, he later became known as Prince Henry the Navigator.

In 1418, Prince Henry set up an informal school for sailors at Sagres (SAH grehz). From there, he sent ships to explore the coast of West Africa.

Sea voyages were difficult and dangerous. Captains knew how to sail with the wind but could not sail well against it. To solve this problem, the Portuguese designed better ships, called caravels (KAR uh vehls). A *caravel* had a rudder for steering and triangular sails. The rudder and triangular sails helped a caravel sail against the wind.

Another problem was getting lost at sea. Captains could steer only by the sun. Also, there were no good maps of the coast of Africa. To reduce the risk of getting lost at sea, Prince Henry invited mapmakers and astronomers to Sagres. They drew up new maps and charts based on information from sea captains.

New instruments. Two new instruments also helped sailors. One was the *magnetic compass,* a Chinese invention brought to Europe by the Arabs. The magnetic compass showed which

direction was north. With a compass, a captain could steer a straight course. The other instrument was the astrolabe (AS truh layb). The *astrolabe* was used to measure the positions of stars. With it, a sailor could figure out his latitude at sea.

By 1460, the year Prince Henry died, the Portuguese had explored a long stretch of the African coast. They brought back gold, ivory—and slaves. Before long, other nations joined Portugal in the African slave trade.

Gold Kingdoms of Africa

In the 1400s, Europeans knew little about Africa or the many peoples who lived on that large continent. A Spanish map showed an African ruler in the middle of the Sahara Desert. The caption read: "This Negro lord is called Musa Mali. So abundant is the gold in his country that he is the richest and most noble king in all the land."

In fact, Musa Mali's real name was Mansa Musa. He ruled Mali, a kingdom in West Africa. The kingdom of Mali flourished from about 1200 to 1400. In 1324, Mansa Musa traveled from Mali across North Africa to Egypt and the Middle East. He so dazzled the Egyptians with his great wealth that news of his visit reached Europe. Mali's wealth came from trade in gold and salt.

Mali was one of several kingdoms that rose in West Africa. (See the map on page 57.) After Mansa Musa's death, Mali declined. In the late 1400s, Songhai (SAWNG hī) became the most powerful kingdom in West Africa. Timbuktu, located on the Niger River, was a thriving center of trade and learning. The University of Sankore in Timbuktu produced many fine scholars.

Around Africa to India

To Europeans like Prince Henry, Africa meant gold. In fact, they named part of West Africa the *Gold Coast*. The

New instruments and accurate maps helped sailors in the 1400s. This picture shows a geographer at work.

African artists created fine works of art. This bronze sculpture of a woman was made in the African city-state of Benin. The Portuguese traded with Benin in the late 1400s.

heard about the voyage, he realized that Portugal had at last found a sea route to India. So he renamed the Cape of Storms the *Cape of Good Hope.*

In 1497, King John sent off four ships under the command of Vasco da Gama. His orders were to "make discoveries and go in search of spices." In May 1498, after sailing around Africa and across the Indian Ocean, da Gama reached India. (See the map on page 57.)

The Portuguese had achieved their goal. From India, they sailed on to the East Indies, the source of spices. And within a few years, they built a rich trading empire in Asia.

Spain Joins the Search

Like Portugal, Spain wanted a share of the spice trade. But Spain was busy fighting to expel the Arabs. In 1492, the last Arab stronghold fell to the armies of King Ferdinand and Queen Isabella. That same year, Isabella sent a daring sea captain on a voyage of discovery.

Christopher Columbus. The sea captain was an Italian named Christopher Columbus. Columbus grew up in Genoa, a busy seaport. As a young man, he sailed on several voyages in the Mediterranean. Later, on a voyage to England, his ship was attacked and sunk off the coast of Portugal. Columbus was wounded but was able to float to shore on an oar.

In Portugal, Columbus heard about the discoveries being made along the coast of Africa. He began studying Portuguese maps and charts. Slowly, he developed his own ideas about how to reach the Indies.

A plan for sailing west. Like all educated people of his day, Columbus knew the earth was round. He was convinced that he could reach Asia by sailing west. With favorable winds, he believed, a sailing ship could reach Asia within two months.

Portuguese built forts on the Gold Coast to protect their trade in gold, ivory, and slaves. Before long, they looked beyond Africa to India. They believed that by sailing around Africa, they would reach India and win a share of the silk and spice trade.

In 1488, Bartholomeu Dias (DEE uhsh) sailed around the southern tip of Africa. Dias called the tip the Cape of Storms because of its rough seas. He wanted to sail on to India, but his frightened crew forced him to return home. When King John of Portugal

To locate places exactly, mapmakers draw lines around the globe. Some lines run east and west. Other lines run north and south. Lines that run east and west are called **lines of latitude.** Each line is numbered in degrees (°). The line of latitude that runs east and west around the center of the earth is called the **Equator.** See the map at right.

Lines that run north and south are called **lines of longitude.** The line of longitude that runs north and south through Greenwich (GREHN ihch), England, is called the **Prime Meridian** (muh RIHD ee uhn).

1. **Locate lines of latitude.** Lines of latitude measure distances north or south of the Equator. The Equator is at 0° latitude. North of the Equator, lines of latitude are numbered from 1° to 90°N, where the North Pole is located. South of the Equator, they are numbered from 1° to 90°S, where the South Pole is located. (a) Which label on the map at right is closest to 20°N? (b) Is Lisbon closest to 20°S? 20°N? 40°N?

2. **Locate lines of longitude.** Lines of longitude measure distances east or west of the Prime Meridian. The Prime Meridian is at 0° longitude. Lines of longitude are numbered from 1° to 180° east or west longitude. (a) What continent or continents does 20°E cross? (b) At what longitude is Cape Bojador?

3. **Locate places using latitude and longitude.** To locate places, you need to combine latitude and longitude. For example, Sagres is located at about 38° north latitude and 8° west longitude (38°N/8°W). (a) What is the latitude and longitude of the Cape of Good Hope? (b) At what latitude and longitude did Vasco da Gama reach India? (c) Which explorer sailed past 20°S/20°W?

Columbus asked the king of Portugal for money and ships for the voyage. The king consulted his experts. They disagreed with Columbus about the length of the voyage, claiming that it would take at least four months. Besides, the Portuguese preferred to explore the route around Africa. So the king turned down his request.

Columbus moved to Spain and set his plan before Queen Isabella. She seemed interested, but it took six years of pleading before she finally agreed to provide ships for the voyage.

A voyage of discovery. On August 3, 1492, Columbus set sail. His crew included 90 sailors aboard 3 tiny ships. Columbus commanded the largest ship, the *Santa María.* The other ships were the *Niña* and *Pinta.*

At first, the ships had fair winds. They stopped for repairs in the Canary Islands off the coast of Africa. On September 6, Columbus set his course due west. For a month, the crew saw no land. They grew restless because in those days sailors were never out of sight of land for more than three weeks. Columbus held firm against threats of mutiny.

On October 7, sailors saw flocks of birds flying southwest. Columbus changed course to follow the birds. A few days later, crew members spotted branches floating in the water. A storm blew up, but on the night of October 11,

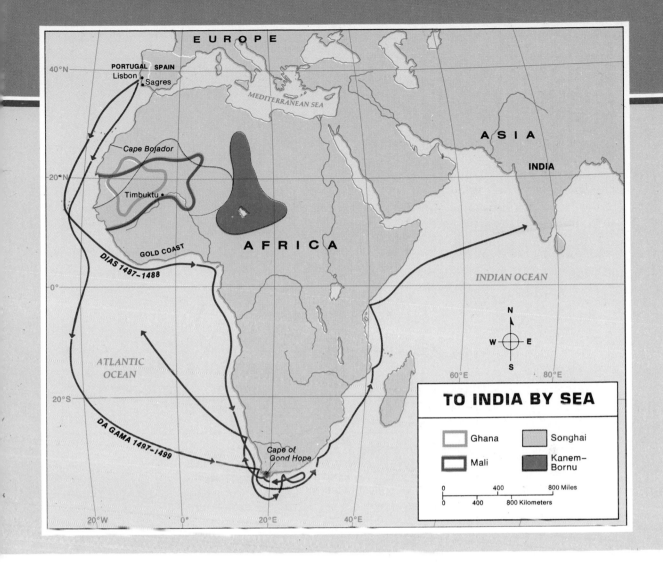

The New Land

Columbus felt sure he had reached the East Indies. So when the local people paddled their canoes out to his ships, he called them Indians. But the new land left Columbus puzzled. The islanders called themselves Arawaks and wore few clothes. Where were the silks, palaces, and cities of China?

When the local people brought Columbus gold ornaments, he concluded that China must be close. Columbus spent three months exploring nearby islands. He visited Hispaniola* and Cuba. Today, these and other islands in the Caribbean Sea are called the West Indies.

Later voyages. In January 1493, Columbus sailed for home. He received riches and honor from Queen Isabella, who named him Admiral of the Ocean Sea and Viceroy of the Indies. The Spanish ruler agreed to finance another voyage.

Columbus made three more voyages to the West Indies. On his second

the moon shone brightly. At 2:00 A.M. on October 12, Rodrigo Triana, the lookout on the *Pinta*, spotted cliffs in the moonlight. "Tierra! Tierra!" he shouted. "Land! Land!"

*Today, Haiti and the Dominican Republic are located on the island of Hispaniola.

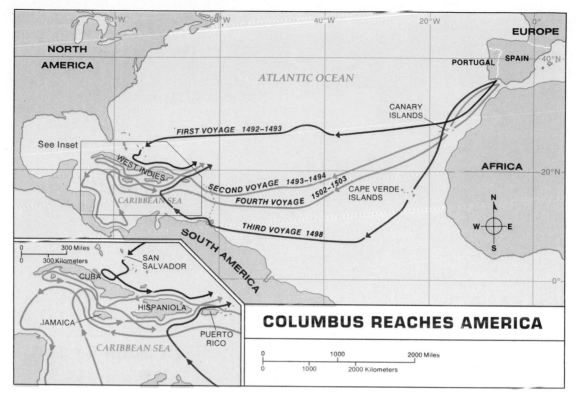

MAP SKILL Columbus made four voyages to the Americas, as this map shows. The weather on the first voyage was so fair that sailors worried that their good luck was too good. On which voyage did Columbus reach Puerto Rico? On which voyage did he sail farthest to the south?

trip, he discovered other islands, including Puerto Rico. He set up the first Spanish colony in the New World at Hispaniola. A *colony* is a group of people settled in a distant land who are ruled by the government of their native land.

Columbus had little success on his later voyages. He quarreled with the colonists and was called back to Spain in disgrace. When he died in 1506, he still believed that the land he had discovered was part of Asia.

Trouble in the conquered lands. The colonists soon grew discontent because they did not find enough gold to make them rich. They forced the Indians to work for them. When the Indians revolted, colonists killed or enslaved them.

The Indians resisted the Spanish in different ways. The Tainos of Puerto Rico grew angry with Spanish treatment. At first, they did not rebel because they believed that the Spanish were gods who could not be killed.

One old chief decided to test whether the Spanish were gods or mortals. A Spanish colonist ordered some Tainos to carry him across a river. Halfway across, the Tainos let the colonist fall into the water and kept him under for a few hours. For several days, they watched—praying forgiveness from their gods all the while—to see if he would come back to life. When he did not, they spread the news that the Spanish were not gods. A rebellion broke out against the Spanish in which thousands of Tainos were killed.

Christopher Columbus was showered with honors when he returned to Spain after his first voyage. Later, he lost the respect of Queen Isabella because he did not bring back riches from the Indies.

Naming the New World. Many explorers followed the route charted by Columbus. They soon realized that the new land was not Asia as Columbus had claimed. In 1499, an Italian merchant named Amerigo Vespucci (vehs PYOOT chee) sailed along the northern coast of South America. When he returned home, he wrote a letter describing "a New World . . . more densely peopled and full of animals than our Europe or Asia or Africa."

In 1507, a German mapmaker read this letter. On a map, he then labeled the new land America, after Amerigo. In this way, America was named after Amerigo Vespucci, not after Christopher Columbus.

═══ SECTION REVIEW ═══

1. **Locate:** Portugal, Spain, Sagres, Mali, Songhai, Timbuktu, Cape of Good Hope, Indian Ocean, India, West Indies, Hispaniola, Puerto Rico.
2. **Define:** navigation, caravel, magnetic compass, astrolabe, colony.
3. How did Prince Henry encourage exploration?
4. Why were Egyptians and Europeans so impressed with Mansa Musa?
5. **What Do You Think?** Why do you think Columbus risked great danger to sail across the Atlantic Ocean?

3 Exploring the New World

Read to Learn

★ How did Spain and Portugal divide up the world?
★ What areas did Balboa and Magellan explore?
★ How did Spain win an empire in the New World?
★ What does this word mean: conquistador?

After 1492, many explorers crossed the Atlantic. They risked great dangers in their search for a way to the rich empires of Asia. The explorers did not reach China or India. But they did discover that the New World had its own rich empires. In the 1500s, Spain won an empire in the Americas that made it the richest nation in Europe.

Dividing Up the World

When the news of Columbus' first voyage reached King John of Portugal, he refused to recognize Spanish claims to the new lands. He said that Columbus had simply found a few islands in the Atlantic Ocean that already belonged to Portugal. To prevent war between Spain and Portugal, the Pope offered to settle the dispute. In 1494, he had them sign the Treaty of Tordesillas. The treaty drew a *Line of Demarcation* (dee mahr KAY shuhn) that divided up the world. (See the map on page 61.)

The treaty gave Spain the right to colonize and trade with the lands west of the line. Spain, therefore, claimed North and South America. The treaty gave Portugal the right to colonize and trade with the lands east of the line. Portugal, therefore, controlled trade with China and the East Indies. The treaty, of course, ignored the interests or wishes of the peoples living in these lands.

Almost by chance, Portugal gained a foothold in South America. In 1500, Pedro Álvares Cabral (kuh BRAHL) set sail for India around Africa. Strong winds blew his ship far off course, and he landed on the coast of Brazil. Cabral realized that this part of South America was east of the Line of Demarcation. So he claimed the land for Portugal.

Balboa Sees the Pacific

In the early 1500s, Spanish sailors explored the coasts of North and South America, looking for a western route to Asia. Once they realized that these large continents blocked the way, they searched for a route across or around the Americas.

In 1513, Vasco Núñez de Balboa (bal BOH uh) decided to find such a route. Balboa heard from the people of Panama that a large body of water lay to the west. So he set out with 190 men to cross the Isthmus of Panama.

The isthmus was only 45 miles (72 km) wide, but it was covered by a thick, steaming jungle. The explorers hacked a trail through the jungle and waded across swamps filled with mosquitoes. Finally, Balboa climbed a mountain and looked out on a huge ocean. The next day, sword in hand, he waded into the water and claimed the ocean for Spain. He called it the South Sea because he thought it was south of Asia. In fact, he was looking out on the Pacific Ocean.

A Voyage Around the World

When Balboa saw the Pacific, he thought that the East Indies were nearby. He had no idea how wide the ocean was. Before long, however, Ferdinand Magellan (muh JEHL uhn) discovered the true size of the Pacific.

Magellan was a Portuguese sea captain who made several voyages around Africa to India and the East Indies. He believed that he could find a shorter route to Asia by sailing around South America.

Departure. In August 1519, an eager and hopeful Magellan sailed out of Seville harbor in Spain. He was in command of 5 ships and 268 men. When the fleet reached Brazil, problems arose. One ship was destroyed in a storm. The other ships tried to sail around Cape Horn, the tip of South America. But fierce storms drove them back.

For five long months, Magellan waited for better weather. The frightened officers tried to force him to return home. But he boldly crushed the mutiny, leaving the ringleaders to die on the bleak South American coast. Finally, Magellan discovered a passage around Cape Horn. The passage is now called the Strait of Magellan. In November 1520, Magellan led his three remaining ships into the large ocean Balboa had seen earlier. Magellan called it the Pacific Ocean because it was so peaceful compared to the stormy Atlantic.

Crossing the Pacific. The Pacific posed new problems because it was so huge. "We remained 3 months and 20 days," wrote one sailor, "without taking on any food or refreshment. We ate only old biscuit reduced to powder and full of grubs . . . and we drank water that was yellow and stinking." Sailors caught rats to eat. When there were no more rats, they ate sawdust and leather so tough that they had to soak it for days before it was soft enough to chew.

Magellan finally reached the Philippine Islands. (Find Magellan's route on the map below.) There, he was killed in a battle with the local people. Magellan's crew sailed on. In 1522, one ship and 18 sailors reached Spain. These survivors were the first Europeans to circle the globe. Magellan's voyage proved that ships could reach Asia by sailing west.

Spain Wins an Empire

In 1519, the year Magellan set out from Spain, Hernando Cortés (kawr TEHZ), a Spanish adventurer, landed on the coast of Mexico. Cortés had heard

MAP SKILL In the 1400s and 1500s, European sailors explored the oceans of the world. They wanted to find an easy sea route to Asia. Follow the route Magellan pioneered on his voyage of discovery. At what latitude did he cross the Line of Demarcation?

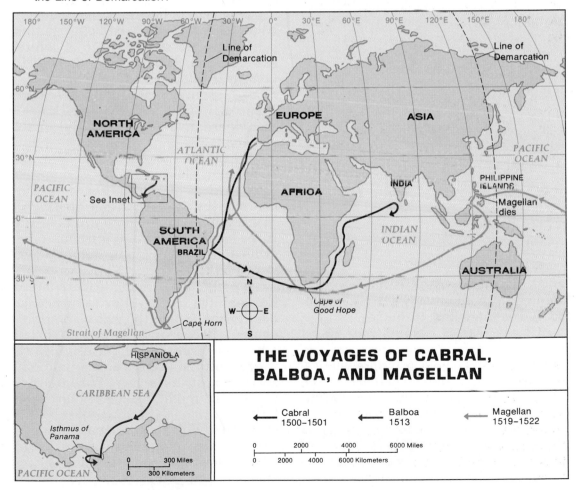

THE VOYAGES OF CABRAL, BALBOA, AND MAGELLAN

Doña Marina

A Native American woman known to the Spanish as Doña Marina helped Cortés in his victory over the Aztecs. Although she was of royal birth, Doña Marina was given as a slave to Cortés. She learned Spanish quickly and became an interpreter for Cortés. When Doña Marina heard of a plot by Montezuma to kill the Spanish, she told Cortés, saving him from death.

set up outposts in the Americas. In exchange, the conquistadors agreed to give Spain one fifth of any gold or treasure they captured.

Cortés takes Tenochtitlan. Soon after Cortés reached shore, messengers carried word of his landing to Montezuma (mahn tuh ZYOO muh), the Aztec emperor. They reported that fair-skinned strangers had come from the east. The strangers, they said, had come across the sea. The fair-skinned men wore metal armor and had powerful weapons that made loud noises and shattered trees into splinters. (The weapons were cannons.) The messengers also reported that the Spanish had "deer that carry them on their backs wherever they wish to go." (The "deer" were horses, which the Aztecs had never seen before.)

Montezuma hesitated, not knowing what to do. The Aztecs believed that they were descended from a white-skinned god, Quetzalcoatl (keht sahl koh AH tuhl). The god was expected to return to their land from the east. What if Cortés and his fair-skinned men were messengers of the Aztec god?

When the newcomers neared Tenochtitlan, Montezuma decided to welcome them as his guests. For more than six months, Cortés negotiated with Montezuma. But he actually held the Aztec leader almost as a prisoner in his own capital. Still, Montezuma refused to call out his army.

Finally, other Aztec leaders forced Cortés out of the city. Cortés turned for help to the people the Aztecs had conquered. Because these people hated Aztec rule, they joined Cortés. In 1521, they captured Tenochtitlan and destroyed most of the city. Within a few years, the mighty Aztec empire had fallen.

Pizarro defeats the Incas. Rumors of other rich empires attracted more conquistadors to the Americas. Fran-

about the mighty Aztec empire. Now he wanted to conquer it. His army included 400 soldiers and 16 horses.

Cortés was a *conquistador* (kohn KEES tah dohr), or conqueror. The conquistadors were bold warriors, successors to the knights who had driven the Muslims out of Spain. One knight summed up the motives of the conquistadors. "We came here to serve God and the king and also to get rich." Spanish rulers gave conquistadors the right to

cisco Pizarro (pee ZAHR oh) heard about the Inca empire when he marched with Balboa across Panama. After several unsuccessful attempts, Pizarro reached Cuzco, the Inca capital, in 1532.

Pizarro found the Incas divided by civil war. He launched a surprise attack and killed the Inca ruler, Atahualpa (ah tah WAHL pah). By 1535, Pizarro had taken control of much of the Inca empire.

Reasons for success. Why were Cortés and Pizarro able to conquer two powerful empires with only a handful of soldiers? First, the Spanish had better weapons. They used guns and cannons against the Indians' bows, arrows, and spears. Second, the Aztecs and Incas had never seen horses and were frightened by the mounted Spanish knights. Third, Native Americans like the Aztecs and Incas at first thought the Spanish were gods.

Finally, diseases such as chicken pox, measles, and influenza helped the Spanish. The Aztecs and Incas had no resistance to these European diseases. They caught the diseases from the Spanish and died by the thousands. Many Aztec warriors caught smallpox and dropped dead in battle. The Spanish claimed that the hand of God was striking the Aztecs down.

Aztec and Inca treasures made the conquistadors rich. Spain grew rich, too, especially after gold and silver mines were discovered in Mexico and Peru.

Spain Looks North

While Cortés and Pizarro were winning riches in Central and South America, other conquistadors explored North America. One was Juan Ponce de León (PAWN say day lay AWN). Ponce de León explored an island Columbus had visited. When Ponce de León saw a beautiful bay in the north, he called it Puerto Rico, or rich port. Later, he put down

A Spanish priest copied this picture from an Aztec painting. It shows how the Aztecs saw the Spanish. The Aztecs were awed by Spanish horsemen. Some thought that a man on horseback was a new kind of animal—half man, half beast.

the Taino rebellion on Puerto Rico and became the island's first governor.

In 1513, Ponce de León explored Florida, hoping to find the Fountain of Youth. This magical fountain, he had heard, would make anyone who bathed in it young forever. He found no fountain or rich kingdoms. But he did take many Indian slaves from Florida to Puerto Rico to replace those who had died or been killed by the Spanish.

Two other conquistadors, Francisco Coronado (koh roh NAH doh) and Hernando De Soto, heard stories of the Seven Cities of Gold. The streets of these cities were said to be paved with gold. Coronado's search led him into New Mexico. In 1540, after great hardships, he found villages of the Zuñis, but no

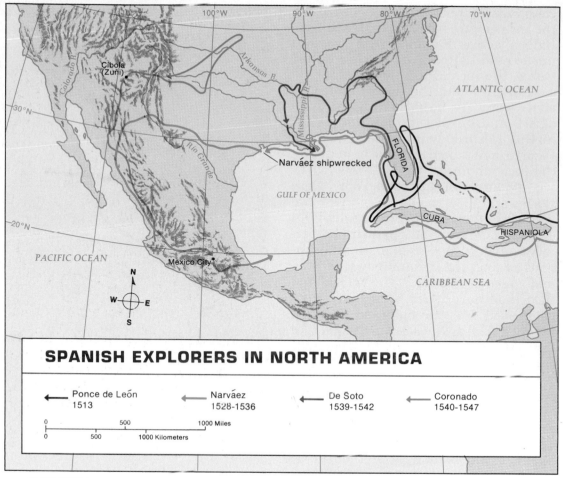

SPANISH EXPLORERS IN NORTH AMERICA

← Ponce de León 1513
← Narváez 1528-1536
← De Soto 1539-1542
← Coronado 1540-1547

| 0 | 500 | 1000 Miles |
| 0 | 500 | 1000 Kilometers |

MAP SKILL Conquistadors explored parts of North America in the 1500s. They did not find the Seven Cities of Gold as they hoped. But they mapped routes that Spanish missionaries and settlers followed. Which explorer was the first to visit Florida?

gold. From 1539 to 1542, De Soto explored the southeast of the present-day United States. But he died without finding gold. Follow the routes taken by Ponce de León, Coronado, and De Soto on the map above.

At first, the conquistadors were welcomed by the local Indians they met. But when the Spanish started to kill, rob, and enslave the Indians, the Indians fought back. This fierce Indian resistance forced Spain to back off from North America. Instead, Spain concentrated on its empire in the south. Before long, other nations began to claim lands in North America.

SECTION REVIEW

1. **Locate:** Line of Demarcation, Brazil, Isthmus of Panama, Cape Horn, Pacific Ocean, Philippine Islands, Puerto Rico, Florida.

2. **Define:** conquistador.

3. What nations signed the Treaty of Tordesillas?

4. Why did conquistadors go to the Americas?

5. How did disease help the Spanish defeat the Aztecs?

6. **What Do You Think?** How do you think Magellan's voyage affected the way Europeans saw the world?

Among the conquistadors was an African called Estevanico (ehs tay vahn EE koh). He was brought as a slave from Morocco to the New World. In 1528, he sailed to Florida with 300 Spanish soldiers and their servants. Under their leader, Pánfilo de Narváez (nahr VAH ehs), the group hoped to find the Seven Cities of Gold.

Disaster struck early. Almost everyone, including Narváez, was killed in battle with Indians, died of disease, or drowned crossing the Gulf of Mexico. Only Estevanico and three other men survived. For eight years, they wandered through Texas, Arizona, and New Mexico, hunting for the cities of gold.

Estevanico learned Native American languages, so he was able to lead the others in their search. Several times, the four men were taken as slaves by Native Americans. Estevanico helped his companions to escape or win freedom.

The four survivors finally reached Spanish settlements in western Mexico.

In 1539, Estevanico again set out to hunt for the cities of gold. He reached the edges of a Zuñi pueblo that shimmered like gold in the sun. But he was killed in battle before he learned whether the city was full of riches.

★ Find the areas Estevanico explored on the map on page 64.

4 Early Claims to North America

Read to Learn
★ What explorers searched for a northwest passage?
★ How did the Protestant Reformation affect Europeans?
★ Why were Spain and England rivals?
★ What do these words mean: northwest passage?

When other European nations saw the rich empire Spain was winning in the New World, they, too, wanted a share. Soon, England, France, and the Netherlands outfitted their own voyages of discovery.

Search for a Northwest Passage

To the nations of Europe, spices from Asia were still more valuable than land in the New World. But what was the quickest route to Asia? Magellan's passage around South America was too long and dangerous. So English, French, and Dutch explorers looked for a *northwest passage,* or a waterway through or around North America.

John Cabot. In 1497, five years after Columbus' first voyage, King Henry VII of England sent John Cabot on a voyage of discovery. Cabot was sure he could find a shorter route across the Atlantic by sailing farther north. He left Bristol, England, on May 2, 1497. On June 24, he reached land, probably an island off Nova Scotia. Like Columbus, he thought that he had reached Asia. He claimed the land for England. On a second voyage, Cabot explored the eastern coast of North America, still thinking he was exploring Asia.

French explorers. In 1524, France sent an Italian sailor, Giovanni da Verrazano (vehr rah TSAH noh), on a voyage of discovery. Verrazano searched the coast of North America for a northwest passage. He probably sailed into New York harbor, where a bridge named after him stands today.

France outfitted several more voyages. In the 1530s, Jacques Cartier (kahr tee YAY) sailed past Newfoundland and found the broad opening where the St. Lawrence River flows into the Atlantic. (See the map below.) The opening looked to him like a passage that might lead to China.

Cartier sailed up the St. Lawrence and met a group of Iroquois. They told him about the kingdom of Saguenay (sag uh NAY). The Saguenay, they said,

MAP SKILL The search for a northwest passage sent explorers from many nations across the Atlantic. Find the route Hudson took in 1610. What nation sent Hudson on that voyage? What body of water did he explore in 1610?

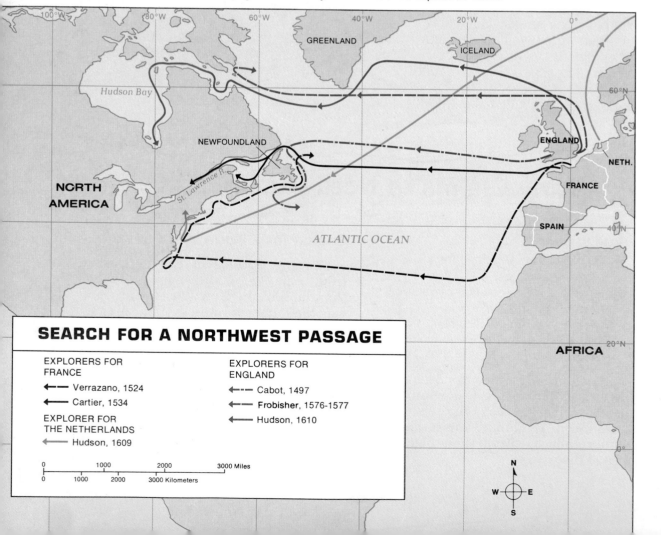

SEARCH FOR A NORTHWEST PASSAGE

EXPLORERS FOR FRANCE
←— Verrazano, 1524
←— Cartier, 1534

EXPLORER FOR THE NETHERLANDS
←— Hudson, 1609

EXPLORERS FOR ENGLAND
←-— Cabot, 1497
←— Frobisher, 1576-1577
←— Hudson, 1610

0   1000   2000   3000 Miles
0 1000 2000 3000 Kilometers

Native Americans sometimes tried to stop European explorers from invading their lands. Here, Martin Frobisher and his sailors battle with Eskimos.

had rich gold and silver mines. Some of the people, they added, hopped around on one leg or flew like bats.

Cartier believed these fabulous stories. In 1541, he left home again to hunt for the Saguenay. As he sailed up the St. Lawrence River, he kept getting reports that the Saguenay were just a bit farther away. In the end, Cartier returned to France without finding the Saguenay or a northwest passage. He did, however, claim many lands for France. Also, he helped build the first French settlements in Canada.

Frobisher and Hudson. Two English explorers, Martin Frobisher and Henry Hudson, also searched for a northwest passage. Between 1576 and 1578, Frobisher made three voyages to North America. Although he failed in his main purpose, Frobisher explored parts of northern Canada. Before returning home on one trip, he filled his ship with tons of sparkling ore that he thought was gold ore. The ore proved to be iron pyrite, or fool's gold, which had no value.

Henry Hudson made two trips to North America for England, exploring regions in the far north. Then, in 1609, he agreed to explore for the Dutch. In a small ship, the *Half Moon*, Hudson discovered a wide bay. He hoped that it was a northwest passage. But it turned out to be the river that now bears his name. Hudson sailed up the river about 150 miles (240 km) to where Albany, New York, stands today.

On Hudson's fourth voyage, he sailed again for England. He explored

Hudson Bay, which was named after him. On the way home, Hudson's crew rebelled. They put Hudson, his son, and seven loyal sailors into a small boat and set it adrift. The small boat and its crew were never seen again.

Explorers kept looking for a northwest passage in the 1700s and 1800s. A route to the Pacific Ocean across the top of North America does exist. But it is blocked with ice for most of the year. The first successful trip through this passage was finally made in 1906.

Rivalries Among European Nations

During the 1500s and 1600s, European nations fought many wars over religion. Until the 1500s, the Catholic Church was the only church in Western Europe. But in 1517, a German monk named Martin Luther called for reforms in the Catholic Church. His call split the Church.

Luther's followers became known as Protestants because of their protests against the Catholic Church. The movement to reform the Church was called the *Protestant Reformation.* In the 1500s, many different Protestant churches were formed. Believers took their faith so seriously that Catholics and Protestants tortured and killed each other in many wars. These religious wars became mixed up with political wars—wars fought for power and territory. When European nations expanded overseas, their wars were carried to these new lands, too.

Spain and England. In the late 1500s, Spain was the most powerful Catholic nation in Europe. The Spanish king, Philip II, wanted to force Protestants to return to the Catholic Church. He faced fierce opposition, however.

England was the strongest Protestant nation. But it was not nearly as powerful as Spain. The queen of England, Elizabeth I, was head of the Church of England. She feared the power of Catholic Spain and was determined to prevent Philip from conquering England.

English Sea Dogs. Elizabeth knew England was no match for Spain. Yet she allowed daring English sailors to attack Spanish treasure fleets and to raid Spanish colonies in the New World. These adventurers were known in England as Sea Dogs—though the Spanish called them pirates!

Like the conquistadors, the English Sea Dogs wanted to win fame and fortune for themselves. But they also fought for their country against Spain. One Sea Dog, Sir Humphrey Gilbert, joined the search for a northwest passage. Gilbert planned to set up a colony in North America to use as a base for his search and for raids on Spanish treasure ships. He wrote a book for Queen Elizabeth called *How Her Majesty May Annoy the King of Spain.*

Sir Francis Drake. Perhaps the boldest Sea Dog was Sir Francis Drake. In 1577, Drake took Magellan's route around Cape Horn. He attacked Spanish settlements in Peru. At one port, Drake's crew grabbed up treasure while Drake forced helpless Spanish officials to dine with him on board his ship, the *Golden Hind.* During the meal, crew members played violins. Drake explored farther up the Pacific coast before sailing west across the Pacific Ocean.

In 1580, Drake returned to England after circling the globe. He received a hero's welcome, especially since the *Golden Hind* was filled with Spanish gold. Queen Elizabeth visited Drake on board his ship. There, she knighted him—Sir Francis Drake—as a reward for his services. King Philip of Spain was furious when he heard this. He demanded that Elizabeth return the stolen Spanish treasure. When Elizabeth refused, Philip prepared for war.

Queen Elizabeth I knighted Drake on board the *Golden Hind*. Drake won his greatest prize when he captured the Spanish ship *Glory of the South Sea*. It carried many chests of gold, silver, and jewels.

The Spanish Armada. In 1588, Spain sent a huge fleet, called the **Spanish Armada,** against England. The English were greatly outnumbered, but their ships were faster than the heavy Spanish galleons. During the battle, a violent storm blew up, scattering the Spanish Armada.

The defeat of the Spanish Armada did not mean the end of Spanish power. Spain continued to profit from its colonies in the New World. However, in the years after 1588, England, France, and other nations began setting up their own colonies in the Americas.

SECTION REVIEW

1. **Locate:** Newfoundland, St. Lawrence River, Hudson Bay.
2. **Define:** northwest passage.
3. What dangers did explorers face in looking for a northwest passage?
4. Why were Martin Luther's followers called Protestants?
5. (a) How did the English Sea Dogs anger Spain? (b) Why did Queen Elizabeth knight Drake?
6. **What Do You Think?** Why do you think finding a northwest passage was so important?

Chapter 3 Review

★ Summary ★

About the year 1000, the Vikings reached North America. But news of their voyages did not spread to other parts of Europe during the Middle Ages. In the Renaissance, however, European nations began to look overseas. Portugal led the way in looking for a sea route to India.

Christopher Columbus reached the West Indies in 1492. He claimed the land for Spain. In the 1500s, the conquistadors helped Spain win a huge empire in the Americas.

Sailors from many nations explored the oceans of the world in the 1500s and 1600s. Magellan found a route around South America to the Pacific. Other explorers hunted for a northwest passage to the Pacific and Asia.

★ Reviewing the Facts ★ *3 pts. each*

Key Terms. Match each term in Column 1 with the correct definition in Column 2.

Column 1	Column 2
1. feudalism	**a.** instrument used to measure the positions of stars
2. caravel	**b.** system of rule by lords who owe loyalty to their king
3. astrolabe	**c.** group of people settled in a distant land who are ruled by the government of their native land
4. colony	**d.** conqueror
5. conquistador	**e.** ship with a rudder and triangular sails

Key People, Events, and Ideas. Identify each of the following.

1. Leif Ericson
2. Crusades
3. Renaissance
4. Prince Henry
5. Vasco da Gama
6. Queen Isabella
7. Ferdinand Magellan
8. Hernando Cortés
9. Francisco Pizarro
10. Francisco Coronado
11. Jacques Cartier
12. Henry Hudson
13. Protestant Reformation
14. Queen Elizabeth I
15. Sir Francis Drake

★ Chapter Checkup ★ *5 points each*

1. (a) Describe life on a manor during the Middle Ages. (b) What changes were taking place by 1050?
2. (a) Why did the Pope call for a crusade? (b) List three results of the Crusades.
3. What improvements were made in sailing in the 1400s?
4. (a) Why did the king of Portugal refuse to help Columbus? (b) What ruler supported Columbus? (c) Why did Columbus' crew rebel during his first voyage?
5. (a) What body of water did Balboa find? (b) Why did he call it the South Sea?
6. Why did Montezuma hesitate to fight the Spanish?
7. Give three reasons why the Spanish were able to conquer the Aztecs and Incas.
8. (a) List three sailors who explored the coasts of North America. (b) What did Cartier hope to find on his voyage up the St. Lawrence?

1. **Relating past to present.** (a) What two nations divided up the world in 1494? (b) What two nations today are competing for influence around the world? (c) Compare these situations.

2. **Analyzing a quotation.** Columbus told his crew: "It is useless to complain, since I have come to find the [East] Indies and so will continue until I find them." How might these words have affected the crew?

3. **Expressing an opinion.** Review the story of Doña Marina on page 62. Do you think Doña Marina was a traitor to her people or a hero? Explain your opinion.

4. **Applying information.** (a) What motives led Portugal and Spain to explore the oceans of the world? (b) How did these motives affect their treatment of the peoples they met?

★ **Using Your Skills** ★

1. **Map reading.** Review the map-reading steps in Skill Lesson 3 (page 56). Then study the map on page 66. (a) At about what latitude did Cabot cross the Atlantic? (b) Who explored farthest south in North America? (c) What is the latitude and longitude of the southernmost point this explorer reached?

2. **Placing events in time.** The time lines at the beginning of each chapter show when important events took place. Study the time line on page 48. (a) When did Leif Ericson reach Vinland? (b) In what year did Marco Polo leave for China? (c) Which of these events took place first?

3. **Ranking.** Review the explorers mentioned in this chapter. Then choose five explorers and rank them according to whose voyages you think had the most important results. Explain your ranking.

4. **Using a painting as a primary source.** Review the steps for using a painting as a primary source in Skill Lesson 2 (page 43). Then study the painting on page 63. (a) What is the subject of the painting? (b) How does the artist show the Spanish? (c) What do you think the artist thought of the Spanish? Explain your answer.

5. **Making a review chart.** Make a large chart with four headings across the top: Explorer, Date(s) of Voyage(s), For What Country, Results of Voyage(s). Fill in the chart for all explorers mentioned in this chapter. Use other books, if necessary, to complete the chart.

★ **More to Do** ★

1. **Preparing a newspaper advertisement.** Prepare a newspaper advertisement that Magellan could have used to get sailors to join his voyage of discovery.

2. **Writing a dialogue.** Write a dialogue that might have taken place between Montezuma and Cortés when they first met.

3. **Drawing a cartoon.** Draw a cartoon showing what Native Americans might have thought of the first Europeans they saw.

4. **Exploring local history.** Find out if Europeans explored your local area. Then prepare a map showing the route they took during their exploration.

Unit 1 Review

★ Unit Summary ★

Chapter 1 The first Americans probably crossed a land bridge from Asia to North America about 70,000 years ago. They found many different physical regions and climates in the Americas. People who settled the land learned to adapt to the geography of each region.

Chapter 2 Archaeologists have studied the cultures of the first Americans. Native American groups settled in different parts of North America. Each people had its own culture. The Mayas, Aztecs, and Incas built empires in the Americas.

Chapter 3 During the Renaissance, Europeans explored the oceans of the world. Sailors like Columbus and Magellan charted new routes across the oceans. Other explorers claimed large parts of the Americas for Portugal, Spain, France, and England.

★ Unit Checkup ★

Choose the word or phrase that best completes each of the following statements.

1. During the last ice age, much of North America was covered by
   (a) glaciers.
   (b) plateaus.
   (c) tributaries.

2. The climate of the Southeast is
   (a) desert.
   (b) steppe.
   (c) humid subtropical.

3. Archaeologists study
   (a) weather and climate.
   (b) natural resources.
   (c) evidence of early people.

4. The Navajos lived in the
   (a) Pacific Northwest.
   (b) Eastern Woodlands.
   (c) Southwest.

5. The Aztecs built their capital city at
   (a) Tikal.
   (b) Cuzco.
   (c) Tenochtitlan.

★ Building American Citizenship ★

1. Over the years, Americans have benefited from the rich resources of the land. Today, many private citizens as well as the United States government are concerned about protecting the American land. How are people trying to protect the land and its resources?

2. Millions of Native Americans lived in North and South America before 1492. As you learned, they developed many different cultures. Today, Native Americans are proud of their traditions and cultures. Choose one Native American group you read about in this unit. Find out more about the group's history and culture. Then describe how the traditions of the group have survived.

3. During the Renaissance, explorers sailed into unmapped waters. Today, American space explorers are making voyages into new regions. What qualities did Renaissance explorers have that space explorers of today have?

The picture at right was drawn by an Aztec artist in the 1500s. It shows the effects of smallpox on the Aztecs. Study the picture. Then answer the following questions.

1. How does the artist show the effects of smallpox?

2. What do you think the picture in the top part of the drawing represents?

3. Why do you think the artist made the drawing?

4. What does the drawing tell you about the Aztecs?

5. What title would you give this Aztec drawing?

History Writer's Handbook

Analyzing a Question Before Writing

Before writing an answer to a question, study the question. Look for the key word and other clues in the question that will help you prepare a good answer.

The *key word* in a question tells you what to do with the topic. Often the key word is an instruction word. Some common instruction words and their meanings are listed below.

Explain: tell how or why
Compare: give similarities and differences
Describe: give details or features
Summarize: tell important ideas in as few words as possible

Sometimes the key word is a question word. Some common question words and their meanings are listed below.

Why: give reasons
How: tell in what way or by what means
What: give specific examples

Other clues in a question are words or phrases that limit the topic. A clue might tell you to limit the topic to a certain person, event, geographic area, or time period. Or it might tell you the number of examples or ideas you need to include.

Practice Analyze the following question: *How did the geography of the Far North affect the way of life of Eskimos?*

1. What is the key word in the question?

2. What does the key word tell you to do?

3. What clue tells you to limit the topic to a geographic area?

4. What does the clue *of Eskimos* tell you?

Unit 2

SETTLING THE NEW WORLD

1520		1560		1600		1640

1521 Cortés conquers Aztecs
1532 Pizarro defeats Incas
1535 Government of New Spain set up in the Americas
1544 Laws passed to protect Indians in New Spain

1565 St. Augustine, Florida, settled
1587 John White sets up colony at Roanoke

1607 Jamestown settled by English
1608 Quebec settled by French
1619 First Africans brought to Jamestown
1620 Pilgrims settle Plymouth Colony
1626 New Netherland settled by Dutch

1520		1560		1600		1640

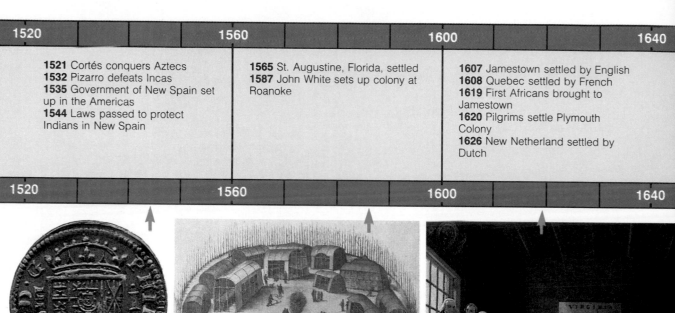

Mid-1500s The Spanish made coins from the gold of the New World.

Late 1580s The English artist John White painted this Algonquin village.

1619 The first House of Burgesses was set up in Virginia.

UNIT OUTLINE

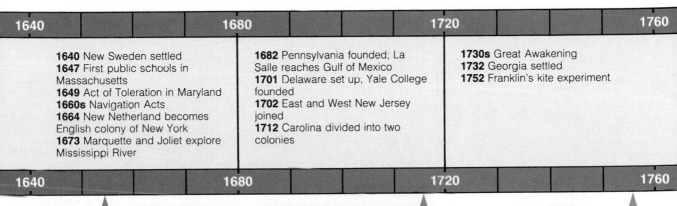

1640	1680	1720	1760

1640 New Sweden settled
1647 First public schools in Massachusetts
1649 Act of Toleration in Maryland
1660s Navigation Acts
1664 New Netherland becomes English colony of New York
1673 Marquette and Joliet explore Mississippi River

1682 Pennsylvania founded; La Salle reaches Gulf of Mexico
1701 Delaware set up, Yale College founded
1702 East and West New Jersey joined
1712 Carolina divided into two colonies

1730s Great Awakening
1732 Georgia settled
1752 Franklin's kite experiment

1640	1680	1720	1760

1600s and 1700s French fur traders explored much of North America.

1700s Prudence Punderson embroiders at home.

1700s Colonists developed their own industries, such as glassmaking and forging iron.

CHAPTER
4
Planting Colonies (1530–1690)

Chapter Outline

1 Spain Builds a Large Empire
2 French and Dutch Colonies
3 English Settlers in Virginia
4 The Pilgrims at Plymouth

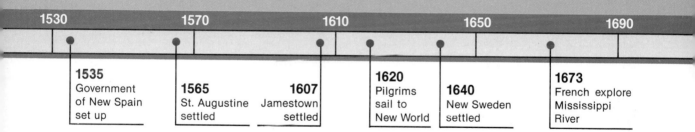

1530   1570   1610   1650   1690

1535 Government of New Spain set up

1565 St. Augustine settled

1607 Jamestown settled

1620 Pilgrims sail to New World

1640 New Sweden settled

1673 French explore Mississippi River

About This Chapter

In 1584, Richard Hakluyt wrote a pamphlet urging Queen Elizabeth I of England to plant colonies in America. He argued that "if England possesses these places in America, Her Majesty will have good harbors, plenty of excellent trees for masts, good timber to build ships . . . all things needed for a royal navy, and all for no price."

Further, he argued that the English would be able to trade with Native Americans, exchanging "cheap English goods for things of great value that are not thought to be worth much by the natives of America." This trade, he said, would make England very rich. The Queen was not convinced by Hakluyt's arguments. But England's rival, Spain, was already setting up colonies in America.

In the 1500s and 1600s, Spain, France, the Netherlands, and Sweden planted colonies in the New World. Despite a slow start, England, too, set up its own colonies.

Early colonists faced terrible hardships. The long journey across the Atlantic used up their food supplies and left many weak and ill. In the New World, settlers had to build homes, grow food, and make everything they needed. Despite the hardships, most early colonies survived with the help of friendly Native Americans.

The New World colonies differed from each other. These differences were due in part to geography and to the varied cultures from which settlers came.

Study the time line above. When was Jamestown settled?

Pilgrims were among the earliest English settlers in North America. Almost 250 years later, George Boughton painted *Pilgrims Going to Church.*

1 Spain Builds a Large Empire

Read to Learn

★ How did Spain govern its colonies?
★ What social classes existed in New Spain?
★ What was Spanish culture like in the New World?
★ What do these words mean: viceroy, pueblo, presidio, mission, peninsular, creole, mestizo, encomienda, plantation?

Between 1492 and 1535, conquistadors won a large empire for Spain. During that time, Spain encouraged them with words but gave them little money for their voyages to the New World. Once Spain began to profit from the riches of the Americas, it paid close attention to its colonies there.

Governing an Empire

In 1535, the Spanish king, Charles V, set up a system of government in the Americas that lasted for nearly 300 years. He divided his empire into New Spain and Peru. (See the map on page 78.) New Spain included Spanish colonies in the West Indies, Central America, and North America. Peru included all Spanish lands in South America.

The king put a viceroy in charge of each region. A *viceroy* is an official who rules an area in the name of a king or queen. Colonists had little say in their government. The viceroy and other officials chosen by the king enforced a series of laws called the Laws of the Indies.

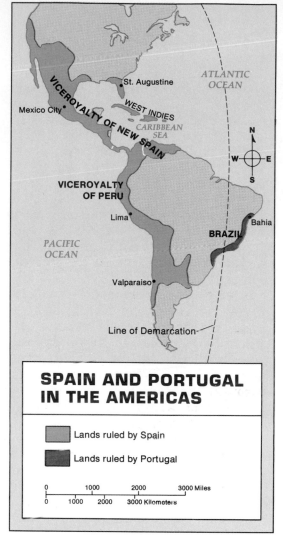

SPAIN AND PORTUGAL IN THE AMERICAS

Lands ruled by Spain

Lands ruled by Portugal

MAP SKILL Both Spain and Portugal built empires in the New World, as this map shows. The Spanish empire included the viceroyalties of New Spain and Peru. Name two settlements in New Spain.

sidios (pray SIH dee ohs), and missions. *Pueblos* were towns that were centers for farming and trade. At the center of the town was the plaza, a large open space. Here, townspeople and farmers gathered on important occasions. At one end of the plaza stood the church, usually the largest building in town. Shops and private homes lined both sides of the plaza.

Presidios were forts that housed soldiers. A presidio formed a rectangle and was surrounded by high mud brick walls. Inside the walls were shops, stables for horses, and storehouses for food. Most soldiers lived in large barracks. Farmers settled outside the walls of the presidios and were glad to have military help nearby.

Missions were religious settlements run by Catholic priests and friars. Like other Europeans who settled in the New World, the Spanish had no use for Indian religious beliefs. They believed it was their duty to convert the Indians to Christianity.

Priests set up missions throughout New Spain. They forced Indians to live in the missions and learn about Christianity. Each mission supported itself through the work of Indians. With a presidio nearby, priests had soldiers to back up their demands for Indian labor and to put down revolts. By setting up presidios and missions, the Laws of the Indies allowed Spain to rule the conquered Indians.

Social Classes

Under the Laws of the Indies, people were divided into social classes. At the top were the *peninsulares* (puh nihn suh LAHR ays). They were born in Spain and were sent by the Spanish government to rule the colonies. Only peninsulares could hold the highest jobs in government and the Catholic Church. Although peninsulares were wealthy landowners, most lived in the cities.

The *Laws of the Indies* allowed Spain to keep strict control over its colonies. The laws said how the colonies should be ruled. They told farmers what to plant and how to raise cattle. They said how and where towns should be built. For example, a town had to be built on high ground with good farmland, woods, and a plentiful water supply nearby.

Under the laws, three kinds of settlements were organized: pueblos, pre-

Creoles. Below the peninsulares were the *creoles* (KREE ohls). They were descended from Spanish settlers who were born in the Americas. Many creoles were wealthy and well educated. But they could not hold the jobs that were kept for the peninsulares. This policy made the creoles resent the peninsulares.

Many creoles owned large farms. There, they grew crops that were in demand in Europe, including bananas, rice, melons, and wheat. Creoles also raised crops that were new to Europeans but that Native Americans had grown for years. These included corn, beans, tomatoes, potatoes, squash, and tobacco. Many creoles took up ranching. They raised horses, sheep, cattle, and pigs on large ranches that stretched for many miles.

Mestizos and Native Americans. Below the creoles were the *mestizos* (mehs TEE zohs). These people were of mixed Spanish and Indian background. Mestizos worked on farms and ranches owned by creoles. In the cities, they worked as carpenters, shoemakers, tailors, and bakers. In the 1600s and 1700s, the mestizo population grew rapidly.

The lowest class in the colonies were the Native Americans. Under the strict social system set up by the Spanish, Indians were kept in poverty for hundreds of years.

Tragedy for Native Americans

Most Spanish settlers hoped to become rich in the New World. To do so, they needed workers to make their ranches, mines, and farmlands profitable. The Spanish government helped settlers by giving them *encomiendas* (ehn koh mee EHN dahs), or the right to demand taxes or labor from Native Americans living on the land.

In the West Indies, the Spanish learned that the best profits could be made by setting up *plantations,* or large estates farmed by many workers. Indians were forced to work on the plantations. They grew sugar cane and tobacco, which plantation owners sent to Spain. Sugar cane was especially valuable because it could be made into sugar, molasses, and rum.

When the Spanish found gold and silver in Peru and Mexico, they forced Native Americans to work the mines. Spanish soldiers marched Indians hundreds of miles from their homes. In the mines, Indians were forced to dig deep, narrow underground tunnels. They worked 12 hours a day, hacking out the rich ore.

Death from disease. Thousands of Native Americans died from overwork, mine accidents, and horrible conditions in the mines. European diseases killed millions more. As you have read, Native Americans had no resistance to European diseases. Smallpox, measles, and typhoid wiped out entire towns. (See the graph on page 81.)

Often, there were too few people left in a village to bury those who had died. One Aztec wrote that in village after village, people "could not walk. They only lay in their resting places and beds. They could not move. They could not stir."

Bartolomé de Las Casas. Spanish missionaries were concerned about the cruel treatment and high death rate among the Indians. One priest, Bartolomé de Las Casas (day lahs KAH sahs), worked hard to improve conditions for them.

As a young man, Las Casas visited Cuba, Puerto Rico, and other Spanish colonies. Everywhere, he saw Indians dying of hunger, disease, and mistreatment. Horrified, Las Casas returned to Spain and asked the king for laws to protect the Indians.

Spain looked on the Indians as loyal subjects. So in 1544, it passed laws to protect them. The laws said that Native Americans could not be made slaves and allowed them to own cattle and

Spain forced Native Americans to work long hours in gold and silver mines. This painting, done around 1584, shows a silver mine and processing plant in Potosí, Peru. For a time, Potosí was the largest city in the New World because of its rich silver mine.

grow crops. The new laws helped a little but did not end the disease or the mistreatment.

Slaves From Africa

Las Casas made another suggestion to help the Indians. He advised the Spanish to replace Indians with slaves from Africa. Africans, he said, did not suffer from European diseases as Indians did. Also, many Africans were farmers in their own lands. So they already had useful farming skills.

Spanish colonists agreed with Las Casas. They needed workers for their plantations. Bringing in African slaves seemed like a good way to replace the Indians who were dying off in such large numbers. Europeans had been taking slaves in Africa since the 1460s. Soon, ships were bringing thousands of African men, women, and children to be sold as slaves in the New World.

Before he died, Las Casas regretted his suggestion. He saw that African slaves suffered as much as the Indians. By that time, however, the plantation system had taken hold. In the years ahead, the African slave trade grew. Like the Spanish, other European colonists set up plantations in the New World and brought in African slaves to make them profitable.

Spanish Culture in the New World

By the mid-1500s, the Spanish had firmly planted their culture in the Americas. They brought with them their language, laws, religion, and learning.

Native Americans also influenced the culture of New Spain. They introduced colonists to new foods, including corn, tomatoes, chocolate, and potatoes. The Spanish wore Indian clothing such as the poncho, a coatlike blanket with a

Skill Lesson 4   Reading a Line Graph

Historians use graphs to show trends, or developments over time. Graphs are a way of showing **statistics,** or facts in number form. The most commonly used kind of graph is a **line graph.** Other kinds are circle and bar graphs.

A line graph has a grid that is made up of horizontal and vertical lines. A **horizontal axis** runs across the bottom of the grid. A **vertical axis** runs up and down one side of the grid. Information is put on the grid with dots. The dots are then connected to make a **curve.** The curve shows changes taking place over a period of time.

The curve on a line graph shows a trend. If the curve goes up, the graph is showing an upward trend. If the curve goes down, the graph is showing a downward trend. On some line graphs, you might see both upward and downward trends.

Use the steps below to read the line graph at right.

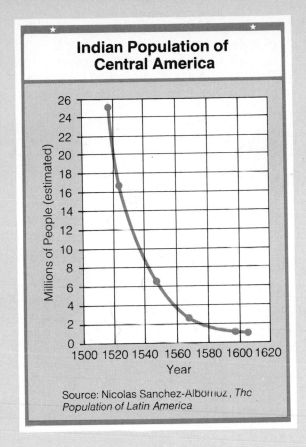

Indian Population of Central America

Source: Nicolas Sanchez-Albornoz, *The Population of Latin America*

1. **Identify the type of information shown on the line graph.** Most graphs have a title, date, and source. The title tells you what the subject is. The date tells you what time period is covered. The source tells you where the information was found. (a) What is the title of the graph? (b) What time period does the graph cover? (c) What is the source of the graph?

2. **Study the labels on the graph.** Both the horizontal axis and the vertical axis have labels. (a) What do the numbers on the horizontal axis show? (b) What do the numbers on the vertical axis show?

3. **Practice reading the line graph.** The dates on the horizontal axis are spaced evenly. The numbers on the vertical axis are also spaced evenly apart and usually begin at zero. A line graph may show numbers in thousands or millions. (a) About how many Native Americans lived in Central America in 1520? (b) About how many lived there in 1540? in 1600? (c) During which period did the population fall the most?

4. **Draw conclusions from the information shown on the graph.** Use the line graph and your reading in this chapter to answer the following questions. (a) In your own words, describe what happened to the population of Native Americans living in Central America between 1520 and 1600. (b) Why did the Indian population in Central America decline so rapidly? (c) What effect do you think the death of so many people might have had on those who survived?

Sor Juana

The most famous poet of New Spain was Juana Inés de la Cruz. Born in 1651, she was a brilliant child who could read by age 3. When she was 14, she begged to be allowed to study at the University of Mexico like the men. But she was refused.

Juana Inés became lady-in-waiting to the wife of the viceroy. After a short time, however, she decided to become a nun so that she could go on with her studies in the peace of the convent. As Sor Juana, or Sister Juana, she read widely and learned several languages. She wrote many poems and plays and published essays on science, music, and mathematics.

Sor Juana became well known for her brilliant mind. Educated men and women pleaded for the right to talk to her at the convent. However, some people envied her success. They criticized her for seeking knowledge instead of doing good works. In 1693, Sor Juana sold her library

and went out to care for the sick. A great plague swept Mexico a few years later. While helping victims of the plague, she herself became ill and died.

★ How did Sor Juana contribute to the arts in America?

hole in the middle for the head. Indian words such as canoe, tobacco, and hurricane came into Spanish and English. The word hurricane, for example, came from the Tainos of Puerto Rico. To the Tainos, Juracan was a god who acted like a devil.

The Spanish built their cities on the foundations of Aztec and Inca cities. Mexico City, capital of New Spain, rose on the site of Tenochtitlan. Like the Aztec city, the new Spanish capital had paved and lighted streets, a police department, and a public water system.

Spanish settlers built libraries, theaters, and fine churches. Indian artists decorated Christian churches with paintings of their harvests and other traditions. Printing presses turned out the first European books published in the New World.* By 1551, Spanish colonists had opened universities in the West Indies, Mexico, Ecuador, and Peru. People like Sor Juana (see the picture above) were contributing to the arts in America.

Missionaries and explorers spread Spanish culture across the New World. They trekked as far north as Oregon and as far south as the tip of South America. In fact, Spanish colonies in the Americas became the basis for the

---

*Indians produced books before the Spanish arrived. But most of these were burned by Spanish soldiers and priests.

independent nations of Latin America today.

The Spanish also built settlements in the American Southwest. Spanish settlers were used to its dry climate because it was similar to the climate of Spain. They brought the first horses, cattle, pigs, goats, and chickens to the Southwest. And they planted many kinds of fruit and nut trees.

In 1565, the Spanish built a presidio at St. Augustine, Florida. St. Augustine is the oldest European settlement in the United States.

Place names in the United States show the widespread influence of Spanish culture. States such as Nevada, Colorado, and Montana have Spanish names. Cities in the Southwest such as Los Angeles, El Paso, Santa Fe, San Carlos, and San Antonio were first settled by Spanish missionaries.

━━ SECTION REVIEW ━━

1. **Locate:** New Spain, Peru, Mexico City, Cuba, Puerto Rico, St. Augustine.
2. **Define:** viceroy, pueblo, presidio, mission, peninsular, creole, mestizo, encomienda, plantation.
3. What were the Laws of the Indies?
4. How did Bartolomé de Las Casas try to help Native Americans?
5. **What Do You Think?** How do you think slavery affected the economy of Spanish colonies?

2 French and Dutch Colonies

Read to Learn

★ What regions did the French explore?
★ Who set up New Netherland?
★ How did Europeans treat the Indians in North America?
★ What do these words mean: coureur de bois?

Spain's rich gold and silver mines in Mexico and Peru made it the envy of other European nations. France, England, Sweden, and the Netherlands sent their own explorers to hunt for treasures in the New World. Although they found no treasure, they all planted colonies in North America.

The First French Settlements

In the early 1500s, French fishermen discovered rich fishing grounds off the coast of Newfoundland. Each summer, fishermen sailed across the Atlantic and caught tons of cod. They dried the fish on shore before sailing back to France with their catch.

The fishermen did not settle in Newfoundland. But they did trade with Native Americans. They exchanged knives, kettles, and cloth for furs, especially beaver skins. These furs sold for high prices in Europe.

Samuel de Champlain. In the early 1600s, France took steps to encourage the fur trade. In 1603, it sent Samuel de Champlain (sham PLAYN) to North America. He brought settlers to the coast of Maine. The climate was so harsh that the settlers soon left. A year later, Champlain set up a colony at Port Royal, Nova Scotia.

In 1608, Champlain followed Cartier's route up the St. Lawrence. He built a trading post under a rocky cliff above the river. The settlement was called Quebec (kwee BEHK). It quickly grew into the center of a thriving fur trade.

Fur trappers and traders. Most French colonists were trappers and traders. Because they lived in the woods, they became known as *coureurs* *de bois* (koo RUHR duh BWAH), or runners of the woods.

Coureurs de bois learned how to trap and survive in the woods from Native Americans. Many married Indian women. Indians showed the French how to build and use canoes. In the fall, Indians and trappers paddled up the St. Lawrence to winter trapping grounds. The trip was difficult because they had to carry canoes around rapids.

Indians taught trappers how to make snowshoes. Wearing snowshoes, they climbed through deep snow to find their traps. Trappers slept in wigwams, or Indian houses made of poles and birchbark.

When the snows melted, trappers loaded furs into their canoes for the trip down the St. Lawrence. At the French settlements, they traded the furs for blankets, kettles, and other goods they would use the next winter.

A Route to the West

The St. Lawrence River was very important to the French in North America. The Appalachian Mountains blocked most routes inland from the Atlantic. However, the St. Lawrence led deep into the heart of America. Led by Indian guides, French trappers and traders explored the St. Lawrence to the Great Lakes.

French Catholic missionaries often traveled with the fur traders. The missionaries were determined to make Native Americans accept Christianity. They set up missions, drew maps, and wrote about the newly explored lands. In 1673, Father Jacques Marquette (mahr KEHT), a priest, and Louis Joliet (JOH lee eht), a fur trader, set out in canoes across Lake Michigan. With the help of Indian guides, they explored south and west until they reached the Mississippi River. They were excited by this discovery, hoping at last to have found a passage to Asia.

After paddling over 700 miles (1,100 km), Marquette and Joliet realized that the Mississippi emptied into the Gulf of Mexico, not into the Pacific. Disappointed, they returned north before they reached the Gulf. Their journey was important, however, because it opened the way for other explorers.

In 1682, Robert La Salle (lah SAHL) explored the Mississippi down to the Gulf of Mexico. La Salle boldly claimed the entire Mississippi Valley for France. He named the region *Louisiana* for the French king, Louis XIV.

To keep Spain and England out of Louisiana, the French built forts along the Mississippi. In the north, Antoine Cadillac built Fort Detroit near Lake Erie. In the south, the French built New Orleans at the mouth of the Mississippi. New Orleans soon grew into a busy trading center.

New France

The French colony of *New France* grew slowly. Aside from trappers and traders, few French settled there. In the 1660s, however, Louis XIV decided to encourage farmers to go to New France.

An attempt at farming. The king put a new governor in charge of the colony. In 1665, the governor set sail for New France with 1,000 farmers. To encourage family life, the governor brought many young women to New France. Some were noble. Others came from middle class or peasant families. Most women were single, but they soon found husbands among the settlers. Peasant women were the most popular because they were used to the hard work of farming.

Despite efforts to encourage farming, trappers still outnumbered farmers. People made more money trapping than farming. Also, only nobles owned the land. Because farmers could not own their own land, they either had to work for the nobles directly or else pay them rent.

Like Spain, France ruled its colony strictly. It gave settlers little freedom. Farmers lived under the close watch of French officials. Coureurs de bois, however, enjoyed more freedom because they lived far from French settlements.

French influence. As they hunted for fur, the French explored large parts of North America. Following Indian trails, they mapped routes from the Gulf of Mexico to northern Canada. In

MAP SKILL French explorers trekked across large parts of North America on foot and by canoe. Find the route taken by Marquette and Joliet. About how many miles did they travel along the Mississippi River?

THE FRENCH EXPLORE NORTH AMERICA

← Champlain, 1608

← Marquette and Joliet, 1673

← La Salle, 1682

Father Jacques Marquette and Louis Joliet traveled from Lake Michigan into the Fox River and upstream to Portage, Wisconsin. There, they portaged, or carried, their canoes overland to the Wisconsin River and then paddled downriver to the Mississippi.

1743, French explorers saw the Rocky Mountains for the first time.

The French built towns and trading posts across their large colony. French influence is seen today in place names such as Vermont—green mountain, Terre Haute—high land, and Baton Rouge—red stick.

New Netherland

In the 1600s, the Dutch set up the colony of *New Netherland* in North America. As you read, the English explorer Henry Hudson made one voyage for the Dutch. In 1609, he found the mouth of a river, today called the Hudson River. The Dutch paid little attention to Hudson's discovery at first. Then in 1626, Peter Minuit (MIHN yoo wiht) led a group of Dutch settlers to North America. In a famous deal, he bought Manhattan Island at the mouth of the Hudson from local Indians.

Minuit called his settlement New Amsterdam. From a tiny group of 30 houses, it grew into a busy port where ships docked from all over the world. The Dutch built trading posts along the Hudson River. The most important one was Fort Orange. Today, Fort Orange is called Albany.

Fur trading. The Dutch entered the fur trade. They became fierce rivals of the French and their Indian allies, the Algonquins (al GAHN kwihnz). The Dutch made friends with the Iroquois, longtime rivals of the Algonquins. They gave guns to the Iroquois to fight the Algonquins. With Iroquois help, the Dutch brought furs down the Hudson to New Amsterdam. The French and Algonquins fought back, however. For many years, fighting raged among Europeans and their Indian allies.

New Sweden is taken over. About 1640, Swedish settlers arrived in North America. They set up the colony of *New Sweden* along the Delaware River. Swedes built a town where Wilmington stands today. Some Dutch settlers helped their Swedish neighbors, but most Dutch resented the nearby Swedish colony. Fighting broke out between the colonists. In 1655, the Dutch took over New Sweden.

Dutch influence. As you will read, England conquered New Netherland in 1664 and made it an English colony. Still, many Dutch customs survived. The Dutch introduced Saint Nicholas to the New World. Every year on the saint's birthday, children put out their shoes to be filled with presents. Later, "Saint Nick" became Santa Claus, and the custom of giving gifts was moved to Christmas Eve.

Many Dutch words entered the English language. A Dutch master was a "boss." The people of New Amsterdam sailed in "yachts." Dutch children munched on "cookies" and "crullers" and listened to ghost stories about "spooks."

Newcomers and Native Americans

In North America, as in New Spain, European diseases killed thousands of Native Americans. Indians told one Dutch explorer that their people were "melted down" by disease. "Before the smallpox broke out among them," the explorer said, "they were ten times as numerous as they now are."

Rivalry between French and Dutch fur traders also affected the Indians. Each group encouraged its Indian allies to attack the other. Besides, the scramble for fur led to overtrapping. By 1640, beavers had almost been wiped out in the Iroquois lands of upstate New York.

The arrival of European settlers affected Native Americans in other

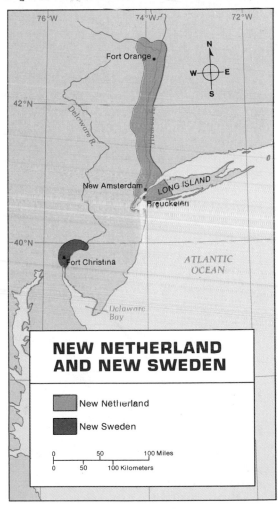

MAP SKILL The Netherlands and Sweden both claimed lands in North America. The Dutch settlement at Breuckelen was later called Brooklyn. What is the latitude and longitude of Breuckelen?

When the Dutch settled the southern tip of Manhattan Island, they called their settlement New Amsterdam. This picture shows New Amsterdam about 1655. Notice the windmill, which produced energy to grind corn.

ways. Missionaries tried to convert Indians to Christianity. Indians gave up hunting with bows and arrows in favor of muskets and gunpowder bought from Europeans. Alcohol sold by European traders had a terrible effect on Indian life.

The French, Dutch, and English influenced fewer Indians than the Spanish because there were fewer Indians where they settled. However, they all seized Indian lands. And settlers from all three nations enslaved Indians and sold them to plantations in the West Indies.

SECTION REVIEW

1. **Locate:** Nova Scotia, St. Lawrence River, Quebec, Great Lakes, Gulf of Mexico, New France, Hudson River, New Amsterdam, New Netherland, Fort Orange, New Sweden.
2. **Define:** coureur de bois.
3. How did most French colonists make a living?
4. Why did the Dutch become allies of the Iroquois?
5. **What Do You Think?** Why do you think Indians came to see European settlers as invaders?

3 English Settlers in Virginia

Read to Learn

★ Why is Roanoke known as the "lost colony"?
★ What problems did the Jamestown Colony face?

★ How did life improve for the colonists by the 1620s?
★ What do these words mean: charter, joint stock company, capital, burgess, representative government, stockade?

In the early 1500s, England had little interest in setting up colonies in North America. English explorers searched for a northwest passage and raided Spanish treasure ships. By the late 1500s, however, a few people began to dream of planting colonies.

The Lost Colony of Roanoke

In 1585, Sir Walter Raleigh raised enough money to send seven English ships to America. The ships reached Roanoke (ROH uh nohk) Island off the coast of North Carolina, but the colonists did not stay in America. In 1587, John White, an artist who had sailed on the first voyage, returned to Roanoke to try again to build a colony. Among the settlers with him were his daughter, Ellinor Dare, and her husband. In Roanoke, Ellinor Dare gave birth to the first English child born in North America, Virginia Dare.

When supplies ran low, White returned to England. But 117 settlers, including his daughter and granddaughter, stayed behind. Before he left, White told the settlers to leave a message carved on a tree if they moved to another place. If they were attacked, they were to carve a cross.

Because of war between England and Spain, White was unable to return to Roanoke until 1590. As White rowed to shore, a sailor played English songs on a trumpet to let the settlers know they were coming. No one answered.

On shore, White found books and rusty armor scattered about the fort the colonists had built. He thought that Indians had dug these up after the colonists left. Then he saw carved on a tree the letters C R O A T O A N—but no cross. On his earlier voyage, White had visited Croatoan Island. The Indians there had been friendly. Bad weather kept White from sailing to the island to look for his family and the settlers. He returned to England without ever finding them.

To this day, no one knows what happened to the "lost colony" of Roanoke. Did they join the Croatoans? Did they starve? Or were they killed by other Indians whose chief had been murdered by the English? The failure of Roanoke and the cost of setting up a colony discouraged other settlements for a time. In the 1600s, however, the English found new ways to raise money to set up colonies in the New World.

The Jamestown Colony

In 1606, the *Virginia Company* of London received a charter from King James I. A *charter* is a legal document giving certain rights to a person or

In 1590, John White painted this map of Roanoke Island, located off the coast of North Carolina. On earlier trips, White painted scenes of Indian life as well as plants and animals of the New World.

company. The charter gave the company the right to colonize the land between the Potomac River and North Carolina. The land was called Virginia. The charter gave colonists the same rights as people in England.

Financing the colony. The Virginia Company was a *joint stock company,* a private trading company that sold shares to investors. For years, merchants had used joint stock companies to finance trading voyages. In a joint stock company, a group of merchants pooled their funds to form a company. Each merchant got shares of stock for the money he put in.

When the company raised enough *capital,* or money for investment, it outfitted ships for a trading voyage. If ships returned safely, the cargoes were sold. Each investor then received a share of the profits.

The Virginia Company financed, or paid for, the first successful English colony. Investors in the company hoped that colonists would find gold mines like those in New Spain.

Early problems. The Virginia Company sent its first group of colonists across the Atlantic in 1607. The colonists sailed their three small ships into Chesapeake Bay and up a river they called the James. After landing in a wooded area, they began to build homes. They called their settlement *Jamestown,* after King James 1. From the start, they ran into problems. The land was swampy. Mosquitoes were everywhere, and the drinking water was bad. Before long, many colonists died from diseases.

Governing the colony was also a problem. The London merchants were supposed to make laws for the colony. Because the merchants were far away, they chose a council of 13 men to rule the colony. But members of the council quarreled with each other. As a result, little was done to make the colony strong. Colonists spent their days hunting for gold instead of planting crops.

Captain John Smith. The Jamestown Colony almost failed that first year. It was saved from disaster by Captain John Smith. Smith, the son of a farmer, had already lived through many adventures in Europe before sailing to America. He grew disgusted with the Jamestown colonists. "No talk, no hope, nor work," he complained. People only wanted to "dig gold, wash gold, refine gold, load gold." But no one found gold, and the colony was running out of food.

Smith then took matters into his own hands. He visited nearby Indian villages to trade for food. Powhatan, a powerful chief who was angry with the English, took Smith prisoner and ordered him put to death. According to Smith, Powhatan's 10-year-old daughter, Pocahontas (poh kuh HAHN tuhs), begged her father to spare him. Powhatan agreed and even sold corn to Smith to feed the hungry colonists at Jamestown.

Because of his success with the Indians, the council put Smith in charge of the colony. Smith told people that they would only get food if they worked. Life in the colony improved when colonists began planting crops. But in 1609, Smith was injured in an accident. After he returned to England, the colony again fell on hard times.

The Starving Time

The Virginia Company sent more settlers to Jamestown, but most died from disease and starvation. Of 900 settlers who arrived between 1606 and 1609, only 150 survived. During the winter of 1609–1610, these survivors faced "the starving time." They ran out of food and were forced to live on "dogs, cats, snakes, toadstools, horsehides, and what not." By spring, only 60 were still alive.

When it learned of the tragedy, the Virginia Company put a military governor in charge of the colony. The governor had power to make any laws he felt were needed.

Colonists complained that military rule was too strict. One settler was executed for killing a chicken without permission. Another, who stole a few cups of oatmeal, was chained to a tree until he starved to death. Despite military rule, Jamestown remained in trouble. Investors in the Virginia Company feared that they would never make a profit.

Profits From Tobacco

Several events helped the colony survive and even prosper. First, colonists began to grow tobacco. Europeans learned about tobacco and pipe smoking from Native Americans. One colonist, John Rolfe, learned from the Indians that the Virginia soil was excellent for growing tobacco. Rolfe developed a blend of tobaccos that became popular in Europe.

At first, tobacco helped the young colony prosper, especially when the demand for tobacco grew in Europe. Settlers cleared new land outside Jamestown. For the first time, ships of the Virginia Company returned to England filled with profitable cargoes. But later on, planters produced too much tobacco, and prices fell.

Growing tobacco was hard work. Settlers tried to make Indians work the tobacco plantations. When Indians ran off into the forests, planters looked for other workers. In 1619, a Dutch ship arrived in Jamestown with 20 Africans on board. At least 3 of the Africans were women. The Dutch had seized these men and women in Africa to sell as servants or slaves.

The first Africans in Virginia may have worked as servants and earned their freedom. However, by the late 1600s, Virginia planters had come to depend on a cruel system of slave labor to produce their crops. The system lasted for over 200 years.

Ætatis suæ 21. Aº 1616.

AMERICANS WHO DARED

Pocahontas

Pocahontas was the daughter of Powhatan, an Indian leader in Virginia. Pocahontas was her nickname, meaning "playful one." Her real name was Matoaka. Captain John Smith said that she not only saved his life but also saved the Jamestown Colony from "death and famine." In 1614, Pocahontas married John Rolfe, a planter. Soon after, she visited England. An artist painted this portrait of her dressed like an upper class English woman. Sadly, Pocahontas died in England just before she was to sail home.

Representative Government

The second event that helped Virginia was a new form of government. In 1619, the Virginia Company sent a governor to the colony with orders to consult settlers on important matters. Settlers who owned land were allowed to elect *burgesses,* or representatives. The burgesses met in an assembly called the *House of Burgesses.* Together with the governor, they made laws for the colony.

The House of Burgesses brought representative government to the English colonies. A *representative government* is one in which voters elect representatives to make laws for them. Although only wealthy men who were landowners could vote, the idea grew up that settlers had a say in how they were governed.

The idea of representative government was deeply rooted in English history. In 1215, English nobles forced King John to sign the *Magna Carta,* or Great Charter. This document gave nobles certain rights. It said that the king could not raise new taxes without first consulting the Great Council made up of nobles and church leaders. Most important, it showed that the king had to obey the law.

Gradually, the rights won by nobles were given to other English people. The Great Council grew into Parliament, a representative assembly. By the 1600s, Parliament was divided into the House of Lords, made up of nobles, and the House of Commons. Members of the House of Commons were elected to office. Only a few wealthy men had the right to vote. Still, English people firmly believed that the ruler must consult Parliament on money matters and obey the law.

Women in Virginia

The third event that helped the colony was the arrival of women. Most early settlers in Jamestown were men. The first English women in Jamestown were Anne Forest, who came with her husband, and Anne Burras, her young maid. They were on board a supply ship that arrived in 1608. A small number of women lived in the colony during "the starving time."

In 1619, the Virginia Company decided to send 100 women to Virginia to "make the men more settled." The women quickly found husbands among the settlers. The Virginia Company profited from the marriages because it charged each man who found a wife 150 pounds of tobacco.

Life in Virginia was hard. Women had to make everything from scratch—food, clothing, even medicines. Still, after women arrived, settlers took hope that the colony would survive.

Friend or Enemy

The Indians who lived around Jamestown were farmers. At first, they did not see the English as a threat. In fact, they often felt sorry for the half-starved white settlers who did not know how to grow corn or trap animals.

The English, on the other hand, were suspicious of the Indians. They called the Indians heathens, or non-Christians. They looked down on Indian customs, which were so different from their own. Because they feared attacks by the Indians, settlers built their homes close together. They surrounded their homes with a *stockade,* a high fence made of wooden posts.

As more colonists arrived, they needed land. Because growing tobacco wore out the soil quickly, colonists kept clearing new land. More and more settlements sprang up in Virginia. The Indians soon began to see the colonists as invaders who were taking over their land and giving it out to white settlers from across the Atlantic. They tried without success to negotiate with white officials.

In 1622, Indians attacked and killed about 350 settlers in Virginia. The English, in turn, killed or enslaved the Indians. In the 1600s, the English made many treaties with the Indians in which they agreed to respect Indian land. But in the end, the English

Jamestown settlers welcomed the arrival of supply ships such as this one. Without supplies from England, settlers would have suffered even worse hardships than they did. The two women at left may have been Anne Forest and Anne Burras, who reached Jamestown in 1608.

ignored these treaties. So the fighting continued. More and more Indians were either killed or pushed inland.

SECTION REVIEW

1. **Locate:** Roanoke, Chesapeake Bay, Jamestown.
2. **Define:** charter, joint stock company, capital, burgess, representative government, stockade.
3. (a) List three problems the Jamestown colonists faced. (b) What product helped Jamestown prosper?
4. How was representative government set up in Virginia?
5. How did Native Americans help the Jamestown colonists?
6. **What Do You Think?** How do you think the arrival of women helped the Jamestown Colony survive?

4 The Pilgrims at Plymouth

Read to Learn

★ Who were the Pilgrims?
★ What did the Mayflower Compact say?
★ How did the Pilgrims survive their first winter?

In 1620, a year after the House of Burgesses was set up in Virginia, another band of settlers sailed to America. They were known as Separatists because they wanted to set up their own church separate from the Church of England. Later, the Separatists were called *Pilgrims.*

Search for Religious Freedom

The Pilgrims were looking for a place where they could live and worship in their own way. Queen Elizabeth and her successor, King James I, disliked any group that refused to follow

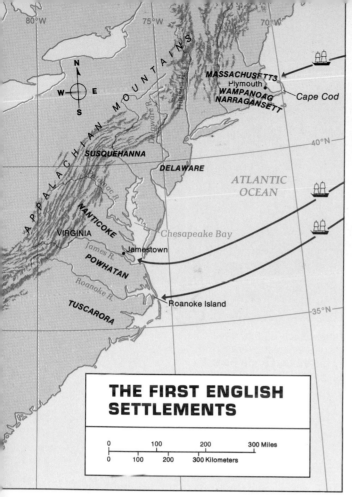

MAP SKILL In the early 1600s, English settlers planted colonies in Roanoke, Jamestown, and Plymouth. The colony at Roanoke ended in failure. Which of these three colonies was farthest north? What Indians lived near the Jamestown colonists?

the official religion, the Church of England. King James vowed to "harry them [the Pilgrims] out of the land." As a result, the Pilgrims were persecuted, or attacked, for their beliefs.

From England to Leyden. In the early 1600s, the Pilgrims left England for Leyden, a city in the Netherlands. The Dutch allowed the newcomers to worship freely. But the Pilgrims did not feel at home in Leyden. They were farmers and did not like city life. They worried, too, because their children were growing up speaking Dutch, not English.

The Pilgrims and some other English people got a charter to set up a colony in Virginia. In September 1620, 101 men, women, and children set sail for Virginia. On the voyage, a storm blew their small, leaky ship, the *Mayflower,* off course. They landed far north of Virginia, at a spot near Cape Cod.

The Mayflower Compact. The Pilgrims explored the coast and decided to stay where they were instead of sailing south to Virginia. But their charter did not apply to a colony outside Virginia. So before they went ashore, they drew up an agreement on how they would govern their colony.

Forty-one Pilgrims signed the *Mayflower Compact.* In it, they agreed to consult each other about laws for the colony and promised to work together to make the colony succeed.

The Mayflower Compact began:

We, whose names are underwritten . . . Having undertaken for the Glory of God, and Advancement of the Christian Faith . . . a Voyage to plant the first colony in the northern parts of Virginia . . . do enact, constitute, and frame, such just and equal Laws . . . as shall be thought most meet [fitting] and convenient for the general Good of the Colony.

Later, when the colony grew too large for everyone to consult together, the settlers chose representatives to an assembly. The assembly made laws for the colony.

Hard Times—and Success

The Pilgrims called their settlement *Plymouth* because they had sailed from Plymouth, England. When they landed in December, it was too late to plant crops. So they had to live off wild game and whatever food they had left from the voyage.

The Pilgrims spent their first winter in sod houses quickly thrown together. William Bradford, an early governor of Plymouth, wrote that some Pilgrims lived in caves "half a pit and half a tent of earth supported by branches . . . nasty, dank and cold."

In July 1620, the Pilgrims left Holland on the first stage of their voyage to the New World. This painting shows them at prayer as their ship sets sail. Religious faith made the Pilgrims confident of success. "Their condition was not ordinary," wrote one. "Their ends were good and honorable; their calling lawful and urgent, and therefore they might expect the blessing of God."

Bradford described the hardships of that winter. The Pilgrims "had no friends to welcome them, nor inns to entertain or refresh their weatherbeaten bodies," he wrote. "If they looked behind them, there was the mighty ocean which they had passed. . . .What could now sustain them, but the Spirit of God and His grace?"

The Pilgrims had a strong religious faith. They believed that it was the will of God for them to stay in Plymouth. By the spring, almost half the settlers had died of disease or starvation. The survivors refused to give up. They cleared land and planted crops.

Samoset, a Pemaquid Indian from Maine, helped the Pilgrims. He had learned some English a few years before from explorers sailing along the coast. Samoset and other Indians taught the Pilgrims to plant corn and trap animals for furs.

Samoset brought Squanto, a Wampanoag who spoke English, to the Pilgrims. Squanto gave the Pilgrims good advice on planting crops. He showed them how to catch eels from nearby rivers. By treading water, he stirred up eels from the river bottom and then snatched them up with his hands.

In the fall, the Pilgrims had a good harvest. The colony was saved! Because they believed that God gave them this harvest, they set aside a day for giving thanks to God. In the years ahead, the Pilgrims celebrated the end of the harvest with a day of thanksgiving. Americans today celebrate *Thanksgiving* as a national holiday.

SECTION REVIEW

1. **Locate:** Cape Cod, Plymouth.
2. (a) Why did the Pilgrims leave England for Leyden? (b) Why did they leave Leyden for the New World?
3. Why did the Pilgrims write the Mayflower Compact?
4. **What Do You Think?** Do you think the Pilgrims could have survived without the help of the Indians? Explain.

Chapter 4 Review

★ Summary ★

Spain was the first European nation to build an empire in the Americas. In the 1500s, Spain set up a government that kept its colonies under firm control. A rich culture based on Spanish and Indian traditions grew up in New Spain.

French, Dutch, and Swedish settlers also planted colonies in North America. French settlers were mostly trappers and traders. The Dutch settled along the Hudson River and competed with the French and Indians for control of the rich fur trade.

The first permanent English colony was set up at Jamestown, Virginia. After a desperate struggle to survive, the colony began to prosper. To the north, the Pilgrims built the Plymouth Colony. They, too, suffered through hard times but were helped by friendly Indians.

★ Reviewing the Facts ★   *2 points each*

Key Terms. Match each term in Column 1 with the correct definition in Column 2.

Column 1	Column 2
1. viceroy	**a.** money for reinvestment
2. mestizo	**b.** runner of the forest
3. coureur de bois	**c.** document giving certain rights to a person or company
4. charter	**d.** person of mixed Indian and Spanish background
5. capital	**e.** royal official who rules a colony in the name of a king or queen

Key People, Events, and Ideas. Identify each of the following.

1. Bartolomé de Las Casas
2. Samuel de Champlain
3. Jacques Marquette
4. Louis Joliet
5. Robert La Salle
6. Peter Minuit
7. Virginia Company
8. John Smith
9. Pocahontas
10. John Rolfe
11. House of Burgesses
12. Magna Carta
13. Pilgrims
14. Mayflower Compact
15. Squanto

★ Chapter Checkup ★   *5 points each*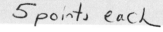

1. Why did the Spanish build missions?

2. (a) List the four social classes in New Spain. (b) How did each earn a living?

3. Describe three things the coureurs de bois learned from the Indians.

4. Why did settlers in New France prefer trapping to farming?

5. In what part of North America did the Dutch settle?

6. How did the English finance the Jamestown Colony?

7. (a) Why did the Indians feel sorry for the first Jamestown settlers? (b) How did their view change?

8. Why did the Pilgrims decide to stay in Plymouth despite the hard times they suffered?

1. **Relating past to present.** Describe one custom or idea that Americans have inherited from each of the following: (a) Spanish; (b) French; (c) Dutch; (d) English; (e) Indians.

2. **Defending a position.** Bartolomé de Las Casas did more harm than good when he tried to help Native Americans. Defend or criticize this statement.

3. **Learning about citizenship.** Review the descriptions of the governments of New Spain and Virginia. (a) In which colony did people have more say over their government? (b) Why?

4. **Comparing.** Compare the early years of settlers in Jamestown and Plymouth. (a) How were their experiences similar? (b) How were they different?

5. **Analyzing a quotation.** Review the quotation from the Mayflower Compact on page 94. (a) Why did the Pilgrims undertake their voyage? (b) What kinds of laws did they plan to make for the Plymouth Colony?

★ **Using Your Skills** ★

1. **Map reading.** Study the map on page 78. (a) What lands did Spain rule? (b) What lands did Portugal rule? (c) Describe the location of St. Augustine in terms of latitude and longitude.

2. **Map reading.** Study the map on page 85. (a) Which explorer or explorers traveled along the Mississippi River? (b) Which French explorer or explorers sailed up the St. Lawrence River first? (c) Using this map and your reading in this chapter, why do you think French explorers traveled where they did?

3. **Making a generalization.** Review the description of relations between Native Americans and Europeans on pages 79, 84, and 87. (a) Make a generalization about the way Europeans behaved toward Native Americans. (b) List three facts to support your generalization.

4. **Outlining.** Review the outlining steps you learned on page 31. Then outline the section "French and Dutch Colonies" on pages 83–88.

★ **More to Do** ★

1. **Creating a map.** On a blank map of North and South America, use different colors to show what lands each of the following countries claimed around 1650: Spain, Portugal, France, the Netherlands, Sweden, and England. Label the main cities or towns in each colony.

2. **Writing a diary.** Write several diary entries of a woman who sailed to Jamestown in 1619. Include her trip across the Atlantic and her first years in Jamestown.

3. **Interviewing.** Imagine that you are a reporter who is interviewing either Squanto or Samoset. Do background research to find out where he came from and what he thought of the Pilgrims. Write up your interview or give it as an oral report.

4. **Exploring local history.** Find out about any monuments in your local area that honor European explorers. Prepare a brochure encouraging people to visit these monuments.

5
English Colonies Take Root (1630–1750)

Chapter Outline

1 New England Colonies
2 Middle Colonies
3 Southern Colonies
4 Governing the Colonies

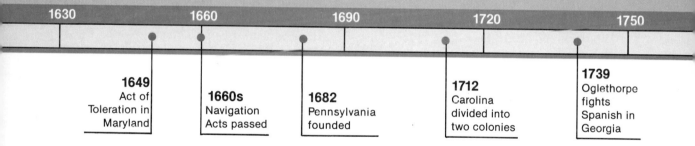

1630	1660	1690	1720	1750

1649
Act of Toleration in Maryland

1660s
Navigation Acts passed

1682
Pennsylvania founded

1712
Carolina divided into two colonies

1739
Oglethorpe fights Spanish in Georgia

About This Chapter

Young William Penn spurred his horse toward London. Even though it was night, he rode fast because he carried an important message for King Charles II. At dawn, Penn reached the king's palace. He insisted on delivering his message to the sleepy king. The message came from Penn's father, Sir William, an admiral in the royal navy.

Penn's meeting with the king lasted only a short time. But years later it helped Penn to have served as a messenger to the king. While a student at Oxford University, Penn joined the Quakers, a religious group that the Church of England hated. Penn was jailed for his beliefs even though he was wellborn and the son of an admiral. To avoid further trouble, Penn decided to move to America.

The king owed Penn's father a lot of money. Instead of asking for the money, Penn asked for a royal charter granting him lands to start a colony in America. The king agreed. As Penn said, "The government at home was glad to be rid of us [the Quakers] at so cheap a rate." In 1682, Penn sailed for America, determined to make his colony a place where Quakers could live in peace.

In this chapter, you will read about the colonies England planted along the Atlantic coast of North America. Slowly, the scattered villages and towns grew into 13 English colonies. Each colony had its own story.

Study the time line above. Was Pennsylvania founded before or after Maryland's Act of Toleration?

The English planted 13 colonies in North America. This painting shows Baltimore, Maryland, which grew into a busy harbor in the 1700s.

1 New England Colonies

Read to Learn

★ Why did the Puritans leave England?
★ How were Massachusetts, Connecticut, and Rhode Island founded?
★ Why did fighting break out between settlers and Indians?
★ What do these words mean: emigrate, democratic government, toleration?

During the 1600s, the English set up 13 colonies along the eastern coast of North America. Although each colony was different, they were grouped together by location. From north to south, they were the New England Colonies, Middle Colonies, and Southern Colonies. The first New England Colony was Plymouth, settled by the Pilgrims in 1620. Within a few years, other settlers braved the dangerous trip across the Atlantic to build homes in America.

Reasons for Leaving Home

Settlers had many reasons for leaving England. Some, like those who went to Jamestown, wanted to get rich by finding gold. Others hoped to improve their lives by owning land. In England, the oldest son usually inherited his father's land. Younger sons had little hope of having land. The colonies offered such people large amounts of land. They gave little thought to the Indians already living there.

For many settlers, religious reasons were as strong as economic ones. As you have read, the Pilgrims left England because they could not worship as they pleased. Other religious groups soon followed.

Evil and declining times. Among these groups were the Puritans. *Puritans* were Protestants who wanted the Church of England to become purer by getting rid of Catholic practices. They opposed organ music and the special clothes worn by priests. Unlike the Pilgrims, the Puritans did not want to separate from the Church of England. But they did want reforms made.

Puritans were a powerful group in England. Many were well-educated and successful merchants or landowners. Because they held seats in Parliament, they could make their views known.

King James I disliked Puritans as much as he did Pilgrims, and he made their lives difficult. After he died in 1625, his son, Charles I, moved even more firmly against the Puritans. When Puritans and their supporters in Parliament fought back, Charles dismissed Parliament. He said that he would rule without it. He threatened Puritans with harsh punishments if they did not obey bishops of the Church of England. Puritan leaders decided that England had fallen on "evil and declining times." So they made plans to *emigrate,* or leave their country and settle elsewhere.

The Great Migration. The Puritans got a charter from the king to form the Massachusetts Bay Company. The charter gave land in New England to the company. During the winter of 1629, the Puritans prepared to leave home.

The next year, over 1,000 men, women, and children sailed in 17 ships for the *Massachusetts Bay Colony*. Some joined a small group of Puritans who had already settled in Salem. Many went to Boston, which soon grew into the largest town in the colony. Villages sprang up as people flocked to the new colony. Between 1629 and 1640, more than 20,000 settlers arrived in Massachusetts Bay. The movement became known as the *Great Migration*.

The Massachusetts Bay Colony

Puritans held strong beliefs about how people should live and govern themselves. They felt they had a mis-

In the 1600s, economic conditions in England forced many farm workers off the land. Homeless farmers poured into the cities. When they could not find jobs, some became beggars. English officials urged poor families like this one to go to the New World.

sion to build a new society in the Massachusetts Bay Colony. The new society was to be based on the laws of God. If they obeyed God's laws, Puritans believed, God would protect them. John Winthrop, a leading Puritan, told the settlers "that we shall be as a city upon a hill. The eyes of all people are upon us."

Winthrop, a well-to-do lawyer, helped organize the new colony. He and other officials of the Massachusetts Bay Company had to decide who could take part in the government of the new colony. Under the company charter, only stockholders had the right to govern. At first, Winthrop and a few others tried to follow this rule. But most settlers were not stockholders.

Before long, Winthrop realized that the colony would run more smoothly if more settlers could take part. As a result, all men who were church members were allowed to vote for a governor and for representatives to an assembly called the *General Court*. In fact, only a limited number of men could vote. Still, the idea of representative government was planted in the Massachusetts Bay Colony.

Winthrop was a practical man who listened to others. He was elected governor of Massachusetts Bay many times. Under his leadership, the colony grew and prospered.

The Path to Connecticut

As the elected governor, Winthrop believed that he had the right to rule the colony as he thought best. Some Puritans disagreed. Thomas Hooker, a minister, argued that an official like Winthrop might mean well but still govern badly. Hooker wanted laws to limit the governor's power.

Rivalry grew up between Winthrop and Hooker. In 1636, Hooker and about 100 supporters decided to leave the Massachusetts Bay Colony. A handful of Puritans had already moved into the fertile Connecticut River valley. Hook-

AMERICANS WHO DARED

John Winthrop

John Winthrop, first governor of the Massachusetts Bay Colony, was reelected many times between 1630 and 1649. He led 1,000 people to Boston in the first wave of the Great Migration. Winthrop firmly believed that people should act according to Christian principles. As a devout Puritan, he commanded the respect of other colonists.

er and his friends took the same path. They drove their cattle, goats, and pigs along Indian trails that cut through thick forests. At last, they reached the Connecticut River valley. There, they built the town of Hartford. Other colonists soon followed Hooker into Connecticut. They set up many new towns along the river.

In 1639, the settlers wrote rules called the *Fundamental Orders of Connecticut*. The Fundamental Orders set

of the people." These two ideas are central to a democratic government. A *democratic government* is one in which the people hold power and exercise it by choosing representatives in free elections.

Connecticut became a separate colony in 1662. That year, the towns along the Connecticut River were joined, and the king gave the colony a royal charter. (See the map at left.)

Escape to Rhode Island

In the 1630s, other differences grew up among the Puritans in Massachusetts. A young Salem minister, Roger Williams, challenged the governor's authority. Williams was a gentle, friendly man. But his ideas greatly worried Puritan leaders.

Dangerous ideas. Williams said that the king of England did not have the right to give land in North America to Puritans or anyone else. The land, he said, belonged to the Indians. English settlers should buy their land from the Indians. Puritan leaders were horrified by Williams' ideas. They saw him as a dangerous troublemaker.

Williams had other ideas that were troubling to Puritan leaders. He said that the business of church and state should be completely separate from each other. He also believed in toleration. *Toleration* means willingness to let others practice their own beliefs. In Massachusetts, Puritans refused to let people with different religious beliefs worship freely. Williams even wanted to allow men who were not church members to vote.

Flight in winter. In 1635, leaders of the Massachusetts Bay Colony ordered Williams to return to England. Before Williams could leave, Governor Winthrop took pity on him. He secretly advised Williams to flee. Williams took this advice, escaping in the winter through frozen forests to Narragansett Bay. He stayed with Indians and in the

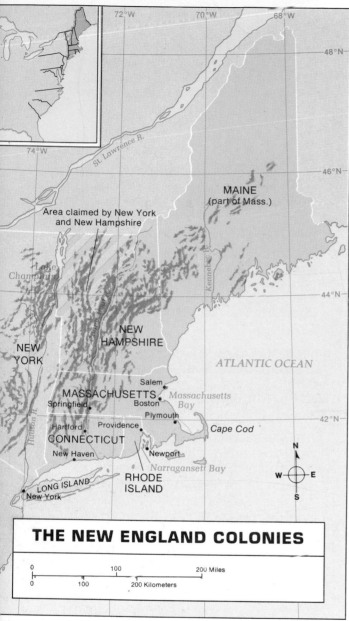

MAP SKILL The New England Colonies were among the first colonies the English set up in America. Name the four New England Colonies. At what latitude is Plymouth?

up a government similar to that of Massachusetts. But the power of the governor was limited. Hooker believed that the people should set limits on the power of the government. Its power, he said, came only from "the free consent

spring bought land from them for a settlement.

In 1644, Williams went to England to get a charter for his colony. At first, the colony was called the Providence Plantations. Later, Providence and other towns became the colony of *Rhode Island*.

Religious freedom. In Rhode Island, Williams put his beliefs into practice. He made sure that the church was separate from the state and allowed settlers to worship as they pleased. This drew Catholic and Jewish settlers to Rhode Island. Williams also allowed all white men to vote, even if they were not church members.

Anne Hutchinson on Trial

Among those who fled to Rhode Island was Anne Hutchinson. Hutchinson and her husband, William, arrived in Boston in 1634. She worked as a midwife, helping to deliver babies. She was herself the mother of 14 children.

Hutchinson was an intelligent and devout churchgoer. Often, she met with friends at her home after church to discuss the minister's sermon. These meetings worried Puritan officials. They believed that only clergymen were qualified to explain God's law. When Hutchinson claimed that many ministers were teaching incorrect beliefs, she was put on trial.

At her trial, Hutchinson answered the questions put to her by Governor Winthrop and other Puritan officials. Winthrop found that she had "a nimble wit and active spirit." Time after time, she showed up the weakness in his arguments. And he could not prove that she had broken any Puritan laws or religious teachings. Finally, after two days of questioning, Hutchinson made a mistake. She said that God had spoken directly to her. To Puritans, this was a terrible error. They believed that God spoke only through the Bible, not to individuals.

In 1638, the General Court sent Hutchinson away from the colony. With her family and supporters, she went to Rhode Island. Later, she moved to the Dutch colony of New Netherland, where she and most of her family were killed by Indians.

Conflict Over the Land

Massachusetts was the largest colony in New England. It controlled trading and fishing villages along the coast

Anne Hutchinson, shown here, courageously faced her accusers. During her trial, she claimed that she had received "an immediate revelation" from God. Because this claim violated Puritan beliefs, Hutchinson was sent out of the colony along with her husband and 14 children.

Tensions ran high in Salem Village, Massachusetts, in 1692. In the eastern part of the village, commerce was booming. Merchants living there enjoyed economic success and growing political power. But farmers in the western part of the village resented the merchants. They faced hard times and had lost political influence. Historians think that this east-west conflict fueled a terrible panic known as the Salem witch hunt.

The panic broke out when two girls began to suffer strange fits. When coaxed to explain their behavior, the girls accused neighbors of casting spells on them. People were quick to believe that the Devil was at work. Soon, accusations of witchcraft spread like wildfire through all of Salem. Before officials ended the witch hunt 10 months later, at least 200 people were named as witches. Of those put on trial, 20 were hanged.

What role did east-west conflict play in the witch hunt? A map study of Salem Village showed a striking split. Most of the accused witches lived in the eastern part. Most of the accusers lived in the western part. Historians have concluded that the witch hunt was in part a subconscious reaction to east-west conflict. Farmers lashed out against merchants and others in the eastern part by accusing them of witchcraft.

★ What caused east-west conflict in Salem Village?

north of Boston. In 1680, the king of England made these settlements into a separate colony called *New Hampshire.* However, in 1691, Massachusetts absorbed the towns and villages of the smaller Plymouth Colony.

As settlers streamed into the colonies, they took over Indian lands. They argued that Indians had no right to the land because they were not farming it. In fact, most Indians were farmers, even though they did not farm all the land. They also depended on the land for hunting to add meat to their diet.

Pequot War. When settlers ignored Indian land claims, fighting broke out. In the 1630s, the English accused the Pequots (PEE kwahts) of killing two traders in the Connecticut Valley. Colonists decided to punish the Pequots. They attacked a Pequot town when most of the men were away and killed hundreds of unarmed men, women, and children.

In the war that followed, most of the Pequots were killed, and the English took over the rich lands of the Connecticut Valley.

King Philip's War. In 1675, a Wampanoag leader, Metacom, took a stand against the English who were moving onto Indian lands near Plymouth. Metacom was called King Philip by the English.

In *King Philip's War,* which lasted for 15 months, both sides committed terrible acts. In the end, Metacom was captured and killed. His family and about 1,000 other Indians were sold into slavery in the West Indies. Many Indians were forced to leave their homes and starved to death. As in Connecticut, colonists soon expanded into Indian lands.

This pattern of expansion and war between colonists and Indians was repeated throughout the colonies. And it continued even after the colonies won independence.

═ SECTION REVIEW ═

1. **Locate:** Massachusetts, Connecticut, Rhode Island, New Hampshire.
2. **Define:** emigrate, democratic government, toleration.
3. How did Puritans disagree with the Church of England?
4. List one way each of the following differed with the Puritan leaders of Massachusetts Bay: (a) Thomas Hooker; (b) Roger Williams; (c) Anne Hutchinson.
5. **What Do You Think?** Do you think settlers and Indians could have avoided war? Explain.

2 Middle Colonies

Read to Learn
★ How did England gain New York?
★ What ideas did William Penn have for his colony?
★ What do these words mean: patroon, proprietary colony, royal colony?

South of New England were the Middle Colonies. The Middle Colonies were unlike the other English colonies, which were settled mostly by English people. Many different people settled in the Middle Colonies. Among them were the Dutch and Swedes who lived along the Hudson and Delaware rivers.

New Netherland Becomes New York

The Dutch colony of New Netherland attracted settlers from many parts of the world. One visitor told of hearing 16 different languages spoken along the busy docks of New Amsterdam.

Patroons rule the land. To encourage farming in New Netherland, the Dutch granted huge parcels of land to a few rich families. A single land grant stretched many miles along the Hudson. One grant was the size of Rhode Island. Owners of these manors, or estates, were called *patroons.* In return for land, each patroon agreed to bring over 50 farm families from Europe.

Patroons ruled the lives of settlers on their land. They decided how much land each family would farm and how much rent each must pay. They held their own courts and gave out punishments for any crime committed on their land. Because few farmers wanted to live under the harsh rule of the patroons, the population of New Netherland remained small.

Peter Stuyvesant. The Dutch West India Company ran the colony. To improve profits, it gave the governor almost absolute power. One governor, Peter Stuyvesant, was a hard-nosed man who had lost a leg fighting in the West Indies. He believed that New Netherland needed strong rule to survive. So he punished lawbreakers with heavy fines or whippings.

Stuyvesant drove the colony into debt by carrying on many costly wars against the Indians. To pay expenses, he taxed most goods that people bought. When colonists demanded a voice in the government, Stuyvesant told them his authority came "from God and the West India Company, not from the pleasure of a few ignorant subjects."

The English move in. In the 1660s, rivalry between England and the Netherlands led to war in Europe. King Charles II of England saw that New Netherland stood between New England and English settlements in Virginia. So in 1664, he sent English warships to New Amsterdam.

Even when the English aimed guns at the city, Stuyvesant swore not to give up. But he had few weapons and little gunpowder. Also, he was so unpopular and had spent so much money fighting Indians that Dutch colonists refused to help him. In the end, he had to surrender without firing a shot.

When King Charles gave New Netherland to his brother, the Duke of York, the colony was renamed *New York* in his honor. For a time, the Duke of York ruled the colony much as the Dutch had. But New Yorkers, especially Puritans who moved to New York from New England, demanded the right to choose an assembly to make laws for the colony. In 1683, the Duke of York finally allowed New York to have its own assembly.

New Jersey

In 1664, New York stretched as far south as the Delaware River. The Duke of York decided to give part of the colony to two friends, Lord Berkeley and Sir George Carteret. These men set up a proprietary (pruh PRĪ uh tehr ee) colony, called *New Jersey.*

In a *proprietary colony,* the king gave land to one or more people, called proprietors. In return, proprietors gave the king a yearly payment and accepted his authority. Proprietors then divided up the land and rented it to oth-

Peter Stuyvesant was known for his temper and stubbornness. He let no one question his judgment. When one settler criticized him, Stuyvesant replied, "I will make him a foot shorter and send the pieces to Holland."

ers. They made laws for the colony but had to respect the rights people had under English law.

New Jersey occupied the fertile land between the Hudson and Delaware rivers. Like New York, New Jersey was settled by people from many nations. Puritans, French Protestants, Scots, Irish, Swedes, Dutch, and Finns mingled in New Jersey. For a time, the colony was divided into two parts: East Jersey and West Jersey. In 1702, East and West Jersey were joined, and New Jersey became a *royal colony* under the king's control. The colony had a charter that protected religious freedom and an assembly that voted on local matters.

William Penn's Holy Experiment

Religious freedom was on the mind of William Penn when he founded a colony in 1682. Penn belonged to the Religious Society of Friends, a group organized by George Fox. The group was known as the *Quakers.*

Religious freedom. Like the Pilgrims and Puritans, the Quakers were Protestant reformers. But their reforms went further than those of other Protestants. Quakers believed that men and women were equal in God's sight. They saw no need for ministers or priests and refused to pay taxes to the Church of England. They had no use for church ceremonies and felt that it was wrong to wear fancy clothes. Quakers also believed that wars were wrong, and they refused to serve in the army.

In both England and New England, Quakers were arrested, fined, and even executed for their beliefs. As you read at the beginning of this chapter, Penn was jailed for his beliefs. So Penn wanted his colony to protect the religious freedom of Quakers as well as other groups.

Penn named his colony Sylvania, meaning woodlands. But the king changed the name to *Pennsylvania,* or

THE MIDDLE COLONIES

MAP SKILL What are the four Middle Colonies shown on this map? Why do you think these colonies were called the Middle Colonies?

Penn's woodlands, to honor William Penn's father, a well-known admiral.

The Frame of Government. Penn wrote the *Frame of Government* to explain how the colony would be run. A governor appointed by Penn and a council of advisers made laws for the colony. A representative assembly accepted or rejected these laws. Later, the assembly won the right to make laws itself. Any white man who owned land or paid taxes had the right to vote.

Penn thought of his colony as a "holy experiment." It was meant to be a model of religious freedom, peace, and Christian living. The Frame of Government allowed freedom of worship for anyone who believed in God. Protestants, Catholics, and Jews went to Pennsylvania to escape persecution.* Penn's beliefs also led him to oppose slavery and act fairly toward Native Americans.

Like Roger Williams in Rhode Island, Penn believed that the land belonged to the Indians. He said that settlers should pay for the land. Native Americans respected Penn for this policy. As a result, the colony enjoyed many years of peace with its Indian neighbors.

Penn advertised for settlers by sending pamphlets all over Europe. Many settlers came from England, Wales, Scotland, and Ireland. Pamphlets were translated into German, French, and Dutch. A large number of German-speaking Protestants moved

---

*Later, English officials forced Penn to turn away Catholic and Jewish settlers.

to Pennsylvania. They were called the Deutsch (doich), or Germans. Later, the Pennsylvania Deutsch became known as the Pennsylvania Dutch.

City of brotherly love. Penn looked up the Delaware River for a spot to build his capital that was "high, dry, and healthy." He had grown up in London, a dirty city with houses crowded close together. Under such conditions, fires were a constant danger. Penn wanted his capital to be "a green country town, which will never be burnt and always be wholesome."

Penn called his capital Philadelphia, a Greek word meaning brotherly love. He drew up a plan for the city. Houses had to leave "ground on each side for gardens or orchards or fields." In the 1700s, Philadelphia grew into the largest, most prosperous city in the English colonies.

The Lower Counties become Delaware. Pennsylvania had no outlet on the coast. So Penn asked the Duke of York to give up some land on the lower Delaware River. The duke agreed, giving Penn an area known as the Lower Counties. Settlers in the Lower Coun-

William Penn treated the Delaware Indians with respect. Friendly relations between settlers and Indians helped Pennsylvania prosper. In this painting, Penn and other Quakers present gifts to the Indians as part of a treaty agreement.

ties did not like this change. They did not want to send representatives all the way to Philadelphia to meet in the assembly. So in 1701, Penn gave them their own assembly. The new colony was called **Delaware.** (See the map on page 107.)

(See the map on page 107.)

SECTION REVIEW

1. **Locate:** Middle Colonies, New York, Hudson River, New Jersey, Delaware River, Pennsylvania, Philadelphia, Delaware.

2. **Define:** patroon, proprietary colony, royal colony.

3. (a) Why did few Dutch settle in New Netherland? (b) Why were the English able to seize the Dutch colony so easily?

4. How was each of these colonies formed: (a) New Jersey; (b) Delaware?

5. **What Do You Think?** In what ways do you think William Penn's "holy experiment" was successful?

3 Southern Colonies

Read to Learn

★ Why did Lord Baltimore want to set up a colony?

★ How was North Carolina different from South Carolina?

★ What plans did General Oglethorpe have for Georgia?

Virginia was the first Southern Colony. In the 1600s and 1700s, English settlers established four other Southern Colonies: Maryland, North Carolina, South Carolina, and Georgia. (See the map on page 112.)

(See the map on page 112.)

A Safe Place for Catholics

In the 1600s, English Catholics had to worship in secret, facing jail or death if they were caught. A Catholic noble, Sir George Calvert, decided to start a colony in America where Catholics could worship in peace.

Lord Baltimore. Calvert's title was Lord Baltimore. He escaped persecution because he was a friend of King Charles I. In 1632, Charles gave him 10 million acres of land north of Virginia. Lord Baltimore named his colony **Maryland** in honor of Queen Henrietta Maria, wife of Charles I. Lord Baltimore died before his colony got under way. But his son, the second Lord Baltimore, sent settlers to Maryland in 1634.

The settlers found much to please them. Chesapeake Bay was full of fish, oysters, and crabs. They could grow tobacco and other crops on the fertile land. When they saw a brightly colored bird, they named it the Baltimore-Bird "because the Colors of Lord Baltimore's Coat of Arms are black and yellow."

The early years. Lord Baltimore never visited Maryland, but he made careful plans for the colony. He appointed a governor and council of advisers and set up an elected assembly. He offered land to any man who brought settlers to the colony. A man received 100 acres for bringing over a healthy male servant and 50 acres for each woman or child.

Among those who settled in the colony were a few women like Margaret Brent. Because she brought her own servants, Brent was given land. She started a plantation and managed it so well that she won the respect of other planters, including the governor.

In 1647, when the governor was dying, he asked Brent to take charge of his estate. She did. She also helped prevent a rebellion in Maryland. The

Although Lord Baltimore, shown here, never visited Maryland, he influenced the life of the colony. He strongly supported the Act of Toleration, which gave freedom of worship to people in his colony.

tlers permission "to root out [the Indians] from any longer being a people."

In the 1640s, Indian and white leaders agreed to divide the land. Both peoples enjoyed peace for about 30 years. But as more settlers arrived and took land, fighting broke out again.

In 1676, Nathaniel Bacon, a 29-year-old planter, organized men and women on the frontier. They wanted the governor to do more to protect them from the Indians. When the governor refused, Bacon and his followers raided Indian villages. They then marched on Jamestown, burning the capital. *Bacon's Rebellion* lasted only a short time. When Bacon died soon after, the revolt fell apart. But it showed that frontier settlers were determined to stay and push even deeper into Indian lands.

Maryland assembly praised her efforts, saying that "the colony's safety at that time [was better] in her hands than in any man's." But when Brent asked for a place in the Maryland assembly, her request was refused because she was a woman.

Although many Catholics settled in Maryland, Protestants also came to the colony. To avoid problems over religion, Lord Baltimore asked the Maryland assembly to approve an *Act of Toleration* in 1649. The act gave religious freedom to all Christians. However, it did not protect the rights of Jews.

Rebellion in Virginia

In Virginia, waves of settlers joined the survivors of the early years. Wealthy tobacco planters controlled the best land near the coast. Newcomers could only get land by taking over Indian lands in the interior. When clashes occurred between Indians and settlers, officials in London gave set-

The Carolinas

In 1663, King Charles II granted eight nobles a huge tract of land that stretched from Virginia to Spanish Florida. The nobles set up a colony called Carolina, the Latin name for Charles. They had grand plans for Carolina. People who bought land would be given noble titles such as Lord High Chamberlain. The new nobles would have serfs and slaves to work for them. These grand plans did not work out. Instead, settlers set up a government like that of Virginia and Maryland with a governor and elected assembly.

People settled in two different areas of the Carolinas. The areas were far apart and had little contact with each other. In the north, tobacco farmers trickled in from Virginia. They tended to have small farms.

In the south, the first settlers built Charles Town, later called Charleston, where the Ashley and Cooper rivers meet. They tried to raise grapes, oranges, and lemons. But these crops did not do well. So they grew rice, which soon became a major crop.

Planters in the south had large estates worked by slaves.* By the early 1700s, thousands of slaves had been brought to the southern part of Carolina. The northern part had fewer slaves. In 1712, Carolina was divided into two colonies: *North Carolina* and *South Carolina.*

The Last Colony

In 1732, King George II gave the southern part of South Carolina to

*In the 1600s, the slave system brought to the West Indies by Spain spread to the English colonies. English, Dutch, and French merchants competed for control of the slave trade.

General James Oglethorpe (OH guhl thawrp). The general was a respected soldier and an energetic reformer. Oglethorpe named his colony *Georgia* in honor of the king. Georgia was the last of the 13 English colonies set up in America.

Oglethorpe was concerned about people imprisoned in England for debt. Under English law, debtors could be jailed until they paid what they owed. Conditions in prison were awful. When debtors came out of prison, they often had no money and nowhere to live. Oglethorpe wanted to help debtors and other poor people by paying their passage to Georgia. He believed that in

In 1734, James Oglethorpe returned to England to get support for his colony in Georgia. He brought along a group of Indians, shown at right, who had sold land to him. In England, Oglethorpe got new rules forbidding slavery and rum in the colony. However, the rules were unpopular in the colony and were later dropped.

Georgia the freed debtors could make a new start in a new home.

A slow start. In 1733, Oglethorpe and 120 settlers sailed from England to Georgia. They built the town of Savannah above the river of the same name.

Oglethorpe set out strict rules for these first settlers. He limited farms to 500 acres and outlawed slavery. He did not allow the sale of rum in the colony. Under these rules, the colony grew slowly. Some settlers moved to other colonies, where they could own large plantations and slaves. When Oglethorpe eased the rules and allowed slavery, Georgia grew more quickly.

King George II supported Oglethorpe's plan for Georgia, mainly because he wanted a strong English colony on the border of Spanish Florida. Spain was still a rival of England in America. And both countries claimed the land between South Carolina and Florida.

War with Spain. General Oglethorpe put his military experience to work. In 1739, Parliament declared war on Spain. Oglethorpe led English forces against the Spanish in Florida. Spain responded by invading Georgia. With the help of the Creek Indians, Oglethorpe and his army forced the Spanish to retreat.

During this time, Mary Musgrove greatly helped Oglethorpe. Musgrove was the daughter of a Creek mother and an English father. She married a planter, John Musgrove, and together they ran a successful plantation.

Because Mary Musgrove spoke both English and Creek, she helped to keep up the friendship between the Creeks and settlers in Georgia. Also, she informed Oglethorpe of Spanish movements on the border between Georgia and Florida.

MAP SKILL The Southern Colonies stretched from Maryland to Georgia. Name three ports in the Southern Colonies. Who ruled the land south of Georgia?

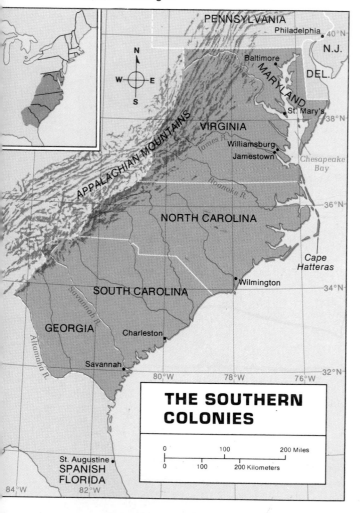

THE SOUTHERN COLONIES

0   100   200 Miles
0 100 200 Kilometers

SECTION REVIEW

1. **Locate:** Maryland, Chesapeake Bay, Virginia, Charleston, North Carolina, South Carolina, Georgia, Savannah, Spanish Florida.

2. (a) Why was Maryland founded? (b) What was the purpose of Maryland's Act of Toleration?

3. Why did Nathaniel Bacon and other frontier settlers rebel in Virginia?

4. Name one difference between North Carolina and South Carolina.

5. **What Do You Think?** Why do you think England wanted a military man like General Oglethorpe to lead Georgia?

4 Governing the Colonies

Read to Learn

★ Why did England pass the Navigation Acts?
★ What were colonial governments like?
★ What do these words mean: mercantilism, import, export, enumerated article, legislature, indentured servant?

At first, English officials paid little attention to the small, struggling settlements in North America. In time, however, all the colonies except Pennsylvania and Maryland came under royal control. For the most part, England left the colonies to themselves. But it did take a strong interest in trade with the colonies.

Trade Between England and the Colonies

Like other European countries, England believed that colonies existed for the benefit of the parent country. This belief was part of the economic theory of *mercantilism* (MER kuhn tihl ihz'm). According to this theory, a nation became strong by building up its gold supplies and expanding its trade.

Trade occurs when goods are exchanged. *Imports* are goods brought into a country. *Exports* are goods sent to markets outside a country. Because exports help a country earn money, mercantilists thought that a country should export more than it imports.

The Navigation Acts. In the 1660s, Parliament passed a series of laws that governed trade between England and its colonies. These laws were known as the *Navigation Acts*. The purpose of the Navigation Acts was to strengthen England and make it richer.

One law said that only ships built in England or the colonies could carry goods to and from the colonies. Also, it said that most of the sailors on the ships had to be from England or the colonies. This law was designed to keep trade in English hands and train sailors who could serve in the navy in wartime.

Another law required any ship carrying European goods to America to stop first in England. The English collected taxes on the goods before they were sent to the colonies. This law allowed England to profit from trade between its colonies and other nations. Other laws listed certain goods from the colonies that could be sold only in England. These goods included tobacco, cotton, and sugar and were known as the *enumerated articles*. In this way, the laws protected the supply of raw materials that English merchants and workers made into finished goods.

Benefits and drawbacks. The Navigation Acts were good for England. In general, they were good for the colonists, too.

The law that limited trade to English or colonial ships encouraged colonists to build their own ships. New England became a center for shipbuilding, and shipbuilders in the colonies made good profits. The colonies benefited from the strong English navy that protected trade. Also, colonial merchants did not need to compete with foreign merchants because they were sure of a market for their goods in England.

Still, many colonists resented the Navigation Acts. They felt that England was treating them like children by telling them what they could or could not do. Also, European goods cost more because they had to be shipped to England first. There, they were taxed before being sent to the colonies.

In the end, many colonists ignored the Navigation Acts or found ways to

Trade between England and the colonies grew in the 1600s and 1700s. Because of the Navigation Acts, ports such as Bristol, England, shown here, bustled with activity.

get around them. Smuggling goods in and out of the colonies became a way of life for some New Englanders. For a time, English officials did little to stop the smuggling. When illegal trade increased, however, England looked for ways to enforce the Navigation Acts.

The Dominion of New England

In the 1680s, England tried to enforce the Navigation Acts, especially in Massachusetts where smuggling was widespread. In 1686, King James II combined all the colonies from Massachusetts to New Jersey into the *Dominion of New England.* He dismissed their assemblies and appointed Sir Edmund Andros to rule the colonies. Andros did not like Puritans. He

soon made himself very unpopular in New England.

Events in England helped the colonists. In 1688, King James was overthrown in the Glorious Revolution. The new king and queen, William and Mary, ended the Dominion of New England and restored elected assemblies in the colonies.

The revolution in England had another effect. In 1689, William and Mary signed the *English Bill of Rights.* It protected the rights of individuals and gave anyone accused of a crime the right to trial by jury. It outlawed cruel punishments. Also, it said that a ruler could not raise taxes or an army without the approval of Parliament. As English men and women, colonists were protected by this bill.

Governors and Assemblies

By the late 1600s, each colony had developed its own form of government. Still, the basic setup of each was the same. A governor was sent from England to direct the affairs of the colony. He enforced the laws and appointed a council of advisers to help him rule.

Elected assemblies. Each colony had a legislature. A *legislature* is a group of people who have the power to make laws. In most colonies, the legislature had an upper house and a lower house. The upper house was made up of the governor's council. The lower house was an elected assembly. It approved laws and protected the rights of citizens. Just as important, it had the right to approve any taxes the governor wanted.

Sometimes, a governor and assembly disagreed. But an assembly controlled the money. So it could refuse to

CHART SKILL The 13 colonies were founded over a period of 125 years. What were the main reasons why the colonies were founded?

Founding of the Colonies

Colony/Date Founded	Leader	Reasons Founded
New England Colonies		

Massachusetts
  Plymouth/1620
  Massachusetts Bay/1630
	William Bradford
	John Winthrop
		Religious freedom
		Religious freedom

New Hampshire/1622	Ferdinando Gorges John Mason	Profit from trade and fishing

Connecticut
  Hartford/1636
  New Haven/1639
	Thomas Hooker	Expand trade; religious and political freedom

Rhode Island/1636	Roger Williams	Religious freedom
Middle Colonies		
New York/1624	Peter Minuit	Expand trade
Delaware/1638	Swedish settlers	Expand trade
New Jersey/1664	John Berkeley George Carteret	Profit from land sales; religious and political freedom
Pennsylvania/1682	William Penn	Profit from land sales; religious and political freedom
Southern Colonies		
Virginia/1607	John Smith	Trade and farming
Maryland/1632	Lord Baltimore	Profit from land sales; religious and political freedom

The Carolinas/1663
  North Carolina/1712
  South Carolina/1712
	Group of eight proprietors	Trade and farming; religious freedom

Georgia/1732	James Oglethorpe	Profit; home for debtors; buffer against Spanish Florida

Among the many kinds of primary sources are photographs and written records. Written records are primary sources if they are firsthand information from people who were involved in an event. Letters, diaries, contracts, laws, and treaties are all primary sources.

The excerpt below is adapted from Gottlieb Mittelberger's *Journey to Pennsylvania*. The book was published after a trip in 1750. Follow these steps to practice using a primary source.

1. **Identify the source by asking who, what, when, and where.** (a) Who wrote the source? (b) What is it about? (c) About when was it written? (d) Where does it take place?

2. **Recognize the author's point of view.** Many eyewitnesses have a particular reason for writing about an event. And they want to share their views with their readers. When you read a primary source, you need to recognize the author's point of view. (a) What is Mittelberger's opinion about the journey to Pennsylvania? (b) What words or phrases show you that he feels strongly about the journey?

3. **Decide whether the source is reliable.** (a) Do you think that Mittelberger gives an accurate view of the journey? Why? (b) Do you think that there is anything left out of his account? (c) Would you say that this is a reliable source for learning about crossing the Atlantic in the mid-1700s? Explain.

 Journey to Pennsylvania

When the ships have weighed anchor, the real misery begins. Unless they have good wind, ships must often sail 8, 9, 10 or 12 weeks before they reach Philadelphia. Even with the best wind, the voyage lasts 7 weeks. . . . During the voyage people suffer terrible misery, stench, many kinds of seasickness, fever, dysentery, boils, scurvy, cancer, and the like, all of which come from old, sharply-salted food and meat and from very bad, foul water so that many die miserably.

Add to this misery, the lack of food, hunger, thirst, frost, heat, dampness, and fear. The misery reaches a peak when a gale rages for two or three nights and days so that every one believes that the ship will go to the bottom with all human beings on board.

When ships land at Philadelphia after the long voyage, only those who have paid for their passage are allowed to leave. Those who cannot pay must stay on board until they are bought and released from the ships by their buyers. . . . The sale of human beings in the market on board ship goes like this. English, Dutch, and Germans come on board to choose among the healthy passengers and bargain with them how long they will serve for their passage money. Adults bind themselves to serve anywhere from 3 to 6 years. Young people must serve until they are 21 years old.

Many parents must sell and trade away their children like so many head of cattle. It often happens that whole families are sold to different buyers.

Work and labor in this new and wild land are very hard. Work mostly consists of cutting wood, felling oak trees, and clearing large tracts of forest.

pay the governor's salary until he met its demands.

On voting day. Each colony had its own rules about who could vote. In all colonies, only white Christian men over age 21 could vote. In some, only Protestants or members of a particular church could vote. All voters had to own property. Colonial leaders believed that only property owners knew what was best for the colony. A newcomer had to live in the colony for a certain time before he could vote. There were fewer rules for local elections. Often, any law-abiding white man could vote for local officials.

On election day, voters and their families met in towns and villages. Excitement filled the air as people exchanged news and gossip. Candidates greeted voters and offered to buy them drinks. Finally, the sheriff called the voters together. One by one, he read out their names. When called, a voter announced his choice in front of everyone. The candidate often thanked the voter for his support. One observer recorded this election day scene:

Sheriff: "Mr. Blair, who do you vote for?"
Blair: "John Marshall."
Marshall: "Your vote is appreciated, Mr. Blair."
Sheriff: "Who do you vote for, Mr. Buchanan?"
Buchanan: "For Mr. John Clopton."
Clopton: "Mr. Buchanan, I shall treasure that vote in my memory. It will be regarded as a feather in my cap forever."

Limited Rights for Many

The right to vote was limited to a few white men. Nonwhites such as blacks and Indians had few rights. Also, women and white servants had limited rights.

Women. Like women in Europe at that time, women in the colonies had few legal rights. A woman's father or husband was supposed to protect her. Women were expected to marry at an early age. A married woman could not start a business of her own or sign a contract unless her husband approved of the arrangement.

In most colonies, unmarried women and widows had more rights. They could make contracts and sue in court. In Maryland and the Carolinas, women settlers who were heads of families were offered land on the same terms as men. Margaret Brent, you remember, won respect for managing her plantation so well.

Indentured servants. Many men and women who were eager to go to America could not pay for the voyage. So they became indentured servants. An *indentured servant* signed a contract, agreeing to work for a certain length of time for whoever paid his or her way to the colony. The time was usually between four and seven years. At the end of that time, an indentured servant received a set of clothes, tools, 50 acres of land, and freedom. More men than women were indentured servants. Because there were so few women in the New World, women often shortened their terms of service by marrying.

Thousands of men, women, and children came to America as indentured servants. After completing their service, they supported themselves as farmers, merchants, and craftworkers. Some became successful and rose to positions of respect in the colonies.

═ SECTION REVIEW ═

1. **Define:** mercantilism, import, export, enumerated article, legislature, indentured servant.
2. Describe three laws included in the Navigation Acts.
3. How did the English Bill of Rights limit the power of the ruler?
4. How was the legislature organized in most colonies?
5. **What Do You Think?** Why do you think there were fewer rules for voting in local elections than in assembly elections?

Chapter 5 Review

★ Summary ★

Between 1607 and 1732, the English set up 13 colonies along the Atlantic coast of North America. People had many reasons for settling in the colonies.

Puritans, Quakers, and Catholics emigrated to find religious freedom. Others left for economic reasons. People like William Penn and James Oglethorpe founded colonies, hoping to make them models of peaceful living and hard work.

In general, England left the colonies alone. In the 1600s and 1700s, each colony had its own government and laws about voting. However, England regulated the trade of the colonies. The Navigation Acts strengthened England's economy. At the same time, the colonies also benefited from these acts. By the mid-1700s, the English colonies were firmly rooted in America.

★ Reviewing the Facts ★   *2 pts. each*

Key Terms. Match each term in Column 1 with the correct definition in Column 2.

Column 1
1. emigrate
2. toleration
3. patroon
4. proprietary colony
5. indentured servant

Column 2
a. someone under contract to work for a certain length of time in exchange for passage to the colonies
b. owner of a manor in New Netherland
c. leave one country to settle in another
d. willingness to let others have their own beliefs
e. land granted by the king to one or more people

Key People, Events, and Ideas. Identify each of the following.

1. Great Migration
2. John Winthrop
3. Thomas Hooker
4. Roger Williams
5. Anne Hutchinson
6. Metacom
7. Peter Stuyvesant
8. William Penn
9. Quakers
10. George Calvert
11. Act of Toleration
12. Margaret Brent
13. James Oglethorpe
14. Mary Musgrove
15. Navigation Acts

★ Chapter Checkup ★   *5 points each*

1. Why did Puritans declare that England had fallen on "evil and declining times"?
2. Why was Roger Williams seen as a dangerous troublemaker?
3. (a) How were the Middle Colonies different from the other English colonies? (b) Name five groups that settled in the Middle Colonies.
4. (a) What beliefs did the Quakers teach? (b) How did William Penn get settlers for his colony?
5. Why did Lord Baltimore want to start a colony in America?
6. (a) What rules did James Oglethorpe set up for his colony? (b) Why did he change these rules?
7. (a) How did the Navigation Acts help England? (b) How did they help the colonies? (c) Why did the colonies resent them?
8. Describe how a person became an indentured servant.

1. **Relating past to present.** (a) Why do you think Puritan leaders saw Roger Williams as a threat to the Massachusetts Bay Colony? (b) Do you think he would be considered a dangerous person today? Explain.

2. **Analyzing a quotation.** James Oglethorpe believed that once debtors reached Georgia, they could work "in a land of liberty and plenty, where . . . they are unfortunate indeed if they can't forget their sorrows." What do you think he meant by this?

3. **Learning about citizenship.** (a) Which colony or colonies were started by people seeking religious freedom? (b) How did each of these colonies treat other religious groups? (c) Do you think religious toleration was widely accepted in the 1600s and 1700s? Explain.

4. **Evaluating.** As colonies grew, relations between settlers and Indians worsened. War often broke out between the two groups. (a) Why did Indians like Metacom take a stand against the English? (b) How did the views of Roger Williams and William Penn differ from the views of other colonists?

★ **Using Your Skills** ★

1. **Map reading.** Study the map on page 107. (a) Which of the Middle Colonies was farthest north? (b) Which of the Middle Colonies was farthest south? (c) Why do you think the 13 colonies were all on the coast?

2. **Placing events in time.** Review the time line on page 98. (a) What event appears first on the time line? (b) What event appears last? (c) During what period were the Navigation Acts passed?

3. **Comparing.** Compare the way Rhode Island and Pennsylvania were founded.

(a) Who founded each colony? (b) What ideas did each founder have? (c) How were their ideas similar? (d) How were their ideas different?

4. **Chart reading.** A chart shows a lot of information in a clear and simple way. Review the chart on page 115 about the founding of the colonies. (a) Which colony was founded first? (b) During what time period were the Southern Colonies founded? (c) How many colonies were founded by individuals?

★ **More to Do** ★

1. **Writing a play.** As a group project, write a brief play about the trial of Anne Hutchinson and act it out.

2. **Preparing a pamphlet.** Prepare a pamphlet William Penn might have used to attract settlers to his colony.

3. **Exploring local history.** Interview someone who has recently immigrated to your community from another country. Write a report comparing their reasons for leaving their home with the reasons of Europeans in the 1600s and 1700s.

4. **Organizing a debate.** Organize a debate on this statement: "Governments in the early colonies were undemocratic." One group should find information to support the statement. The other group should find information to disprove it.

6

Life in the Colonies (1630–1775)

Chapter Outline

1 The New England Way of Life
2 The Breadbasket Colonies
3 Two Ways of Life in the South
4 A New American Culture
5 Growth and Change

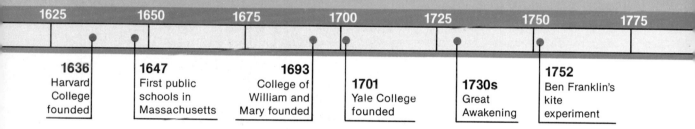

1625	1650	1675	1700	1725	1750	1775

1636 Harvard College founded

1647 First public schools in Massachusetts

1693 College of William and Mary founded

1701 Yale College founded

1730s Great Awakening

1752 Ben Franklin's kite experiment

About This Chapter

In the 1600s and 1700s, thousands of settlers flocked to the English colonies. They found a world very different from their old ones. From New England to the South, settlers experimented with new crops, new building materials, and new ideas. In the end, each region developed its own way of life.

In the 1600s, life was very hard for the newcomers. People in the different colonies knew little about one another. By the 1700s, however, the colonies were well established. Improved trade and travel allowed colonists to learn more about each other.

Even after conditions improved, people worked hard at many tasks. At an early age, children took on important jobs. In 1775, a Connecticut girl wrote this description of her day's work.

Fixed gown . . . mended Mother's Riding-hood, spun short thread, fixed two gowns for Welsh's girls . . . spun linen, worked on cheesebasket, [combed] flax with Hannah, we did 51 lbs. apiece. Pleated and ironed, read a sermon of Dodridge's, spooled a piece, milked the cows, spun linen, did 50 knots, made a broom of guinea wheat straw, spun thread to whiten, set a red dye, [visited with] two scholars from Mrs. Taylor's, I carded two pounds of whole wool [and then] spun harness twine and scoured the pewter.

Study the time line above. Name three colleges founded in the colonies.

Plantations in the South were often built along rivers. Planters loaded goods on ships bound for England, the West Indies, and Europe.

1 The New England Way of Life

Read to Learn

★ How did geography affect colonists in New England?

★ Why was the meetinghouse the center of town life?

★ What tasks did women perform?

★ What do these words mean: subsistence farmer, surplus, stocks?

The New England Colonies were settled mostly by Puritans and their offspring. Puritan attitudes and beliefs influenced the way of life in these colonies. But geography also affected life in New England.

The Land and Climate

When the Pilgrims arrived off Cape Cod, William Bradford described the new land as a "country, full of woods and thickets," that had a "wild and savage" look. Settlers soon discovered that New England was, indeed, a land of forests. They organized chopping bees to clear away trees and haul off large boulders that dotted the land.

The rocky soil was not very fertile, and farming methods were crude. As a result, the land wore out. So every few years, farmers needed to clear new land. Most settlers were **subsistence farmers.** That is, they had small plots of land on which they grew enough food for their own needs. When they did produce **surpluses,** or extra food, they traded it for such goods as tools and kettles.

The climate of New England was quite harsh. During the short growing season, families worked from dawn to dusk in the fields. During the long cold winters, deep snows sometimes cut towns off from each other.

Yet sometimes, snow helped farmers. Once farmers began producing more goods, they often waited until the winter to take these goods to the nearest port. When the roads were covered with snow, they loaded butter, maple sugar, and other products onto sleds drawn by oxen. Because the sleds slipped smoothly over the packed snow, the trips were quicker than at other times of the year.

Using the Land's Resources

New Englanders made good use of their limited resources. The large forests provided lots of timber. Fish and furs were plentiful, and the jagged coastline offered many good harbors.

Shipbuilding. Settlers in New England used the forests to supply timber to a busy shipbuilding industry. Lumber was brought from New Hampshire to shipbuilders in Boston. Portsmouth, New Hampshire, and Newburyport, Massachusetts, later became major shipbuilding ports.

The tallest trees were made into masts. Other products used in shipbuilding such as pitch and tar also came from the forests. England encouraged shipbuilding in the colonies. It needed ships for its navy, and its own forests had been cut down years before.

Fishing and whaling. Although most New Englanders were farmers, many fished the coastal waters. Fishing people hauled in huge catches. When Captain John Smith visited New England, he caught 60,000 cod in just one month. One New Englander reported, "I myself . . . have seen such multitudes of sea bass that it seemed to me that one might go over their backs without getting one's feet wet." Catches included oysters over a foot long and lobsters over five feet.

Fishing was hard work. When the fish were running, fishermen did not stop to eat or sleep. A cook held food in front of the fishermen so that they could eat while they worked. After fishing boats returned to shore, fish were dried in the sun and sent to other colonies or to England.

MAP SKILL Farming, shipbuilding, and fishing were among the economic activities of New England colonists. Study the map and the key. Name one city where ships were built.

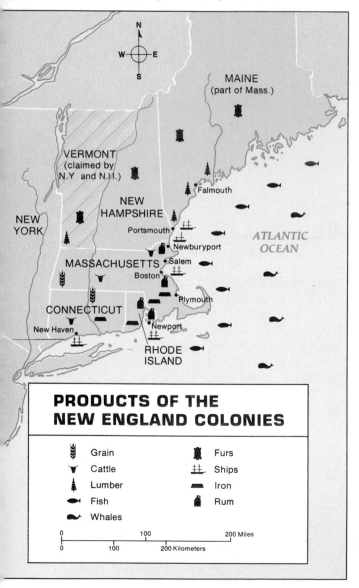

PRODUCTS OF THE NEW ENGLAND COLONIES

- Grain
- Cattle
- Lumber
- Fish
- Whales
- Furs
- Ships
- Iron
- Rum

In the 1600s, New Englanders began to hunt whales. Whales supplied settlers with products such as ivory and oil for lamps. Whaling grew into a big business in the 1700s and 1800s.

New England Towns

New England was a land of towns and villages. Farm families lived in towns and went each day to their fields outside the towns. Puritans thought people should live in towns so that they could worship and take care of local matters as a community.

What did a New England town look like? At the center of most towns was the common, an open field where cattle grazed. Nearby was the meetinghouse. The meetinghouse was the center of town life. As one New Englander observed, it was "built by our own vote, framed by our own hammers and saws, and by our own hands set in the most convenient place for all." The meetinghouse served two purposes. It was the church where Puritans met to worship. It was also used for town meetings.

On the common outside the meetinghouse, many towns set up stocks. *Stocks* were wooden frames with holes for the arms and legs. They were used to punish people found guilty of crimes such as drunkenness and swearing. People could be sentenced to spend a few hours or a few days in the stocks. Passers-by laughed at prisoners and threw rotten eggs or stones at them.

Wooden houses with steep roofs lined both sides of the narrow streets of a town. Often, the second floor of a house was built out over the street. This overhang gave the second-floor rooms more space and protected the first-floor walls from rain.

Church services. Religion was at the center of Puritan life. The church enforced rules about behavior, clothing, and education. Attendance at church was required. Services were very different from those of today. Sun-

Puritans used stocks such as those shown here to punish people who broke their strict moral code. Sometimes, people were sentenced to stand with their head and arms in stocks. The public shame and discomfort in the stocks made people think twice about breaking the law.

day services lasted all day. In the morning, the meetinghouse bell rang to call everyone to worship. At midday, people had an hour for lunch and then returned for the afternoon service.

In church, Puritans sat on hard wooden benches. The wealthy sat apart in boxlike enclosures with high walls. During the 1600s, women were seated on one side of the house and men on the other. Children had their own separate section. It was hard for them to keep quiet during the long services. One Connecticut boy was scolded for his "rude and idle behavior in the meetinghouse such as laughing and smiling . . . or pulling the hair of his neighbor."

Town meetings. Church services were solemn times, but town meetings could be noisy. Citizens met to discuss questions that affected the town—what roads to build, what fences to repair, how much to pay the schoolmaster. Townspeople argued and then voted on these issues.

Town meetings gave New Englanders a chance to speak out on issues. Unlike the Spanish or French colonists in the Americas, the English colonists had a say in government. This early experience encouraged the growth of democratic ideas in the New England Colonies.

At Home With the Family

During the long, cold New England winters, life at home centered around the huge kitchen fireplace. The fire-place covered an entire wall of the kitchen. Despite the size of the fire-place, the room was cold because winds blew down the chimney. One New Englander described how the ink in his pen froze even as he sat writing right inside his fireplace.

If the kitchen was chilly, bedrooms were even colder. Thick drapes hung from four posts at each corner of a bed. The drapes helped keep out the cold. Before going to sleep, people put a metal warming pan filled with hot coals in their beds to heat the sheets.

In the 1600s, New Englanders sat on narrow benches at long tables to eat their meals. Instead of plates, they used trenchers. A trencher was a block of wood hollowed out for food. Two people shared a trencher. In the 1700s, people began to use pewter or china plates.

At meals, children were supposed to eat quickly and remain silent. In some homes, children had to eat standing by

In colonial times, the fireplace was the center of family life. It was used for both cooking and heating the home. In this picture, children inside the fireplace are sitting on the warming bench. Why do you think the warming bench was a popular spot?

Women worked hard raising their families, keeping the house, and doing chores on the farm. This picture shows women on a typical washday. At left, one woman boils water. The others beat and rinse clothes in the stream.

the table or behind their parents, who handed them food! One book of table manners advised children: "Look not earnestly at any other person that is eating." And it warned them not to throw bones under the table.

A Busy Life for Women

In New England and in other colonies, women worked at many tasks from sunrise to sunset. Although a woman had few legal rights, she worked as an equal partner with her husband to provide for her family. Women helped clear the land. They planted and harvested crops. They ground corn, skinned and cleaned animals, and dried fruits and vegetables such as peppers, pumpkins, and apples. Many women kept geese, and they plucked goose feathers for pillows and mattresses.

In the fall, women made candles for the long winter evenings ahead. First, they melted animal fat in a huge pot. Then, they dipped candlewicks into the fat, letting it cool on the wick. On a good day, a woman could make about 200 candles.

Women spent a lot of time making clothes for the family. They began with wool from sheep and flax from a plant. Wool had to be dyed, greased, and combed before it was spun into thread. Women then wove the thread into cloth or knitted it into socks or mittens. Flax had to be cut, beaten, combed, and sorted before it was spun into linen thread.

Women worked at many jobs outside the home. They were blacksmiths, tinmakers, and weavers as well as innkeepers, merchants, and barbers. They also worked as nurses, midwives, and doctors.

SECTION REVIEW

1. **Define:** subsistence farmer, surplus, stocks.
2. Why did New England farmers have a hard time producing good harvests?
3. List three ways that colonists made a living in New England.
4. What was the purpose of town meetings?
5. **What Do You Think?** Do you think women in the New England Colonies had harder lives than women of today? Explain your answer.

2 The Breadbasket Colonies

Read to Learn
★ How did geography affect people in the Middle Colonies?
★ How did Swedish, Dutch, and German settlers influence the Middle Colonies?
★ What do these words mean: cash crop, tenant farmer, backcountry?

New Englanders visiting the Middle Colonies saw much that was familiar. But they also found differences. Farms were larger and more spread out. Towns were not the center of life. Unlike New Englanders, who came mostly from England, settlers in the Middle Colonies came from many European countries.

The Land and Climate

The land and climate of the Middle Colonies were different from those of New England. In the fertile lands of the Hudson and Delaware river valleys, farmers prospered. Winters were less harsh. Summers were warmer, and the growing season lasted longer.

Cash crops. Unlike the subsistence farmers of New England, farmers in the Middle Colonies produced surpluses of wheat, barley, and rye. These became *cash crops,* or crops that are sold for money on the world market. The Middle Colonies became known as the *Breadbasket Colonies* because they exported so much wheat and other grain.

Farmers also raised cattle and pigs. Every year, they sent tons of beef, pork, and butter to the ports of New York and Philadelphia. From there, the food was shipped to New England and the South or to the West Indies, England, and other parts of Europe.

Manufacturing and crafts. The Middle Colonies produced many kinds of manufactured goods. A visitor to Pennsylvania mentioned that he saw workshops turn out "most kinds of hardware, clocks, watches, locks, guns, flints, glass, stoneware, nails, paper." Pennsylvania became a center of manufacturing and crafts, in part because William Penn had encouraged many German settlers with valuable skills to set up shop there.

Colonists in the Delaware River valley made household and farm tools because they had large supplies of iron ore. They built furnaces to heat the iron ore and turn it into pig iron. At forges, or smaller furnaces, ironworkers puri-

Iron products made at forges were important to daily life in the colonies. Pat Lyon, owner of this forge, was a very successful businessman.

fied the pig iron and made nails, farm tools, and parts for guns.

Manor life in New York. In New Jersey, Pennsylvania, and Delaware, farmers earned a legal right to land by clearing, planting, and living on it. In New York, however, a different system existed.

As you read, Dutch patroons owned huge manors along the Hudson River. *Tenant farmers* worked the land and paid rent to the landowner. The manor system did not change when the English took over New Netherland, even though many tenant farmers were unhappy with it. They felt that rents were too high. They resented having to use their own oxen to clear or plow the landowner's fields. At harvest time, they had to leave their own crops in the field while they harvested the landowner's crops.

Several times, angry tenant farmers rioted and attacked manor houses. Many tenant farmers simply left New York. They moved to Pennsylvania or New Jersey, where they could work their own land. Others went north to farm the land in the area that later became Vermont.

Comfortable Homes

The different peoples who settled the Middle Colonies had their own styles of building. Some colonists built log cabins, which were introduced to America by the Swedes. Sweden was a land of forests. Swedes had built log cabins there long before Swedish settlers came to America.

Dutch houses were common in the towns and cities of New York. The Dutch used brick for building their homes. Their houses had steep roofs topped by weather vanes. Front doors were split across the middle. The top half was opened to let in air and light. The bottom half was closed to keep out geese and pigs. In front, the Dutch built

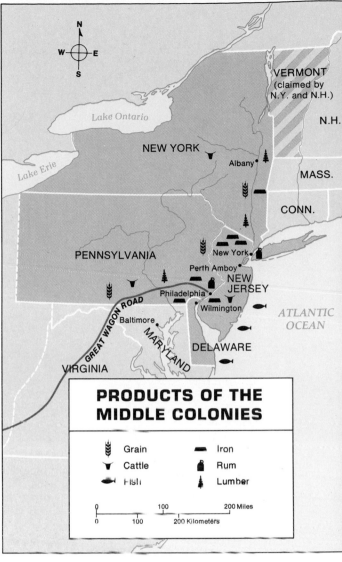

MAP SKILL Compare this map of the Middle Colonies to the map of the New England Colonies on page 122. What similarities do you find in the products of the two regions? What differences do you find?

a wooden porch, which they called a stoop.

German settlers developed a new kind of woodburning stove. It heated a home better than a fireplace, which let blasts of cold air leak down the chimney. Other colonists copied the German stove.

Visitors to the Middle Colonies remarked on the comfortable life of

This painting shows a flax-scutching bee in the Middle Colonies. Flax is a plant with fibers that are spun into linen thread. A bee was a party where many people worked together at a task. The man at far left is breaking the tough stalks of the flax plant. Other men and women pound the stalks to get at the fibers. At bees such as this one, colonists exchanged news with friends and neighbors.

many farm families. A New Englander who stayed with a Quaker family in Philadelphia reported that the people dressed simply, according to Quaker custom. But he marveled at the supper he was served, which included "ducks, hams, chickens, beef, pig, tarts, creams, custards, [and] jellies."

Moving West

In the 1700s, thousands of Scotch-Irish and German settlers arrived in the Middle Colonies. They set out from Philadelphia and other cities for frontier lands farther west. As settlers pushed the Indians out, they built new towns such as Haverford, Lancaster, and York. When they ran up against the Appalachian Mountains, many turned south and settled in western Maryland and Virginia. This area along the Appalachians was called the *backcountry.*

The Great Wagon Road. The route to the backcountry was known as the *Great Wagon Road.* Like most roads, it was rough and rutted with deep mudholes.

Settlers built large wagons, called *Conestoga* (kahn uh STOH guh) wagons, to carry goods along the road. A Conestoga wagon had large wheels that kept goods from getting wet as the wagon bumped through mudholes. The floor curved up at both ends so that goods would not fall out as the wagon went up or down steep hills. A cloth cover stretched over hoops of wood kept out rain and snow.

Life in the backcountry. The first settlers in the backcountry took over lands already cleared by Indians. Later settlers had to clear thick forests themselves before they could farm the land. To do this, they used a method they had learned from the Indians. They girdled trees, or cut the bark around tree trunks with axes. Sometimes, they burned around the roots. Both methods killed the trees. Farmers then planted seeds between the dead trees. After a year or two, they cleared away the dead trees.

People used the forests for many of their needs. They built log cabins and made wooden shutters. Indians showed them how to use knots from pine trees to make candles to light their homes. Settlers gathered wild honey from hollow logs and hunted animals for food. Sharpshooters brought home deer, bear, and wild turkey.

SECTION REVIEW

1. **Locate:** Hudson River, Delaware River, Philadelphia, Appalachian Mountains, Great Wagon Road.
2. **Define:** cash crop, tenant farmer, backcountry.
3. Why were the Middle Colonies known as the Breadbasket Colonies?
4. Why were tenant farmers in New York unhappy with life on the manors?
5. **What Do You Think?** Why do you think settlers pushed into the backcountry rather than stay in the east?

---

3 Two Ways of Life in the South

Read to Learn

★ How did geography affect settlers in the Southern Colonies?
★ Why did planters turn to slave labor?
★ How was plantation life different from life in the backcountry?
★ What do these words mean: tidewater, slave code, racism?

Settlers in the Southern Colonies developed a way of life different from that of other English colonies. The difference was due in part to climate and geography.

The Land and Climate

In the South, the climate was warmer than elsewhere along the coast of North America. As you have read, Jamestown settlers learned that the climate and soil of Virginia were well suited to growing tobacco. At first, small farmers grew tobacco along with food crops. But tobacco soon wore out the soil. As a result, plantations often replaced small tobacco farms. Plantation owners could rotate crops and leave part of their land idle each year. This way, the soil did not wear out so quickly.

Settlers in other Southern Colonies followed the example of Virginia. By the 1700s, Virginia, Maryland, and parts of North Carolina had become major tobacco-growing areas. South Carolina and Georgia produced rice and indigo. In busy Charleston harbor, ships loaded cargoes of tobacco, rice, and indigo for markets overseas.

Geography affected where southerners built their plantations. They settled along the coast and fertile river valleys because these low-lying areas were good for growing rice. Rivers gave inland planters an easy way to ship their harvests. At harvest time, crops were brought to the river bank and loaded onto ships bound for England or the West Indies.

Along the coastal plain, ocean tides swept up river for quite a distance. As a result, the coastal plain was known as the *tidewater.* The tidewater was a region of plantations. Farther inland,

the land was hilly and covered with thick forests. As in the Middle Colonies, this inland area was called the backcountry. Two ways of life grew up in the South, one in the tidewater and the other in the backcountry.

Growth of Slavery

Tidewater planters needed many workers to make their land profitable. At first, they tried to make Indians work the land. Or they brought indentured servants from England. By the late 1600s, however, planters were buying large numbers of African slaves. Although people in other colonies owned some slaves, most slaves lived in the South.

Reasons. Why did southern planters turn to African slave labor? The English saw how slave labor earned profits for the Spanish colonists. Planters believed that Africans were used to warm climates. Then, too, it was hard for blacks to escape because their skin color made it easy to find them. Unlike the Indians, Africans did not know the forests of North America.

Planters preferred slaves to indentured servants because buying a slave was a one-time expense. Indentured servants could leave after they completed their years of service. But planters owned and controlled their slaves as well as their slaves' children forever. Colonists passed *slave codes,* or laws that controlled the behavior of slaves and denied them basic rights. Slaves were seen as property, not as human beings.

Most English colonists accepted slavery. They did not question the justice of owning slaves because of racism. *Racism* is the belief that one race is superior to another. White Europeans believed that black Africans were inferior to them. They claimed to be helping their slaves by teaching them Christian beliefs. A few colonists, however, protested that slavery was unjust.

MAP SKILL Study this map of the Southern Colonies. What are the major products of the tidewater, or coastal areas? What are the major products of the backcountry?

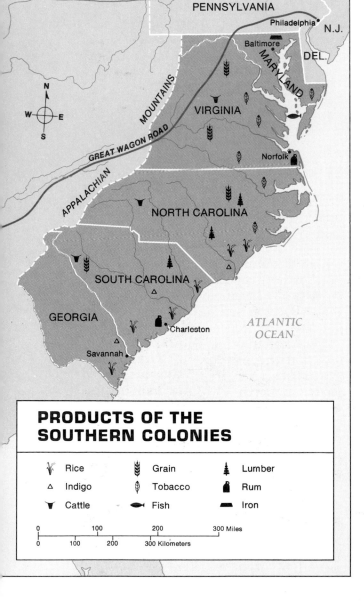

PRODUCTS OF THE SOUTHERN COLONIES

Rice	Grain	Lumber	
Indigo	Tobacco	Rum	
Cattle	Fish	Iron	

0   100   200   300 Miles

0   100   200   300 Kilometers

Quakers spoke out against slavery, and some New Englanders criticized merchants who grew rich from the slave trade.

The Middle Passage. During the 1700s, the slave trade grew into a major business. Portuguese, Spanish, Dutch, English, and French ships brought about 100,000 Africans to the Americas each year.

White slave traders built forts on the African coast. They offered guns and other goods to African rulers who brought slaves to the coast. Slaves were forced on board ships and packed into small spaces below decks with hardly enough room to sit up. Often, they were chained together two by two. Once or twice a day, they were taken up on deck to eat and exercise.

Some Africans fought for their freedom during the trip. Others refused to eat. But sailors pried open their mouths and forced them to swallow food. Still others leaped overboard. They chose to die rather than to live as slaves. Many died of diseases that spread quickly in the hot, filthy air below deck.

The horrible trip from Africa to the Americas was called the *Middle Passage.* When slave ships reached American ports, captains sold their human cargo in the marketplace. Planters inspected the slaves to find healthy, strong workers. On the plantation, slaves had to adjust to a strange language and culture—and to a life without freedom.

Slaves helped the Southern Colonies grow. They cleared the land, worked the crops, and tended the livestock. They showed white colonists how to grow rice. Still as slaves, some became fur trappers, sailors, and soldiers. But many did not accept their lot. Sometimes, they tried to escape, attacked their owners, or damaged crops in protest.

This painting was done by an Englishman who served as an officer on a slave ship. Captains crammed their human cargo into the holds below deck. Many slaves died of diseases that spread quickly in the overcrowded and filthy holds.

Life on a Plantation

Many plantations were almost self-sufficient. People on the plantation produced most of the food and other goods they needed. On a typical plantation, the largest building was the Great House, where the planter and his family lived. Houses were made of wood or brick. The inside walls were plastered with lime ground from oyster shells.

Wealthy planters copied the styles of English manor houses. A planter's house had a parlor for visitors, a dining room, a library or music room, bedrooms for family members, and guest bedrooms. Some houses also had large ballrooms for dancing. The kitchen was often a separate building so that the Great House remained "cool and sweet." As one planter explained, "The Smell of hot Victuals [food]" was "offensive in hot Weather."

Planters made all decisions about the land. They decided which fields to plant, what crops to grow, and when to harvest the crops and take them to market. They also directed the lives of slaves. A planter might own from 20 to 100 slaves. Most slaves worked in the fields. However, some were skilled workers. Black carpenters, barrelmakers, blacksmiths, and brickmakers produced goods the plantation needed. Other slaves worked in the Great House as cooks, cleaners, or servants.

In the Great House on a plantation, Southerners lived in simple elegance. Here, family members enjoy music and dancing. At an early age, children of wealthy planters learned to play musical instruments and practiced graceful dancing steps.

Free Enterprise in Action

Eliza Lucas and Indigo

Eliza Lucas was 17 years old when her parents moved to South Carolina from the West Indies. Her father, an army colonel, soon had to leave his family to serve overseas. Because her mother was ill, Eliza Lucas took over the family plantation. The Lucases grew rice in low-lying fields. But Colonel Lucas also owned land where rice could not be grown. He and his daughter wanted to put that land to good use.

Colonel Lucas sent home seeds and plants from all over the world, including ginger, cotton, figs, and indigo. Indigo is a plant whose leaves produce a blue dye. Indigo was grown in the West Indies and sold well in England, where it was used to dye cloth.

Eliza Lucas successfully raised a few indigo plants. So her father sent an overseer, or manager, from the West Indies to help her raise a full crop. But the overseer made a dye of poor quality from the indigo. The young woman found out that the overseer was spoiling the dye on purpose. He was afraid that if she succeeded in growing indigo, West Indian planters would lose business.

Colonel Lucas then sent a black slave skilled at growing indigo to help his daughter. The man showed slaves on the plantation how to raise a good crop. Eliza Lucas then gave indigo seeds to her neighbors. Indigo succeeded beyond her wildest dreams. By 1754, South Carolina was shipping many tons of indigo to England every year. By then, Eliza Lucas had married Charles Pinckney. For the next 40 years, she continued to raise indigo and other crops.

★ How do you think growing indigo helped the economy of the South?

Women kept the household running smoothly. They were in charge of the house slaves and made sure daily tasks were done. These tasks included weeding the vegetable garden, milking the cows, and collecting eggs. Women ran the plantation if their husbands were away or died.

The Backcountry South

In the backcountry of the South, settlers developed a different way of life from tidewater planters. Many backcountry people came from Pennsylvania along the Great Wagon Road. (See the map on page 127.) They settled in western Maryland, Virginia, and the Carolinas. Many went on to the Shenandoah Valley, where they found rich lands for farming.

In the backcountry, people built log cabins and raised cattle and pigs. Once a year, they rounded up their animals and drove them to markets in Baltimore, Petersburg, or Charleston.

The backcountry was more democratic than the tidewater. There were few very rich families on the frontier. Settlers treated each other as equals. As one visitor noted, "Every man . . . calls his wife, brother, neighbor, or acquaintance by their proper name of Sally, John, James, or Michael." By contrast, tidewater people used terms such as "My dear sir," "Madam," or "Mister." Also, backcountry people wore simple clothes suited to frontier life, not the silks and velvets worn by tidewater families.

Backcountry settlers often quarreled with their governments in the east. These frontier settlers did not elect as many representatives to colonial assemblies as tidewater planters did. So when the government passed laws that were unpopular in the backcountry, settlers there sometimes rebelled to defend their rights.

===SECTION REVIEW===

1. **Define:** tidewater, slave code, racism.
2. What cash crops did the South grow?
3. Why did planters prefer slaves to indentured servants?
4. (a) What kinds of decisions did planters make? (b) What kinds of jobs did women do on plantations?
5. **What Do You Think?** Why do you think settlers in the backcountry resented tidewater planters?

4 A New American Culture

Read to Learn
★ How did children in the colonies get an education?
★ What were the social classes in the colonies?
★ Why did Benjamin Franklin become famous?
★ What do these words mean: public school, apprentice, gentry, almanac?

By the mid-1700s, the English colonies had developed a culture different from that of England. Settlers from many lands contributed to the new American culture.

Education in the Colonies

From the start, colonists worried about how to teach their children what they needed to know in the New World. New England led the way in education. Many Puritans were well educated. They believed that all people should learn to read so that they could study the Bible. As a result, the Massachusetts assembly passed a law ordering all parents to teach their children "to read and understand the principles of religion."

The first public schools. In 1647, Massachusetts required all towns with 50 families to hire a school teacher for their children. A town with 100 families had to set up a grammar school for boys to prepare them for college. The law set up the first *public schools,* or schools supported by taxes. Public schools were important because they allowed children from both poor and rich families to get an education.

The first New England schools had only one room for students of all ages. Because there were few coins in the colonies, parents paid the schoolteacher with furs, fruit, green vegetables, and corn.

Other schools and colleges. In the Middle Colonies, churches and individual families set up private schools. These schools charged fees. So only children of well-to-do families could afford to attend. In the Southern Colonies, people lived too far apart to bring children together in a school. Planters hired tutors, or private teachers, for their children. Sometimes, a school was set up in an old tobacco shed in the fields. Children rode on horseback or rowed up a river to school.

In 1636, Massachusetts set up the first college to train Puritan ministers. Two years later, John Harvard, a minister, left his library to the college, which then took his name. Puritans in Connecticut set up Yale College in 1701. In Virginia, the College of William and Mary was organized in 1693 to train ministers of the Church of England. Before long, colleges also began training lawyers, doctors, and teachers.

A	In *Adam's* Fall We finned all.
B	Thy Life to mend This Book attend.
C	The Cat doth play And after flay.
D	A Dog will bite A Thief at Night.
E	The Eagle's Flight Is out of Sight.
F	The idle Fool Is whipt at School.

A New England schoolbook, or primer, not only taught students to read but also gave moral lessons. From a book such as this one, children learned the alphabet, reading, and spelling. In school, they also studied arithmetic, history, and geography.

Learning on the job. Many children had no formal schooling. They learned the skills they needed on the job. In farm families, children learned from their parents and older brothers and sisters.

Children also served as apprentices (uh PREHN tihs ehz). An *apprentice* worked for a master craftsman to learn a trade or craft. For example, when a boy reached age 12 or 13, his parents might apprentice him to a master glassmaker. The young apprentice lived in the glassmaker's home for six or seven years. The glassmaker gave him food and clothing and treated him like one of the family. He was also supposed to teach the boy to read and write and give him religious training.

In return, the apprentice worked without pay in the glassmaker's shop and learned the skills he needed to become a master glassmaker. He was then ready to start his own shop as a glassmaker. Boys were apprenticed to many trades. They became papermakers, printers, clockmakers, or leather tanners.

Education for girls. Girls, too, became apprentices, although they had a smaller choice of trades. A girl's parents might send her to become a cook, a needleworker, or a housemaid. However, women learned other trades from their fathers, brothers, or husbands. They worked as shoemakers, silversmiths, and butchers. Quite a few women became printers. A woman often took over her husband's business after his death.

Most schools accepted only boys. In New England, however, girls attended dame schools, or private schools run by women in their own homes. Girls learned many skills at home by helping their mothers to dry meat and vegetables, spin wool, weave, and embroider. Often, parents taught their daughters to read and write.

Bigwigs and the Meaner Sort

Colonists enjoyed more social equality than people in England. But social classes did exist in the colonies. At the top stood the *gentry.* They included wealthy planters, merchants, ministers, successful lawyers, and royal officials. Below the gentry was the middle class. It included farmers who worked their own land, skilled craftworkers, and some tradespeople. The lowest class, often called the "meaner sort," included hired farmhands, indentured servants, and slaves.

People dressed according to their social class. The gentry showed off their wealth by wearing silks with lace ruffles. People of the "meaner sort" could be fined for dressing like the gentry. Instead of silks, they wore simple clothes made of homespun linen or wool.

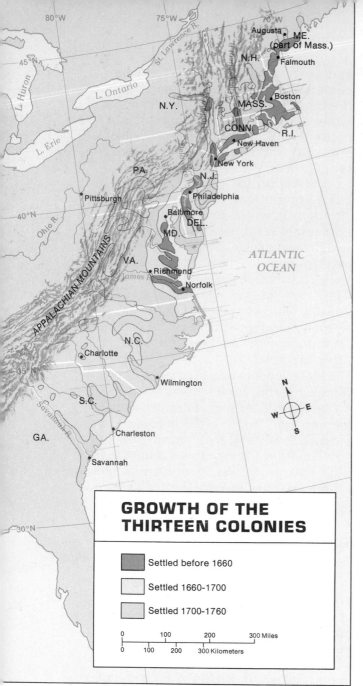

GROWTH OF THE THIRTEEN COLONIES

■ Settled before 1660

□ Settled 1660-1700

▨ Settled 1700-1760

0   100   200   300 Miles

0 100 200 300 Kilometers

MAP SKILL The 13 colonies grew and expanded in the 1600s and 1700s. In which direction did settlers move as the colonies grew? What barriers to settlement did they have to overcome?

The gentry and middle class copied the popular styles of London. In the 1600s, long curly wigs were in fashion. Wealthy colonists who wore these fancy wigs became known as "bigwigs." By the mid-1700s, men wore smaller wigs tied at the back with a ribbon.

Benjamin Franklin: An American Genius

People in the colonies could climb the social ladder more easily than in England. One such person was Benjamin Franklin, the son of a poor Boston soap and candle maker. Franklin was born in 1706 and died in 1790. In his long life, he rose from poverty to become famous throughout the world.

Successful printer. Franklin was one of 17 children. He left school at age 10 to work for his father. Later, he was apprenticed to his brother James, a printer. Although Franklin had only two years of formal schooling, he never stopped learning. He used his spare time to read and study literature, mathematics, and foreign languages.

At age 17, Franklin ran away from Boston and made his way to Philadelphia. He set up a printing shop that he turned into a thriving business. He published pamphlets, newspapers, and *almanacs,* or books containing calendars and other useful information. Franklin's best-known book was *Poor Richard's Almanac.* Many of its sayings are still quoted today: "Early to bed and early to rise makes a man healthy, wealthy, and wise" and "The sleeping fox catches no poultry."

Scientist and inventor. From an early age, Franklin was curious about how things worked. And he was full of ideas for improving things. In 1740, he invented the Franklin stove. It burned less wood and heated homes better than other stoves. He invented the bifocal lens, which let people wear one pair of glasses for both distance and closeup work.

Franklin experimented with electricity. In 1752, he proved that lightning was a form of electricity. To do this, he flew a kite during a thunderstorm. When lightning struck the kite, electricity flowed down a wire attached to the kite. Franklin then invented the lightning rod to protect buildings against damage from lightning.

Benjamin Franklin is shown here conducting his famous experiment with lightning. Franklin became known throughout America and Europe for his work. In 1754, a French scientist wrote him: "We are all waiting with the greatest eagerness to hear from you." Today, scientists say that Franklin was lucky he was not electrocuted when he flew the kite in a storm.

Energetic leader. Franklin had ideas about improving city life. He convinced Philadelphia to pave its streets with cobblestones, organize a police force, and set up a fire company. Eager to promote education, he organized the first lending library in America and an academy that later became the University of Pennsylvania.

Franklin had a rich career as a public leader and diplomat, as you will read later on. His practical inventions helped people, and his fame worldwide gave colonists reason to be proud of their home-grown genius.

The Great Awakening

In the 1730s and 1740s, a religious movement, known as the *Great Awakening,* swept through the colonies. In New England, the Puritan preacher Jonathan Edwards called on listeners to examine their lives and give up their unholy ways. In a famous sermon, "Sinners in the Hands of an Angry God," Edwards described the fiery torments of hell that awaited evildoers.

Between 1738 and 1770, an English minister, George Whitefield (HWIHT feeld), drew huge crowds to outdoor meetings from Massachusetts to Georgia. Whitefield was a powerful speaker.

His voice rang with feeling as he called on sinners to reform. "It was wonderful to see the change soon made in the manner of our inhabitants," reported Benjamin Franklin after hearing Whitefield preach.

The Great Awakening aroused bitter debate. Some people strongly supported it. They listened to traveling preachers and formed many new churches. Other people opposed the movement. They supported established churches.

The movement brought other changes. The growth of new churches forced people to be more tolerant. The clergy lost influence in part because the Great Awakening emphasized a person's own experience in religion.

SECTION REVIEW

1. **Define:** public school, apprentice, gentry, almanac.
2. Why did Puritans want their children to get an education?
3. What classes existed in the colonies?
4. Describe two ways Benjamin Franklin influenced the colonies.
5. **What Do You Think?** Why do you think the Great Awakening had such an important effect on colonists?

5 Growth and Change

Read to Learn
★ What was travel like in the colonies?
★ How did trade affect the colonies?
★ What was life like in cities of the colonies?
★ What do these words mean: triangular trade?

In the 1600s, the English colonies had little contact with each other. As the colonies grew, however, people learned more about their neighbors. By the mid-1700s, people from different colonies discovered that they had many interests in common.

Improvements in Travel

In the 1600s and early 1700s, travel was slow and dangerous. There were few roads. Travelers followed Indian trails through the forests. Even when trails were widened into roads, they were dusty in summer and muddy in winter. Often, there were no bridges across streams and rivers. Early visitors to Boston had to cross the Charles River on a small ferry. Their carriages were taken apart to fit onto the ferry, and their horses swam along behind the boat.

Because travel was so difficult, colonists stayed close to home. Settlers seldom heard from friends or relatives in other colonies. A postal service grew up, but it was slow. In 1717, it took one month for a letter to get from Boston to Williamsburg, a town in Virginia— and two months in winter.

Franklin's milestones. In the mid-1700s, colonists tried to improve travel and communication. Ben Franklin had milestones placed along the road between Boston and Philadelphia so that people would know how far they had traveled. He invented a machine that recorded distances as it was wheeled along behind his wagon. At each mile,

he left a large stone on the ground. Roadworkers then put the stone firmly in place.

Along with better roads came better mail service. In 1753, Franklin was appointed postmaster general for the colonies. He set up relay stations along the mail roads. At the relays, mail carriers changed tired horses for fresh ones. As a result, mail moved more quickly.

The spread of ideas. As travel and mail service improved, colonists learned more about their neighbors. Taverns sprang up along main roads and in towns and cities. Travelers stopped in taverns to exchange news and gossip with local people.

News and ideas were also spread through pamphlets, newspapers, and books turned out by printing presses in the colonies. The first printing press was set up at Harvard College in 1639. Early presses printed religious books along with histories and travelers' stories. In the 1700s, presses printed pamphlets and newspapers.

Colonial newspapers were short, often only four pages long. They carried news about the other colonies and about England and Europe. This news was often several months old by the time it reached other colonies.

Trade Expands

The colonies developed a greater sense of unity through trade. As trade expanded, the colonies grew prosperous and strong. Ships of every kind bustled up and down the Atlantic coast. They carried fish, lumber, and other products from New England to the Middle Colonies and the South. The Middle Colonies shipped grain and flour to New England and the South. The Southern Colonies exported rice, indigo, and tobacco to colonies in the north.

Yankee traders. Merchants from New England dominated colonial trade. They were known as *Yankees,* a nickname that implied sharp, clever, hard-working people. Yankee traders won a reputation for always getting a good buy and profiting from any deal.

A Yankee ship, wrote one observer, arrived in Puerto Rico loaded with horses and other goods. The crew quickly unloaded the horses. Then, Yankee traders turned their ship "into retail shops, where they dealt out their onions, potatoes, salt fish, and apples, an article which brought a very high price."

The triangular trade. Colonial merchants developed many trade routes. One series of routes was known as the *triangular trade* because the three routes formed a triangle. (See the map on page 141.) On the first leg of the journey, New England ships carried fish, lumber, and other goods to the West Indies. There, they picked up sugar and molasses. Molasses was a dark brown syrup made from sugar cane. New Englanders used molasses to make rum. Much of the rum was sold in New England, but some was used to trade.

On the second leg, merchants carried rum, guns, gunpowder, cloth, and tools from New England to West Africa. They used these goods to buy slaves. On the final leg, traders carried slaves to the West Indies. With the profits from selling the slaves, Yankee traders bought more molasses.

Many New England merchants grew wealthy from the triangular trade. In doing so, they often disobeyed the Navigation Acts. Traders were supposed to buy sugar and molasses only from English colonies in the West Indies. But the demand for molasses was so high that New Englanders bought from the Dutch, French, and Spanish West Indies. Although England opposed this illegal trade, bribes could make customs officials look the other way.

AMERICANS WHO DARED

Paul Cuffe

The 42-ton whaling ship sailed proudly into port. Its captain-owner, Paul Cuffe, and the all-black crew welcomed the sight of home. Cuffe, the son of a free black man and Native American woman, grew up in Massachusetts. At age 16, he went to sea on a whaling ship. After years of struggle, he owned a small fleet of trading ships and made a fortune. Even while he succeeded in business, Cuffe worked hard to win freedom and equality for blacks.

Growing Cities

Port cities grew as trade expanded. Sailors hurried along docks and piers that were piled high with cargoes. On nearby streets, merchants and craftworkers showed off their goods. Boston, the busiest port in the colonies, had more than 40 wharves.

New York City prospered from trade, too. Its streets were even lighted at night. As daylight faded, a night

Skill Lesson 6   Reading a Bar Graph

As you learned in Skill Lesson 4 (page 81), graphs show statistics in picture form. A bar graph is useful because it shows changes in one or more sets of numbers over time.

The bar graph at right shows the growth of trade between England and the 13 colonies during the period from 1700 to 1750.

There are two kinds of bar graphs. In a vertical bar graph, the bars go up and down. In a horizontal bar graph, the bars go from side to side. Some bar graphs have two or more bars in different colors so that you can make comparisons.

Study the bar graph at right. Then use the following steps to read the bar graph.

1. **Identify the subject of the bar graph.** Like a line graph, a bar graph has a title as well as a horizontal axis and a vertical axis. Each axis is labeled with numbers or dates. Often, a label says that the numbers are in thousands. In this case, you add three zeros to the numbers shown. If the numbers are in millions, you add six zeros. (a) What is the title of the graph? (b) What do the numbers on the vertical axis show? (c) What dates are shown on the horizontal axis? (d) What is the source of the information shown on this graph?

2. **Practice reading the facts on the bar graph.** Notice that the intervals, or spaces, between the numbers and dates are always equal. Also, the numbers on the vertical axis always start with zero. (a) What are the intervals between the dates on the graph? (b) What was the value of trade with England in 1700? (c) What was its value in 1740? (d) In what year was trade worth most? (e) In what year was it worth least?

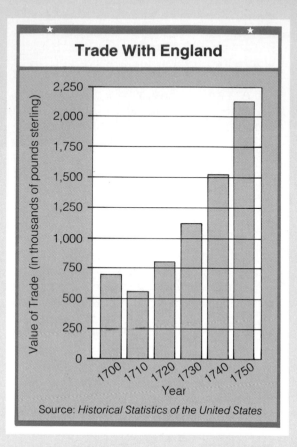

Trade With England

Value of Trade (in thousands of pounds sterling)

Year

Source: *Historical Statistics of the United States*

3. **Make a generalization based on the facts on the bar graph.** Study the graph to find facts to support a generalization. (a) Between what years did trade increase the most? (b) Between what years did it decrease? (c) Make a generalization about trade with England between 1710 and 1750.

4. **Interpret the information.** Use the bar graph, the map on page 141, and your reading in the chapter to interpret the information about trade. (a) Why do you think trade was important to England? (b) Why do you think it was important to the colonies? (c) What goods were traded between England and the colonies?

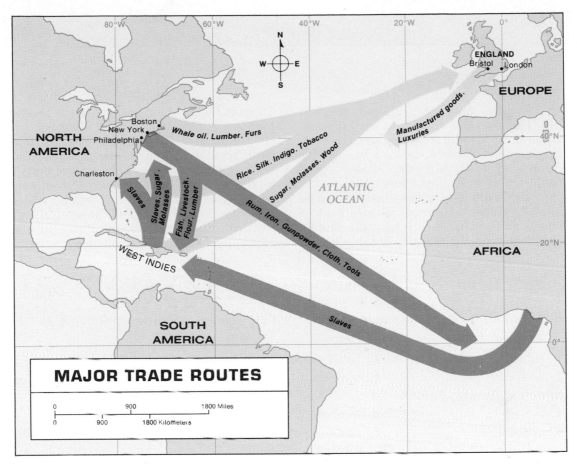

80°W 60°W 40°W 20°W 0°

N
W—E
S

ENGLAND
Bristol London

EUROPE

NORTH
AMERICA

Boston
New York
Philadelphia

Whale oil, Lumber, Furs

Manufactured goods,
Luxuries

40°N

Charleston

Rice, Silk, Indigo, Tobacco

ATLANTIC
OCEAN

Slaves, Sugar,
Molasses

Slaves

Fish, Livestock,
Flour, Lumber

Sugar, Molasses, Wood

Rum, Iron, Gunpowder, Cloth, Tools

WEST INDIES

20°N

AFRICA

SOUTH
AMERICA

Slaves

0°

MAJOR TRADE ROUTES

0   900   1800 Miles

0   900   1800 Kilometers

MAP SKILL Colonists traded with the West Indies, Africa, and Europe in a series of triangular trade routes. Find a three-sided trade route. What goods were traded at each place along the route?

watchman called out: "Lanthorn, and a whole candell-light. Hang out your lights." During the night, he checked the lights, calling out the time and weather. "Two o'clock and fair winds!" Or "Five o'clock and cloudy skies!"

The fastest growing city was Philadelphia. By 1760, its population was the largest in North America. Thanks to Ben Franklin, it boasted the only hospital in North America. It had three libraries and three newspapers—one in German.

In the South, the largest cities were Baltimore and Charleston. Charleston was known as the most elegant colonial city. Wealthy rice planters and their families lived in beautiful mansions and dressed in the latest fashions from London and Paris.

Most Americans lived on farms. Yet cities were important centers. There, people met in great numbers and exchanged news and ideas that would shape events in the years ahead.

SECTION REVIEW

1. **Define:** triangular trade.
2. Why was travel difficult in the colonies?
3. Name two ways people learned about what was going on in other colonies.
4. Why was molasses important in the triangular trade?
5. **What Do You Think?** How do you think the growth of trade was related to the growth of cities?

Chapter 6 Review

★ Summary ★

Colonists developed different ways of life. This was due in part to the land and climate of the different regions. In New England, for example, the land was poor for farming. The Puritan religion also helped shape the New England way of life.

The fertile land of the Middle Colonies allowed settlers to produce surpluses of wheat and grain. As a result, the Middle Colonies exported foods to other colonies.

To meet the need for workers in the South, planters imported thousands of slaves.

Children in the colonies were educated in different ways. Some learned to read and write in public schools. Others were taught by tutors. Many children learned trades as apprentices. As roads and mail service improved, colonists in different regions learned more about each other. In the 1700s, trade helped the colonies prosper.

★ Reviewing the Facts   2 8 points   30 ★

Key Terms. Match each term in Column 1 with the correct definition in Column 2.

Column 1

1. subsistence farmer
2. cash crop
3. tenant farmer
4. racism
5. apprentice

Column 2

a. belief that one race is superior to another
b. someone who learns a trade from a master craftsworker
c. goods sold for money on the world market
d. someone who grows just enough food to live on
e. someone who works and pays rent for land owned by another

Key People, Events, and Ideas. Identify each of the following.

1. Breadbasket Colonies
2. Great Wagon Road
3. Middle Passage
4. John Harvard
5. Benjamin Franklin
6. *Poor Richard's Almanac*
7. Great Awakening
8. Jonathan Edwards
9. George Whitefield
10. Yankee

★ Chapter Checkup   4/ 5 points   40 ★

1. How did New England colonists make use of the forests?
2. (a) Describe a typical New England town. (b) Why did Puritans want to live in towns?
3. (a) What manufactured goods did the Middle Colonies produce? (b) Why did Pennsylvania become a center of manufacturing?
4. Why was the Conestoga wagon useful?
5. Give three examples of how plantations were self-sufficient.
6. Why were public schools important?
7. Explain three ways girls got an education in the colonies.
8. (a) How was travel made easier in the 1700s? (b) How did improved travel affect the colonies?
9. What products did each of the following regions export to other parts of the world: (a) New England; (b) Middle Colonies; (c) South.
10. Describe two cities in two different colonies.

★ Thinking About History

6 pts. ★(30)

1. **Relating past to present.** Review the description of New England homes and family life on pages 123–125. (a) How was life similar to that of today? (b) How was it different?

2. **Applying information.** Why do you think New Englanders came to dominate trade in the colonies?

3. **Evaluating.** Do you think racism was a major or minor factor in the growth of slavery? Explain your answer.

4. **Comparing.** (a) Compare the ways of life of tidewater planters and people living in the backcountry. (b) What do you think were the most important differences between the two groups?

5. **Analyzing a quotation.** A popular saying Ben Franklin included in *Poor Richard's Almanac* went: "An ounce of prevention is worth a pound of cure." Give an example to show what this means.

Done

★ Using Your Skills ★

1. **Map reading.** Study the map on page 136. (a) What does this map show? (b) What areas were settled before 1660? (c) What areas were settled between 1660 and 1700? (d) Why do you think settlers moved inland?

2. **Map reading.** Study the map on page 141. (a) What products did New Englanders export to the West Indies? (b) What products did colonists import from Europe? (c) How were slaves part of the triangular trade?

3. **Making a review chart.** Make a large chart with three columns and three rows. Title the columns New England Colonies, Middle Colonies, and Southern Colonies. Title the rows Land, Climate, and Products. Fill in the chart, using the maps on pages 122, 127, and 130 and your reading in this chapter. (a) How was the land in New England different from that in the Middle Colonies? (b) What crops were produced only in the South? (c) How do you think the land and climate affected the crops and products of the three regions?

4. **Using a painting as a primary source.** Study the painting on page 121. (a) Which building do you think was the Great House? Why? (b) Which building or buildings were the slaves' houses? Why? (c) How do the hill and the houses on it show the different classes in the South?

★ More to Do ★

1. **Preparing an oral history.** In groups of two, prepare an oral history in which one student interviews the other about what it was like to be captured as a slave in Africa and sent to the New World.

2. **Researching a report.** Research and write a report on one of the following aspects of daily life in the colonies: (a) food; (b) clothing; (c) games.

3. **Exploring local history.** Prepare a skit about the experiences of early settlers in your community.

4. **Making a model.** Create a model of a New England town or a southern plantation in about 1750.

5. **Eyewitness reporting.** As an eyewitness, describe Benjamin Franklin's experiment with flying his kite during a thunderstorm.

Unit 2 Review

★ Unit Summary ★

Chapter 4 In the 1500s, Spain built a large empire in the Americas. France, too, explored and claimed lands in North America. Although the first English colony at Roanoke failed, Jamestown was settled in 1606. To the north, Pilgrims planted the Plymouth Colony in 1620.

Chapter 5 In the 1600s and 1700s, the English set up 13 colonies in North America. Many colonists came to America for religious or economic reasons. Each colony had its own government with a royal governor and an elected assembly. However, many people, including women and slaves, did not have the right to vote.

Chapter 6 The New England, Middle, and Southern colonies differed from each other, in part because of geography. Although each colony had its own way of life, trade and travel helped colonists learn about one another.

★ Unit Checkup ★

Choose the word or phrase that best completes each of the following statements.

1. Most settlers in New France were
   (a) farmers.
   (b) fur traders.
   (c) plantation owners.

2. Many of the early English colonies were financed by
   (a) joint stock companies.
   (b) cash crops.
   (c) subsistence farmers.

3. England regulated trade with the colonies in the
   (a) Frame of Government.
   (b) Fundamental Orders of Connecticut.
   (c) Navigation Acts.

4. The Breadbasket Colonies were the
   (a) New England Colonies.
   (b) Middle Colonies.
   (c) Southern Colonies.

5. A successful American printer, scientist, and inventor was
   (a) Benjamin Franklin.
   (b) Jonathan Edwards.
   (c) Mary Musgrove.

★ Building American Citizenship ★

1. Many people settled in the 13 colonies to find religious freedom. (a) How did some colonies protect religious freedom? (b) Is religious freedom still a concern of Americans today? Explain your answer.

2. Colonial governments based the right to vote on age, property, religion, race, and sex. What is the right to vote based on today?

3. Town meetings gave New Englanders a chance to speak out on issues. How can Americans today make sure their voices are heard?

4. Racism allowed white settlers to justify slavery in America. (a) How did racism affect relations between settlers and Indians? (b) Why do you think American leaders today speak out against racism?

The line graph at right shows the growth of population in the 13 colonies between 1650 and 1750. Study the graph. Then answer the following questions. (Note that the numbers on the vertical axis are in thousands. So you have to add three zeros to them to get the correct population.)

1. How many people lived in the colonies in 1650?

2. What was the population of the colonies in 1700?

3. When did the population reach one million?

4. (a) Did more people settle in the colonies between 1650 and 1700 or between 1700 and 1750? (b) Why do you think more came in that time period?

5. Why do you think the colonies were anxious to get more settlers?

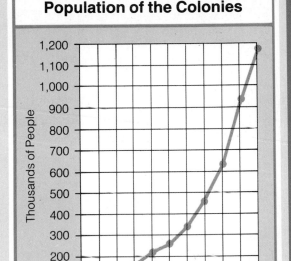

Population of the Colonies

Source: *Historical Statistics of the United States*

History Writer's Handbook

Identifying Parts of a One-Paragraph Answer

Study the following question. *What ideas of Roger Williams did the Puritans see as dangerous?* To answer the question, you might write a paragraph, or a group of sentences that develop the main idea of the answer.

Begin the one-paragraph answer with a *topic sentence* that states the main idea of the answer. For example: *The Puritans saw three ideas of Roger Williams as dangerous.*

Next, write *detail sentences* that give information to support the main idea. For example: *Williams wanted to pay the Indians for their land. He argued for separation of church and state. He also supported freedom of worship.*

Practice Study the following question. *How did John Smith save the Jamestown Colony?* Now study the following one-paragraph answer.

John Smith used strong means to save the Jamestown Colony. He bought corn from the Indians to feed the starving colonists. Then he told the people they would only get food if they worked.

Identify the topic sentence and the detail sentences in the answer.

Unit 3
THE STRUGGLE FOR INDEPENDENCE

| 1740 | | 1750 | | 1760 | | 1770 |

1740s English settlers and traders move into Ohio River valley

1754 French and Indian War begins; Albany Plan of Union
1759 English take Quebec

1763 Treaty of Paris ends French and Indian War; Pontiac's War
1765 Stamp Act
1766 Stamp Act repealed
1767 Townshend Acts

| 1740 | | 1750 | | 1760 | | 1770 |

JOIN, or DIE.

No Stamp Act.

1700s England and France battled for control of North America.

1760s Benjamin Franklin's cartoon, "Join, or Die," came to have more meaning when the colonists protested British efforts to tax them.

UNIT OUTLINE

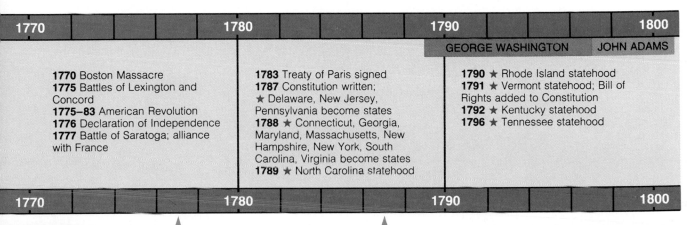

1770	1780	1790	1800

GEORGE WASHINGTON   JOHN ADAMS

1770 Boston Massacre
1775 Battles of Lexington and Concord
1775–83 American Revolution
1776 Declaration of Independence
1777 Battle of Saratoga; alliance with France

1783 Treaty of Paris signed
1787 Constitution written;
★ Delaware, New Jersey, Pennsylvania become states
1788 ★ Connecticut, Georgia, Maryland, Massachusetts, New Hampshire, New York, South Carolina, Virginia become states
1789 ★ North Carolina statehood

1790 ★ Rhode Island statehood
1791 ★ Vermont statehood; Bill of Rights added to Constitution
1792 ★ Kentucky statehood
1796 ★ Tennessee statehood

1770	1780	1790	1800

1777 George Washington at the Battle of Princeton.

1787 The Constitution of the United States.

CHAPTER

7

Crisis in
the Colonies (1745–1775)

Chapter Outline

1 Competing for Empire
2 Showdown in North America
3 Trouble Over Taxes
4 The Split Widens
5 The Shot Heard 'Round the World

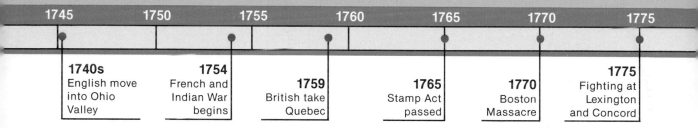

1745	1750	1755	1760	1765	1770	1775

1740s
English move
into Ohio
Valley

1754
French and
Indian War
begins

1759
British take
Quebec

1765
Stamp Act
passed

1770
Boston
Massacre

1775
Fighting at
Lexington
and Concord

About This Chapter

In the 1760s, colonists faced a deep crisis over this question: Did England have the right to tax them? In August 1765, Thomas Hutchinson, the lieutenant governor of Massachusetts, found himself in the middle of the storm. A few months earlier, Parliament had passed the Stamp Act, which taxed certain goods. Many colonists in Boston were furious about the tax. In fact, some colonists were angry enough to take violent action.

On August 26, Hutchinson and his family were having supper when a messenger burst in. "The mob is coming!" he cried. Hutchinson knew that the mob was after him because he was a royal official. He told his children to go to a neighbor's house, and he prepared to face the mob. But his oldest daughter "protested that she would not quit the house unless I did," recalled Hutchinson. "I could not stand against this and withdrew with her to a neighboring house."

Within minutes, the mob "fell upon my house with the rage of devils." When the mob realized that Hutchinson had fled, they rushed off to find him. Hutchinson hid all night. At dawn, he returned to find his home destroyed.

The violence shocked many colonists. But it was only the beginning. Anger over the Stamp Act grew. So, too, did the quarrel between England and its American colonies. By 1775, the quarrel had reached a point where it could be decided only by war.

Study the time line above. Name two events that happened in the years after the Stamp Act was passed.

Disputes between colonists and England led to a crisis. Here, angry New Yorkers destroy a statue of King George III.

1 Competing for Empire

Read to Learn
★ What nations claimed land in North America?
★ Where did France build forts?
★ Why did Indian nations take sides in the struggle between England and France?

During the 1700s, Spain, France, and England competed for empire around the world. In North America, the 13 English colonies were caught up in these rivalries.

Rivals for North America

By the late 1600s, England had two rivals in North America: Spain and France. Spanish settlers had expanded slowly into North America. Missionaries led the way into California, New Mexico, and Arizona. Because those settlements were far away from its colonies on the Atlantic coast, England did not see them as a threat.

However, Spain and England often clashed in the West Indies and along the border between Georgia and Spanish Florida. As you learned, Georgia was set up to stop Spain from expanding north from Florida. For years, Spain and England eyed each other with distrust across this border.

The key to a large empire. England's other rival was France. France claimed all the land along the Mississippi River. Find New France on the map on page 150. To back their

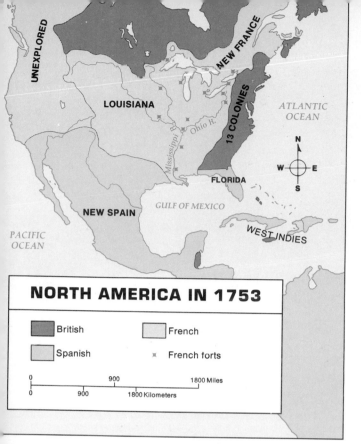

NORTH AMERICA IN 1753

- British
- Spanish
- French
- ✕ French forts

0   900   1800 Miles
0 900 1800 Kilometers

MAP SKILL France and Spain claimed land to the north and south of the 13 English colonies in North America. Who claimed land along the Mississippi River?

claim, the French built forts from the Great Lakes to New Orleans. These forts gave France the key to a large empire and blocked the English colonies from expanding to the west.

To the north, France controlled Canada with a string of forts along the St. Lawrence River. These forts were meant to keep an enemy from sailing up the river into New France. Also, the forts protected the rich fishing grounds off Newfoundland and the fur trade around the Great Lakes.

By right of arms. English settlers lived in the area between the Atlantic Ocean and the Appalachian Mountains. By the 1740s, however, English traders were moving west from New York and Pennsylvania into the Ohio River valley.

At first, the French tried to scare off the English. In 1749, French soldiers moved down the Allegheny and Ohio rivers. Wherever a stream joined these two rivers, the French put up a sign warning that the land belonged to France "by right of arms."

English traders ignored these warnings. So the governor of New France, the Marquis Duquesne (mahr KEE doo KAYN), had forts built in the Ohio River valley to keep the English out of the French empire.

Native Americans Take Sides

The lands that Spain, France, and England claimed in North America were not empty. Native Americans hunted and grew crops on these lands. They did not want to give up the land to European settlers. In the 1700s, some Native Americans decided that the only way to protect their way of life was to take sides in the struggle between England and France.

Indians controlled fur trade in the heart of North America. So both France and England looked for allies among the Indians. The French expected the Indians to side with them. Most French in North America were trappers and traders, not farmers. Trappers did not destroy hunting grounds by clearing forests for farms. Also, many French trappers married Indian women and adopted Indian ways.

On the other hand, English settlers were mostly farm families. They cleared land, often ignoring Indian rights. Because the English believed that their culture was superior, they looked down on Indian ways. As English settlers expanded onto Indian lands, Indians fought back.

In the end, both France and England found allies. France's strongest allies were the Algonquins and Hurons. The English looked for help to the powerful Iroquois nations, old enemies of the Algonquins.

An English trader and official, William Johnson, won the respect of the Mohawks, one of the Iroquois nations.

The English invited friendly Iroquois leaders to visit London. A Dutch artist, John Verelst, painted this portrait of the Iroquois leader Ho Nee Yeath Taw No Row. The English called him John Wolf Clan.

Johnson was one of the few English men to marry an Indian woman. His wife, Molly Brant, was the daughter of a Mohawk chief. Johnson urged his Iroquois friends to become allies of the English.

The English also won the help of Indians in the Ohio Valley by charging lower prices for trade goods than the French. Many Indians began buying from English traders. The loss of Indian trade angered the French, who were determined to defend their claims in the Ohio River valley.

SECTION REVIEW

1. **Locate:** Florida, Mississippi River, Gulf of Mexico, New Orleans, Canada, St. Lawrence River, Ohio River.
2. How did France protect its claim to land in North America?
3. Why did some Indians in the Ohio River valley prefer to trade with the English?
4. **What Do You Think?** How do you think the actions of both England and France increased tensions in North America?

2 Showdown in North America

Read to Learn

★ What role did George Washington play in the French and Indian War?
★ Why did the colonies reject the Albany Plan of Union?
★ What lands did Britain gain by the Treaty of Paris?
★ What does this word mean: population?

Three times between 1689 and 1748, France and Great Britain* went to war. Battles raged in both Europe and North America. English colonists named the wars after the ruling king or queen. There was King William's War, Queen Anne's War, and King George's War. Each war ended with an uneasy peace. In 1754, fighting broke out again in a long conflict, called the *French and Indian War.*

Drama at Fort Necessity

Scuffles between France and Britain in the Ohio River valley triggered the opening shots of the French and Indian War. Some wealthy Virginians claimed land in the upper Ohio River valley. To protect their claims, they urged the governor of Virginia to build a fort where the Monongahela

*In 1707, England and Scotland were joined into the United Kingdom of Great Britain. After that date, the terms Great Britain and British were used to describe the country and its people. However, the terms England and English were still used in the 1700s.

and Allegheny rivers meet. (See the map on page 154.) The governor sent a young officer, George Washington, to carry out this task.

Washington was only 22 years old at the time, but he was an able and brave soldier. Washington grew up on a plantation in Virginia. At age 15, he began work as a surveyor. He later explored frontier lands in western Virginia. In 1753, Washington carried a message to the French in Ohio warning them to pull back their forces. On this dangerous mission, young Washington narrowly escaped death.

In 1754, Washington again headed west from Virginia. This time, he led 150 soldiers to carry out the governor's order to build the new fort. On the way, Washington heard that the French had already built Fort Duquesne where the two rivers meet. But he continued on.

When Washington learned that a French scouting party was camped in the woods ahead, he made a quiet march at night and surprised them. In a brief battle, Washington's troops scattered the French.

Defeat soon followed success. The Virginians, expecting the French to counterattack, hastily put up a stockade. They called it Fort Necessity. A strong force of French troops and Indians surrounded the fort. Trapped and outnumbered, the Virginians surrendered. Later, Washington was released

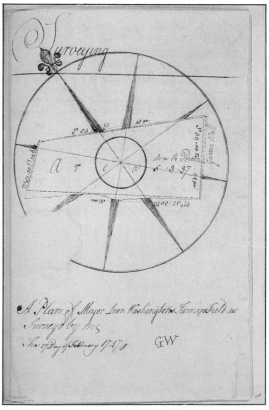

By age 17, George Washington, at left, was the official surveyor for Culpeper County, Virginia. He drew the plan, shown below, of his brother Lawrence Washington's turnip field.

and rode back to Virginia. The clash at Fort Necessity was the first battle of the French and Indian War.

A Plan of Union

While Washington was defending Fort Necessity, delegates from seven of the English colonies were meeting in Albany, New York. They came together for two main reasons. They wanted the Iroquois to help them against the French. And they wanted to plan a united defense against the French.

The Iroquois leaders who came to the meeting had not decided whether to help the British. They thought that the French were stronger and had more forts than the British. The Iroquois left without agreeing to help, but later they did fight with the British.

The delegates in Albany knew that the colonies needed to work together against the French. Benjamin Franklin proposed the Albany *Plan of Union.* The plan called for a Grand Council with representatives from each colony. The Grand Council would make laws, raise taxes, and set up the defense of the colonies. The delegates approved the Plan of Union. But the colonial assemblies rejected it because they did not want to give up any of their own powers.

The Balance of Power

The French and Indian War, which began in 1754, lasted until 1763. The war went badly for the British at first. The French had several advantages. For example, New France had a single government that could make decisions more quickly than the 13 separate English colonies. Also, the French had many Indian allies to help in the fight against the British.

But Britain had some advantages. It, too, had Indian allies. In the 13 colonies, the *population,* or number of people, was 20 times greater than that of New France. The English colonies were easier to defend than New France. And the British navy ruled the seas.

English setbacks. In 1755, General Edward Braddock led British and colonial troops to attack Fort Duquesne. General Braddock knew how to fight a war in Europe, but he had never fought in the wilderness of North America. A stubborn man, Braddock was called "Bulldog" behind his back.

The British moved slowly because they had to clear a road through thick forests for their cannons and other heavy gear. Washington, who went with Braddock, was upset at the slow pace. Indian scouts warned Braddock that he was heading for disaster. But he ignored their warning.

When the British neared Fort Duquesne, the French and their Indian allies launched a surprise attack. French and Indian sharpshooters hid in the forest and picked off British soldiers, who wore bright red uniforms. Braddock had five horses shot out from under him before he fell, fatally wounded. Washington was luckier. As he later reported, he "escaped without a wound, although I had four bullets through my coat."

Almost half the British were killed or wounded. Washington and other survivors returned to Virginia with news of Braddock's defeat. Washington then took command of a small force. During the rest of the war, he tried to guard the long Virginia frontier against Indian attacks.

For the next two years, the French and their Indian allies won a string of victories. The French captured Fort Oswego on Lake Ontario and took Fort William Henry on Lake George. (See the map on page 154.)

A confident leader. In 1757, a new prime minister, William Pitt, took over the British government. Pitt was a bold leader. "I believe that I can save this nation and that no one else can," he claimed with confidence. Pitt decided to try to win the war in North America first.* He sent Britain's best generals to the colonies. Then, he encouraged the colonists to support the war by promising to pay high prices for all goods they supplied to the troops.

Under Pitt's leadership, the tide of battle turned. In 1758, Lord Jeffrey Amherst captured the French fort at Louisbourg. That year, too, the Iroquois persuaded the Delawares to stop

fighting the British. Without the Delawares, the French could not hold Fort Duquesne. When the British took the fort, they renamed it **Fort Pitt,** after the British prime minister. It later became the city of Pittsburgh.

On the Plains of Abraham

The British kept up the offensive. With the help of their Indian allies, they took Fort Niagara. In 1759, Pitt sent General James Wolfe to attack Quebec, capital of New France. If Britain captured Quebec, France could no longer supply its forts farther up the

---

*By 1756, the French and Indian War had spread from North America to Europe. There, it became known as the Seven Years War. The British and French also fought in India, where the British suffered defeats at first.

MAP SKILL During the French and Indian War, Britain and France battled for control of North America. Find Louisbourg, Quebec, and Fort Duquesne on the map. Why do you think Britain wanted to capture these places?

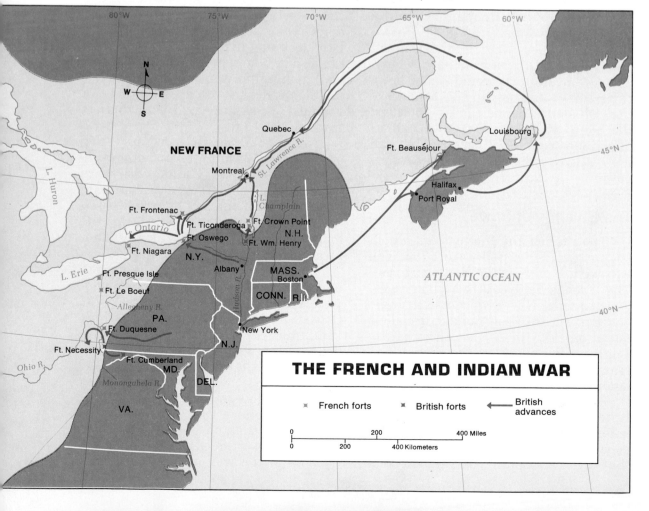

THE FRENCH AND INDIAN WAR

× French forts × British forts ← British advances

0   200   400 Miles
0   200   400 Kilometers

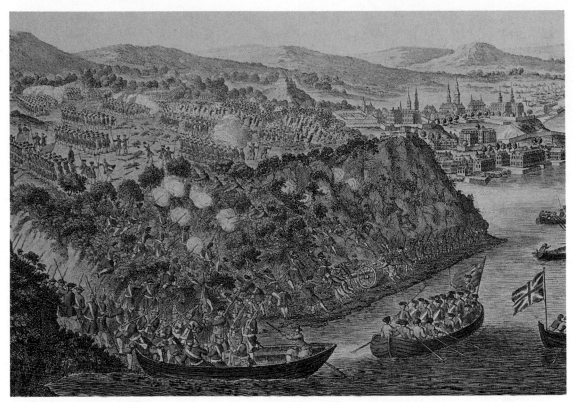

This painting by Sigmund Samuel shows British troops climbing up to the Plains of Abraham. When General Wolfe first saw the cliffs, he said, "I don't think we can by any possible means get up here; however, we must use our best endeavour." They succeeded and surprised the French in Quebec.

St. Lawrence River. Thus, the war would be won. But Quebec was well defended. It sat atop a steep cliff above the St. Lawrence. An able French general, the Marquis de Montcalm, was prepared to fight off a British attack.

Wolfe devised a daring plan to take Quebec. He knew that Montcalm had only a few soldiers guarding the cliff because the French thought that it was too steep to climb. Late one night, Wolfe secretly moved his troops in small boats to the foot of the cliff. British soldiers swarmed ashore and scrambled up the steep cliff onto the **Plains of Abraham** outside the city.

When the sun rose, Montcalm woke to hear that 4,000 British troops were waiting to go into battle. He quickly marched his own troops out to meet them. In the fierce battle that followed, both Wolfe and Montcalm were killed. But Wolfe lived long enough to see the British win.

British Gains

When news of the British victory reached the 13 colonies, church bells rang out in celebration. The fall of Quebec sealed the fate of New France. In 1760, the British took Montreal, and the war in North America ended. Fighting dragged on in Europe until Britain and France signed the **Treaty of Paris** in 1763.

By this treaty, Britain gained Canada and all French lands east of the

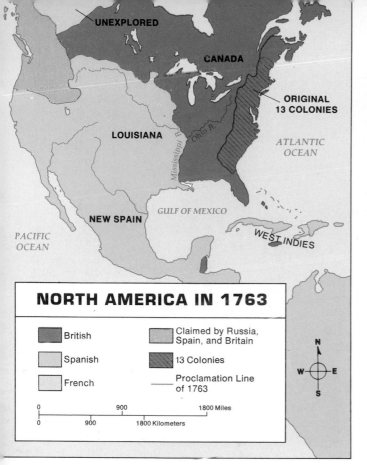

NORTH AMERICA IN 1763

	British		Claimed by Russia, Spain, and Britain
	Spanish		13 Colonies
	French		Proclamation Line of 1763

0   900   1800 Miles
0   900   1800 Kilometers

MAP SKILL Compare this map to the map on page 150. How was North America in 1763 different from what it had been in 1753?

Mississippi River. (This area is shown on the map at left.) In the New World, France kept only a few sugar-growing islands in the West Indies. Spain, which had entered the war on the French side in 1762, had to give Florida to Britain. However, Spain kept its lands west of the Mississippi, as well as its empire in Central and South America.

After years of fighting, peace returned to North America. Yet within a few years, a new struggle broke out. This time, the struggle pitted Britain against its own colonies.

▬▬▬ **SECTION REVIEW** ▬▬▬

1. **Locate:** Fort Duquesne, Fort Oswego, Louisbourg, Quebec, Montreal.
2. **Define:** population.
3. (a) What was the Albany Plan of Union? (b) Why was it rejected?
4. How did the British victory at Quebec affect the outcome of the war?
5. **What Do You Think?** Why do you think the British were able to win so much of North America by 1763?

3 Trouble Over Taxes

Read to Learn

★ Why did Pontiac fight the British?
★ How did Britain try to get money to repay its debts?
★ Why did colonists object to the Stamp Act?
★ What do these words mean: boycott, repeal?

Britain was pleased with its victory. So, too, were the colonists. They were free of the French threat and could go back to their everyday lives. Their soldiers had fought well, and they had developed good officers like George Washington.

But with victory came problems. How would Britain govern the lands it won from France? How would Britain treat French settlers and their Indian allies? Even more urgent, how would Britain repay the money it had borrowed to win the French and Indian War?

Fighting on the Frontier

Even before the war between Britain and France ended, trouble flared up in the Ohio Valley. English colonists crossed the Appalachians to settle in the former French lands. Yet

Native American nations already lived there. They included the Senecas, Delawares, Shawnees, Ottawas, Miamis, and Hurons.

The British sent Lord Jeffrey Amherst to the frontier to keep order. In the past, French traders treated Native Americans with respect, holding feasts and giving presents. Amherst refused to do this. He raised the prices on goods traded to the Indians because the British no longer had to compete with the French. Also, he allowed English settlers to build forts on land given to the Indians by treaties.

Pontiac's War. Amherst's actions angered Native Americans. They found a leader in Pontiac, an Ottawa chief. One English trader described Pontiac as "a shrewd, sensible Indian of few words, [who] commands more respect amongst these nations than any Indian I ever saw." (See the picture at right.)

War broke out when Pontiac attacked British troops at Fort Detroit. He then called on other Indian nations to join the fight. A number of Indian nations responded to his call. In a few months, they overran most British forts on the frontier. British and colonial troops fought back and regained much they had lost.

In October 1763, Pontiac learned that the Treaty of Paris had been signed. The treaty ended the Indians' hope of receiving French aid. One by one, the Indian nations stopped fighting and returned home. "All my young men have buried their hatchets," said Pontiac. By December, the British again controlled the frontier.

Proclamation of 1763. Pontiac's War convinced the British that they must stop settlers from moving onto Indian lands. So the British issued the *Proclamation of 1763.* It drew a line along the Appalachian Mountains and forbade colonists to settle west of that line. Settlers already living west of the line had to leave.

AMERICANS WHO DARED

Pontiac

Pontiac was a strong, proud man and the leader of the Ottawas. He was determined to hold the Ohio Valley against the British. Pontiac believed that Indians could save their land only by returning to their old ways. He carried this message to his followers. A skillful organizer, Pontiac brought many Indian nations together to fight the British.

The proclamation was meant to protect Native Americans and fur traders in the western lands. Britain sent 10,000 troops to America to enforce it. The troops were supposed to patrol the frontier. However, most stayed in cities on the Atlantic coast.

The proclamation angered colonists because it stopped them from moving west. Also, colonists had to help pay for the British troops. Many settlers simply ignored the proclamation and moved west anyway.

An Urgent Need for Money

Britain faced another problem after the French and Indian War. It was deeply in debt. The British prime minister, George Grenville, decided that the colonists must help pay the debt since they gained the most from the war.

Sugar Act. In 1764, Prime Minister Grenville asked Parliament to approve the Sugar Act, which put a new tax on molasses. Molasses, you will remember, was a valuable item in the triangular trade. (See page 141.)

The *Sugar Act* of 1764 replaced an earlier tax on molasses. The earlier tax was so high that any merchant who paid it would have been driven out of business. So most merchants simply avoided the tax by smuggling molasses into the colonies. Often, they bribed tax collectors to look the other way. The Sugar Act of 1764 lowered the tax. But Grenville demanded that the smuggling and bribes be stopped. And he wanted the tax paid.

Stamp Act. In 1765, Grenville persuaded Parliament to pass the *Stamp Act.* It put a tax on legal documents such as wills or marriage papers, as well as on newspapers, almanacs, playing cards, and even dice. The Stamp Act required that all legal documents and dozens of other items carry a stamp to show that the tax had been paid. Stamp taxes were used in Britain and other countries to raise money. But Britain had never required its colonies to pay such a tax.

No Taxation Without Representation

To the surprise of the British, the colonists responded violently to the Stamp Act. Riots broke out in New York City, Newport, and Charleston. In Boston, angry mobs destroyed the homes of royal officials. Agents who were supposed to collect the unpopular stamp tax were run out of town.

The British prime minister, George Grenville, thought the Stamp Act was a fair tax. To his surprise, the colonists claimed it was completely unfair. The stamp, above, was used on wills and insurance policies to show that a five-shilling tax had been paid.

John Adams, a Massachusetts lawyer, noted that the rage of the people was felt in every colony. "Our presses have groaned, our pulpits have thundered, our legislatures have resolved, our towns have voted, the crown officers everywhere trembled."

Why were the colonists so angry at the taxes? After all, Britain had spent a lot of money to protect them during the recent war. And British citizens were paying much higher taxes than the American colonists.

Colonists objected to the taxes because they believed in the principle of no taxation without representation. This principle had its roots in English traditions going back to the Magna Carta. (Review page 92.) Colonists claimed that only they or their representatives had the right to pass taxes. They argued that they did not elect any representatives to Parliament. So Parliament had no right to tax them. The colonists were willing to pay taxes—if the taxes were passed by their own colonial legislatures.

The Stamp Act Congress

Colonists began to organize against the Stamp Act. In October 1765, nine colonies sent delegates to the *Stamp Act Congress,* which met in New York City. The congress sent petitions, or letters, to King George III and Parliament. In these petitions, the delegates declared that the Stamp and Sugar acts were unjust because Parliament had no right to tax the colonies.

Parliament was in no mood to listen to the petitions of the Stamp Act Congress. But colonists took another action that was more effective. They joined together to boycott British goods. To *boycott* means to refuse to buy certain goods or services. The boycott of British goods took its toll. Trade fell off by 14 percent. British merchants suffered. So, too, did British workers who made goods for the colonies.

Finally, in 1766, Parliament *repealed,* or canceled, the Stamp Act. At the same time, however, it passed the Declaratory Act. In this act, Parliament said that it had the right to make laws and raise taxes in "all cases whatsoever."

When colonists heard that the Stamp Act had been repealed, they were overjoyed. They paid little attention to the Declaratory Act. But the dispute over taxes was not settled. Before long, colonists would face other crises when Parliament again tried to tax them.

━━ **SECTION REVIEW** ━━

1. **Locate:** Appalachian Mountains, New York, Charleston, Boston.
2. **Define:** boycott, repeal.
3. What was the goal of the Proclamation of 1763?
4. Why did colonists object to the Stamp Act?
5. **What Do You Think?** Do you think the Stamp Act was unjust? Explain.

4 The Split Widens

Read to Learn

★ How did the colonists respond to the Townshend Acts?
★ What leaders emerged in the colonies?
★ What happened during the Boston Massacre?
★ What do these words mean: writ of assistance, nonimportation agreement, committee of correspondence?

The repeal of the Stamp Act left Britain with its war debt still unpaid. So Parliament passed new taxes, which colonists again protested. As tensions built, violence broke out again.

The Townshend Acts

In May 1767, Parliament debated the issue of taxing the colonists. During the debate, George Grenville, now a member of Parliament, challenged Charles Townshend, who was in charge of the British treasury.

"You are cowards, you are afraid of the Americans, you dare not tax America!" shouted Grenville.

"Fear? Cowards?" snapped Townshend, "I dare tax America!"

"Dare you tax America?" cried Grenville. "I wish I could see it!"

"I will, I will!" replied Townshend.

The next month, Parliament passed the **Townshend Acts**, which taxed goods such as glass, paper, silk, lead, and tea. Although the taxes were fairly low, Americans still claimed that Parliament did not have the right to tax them.

The Townshend Acts set up new ways to collect the taxes. Customs officers were sent to American ports with orders to stop smugglers. They were allowed to use writs of assistance in their work. A **writ of assistance** was a legal document. It let a customs officer inspect a ship's cargo without giving any reason for the search. Sometimes, customs officers used these writs to keep ships from leaving port until merchants paid them bribes.

Colonists protested the writs of assistance. They said that the writs violated their rights as British citizens. Under British law, an official could not search someone's property without giving a good reason for suspecting that person.

A Tough Response

The colonists' answer to the Townshend Acts was loud and clear. From New Hampshire to Georgia, merchants and planters signed *nonimportation agreements*. In these agreements, they promised to stop importing goods taxed by the Townshend Acts. They hoped that British merchants who were hurt by the loss of business would force Parliament to repeal the new taxes.

Colonists carried their fight to the newspapers. They wrote letters warning fellow citizens of the danger of letting Parliament tax them. Newspapers in one colony printed letters sent to newspapers in other colonies.

Many angry colonists joined the *Sons of Liberty*. This group was formed during the Stamp Act protests. Members met to talk about ways to protest British policies and protect colonial liberties. The Sons of Liberty agreed to stop using any goods that were taxed and to stop drinking British tea.

Women formed the *Daughters of Liberty*. They pledged to wear dresses of homespun cloth rather than of cloth imported from England. In Rowley, Massachusetts, "thirty-three respectable ladies of the town met at sunrise with their [spinning] wheels to spend the day at the house of the Reverend Jedediah Jewell." At sunset, the women appeared "neatly dressed . . . in homespun."

In cities such as Boston and Charleston, Sons and Daughters of Liberty hung lanterns in large trees,

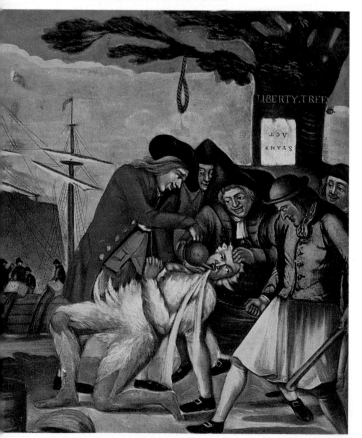

Some colonists tarred and feathered tax collectors to protest British taxes. This drawing by a British artist shows colonists pouring tea down the throat of a tax collector who has been tarred and feathered.

which then became known as Liberty Trees. From these trees, they hung cloth or straw statues dressed like British officials. The statues served as warnings to the officials not to try to collect the unpopular taxes. Sons and Daughters of Liberty visited merchants to persuade them to sign the nonimportation agreements.

Colonists Find Leaders

During the quarrel with Britain, leaders emerged in all the colonies. In Massachusetts, Samuel Adams of Boston took the lead against Britain. Sam Adams seemed an unlikely leader. He was a failure in business and a poor public speaker. But he loved politics. He was always present at Boston town meetings and Sons of Liberty rallies.

Sam Adams "eats little, sleeps little, thinks much," reported one colonist. "He is most decisive . . . in the pursuit of his objects." Adams worked day and night against Britain. He published a lot of pamphlets and wrote many letters to the newspapers. His fiery arguments made colonists aware of the dangers of British rule.

Another Massachusetts leader was John Adams. John Adams, a lawyer, was more cautious than his second cousin, Sam. His knowledge of British law earned him the respect of many colonists.

In Virginia, George Washington was a member of the House of Burgesses when it protested the Townshend Acts. Another Virginian, Patrick Henry, was well known for speeches that moved listeners to both tears and anger. In a speech against the Stamp Act, Henry attacked Britain so furiously that some people called out, "Treason!" Henry replied, "If this be treason, make the most of it!" Henry's words moved a young listener, Thomas Jefferson. At the time, Jefferson was a 22-year-old law student. Later, he joined the ranks of American leaders.

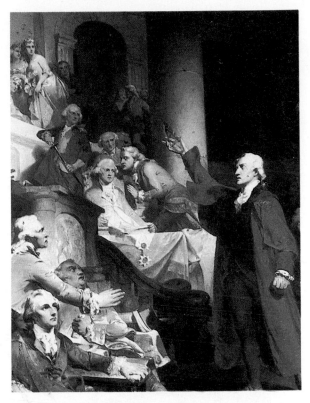

Among the colonial leaders, Patrick Henry won fame for his spellbinding speeches. Here, he addresses fellow Virginians in the House of Burgesses.

Women like Mercy Otis Warren also took leading roles. Warren wrote plays that made fun of royal officials. The plays were published in newspapers and widely read. Warren's home in Plymouth, Massachusetts, was a meeting place for colonists opposed to British policies.

Trouble in the Cities

New York and Boston were centers of protest. In 1766, the New York assembly refused to obey the Quartering Act. The *Quartering Act* said that colonists had to pay for the housing of British soldiers. New Yorkers argued that the Quartering Act was just another way of taxing them without their consent. When news of New York's action reached Britain, royal officials angrily dismissed the assembly.

In Boston, too, tempers were rising. The governor dismissed the Massachusetts assembly in 1768 because it asked to have the Townshend Acts repealed. Soon after, two regiments of British soldiers arrived in Boston to protect customs officers from outraged citizens.

To many people, the soldiers' tents set up on the Boston Common were daily reminders that Britain was trying to bully them into paying unjust taxes. When the soldiers walked along the streets of Boston, they risked insults, snowballs, or beatings. The time was ripe for disaster.

The Boston Massacre

On the night of March 5, 1770, a crowd gathered outside the Boston customs house. Colonists shouted insults at the "lobsterbacks," their name for the redcoated soldiers who guarded the building. Then, they began throwing snowballs, oyster shells, and sticks at the soldiers.

The soldiers stood their ground. Suddenly, a shot rang out—no one knows whether from the soldiers or the crowd. The soldiers fired into the crowd. When the smoke from the musket volley cleared, five people lay dead or dying. Among them was Crispus

Paul Revere, a Boston silversmith, engraved and printed this scene of the Boston Massacre. The picture circulated widely in the colonies. It helped stir up anger against Britain. Revere shows Captain Thomas Preston, at right, ordering his troops to fire on the colonists.

Attucks, a black sailor who was active in the Sons of Liberty.

Sam Adams quickly wrote to the other colonies about the shooting, which he called the **Boston Massacre**. Paul Revere, a Boston silversmith, made an engraving of it. The engraving vividly showed the dead and wounded colonists. As news of the Boston Massacre spread, colonists' outrage grew.

The soldiers were put on trial for the shooting. John Adams agreed to defend them, saying that they deserved a fair trial. He wanted to show the world that Americans believed in justice, even if the British government did not. At the trial, Adams argued that the crowd had provoked the soldiers. His arguments convinced the jury, and the soldiers received light sentences.

Parliament Backs Down

On the day of the Boston Massacre, Parliament was meeting in London. The nonimportation agreements had crippled trade with the colonies. Under pressure from British merchants, Parliament repealed most of the Townshend taxes. But it left in place the tax on tea. The colonists, it said, must accept the fact that Parliament had the right to tax them.

Americans were delighted with the repeal. So they paid little attention to the tax on tea. They ended their boycott of British goods, and for a few years, calm returned to the colonies. But memories of the disputes left Americans uneasy.

During this period of calm, Sam Adams set up the first **committees of correspondence** to keep colonists informed of British actions. The committees wrote letters and pamphlets to spread the alarm whenever Britain tried to enforce unpopular acts of Parliament. In this way, the committees helped unite the colonists against Britain.

SECTION REVIEW

1. **Define:** writ of assistance, nonimportation agreement, committee of correspondence.
2. (a) Why did some colonists join the Sons and Daughters of Liberty? (b) What actions did these groups take?
3. How did Samuel Adams work for the colonists' cause?
4. Why did New Yorkers protest against the Quartering Act?
5. **What Do You Think?** Why do you think Sam Adams called the shooting at the customs house the Boston Massacre?

5 The Shot Heard 'Round the World

Read to Learn
★ Why did Americans protest the Tea Act?
★ How did Britain respond to the Boston Tea Party?
★ Why did General Gage send troops to Concord?
★ What do these words mean: militia, minuteman?

Between 1765 and 1770, Parliament twice passed and then repealed taxes. In 1773, a new conflict over taxes exploded. This time, colonists began to think the unthinkable. Perhaps the time had come to throw off British rule and declare their independence.

Trouble Over Tea

The new trouble began over tea. Colonists enjoyed drinking tea. Most of it came from the British East India

In the early 1770s, the *Gaspee*, a British ship, patrolled the waters off Providence, Rhode Island, to prevent smuggling. Its commander, William Dudingston, often angered colonists when he stopped small fishing boats at gunpoint.

On June 9, 1772, the *Gaspee* ran aground while chasing a local ship. On hearing this news, a group of Providence merchants rowed out to the stranded ship. Swiftly, they swarmed on board the *Gaspee*. They sent Dudingston and his crew ashore and then set fire to the *Gaspee*.

News of the *Gaspee* affair ignited a storm in London. The king ordered a secret commission to look into the affair. However, colonists learned about the commission. When commission members arrived in Rhode Island, they ran into a wall of silence. They offered a reward for information leading to the arrest and conviction of the guilty parties. But there were no arrests.

In the end, the commission members returned to England empty-handed. Still, colonists saw their coming to the colonies as yet another British attack on American liberties. Committees of correspondence sprang up throughout the colonies to discuss the fears aroused by the *Gaspee* affair.

★ How did the *Gaspee* affair increase tension in the colonies?

Company. The company sold its tea to American tea merchants. In turn, these tea merchants sold the tea to the colonists.

In the 1770s, the British East India Company was in financial trouble. Over 15 million pounds of its tea sat unsold in British warehouses. In 1773, Parliament tried to help the troubled company by passing the ***Tea Act***. The act removed some taxes paid by the British East India Company. It also let the company sell tea directly to colonists instead of to American tea merchants. These steps were meant to lower the price of tea so that Americans would buy more of it.

To the surprise of Parliament, colonists protested the Tea Act. American tea merchants were angry because they were cut out of the tea trade. If Parliament ruined tea merchants today, they warned, it might turn on other businesses tomorrow. Even tea drinkers, who would have paid less for tea, scorned the Tea Act. They believed that it was a trick to make them agree to Parliament's right to tax the colonies.

Once again, Americans responded with a boycott. "Do not suffer yourself to sip the accursed, dutied *STUFF*," said one newspaper. "For if you do, the devil will immediately enter into you, and you will instantly become a traitor to your country." Daughters of Liberty brewed homemade "liberty tea" from raspberry leaves. At some ports, colonists refused to let ships unload their cargoes of tea.

The Boston Tea Party

When three ships loaded with tea reached Boston, Massachusetts, Governor Thomas Hutchinson insisted that the ships unload their cargo. But Sam Adams and other Sons of Liberty had their own plans. On the night of December 16, they met in Old South Church. They sent a message to the governor, demanding that the ships leave the harbor. The messenger returned with the governor's reply. The ships must stay and unload their cargo. Adams stood up and declared, "This meeting can do nothing further to save the country."

His words were a signal. One by one, people left the meeting. A little while later, a crowd of about 50 people dressed as Indians swarmed down to the harbor and boarded the tea ships. "We then were ordered by our commander to open the ship's hatches," recalled one colonist, "and take out all the chests of tea and throw them overboard . . . first cutting and splitting the chests with our tomahawks."

News of the Boston Tea Party, shown here, spread quickly. Other seaports held "tea parties" of their own. Some colonists celebrated the event, but others feared that it would lead to more trouble with Britain.

In three hours, the job was done. The contents of 342 chests of tea floated in Boston harbor. The next day, the cautious John Adams wrote about the event in his diary:

> The people should never rise without doing something to be remembered, something notable and striking. This destruction of the tea is so bold, so daring, so firm . . . it must have such important and lasting consequences that I can't help considering it a turning point in history.

Britain Responds

Colonists had mixed reactions to the *Boston Tea Party*. Some cheered this firm protest of British rule. Others worried that such action would encourage lawlessness in the colonies. But even those who condemned the Boston Tea Party were shocked at Britain's response to it.

The Intolerable Acts. Parliament and King George III felt that the people of Boston needed to be punished. In 1774, Parliament passed a series of laws directed against Massachusetts. First, it shut down the port of Boston. No ship could enter or leave the harbor—not even a small boat. The harbor would remain closed until the colonists paid for the tea and showed that they were sorry for what they had done.

Second, Parliament said that town meetings could be held only once a year unless the governor gave permission for other meetings. In the past, colonists had called town meetings whenever they wished.

Third, Parliament allowed customs officers and other officials who might be charged with major crimes to be tried in England instead of in Massachusetts. Colonists protested. They said that a dishonest official could break the law in America and avoid punishment "by being tried, where no evidence can pursue him."

Fourth, Parliament passed a new Quartering Act. No longer would red-coats camp in tents on the Boston Commons. Instead, commanders could force citizens to house troops in their homes. The colonists called these laws the *Intolerable Acts* because they were so harsh.

Quebec Act. About the same time, Parliament also passed the *Quebec Act.* It set up a government for Canada and protected the rights of French Catholics. The Quebec Act included the land between the Ohio and Missouri rivers as part of Canada. The act pleased French Canadians. But it angered the American colonists, in part because the new government in Canada did not include an elected assembly. American colonists were especially upset that western lands, which they claimed, were made part of Canada.

Colonists react. The committees of correspondence spread the news of the Intolerable Acts and wrote angrily about the Quebec Act. People from other colonies sent aid to Boston, where the people faced hunger while their port was closed. Carts rolled into Boston with rice from South Carolina, corn from Virginia, flour from Pennsylvania, and sheep from Connecticut.

In the Virginia assembly, young Thomas Jefferson suggested that a day be set aside to mark the shame of the Intolerable Acts. The royal governor of Virginia did not like the idea and dismissed the assembly. But the colonies went ahead with the idea anyway. On June 1, 1774, church bells rang slowly. Merchants closed their shops. Many colonists prayed and fasted all day.

The First Continental Congress

As sympathy for Massachusetts grew, leaders from the colonies decided to meet. They wanted to unite against the Intolerable Acts. In September 1774, delegates from 12 colonies gathered in Philadelphia at the *First Continental Congress.* Only Georgia did not send delegates.

Skill Lesson 7   Using a Time Line

Historians study events that happened in the past. They often look at these events in **chronological order,** or the order in which they occurred. In this way, they can judge whether or not events are related.

A **time line** is one way to show the relationship between events over time. A time line also shows the dates when events happened.

A time line appears at the beginning of each unit and at the beginning of each chapter in this book. These time lines are called horizontal time lines because they set out dates and events on a line from left to right.

Study the time line below. Then use these steps to read the time line.

1. **Identify the time period covered in the time line.** (a) What is the earliest date shown on the time line below? (b) What is the latest date? (c) What is the period covered by this time line?

2. **Decide how the time line is divided.** Time lines are always divided into equal parts or time periods. Some time lines are divided into 10-year periods. A 10-year period is called a **decade.**

Some time lines are divided into 100-year periods. A 100-year period is called a **century.** The period from

1700 to 1799, for example, is called the 18th century. We live in the 20th century, or the period from 1900 to 1999. (a) List the dates on the top of the time line below. (b) How many years are there between each date? (c) What events occurred during the decade of the 1760s? (d) What century is shown on this time line?

3. **Study the time line to discover how events are related.** Use your reading in this chapter and the time line to answer these questions. (a) When did the Boston Tea Party take place? (b) Was the Tea Act passed before or after the Boston Tea Party? (c) Was there a relationship between these two events? Explain your answer.

4. **Draw conclusions.** Compare the time line below to the one on page 148. Then use your reading in this chapter and the two time lines to draw conclusions about events taking place during this period. (a) What time period is shown on page 148? (b) Which time line shows the longer period of time? (c) What events took place between 1745 and 1763? (d) How do you think these events affected what happened after 1763?

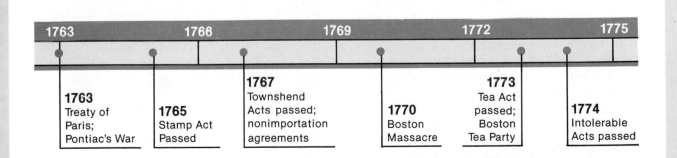

| 1763 | 1766 | 1769 | 1772 | 1775 |

1763
Treaty of Paris; Pontiac's War

1765
Stamp Act Passed

1767
Townshend Acts passed; nonimportation agreements

1770
Boston Massacre

1773
Tea Act passed; Boston Tea Party

1774
Intolerable Acts passed

Delegates had different views about what the Continental Congress should do. Some wanted to patch up the quarrel with Britain by getting Parliament to guarantee their rights. Others argued that the Intolerable Acts proved that Britain would destroy their rights whenever it chose. They urged colonists to stand together firmly against Britain.

After much debate, the delegates passed a resolution backing Massachusetts in its struggle against the Intolerable Acts. They agreed to boycott all British goods and stop exporting American goods to Britain until the acts were repealed. They urged each colony to set up and train its own militia (muh LIHSH uh). A *militia* is an army of citizens who serve as soldiers during an emergency.

Before leaving Philadelphia in October 1774, the delegates agreed to meet again the next May. By May 1775, however, events would set the colonists on a new course.

The British Are Coming!

In Massachusetts, colonists were already preparing to resist Britain. Volunteers, known as *minutemen,* trained regularly. Minutemen kept their muskets at hand, ready to fight at a minute's notice. In towns near Boston, they collected weapons and gunpowder.

Meanwhile, Britain built up its forces. More redcoats landed at Boston, bringing the total number of troops to 4,000. Early in 1775, General Thomas Gage, who commanded the British troops, sent scouts to the towns near Boston. They reported that minutemen had a large store of arms in Concord, a village 18 miles (29 km) from Boston. On April 18, Gage sent about 700 troops to seize the arms by surprise. The troops left Boston quietly at night. But eagle eyes saw them leave. Sons of

Liberty hung two lamps from the Old North Church in Boston. The lamps were a signal to other watchers.

Paul Revere's ride. Across the Charles River, Paul Revere and other Sons of Liberty saw the signal. They mounted their horses and rode toward Concord. As Revere passed through each sleepy village, he shouted: "The British are coming! The British are coming!"

In the early morning of April 19, the redcoats reached the common at Lexington, a town near Concord. There, 70 armed minutemen waited under the command of Captain John Parker. The British ordered the minutemen to go home. They refused. A shot broke through the chill air. Later reports disagree over who fired it. (See the two reports on page 217.) In the brief struggle that followed, eight colonists were killed, and one British soldier was wounded.

The British went on to Concord but found no arms or supplies. When they turned back to Boston, they met 300 more minutemen on a bridge outside Concord. Fighting broke out again. This time, the British were forced to retreat. As they withdrew through the woods and fields, colonial sharpshooters took deadly aim at them. Before they reached Boston, the British lost 73 men. Another 200 were wounded or missing.

Fading hopes for peace. News of the battles at Lexington and Concord traveled fast. Many colonists saw their hopes of reaching an agreement with Britain fade. Only war would decide the future of the 13 colonies.

More than 60 years after the battles, a monument was set up in Concord. A well-known New England poet, Ralph Waldo Emerson, wrote a poem to be sung at the opening ceremony. In the "Concord Hymn," he created a vivid picture of the clash at Concord. It begins:

MAP SKILL In the picture at right, British redcoats fire on minutemen at Lexington. The fighting at Lexington and Concord lasted only a few minutes, but the return to Boston was costly for the British. They faced angry colonists as they retreated. What towns did the British pass through on their way to Concord?

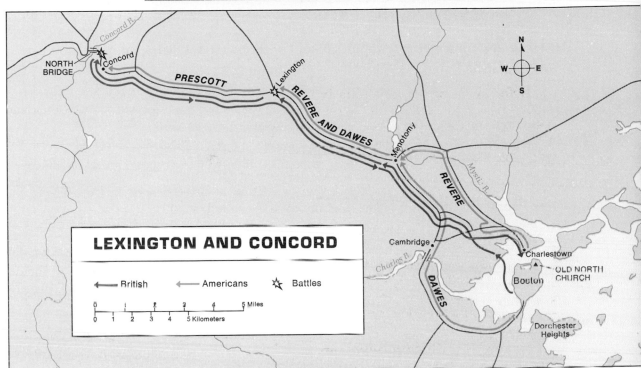

LEXINGTON AND CONCORD

← British   ← Americans   ✫ Battles

0   1   2   3   4   5 Miles
0 1 2 3 4 5 Kilometers

By the rude bridge that arched the flood,
Their flag to April's breeze unfurled,
Here once the embattled farmers stood,
And fired the shot heard round the world.

The "embattled farmers" faced long years of war. But at the war's end, the 13 colonies would stand firm as a new, independent nation.

═ SECTION REVIEW ═

1. **Locate:** Boston, Lexington, Concord.
2. **Define:** militia, minuteman.
3. What was the goal of the Tea Act?
4. Describe three of the Intolerable Acts.
5. **What Do You Think?** Why do you think delegates to the first Continental Congress were divided over how to respond to the Intolerable Acts?

Chapter 7 Review

★ Summary ★

In the mid-1700s, competition between France and England resulted in the struggle known as the French and Indian War. By 1763, Britain had won control of the French empire in North America.

The war left Britain deeply in debt. So Parliament decided to tax the colonies to help repay this debt. Colonists protested against the taxes passed by Parliament.

To protest the Tea Act, a group of colonists dumped tea into Boston harbor. Britain responded by passing the Intolerable Acts. In September 1774, leaders from 12 colonies met at the First Continental Congress. They planned to meet again in 1775. But by then, minutemen and British troops had clashed at the battles of Lexington and Concord.

★ Reviewing the Facts ★

2 pts.

Key Terms. Match each term in Column 1 with the correct definition in Column 2.

Column 1

1. boycott
2. repeal
3. writ of assistance
4. committee of correspondence
5. militia

Column 2

a. document letting officials make a search
b. group that informed colonists of British actions
c. army of citizen soldiers
d. cancel
e. refusal to buy or use certain goods or services

Key People, Events, and Ideas. Identify each of the following.

1. Plan of Union
2. Pontiac
3. Proclamation of 1763
4. Stamp Act
5. Stamp Act Congress
6. Townshend Acts
7. Quartering Act
8. Samuel Adams
9. Patrick Henry
10. Mercy Otis Warren
11. Boston Massacre
12. Tea Act
13. Quebec Act
14. First Continental Congress
15. Paul Revere

★ Chapter Checkup ★

5 pts.

1. (a) Which Indian nations sided with France in the 1700s? (b) Who helped Britain? (c) Why did Native Americans take sides in the struggle between Britain and France?

2. (a) Why did George Washington lead troops into the Ohio Valley in 1754? (b) What happened at Fort Necessity?

3. Describe the role each of the following played in the French and Indian War: (a) Edward Braddock; (b) William Pitt; (c) James Wolfe.

4. Why did Pontiac fight the British?

5. (a) List three ways Parliament tried to tax the colonies. (b) Describe how colonists responded to each.

6. Why did the colonists protest taxes passed by Parliament?

7. (a) What was the Boston Tea Party? (b) What different reactions did colonists have to it?

8. (a) Why did General Gage send troops to Concord? (b) What happened to them when they reached Lexington?

★ Thinking About History ★

5 pts.

1. **Drawing a conclusion.** (a) How did Britain try to prevent clashes between Native Americans and settlers on the frontier? (b) Do you think this policy was likely to succeed? Explain.

2. **Learning about citizenship.** Parliament claimed that it represented all British subjects and had the right to tax the colonies. Colonists replied that only their own representatives had that right. With which side do you agree? Explain.

3. **Relating past to present.** Compare the ways colonists protested unpopular acts of Parliament to the ways people protest unpopular laws today. (a) How are they similar? (b) How are they different?

4. **Analyzing a quotation.** In early April 1775, a British scout near Boston talked to an old man cleaning his musket. "I asked him what he was going to kill. He said there was a flock of redcoats at Boston, which he expected would be here soon; he meant to try and hit some of them, as he expected they would be very good marks." (a) What did the old man mean by "a flock of redcoats"? (b) Was his prediction true? Explain.

5. **Understanding the economy.** Describe two economic reasons why colonists protested British policies.

★ Using Your Skills ★

5 pts.

1. **Map reading.** Study the map on page 150. (a) How many countries claimed land in North America? (b) Which country held land around the Great Lakes? (c) What country had control of Florida in 1753?

2. **Map reading.** Study the map on page 169. (a) In what direction did Paul Revere ride when he left Boston? (b) About how far is Lexington from Concord? (c) In what direction did the British travel when they retreated from Concord?

3. **Placing events in time.** Study the time line on page 167 and review your reading in this chapter. (a) Were the Intolerable Acts passed before or after the Boston Tea Party? (b) What was the link between these two events?

4. **Making a generalization.** (a) List three facts about events leading up to the Boston Massacre. (b) Make a generalization based on these facts about the Boston Massacre.

★ More to Do ★

1. **Writing a diary.** Write several entries for a diary George Washington might have kept on his way to the Ohio Valley in 1754.

2. **Exploring local history.** Use the maps on pages 150 and 156 and a blank map to show whether your local area was part of the territory claimed by Britain, France, or Spain in 1753. In 1763.

3. **Drawing a cartoon.** Draw a cartoon showing a British view of the Sons or Daughters of Liberty.

4. **Giving a speech.** Give a speech that Patrick Henry might have made in the Virginia assembly after hearing about the battles of Lexington and Concord.

8

The American Revolution (1775–1783)

Chapter Outline

1 Fighting Begins
2 Declaring Independence
3 Dark Days of the War
4 Other Battlefronts
5 Victory at Last

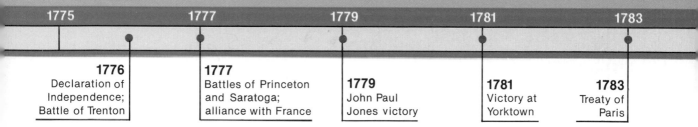

1775	1777	1779	1781	1783
1776 Declaration of Independence; Battle of Trenton	**1777** Battles of Princeton and Saratoga; alliance with France	**1779** John Paul Jones victory	**1781** Victory at Yorktown	**1783** Treaty of Paris

About This Chapter

Early in 1775, debate raged across the colonies. A few outspoken leaders called on the colonies to declare their independence from Britain. But most leaders were more cautious. They hoped to get Britain to change its conduct toward the colonies. Still, the issue was discussed everywhere.

In March 1775, Patrick Henry made a passionate speech to his fellow Virginians. "There is no longer any room for hope," he cried. "We have done everything that could be done to avert [prevent] the storm which is now coming on." Henry declared that the colonists must fight to protect their rights. Britain, he said, was not to be trusted. Its army and navy were being sent to America with one purpose—to enslave the colonists.

To those people who argued that the colonies were too weak to fight Britain, Henry replied: "But when shall we be stronger. Will it be the next week or the next year? Will it be when we are totally disarmed? . . . Shall we gather strength by irresolution [lack of decision] and inaction?" Henry's voice rose as he uttered these last words: "I know not what course others may take. But as for me, give me liberty, or give me death!"

Henry's words echoed through the colonies in the days ahead. Between 1775 and 1783, thousands of colonists took up the challenge—to fight for liberty.

Study the time line above. How do you think Patrick Henry's speech might have influenced events in 1776?

John Trumbull painted this picture, *The Battle of Bunker Hill.* In the battle, colonists showed they would fight for their liberties.

1 Fighting Begins

Read to Learn

★ What did the Second Continental Congress do?
★ How did the colonists defend Bunker Hill?
★ Why did the British leave Boston?
★ What does this word mean: blockade?

Lexington and Concord were the first battles of the American Revolution. In April 1775, no one knew how long the fighting would last. King George III believed that he could soon restore order in the colonies. Meantime, colonists wondered what chance they had of defeating a well-armed, powerful nation like Britain.

Victory at Ticonderoga

In 1775, each colony had its own small militia. But the colonies had no army to face the British. Even so, less than a month after Lexington and Concord, a daring band of colonists made a surprise attack on Fort Ticonderoga (tī kahn duh ROH guh). The fort stood at the southern end of Lake Champlain and protected the water route to Canada. (See the map on page 175.)

Leading the attack was Ethan Allen, a blacksmith famous for his strength and fierce temper. Allen knew that the fort had many cannons the Americans needed. Allen's followers came from the nearby Green Mountains of Vermont.

Early on May 10, Allen and his **Green Mountain Boys** slipped through the morning mists at Fort Ticonderoga. Quickly, they overpowered the one guard on duty at the gate and entered the fort. Allen went straight to the rooms where the officers slept. In a loud voice, he called out to the British commander, "Come out, you old rat!"

The commander pulled on his uniform and demanded to know on whose authority Allen acted. "In the name of the Great Jehovah [God] and the Continental Congress!" replied Allen. The commander had no choice but to surrender the fort with its supply of gunpowder and about 100 cannons.

The Second Continental Congress

On the day that Ethan Allen took Ticonderoga, the Second Continental Congress met in Philadelphia. This time, all 13 colonies sent delegates. The situation was very different from what it had been in September 1774. Now, the colonists were actually fighting the British.

Still, the delegates were divided over what to do. A few, like Sam Adams and John Adams, secretly wanted the colonies to declare their independence. But most delegates hoped to avoid a break with Britain. After much debate, the Continental Congress voted to try to patch up the quarrel with Britain. Delegates sent King George III the **Olive Branch Petition**. In it, they declared their loyalty to him. But they asked him to repeal the Intolerable Acts and end the fighting.

At the same time, the Congress took a bold step. It set up the Continental Army and named George Washington as its commander in chief.

The Balance of Forces

Without wasting time, Washington left Philadelphia for Boston. Riding north, the new American commander knew that he faced a long, hard struggle. The British army was disciplined and experienced. Washington's army was untrained and had little gunpowder and few cannons. Britain was a powerful nation with a strong navy. Its ships could move soldiers quickly up and down the coast. The Americans had no navy to match the British fleet.

Despite these advantages, Britain faced some serious problems. Its soldiers were fighting 3,000 miles (4,800 km) from home. It took months for news to reach Britain or for supplies and fresh troops to reach America. Also, British soldiers often risked attack by colonists once they marched out of the cities into the countryside.

Still, the Americans had certain strengths. They had every reason to fight because they were defending their own homes, farms, and shops. Reuben Stebbins of Williamstown, Massachusetts, was typical of many soldiers. When he heard the British were near his home, he rode off to battle. "We'll see who's goin' t' own this farm!" he cried.

Even though few Americans were trained as soldiers, many owned rifles and were good shots. Also, the Americans were fortunate to have George Washington, who proved to be an excellent leader.

Battle of Bunker Hill

Even before Washington reached Boston, American forces fought a fierce battle there. Minutemen kept close watch on the British troops under General Gage. They wanted to keep the British from leaving the city.

Digging in. At sunset on June 16, 1775, Colonel William Prescott led 1,200 American troops to take up position on Bunker Hill in Charlestown. (See the map on page 175.) From this position, they could fire on British ships in Boston Harbor. Prescott soon saw that nearby Breed's Hill was a bet-

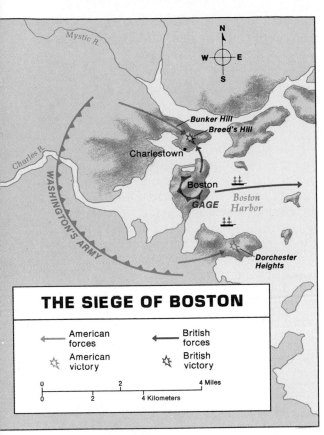

THE SIEGE OF BOSTON

| American forces ← | British forces ← |
| American victory ☆ | British victory ☆ |

0 ... 2 ... 4 Miles
0 ... 2 ... 4 Kilometers

MAP SKILL Early in the American Revolution, several battles took place in and around Boston, as the map above shows. After fierce fighting, colonists were forced to leave Bunker Hill and Breed's Hill. Later, they took Dorchester Heights. In 1775 and 1776, fighting took place elsewhere in New England and Canada, as the map at right shows. Name two American victories early in the Revolution.

THE FIGHT FOR INDEPENDENCE BEGINS

| American forces ← | British forces ← |
| American victories ☆ | British victories ☆ |

0 ... 50 ... 100 ... 150 Miles
0 ... 50 ... 100 ... 150 Kilometers

ter position. So he put his men to work digging trenches there. "Dig, men, dig," he urged. "Dig for your lives." Prescott knew that the trenches must be finished before dawn. Otherwise, the British could easily force them off the hill.

At dawn, the British general, William Howe, spotted the Americans. He ferried about 2,400 redcoats across the harbor to Charlestown. There, the British had to cross rough fields broken by fences to climb Breed's Hill. Each soldier carried a heavy pack that weighed about 125 pounds. It was hot, exhausting work, and the soldiers moved slowly.

The Americans waited in their trenches, watching the British struggle up the hill. Because the colonists had only a small amount of gunpowder, the American commanders warned, "Don't shoot until you see the whites of their eyes!"

A hot fire. As the enemy advanced, "we gave them such a hot fire that they were obliged to retire nearly 150 yards before they could rally," recalled Colonel Prescott. Twice, the British advanced up the hill. Twice, they had to retreat from American musket fire. "The oldest officers say they never saw a sharper action," reported Francis Rawdon, a young redcoat.

On the third try, the British pushed over the top. By then, the Americans had run out of gunpowder. Although the British took both Bunker and Breed's hills, it was a costly victory. Over 1,000 redcoats lay dead or wounded. The Americans lost 400.

The *Battle of Bunker Hill* was the first major battle of the war. It showed that the American army would not collapse at the first sound of battle. On the other hand, it showed that the British would not be easy to defeat.

The British Leave Boston

Washington reached Boston a few weeks after the Battle of Bunker Hill. All through the summer and fall, he struggled to make an army out of soldiers from different colonies. "Connecticut wants no Massachusetts men in her corps," he wrote. And "Massachusetts thinks there is no necessity for a Rhode Islander to be introduced into her." Slowly, Washington won the respect of the troops. The army learned to obey orders and work together.

By January 1776, the Continental Army surrounded the British in Boston. The cannons captured at Fort Ticonderoga were dragged on sleds

After the Green Mountain Boys took Fort Ticonderoga, they dragged cannons they had captured across the snow-covered Green Mountains to Boston. There, the cannons were used to fortify Dorchester Heights, which overlooked the city. What problems do you think the Green Mountain Boys faced in bringing the cannons to Boston?

across mountains and forests to Boston. Washington put the cannons on Dorchester Heights, a hill overlooking Boston and its harbor. The British realized that the Americans were dug in too well to be forced out. So in March 1776, General Howe ordered his troops to leave Boston for Halifax, Canada.

Although the British left New England, Washington knew that the war was far from over. King George III ordered a blockade of all colonial ports. A *blockade* is the shutting off of a port by ships to keep people or supplies from moving in or out. Also, the king hired Hessian troops from Germany to help British soldiers fight the colonists.

Invasion of Canada

While Washington was training one army outside Boston, two other American armies were moving north into Canada. (See the map on page 175). One, led by Richard Montgomery, left from Fort Ticonderoga. The other, led by Benedict Arnold, moved north through Maine. Americans expected French Canadians to help them force the British out of Canada.

Montgomery seized Montreal in November 1775. Then he moved down the St. Lawrence toward the city of Quebec. Arnold had a terrible journey through the Maine woods in winter. His troops were forced to boil candles, bark, and shoe leather for food. Finally, they, too, reached Quebec. But the Americans were disappointed because French Canadians did not come to their aid.

On December 31, 1775, the Americans attacked Quebec during a driving snowstorm. The attack was turned back. Montgomery was killed, and Arnold was wounded. The Americans stayed outside Quebec until May 1776, when the British landed new forces in Canada. Weakened by disease and hunger, the Americans withdrew, leaving Canada to the British.

SECTION REVIEW

1. **Locate:** Lake Champlain, Fort Ticonderoga, Boston, Bunker Hill, Breed's Hill, Boston Harbor, Montreal, Quebec.
2. **Define:** blockade.
3. Why was Ethan Allen able to take Fort Ticonderoga so easily?
4. How did colonists try to patch up the quarrel with Britain in 1775?
5. **What Do You Think?** How do you think the Battle of Bunker Hill affected the American cause?

2 Declaring Independence

Read to Learn
★ What did Paine argue for in *Common Sense?*
★ What are the main parts of the Declaration of Independence?
★ Who were the Loyalists?
★ What does this word mean: traitor?

Late in 1775, the Continental Congress learned that the king had rejected the Olive Branch Petition and set up the blockade. To many Americans, these actions showed that the colonists could no longer hope to settle their differences with Britain. Still, many colonists did not want to take the final step and declare their independence.

The Voice of *Common Sense*

Although many colonists thought that the king had ignored their rights, they were still loyal to Britain. Then, in

January 1776, Thomas Paine wrote a pamphlet called *Common Sense*. Paine had only recently moved to Philadelphia from England. But he believed that the colonists should declare independence.

The pamphlet created a great stir in the colonies. In it, Paine answered the colonists' worries about breaking with Britain. He argued that it was foolish "to be always running three or four thousand miles with a tale or petition, waiting four or five months for an answer, which when obtained requires five or six more to explain it in."

Paine asked anyone "to show a single advantage this continent can reap, by being connected with Britain." Besides, he said, America was already at war with Britain. And "since nothing but blows will do . . . let us come to a final separation!"

Between January and July 1776, 500,000 copies of *Common Sense* were sold in the colonies. George Washington wrote that "*Common Sense* is working a powerful change in the minds of men." The pamphlet even changed Washington's habits. Until 1776, he followed the custom of drinking a toast to the king at official dinners. After reading Paine's pamphlet, he dropped this custom.

Congress Acts

Paine's pamphlet had an effect on the Continental Congress, too. More and more delegates came to believe that the colonies must declare independence. In June 1776, Richard Henry Lee from Virginia offered a resolution saying that "these United Colonies are, and of right ought to be, free and independent States." It was a tense moment. Delegates knew that there would be no turning back once they declared independence. If Britain won the war, they would be hanged as traitors. A *traitor* is a person who betrays his or her country.

In the end, the delegates appointed a committee to draw up a declaration of independence. The committee included John Adams, Benjamin Franklin, Thomas Jefferson, Robert Livingston, and Roger Sherman. Their job was to explain to the world why the colonies were taking such a drastic step. The committee asked Jefferson to prepare the document.

Jefferson was one of the youngest delegates in the Congress. Tall, slender, and quiet, he spoke little in the Congress. But among his friends, he liked to sprawl in a chair with his long legs stretched out and talk for hours. In late June, Jefferson completed the declaration, and it was read to the Congress. The delegates made a few changes.*

On July 2, the Continental Congress voted that the 13 colonies were "free and independent States." Two days later, on July 4, 1776, the delegates accepted the *Declaration of Independence*. Since then, Americans have celebrated July 4th as Independence Day.

The Declaration of Independence

The Declaration of Independence has three main parts. (An introduction and the text of the Declaration is printed on pages 793–796.) The first part explains the basic rights on which the nation is founded. "We hold these truths to be self-evident," wrote Jefferson, "that all men are created equal, that they are endowed by their Creator with certain unalienable rights, that among these are life, liberty, and the pursuit of happiness."

How do people protect these basic rights? By forming governments, the Declaration said. Governments could exist only if they had the "consent of

---

*One change involved slavery. The delegates dropped a statement that condemned King George for continuing slavery in the colonies.

The signing of the Declaration of Independence was a solemn occasion. But John Adams felt that future Americans would celebrate the event "with pomp and parade, with shows, games, sports, guns, bells, bonfires, and illuminations from one end of this continent to the other."

the governed." If a government took away its citizens' rights, then it was the people's right and "their duty, to throw off such government, and provide new guards for their future security."

The second part of the Declaration lists the wrongs committed by Britain. In the long list, Jefferson showed how the king had abused his power. It backed up the colonists' argument that they had a right to revolt.

The last section declares that the colonies had become "the United States of America." All ties with Britain were cut. As a free and independent nation, the United States could now make alliances and trade with other countries.

John Hancock, the president of the Continental Congress, was the first to sign the Declaration. He signed his name in large, bold handwriting. Other delegates added their names.

Patriots and Loyalists

John Dunlap of Philadelphia published the Declaration of Independence late on July 4, 1776. Later, Mary Katherine Goddard, a Baltimore printer, produced the first copies of the Declaration that included the names of all the signers. When copies of the Declaration reached towns and villages, people had to decide whether to support the new nation or remain loyal to Britain.

The nation was divided. On one side were *Patriots,* people who supported independence. On the other were *Loyalists,* people who stayed loyal to the king. Many families were split. Ben Franklin, for example, was a Patriot. His son, the royal governor of New Jersey, remained loyal to George III. Loyalists included royal officials as well as many merchants and farmers.

Skill Lesson 8   Comparing Two Points of View

As you learned in Skill Lesson 5 (page 116), people usually have a reason for writing about events or developments in which they are involved. As a result, a primary source, or firsthand account, reflects the author's point of view. Two people writing about the same subject can have different points of view.

The letters below are written by Abigail and John Adams. During the Revolution, John Adams was away from home for long periods. His wife, Abigail Adams, wrote to him often. She kept him informed about their children and their farm, which she kept going. When the Continental Congress was preparing the Declaration of Independence, she wrote her husband the first letter reprinted below. The second letter is John Adams' reply to his wife.

Read the letters. Then compare the two points of view.

1. **Study the contents of each source.** (a) What does Abigail Adams want her husband to do? (b) What is John Adams' response to her request? (c) Who does John Adams mean when he says "another tribe, more numerous and powerful than all the rest"?

2. **Compare the points of view.** (a) What does Abigail Adams think men are like? (b) Does John Adams agree with his wife's view of men? Explain.

3. **Evaluate the usefulness of these sources.** (a) What do these letters tell you about American society in 1776? (b) Do you think these letters are a reliable source of information? Explain.

 Abigail Adams wrote:

I long to hear that you have declared independence. And by the way, in the new code of laws that I suppose you will make, I wish you would remember the ladies and be more generous and favorable to them than your ancestors. Do not put such unlimited power in the hands of husbands. Remember, all men would be tyrants if they could. If particular care and attention is not paid to the ladies, we are determined to stir up a rebellion and will not regard ourselves as bound by any laws in which we have had no voice or representation.

 John Adams replied:

As to your extraordinary code of laws, I can't help laughing. We have been told that our struggle has loosened the bonds of government everywhere, that children and apprentices were disobedient, that schools and colleges had grown turbulent, that Indians slighted their guardians and Negroes grow insolent to their masters. But your letter was the first hint that another tribe, more numerous and powerful than all the rest, had grown discontented.

Depend upon it, we know better than to repeal our masculine systems. Although they are in full force, you know they are little more than theory . . . in practice, you know, we are the subjects. We have only the title of masters, and rather than give this up, which would subject us completely to the power of the petticoat, I hope General Washington and all our brave heroes would fight.

During the war, many thousands of Loyalists supported the British. There were more Loyalists in the Middle States and the South than in New England. But life was difficult for Loyalists everywhere. Patriots tarred and feathered people who spoke in favor of Britain. Many Loyalists fled to England or Canada. Those who fled lost their homes, stores, and farms.

SECTION REVIEW

1. **Define:** traitor.

2. Give two reasons Paine thought the colonies should become independent.

3. What are the basic rights set out in the Declaration of Independence?

4. **What Do You Think?** Why do you think many colonists remained loyal to Britain?

3 Dark Days of the War

Read to Learn
- ★ What major battles were fought in the Middle States?
- ★ Why was the Battle of Saratoga a turning point in the Revolution?
- ★ How did foreigners help the Americans during the Revolution?
- ★ What does this word mean: cavalry?

Most of the early battles of the American Revolution were fought in New England. After General Howe left Boston in March 1776, however, the heavy fighting moved to the Middle States. For the next two years, Americans battled the British in New York, New Jersey, and Pennsylvania. During this time, Americans faced the darkest days of the war.

Battle for New York

When General Howe left Boston, he by no means gave up fighting. He reorganized his forces in Halifax and then sailed for New York City. Washington expected Howe's move. He marched from Boston to New York to defend the city. But he faced a grim situation. Howe had 34,000 troops, 10,000 sailors, 30 warships, and 400 smaller boats to ferry his troops ashore. Washington had only 20,000 troops. Most of them had little training and no experience in battle. And he had no navy.

Washington divided his troops because he did not know where Howe would land. He sent some to Long Island. In August 1776, Howe made a surprise attack on these troops. In the *Battle of Long Island,* more than 1,400 Americans were killed, wounded, or captured. The rest retreated across the East River to Manhattan.

Washington realized that he could not defend New York against Howe. So he retreated north. All through the fall, he fought running battles with Howe's army. In November, Washington crossed the Hudson River into New Jersey. The British followed, chasing the Americans across the Delaware River into Pennsylvania. (See the map on page 182.)

During the battle for New York, Washington needed information about Howe's forces. Nathan Hale, a young Connecticut officer, offered to go behind British lines. Hale got the information but was captured by the British. He was tried and condemned to death.

"He behaved with great composure," wrote a British soldier, "saying he thought it the duty of every good officer to obey any orders given him by his Commander in Chief." Later, it was reported that Hale's last words were "I only regret that I have but one life to lose for my country."

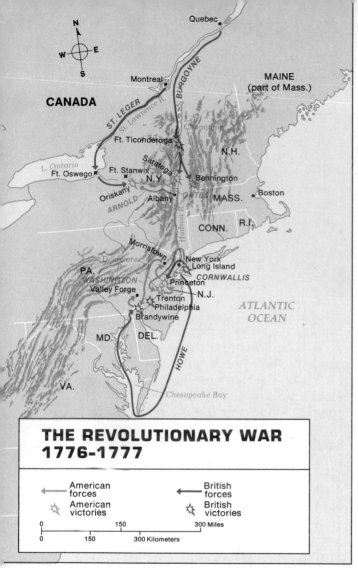

THE REVOLUTIONARY WAR 1776-1777

← American forces
⭐ American victories

← British forces
⭐ British victories

0 — 150 — 300 Miles
0 — 150 — 300 Kilometers

MAP SKILL In 1776 and 1777, American and British forces fought many battles, as this map shows. In October 1777, Americans won an important victory at the Battle of Saratoga. Describe the route taken by General Burgoyne's army to reach Saratoga.

A Much-Needed Victory

By December 1776, Washington was very discouraged. "I am wearied to death," he admitted. "I think the game is pretty near up." The Continental Congress fled from Philadelphia, fearing a British attack. Washington's troops were discouraged, too. They were cold and hungry. Every day, soldiers left the army to return home.

Tom Paine, author of *Common Sense*, wrote a new pamphlet, called *The Crisis*. In it, he wrote:

These are the times that try men's souls. The summer soldier and the sunshine patriot will, in this crisis, shrink from the service of their country; but he that stands *now*, deserves the love and thanks of men and women.

Attack on Trenton. Washington had Paine's words read aloud to his troops. The Americans needed more than words, however. So Washington decided on a bold move. He planned a surprise attack on Trenton.

On Christmas night, Washington secretly led his troops across the icy Delaware River. Soldiers huddled in the boats as the spray from the river froze on their faces. Once across the river, the troops marched through the swirling snow. General Washington rode up and down the lines. "Soldiers, keep by your officers," he urged.

Early on December 26, the Americans surprised the Hessian troops guarding Trenton and took most of them prisoner. After the *Battle of Trenton,* one American wrote in his diary: "Hessian population of Trenton at 8 A.M.—1,408 men and 39 officers; Hessian population at 9 A.M.—0." Most were then prisoners of the Americans.

Victory at Princeton. After the Battle of Trenton, the British sent General Charles Cornwallis to recapture the city. In the evening of January 2, Cornwallis saw the lights of Washington's campfires. "At last we have run down the old fox and we will bag him in the morning," he said.

But Washington fooled Cornwallis. Washington left his fires burning and marched behind British lines to attack Princeton. There, he won another victory. From Princeton, Washington moved on to Morristown, where the army spent the winter. The victories at Trenton and Princeton gave the army new hope and confidence.

A British Plan of Attack

Early in 1777, General John Burgoyne (buhr GOIN) convinced King George to try a new plan of attack. Burgoyne told the king that if the British could cut off New England from the other colonies, the war would soon be over.

Burgoyne's plan called for three British armies to march on Albany from different directions. New England would be cut off when the three armies met in Albany. Britain then would control all the land from Canada to New York. The king and his advisers approved the plan. However, they ordered General Howe to take Philadelphia before he marched to Albany.

Brandywine and Germantown. Burgoyne's plan might have worked if General Howe had taken Philadelphia quickly. But he did not. In July 1777, he sailed from New York to the Chesapeake Bay. (See the map on page 182.) As he marched toward Philadelphia, Washington tried to stop him. At the *Battle of Brandywine*, the Americans were defeated.

Howe entered Philadelphia in late September. Washington again attacked the redcoats, this time at Germantown, just outside Philadelphia. But the Americans again met defeat. Washington retreated to Valley Forge, where he set up winter quarters.

Meanwhile, two other British armies under Barry St. Leger (lay ZHAIR) and Burgoyne moved south from Canada on their way to Albany. St. Leger tried to take Fort Stanwix. He had to retreat when Benedict Arnold arrived with a strong American army. General Burgoyne retook Fort Ticonderoga without firing a shot. But his army moved slowly because they had to drag many baggage carts through the woods.

Turning point at Saratoga. Burgoyne sent soldiers into Vermont to find food and horses. Patriots attacked and defeated these troops at the *Battle of Bennington.*

Burgoyne's troubles grew. The Green Mountain Boys hurried into New York to help the American army led by General Horatio Gates. At the

In October 1777, Washington attacked the British army, shown here at Germantown. The day was not as clear as this later painting shows. Fog covered the battlefield. The fog caused confusion and kept the Americans from winning a victory.

village of Saratoga, Gates surrounded the British. Twice, Burgoyne tried to break through the American lines. Both times, he was driven back by General Benedict Arnold. Realizing he was trapped, General Burgoyne surrendered his entire army to the Americans on October 17, 1777.

Alliance With France

The American victory at the **Battle of Saratoga** was a turning point in the war. It ended the British threat to New England and encouraged Americans at a time when Washington's army in Pennsylvania was suffering defeats. More important, it convinced France to sign a treaty with the United States.

In 1776, the Continental Congress had sent Benjamin Franklin to Paris to get help from the French king, Louis XVI. The Americans were in desperate need of weapons and other supplies. They also wanted France to declare war on Britain. France had a strong navy that could be used against the British.

Franklin knew that many French people favored the American cause. France and Britain were longtime rivals. And the French were still unhappy about their defeat by the British in the French and Indian War. Still, Franklin had a hard time. Louis XVI secretly sent some weapons and supplies. Yet the French king did not want to help the Americans openly until he saw that they were likely to win.

The Battle of Saratoga convinced him to help the struggling young nation. In February 1778, France became the first nation to sign a treaty with the United States. In it, Louis XVI recognized the new nation and agreed to give it military aid.

The Winter at Valley Forge

French aid came too late to help Washington and his army at Valley Forge. During the long, cold winter of 1777–1778, they suffered terrible hard-

ships, while the British in Philadelphia were warm, comfortable, and well fed.

The Americans had little food or clothing. As the winter wore on, soldiers suffered from frostbite and disease. A Rhode Island officer wrote home to beg the governor to send food and clothes. His troops were so ragged looking, he wrote, that others called them "the naked regiment." Some soldiers stood on guard wrapped only in blankets. Many had no shoes and wrapped bits of cloth around their feet.

When news of the army's suffering spread, Americans sent food and clothing to Valley Forge. Women were especially active. They gathered medicine, food, clothing, and ammunition for the army. They raised money to buy other supplies and collected lead objects to be melted into bullets. (See the picture of Laura Wolcott on page 188.)

Help From Overseas

Help also came from overseas. In 1777, the Marquis de Lafayette (lah fih YET), a French noble, brought many professional soldiers to America. He fought at Brandywine and spent the winter at Valley Forge. The young Frenchman became a trusted friend of General Washington.

Two Polish officers helped the Americans. They were Thaddeus Kosciusko (kahs ee USH koh) and Casimir Pulaski (poo LAHS kee). Kosciusko, an engineer, helped build forts and other defenses. Pulaski trained *cavalry,* or troops on horseback.

Help came from New Spain, too. Bernardo de Galvez* was governor of the Spanish lands of Louisiana during the Revolution. He supplied cattle from Spanish herds in Texas to the Americans. Also, he attacked the British in Florida.

Friedrich von Steuben (STOO buhn) from Prussia improved discipline in the

---

*The city of Galveston, Texas, is named after Bernardo de Galvez.

The harsh winter at Valley Forge was a severe test of Washington's leadership. He kept the army together despite great hardships. Washington had to plead with local merchants and farmers for food supplies. And he wrote daily to Congress to send supplies and new recruits.

American army. Steuben once served in the Prussian army, the best-trained army in Europe. A lively person, Steuben kept everybody in good spirits. He showed the Americans how to use bayonets. Most soldiers had not fought with bayonets. So they used them to roast meat over the fire.

Although Steuben spoke little English, he soon taught Washington's troops how to march. He ordered each soldier to put his left hand on the shoulder of the man in front of him. Then, Steuben called out in his German accent: "Fooorrvarrd march! Von, Two, Tree, Four!"

By the spring of 1778, the army at Valley Forge was more hopeful. "The army grows stronger every day," wrote one New Jersey soldier. "The troops are instructed in a new and so happy a method of marching that they will soon be able to advance with the utmost regularity, even without music and on the roughest grounds." While soldiers drilled, Washington and his staff planned new campaigns against the British.

SECTION REVIEW

1. **Locate:** New York, Philadelphia, Trenton, Delaware River, Princeton, Albany, Brandywine, Saratoga, Valley Forge.

2. **Define:** cavalry.

3. (a) Name three battles fought in the Middle States. (b) What was the result of each?

4. Why did Americans want an alliance with France?

5. **What Do You Think?** Why do you think foreigners like Lafayette and Steuben helped the Americans?

4 Other Battlefronts

Read to Learn

★ Why did some Indians help the British?
★ How did John Paul Jones become a hero?
★ What role did black Americans and women play in the Revolution?
★ What does this word mean: neutral?

The Revolution was fought on many fronts. While the Continental Army battled in the east, other Patriots fought in the west and at sea.

War in the West

During the war, Americans continued to move west. In Kentucky, they named one new settlement Lexington, after the first battle of the Revolution. Another settlement was called Louisville, after America's ally, King Louis XVI of France. But as settlers moved west, they often clashed with Native Americans whose lands they were invading.

Native Americans. When the Revolution began, many Native Americans wanted to stay *neutral,* or not fight for either side. Yet some Indians did fight. Indian nations such as the Algonquins and Iroquois were divided over which side to help. In Massachusetts, Algonquins helped the Patriots. But west of the Appalachians, some Algonquins helped the British because Patriots were seizing their lands.

In Tennessee, most Cherokees wanted to stay neutral or favored the Patriots. Nancy Ward, a Cherokee leader, warned Patriot settlers of a raid planned by a small group of Cherokees. Settlers responded to the warning by attacking all the Cherokees. This betrayal of trust forced the Cherokees to join the British.

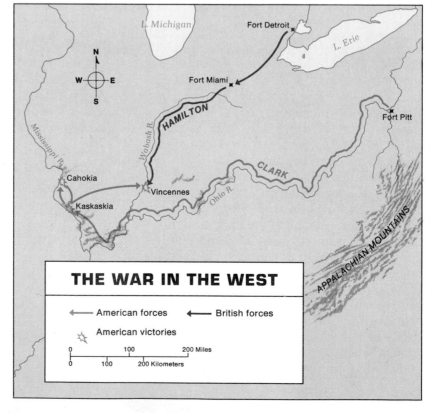

MAP SKILL American and British forces fought for control of lands west of the Appalachian Mountains. Find the route George Rogers Clark took from Fort Pitt to Vincennes. In which direction or directions did he march to reach Vincennes?

THE WAR IN THE WEST

← American forces   ← British forces

American victories

0   100   200 Miles
0   100   200 Kilometers

In this picture of a famous naval battle, the *Bonhomme Richard,* commanded by John Paul Jones, fires on the *Serapis.* After winning the battle, Jones climbed on board the captured *Serapis* and watched his own damaged ship sink.

The British found other Indian allies and supplied them with weapons. The Indians who joined the British did so to protect their homes against white settlers.

Clark's victories. In 1778, George Rogers Clark led Virginia frontiersmen against the British in the Ohio River valley. With the help of Miami Indians, Clark captured the British forts at Kaskaskia and Cahokia. (See the map on page 186.)

Clark wanted to take Vincennes, but British forces there far outnumbered the Virginians. So he planned a surprise attack. During the winter, he marched 150 miles (240 km) through heavy rains, swamps, and icy rivers. When Clark's small band of men reached the fort, they spread out through the woods to appear greater in number than they really were. The trick worked. The British commander thought that it was useless to fight so many Americans. In February 1779, he surrendered Vincennes to Clark.

War at Sea

With its strong navy, Britain was able to blockade and patrol the Atlantic coast. Although the American navy remained small, American ships attacked and captured British ships at sea. One daring American captain, John Paul Jones, even raided the English coast.

In September 1779, Jones fought the most famous sea battle of the war. The battle took place in the North Sea off the coast of Britain. Jones was in command of the *Bonhomme Richard*—named after Franklin's *Poor Richard's Almanac*—when he saw 39 merchant ships guarded by a British warship, the *Serapis.* He attacked the *Serapis* even though it was larger than his ship.

During the battle, British cannon balls ripped through the *Bonhomme Richard,* setting it on fire. The British commander called on Jones to surrender. "I have not yet begun to fight!" replied Jones. He brought his ship in close to the enemy. Americans jumped aboard the *Serapis* and defeated the British in hand-to-hand fighting. The victory made Jones a popular hero.

Black Americans in the War

By 1775, many blacks had gained their freedom through loyal service.

AMERICANS WHO DARED

Laura Wolcott

Laura Wolcott lived in Litchfield, Connecticut, where her family were Patriots. At age 15, she made her own contribution to the cause. In July 1776, New Yorkers tore down a statue of King George III. Pieces of lead from the statue were sent to Litchfield. Women made them into cartridges for Washington's army. Wolcott made at least 4,250 cartridges.

Slavery was declining in the North,* where a number of free blacks lived. Black Patriots hoped that the Revolution would lead to equality. The Declaration of Independence stated that "all men are created equal." Black Americans expected the new nation to live up to this goal and end slavery.

Some white Americans supported the idea of freedom for slaves. James

*In the 1760s, two surveyors, Charles Mason and Jeremiah Dixon, marked the official border between Pennsylvania and Maryland at 39°43′N. The border, known as the Mason–Dixon Line, came to be seen as the dividing line between the North and South.

Otis of Massachusetts wrote that "the colonists are by the law of nature free born, as indeed all men are, white or black." By 1783, Vermont, Massachusetts, and New Hampshire had outlawed slavery. During the war, other states debated the issue.

When the Revolution began, the British tried to win the support of blacks. In 1775, the governor of Virginia stated that all slaves who served the king would be given their freedom. This offer encouraged thousands of slaves to join the British.

Meantime, many free blacks and slaves supported the Revolution. At least seven blacks were among the minutemen who fought at Lexington and Concord. Other black Patriots marched into battle at Ticonderoga and Bunker Hill.

For a time, the Continental Congress refused to let slaves or free blacks serve officially in the army. However, the British success in recruiting slaves made the Congress change its mind. By 1778, both free blacks and slaves were allowed to serve in the Continental Army. They formed all-black fighting regiments and served in white regiments as drummers, fifers, spies, and guides.

Women in the Revolution

Women supported the Patriot cause in many ways. They worked on the home front, making guns and other weapons. One woman, known as "Handy Betsy the Blacksmith," was famous for supplying cannons and guns to the army.

Women raised money to supply the army with food, clothing, and medicine. They also took over work usually done by men. They farmed the land alone and grew the food so badly needed by the Continental Army.

Women made shoes and wove cloth for blankets and uniforms. Betsy Ross of Philadelphia was one of many women who sewed flags for Washing-

As a child, Phillis Wheatley was brought from Africa to America and sold as a slave. Later, she managed to teach herself Greek and Latin and wrote fine poetry. In one well-known poem, she praised the leadership of General Washington.

Many women joined their soldier-husbands at the front. There, they washed clothes, cooked, and cared for the wounded. Martha Washington joined her husband as often as possible. She and other women helped raise the army's spirits.

A few women took part in battle. During the Battle of Monmouth in 1778, Mary Ludwig Hays carried water to her husband and other soldiers. The soldiers called her "Moll of the Pitcher" or Molly Pitcher. When her husband was wounded, she took his place, loading and firing a cannon. Deborah Sampson of Massachusetts dressed as a man and fought in several battles. Later, she wrote about her life in the army.

▬ SECTION REVIEW ▬

1. **Locate:** Ohio River, Kaskaskia, Cahokia, Vincennes.
2. **Define:** neutral.
3. Which side did Native Americans take in the Revolution?
4. Why did black Americans support the Revolution?
5. **What Do You Think?** Why do you think women were as important as men in the war effort?

ton's forces. Long after the war, the story grew up that Washington asked Ross to make the first American flag of stars and stripes. But the story cannot be proved.

5 Victory at Last

Read to Learn

★ What battles were fought in the South?
★ How were the British trapped at Yorktown?
★ What were the terms of the Treaty of Paris?
★ What does this word mean: ratify?

In 1778, the war entered a new stage. The fighting, which had begun in New England and shifted to the Middle States, now moved into the South.

Battlefields in the South

Fighting began in the South in the early days of the Revolution. In February 1776, North Carolina Patriots defeated a Loyalist army at the **Battle of Moore's Creek Bridge.** This victory has sometimes been called the Lexington and Concord of the South.

After the French entered the war, the British decided to put their main effort in the South. They counted on the support of Loyalists there. For a time, the British met with success. In December 1779, British troops seized Savannah, Georgia. They later took Charleston, South Carolina. The Americans suffered one blow after another at the hands of the British. "I have almost ceased to hope," wrote Washington after hearing of these American losses.

Tale of a traitor. In the summer of 1780, Washington got more bad news. He learned that Benedict Arnold, one of his most talented generals, had gone over to the British side. Arnold had fought bravely in many battles. One soldier recalled that Arnold always led—never followed—his men into battle. "It was 'Come on, boys!' not 'Go on, boys!' He didn't care for nothin'. He'd ride right in."

In 1780, Arnold was in command of the American fort at West Point. Because he felt that he had not received credit for his successes, Arnold offered to turn West Point over to the British. The plot almost succeeded. American soldiers caught the messenger carrying Arnold's offer. West Point was saved. Arnold himself escaped and joined the British.*

The tide turns. In the fall of 1780, the Americans began to stem the tide of British victories in the South. Patriots organized hit-and-run attacks on the redcoats. Francis Marion of South Carolina led a small band of men who slept by day and traveled by night. Marion was known as the *Swamp Fox*. He

---

*In America, the name Benedict Arnold came to mean a traitor.

Francis Marion's hit-and-run attacks earned him the nickname Swamp Fox. Banastre Tarleton, a British colonel, claimed that "the devil himself could not catch Marion." Here, Marion and his men cross the Pee Dee River in South Carolina.

appeared suddenly out of the swamps, attacked the British, and then retreated into the swamps. His attacks kept the British off balance.

Two American generals, Daniel Morgan and Nathanael Greene, helped the Patriots to victory in the South. Morgan, a Virginian, commanded a company at the Battle of Saratoga in New York. In January 1781, he defeated a Loyalist and British army at the **Battle of Cowpens** in South Carolina.

Joining Morgan, General Greene used the same hit-and-run tactics as Francis Marion. He won few outright victories, but he did wear down the British. The American successes made the British general, Charles Cornwallis, decide to leave the Carolinas. In April 1781, Cornwallis took his army north into Virginia.

Victory at Yorktown

At first, Cornwallis was successful in Virginia. Secretly, he sent Loyalist troops to attack Charlottesville, where the Virginia legislature was meeting. Loyalist soldiers almost captured the lawmakers, including Virginia's governor, Thomas Jefferson.

American troops under Lafayette fought back by making raids on the British. Lafayette did not have enough troops to fight a real battle. Still, the American raids forced Cornwallis to pull his troops back to Yorktown, on a peninsula between the James and York rivers. Cornwallis felt safe at Yorktown because he counted on the British navy to supply his troops. But a French fleet under Admiral de Grasse drove the British ships out of the Chesapeake Bay. French troops under the Comte de Rochambeau (roh shahm BOH) had just landed from France. They joined General Washington in New York. Together, they marched into Virginia, boxing in the British army.

Cornwallis held out for three weeks before he surrendered his entire army

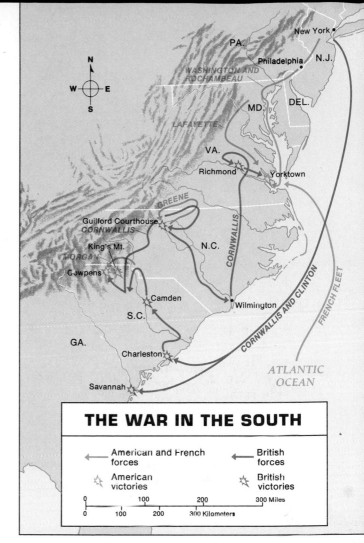

THE WAR IN THE SOUTH

← American and French forces   ← British forces

☆ American victories   ☆ British victories

0   100   200   300 Miles
0   100   200   300 Kilometers

MAP SKILL Britain won a string of victories in the south in 1779 and 1780. Slowly, Americans turned the tide. In October 1781, French and American forces trapped Cornwallis at Yorktown, forcing him to surrender. How do you think the French fleet helped the American victory at Yorktown?

on October 17, 1781. Two days later, the defeated British soldiers turned over their muskets to the Americans. During the ceremony, the British army band played the song "The World Turned Upside Down."

A Time for Peace

News of the American victory at Yorktown stunned the British. "It is all over," cried the British prime minister, Lord North. The defeat of Cornwallis convinced the British to negotiate for

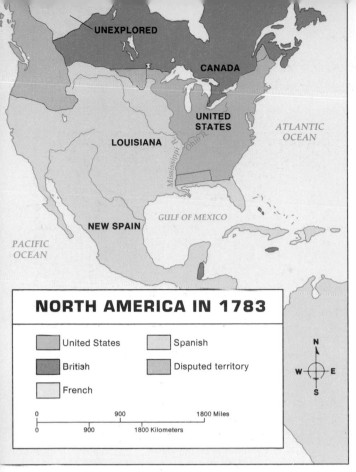

NORTH AMERICA IN 1783

- United States
- British
- French
- Spanish
- Disputed territory

```
0        900            1800 Miles
0     900      1800 Kilometers
```

MAP SKILL By the Treaty of Paris, Britain recognized the United States as an independent nation. What nations held land on the borders of the United States?

peace. Peace did not come at once, however.

Peace talks began in Paris in 1782. Congress sent Benjamin Franklin and John Adams, along with John Jay of New York and Henry Laurens of Virginia, to work out a peace treaty. Because the British wanted to end the war, the Americans got most of what they wanted.

The Treaty of Paris. Britain agreed to recognize the United States as a free and independent nation. It recognized the borders of the new nation. The United States extended from the Atlantic Ocean to the Mississippi River. The southern border stopped at Florida, which now belonged to Spain again.

For their part, the Americans agreed to ask state legislatures to pay Loyalists for the property they lost in the war. In the end, however, most state legislatures ignored Loyalist claims. On April 19, 1783, Congress *ratified,* or approved, the Treaty of Paris. This date was exactly eight years after the first shots were fired at Lexington and Concord.

Cooperation between General Washington and the Marquis de Lafayette helped win the war. This painting shows the two men at the Battle of Yorktown in 1781. Reuben Law Reed painted this picture many years after the war from the description of an eyewitness.

Thousands of men and women fought for the American cause. Some joined the Continental Army. Others helped from behind the lines. Among the heroes of the Revolution are the four people shown on these stamps.

In 1777, young Sybil Ludington made a midnight ride like that of Paul Revere. She warned Patriot soldiers of a British attack on Danbury, Connecticut.

Salem Poor, a black soldier, fought at Lexington and Concord and at the Battle of Bunker Hill. After Bunker Hill, Colonel Prescott and other officers asked the Continental Congress to reward Poor as a "brave and gallant soldier."

Haym Salomon, a Jew, left Poland because of religious persecution. In America, he joined the Sons of Liberty and was arrested by the British. Later, he made a fortune in business. When the Continental Congress was desperate for money, Salomon spent his own fortune to help the American cause.

Sybil Ludington — *Youthful Heroine*
Salem Poor — *Gallant Soldier*
Haym Salomon — *Financial Hero*
Peter Francisco — *Fighter Extraordinary*

At age 16, Peter Francisco fought at the Battle of Brandywine. In the next four years, he fought in many other battles and was wounded four times. In one battle, he is credited with carrying a 1,000-pound cannon to keep it from falling into British hands.

★ How did the deeds of men and women like these four help the American cause?

Washington retires. The war was a long and difficult struggle. Patriots fought against better-armed and better-trained soldiers. French money, arms, and soldiers helped the Americans win major battles. The strength and courage of leaders like Washington were also important to the American victory. In 1781, when Washington marched from New York to Yorktown, men, women, and children turned out along the road to see the commander in chief. People quietly touched his horse or his cloak as he passed.

When peace came, Washington bid farewell to his soldiers and retired to his home in Mount Vernon, Virginia. The new nation still faced difficult tests, however. Americans would once again call on Washington to lead the nation.

SECTION REVIEW

1. **Locate:** Savannah, Charleston, Cowpens, Yorktown.

2. **Define:** ratify.

3. How did each of the following help the Patriots: (a) Francis Marion; (b) Daniel Morgan; (c) Nathanael Greene?

4. How did the French help the Americans at Yorktown?

5. **What Do You Think?** Why do you think people touched George Washington's cloak as he rode by on his way to Yorktown?

Chapter 8 Review

★ Summary ★

When the Second Continental Congress met in 1775, members had to decide whether the colonies should declare independence. Thomas Paine's pamphlet, *Common Sense,* helped convince them to draw up the Declaration of Independence. The Declaration explained why the colonies were breaking away from England.

The revolution was fought on many fronts—in New England, the Middle States, and the South. George Washington led Patriot armies through difficult times. The American victory at Saratoga was a turning point because it brought France into the war on the American side. In October 1781, Washington defeated Cornwallis at the Battle of Yorktown, the last major battle of the war. In the Treaty of Paris, Britain agreed to recognize the United States as an independent nation.

★ Reviewing the Facts ★

Key Terms. Match each term in Column 1 with the correct definition in Column 2.

Column 1	Column 2
1. blockade	a. troops on horseback
2. traitor	b. approve
3. cavalry	c. not fight for either side in a war
4. neutral	d. someone who betrays his or her country
5. ratify	e. shutting off of a port to keep supplies from moving in or out

Key People, Events, and Ideas. Identify each of the following.

1. Ethan Allen	6. Patriot	11. John Paul Jones
2. Olive Branch Petition	7. Loyalist	12. Molly Pitcher
3. Thomas Paine	8. Nathan Hale	13. Phillis Wheatley
4. Thomas Jefferson	9. John Burgoyne	14. Benedict Arnold
5. John Hancock	10. Marquis de Lafayette	15. Admiral de Grasse

★ Chapter Checkup ★

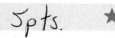

1. (a) What advantages did the British have during the Revolution? (b) What advantages did the Americans have?

2. How did the Patriot stand at Bunker Hill help the Americans?

3. (a) What are the three main parts of the Declaration of Independence? (b) What does each part say?

4. Why are the years from 1776 to 1778 often called the dark days of the war?

5. How did France help the United States?

6. How did each of the following people help the Patriot cause: (a) Nancy Ward; (b) George Rogers Clark; (c) Deborah Sampson?

7. (a) Who was the Swamp Fox? (b) How did he help the Americans?

8. What were the terms of the Treaty of Paris?

1. **Taking a stand.** Loyalists believed that the colonists were betraying their country by declaring independence. Do you agree? Explain.

2. **Relating past to present.** Reread the Declaration of Independence on pages 793–796. In 1776, colonists said that a government must respect certain basic rights of its citizens. Today, these rights are called human rights. (a) According to the Declaration, how did Britain violate, or fail to protect, these rights? (b) Do any countries today violate the human rights of their citizens? Explain.

3. **Analyzing a quotation.** When Cornwallis moved his army to Yorktown, Lafayette saw a chance to trap the British. "Why haven't we a fleet here?" he cried. "If the French army could fall from the clouds into Virginia and be supported by a squadron [of ships] we should do some very good things." (a) What did Lafayette mean by "some very good things"? (b) Did his wish come true? Explain.

4. **Understanding geography.** How do you think geography played a role in each of the following battles: (a) Battle of Bunker Hill; (b) Battle of Trenton?

Stop

★ **Using Your Skills**   *Extra Credit*   ★

1. **Map reading.** Study the map at right on page 175. (a) What British general's route is shown on this map? (b) In what direction did Benedict Arnold march to reach Quebec? (c) About how far did Montgomery have to travel from Fort Ticonderoga to Quebec?   *#1 5 pts.* the time line by writing the names of major battles or other events next to the year in which they happened. (a) What is the first event of the Revolution? (b) What is the last event? (c) During what period were most of the major battles fought?

2. **Constructing a time line.** Make a time line for the American Revolution. To construct a time line, draw a horizontal line on a blank sheet of paper. Label the left end 1775 and the right end 1783. Divide the line into eight equal parts, each representing one year. Complete

3. **Outlining.** Review the outlining skill you learned on page 31. Then prepare an outline of the first two sections of this chapter on pages 173–181. Using your outline, write a summary of what happened during the early years of the American Revolution.

★ **More to Do**   ★

1. **Drawing a cartoon.** Draw a cartoon about the American victory at Fort Ticonderoga in 1775.

2. **Making a poster.** Make a poster to recruit soldiers for Washington's army.

3. **Organizing a debate.** As a group project, prepare a debate among delegates to the Continental Congress on the following question: "Should the colonies declare their independence from Britain?"

4. **Interviewing.** In small groups, prepare skits in which you interview survivors of the winter at Valley Forge.

5. **Exploring local history.** Write a pamphlet describing how your local area honors events and heroes of the American Revolution.

9

Creating a Government (1776–1790)

Chapter Outline

1 The First American Government
2 The Constitutional Convention
3 We, the People
4 Ratifying the Constitution

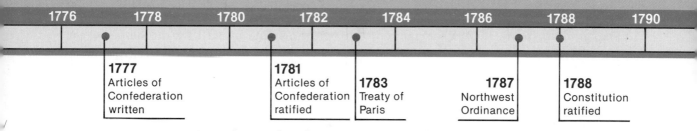

| 1776 | 1778 | 1780 | 1782 | 1784 | 1786 | 1788 | 1790 |

1777
Articles of Confederation written

1781
Articles of Confederation ratified

1783
Treaty of Paris

1787
Northwest Ordinance

1788
Constitution ratified

About This Chapter

During the American Revolution, the nation set up its first government under the Articles of Confederation. By 1787, however, many Americans were dissatisfied with the Articles. In May 1787, delegates met in Philadelphia to write a new constitution for the United States.

James Madison was one of the men who attended the Constitutional Convention. He decided to keep "an exact account of what might pass in the Convention." The notes, he felt, would be an important record for future generations.

"I chose a seat in front of the presiding member, with the other members on my right and left hand," reported Madison. In this central place, he could hear all that was said.

He carefully noted "what was read from the chair or spoken by the members." At the end of each day, he wrote up his notes.

Madison claimed his notes were complete. "I was not absent a single day," he wrote, "nor more than a fraction of an hour in any day so that I could not have lost a single speech, unless a very short one."

Thanks to Madison's hard work, we have a full record of the debates that went on at the Constitutional Convention. From his notes, we can see how the Constitution was shaped. The Constitution, written in 1787, still forms the basis of our government.

Study the time line above. Was the Constitution ratified before or after the Treaty of Paris?

With the sun rising behind his chair, George Washington watches as delegates sign the Constitution of the United States.

1 The First American Government

Read to Learn

★ Why did the states want written constitutions?

★ What problems did the United States face under the Articles of Confederation?

★ What do these words mean: constitution, execute, bill of rights, economic depression?

In 1776, the Declaration of Independence created a new nation made up of 13 independent states. The states faced a long, uphill battle against Britain. The struggle was made even harder because the states had little experience in working together. In the past, Britain made decisions for the colonies as a whole. Now, the new states had to set up not only their own governments but also a national government.

State Governments

In forming its government, each state wrote a constitution. A *constitution* is a document that sets out the laws and principles of a government. Some states, such as Connecticut and Rhode Island, revised the charters they had before the Revolution. Others, such as Massachusetts, wrote new constitutions, which voters approved.

Americans wanted written constitutions for two reasons. First, a written constitution would clearly spell out the rights of all citizens. Second, it would limit the power of government.

The new state governments were similar to colonial governments. All the states had a legislature elected by voters. Most legislatures had an upper house, called a senate, and a lower house. Every state except Pennsylvania had a governor, who *executed,* or carried out, the laws.

Virginia included a bill of rights in its new constitution. A *bill of rights* lists freedoms the government has to protect. In Virginia, the bill of rights protected freedom of speech, freedom of religion, and freedom of the press. Citizens also had the right to a trial by jury. Other states followed Virginia's lead and included bills of rights in their constitutions.

The new state constitutions expanded the number of citizens who had the right to vote. To vote, a citizen had to be male and over age 21. He had to own a certain amount of property or pay a certain amount of taxes. For a time, women in New Jersey could vote. (See the picture below.) In a few states,

Even after the Revolution, American women had limited political and legal rights. For a time, New Jersey let women vote, as this picture shows. But this right was taken away in 1807.

free black men could vote. But slaves could not vote in any state.

The Articles of Confederation

While the states were forming their governments, the Continental Congress wrote a constitution for the nation as a whole. Writing a constitution that all the states would approve was a difficult job. In 1776, few Americans thought of themselves as citizens of one nation. Instead, they felt loyal to their own states.

A weak national government. The new states were unwilling to give too much power to a national government. They were already fighting Britain. And they did not want to replace one harsh ruler with another. After much debate, the first American constitution, called the *Articles of Confederation,* was completed in 1777. Under the Articles, the 13 states agreed to send delegates to Congress. Each state had one vote in Congress. The Articles gave Congress the power to declare war, appoint military officers, and coin money. Congress was also responsible for foreign affairs.

The Articles of Confederation limited the powers of Congress by giving the states final authority. Although Congress could pass laws, at least 9 of the 13 states had to approve a law before it went into effect. Congress could not regulate trade between states or even between states and foreign countries. Congress could not pass any laws regarding taxes. To get money, Congress had to ask each state for it. No state could be forced to pay.

The Articles created a loose alliance among the 13 states. The national government was weak, in part because it had no president to carry out laws passed by Congress. This weak national government might have worked if the states had been able to get along with each other. But many disputes arose, and there was no way of settling them because the Articles did not set up a system of courts.

Conflict over western lands. The first dispute arose even before the Articles went into effect. Every state had to approve the Articles. But Maryland refused. It wanted the land between the Appalachian Mountains and the Mississippi River turned over to Congress.

Virginia and several other large states claimed these western lands. (See the map at right.) As a small state, Maryland worried that the large states would become too powerful unless they gave up their land claims.

At first, Virginia and the other states refused to give up their claims. But Thomas Jefferson and other leading Virginians saw the need for a national government. So they convinced the Virginia legislature to give up its claims. Other large states followed Virginia's lead. Finally, in 1781, Maryland ratified the Articles of Confederation, and the first American government went into effect.

Many Troubles

The new government faced many troubles. Massachusetts, New Hampshire, and New York all claimed Vermont, but they had no way of settling their dispute. Foreign countries took advantage of the new government's weakness. For example, Britain refused to withdraw its troops from the Ohio Valley as it had agreed to do under the peace treaty. Spain, too, challenged the new nation. It closed the port of New Orleans to American farmers. The port was important to them because they used it to ship goods to the east.

The most difficult problem for the new government was raising money. Congress did not have the power to pass tax laws, and the states did not contribute enough money to meet the government's expenses.

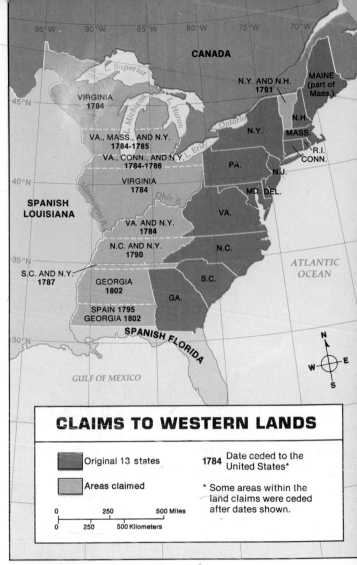

CLAIMS TO WESTERN LANDS

- ■ Original 13 states
- ■ Areas claimed
- **1784** Date ceded to the United States*
- * Some areas within the land claims were ceded after dates shown.

0 — 250 — 500 Miles
0 — 250 — 500 Kilometers

MAP SKILL By 1783, a number of states claimed lands west of the Appalachians. Which states claimed the most land? Which states had no land claims in the West?

During the Revolution, the Continental Congress tried to raise money simply by printing paper money. Paper money is valuable only if it is backed by reserves such as gold or silver or by confidence in the government. The Continental dollars Congress printed had no gold or silver backing. Also, few people believed that the government could pay its debts. So Continental dollars soon became worthless.

When Continental dollars became worthless, states printed their own paper money. This caused a great deal

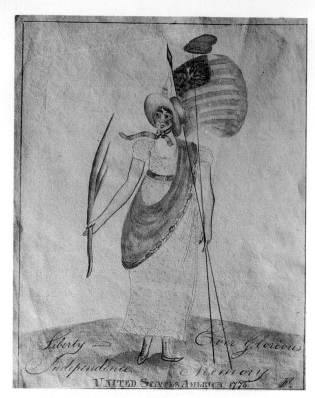

Liberty ~ Ever Glorious
Independence ~ e Memory
UNITED STATES AMERICA 1776

Despite the problems the new nation faced, Americans felt great patriotic pride. This pride was seen in the symbols of the nation. Miss Liberty, who is shown here carrying a flag, stood as a symbol of freedom.

of confusion. How much was a North Carolina dollar worth? Was a Virginia dollar just as valuable? Most states refused to accept money from other states. As a result, trade between states became difficult.

Congress tried to pass a law taxing imported goods. But every state had to approve the tax before it could go into effect. When only 12 states approved it, the tax was defeated.

Organizing the Northwest Territory

Despite its troubles, Congress did pass two important laws. Both concerned the Northwest Territory,* lands

---

*Americans used the word territory to mean an area that was not yet organized into a state.

lying north of the Ohio River and east of the Mississippi. (See the map on page 201.) Many settlers lived in this region. Every year, more headed west to clear land for farms.

To set up a system for settling the Northwest Territory, Congress passed the **Land Ordinance of 1785.** The ordinance called for the land to be surveyed and divided into townships. Each township would have 36 sections. A section was one square mile and contained 640 acres. (See the diagram on page 201.) Congress planned to sell sections to settlers for $640 each. One section in every township was set aside to support public schools.

Two years later, in 1787, Congress passed the **Northwest Ordinance.** This ordinance set up a government for the Northwest Territory and outlawed slavery there. It allowed the region to be divided into separate territories. Once a territory had a population of 60,000 free citizens, it could ask Congress to be admitted as a new state. The new state would then be "on an equal footing with the original states in all respects whatsoever."

The Northwest Ordinance was important because it set up a way for new states to be admitted to the United States. It guaranteed that new states would be treated just the same as the original 13 states. Eventually, the Northwest Territory was carved into five states: Ohio, Indiana, Illinois, Michigan, and Wisconsin.

Shays' Rebellion

While Congress dealt successfully with the Northwest Territory, it failed to solve other problems. Among the most serious were the problems of farmers.

During the Revolution, the demand for farm products was high. Farmers borrowed money for land, seed, animals, and tools. But after the war, the nation suffered an economic depres-

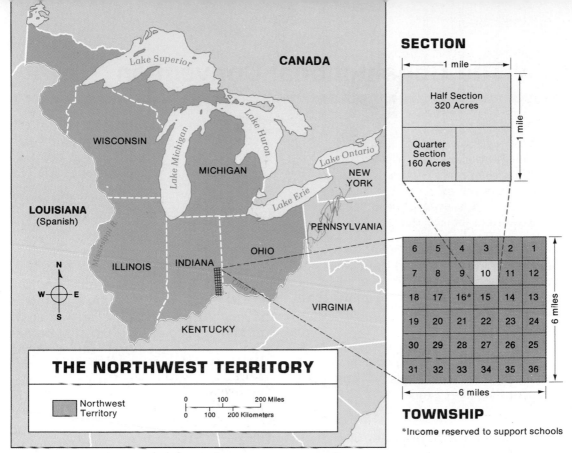

SECTION

1 mile

Half Section
320 Acres

1 mile

Quarter
Section
160 Acres

6	5	4	3	2	1
7	8	9	10	11	12
18	17	16*	15	14	13
19	20	21	22	23	24
30	29	28	27	26	25
31	32	33	34	35	36

6 miles

6 miles

TOWNSHIP

*Income reserved to support schools

MAP SKILL The Northwest Territory included lands between the Ohio and Mississippi rivers. In the 1780s, Congress set up a system for settling the area. How is each township within the Northwest Territory divided up?

sion. An *economic depression* is a period when business activity slows, prices and wages fall, and unemployment rises. When prices for farm goods fell, farmers could not repay their loans.

Farmers in western Massachusetts were hard hit by falling farm prices. To make matters worse, Massachusetts raised taxes. The courts threatened to seize the farms of people who did not pay their loans and taxes.

Captain Daniel Shays was a Massachusetts farmer who had fought in the Revolution. In 1786, Shays gathered a force of about 1,000 angry farmers. They attacked courthouses and tried to take a warehouse full of rifles and gunpowder. Massachusetts quickly raised an army and ended the rebellion.

Shays' Rebellion worried many Americans. It was a sign that the Arti-

cles of Confederation were not working. Leaders of several states called for a convention to discuss ways of reforming the Articles. They decided to meet in Philadelphia in May 1787. When they met, however, they took more drastic action.

SECTION REVIEW

1. **Locate:** Maryland, Virginia, Northwest Territory.
2. **Define:** constitution, execute, bill of rights, economic depression.
3. Why did states want to limit the power of the national government?
4. Describe three problems the nation had faced under the Articles of Confederation.
5. **What Do You Think?** Why do you think Americans in the 1770s and 1780s thought state governments were more important than the national government?

2 The Constitutional Convention

Read to Learn
★ Who were the leaders of the Constitutional Convention?
★ What compromises were worked out at the Convention?
★ What do these words mean: legislative, executive, judicial, compromise?

The delegates who went to Philadelphia in May 1787 had their work cut out for them. Soon after the meeting began, they decided to do more than revise the Articles of Confederation. They chose to write a new constitution for the United States. Between May and September, they forged a document that has been the basis of American government ever since.

The Convention Opens

The *Constitutional Convention* met in Philadelphia. Every state was supposed to send delegates, but Rhode Island refused. Thus, only 12 of the 13 states were represented.* The meeting took place in the Pennsylvania State House, the same place where the Declaration of Independence had been signed 11 years before.

Who was there? The 55 delegates included many leaders from the Revolution. Benjamin Franklin, at age 81, was the senior statesman. George Washington traveled north from his home in Mount Vernon, Virginia. Washington was so well respected by the delegates in Philadelphia that he was at once elected president of the Constitutional Convention.

Quite a few delegates were young men in their 20s and 30s. Among them was Alexander Hamilton of New York.

---

*New Hampshire was reluctant to send delegates. It did not do so until the Convention was half over.

During the Revolution, Hamilton served for a time as Washington's private secretary. Hamilton did not like the Articles of Confederation, which he said were "fit neither for war nor peace." The nation, he wrote, "is sick and wants powerful remedies." The powerful remedy he prescribed was a strong national government.

Another member of the Constitutional Convention was James Madison of Virginia. At first glance, Madison did not impress people. He was short and thin and spoke so softly that he was often asked to speak up. But Madison had much worth saying. He had served in Congress and in the Virginia legislature. A hard worker, he was always eager to learn. Before going to Philadelphia, he collected the latest books on government and politics. Madison arrived in Philadelphia a week early so that he would have time to read and organize his thoughts.

Need for secrecy. When the meeting began, the delegates decided to keep their talks secret. They wanted to be free to speak their minds without seeing their words printed in newspapers. "My wish," wrote Washington, "is that the Convention may . . . probe the defects of the Constitution to the bottom, and provide radical cures." He and other delegates wanted to explore every issue and solution, without pressure from outside.

To ensure secrecy, guards stood at the door, admitting only the delegates. The windows were kept closed to keep passers-by from overhearing the debates. But the closed windows made the room terribly hot. As it was, the summer of 1787 was the hottest in many years. New Englanders in their woolen suits suffered terribly. Southerners were more used to the heat and wore lighter clothes.

In 1787, delegates to the Constitutional Convention met in the Pennsylvania State House, renamed Independence Hall. Both the Declaration of Independence and the Constitution were signed here.

Heated Debate

On May 25, George Washington took his place as president of the Convention. He sat in a high-backed chair at the front of the room. The other delegates sat at tables covered by green cloth. Everyone agreed on the need for action. By May 30, the delegates had voted to write a new constitution instead of revising the Articles of Confederation.

Virginia Plan. Early on, Edmund Randolph and James Madison, both of Virginia, presented a plan for the new government. It became known as the *Virginia Plan.* In the end, much of the Virginia Plan was included in the new constitution.

The Virginia Plan called for a strong national government with three branches: legislative, executive, and judicial (jyoo DIHSH uhl). In general, the *legislative branch* of a government passes the laws. The *executive branch* carries out the laws. And the *judicial branch,* or system of courts, decides if laws are carried out fairly.

The Virginia Plan also called for a two-house legislature with a lower house and an upper house. Seats in both houses would be divided up according to the population of each state. States with large populations would elect more representatives than states with small populations. This differed from the Articles of Confederation. Under the Articles, each state had one vote in Congress, no matter what its population.

Small states at once protested this plan. They were afraid that large states would outvote them. Supporters of the Virginia Plan said that it was only fair for a state with more people to have more representatives.

New Jersey Plan. The debate over the Virginia Plan almost caused the Convention to fall apart. In June 1787, William Paterson of New Jersey presented a plan that had the support of the small states. The *New Jersey Plan* also called for three branches of government. But it called for a legislature with only one house. Each state would have one vote, no matter what its population was.

The Great Compromise

The delegates argued to a standstill. The heat caused tempers to rise. Finally, Roger Sherman of Connecticut worked out a compromise between the large and small states. A *compromise* is a settlement in which each side gives up some of its demands in order to reach an agreement.

Sherman's compromise called for a legislature with a lower and an upper house. Members of the lower house, known as the *House of Representatives,* would be chosen by all men who could vote. Seats would be divided up according to the population of each state. The large states liked this part of the compromise because it was similar to the Virginia Plan.

Members of the upper house, called the *Senate,* would be chosen by state legislatures. Each state would have two senators. Small states supported this part of the compromise. Together, the two houses would be the Congress of the United States.

On July 16, delegates narrowly accepted Sherman's plan, which became known as the *Great Compromise.* Each side gave up some demands in favor of the nation as a whole. If the delegates had not agreed to the Great Compromise, the Convention might have broken up without solving the problems facing the United States.

Compromises Over Slavery

After accepting the Great Compromise, the delegates faced a new question. Would slaves be counted as part of the population? The answer to this question was important because it affected the number of representatives a state would have in the House of Representatives.

The slavery question led to bitter arguments between the North and South. Southerners wanted to include slaves in the population count even though they would not let slaves vote. Northerners protested. They realized that if slaves were counted, southern states would have more representatives than northern states. Northerners argued that since slaves could not vote, they should not be counted.

The debate raged on until the delegates worked out a new compromise. They agreed that three fifths of the slaves in any state would be counted. In other words, if a state had 5,000 slaves, 3,000 of them would be included in the state's population count. This agreement was known as the *Three Fifths Compromise.*

Northerners and Southerners disagreed over another issue related to slavery. By 1787, some northern states had banned the slave trade within their borders. They wanted the new Congress to ban the slave trade in the entire nation. Southerners warned that their economy would be ruined if Congress outlawed the slave trade.

In the end, the two sides compromised. Northerners agreed to let the slave trade continue for at least 20 years. After that, Congress could regulate it if it wished.

The Final Weeks

Throughout the summer, the delegates made many more decisions about the new constitution. How many years should the President, head of the executive branch, serve? How should the courts be organized? Would members of Congress be paid?

Finally, on September 17, the Constitution was ready. Delegates from each state came forward to sign the document. Washington and the other members of the Constitutional Convention had done a remarkable thing. In a few months, they had set up the framework for a lasting government. Their next job was to win approval for the Constitution.

SECTION REVIEW

1. **Define:** legislative, executive, judicial, compromise.
2. Why did delegates decide to keep their talks secret?
3. Why did delegates from small states object to the Virginia Plan?
4. What was the Great Compromise?
5. **What Do You Think?** Do you think the Three Fifths Compromise was a reasonable solution? Explain.

AMERICANS WHO DARED

James Forten

James Forten of Philadelphia was a free black. During the Revolution, he served as a powder boy on an American ship—even though he was only 15 years old. After the war, he became a sailmaker and invented a device for handling sails. He bought his own sail shop and earned a large fortune. Forten devoted his life to ending slavery and urging equal rights for free blacks. He refused to sell sails and rigging to slave ships and used his wealth in the cause of ending slavery.

3 We, the People

Read to Learn

★ How does the Constitution divide powers between the federal government and the states?
★ How does separation of powers work?
★ What do these words mean: republic, federalism, separation of powers, electoral college, checks and balances, bill, veto, override, impeach?

In September 1787, after months of debate and many compromises, the framers of the Constitution returned to their home states. The people of the United States now had their first look at the Constitution. (The complete text of the Constitution is printed on pages 810–831.) The Constitution created a republic. A *republic* is a nation in which the voters elect representatives to govern them.

"We, the people of the United States," the document begins, "do ordain and establish this Constitution for the United States of America." By starting this way, the Constitution makes clear that the power of the government comes from the American people.

Federalism: A Framework of Government

All over the land, people read the Constitution. They were curious to see how it differed from the Articles of Confederation. A major issue they were interested in was what powers the national government would have and what powers the states would have.

Under the Articles of Confederation, the states had more power than the Congress. But this system had caused problems. Under the new Constitution, the states delegated, or gave up, some powers to the national govern-

ment. At the same time, the states reserved, or kept, power in other areas. This sharing of power between the states and the national government is called *federalism*. The system of federalism is shown in the diagram below.

Federalism has given Americans a flexible system of government. The people have power because they elect both national and state officials. The federal, or national, government has the power to act for the nation as a whole. And the states have power over important local matters.

Powers of the federal government. The Constitution spells out the powers of the federal government. For example, only the federal government has the power to coin money. So states could no longer issue money as they had under the Articles of Confederation. The federal government has the power to regulate trade between states and with other countries. Also, the federal government has the power to declare war.

CHART SKILL Under the federal system, states and the national government divide up power. Name two powers shared by both national and state governments. Who has the power to set up schools?

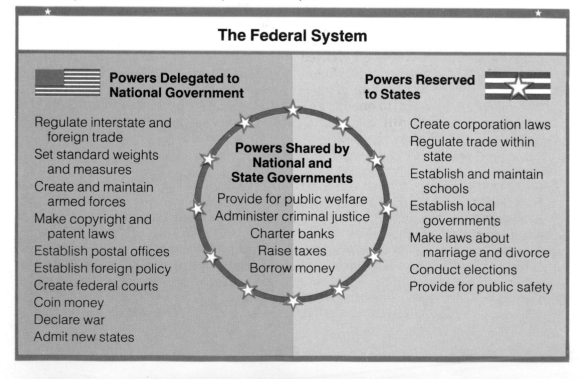

The Federal System

Powers Delegated to National Government

Regulate interstate and foreign trade
Set standard weights and measures
Create and maintain armed forces
Make copyright and patent laws
Establish postal offices
Establish foreign policy
Create federal courts
Coin money
Declare war
Admit new states

Powers Shared by National and State Governments

Provide for public welfare
Administer criminal justice
Charter banks
Raise taxes
Borrow money

Powers Reserved to States

Create corporation laws
Regulate trade within state
Establish and maintain schools
Establish local governments
Make laws about marriage and divorce
Conduct elections
Provide for public safety

Powers of the states. Under the Constitution, states have the power to regulate trade within their borders. They can decide who votes in state elections. They have power over schools and local governments. Also, the Constitution says that powers not given to the federal government belong to the states. This point pleased people in small states who were afraid that the federal government might become too powerful.

Shared powers. The Constitution states that some powers are to be shared by federal and state governments. Both governments have the power to build roads. Today, for example, federal roads are called U.S. 169 or Interstate 40. State roads are labeled Connecticut 47 or Arizona 85.

The framers of the Constitution had to decide how the states and the federal government would settle any future disagreement. To do this, they made the Constitution "the supreme law of the land." This means that in any dispute, the Constitution is the final authority.

Separation of Powers

The Constitution set up a strong federal government. To keep the government from becoming too powerful, the framers of the Constitution created three branches of government. Then, through a system of separation of powers, they made sure that no one branch could become too powerful. *Separation of powers* means that each branch of government has its own powers. The powers are clearly described in the Constitution. (Look at the diagram on page 208.)

Congress. Congress is the legislative branch of government. It is made up of the House of Representatives and the Senate. Members of the House are elected for two-year terms. Senators are elected for six-year terms.

Under the Constitution, voters in each state elect members of the House of Representatives. Delegates at the Constitutional Convention wanted the House to represent the interests of ordinary people. At first, the Constitution said that senators were to be chosen by state legislatures. In 1913, this was changed. Today, senators are elected in the same way as House members.

Article I of the Constitution sets out the powers of Congress. Among them, Congress has the power to collect taxes. It can "regulate commerce with foreign nations, and among the several states." In foreign affairs, it has the right to declare war and "raise and support armies."

The President. Article II of the Constitution sets up the executive branch of government. It is headed by the President. The executive branch also includes the Vice President and any advisers appointed by the President. The President and Vice President serve four-year terms.

The President is responsible for carrying out all laws passed by Congress. The President is also commander in chief of the armed forces and is responsible for foreign relations.

The courts. Article III calls for a Supreme Court. The article allowed Congress to set up other federal courts under the Supreme Court. The Supreme Court and other federal courts hear cases that involve the Constitution or any laws passed by Congress. They also hear cases arising between two or more states.

Electoral College

The framers of the Constitution debated whether to let voters elect the President directly. But this idea worried them. In the late 1700s, news traveled slowly. The framers argued that New Englanders would probably know little about a candidate for President

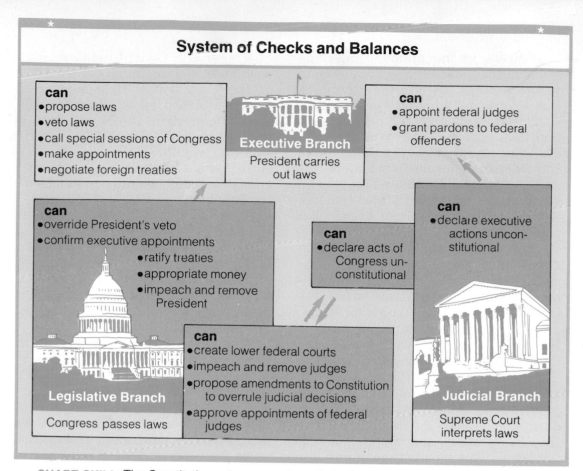

System of Checks and Balances

Executive Branch
President carries out laws

can
- propose laws
- veto laws
- call special sessions of Congress
- make appointments
- negotiate foreign treaties

can
- appoint federal judges
- grant pardons to federal offenders

Legislative Branch
Congress passes laws

can
- override President's veto
- confirm executive appointments
  - ratify treaties
  - appropriate money
  - impeach and remove President

can
- create lower federal courts
- impeach and remove judges
- propose amendments to Constitution to overrule judicial decisions
- approve appointments of federal judges

Judicial Branch
Supreme Court interprets laws

can
- declare acts of Congress unconstitutional

can
- declare executive actions unconstitutional

CHART SKILL The Constitution sets up a system of checks and balances among the three branches of government. Name one way Congress checks the President. What power does the Supreme Court have to check Congress?

from the South. And a candidate from Pennsylvania would be unknown to voters in Massachusetts or Georgia. So how could voters choose the best candidate for the job?

To solve this problem, the Constitution set up a system for electors from each state to choose the President. State legislatures would decide how to choose their electors. Every four years, the electors met as a group, called the *electoral college.* The electoral college voted for the President and Vice President of the United States.

The framers of the Constitution expected that electors would be well-informed citizens who were familiar with the national government. They believed that such men would choose a

President wisely. The electoral college still meets today, but its function has changed somewhat from the original system.

Checks and Balances

The Constitution set up a system of *checks and balances.* Under this system, each branch of the federal government has some way to check, or control, the other two branches. The system of checks and balances is another way in which the Constitution limits the power of government.

To do its work, Congress passes *bills,* or proposed laws. A bill then goes to the President to be signed into law. (Study the flow chart at right.) The

Skill Lesson 9　Reading a Flow Chart

A *flow chart* is used to give a lot of information in a simple and easy-to-understand way. A flow chart shows developments in a step-by-step manner. For example, under the Constitution of the United States, Congress has the power to pass bills, which the President signs into law. Over the years, a complicated process has developed whereby a bill actually becomes a law.

Study the flow chart to see the steps through which a bill has to pass before it can become a law.

1. **Identify the parts of the flow chart.** (a) What is the title of the flow chart? (b) What does each of the four columns show? (c) What do the black arrows show? (d) What color shows House action? Senate action?

2. **Practice reading the flow chart.** (a) Where is a bill usually introduced? (b) What happens to a bill after it has been introduced? (c) What happens after the House and Senate have both passed their own forms of a bill? (d) What is the last step a bill goes through before it becomes a law?

3. **Evaluate the information shown on the flow chart.** Every year, about 10,000 bills are introduced in Congress. Only about 1,000 ever make it through the many steps to become laws. (a) Why do you think House and Senate committees hold hearings on bills that have been introduced? (b) Using the flow chart, why do you think only a few bills actually become laws?

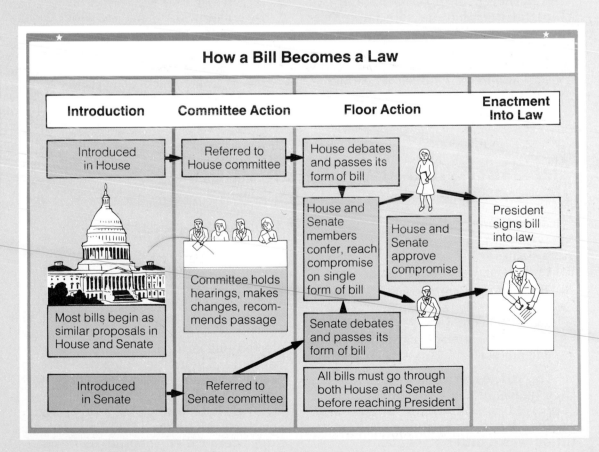

How a Bill Becomes a Law

Introduction	Committee Action	Floor Action	Enactment Into Law

Introduced in House

Referred to House committee

House debates and passes its form of bill

House and Senate members confer, reach compromise on single form of bill

House and Senate approve compromise

President signs bill into law

Committee holds hearings, makes changes, recommends passage

Most bills begin as similar proposals in House and Senate

Senate debates and passes its form of bill

Introduced in Senate

Referred to Senate committee

All bills must go through both House and Senate before reaching President

President can check the power of Congress by *vetoing,* or rejecting, a bill. On the other hand, Congress can check the President by *overriding,* or overruling, the President's veto. To override a veto, two thirds of both houses of Congress must vote for the bill again.

Congress has other checks on the President. The President appoints officials such as judges and ambassadors. But the Senate must approve these appointments. The President has the power to negotiate treaties with other nations. But two thirds of the Senate have to approve a treaty before it can become law.

Congress also has the power to remove the President from office if it finds the President guilty of a serious crime. The Constitution describes how this can be done. First, the House of Representatives must *impeach,* or bring charges, against the President. A trial is then held in the Senate. If two thirds of the senators vote for conviction, the President must leave office.

Congress and the President have checks on the power of the courts. The President appoints judges, who must be approved by the Senate. If judges misbehave, Congress may remove them from office.

The Constitution offers a remarkable balance among the three branches of the federal government and between state governments and the federal government. This balance has helped it work for nearly 200 years, longer than any other written constitution in the world. The Constitution has survived, too, because it is a living document. As you will read in this and later chapters, it can be changed to meet new conditions in the United States.

SECTION REVIEW

1. **Define:** republic, federalism, separation of powers, electoral college, checks and balances, bill, veto, override, impeach.
2. (a) List three powers delegated to the national government. (b) List three powers reserved to the states.
3. (a) List the three branches of the federal government. (b) Name one power given to each.
4. Why was the electoral college set up?
5. **What Do You Think?** How do you think the system of checks and balances limits the power of government?

4 Ratifying the Constitution

Read to Learn

★ What did Federalists and Antifederalists say about the Constitution?
★ How can the Constitution be amended?
★ What rights do the first ten amendments protect?
★ What do these words mean: amend, due process?

In 1787, Americans were divided in their views of the Constitution. Many supported it. But many others were shocked by it. So ratifying the Constitution was a bitter struggle.

The Debate Goes On

The framers of the Constitution set up a process for the states to decide on the new government. At least 9 of the 13 states had to approve the Constitution before it could go into effect. In 1787 and 1788, voters in each state elected delegates to special state conventions. Then, the delegates met to decide whether or not to ratify the new Constitution.

The two sides. In every state, debates went on over the Constitution. Supporters called themselves *Federal-*

Spirit of America

Need for a Bill of Rights: Spirit of Religion

For Americans in 1776, the Revolution was not just a struggle for freedom from British control. It was a struggle for freedom in general. For many, the idea of freedom included the right to worship as they pleased.

The original Constitution contained no protection of religious freedom. Americans were worried. Under the newly formed government, how free would they be to worship, or not to worship, as they pleased?

After George Washington became President in 1789, several religious groups wrote to him. Baptists, Quakers, Jews, Presbyterians, Catholics, and others all expressed hopes that he would safeguard their religious freedom.

In his responses, Washington hailed the importance of religion to the new nation. Religion, he said, promoted good deeds, honesty, hard work, and thrift. He promised that the new government would support religious freedom. In one letter, he wrote, "Every man . . . ought to be protected in worshipping the Deity according to the dictates of his own conscience."

Religious freedom became law in 1791. In that year, the Bill of Rights was added to the Constitution. The First Amendment guaranteed religious freedom by stating, "Congress shall make no law respecting an establishment of religion, or prohibiting the free exercise thereof."

★ Why did religious groups write to President Washington?

---

ists. They called people who opposed the Constitution *Antifederalists.*

Federalists favored a strong national government. The best-known Federalists were James Madison, Alexander Hamilton, and John Jay. They wrote a series of letters, called *The Federalist Papers,* defending the Constitution. They signed their letters with the names of ancient Roman heroes such as Publius or Cato. People generally knew who the letter writers really were, but it was the custom of the time to use pen names.

Antifederalists opposed the Constitution for many reasons. They felt that it made the national government too strong and left the states too weak. They thought that the Constitution gave the President too much power. Most people expected George Washington to be elected President. Antifederalists admired him. But they warned that in the future a less desirable person might be elected. So they did not want the office to be too powerful.

Call for a bill of rights. The main argument of the Antifederalists was that the Constitution had no bill of rights. Americans had just fought a revolution to protect their freedoms. They wanted to include a bill of rights in the Constitution that spelled out these basic freedoms.

Federalists answered that the Constitution protected citizens very well without a bill of rights. Anyway, they argued, it would be impossible to list all the natural rights of people. Antifederalists replied that if rights were not clearly written down, it would be easy to ignore them. Several state conventions refused to approve the Constitution until they were promised that a bill of rights would be added.

Approval at last. On December 7, 1787, Delaware became the first state to ratify the Constitution. In June 1788, New Hampshire became the ninth state to approve it. The Constitution could go into effect.

Still, the future of the United States remained in doubt. It was important that all states support the Constitution. But New York and Virginia, two of the largest, had not yet ratified the Constitution. In both states, Federalists and Antifederalists were closely matched. In Virginia, Patrick Henry argued strongly against the Constitution. "There will be no checks, no real balances in this government," he cried. Henry was popular in Virginia. But in the end, Washington, Madison, and other Federalists turned the tide in favor of the Constitution. In late June, Virginia ratified the Constitution.

In New York, the struggle went on for another month. Finally, in July 1788, the state convention voted in favor of the Constitution. North Carolina ratified it in November. Rhode Island, the last state to ratify the Constitution, did so in May 1790.

We Have Become a Nation

When Americans heard that the Constitution was approved, they held great celebrations. The city of Philadelphia set its celebration for July 4, 1788. As the sun rose that day, church bells rang. In the harbor, the ship *Rising Sun* boomed a salute from its cannons. A huge parade snaked along Market Street, led by soldiers who had served in the Revolution. Horses wore bright ribbons, and bands played popular songs.

As usual, watchmen announced the hour and the weather. But on this day, they added, "10 o'clock, and a glorious star-light morning." They meant that ten stars (or states) had ratified the Constitution. Thousands watched as six horses pulled a blue carriage shaped like an eagle. Thirteen stars and stripes were painted on the front, and the Constitution was raised proudly above it.

Americans celebrated their independence and their new Constitution with parades and picnics. Here, patriotic Americans raise a Liberty Pole as their families watch.

That night, even the skies seemed to celebrate. The northern lights, vivid bands of color, lit up the sky above the city. Benjamin Rush, a Philadelphia doctor and strong supporter of the Constitution, wrote to a friend: "Tis done. We have become a nation."

The nation held its first election under the Constitution in January 1789. The first President was, of course, George Washington. John Adams was elected Vice President. The first Congress was made up of 59 representatives and 26 senators. It met in New York City, the nation's first capital.

Amending the Constitution

The first Congress turned its attention quickly to the need for including a bill of rights in the Constitution. The framers had provided a way to *amend,* or change, the Constitution. They wanted to make the Constitution flexible enough to change as the times changed. But they did not want changes made lightly. So they made the process fairly difficult.

The first step is to propose an amendment. This can be done in two ways. Two thirds of both houses of Congress can vote to propose an amendment. Or two thirds of the states, meeting in special conventions, can propose an amendment. The next step is to ratify the amendment. Three fourths of the states must vote for the amendment before it can become part of the Constitution.

In the 200 years since the Constitution was adopted, only 26 amendments have been made. Ten of these amendments were added in the first years of the Constitution.

The Bill of Rights

In 1789, the first Congress passed a series of amendments. By December 1791, three fourths of the states had ratified ten amendments. These ten amendments became part of the Constitution and are known as the ***Bill of Rights.***

The Bill of Rights protects certain basic rights. James Madison, who wrote the amendments, said that the Bill of Rights does not *give* Americans these rights. People already have these rights. They are natural rights, he said, that belong to all human beings. The Bill of Rights simply prevents the government from taking away these rights.

The First Amendment guarantees the basic rights of freedom of religion, freedom of speech, freedom of the press, and freedom of assembly, or the right to meet in groups. The next three amendments came out of the colonists' struggle with Britain. For example, the Third Amendment prevents Congress from forcing citizens to keep troops in their homes. Before the Revolution, you will remember, Britain tried to make colonists house soldiers.

Amendments 5 through 8 protect citizens who are accused of crimes and are brought to trial. Every citizen has the right to due process of law. ***Due process*** means that the government must follow the same fair rules in all cases brought to trial. These rules include the right to trial by jury, the right to be defended by a lawyer, and the right to a speedy trial. The last two amendments limit the powers of the federal government to those that are granted in the Constitution.

▬SECTION REVIEW▬

1. **Define:** amend, due process.
2. Why did Antifederalists oppose the Constitution?
3. How can an amendment be made to the Constitution?
4. List three rights protected in the Bill of Rights.
5. **What Do You Think?** What do you think Dr. Rush meant when he said, "We have become a nation"?

Chapter 9 Review

★ Summary ★

After independence, each state organized its own government. The first national government was set up under the Articles of Confederation. Under the Articles, however, states had final say over most issues. This left the national government too weak to work effectively.

In 1787, delegates from 12 states met at the Constitutional Convention in Philadelphia. They drew up a new constitution, which has been the basis for the government of the United States ever since. The Constitution set up a system of sharing powers between state governments and the federal government. Within the federal government, separation of powers and a system of checks and balances limit the powers of each branch of government. Soon after the Constitution was ratified in 1789, the Bill of Rights was added.

46   ## ★ Reviewing the Facts   2 pts. ★

Key Terms. Match each term in Column 1 with the correct definition in Column 2.

Column 1

1. constitution
2. compromise
3. republic
4. federalism
5. impeach

Column 2

a. settlement in which each side gives up something
b. document that sets out the basic laws of a government
c. bring charges against someone
d. sharing of power between the national and state governments
e. nation where voters choose representatives to govern them

Key People, Events, and Ideas. Identify each of the following.

1. Articles of Confederation
2. Northwest Ordinance
3. Shays' Rebellion
4. Alexander Hamilton
5. James Madison
6. Constitutional Convention
7. Virginia Plan
8. New Jersey Plan
9. House of Representatives
10. Senate
11. Great Compromise
12. Three Fifths Compromise
13. Federalist
14. Antifederalist
15. Bill of Rights

32   ## ★ Chapter Checkup   4 pts. ★

1. Describe three problems under the Articles of Confederation.
2. Describe one cause and one result of Shays' Rebellion.
3. Compare the Virginia Plan to the New Jersey Plan.
4. What two issues divided northern and southern states during the Constitutional Convention?
5. Why did the framers of the Constitution set up each of the following: (a) separation of powers; (b) checks and balances?
6. How was the Constitution ratified?
7. (a) Why did Antifederalists want a bill of rights in the Constitution? (b) How did Federalists respond to this demand?
8. How does the Bill of Rights protect citizens who are accused of crimes?

★ Thinking About History

10 pts.

1. Understanding the economy. (a) What money troubles did the national government face under the Articles of Confederation? (b) Why did the government print paper money? (c) Why did Continental dollars become worthless?

2. Relating past to present. (a) On what issues did the Constitutional Convention have to compromise? (b) Why do you think these compromises were necessary? (c) Describe one local or national issue today on which you think compromise is necessary.

3. Analyzing information. Explain how the system of federalism set up by the Constitution solved some of the problems the government faced under the Articles of Confederation.

4. Learning about citizenship. How does the Constitution set up a balance between the powers of the states and the powers of the national government?

★ Using Your Skills

(1-2)

Extra Credit - 2 pts. each

1. Map reading. Study the map on page 199. (a) What state or states claimed land around the Great Lakes? (b) Who owned the land west of the Mississippi River? (c) What state or states claimed land directly south of Lake Superior?

2. Using a diagram. Study the diagram on page 201. (a) How large is a township? (b) How many sections are there in a township? (c) How large is a section? (d) Can a section be subdivided? Explain.

3. Making a review chart. Information that is organized in a chart can be easily reviewed and compared. Make a chart with two columns and three rows. Title the columns Articles of Confederation and Constitution. Title the rows Legislative Branch, Executive Branch, and Judicial Branch. Complete the chart with information from the chapter. (a) What were the major differences between the Articles of Confederation and the Constitution? (b) Were there any similarities? Explain.

4. Ranking. Review the Bill of Rights on pages 822–824. Then choose five rights and rank them according to which you think is most important. Explain your ranking.

★ More to Do

1. Exploring local history. Research and write a report describing the adoption of your state's first constitution.

2. Researching. Find out more about one of the delegates at the Constitutional Convention. Describe his background and how he came to be a delegate.

3. Creating headlines. Create a series of headlines announcing the completion of work on the Constitution.

4. Organizing a debate. As a group project, organize a debate between Federalists and Antifederalists. Set up the debate at a state convention called to ratify the Constitution.

5. Preparing a report. Write a report about some aspect of American life after the Revolution. You might describe songs, dress styles, schools, or churches.

Unit 3 Review

Chapter 7 During the French and Indian War, Britain drove the French out of North America. After the war, Britain tried to raise money to pay off its debts by taxing the 13 colonies. Colonists protested the new taxes. They claimed that Parliament did not have the right to tax them. The crisis over taxes slowly led to war.

Chapter 8 In July 1776, a year after the American Revolution began, colonists declared their independence from Britain. George Washington led the Americans in their struggle for independence. Americans suffered many setbacks at first. Finally, with French help, they defeated the British. By the Treaty of Paris, Britain recognized the American nation.

Chapter 9 The Articles of Confederation set up the first American government. In 1787, however, Americans decided to replace the Articles with a new constitution. Under the new government, states and the national government shared power. Each of the three branches of the federal government had checks on the power of the other.

★ **Unit Checkup** ★

Choose the word or phrase that best completes each of the following statements.

1. Colonists protested against the Sugar and Stamp acts by declaring a
   (a) blockade.
   (b) compromise.
   (c) boycott.

2. Britain responded to the Boston Tea Party by passing the
   (a) Tea Act.
   (b) Intolerable Acts.
   (c) Stamp Act.

3. Colonists who supported Britain during the American Revolution were called
   (a) Loyalists.
   (b) Patriots.
   (c) Federalists.

4. France agreed to help the Americans after the Battle of
   (a) Saratoga.
   (b) Bunker Hill.
   (c) Yorktown.

5. During the Constitutional Convention, the Three Fifths Compromise had to do with
   (a) slaves.
   (b) money.
   (c) land claims.

★ **Building American Citizenship** ★

1. Colonists protested British efforts to tax them because they did not elect representatives to Parliament. (a) Who decides on taxes in this country today? (b) How can people influence what taxes are passed?

2. In 1776, Americans believed that they should explain to the world why they were breaking away from Britain. They did so in the Declaration of Independence. How do people today make known their disagreements with the government?

3. The Constitution set up a federal system. (a) Describe decisions your state government makes that affect your life. (b) Describe decisions the United States government makes that affect your life.

Read the two reports on the Battle of Lexington. Then answer the questions below.

1. On what issue or issues do the two reports differ?
2. Is William Sutherland writing from the British or colonists' point of view?
3. How can you tell which side the Reverend Jonas Clark favors?
4. Can you tell if one of these reports is more reliable than the other? Explain.

 William Sutherland reported:

We still went on farther when three shots more were fired, which we did not return. . . . When we came up to the main body, several of our officers called out, "Throw down your arms and you shall come to no harm," or words to that effect. They refused to do this. I heard Major Pitcairn call out, "Soldiers, don't fire. Keep your ranks. Form and surround them." Instantly, some of the villains, who got over the hedge, fired at us, which our men for the first time returned.

 Rev. Jonas Clark reported:

Three officers advanced on horseback to the front of the body. One of them cried out, "Villains, rebels, disperse!"—or words to this effect. One of them said, "Lay down your arms . . . why don't you lay down your arms!" About this time, the second of these officers fired a pistol toward the militia as they were dispersing. Another pointed toward our men and with a loud voice said to the troops, "Fire!" which was instantly followed by a discharge of arms.

History Writer's Handbook

Rewording a Question as a Topic Sentence

The topic sentence in a one-paragraph answer states the main idea of the answer. You can often write a topic sentence by rewording the question.

Look at the following question. *Why was the American victory at Saratoga a turning point in the American Revolution?* By rewording the question, you might write the following topic sentence. *The American victory at Saratoga was a turning point in the American Revolution for three reasons.*

Note that the topic sentence includes the clues in the question. The phrase *for three reasons* covers what the key word *Why* in the question is telling you to do (give reasons). The phrases *at Saratoga* and *in the American Revolution* repeat the clues that limit the topic.

You may reword the question as a topic sentence without covering the key word. For example: *The American victory at Saratoga was a turning point in the American Revolution.* But keep the key word in mind when you later select information for detail sentences.

Practice Reword each of the following questions as a topic sentence for a one-paragraph answer.

1. Describe the three parts of the Declaration of Independence.
2. Compare the legislative branches of the Virginia Plan and the New Jersey Plan.

Unit 4

STRENGTHENING THE NEW NATION

1780	1790	1800	1810

GEORGE WASHINGTON | JOHN ADAMS | THOMAS JEFFERSON

1787 Northwest Ordinance; Constitution written; ★ Delaware, New Jersey, Pennsylvania become states
1788 ★ Connecticut, Georgia, Maryland, Massachusetts, New Hampshire, New York, South Carolina, Virginia become states
1789 ★ North Carolina statehood

1790s Lancaster Turnpike built
1790 ★ Rhode Island statehood
1791 ★ Vermont statehood; Bank of the United States set up; Bill of Rights
1792 ★ Kentucky statehood
1793 Cotton gin invented
1795 Treaty of Greenville
1796 ★ Tennessee statehood

1800s Whitney develops interchangeable parts
1803 ★ Ohio statehood; Louisiana Purchase
1804–06 Lewis and Clark explore Louisiana Purchase
1807 Embargo Act; *Clermont* launched

1780	1790	1800	1810

Late 1700s Columbia was an early symbol of the United States.

1790s *Daniel Boone Escorting a Band of Pioneers Into the Western Country* by George Caleb Bingham.

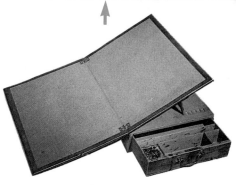

Early 1800s Thomas Jefferson designed this portable writing desk.

1810	1820	1830	1840

AMES MADISON   JAMES MONROE   ANDREW JACKSON

JOHN QUINCY ADAMS   MARTIN VAN BUREN

1812 ★ Louisiana statehood
1812–14 War of 1812
1815 Battle of New Orleans
1816 ★ Indiana statehood; Era of Good Feelings begins
1817 ★ Mississippi statehood
1818 ★ Illinois statehood
1819 ★ Alabama statehood

1820 ★ Maine statehood
1821 ★ Missouri statehood
1825 Erie Canal completed

1836 ★ Arkansas statehood
1837 ★ Michigan statehood

1810	1820	1830	1840

1813 During the Battle of Lake Erie, Oliver Perry's ship was crippled by British gunfire. The American commander rowed through heavy fire to another ship.

1800s Philadelphia was one of the largest cities in the nation. Here, a Philadelphia man sells oysters outside the Chestnut Street Theater.

10

The First Presidents (1789–1800)

Chapter Outline

1 The New Government at Work
2 Staying Neutral
3 Political Parties
4 Adams Takes a Firm Stand

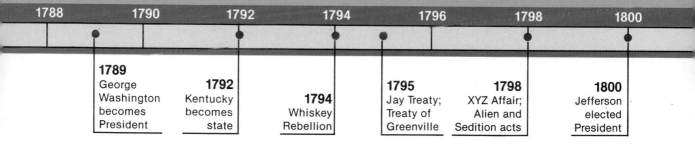

1788	1790	1792	1794	1796	1798	1800

1789
George Washington becomes President

1792
Kentucky becomes state

1794
Whiskey Rebellion

1795
Jay Treaty; Treaty of Greenville

1798
XYZ Affair; Alien and Sedition acts

1800
Jefferson elected President

About This Chapter

Early on April 30, 1789, crowds gathered in the streets of New York. They were there to see George Washington take the oath of office as President of the United States. Around noon, Washington arrived at Federal Hall.

Vice President John Adams stepped forward to greet him. Adams had a speech ready, but he was so nervous that he forgot every word of it. Finally, he said, "Sir, the Senate and House of Representatives are ready to attend you to take the oath required by the Constitution." Then, he led Washington out onto a balcony where the crowds could watch the ceremony.

After taking the oath, Washington went inside to make a speech. He looked "grave, almost to sadness," recalled one senator. His voice broke with emotion, said another. "This great man was agitated and embarrassed more than ever he was by the leveled cannon or pointed musket."

Why was President Washington so grave and serious on the day he took office? In 1789, Washington did not know that the nation would grow and prosper. He was the first President of a new nation that many people, especially the British, thought would fail. Washington proved them wrong when he led the nation firmly and set it on the path to greatness.

Study the time line above. In what century did Washington take office?

—220—

In 1789, George Washington rode from Virginia to New York to take office. Here, he passes through Trenton, New Jersey.

1 The New Government at Work

Read to Learn

★ Who was in Washington's cabinet?

★ How did Hamilton plan to strengthen the nation's economy?

★ What do these words mean: precedent, cabinet, bond, national debt, speculator, tariff?

In April 1789, the newly elected President and members of Congress set about the task of governing the United States.

Washington in Office

When George Washington took office, he had few guidelines to follow. The Constitution set up a framework of government but did not say just how the government would work. Every action or decision the first President made set a precedent (PREHS uh duhnt). A *precedent* is an act or decision that sets an example for others to follow.

A dignified leader. Washington was determined to set an example as a formal, dignified President. When he rode, he mounted a white horse with a leopard-skin saddlecloth. When he drove, he used a carriage pulled by six cream-colored horses. People recognized the President's carriage and greeted him with respect.

Washington was a strong leader. When problems developed, he stepped in to resolve them. But he was careful

President Washington and First Lady Martha Washington, standing on the dais at left, often held formal receptions. Washington received visitors on Tuesday afternoons from 3 P.M. to 5 P.M. Anyone who was properly dressed could come. The First Lady also held teas every Friday evening.

to stay out of day-to-day political battles. As a result, people came to see him as a man who could lead the nation with dignity.

At the end of Washington's first term, the President wanted to retire to Mount Vernon. However, his friends persuaded him to run for reelection. He won easily. When his second term ended in 1796, Washington refused to run for a third term. In doing this, he set a precedent that other Presidents followed until 1940.

Choosing a cabinet. The Constitution said very little about how the executive branch of government should be organized. But it was clear that the President needed people to help him carry out his duties. When the first Congress met in 1789, it quickly set up five departments to help the President. They were the State Department, the Treasury Department, the War Depart-

ment, and the offices of the Attorney General and Postmaster General.

Washington chose talented men to head the five departments. This group of officials became known as the *cabinet.* Washington's cabinet included Thomas Jefferson as Secretary of State, Alexander Hamilton as Secretary of the Treasury, Henry Knox as Secretary of War, Edmund Randolph as Attorney General, and Samuel Osgood as Postmaster General.

Organizing the federal courts. The Constitution called for a Supreme Court. But it gave Congress the job of organizing the federal court system. In 1789, Congress passed the *Judiciary Act.* The act said that the Supreme Court should have a Chief Justice and five Associate Justices.* It also set up a

---

*Today, the Supreme Court has been expanded to include eight Associate Justices.

system of district courts and circuit courts. Decisions made in these lower courts could be appealed to the Supreme Court.

Washington chose John Jay as the first Chief Justice of the Supreme Court. The justices wore black and scarlet robes like judges in England. But Jefferson convinced them not to wear white wigs like English judges.

Restoring Confidence

As Secretary of the Treasury, Alexander Hamilton wanted to put the nation's finances on a firm footing. Yet he faced grave problems. During the Revolution, the national government and individual states borrowed a lot of money from foreign countries and from ordinary citizens. Governments borrow money by issuing bonds. A *bond* is a certificate that promises to pay the holder a certain sum of money plus interest on a certain date. For example, if a person pays $100 for a government bond, the government agrees to repay that money with interest in five or ten years. The money a government owes is called the *national debt*.

By 1789, most southern states had paid off their debts from the Revolution. But other states and the federal government had not. When Alexander Hamilton became Secretary of the Treasury, he wanted to make sure that these debts were paid. After all, he said, who would lend money to the United States in the future if the country did not pay its old debts?

Hamilton's plan. Hamilton was an energetic young man who wanted to make a name for himself. He suggested a two-step plan for paying off both the national debt and state debts.

First, he wanted to buy up the government's old bonds and issue new bonds. When the nation's finances improved, the government would be able to pay off the new bonds. Second, Hamilton wanted the national government to pay off debts owed by states.

Alexander Hamilton was only 32 years old when he became Secretary of the Treasury. He strongly supported the Bank of the United States, above. The Bank was located on Third Street in Philadelphia, then the nation's largest city.

Opposition to the plan. In Congress, James Madison led the opposition to Hamilton's plan. During the Revolution, soldiers and other people were paid for their services with government bonds. Many of these people needed cash. So they sold their bonds to speculators. A *speculator* is someone who is willing to invest in a risky venture on the chance of making a large profit.

Speculators usually paid bondholders only 10 or 15 cents for a bond worth one dollar. If the government repaid the bonds at their full value, speculators stood to make large profits. Madison argued that speculators should not be paid full value for the bonds. After bitter debate, Hamilton managed to convince Congress to accept his plan and repay the national debt in full.

CHART SKILL As Secretary of the Treasury, Hamilton had to set up a way for the government to meet its expenses. What was the government's income in 1789? How much did it owe?

Money Problems of the New Nation

1789 – 1791

Amount Owed

Income

$77,228,000 debt

$4,269,000 to run government

$4,399,000 from tariffs

$19,000 from other sources

Total: $81,497,000

Total: $4,419,000

Source: *Historical Statistics of the United States*

Many southern states opposed Hamilton's idea of repaying the debts owed by the states because they had already paid their debts. Once again, Madison led the fight against Hamilton. When Hamilton saw that Madison had enough votes in Congress to defeat him, he offered the southern states a compromise.

The compromise. Hamilton knew that many Southerners wanted to move the nation's capital from New York City to Virginia. Hamilton offered to get his New England friends to vote for a capital in the South if Southerners would support his plan for repaying state debts.

Southerners, including Madison, finally agreed. In July 1790, Congress passed a bill taking over state debts and making plans for the new capital city. Congress decided that the capital should not be part of any state. Instead, it set aside a piece of land on the Potomac River, which it called the District of Columbia. Congress expected the new capital city, called the Federal City, to be ready by 1800. (See page 234.) Meanwhile, it made Philadelphia the nation's capital.

Meeting Government Expenses

Another part of Hamilton's program to strengthen the nation's economy was to create a national bank. In 1791, Congress passed a bill setting up the *Bank of the United States.* The government deposited the taxes it collected into the Bank. In turn, the Bank issued paper money and paid government bills. By making loans to citizens, the Bank encouraged the growth of new businesses.

The new government had many expenses. It had to pay its employees, build the new Federal City, and keep up the army and navy. As Secretary of the Treasury, Hamilton had to find ways to raise money for the government. The Constitution, you remember, gave Congress the right to pass tax

To put down the Whiskey Rebellion, President Washington called out the state militias. Nearly 15,000 troops responded. Here, Washington reviews some of the troops at Fort Cumberland, Maryland.

laws. So Hamilton asked Congress to pass several tax laws. See the chart on page 224.

One law was a *tariff,* or tax, on all foreign goods brought into the country. Hamilton hoped that a tariff would help American manufacturers by making imported goods more expensive than American goods. The tariff was meant to encourage people to buy American goods.

The tariff was more popular in the North than in the South. Industries were growing in the North, and the tariff protected northern manufacturers from foreign competition. Southerners were mostly farmers. They bought more foreign goods than Northerners. They resented the tariff because it made these goods more expensive.

Congress also passed a bill that taxed all liquor made and sold in the United States. Hamilton wanted this tax to raise money for the Treasury. Instead, it led to a rebellion.

The Whiskey Rebellion

Many farmers in the backcountry raised corn. Corn was too bulky to haul to markets in the East. But whiskey could be carried easily in barrels. So farmers made corn into whiskey and sold the whiskey to earn money. When backcountry farmers heard about the tax on whiskey, they compared it to the unfair taxes the British Parliament had passed in the 1760s. They refused to pay it.

When officials in western Pennsylvania tried to collect the unpopular tax in 1794, farmers rebelled. Soon, thousands of farmers were marching through Pittsburgh. Supporters of the *Whiskey Rebellion* set up Liberty Trees and sang revolutionary songs.

Washington acted quickly. He called up the militia and took charge of the troops himself. When the farmers heard that 15,000 troops were marching against them, they surrendered peacefully. Hamilton wanted the leaders executed. Washington disagreed and pardoned them. He felt that the government had showed its strength. Now that the crisis was over, he wisely decided to show mercy.

SECTION REVIEW

1. **Define:** precedent, cabinet, bond, national debt, speculator, tariff.
2. Why did Washington need a cabinet?
3. What did Hamilton want to do about debts owed since the Revolution?
4. Describe two ways Congress tried to raise money.
5. **What Do You Think?** Why do you think Washington chose to stay out of day-to-day political battles?

2 Staying Neutral

Read to Learn

★ How did the French Revolution affect the United States?

★ What was the purpose of the Neutrality Proclamation?

★ Why did war break out on the western frontier?

★ What advice did Washington give in his Farewell Address?

In its early years, the new nation faced many challenges both at home and abroad. Spain, Britain, and Native American nations ruled the lands that bordered the United States. President Washington had to decide how the United States would deal with these other powers.

The French Revolution

Events in Europe posed unexpected problems for the United States. Late in 1789, ships arriving at American ports brought surprising news from France. On July 14, 1789, a mob in Paris had attacked the Bastille (bah STEEL), a huge prison. Only a few prisoners were held there. But the attack on the Bastille marked the beginning of the *French Revolution.*

The French people had many reasons for rebelling against their king and the nobles who ruled their country. They wanted a constitution and rights similar to those that Americans had just won in their Revolution.

The storming of the Bastille, shown here, marked the beginning of the French Revolution. Lafayette sent Washington the key to the Bastille to show the close ties between the French and American revolutions. Differing reactions to the French Revolution caused divisions in Washington's cabinet.

At first, most Americans supported the French Revolution. They knew what it meant to fight for liberty. Besides, France was America's first ally. And people like the Marquis de Lafayette were working for the cause of liberty in France. Lafayette, you remember, had helped Americans in their fight for independence.

Like most revolutions, the French Revolution soon took a violent course. The French king, Louis XVI, and his family were imprisoned and then executed. In America, opinion was divided. People like Hamilton were horrified at the Reign of Terror that swept France and killed thousands of people. Thomas Jefferson condemned the terror but thought that the violence was necessary for the French to win their freedom. John Adams disagreed. He claimed that the French had no more chance of creating a free government "than a snowball can exist in the streets of Philadelphia under a burning sun."

Washington Avoids War

The French Revolution worried rulers and nobles all over Europe. They were afraid that revolutionary ideas would spread to their own lands. To prevent this, Britain, Austria, Prussia, the Netherlands, and Spain joined in a war against France. The fighting continued on and off from 1792 to 1815.

The war in Europe affected the United States. In 1778, the United States and France had signed a treaty of friendship. Under the treaty, France could use American ports. Now that France was at war with Britain, it wanted to use American ports to supply its ships and attack British ships.

Washington's cabinet was divided over what course to follow. Alexander Hamilton argued that America's treaty with France was signed with King Louis XVI. Since the king was dead, he went on, the treaty was no longer in force. However, Thomas Jefferson favored the French cause. He was suspicious of Hamilton, who wanted friendly relations with Britain, America's old enemy.

The Neutrality Proclamation. Washington wanted to keep the nation from being dragged into a European war. So in April 1793, he issued the *Neutrality Proclamation.* It stated that the United States would not support either side in the war. Also, it forbade Americans from taking any warlike action against either Britain or France.

Despite the Neutrality Proclamation, problems arose. American merchants wanted to trade with both Britain and France. But each of these countries wanted to stop Americans from trading with its enemy.

Jay's Treaty. In 1793, the British began attacking American ships that traded with the French colonies in the West Indies. Well-armed British warships chased and captured American merchant ships. On the small French island of St. Eustacia, the British took 130 American ships. When Americans learned of Britain's high-handed action, many wanted to declare war. Washington knew that the United States was in no position to fight a war. So he sent Chief Justice John Jay to Britain for talks.

After much hard bargaining, Jay worked out a treaty in 1794. The British agreed to pay damages for the ships taken in the West Indies. But they refused to make any promises about future attacks. Jay also wanted the British to give up the forts they still held in the Ohio Valley. Britain agreed to do this only after the Americans paid the debts owed to British merchants since the Revolution.

The Senate was unhappy with *Jay's Treaty.* But at Washington's request, it ratified the treaty in 1795. Although the treaty was unpopular, Washington was satisfied that he had avoided war with Britain.

In rural areas, people got together for many occasions. Quilting parties such as this one were popular. They often doubled as engagement parties. The quilt made at the party was presented as a gift to the engaged couple.

War on the Frontier

During the 1790s, thousands of settlers moved into the Northwest Territory. The large number of white settlers in the Northwest Territory created serious problems. The United States had signed treaties with the Indian nations who lived there. Most settlers ignored the treaties and took land wherever they pleased.

Indians fight back. Native Americans resented the people who were invading their lands. As a result, clashes occurred between settlers and Indians. Indians attacked white families who lived far from a fort. White settlers took revenge on Indians, even on those who had not taken part in the attacks. The violence spread.

In 1791, the Miami Indians in Ohio joined with other Indian nations to drive settlers off their land. The Miamis were led by a skillful fighter, Little Turtle. The British in the Ohio Valley encouraged the Indians by supplying them with rifles and gunpowder. When Washington heard the news, he sent General Arthur St. Clair with 3,000 soldiers to fight the Indians. Little Turtle defeated St. Clair's forces.

Battle of Fallen Timbers. Washington replaced St. Clair with General Anthony Wayne. Wayne drilled his troops well. In 1794, he marched into Miami territory. A Shawnee leader, Blue Jacket, had taken over from Little Turtle. He gathered his forces at a place called Fallen Timbers. It got this name because a violent windstorm had blown down many trees and created a tangle of logs. The Indians thought that Wayne would have trouble fighting on this ground. But Wayne's troops pushed through the underbrush and defeated the Indians.

The next year, 12 Indian nations signed the *Treaty of Greenville* with the United States. They had to give up about 25,000 square miles (65,000 square km) of land. In return, they received $20,000 and a promise of more payments if they kept the peace.

Washington's Farewell Address

During his years as President, Washington kept a measure of peace in the new nation. Before he left office in 1796, he wrote some words of advice for his fellow citizens. Washington's *Farewell Address* was printed in newspapers across the country.

In the address, he warned the country against becoming involved in European affairs: "'Tis our true policy to steer clear of permanent alliances with any portion of the foreign world."

To Washington, the United States was a young nation struggling to get on its feet. It should concentrate on the business of governing at home. However, Washington did support trade with other nations because trade helped the American economy.

Washington's Farewell Address became a guiding principle of American foreign policy. Future Presidents tried to follow his advice though with mixed results.

After Fallen Timbers, Indian leaders had to sign the Treaty of Greenville. Find Anthony Wayne's signature on the treaty above. English names were written next to the symbols marked by each Indian leader.

SECTION REVIEW

1. (a) What did most Americans think of the French Revolution when it began? (b) How did their views change?
2. What did the Neutrality Proclamation say?
3. Why did Washington send Chief Justice Jay to Britain?
4. Describe one result of the Battle of Fallen Timbers.
5. **What Do You Think?** Why do you think Washington advised Americans to "steer clear of permanent alliances"?

3 Political Parties

Read to Learn

★ Why did political parties form in the United States?
★ What ideas did each party support?
★ How did newspapers influence politics?
★ Who was elected the second President of the United States?

In 1789, there were no political parties in the United States as there are today. In fact, President Washington and other leaders of the new nation mistrusted political parties. Yet before Washington left office in 1796, two parties had developed.

Against All Warnings

During the 1700s, most Americans distrusted political parties. In his Farewell Address, Washington warned that parties caused "jealousies and false alarms." Jefferson echoed this warning. He said, "If I could not go to heaven but with a party, I would not go at all."

Americans had good reason to distrust political parties. They had seen how parties worked in Britain. Parties, called factions in Britain, were made up of a few people who schemed to win favors from the government. They were more interested in personal profit than in the public good. American leaders wanted to keep factions from forming. But disagreements between two of Washington's chief advisers spurred the growth of political parties.

The two parties that developed in the 1790s were led by Secretary of the Treasury Alexander Hamilton and Secretary of State Thomas Jefferson. Hamilton and Jefferson were different in many ways. Hamilton was a short, slender man. He spoke forcefully, dressed elegantly, and sparkled with energy. He was much in demand at formal parties.

Jefferson was tall and a bit gawky. Although he was a Virginia aristocrat, he dressed and spoke informally. "He spoke almost without ceasing," recalled one senator. "Yet he scattered information wherever he went" and sparkled with brilliant ideas.

Two Views on Government

Hamilton and Jefferson had very different views about what was good for the country. Hamilton wanted the federal government to be stronger than state governments. Jefferson believed that state governments should be stronger.

Hamilton supported the Bank of the United States. Jefferson opposed it because he felt that it gave too much power to wealthy investors who would help run it. Also, Jefferson interpreted the Constitution strictly. He argued that nowhere did the Constitution give the federal government the power to create a national bank.

Hamilton interpreted the Constitution more loosely. He pointed out that the Constitution gave Congress the power to make all laws "necessary and proper" to carry out its duties. He reasoned that since Congress had the right to collect taxes and the Bank was necessary to collect taxes, then Congress had the right to create the Bank.

Hamilton wanted the government to encourage economic growth. His programs favored the growth of trade, manufacturing, and cities. He favored business leaders and mistrusted the common people. Jefferson believed that the common people, especially farmers, were the backbone of the nation. He thought that crowded cities and manufacturing might corrupt American life.

Finally, Hamilton favored Britain, an important trading partner of the United States. Jefferson favored France, America's first ally and a nation whose people were struggling for liberty and freedom.

Parties Take Shape

At first, Jefferson and Hamilton disagreed only in private. But when Congress began passing Hamilton's program, Jefferson and his friend, James Madison, decided to organize support for their views. They moved quietly and cautiously at first.

In 1791, they went to New York State, telling people that they were going to study its wildlife. In fact, Jefferson was interested in nature and traveled as far north as Lake George. But he and Madison also met with such important New York politicians as Governor George Clinton and Aaron

Burr, a strong critic of Hamilton. Jefferson asked Clinton and Burr to help defeat Hamilton's program by getting New Yorkers to vote for Jefferson's supporters at the next election.

Republicans and Federalists. Before long, leaders in other states began organizing to support either Jefferson or Hamilton. Jefferson's supporters called themselves *Democratic Republicans.* Often, the name was shortened to Republicans.* Hamilton and his supporters were known as *Federalists* because they favored a strong federal government. Federalists had the support of merchants and shipowners in the Northeast and some planters in the South. Small farmers, craftworkers, and some wealthier landowners supported the Republicans.

Newspapers wave the banner. Newspapers influenced the growth of political parties. Newspaper publishers took sides on the issues. The most influential newspaper, the *Gazette of the United States,* was published in Philadelphia, which was still the nation's capital in the 1790s. John Fenno, publisher of the *Gazette,* strongly supported Hamilton's programs. Jefferson's friend Philip Freneau started a rival paper, called the *National Gazette.* It published articles supporting the Republicans. (See Skill Lesson 10 on page 232.)

Between 1790 and 1800, the number of American newspapers more than doubled—from about 100 to over 230. These newspapers played an essential role in the new nation. They kept people informed and helped shape public opinion.

---

*Jefferson's Republican party was not the same as today's Republican Party. In fact, Jefferson's Republican Party later grew into today's Democratic Party.

CHART SKILL By the 1790s, two political parties had formed. Describe two differences between the parties on economic issues.

The First Political Parties

Federalists	Republicans
1. Led by A. Hamilton	1. Led by T. Jefferson
2. Wealthy and well-educated should lead nation	2. People should have political power
3. Strong central government	3. Strong state governments
4. Emphasis on manufacturing, shipping, and trade	4. Emphasis on agriculture
5. Loose interpretation of Constitution	5. Strict interpretation of Constitution
6. Pro-British	6. Pro-French
7. Favored national bank	7. Opposed national bank
8. Favored protective tariff	8. Opposed protective tariff

Choosing the Second President

When Washington retired in 1796, political parties played an important part in choosing his successor. The election of 1796 was the first in which political parties played a role. Each party put forward its own candidates. The Republicans chose Jefferson as their candidate for President and Aaron Burr for Vice President. The Federalists chose John Adams for President and Thomas Pinckney for Vice President.

The election of 1796 had an unusual result. According to the Constitution, each elector cast two votes. He could cast them for any two candidates. The person receiving the most votes would become President. The person with the next highest total would become Vice President.

Many primary sources, such as letters, diaries, and speeches, express the opinions of the people who wrote them. Therefore, when historians study primary sources, they have to recognize fact and opinion. A **fact** is something that actually happened. It is known to be true because it can be proved or observed. An **opinion** is a judgment that reflects a person's beliefs or feelings. It is not necessarily true.

Often, writers present a series of facts to back up an opinion. For example, in the Declaration of Independence, Jefferson listed facts to support the opinion that George III had tried to establish "an absolute tyranny over these states."

In the letter below, Alexander Hamilton writes about political differences between himself and the party led by Madison and Jefferson.

1. **Determine which statements are facts.** Remember that facts can be checked and thereby can be proved.

Use your reading in this chapter to help answer these questions. (a) Choose two statements of fact in Hamilton's letter. (b) How might you prove that each statement is a fact?

2. **Determine which statements are opinions.** Writers often show that they are giving an opinion by saying "in my view" or "I think" or "I believe." (a) Choose two statements in which Hamilton gives his opinion. (b) How can you tell each is an opinion?

3. **Determine how a writer mixes fact and opinion.** Reread the last sentence of the letter. (a) What did Hamilton mean by a "womanish attachment to France and a womanish resentment against Great Britain"? (b) Is it true that Jefferson supported France and opposed Britain? (c) What country did Hamilton want the United States to support? (d) Why do you think Hamilton mixed fact and opinion in the statement?

 Alexander Hamilton wrote:

It was not until the last session of Congress that I became completely convinced that Mr. Madison and Mr. Jefferson are at the head of a faction that is hostile toward me. They are motivated by views that, in my judgment, will undermine the principles of good government and are dangerous to the peace and happiness of the country.

Freneau, the present publisher of the *National Gazette,* was a known Antifederalist. It is certain that he was brought to Philadelphia by Mr. Jefferson to be the publisher of a newspaper. At the same time as he was starting his paper, he was also a clerk in the Department of State.

His paper is devoted to opposing me and the measures that I have supported. And the paper has a general unfriendly attitude toward the government of the United States.

On almost all questions, great and small, which have come up since the first session of Congress, Mr. Jefferson and Mr. Madison have been found among those who want to limit federal power. In respect to foreign policy, the views of these gentlemen are, in my judgment, equally unsound and dangerous. They have a womanish attachment to France and a womanish resentment against Great Britain.

Abigail and John Adams are shown here soon after they married. During the Revolution, they were often apart. Abigail Adams' letters to her husband give a fascinating look at these two brilliant people and the early years of the new nation.

When the ballots of the electoral college were counted, John Adams had 71 votes. So Adams, a Federalist, became President. Thomas Jefferson had 68 votes. So Jefferson, a Republican, became Vice President. In 1804, the system was changed by the Twelfth Amendment. It required electors to vote separately for the President and Vice President. Meanwhile, Adams took office in March 1797 as the second President of the United States.

■ SECTION REVIEW ■

1. Why did American leaders distrust political parties?
2. (a) Name the two political parties that developed in the 1790s. (b) Who was the leader of each?
3. Describe one issue on which Hamilton and Jefferson disagreed.
4. **What Do You Think?** Why do you think political parties emerged even though American leaders warned against them?

4 Adams Takes a Firm Stand

Read to Learn
★ Why did many Americans want war with France?
★ Why did Adams become unpopular with his own Federalist Party?
★ What were the Alien and Sedition acts?
★ What do these words mean: alien, sedition, unconstitutional, nullify?

Like Washington, John Adams faced many problems when he took office. But Washington had been very popular and was respected as "the father of his country." When George Washington died in 1799, Henry Lee of Virginia wrote that he was "first in war, first in peace, first in the hearts of

Soon after taking office, President Washington chose the exact location on the Potomac River for the Federal City, as the capital was then called. Although the area was wilderness, it offered advantages. It was within reach of states in the North and West as well as in the South. And it was safe from attack.

Hoping to turn the wilderness into a beautiful city, President Washington

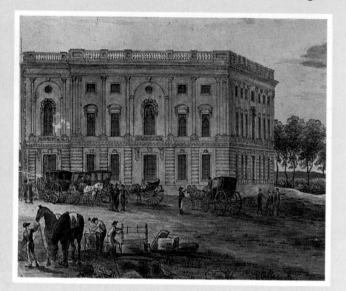

hired the French architect Pierre Charles l'Enfant to draw up plans. L'Enfant designed a capital he said would be "magnificent enough to grace a grand nation."

Besides a design, building a new capital called for money and labor. But business people and workers did not see the wilderness as pleasant or profitable. They chose to stay in Philadelphia and other older cities. So work on the city went slowly.

In 1800, President Adams and the government moved from Philadelphia to the Federal City. Instead of a magnificent city, members of Congress found a village of muddy wagon tracks, unfinished buildings, and swampy fields. One member called the capital "wilderness city." Another described it as "a mud hole."

Renamed Washington, D.C., the capital was slowly finished. Like the nation itself, it grew out of the wilderness and became a source of pride to Americans. Its broad avenues and stately buildings were a dream come true.

★ Why did it take a long time to build the nation's capital?

his countrymen." Adams did not enjoy the same high level of fame and respect.

The XYZ Affair

Foreign affairs occupied much of President Adams' attention. When the United States ratified Jay's Treaty with Britain in 1795, France had responded with anger. French warships seized some American ships in the West Indies. When the United States sent an ambassador to Paris to discuss the problem of neutral rights, the French refused to see him.

Adams was determined to work out a solution. In 1797, he sent three new ambassadors to Paris. This time, the Americans were received. But the French foreign minister, Maurice de Talleyrand, said that there would be delays before talks could begin.

A secret offer. Talleyrand was a shrewd man but not very honest. He sent three secret agents to offer the Americans a deal. The agents were blunt. "You must pay money," they told the Americans. "You must pay a great deal of money." Talleyrand wanted $250,000 for himself and a loan to

France of $10 million. "Not a sixpence!" replied one of the Americans angrily.

The Americans reported the incident to President Adams, referring to the agents as X, Y, and Z. When Adams made the *XYZ Affair* public in 1798, most Americans were outraged. People repeated the slogan "Millions for defense, but not one cent for tribute!" They were willing to spend money to defend America, but they would not pay bribes to another nation.

Spending for defense. The XYZ Affair ignited war fever in the United States. But President Adams resisted the pressure to declare war on France. Like Washington, he wanted to keep the country out of European affairs. Still, he could not ignore French attacks on American ships. So he moved to strengthen the American navy. At the same time, Congress created the Department of the Navy.

Up and down the coast, shipyards fitted out small boats with guns and cannons. They built nearly a dozen frigates. Frigates were large, fast sailing ships that carried as many as 44 guns. The best-known frigate, the U.S.S. *Constitution,* was launched in 1797 (before the XYZ Affair).* Later, it was nicknamed "Old Ironsides" because its wooden hull was so strong that it seemed to be made of iron.

Talleyrand was so impressed by the new American navy that he stopped attacking American ships. He also assured Adams that if American ambassadors came to France, they would be treated with respect.

A Split in the Federalist Party

Many Federalists, led by Alexander Hamilton, wanted to ignore Talleyrand's offer to negotiate. They thought that the United States would benefit from a war with France. War, they said, would force the United States to build a strong army as well as a navy. These Federalists also hoped that war with France would weaken support for Jefferson and the Republicans, who were sympathetic to the French.

President Adams was a Federalist, but he disagreed with Hamilton's wish for war. The growing disagreement between Adams and Hamilton led to a split in the Federalist Party. Hamilton and his supporters were called *High Federalists.*

Adams delayed building up an American army. Instead, he sent new ambassadors to France. Although

In the late 1790s, fears of war led the new nation to strengthen its navy. This print shows the building of the frigate *Philadelphia.*

*After 100 years of service, the U.S.S. *Constitution* was retired from active service in 1897. It can be visited today in the Boston Navy Yard.

Hamilton no longer held office, he attacked Adams, calling him "unfit for a President." Hamilton urged Federalists in the Senate to block approval of the ambassadors to France. In turn, Adams threatened to resign and let Vice President Jefferson take office. At the thought of a Republican President, Hamilton backed down.

When the American ambassadors reached France, they found a young army officer, Napoleon Bonaparte, in power. Napoleon was interested in expanding French power in Europe. He did not want to be bothered fighting the United States. So he signed an agreement known as the *Convention of 1800.* In it, France agreed to stop seizing American ships.

Adams kept the nation out of war. But peace cost him the support of many Federalists and split his party.

The Alien and Sedition Acts

In 1798, while talks were still going on with France, the High Federalists in Congress passed several strict laws. The laws were known as the Alien and Sedition acts. They were meant to protect the United States in case of war.

The *Alien Act* allowed the President to expel any *alien,* or foreigner, who was thought to be dangerous to the country. Another law made it harder for immigrants to become citizens. Before 1798, a white male immigrant could become a citizen after living in the United States for 5 years. Under the new law, immigrants had to live in America for 14 years before they could become citizens.

The High Federalists passed this act because many recent immigrants supported Jefferson and the Republicans. The act would keep these immigrants from voting for years.

Republicans hated these laws. They were even more outraged by the *Sedition Act. Sedition* (sih DISH uhn) means the stirring up of rebellion against a government. The Sedition Act said that citizens could be fined and jailed if they criticized public officials.

Republicans argued that the Sedition Act violated the Constitution. The First Amendment, they said, protected an American's freedom of speech. One Republican warned that the act would make it a crime to "laugh at the cut of a congressman's coat" or "give dinner to a Frenchman." Republican fears were confirmed when several Republican newspaper editors and even a congressman were fined and jailed for their opinions.

The Kentucky and Virginia Resolutions

Vice President Jefferson believed that the Alien and Sedition acts were *unconstitutional,* that is, not permitted by the Constitution. Jefferson could not turn to the courts for help because the Federalists controlled them. Instead, he called on the states to act. He argued that a state had the right to *nullify,* or cancel, a law passed by the federal government.

Urged on by Jefferson, the Kentucky and Virginia legislatures passed a series of resolutions in 1798 and 1799. The *Kentucky and Virginia resolutions* said that each state "has an equal right to judge for itself" whether a law is constitutional. If a state decides that a law is unconstitutional, Jefferson said, it has the power to nullify the law.

The Kentucky and Virginia resolutions raised important questions. Did states have the power to decide if laws were constitutional? Did states have the power to nullify laws passed by Congress? These questions were left unanswered at the time because other states did not support the movement to nullify the Alien and Sedition acts. In the end, the Alien and Sedition acts were changed or dropped. However, the question of a state's right to nullify laws would come up again.

Election of 1800

By 1800, the fear of war with France had died down. As it did, Federalist power declined. The Republicans hoped to sweep the Federalists out of office. In the election of 1800, they pointed out that Federalists had raised taxes to prepare for war with France. Also, they made an issue of the unpopular Alien and Sedition acts.

Jefferson ran as the Republican candidate for President. Aaron Burr ran for Vice President. Adams was again the Federalist candidate with Charles Pinckney for Vice President.

A tie vote. Republicans won a large victory in Congress. In the race for President, Republicans beat the Federalists. But when the electoral college voted, Jefferson and Burr each received 73 votes. The tie vote raised this question: Who would be President—Jefferson or Burr?

According to the Constitution, in the case of a tie vote, the House of Representatives decides the election. The House voted 35 times. Each time, the vote remained a tie. Even though the people clearly meant Jefferson to be President, Burr would not step aside. At last, the House made Jefferson President. Burr became Vice President.

Congress took steps to prevent another confusing election. It passed the Twelfth Amendment, which was ratified in 1804. The amendment required electors to vote separately for President and Vice President.

Federalist power fades. With the election of a Republican President, the Federalist era came to an end. After 1800, Federalists won fewer seats in Congress. In 1804, the Federalist leader, Alexander Hamilton, was killed in a duel with Aaron Burr.

The Federalist Party lost power largely because it distrusted the ordinary citizen. Although the party declined slowly after 1800, it left its mark. Federalists helped the nation

AMERICANS WHO DARED

Benjamin Banneker

Benjamin Banneker, the son of a freed slave, became a respected astronomer and mathematician. He was largely self-taught. From studying books, he made a clock—without ever seeing one. In 1790, he was chosen as a surveyor for the Federal City. But he gained more fame from his almanacs, which were full of useful scientific information.

during its early years. And a Federalist President, John Adams, kept the nation out of war.

═══ SECTION REVIEW ═══

1. **Define:** alien, sedition, unconstitutional, nullify.
2. How did Talleyrand insult the United States?
3. How did Adams and Hamilton differ on the question of war with France?
4. (a) Why did the Federalists support the Alien and Sedition acts? (b) Why did the Republicans oppose them?
5. **What Do You Think?** How do you think the Kentucky and Virginia resolutions fit in with Jefferson's ideas on government?

Chapter 10 Review

★ Summary ★

In 1789, George Washington took office as the first President of the United States. Although he faced many problems during his two terms, he led the nation on a course of peaceful growth. Washington chose able men to serve in his cabinet. As Secretary of the Treasury, Hamilton tried to strengthen the nation's finances.

Foreign affairs occupied the attention of both Washington and Adams, the second President of the United States. Both Presidents kept the United States out of war. But Adams did this at the cost of splitting his party.

In 1800, Thomas Jefferson was elected as the third President of the United States. By this time, political parties were playing a major role in American politics.

★ Reviewing the Facts *2 pts. each* ★

Key Terms. Match each term in Column 1 with the correct definition in Column 2.

Column 1
1. cabinet
2. tariff
3. alien
4. sedition
5. nullify

Column 2
a. tax
b. foreigner
c. cancel
d. stirring up of rebellion against a government
e. group of officials who head up executive departments

Key People, Events, and Ideas. Identify each of the following.

1. Judiciary Act
2. Bank of the United States
3. Whiskey Rebellion
4. Neutrality Proclamation
5. Jay's Treaty
6. Treaty of Greenville
7. Farewell Address
8. Alexander Hamilton
9. Thomas Jefferson
10. XYZ Affair
11. John Adams
12. Convention of 1800
13. Alien Act
14. Sedition Act
15. Kentucky and Virginia resolutions

★ Chapter Checkup ★ *5 pts. each*

1. (a) Describe Hamilton's plan for paying off state and national debts. (b) Who objected to his plan? (c) Why did they object?
2. What was the cause of the Whiskey Rebellion?
3. Why did Washington issue the Neutrality Proclamation?
4. Describe one cause and one result of war on the frontier in the 1790s.
5. (a) How did political parties develop? (b) Who supported the Federalists? (c) Who supported the Republicans?
6. Describe two results of the XYZ Affair.
7. How did differences between Adams and Hamilton affect the Federalist Party?
8. What important issue was raised by the Kentucky and Virginia resolutions?

★ Thinking About History

Answer 1,3 10pts. ★

(1.) Understanding the economy. (a) Why did Hamilton want to pay off the nation's debts? (b) How did speculators stand to make a large profit from this plan?

2. Relating past to present. (a) What advice did Washington give in his Farewell Address? (b) Do you think Americans today would still agree with his advice? Explain.

(3.) Expressing an opinion. Do you think the Alien and Sedition acts were necessary to protect the nation? Why?

→4. Learning about citizenship. (a) What problems did the first Presidents of the United States face? (b) Give two examples of how strong leadership helped the new nation.

Ex. = *Sports*

★ Using Your Skills

1. Placing events in time. Make a horizontal time line. Label the left end 1789 and the right end 1800. Divide the time line into 11 equal parts, each representing one year. Then write each major event from this chapter below the year in which it happened. (a) What event or events took place in 1794? (b) Were the Alien and Sedition acts passed before or after the Kentucky and Virginia resolutions? (c) How were these two events related?

2. Skimming a chapter. Skimming is a useful reading skill. When you skim a chapter, you read the chapter quickly to get a general idea of what it is about. To skim a chapter in this book, look first at the Chapter Outline at the beginning of each chapter. The Chapter Outline lists all the sections in the chapter. Next, look at the boldface heads that show you the main topics in each section. Finally, quickly read the first and last sentence of each paragraph.

Skim the first part of this chapter (pages 220–225). (a) What does the Chapter Outline tell you about the chapter? (b) List the main topics covered in the section "The New Government at Work." (c) What do you think the general idea of this section is?

★ More to Do

1. Organizing a debate. As a group project, prepare a debate between Alexander Hamilton and Thomas Jefferson on whether the Bank of the United States was constitutional.

2. Interviewing. In small groups, prepare an interview with President Washington on his last day in office. Ask one person in the group to imagine he or she is George Washington. Find out which of Washington's achievements he values most and what he thinks lies ahead for the new nation.

3. Exploring local history. Make a chart with three headings: Position, Name, Party. Fill in the chart for your state's governor, senators, and representatives and for your local government officials, including the mayor or council.

4. Making a speech. When the election of 1800 was being decided in the House of Representatives, members had to choose between Aaron Burr and Thomas Jefferson. Imagine that you are a representative and write a speech to give in support of Aaron Burr as President.

CHAPTER

11

Age of Jefferson (1801–1816)

Chapter Outline

1 Jefferson Takes Office
2 The Nation Doubles in Size
3 Dangers at Sea
4 War Fever
5 The War of 1812

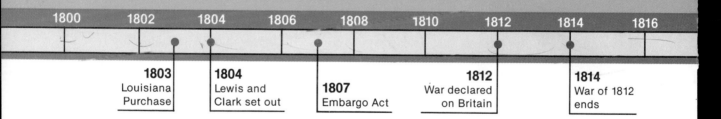

1800   1802   1804   1806   1808   1810   1812   1814   1816

1803 Louisiana Purchase

1804 Lewis and Clark set out

1807 Embargo Act

1812 War declared on Britain

1814 War of 1812 ends

About This Chapter

On March 4, 1801, Thomas Jefferson walked along the muddy streets of the new capital city. Washington, D.C., was still only half finished. The newly elected President was on his way to his inauguration. He deliberately kept the event simple. No guard of honor or servants accompanied him when he went inside the unfinished Capitol building. He took the oath of office and walked back to the boardinghouse where he was living.

Jefferson was the first President of the United States to take office in the new capital city. He was also the first Republican President. Federalists worried about how Jefferson would use his power. They soon found out what the new President and the new century would bring.

In fact, Jefferson did not see his election as his greatest success. For him, drafting the Declaration of Independence was more important. Once, some friends wanted to hold a public celebration for his birthday. Jefferson said, "The only birthday I ever commemorate is that of our Independence, the Fourth of July." As President, Jefferson tried to live up to the ideals of the Declaration.

After he left office, the next two Presidents, James Madison and James Monroe, carried on the traditions set down by Jefferson. His influence was so great that this period is often called the Age of Jefferson.

Study the time line above. Name two events that occurred after Jefferson took office.

During the War of 1812, the *Constitution* defeated the British frigate *Guerrière*. This painting celebrates that American victory.

1 Jefferson Takes Office

Read to Learn

★ How did Jefferson treat the Federalists?
★ What were Jefferson's views on government?
★ Why was *Marbury* v. *Madison* an important case?
★ What do these words mean: democratic, laissez faire, judicial review?

Thomas Jefferson was a wealthy plantation and slave owner and a respected scholar. He had more than 6,000 books in his library at Monticello. He knew Greek, Latin, French, and Italian and was familiar with many Native American languages.

Even though Jefferson was a member of the upper class, he believed that his election was a victory for ordinary American citizens. In Europe, kings and nobles still ruled, but Jefferson was proud that the United States was a republic. He vowed to serve as President without fancy ceremonies. Once in office, Jefferson was determined to live up to his own principles.

A More Democratic Style

As President, Thomas Jefferson was different from Washington or Adams. Because he wanted to represent ordinary citizens, Jefferson vowed to make the government more democratic.

Thomas Jefferson, third President of the United States, made many inventions. Among them was this polygraph machine. The machine copied a letter as the President wrote it. Jefferson wrote hundreds of letters. With this machine, he could keep a copy for his records.

Democratic means ensuring that all people have the same rights. Jefferson was determined to end the special privileges the rich and well-born enjoyed under the Federalists.

Jefferson's personal style matched his democratic beliefs. He preferred informal dinners to the formal parties held by Washington and Adams. He greeted people by shaking hands instead of bowing. European officials were shocked when Jefferson appeared in wrinkled clothes and slippers to receive them. By being informal, Jefferson was showing that the President was an ordinary person.

Federalists feared Jefferson's democratic beliefs. They knew that he supported the French Revolution, and they worried that he would lead a revolution in America. Also, they were afraid that he might punish them because they had used the Alien and Sedition acts to jail Republicans.

In his inaugural speech, Jefferson tried to ease these fears. He pointed out that although Republicans were in the majority, he would not treat the Federalists harshly. "The minority possess their equal rights, which equal law must protect," he stated. Americans must "unite with one heart and one mind." He concluded, "We are all Republicans, we are all Federalists."

Old and New Programs

Jefferson's first job as President was to choose a cabinet that shared his views. He appointed his good friend, James Madison, as Secretary of State. Madison had worked closely with Jefferson to organize the Republican Party. The President chose Albert Gallatin as Secretary of the Treasury. Gallatin was a wizard with finances. Through careful management, he helped Jefferson reduce government expenses.

A few changes. As President, Jefferson kept some Federalist programs but changed others. On Gallatin's advice, Jefferson decided to keep the

Bank of the United States, which he once opposed. (See page 230.) He continued to pay off state debts and let many Federalists keep their government jobs. However, the President and Gallatin disliked the whiskey tax, so it was repealed.

Jefferson also let the Alien and Sedition acts expire, or run out. He freed citizens jailed under the acts and returned to the law that allowed immigrants to become citizens after five years in the country.

Keeping government small. Jefferson believed that the government should protect the rights of its citizens. After that, he believed, government should not interfere in people's lives. This idea is known as *laissez faire* (LEHS AY fehr), from the French term for "let alone." Jefferson put this idea into practice when he reduced the number of people in government and made the navy smaller.

Jefferson's policy of laissez faire was very different from Hamilton's view of government. Federalists, like Hamilton, wanted the government to promote trade, commerce, and manufacturing. They also wanted a strong army and navy.

John Marshall and the Supreme Court

President Jefferson's programs were popular, and his Republican followers controlled Congress. But the Federalists remained powerful in the federal courts. Before leaving office in 1800, President John Adams appointed a number of new judges. Among them was John Marshall, the Chief Justice of the Supreme Court. So when Jefferson became President, he found John Marshall, a strong Federalist, at the head of the Supreme Court.

The early court. Although Jefferson and Marshall differed over politics, they were similar in some ways. Both men were well educated, bright, and owned plantations in Virginia. In fact, they were cousins. Both acted informally. Indeed, Marshall was absent-minded to the point that he sometimes even forgot to comb his hair.

In 1801, Marshall arrived in Washington. At the time, there was no Supreme Court building. The place where it was to be built was still a marsh covered with brambles. So the justices met in the basement of the Capitol.

The six justices kept mostly to themselves. They lived in the same small boardinghouse, ate together, and seldom went to parties. Members of Congress and other government officials scarcely knew them. In fact, Justice William Paterson and President Jefferson once traveled all day on the same stagecoach without either man recognizing the other!

Marbury* v. *Madison. John Marshall strongly influenced the decisions

John Marshall served as Chief Justice of the Supreme Court for 34 years. During that time, he wrote more than 500 decisions. His ideas influenced the shape of the national government, which he believed should be more powerful than state governments.

of the Supreme Court for over 30 years. He made his most important decision in an 1803 case known as **Marbury v. Madison.***

The case—a complicated one—involved the Judiciary Act. Under this act, President Adams had appointed many new judges just before he left office. The Supreme Court decided *Marbury* v. *Madison* by striking down the Judiciary Act. The law, said the Court, was unconstitutional. Congress had no right to pass it.

The Court's decision, written by Chief Justice Marshall, set an important precedent. The decision established the right of the Supreme Court to judge any law made by Congress and to declare that law unconstitutional. The right of the Court to review laws is known as *judicial review.*

When Jefferson heard of the decision, he worried that the Supreme Court was growing too powerful. But Marshall used the Court's power carefully. Today, the Supreme Court still exercises the right of judicial review.

━━ SECTION REVIEW ━━

1. **Define:** democratic, laissez faire, judicial review.
2. How did Jefferson try to reassure the Federalists?
3. (a) Name two Federalist programs Jefferson did not change. (b) Describe one change he did make.
4. What branch of government did John Marshall influence?
5. **What Do You Think?** Why do you think Jefferson was afraid the Supreme Court might get too much power?

---

*Every case brought before a court has two parties. One is the plaintiff, or person with a complaint. The other is the defendant, or person who must defend against the complaint. The plaintiff's name appears first, followed by the defendant's name. The v. means versus, or against.

2 The Nation Doubles in Size

Read to Learn

★ Why was the Mississippi River important to western farmers?
★ How did the United States get Louisiana?
★ What lands did Lewis and Clark explore?
★ What do these words mean: continental divide?

The United States gained most of the land east of the Mississippi in 1783. Spain still owned the land to the west, known as Louisiana.* Many American settlers looked eagerly at Louisiana. In 1803, President Jefferson took a step that doubled the nation in size and set it on a course of expansion for years to come.

Control of the Mississippi

By 1800, almost one million Americans lived between the Appalachians and the Mississippi River. Most were farmers. The cheapest way to get their goods to markets on the east coast was to ship them down the Mississippi to New Orleans. Goods were stored in warehouses there until they could be loaded onto ships. Of course, farmers in the West were very concerned about who controlled the Mississippi and the port of New Orleans.

From time to time, Spain threatened to close New Orleans to Americans. In 1795, President Washington

---

*In 1763, Spain gained control of the Mississippi River from France. It also gained lands west of the Mississippi, known as Louisiana.

sent Thomas Pinckney to Spain to find a way to keep the port open. Pinckney negotiated a treaty with Spain. In the **Pinckney Treaty,** Spain agreed to let Americans ship their goods down the Mississippi and store them in New Orleans. The treaty also settled a dispute over the northern border of Spanish Florida.

For a time, Americans sent their goods to New Orleans without problem. Then, in 1800, Spain signed a secret treaty with Napoleon Bonaparte of France. The Spanish gave Louisiana back to France. When President Jefferson learned about the treaty, he was alarmed. Napoleon was an amibitious empire builder. His armies were winning battles all across Europe. Jefferson was afraid that Napoleon might want to build an empire in North America as well as in Europe.

Revolt in Haiti

Jefferson had reason to worry. Napoleon had plans to increase French power in America. He wanted to ship food from Louisiana to French islands in the West Indies. But his plan soon ran into trouble because of events in Haiti.*

Haiti was a French colony in the Caribbean. White French planters in Haiti grew rich from growing and exporting sugar. During the French Revolution, however, black slaves who worked the sugar plantations fought for their freedom. They were led by Toussaint L'Ouverture (too SAN loo vehr TYOOR). By 1801, Toussaint had forced the French out of Haiti.

Napoleon sent troops to regain control of Haiti. He expected to win easily, but the Haitians resisted fiercely. Many French soldiers died from yellow fever. Although Toussaint was taken prisoner, the French were unable to conquer the island.

---

*Haiti occupies the western half of Hispaniola, one of the islands Columbus explored.

In 1791, Toussaint L'Ouverture led slaves in Haiti in a revolt against French rule. After 13 years of fighting, L'Ouverture was captured. Although he died in a French prison, his followers won independence for Haiti in 1804.

The Louisiana Purchase

Napoleon's troubles in Haiti benefited the United States. About the time that the French were losing in Haiti, President Jefferson sent Robert Livingston and James Monroe to France. Jefferson wanted to buy New Orleans from Napoleon to be sure that Americans could always use the city. The President told Livingston and Monroe to offer up to $10 million for the city.

The Americans talked to Napoleon's foreign minister, Talleyrand. At first, Talleyrand showed little interest in the offer. But then, French defeats in Haiti ruined Napoleon's dreams of empire in America. Also, Napoleon needed money to fight his wars in Europe. Suddenly, Talleyrand asked Livingston if the United States wanted to buy all of Louisiana, not just New Orleans.

Livingston and Monroe could hardly believe their ears. They did not have orders to buy all of Louisiana. But they knew Jefferson wanted control of the Mississippi. In the end, they agreed to pay the French $15 million for Louisiana. Neither the French nor the Americans consulted the various Indian nations who lived on the land about the purchase.

Jefferson was delighted when he heard the news. Like many other Americans, he was sure that Louisiana would help make the United States a great nation. He had one doubt, however. Did the Constitution give the President the right to buy land?

After much thought, he decided that the President did have the power to buy land because the Constitution allowed the President to make treaties. In 1803, the Senate agreed when it approved the *Louisiana Purchase*. The United States took control of vast new lands west of the Mississippi.

Lewis and Clark Set Out

In 1803, Congress provided money for a team of explorers to study the newly bought land. Jefferson chose Meriwether Lewis, his Virginia neighbor and his private secretary, to head the team. Lewis asked another Virginian, William Clark, to join him. Lewis and Clark chose about 40 men to go with them.

Jefferson gave Lewis and Clark careful instructions. He asked them to map the country and make notes about the Native American peoples they met. They were to study the climate, wildlife, and mineral resources of the land. The President hoped that the explorers would find a route to the Pacific and develop trade with the Indians.

In May 1804, Lewis and Clark started up the Missouri River from St. Louis on a journey that would take them all the way to the Pacific. (Follow their route on the map at right.) At first, progress was slow. The lower Missouri was full of tree limbs and stumps that snagged their boats. Also, they were traveling against the swift current. One night, the current tore away the riverbank where they were camping. The party had to scramble into their boats to avoid being washed downstream.

Lewis and Clark kept journals on their travels. They marveled at the broad, grassy plains that stretched "as far as the eye can reach." Everywhere, they saw "immense herds of buffalo, deer, elk, and antelopes." In their journals, they described flocks of pelicans on the river banks and prairie dogs digging burrows.

Lewis and Clark met people from many different Indian nations. They gave medals with the seal of the United States government to Indian leaders. The leaders often invited Lewis and Clark to their villages and had them carried on buffalo hides as a sign of friendship.

Ahead to the Rockies

During the first winter, Lewis and Clark set up a camp with the Mandan Indians near Bismarck, North Dakota. The explorers planned to continue up the Missouri in the spring. But they worried about how they would cross the steep Rocky Mountains. Luckily, Sacajawea (sahk uh juh WEE uh), a Shoshone Indian, and her French Canadian husband were staying with the Mandans that winter. The Shoshones (shoh SHOH neez) lived in the Rocky Mountains, and Sacajawea offered to act as guide and interpreter.

In April 1805, the party traveled up the Missouri past the Yellowstone River. Lewis described the Great Falls of the Missouri as "the grandest sight I ever beheld." In the foothills of the Rockies, the country changed. Bighorn sheep ran along the high hills. The climate was drier. The sharp thorns of

Every map tells a story. Many maps in this book tell the story of explorers moving across the land and sea. See, for example, the routes of Dias and da Gama on page 57. Other maps show the movements of troops or ships during a war. See the battle maps on pages 182 and 186.

When Lewis and Clark set out in 1804, their job was to map the lands in the Louisiana Purchase.

1. **Study the map to see what it shows.** (a) What is the subject of this map? (b) What color shows the route of Lewis and Clark?

2. **Practice reading directions on the map.** To follow a route on a map, you need to determine in what direction or directions the route goes. Find the directional arrow that shows, N, S, E, and W. Sometimes, you need to combine directions when explorers travel in a direction between north and east. In this case, they are said to be traveling northeast (NE). They could also travel to the northwest (NW), southeast (SE), or southwest (SW). (a) In what direction did Lewis and Clark travel after they left St. Louis? (b) In what direction did they travel along the Columbia River?

3. **Describe movements on a map in terms of direction.** Maps like this one show movement. (a) Describe the directions in which Pike traveled during 1806 and 1807. (b) What city did he reach at the end of his trip?

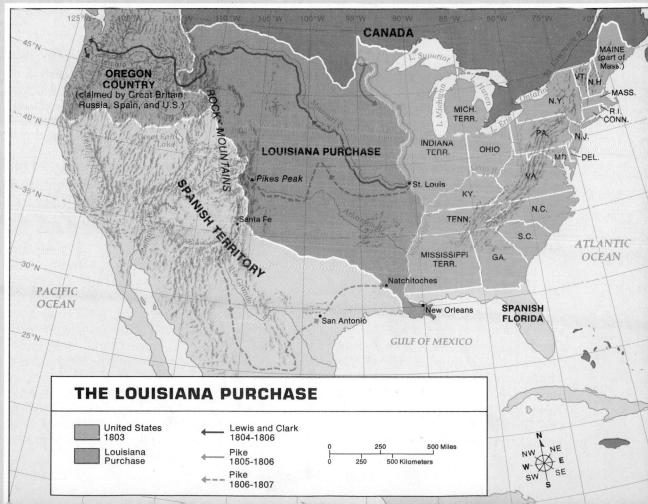

THE LOUISIANA PURCHASE

United States 1803

Louisiana Purchase

→ Lewis and Clark 1804-1806

← Pike 1805-1806

⇠ Pike 1806-1807

0   250   500 Miles
0   250   500 Kilometers

Here, Lewis and Clark look out on the Great Falls of the Missouri River. With them are Sacajawea, their Native American guide, and York, Clark's black servant. Lewis and Clark's account of the animals and lands in the Louisiana Purchase created much enthusiasm back east.

prickly pears jabbed through the explorers' moccasins. Once, a grizzly bear chased Lewis when he was exploring alone.

As they neared the Rockies, Sacajawea recognized the lands of her people. One day, Lewis returned to camp with some Indian leaders. Sacajawea began "to dance and show every mark of the most extravagant joy." One of the men was her brother. Lewis and Clark bought horses from the Shoshones and found out from them the best route to follow across the mountains.

On to the Pacific

In the Rockies, the explorers found rivers that flowed west toward the Pacific. They realized that they had crossed a continental divide. A *continental divide* is a mountain ridge that separates river systems. In North America, the continental divide is in the Rockies. Rivers east of the continental divide flow into the Mississippi and the Gulf of Mexico. West of the continental divide, rivers flow into the Pacific Ocean and Gulf of California.

Lewis and Clark found a large river flowing west. They built canoes and headed downstream until they reached the Columbia River.

In the Pacific Northwest, Lewis and Clark met the Nez Percé (NEHZ puhr SAY) Indians. The explorers wanted to learn about the Nez Percés, but every question had to go through four translators. First, their English words were translated into French for Sacajawea's husband. He then translated the French into Mandan. Sacajawea translated the Mandan into Shoshone. Then, a Shoshone who lived with the Nez Percés translated the question into Nez Percé. Of course, every answer went through the same process in reverse.

On November 7, 1805, Lewis and Clark reached their goal. Lewis wrote in his journal: "Great joy in camp. We are in view of the ocean, this great

Pacific Ocean which we have been so long anxious to see." On a nearby tree, Clark carved, "By Land from the U. States in 1804 & 5."

The trip back to St. Louis took another year. In 1806, Americans celebrated the news of the return of Lewis and Clark. The explorers brought back much valuable information about the Louisiana Purchase. They lost only one man from sickness. Except for one small battle, they got along peacefully with Native Americans in the West.

Pike's Route West

Even before Lewis and Clark returned, another explorer, Zebulon Pike, set out from St. Louis. From 1805 to 1807, he explored the upper Mississippi River, the Kansas and Arkansas rivers, and parts of Colorado and New Mexico. On Thanksgiving Day 1806, Pike saw a tall mountain, today called Pikes Peak, in Colorado. Later, he headed into Spanish lands in the Southwest. The Spanish arrested him. In the end, Pike made his way home with news of the lands he had visited.

Many Indians lived in the lands that Lewis, Clark, and Pike visited. White settlers did not push onto these lands right away. But the area around New Orleans soon had a large enough white population to apply for statehood. In 1812, this area entered the Union as the state of Louisiana.

SECTION REVIEW

1. **Locate:** Mississippi River, New Orleans, Haiti, Louisiana Purchase, Missouri River, Rocky Mountains, Columbia River, Pacific Ocean, Pikes Peak.

2. **Define:** continental divide.

3. (a) What was the purpose of the journey of Lewis and Clark? (b) How did Sacajawea help them?

4. What areas did Zebulon Pike explore?

5. **What Do You Think?** Why do you think Jefferson was both praised and criticized for the Louisiana Purchase?

3 Dangers at Sea

Read to Learn

★ How was American trade threatened in the early 1800s?

★ Why did British warships seize American sailors?

★ Why were the Embargo and Nonintercourse acts unpopular?

★ What do these words mean: impressment, embargo?

Jefferson won popular support for the Louisiana Purchase. The nation was growing rapidly, and Americans were looking for new lands to settle. During this time, too, Americans were reaching out overseas. American traders looked for new markets. Yankee ships sailed to Europe, the West Indies, and even China.

Yankee Traders

In the years after the Revolution, American trade grew rapidly. Ships sailed out of New England ports on voyages that sometimes lasted three years. When captains put into foreign ports, they kept a sharp lookout for trade goods and new markets in which to sell. Traders often took big risks, hoping for bigger profits in return. One clever trader sawed up the winter ice from New England ponds, packed it deep in sawdust, and carried it to India. There, he traded the ice for silks and spices.

In 1784, the *Empress of China* became the first American ship to trade with China. Before long, New England merchants built up a profitable trade with China. Yankee traders took ginseng, a plant that grew wild in New England, and exchanged it for Chinese silks and tea. The Chinese used the roots of the ginseng plant for medicines.

In the 1790s, Yankee ships sailed up the Pacific coast of North America. In fact, Yankee traders visited the Columbia River more than ten years before Lewis and Clark reached it by land. For a time, traders from Boston were so common in the Pacific Northwest that Native Americans called every white man "Boston." Traders bought furs from Native Americans. They then sold the furs for large profits in China.

War With Tripoli

American trading ships ran great risks, especially in the Mediterranean Sea. For many years, the rulers of the Barbary States on the coast of North Africa attacked American and European ships. The United States and many European countries were forced to pay a yearly tribute, or bribe, to protect their ships from attack. (See the map below.)

The ruler of Tripoli, one of the Barbary States, wanted the United States to pay an even bigger bribe. When President Jefferson refused, Tripoli declared war on the United States. In response, Jefferson ordered American ships to blockade the port of Tripoli.

One of the American ships, the *Philadelphia,* ran aground near Tripoli. Tripoli pirates swarmed on board and imprisoned the crew. The pirates planned to use the *Philadelphia* to attack other ships. But a brave American officer, Lieutenant Stephen Decatur, had other plans. Late one night, Decatur and his crew sailed quietly into Tripoli harbor. They boarded the captured ship and set it on fire so that the pirates could not use it.

Meanwhile, a force of American marines marched 500 miles (800 km) across North Africa to make a surprise attack on Tripoli. The war with Tripoli lasted until 1805. In the end, the ruler of Tripoli signed a treaty promising to let American ships alone.

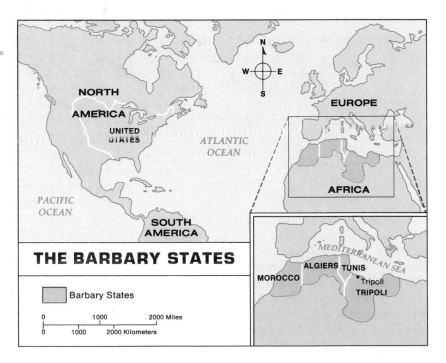

MAP SKILL President Jefferson wanted to end the practice of paying tribute to the Barbary States. Where were the Barbary States located?

In a daring nighttime raid, Decatur boarded a captured ship in Tripoli harbor and set it on fire. Americans looked on Decatur as a national hero. Even the great British admiral, Lord Nelson, called Decatur's deed "the most . . . daring act of the age."

More Troubles at Sea

During the early 1800s, American ships faced another problem at sea. In 1803, Britain and France went to war again. At first, Americans profited from the war. British and French ships were so busy fighting that they could not engage in trade. American merchants took advantage of the war to trade with both sides. As trade increased, American shipbuilders hurried to build new ships.

Neutral ships are seized. Then, Britain and France each tried to cut off trade to the other country. Americans claimed that they were neutral. But the warring countries ignored this claim as they had in the 1790s. (See page 227.) Napoleon seized American ships bound for England. At the same time, the British seized American ships carrying goods to and from France. Between 1805 and 1807, hundreds of American ships were seized.

Impressment of American sailors. Not only did Britain seize American ships, but it also took American sailors and forced them to serve on British ships. This practice was called *impressment.* The practice was common in Britain. For centuries, impressment gangs had raided villages and forced young men to serve in the navy.

In the early 1800s, many British sailors preferred to sail on American ships. They earned better wages, and conditions on American ships were less harsh. Once, the entire crew of a British ship that was docked at Norfolk, Virginia, deserted to join an American ship.

Because of the war with France, the British navy needed all the sailors it

American Foreign Trade, 1800–1812

Millions of Dollars vs. Year

Source: *Historical Statistics of the United States*

GRAPH SKILL In the early 1800s, trade was important to the new nation, especially to New Englanders. Why do you think trade was increasing up to 1807?

could find. Its warships began stopping and searching American merchant ships. If a British officer found English sailors on board a ship, he forced them off and made them serve in the British navy. If a sailor claimed to have become an American citizen, the officer impressed him anyway. "Once an Englishman, always an Englishman," the British claimed. Even worse, the British impressed thousands of American sailors.

One young American, James Brown, secretly sent a letter to his brother. "Being on shore one day in Lisbon, in Portugal," he wrote, "I was impressed by a gang and brought on board the [British ship] *Conqueror*, where I am still confined. Never have I been allowed to put my foot on shore since I was brought on board, which is now three years."

Two Unpopular Acts

Americans were furious with the British for impressing their sailors and attacking their ships. Many wanted to declare war on Britain. Like Washing-

Americans resented the highhanded way in which British officers seized American sailors at sea. The British defended impressment by saying they were only taking deserters from their own navy. The British often ignored documents Congress gave sailors to prove they were American citizens.

In the early 1800s, the United States watched events in Europe with growing concern. As this 1805 cartoon shows, Americans feared that King George III of Britain and Napoleon Bonaparte of France were carving up the world. Napoleon controlled much of Europe. The British ruled the seas.

ton and Adams, President Jefferson wanted to avoid war. He knew that the small American navy could not match the powerful British fleet.

Instead, in 1807, he convinced Congress to pass the Embargo Act. An *embargo* is a ban on trade with another country. The *Embargo Act* forbade Americans to export or import any goods. Jefferson hoped that the embargo would hurt France and Britain because they would be unable to get badly needed goods. He could then offer to end the embargo if they would let Americans trade in peace.

Britain and France were hurt by the embargo. But Americans suffered even more. American sailors lost their jobs. Farmers were hurt because they could not ship wheat abroad. Docks in the South were piled high with cotton and tobacco. Ordinary citizens were unable to get imports such as sugar, salt, tea, and molasses.

The Embargo Act hurt New England merchants most, and they protested strongly. Finally, Jefferson admitted that the Embargo Act was a mistake. In 1809, Congress replaced it

with the *Nonintercourse Act.* Under this act, Americans could trade with all nations except Britain and France. Also, if either Britain or France agreed to stop seizing American ships and sailors, the President could restore trade with that country.

Jefferson signed the Nonintercourse Act a few days before his second term ended. The year before, he had decided not to run for a third term as President. James Madison, his friend, ran and won an easy victory. When Madison took office in 1809, he hoped that Britain and France would soon give in to American pressure.

SECTION REVIEW

1. **Define:** impressment, embargo.
2. (a) Why did Jefferson blockade Tripoli? (b) Describe one result of the war.
3. How did Britain anger the United States in the early 1800s?
4. (a) What was the purpose of the Embargo Act? (b) Why was it replaced?
5. **What Do You Think?** How do you think Jefferson's limits on trade hurt the American economy?

4 War Fever

★ Why did the War Hawks want to fight Britain?

★ How did Tecumseh win the respect of the Indians?

★ What does this word mean: nationalism?

Like other Presidents, James Madison wanted to keep the nation out of war. But events at home and abroad proved to be beyond his control. France and Britain continued to seize American ships. By 1812, much of the nation had caught war fever.

The War Hawks

In 1810, Napoleon promised to respect the rights of American ships. So Madison let Americans trade with France again. Britain refused to make a similar promise. So the embargo against Britain went on.

In Congress, feelings ran strongly against Britain. Only New Englanders wanted trade with Britain to be restored. Many representatives from the South and West wanted war with Britain. They were known as the *War Hawks.* The War Hawks had a strong sense of nationalism. *Nationalism* is pride in or devotion to one's own country. The War Hawks felt that Britain was insulting the United States by seizing American ships and sailors.

The most outspoken War Hawk was Henry Clay of Kentucky. Clay wanted war for two main reasons. He wanted revenge on Britain for attacking American ships. Also, he wanted an excuse to conquer Canada. "The militia of Kentucky are alone competent [able] to place Montreal and Upper Canada at your feet," Clay boasted to Congress.

Westward Expansion

The War Hawks had yet another reason for wanting war with Britain. They claimed that Britain was arming Indians on the frontier and encouraging them to attack American settlers. In fact, this time it was not British meddling but rather American expansion that caused new fighting between Native Americans and settlers.

Under the Treaty of Greenville, Native Americans were forced to sell much of their Ohio land in 1795. (See page 229.) In 1803, Ohio was admitted to the Union. By then, thousands of settlers were pushing farther west into the Indiana Territory. These settlers began taking over Indian lands.

William Henry Harrison, governor of the Indiana Territory, supported the settlers' desire for land. Harrison looked down on Indians, calling them "wretched savages." In 1809, he tricked a few Indian leaders into signing a treaty. In it, they gave up 3 million acres for less than half a cent an acre.

Tecumseh Takes a Stand

Many Native Americans were furious over this treaty. They claimed that the men who signed it did not have the right to sell the land. Among those angered by the sale were two Shawnee leaders: Tecumseh (tih KUM suh) and his brother, called the Prophet. The two men wanted to keep settlers from taking more Indian land.

Strong leaders. Tecumseh had fought at the Battle of Fallen Timbers. In the early 1800s, he organized many Native American nations into a confederation. The Prophet provided spiritual leadership for the confederation.

Tecumseh and the Prophet urged Native Americans to preserve their traditional ways. Many white customs, they said, were corrupting the Indian way of life. They took a strong stand against whiskey. White traders used gifts of whiskey to trick Indians into selling land and furs cheaply.

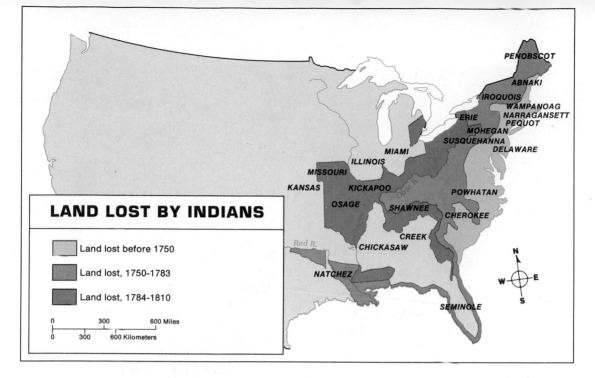

LAND LOST BY INDIANS

Land lost before 1750

Land lost, 1750-1783

Land lost, 1784-1810

0 300 600 Miles
0 300 600 Kilometers

PENOBSCOT
ABNAKI
IROQUOIS
WAMPANOAG
NARRAGANSETT
PEQUOT
ERIE
MOHEGAN
SUSQUEHANNA
DELAWARE
MIAMI
ILLINOIS
MISSOURI
KANSAS
KICKAPOO
OSAGE
SHAWNEE
POWHATAN
CHEROKEE
CREEK
CHICKASAW
Red R.
Ohio R.
NATCHEZ
SEMINOLE

N S E W

MAP SKILL As settlers moved west, they took over Indian lands. When did Indians in the East lose their lands? Which Native American groups in the West lost lands between 1784 and 1810?

Tecumseh earned the respect of Native Americans. He convinced them to unite against white settlers. "Until lately," he said, "there was no white man on this continent. . . . It all belonged to red men." The whites have "driven us from the great salt water, forced us over the mountains. . . . The way—and the only way— to check and to stop this evil is for all the red men to unite in claiming a common equal right in the land."

Even white leaders saw how much influence Tecumseh had among Native Americans. Harrison grudgingly admitted, "He is one of those uncommon geniuses which spring up occasionally to produce revolutions and overturn the established order of things."

Battle of Tippecanoe. Rivalries between Indian nations prevented Tecumseh from uniting all the Indians east of the Mississippi River. Still, white settlers were alarmed at his success. In 1811, they convinced Governor Harrison to march on Tecumseh's settlement at Tippecanoe Creek in Indiana. At the time, Tecumseh was away meeting with Indian leaders to the south. His brother was in charge.

The Prophet decided to meet the danger by leading a surprise night attack on Harrison's troops. In the battle that followed, neither side won a real victory. But white people in the East celebrated the *Battle of Tippecanoe* as a major victory.

The next year, war between Britain and the United States appeared likely. Tecumseh went north to speak to the British in Canada. He offered to lead his Indian confederation against the Americans if war broke out.

War Is Declared

The Battle of Tippecanoe marked the beginning of a long, deadly war between Native Americans and white settlers on the frontier. It also added fuel to the claim of the War Hawks that Britain was arming the Indians.

Using this claim, the War Hawks stepped up the pressure for war. They

Tecumseh, at left, and the Prophet, at right, called on Indian nations to stop selling land to the United States government. Tecumseh argued that the land belonged to all Indians and should not be divided or sold unless all agreed.

brought up other arguments, too. The United States must defend its rights at sea and end impressment. They urged Americans to conquer not only Canada but also Florida, which belonged to Spain, Britain's ally.

Finally, on June 18, 1812, President Madison gave in to the pressure. He asked Congress to declare war on Britain. Congress quickly agreed. Americans soon discovered that winning the war would not be as easy as they thought.

SECTION REVIEW

1. **Locate:** Ohio, Indiana Territory, Canada, Spanish Florida.
2. **Define:** nationalism.
3. What did the War Hawks hope to gain from a war with Britain?
4. (a) Who was Tecumseh? (b) What did he think the Indians should do to save their lands?
5. **What Do You Think?** Why do you think President Madison was unable to avoid war with Britain?

5 The War of 1812

Read to Learn
★ What were the major battles in the War of 1812?
★ How did the Indians help the British?
★ What issues did the peace treaty settle?

Despite the eagerness of the War Hawks, the nation was deeply divided over the war. People in the South and West generally supported the war. New Englanders mostly opposed it. British impressment hurt trade, but New Englanders knew that war would disrupt trade even more. They spoke with scorn of "Mr. Madison's war."

The War at Sea

The nation was not ready for war. The American army was small and poorly trained. Its navy had only 16 ships fit to fight against the huge British navy. Yet Britain, too, had problems. It was locked in a deadly struggle with Napoleon in Europe and could spare few troops to defend Canada.

When the war began, Britain used its powerful navy to blockade American ports. It wanted to stop Americans from trading with other countries. The American navy was too small to break the blockade. Still, the Americans had several talented young captains who won stunning battles at sea.

One famous battle took place in August 1812. Captain Isaac Hull was in command of the *Constitution* when he saw a British frigate, the *Guerrière* (gair ee AIR), south of Newfoundland. For close to an hour, the two ships maneuvered into position. The *Guerrière* fired on the *Constitution* several times. Captain Hull ordered his sailors to hold their fire. When he finally got close enough, Hull bent over to shout to the sailors below, "Now boys, you may fire!" He bent over so forcefully that his trousers split at the seams!

The guns of the *Constitution* roared into action. They ripped large holes in the *Guerrière* and shot off both masts. When the smoke cleared, Hull asked the British captain if he had "struck" his flag—that is, surrendered by lowering his flag. The British captain was stunned by the attack. He could only reply: "Well, I don't know. Our mizzenmast is gone, our mainmast is gone. And, upon the whole, you may say we *have* struck our flag."

During the war, American ships won other victories at sea. Although these victories cheered Americans, they did little to help win the war.

Fighting in the West

In 1812, the War Hawks demanded an invasion of Canada. They expected Canadians to welcome the chance to throw off British rule. They also thought that Americans could easily defeat the British troops in Canada.

The United States planned to invade Canada at three points: Detroit, Niagara Falls, and Montreal. To the surprise of the War Hawks, Canadians did not welcome the Americans. Instead, they fought back fiercely and forced Americans to retreat.

Invasion of Canada. In the West, William Hull led American forces from Detroit into Canada. The Canadians had only a few untrained troops there. To trick the Americans, General Isaac Brock paraded his soldiers in red cloaks to make Hull think that they were experienced British regulars. Tecumseh helped the Canadians by making raids on Hull's troops. As another trick, Brock allowed false "secret" messages to fall into American hands. One such message said that 5,000 Indians were helping him when, in fact, the number was far less.

Brock's tricks worked, and Hull retreated from Canada. The British followed him and captured Detroit. The Americans were unable to retake Detroit because the British controlled Lake Erie.

The battle for Lake Erie. In 1813, the Americans set out to win control of Lake Erie. Captain Oliver Hazard Perry had no fleet. So he designed and built his own ships. In September 1813, he sailed his tiny fleet into battle against the British.

During the battle, Perry's own ship was battered by the British and left helpless. Perry took his flag down and rowed over to another American ship. There, he hoisted the colors again and continued to fight. The battle ended with an American victory. Perry wrote his message of victory on the back of an envelope. "We have met the enemy and they are ours."

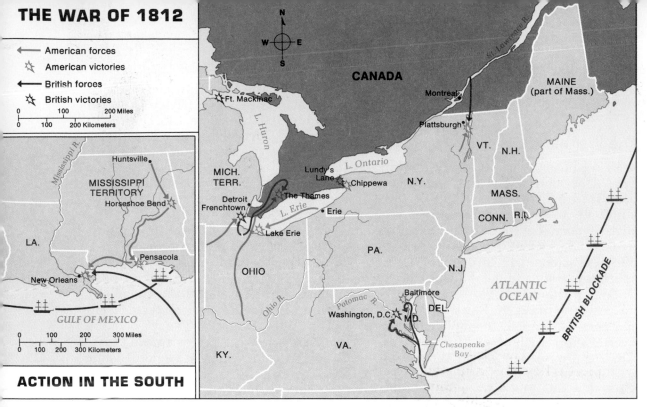

THE WAR OF 1812

Legend:
- ← American forces
- ☆ American victories
- ← British forces
- ☆ British victories

0   100   200 Miles
0   100   200 Kilometers

ACTION IN THE SOUTH

(Map labels — Main map:) CANADA, MAINE (part of Mass.), St. Lawrence R., Montreal, Plattsburgh, Ft. Mackinac, L. Huron, L. Ontario, Lundy's Lane, Chippewa, VT., N.H., MICH. TERR., Detroit, Frenchtown, The Thames, L. Erie, Erie, Lake Erie, N.Y., MASS., CONN., R.I., N.J., OHIO, PA., Ohio R., Potomac R., Baltimore, Washington, D.C., MD., DEL., ATLANTIC OCEAN, Chesapeake Bay, VA., KY., BRITISH BLOCKADE

(Map labels — Action in the South inset:) Mississippi R., Huntsville, MISSISSIPPI TERRITORY, Horseshoe Bend, LA., Pensacola, New Orleans, GULF OF MEXICO

0   100   200   300 Miles
0   100   200   300 Kilometers

MAP SKILL The War of 1812 was fought on several fronts. What battles took place in or near Canada? Which of these were American victories?

Indian losses. With Lake Erie in American hands, Tecumseh and the British were forced to abandon Detroit. General Harrison pursued them into Canada. At the ***Battle of the Thames,*** the Americans won a decisive victory. Tecumseh died in the fighting. With Tecumseh gone, the Indian confederation he had organized fell apart. Rivalries among the Indians led to more disasters.

The Creeks, Tecumseh's allies to the south, were divided over what to do. Some wanted to keep up the battle against white settlers. They were known as the Red Stick—a symbol for war—faction. During the fighting, both settlers and Indians committed brutal acts. Many were killed on both sides. A Tennessee officer, Andrew Jackson, took command of American forces in the Creek War.

In 1814, Jackson led his forces against the Creeks. With the help of the Cherokees, Jackson won a decisive victory at the ***Battle of Horseshoe***

Bend. The battle ended the fighting for the moment. Once again, the Indians had to give up land to white settlers.

Burning of Washington

In 1814, Britain and its allies finally defeated Napoleon. With the fighting over in Europe, Britain began sending its best troops to America. The British planned to invade the United States from Canada in the north and from New Orleans in the south. At the same time, they began raiding American cities along the east coast. (See the map above.)

British ships sailed into Chesapeake Bay in August 1814. They put troops ashore about 30 miles (48 km) from Washington. American troops met the British at Bladensburg, Maryland. President Madison rode out to watch, carrying a set of dueling pistols in case of trouble. What he saw disappointed him. The experienced British soldiers quickly scattered the poorly

—258—

trained Americans. Washington was left undefended.

In the President's mansion, Dolley Madison anxiously waited for her husband to return. Her guard of soldiers disappeared. She scrawled a note to her sister Anna: "Will you believe it, my sister? We have had a battle or skirmish near Bladensburg and here I am still within sound of the cannon! Mr. Madison comes not. May God protect us. Two messengers covered with dust come to bid me fly. But here I mean to wait for him."

As British troops marched into the city, Dolley Madison gathered up important papers of the President and a fine portrait of George Washington. She fled south. The British captured the capital. They set fire to the President's mansion and other public buildings before leaving Washington.*

From Washington, the British marched north toward Baltimore. However, Baltimore was well defended, and the British were forced to give up the attack. (Read "The Star-Spangled Banner" on page 261.)

Battle of New Orleans

Meanwhile, another British force was threatening the United States in the south. In late 1814, the British decided to attack New Orleans. From there, they hoped to sail up the Mississippi. But Andrew Jackson was waiting for them. Jackson had turned his frontier fighters into a strong army. He took Pensacola in Spanish Florida to keep the British from using it as a base. He then marched through Mobile and set up camp in New Orleans.

On Christmas Eve 1814, Jackson's troops surprised the British invaders outside New Orleans. After a brief battle, the Americans withdrew. They dug trenches to defend themselves. During

---

*When Washington was rebuilt after the fire, the President's mansion was given a coat of whitewash to cover the black charring. After that, it became known as the White House.

AMERICANS WHO DARED

Dolley Madison

Dolley Madison influenced the social life of Washington for almost 50 years. Her career there began when her husband, James Madison, became Secretary of State to President Jefferson. She served as hostess for the widowed Jefferson. When James Madison was elected President, she held the first inaugural ball in Washington. Dolley Madison returned to the Capitol after the British burnt it and managed to entertain visitors as well as ever. Many times, her social skills helped to smooth over quarrels between political leaders.

the first week of January, the British tried to overrun Jackson's defenses. Then, on January 8, 1815, the British launched an all-out attack. In the battle that followed, the British bravely charged forward again and again. Over 2,000 redcoats fell before the deadly fire of American sharpshooters and cannons. Fewer than a dozen American lives were lost.

The **Battle of New Orleans** ended with a complete American victory. In parts of the country, Jackson became a

The bloodiest engagement of the War of 1812 was the Battle of New Orleans, shown here. Andrew Jackson's overwhelming victory made him a popular hero.

popular hero, second only to George Washington. However, Americans later learned that this bloody battle might have been avoided. It took place two weeks after the United States and Britain had signed a peace treaty in Europe.

An End to the War

It took weeks for news to cross the Atlantic in the early 1800s. By late 1814, Americans knew that peace talks had begun. But no one knew how long they would last. While Jackson was preparing to fight the British at New Orleans, New Englanders were meeting to protest "Mr. Madison's war."

The Hartford Convention. In December 1814, delegates from several New England states met in Hartford, Connecticut. Most were Federalists. They disliked the Republican President and the war. The British blockade hurt New England trade. Also, many New

Englanders felt that the South and West would benefit if the nation won land in Canada and Florida. If new states were carved out of these lands, New England would lose influence.

Delegates to the *Hartford Convention* threatened to leave the Union if the war went on. While the convention debated what to do, news of the peace treaty arrived. With the war over, the Hartford Convention quickly ended.

The peace treaty. Peace talks took place in Ghent, Belgium. The *Treaty of Ghent* was signed on December 24, 1814. John Quincy Adams, one of the Americans there, summed up the treaty in these words: "Nothing was adjusted, nothing was settled." Both sides agreed to return to prewar conditions. The treaty did not say anything about impressment or neutral rights. But since Britain was no longer fighting France, these issues had faded.

Other issues, such as who would control the Great Lakes, were settled later through negotiation. In 1817, the

Voices of Freedom

The Star-Spangled Banner

On September 13, 1814, Francis Scott Key was on board a British warship near Baltimore to negotiate the release of an American prisoner. That day, the British began their attack on Fort McHenry, the key to Baltimore's defense.

Key spent a sleepless night on deck. He watched British rockets exploding across the harbor. By dawn on September 14, the bombing had stopped. When the early morning fog lifted, Key was delighted to see that the American flag—the stars and stripes—still waved over Fort McHenry.

Soon after, Key wrote "The Star-Spangled Banner." The poem told the story of his night's watch. Before long, the poem was set to a popular tune and was sung widely. In 1931, Congress made it the national anthem of the United States. The poem begins:

Oh, say, can you see by the dawn's early
    light,
What so proudly we hailed at the twilight's
    last gleaming?
Whose broad stripes and bright stars,
    through the perilous fight,
O'er the ramparts we watched were so
    gallantly streaming?

And the rockets' red glare, the bombs
    bursting in air,
Gave proof through the night that our flag
    was still there.
Oh, say, does that star-spangled banner
    yet wave
O'er the land of the free and the home of
    the brave?

★ How does Key's poem reflect his experiences?

United States and Britain signed the **Rush–Bagot Agreement.** It forbade warships on the Great Lakes. In 1818, the two countries agreed to set much of the border between Canada and the United States at 49°N latitude.

The War of 1812 did benefit the United States in some ways. Britain and other European nations were forced to treat the young republic with respect. Also, the success of heroes like Oliver Hazard Perry and Andrew Jackson gave Americans great pride in their country.

SECTION REVIEW

1. **Locate:** Detroit, Montreal, Lake Erie, Horseshoe Bend, Washington, D.C., Baltimore, New Orleans, Hartford.
2. What unexpected problems did Americans face when they invaded Canada?
3. Why did many New Englanders oppose the war?
4. What did Dolley Madison rescue from Washington?
5. **What Do You Think?** Why do you think the Americans and British fought so hard for control of Lake Erie?

Chapter 11 Review

★ Summary ★

President Thomas Jefferson, a Republican, kept some Federalist programs but changed others. In 1802, he doubled the size of the United States with the Louisiana Purchase. Lewis and Clark explored the newly acquired land.

In the early 1800s, American ships faced many dangers. The French and British ignored the rights of neutral ships. And the British seized American sailors. In 1812, President Madison gave in to pressure from the War Hawks and declared war on Britain.

During the War of 1812, the United States was unable to conquer Canada. There was fierce fighting on the frontier, where Indians tried to defend their lands against white settlers. Andrew Jackson's stunning victory at New Orleans took place two weeks after a peace treaty had been signed but before news of the treaty reached the United States.

★ Reviewing the Facts ★

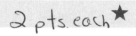
2 pts. each

Key Terms. Match each term in Column 1 with the correct definition in Column 2.

Column 1
1. laissez faire
2. continental divide
3. impressment
4. embargo
5. nationalism

Column 2
a. forcing American sailors to serve on British ships
b. mountain range that separates river systems
c. devotion to one's country
d. ban on trade with another country
e. let alone

Key People, Events, and Ideas. Identify each of the following.
1. Albert Gallatin
2. John Marshall
3. *Marbury* v. *Madison*
4. Toussaint L'Ouverture
5. Meriwether Lewis
6. William Clark
7. Sacajawea
8. Embargo Act
9. War Hawks
10. Henry Clay
11. Tecumseh
12. Oliver Hazard Perry
13. Dolley Madison
14. Hartford Convention
15. Treaty of Ghent

★ Chapter Checkup ★

5 pts. each

1. What precedent did John Marshall set for the Supreme Court?
2. Why did Americans want to control the Mississippi River? (b) How did the revolt in Haiti influence Napoleon's decision to sell Louisiana?
3. (a) Name three parts of the world that American trading ships visited in the early 1800s. (b) Why did President Jefferson blockade Tripoli in 1801?
4. (a) Why did British ships seize American sailors? (b) How did Jefferson try to stop France and Britain from seizing American ships?
5. Describe three causes of the War of 1812.
6. Explain why each of the following was important to Indians in the West: (a) the Prophet; (b) Battle of Tippecanoe; (c) Battle of Horseshoe Bend.

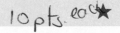
★ Thinking About History

1. **Understanding geography.** (a) How did the Louisiana Purchase affect the size of the United States? (b) What did the journey of Lewis and Clark prove? (c) How do you think these two events could have affected the view Americans had of their country?

2. **Taking a stand.** Do you think that Americans had good reason to invade Canada during the War of 1812? Explain your stand.

3. **Analyzing information.** Review the discussion of relations between white settlers and Indians on pages 92, 104–105, 156–157, 186–187, and 228–229. (a) How did these relations change over time? (b) Why do you think clashes continued to take place between these groups?

4. **Relating past to present.** Reread "The Star-Spangled Banner" on page 261. Why do you think this poem became the national anthem of the United States?

★ Using Your Skills ★

1. **Using visual evidence.** Study the picture on page 248. (a) Who is shown in the picture? (b) What part of the country are they exploring? (c) What geographical features are shown in the picture? (d) Why do you think it took the explorers almost a month to cross this river?

2. **Graph reading.** Study the graph on page 252. (a) What was the value of American foreign trade in 1807? (b) What was its value in 1812? (c) What event or events caused the change?

3. **Map reading.** Study the map on page 258. (a) What British victories are shown on this map? (b) What American victories are shown? (c) Where was the British blockade?

4. **Outlining.** Prepare an outline for Section 4 on pages 254–256. Then write a paragraph summarizing the events leading up to the War of 1812.

5. **Skimming a chapter.** Review the skill on skimming a chapter on page 239. Then practice skimming this chapter. (a) What are the main topics covered in this chapter? (b) What is the general idea of the section called "Dangers at Sea" (pages 249–253)?

★ More to Do ★

1. **Eyewitness reporting.** Prepare an eyewitness report from the point of view of an Indian meeting Lewis and Clark.

2. **Exploring local history.** Study the map on page 247 to determine what part of North America your state belonged to in 1803. Did the Lewis and Clark or the Pike expedition pass through your state? If so, draw the route of the expedition on an outline map of your state. Add to your map the locations of any local monuments to the explorers.

3. **Creating headlines.** Create headlines for newspapers supporting the War Hawks in the early 1800s.

4. **Writing a skit.** As a group project, prepare a short skit in which a British ship stops an American ship at sea. Have students imagine they are British officers planning to impress American sailors into the British navy.

5. **Researching.** Prepare a short biography of Dolley Madison. Explain why she is one of the best-known First Ladies.

CHAPTER

12

The Nation Prospers (1790–1825)

Chapter Outline

1 The Industrial Revolution
2 The Way West
3 Changing Times
4 America's Neighbors

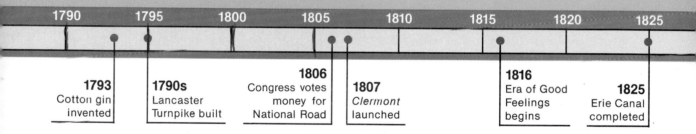

| 1790 | 1795 | 1800 | 1805 | 1810 | 1815 | 1820 | 1825 |

1793
Cotton gin invented

1790s
Lancaster Turnpike built

1806
Congress votes money for National Road

1807
Clermont launched

1816
Era of Good Feelings begins

1825
Erie Canal completed

About This Chapter

After the War of 1812, thousands of Americans moved west. Many of the settlers were immigrants from Britain. Elias Pym Fordham, an Englishman, settled in Illinois. He wrote to friends in England about his new home.

The territory is "peopling so fast that very soon our country will be backed up," Fordham wrote. "Mr. Birkbeck is laying out a farm of 1,600 acres in the midst of his estate of 4,000 acres. My little estate lies on and between two small hills, from which descend several small streams that unite in the valley and flow on through the prairie."

Travel through the western lands was difficult. "I am going down the river in a boat," wrote Fordham. "I went down last autumn in two boats, in one of which I had two horses. To confess the truth, I nearly lost the boats and all the property. It was in the night and a most tremendous thunderstorm came on. The intervals between the flashes of lightning were so dark that we could not see some rocks, which we ran into and hung to all night."

In the early 1800s, America was changing in many ways. The Industrial Revolution was beginning. With the growth of industry, cities expanded rapidly. Many people left farms to work in the growing cities.

Study the time line above. Which events occurred after the War of 1812?

In the early 1800s, thousands of Americans moved west. The National Road, above, was sometimes jammed with people, wagons, and cattle.

1 The Industrial Revolution

Read to Learn

★ What inventions helped start the Industrial Revolution?
★ How did the Industrial Revolution begin in America?
★ What was life like in the Lowell mills?
★ What do these words mean: spinning jenny, cotton gin, capitalist, factory system, interchangeable parts?

The early 1800s brought a new revolution to the United States. Unlike the revolution against British rule, this one had no battles and no fixed dates. Instead, it was a long, slow process that completely changed the way goods were produced.

The Revolution Begins

The new revolution was called the Industrial Revolution. Before the Industrial Revolution, most goods were produced by hand, and most people were farmers. As the *Industrial Revolution* got under way, machines replaced hand tools, and new sources of power, such as steam and electricity, replaced human and animal power. During the Industrial Revolution, the economy shifted from farming to manufacturing, and people moved from farms to the cities.

New ways to spin and weave. The Industrial Revolution began in Britain in the mid-1700s. There, a series of inventions brought a revolution to the textile industry. The spinning of thread and weaving of cloth became mechanized. Before 1750, family members spun fibers into thread and wove it into cloth by hand in their homes. They used simple spinning wheels and hand looms. By the early 1800s, this system had changed.

In 1765, James Hargreaves developed the spinning jenny. With the *spinning jenny,* a person spun several threads at once, not just one thread as on a spinning wheel. In 1769, Richard Arkwright invented a machine that held 100 spindles of thread. This machine was too heavy to be operated by hand. So he used water power to turn it. The new machine was called the water frame.

Other inventions speeded up the process of weaving. In 1785, Edward Cartwright built a loom powered by water. Using this power loom, a worker could produce 200 times more cloth in a day than was possible before. In 1793, an American, Eli Whitney, gave a further boost to the textile industry. Whitney invented the *cotton gin,* a machine that speeded up the process of cleaning cotton fibers. (You will read more about the cotton gin in Chapter 15.)

The factory system. New machines like the water frame had to be set up near rivers because they needed running water to power them.* They were expensive to build. So most were owned by *capitalists,* people with capital, or money, to invest in business to make a profit. Early capitalists built spinning mills and hired hundreds of workers to run the machines.

The spinning mills were the beginning of a new system of production in Britain. Instead of spinning and weaving at home, people went to work in factories. The *factory system* brought workers and machines together in one place to produce goods. In factories, everyone had to work a certain number of hours each day. Workers were paid daily or weekly wages.

Americans Build Factories

Britain led the way in the Industrial Revolution. In the late 1700s, Britain tried to keep its inventions secret from other countries. Parliament passed a law forbidding anyone from taking plans of Arkwright's water frame out of the country. It also said that factory workers could not leave the country.

Enforcing these laws was almost impossible, as Samuel Slater proved. Slater was a bright mechanic who worked in one of Arkwright's mills. He decided to seek his fortune in America, where several states were offering rewards for information about British inventions. Slater knew that British officials often searched the baggage of people sailing to America. So he memorized the design of Arkwright's mill before he sailed for New York in 1789.

In America, Slater heard that Moses Brown, a Quaker merchant, wanted to build a spinning factory in Rhode Island. Slater offered to help Brown. "If I do not make as good yarn as they do in England," he vowed confidently, "I will have nothing for my services, but will throw the whole of what I have attempted over the bridge." Brown hired him.

In 1790, Moses Brown opened his mill in Pawtucket, Rhode Island. It was the first factory in America. Slater worked hard to make the factory succeed. He improved on the machines he had worked with in Britain. In the winter, he was up before daybreak, chopping ice from the water wheel. Slater's wife Hannah helped, too. She developed a way to make stronger thread. Before long, other manufacturers were building mills, using Slater's ideas.

---

*Water flowing down a stream or a waterfall turned a water wheel that produced the power to run the machines.

Rivers powered the textile mills that sprang up across New England during the Industrial Revolution. Here, the building with the smokestack is one of the first American textile mills. Water power turned the wheels that ran machines in this early factory.

At first, American factories only spun threads. Weaving was still done on hand looms. By the early 1800s, Cartwright's power loom found its way to America.

The Lowell Experiment

The War of 1812 gave a boost to American industry. Because the British were blockading the Atlantic coast, Americans started to make goods they had once imported from Europe.

During the war, a clever New England merchant named Francis Cabot Lowell improved on British textile mills. In Britain, spinning was done in one factory and weaving in another. Lowell decided to combine spinning and weaving under one roof.

In 1813, Lowell and several partners formed the *Boston Associates.* They raised about $1 million—a huge sum in those days—to build a textile factory in Waltham, Massachusetts. The new factory had all the machines needed to turn raw cotton into finished cloth. The machines were powered by water from the nearby Charles River.

Life in the Lowell mills. After Lowell's death, the Boston Associates built a factory town and named it after him. In 1821, Lowell, Massachusetts, was a village with only five farm families. By 1836, it was a bustling city of 18,000 people.

The Boston Associates hired young women from nearby farms to work in the Lowell mills. Young women often worked in factories in towns for a few years before they returned to the country to marry. They sent their wages home to help their parents.

At first, farm families hesitated to let their daughters go to work in the Lowell mills. To reassure parents, the Boston Associates built clean boarding-houses for their employees. They hired housemothers to run the houses. The company also planted thousands of shade trees, built churches, and made rules to protect the women.

In the early 1800s, conditions in the Lowell mills were much better than in most factories in Europe. As a result, the Lowell mills were seen by some as a symbol of progress brought about by the Industrial Revolution. But as the factory system spread, conditions grew worse and wages dropped.

Children at work. In the early factories, most workers were women and children. They could be paid less than men.

Children were especially useful in spinning factories. Because they were quick and small, they could easily scamper around machines to change the spindles. For his mill, Samuel Slater hired seven boys and two girls, ranging in age from 7 to 12.

Working hours were long—12 hours a day, 6 days a week. By today's standards, it seems cruel that those children worked such long hours. But in those days, most boys and girls worked long hours on the family farm. Therefore, farm families often let their children work in factories so that they could earn money needed at home.

Interchangeable Parts

In the early 1800s, Eli Whitney came up with an idea that had a great impact on the way goods were produced. Most goods were produced by skilled workers. Whitney knew, for example, that a gunsmith spent many hours making the stock, barrel, and trigger of a rifle. Each rifle was slightly different from the next because each part was made by hand. If a rifle part broke, a gunsmith had to make a new part to fit that gun. This method of making and repairing goods was very slow.

Whitney's idea was to build machines that made each separate part of the gun. Every part would then be exactly alike. All the stocks would be the same size and shape. All the barrels would be the same length. If a trigger broke, it could easily be replaced with another machine-made trigger. Whitney introduced this idea of *interchangeable parts* in making guns. It was a big step forward. Interchangeable parts made it possible to put together and repair goods such as guns quickly.

The use of interchangeable parts spread slowly to other industries. Factories began to produce clocks, knives,

Before the Industrial Revolution, women had spun cloth at home. In the early 1800s, women did much of the work in the new textile factories. They were paid less than men for the same work.

As the new nation grew, Americans celebrated July 4th, or Independence Day, in many ways. By the early 1800s, people celebrated the Fourth with parades, picnics, and patriotic speeches. Symbols such as the American flag with its stars and stripes and the bald eagle became popular.

Americans chose the bald eagle as a symbol of the new republic because of its power. The bald eagle is found only in North America. It is not, in fact, bald but has white feathers on top of its head. Early settlers used the word bald because at a distance the eagle looked bareheaded without brown feathers on top.

Americans soon adopted other symbols. One was the Liberty Bell that was hung in the State House in Philadelphia in 1752. On one side, the bell has these words from the Bible: "Proclaim liberty throughout the land to all the inhabitants thereof." On July 8, 1776, the bell announced the first public reading of the Declaration of Independence.

Uncle Sam is another patriotic symbol. Uncle Sam was a real person— Samuel Wilson of Massachusetts. During the War of 1812, he supplied meat to the army and stamped each barrel U.S. When asked what the initials U.S. stood

for, one of Sam Wilson's employees replied, "Uncle Sam"—meaning Uncle Sam Wilson. The idea that food, uniforms, and other supplies came from Uncle Sam caught on. At first, Uncle Sam appeared in cartoons as a young man with stars and stripes on his shirt. Later, cartoonists drew him with the familiar gray hair, beard, top hat, and tailcoat we see today.

★ Why do you think symbols were important to the new nation?

pistols, locks, and other items with interchangeable parts.

City Life

In the early 1800s, people moved to cities to work in factories. By today's standards, cities were small. A person could walk from one end of a city to the other in 30 minutes. Buildings were only a few stories high. Houses were built of wood, heated by fireplaces, and lit by lamps. As the factory system spread, cities grew.

Dangers. Growing cities had many problems. Fire was a constant threat. If a chimney caught fire, a blaze spread quickly from one wooden house to the next. In most cities, Americans set up volunteer fire departments. New York City had over 1,300 volunteers and 42 hand-drawn or horse-drawn engines. Volunteer fire companies competed fiercely to be first to the scene of a blaze. Sometimes, the rivalry between two companies was so fierce that they brawled in the street while the fire burned on.

Cities had other hazards. Dirt and gravel streets were muddy when it rained. Cities had no sewers, and garbage was thrown into the street. An English visitor to New York reported:

> The streets are filthy, and the stranger is not a little surprised to meet the hogs walking about in them, for the purpose of devouring the vegetables and trash thrown into the gutter.

Because people lived close together in cities, disease spread easily. Yellow fever and cholera epidemics raged through cities, killing hundreds.

Advantages. Despite these problems, cities had much to offer. There were plays to see and museums to visit. Circuses came from time to time. In the 1840s, city dwellers flocked to see hot air balloons carry a few daring passengers into the sky.

Fashions from Europe arrived first in the cities. In the early 1800s, most older American men still wore styles popular in colonial days, including wigs. Some younger men sported loose, full-length trousers instead of tight knee breeches. They wore their own hair, letting it curl down over the forehead. One critic complained that the new hair style looked "as if you had been fighting a hurricane backward."

Beginning in the 1790s, a revolution took place in women's fashion. The high-waisted, narrow lines of the French "Empire" style replaced the older style of full skirts and tightly laced dresses. In the 1840s, however, tight-waisted, restrictive clothing for women again became the fashion.

═══ SECTION REVIEW ═══

1. **Define:** spinning jenny, cotton gin, capitalist, factory system, interchangeable parts.
2. (a) List three inventions of the Industrial Revolution. (b) Briefly explain how each changed the ways goods were produced.
3. How did Samuel Slater contribute to the Industrial Revolution in America?
4. Why were early workers in the factories mostly women and children?
5. **What Do You Think?** Why do you think capitalists were necessary to the Industrial Revolution?

2 The Way West

Read to Learn

★ What routes did settlers take to move west?
★ How were roads improved?
★ Why were steamboats useful?
★ What do these words mean: turnpike, corduroy road, canal?

In the early 1800s, America was a nation on the move. Thousands of settlers headed west. As the nation grew, settlers needed ways to stay in touch with people in the East and transport their goods to market. As a result, Americans turned their attention to improving transportation.

A Flood of Settlers

"Old America seems to be breaking up and moving westward," noted a visitor to the United States in 1817. At that time, the West was the land between the Appalachians and the Mississippi. Settlers had been moving west throughout the 1700s. Even during the Revolution, settlers continued to cross the Appalachians.

In the 1800s, the stream of pioneers heading west turned into a flood. By 1820, so many people had moved west that the population of most of the original 13 states had declined.

Crossing the Appalachian Mountains was hard for settlers. In 1750, however, Thomas Walker pioneered a route through a gap in the mountains near the Cumberland River. The *Cumberland Gap* was a natural gateway for settlers moving into Kentucky and Tennessee.

The rich, black soil of Alabama and Mississippi attracted settlers from Georgia and South Carolina. New Englanders, "Yorkers," and Pennsylvanians pushed into the Northwest Territory along several different routes. One route ran from Albany, New York, west along the Mohawk River through a gap in the Appalachians. (See the map on page 272.) Settlers then followed Indian trails west around Lake Erie. Some took boats across Lake Erie into Ohio.

Another route west was the Great Wagon Road through Pennsylvania that was built in colonial times. At the foothills of the Appalachians, settlers unloaded their wagons and used packhorses to carry their goods across the steep mountain trails to Pittsburgh. There, they loaded their goods onto large flatboats to carry them down the Ohio River into Indiana, Kentucky, and Illinois. Flatboats were well suited to the shallow rivers of the region. Even with a heavy load, they did not sink very deep.

With the flood of settlers, the western lands soon had enough people to apply for statehood. Between 1792 and 1819, eight new states joined the Union: Kentucky (1792), Tennessee (1796), Ohio (1803), Louisiana (1812), Indiana (1816), Mississippi (1817), Illinois (1818), and Alabama (1819).

Improving the Roads

Settlers faced many hardships as they moved west. Among them was poor roads. What people called roads were little more than trails that were too narrow for even a single wagon. Trails often plunged through muddy swamps. Tree stumps stuck up through

AMERICANS WHO DARED

Daniel Boone

As a young man, Daniel Boone learned from Indians how to survive in the wilderness. Dressed in deerskins and carrying a tomahawk, hunting knife, and long rifle, he led pioneers west into Kentucky in 1769. Later, he led settlers along an old Indian path, renamed the Wilderness Road. Boone fought battles with the Indians to protect his new settlement of Boonesboro, Kentucky. In the 1800s, other settlers took the route Boone pioneered.

the road and broke axles on the wagons of careless travelers.

Turnpikes. Perhaps the best road in America was the *Lancaster Turnpike*. It was built in the 1790s between Philadelphia and Lancaster in Pennsylvania. The road was set on a bed of gravel, so rains drained off easily. It was topped with smooth, flat stones.

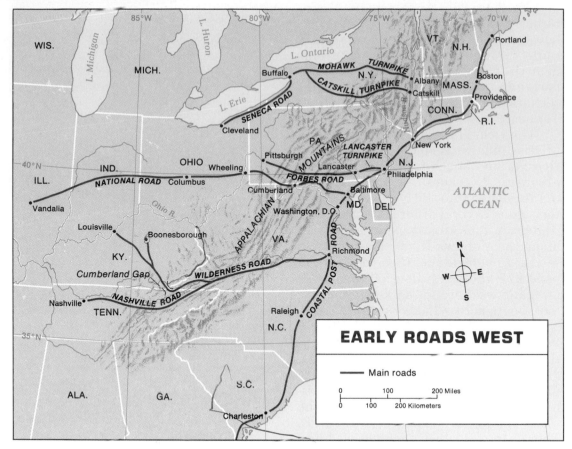

MAP SKILL In the early 1800s, settlers took new roads into the West. Private companies built turnpikes. The National Road was the first road built by the federal government. Today, the National Road is U.S. Highway 40. Through what states did the National Road run in the 1800s?

The Lancaster Turnpike was built by a private company. Other companies also built gravel and stone roads that helped improve travel. To pay for the roads, the companies collected tolls. At certain places along a road, a pole, called a pike, blocked the road. After a wagon paid a toll, the pike was turned aside. Roads with these pikes were called *turnpikes,* often shortened to pikes.

Gravel and stone roads were expensive to build. So many roads were made of logs instead. Such roads were called *corduroy roads* because the logs set side by side looked like corduroy cloth. Corduroy roads had fewer ruts and pot-holes than dirt roads, but they made for a very noisy and bumpy ride.

Bridges. A major problem in improving roads was bridging rivers. Stone bridges were expensive to build, but wooden ones rotted quickly. A Massachusetts carpenter finally designed a wooden bridge that could be built cheaply and easily. He found that putting a roof over a bridge protected it from the weather.

Covered bridges lasted four times longer than open ones. Soon, covered wooden bridges were being put up in many places. Today, a few covered bridges can still be seen on back roads in the East.

The National Road. Some states set aside money to improve roads and build new ones. In 1806, for the first time, Congress approved spending money to build a national road. The road was to run from Cumberland, Maryland, to Wheeling, Virginia.*

Because of the War of 1812, the National Road was not finished until 1818. Later, it was extended across Ohio and Indiana into Illinois. As each new part was built, settlers eagerly used it to drive their wagons west.

The Sound of Steamboats

To settlers on the move, rivers were as useful as roads for transportation. In fact, floating downstream on a boat was often easier than traveling overland by wagon. The problem with river travel was moving upstream against the current. On parts of the Mississippi and Ohio rivers, the downstream current was very strong. Boats with sails could

---

*Today, Wheeling is in West Virginia.

beat their way upstream, but that was slow work. People sometimes used paddles or long poles to push boats upstream. Or they hauled them upstream from the shore with ropes. Yet none of these methods worked well.

Fitch and Fulton. The key to river travel by the 1800s was the steamboat. John Fitch, a Yankee from Connecticut, improved on steam engines that had been built in Britain. Fitch's steam engine turned paddle wheels that moved a boat upstream against the current.

Fitch tested his first steamboat on the Delaware River in 1787. At the time, the Constitutional Convention was meeting in Philadelphia. Fitch took several delegates for a ride on his new steamboat. Soon after, Fitch started a ferry service on the river. His business failed because few people used the ferry.

Twenty years later, Robert Fulton succeeded where Fitch had failed. Fulton grew up in Philadelphia and probably saw Fitch's steamboat. In 1807, he

Before new roads were built, travel was slow and uncomfortable. Tree stumps stuck up through the roads. The phrase "I'm stumped" may have come from coaches breaking down on these half-cleared tree stumps. At the far right of this picture, notice the corduroy road, where logs were set over marshy patches.

Circle graphs are one way of showing statistics. (See Skill Lesson 4 on page 81 and Skill Lesson 6 on page 140.) A circle graph is sometimes called a pie graph because it is divided into wedges, like a pie. Each wedge, or part, can be compared to every other part. A circle graph shows the relationship between each of the parts and the whole.

To compare information over time, two or more circle graphs can be used. A circle graph can also be used with a line or bar graph.

1. **Identify the information shown on the graphs.** (a) What year does the circle graph on the left show? (b) What do the colors represent? (c) What year does the circle graph on the right show? (d) What do the colors represent?

2. **Practice reading the graphs.** In a circle graph, you can compare any part with every other part or with the whole graph. The graph shows each part as a percentage of the whole. The whole graph is 100 percent. (a) What percent of the population lived in the North in 1800? (b) Which section of the country had the largest percent of the population in 1800? (c) Which section had the smallest percent of the population in 1800? (d) What percent of the population lived in the West in 1830? In the East? In the South?

3. **Interpret the information shown on the graphs.** Compare the two graphs. (a) Which section of the country gained the largest percent of the population between 1800 and 1830? (b) Which section of the country lost the greatest percent in this period? (c) Why do you think this section did not grow as fast as the West in this period? (d) Using your reading in the chapter and these graphs, make a generalization about what was happening to the population of the United States between 1800 and 1830.

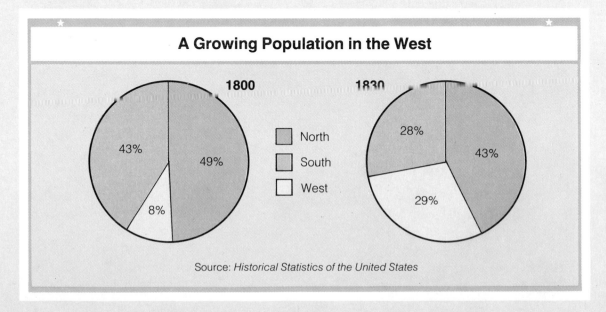

A Growing Population in the West

1800

1830

43% 49% 8%

North South West

28% 43% 29%

Source: *Historical Statistics of the United States*

MAJOR CANALS

Canals

| 0 | 150 | 300 Miles |

| 0 | 150 | 300 Kilometers |

CANADA

MAINE

L. Champlain

VT. N.H.

ERIE CANAL

CHAMPLAIN CANAL

L. Ontario

Troy

N.Y. Albany

MASS.

Buffalo

CONN. R.I.

ILLINOIS AND MICHIGAN CANAL

Chicago

L. Erie

New York

La Salle

Toledo

Cleveland

PA.

PENNSYLVANIA CANAL

Miami R.

WABASH AND ERIE CANAL

Pittsburgh

N.J.

Philadelphia

IND.

OHIO

CHESAPEAKE AND OHIO CANAL

ILL.

MIAMI AND ERIE CANAL

Cincinnati

OHIO AND ERIE CANAL

Potomac R.

MD. DEL.

Washington, D.C.

ATLANTIC OCEAN

Wabash R.

Ohio R.

Evansville

VA.

Richmond

Mississippi R.

Illinois R.

KY.

JAMES AND KANAWHA CANAL

N E S W

MAP SKILL The building of the Erie Canal set off an age of canal building across the new nation. Canals linked lakes and rivers and made inland travel easier. What is the longest canal shown on this map? In what direction does it run?

launched his steamboat, the *Clermont,* on the Hudson River. On his first run, Fulton took on passengers in New York City and headed upriver to Albany. The *Clermont* made the 300-mile (480 km) trip to Albany and back in just 62 hours. Within 3 months, the *Clermont* was making a profit for its owner.

Western steamboats. Fulton's success showed that a steamboat line could be profitable. Other steamboat lines quickly opened up river travel. Steamboats turned the Mississippi, Ohio, and Missouri rivers into busy routes for trade goods and travelers.

Western rivers were shallow compared with those in the East. They needed a special kind of boat. Henry Shreve, a pioneer steamboat captain, designed a flat-bottomed steamboat. It could carry heavy loads without getting stuck on sand bars.

By the 1830s, the booming of steamboat engines and the black smoke from their stacks were familiar sounds and sights along the Mississippi. At night, sparks lit up the sky as boats docked with a toot of the whistle. Although steamboats had comfortable cabins, they could be dangerous. Often, steam boilers exploded or sparks from smokestacks kindled raging fires. Even the best riverboat captains found them-selves stuck on sand bars now and then.

An Age of Canal Building

Rivers helped move people and their goods. Still, rivers did not exist everywhere they were needed. So Americans built canals to improve trade and travel. A *canal* is a channel dug and filled with water to allow ships to cross a stretch of land.

The first canals were only a few miles long. Some provided routes around waterfalls on a river. Others linked a river to a nearby lake. In the early 1800s, however, Americans began building longer canals.

An ambitious plan. One long canal was the *Erie Canal*, which connected the Hudson River with Lake Erie. (See the map above.) New Yorkers were eager to see this canal built. With it, goods could be moved across the Great Lakes and along the Mohawk and Hudson rivers into New York and back. New York City stood to gain much trade from the West. All the towns along the canal would prosper.

At first, many people thought that the plan was too ambitious. When a New Yorker told President Jefferson about it, the President remarked,

Canals helped link the West to the East in the early 1800s. Often, a team of horses dragged a boat along the canal, as you can see here. Boats had shelflike sleeping platforms for overnight passengers. During the day, passengers sat on top, ducking when a boat passed under a low bridge.

"Why, sir, you talk of making a canal 350 miles through the wilderness—it is little short of madness to think of it at this day!"

The Erie Canal. Governor DeWitt Clinton of New York disagreed. He convinced the state legislature to provide money for the canal. In 1817, workers began digging "Clinton's Ditch." Within a year, they had finished 69 miles (110 km) of the canal.

An immense task still remained to be done. To speed up the work, the canal builders invented new equipment. A machine was developed that could pull out nearly 40 tree stumps a day. In two places, the canal had to cross over rivers. Workers built stone aqueducts, or bridges, that carried the canal over the rivers.

When the Erie Canal was completed in 1825, trade flowed from the Great Lakes into New York. With the canal, shipping costs dropped, and travel time was greatly reduced. The canal helped make New York City the nation's leading center of commerce.

The success of the Erie Canal encouraged other states to build canals. As a result, canals helped link the nation together.

SECTION REVIEW

1. **Locate:** Cumberland Gap, Kentucky, Tennessee, Alabama, Mississippi, Lake Erie, Ohio, Indiana, Illinois, Lancaster Turnpike, National Road, Erie Canal.
2. **Define:** turnpike, corduroy road, canal.
3. Describe one route settlers used to move west.
4. List three ways travel improved in the early 1800s.
5. **What Do You Think?** Why do you think the Erie Canal was such an important achievement?

3 Changing Times

Read to Learn
★ What was the Era of Good Feelings?
★ How did Congress help American industry after the War of 1812?
★ What do these words mean: dumping, protective tariff?

In the years after the War of 1812, many Americans were in a hopeful mood. The nation was growing and changing. New factories were built. Settlers were carving up western lands into new states. Changes were taking place in politics, too.

An Era of Good Feelings

In 1816, a Republican President, James Madison, and a Republican majority in Congress firmly controlled the nation. By then, the Federalist Party was declining. Some Federalists joined the Republican Party. When Madison's second term ended, the Republicans nominated James Monroe to succeed him. Federalists chose Rufus King of New York. In the election, Monroe got 183 electoral votes and King only 34.

President Monroe belonged to the generation of Jefferson and Madison. He was over 60 years old when he took office. The new President still followed the fashions of the early 1800s. He powdered his hair and tied it back in a tail at a time when younger men wore their hair loose. He also preferred knee breeches and stockings to the full-length trousers of the new generation.

Still, Americans were fond of their old-fashioned President. Soon after taking office, Monroe toured New England, once the center of Federalist support. During the tour, New Englanders greeted Monroe so warmly that one Boston newspaper wrote about a new "Era of Good Feelings." When Monroe ran for a second term in 1820, no one ran against him. The easy Republican victory marked the end of the Federalist Party.

Webster, Calhoun, and Clay

The disappearance of the Federalists did not mean an end to political differences. In Congress, a group of bright young leaders was taking center stage. They were Daniel Webster of Massachusetts, John C. Calhoun of South Carolina, and Henry Clay of Kentucky. Each came from a different section of the United States. All three played critical roles in Congress for more than 30 years.

Daniel Webster spoke for the North. He was one of the most powerful

Young Daniel Webster was a splendid speaker who could shed tears at will. As a New Englander, he opposed the War of 1812 in Congress. After the war, he backed measures to help trade and industry in New England.

speakers of his day, and he was proud of it. "He will not be outdone by any man, if it is within his power to avoid it," remarked a friend. His dark hair and eyebrows earned him the nickname of "Black Dan." Webster served as a representative in the House and later as a senator from Massachusetts.

John C. Calhoun spoke for the South. Like Webster, he served as a representative and a senator from his state. He, too, was a powerful speaker. He was trained at Yale College and always worked out his ideas clearly. Slim and handsome, he had deep-set eyes and a high forehead. His way of speaking was so intense that some people found themselves uncomfortable in his presence.

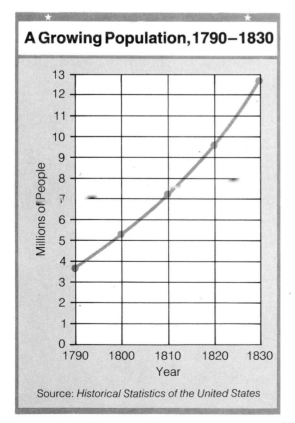

GRAPH SKILL The years after the War of 1812 were a time of economic growth. The nation's population grew, too, as this graph shows. About how much did the population increase between 1810 and 1820?

A Growing Population, 1790–1830

Source: *Historical Statistics of the United States*

In contrast, Henry Clay was full of charm and grace. Clay spoke for the West. As you read in Chapter 11, he was a War Hawk in 1812. Clay had simple, informal manners. He enjoyed staying up late at night to talk about politics or play cards. Like Webster and Calhoun, Clay's speeches could move people to laughter or tears.

Help for American Industry

In the years after the War of 1812, congressmen like Webster, Calhoun, and Clay often debated economic issues. Despite the nation's physical growth, its economy faced severe problems. One problem was the absence of a national bank. Another was foreign competition.

The second Bank of the United States. The charter that set up the first Bank of the United States ran out in 1811. The Bank had loaned money and regulated the nation's money supply. Without it, the economy suffered. State banks made loans and issued money. But they put too much money into circulation, which caused prices to rise rapidly.

To solve the problem, Congress chartered the second Bank of the United States in 1816. By lending money to individuals and restoring order to the money supply, the Bank helped American businesses grow.

Foreign competition. American industry grew quickly between 1807 and 1814. First the Embargo Act and then the War of 1812 kept most British goods out of the United States. As a result, American manufacturers opened many new mills and factories.

In 1814, British goods again flooded into America. The British could make and sell goods more cheaply than Americans, who had to charge for building their new factories. As a result, American goods cost more. British manufacturers knew this. So they tried to put the new American factories out of business by dumping goods. *Dumping* means selling goods in another country at very low prices. Dumping caused dozens of New England businesses to fail. Angry factory owners turned to Congress for help.

Tariff of 1816. Congress responded by putting a high tariff on goods imported from Europe. The Tariff of 1816 increased tariffs to 25 percent. The increase made goods imported from Europe more expensive than American-made goods. (See the diagram at right.) This kind of tariff is called a *protective tariff* because it is meant to protect a country's industries from foreign competition.

The Tariff of 1816 sailed through Congress. In 1818 and 1824, Congress passed even higher tariffs. By then, some people, especially Southerners, began to resent the tariff. Southerners had built few factories, so the tariff did not help them. In fact, it forced them to buy more expensive American-made goods. John C. Calhoun became a bitter foe of the tariff. To Southerners like Calhoun, the tariff seemed to make northern manufacturers rich at the expense of the South.

Clay's American System

As the debate over tariffs heated up, Henry Clay came up with a plan to help the economy of each section of the country. In 1824, he set out his ideas. Under Clay's *American System,* tariffs on imports would be kept high. High tariffs would help industry in the North expand. With wealth from expanding industry, Northerners would have the money to buy farm products from the West and South.

The other part of Clay's American System concerned internal improvements—the building of roads, bridges, and canals. Clay wanted Congress to spend money earned from the tariff on internal improvements. Such improvements, he said, would help the West and South by making it easier to ship goods to city markets.

Clay's American System was never really put into effect. Tariffs stayed

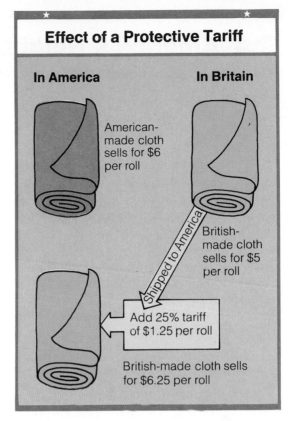

Effect of a Protective Tariff

In America — American-made cloth sells for $6 per roll

In Britain — British-made cloth sells for $5 per roll

Shipped to America

Add 25% tariff of $1.25 per roll

British-made cloth sells for $6.25 per roll

DIAGRAM SKILL In 1816, the government passed a protective tariff to help American factory owners rather than to raise money. As this diagram shows, the tariff made British goods more expensive than American goods. Why do you think Southerners said that the tariff was unfair?

high, but Congress did not spend much money for internal improvements. Southerners found little to like in the American System. They did not support government building of roads and canals because the South could ship most goods by river.

SECTION REVIEW

1. **Define:** dumping, protective tariff.
2. What section of the country did each of the following represent: (a) Daniel Webster; (b) John C. Calhoun; (c) Henry Clay?
3. Why did Congress pass the Tariff of 1816?
4. **What Do You Think?** What do you think were the major problems with Clay's American System?

4 America's Neighbors

Read to Learn
★ How did Canada achieve self-rule?
★ How did Latin American nations win independence?
★ What was the Monroe Doctrine?

As the United States grew and changed, so, too, did its neighbors to the north and south. To the north, Canada became an independent nation. To the south, the colonies of Spain and Portugal fought their own revolutions. These revolutions were inspired in part by the American Revolution. In this way, the United States served as an example to the nations around it.

Canada Becomes a Nation

The population of Canada was a mix of Indian, French, and English. The first white settlers in Canada were French. In 1763, however, the British won Canada. During and after the American Revolution, thousands of Loyalists fled to Canada from the United States. They settled mainly in Nova Scotia, New Brunswick, Prince Edward Island, and the area north of the Great Lakes.

A divided land. French Canadians and English Canadians distrusted one another. They not only spoke different languages but practiced different religions. Most English settlers were Protestants. Most French settlers were Catholics.

In 1791, Britain decided to rule the two groups separately. It divided Canada into Upper and Lower Canada. Upper Canada included the area around the Great Lakes settled by English-speaking people. Lower Canada included the region along the St. Lawrence River settled by the French. Although each province had its own government, Britain made most of the important decisions for its colony.

During the early 1800s, Canadians grew discontent with British rule. In 1837, rebellions broke out. Britain did not want another revolution like the one in the 13 colonies. Lord Durham, the governor of Canada, recommended that Upper and Lower Canada be united. In a report to Parliament, he said that Canadians should be given control over local affairs. Britain would control only Canada's foreign affairs. The Durham Report became the basis for Canadian self-rule.

The Dominion of Canada. Canadians slowly gained control over their own affairs. In 1867, the provinces of Nova Scotia, New Brunswick, Ontario, and Quebec were joined into the *Dominion of Canada.* Later, Prince Edward Island, Manitoba, Alberta, Saskatchewan, and British Columbia joined the Dominion.

By slow and generally peaceful means, Canada became a nation. The government of Canada was similar to the British government. Canadians had an elected parliament and a prime minister. A governor general represented the British ruler but had little power.

Revolutions in Latin America

To the south of the United States, Spanish colonists were eager for independence. They had many reasons to dislike Spanish rule. Most people had no say in government. The American and French revolutions encouraged the peoples of Latin America* to fight for control of their own affairs.

---

*Latin America refers to the parts of the Western Hemisphere where Latin languages such as Spanish, French, and Portuguese are spoken. It includes Mexico, Central and South America, and the West Indies.

Simón Bolívar. Perhaps the best known revolutionary leader was Simón Bolívar (see MOHN BAHL uh vuhr). He is often called the Liberator for his role in the Latin American wars of independence. Bolívar was born into a wealthy creole family in Venezuela. As a young man, he took up the cause of Latin American independence. "I will never allow my hands to be idle," he vowed, "nor my soul to rest until I have broken the shackles which chain us to Spain."

Bolívar visited the United States because he admired its form of government. When he returned to Venezuela, he led rebel armies in a long stuggle against Spain. In August 1819, Bolívar led an army on a daring march from Venezuela over the ice-capped Andes Mountains and into Colombia. There, he defeated the Spanish. Soon after, he became president of the independent Republic of Great Colombia. It included today's nations of Venezuela, Colombia, Ecuador, and Panama.

José de San Martín. Another daring leader was José de San Martín. He helped Argentina in its struggle for independence. Argentina won its freedom in 1816. San Martín also helped Chile, Peru, and Ecuador win their independence.

Mexico wins independence. During the early 1800s, Mexicans also fought for freedom from Spain. Among the heroes of these struggles were two priests: Miguel Hidalgo (hih DAL goh) and José Morelos (maw REH lohs).

In 1810, Father Hidalgo organized an army of Indians that freed several Mexican provinces. He then set up a government that outlawed slavery and returned land to the Indians. However, in 1811, Hidalgo was captured and executed by troops loyal to Spain. Morelos continued to fight for equal rights for all races and to give land to poor peasants. Wealthy Mexicans opposed his ideas and helped Spanish troops capture him.

Simón Bolívar, shown here, helped six Latin American nations win their freedom from Spanish rule. He accepted the title of Liberator but refused to exchange it for the title of king or emperor.

Mexicans finally won independence in 1821. A few years later, Mexican leaders wrote a constitution that made Mexico a republic.

Other Nations Are Formed

In 1821, the people of Central America declared their independence from Spain. Two years later, they formed the United Provinces of Central America. It included today's nations of Nicaragua, Costa Rica, El Salvador, Honduras, and Guatemala.

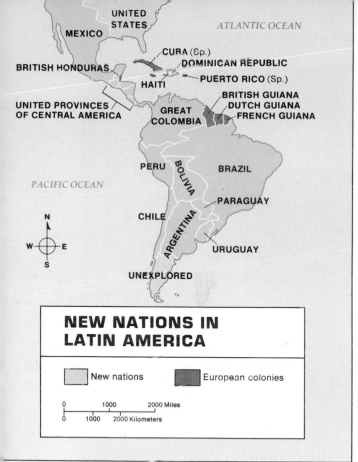

NEW NATIONS IN LATIN AMERICA

New nations
European colonies

0   1000   2000 Miles
0   1000   2000 Kilometers

MAP SKILL The wars of independence in Latin America led to the creation of many new nations. Look at Central America on the map on page 758. What nations were carved out of the United Provinces of Central America?

The Portuguese colony of Brazil also won its independence—but without having to fight for it. Instead, the people asked Prince Pedro, son of the Portuguese king, to be their ruler. He accepted. In 1822, he declared Brazil's independence.

By 1825, most colonies in Latin America had thrown off European rule. Unlike the 13 colonies, however, the colonies of Latin America did not unite into a single country. Instead, they set up many different nations. One reason for this was geography. The Andes Mountains, for example, were a serious barrier to travel and communication. Also, the Spanish colonies were spread out over a huge area.

Like the United States, the new nations of Latin America faced many problems. They wanted to set up stable governments. But, as colonies, they had not been allowed to elect assemblies as the 13 American colonies had. So they had no experience in self-government. As a result, many of these nations were unable to achieve their goal of democratic rule.

The United States Gains Florida

Although Spain lost many of its colonies, it held on to Puerto Rico, Cuba, and Florida. Many Americans thought that Florida should be added to the United States. As early as 1810, President Madison claimed West Florida, the land along the Gulf of Mexico.

Concern over Spanish Florida grew, especially among Southerners. Slaves from Georgia and other southern states often fled into Florida. Also, Creek and Seminole Indians in Florida raided settlements in Georgia. The Spanish did little to stop these raids. So in 1818, President Monroe sent Andrew Jackson into Florida to attack the Seminoles. Jackson's war against the Seminoles angered the Spanish. The United States replied that the Spanish had brought the trouble on themselves.

Because Spain was already fighting rebels in Mexico and elsewhere, it did not want war with the United States. John Quincy Adams, son of the second President of the United States, was Monroe's Secretary of State. Adams worked out a treaty with Spain that went into effect in 1821. In the *Adams–Onís Treaty,* Spain gave Florida to the United States in return for a payment of $5 million.

The Monroe Doctrine

Even while Americans cheered the Adams–Onís Treaty, Monroe and Adams worried that European nations would interfere in North and South America. In 1815, Russia, Prussia, Austria, and France formed the Holy Alliance. Its aim was to crush any rev-

By the 1820s, the growth of American trade made shipbuilding even more important than it had been in colonial times. Here, Americans celebrate the launching of a new ship, *Fame.*

olution that sprang up in Europe. Monroe and Adams feared that members of the alliance might help Spain regain its old colonies. Russia also claimed lands on the Pacific coast of North America.

The British, too, worried about other European nations meddling in the affairs of North and South America. So they suggested that the United States and Britain issue a joint statement guaranteeing the freedom of the new nations of Latin America. Secretary of State Adams boldly advised Monroe to issue his own statement. Joining with the British, he warned, would make the United States appear "to come in as a [small] boat in the wake of the British man-of-war." Monroe agreed.

In a message to Congress in 1823, the President made a statement on foreign policy that is known as the *Monroe Doctrine.* The United States, he said, would not interfere in the affairs of European nations or European colonies in the Americas. In return, he warned European nations not to interfere with the newly independent nations of Latin America. The Monroe Doctrine also declared that the United States would

oppose the building of any new colonies in the Americas.

Monroe's message showed that the United States was determined to keep Europeans out of the Western Hemisphere. In 1823, the United States did not have the power to enforce the Monroe Doctrine. However, Britain supported the Monroe Doctrine. Its powerful navy kept Europeans from trying to build new colonies in the Americas.

SECTION REVIEW

1. **Locate:** Canada, Venezuela, Argentina, Chile, Peru, Colombia, Ecuador, Mexico, Nicaragua, Costa Rica, El Salvador, Honduras, Guatemala, Brazil.

2. (a) Why did Britain divide Canada in 1791? (b) What did Lord Durham recommend in his report to Parliament?

3. What role did each of the following play in Latin America: (a) Simón Bolívar; (b) José de San Martín; (c) Miguel Hidalgo?

4. How did Florida become part of the United States?

5. **What Do You Think?** Do you think the Monroe Doctrine is still important today? Why or why not?

Chapter 12 Review

★ Summary ★

In the early 1800s, America was growing and changing. The Industrial Revolution brought the factory system and new machines to replace older ways of producing goods. New roads and canals and the use of steamboats helped improve transportation. To help the economy, Congress chartered the second Bank of the United States and passed a protective tariff.

America's neighbors struggled for independence during this period. Canada achieved self-rule through slow, peaceful means. In Latin America, however, Spanish colonies fought hard for their freedom. In 1823, the United States announced the Monroe Doctrine. It warned European nations to stay out of the affairs of the Western Hemisphere.

★ Reviewing the Facts ★

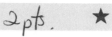

Key Terms. Match each term in Column 1 with the correct definition in Column 2.

Column 1	Column 2
1. capitalist	**a.** selling goods in another country at very low prices
2. factory system	**b.** channel filled with water that lets ships cross land
3. canal	**c.** person with money to invest in business to make a profit
4. dumping	**d.** tax to help home industries against foreign competition
5. protective tariff	**e.** way of bringing workers and machines together in one place to produce goods

Key People, Events, and Ideas. Identify each of the following.

1. Industrial Revolution
2. Eli Whitney
3. Samuel Slater
4. Francis Cabot Lowell
5. Lancaster Turnpike
6. John Fitch
7. Robert Fulton
8. Erie Canal
9. James Monroe
10. Era of Good Feelings
11. Tariff of 1816
12. American System
13. Simón Bolívar
14. Miguel Hidalgo
15. Adams–Onís Treaty

★ Chapter Checkup ★

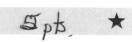

1. (a) What industry was most affected by the inventions of the early Industrial Revolution? (b) How did the War of 1812 speed up the Industrial Revolution in America?

2. (a) Why did the Boston Associates hire women to work in the Lowell mills? (b) How did they try to attract women from farm families?

3. Explain how interchangeable parts improved the way goods were produced.

4. Explain how each of the following helped settlers moving west: (a) turnpikes; (b) steamboats; (c) Erie Canal.

5. (a) Why did northern manufacturers want a protective tariff? (b) How did Southerners respond to the tariff?

6. (a) Why did the United States fear that European nations might interfere in the Western Hemisphere? (b) What other nation supported the Monroe Doctrine? (c) Why was its support important?

★ Thinking About History

10 pts. each ★

1. **Understanding the economy.** (a) How did the invention of new machines lead to the factory system? (b) Why were early factories set up near rivers?

2. **Relating past to present.** (a) Why were cities dangerous places to live in the early 1800s? (b) What advantages did they offer? (c) Do cities today still have the same dangers and advantages? Explain your answer.

3. **Understanding geography.** (a) How did geography make travel to the West difficult? (b) How did settlers overcome these difficulties?

4. **Comparing.** (a) Compare the way Canada won its independence to the way the Spanish colonies won theirs. (b) Suggest some reasons why their experiences were different.

★ Using Your Skills ★

Extra credit (+3)

1. **Map reading.** Study the map on page 272. (a) What city or cities in the West were located on major roads? (b) Describe one road that ran north–south. Name the city or state where the road began and where it ended. (c) What states did it cross?

2. **Reading for the main idea.** Each paragraph or group of paragraphs in this book has a main idea. The *main idea* is the generalization that underlies all the facts and examples. It ties them together. Often, the main idea is the topic sentence, or first sentence, of a paragraph. Facts are then given to support the main idea. Sometimes, the main idea is in the middle or end of a paragraph.

Read the first paragraph on page 270 under the heading "A Flood of Settlers."

(a) What is the main idea of the paragraph? (b) What facts are given in that paragraph and the next one to support the main idea?

3. **Making a review chart.** Make a review chart with three vertical columns. Label the columns Inventor, Invention, and Importance. Then complete the chart by including all the inventors discussed in this chapter.

4. **Graph reading.** Study the graph on page 278. (a) What is the subject of the graph? (b) What was the population of the United States in 1800? 1820? 1830? (c) Compare this graph to the circle graphs on page 274. About how many people lived in the West in 1830?

★ More to Do ★

1. **Exploring local history.** Research and write a report about industries that developed in your local community during the early 1800s. Describe the effect the industries had on the way of life in the community.

2. **Eyewitness reporting.** Imagine that you are a reporter for an eastern newspaper and that you are traveling west with a family of settlers. Prepare an article on the hardships of travel to send to your paper in the East.

3. **Building a model.** As a group project, build a model of an early steamboat.

4. **Researching.** Find out more about one of the leaders in the Latin American struggles for independence. Describe the leader's background, ideas, and efforts in the battle for freedom.

Unit 4 Review

★ Unit Summary ★

Chapter 10 George Washington, the first President of the United States, guided the nation through its early years. During his second term, political parties took shape. Both Washington and Adams, the second President, managed to keep the United States out of foreign wars.

Chapter 11 Thomas Jefferson had a more democratic style than the first two Presidents. During his time in office, the United States doubled in size. But British impressment of American sailors and the pressure of the War Hawks led President Madison into war in 1812.

Chapter 12 The years after the War of 1812 were a time of change. The Industrial Revolution changed the way goods were made. Thousands of Americans moved west. New roads and canals were built to help the growing nation. Also, the nations of Latin America won their independence, and the United States warned European nations not to meddle in affairs of the Western Hemisphere.

★ Unit Checkup ★

Choose the word or phrase that best completes each of the following statements.

1. Washington warned Americans against becoming involved in European affairs in the
   (a) Neutrality Proclamation.
   (b) Farewell Address.
   (c) Treaty of Greenville.

2. Hamilton's program to strengthen the economy included the
   (a) Alien and Sedition acts.
   (b) Tariff of 1816.
   (c) Bank of the United States.

3. Lewis and Clark explored the
   (a) Louisiana Purchase.
   (b) Northwest Territory.
   (c) Cumberland Gap.

4. One cause of the War of 1812 was the
   (a) burning of Washington.
   (b) attack on Fort McHenry.
   (c) impressment of American sailors.

5. Eli Whitney developed the
   (a) idea of interchangeable parts.
   (b) spinning jenny.
   (c) water frame.

★ Building American Citizenship ★

1. Newspapers influenced the growth of political parties in the 1790s by supporting one party or the other. Do you think newspapers play an important role in politics today? How? Why is freedom of the press important to a democratic government?

2. Thomas Jefferson supported such democratic beliefs as the rights and freedom of the individual. He once said, "The minority possess their equal rights, which equal law must protect." (See page 242.) How can a government elected by majority vote still protect the rights of a minority?

3. Why are good roads and transportation as important to the United States today as they were in the early 1800s?

Time lines can be horizontal, as on pages 146 and 264. Or they can be vertical, like the one at right. Study this vertical time line. Then answer the following questions.

1. What Presidents are shown on the time line?
2. Who was President when the Embargo Act was passed?
3. Who was President during the War of 1812?
4. Did Madison become President before or after Jefferson?
5. Describe how each event on the time line affected relations between the United States and other nations.

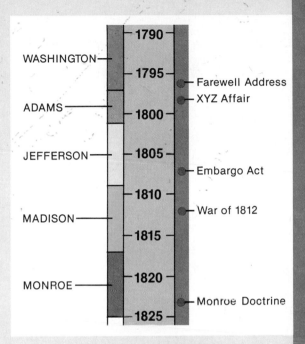

History Writer's Handbook

Selecting Supporting Information

Detail sentences in a one-paragraph answer give information to support the main idea. The information may be details, facts, examples, reasons, or incidents. The topic sentence often helps you decide what kind of information you need.

Look at the following topic sentence. *Hamilton's two step plan for paying off the national debt and state debts may be described as follows.* The information you need is details about each step of Hamilton's plan. For example: *The national government would buy up the government's old bonds and issue new ones. The national government would also pay off debts owed by the states.*

Make sure you have enough information. Also make sure the information you select supports the main idea. Look at the following topic sentence. *Southerners resented the tariff of 1816 for two reasons.* The following information would not support the main idea. *In 1816, Congress passed a high tariff. In 1816, Congress chartered the second Bank of the United States.* Neither piece of information gives or explains a reason why Southerners resented the tariff of 1816. And the second piece of information does not even relate to the topic.

Practice Look at the following topic sentence for a one-paragraph answer. *Many Federalists favored war with France for two reasons.*

1. What kind of information should the detail sentences give?
2. Select information to include in the detail sentences. (See page 235.)

Unit 5

A GROWING NATION

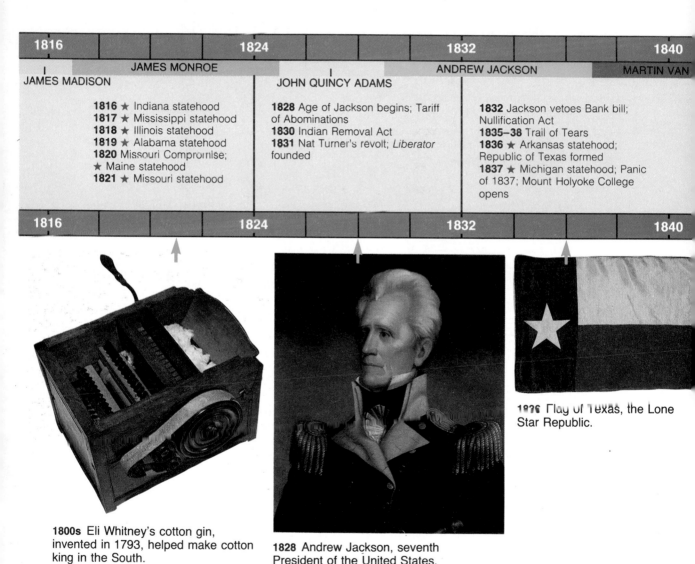

1816		1824		1832		1840

JAMES MONROE

JAMES MADISON

JOHN QUINCY ADAMS

ANDREW JACKSON

MARTIN VAN

1816 ★ Indiana statehood
1817 ★ Mississippi statehood
1818 ★ Illinois statehood
1819 ★ Alabama statehood
1820 Missouri Compromise;
★ Maine statehood
1821 ★ Missouri statehood

1828 Age of Jackson begins; Tariff of Abominations
1830 Indian Removal Act
1831 Nat Turner's revolt; *Liberator* founded

1832 Jackson vetoes Bank bill; Nullification Act
1835–38 Trail of Tears
1836 ★ Arkansas statehood; Republic of Texas formed
1837 ★ Michigan statehood; Panic of 1837; Mount Holyoke College opens

1816		1824		1832		1840

1800s Eli Whitney's cotton gin, invented in 1793, helped make cotton king in the South.

1828 Andrew Jackson, seventh President of the United States.

1836 Flag of Texas, the Lone Star Republic.

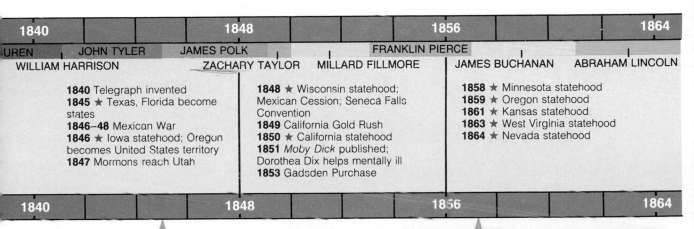

1840		1848		1856		1864

UREN | JOHN TYLER | JAMES POLK | FRANKLIN PIERCE |

WILLIAM HARRISON | ZACHARY TAYLOR | MILLARD FILLMORE | JAMES BUCHANAN | ABRAHAM LINCOLN

1840 Telegraph invented
1845 ★ Texas, Florida become states
1846–48 Mexican War
1846 ★ Iowa statehood; Oregon becomes United States territory
1847 Mormons reach Utah

1848 ★ Wisconsin statehood; Mexican Cession; Seneca Falls Convention
1849 California Gold Rush
1850 ★ California statehood
1851 *Moby Dick* published; Dorothea Dix helps mentally ill
1853 Gadsden Purchase

1858 ★ Minnesota statehood
1859 ★ Oregon statehood
1861 ★ Kansas statehood
1863 ★ West Virginia statehood
1864 ★ Nevada statehood

1840		1848		1856		1864

Mid-1800s Settlers going west often traveled by boat along the upper Missouri River.

Mid-1800s Lucretia Mott, an abolitionist and crusader for women's rights.

CHAPTER

13

Age of Jackson (1824–1840)

Chapter Outline

1 The People's Choice
2 Jackson Takes Office
3 Tests of Strength
4 Jackson's Successors

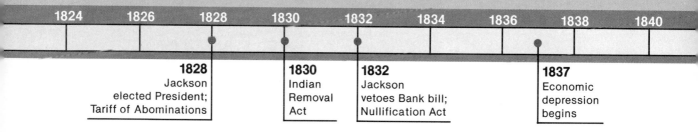

1824	1826	1828	1830	1832	1834	1836	1838	1840

1828
Jackson
elected President;
Tariff of Abominations

1830
Indian
Removal
Act

1832
Jackson
vetoes Bank bill;
Nullification Act

1837
Economic
depression
begins

About This Chapter

Andrew Jackson was elected President in 1828. Jackson was a new kind of President. He was a self-made man and a frontiersman who was famous for his fearlessness. One story illustrates Jackson's grit.

Many years before he became President, Andrew Jackson served as a judge on the Tennessee frontier. One day, he faced an outlaw named Russell Bean. Bean had scared off the town sheriff by promising to shoot "the first skunk that came within ten feet." But when Andrew Jackson came roaring out of the courthouse, Bean changed his mind. "I looked [Jackson] in the eye and saw shoot," the outlaw explained. Bean decided to leave town rather than face Jackson's wrath.

Jackson made as strong a President as he had a judge. He faced a number of serious problems during his time in office. The President handled each crisis firmly. Because Jackson had such an influence on the country, the period from 1824 to 1840 is called the Age of Jackson.

During the Age of Jackson, the common people gained a new voice in politics. Farm hands, craftsworkers, small merchants, and other average Americans saw Jackson as one of them. Their votes made him President. The common people gave Andrew Jackson their loyal support throughout his years in office.

Study the time line above. What action did President Jackson take in 1832?

Voting Day, by George Bingham, catches the spirit of the Age of Jackson. By 1828, more people had a voice in government than ever before.

1 The People's Choice

Read to Learn
★ Why was the election of 1824 disputed?
★ What plans did President Adams have for the nation?
★ How did democracy grow in the 1820s?
★ What do these words mean: suffrage, caucus, nominating convention?

Andrew Jackson, hero of many battles, was the people's choice for President in 1824. More people voted for Jackson than for any other candidate. But Jackson did not become President in 1824. How did this happen?

The Election of 1824

In 1824, four men ran for President. All four were Republicans, but each drew support from different parts of the country. John Quincy Adams was most popular in the East. Henry Clay and Andrew Jackson had support in the West. William Crawford was favored in the South, but he was too ill to campaign much.

The candidates. John Quincy Adams of Massachusetts was the son of Abigail and John Adams, the second President. The younger Adams was a Harvard graduate and a talented diplomat. He helped end the War of 1812 and was Secretary of State under President James Monroe.

People admired Adams for his intelligence and strict morals. However, as a critic said, he was "hard as a piece of granite and cold as a lump of ice." This

John Quincy Adams was the first President to be photographed. He sat for this portrait in 1847, more than 20 years after he entered the White House.

of the electoral votes. Jackson led with 38 percent. Adams was second, Crawford third, and Clay fourth. Under the Constitution, the House of Representatives had to choose the President from the top three candidates. Clay could not be elected. But as Speaker of the House, he used his influence to help Adams.

With Clay's help, Adams was elected President. Soon after the election, President Adams named Henry Clay as Secretary of State. Angry Jackson supporters claimed that Adams and Clay had made a deal and stolen the election from Jackson. As Jackson rode home to Tennessee, he met an old friend. "Well, General," said the friend, "we did all we could for you here, but the rascals at Washington cheated you out of it."

"Indeed, my old friend," replied Jackson, "there was *cheating* and *corruption,* and *bribery,* too." In fact, nothing so dishonest had taken place. The election had been decided as the Constitution said. But Jackson and his followers were angry.

Adams as President

John Quincy Adams had ambitious plans for the nation. Above all, the new President thought that the federal government should help the economy of the young republic grow.

Plans for national growth. President Adams wanted the government to pay for new roads and canals. He planned to set up a national university in Washington and build an observatory for astronomers. And he wanted the government to support projects to improve farming, manufacturing, trade, science, and the arts.

Adams' plans for national growth were not popular. Many people objected to spending federal money on such projects. Even the President's supporters found his many projects too costly. Congress approved money for a national road and for some canals. But it turned down all Adams' other plans.

coldness kept him from being well liked.

Henry Clay was Speaker of the House of Representatives. He was a skillful negotiator and helped work out important compromises in Congress. Clay was from Kentucky, a western state. But he was not nearly as popular as the other candidate from the West, Andrew Jackson.

To most Americans, Andrew Jackson was the hero of the Battle of New Orleans. He was also a fine example of a self-made man. He had risen from a poor boyhood to become a successful businessman. As a result, he won the support of self-made men everywhere, especially in the frontier areas of the West.

Adams is elected. The results of the 1824 election created a problem. Jackson won the popular vote. But none of the candidates won a majority

A bitter campaign. Adams ran for reelection in 1828. This time, Andrew Jackson was his only opponent. Few issues were discussed during the campaign. Instead, it became a name-calling contest. Jackson supporters said that Adams had become President only because of the "corrupt bargain" with Clay in 1824.

Adams' supporters fought back. They called Jackson a murderer and handed out leaflets with coffins printed on them. Jackson had killed men in duels, they pointed out. Also, he had executed soldiers for deserting in battle. Some people even criticized Jackson's wife during the campaign.

Adams faced an uphill battle. His policies were unpopular, and even his background hurt him. Adams was seen as an aristocrat, a member of the upper class. A democratic spirit was sweeping the nation in the 1820s. Many people felt that aristocrats like Adams had run the nation long enough.

Jackson easily won the election. His supporters called his success a victory for the common people. By common people they meant farmers in the West and South and working people in the cities of the East.

Growth of Democracy

The election of 1828 showed how America was changing. The nation was growing quickly. Three times more people voted in 1828 than in 1824. Many of the new voters lived in the frontier states between the Appalachians and the Mississippi River. Life on the frontier encouraged a democratic spirit. This spirit was reflected in the voting laws of the western states. Any white man over age 21 could vote.

New voters. The new voters in the western states were a rugged group of people. They often began life very poor. But through hard work, they prospered. Most white men in the West were on an equal footing. There were fewer rich, old families than in the East. As a result, westerners thought that any honest, hard-working person could be successful.

There were also new voters in the East. Voting laws there were becoming more democratic. Several states dropped the requirement that voters own land. Thus, a large number of craftsworkers and shopkeepers won **suffrage,** the right to vote, for the first time. Despite these changes, many Americans still did not have the right to vote. They included women, Native

MAP SKILL In the election of 1828, Andrew Jackson won a clear majority of the popular and electoral vote. What part of the country supported John Quincy Adams?

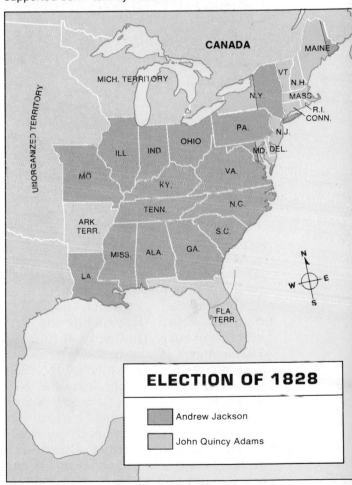

ELECTION OF 1828

Andrew Jackson

John Quincy Adams

When Andrew Jackson was sworn into office in March 1829, thousands of his supporters flooded the capital to cheer their hero. Many in the throng were rugged frontier people. After Jackson's swearing in, the crowd moved noisily to the White House for a party. One eyewitness wrote:

On their arrival at the White House, the . . . crowd clamored for refreshments and soon drained the barrels of punch. A great deal of china and glassware was broken, and the East Room was filled with a noisy mob. . . . Such a scene had never before been witnessed at the White House, and the aristocratic old Federalists saw, to their disgust, men whose boots were covered with the red mud of the unpaved streets standing on the satin-covered chairs to get a sight at the President of their choice.

Another eyewitness managed to get inside the crowded White House. She noted that "ladies fainted, men were seen with bloody noses." She added, with disapproval, "But it was the people's day, and the people's President, and the people would rule."

In the end, no one was badly hurt, but many were shocked. The party showed that a new kind of voter had chosen a new kind of President.

★ How do you think Andrew Jackson was different from "the aristocratic old Federalists"?

Americans, and most black Americans. Slaves had no political rights.

In the early years of the nation, most northern states allowed free blacks to vote. However, during the 1820s, most of these states took the vote away from free blacks. By 1830, blacks could vote only in a few New England states. To most white Americans at the time, it seemed natural that only white men took part in politics.

New political parties. By the late 1820s, new political parties had grown up. The Republican Party had been the major party for many years. But the differences between John Quincy Adams and Andrew Jackson showed a split in the Republican Party after 1824.

People who supported Adams and his plans for national growth called themselves National Republicans. Later, they took the name **Whigs.** Many business people in the East as well as some planters in the South were Whigs.

Jackson and his supporters formed a new party. They called themselves

Democrats. Most support for the Democratic Party came from frontier farmers and factory workers in the East.

Choosing a candidate. The new parties developed a more open way of choosing candidates for President. In the past, a few members of each party had held a *caucus,* or private meeting. At the caucus, party leaders chose the candidate. Many people thought that the system was undemocratic because very few people took part in it.

In the late 1820s, both political parties began holding *nominating conventions.* Delegates from all the states went to their party's nominating convention. The delegates then selected the party's candidate for President.

This gave people a more direct voice in choosing candidates. Today, the major political parties still hold conventions.

SECTION REVIEW

1. **Define:** suffrage, caucus, nominating convention.
2. Why was the election of 1824 decided in the House of Representatives?
3. How did frontier life encourage a democratic spirit?
4. What new political parties grew up in the late 1820s?
5. **What Do You Think?** Why do you think many people felt there was a "corrupt bargain" between Henry Clay and John Quincy Adams in 1824?

2 Jackson Takes Office

Read to Learn

★ How did Andrew Jackson become a national leader?

★ Why did Jackson replace many officeholders?

★ Why did Jackson oppose a national bank?

★ What do these words mean: spoils system, kitchen cabinet, pet bank?

In March 1829, Andrew Jackson took office as the seventh President of the United States. Jackson was different from earlier Presidents. All of them had come from wealthy, powerful families in Virginia or New England. Jackson came from the West. He brought the spirit of the frontier to the office of President. His motto was "Let the people rule."

Old Hickory

Jackson won the election of 1828 with the support of the common people. Like many of them, he was born in a log cabin. Jackson's parents moved from Ireland to the Carolina frontier two years before he was born. Young Andrew had to grow up quickly. His father died a few days before Andrew was born. His mother died when Jackson was 14 years old.

At age 13, Jackson fought in the American Revolution and was captured by the British. When ordered to clean a British officer's boots, Jackson proudly refused. The officer slashed Jackson's hand and face with a sword. Jackson bore the scars of these wounds for the rest of his life.

After the Revolution, Jackson studied law. He moved to the Tennessee frontier and built a successful law practice. Soon, he was rich enough to buy land and slaves. In 1796, Andrew Jackson was elected to the House of Representatives.

Jackson won national fame during the War of 1812. As commander of the United States forces, he defeated the British at New Orleans. To settlers on

This painting shows Andrew Jackson at the Battle of New Orleans. Although Jackson became one of the richest men in Tennessee, he was a hero to the common people. Jackson called himself "the direct representative of the American people."

the frontier, Jackson was also a hero of wars against the Indians. He defeated the Creek Indians at the Battle of Horseshoe Bend and forced them to give up millions of acres of land in Georgia and Alabama.

Jackson was a strong leader with a forceful personality. His enemies knew him as a fierce opponent. The Creeks that Jackson defeated called him Sharp Knife. But his own troops gave him a nickname that stuck. To them, he was as hard and tough as the wood of a hickory tree. They called him *Old Hickory*.

Spoils to the Victor

Soon after Andrew Jackson took office, he fired many government employees. Some of these people had held their jobs since George Washington's time. The new President said that he was dismissing people who held their jobs as a privilege.

The spoils system. Jackson replaced officials with his own supporters. Some people saw this practice as a step toward greater democracy. They claimed it gave more people a chance to work in the government. Others disagreed. They said that Jackson gave jobs to loyal Democrats who helped elect him, not to people who could do the job well.

A Jackson supporter explained the practice this way: "To the victors belong the spoils." Spoils are profits or benefits. The practice of giving jobs to loyal supporters is called the *spoils system*. Politicians before Jackson had given jobs to supporters. But Jackson was the first President to do so on a large scale. After Jackson, the spoils system became an important part of American politics.

Kitchen cabinet. Jackson rewarded some of his supporters with cabinet jobs. Only Secretary of State Martin

Van Buren was really qualified for his post. As a result, Jackson seldom met with his official cabinet. Instead, he had a group of unofficial advisers. They included Democratic leaders and newspaper editors.

The group met in the White House kitchen and became known as the **kitchen cabinet.** The kitchen cabinet was made up of rough-and-ready men. They chewed tobacco and spat at the woodstove while they discussed politics. Despite their rough manners, these men were well informed. They kept Jackson up to date on the mood of the country.

Jackson and the Bank

During Jackson's first term, a major political battle raged over the Bank of the United States. Like many people from the West, Jackson disliked the Bank. He thought that it had too much power. For example, the Bank regulated loans made by state banks. When the Bank's directors decided that state banks were making too many loans, it cut back the amount of money these banks could lend. This angered people in the South and West because they wanted to borrow money to buy land.

Jackson saw the Bank as a tool the rich used to help each other. He especially disliked Nicholas Biddle, president of the Bank since 1823. Biddle stood for everything Jackson and the Democrats mistrusted. He was rich and came from an aristocratic Philadelphia family.

I will kill it! Biddle worried that President Jackson might try to destroy the Bank. Two senators, Henry Clay and Daniel Webster, came up with a plan to save the Bank and defeat Jackson at the same time.

The Bank's charter did not have to be renewed until 1836. But Clay and Webster wanted the Bank to be an issue in the 1832 election. So they convinced Biddle to apply for renewal early. They were sure that most Americans supported the Bank. Thus, if Jackson vetoed the bill to renew the Bank's charter, he would lose popularity—and the election.

Clay pushed the recharter bill through Congress in 1832. Word that Congress had passed the bill reached Jackson when he was sick in bed. The President vowed, "The Bank . . . is trying to kill me, but I will kill it!"

Jackson's veto. When the Bank bill reached the President, he vetoed it at once. Jackson claimed that the Bank was unconstitutional. Earlier, the Supreme Court had ruled that the Bank was constitutional. In his veto message, Jackson challenged this ruling. He argued that only states, not the federal government, had the right to charter banks.

Republicans were sure that the President had blundered. To take advantage of the Bank issue, they chose Henry Clay to run against Jackson. When the votes were counted, however, the Republicans were stunned. Jackson

Whigs expected to beat Jackson in the election of 1832 because of the Bank issue. In this campaign cartoon, Jackson and Clay race toward the White House. As Jackson's horse stumbles on the Bank, Clay pulls ahead. In the end, however, Jackson won. Why do you think Jackson is swinging a club labeled "veto"?

Political cartoons can tell you a great deal about the past. For many years, cartoonists have tried to influence public feeling about important issues. To do so, they may exaggerate the facts. This is one reason why cartoons can often make a point more strongly than words can.

BORN TO COMMAND.

KING ANDREW THE FIRST.

Study the cartoon at left, which was published in the 1830s. Ask yourself what point about Andrew Jackson the cartoonist was trying to make. Then answer the following questions.

1. **Identify the symbols used in the cartoon.** Cartoons often use symbols. A *symbol* is something that stands for something else. For example, a skull and crossbones is a symbol for death. A dove is a symbol for peace. To understand a cartoon, you must know what its symbols mean.

    Figure out what the symbols in this cartoon stand for. (a) Who is pictured in the cartoon? (b) What is he holding in each hand? (c) What do these symbols stand for? (d) What is he wearing on his head? (e) What does this symbol stand for? (f) What is he standing on?

2. **Analyze the meaning of the symbols.** Use your reading of this chapter and the cartoon to decide what the symbols refer to. (a) What incident is probably referred to by the object in Jackson's left hand? (b) What event might the cartoonist have had in mind when he showed Jackson standing on the Constitution?

🔵 **Interpret the cartoon.** Draw conclusions about the cartoonist's point of view. (a) What do you think the cartoonist thought of President Jackson? Why? (b) How was the cartoonist trying to influence the public's attitude toward Jackson? (c) Does the cartoon give a balanced view of Jackson as President? Explain. (d) Study the painting of Jackson on page 296. Does the painting express an attitude toward Jackson different from that of the cartoon?

won by a large margin. Most voters stood solidly behind Jackson's veto of the Bank bill.

Pet banks. The Bank was due to close its doors in 1836. But Jackson wanted to send the Bank to an early grave. He ordered the Secretary of the Treasury, Roger Taney, to stop putting government money in the Bank. Instead, Taney put the money into state banks. These became known as *pet banks* because Taney and his friends owned shares in many of them. The loss of federal money crippled the Bank of the United States. When the Bank's charter ran out in 1836, Jackson's victory was complete.

━━ SECTION REVIEW ━━

1. **Define:** spoils system, kitchen cabinet, pet bank.
2. (a) What were the benefits of the spoils system? (b) What were its drawbacks?
3. Why did President Jackson dislike the Bank of the United States?
4. How did Clay and Webster make an election issue of the Bank?
5. **What Do You Think?** How do you think Andrew Jackson's background helped make him a strong President?

3 Tests of Strength

Read to Learn

★ How did a high tariff cause a crisis in 1832?
★ Why were Native Americans forced off their land?
★ How did life become more democratic in the 1820s?
★ What do these words mean: nullification, states' rights, secede, discrimination?

The fight over the Bank increased Jackson's support among the people. By using the veto, Jackson showed that he was a strong President. In other tests of strength, Jackson took actions that made the office of the President more powerful.

Debate Over Tariffs

Soon after Jackson won reelection in 1832, he faced another major crisis. The root of the crisis was a tariff bill passed by Congress in 1828. It was the highest tariff ever made law. Southerners called it the *Tariff of Abominations*. An abomination is something that is hated.

Like earlier tariffs, the tariff of 1828 helped manufacturers in the North by making European imports more expensive than American-made goods. (See page 279.) But the tariff hurt Southerners. They exported cotton to Europe and bought European-made goods in return. High tariffs made these imported goods more expensive for Southerners.

Calhoun defends states' rights. John C. Calhoun led the South's fight against the tariff. He used an idea Thomas Jefferson had developed for the Kentucky and Virginia resolutions. (See page 236.) Like Jefferson, Calhoun argued that a state had the right to cancel a federal law it considered unconstitutional. The idea of declaring a federal law illegal is called *nullification*.

Calhoun raised a serious issue. Did the states have the right to limit the power of the federal government? Or did the federal government have final say? Calhoun supported *states' rights,* the right of the states to limit the power of the federal government.

Webster takes the floor. Daniel Webster took a different position. In 1830, he attacked the idea of nullification on the Senate floor. If states had the right to nullify federal laws, he declared, the nation would be ripped apart. At the end of a long speech, his words rang out clearly: "Liberty and Union, now and forever, one and inseparable."

A challenge to Jackson. Many Southerners hoped that President Jackson would speak out for states' rights. After all, he was born in the South and lived in the West. In both sections, support for states' rights was strong. Also, Calhoun was Jackson's Vice President.

In 1830, Jackson and Calhoun attended a dinner party sponsored by southern congressmen. Several congressmen made toasts in favor of states' rights. Finally, it was Jackson's turn to make a toast. Everyone fell silent. Old Hickory raised his glass and turned to face Calhoun, the leading spokesman for states' rights. Jackson looked his Vice President in the eye and said, "Our Union—it must be preserved!"

The drama continued as Calhoun raised his glass. "The Union—next to our liberty, the most dear," he replied. The challenge was clear. Calhoun meant that the liberty of a state was more important than saving the Union.

The debate between supporters of states' rights and defenders of the Union would rage on for years. Because he disagreed with Jackson, Calhoun eventually resigned the office of Vice President. He then was elected senator from South Carolina.

The Nullification Crisis

In 1832, the debate over states' rights heated up when Congress passed a new tariff. South Carolina responded by passing the Nullification Act. It declared that the tariffs of 1828 and 1832 were illegal. At the same time, the state prepared to defend itself. It threatened to *secede,* or withdraw, from the Union if challenged.

Jackson was furious when he heard the news from South Carolina. He said in private, "If one drop of blood be shed there in defiance of the laws of the United States, I will hang the first man of them I can get my hands on to the first tree I can find." Officially, the President was cooler. He supported a compromise tariff bill that Henry Clay suggested. The bill called for lower tariffs. At the same time, Jackson got Congress to pass a force bill. It allowed him to use the army, if necessary, to enforce the law.

Jackson's firm stand had its effect. No other state came forward to support South Carolina. Calhoun gave in and agreed to Clay's compromise tariff. South Carolina repealed the Nullification Act. Because of the President's

The determination of young John C. Calhoun shows clearly in this painting. When Calhoun entered Congress in 1812, fellow congressmen called him "the young Hercules." Hercules was a hero in Greek mythology who was famous for his superhuman strength.

strong leadership, the *Nullification Crisis* passed. Yet, troubling differences remained between the North and South. They would surface again in the years ahead.

Tragedy for Native Americans

Jackson's stand on another issue had tragic results for Native Americans. Since Europeans first arrived in North America, they had steadily pushed Native Americans off the land. From New York to Florida, Indians were forced to move west. Indian leaders like Pontiac and Tecumseh tried to stop settlers from invading their lands. But their efforts ended in defeat.

The Southeast Indians. By the 1820s, only about 125,000 Indians still lived east of the Mississippi. Most belonged to the Creek, Chickasaw, Cherokee, Choctaw, and Seminole nations. The people of these five nations lived in the Southeast. Many had adopted the customs of white settlers. The Cherokees, for example, wrote their own constitution and published a newspaper.

Indians like the Cherokees wanted to live in peace with their white neighbors. But the rich land they owned in the Southeast was ideal for growing cotton. Land-hungry settlers wanted the land for themselves. President Jackson sympathized with the settlers. He believed that all Indians should move west of the Mississippi River.

The Supreme Court rules. Soon after Jackson took office, the state of Georgia claimed the right to seize Cherokee lands. The Cherokees went to court to defend their land. They had signed a treaty with the federal government that protected their property. Therefore, they argued, Georgia did not have the right to take the land away. The Cherokee case reached the Supreme Court. Chief Justice John Marshall upheld the right of the Cherokees to keep their land.

AMERICANS WHO DARED

Sequoyah

Sequoyah (sih KWOI uh), a Cherokee born in Tennessee, was a skilled hunter and trapper. After an accident crippled him, he worked for 12 years to create a written alphabet for his people. The alphabet had 86 symbols and used Greek, English, and Hebrew letters. In the 1820s, Cherokee children learned to read and write using Sequoyah's letters. The Cherokees also used his alphabet to write a constitution.

This time, President Jackson defended states' rights. He said that the federal government could not stop Georgia from moving the Indians. "John Marshall has made his decision," Jackson is reported to have said. "Now let him enforce it." The President then refused to use federal power to protect the Cherokees.

Indian Removal Act. Since the Supreme Court ruling was not enforced, the Indians had no protection. In 1830, Congress passed the *Indian Removal Act.* It stated that Native Americans had to move west of the Mississippi.

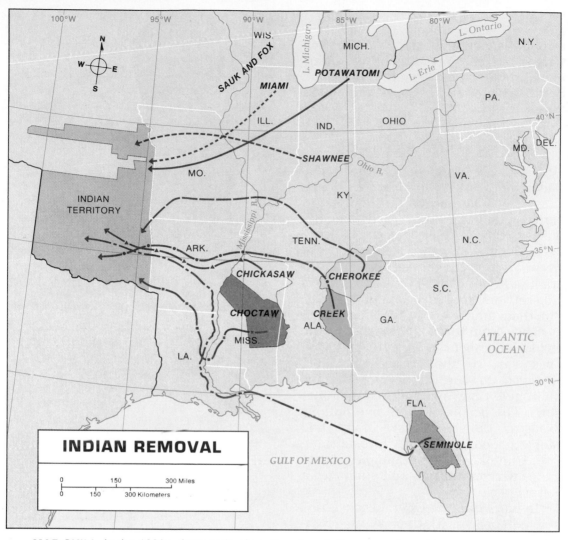

text within map:
100°W 95°W 90°W 85°W 80°W
WIS.
L. Ontario
N.Y.
MICH.
POTAWATOMI
L. Erie
L. Michigan
SAUK AND FOX
MIAMI
ILL.
IND.
OHIO
PA.
40°N
MD. DEL.
SHAWNEE
Ohio R.
MO.
VA.
KY.
N.C.
35°N
INDIAN
TERRITORY
Mississippi R.
ARK.
TENN.
S.C.
CHICKASAW
CHEROKEE
CHOCTAW
CREEK
ALA.
GA.
ATLANTIC
OCEAN
MISS.
LA.
30°N
FLA.
SEMINOLE
N W E S

INDIAN REMOVAL

0   150   300 Miles
0   150   300 Kilometers

GULF OF MEXICO

MAP SKILL In the 1830s, thousands of southeastern Indians were forced to march along the Trail of Tears. They had to move into the Indian Territory west of the Mississippi River. Besides the five southeastern nations, what other Indian peoples were forced to move west?

Most Americans had heard that the land there was a vast desert. So they did not mind turning the area over to the Indians.

The Trail of Tears

The Cherokees and other Indian nations did not want to move west. But they had no choice. Between 1835 and 1838, the United States army forced them to leave at gunpoint. Their long, sad journey west became known as the *Trail of Tears*. One eyewitness described the scene:

The Cherokees are nearly all prisoners. They had been dragged from their homes and encamped at the forts and military places, all over the nation. In Georgia especially, multitudes were allowed no time to take anything with them except the clothes they had on. . . . The property of many has been taken and sold before their eyes for almost nothing.

The Indians marched hundreds of miles to lands they had never seen before. (See the map above.) They had little food and no shelter. Many children and older people perished. In all, about one quarter of the Indians died.

The Seminole Indians in Florida fought fiercely against removal. They were led by Chief Osceola. The Seminoles battled the United States army from 1835 to 1842. In the end, they were defeated. But the *Seminole War* was the costliest battle the United States fought to gain Indian lands. By 1844, only a few thousand Indians were left east of the Mississippi River.

A Growing Spirit of Equality

During Jackson's two terms in the White House, changes begun earlier came into full swing. You have read how politics became more democratic in the 1820s. The democratic spirit also grew stronger in other ways. Americans talked and acted with a new spirit of equality.

In America, servants expected to be treated as equals. Butlers and maids refused to be called with bells, as was done in Europe. In fact, they did not like to be called servants at all. One coach driver complained that his employer "had had private meals every day and not asked him to the table." Americans were so keen on equality that Europeans found them downright rude.

The spirit of equality left out many Americans, however. The Indian Removal Act denied the most basic rights to Native Americans. Women could not vote or hold office. Their right to own property was limited. Black Americans actually lost rights in the 1820s. In both the North and South, free blacks faced growing discrimination, as you will read in Chapter 15. *Discrimination* is a policy or an attitude that denies equal rights to certain people. Despite the limits on equality, democracy grew during the Age of Jackson.

This painting by Mary Ann Thompson shows Cherokees on the Trail of Tears. More than 4,000 Cherokees died from freezing weather, disease, and cruel treatment on the long march west.

1. **Locate:** South Carolina, Georgia, Mississippi River.
2. **Define:** nullification, states' rights, secede, discrimination.
3. (a) What section of the country benefited most from high tariffs? (b) What section opposed high tariffs?
4. (a) Why did white settlers want to take over Indian lands in the Southeast? (b) How did the Cherokees try to defend their land?
5. **What Do You Think?** What do you think Andrew Jackson would have done if South Carolina had tried to secede from the United States during the Nullification Crisis?

4 Jackson's Successors

Read to Learn

★ What caused the Panic of 1837?
★ How did William Henry Harrison become President?
★ What problems did John Tyler have as President?

Andrew Jackson did not run again in 1836. But he helped Vice President Martin Van Buren to follow him into the White House. When Van Buren took the oath of office, Jackson stood at his side. The crowd turned its gaze to the outgoing President, not Van Buren. As Old Hickory stepped down from the platform, a rousing cheer rose from the crowd. In that roar, the people expressed their loyalty to Andrew Jackson.

The Panic of 1837

As Jackson's chosen successor, Martin Van Buren rode into office on a wave of popular support. But within two months of taking office, Van Buren faced the worst economic crisis the nation had known. The crisis is called the *Panic of 1837*.

Causes. The Panic of 1837 came about for several reasons. During the 1830s, the government sold millions of acres of public land in the West. Farmers bought some land, but speculators bought even more.

To pay for the land, speculators borrowed money from state banks, especially western banks. There was no national bank to restrict lending. As a result, state banks printed more and more paper money to meet the demand for loans. Often, the paper money was not backed by gold or silver.

In 1836, President Jackson had become alarmed at the wild speculation in land. To slow it down, he ordered that anyone buying public land had to pay with gold or silver, not with paper money. Speculators and others went to the state banks to exchange their paper money for gold and silver. But they found that the banks did not have gold and silver.

Hard times. Very quickly, the panic began. More and more people hurried to banks to try to get gold and silver for their paper money. In New York, one bank "was jammed with depositors crying 'Pay, pay!' " a witness said. Hundreds of banks failed. They had to lock their doors because they could not meet the demand.

About the same time, the price of cotton fell because of an oversupply. Cotton planters could not repay their bank loans. This caused more banks to fail. As a result, business slowed, and the nation moved into an economic depression.

The depression lasted three years. At its height, 90 percent of the nation's factories were closed. Thousands of people were thrown out of work. In some cities, hungry people broke into warehouses and stole food.

It was easy for people to blame Van Buren for the Panic of 1837. The President did not believe that the government should interfere with business, even during a depression. So Van Buren did little to ease the impact of the Panic. He did cut back expenses at the White House. When he entertained visitors, they were served simple dinners. But as the depression dragged on, Van Buren became less popular.

Tippecanoe and Tyler Too

Even though Van Buren lost support, the Democrats nominated him to carry the party banner in 1840. The Whigs chose William Henry Harrison of Ohio. Harrison was well known as the hero of the Battle of Tippecanoe. (See page 259.) The Whigs named John Tyler as their candidate for Vice President. They used "Tippecanoe and Tyler too" as their campaign slogan.

The Whigs had learned a lot about campaigning from their old foe, Andrew Jackson. They wanted to win the votes of common people. So they presented Harrison as a simple Ohio farmer who lived in a log cabin. In fact, he came from a wealthy and powerful Virginia family. His father had been governor of Virginia and a signer of the Declaration of Independence.

Harrison won easily and forced the Democrats out of the White House for the first time in 12 years. The Whigs arrived in Washington with a clear-cut program. They wanted to set up a new Bank of the United States. They planned to spend federal money for roads, canals, and other improvements. And they wanted a high tariff. But the Whigs' hopes were soon dashed. After less than a month in office, President Harrison died of pneumonia.

John Tyler was the first Vice President to succeed a President who died in office. As President, his actions shocked and disappointed leaders of the Whig Party. Tyler had once been a

This campaign banner shows William Henry Harrison's log cabin symbol. During the campaign, Whigs tried new ways to stir up public support for their candidate. They held huge outdoor meetings and built log cabins in public places to get people to vote for Harrison.

Democrat. He disagreed with the Whigs on almost every issue. When Whigs in Congress passed a bill to recharter the Bank of the United States, Tyler vetoed it.

As a result, Tyler's whole cabinet resigned, except for Daniel Webster. The Whigs threw Tyler out of their party. Democrats were delighted with the Whigs' problem. "Tyler is heartily despised by everyone," reported one observer. "He has no influence at all." With few supporters, Tyler did little during his years in office.

SECTION REVIEW

1. What did President Jackson do to stop land speculation in 1836?
2. What were the causes of the Panic of 1837?
3. How did the Whigs try to win the votes of common people in 1840?
4. Why were Whigs disappointed with John Tyler?
5. **What Do You Think?** What do you think President Van Buren could have done to ease the Panic of 1837?

Chapter 13 Review

★ Summary ★

In the 1820s, common people began to play a new role in government. In 1824, their choice for President was Andrew Jackson. Jackson was a Tennessee frontiersman, self-taught and self-made.

Jackson was not elected President until 1828. He took bold actions on several issues. Jackson undermined the national Bank. He kept South Carolina in the Union. And he allowed Indian removal despite a Supreme Court ruling against it.

Jackson's successor, Martin Van Buren, lost support because of the Panic of 1837. In 1840, Van Buren was beaten by William Henry Harrison. Harrison died after a month in office, leaving John Tyler to serve out an uneventful term.

★ Reviewing the Facts ★   *2 pts.*

Key Terms. Match each term in Column 1 with the correct definition in Column 2.

Column 1	Column 2
1. suffrage	**a.** private meeting to choose a candidate
2. caucus	**b.** right to vote
3. states' rights	**c.** right of states to limit federal power
4. secede	**d.** policy or attitude that denies equal rights to some people
5. discrimination	**e.** withdraw

Key People, Events, and Ideas. Identify each of the following.

1. John Quincy Adams
2. Henry Clay
3. Whig
4. Democrat
5. Old Hickory
6. John C. Calhoun
7. Tariff of Abominations
8. Daniel Webster
9. Nullification Crisis
10. Indian Removal Act
11. Trail of Tears
12. Osceola
13. Seminole War
14. Martin Van Buren
15. Panic of 1837

★ Chapter Checkup ★   *5 pts.*

1. (a) Describe President John Quincy Adams' plans for national growth. (b) Were his plans carried out? Explain.
2. Why were there many more voters in 1828 than in 1824?
3. (a) What political parties grew in the 1820s? (b) Who supported each party?
4. (a) What is a nominating convention? (b) How is it more democratic than a caucus?
5. What did each of the following do during the struggle over the Bank: (a) Nicholas Biddle; (b) Henry Clay; (c) Andrew Jackson.
6. (a) Why did South Carolina try to nullify the tariffs of 1828 and 1832? (b) How did President Jackson respond?
7. (a) Why did settlers want to force Indians to move west? (b) How did Andrew Jackson help them achieve their goal?
8. (a) Describe the causes of the Panic of 1837. (b) How did it affect the 1840 presidential election?

1. **Relating past to present.** European visitors to the United States in the 1830s commented on the social and political equality of the people. (a) What groups of Americans gained more rights in the 1820s? (b) What groups of Americans have gained more rights since then?

2. **Expressing an opinion.** If Congress had approved the roads, canals, and other improvements planned by John Quincy Adams, the economy of the nation would have grown faster. Do you agree or disagree with this statement? Explain.

3. **Understanding the economy.** When the Bank of the United States limited lending in the 1820s, people in the West and South were hurt most. Why did people living near the frontier need to borrow money?

4. **Learning about citizenship.** During the Age of Jackson, how did common people play a more important role than ever before in American politics?

★ **Using Your Skills**

1. **Recognizing points of view.** Review Skill Lesson 5 on page 116. Then reread "The People's President" on page 294. (a) Do you think the first eyewitness supported Jackson? Why or why not? (b) Do you think the second eyewitness supported Jackson? Explain.

2. **Comparing.** Draw a chart with two columns and three rows. Label the columns John Quincy Adams and Andrew Jackson. Label the rows Family, Education, and Experience in Public Life. Fill out the chart. (a) What were the differences between Jackson and Adams? (b) How do the differences show the changes in American politics in the 1820s?

3. **Using a painting as a primary source.** Look at the painting on page 291. (a) What are the people in the picture getting ready to do? (b) What might the three men at right be talking about? (c) What groups of Americans are not shown in the painting? Why not?

4. **Placing events in time.** Study the time line on page 290. (a) When was the Tariff of Abominations passed? (b) When did South Carolina pass the Nullification Act? (c) What is the relationship between the two events?

★ **More to Do**

1. **Writing a letter.** Imagine that you are John C. Calhoun after the toast incident described on page 300. Write a letter of resignation to President Jackson explaining why you no longer wish to serve as his Vice President.

2. **Preparing a newspaper editorial.** Imagine that you are the editor of a Cherokee newspaper during the early 1830s. Write an editorial commenting on passage of the Indian Removal Act by Congress. Include a headline for your editorial.

3. **Exploring local history.** On an outline map of your state, mark the location of any cities, towns, monuments, parks, and other places named in memory of Andrew Jackson.

CHAPTER

14

Westward Ho! (1820–1860)

Chapter Outline

1 Oregon Country
2 The Lone Star Republic
3 Looking Toward the West
4 War With Mexico
5 From Sea to Shining Sea

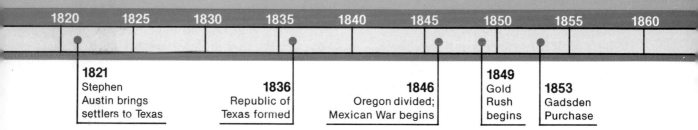

| 1820 | 1825 | 1830 | 1835 | 1840 | 1845 | 1850 | 1855 | 1860 |

1821
Stephen
Austin brings
settlers to Texas

1836
Republic of
Texas formed

1846
Oregon divided;
Mexican War begins

1849
Gold
Rush
begins

1853
Gadsden
Purchase

About This Chapter

From its beginning, America has been a nation on the move. The country began as a group of small colonies dotting the east coast. As these colonies grew, they slowly spread inland. After the Revolution, many Americans moved across the Appalachians. By the 1830s, they had carved up the land east of the Mississippi River.

Settlers continued to push west in the 1840s. They opened up lands in the West and the Southwest. In 1846, a New York newspaper editor named Horace Greeley published the article "To Aspiring Young Men." In it, Greeley offered this advice to young people: "If you have no family or friends to aid you . . . turn your face to the great West and there build up your home and fortune."

Greeley's advice exactly suited the spirit of the times. Soon, his statement was boiled down to the famous message "Go west, young man." And thousands upon thousands of American men and women rallied to the cry "Westward Ho!"

As more Americans moved west, the idea grew that the United States should expand all the way to the Pacific Ocean. During the 1840s, the nation added huge stretches of land to its area. Oregon, California, New Mexico, and Texas all became part of the United States. By 1850, the country reached from sea to sea.

Study the time line above. How long after Stephen Austin first led settlers into Texas did Texans establish the Republic of Texas?

In the mid-1800s, thousands of Americans headed west to find new opportunities. Here, pioneer families bed down after a long day on the trail.

1 Oregon Country

Read to Learn

★ Who were the first American settlers in Oregon Country?

★ Why did Oregon fever sweep the United States?

★ What hardships did travelers on the Oregon Trail face?

★ What does this word mean: rendezvous?

By the 1820s, settlers had filled in much of the land east of the Mississippi. Americans continued to move west. However, few settled on the Great Plains between the Mississippi and the Rockies. Instead, they were drawn to lands farther west.

Beyond the Rockies

In the early 1800s, people began to hear about a land beyond the Rocky Mountains called Oregon Country. At that time, *Oregon Country* meant the whole Pacific Northwest plus part of the Intermountain region and the Rockies. Today, this land includes the states of Oregon, Washington, Idaho, and parts of Montana and Canada. (See the map on page 310.)

Land and climate. The area once called Oregon Country has a varied climate and geography. Along the Pacific Coast, the land is fertile and gets lots of rain. Early white settlers found fine

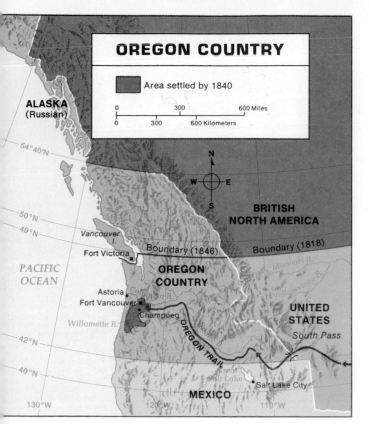

OREGON COUNTRY

Area settled by 1840

ALASKA
(Russian)

54°40'N

50°N
49°N

BRITISH
NORTH AMERICA

Vancouver I.
Fort Victoria

Boundary (1846)   Boundary (1818)

PACIFIC
OCEAN

OREGON
COUNTRY

Missouri R.

Astoria
Fort Vancouver

Yellowstone R.

UNITED
STATES

Champoeg

Willamette R.

42°N

OREGON TRAIL

South Pass

40°N

Salt Lake

Salt Lake City

MEXICO

130°W   120°W   110°W

MAP SKILL Oregon Country was the first area
in the Far West to draw settlers from the
United States. What two rivers did the Oregon
Trail follow as it wound into Oregon Country?

farmland in the Willamette River valley and the lowlands around Puget
Sound. Also, the Pacific Ocean keeps
temperatures mild all year. Farther
inland is a coastal mountain range that
has dense forests. In the 1800s, these
forests held bears and beavers that
lured trappers to the West.

Between the coastal mountains and
the Rockies is a high plateau. This
Intermountain region is much drier
than the coast and has scattered desert
areas. Temperatures are also more
extreme. At the eastern edge of Oregon
Country were the Rocky Mountains.
There, trappers found beavers and other valuable animals.

Conflicting claims. Several countries claimed Oregon in the early
1800s: the United States, Great
Britain, Spain, and Russia. They paid

no attention to the rights of the Indians
in Oregon.

The United States based its claim
on the voyage of Robert Gray. A sea
captain from Boston, Gray visited the
coast of Oregon and named the Columbia River in 1792. The journey of Lewis
and Clark through Oregon further supported American claims to the land.

John Jacob Astor, an American fur
trader, sent a shipload of men and supplies around South America to Oregon
in 1811. They built the town of Astoria
at the mouth of the Columbia River.
Astor's fur traders stayed only a short
time, but they gave Americans another
claim to Oregon.

The British claim to Oregon dated
back to a visit by Sir Francis Drake in
1577. In the early 1800s, many British
fur traders roamed Oregon. Britain
also had Fort Vancouver, the only permanent outpost in Oregon. (See the
map at left.)

In 1818, the United States and
Britain agreed to occupy Oregon jointly. Citizens of both nations would have
equal rights in Oregon. Spain and Russia had few settlers in the area. So they
dropped their claims to Oregon.

Mountain Men

In the early 1800s, a few hardy
trappers followed Indian trails across
the Rockies into Oregon. They wandered through the area, trapping furs
and living off the land. The tough, lone
adventurers were called *Mountain Men.*

Mountain Men were a colorful group.
They dressed in shirts and trousers
made of leather. Porcupine quills decorated their shirts. Around their neck
hung a "possibles sack." Inside the sack
were a pipe, some tobacco, a mold to
make bullets, and other useful items.

Living in the wild. When game was
plentiful, the trappers gorged themselves with food. They ate raw buffalo
liver and gnawed buffalo steaks roasted over an open fire. During lean times,
the trappers lived off the land as well as

they could. "I have held my hands in an anthill until they were covered with ants, then greedily licked them off," recalled one Mountain Man. During harsh winters, Mountain Men often lived with Indians. In fact, they learned many of their survival methods from Indians.

In their hunt for furs, Mountain Men made many useful discoveries. Jedediah Smith found South Pass in Wyoming in 1823. This broad plateau offered an easy way to cross the Rocky Mountains. Manuel Lisa, a Spanish American trapper, led a trip up the Missouri River in 1807. He founded Fort Manuel, the first outpost on the upper Missouri.

The rendezvous. Through the fall and spring, Mountain Men tended their traps. In July, they came out of the wilderness. They met fur traders at a place chosen the year before, called the *rendezvous* (RAHN day voo), or get-together.

The rendezvous was a wild event. One Mountain Man described it as a time of "mirth, songs, dancing, shouting, trading, running, jumping, singing, racing, target-shooting, yarns, [and] frolic." After the first day, the Mountain Men bargained with the fur traders. Beaver hats were popular in the East and in Europe, so Mountain Men got a good price for their furs. But the traders charged high prices for the flour, bullets, and other supplies they hauled to the rendezvous.

In the late 1830s, the fur trade declined. Trappers killed so many beavers that the animals became scarce. Also, beaver hats went out of fashion. However, Mountain Men took on a new job—leading settlers across the rugged trails into Oregon.

Early Settlers in Oregon

The first white Americans to build permanent homes in Oregon were missionaries. Marcus and Narcissa Whitman were among the first missionaries

AMERICANS WHO DARED

James Beckwourth

James Beckwourth was one of the best-known Mountain Men. Beckwourth, the son of a Virginia slave, headed west to escape slavery. He discovered a pass through the Sierra Nevada into California that was named for him. In 1856, Beckwourth added to his own legend by publishing his life story.

to reach Oregon. They had heard that Indians in Oregon were eager to accept Christianity. After the Whitmans married in 1836, their honeymoon was the seven-month journey to Oregon. Narcissa Whitman was one of the first white women to cross the Rocky Mountains.

The Whitmans built their mission near the Columbia River and began to work with the Cayuse (KĪ oos) Indians. Marcus Whitman was a doctor. Narcissa Whitman set up a mission school. Soon, other missionaries and settlers joined the Whitmans. As more settlers arrived and took over Indian lands, trouble arose with the Cayuses. Even worse, settlers brought diseases that often killed the Indians.

Narcissa Whitman, shown here, rejoiced when she and her husband finally reached the Columbia River valley in Oregon Country. "The beauty of this extensive valley," she wrote, "at this hour of twilight was enchanting and [turned] my mind from the fatigue under which I was laboring."

In 1847, tragedy struck the Whitmans' mission. An outbreak of measles among the settlers spread to the Cayuses. Dr. Whitman tended both white and Indian children, but many Cayuse children died. The angry Cayuses blamed the settlers for the disease. A band of Cayuses attacked the mission, killing the Whitmans and 12 others.

The Oregon Trail

Despite the Whitmans' death, other bold pioneers set out on the long trek to Oregon. News about Oregon began to trickle back to the United States. There, farmers marvelled at stories of wheat that grew taller than a man and Oregon turnips five feet around. Stories like these touched off an outbreak of Oregon fever.

Oregon fever spread quickly. Soon, the trails west were clogged with pioneers. Beginning in 1843, wagon trains left every spring for Oregon. The route taken by these settlers was called the *Oregon Trail.* (See the map on page 320.)

Families planning to go west met at Independence, Missouri, in the early spring. Because most families had cattle or other animals, they camped outside town. When enough families had gathered, they formed a wagon train. Each wagon train elected leaders to make decisions along the trail.

Life on the Trail

Wagon trains left Independence in May. The pioneers traveled quickly to reach Oregon before early October, when snow began to fall in the mountains. This meant that they had to cover 2,000 miles (3,200 km) on foot in 5 months. In the 1840s, traveling 15 miles a day was considered good time.

Daily routine. Families adapted quickly to life on the trail. At dawn, everyone woke to a bugle blast. Each person had a job to do. Young girls helped their mothers prepare breakfast. Men and boys harnessed the horses or oxen. By 6:00 A.M., the cry of "Wagons ho!" rang out on the plains.

The pioneers made a brief stop at noon for lunch. Then, they returned to the trail until 6:00 or 7:00 P.M. At night, the wagons were pulled in a circle. This kept the cattle from wandering off to find grass.

Pioneers often brought too much equipment. It was dangerous to ford streams and cross mountains with heavy wagons. To lighten the wagons, travelers threw away gear. Soon, the trails were littered with junk.

One traveler wrote home that the Oregon Trail was strewn with "large blacksmiths' anvils, ploughs, large grind-stones, baking ovens, kegs, barrels, harness, [and] clothing." Some

A diary is often a useful primary source because it tells you what the writer saw, heard, said, thought, and felt. It gives you firsthand information about people, places, and events. Because diaries are private, writers often say what they honestly think.

The excerpts below are from a diary kept by Amelia Stewart Knight. With her husband and children, she traveled the Oregon Trail in 1853. Her diary tells about the hardships the family faced on their way to a new life in Oregon.

1. **Identify the primary source.** (a) Who wrote the diary? (b) Under what conditions was it written? (c) Why do you think the writer wrote it?

2. **Analyze the information in the primary source.** Study the diary for information about how the writer lived. (a) What does Knight say about hardships on the Oregon Trail? (b) Describe the geography of the area the Knight family traveled through. (c) What chores did Amelia Knight do? (d) What chores did the children do?

3. **Draw conclusions about the writer's point of view.** Decide how the writer felt about making the overland journey west. (a) How do you think Amelia Knight felt about the hardships of the journey? (b) How might keeping the diary have helped her face these hardships? (c) What personal qualities did a person need to make the journey? (d) Study the painting on page 309. What activities described in the diary can you see in the painting? (e) What other activities does the painting show?

 Amelia Stewart Knight's Diary

Monday, April 18th   Cold; breaking fast the first thing; very disagreeable weather; wind east cold and rainy, no fire. We are on a very large prairie, no timber to be seen as far as the eye can reach. Evening—Have crossed several bad streams today, and more than once have been stuck in the mud.

Saturday, April 23rd   Still in camp, it rained hard all night, and blew a hurricane almost. All the tents were blown down, and some wagons capsized. Evening—It has been raining hard all day; everything is wet and muddy. One of the oxen missing; the boys have been hunting him all day. (Dreary times, wet and muddy, and crowded in the tent, cold and wet and uncomfortable in the wagon. No place for the poor children.) I have been busy cooking, roasting coffee, etc. today, and have come into the wagon to write this and make our bed.

Friday, May 6th   We passed a train of wagons on their way back, the head man had drowned a few days before, in a river called the Elkhorn, while getting some cattle across. With sadness and pity I passed those who a few days before had been well and happy as ourselves.

Friday, August 19th   After looking in vain for water, we were about to give up, when husband came across a company of friendly Cayuse Indians, who showed him where to find water. The men and boys have driven the cattle down to water and I am waiting to get supper. We bought a few potatoes from an Indian, which will be a treat for our supper.

This painting shows a wagon train on the Oregon Trail fording the Platte River. At times, so many travelers crowded the trails west that the lead wagon of one train was just a few yards behind the last wagon in the train ahead.

travelers changed their dirty clothes for clean sets they found beside the trail. Pioneers also used the "plains library." They picked up a book, read it, and then left it beside the trail for later travelers to read.

Hardships. The long journey held many dangers. During the spring rains, travelers risked their lives floating wagons across swollen rivers. In the summer, they faced blistering heat on the plains. In the fall, they ran into early snow that blocked passes through the mountains. The greatest danger was illness. Cholera (KAHL er uh) and other diseases wiped out whole wagon trains.

Indians. As they moved west toward the Rockies, pioneers saw Indians often. At times, Indians attacked the whites trespassing on their land. More often, Indians traded with the travelers. Some pioneers depended on food they bought from Indians. One pioneer wrote: "Whenever we camp near any Indian village, we are no sooner stopped than a whole crowd may be seen coming galloping into our camp. The squaws do all the swapping."

Despite the hardships of the trip, more than 50,000 people reached Oregon between 1840 and 1860. Their wagon wheels cut so deeply into the plains that the ruts can still be seen today.

By the 1840s, Americans greatly outnumbered the British in Oregon. In 1818, the two nations had agreed to occupy Oregon jointly. However, many Americans began to feel that Oregon should be part of the United States. Arguments over the future of Oregon nearly led to war with Britain.

1. **Locate:** Oregon Country, Willamette River, Oregon Trail, Independence, South Pass.
2. **Define:** rendezvous.
3. What were Mountain Men looking for in the West?

4. Who were the first white Americans to build permanent homes in Oregon?
5. (a) Why did pioneers begin moving to Oregon Country? (b) What hardships did they face along the way?
6. **What Do You Think?** What qualities do you think Mountain Men needed to survive in the wilderness?

2 The Lone Star Republic

Read to Learn
★ Who were the first settlers from the United States in Texas?
★ How did Texans win independence?
★ What problems did the Republic of Texas face?
★ What does this word mean: annex?

Even before pioneers began moving west along the Oregon Trail, other Americans were pushing into the Southwest. In the 1820s and 1830s, Americans settled on the fertile plains of central and southern Texas.

Americans Settle in Texas

Since the early 1800s, American farmers had looked eagerly at Spanish lands in the Southwest. But Spain refused to let Americans settle in Texas until 1820. That year, Spain gave Moses Austin a land grant in Texas. But Austin died before he could set up a colony. His son, Stephen Austin, took up the work.

In 1821, Mexico gained its independence from Spain (see page 281). The new nation gladly let Stephen Austin lead settlers into Texas, its northern province. Only about 4,000 Mexicans lived in Texas. The Mexican government thought that the Americans would help develop the land. It also hoped that American settlers would help control Indian attacks.

Thousands of Indians lived in Texas. They included hunters such as the Comanches and Apaches as well as the Pueblos and other farming people. For 200 years, Spanish missionaries had tried to convert the Indians to Christianity. But they had little success. In fact, some Indian groups fiercely resisted the missionaries.

Mexico granted Austin and each settler 640 acres of land. The settlers agreed to become citizens of Mexico, obey its laws, and worship in the Catholic Church. Austin carefully chose 300 families to settle in Texas. He looked for hard-working people who could take care of themselves. In 1821, they began moving to Texas. Under Austin's wise leadership, the colony grew. By 1830, the number of Americans in Texas had reached 20,000.

Parts of Texas were ideal for cattle raising. Other parts had land good for growing cotton. Many Americans moved to Texas from the South. Some built large cotton plantations and brought in thousands of slaves to work the land.

Problems With Mexico

Stephen Austin and his settlers had agreed to become Mexican citizens and Catholics. But other Americans flooding into Texas were Protestants. They spoke only a few words of Spanish, the

Stephen Austin seemed an unlikely pioneer. A sensitive and shy man, Austin enjoyed playing the flute and reading. But he was a man of action, too. In this painting, Austin reacts to news from a scout about a battle between Indians and settlers.

official language of Mexico, and they felt no loyalty to Mexico. Problems soon developed between settlers and the Mexican government.

In 1830, Mexico passed a law forbidding any more Americans to move to Texas. Mexico feared that the Americans wanted to make Texas part of the United States. In fact, the United States had already tried to buy Texas from Mexico.

The Mexican government also decided to make settlers obey laws that had been ignored for years. One law outlawed slavery in Texas. Another required Texans to worship in the Catholic Church. Texans resented the laws and the Mexican troops who came north to enforce them.

In 1832, General Antonio López de Santa Anna rose to power in Mexico. Two years later, Santa Anna threw out the Mexican constitution. Americans feared that Santa Anna might try to drive them out of Texas.

The Fight for Independence

Americans in Texas believed that the time for action had come. In October 1835, Texans in the town of Gonzales (gon ZAH lehs) fought with Mexican troops. The Texans won. (See the map on page 317.) The fight at Gonzales is called "the Lexington of Texas," after the battle that began the American Revolution.

Two months after Gonzales, Texans forced Mexican troops out of San Antonio. News of the two Mexican defeats angered General Santa Anna. He marched north at the head of a large army, determined to crush the rebellion in Texas.

On March 2, 1836, Texans met in Washington-on-the-Brazos (BRAH zohs). There they declared their independence from Mexico. Texans set up the *Republic of Texas* and asked Sam Houston to command the army. Houston's army was small and untrained. So he decided to fall back as Santa Anna advanced.

The Alamo. At the same time that Texans were declaring their independence, a heroic fight was raging in San Antonio. There, 188 Texans, including both Americans and Mexicans, were trying to hold off Santa Anna's army. They took cover in the *Alamo,* an old Spanish mission. Thousands of Mexican troops surrounded the Alamo.

For 12 days, the Mexicans shelled the Alamo. The outnumbered Texans held out bravely. At last, on March 6, the Mexicans launched an all-out attack. Mexican soldiers poured over the walls of the old mission. In furious hand-to-hand fighting, all the defenders died. But hundreds of Mexican soldiers were killed in the battle. And the defenders of the Alamo had given Sam Houston time to organize his army. (See page 318.)

Victory. The slaughter at the Alamo both angered and inspired Texans. It brought a flood of volunteers into Sam Houston's army. They came from the United States as well as from Texas.

On April 21, 1836, Houston decided that the moment to attack had come. Santa Anna's army was camped near the San Jacinto (jeh SEEN toh) River. Texans charged into the Mexican camp, crying "Remember the Alamo!"

The **Battle of San Jacinto** lasted only 15 minutes. Texans killed 630 Mexicans and captured 700 more. The next day, Texans captured Santa Anna himself. They forced him to sign a treaty granting Texas its independence.

The Republic of Texas

At the Battle of San Jacinto, Texans carried a flag with a single white star. After the battle, Texans began calling their nation the **Lone Star Republic.** They drew up a constitution like that of the United States and elected Sam Houston president.

MAP SKILL The Texas war of independence was brief but bloody. Three weeks after the Alamo defenders died, General Urrea of Mexico executed 300 Texans captured at Goliad. How do you think the events at the Alamo and Goliad affected Texans? Where did Texans finally defeat and capture General Santa Anna?

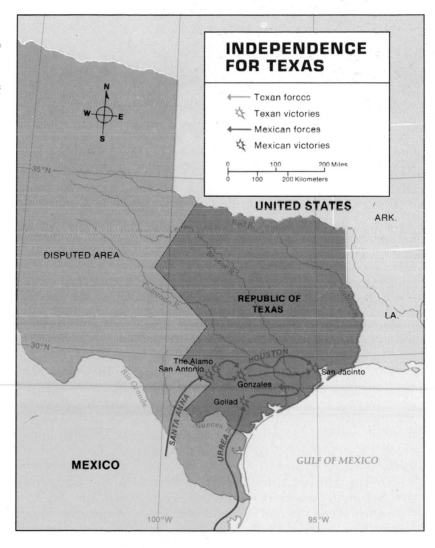

INDEPENDENCE FOR TEXAS

← Texan forces
✪ Texan victories
← Mexican forces
✪ Mexican victories

0   100   200 Miles
0   100   200 Kilometers

UNITED STATES

ARK.

DISPUTED AREA

REPUBLIC OF TEXAS

LA.

Red R.

Brazos R.

Colorado R.

The Alamo
San Antonio

Gonzales

Goliad

HOUSTON

San Jacinto

Rio Grande

SANTA ANNA

URREA

Nueces R.

MEXICO

GULF OF MEXICO

100°W   95°W

35°N

30°N

William B. Travis commanded the Texans defending the Alamo. The group included the famous frontiersmen Jim Bowie and Davy Crockett as well as several women.

Travis wrote the following letter while he and his troops were trapped inside

the Alamo. He addressed it "To the People of Texas and all Americans in the world." Perhaps Travis realized that the defense of the Alamo would rally both Texans and Americans to fight for Texas independence.

> Fellow citizens and compatriots—I am besieged by a thousand or more of the Mexicans under Santa Anna. I have sustained a continual Bombardment and cannonade for 24 hours and have not lost a man. The enemy has demanded a surrender . . . otherwise the garrison are to be put to the *sword,* if the fort is taken. I have answered the demand with a cannon shot, and our flag still waves proudly from the walls.
>
> I shall never surrender or retreat. . . . I am determined to sustain myself as long as possible and die like a soldier who never forgets what is due to his honor and that of his country.

> VICTORY OR DEATH
> William Barret Travis

★ Why do you think the defenders of the Alamo fought to the death?

The new country faced huge problems. First, the government of Mexico did not accept the treaty signed by Santa Anna. Mexicans still considered Texas part of their country. Second, Texas was almost bankrupt. Sam Houston once gave a formal speech dressed in a blanket to show how badly Texas needed money. Most Texans hoped to solve these problems by becoming part of the United States.

In the United States, people were divided about whether to annex Texas. To *annex* means to add on. Southerners favored annexing Texas. Northerners

were against it. At issue was slavery. Northerners knew that slave owners lived in Texas. Many Northerners opposed slavery and did not want to annex an area that allowed slavery. President Jackson also worried that annexing Texas would lead to war with Mexico. As a result, the United States refused to annex Texas.

Over the next ten years, the Lone Star Republic survived and prospered under Sam Houston's leadership. During the Panic of 1837, thousands of Americans moved to Texas. They went to find land and start businesses. Settlers from Germany and Switzerland swelled the population. By the 1840s, there were 140,000 people in Texas, including many Mexicans and black Americans.

Both free blacks and slaves had fought for Texas independence. After independence, however, slave owners wanted to drive free blacks out of the country. They claimed that free blacks caused unrest among the slaves. Despite pressure to leave, some free blacks stayed in Texas.

3 Looking Toward the West

Read to Learn

★ What were the landforms and climate of the West?
★ Who were the first white settlers in the West?
★ How did the Spanish treat Native Americans in California?
★ What did Americans mean by the term Manifest Destiny?

In the 1840s, Americans began to talk about expanding the nation all the way to the Pacific Ocean. They looked with new interest toward California and the Southwest, both part of Mexico.

The Southwest

The Southwest was part of Mexico in the 1840s. This huge region was known as the *New Mexico Territory.* It included most of New Mexico and Arizona as well as parts of Nevada, Utah, and Colorado. The capital of the territory was Santa Fe.

Land and climate. The Southwest is hot and dry. Thin grasses grow in some parts. Other parts are desert. Before the Spanish came, the Pueblos and Zuñis irrigated the land and farmed it. Other Indians, such as the Apaches and Yumas, were hunters.

A Spanish explorer, Juan de Oñate (oh NAH tay), traveled across New Mexico in 1598. He built the first white settlement at Santa Fe. When more Spanish settlers arrived, they set up huge sheep ranches. A few rich families owned the sheep ranches. Indians tended the herds.

Santa Fe Trail. Under the Spanish, Santa Fe became a busy trading town. However, Spain refused to let Americans settle in New Mexico. Only after Mexico won its independence were Americans welcome there.

William Becknell, a businessman and adventurer, was the first American to head for Santa Fe. Becknell set out from St. Louis in 1821, carrying tools and rolls of cloth. He led a group of traders on the long trip across the plains. When they reached Santa Fe, they found Mexicans eager to buy their goods. Other Americans soon followed Becknell's route from Independence to Santa Fe. The route became known as the *Santa Fe Trail.* (Trace the Santa Fe Trail on the map on page 320.)

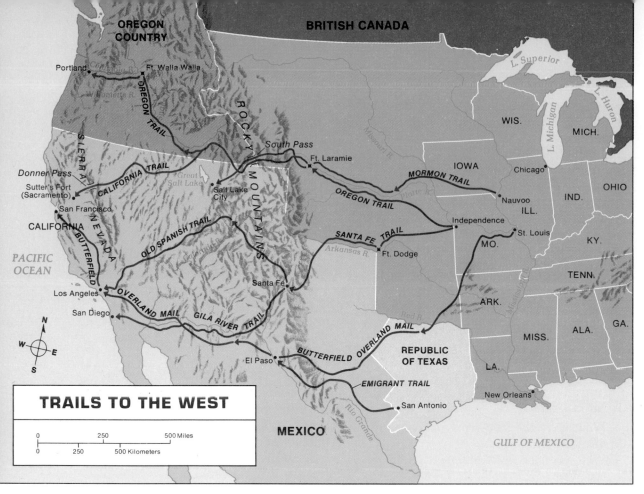

MAP SKILL Americans followed a number of trails to reach the West, as this map shows. Which overland trails ended in cities in California?

California

Like New Mexico, California was part of Mexico in the early 1840s. Spain had claimed this land 100 years before English colonists built homes in Jamestown. As a result, Spanish culture shaped life in California.

Land and climate. California has a dramatic landscape. Two tall mountain ranges slice through the area. One hugs the coast. The other sits inland on the border of Nevada and Arizona. Between these two ranges is California's fertile central valley.

Northern California receives plenty of rain. In the south, water is scarce, and much of the land is desert. California enjoys mild temperatures all year, except in the high mountains.

Spanish missions. Spanish soldiers and missionaries built the first permanent European settlements in California. In 1769, Captain Gaspar de Portolá led a group of soldiers and missionaries up the Pacific coast. The chief missionary was Father Junípero Serra (hoo NEE peh roh SEHR rah).

Father Serra built his first mission at San Diego. He went on to build 20 other missions along the California coast. Each mission claimed the surrounding land and soon became self-sufficient. Spanish soldiers built forts near the missions.

Treatment of Native Americans. Soldiers forced local Indians to work for the missions. Resistance was limited because the California Indians were peaceful people. Also, they lived in small groups rather than large nations.

At the missions, Indians herded sheep and cattle and tended farmland. In return, they learned the Catholic religion and lived at the mission. Many missionaries were truly concerned with converting the Indians. However, life on the missions was hard. Thousands of Indians died from overwork and disease.

Life for Indians became even worse after Mexico won its independence from Spain. The Mexican government offered mission land to ranchers. Some ranchers cruelly mistreated the Indians. If Indians tried to run away, ranchers hunted them down. The harsh conditions had a deadly effect. Between 1770 and 1850, the number of Indians in California fell from 310,000 to 100,000.

A Confident Nation

In the mid-1840s, only about 700 people from the United States lived in California. But more and more Americans were looking toward the West. Many heard tall tales about a pioneers' paradise in California. Also, Americans knew that their government had tried to buy California from Mexico several times. Officials were especially interested in the fine ports at San Diego and San Francisco.

Manifest Destiny. Americans felt confident in the 1840s. They believed that their democratic government was the best in the world. Many Americans wanted the United States to spread all the way across the continent.

In the 1840s, a New York newspaper coined a phrase for that feeling— *Manifest Destiny.* Manifest means

Spanish ranchers in North America lived an elegant life. Here, a hacendado, or landowner, and his wife ride out to greet visitors. Notice their rich clothing. Since hacendados lived many miles from their neighbors, they gave visitors a lavish welcome. One traveler commented on a feast he attended: "The dishes followed each other in such numbers that I am almost afraid to mention them."

clear or obvious. Destiny means something that is sure to happen. Americans who believed in Manifest Destiny thought that America was "obviously" meant to expand to the Pacific.

Manifest Destiny had another side, however. Some Americans thought they were better than Native Americans and Mexicans. For these Americans, racism justified taking over lands owned by Indians and Mexicans.

Election of 1844. Manifest Destiny played an important role in the election of 1844. The Whigs nominated Henry Clay for President. Clay was a famous and respected national leader. The Democrats chose a relative unknown, James Polk.

People soon knew Polk as the candidate who favored expansion. Polk demanded that California, New Mexico, Texas, and Oregon be added to the United States. The Democrats made Oregon a special issue. Even though Oregon was held jointly with Britain, they demanded the whole area all the way to its northern border at latitude 54°40'N. "Fifty-four forty or fight!" was their campaign slogan. Americans approved of Polk's goals, and he won the election.

═══ **SECTION REVIEW** ═══

1. **Locate:** Santa Fe, Santa Fe Trail, San Diego.
2. What did William Becknell find when he arrived in Santa Fe?
3. Who were the first white settlers in California?
4. **What Do You Think?** Why do you think so many Americans believed in Manifest Destiny?

4 War With Mexico

Read to Learn

★ How did Oregon become part of the United States?
★ Why did the United States go to war with Mexico?
★ How did Spanish and Indian cultures influence Americans?
★ What does this word mean: cede?

James Polk rode into the White House on a wave of support for expansion. The new President firmly believed in Manifest Destiny. To fulfill this dream, however, he faced a showdown with Britain and a war with Mexico.

Expanding the Nation's Borders

By 1844, Americans were willing to reconsider the idea of annexing Texas. Expansionist feeling in the United States was running high, as Polk's election showed.

Annexing Texas. In 1844, Sam Houston signed a treaty of annexation with the United States, but the Senate refused to ratify it. Many people still feared that the treaty would lead to war with Mexico. Houston was disappointed. But he kept up hope and thought of a plan. To convince Congress to annex Texas, he let Americans think that Texas might become an ally of Britain. The trick worked. In March 1845, Congress passed a joint resolution admitting Texas to the Union.

Annexing Texas led at once to a dispute with Mexico. The dispute was over the southern border of Texas, now part of the United States. Texas said that its border was the Rio Grande. Mexico replied that the Nueces (noo AY says) River was the southern border of Texas. (See the map on page 324.)

Oregon divided. The dispute over the Texas border was not the only problem facing Polk when he took office in 1845. As he had promised in his campaign, Polk moved to gain control of Oregon. For a time, war between Britain and the United States seemed likely.

President Polk did not really want a war with Britain. So in 1846, he agreed to a compromise. Oregon was divided at latitude 49°N. Britain took the lands north of this line. The United States took the lands south of it and called them the Oregon Territory. This territory was later divided into three states. Oregon became a state in 1859, Washington in 1889, and Idaho in 1890.

The Mexican War

In 1845, the United States and Mexico stood on the brink of war. Mexicans were furious when the United States annexed Texas. They had never accepted the independence of Texas. Also, they were afraid that Americans in California and New Mexico might rebel, as the Texans had done.

Americans, in turn, were angry with Mexico. President Polk offered to buy California and New Mexico from the Mexicans. But Mexico refused. Americans felt that Mexico was standing in the way of Manifest Destiny.

American blood on American soil. In January 1846, President Polk sent General Zachary Taylor to Texas. Taylor's mission was to cross the Nueces River and set up posts along the Rio Grande. Polk knew that Mexico claimed this land and that the move might push Mexico into war. In April 1846, Mexican troops crossed the Rio Grande and fought a brief battle with the Americans. Soldiers on both sides were killed.

President Polk claimed that Mexico had "shed American blood on American soil." He asked Congress to declare war on Mexico. Congress did as Polk wanted, but America was divided over the war. Many people in the South and

West were eager to fight because they wanted more land. People in the North opposed the war. They saw it as a southern plot to add more slave states to the Union.

Early battles. When the *Mexican War* began, Americans attacked on several fronts. General Taylor crossed the Rio Grande into Mexico. He won several battles against the Mexican army. In February 1847, he defeated General Santa Anna at the Battle of Buena Vista. (See the map on page 324.)

Meanwhile, General Winfield Scott landed another American army at the Mexican port of Veracruz. After a long battle, the Americans took the city. Scott then marched toward Mexico City. He followed the same route taken by Hernando Cortés more than 300 years earlier.

The Bear Flag Republic. A third American army, led by General Stephen Kearny, headed west along the Santa Fe Trail. It reached San Diego in the fall of 1846. After several battles, Kearny took control of southern California.

Earlier, Americans in northern California had rebelled against Mexican rule. Captain John Frémont and a band of frontiersmen led the rebels. On June 15, 1846, they declared California an independent republic. The rebels raised a handmade flag showing a grizzly bear. They called their new nation the *Bear Flag Republic.* During the Mexican War, Frémont joined forces with the United States army.

On to Victory

By 1847, the United States controlled all of New Mexico and California. Meantime, General Scott reached the outskirts of Mexico City. He hoped simply to walk into the Mexican capital. Instead, he had to fight a fierce battle. Young Mexican soldiers made a heroic last stand at Chapultepec (chah

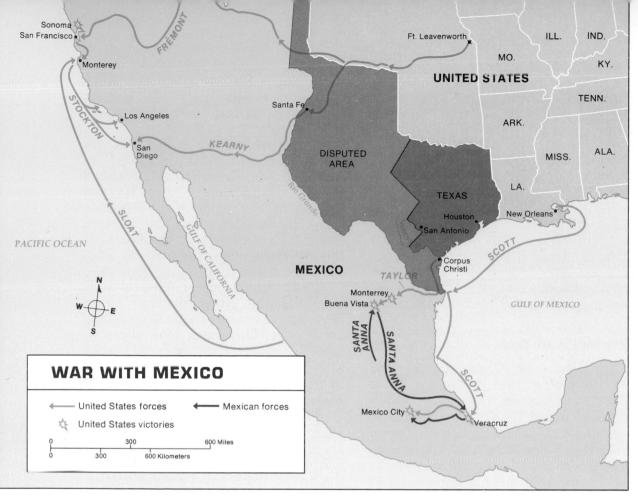

← United States forces   ← Mexican forces

☆ United States victories

| 0 | 300 | 600 Miles |
| 0 | 300 | 600 Kilometers |

MAP SKILL Fighting on the Texas border triggered the Mexican War. But the rest of the war took place in Mexico, as this map shows. Locate the two rivers that border the area disputed by Mexico and the United States at the start of the war. What are the two rivers?

POOL tuh pek), the fort that guarded Mexico City. Like the American defenders of the Alamo, the young Mexicans at Chapultepec fought to the last. Today, Mexicans still celebrate these young men as heroes.

The peace treaty. With the American army in Mexico City, the Mexican government had to make peace. In 1848, Mexico signed the Treaty of Guadalupe Hidalgo (gwah duh LOOP ay ih DAHL goh). Under the treaty, Mexico *ceded,* or gave, all of California and the New Mexico Territory to the United States. These lands were called the *Mexican Cession.* (See the map on page 326.) In return, the United States paid Mexico $15 million and agreed to respect the rights of Spanish-speaking people in the Mexican Cession.

Gadsden Purchase. A few years after the Mexican War, the United States completed its expansion across the continent. In 1853, it paid Mexico $10 million for a strip of land now in Arizona and New Mexico. The land was called the *Gadsden Purchase.* Americans rejoiced. Their dreams of Manifest Destiny had come true.

Mexican and Indian Heritage

Texas and the Mexican Cession added vast new lands to the United States. In these new lands, Americans found a rich culture that blended Spanish and Indian traditions.

When English-speaking settlers flooded into the Southwest, they brought their own culture with them, including ideas about democratic government. At the same time, they learned much from the older residents of the area. Mexican Americans taught the newcomers, whom they called Anglos, how to irrigate the soil. They also showed the Americans how to mine silver and other minerals. Many Spanish and Indian words became part of the English language. They included stampede, buffalo, soda, and tornado.

Americans kept some Mexican laws. One law said that a husband and wife owned property jointly. In the rest of the United States, married women could not own property. Another law said that landowners could not cut off water to their neighbors. This law was important in the dry Southwest.

Americans often did not treat Mexican Americans and Indians well. These older residents of the Southwest struggled to protect their traditions and rights. But Americans ignored old land claims. If Mexican Americans went to court to defend their property, they found that American judges rarely upheld their claims. "The Americans say they have come for our good," one Mexican American explained. "Yes, for all our goods."

SECTION REVIEW

1. **Locate:** Rio Grande, Nueces River, Buena Vista, Veracruz, Mexico City, Mexican Cession, Gadsden Purchase.
2. **Define:** cede.
3. How did the United States gain the Oregon Territory?
4. What lands did the United States gain from the Mexican War?
5. **What Do You Think?** Why do you think Americans ignored the land claims of Mexican Americans?

5 From Sea to Shining Sea

Read to Learn
★ Why did Mormons settle in Utah?
★ How did the Gold Rush change life in California?
★ Why did California have a mix of people?
★ What do these words mean: forty-niner, vigilante?

In 1848, the United States finally stretched "from sea to shining sea." The Stars and Stripes flew from the ports of New England to the sun-baked missions of San Diego. Restless pioneers soon headed into these lands to build homes and seek their fortunes.

Mormons Move West

Among the early pioneers to settle in the Mexican Cession were the *Mormons*. The Mormons belonged to the Church of Jesus Christ of Latter Day Saints. The church was founded in the 1820s by Joseph Smith. Smith, a farmer who lived in upstate New York, won many followers.

Early years. Smith was an energetic and well-liked man. But some of his teachings angered non-Mormons. For example, at first Mormons believed in owning property in common. Smith also said that a man could have more than one wife.* The Mormons were forced to move from New York to Ohio, then to Missouri, and later to Illinois.

In the 1840s, the Mormons built the town of Nauvoo, Illinois, on the banks

---

*In 1890, Mormons gave up the practice of allowing a man to have more than one wife.

of the Mississippi River. The Mormons worked together for the good of their community. They ran successful farms and industries. By 1844, Nauvoo was the largest town in Illinois. Its clean streets were lined with neat brick houses.

However, the Mormons again had trouble with their neighbors. In 1844, a mob attacked Nauvoo and killed Joseph Smith. The Mormons quickly chose Brigham Young as their new leader. Young realized that the Mormons needed a home where they would be safe. He had read about a valley between the Rocky Mountains and the Great Salt Lake in Utah. Young decided that the isolated valley would make a safe home for the Mormons.

An impossible task. To move 15,000 men, women, and children from Illinois to Utah seemed an impossible task. Young relied on faith and careful planning to achieve his goal. In 1847, he led an advance party into the Great Salt Lake valley. For two years, Mormon wagon trains struggled across the plains and over the steep Rockies.

Once they reached Utah, the Mormons had to survive in the desert climate of the valley. Once again, Young proved to be a gifted leader. He planned an irrigation system to bring water to farms. Young also drew up plans for a large city, called *Salt Lake City,* to be built in the desert.

The Mormon settlement in Utah grew quickly. Like other white settlers,

MAP SKILL By 1848, the United States stretched all the way from the Atlantic to the Pacific Ocean. What area on the map was the last to become part of the United States? When was it added?

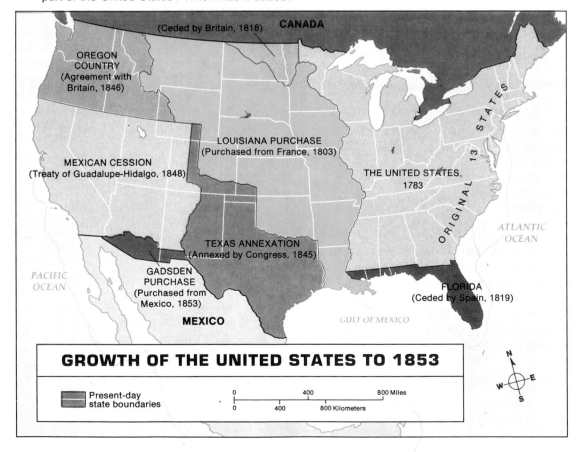

GROWTH OF THE UNITED STATES TO 1853

Mormons often suffered violence at the hands of their neighbors. Here, non-Mormons attack a Mormon settlement near Independence, Missouri, in 1833. The violence ruined the settlement, which Joseph Smith had hoped would one day be "the chief city in the Western Hemisphere."

Mormons took over thousands of acres of Indian land, usually without paying anything for it. Congress recognized Brigham Young as governor of the Utah Territory in 1850. Trouble broke out when non-Mormons moved to the area. In the end, peace was restored, and Utah became a state in 1896.

The Gold Rush

While the Mormons were trekking into Utah, news reached the East that sent thousands of people hurrying along trails west. The news was the discovery of gold in California.

Sutter's Mill. John Sutter, a Swiss immigrant, was building a sawmill on the American River north of Sacramento in 1848. James Marshall was in charge of the job. One morning, Marshall saw a gleaming yellow rock in the river. He reached into the icy water and picked up the yellow lump. He held it in the sunlight. For a moment, Marshall could not speak. Then, a single word came to his lips: "Gold."

In a few days, news of the gold strike spread to San Francisco. Carpenters dropped their saws. Bakers left bread in their ovens. Schools emptied as teachers and students joined the rush to the gold fields. From California, the news sped eastward. Thousands of Americans caught gold fever. They spent their hard-earned savings to set out for the gold fields of California. The California Gold Rush had begun.

The Gold Rush drew people from all over the world in 1849. They were called *forty-niners*. If forty-niners had money, they traveled to California by sea because it was faster. But most traveled overland. Many passed through Salt Lake City. There, the Mormons prospered by selling food and horses to weary travelers. In 1849, more than 80,000 people made the long journey to California.

Panning for gold. At first, mining took little skill. The gold was near the surface of the earth. Miners used knives to dig for gold in riverbeds. Soon, they found a better way. They loaded gravel from the riverbed into a washing pan. They held the pan under water and swirled it gently. The river water washed away lighter gravel, leaving the heavier gold in the pan.

MAP SKILL During 1849 alone, some 80,000 people rushed to California. The population of San Francisco and other cities jumped. What cities were near to the gold mines in northern California?

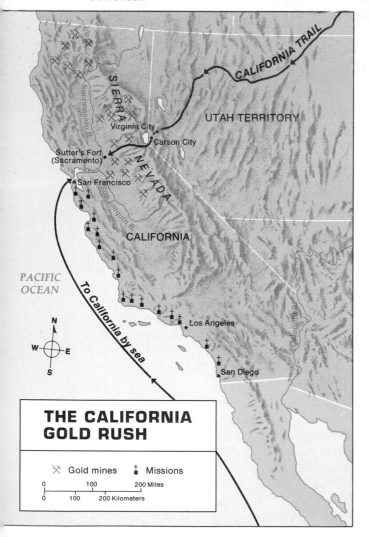

THE CALIFORNIA GOLD RUSH

⚒ Gold mines   ✝ Missions

0   100   200 Miles
0   100   200 Kilometers

Only a few miners struck it rich. Most went broke trying to make their fortunes. These people often had to leave the gold fields. Many found other jobs and helped to build up the economy of California.

California joins the Union. The Gold Rush changed life in California. Almost overnight, places like San Francisco grew from sleepy towns into bustling cities. The Gold Rush also created problems. Greed turned some forty-niners into criminals. Murders and robberies plagued many mining camps. To reduce crime, miners formed vigilance committees. *Vigilantes* (vihj uh LAN teez) dealt out punishment even though they had no legal power to do so. Sometimes, the accused criminal was lynched, or hanged, without a legal trial.

Californians realized that they needed a government to stop the lawlessness. In 1849, they drafted a state constitution. They then asked to be admitted to the Union. California's request created an uproar in the United States. The issue was whether the new state would allow slavery or not. You will read about this issue in Chapter 17. After much debate in Congress, California was finally admitted to the Union in 1850.

A Mix of Peoples

California's population grew rapidly in the next few years. Most newcomers were white Americans. During the wild days of the Gold Rush, they often ignored the rights of other Californians.

Native Americans. Indians fared worst of all. Many were driven off their lands and died of starvation and disease. Others were murdered. In 1850, the Indian population in California was about 100,000. By the 1870s, there were only 17,000 Indians left in the state.

Forty-niners, like the men and woman here, worked hard to find gold. First, they used picks to break up a streambed. Then, they shoveled the mud and gravel into wooden placers such as the one in this photograph. The miners used water from the stream to wash away everything but the gold. Because it was heavier, gold stayed in the placer.

Mexican Americans. Often, Mexican Americans lost land they had owned for years. Many fought to preserve the laws and customs of their people. Jose Carillo (cah REE yoh) was from one of the oldest Mexican families in California. In part because of his efforts, the state's constitution was written in both Spanish and English.

Chinese Americans. Chinese settlers began coming to California in 1848. They were welcomed at first because California needed laborers. But when the Chinese staked claims in the gold fields, resentment grew. White miners often drove off the Chinese. But the Chinese stayed in California and helped the state grow.

Black Americans. Like other forty-niners, free blacks went to California hoping to strike it rich. Some did become wealthy. In fact, California had the wealthiest black population of any state by the 1850s. But blacks still faced discrimination. For example, California law denied blacks the right to testify against whites in court. In 1863, after a long struggle, blacks won the repeal of this law.

In spite of these problems, California thrived and grew. Settlers continued to pour into the state. By 1860, it had 100,000 citizens. The mix of peoples in California gave it a unique culture.

SECTION REVIEW

1. **Locate:** Salt Lake City, Sutter's Mill, Sacramento, San Francisco.
2. **Define:** forty-niner, vigilante.
3. (a) Why did Brigham Young choose the Salt Lake River valley as the new home of the Mormons? (b) What hardships did the Mormons face when they reached Utah?
4. Describe what happened during the California Gold Rush.
5. **What Do You Think?** Why do you think the Mormon settlement in Utah was more orderly than mining camps in California?

Chapter 14 Review

★ Summary ★

During the mid-1800s, the nation grew rapidly. Settlers followed Mountain Men and missionaries into Oregon Country. In 1845, after a standoff with Britain, the United States took over part of Oregon.

In the 1820s, Americans began to move to Texas. In 1835, Texans rebelled against Mexico. They formed a republic in 1836. When Texas joined the Union in 1846, war with Mexico resulted. Mexico lost and gave up California and the Southwest.

In 1849, thousands of gold miners rushed to California. The population boom led California to join the Union in 1850.

30 ★ **Reviewing the Facts** ★

2 pts. each

Key Terms. Match each term in Column 1 with the correct definition in Column 2.

Column 1
1. rendezvous
2. annex
3. cede
4. forty-niner
5. vigilante

Column 2
a. give
b. someone who went to California during the Gold Rush
c. add on
d. someone who punishes a suspected criminal even though he has no legal power to do so
e. get-together

Key People, Events, and Ideas. Identify each of the following.

1. Mountain Men
2. Narcissa Whitman
3. Oregon Trail
4. Stephen Austin
5. Antonio López de Santa Anna
6. Sam Houston
7. Alamo
8. Lone Star Republic
9. Santa Fe Trail
10. Junípero Serra
11. Manifest Destiny
12. James Polk
13. Bear Flag Republic
14. Mexican Cession
15. Joseph Smith

40 ★ **Chapter Checkup** ★

5 pts. each

1. (a) Why were many Americans attracted to the Oregon Country? (b) How did they travel there?
2. Explain how each of the following helped to open the West: (a) Mountain Men; (b) missionaries; (c) forty-niners.
3. Why did settlers in Texas rebel against the Mexican government?
4. (a) Describe the life of Indians on missions in California. (b) How did their lives change after Mexican independence?
5. How did the idea of Manifest Destiny influence the election of 1844?
6. List three ways older residents of the Southwest influenced American settlers.
7. (a) Why did the Mormons move west from Illinois? (b) Why did they choose to settle in the Great Salt Lake valley?
8. (a) Describe the mix of cultures in California after the Gold Rush. (b) How did the search for gold cause problems for some groups?

1. **Drawing a conclusion.** How was the defeat at the Alamo also a victory for Texans?

2. **Analyzing a quotation.** One army officer who fought against Mexico called the Mexican War "one of the most unjust ever waged by a stronger against a weaker nation." (a) What did he mean? (b) Do you agree or disagree with his statement? Explain.

3. **Understanding geography.** (a) What lands did the Mormons cross on their way from Illinois to the Great Salt Lake valley? (b) How did Mormons turn the desert into farmland?

4. **Relating past to present.** (a) Why do you think forty-niners were ready to risk their savings and their lives looking for gold in California? (b) Can you think of people today who take risks to make a fortune? Explain.

5. **Understanding the economy.** How do you think the Gold Rush helped to make settlements in the West grow?

extra credit

★ **Using Your Skills** ★

1. **Identifying immediate and long-range causes.** Wars and other events in history have both immediate and long-range causes. An *immediate cause* is an event that triggers a war. *Long-range causes* are problems or conflicts that build up over a period of time. Long-range causes of a war often create a mood of bad feeling between two countries. Review the events leading up to the Mexican War. (a) What was the immediate cause of war with Mexico? (b) What were the long range causes?

2. **Making a review chart.** Make a review chart with three columns and four rows. Label the columns Oregon, Texas, and California. Label the rows First European Settlers, First Settlers From the United States, Date Became a Territory, and Date Became a State. Then complete the chart for the three areas.

3. **Map reading.** Study the map on page 324. (a) Who commanded the American troops that landed at Veracruz? (b) About how many miles is it from Veracruz to Mexico City? (c) What city in California did Kearny's troops capture?

4. **Placing events in time.** Study the time line on page 308. (a) When did the Mexican War begin? (b) How many years later did the Gold Rush begin? (c) Can you think of a way the first event affected the second?

★ **More to Do** ★

1. **Writing a diary.** Imagine that you are a Mountain Man living in the Rocky Mountains in the 1830s. Write diary entries for seven days.

2. **Making a poster.** Make a poster to rally Texans to fight for independence from Mexico in March 1836.

3. **Exploring local history.** Write a report about any people who left your local area for the West during the 1830s or 1840s. If you live in the West, find out about people who arrived during this period.

4. **Drawing a cartoon.** Draw a cartoon about the Gold Rush to California.

5. **Researching.** Find out more about the Gadsden Purchase. Why did people want to purchase this area?

15

Two Ways of Life (1820–1860)

Chapter Outline

1 Industry in the North
2 Life in the North
3 The Cotton Kingdom
4 Life in the South

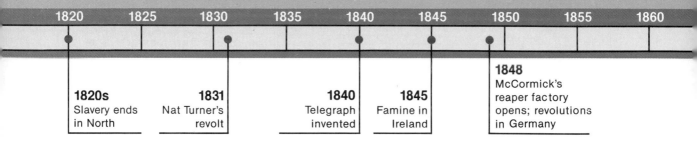

| 1820 | 1825 | 1830 | 1835 | 1840 | 1845 | 1850 | 1855 | 1860 |

1820s
Slavery ends in North

1831
Nat Turner's revolt

1840
Telegraph invented

1845
Famine in Ireland

1848
McCormick's reaper factory opens; revolutions in Germany

About This Chapter

The first half of the 1800s was a time of rapid change in America. In the North, factories sprang up in cities and villages. Factories brought a new way of life to the North. Cities grew, swollen by the arrival of immigrants from Europe.

One such immigrant was Jacob Lanzit. He came to America from Austria in the 1850s. To make a living, Lanzit tried various jobs. He sold cigars, peddled stationery, sewed clothing, and ran a dry goods store. Life in the New World was not as easy as Lanzit had hoped. "However," he wrote, "I can make a living. It is hard work, to be sure, but I am now in America; that means working."

Immigrants faced hardships, but had opportunities as well. Most made places for themselves in the bustling cities of the North. Jacob Lanzit went on to open his own printing shop and raise a family in New York City.

The South grew also, but in a different way. Few factories were built there. Farming, especially growing cotton, dominated southern life. Slavery spread as Southerners planted more land with cotton.

As the North and South grew, they developed distinct ways of life. To some people, the North and South seemed like two different countries.

Study the time line above. What event on the time line do you think encouraged people in Ireland to come to the United States?

Wealthy southern planters created an elegant way of life, as this painting of a plantation in Louisiana shows.

1 Industry in the North

Read to Learn

★ What inventions helped the northern economy?
★ How did railroads help business?
★ What do these words mean: telegraph, clipper ship?

In the early 1800s, life was changing in the North. Factories were springing up on lands where cows once grazed. Peaceful New England towns were changed forever by the whir and clatter of new machines. Most Northerners still lived on farms. But more and more, the northern economy centered on manufacturing and trade.

New Machines

The Industrial Revolution reached America in the early 1800s, as you read in Chapter 12. Inventions continued to spark the growth of new industries in the 1840s and 1850s. For example, Elias Howe patented a sewing machine in 1846. A few years later, Isaac Singer improved on Howe's sewing machine. He then advertised to increase demand for it.

The invention of the sewing machine had far-reaching effects. Factories were set up with hundreds of sewing machines. They produced dozens of shirts in the time it took a tailor to sew a few seams by hand.

New farm tools. Other inventions helped farmers. For example, John Deere invented a lightweight steel plow. In the past, plows were made of wood or iron. They were so heavy that they had to be pulled by slow-moving oxen. John Deere's plow was light enough for a horse to pull.

In 1848, Cyrus McCormick opened a factory in Chicago that made mechanical reapers. McCormick's reaper was a horse-drawn machine that mowed wheat and other grains. The new reaper could do the work of five people using hand tools.

Machines such as the reaper and steel plow helped farmers. Farmers produced more grain and needed fewer farm hands. As a result, thousands of farm workers left the countryside. Many took jobs in the new factories that were opening in cities and towns.

Messages by Wire

Another invention gave Americans a new way to keep in touch. In 1840, Samuel F. B. Morse received a patent for his "talking wire," or telegraph. The *telegraph* was a machine that sent electrical signals along a wire. The signals were based on a code of dots and dashes. Each group of dots and dashes stood for a different letter of the alphabet. Later, this code was called the Morse code.

The telegraph was an instant success. Telegraph companies sprang up everywhere and strung thousands of miles of wire. Messages traveled over

MAP SKILL Farming, especially wheat and other grains, remained vital to the northern economy, as this product map shows. At the same time, industry became more important every year. Which states produced textiles? Which states had an important mining industry?

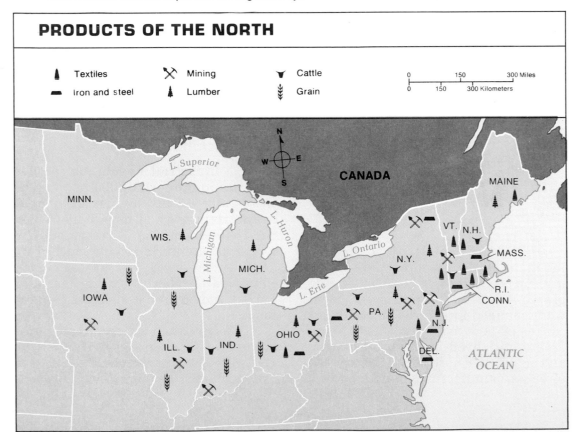

PRODUCTS OF THE NORTH

long distances in a matter of minutes. Newspaper reporters used telegraphs to wire in stories about major events such as the Mexican War. The telegraph helped business grow by making it easier for merchants to find out about the supply and price of goods.

The Iron Horse

A further boost to the economy came as transportation improved. Americans continued to build new roads and canals. But the greatest change came with the railroad.

The first railroads had wood rails covered with a strip of iron. Horses pulled cars along the rails. Then, in 1829, the Stephenson family in England developed a steam-powered engine for pulling rail cars. The engine, called the *Rocket*, barreled along at 30 miles (48 km) per hour, an astonishing speed at the time. In America, people laughed at the noisy clatter of these "iron horses." Some were terrified by sparks that flew out of the engines, burning passengers' clothes and setting buildings on fire.

Many Americans believed that horse-drawn rail cars were safer and faster than steam-powered engines. In 1830, a race was held to settle the question.

A huge crowd gathered in Baltimore to watch a horse-drawn rail car race a steam engine called the *Tom Thumb*. One onlooker described the *Tom Thumb* as "a teakettle on a truck." When the race began, the horse labored to keep up with the chugging *Tom Thumb*. Suddenly, the steam engine broke down. The crowd cheered as the horse crossed the finish line first. But *Tom Thumb*'s defeat was not the end of the steam engine.

Engineers developed better rails and engines. Soon, private companies started building railroads. By the late 1850s, railroads connected the East to cities such as Chicago in the Midwest. Cities at hubs of the railroad network

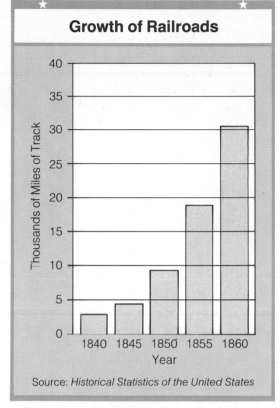

Growth of Railroads

Thousands of Miles of Track vs. *Year*

Source: *Historical Statistics of the United States*

GRAPH SKILL Railroads expanded rapidly after 1840. The surge in railroad mileage came about mainly from track laid in the North and Midwest. Southerners did build thousands of miles of railroads, but they lagged behind Northerners. During which five-year period did the country's total railroad mileage pass 20,000 miles?

grew quickly. (See the map on page 369.)

Golden Age of Sail

While railroads were boosting the economy on land, American ships were capturing much of the world's trade at sea. At busy seaports on the east coast, captains loaded their ships with wheat, cotton, lumber, furs, and tobacco.

Speed was the key to successful trade at sea. In 1845, an American named John Griffith launched the *Rainbow,* the first of the *clipper ships.* These elegant ships had tall masts and huge sails that caught every gust of wind. With their narrow hulls, they clipped swiftly through the water.

The most daring of all seafarers were whalers. In the 1850s, eight out of ten of the world's whaling ships sailed from New England. Many crew members were Americans. Others came from as far away as Portugal and Hawaii. Native Americans proved to be good harpooners. In a whaling port, it seemed that every language of the world could be heard.

Once at sea, crew members ignored differences in language and culture. They worked together as a team. When a whale was sighted, small rowboats went out from the ship. The harpooners stood in front. They threw harpoons with strong ropes tied to them. These stuck in the whale, which usually dove deep under the waves. The whale pulled rope out from the boats so fast that the crews had to pour water on it. Otherwise, friction would set the boats afire! When the whale resurfaced, it often dragged the boats for miles.

Slowly, the whale grew tired. Crews pulled in the ropes, drawing the boats closer to the huge animal. The harpooners stood once again. This time, they aimed sharp lances at the whale's heart. If they missed, the wounded whale might turn and crush the boats. If they struck true, the sea boiled red, and the whale died in minutes.

Whaling made many New England seaports prosper. Whale oil was sold as lamp fuel. Whalebone was used in umbrellas. Ambergris, found in male whales, was used in perfumes.

★ How do you think whaling affected the New England economy?

In the 1840s, shipbuilders like Donald McKay launched dozens of clipper ships. American clipper ships broke every speed record. They sailed from New York to Hong Kong in 81 days, flying past older ships that took 5 months to reach China. The speed of the clipper ships helped the United States win a large share of foreign trade during the 1840s and 1850s.

The triumph of the graceful clippers was short-lived. In the 1850s, clipper ships lost their advantage when the British launched the first ocean-going steamships. These sturdy iron vessels carried more cargo and traveled faster than clippers.

An Expanding Economy

Northern industry grew steadily in the mid-1800s. In the 1830s, factories began to use steam power instead of water power.

Steam power helped the factory system to spread. It allowed manufacturers to build anywhere, not just near rivers. This was important because the best river sites had been taken in the North. Steam-driven machines were powerful and cheap to run. Soon, textile mills and other factories were using them.

With new machines, northern factory owners produced goods more cheaply and quickly than ever before. The low-priced goods found eager buyers. As demand increased, owners built larger factories. They hired dozens of workers to run machines.

Railroads also contributed to rapid industrial growth in the North. Railroads helped manufacturers ship raw materials and finished goods quickly and cheaply. They created new markets by opening up distant sections of the country to trade.

Railroads had an important effect on northern farming, too. Since colonial days, farmers in New England had scratched a living from poor, rocky soil. With the growth of railroads, farming in the richer soils of the West boomed. Western farmers shipped grain and other foods east by rail. As a result, New Englanders turned to manufacturing and trade.

SECTION REVIEW

1. **Define:** telegraph, clipper ship.
2. List two inventions that helped farmers.
3. Why was the telegraph important?
4. How did railroads contribute to industrial growth in the North?
5. **What Do You Think?** Why do you think the Industrial Revolution caught on in the North?

2 Life in the North

Read to Learn

★ What was life like for factory workers?
★ Why did workers organize unions?
★ What do these words mean: skilled worker, trade union, strike, unskilled worker, immigrant, famine, nativist, prejudice?

Most people in the North continued to live as farmers. However, life in the North was changing because of the growth of industry and cities.

Working in Factories

Factories in the 1840s were different from the textile mills of the early 1800s. Owners built bigger factories and used steam-powered machines. They hired more workers to tend the machines. For these workers, wages remained low and hours long.

A long day. As the demand for workers grew, entire families signed on to work in factories. They needed the earnings of every member to pay for their food and housing.

A family's day began early—when the factory whistle sounded at 4:00 A.M. Father, mother, and children dressed in the dark before dawn and headed off to work. The whistle blew at 7:30 A.M. and again at noon to announce breakfast and lunch breaks. The day did not end until 7:30 P.M. when the final whistle sent workers home.

Poor conditions. During the long day, factory workers faced many dangers. Owners often paid little attention to bad working conditions. Few factories had windows or heating systems. The heat in summer was stifling. In winter, the cold contributed to sickness.

Poor lighting led to accidents. Also, machines had no safety devices. From time to time, workers' hands or arms were crushed by machines. Injured workers lost their jobs, and there was no insurance to make up for lost wages.

This painting shows a thriving New England town in the 1840s. Many small towns in the North had textile mills and other factories by this time. At first, factories drew their workers from men, women, and children living on nearby farms.

Despite the long hours and dangers, factory workers in America were better off than those in Europe. American workers could usually find jobs and earn regular wages. European workers often had no work at all.

Workers Organize

Poor working conditions and low wages led workers to organize. The first to do so were skilled workers. *Skilled workers* were people who had learned a trade, such as carpenters and shoemakers. In the 1820s and 1830s, skilled workers in each trade banded together to form *trade unions.*

Trade unions called for a shorter work day, better wages, and safer working conditions. They sometimes pressed their demands by going on strike. In a *strike,* union workers refuse to do their jobs. But strikes were illegal in the United States. Strikers faced fines or jail sentences. And strike leaders were fired from their jobs.

Slowly, however, workers made progress. In 1840, they won a major victory when President Van Buren approved a 10-hour workday for government employees. Other workers still worked 12 to 15 hours a day. But they kept pressing their demands until they won the same hours as government workers. Workers celebrated another victory in 1842 when a Massachusetts court declared that they had the right to strike.

While skilled workers slowly won better pay, unskilled workers could not bargain for better wages. *Unskilled workers* did jobs that required little or no training. So they were easily replaced. As a result, employers were unwilling to listen to their demands for better pay.

Women Speak Up

Thousands of women held jobs in factories. By the 1840s, conditions for women were getting worse at Lowell and other mills. For example, some mills charged fines if workers were late. They forbade women to talk on the job. Like men, women workers organized. They used strikes to protest cuts in wages and unfair work rules.

At first, few strikes succeeded. Employers fired strike leaders. They threatened to dismiss any workers who went on strike. Single women could return home to their families, but their pay was often badly needed. Married women knew that their children would suffer if they lost their jobs.

Sometimes, a strike succeeded. In 1831, mill workers in Exeter, New Hampshire, went on strike. They were protesting against an overseer who turned the clocks back every day. The women were working longer without getting extra pay. After they struck, the factory owner agreed to make the overseer stop the practice.

Despite many setbacks, women refused to remain silent. One group compared their struggle to the American Revolution: "As our fathers resisted . . . the lordly [greed] of the British, so we, their daughters, never will wear the yoke [of slavery] which has been prepared for us."

A Flood of New Americans

Many of the new workers in the factories of the North were immigrants. An *immigrant* is a person who comes from his or her homeland and settles in another country. During the 1840s and 1850s, 4 million immigrants flooded into the United States.

Potato famine. In the 1840s, many immigrants came from Ireland. A disease rotted the potato crop in Europe in 1845. The loss of this crop caused a *famine,* or severe food shortage, especially in Ireland. Irish peasants depended on the potato. Without it, many starved.

Over 1.5 million Irish fled to America between 1845 and 1860. Most were too poor to buy farmland. So they settled in the cities where they landed. In

This engraving shows people on their way to work at a factory. Many of the workers carry their lunch in a basket or a lunch pail. Women and children often earned only one half or one third of what men earned for the same work.

New York City and Boston, thousands of Irish crowded into slums. They took any job they could find.

Fleeing Germany. Another group of immigrants came from Germany. Between 1850 and 1860, nearly one million Germans arrived in America. Many were fleeing from repression. In 1848, revolutions broke out in several parts of Germany. The rebels fought for democratic government. When the revolutions failed, thousands had to flee for their lives.

Contributions. Newcomers from many lands helped the American economy grow rapidly. Irish workers kept northern factories humming. Craftsworkers from Britain and Germany brought useful skills to America. Each group left its imprint on American life. Irish immigrants brought their lively music and dances. German immigrants brought the custom of decorating the Christmas tree. Immigrants from other nations enriched America with their language, foods, and customs.

America for Americans

The flood of immigrants alarmed many Americans. Some Americans, called *nativists,* wanted to preserve the country for native-born white citizens. Nativists trumpeted the idea of "America for Americans" and favored laws to limit immigration. They also wanted to deny newcomers the right to vote until they had lived in America for 21 years. At the time, immigrants had to live here only 5 years to vote.

Nativists had many reasons for disliking immigrants. American workers resented immigrants because the newcomers worked for low pay. Other nativists disliked the newcomers because of prejudice. *Prejudice* is an unfavorable opinion about people who are of a different religion, race, or nationality. For example, some Protestants mistrusted Irish and German immigrants who were Catholics.

In the 1850s, nativists organized the ***Know-Nothing Party.*** This name came from the answer party members gave when asked about their activities. They replied, "I know nothing." In 1856, the Know-Nothing candidate for President won 21 percent of the popular vote. Soon after, the party died out.

Free Blacks

Free blacks in the North faced worse prejudice than immigrants did. They had few rights. As one writer stated, black Americans were denied "the ballot-box, the jury box, the halls of legislature, the army, the public lands, the school, and the church."

Free blacks also faced discrimination on the job. One black carpenter was turned away by every furniture maker in Cincinnati. "At last," a study on free blacks reported, "he found a shop carried on by an Englishman, who agreed to employ him—but on entering the shop, the workmen threw down their tools and declared that he should leave or they would." As a result of prejudice, skilled blacks often took low-paying jobs as laborers.

Despite prejudice, some free blacks moved ahead. James Forten grew rich manufacturing sails. (See page 205.) Other blacks became lawyers, actors, and scientists.

━━ SECTION REVIEW ━━

1. **Define:** skilled worker, trade union, strike, unskilled worker, immigrant, famine, nativist, prejudice.

2. (a) How did factory conditions get worse in the 1800s? (b) What benefits did early unions ask for?

3. (a) Where did most immigrants come from in the 1840s and 1850s? (b) Why did they leave their homelands?

4. What problems did free blacks face in the North?

5. **What Do You Think?** Why do you think most factory owners were happy to hire immigrants?

3 The Cotton Kingdom

Read to Learn

★ How did the cotton gin change the South?
★ Why was the South known as the Cotton Kingdom?
★ What industries grew in the South?

While factories sprouted up in towns and cities of the North, the South also enjoyed economic growth. Southerners shipped tons of tobacco, rice, and sugar to the North and to Europe. But one crop—cotton—came to dominate the southern economy.

Eli Whitney's Invention

The Industrial Revolution greatly increased the demand for southern cotton. Textile mills in the North and in Britain could handle more and more cotton. At first, planters could not keep up with demand. They could grow plenty of cotton, but cleaning it took time. Removing the seeds from the cotton fibers was a slow task. Planters badly needed a new way to clean cotton.

In 1793, Eli Whitney built the first cotton gin, a machine for cleaning cotton. (Gin was short for engine.) The cotton gin had two wooden rollers with thin wire teeth. When cotton was swept between the rollers, the wire teeth pulled the fibers clear of the seeds. (See the picture on page 288.)

The cotton gin was a simple but important invention. With a gin, one worker could do the work of 1,000 people cleaning cotton by hand. News of Whitney's invention spread quickly. In fact, thieves broke into his workshop to steal an early model. Because of the gin, Southerners grew more cotton.

The Cotton Kingdom

Planters soon learned that land planted with cotton year after year

Harvesting cotton took long hours of backbreaking work. On most big plantations, a white overseer directed the work of slaves, as this painting by Mary Williams shows. Because cotton soon exhausted the soil, planters often sold their land and moved west. As planters moved westward in the 1800s, so did slavery.

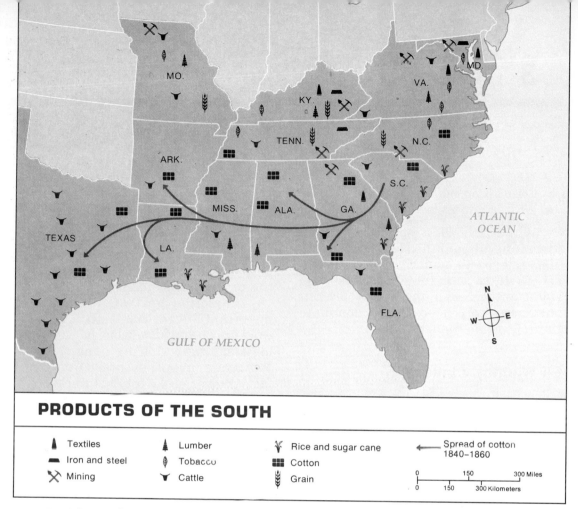

PRODUCTS OF THE SOUTH

▲ Textiles	♠ Rice and sugar cane	← Spread of cotton 1840–1860
▬ Iron and steel	♣ Tobacco	
✗ Mining	▦ Cotton	
⊤ Cattle	♠ Grain	

0   150   300 Miles
0   150   300 Kilometers

MAP SKILL Southerners produced many different goods by the mid-1800s.
Tobacco and rice were important crops. Livestock was a major source of
income, too. But cotton overshadowed every other product of the South. To
what areas did cotton growing spread between 1840 and 1860?

wore out. This forced them to find new land to cultivate.

After the War of 1812, planters headed west. They built farms on the fertile land of Alabama, Mississippi, and Louisiana. Some moved even farther west into Texas. Soon, cotton plantations stretched in a wide band from South Carolina and Georgia to Texas. This area became known as the *Cotton Kingdom.* (See the map above.)

Production boomed in the Cotton Kingdom. The boom helped the economy of the South and the nation as a whole. By the 1850s, the United States earned millions of dollars every year from cotton exports.

The increased demand for cotton had a tragic side, however. As the Cotton Kingdom spread, the demand for slaves grew. Slaves planted and picked the cotton. As slaves produced more cotton, planters earned the money to buy more land and more slaves.

The number of slaves in the South grew steadily after 1800. (See page 345.) Yet, most families owned no slaves at all. Of those who did, most had only one or two.

Other Industries

Cotton was the major cash crop grown in the South. But tobacco, rice, and sugar cane were important money-making crops as well. Southerners also raised much of the nation's livestock. They shipped hogs and cattle to northern cities. Horses, oxen, and mules bred in the South pulled carts and dragged plows all around the nation.

The South took some steps to encourage industry. In the 1800s, Southerners built factories to process sugar and tobacco. They also built textile mills. William Gregg modeled his cotton mill in South Carolina on the Lowell mills in Massachusetts. Gregg built houses and gardens for his workers and schools for their children.

Even so, the South lagged far behind the North in industry. Wealthy Southerners put their money into land and slaves rather than factories. Southerners depended on the North and Europe for finished goods such as cloth and tools. Many resented this fact. One Southerner wrote that "slaveholders themselves are enslaved to the products of northern industry." Still, most Southerners were proud of their booming cotton industry. As long as cotton remained king, Southerners could look to the future with confidence.

AMERICANS WHO DARED

Eli Whitney

Eli Whitney grew up in Massachusetts at the time of the American Revolution. After college, Whitney spent time on a South Carolina plantation owned by Catherine Greene. One day, some planters complained that they needed a better way to clean cotton. Catherine Greene suggested they ask Whitney. Using odds and ends, Whitney built the first cotton gin in only 10 days.

SECTION REVIEW

1. **Locate:** Alabama, Mississippi, Louisiana, Texas.
2. How did the cotton gin help planters?
3. Why did planters need more and more new land to cultivate?

4. What crops besides cotton were grown in the South?
5. **What Do You Think?** Why do you think the demand for cotton rose steadily in the 1800s?

4 Life in the South

Read to Learn
★ How did white Southerners live?
★ How did free blacks live in the South?
★ What was life like for slaves?
★ What do these words mean: extended family?

The wealthiest Southerners were plantation owners. They lived off the unpaid labor of slaves. Most Southerners, however, did not own slaves. They had small farms and worked hard to provide for themselves.

Southern Whites

White Southerners were divided into three groups. They were wealthy planters, farmers who worked their own land, and poor whites.

Planters. Planters were few in number, but their views and way of life dominated the South. A planter was someone who owned at least 20 slaves. Of the 5.5 million whites in the South, only 50,000 were planters in 1860. Still, planters had power over the lives of many people.

The richest planters built elegant homes and filled them with fine European furniture. They entertained lavishly, dressing and behaving like the nobility of Europe.

Planters had responsibilities, too. They had to make important decisions about when to plant and harvest their crops. Because of their wealth and influence, owners of large plantations often became political leaders. They devoted many hours to local and state politics. As a result, they hired men to oversee the work of slaves.

Small farmers. About 75 percent of southern whites were small farmers. These "plain folk," as they called themselves, owned land and perhaps one or two slaves. Unlike planters, plain folk usually worked in the cotton fields alongside their slaves.

Among small farmers, helping each other out was an important duty. "People who lived miles apart counted themselves as neighbors," wrote a farmer in Mississippi. "And in case of sorrow or sickness or need of any kind, there was no limit to the ready service neighbors provided."

Poor whites. A small group of poor whites clung to the bottom of the social ladder. They farmed but did not own land. Instead, they rented it. Many barely kept themselves and their families from starving.

Poor whites often lived in the hills and wooded areas of the South. They planted corn, potatoes, and other vegetables. Like their better-off neighbors, they herded cattle and pigs. Despite their difficult lives, poor whites enjoyed rights that were denied to free blacks and slaves.

Southern Blacks

The black population of the South included free blacks and slaves. Although legally free, free blacks faced harsh discrimination. And slaves had no rights at all.

Free blacks. Many free blacks were descended from slaves freed during and after the Revolution. Others had bought their freedom or been granted it by their owners. But as the number of slaves grew, fewer earned their freedom. Slave owners did not like to have free blacks living near slaves. They thought free blacks encouraged slaves to rebel.

Still, by 1860, about 215,000 free blacks lived in the South. Many worked as servants and farm laborers. Some practiced skilled trades such as shoemaking.

Free blacks made valuable contributions to southern life. Norbert Rillieux (RIHL yoo), a free black in New Orleans, invented a machine that revolutionized sugar making. Henry Blair patented a seed planter.

Despite these successes, free blacks had difficult lives. They were denied basic rights, such as the right to vote or travel. Free blacks also feared being kidnapped and sold into slavery.

Slaves. By 1860, slaves made up one third of the population of the South. Most worked as field hands on cotton plantations. Men and women did backbreaking labor in the field. They cleared new land, planted, and harvested crops. Teenagers worked alongside adults in the fields. Children pulled weeds, picked insects from crops, and carried water to other workers.

Some slaves became skilled workers such as blacksmiths and carpenters. Planters often hired these skilled

Skill Lesson 15 Comparing Two Line Graphs

Historians use graphs to show trends, or developments over time, as you learned in Skill Lesson 4 (page 81). Often, historians use two or more graphs to compare different kinds of information. They can compare a line graph and a circle graph. They can also use two line, bar, or circle graphs.

By comparing graphs, historians can often begin to draw conclusions about two or more developments. For example, suppose one graph shows an increase in population during a certain period. Another graph shows a decrease in disease for the same period. Historians looking at the graphs might think that population increased because disease decreased. They would need to know more information before they could be certain, however.

The graphs below are both line graphs. Each shows a trend that took place over a number of years. By comparing the two graphs and thinking about what you read in this chapter, you can draw conclusions about the two developments.

1. **Identify the information shown on the graphs.** (a) What is the title of the graph at left? (b) What is the title of the graph at right? (c) What do the numbers on the horizontal axis and vertical axis of the graph at left show? (d) What do the numbers on each axis of the graph at right show?

2. **Practice reading the graphs.** Notice that the numbers given on the vertical axis are in thousands. (a) About how many thousands of bales of cotton were produced in 1830? In 1860? (b) What was the slave population in 1830? In 1860?

3. **Compare the information shown on the graphs.** Use the graphs and your reading of this chapter to answer these questions. (a) Was there an upward or downward trend in cotton production between 1800 and 1860? (b) Was there an upward or downward trend in slave population in the same period? (c) How do you think the trend in cotton production is related to the trend in slave population?

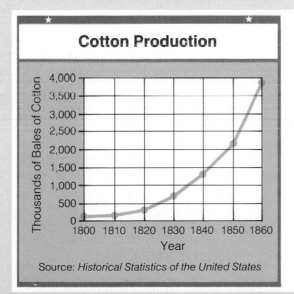

Cotton Production

Source: *Historical Statistics of the United States*

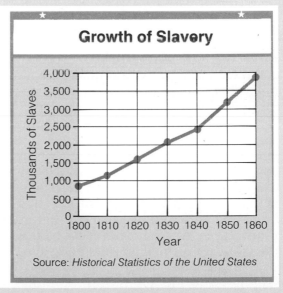

Growth of Slavery

Source: *Historical Statistics of the United States*

workers out to other plantations. Some slaves worked in cities and lived almost as if they were free blacks. But their earnings belonged to their owners.

Older slaves, especially women, worked as servants in the planter's house. They cooked, cleaned, and did other chores under the supervision of the planter's wife.

The Life of Slaves

The slave's life depended on individual owners. Some owners treated their slaves well. They made sure that their slaves had decent food, clean houses, and warm clothes. Other planters spent as little as possible to feed, clothe, and shelter slaves.

Hard work. Many planters were determined to get the most work possible from their slaves. As a result, slaves worked from sunup to sundown, as much as 16 hours a day. Frederick Douglass, an escaped slave, recalled his life under one harsh master:

> We were worked in all weathers. It was never too hot or too cold; it could never rain, blow, hail, or snow too hard for us to work in the field. Work, work, work. . . . The longest days were too short for him and the shortest nights too long for him.

Slaves sometimes suffered whippings and other cruel punishments. They had only one real protection against such treatment. Owners saw their slaves as valuable property. Therefore, most slave owners wanted to keep this human property healthy and productive.

Slave families. Keeping a family together was difficult for slaves. Because slaves were property, owners could buy and sell them at will. The law did not even recognize slave marriages or slave families. As a result, a husband and wife could be sold to different plantations. And children could be taken away from their parents and sold.

Nevertheless, family life provided a feeling of pride for slaves. Families gathered together during their precious time away from work. They kept small gardens. Parents and grandparents took care of children.

Slaves preserved some African customs. For example, grandparents, parents, children, aunts, uncles, and cousins formed a close-knit family group. This idea of an **extended family** had its roots in Africa. Slaves also handed down stories and songs to their children. In African cultures, parents taught children songs as a way to pass on their history and moral ideas.

Faith in God helped slaves cope with the harshness of daily life. Bible stories about how the ancient Israelites were freed from slavery inspired many slave songs. As they toiled in the fields, slaves sang about a coming day of freedom. One slave song, "Go Down, Moses," includes the lines:

> We need not always weep and moan,
>   Let my people go;
> And wear these slavery chains forlorn,
>   Let my people go.

Resisting Slavery

Slaves actively fought against the system that denied them freedom. Some slaves resisted by breaking tools and destroying crops. Others pretended to be sick. Another way to resist was to run away. But escapes were seldom successful.

At times, slaves reacted with violence to the brutal system under which they lived. Denmark Vesey, a free black, planned a revolt in 1822. Vesey was betrayed before the revolt began. He and 35 others were executed.

In 1831, a slave preacher named Nat Turner led his followers through Virginia, killing more than 60 whites. Terrified whites hunted the countryside for Turner and his followers. They killed many innocent blacks before catching and hanging Turner.

Nat Turner's revolt increased southern fears of slave uprisings. But

These two pictures show the sorrow and the dignity of slave life. The slave auction at left shows a mother and her infant being sold in Missouri. Slave families were often broken up at auctions. The early photograph at right shows that some slave families succeeded in staying together. The grandparents, parents, and children in this family lived and worked together on a South Carolina plantation.

revolts were rare. Slaves had little chance to organize or arm themselves.

Slave Codes

To keep control of the growing number of slaves, Southerners passed laws known as slave codes (see page 130). These laws were designed to keep slaves from rebelling or running away. Under the slave codes, slaves were not allowed outside after dark. They could not gather in groups of more than three or four. They could not leave their owner's land without a written pass. They could not own weapons.

Slave codes also made it a crime for slaves to learn to read and write. By limiting education for slaves, owners hoped to keep them from escaping. If slaves did escape, they had trouble finding their way north. Few runaway slaves could use maps or read train schedules.

Other laws were meant to protect slaves. For example, owners were forbidden to mistreat slaves. But slaves did not have the right to testify in court. So they could not bring charges against cruel owners.

As slavery grew, the economic ties between the North and South became stronger. Northern mill owners needed cotton from the South. And Southerners relied on goods from northern factories. Yet Americans saw that the two sections had different ways of life. Slavery seemed to be the key difference between them.

SECTION REVIEW

1. **Define:** extended family.
2. Why did planters dominate southern life?
3. Describe the daily life of slaves.
4. How did Nat Turner's revolt affect white Southerners?
5. **What Do You Think?** How do you think denying education to slaves helped prevent escape attempts?

Chapter 15 Review

★ Summary ★

By the 1840s, the North and South were taking different paths. In the North, machines hummed inside new factories. People from farms and immigrants poured into cities to find jobs. As factory conditions got worse, men and women workers formed unions. They made few gains at first.

In the South, cotton growing spread, as did slavery. Most Southerners owned no slaves. Yet large planters dominated southern life and politics.

Slaves worked long hours for no pay, and slave codes made escape difficult. Family ties and religion eased some of the pain of slavery. Slavery was the key difference between the ways of life in the North and South.

★ Reviewing the Facts ★

2 pts.

Key Terms. Match each term in Column 1 with the correct definition in Column 2.

Column 1
1. trade union
2. strike
3. famine
4. nativist
5. prejudice

Column 2
a. someone who wanted to limit immigration
b. refusal by workers to do their jobs
c. unfavorable opinion about people of a different religion, race, or nationality
d. organization of skilled workers
e. severe food shortage

Key People, Events, and Ideas. Identify each of the following.

1. Isaac Singer
2. Cyrus McCormick
3. Samuel F. B. Morse
4. Donald McKay
5. Know-Nothing Party
6. Eli Whitney
7. Cotton Kingdom
8. Norbert Rillieux
9. Denmark Vesey
10. Nat Turner

★ Chapter Checkup ★

5 pts

1. (a) What inventions improved farming in the 1830s and 1840s? (b) How did these inventions help factories grow?

2. (a) What inventions changed the way people kept in touch and traveled? (b) How did these inventions help the economy expand?

3. (a) How did clipper ships help the United States capture sea trade? (b) What cut short the age of clipper ships?

4. (a) How were conditions in factories changing by the 1840s? (b) How did factory workers respond to these changes?

5. (a) Why did immigration to the United States increase in the 1840s? (b) How did some native-born Americans respond?

6. (a) What was the Southern economy based on? (b) Why did slavery grow in the South through the mid-1800s?

7. (a) What were the three groups of white Southerners? (b) Which group was the most influential? Why?

8. (a) Why was family life important to slaves? (b) Why was it difficult for slave families to stay together?

Understanding geography. A Norwegian farmer who came to the United States in the 1830s wrote, "Here in America, it is the railroads that build up the whole country." (a) How did railroads help the country grow? (b) What sections of the country did railroads help most?

 Relating past to present. (a) How did the Industrial Revolution in the early 1800s change the way of life for many Northerners? (b) What major change is taking place in industry today? (c) How is it changing the way of life for many people?

3. **Learning about citizenship.** Why do you think Germans fleeing their country after 1848 wanted to come to the United States?

 Understanding the economy. In the 1840s, a Southerner wrote this description of a southern gentleman: "See him with northern pen and ink, writing letters on northern paper, and sending them away in northern envelopes, sealed with northern wax, and impressed with a northern stamp." What point about the South do you think the writer was making?

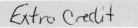

1. **Placing events in time.** Study the time line on page 332. (a) When did slavery end in the North? (b) What event on the time line was a response to slavery in the South? (c) From your reading of the chapter, did the number of slaves in the South shrink or grow from 1820 to 1860?

2. **Comparing.** Review the descriptions of how free blacks lived in the North and South on pages 340 and 344. (a) In which section of the country did free blacks have more freedom? (b) Why do you think free blacks had more freedom there? (c) What basic rights were denied to free blacks in both sections?

3. **Using a painting as a primary source.** Study the painting on page 338. (a) What does the painting show? (b) How can you tell it was painted after 1800? (c) Do you think a painting of a town in the South would look different? Explain.

4. **Map reading.** Study the product maps on pages 334 and 342. (a) What products did both the North and South produce? (a) What products did the South alone produce? Why?

1. **Preparing a report.** Write a report about the potato—where it was first grown, how it was used, and why it was important in Ireland. Use information from encyclopedias and books.

2. **Drawing a cartoon.** Draw a cartoon that either supports or criticizes the attitude of nativists toward immigrants in the 1850s.

3. **Writing a dialogue.** Write a dialogue between one Southerner who wants to invest in land to grow cotton and another Southerner who wants to build a textile mill.

4. **Exploring local history.** Prepare an oral report about the legal status of blacks in your local area during the 1850s.

16
The Reforming Spirit (1820–1860)

Chapter Outline

1 Crusade Against Slavery
2 Rights for Women
3 Reform Marches On
4 Creating an American Culture

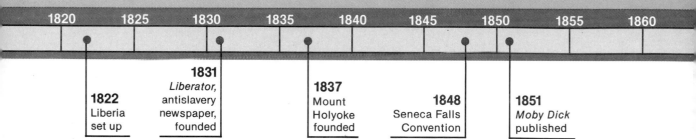

| 1820 | 1825 | 1830 | 1835 | 1840 | 1845 | 1850 | 1855 | 1860 |

1822
Liberia
set up

1831
Liberator,
antislavery
newspaper,
founded

1837
Mount
Holyoke
founded

1848
Seneca Falls
Convention

1851
Moby Dick
published

About This Chapter

In the mid-1800s, a spirit of reform spread across the nation. People joined together to make others aware of America's problems and try to cure them. Some reformers called for better schools. Others tried to win basic rights for women. Many joined the movement to end slavery.

An important event in the antislavery movement came in 1829. That year, a free black named David Walker published his *Appeal to the Coloured Citizens of the World.* Walker urged slaves to throw off their chains by any means necessary. "Remember, Americans, that we must and shall be free," Walker warned. If slaves were not given their freedom, they would seize it by force, he threatened. "Will you wait until we shall,

under God, obtain our liberty by the crushing arm of power? Will it not be dreadful for you?" he asked white Americans.

Walker's book created a sensation in both the North and South. Many people, especially Southerners, were horrified by the threat of a slave revolt. Some Southerners refused even to listen to arguments against slavery from that point on.

Few antislavery reformers went as far as Walker did. Most hoped to end slavery gradually. Like other reformers, their goal was to make America a better place. In many cases, the efforts of these reformers succeeded.

Study the time line above. Which event do you think was an advance for the antislavery movement?

In the 1840s, more American children began going to school. Winslow Homer painted these schoolchildren playing a game called Snap the Whip.

1 Crusade Against Slavery

Read to Learn

★ How did the antislavery movement grow?

★ What did antislavery groups do to help slaves?

★ How did Americans react to the antislavery crusade?

★ What do these words mean: abolition, underground railroad?

In the Age of Jackson, many Americans pointed proudly to the growth of democracy in their country. More people could vote and take part in government than before. But some Americans felt that democracy was still far from complete. Their voices rang out strongly against slavery. An English visitor summed up the problem slavery posed for Americans: "You will see them with one hand hoisting the cap of liberty, and with the other flogging their slaves."

The Reforming Spirit

The idea that slavery was wrong grew out of two different backgrounds. One was political. The other was religious.

Background. The political reason for opposing slavery went back to the American Revolution. In the Declaration of Independence, Thomas Jefferson wrote that "all men are created equal." Yet many white Americans, including

Jefferson, did not think that the statement applied to slaves. Reformers felt that this situation had to change.

The second reason for opposing slavery was religious. Since colonial times, Quakers had spoken out against slavery. All men and women were equal in the eyes of God, they said. It was sinful for one human being to own another.

Ending northern slavery. In the North, other religious leaders followed the Quakers' example and opposed slavery. Preachers described the evils of slavery in vivid detail. Their sermons convinced many Northerners to take a stand. The campaign against slavery succeeded in the North. By 1804, all states from Pennsylvania north had promised to free slaves within their borders.

Slavery in the North ended without a big struggle. For one thing, there were only 50,000 slaves in the North in 1800, compared to nearly one million in the South. Even so, many whites worried about what would happen to the freed slaves.

Liberia. The *American Colonization Society* provided an answer. The society, founded in 1817, wanted to set up a colony in Africa for free blacks. In 1822, President Monroe helped the society establish *Liberia* in western Africa. Liberia was an independent nation in Africa. Its name comes from the Latin word for free.

Free blacks had mixed feelings about Liberia. Some believed that blacks should go to Africa because they would never have equal rights in America. But most blacks wanted to stay in America, their homeland. If free blacks left America, they said, slavery would grow stronger than ever.

At one meeting in Pittsburgh, blacks declared, "African colonization is a scheme to drain the better-informed part of the colored people out of these United States so that the chain of slavery may be riveted more tightly." In the end, only a few thousand blacks settled in Liberia.

Call for Abolition

By the mid-1800s, the abolition movement was in full swing. *Abolition* means ending something completely. Abolitionists called for an end to slavery everywhere in the United States. Some supported a gradual end to slavery. They hoped that slavery would die out if it was kept out of the new western lands. Others insisted on an immediate end to slavery.

Black abolitionists. From the first, blacks played a major part in the abolition movement. Through lawsuits and petitions, blacks tried to abolish slavery. In the 1820s, Samuel Cornish and John Russwurm set up an antislavery newspaper, *Freedom's Journal*. They attacked slavery by publishing stories about the brutal treatment of slaves in the South. James Forten and other successful blacks gave generously to support this paper and other antislavery efforts.

Frederick Douglass. The best-known black leader was Frederick Douglass. Douglass had been born into slavery. He secretly taught himself to read, even though it was forbidden by the slave codes. Because he could not own books, Douglass picked through "the mud and filth of the gutter" to find pages from books.

In 1838, Douglass escaped from his owner in Maryland. He fled north to Massachusetts. There, Douglass attended an antislavery meeting. As he listened to the speakers, he felt that he must stand up and speak. In a powerful voice, he told the audience what freedom meant to a slave. Douglass made such a strong impression on the people at the meeting that he was asked to become a lecturer against slavery.

William Lloyd Garrison

The most outspoken white abolitionist was a fiery young man from Boston, William Lloyd Garrison. In 1831, Garrison launched an antislavery newspaper, *The Liberator*. In the first issue, he told his readers that he would not rest until slavery ended. "I am in earnest. . . . I will not excuse—I will not retreat a single inch—AND I WILL BE HEARD." A year after starting *The Liberator,* Garrison organized the *New England Anti-Slavery Society* to press the crusade against slavery.

Garrison attracted other reformers to the cause. Theodore Weld, a minister, worked with Garrison in the 1830s. Weld added the zest of a religious crusade to antislavery meetings. In 1836, Theodore Weld married Angelina Grimké, a southern woman who despised slavery. They toured the North, convincing thousands to join the cause.

The Underground Railroad

Abolitionists did more than write books and give speeches. Some risked prison and death by helping slaves escape from the South.

Brave men and women formed the underground railroad. This was not a real railroad. The *underground railroad* was a secret network of abolitionists. They worked together to help runaway slaves reach freedom in the North or Canada.

Free blacks and whites served as "conductors" on the underground railroad. Conductors guided escaping slaves to "stations" where they could sleep for the night. Some stations were the houses of abolitionists. Others were churches or even caves. Fleeing slaves hid in wagons that had false bottoms or under loads of hay. The trip was dangerous and difficult.

AMERICANS WHO DARED

Frederick Douglass

Frederick Douglass escaped from slavery in Maryland. He became a famous abolitionist speaker in the North. On one occasion, he told an audience: "I expose slavery . . . because to expose it is to kill it. Slavery is one of those monsters of darkness to whom the light of truth is death. Expose slavery and it dies. . . . All the slaveholder asks of me is silence."

One daring conductor, Harriet Tubman, was an escaped slave herself. Tubman risked her life by returning 19 times to the South. She led hundreds of slaves to the North. On one of her last trips, Tubman led her aged parents to freedom.

Despite such efforts, the underground railroad could help only about 1,000 slaves a year to escape. Thus, only a few of the millions of southern slaves reached freedom along the underground railroad.

This painting shows a station on the underground railroad. The escaping slaves have traveled by wagon, hidden under a load of hay. Here, they are taken into a house by a white conductor.

Responses to the Crusade

Abolitionists like William Lloyd Garrison were unpopular in both the North and South. Northern mill owners and bankers depended on cotton from the South. They saw Garrison's attacks on slavery as a threat to their prosperity. And many northern workers were afraid that freed slaves would come to the North and take their jobs by working for low wages.

In northern cities, mobs sometimes broke up antislavery meetings. They beat abolitionists and pelted them with stones. At times, these attacks backfired and won support for the abolitionists. One night, a Boston mob dragged Garrison through the streets at the end of a rope. A doctor who saw the attack wrote, "I am an abolitionist from this very moment."

The movement to end slavery made Southerners very uneasy. They accused abolitionists of preaching violence. David Walker's call for a slave revolt seemed to confirm the worst fears of the South. (See page 350.) Southern postmasters refused to deliver abolitionist newspapers. Many Southerners blamed Nat Turner's revolt in 1831 on Garrison. He had founded *The Liberator* only a few months before Turner's rebellion.

In response to the antislavery crusade, many slave owners defended slavery. One wrote that with good food, clothing, and houses, "the slaves will love their master and serve him cheerfully, diligently, and faithfully." Others argued that slaves were better off than northern workers who toiled in dusty, airless factories.

The antislavery movement grew in the 1840s and 1850s. It deepened the division between the North and South.

Even Southerners who owned no slaves felt that slavery had to be defended. To them, slavery was an essential part of the southern economy. Southerners tended to exaggerate northern support for the antislavery movement. They began to believe that Northerners wanted to destroy their way of life.

SECTION REVIEW

1. **Define:** abolition, underground railroad.
2. Give two reasons why Americans opposed slavery.
3. (a) When did northern states end slavery? (b) Why did slavery there end without a big struggle?
4. (a) What was the goal of the American Colonization Society? (b) Why did many free blacks oppose colonization?
5. **What Do You Think?** Why do you think escaped slaves like Frederick Douglass made good antislavery speakers?

2 Rights for Women

Read to Learn

★ What rights did women want in the mid-1800s?
★ Who were the leaders of the women's rights movement?
★ What did the Seneca Falls Convention achieve?

Both black and white women were active in the antislavery crusade. They held meetings, signed petitions, and wrote letters to Congress. As they worked to end slavery, women realized that they could make few changes because they lacked full social and political rights. As a result, many women abolitionists became crusaders for women's rights.

Women's Rights Movement

In the 1800s, women had few political or legal rights. They could not vote or hold office. When a woman married, her property passed to her husband. If a woman held a job, her earnings belonged to her husband. A man also had the right to punish his wife as long as he did not seriously injure her.

The Grimké sisters. Women in the antislavery movement saw all too clearly how limited their rights were. Among the first to speak out on the subject were the Grimké sisters. Angelina and Sarah Grimké came from a slave-owning family in South Carolina. They grew to hate slavery and moved to the North to work for abolition. Their firsthand knowledge of slavery made them powerful speakers, and they drew large crowds in northern cities.

Some Northerners were shocked at the boldness of the Grimkés. Women rarely stood on stage and addressed an audience that included men. Preachers scolded the Grimkés. "When [a woman] assumes the place and tone of a man as a public reformer," warned several preachers, "her character becomes unnatural."

The Grimkés did not give up their crusade, however. Instead, Angelina Grimké answered critics in letters and pamphlets. She insisted on discussing women's rights as well as abolition: "What then can woman do for the slave, when she herself is under the feet of man and shamed into silence?"

Sojourner Truth. Black women also struggled for women's rights. Sojourner Truth was born into slavery in New York State. She ran away from her owner just before state law would have freed her. Truth was a spellbinding speaker. Once, she listened to a man claiming that women needed to be protected. Truth stood up and replied:

Sojourner Truth was born Isabella Baumfree in New York State. In 1827, she took her new name, claiming that God had sent her to tell the truth about slavery. Although she could not read, Truth was a powerful speaker for abolition and women's rights.

Nobody ever helps me into carriages, or over mudpuddles, or gives me any best place! And ain't I a woman? . . . I have borne thirteen children, and seen them most all sold off into slavery, and when I cried out with my mother's grief, none but Jesus heard me! And ain't I a woman?

Others speak for equality. Inspired by the Grimkés and Sojourner Truth, other women spoke up for women's rights. Many of these leaders came out of the antislavery movement. One group of women, including Lucretia Mott and Elizabeth Cady Stanton, traveled to London in 1840 for the World Antislavery Convention. When they arrived, they found that they were not welcome. Women were barred from the meeting!

After returning home, Mott and Stanton took up the cause of women's rights with new zeal. Mott was a Quaker minister and the mother of five children. A quiet speaker, her logic won the respect of many listeners. Elizabeth Cady Stanton was the daughter of a well-known New York judge. When she was growing up, clerks in her father's law office teased Stanton. They read her laws that denied basic rights to women. This teasing helped make Stanton a lifelong foe of inequality.

Another energetic organizer was Susan B. Anthony. She was ready to go anywhere at any time to speak for the cause. Even when an audience heckled her and threw eggs, Anthony always finished her speech. Anthony joined forces with Stanton and other women's rights leaders.

Elizabeth Cady Stanton, at left, and Susan B. Anthony, at right, dedicated their lives to the women's rights movement. Anthony was a superb organizer. In fact, one woman called her "the Napoleon of the movement," after the French military genius.

The Seneca Falls Convention

Mott and Stanton decided to hold a national convention for women's rights. They wanted to draw attention to the problems women faced.

In 1848, the convention met in Seneca Falls, New York. At the *Seneca Falls Convention,* leaders of the women's rights movement voted on a plan of action. They called their plan the Declaration of Sentiments. It was modeled on the Declaration of Independence. The new declaration proclaimed, "We hold these truths to be self-evident: that all men and women are created equal."

The men and women at Seneca Falls approved resolutions demanding equality for women at work, school, church, and before the law. All the resolutions passed without a no vote, except for one. It demanded that women be allowed to vote in elections. Even the women at Seneca Falls hesitated to make this bold demand. In the

Many American women had little interest in the movement for women's rights. They were busy with traditional duties such as raising children, keeping house, and helping their husbands. As this print shows, getting produce from the farm to market was a task that needed the help of the whole family.

end, they approved the demand by a slim majority.

The Seneca Falls Convention marked the beginning of an organized women's rights movement. In the years after 1848, women worked for change in many areas. They won more legal rights in some states. New York State passed laws allowing women to keep property and earnings when they married. But progress was slow. Many men and women opposed the women's rights movement. The struggle for equal rights would be long.

Improving Women's Education

A major concern of women at Seneca Falls was education. At the time, poor white and black women had little hope of even learning to read and write.

Middle class families could often afford to send their daughters to school. However, young women learned dancing and drawing, not mathematics or science, as young men did. Since women were expected to marry and take care of families, people thought that they did not need to learn such subjects.

Reformers like Emma Willard and Mary Lyon worked hard to improve education for women. Willard opened a high school for women in Troy, New York, that taught all subjects. Lyon spent years raising money to build Mount Holyoke Female Seminary. She avoided calling the school a college because many people thought that sending women to college was wrong. But Mount Holyoke, which opened in 1837, was the first women's college in America.

Twenty-nine medical schools refused to admit Elizabeth Blackwell because she was a woman. Friends advised her to take a man's name and clothing in order to reach her goal. Blackwell refused. Later, she was accepted at Geneva Medical College. In 1857, Blackwell set up a hospital for the poor in New York City.

Women also struggled to get an education in fields such as medicine. Elizabeth Blackwell applied to medical school at Geneva College in New York. She was accepted, even though most school officials thought that she would fail. To their surprise, Blackwell graduated first in her class. Many women had practiced medicine since colonial times, but Blackwell was the first woman doctor with a medical degree. She later set up the first nursing school in the United States.

At about the same time, a few men's colleges began to admit women. As women's education improved, women found jobs teaching, especially in grade schools.

═══ SECTION REVIEW ═══

1. What did women abolitionists realize about their rights?
2. Describe the role each of the following played in the women's rights movement: (a) Sojourner Truth; (b) Lucretia Mott; (c) Susan B. Anthony.
3. (a) What was the first women's college in the United States? (b) When did it open?
4. **What Do You Think?** Why do you think women at the Seneca Falls Convention modeled their declaration on the Declaration of Independence?

3 Reform Marches On

Read to Learn
★ What reforms did Dorothea Dix seek?
★ How did public schools change in the 1800s?
★ What do these words mean: temperance movement?

The 1830s and 1840s were a busy period of reform. Hundreds of groups sprang up to urge improvements in everything from schools to prisons.

Dorothea Dix

One Sunday in 1851, Dorothea Dix, a Massachusetts schoolteacher, was invited to read to prisoners in the local jail. When she entered the jail, Dix was horrified by what she found. A group of mentally ill people were locked up alongside the criminals. They were dressed in rags and kept in unheated cells. When Dorothea Dix left the jail, she decided she had to take action.

Help for the mentally ill. During the next 18 months, Dix visited every jail and asylum for the mentally ill in Massachusetts. In a report to the Massachusetts legislature, Dix listed the horrors she had seen. She told of inmates kept in "cages, closets, cellars, stalls, [and] pens." She pointed out that these people were ill and should be treated as patients, not criminals.

In response to her report, the legislature voted to improve care for the mentally ill. Dix took her crusade to many other states. In almost every one, her reports resulted in action to help the mentally ill.

Prison reform. Dix also criticized the horrible conditions in the prisons she visited. Prisoners were often stuffed into tiny, cold, damp rooms. Men, women, and children shared the same crowded quarters. If food was in short supply, prisoners went hungry unless they had money to buy meals from the jailers.

In the 1800s, people were jailed even for minor crimes such as owing money. In 1830, five out of six people in northern jails were debtors. Most owed less than $20. For more serious crimes, people suffered severe punishments such as whipping and branding.

Dorothea Dix's report to the Massachusetts legislature on the mentally ill pulled no punches. Dix wrote, "The condition of human beings, reduced to the extremist state of misery, cannot be told in softened language." Although her report shocked some legislators, it got quick action.

Reformers like Dix called for changes in the prison system. As a result, some states built new prisons housing one or two inmates to a cell. People convicted of minor crimes received shorter sentences. Cruel punishments were forbidden. And slowly, states stopped treating debtors as criminals.

A Better Education

Reformers believed that all people needed an education. As more men won the right to vote, reformers felt they needed to be well informed.

However, few American children went to school before the 1820s. Where public schools existed, they were often old and run-down. Schools had little money for books. Teachers were poorly paid and trained. Students of all ages crowded together in a single room. Faced with a class of 80 students, many teachers worried more about controlling their students than teaching them.

Growth of public schools. In the 1820s, New York State led the way in public education. The state ordered every town to set up an elementary school. The new public schools were not totally free. Parents had to pay something for their children to attend. But it was a start. Before long, other states passed similar laws requiring towns to support public schools.

Horace Mann led the fight for public schools in Massachusetts. In 1837, Mann was put in charge of education in the state. He hounded legislators to provide money for new and better elementary schools. Under Mann's leadership, Massachusetts built new schools, extended the school year, and paid teachers better. The state also opened three colleges to train teachers.

Reformers in other states pressed their legislatures to follow the lead of Massachusetts. By the 1850s, most northern states had free, tax-supported elementary schools. Schools in the

South improved, but more slowly. In both the North and South, schooling stopped after eighth grade. There were very few public high schools.

Schools for black Americans. Free black children had little chance for an education. A few cities, such as Boston and New York, set up separate schools for black students. But these schools got less money than schools for white students. Even so, some blacks did get good educations. A few attended private colleges such as Harvard, Dartmouth, and Oberlin. In the 1850s, several colleges for black students opened in the North.

Education for the disabled. A few reformers worked to improve education for the physically disabled. In 1815, the Reverend Thomas Gallaudet (gal uh DEHT) set up a school for the deaf in Hartford, Connecticut. Gallaudet showed that deaf children could learn like other children. A few years later, Dr. Samuel Gridley Howe directed the first school for the blind. Howe invented a way to print books with raised letters. Blind students could read the letters by using their fingers.

Fighting Demon Rum

In the 1800s, drinking alcohol was a widespread problem. At political rallies, weddings, and even funerals, men, women, and sometimes children drank alcohol. Often they drank heavily.

Reformers cried out against "demon rum." They linked alcohol to crime, the breakup of families, and mental illness. The campaign against drinking was called the *temperance movement.*

As new schools were built in the 1840s and 1850s, talented young women went into teaching. By 1860, most of the country's elementary school teachers were women. Why do you think women wanted to become teachers?

Some temperance groups wanted to persuade people to limit their drinking. Others demanded that states prohibit the sale of alcohol.

In the 1850s, Maine banned the sale of alcohol, and eight other states soon followed. However, many Americans opposed these laws, and most were repealed. Still, temperance crusaders pressed on. The movement gained new strength in the late 1800s.

Reform movements did much to improve life in America. Many states built new schools and provided better care for prisoners and the mentally ill. The public became more aware of the dangers of alcohol. Not all reforms succeeded. But in general, Americans had a renewed concern with improving society. And the work of Horace Mann, Dorothea Dix, and others paved the way for later reformers.

"Father, come home!" is the title of this engraving. It shows a young girl leading her father away from a barroom. The picture appeared in an 1854 best-seller exposing the evils of alcohol. The book led many drinkers to give up liquor and "come home" for good.

SECTION REVIEW

1. **Define:** temperance movement.
2. (a) List two problems Dorothea Dix uncovered. (b) What did she do to correct them?
3. Why did reformers feel that the growth of democracy made education even more important?
4. (a) Who led the fight for better public schools in Massachusetts? (b) What improvements in public education did Massachusetts make?
5. **What Do You Think?** What hopes do you think reformers in various movements shared? Why?

4 Creating an American Culture

Read to Learn
★ What themes did American writers use?
★ Which women writers enjoyed great popularity?
★ How did an American style of painting develop?

In the 1800s, writers and artists were creating a new vision of America. They broke free of European traditions and created styles that were truly American.

American Writers

After 1820, American writers began to write stories with American themes. New York and Boston were home to many of the nation's writers.

Early writers. Washington Irving was the first American writer to become well known in Europe as well as America. Irving, a New Yorker, published his first works in the 1820s. His two most famous stories are "Rip Van Winkle" and "The Legend of Sleepy

Hollow." The stories appeared in a collection of stories called *The Sketch Book*. Both take place in the Hudson River valley north of New York City.

"Rip Van Winkle" is based on an old Dutch legend. Rip is a simple farmer in the days before the American Revolution. One day, he is put under a magic spell. He sleeps for 20 years. He awakes to find that his quiet village has changed into a bustling town. The town buzzes with talk about "rights of citizens—elections—members of congress—Bunker's Hill—heroes of seventy-six—and other words, which . . . bewildered Van Winkle." Readers appreciated the way Irving poked fun at Rip, who had slept through the entire American Revolution.

In the 1820s, James Fenimore Cooper began to publish a series of popular novels that were set on the American frontier. In *The Last of the Mohicans* and *The Deerslayer,* Cooper gave a romantic, or idealized, view of how whites and Indians got along. However, his stories were so full of exciting adventures that few readers cared whether they were true to life.

Later novelists. New England writers like Nathaniel Hawthorne often turned to historical themes. Hawthorne was descended from the Puritans of Salem, Massachusetts. America's Puritan past fascinated him. His best-known novel is *The Scarlet Letter,* published in 1850.

Herman Melville admired Hawthorne's works, and the two men became friends. In 1851, Melville published *Moby Dick,* which ranks among America's greatest novels. *Moby Dick* tells about a voyage of the *Pequod,* a whaling ship commanded by Captain Ahab. Ahab has vowed to kill the great white whale that bit off his leg years earlier. The novel had limited success in the 1800s. Today, however, this dramatic story of a whale hunt is seen as a symbolic struggle between good and evil.

In 1853, William Wells Brown published *Clotel,* a novel about slave life in America. Brown was America's first black novelist and the first black to earn his living as a writer.

American poets. John Greenleaf Whittier, a Quaker from Massachusetts, wanted to write poetry about early American history. But with the urging of his friend, William Lloyd Garrison, he found himself drawn to the antislavery cause. In many poems, Whittier sought to make people aware of the evils of slavery.

Of all American poets from this period, Walt Whitman is probably read more often today than any other. He published only one book of poems, *Leaves of Grass.* However, he added poems to this book over a period of 37 years. His bold, emotional language made his poetry different from any written before it. In his poems, Whitman praised America's land and celebrated the many different people that made America great.

Emerson and His Circle

Perhaps the most widely read American writer in the mid-1800s was Ralph Waldo Emerson. In essays and poems, Emerson emphasized the importance of the individual. He believed that every person had an "inner light" that is part of God. Emerson urged people to rely on this inner light to guide their lives. In 1837, he composed his famous "Concord Hymn." It was dedicated to the first battle of the American Revolution.

Emerson influenced many writers, including Henry David Thoreau (THOR oh). Thoreau's best-known work is *Walden,* which tells about a year he spent living alone in a cabin in Massachusetts. Like Emerson, Thoreau thought that every person must judge what is right and wrong. He wrote: "If a man does not keep pace with his companions, perhaps it is because he hears a

Henry Wadsworth Longfellow was America's best-loved poet during the 1800s. He based many of his poems loosely on events from America's past. For example, *The Song of Hiawatha* tells about an Indian chief who lived by Lake Superior in the 1600s. Another poem, *The Courtship of Miles Standish,* weaves its story around a leader of the Plymouth Colony in Massachusetts.

By writing about American themes, Longfellow deepened the feeling Americans had for their past. He also helped to create a sense of identity for Americans. Probably his most famous patriotic poem is "Paul Revere's Ride." The poem is set at the beginning of the American Revolution. It tells about the exciting ride Paul Revere made to alert colonists that British soldiers were on the march. The poem begins:

Listen, my children, and you shall hear
Of the midnight ride of Paul Revere,
On the eighteenth of April, in Seventy-
five;
Hardly a man is now alive
Who remembers that famous day and
year.
He said to his friend, "If the British
march
By land or sea from the town to-night,
Hang a lantern aloft in the belfry arch
Of the North Church tower as a signal
light,—
One, if by land, and two, if by sea;
And I on the opposite shore will be,
Ready to ride and spread the alarm
Through every Middlesex village and
farm,
For the country folk to be up and to
arm."

★ Why do you think Longfellow's poems appealed to Americans in the mid-1800s?

different drummer. Let him step to the music which he hears." Thoreau hated slavery and was a conductor on the underground railroad.

Women Writers

Women writers published many books in the 1800s. Margaret Fuller, a friend of Emerson's, wrote *Woman in the Nineteenth Century*. This book strongly influenced the women's rights movement. Women also wrote many of the best-selling novels of the time. These novels often told about young women who gained wealth and happiness by honesty and self-sacrifice. Some novels were more true to life. They showed the hardship faced by widows and orphans.

Few of these novels are read today. But writers like Catharine Sedgwick and Fanny Fern earned far more money than Nathaniel Hawthorne or Herman Melville. In fact, Hawthorne complained bitterly about the success of women writers. "America is now wholly given over to a . . . mob of scribbling women," he once wrote.

The Artists' View

Most American painters studied in Europe. Their paintings reflected European styles. Benjamin West was a portrait painter in Philadelphia in his youth. Later, he settled in London. West became famous for his historical paintings. In fact, King George III admired his work.

You will sometimes need to research information using books in the library. Every library has a card catalog. The card catalog helps you find the books you need quickly.

1. Study the parts of the card catalog. The *card catalog* is a set of drawers holding small cards. The cards are in alphabetical order. Every nonfiction, or factual, book has at least three cards. The author card lists the book by the author's last name. The title card lists the book by its title. The subject card lists the book by its subject—for example, Baseball or American history.

You can tell what kind of card you are looking at by reading the top line. The top line will show either the author's last name, the title of the book, or the subject heading. Usually, author and title cards are kept together in one set of drawers. Subject cards are kept in another set of drawers.

Look at Card A. (a) Is this an author, title, or subject card? (b) Who is the author of the book? (c) What is the title of the book? (d) What is the subject of the book?

2. Practice using the call number. Every card for a nonfiction book has a number in the top left corner. This is the call number of the book. The *call number* tells you where you will find the book on the library shelves. Each nonfiction book has its call number printed on the spine, or narrow back edge. Nonfiction books are arranged on the shelves in numerical order. The letters after the number are the first letters of the author's last name. Look at Card A. (a) What is the call number of the book? (b) What do the letters "Dul" printed below the call number mean?

3. Use other cards in the card catalog. Look at Cards B and C. (a) Is Card B an author, title, or subject card? (b) Is Card C an author, title, or subject card? (c) Why do the two cards have the same call number?

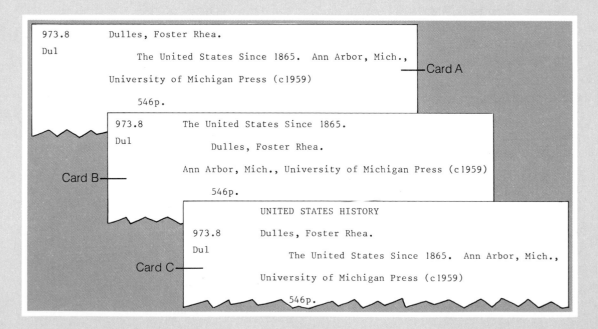

```
973.8        Dulles, Foster Rhea.
Dul
                  The United States Since 1865.  Ann Arbor, Mich.,
        University of Michigan Press (c1959)                         ——Card A
                  546p.
```

```
973.8        The United States Since 1865.
Dul
                  Dulles, Foster Rhea.
        Ann Arbor, Mich., University of Michigan Press (c1959)
Card B——              546p.
```

```
                  UNITED STATES HISTORY
        973.8        Dulles, Foster Rhea.
        Dul
                          The United States Since 1865.  Ann Arbor, Mich.,
Card C——      University of Michigan Press (c1959)
                  546p.
```

George Caleb Bingham captured the mood and details of life on the American frontier, as this painting, *Fur Traders Descending the Missouri*, shows. Bingham said that he painted so that "our social and political characteristics . . . will not be lost."

Many young American artists studied with West in London. They included Charles Wilson Peale, Gilbert Stuart, and John Singleton Copley. Both Peale and Stuart painted well-known portraits of George Washington.

By the mid-1800s, American artists began to develop their own style. The first group of artists to do so belonged to the *Hudson River School.* Artists like Thomas Cole and Asher Durand painted landscapes of the Hudson River and Catskill Mountains of New York.

Other American artists painted scenes of fertile farmlands and hard-working farm families. George Caleb Bingham was inspired by his native Missouri. Bingham's paintings show frontier life along the rivers that feed the great Mississippi.

Artists celebrated the vast American landscape. They expressed confidence in America and its future. This confidence was shared by reformers and by the thousands of Americans opening up new frontiers in the West.

SECTION REVIEW

1. (a) List three American novelists. (b) Which American writer first became well known in Europe?
2. (a) Who wrote *Leaves of Grass?* (b) What is unusual about this book of poems?
3. What women writers were popular in the mid-1800s?
4. What did artists of the Hudson River School paint?
5. **What Do You Think?** Why do you think Americans only developed a style of painting in the mid-1800s?

Chapter 16 Review

★ Summary ★

By the 1830s, reformers were busy trying to improve American life. Many joined the antislavery crusade. Northern abolitionists strongly attacked slavery. Some risked their lives to help slaves escape on the underground railroad.

Women abolitionists saw how their own rights were limited. In 1848, women's rights supporters held a convention at Seneca Falls. There, they drew up a list of demands. Other reformers called for more schools, improved care for the mentally ill, prison reform, and temperance.

At the same time, a new generation of writers and artists developed American themes. Together, the reformers, writers, and artists showed how the nation was maturing. Americans set out with confidence to cure the country's ills and to define what America was.

★ Reviewing the Facts ★

Key Terms. Match each term in Column 1 with the correct definition in Column 2.

Column 1
1. abolition
2. underground railroad
3. temperance movement

Column 2
a. ending something completely
b. campaign against drinking
c. secret network of people who helped runaway slaves

Key People, Events, and Ideas. Identify each of the following.

1. Liberia
2. Frederick Douglass
3. William Lloyd Garrison
4. Angelina Grimké
5. Sojourner Truth
6. Lucretia Mott
7. Seneca Falls Convention
8. Dorothea Dix
9. Horace Mann
10. Washington Irving
11. William Wells Brown
12. Walt Whitman
13. Margaret Fuller
14. Benjamin West
15. Hudson River School

★ Chapter Checkup ★

1. (a) What were the political roots of the antislavery movement? (b) What were the religious roots of the antislavery movement?

2. (a) Who were leaders of the abolition movement? (b) How did they try to end slavery?

3. (a) Why did some Northerners oppose the antislavery movement? (b) How did most white Southerners respond to the movement?

4. (a) How were women's rights limited in the 1800s? (b) What did women at the Seneca Falls Convention demand?

5. (a) What was the condition of public schools in the early 1800s? (b) How was education improved in the mid-1800s?

6. (a) How did opportunities for higher education for women change after 1820? (b) How did education for blacks change after 1820?

7. What theme did each of the following write about: (a) Washington Irving; (b) James Fenimore Cooper; (c) Walt Whitman?

8. What themes did American painters in the mid-1800s take up?

★ Thinking About History ★

1. **Relating past to present.** (a) How did antislavery leaders try to win support of the public? (b) How do reform leaders today try to win support for their causes?

2. **Understanding the economy.** By the mid-1800s, factories supplied many household items once made by hand. As a result, middle class women had more free time. (a) How does this fact help explain why some women became active reformers? (b) How does it explain why writers like Fanny Fern were so popular?

3. **Analyzing information.** American writers in the 1800s stressed the importance of the individual. How does the history of the United States help explain this emphasis on the individual?

4. **Learning about citizenship.** During the mid-1800s, Americans worked to reform many aspects of American life. (a) What new roles do you think women and black reformers took on? (b) How do you think the actions of abolitionists, women's rights supporters, and other reformers made Americans look at their society in a new way?

★ Using Your Skills ★

1. **Making a review chart.** Make a review chart with five columns and three rows. Label the columns Abolition, Women's Rights, Care for Mentally Ill, Prison Reform, and Education Reform. Label the rows Problems to Solve, Leaders, and Achievements. Then complete the chart. (a) According to the chart, how many people were leaders of more than one movement? (b) Which movement do you think achieved the most?

2. **Using a painting as a primary source.** Study the painting on page 360. (a) When was the painting done? (b) How does the classroom in the painting differ from a classroom today? (c) How is it similar?

3. **Placing events in time.** Study the time line on page 350. (a) When did William Lloyd Garrison begin publishing *The Liberator?* (b) When was the first women's college opened? (c) When was the Seneca Falls Convention held?

★ More to Do ★

1. **Inventing a story.** Imagine that you are a slave escaping to the North. Invent a story explaining why you are traveling alone.

2. **Writing a dialogue.** Write a dialogue between Sojourner Truth and the man she was answering in the incident described on pages 355 and 356.

3. **Drawing a cartoon.** Draw a cartoon criticizing the practice of putting debtors in prison.

4. **Writing a report.** Read Washington Irving's "Rip Van Winkle" or "The Legend of Sleepy Hollow." Write a report telling what happens in the story. What information does the story give about life in America?

5. **Exploring local history.** Write a report about efforts to reform slavery, women's rights, prisoners' rights, education, or mental health care in your local area during the mid-1800s.

Unit 5 Review

Chapter 13 Andrew Jackson became President in 1828. His bold actions made the office of President stronger. Despite conflicts, Jackson was a hero to common people just gaining a voice in politics.

Chapter 14 America expanded quickly after 1820. Settlers moved to Texas and Oregon, which both became part of the United States in the mid-1840s. The Mexican War added California and the Southwest to the Union. By 1850, America stretched from sea to sea.

Chapter 15 The North and South developed different ways of life through the mid-1800s. Industry and trade thrived in northern cities. In the South, the Cotton Kingdom spread and slavery grew.

Chapter 16 By the 1830s, many reformers were working to improve America. Abolitionists tried to end slavery, women demanded basic rights, and other reformers sought to improve schools, prisons, and care for the mentally ill. New writers and artists helped shape American culture.

★ Unit Checkup ★

Choose the word or phrase that best completes each of the following statements.

1. President Martin Van Buren lost support because of the
   (a) Nullification Crisis.
   (b) Panic of 1837.
   (c) Indian Removal Act.

2. From 1818 to 1845, the United States occupied Oregon jointly with
   (a) Britain.
   (b) Russia.
   (c) France.

3. When Texans charged at the Battle of San Jacinto, they shouted,
   (a) "Fifty-four forty or fight!"
   (b) "Tippecanoe and Tyler too!"
   (c) "Remember the Alamo!"

4. Because of the potato famine of 1845, thousands of people came to America from
   (a) Germany.
   (b) Ireland.
   (c) France.

5. Helping free blacks move to Liberia was the goal of the
   (a) New England Anti-Slavery Society.
   (b) Seneca Falls Convention.
   (c) American Colonization Society.

★ Building American Citizenship ★

1. Many Irish and German immigrants came to the United States in the mid-1800s. (a) Why did nativists want to limit immigration? (b) What reasons do people today give for putting limits on immigration?

2. The black population of the 1800s included free blacks as well as slaves. (a) Why do you think free blacks worked to end slavery? (b) How do you think free blacks in the South felt about the antislavery movement?

3. Through family life, slaves passed on to their children pride in their history and moral ideas. Why do you think Americans today see family life as important to the nation?

The map at right shows the growth of railroads between 1840 and 1860. Study the map. Then answer the following questions.

1. Were there more railroads in the North or South in 1840? In 1860?

2. (a) Which northern states had the most miles of railroad track in 1840? In 1860? (b) What can you conclude about the growth of the country's population?

3. Why do you think there were no railroads in western Virginia and eastern Kentucky?

4. Besides the railroads, what transportation advantages did Buffalo, Cleveland, Detroit, Chicago, and Milwaukee share?

5. How do you think the growth of factories in the North affected the building of railroads?

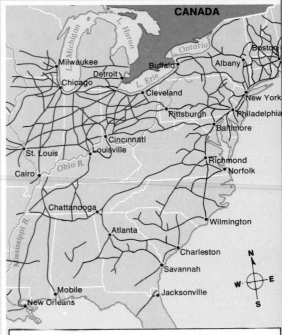

GROWTH OF RAILROADS

—— Railroads in 1840

—— Railroads built, 1840–1860

0   300   600 Miles

0   300   600 Kilometers

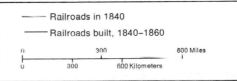

History Writer's Handbook

Arranging Supporting Information

Arrange supporting information for detail sentences in a logical order. Common orders are described below.

Time order is arrangement in order of occurrence. *Comparison order* is arrangement according to similarities and differences. *Order of importance* is arrangement from most important to least important, or vice versa. *Cause-and-effect* order is arrangement to show a chain reaction of causes and effects.

Practice Look at the following topic sentence. *Americans based their claim to Oregon on three events.* The following is supporting information. *Lewis and Clark explored Oregon in 1806. Gray visited the Oregon coast in 1792. Astor's fur traders built Astoria in 1811.*

1. Which order might be best to arrange the supporting information?

2. Arrange the information in that order.

Unit 6

THE NATION DIVIDED

1836		1844		1852		1860

MARTIN VAN BUREN   JOHN TYLER   JAMES POLK   FRANKLIN PIERCE   JAMES

ANDREW JACKSON   WILLIAM HARRISON   ZACHARY TAYLOR   MILLARD FILLMORE

1836 ★ Arkansas statehood
1837 ★ Michigan statehood

1845 ★ Texas, Florida become states
1846 ★ Iowa statehood
1846–48 Mexican War
1848 ★ Wisconsin statehood; Free Soil Party formed
1850 Compromise of 1850; ★ California statehood

1852 *Uncle Tom's Cabin* published
1854 Kansas–Nebraska Act; Republican Party formed
1858 ★ Minnesota statehood; Lincoln–Douglas debates
1859 ★ Oregon statehood; raid on Harpers Ferry

1836		1844		1852		1860

Mid-1800s Southern planters at the New Orleans cotton market.

CAUTION!!

COLORED PEOPLE

OF BOSTON, ONE & ALL,

You are hereby respectfully CAUTIONED and advised, to avoid conversing with the

Watchmen and Police Officers of Boston,

For since the recent ORDER OF THE MAYOR & ALDERMEN, they are empowered to act as

KIDNAPPERS

AND

Slave Catchers,

And they have already been actually employed in KIDNAPPING, CATCHING, AND KEEPING SLAVES. Therefore, if you value your LIBERTY, and the *Welfare of the Fugitives* among you, Shun them in every possible manner, as so many *HOUNDS* on the track of the most unfortunate of your race.

Keep a Sharp Look Out for KIDNAPPERS, and have TOP EYE open.

APRIL 24, 1851.

1851 Even in the North, free blacks and runaway slaves faced dangers, as this poster shows.

1857 Dred Scott took his fight for freedom to the Supreme Court—and lost.

UNIT OUTLINE

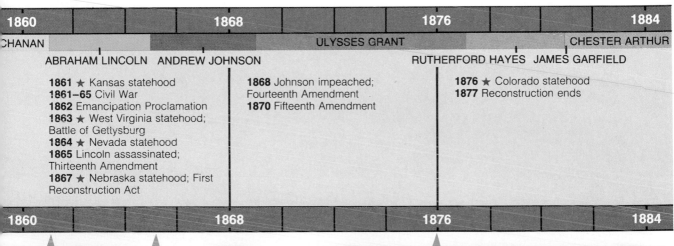

1860	1868	1876	1884

CHANAN ━ ABRAHAM LINCOLN ━ ANDREW JOHNSON ━ ULYSSES GRANT ━ RUTHERFORD HAYES ━ JAMES GARFIELD ━ CHESTER ARTHUR

1861 ★ Kansas statehood
1861–65 Civil War
1862 Emancipation Proclamation
1863 ★ West Virginia statehood; Battle of Gettysburg
1864 ★ Nevada statehood
1865 Lincoln assassinated; Thirteenth Amendment
1867 ★ Nebraska statehood; First Reconstruction Act

1868 Johnson impeached; Fourteenth Amendment
1870 Fifteenth Amendment

1876 ★ Colorado statehood
1877 Reconstruction ends

1860	1868	1876	1884

1861–65 A Confederate drummer boy.

1861–65 A lantern showing President Lincoln.

1865–77 During Reconstruction, freedmen voted in the South.

CHAPTER

17

The Coming of the War (1820–1860)

Chapter Outline

1 Differences Over Slavery
2 A Great Compromise
3 Adding Fuel to the Fire
4 A New Political Party
5 The Union Is Broken

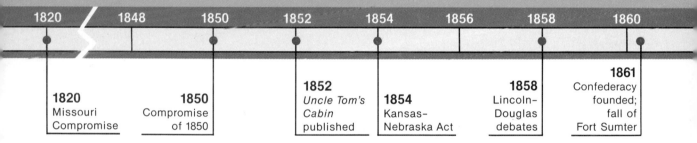

| 1820 | 1848 | 1850 | 1852 | 1854 | 1856 | 1858 | 1860 |

1820
Missouri Compromise

1850
Compromise of 1850

1852
Uncle Tom's Cabin published

1854
Kansas-Nebraska Act

1858
Lincoln-Douglas debates

1861
Confederacy founded; fall of Fort Sumter

About This Chapter

By the mid-1800s, the issue of slavery sharply divided the North and South. Americans continued to move west into the Louisiana Purchase and then the Mexican Cession. As they did, the nation was forced to deal with this question: Should slavery be allowed in the new states carved out of the western territories? Northerners thought that new states should ban slavery and enter the Union as free states. Southerners thought that new states should allow slavery and join the Union as slave states.

The issue first arose when Missouri applied to join the Union as a slave state in December 1818. Northerners angrily objected to adding another slave state. They knew that another slave state would add to the power of the South in the Senate. A bitter debate erupted in Congress. Thomas Jefferson, then retired, wrote that "in the gloomiest moment of the revolutionary war I never had any [fears] equal to what I feel from this source." Jefferson said that the crisis over Missouri, "like a firebell in the night, awakened and filled me with terror."

Americans compromised on the slavery question at first. However, as time went on, feelings grew more heated, and compromise became more difficult.

Study the time line above. How many years passed between the Missouri Compromise and the Compromise of 1850?

In this painting, a slave family escapes from the South. When Northerners refused to return runaway slaves, an explosive situation developed.

1 Differences Over Slavery

Read to Learn

★ How did the spread of slavery become an issue?
★ How did Congress compromise on the slavery question?
★ Why did some people form the Free Soil Party?
★ What do these words mean: sectionalism, popular sovereignty?

Louisiana was the first state created out of the Louisiana Purchase. Because slavery was well established there, Louisiana joined the Union as a slave state with little discussion in 1812. The issue of slavery in the West first came up in 1818. That year, Missouri's request to join the Union as a slave state caused an uproar.

Debate Over Missouri

In 1818, there were 11 free states and 11 slave states. Each state had two senators. So there was a balance between the North and South in the Senate. If Missouri joined the Union as a slave state, the South would have a majority in the Senate. Northerners fought against letting Missouri in as a slave state. For months, Congress argued about what to do.

Finally, Senator Henry Clay proposed a plan that both the North and South accepted. During the debate over Missouri, Maine applied to become a state. Clay called for admitting Missouri as a slave state and Maine as a free state. Clay's plan was known as the

Missouri Compromise. It kept the number of slave and free states equal.

As part of the Missouri Compromise, Congress drew a line across the southern border of Missouri at latitude 36°30'N. Slavery was permitted in the Louisiana Purchase south of that line. But it was banned north of the line. Missouri itself was the only exception. (See the map on page 380.)

Debate Over the Mexican Cession

The Missouri Compromise applied to the Louisiana Purchase only. In 1848, the Mexican War added vast lands in the West to the United States. Would slavery be allowed in the Mexican Cession?

Wilmot Proviso. Many Northerners opposed the war with Mexico, as you read in Chapter 14. They thought that the South wanted to push slavery into the West. Even before the Mexican War was over, a young congressman from Pennsylvania, David Wilmot, raised the slavery question. Wilmot called on Congress to outlaw slavery in any land won from Mexico. Southerners were furious. They argued that Congress had no right to outlaw slavery in the territories.

In 1846, the House passed Wilmot's measure, called the *Wilmot Proviso.* But the Senate defeated it. As a result, the question of slavery in the territories continued to be debated.

Choosing sides. In the 1840s, sectionalism grew stronger. *Sectionalism* means that people feel loyalty to their state or section instead of the whole country. Southerners were united by their support for slavery. To them, the North was a threat. Many Northerners saw the South as a foreign country where American rights and liberties did not exist.

As the debate over slavery in the West heated up, people found it harder not to take sides. Northern abolitionists demanded that slavery be abolished throughout the country. They

In the 1840s, abolitionists stepped up efforts to end slavery. William Whipper, shown here, was a wealthy black lumber merchant who lived in Pennsylvania. He was a leading abolitionist and an ally of William Lloyd Garrison.

insisted that slavery was morally wrong. By the 1840s, a growing number of Northerners agreed with them. Southern slave owners thought that slavery should be allowed in any territory. They also demanded that slaves who escaped to the North be returned to them. Many white Southerners went along with these ideas, even though they owned no slaves.

Between these extreme views were more moderate positions. Some moderates argued that the Missouri Compromise line should be extended across the Mexican Cession all the way to the Pacific. Any new state north of that line would be a free state. Any new state south of the line would be a slave state.

Other moderates supported the idea of popular sovereignty. *Popular sovereignty* means control by the people. In other words, the voters in a territory would decide whether or not to allow slavery. Slaves themselves, of course, could not vote.

Free Soilers. Debate over slavery in the territories led to the birth of a new political party. By 1848, many people in both the Whig and Democratic parties strongly opposed the spread of slavery. However, the leaders of both parties refused to take a stand on the question. They were afraid that the issue would split the nation.

Antislavery Whigs and Democrats met in Buffalo, New York, in 1848. They founded the *Free Soil Party.* Their slogan was "Free soil, free speech, free labor, and free men." The main goal of the new party was to stop the spread of slavery into the territories. Only a few Free Soilers were abolitionists who wanted to end slavery in the South.

Election of 1848

Free Soilers named former President Martin Van Buren as their candidate for President in 1848. Democrats chose Senator Lewis Cass of Michigan.

Cass supported popular sovereignty. Whigs chose Zachary Taylor, hero of the Mexican War. Because Taylor was a slave owner from Louisiana, Whigs believed that he would win many votes in the South.

Taylor easily won the election. But Van Buren, the Free Soil candidate, won 10 percent of the popular vote. And 13 Free Soilers were elected to Congress. The strength of the Free Soilers after only three months of work showed that slavery was a hot political issue.

═SECTION REVIEW═

1. **Locate:** Maine, Missouri, Missouri Compromise line.
2. **Define:** sectionalism, popular sovereignty.
3. Why did Missouri's request for statehood cause conflict in Congress?
4. Why was the Free Soil Party founded?
5. **What Do You Think?** How do you think the growth of the Free Soil Party showed that sectionalism was growing stronger?

2 A Great Compromise

Read to Learn

★ Why did the slavery question flare up again in 1850?
★ How did the North and South again compromise?
★ What law forced Northerners to help catch runaway slaves?
★ What do these words mean: fugitive, civil war?

In 1850, the question of slavery in the West again divided the North and South. That year, California asked to join the Union as a free state. California was the first territory in the Mexican Cession to apply for statehood. Its request threatened the balance between free and slave states once more.

Need for Compromise

Between 1821 and 1850, six states joined the Union. Michigan, Iowa, and Wisconsin joined as free states. Arkansas, Florida, and Texas came in as slave states. (See the diagram on page 377.) If California joined as a free state, the North would have a majority in the Senate. So Southerners angrily opposed admitting a free California. They also feared that more free states might be made out of the Mexican Cession. This would further upset the balance. Some Southerners even talked about seceding from the Union.

Clay's plea. In the midst of the crisis, Congress turned to Senator Henry Clay for help. Clay was known as the

Here, Senators debate the Compromise of 1850. At center, Henry Clay speaks to his fellow senators. Seated behind Clay, Daniel Webster rests his head on his hand. White-haired John C. Calhoun is the third person from the right. When the Senate at last reached a compromise, newspapers printed headlines such as "The Country Saved" and "Most Glorious News."

Great Compromiser because he had worked out the Missouri Compromise. In 1850, the 73-year-old senator was very ill. Still, he pleaded on the Senate floor for the North and South to compromise. If they failed to do so, Clay warned, the nation could fall apart.

Calhoun's speech. Senator John C. Calhoun of South Carolina prepared the southern reply to Clay. Like Clay, Calhoun was aging and ill. He knew that the debate over California was his last battle. Calhoun could not speak loudly enough to address the Senate. So he sat wrapped in a heavy cloak while another senator read his speech.

Calhoun was uncompromising. The slave system could not be changed, he said. Slavery must be allowed in the western territories. Calhoun also brought up the issue of slaves who escaped to the North. Calhoun wanted *fugitive,* or escaped, slaves returned to their owners in the South. Even more, Calhoun wanted Northerners to admit

that Southerners had a right to get their "property" back.

If the North could not agree to southern demands, Calhoun told the Senate, "let the states . . . agree to separate and part in peace. If you are unwilling we should part in peace, tell us so, and we shall know what to do." Calhoun meant that the South would secede from the Union.

Webster for the Union. A plea for unity came from Senator Daniel Webster of Massachusetts. Webster had been Henry Clay's rival for decades. But he stood firmly with Clay on the question of preserving the Union. Webster declared that he spoke to Congress "not as a Massachusetts man, not as a Northern man, but as an American."

Webster was upset by the talk of secession. "There can be no such thing as a peaceable secession," he said. The states could not separate without civil war. *Civil war* is a war between people of the same country.

Webster opposed the spread of slavery into the territories. And he demanded an end to the slave trade in Washington, D.C. But he thought that the South was right to ask for the return of escaped slaves.

Compromise of 1850

In 1850, while the debate still raged, Calhoun died. His last words were: "The South! The South! God knows what will become of her!" President Taylor also died that summer. Taylor had opposed Clay's compromise plan. But the new President, Millard Fillmore, supported it. An agreement finally seemed possible.

Clay was now too sick himself to carry on. Senator Stephen Douglas of Illinois took up the effort. Douglas was smart and energetic. He guided each part of Clay's plan, called the Compromise of 1850, through Congress.

The *Compromise of 1850* had four main parts. First, California was admitted to the Union as a free state. Second, the rest of the Mexican Cession was divided into the New Mexico and Utah territories. In each territory, voters would decide the slavery question according to the idea of popular sovereignty. Third, the slave trade was banned in Washington, D.C. However, Congress declared that it had no right to ban the slave trade between slave states. Fourth, a strict fugitive slave law was passed.

The two sections reached a compromise. But neither side got all it wanted. Northerners were especially angry about the Fugitive Slave Law.

Fugitive Slave Law

Most Northerners had ignored the old Fugitive Slave Law, passed in 1793. Fugitive slaves often lived as free blacks in northern cities.

The *Fugitive Slave Law of 1850* was more strict. The law said that all citizens had to help catch runaway slaves. Anyone who let a fugitive escape could be fined $1,000 and jailed for six months.

Even free blacks were threatened by the new law. Slave catchers kidnapped free blacks and claimed that they were fugitives. In addition, under the new law, a judge received $10 if a person was sent back to slavery but only $5 if a person was freed. Thus, for some judges, it paid to send blacks to the South, whether or not they were runaway slaves. Free or slave, blacks could not testify in their own defense.

GRAPH SKILL Southerners wanted the number of slave and free states to stay equal. This would keep a balance of power in the Senate. The North, with its large population, had a growing majority in the House of Representatives. How did the admission of California affect the balance between free and slave states?

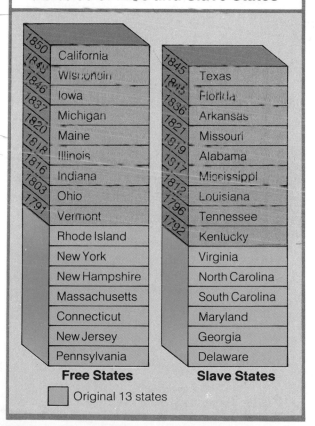

Balance of Free and Slave States

Free States	Slave States
1850 California	1845 Texas
1848 Wisconsin	1845 Florida
1846 Iowa	1836 Arkansas
1837 Michigan	1821 Missouri
1820 Maine	1819 Alabama
1818 Illinois	1817 Mississippi
1816 Indiana	1812 Louisiana
1803 Ohio	1796 Tennessee
1791 Vermont	1792 Kentucky
Rhode Island	Virginia
New York	North Carolina
New Hampshire	South Carolina
Massachusetts	Maryland
Connecticut	Georgia
New Jersey	Delaware
Pennsylvania	

Original 13 states

Voices of Freedom

In the 1850s, city people escaped from their cares in different ways. In New York, P. T. Barnum's American Museum offered 600,000 "curiosities," including wax figures and live animals. During the 1840s and 1850s, many people went to the theater. Shakespeare's plays were popular, and some American playwrights also met with success. A popular type of play was the melodrama. Melodramas were sensational, tragic stories of love and violence. One well-attended play featured a knife duel, a slave auction, and a steamship explosion.

Many Americans went to plays to forget about the country's worsening political mood. Yet the most popular play of the century had a powerful political message. It was a play based on *Uncle Tom's Cabin,* and its message was "Slavery is wrong!"

The Howards, a famous New York family of actors, gave 18 performances a week of *Uncle Tom's Cabin.* At the same time, 5 other versions of *Uncle Tom's Cabin* were playing in New York theaters.

The play had a major impact on how Northerners viewed slavery. Dramatic moments, like the escape of a slave and her child across the partly frozen Ohio River, won sympathy for slaves. And few playgoers left the theater with dry eyes after seeing the agony of Uncle Tom under Simon Legree's lash.

★ How do you think *Uncle Tom's Cabin* added to the tensions of the 1850s?

Southerners were happy with the Fugitive Slave Law, but Northerners hated it. They resented being forced to help capture runaway slaves and thus help slave owners. The sight of helpless people being chained, whipped, and shipped to a life of slavery horrified Northerners. Sometimes, mobs tried to rescue fugitives from their captors. Fights and riots broke out in several northern cities.

Uncle Tom's Cabin

Northern outrage over the Fugitive Slave Law was inflamed by the novel *Uncle Tom's Cabin,* published in 1852. Harriet Beecher Stowe wrote it to show that slavery was evil and that the Fugitive Slave Law was unjust.

Stowe told the story of Uncle Tom, a kindhearted, aging slave. Uncle Tom's owners lose a lot of money and have to sell their land and slaves. A cruel planter, Simon Legree, buys Uncle Tom. Legree badly mistreats his slaves and finally kills Uncle Tom.

In its first year alone, 300,000 copies of *Uncle Tom's Cabin* were sold. The story was published in many different languages. A play based on the book was staged around the world.

Southerners claimed that *Uncle Tom's Cabin* did not give a true picture of slave life. Indeed, Stowe had seen little of slavery firsthand. Yet the book made people see slavery as a moral problem that touched everyone, not just a political question for Congress to settle. More Americans began to ask if it was right for one human being to own another human being. For this reason, *Uncle Tom's Cabin* was one of the most influential books in American history.

━━━ **SECTION REVIEW** ━━━

1. **Locate:** California, New Mexico Territory, Utah Territory.
2. **Define:** fugitive, civil war.
3. How did the Compromise of 1850 settle the question of slavery in California? In New Mexico and Utah?
4. How did the Fugitive Slave Law of 1850 differ from the one of 1793?
5. **What Do You Think?** Why do you think the Fugitive Slave Law of 1850 angered Northerners?

3 Adding Fuel to the Fire

Read to Learn

★ How did slavery become an issue in 1854?
★ Why was Kansas a testing ground for popular sovereignty?
★ How did the Dred Scott decision affect Northerners and Southerners?

Americans hoped that the Compromise of 1850 would end the debate over slavery in the territories. But the Fugitive Slave Law and *Uncle Tom's Cabin* helped keep tensions high. Then, in 1854, the issue of slavery in the territories surfaced again.

Kansas–Nebraska Act

In January 1854, Senator Stephen Douglas introduced a bill to set up a government for the Nebraska Territory. The Nebraska Territory stretched from Texas north to Canada and from Missouri west to Oregon. (See the map on page 380.)

Douglas wanted the territory organized so that a railroad could be built through it from Chicago to California. A railroad would open the West to settlers. It would also help Douglas' home state of Illinois by making Chicago the gateway to the West.

Douglas' plan. Douglas knew that Southerners would not agree to adding another free state to the Union. So he proposed dividing the Nebraska Territory into two territories, Kansas and Nebraska. The question of slavery in the two territories would be decided by popular sovereignty.

Douglas' bill, called the *Kansas–Nebraska Act,* seemed fair to many people. After all, the Compromise of 1850 applied popular sovereignty in New Mexico and Utah. But other people felt that Kansas and Nebraska were different. The Missouri Compromise had already banned slavery in those areas, they said. The Kansas–Nebraska Act would, in effect, undo the Missouri Compromise.

Southerners supported the Kansas–Nebraska Act. They were sure that Kansas would become a slave state because slave owners from Missouri would move west into Kansas. (See the map on page 380.)

President Franklin Pierce, a Democrat elected in 1852, also backed the bill. With the President's help, Douglas pushed the Kansas–Nebraska Act through Congress. He did not realize it at the time, but he had lit a fire under a powder keg.

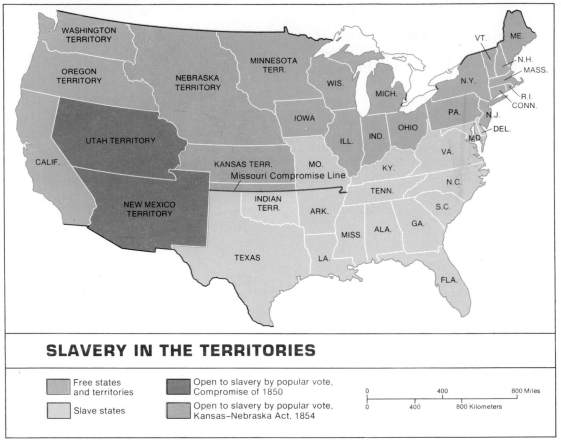

SLAVERY IN THE TERRITORIES

Free states and territories

Slave states

Open to slavery by popular vote, Compromise of 1850

Open to slavery by popular vote, Kansas–Nebraska Act, 1854

0   400   800 Miles
0   400   800 Kilometers

MAP SKILL The issue of slavery in the territories led to conflict between the North and South. In 1850, the North and South agreed to let voters in Utah and New Mexico decide the slavery question for themselves. What territories were opened to slavery in 1854?

Northerners react. Northern reaction to the Kansas–Nebraska Act was swift and angry. Opponents of slavery called the act a "criminal betrayal of precious rights." Now, slavery could spread to areas that had been free for over 30 years.

To protest the act, Northerners openly challenged the Fugitive Slave Law. Two days after the Kansas–Nebraska Act was passed, slave catchers in Boston seized Anthony Burns, an escaped slave. Citizens of Boston poured into the streets to keep Burns from being sent South. Two companies of soldiers had to stop the crowd from freeing Burns. Such incidents showed how deeply Northerners felt about slavery. Events in Kansas soon proved

that the slavery question could stir people to violence.

Bleeding Kansas

In 1854, Kansas became the testing ground for popular sovereignty. Earlier, Kansas settlers had little interest in the question of slavery. Farmers went to Kansas from nearby states looking for cheap land. Few owned slaves. However, after passage of the Kansas–Nebraska Act, a new kind of settler began arriving in Kansas.

Border Ruffians. People from both the North and South wanted control of Kansas. Abolitionists helped more than 1,000 people move there from New England. Proslavery settlers moved

— 380 —

into Kansas, too. Many were from Missouri. They wanted to make sure that New Englanders did not take over the territory. Proslavery bands from Missouri, called **Border Ruffians,** rode across the border. They battled with antislavery settlers.

Two governments. In 1855, Kansas held elections to choose a legislature. Hundreds of Border Ruffians rode to Kansas and voted illegally. They helped elect a proslavery legislature.

The new legislature quickly passed strict laws supporting slavery. One law said that people could receive the death penalty for helping slaves escape. Another made speaking out against slavery punishable by two years of hard labor.

Antislavery settlers refused to accept such laws. They elected their own governor and lawmakers. With two rival governments, Kansas was in chaos. Armed gangs roamed the land looking for trouble.

Bloody battles. In 1856, a drunken band of proslavery men raided the town of Lawrence, an antislavery stronghold. The raiders destroyed homes and smashed the presses of a Free Soil newspaper.

John Brown, a strong abolitionist, decided to strike back. Brown had moved to Kansas to help make it a free state. He claimed that God had sent him to punish supporters of slavery. After the attack on Lawrence, Brown rode with his four sons and two other men to the town of Pottawatomie (pot uh WOT uh mee) Creek. In the middle of the night, Brown and his followers dragged five proslavery settlers from their beds and murdered them.

The murders at Pottawatomie Creek caused more violence. Both sides fought fiercely. By late 1856, over 200 people had been killed. Newspapers called the territory **Bleeding Kansas.**

Violence in the Senate

Even before Brown's attack, the battle over Kansas spilled into the Senate. A sharp-tongued abolitionist, Charles Sumner, took the Senate floor. In one speech, he blasted the actions of the proslavery legislature in Kansas. Then, Sumner viciously criticized his foes, especially Andrew Butler, an elderly senator from South Carolina.

Butler was not in the Senate on the day of Sumner's speech. But the next

In the 1850s, settlers for and against slavery battled one another in Kansas. This print shows the proslavery attack on Lawrence, where antislavery settlers lived. Why do you think the struggle in Kansas was later called a "mini civil war"?

Northern newspapers ran this picture of Preston Brooks beating Charles Sumner with a cane. The picture was intended to outrage Northerners. In the background, it shows southern senators laughing at the brutal act.

day, Congressman Preston Brooks, Butler's nephew, marched into the Senate chamber. Using a heavy cane, Brooks beat Sumner until he fell, bloody and unconscious, to the floor.

Many Southerners believed that Sumner got what he deserved. Brooks received hundreds of canes as gifts from Southerners who supported him. To Northerners, however, the brutal act was just one more proof that slavery led to violence.

Dred Scott Decision

In 1857, a Supreme Court decision pushed the North and South further apart. The decision came in the Dred Scott case.

Dred Scott was a slave who lived in Missouri. Later, Scott moved with his owner to Illinois and then to Wisconsin, both free states. When his owner died, antislavery lawyers helped Scott file a lawsuit. They argued that since Scott had lived in free states, he should be a free man. Eventually, the case reached the Supreme Court.

The Court ruled that Scott could not file a lawsuit because, as a slave, he was not a citizen. The Court stated that slaves were property.

The Court went further. It ruled that Congress could not outlaw slavery in a territory. Only a state legislature could ban slavery, the Court said. As a result, the Missouri Compromise was unconstitutional.

Southerners rejoiced at the *Dred Scott decision*. It meant that slavery was legal except where a state voted to ban it. Northerners were shocked and angry. The Court's ruling made slavery legal in all the territories. Even Northerners who were not abolitionists felt that the Dred Scott decision was unjust.

SECTION REVIEW

1. **Locate:** Kansas Territory, Nebraska Territory, Illinois.
2. How did the Kansas–Nebraska Act undo the Missouri Compromise?
3. Why did proslavery and antislavery forces move into Kansas?
4. What did the Dred Scott decision say?
5. **What Do You Think?** Why do you think the Dred Scott decision shocked Northerners?

4 A New Political Party

Read to Learn
★ What was the main goal of the Republican Party?
★ How did Abraham Lincoln become a national figure?
★ How did the raid on Harpers Ferry drive the North and South apart?
★ What does this word mean: arsenal?

Tension over the slavery question drove a wedge between the North and South. The wedge also split old political parties. Out of these divisions grew a new party.

The Republican Party

In the mid-1850s, people who opposed slavery in the territories were looking for a political voice. The Free Soil Party had weakened. Whigs fought among themselves over the slavery question. Northern and southern Democrats were at odds with each other. Then, in 1854, a group of Free Soilers, northern Democrats, and antislavery Whigs met in Michigan. They formed a new political party, called the *Republican Party.*

The main goal of the Republicans was to keep slavery out of the western territories. Abolitionists supported the party, but they were still a minority. Most Republicans did not expect to end slavery in the South.

The Republican Party grew quickly. In 1856, Republicans chose John Charles Frémont as their candidate for President. Frémont was a frontiersman who had fought for California's independence. (See page 323.) He had never held office, but he opposed the spread of slavery.

Democrats chose James Buchanan of Pennsylvania. He had served as a senator and as Secretary of State. Many Democrats saw Buchanan as a "northern man with southern principles." They hoped that he would attract voters in both the North and South.

Buchanan won the election. However, the voting results alarmed the South. The new Republican Party made a strong showing. Frémont did very well in the North. He nearly won the election without the support of any southern state. Southerners felt that their influence was fading fast.

Abraham Lincoln

Two years later, in 1858, the Illinois Senate race caught the attention of the whole nation. Senator Stephen Douglas was being challenged by Abraham Lincoln, a Republican. The race was important because most Americans thought that Douglas, a Democrat, would run for President in 1860.

Lincoln was not a national figure like Douglas. But he was well known in Illinois as a successful lawyer and politician. Lincoln had spent eight years in the Illinois legislature and then served as a congressman from Illinois.

People liked Lincoln because he was "just folks." He enjoyed swapping stories. Lincoln was known as a good, straightforward speaker. Even so, a listener once complained that he could not understand a speech of Lincoln's. "There are always some fleas a dog can't reach" was Lincoln's reply. Many people admired Lincoln for his honesty. Some called him Honest Abe.

Abraham Lincoln was born in the backwoods of Kentucky. Like many frontier people, his parents moved often in search of better land. They lived in Indiana and later in Illinois. Lincoln spent only a year in school as a child. But he taught himself to read and spent many hours reading by firelight.

After Lincoln left home, he set up a store in Illinois. He learned law on his own and began a career in politics. In 1858, Lincoln decided to run for the Senate because he strongly opposed the Kansas–Nebraska Act.

Lincoln–Douglas Debates

During the Senate campaign, Lincoln challenged Douglas to a series of debates. People thought that Lincoln was foolish because Douglas was one of the greatest speakers in the nation. Douglas had a deep, confident voice. The senator stood only a little over five feet tall, but he seemed taller. People called him the Little Giant.

Abraham Lincoln, on the other hand, was more than six feet tall. He spoke in a high voice with a backwoods accent. He said "git" for "get" and "thar" for "there." He also had a slow, awkward walk.

A house divided. In the *Lincoln–Douglas Debates,* Douglas tried to make Lincoln seem like an abolitionist. Lincoln, in turn, tried to force Douglas to make proslavery statements. In one speech, Lincoln described the nation as "a house divided" over slavery. He warned that the "government cannot endure permanently half slave and half free." Douglas disagreed with Lincoln. He assured the audience that the North and South, free and slave, could get along.

Lincoln's "house divided" speech became famous. It was often quoted by people who wanted to show that Lincoln planned to abolish slavery in the South.

Views on slavery. In fact, Lincoln and Douglas were not so far apart on the slavery question. Douglas saw slavery as a political issue. He wanted to settle the question by popular sovereignty. Lincoln was dead set against slavery in the territories. He believed that blacks were entitled to "life, liberty, and the pursuit of happiness." Slavery was a "moral, social, and political wrong," he said. Even so, Lincoln was not an abolitionist. He had no wish "to interfere with the institution of slavery in the states where it exists."

Douglas won reelection to the Senate. But Abraham Lincoln became known to the nation during the campaign. His careful thinking and down-to-earth manner made him very popular. Two years later, Lincoln and Douglas would again be rivals for office. In the meantime, more bloodshed pushed the North and South further apart.

Abraham Lincoln debated Stephen Douglas, seated at left, seven times during the Senate race of 1858. Lincoln knew that many voters expected Douglas to be elected President in 1860. At one debate, Lincoln pointed to his own "poor, lean, lank face" and said, "Nobody has ever expected me to be President."

Raid on Harpers Ferry

John Brown came into the national spotlight again in 1859. This time, Brown brought his campaign against

Sitting on his own coffin, John Brown rides to the gallows. Horace Pippin, a black artist, painted the scene based on his mother's description. She witnessed Brown's execution on December 2, 1859.

slavery to Virginia. In October, Brown and a group of followers raided the federal *arsenal,* or gun warehouse, at Harpers Ferry, Virginia. Brown planned to give weapons from the arsenal to slaves in the area. This, he hoped, would start a slave revolt.

Brown quickly gained control of the arsenal, but no slave uprising followed. Troops led by Colonel Robert E. Lee surrounded Brown and killed ten of his men. After a day of fighting, Brown was taken prisoner.

Most people in both the North and South thought that Brown's plan to start a slave revolt was insane. But Brown was calm during his trial. He sat quietly as the court found him guilty of murder and treason and sentenced him to death.

Because of the dignity he showed during his trial, Brown became a hero to many Northerners. Church bells rang on the morning of his execution. New Englanders sang a popular tune that began, "John Brown's body lies a mold'ring in the grave, but his soul is marching on." Henry David Thoreau, the well-known writer, praised Brown as "a superior man."

To Southerners, the northern response to John Brown's death was outrageous. To criticize slavery was bad enough. But to sing the praise of a man who hoped to lead a slave revolt was intolerable! Many Southerners became convinced that the North wanted to destroy slavery and the South with it. The nation was poised for a violent clash.

SECTION REVIEW

1. **Define:** arsenal.
2. What was the main goal of the new Republican Party?
3. Why did the Illinois Senate race in 1858 capture the attention of the American people?
4. (a) How did Northerners respond to John Brown's execution? (b) Why did this response anger Southerners?
5. **What Do You Think?** Why do you think the Republican Party did as well as it did in the election of 1856?

5 The Union Is Broken

Read to Learn

★ Why did the election of 1860 make the South feel powerless?

★ Why did seven southern states secede from the Union?

★ What was the immediate cause of the Civil War?

Americans looked toward the election of 1860 with both hope and fear. The nation seemed to be tumbling toward disunion. People hoped that the election would somehow bind the nation together. But no candidate was able to unite Northerners and Southerners. Instead, the nation split along sectional lines.

Election of 1860

The Democratic Party divided in two in 1860. Southern Democrats wanted the party to support slavery in the territories. But northern Democrats refused to do so. One exclaimed, "Gentlemen of the South, you mistake us—you mistake us! We will not do it!"

In the end, northern Democrats picked Stephen Douglas as their candidate for President. Southern Democrats met separately and chose John Breckinridge of Kentucky.

Some Democrats saw the split in their party as a danger signal for the country. They formed the Constitutional Union Party and chose John Bell of Tennessee to run for President. Bell simply wanted to keep the Union together.

Meanwhile, Republicans nominated Abraham Lincoln. The choice of Lincoln panicked Southerners. Many thought that Lincoln really was an abolitionist. After all, Lincoln had said that the country could not survive "half slave and half free." Did that not mean he wanted to end slavery? Lincoln's name was not even on the ballot in ten southern states.

Senator Douglas was sure that Lincoln would win the election. But Douglas believed that Democrats "must try to save the Union." He pleaded with southern voters to stay with the Union, no matter who was elected.

The South Secedes

Lincoln carried the North and won the election. Southern votes did not affect the election at all. Northerners outnumbered Southerners and simply outvoted them. To Southerners, Lincoln's election meant that the South had lost its voice in national government. Southerners believed that the President, the Senate, and the House were now all set against their interests, especially slavery.*

Even before the election, the governor of South Carolina had written to other southern governors. If Lincoln was elected, he wrote, it was the duty of Southerners to quit the Union. With Lincoln in the White House, many Southerners felt that seceding from the Union was their only choice.

Crittenden's last try. Senator John Crittenden of Kentucky made a last effort to save the Union. In December 1860, he introduced a bill to extend the Missouri Compromise line to the Pacific. The bill did not please anyone. By this time, Southerners wanted to be free of the North. "I look upon the whole New England race as meddlers," wrote one Southerner.

South Carolina was the first state to secede. On December 20, 1860, delegates to a special convention in

---

*The North had a slight majority in the House and Senate. But Northerners did not have enough power to force the South to end slavery.

Maps can give you different kinds of information. (See Skill Lesson 1 on page 21.) Some maps give you special kinds of information. An election map shows the results of a presidential election.

Election maps are useful because they show which states each candidate won. Most election maps also have circle graphs to show what percent of the popular vote and electoral vote went to each candidate.

Use the election map and circle graphs below to learn more about the election of 1860.

1. **Decide what is shown on the map and graphs.** (a) What is the subject of the map? (b) What do the four colors stand for? (c) What does the graph at left show? (d) What does the graph at right show?

2. **Practice using information from the map and graphs.** Read the information on the map and graphs. (a) Which party won nearly all the northern states? (b) Which party won all the southern states? (c) What percent of the popular vote did the Republican Party receive? (d) What percent of the electoral vote did the Republican Party receive? (e) Who was the candidate of the Constitutional Union Party? (f) Did he win any states?

3. **Draw conclusions about the election.** Based on the map and graphs, draw conclusions about the election of 1860. (a) How does the map show that sectionalism was important in the election? (b) What did the election seem to show about the political voice of southern voters?

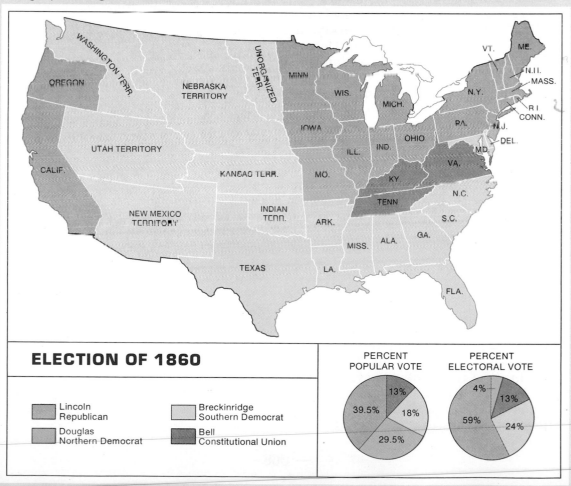

ELECTION OF 1860

Lincoln Republican

Douglas Northern Democrat

Breckinridge Southern Democrat

Bell Constitutional Union

PERCENT POPULAR VOTE

39.5%   13%   18%   29.5%

PERCENT ELECTORAL VOTE

4%   13%   59%   24%

Mary Boykin Chesnut

Mary Boykin Chesnut was born into a wealthy, slave-owning family in South Carolina. In February 1861, she began to keep a diary about the coming war. Early in 1861, Chesnut wrote that she dreaded "this break with so great a power as the United States, but I was ready and willing." She added, "Come what would, I wanted them to fight and stop talking."

Charleston voted for secession. "The state of South Carolina has resumed her position among the nations of the world," the delegates said. By February 1, 1861, six more southern states had seceded. (See the map on page 394.)

The Confederacy. In February 1861, the states that had seceded held a convention in Montgomery, Alabama. They formed a new nation and named it the *Confederate States of America.* Jefferson Davis of Mississippi was named president of the Confederacy.

Many Southerners were joyful and confident about the future. They believed that states had the right to secede. They did not think that the North would fight to keep the South in the Union. And if war did break out, Southerners were sure that they would win.

Opening Shots

When Abraham Lincoln took office as President on March 4, 1861, he warned that "no state . . . can lawfully get out of the Union." At the same time, Lincoln promised that there would not be war with the South unless southern states started it. "We are not enemies, but friends. We must not be enemies," Lincoln told the South.

Seizing federal forts. However, the Confederacy had already begun seizing federal forts and arsenals. It felt that the Union, or federal, forts were a threat because the United States was now a foreign power.

President Lincoln faced a hard choice. Should he allow the Confederates to take over federal property? If he did, it would mean that states would have the right to leave the Union. Or should he use force to protect federal property? If Lincoln sent in troops, he risked losing the support of the four slave states that had not seceded. Such an action might also lose support in the North.

In March 1861, the Confederacy forced Lincoln to make a decision. By then, Confederate troops had taken over nearly all forts, post offices, and other federal buildings in the Confederacy. The Union held only three forts off the Florida coast and Fort Sumter in South Carolina.

Fort Sumter is bombarded. President Lincoln received word from the commander of *Fort Sumter* that food supplies were running low. The President sent a message to the governor of South Carolina. It said that only food would be shipped to Fort Sumter. Lincoln promised not to send any troops or weapons.

Confederate troops, in the foreground, fire cannons across Charleston Harbor at Fort Sumter. At top left is the flag of South Carolina. In the background, smoke rises from Fort Sumter, which flies the United States flag. When Northerners learned of the attack on Sumter, they rallied behind Lincoln and the Union. A New York paper declared, "Fort Sumter is lost, but the country is saved."

To the Confederacy, Fort Sumter was important because it guarded Charleston Harbor. The fort could not be left in Union hands. The Confederates asked for its surrender on April 12, 1861. Major Robert Anderson, the Union commander, would not give in. Confederate guns then opened fire. Major Anderson quickly ran out of ammunition. On April 13, he surrendered Fort Sumter.

Fort Sumter was nearly destroyed by Confederate cannons. But, amazingly, no one was injured. During the battle, people in Charleston flocked to the harbor to watch. To many, it was like a huge fireworks display. No one knew then that the fireworks marked the beginning of a war that would last four terrible years.

SECTION REVIEW

1. Why did Lincoln's victory in 1860 alarm Southerners?
2. (a) When was the Confederacy formed? (b) Why did the Confederacy take over federal property?
3. Why did Lincoln hesitate to use force against the Confederacy?
4. **What Do You Think?** What do you think might have happened if Lincoln had sent troops to retake Fort Sumter?

Chapter 17 Review

★ Summary ★

The issue of slavery in the territories led to conflict between the North and South. The Missouri Compromise settled the issue for a time. After the Mexican War, the North and South again argued about slavery, but compromised in 1850.

In 1854, the Kansas–Nebraska Act canceled the Missouri Compromise and angered Northerners. The Dred Scott decision further inflamed the North. John Brown's raid brought the nation to the edge of war.

After Lincoln's election in 1860, seven states seceded and formed the Confederacy. With the bombardment of Fort Sumter in April 1861, civil war had come.

★ Reviewing the Facts *all* ★

Key Terms. Match each term in Column 1 with the correct definition in Column 2.

Column 1	Column 2
1. sectionalism	a. escaped slave
2. popular sovereignty	b. loyalty to state or section instead of country
3. fugitive	c. control by the voters of a territory
4. civil war	d. warehouse for guns
5. arsenal	e. fight between people of the same country

Key People, Events, and Ideas. Identify each of the following.

1. Missouri Compromise
2. Free Soil Party
3. Stephen Douglas
4. Compromise of 1850
5. Fugitive Slave Law of 1850
6. *Uncle Tom's Cabin*
7. Kansas–Nebraska Act
8. Bleeding Kansas
9. Dred Scott decision
10. Republican Party
11. Abraham Lincoln
12. Lincoln–Douglas Debates
13. John Brown
14. Confederate States of America
15. Fort Sumter

★ Chapter Checkup *all* ★

1. What did the Missouri Compromise say about slavery?

2. (a) Why did the Mexican War raise the question of slavery in the territories? (b) What were two moderate plans to settle the question of slavery in the Mexican Cession?

3. List the four main parts of the Compromise of 1850.

4. (a) Why did Southerners want a strong fugitive slave law? (b) Why did Northerners object to the law?

5. (a) What was the Kansas–Nebraska Act? (b) How did it lead to violence?

6. (a) Why was the Republican Party formed? (b) What did it have in common with the Free Soil Party?

7. (a) What did the Dred Scott decision say about slavery in the territories? (b) Why did it dismay Northerners?

8. (a) Why did two Democrats run for President in 1860? (b) Why did seven states secede after Lincoln's victory?

★ Thinking About History ★

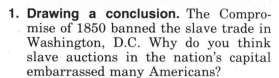

1. **Drawing a conclusion.** The Compromise of 1850 banned the slave trade in Washington, D.C. Why do you think slave auctions in the nation's capital embarrassed many Americans?
2. **Learning about citizenship.** Many Southerners claimed that seceding from the Union was an idea justified by the Declaration of Independence. Study the Declaration of Independence, which begins on page 793. What parts of it could be used to justify secession?
3. **Analyzing information.** Review the discussion of tariffs on pages 279 and 299.

(a) How do you think debates over tariffs added to differences between the North and South? (b) How might disagreement over tariffs have made the South more anxious about keeping power in the Senate?

4. **Relating past to present.** (a) Why do you think the Dred Scott decision had such a great impact on the nation? (b) Can you think of a recent Supreme Court decision that has had a major impact on America?

★ Using Your Skills ★

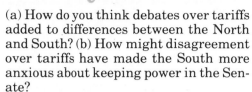

1. **Map reading.** Study the map on page 380. (a) After the Missouri Compromise, what part of the Louisiana Purchase was slave? Free? (b) After the Compromise of 1850, what territories were opened to slavery by popular sovereignty? (c) After the Kansas–Nebraska Act of 1854, what territories were open to slavery by popular sovereignty?
2. **Using a painting as a primary source.** Study the painting on page 385. (a) What is the mood of the crowd pictured? (b) How can you tell the mood? (c) What is the black woman in the right corner

doing? (d) Why might a black artist choose to paint this incident?

3. **Reading for the main idea.** Each paragraph or group of paragraphs in this book has a main idea. The main idea is the generalization that underlies all the facts and examples. Read the subsection called "Fugitive Slave Law" on pages 377–378. (a) What is the main idea of each paragraph? (b) Give two facts that support the main idea of each paragraph. (c) What is the main idea of the subsection?

★ More to Do ★

1. **Exploring local history.** Use the map on page 380 and a blank map to show whether your state was affected by the Missouri Compromise, the Compromise of 1850, or the Kansas-Nebraska Act.
2. **Writing a dialogue.** Write a dialogue between supporters of Lincoln and Douglas during the debates of 1858.
3. **Drawing a political cartoon.** Draw a political cartoon that shows John

Brown's execution from either the northern or southern point of view.

4. **Creating headlines.** Write two sets of headlines—one for a northern paper, one for a southern paper—about these incidents: the Dred Scott decision, the secession of South Carolina, and the bombarding of Fort Sumter.

CHAPTER

18

The Civil War (1860–1865)

Chapter Outline

1 The Call to Arms
2 On the Battle Lines
3 Free at Last
4 Life in Wartime
5 The Tide Turns

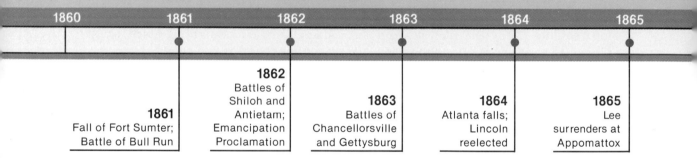

| 1860 | 1861 | 1862 | 1863 | 1864 | 1865 |

1861
Fall of Fort Sumter;
Battle of Bull Run

1862
Battles of
Shiloh and
Antietam;
Emancipation
Proclamation

1863
Battles of
Chancellorsville
and Gettysburg

1864
Atlanta falls;
Lincoln
reelected

1865
Lee
surrenders at
Appomattox

About This Chapter

The Civil War stirred up strong passions. For Southerners, it was a war for independence, like the American Revolution. Northerners fought for an equally important goal— to save the Union.

Strong feelings about the justice of their cause were reflected in the songs of each side. Soldiers often sang to keep their spirits up before going into battle. A popular song in the South was "The Bonnie Blue Flag." One verse began:

Then here's to our Confed'racy,
Strong are we and brave,
Like patriots of old we'll fight
Our heritage to save.

Union soldiers had their own favorite songs. "The Battle-Cry of Freedom" included the rousing chorus:

The Union forever, hurrah! boys, hurrah!
Down with the traitor, up with the star,
While we rally round the flag, boys, rally
    once again,
Shouting the battle-cry of freedom.

With flags held high, soldiers on both sides marched off to war in 1860. They soon learned that war meant more than patriotic songs. More than half a million soldiers would die before the Civil War ended.

Study the time line above. What major southern city was captured in 1864?

More Americans died in the Civil War than in any other war. Many of those killed were young men, often teenagers.

1 The Call to Arms

Read to Learn

★ How did the Civil War tear apart families and states?

★ What strengths and weaknesses did each side have?

★ How were Lincoln and Davis different as leaders?

★ What do these words mean: martial law?

The bombardment of Fort Sumter in April 1861 began the Civil War. As the war started, many American families had divided loyalties. Fathers joined the Union army while their sons volunteered to fight for the Confederacy. Mary Todd Lincoln, President Lincoln's wife, had three brothers who fought for the Confederacy. While General Robert E. Lee led Confederate soldiers, his favorite cousin fought for the Union.

Choosing Sides

Feelings ran high in 1861. People in the Confederacy believed that they had a right to leave the Union. In fact, they called the conflict between the North and South the War for Southern Independence. President Lincoln and other Northerners believed just as strongly that the South had rebelled. Lincoln made it clear that he would do everything in his power to save the Union. Stephen Douglas summed up the way many people in the North felt: "There can be no neutrals in this war; only patriots—or traitors."

Both sides expected to win and to win quickly. Volunteers eagerly signed up, and recruits quickly filled both armies. During the spring of 1861, more than 100,000 men joined the Confederate army. More than 75,000 volunteers answered Lincoln's first call for troops.

Eight slave states were still part of the Union when Lincoln called for volunteers in April 1861. They were called the border states. Virginia,* North

*In the western part of Virginia, many people supported the Union. When Virginia seceded, the Westerners formed their own government. They joined the United States as West Virginia in 1863.

Carolina, Arkansas, and Tennessee soon seceded and joined the Confederacy. (See the map below.)

Opinion was divided in the four border states that remained in the Union. Delaware stayed with the Union from the first. Kentucky and Missouri wavered between the North and South for several months. In the end, both remained in the Union.

Maryland was also divided. In April 1861, pro-Confederate mobs attacked Union troops in Baltimore. President Lincoln responded by declaring martial law in Maryland. ***Martial law*** means rule by the army instead of the elected government. Many people who sided with the South were arrested. Later, the Maryland legislature voted to remain in the Union.

MAP SKILL In early 1861, eight slave states remained in the Union. Which border states eventually seceded?

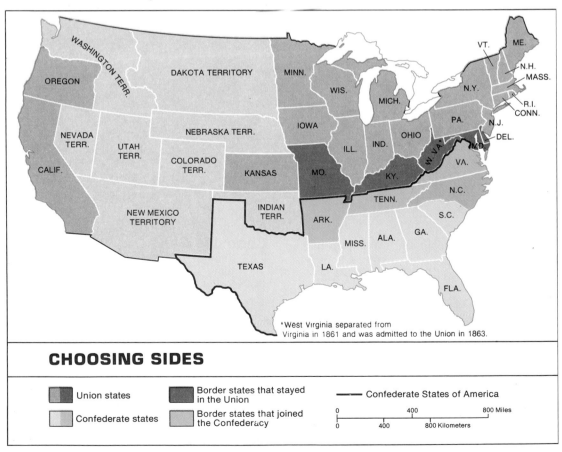

*West Virginia separated from Virginia in 1861 and was admitted to the Union in 1863.

CHOOSING SIDES

- ▇ Union states
- ▢ Confederate states
- ▇ Border states that stayed in the Union
- ▨ Border states that joined the Confederacy
- ▬ Confederate States of America

0   400   800 Miles
0   400   800 Kilometers

Resources

Both sides had advantages and disadvantages as the war began. The South had the strong advantage of fighting a defensive war. If the North did not attack, the Confederacy would remain a separate country. Thus, it was up to the North to attack and defeat the Confederacy. "All we ask," Jefferson Davis said, "is to be left alone."

The South. Fighting a defensive war gave the South an important edge. Southerners were well aware that the North was threatening to invade their homeland. To defend their homes and families, southern soldiers were ready to fight to the bitter end.

Also, many southern men had skills that made them good soldiers. Hunting was an important part of southern life. Thus, young boys learned to ride horses and use guns. Wealthy young men often went to military schools. Southern graduates of West Point* were the most brilliant officers in the army before the war.

The South, however, had serious weaknesses. It had few factories to make guns and supplies. Before the war, Southerners bought such products from the North or from Europe. The South also had few railroads to move troops and supplies. The railroads they had often did not join one another. Tracks simply ran between two points and then stopped.

Also, the South had a small population. Only 9 million people lived there, compared to 22 million in the North. This meant that there were far fewer people in the South to fight and support a war effort than in the North. Besides, over one third of the people in the South were slaves.

The North. The North had almost four times as many free citizens as the South. Thus, it had a large source of volunteers. It also had many people to grow food and make supplies for its armies.

Industry was the North's greatest resource. Northern factories made 90 percent of the nation's manufactured goods. They supplied Union forces with guns, cannons, and ammunition. The North also had a broad railroad network. Almost 75 percent of the nation's rail lines were in the North. (See Skill Lesson 18 on page 396.)

The North had another important advantage over the South. It had a strong navy, while the South had almost no warships. The Union could use its navy to blockade the South and cut off its trade with Europe.

Still, the North had a hard military task. To bring the South back into the Union, northern soldiers had to conquer a huge area. Instead of defending their homes, they were invading unfamiliar land. Also, they needed training in basic fighting skills. Soldiers had to learn how to use weapons and how to survive far from home.

Leadership

When the Civil War began, many people thought that the Confederate president, Jefferson Davis, was a better leader than Abraham Lincoln.

Jefferson Davis. Jefferson Davis was a West Point graduate. He had been an officer in the Mexican War. In addition, Davis served as Secretary of War under President Franklin Pierce. President Davis was respected for his honesty and courage.

However, Davis believed that he alone should direct military plans. He did not like to turn over details to others. When Davis made a decision, he "could not understand any other man coming to a different conclusion," as his wife put it. As a result, Davis wasted time worrying about small matters and arguing with advisers.

Abraham Lincoln. At first, some Northerners had doubts about the ability of Lincoln. He had little experience

---

*West Point, in New York State, is the site of the United States Military Academy. There, future army officers receive training.

Skill Lesson 18　Using a Table

A table is used to present information in a way you can understand quickly and easily. Tables often present numbers or statistics. The numbers are set up in columns and rows.

The table below compares the resources of the North and South in 1861. For both the North and South, the table shows the actual amount of the resource and the percent of the national total. Studying the table can help you understand why the North won the Civil War.

Use the following steps to read and interpret the table.

1. **Identify the information in the table.** Note that the resources in the table are measured in different ways. For example, population is measured in thousands of people. (a) What is the title of the table? (b) How is farmland measured in the table? (c) How is railroad track measured?

2. **Read the information in the table.** Note that the table has five columns. The first column shows what each resource is—farmland, factories, and so on. The second and third columns give the actual amount and percent of each resource that the North had. The fourth and fifth columns give the same information for the South. (a) What was the actual number of factories in the South? (b) What percent of the national total of factories did the South have? (c) What percent of the nation's railroad track did the North have?

3. **Compare the information in the table.** Use the table to compare the resources of the North and South. (a) Did the North or the South have more workers in industry? (b) How many acres of farmland did each side have? (c) In which resource did the South come closest to equaling the North?

4. **Interpret the information based on your reading.** Interpret the information in the table based on your reading of the chapter. (a) Which side had the advantage in each of the resources shown? (b) How might these advantages have helped that side during the war? (c) Which resource do you think was most important during the war? Explain your answer.

Resources of the North and South, 1861

Resources	North		South	
	Number	Percent of Total	Number	Percent of Total
Farmland	105,835 acres	65%	56,832 acres	35%
Railroad Track	21,847 miles	71%	8,947 miles	29%
Value of Manufactured Goods	$1,794,417,000	92%	$155,552,000	8%
Factories	119,500	85%	20,600	15%
Workers in Industry	1,198,000	92%	111,000	8%
Population	22,340,000	63%	9,103,000 (3,954,000 Slaves)	37%

Source: *Historical Statistics of the United States*

in national politics or war. This lack of experience led him to make mistakes. But he learned from his errors. In time, Lincoln proved himself to be a patient but strong leader and a fine war planner.

Day by day, Lincoln gained the respect of those around him. Many liked his sense of humor. Lincoln could joke even when others criticized him. Secretary of War Edwin Stanton once referred to President Lincoln as a fool. When he heard, Lincoln commented: "Did Stanton say I was a fool? Then I must be one, for Stanton is generally right and he always says what he means." His ability to accept criticism helped Lincoln work well with others.

Military leaders. At the outbreak of war, army officers in the South had to make a choice. They could stay with the Union army and fight against their home states. Or, they could join the Confederate forces.

Robert E. Lee faced such a decision when his home state, Virginia, seceded. President Lincoln asked Lee to command the Union army. Lee refused.

"With all my devotion to the Union," Lee explained, "I have not been able to make up my mind to raise my hand against my relatives, my children, my home." Lee later became commander of the Confederate army.

Many of the army's best officers sided with the Confederacy. As a result, President Lincoln had trouble finding generals who could match the South's military leaders. He replaced several commanders before the Union began to win battles.

SECTION REVIEW

1. **Locate:** Virginia, Missouri, Kentucky, Maryland, Delaware.
2. **Define:** martial law.
3. (a) Which four states seceded after April 1861? (b) Which four slave states remained in the Union?
4. Why did many Southerners have skills that made them good soldiers?
5. **What Do You Think?** Why do you think the North's strengths would be more important in a long war than in a short war?

2 On the Battle Lines

Read to Learn
★ What goals did each side have?
★ What battles took place early on?
★ How did the North achieve two of its three goals?

In both the North and South, tens of thousands of young men marched off to war to the cheers of family and friends. In the North, volunteers were urged "On to Richmond," the capital of the Confederacy. The cry in the South was "Forward to Washington!"

Goals of the North and South

The Civil War had three major areas of combat: the East, the West, and at sea. Union war goals involved all three areas.

First, the Union planned to blockade southern ports. This would shut off the South's trade with Europe. Second, in the West, the Union would try to take control of the Mississippi River. This would stop trade on the river and separate Arkansas, Texas, and Louisiana from the rest of the Confederacy. Third, in the East, Union generals hoped to seize Richmond and capture the Confederate government.

The South's goals were simple. It would fight a defensive war. Southerners hoped to wear out Union troops so that they would give up.

The South counted on European money and supplies to help end the war quickly. Cotton was important to the textile mills of England and other countries. Confederates were sure that Europeans wanted to ensure a supply of cotton for their mills.

Fighting in the East

The North hoped for a quick victory, too. In July 1861, Union troops set out for Richmond, which was only about 100 miles (160 km) from Washington, D.C. They clashed with Confederate troops soon after they left. The battle took place near a small stream called Bull Run.

Battle of Bull Run. People from Washington gathered on a hilltop near Bull Run to watch the battle. There was a holiday feeling in the air. Many people carried picnic baskets. They expected to see Union troops crush the Confederates.

But Confederate troops did not turn and run. Under the firm leadership of General Thomas Jackson, they held their ground. Jackson earned the nickname Stonewall because he stood as firmly as a stone wall. In the end, it was Union troops that fled the battlefield. A congressman who watched the retreat said of the panicked Union soldiers:

> Off they went . . . down the highway . . . across fields, towards the woods, anywhere, everywhere, to escape. The further they ran the more frightened they grew. . . . To enable them better to run, they threw away their blankets, knapsacks, canteens, and finally muskets, cartridge-boxes, and everything else.

Instead of pursuing, Confederate soldiers stopped to gather the equipment thrown down by Union troops. The *Battle of Bull Run* showed both sides that they needed to train their soldiers.

An army in training. After Bull Run, President Lincoln made General George McClellan commander of Union armies. McClellan was a superb organizer. He set out to whip the army into shape.

McClellan spent six months training his men. Since the Confederates were fighting a defensive war, little happened in the meantime. Newspapers in the North reported "all quiet along the Potomac" so often that the phrase became a joke. President Lincoln lost patience. He snapped, "If McClellan is not using the army, I should like to borrow it."

In March 1862, McClellan finally moved on Richmond. He and most of his troops went by steamboat from Washington down the Potomac River. (See the map on page 399.) The rest of the army stayed in Washington.

McClellan's troops landed on the peninsula between the York and James rivers. There, McClellan paused. General Lee learned that the Union army was near Richmond. He sent Stonewall Jackson to make a series of attacks near Washington. Because of these raids, troops could not be sent from Washington to help McClellan. When a Confederate cavalry slashed at McClellan's army, the Union general was forced to withdraw. Once again, there was a lull in the war in the East.

War at Sea

The Union navy was far superior to that of the Confederacy. Early in the war, Union ships blockaded southern ports. At first, the Confederates used small ships to slip through the Union blockade. But traffic in southern ports eventually dropped by over 90 percent. The South desperately needed a way to break the Union blockade.

When the war began, the Union had abandoned the *Merrimac,* a warship, in Virginia. Confederates covered the *Merrimac* with iron plates four inches thick. Then they renamed it the *Virginia.* One afternoon in March 1862, the ironclad *Merrimac* defeated three Union ships. Their cannonballs bounced harmlessly off the *Merrimac*'s metal plates.

The Union had developed its own ironclad ship, the *Monitor*. The day after the Confederate victories, the *Monitor* attacked the *Merrimac* in Hampton Roads in Virginia. The Confederate ship boasted more firepower, but the *Monitor* moved more quickly. Neither ship seriously damaged the other, and both withdrew.

Ironclad ships changed naval warfare. Both sides rushed to build more of them. However, the South never mounted a serious attack against the Union navy. The Union blockade held throughout the war.

Battle of Antietam

In September 1862, Robert E. Lee took the offensive. Lee believed that a victory in the North would weaken the Union's will to fight. He began to march north into Maryland. But luck was on the Union's side. A Confederate messenger lost General Lee's battle plans. When a Union soldier found the plans, he turned them over to General McClellan.

With Lee's whole battle plan before him, McClellan moved quickly. He attacked Lee's main force at Antietam (an TEET uhm) on September 17, 1862. In a daylong battle, over 24,000 Union and Confederate soldiers were killed or wounded.

Neither side won a victory at the **Battle of Antietam.** But when the sun rose the day after the battle, Union troops saw that Lee's soldiers had slipped away during the night. McClellan did not pursue Lee. Still, since Lee had withdrawn his forces, the North claimed victory.

Campaign in the West

Until Antietam, the Union army had won few battles in the East. But Union forces had more success in

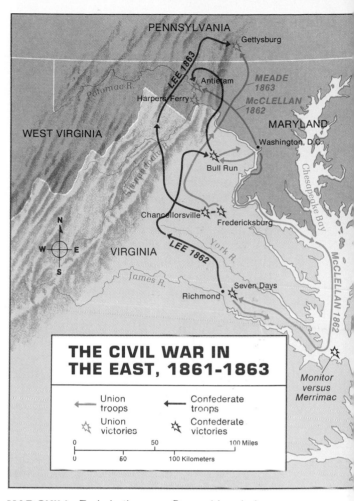

THE CIVIL WAR IN THE EAST, 1861-1863

← Union troops
← Confederate troops
☆ Union victories
☆ Confederate victories

0   50   100 Miles
0   60   100 Kilometers

MAP SKILL Early in the war, General Lee led the Confederate army from one victory to another in the East. Union forces at last claimed victory at the Battle of Antietam. What city in Virginia were Union forces trying to capture?

the West. There, the goal was to take control of the Mississippi River. General Ulysses S. Grant decided to attack Fort Henry and Fort Donelson in Tennessee. These two forts protected Confederate ships on tributaries of the Mississippi. Union troops captured the forts in February 1862. Grant then led his troops south toward the place where the Tennessee and Mississippi rivers join.

Shiloh. In early April, Confederate forces surprised Grant near the town of Shiloh, Tennessee. Union troops won the bloody battle that followed.

The **Battle of Shiloh** was the first of the huge battles that became typical of the Civil War. One Confederate soldier wrote: "It was an awful thing to hear the sing of grape shot, the hum of cannon balls, and the roaring of the bomb shell. . . . O keep me out of such another fight!" More Americans died in one day at Shiloh than in the American Revolution, the War of 1812, and the Mexican War combined. Suddenly, it was clear that the war would not be quick or painless for either side.

Winning the Mississippi. After the capture of Shiloh, the Union gained control of river traffic on the northern Mississippi. In the meantime, the Union navy moved to take the southern part of the river. In April 1862, Union gunboats attacked and captured the port city of New Orleans. Other gunboats took Memphis, Tennessee. The Union was now in control of both ends of the great river. The South could no longer move supplies on the Mississippi.

But Union ships could not safely travel the river either. Confederates still controlled Vicksburg, Mississippi. Vicksburg sat on a high cliff overlooking the Mississippi. Cannons there could shell boats traveling between New Orleans and Memphis. (See the map on page 411.)

General Grant's forces tried again and again to take Vicksburg early in 1863. At last, Grant devised a brilliant trick. Skirting Vicksburg, he marched his troops east to Jackson, Mississippi. After taking that city by surprise, Grant turned around and attacked Vicksburg from the rear. The people of Vicksburg held out for six weeks. Finally, on July 4, 1863, the city fell.

The Union had achieved two of its goals. First, its naval blockade had shut off southern trade. Second, by tak-

As Union troops won victories in the South, they took over houses and plantations. The fine mansion shown here became a signaling station for the Union. From the platform on the roof, Union soldiers used flags to send messages to nearby troops.

ing control of the Mississippi River, the Union had split the Confederacy in two.

■ SECTION REVIEW ■

1. **Locate:** Washington, D.C., Richmond, Mississippi River, Tennessee River, Potomac River, Antietam, Shiloh, New Orleans, Vicksburg.

2. Why was the South fighting a defensive war?
3. What did both sides realize about their troops after the Battle of Bull Run?
4. What battles gave the Union control of the Mississippi River?
5. **What Do You Think?** How do you think news about bloody battles such as Shiloh affected men who were thinking of enlisting in the army?

3 Free at Last

Read to Learn

★ Why did Lincoln free slaves in the Confederacy?
★ How did blacks help the Union?
★ What does this word mean: emancipate?

As the war dragged on, Northerners had to think carefully about why they were fighting. Their main purpose was to restore the Union. But abolitionists argued that the war must also rid the nation of slavery. By 1862, Lincoln and many other Northerners were willing to take this idea seriously.

After all, people asked, was slavery not at the root of the conflict between the North and South? Had thousands of northern boys died to bring a slaveholding South back into the Union? Questions such as these helped change the mood of Northerners.

Emancipation Proclamation

The Civil War did not begin as a war against slavery. The Union included four slave states. President Lincoln did not want to take any action that might force these states to secede. Restoring the Union was his main goal. Lincoln had made this clear earlier: "If I could save the Union without freeing *any* slave, I would do it; and if I could save it by freeing *all* the slaves, I would

do it; and if I could do it by freeing some and leaving others alone, I would also do that."

Broader goals. In mid-1862, it seemed to Lincoln that he could save the Union only by broadening the goals of the war. He decided to free slaves living in the Confederacy. In the four loyal slave states, slaves would not be freed. Nor would slaves be freed in Confederate lands that had already been captured by the Union, such as New Orleans. Lincoln hoped that this action would weaken the South without angering slave owners in the Union.

Lincoln did not want people to think that freeing the slaves was a desperate action. So he waited for a Union victory before announcing his decision. The victory at Antietam gave him the chance he wanted.

The Proclamation. On September 22, 1862, Lincoln issued the *Emancipation Proclamation.* To *emancipate* means to set free. The Proclamation stated that all slaves in states still in rebellion would be free as of January 1, 1863. Since those states were not under Union control, no slaves were set free on that day. But as Union troops won control of areas, slaves were freed.

Still, the Emancipation Proclamation changed the purpose of the war. The abolition of slavery became a Union goal. The Proclamation won the

Blacks came from all over New England to join the 54th Regiment. Here, the regiment storms Fort Wagner on an island off South Carolina. Sergeant William Carney of the 54th won the Congressional Medal of Honor for his bravery during the attack.

Union the sympathy of people in Europe, especially workers. It became less likely that Britain or any other country would back the South. And the Proclamation prompted a wave of support for the Union from free blacks.

Blacks for the Union

When the war began, free blacks in the North had tried to join the Union army. But federal laws kept them from becoming soldiers. So blacks signed up for noncombat tasks.

Meanwhile, Union troops pushed into the South. As they did, thousands of slaves flocked to their side. Some generals wanted to allow the former slaves to become soldiers and fight for the Union.

In the summer of 1862, Congress passed a law allowing blacks to join the army. Both free blacks and escaped slaves rallied to the Union cause. They formed all-black army units in many states. The new units had white commanders. And for more than a year, black soldiers received only half the pay of white soldiers. Even so, over 200,000 blacks fought with the Union during the war. About 68,000 were killed.

Massachusetts was one of the first states to organize all-black regiments. One of them, the 54th, attacked Fort Wagner near Charleston in the summer of 1863. The commander, most of the officers, and almost half the men were killed. The courage and devotion of the 54th Regiment won respect for black soldiers.

Both free blacks and escaped slaves made good soldiers. They went to war to restore the country, as other Union soldiers did. But they also fought to free their people. In a letter to President Lincoln, Secretary of War Stanton said that blacks "have proved themselves among the bravest of the brave, performing deeds of daring and shedding their blood with a heroism unsurpassed by soldiers of any other race."

Blacks in the Confederacy

Slaves found it hard to hide their joy as news of the Emancipation Proclamation filtered into the South. One woman overheard the news just before she was to serve dinner. She asked to be excused so that she could get water from a nearby spring. Once she had reached the quiet of the spring, she shouted: "Glory, glory hallelujah to Jesus! I'm free! I'm free."

Even after the Proclamation, however, slaves had to work on plantations and in factories while whites were fighting. Because factory owners depended on them, slaves gained a few benefits. Some refused to work unless they were paid. Others stopped working if they were threatened with whippings or other punishments. Such "strikes" were often successful.

On many farms and plantations, slaves slowed down their work in the fields. This was one way to undermine the war effort. They knew that when Union troops captured an area, they would be freed.

◼ SECTION REVIEW ◼

1. **Define:** emancipate.
2. (a) Why did Lincoln decide to emancipate the slaves? (b) Which slaves were freed by the Emancipation Proclamation?
3. (a) How did free blacks help the Union at first? (b) How did they help after 1862?
4. **What Do You Think?** How do you think the Emancipation Proclamation helped the Union war effort?

4 Life in Wartime

Read to Learn
* ★ What was life like for soldiers during the Civil War?
* ★ How did each side pay for the war?
* ★ How did women contribute to the war effort?
* ★ What do these words mean: bounty, draft, habeas corpus, inflation, profiteer, tax-in-kind, civilian?

The Civil War touched the life of every American. It was not fought in some far-off land. The war took place on American soil, mainly in the South. Both armies were made up of Americans. And civilians, especially Southerners, suffered the many hardships of war.

Johnny Rebs and Billy Yanks

Early in the war, soldiers on each side came up with nicknames for their enemy. Union troops wore blue uniforms. They were called blues or Billy Yanks, short for Yankees. Gray was the color of the Confederacy. Southern soldiers were called grays or Johnny Rebs, short for rebels.

Becoming soldiers. Troops on both sides were very young men. Most were under 21 years old. But war quickly changed raw recruits into tough veterans. Soldiers put in long hours drilling and marching. They slept on the ground in rain and snow. They scavenged for food, water, and firewood. Nothing hardened the "fresh fish," as new recruits were called, like combat. Boys of 18 learned to stand firm while cannon blasts shook the earth and bullets whizzed past their ears.

Friend or foe. At times, Rebs and Yanks could be friendly enemies. Before one battle, a Confederate hailed a Union soldier with "Say Yank, got something to trade?" After swapping Union coffee for southern tobacco, the soldiers shook hands. "Good luck, Yank!" said the Southerner. "I hope you won't get hurt in any of our fights."

Deadly battles. Soldiers returned to the horrors of combat quickly. New technology made Civil War battles deadly. Cone-shaped bullets replaced

Soldiers often sent photographs to their families to show how they looked in uniform. This photo shows a young Confederate private, Edwin Francis Jenson. Troops for both North and South were often no more than boys.

round musket balls. These bullets made rifles twice as accurate. New cannons could hurl exploding shells several miles. In any battle, one quarter or more of the soldiers were casualties. A casualty is a soldier who is killed or wounded.

In one battle, Union troops knew that they were facing almost certain death. Each soldier wrote his name on a slip of paper and pinned it to his uniform. The soldiers wanted their bodies to be identified when the battle was over.

Other dangers. Soldiers who were sick, wounded, or captured faced different horrors. Medical care in the field was crude. Surgeons cut off the arms and legs of wounded men. Many minor wounds became infected, and there were no medicines to fight infections. As a result, over half the wounded died. And disease killed more men than bullets did.

Prisoners of war on both sides suffered from disease and starvation. At Andersonville, a prison camp in Georgia, more than one Union prisoner out of three died. One prisoner wrote: "There is no such thing as delicacy here. . . . In the middle of last night I was awakened by being kicked by a dying man. He was soon dead. I got up and moved the body off a few feet, and again went to sleep to dream of the hideous sights."

Support Dwindles

Some Northerners had opposed the war all along. Throughout the North, people were against fighting to keep the South in the Union. They were called *Copperheads.* Many people supported the war, but did not like the way Lincoln was managing it. And in the states where slavery existed, many people supported the South.

The draft law. Public support for the war dwindled as the fighting dragged on. To fill its armies, the North took new measures. From the start, the Union gave $100 *bounties,* or payments, to men who joined the army. Later, the bounty was raised to over $300. Even so, the Union was so desperate for soldiers that Congress passed a draft law in 1863. The *draft* required all males between 18 and 45 years old to serve in the military.

The draft law allowed a man to avoid going into the army by paying $300 or by hiring someone to serve in his place. This angered many common people. They called the war "a rich man's war and a poor man's fight." Many draftees deserted, or ran away.

Riots in the North. The draft law went into effect just two months after Lincoln signed the Emancipation Proclamation. As a result, some Northerners felt that they were being forced to fight to end slavery. Riots broke out in several cities. The worst riot, in New York City, lasted for four days in July 1863. White workers turned their

As a boy, Mathew Brady was fascinated with photography, then a new process. While he was a teenager, Brady worked in a photographer's studio in New York. Later, he opened his own studios in New York and Washington. Brady became famous for his fine portraits of business and political leaders.

When the Civil War broke out, Brady was allowed to travel with Union troops. He and his assistants took over 3,500 pictures. Brady used his camera to make a lasting record of the Civil War.

★ Why do you think Brady wanted to photograph the Civil War?

This photograph shows President Lincoln and General McClellan on the battlefield at Antietam.

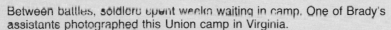
Between battles, soldiers spent weeks waiting in camp. One of Brady's assistants photographed this Union camp in Virginia.

anger against free blacks. They brutally murdered almost 100 blacks.

President Lincoln tried to stop anti-draft riots and other "disloyal practices." Several times, he denied *habeas corpus* (HAY bee uhs KOR puhs), the right to have a trial before being jailed. To those who protested his action, Lincoln quoted the Constitution. It gave him the right, he said, to deny people their rights "when in the cases of rebellion or invasion, the public safety may require it."

States' Rights in the South

In the South, few people openly opposed the war. However, the Confederate constitution caused problems for Jefferson Davis. It guaranteed states' rights. Throughout the war, Davis had trouble getting the states to pay taxes and cooperate on military matters. Governor Joseph Brown of Georgia, for example, insisted that only Georgia officers command Georgia troops. At one point, Georgia threatened to secede from the Confederacy.

The South also had serious problems enlisting soldiers. The South had only 6 million white citizens. As early as 1862, the South passed a draft law. The law said that men who owned more than 20 slaves did not have to serve in the army. This caused much resentment among southern farmers and other plain folk.

Toward the end of the war, the South was unable to replace soldiers killed and wounded in battle. There simply were not enough white men to carry on the war. Robert E. Lee urged the Confederacy to let slaves serve as soldiers. Finally, the Confederacy agreed to Lee's plan. However, the war ended before any slaves put on gray uniforms.

The Wartime Economy

Like all wars, the Civil War was very costly. Both sides had to find ways to pay for it. The war affected the economies of the North and South in different ways.

The North. President Lincoln did not want to raise taxes. He was afraid doing so might lessen support for the war. But the Union needed cash. So in 1861, Congress passed the nation's first income tax law. It required workers to pay a small part of their wages to the federal government. The North also raised millions of dollars more by selling bonds. People who bought bonds in effect lent money to the Union.

The North printed over $400 million in paper money during the war. People called these dollars "greenbacks" because of their color. With so much paper money in use, there was inflation. *Inflation* is a rise in prices as a result of an increase in the amount of money in circulation. With inflation, the dollar loses value. Since each dollar is worth less, merchants ask more for their goods. Between 1860 and 1862, prices for goods doubled in the North.

In some ways, the Civil War helped the northern economy. Because many farmers went off to fight, machines were used to plant and harvest. At least 165,000 reapers were sold during the war, compared to a few thousand a year before it. Farm production actually increased.

Wartime demand for clothing, shoes, guns, ammunition, and other supplies brought a boom to these industries. Some people made fortunes by profiteering. *Profiteers* overcharged the government for supplies desperately needed for the war.

The South. Like the North, the South had to raise money for the war. Its congress passed an income tax and a tax-in-kind. The *tax-in-kind* required farmers to turn over one tenth of their crops to the government. The South also printed paper money. It printed so much, in fact, that wild inflation resulted. By 1865, one Confederate dollar was worth only two cents in gold.

The southern economy suffered greatly because of the war. This was especially true of the cotton trade. Early in the war, Jefferson Davis stopped cotton shipments to Britain. He was sure that the British would side with the South in order to get cotton. But Britain was buying cotton from Egypt and India instead. By stopping the export of cotton, Davis only cut the South's income.

Effect of blockade. The Union blockade had a grim effect on the South. It created severe shortages for soldiers and for *civilians,* or people not in the army. For example, the South bought weapons in Europe, but the blockade kept most from being delivered. When Confederate troops won a battle, they had to scour the field to gather up guns and bullets. Southerners hurried to build weapons factories, but the shortages grew.

Even if supplies were available, they often did not reach the battlefronts. Union armies destroyed many railroad lines, and the South had few parts to make repairs. Breakdowns and delays became common on rail lines. Soldiers waited weeks for food and clothing.

Women in the War Effort

Women played vital roles on both sides during the war. As men left for the battlefields, women took over jobs in industry, in teaching, and on farms. They held bake sales, donated jewelry, and organized fairs to raise money for medical supplies. Some women disguised themselves as soldiers and fought in battle. Others served as spies.

Many women hoped to help their army by working as nurses. Before the Civil War, women nurses were not allowed to take care of men. When war broke out, many women volunteered to care for wounded soldiers. Dorothea Dix was one of the most famous nurses in the North. Dix became superinten-

AMERICANS WHO DARED

Mary Ann Bickerdyke

During the Civil War, Mary Ann Bickerdyke helped care for wounded Union soldiers. Her skill and energy won her the trust of the troops and the nickname "Mother Bickerdyke." Ulysses S. Grant and other generals had great respect for her. Once, she had an officer dismissed for neglecting his duty. The officer asked Major Sherman to help him get his post back. When Sherman learned that the officer had angered Mother Bickerdyke, he replied: "Oh, if it was Mother Bickerdyke, I can do nothing for you. She outranks me."

dent of nurses for the Union army. She set such strict rules for her nurses that some called her Dragon Dix. But Dix toiled day and night alongside the women she enlisted.

Clara Barton earned fame as a Civil War nurse and founder of the American Red Cross. She trained nurses, collected medical supplies, and served on the war front. Barton kept records on hundreds of soldiers. She was able to trace many who were missing. Sojourner

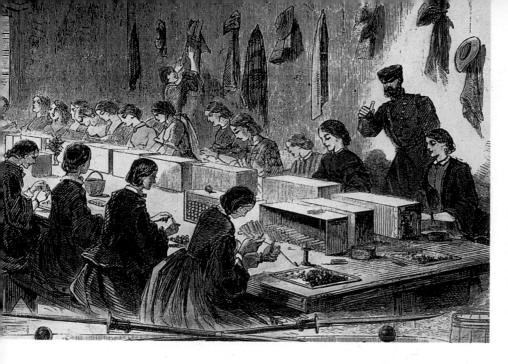

During the Civil War, there was work for every American. Here, women make bullets at an arsenal in Massachusetts. A Union soldier looks on.

Truth, the antislavery speaker, worked in Union hospitals and in camps for freed slaves. She also recruited black soldiers for the Union army.

In the South, Sally Louisa Tompkins opened a successful private hospital in Richmond, Virginia. When private hospitals were ordered to close, Tompkins was made a captain in the cavalry. This way, her hospital could stay open. Of the 1,333 patients treated in Tompkins' hospital, only 73 died—an excellent record for the time.

SECTION REVIEW

1. **Define:** bounty, draft, habeas corpus, inflation, profiteer, tax-in-kind, civilian.
2. (a) Why did support for the war decrease in the North? (b) What did each side do to get more soldiers?
3. Why did the Confederate constitution create problems for Jefferson Davis?
4. How did each side raise money for the war?
5. **What Do You Think?** Why do you think women found more opportunities to work outside the home during the war?

5 The Tide Turns

Read to Learn

★ How did the tide of war turn?
★ How did the Union try to break the South's will to fight?
★ Why did Lee surrender?

The Union claimed victory at Antietam in September 1862. But after Antietam, Robert E. Lee led the Confederate army to smashing victories over Union troops. These were gloomy days in the North. Few people realized that the tide of the war was about to turn.

Later Battles

The war went well for the South in late 1862. In December, General Ambrose Burnside led Union troops against Robert E. Lee outside Fredericksburg, Virginia. Burnside ordered his men to charge six times across an

Robert E. Lee and Ulysses S. Grant differed as much in style as they did in politics. Lee was a perfect southern gentleman, well-dressed and dignified. Grant often wore wrinkled uniforms and appeared unshaven in public. Yet, Grant proved to be the only general who could win against the brilliant tactics of Lee.

open field. The Confederates had dug trenches along the field. From the trenches, they mowed down the Union soldiers. Southerners could hardly believe the bravery of the doomed Union troops. One wrote, "We forgot they were fighting us, and cheer after cheer at their fearlessness went up all along our lines."

Battle of Chancellorsville. Lee and Jackson outfought their Union foes

once again at Chancellorsville, Virginia, in May 1863. But the victory brought an unexpected loss. A Confederate sentry fired at a soldier riding toward him at dusk. Instead of a Union soldier, the rider turned out to be Stonewall Jackson. Jackson died of blood poisoning several days later. Lee said sadly, "I have lost my right arm."

Yet with a victory behind him, Lee could not sit still. He led his troops through the Shenandoah Valley of Virginia into Pennsylvania. Lee hoped to take the Union forces by surprise and then turn south to capture Washington, D.C.

Battle of Gettysburg. By accident, some of Lee's men stumbled on Union troops at the small town of Gettysburg, Pennsylvania. Soon, both sides sent in reinforcements. From July 1 to July 3, over 150,000 soldiers fought outside the town. Union troops under General George Meade gained the high ground on the first day. The Confederates had to charge strong Union positions.

Failing to dislodge his enemy, Lee decided on a last-ditch gamble. He sent 15,000 troops, under General George Pickett, to attack the strongest Union position. *Pickett's Charge,* as the attack was called, fell back under deadly Union fire. Lee withdrew his shattered army into Virginia. The *Battle of Gettysburg* left over 40,000 dead and wounded. For the first time, Union troops had beaten Lee. The greater manpower and resources of the North at last were making a difference. The tide was turning in favor of the Union.

The Gettysburg Address

When the soldiers who died at Gettysburg were buried, their graves stretched as far as the eye could see. On November 20, 1863, Northerners held a ceremony to dedicate this cemetery.

President Lincoln was invited to the ceremony, but he was not the main speaker. At the time, his popularity was at its lowest point. Lincoln waited while another speaker spoke for two hours. Then, the President stood up and spoke for just three minutes.

In his *Gettysburg Address,* Lincoln said that the Civil War tested whether a nation that believed "all men are created equal" could survive. He urged Americans to have the courage to overcome every challenge to their freedom.

Lincoln sat for this photograph just days before he made his speech at Gettysburg. The years of war seemed to increase Lincoln's patience, wisdom, and strength.

Looking at the thousands of graves, Lincoln told the audience:

> We here highly resolve that these dead shall not have died in vain—that this nation, under God, shall have a new birth of freedom—and that government of the people, by the people, for the people, shall not perish from the earth.

Few in the audience listened to Lincoln. Newspapers gave his speech little attention. Lincoln was dismayed by the lack of response. "It is a flat failure," he said of the speech. "The people are disappointed." But later generations have honored Lincoln for his brief speech at Gettysburg.

Union Victories

After Gettysburg, Lincoln made Ulysses S. Grant the commander of Union forces. Grant had a plan for ending the war. He wanted to weaken the

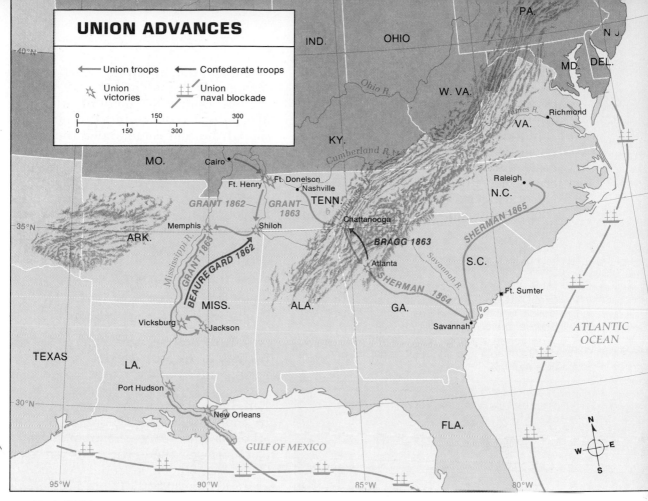

MAP SKILL Union forces in the West met success early in the war. From the West, Union troops under General Sherman pushed into Georgia and the Carolinas. What coastal city did Sherman capture after marching southeast from Atlanta?

South's ability to keep fighting. With 100,000 men, he drove south toward Richmond in May 1864.

At the same time, Grant sent General Philip Sheridan and his cavalry into the rich farmland of the Shenandoah Valley. He told Sheridan: "Leave nothing to invite the enemy to return. Destroy whatever cannot be consumed. Let the valley be left so that crows flying over it will have to carry their rations along with them." Sheridan obeyed. In the summer and fall, he destroyed farms and livestock throughout the valley.

March to the sea. Grant also sent General William Tecumseh Sherman on a march from Atlanta to the Atlantic Ocean. Like Sheridan, Sherman had orders to destroy everything useful to the South. After burning the city of Atlanta in September 1864, Union soldiers began their "march to the sea."

Sherman's men ripped up railroad tracks, built bonfires from the ties, and then melted and twisted the rails. They chopped telegraph wires into small pieces. They slaughtered livestock and burned everything that grew in the soil. They burned barns, homes, and factories. Looking over the destruction, Sherman said: "We have devoured the land. . . . To realize what war is one should follow in our tracks."

Grant, Sherman, and Sheridan had created a new kind of fighting, called total war. Because of it, civilians in the South suffered as much as soldiers.

Lincoln is reelected. But before these Union victories, Lincoln faced a reelection campaign. Many Northerners were unhappy about the war. Northern victory was uncertain. In August, Lincoln commented that his defeat in the upcoming election was "extremely probable."

The Democrats nominated George McClellan to run against Lincoln. Even though he had commanded the Union army, McClellan called for an immediate end to the war.

When Sherman took Atlanta in September, the picture got brighter for Lincoln. In October, Sheridan scored smashing victories in the Shenandoah Valley. These victories turned public opinion around. The popular vote was close, but Lincoln won reelection.

Surrender at Appomattox

Grant had begun his drive to take Richmond in May 1864. Through the spring and summer, Grant fought a series of costly battles in Virginia against Lee. Both sides suffered terrible losses in the Wilderness, Cold Harbor, and other battles. (See the map at left.) Northerners read with horror that Grant lost 60,000 dead and wounded in a single month. Still, Grant pressed his attack. He knew that the Union could replace both men and supplies.

Fall of Richmond. On the other hand, Lee's army was shrinking. To prevent further losses, Lee dug in at the town of Petersburg, Virginia. Petersburg guarded the entrance to Richmond. Here, Grant kept the Southerners under siege for nine months. With a supply of fresh troops, Grant at last attacked Petersburg in March 1865. The town fell on April 3, and Grant captured Richmond the following day. But Jefferson Davis and his cabinet had slipped out of the city earlier.

President Lincoln insisted on visiting Richmond soon after its capture. Lincoln risked his life by walking through the smoldering streets of the city. The President told Southerners that they would be welcomed back into the Union.

Lee surrenders. Robert E. Lee and his army were trapped near a small

MAP SKILL The last battles of the war pitted Grant against Lee in Virginia. In spite of heavy losses, Grant attacked Lee again and again. Short of men and supplies, Lee at last surrendered at Appomattox Courthouse. Where did Grant hold Lee under siege for more than nine months?

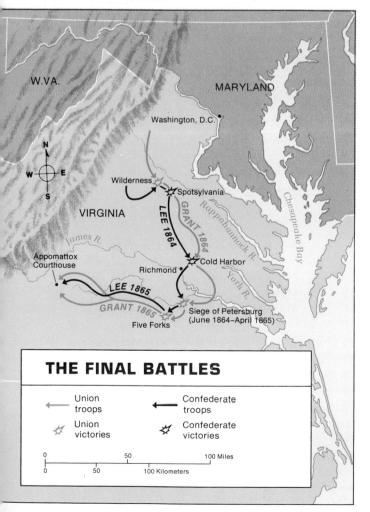

THE FINAL BATTLES

← Union troops

← Confederate troops

✩ Union victories

✩ Confederate victories

0   50   100 Miles

0   50   100 Kilometers

Here, Confederate soldiers weep as they furl their flag for the last time. Defeat was bitter for the southern veterans. Many returned home to find farms and towns devastated by the war.

town in Virginia called **Appomattox Courthouse.** Lee knew that his men would be slaughtered if he ordered them to continue the fight. On April 9, 1865, Lee surrendered.

At Appomattox, Grant's terms of surrender were generous. Confederate troops had to turn over their rifles, but officers could keep their pistols. Troops who had horses could keep them. Grant knew that Southerners would need the animals for spring plowing. As the Confederates surrendered, Union soldiers began to cheer. Grant ordered them to be silent. "The war is over," he said. "The rebels are our countrymen again."

The Civil War made clear that no part of the United States could secede in peace. But putting the nation back together would be a difficult task. Abraham Lincoln's question at Gettysburg still had not been answered. Could a nation dedicated to the idea that "all men are created equal" survive?

===SECTION REVIEW===

1. **Locate:** Fredericksburg, Gettysburg, Atlanta, Appomattox Courthouse.
2. Explain how the actions of each of these generals helped cripple the South's ability to fight: (a) Sheridan; (b) Sherman; (c) Grant.
3. What events helped Lincoln win reelection in November 1864?
4. How were Grant's terms of surrender to Lee generous?
5. **What Do You Think?** What do you think were the most important reasons for the defeat of the South?

Chapter 18 Review

 ★ **Summary** ★

As the Civil War began, the North had three goals: to blockade southern ports, control the Mississippi River, and capture Richmond. The South planned to fight a defensive war.

At first, the war went badly for the Union. But in September 1862, the Union claimed victory at Antietam. President Lincoln used this victory to announce the Emancipation Proclamation. As of January 1, 1863, the war to restore the Union was also a war to end slavery.

In 1864, Grant and Lee fought a series of bloody battles in Virginia. Both sides suffered terrible losses. But only the North could replace its men and supplies. Richmond fell in April 1865, and Lee's army surrendered soon afterward.

 ★ **Reviewing the Facts** ★

Key Terms. Match each term in Column 1 with the correct definition in Column 2.

Column 1	Column 2
1. martial law	a. set free
2. emancipate	b. rule by the army, not by the elected government
3. habeas corpus	c. right to a trial before being jailed
4. profiteer	d. law requiring men to serve in the military
5. draft	e. someone who overcharges the government for war supplies

Key People, Events, and Ideas. Identify each of the following.

1. Robert E. Lee
2. Battle of Bull Run
3. Ulysses S. Grant
4. Stonewall Jackson
5. George McClellan
6. Battle of Antietam
7. Emancipation Proclamation
8. Copperhead
9. Dorothea Dix
10. Sally Louisa Tompkins
11. Pickett's Charge
12. Battle of Gettysburg
13. Gettysburg Address
14. William Tecumseh Sherman
15. Appomattox Courthouse

 ★ **Chapter Checkup** ★

1. (a) What advantages did the South have when the war began? (b) What advantages did the North have?

2. Compare Abraham Lincoln and Jefferson Davis as leaders.

3. (a) What were the three war goals of the North? (b) How did the South hope to win the war?

4. (a) Why did the South expect to get help from Great Britain? (b) Give two reasons why Britain did not help the South.

5. (a) What battles did Grant win in the West? (b) Which war goals had the North achieved by July 1863?

6. Why did Lincoln handle the slave question with caution at first?

7. (a) How did the war affect the economy of the North? (b) How did it affect the economy of the South?

8. Why did Grant order Sherman's "march to the sea"?

★ Thinking About History ★

1. **Understanding the economy.** How did northern industry help the Union win the Civil War?

2. **Expressing an opinion.** Grant's policy of total war was wrong because it hurt civilians in the South as much as it hurt Confederate soldiers. Do you agree or disagree with this statement? Explain your answer.

3. **Drawing a conclusion.** Why did some people in the North and South criticize the Civil War as "a rich man's war and a poor man's fight"?

4. **Learning about citizenship.** Why do you think free blacks were eager to fight for the Union?

5. **Relating past to present.** (a) What advances in technology made Civil War battles deadly? (b) How would a modern war be even more deadly?

★ Using Your Skills ★

1. **Map reading.** Study the map on page 399. (a) What is the distance from Washington to Richmond? (b) Why do you think an army marching from Washington to Richmond would have to travel farther than the distance you measured?

2. **Identifying immediate and long-range causes.** Review the description of immediate and long-range causes on page 331. (a) What was the immediate cause of Lee's surrender at Appomattox Courthouse? (b) What were two long-range causes of Lee's surrender?

3. **Using a painting as a primary source.** Study the painting on page 400. (a) To which army do the soldiers belong? (b) What do you think the soldiers are doing with the pile of furniture at the right? (c) What do you think happened to the owners of the mansion? (d) What does this painting show about life in the South during the Civil War?

4. **Making a generalization.** Reread the section called "Blacks for the Union" on page 402. (a) List three facts about black efforts to help the Union. (b) Using the facts you listed, make a generalization about how blacks helped the Union.

★ More to Do ★

1. **Writing a diary.** Imagine that you are a southern plantation owner whose land and house are occupied by Union troops. Write several diary entries telling what happened when they arrived.

2. **Making a poster.** Make a poster encouraging men to enlist in the army of the Union or the Confederacy.

3. **Drawing a cartoon.** Draw a political cartoon criticizing the draft law of either the North or the South for excusing the rich.

4. **Researching a report.** Research a report on one of the women nurses mentioned in the chapter. (a) Did she work with an organization or on her own? (b) What did she do after the Civil War?

5. **Exploring local history.** Research to find out about any Civil War memorials in your state. Create a brochure that describes the memorials and encourages tourists to visit them.

19

The Road to Reunion (1864–1877)

Chapter Outline

1 Restoring the Union
2 The President and Congress Clash
3 Changes in the South
4 A New Era in National Politics

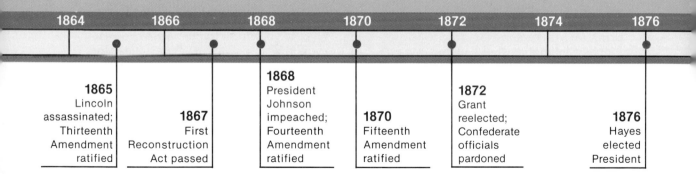

| 1864 | 1866 | 1868 | 1870 | 1872 | 1874 | 1876 |

1865
Lincoln assassinated; Thirteenth Amendment ratified

1867
First Reconstruction Act passed

1868
President Johnson impeached; Fourteenth Amendment ratified

1870
Fifteenth Amendment ratified

1872
Grant reelected; Confederate officials pardoned

1876
Hayes elected President

About This Chapter

In 1865, the Civil War was over. Much of the South lay in ruins, and a whole way of life had ended. Amid the smoldering rubble of Atlanta and Richmond, black and white Southerners wondered about the future. How would the South rebuild its ruined cities, farms, and economy? What role would freed slaves play in southern society?

President Lincoln realized that one question was even more important: How would the North and South be reunited? In his second inaugural address, delivered in March 1865, Lincoln urged Northerners to forgive the South. "With malice toward none, with charity for all," the President said, "let us strive on to bind up the nation's wounds."

Many Northerners disagreed with Lincoln's plea for charity. They felt that the South had to be punished for causing the bloody Civil War. Some wanted Confederate leaders to stand trial for treason. Others wanted to break up southern plantations and give the land to freed slaves.

The years after the Civil War were difficult ones for the South. A bitter political struggle slowed recovery. But in the end, the South rebuilt its cities, economy, and society. The new shape of southern society lasted for almost a century.

Study the time line above. How many amendments to the Constitution were ratified in the period shown?

In 1865, Richmond and other southern cities lay in ruins. Southerners faced two challenges: rebuilding the South and rejoining the Union.

1 Restoring the Union

Read to Learn

★ What was the condition of the South after the war?
★ How did Andrew Johnson become President?
★ Why did President Johnson and Congress clash?
★ What does this word mean: freedman?

Many soldiers who went to fight in the Civil War never returned home. The North lost many more soldiers than the South. However, the farms and cities of the North were hardly touched by the war. In the North, returning soldiers found industry booming and farms prospering. In the South, on the other hand, returning sol-diers found devastated cities and farm-lands.

Conditions in the South

The problems facing the South were staggering. Two thirds of its railroad track had been destroyed. In some areas, 90 percent of all bridges were down. Farms and plantations were a shambles. Thousands of soldiers were disabled. Many southern cities had been destroyed. Much of Charleston, Richmond, Atlanta, and Savannah had been leveled.

After the war, a traveler in Tennes-see described the Tennessee River val-ley. It consisted, he wrote, "for the most part of plantations in a state of semi-ruin, and plantations of which the ruin is for the present total and complete.... The trail of war is visible throughout the valley in burnt up [cotton] gin-houses, ruined bridges, mills, and factories."

The southern financial system was also wrecked. After the war, Confederate money was worthless. Many southern banks closed, and depositors lost all their money. People who had lent money to the Confederacy were never repaid.

Southern society had been changed forever by the war. No longer were there white owners and black slaves. When the war ended, nearly 4 million *freedmen,* or freed slaves, were living in the South. Most had no land, no jobs, and no education. Under slavery, they had been forbidden to own property and to learn to read and write. What would become of them? What rights would freedmen have?

Early Plans for Reconstruction

President Lincoln was worried about rebuilding the South long before the war ended. Lincoln wanted to make it as easy as possible for the South to rejoin the Union. The quicker the nation was reunited, he thought, the faster the South could rebuild.

Lincoln's plan. Lincoln outlined a plan for Reconstruction as early as July 1863. *Reconstruction* refers to the period of the South's rebuilding, as well as the government program to rebuild it. Lincoln's plan called for 10 percent of the voters in each southern state to swear an oath of loyalty to the United States. After this was done, the state could form a new government. The new government then had to abolish slavery. When these three steps were taken, voters could elect members of Congress. The state could once again take part in the national government.

Many Republicans in Congress opposed Lincoln's *Ten Percent Plan.*

They thought that it was too generous toward the South. These Republicans passed their own plan for Reconstruction, called the *Wade–Davis Bill,* in July 1864. It required a majority of white men in the South to swear loyalty to the United States. It denied the right to vote or hold office to any Southerner who had volunteered to fight for the Confederacy.

Freedmen's Bureau. Lincoln refused to sign the Wade–Davis Bill because he felt that it was too harsh. Congress and the President did agree on one step, however. A month before Lee surrendered, Congress set up the Freedmen's Bureau with the support of Lincoln.

The *Freedmen's Bureau* provided food and clothing to former slaves. It sent agents into the South to set up schools. (See page 420.) The bureau provided medical care for over a million people. It also tried to find jobs for freedmen. Because so many Southerners were needy after the war, the bureau helped poor whites as well. One former Confederate was amazed to see "a Government which was lately fighting us with fire, and sword, and shell, now generously feeding our poor and distressed."

Tragedy at Ford's Theater

President Lincoln hoped to convince Congress to support his Reconstruction plan. However, he never got the chance. On April 14, 1865, Lincoln went to Ford's Theater in Washington to see a play. Robert E. Lee had surrendered several days earlier.

As Lincoln watched the play, John Wilkes Booth crept into the President's box. Booth was a Southerner and a former actor. He blamed Lincoln for the South's crushing defeat in the war. Booth shot the President in the head. Lincoln died the next morning without ever regaining consciousness.

The nation had been joyous about the war ending. Now, millions were

Here, Lincoln's funeral procession winds through the streets of New York City. All along the route from Washington, D.C., to Illinois, huge crowds stood silently to pay their respects to the slain President.

plunged into mourning for Lincoln. When Northerners learned that Booth was from the South, they were furious. Many demanded that the South be punished for Lincoln's death. Booth fled the capital. He was caught and killed in a barn outside Washington.

Johnson Is President

Vice President Andrew Johnson became President when Lincoln died. Johnson had been a Democratic senator from Tennessee. When Tennessee seceded in 1861, Johnson remained loyal to the Union. He was put on the Republican ticket in 1864 to win support from Democrats in the North. Like Andrew Jackson, Johnson had started out life poor. He was a fierce enemy of what he called southern aristocrats.

At first, Republicans in Congress thought that Johnson would support a strict Reconstruction plan, as they did. They were encouraged when Johnson said that "traitors must be made impoverished." But the Republicans soon learned that they were wrong. Johnson's plan for Reconstruction was almost as mild as Lincoln's plan.

Johnson's plan called for a majority of the voters in each southern state to pledge loyalty to the United States. It also required each state to ratify the *Thirteenth Amendment.* The Thirteenth Amendment had been passed by Congress in 1864. It officially banned slavery throughout the country. Most southern states ratified the amendment, and it became part of the Constitution in December 1865.

Conflict Over Readmission

The South had done as President Johnson asked. Therefore, in the winter of 1865, Johnson approved the new state governments that Southerners had set up. Voters in the South then chose senators and representatives. Many of those elected had been army officers and high officials under the

By 1869, some 600,000 freed slaves attended schools set up by the Freedmen's Bureau. For teachers, the schools relied mainly on volunteers from the North. About half the teachers were women. Many had been abolitionists before the war.

Teachers found both old and young students eager to learn. Grandmothers and granddaughters sat side by side in the classroom. Some schools stayed open nights so that sharecroppers could attend class after a day's work in the fields. One bureau agent in South Carolina wrote that the freed slaves "will starve themselves, and go without clothes, in order to send their children to school."

The Freedmen's Bureau laid the foundation for the South's public school system. It set up over 4,300 grade schools. The bureau created four universities for black students: Howard, Morehouse, Fisk, and Hampton Institute. The schools gave black students a chance to get a higher education. Many graduates became teachers. By the 1870s, blacks were teaching in grade schools throughout the South.

★ What do you think that the former slaves in the picture at left are learning to do?

Confederacy. Alexander Stephens, the former vice president of the Confederacy, was elected senator from Georgia.

Republicans in Congress were furious. They did not like the way President Johnson had handled the South. Under his plan, the very men who had led the South out of the Union were being elected to the House and Senate. Also, nowhere in the South had blacks been allowed to vote.

Congress met in December 1865. Republicans refused to allow the newly elected representatives from the South to take their seats. Instead, Republicans set up the Joint Committee on Reconstruction to draw up their own plan for dealing with the South. The

stage was set for a showdown between Congress and the President.

SECTION REVIEW

1. **Define:** freedman.
2. How did the Freedmen's Bureau help former slaves and poor whites?
3. How was President Lincoln's Reconstruction plan different from the one proposed by Republicans in the Wade–Davis Bill?
4. (a) Why did some Republicans think Andrew Johnson supported a strict Reconstruction plan? (b) Were they right?
5. **What Do You Think?** Why do you think many Republicans were angry when Southerners elected former Confederate officials to Congress?

2 The President and Congress Clash

Read to Learn

★ What rights did southern states deny freedmen?

★ What did Radical Republicans hope to do in the South?

★ Why was Andrew Johnson impeached?

★ What do these words mean: black code?

In the spring of 1866, the Joint Committee on Reconstruction heard reports on the southern governments formed under Johnson's plan. The committee was outraged at what it learned. Throughout the South, the committee found "evidence of an intense hostility to the federal Union, and an equally intense love of the late Confederacy."

Black Codes

Southern states had ratified the Thirteenth Amendment, which ended slavery. However, white Southerners did not accept the idea of giving blacks real freedom. Throughout the South, legislatures passed *black codes.* These laws severely limited the rights of freedmen.

Black codes varied from state to state. However, all said that blacks could not vote, own guns, or serve on juries. Many allowed blacks to work only as servants or farm laborers. Some codes forced freedmen to sign contracts agreeing to work for a year at a time. Blacks who did not have contracts could be arrested and sentenced to work on a plantation or chain gang. This policy of forced labor was not much different from slavery.

Black codes were not as harsh as slave codes before the Civil War. For example, they gave blacks the right to own some kinds of property and to marry legally. But the codes were clearly meant to keep freedmen from gaining a political voice or achieving any economic power.

Republicans React

Angry about the black codes and the election of Confederate officers, more Republicans turned against President Johnson. Those who took the lead in opposing him were called *Radical Republicans.**

Radical Republicans. Congressman Thaddeus Stevens of Pennsylvania led the Radical Republicans in the House. Charles Sumner of Massachusetts was the Radical Republican voice in the Senate. Other Radical leaders included Senator Benjamin Wade and Congressman Henry Davis. They had sponsored the Wade–Davis Bill.

Radical Republicans had two main goals. They believed that rich southern planters had caused the Civil War. They wanted to make sure that these "aristocrats" did not regain power in the South. "Strip a proud nobility of their bloated estates," Thaddeus Stevens thundered, "send them forth to labor . . . and you will thus humble the proud traitors." Stevens, Sumner, and other Radicals also insisted on protecting the rights of freedmen.

Moderate Republicans. Radical Republicans never controlled Congress during Reconstruction. But they worked together with moderate Republicans. Moderates and Radicals had an important goal in common: keeping power. With Southerners barred from Congress, Republicans controlled both the House and Senate. Most Southerners were Democrats. If southern congressmen were seated, Republicans might lose their majorities.

Moderates agreed with Radical Republicans about some other goals as well. They wanted to keep a high tariff passed during the war. The tariff had

---

*A radical is a person who wants to make drastic changes in society.

You can find information in the library in many sources—books, encyclopedias, and magazines. In Skill Lesson 16 (page 364), you learned how to use the card catalog to find books in the library. Most libraries have several encyclopedias. Encyclopedias present useful overviews of many subjects. **Periodicals,** or magazines, offer up-to-date articles on many subjects.

1. **Find information in an encyclopedia.** Encyclopedias contain articles on many subjects. The articles are arranged in alphabetical order. Imagine that you are writing a report on President Andrew Johnson. Under JOHNSON, ANDREW, you would find the main article. It tells about his life and term in office. At the end of the article are **cross-references** that tell you which other articles in the encyclopedia have information about Andrew Johnson.

   Using an encyclopedia in your classroom or school library, look up Andrew Johnson. Are there any cross-references at the end of the article? What other articles do the cross-references refer you to?

2. **Practice using the Readers' Guide.** The *Readers' Guide to Periodical Literature* is an index, or list, of articles that appear in popular magazines.

The *Readers' Guide* lists every article at least twice, once by the author's last name and again by the subject. Look at the sample from the *Readers' Guide* below at right. (a) What subject entry is shown? (b) How many articles are listed under the subject entry? (c) Which article appears under an author entry?

3. **Look for information in the Readers' Guide.** Each subject entry in the *Readers' Guide* tells you the title of the article and the author's name. It gives the title of the magazine in which the article appears, usually in an abbreviated form. The entry lists the volume number of the magazine, the page numbers of the article, and the date of the magazine. The date is also abbreviated. At the front of the *Readers' Guide* are lists that tell you what the abbreviations stand for.

   Look at the sample from the *Readers' Guide*. (a) In which volume of *Aging* did the article "Candlelight and vintage years" appear? (b) On what page did the article appear? (c) In what magazine did the article "Fairness doctrine for the press" appear? (d) What was the date of the magazine in which the article "First Amendment" appeared? (e) What date do you think is indicated by the abbreviation Ag '77?

Volume: page number

Abbreviated magazine title (Saturday Review)

Abbreviated date (November 25, 1977)

FREEDMAN, Martha H.
  Candlelight and vintage years. Aging 274:11
  Ag '77

FREEDOM of the press
  Fairness doctrine for the press? N. Cousins.
  Sat R   5:4   N 12 '77

First Amendment;   A. Goldstein   Nat R   29:49-50
  N 25 '77

wide support among northern industrialists. They also wanted to help freedmen. But moderates did not think that Congress should interfere too much with the affairs of the South.

Congress Versus the President

Republicans first locked horns with President Johnson in 1866. In April, Congress passed the Civil Rights Act. This act gave citizenship to all blacks. By passing it, Congress hoped to combat black codes and protect the rights of black Americans. President Johnson vetoed the bill. But Republicans in Congress overrode the veto.

The Fourteenth Amendment. Some Republicans worried that the Supreme Court might find the Civil Rights Act unconstitutional. The Court had said in the Dred Scott decision of 1857 that blacks were not citizens. So Republicans proposed the Fourteenth Amendment to the Constitution.

The *Fourteenth Amendment* granted citizenship to all persons born in the United States. This included nearly all blacks. It also encouraged states to allow blacks to vote. It did so by threatening to take representatives away from states that did not let blacks vote. Republicans believed that freedmen would be able to defend their rights if they could vote.

Republicans tried to secure basic rights for southern blacks with the Fourteenth Amendment. But the country had far to go before most Americans would believe in racial equality. Republicans favored giving black Americans the vote. Yet most northern states still denied suffrage to blacks.

Election of 1866. Congress and the President clashed over the Fourteenth Amendment. President Johnson did not want states to ratify the amendment. None of the former Confederate states did, except Tennessee. Before the elections to Congress in November 1866, Johnson decided to take his case to the people. He urged voters to reject the Radical Republicans and stick with his Reconstruction plan.

Johnson traveled around the North, speaking against the Radical Republicans. The President was often heckled by his audience. Furious, Johnson yelled right back. This did not help his cause.

Before the elections, white mobs rioted in New Orleans, killing many freedmen. This convinced many Northerners that the government had to protect the freedmen from violence.

The President had misjudged the temper of the people. In the November election, voters sent large Republican majorities to both houses of Congress.

Radical Reconstruction

With two-thirds majorities in both houses, the Republicans could override Johnson's veto. Johnson became the "dead dog of the White House," as one Republican noted. Republicans enacted their own Reconstruction program. The period that followed is often called *Radical Reconstruction.*

In March 1867, Congress passed the first *Reconstruction Act* over Johnson's veto. The Reconstruction Act threw out the southern state governments that had refused to ratify the Fourteenth Amendment—all the South except Tennessee. It divided the South into five military districts. Each district would be commanded by an army general. Only when the states did what Congress demanded could they rejoin the Union.

The Reconstruction Act required southern states to ratify the Fourteenth Amendment in order to rejoin the Union. Most important, the act stated that blacks must be allowed to vote in all southern states. At the same time, it took the vote away from former Confederate officials and army officers. This included about 10 percent of southern voters.

When elections were held to set up new state governments, many white

Southerners stayed away from the polls. They did so to show their disgust for northern interference. As a result, many Republicans were elected. They won control of the new governments.

Congress passed several Reconstruction acts, each over President Johnson's veto. However, it was Johnson's job to enforce the laws. Many Republicans feared that he would not do so. Therefore, Republicans tried to remove the President from office.

The President on Trial

On February 24, 1868, the House of Representatives voted to impeach the President. As you have read, impeach means to bring an elected official to trial. According to the Constitution, the House can vote to impeach the President for "high crimes and misdemeanors." The case is tried in the Senate. The President is removed from office only if found guilty by two thirds of the senators. (See pages 811 and 818.)

Thaddeus Stevens read the charges against President Johnson on the Senate floor. During the trial, it became clear that the President was not guilty of high crimes and misdemeanors. Charles Sumner admitted that the charges against Johnson were "political in character."

The final Senate vote was 35 to 19. This was one vote short of the two thirds needed to convict the President. Some Republicans refused to vote for conviction. They knew the President had not committed a crime. The Constitution did not intend a President to be dismissed because he disagreed with Congress, they believed. So the President thus served out the few months left in his term.

Grant Takes Office

In 1868, Republicans nominated General Ulysses S. Grant as their candidate for President. Grant was the Union's greatest hero in the Civil War.

By election day in November 1868, most of the southern states had reentered the Union. All of the new southern governments allowed black Americans to vote. During the 1868 elections, about 700,000 southern blacks went to the polls. Nearly all voted for Grant, the Republican.

Republican politicians quickly realized an important fact. If blacks could vote in the North, they would help the Republicans win elections. In 1869, Republican congressmen proposed the *Fifteenth Amendment* to the Constitution. This amendment gave black Americans the right to vote in all states.

Some Republican politicians supported the amendment only because they were eager to win elections. But many other people remembered the great sacrifices made by black soldiers during the war. They felt that it was wrong to let blacks vote in the South but not the North. For these reasons, voters ratified the Fifteenth Amendment in 1870. Black Americans finally had the legal right to vote.

Spectators needed tickets to get into President Johnson's impeachment trial. During the trial, a northern senator waved the bloody shirt of a black beaten by whites. President Johnson was to blame for violence against blacks, the senator claimed. Despite the high emotions, Johnson was not convicted.

1. **Define:** black code.

2. How did black codes limit the freedom of blacks?

3. Who did Radical Republicans blame for the Civil War?

4. (a) What did Andrew Johnson ask voters to do in 1866? (b) Did the voters do as he asked? Explain.

5. **What Do You Think?** Why do you think that nearly all black voters supported the Republican Party during Reconstruction?

3 Changes in the South

Read to Learn

★ Who controlled the South during Reconstruction?

★ What did Reconstruction governments accomplish?

★ How did Conservatives regain control of the South?

★ What do these words mean: scalawag, carpetbagger, sharecropper?

Before the Civil War, a small group of rich planters controlled politics in the South. During Reconstruction, southern politics changed. Many former Confederates could not vote, while blacks could. As a result, new groups dominated the Reconstruction governments.

Governing the South

In the state governments formed during Reconstruction, the leaders of the old South had lost much of their influence. Instead, three other groups dominated the South during Reconstruction. These were white Southerners who supported the Republicans, Northerners who went South after the war, and freedmen.

New governments. Some white Southerners worked with the Republican governments. These Southerners were often business people. Many had not wanted to secede in 1860. They hoped to forget the war and get on with rebuilding the South. But many people in the South thought that any South-erner who worked with the Republicans was a traitor. They called these southern Republicans *scalawags,* a word used for an old, useless horse.

Another important group in the Reconstruction South was Northern-ers. White Southerners called these Northerners *carpetbaggers.* They said that carpetbaggers had left in a hurry to get rich in the South. They only had time to sling a few clothes into cheap cloth suitcases, called carpetbags.

Actually, Northerners went south for different reasons. Many were Union soldiers who had grown to love the fine land of the South. Some were teach-ers—often women—who wanted to help the South recover from the war. Others hoped to open businesses. Still others were reformers who wanted to help the freedmen. And some were for-tune hunters who hoped to profit dur-ing the rebuilding of the South.

Blacks In office. Blacks also had an active part in Reconstruction gov-ernments. As slaves, blacks had no voice at all in southern politics. Now, they were not only voting in large num-bers but also running for office and winning elections.

During Reconstruction, blacks were elected to be congressmen, mayors, and state legislators. Blanche Bruce and Hiram Revels won seats in the United States Senate. However, blacks did not control the Reconstruction South. Only in South Carolina did they make up a majority in the legislature.

During Reconstruction, blacks won election to both the House of Representatives and the Senate. In this painting, Robert Elliot, a black congressman from South Carolina, argues for a civil rights bill.

Success and Failure

Reconstruction governments took important steps to rebuild the South. They built public schools for black as well as white children. Many states gave women the right to own property. They improved care of the mentally and physically handicapped. They rebuilt railroads, telegraph lines, bridges, and roads.

Improvements cost money. So Reconstruction governments passed steep taxes. Before the war, Southerners paid very low taxes. The new taxes created discontent among many Southern whites. So did corruption, which was widespread in the South.

Yet corruption was not limited to the governments of the South. Dishonesty plagued many state and local governments after the war, in both the North and South. Most southern officeholders during the period of Reconstruction served their states well and honestly.

Resisting Reconstruction

Throughout Reconstruction, Southerners who had been powerful before the Civil War tried to regain control of southern politics. Nearly all were Democrats. These leaders, known as *Conservatives,* wanted the South to change as little as possible. Even so, they were willing to let blacks vote and hold a few offices, as long as whites stayed firmly in power.

However, many poor whites, as well as some leaders, took harsher action. These Southerners felt threatened by the millions of freedmen who now competed with them for land and power. They declared war on carpetbaggers, scalawags, and freedmen. As Senator Ben Tillman of South Carolina recalled:

> We reorganized the Democratic Party with one plank, and only one plank, namely, that "this is a white man's country, and white men must govern it." Under that banner we went to battle.

The KKK. Some Southerners organized secret groups to help them regain power. The most effective of these was the *Ku Klux Klan* (KKK). These groups worked to keep blacks and carpetbaggers out of office. White-sheeted klansmen claimed to be the ghosts of Confederate soldiers. They rode at night to the homes of black voters, shouting threats and burning wooden crosses. If threats did not work, the Klan used violence. Klan members murdered hundreds of blacks and their white allies.

Response to terror. Many moderate Southerners condemned the violence of the Klan. But they could do little to stop the Klan's reign of terror.

Blacks turned to the federal government for help. Black voters in Kentucky sent a letter to Congress that said, "We believe you are not familiar with the Ku Klux Klan's riding nightly over the country spreading terror wherever they go by robbing, whipping, and killing our people without provocation."

Congress tried to end the violence of the Klan. In 1870, Congress made it illegal to use force to keep people from voting. The laws did little to undo the damage already done. Some blacks risked their lives by voting and holding office. Many others stayed away from the ballot box.

Life in the South

The South began to rebuild in spite of its political problems. The damage left by the war was repaired, but progress was very slow.

Industry. Between 1865 and 1879, the South laid 7,000 miles (11,200 km) of railroad track. The cotton industry recovered slowly. Not until 1880 did planters grow as much cotton as they had in 1860. The same year, 158 textile mills were operating. Other types of manufacturing also grew during and after Reconstruction. Birmingham, Alabama, became an important steel-making city.

The KKK used threats and violence to try to end Republican rule in the South. This cartoon appeared in an Alabama newspaper. It warned carpetbaggers, pictured here as men from Ohio, to fear for their lives.

Still, the South lagged behind the rest of the nation in industry. In 1900, the South actually produced a smaller part of the nation's manufactured goods than it did in 1860.

Freedmen. Many freedmen left the plantations in the first months after the war ended. For them, moving away from their former owners was a way to prove that they were free. One woman told her ex-owner: "I must go. If I stay here, I'll never know I am free." But there were few opportunities for freedmen. Frederick Douglass noted bitterly that the freedman "was free from the old plantation, but he had nothing but the dusty road under his feet."

At the end of the war, some Radical Republicans talked about giving each freedman "40 acres and a mule." Radicals planned to get the land by breaking up large plantations. However, this never happened. Many freedmen ended up moving back to the same areas where they had been slaves.

Agriculture. Only a small group of planters had held on to their land and wealth during the war. During Reconstruction, these planters owned huge amounts of land. But they no longer had slaves to work the soil.

Many freedmen, as well as many poor whites, went to work for the large planters. They farmed the land owned by planters, using seed, fertilizer, and tools the planters provided. In return, they gave the landowners a share of the crop at harvest time. For this reason, these poor farmers were called *sharecroppers.*

Sharecroppers hoped to own their own land one day. But many faced a

After the Civil War, conditions were hard for both black and white Southerners. Families like this one fell deeply in debt and had to sell their land and homes. Often, they ended up as sharecroppers.

day-to-day struggle just to survive. Most sharecroppers were constantly in debt. They were doing well if they had enough food for themselves and their families.

Even large landowners faced hard times. Each spring, the landowners borrowed money from a bank for supplies. Sometimes, they got supplies on credit from a store owner. In the fall, the bank or store had to be paid back. Often, the harvest did not cover the whole debt. Thus, many landowners sank further and further into debt. Much of the South was locked into a cycle of poverty.

AMERICANS WHO DARED

SECTION REVIEW

1. **Define:** scalawag, carpetbagger, share-cropper.
2. What three groups dominated southern governments during Reconstruction?
3. How did Reconstruction governments help rebuild the South?
4. Why did many poor blacks and whites in the South become sharecroppers?
5. **What Do You Think?** How do you think the Ku Klux Klan helped Conservatives regain power in the South?

Parker Robbins

Parker Robbins was a free black born in North Carolina. When the Civil War came, he enlisted in the Union army. Robbins, shown in a Union officer's uniform, rose to the rank of sergeant major. After the war, Robbins helped frame the new constitution of North Carolina. Later, he was elected to Congress from his home state.

4 A New Era in National Politics

Read to Learn

★ Why did Northerners lose interest in Reconstruction?
★ What happened in the election of 1876?
★ How did southern blacks lose power and rights after 1877?
★ What do these words mean: poll tax, literacy test, grandfather clause, segregation?

As the 1870s wore on, Conservative Democrats regained control of their state governments. At the same time, Northerners began to lose interest in the South.

New Mood of the North

Radical Republicans were losing power in Congress during the 1870s. Thaddeus Stevens died in 1868, and Charles Sumner died in 1874. Many Northerners grew weary of efforts to change the South. They wanted to forget the Civil War. The South should be left alone, they believed.

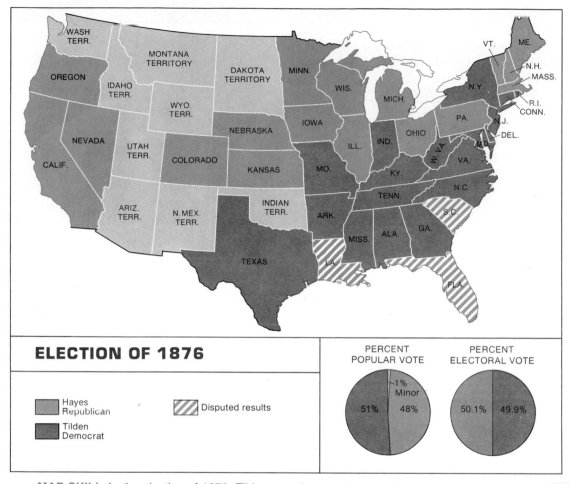

ELECTION OF 1876

- Hayes Republican
- Tilden Democrat
- Disputed results

PERCENT POPULAR VOTE

1% Minor
51% | 48%

PERCENT ELECTORAL VOTE

50.1% | 49.9%

MAP SKILL In the election of 1876, Tilden won the popular vote. But a congressional committee gave the election to Hayes. In return, Hayes agreed to remove the last federal troops from the South. What three states were still occupied by federal troops in 1876?

One reason the Republicans lost support was corruption. President Grant appointed many friends to office. Some took advantage of their jobs by stealing money. Grant kept enough support to win reelection in 1872. But many Northerners lost faith in Republican leaders and policies.

Congress reflected the new mood of the North. In 1872, it passed a law pardoning Confederate officials. As a result, nearly all white Southerners could vote again. They voted solidly Democratic. The Republican state gov-

ernments in the South fell, one by one. By 1876, only three states in the South were under Republican control: South Carolina, Florida, and Louisiana.

Reconstruction Ends

The election of 1876 brought the end of Reconstruction. Democrats nominated Samuel Tilden, governor of New York, for President. Tilden was known as a reformer. He pledged to end corruption. Republicans chose Rutherford B. Hayes, governor of Ohio. Like Tilden, Hayes vowed to fight dishonesty in government.

When the votes were tallied, Tilden had 250,000 more popular votes than Hayes. But Tilden had only 184 electoral votes—one short of the number needed to become President. The election hinged on the votes of the three southern states still under Republican control. In each of these states, Tilden had won. But Republicans claimed that many people, especially blacks, had been kept from voting for Hayes. They said Hayes should have won the three states. In fact, they filed a second set of electoral votes—for Hayes.

Inauguration day drew near, and the country had no one to swear in as President. Congress appointed a special commission to settle the crisis. A majority of the commission members were Republican. So all the disputed votes went to Hayes.

Southern Democrats on the committee could have blocked the election of Hayes. But Hayes had agreed privately to end Reconstruction in the South. Once in office, Hayes removed all federal troops from South Carolina, Florida, and Louisiana. Reconstruction was over.

A Century of Separation

After Hayes' election, white Conservatives tightened their grip on southern governments. Some groups continued to use terror against blacks who tried to vote or hold office. By the late 1880s, southern state governments had found other ways to keep blacks from voting.

Limits on voting. *Poll taxes* required voters to pay a fee each time they voted. Thus, poor freedmen could not afford to vote. *Literacy tests* often asked voters to read and explain a difficult part of the Constitution. Such tests were difficult for most freedmen, who had little education. However,

many southern whites were poor and illiterate, too. They also were kept from voting.

To permit more whites to vote, states passed *grandfather clauses.* If a voter's father or grandfather had voted in 1867, the voter was excused from the poll tax or literacy test. Since no southern blacks could vote in 1867, grandfather clauses kept many blacks from voting.

Segregation. As more blacks lost the vote during the 1890s, segregation became law. *Segregation* means separating people of different races. Southern states passed laws that separated blacks and whites in schools, churches, restaurants, theaters, trains, streetcars, playgrounds, hospitals, beaches, and even cemeteries. These were called *Jim Crow laws.*

Blacks fought segregation by challenging the laws in court. However, in 1896, the Supreme Court made the *Plessy* v. *Ferguson* decision. It allowed segregation as long as separate facilities for blacks and whites were equal. In fact, facilities for blacks were rarely equal.

Reconstruction was a time of both success and failure. Southerners, especially blacks, faced hard times for many years. But at last, all black Americans were citizens. And laws passed during Reconstruction became the basis of the civil rights movement almost 100 years later.

═══ SECTION REVIEW ═══

1. **Define:** poll tax, literacy test, grandfather clause, segregation.
2. (a) How did Hayes become President? (b) What did he agree to do in order to get southern support?
3. (a) What three states were important in the election of 1876? (b) Why?
4. How did segregation develop?
5. **What Do You Think?** Why do you think Northerners lost interest in the problems of the South in the 1870s?

Chapter 19 Review

★ Summary ★

After the Civil War, Americans had to rebuild the ruined South and reunite the two sections of the nation. President Lincoln urged generosity toward the South. However, he was killed before his plan was adopted. Andrew Johnson was also ready to readmit the southern states quickly. But Republicans in Congress objected.

After the election of 1866, Republicans in Congress had enough votes to take over Reconstruction. Freedmen gained the right to vote, while some white Southerners lost it. Republican governments came to power. They took important steps to rebuild the South.

Northerners slowly lost interest in the problems of the South. By the mid-1870s, Democrats were in power in most of the South. Slowly, southern blacks were edged out of politics.

★ Reviewing the Facts 2 pts. ★

Key Terms. Match each term in Column 1 with the correct definition in Column 2.

Column 1
1. freedman
2. carpetbagger
3. sharecropper
4. poll tax
5. segregation

Column 2
a. farmer who pays part of a crop to the landowner
b. fee that voters pay at each election
c. freed slave
d. separation of different races
e. Northerner who went south during Reconstruction

Key People, Events, and Ideas. Identify each of the following.

1. Ten Percent Plan
2. Wade–Davis Bill
3. Freedmen's Bureau
4. John Wilkes Booth
5. Andrew Johnson
6. Thirteenth Amendment
7. Radical Republicans
8. Thaddeus Stevens
9. Charles Sumner
10. Fourteenth Amendment
11. Fifteenth Amendment
12. Ulysses S. Grant
13. Ku Klux Klan
14. Samuel Tilden
15. Rutherford B. Hayes

★ Chapter Checkup 4 pts. ★

1. (a) What problems did the South face after the Civil War? (b) What problems did freedmen face?

2. (a) What was Lincoln's plan for readmitting southern states to the Union? (b) Why did some Republicans object to it?

3. (a) What did Radical Republicans want to achieve during Reconstruction? (b) Which goals did moderates agree with?

4. What were the main parts of the first Reconstruction Act?

5. (a) Why did Congress try to remove President Johnson from office? (b) Why did some Republicans vote against convicting the President?

6. What three groups dominated southern governments during Reconstruction?

7. List three reasons why Northerners went to the South after the Civil War.

8. How did Conservatives regain control of southern governments?

Thinking About History *10 pts.*

1. **Expressing an opinion.** Congress had no right to interfere with the South after the Civil War. Do you agree or disagree with this statement? Explain.

2. **Relating past to present.** (a) What disagreement did Congress and President Johnson have during Reconstruction? (b) Can you think of a recent disagreement between Congress and the President? Explain.

3. **Analyzing a quotation.** After the Civil War, a Mississippi law said: "The Negro is free, whether we like it or not. . . . To be free, however, does not make him a citizen, or entitle him to social or political equality with the white man." (a) What does this law show about attitudes of southern whites toward freedmen? (b) What problems do you think freedmen in Mississippi faced as a result of this law?

4. **Learning about citizenship.** How did the amendments to the Constitution ratified during Reconstruction give black Americans a new role in government?

★ Using Your Skills

1. **Making a generalization.** Reread the discussion of the condition of the South after the Civil War (pages 417 and 418). (a) List three facts about the South after the war. (b) Using the facts you listed, make a generalization about the South after the war.

2. **Placing events in time.** Study the time lines on pages 370–371 and 416. (a) What year did the Civil War end? (b) What two events took place the same year?

3. **Understanding cause and effect.** Many events are connected by cause and effect. A cause is the reason that an event happened. An effect is the result of the cause. Read the three statements below. Decide which one is an effect and which two are causes. Then explain how the causes and the effect are connected.

   (a) Southern states passed black codes.
   (b) Southern states elected former Confederates to Congress.
   (c) Republicans opposed Johnson's plan to readmit southern states.

★ More to Do

1. **Interviewing.** As a group project, conduct interviews with students who imagine that they are freedmen living in the South after the Civil War. If possible, record the interviews and listen to the tape. Do you think the interviews give an accurate picture of life during Reconstruction? Explain.

2. **Drawing a cartoon.** Draw a political cartoon that criticizes the black codes passed in the South after the Civil War.

3. **Writing a letter.** Imagine that you are a Republican senator who voted against convicting Andrew Johnson in 1868. Write a letter to a friend explaining why you voted as you did.

4. **Exploring local history.** Prepare an oral report about life in your local area after the Civil War. If possible, locate photographs or written descriptions of the area during this time period.

Unit 6 Review

Chapter 17 Slavery in the western territories became an emotional issue in the late 1840s. At first, the North and South compromised. But events in the 1850s pushed the two sections further apart. When Abraham Lincoln was elected President in 1860, the South seceded. The Confederacy's bombardment of Fort Sumter signaled the start of the Civil War.

Chapter 18 Both the North and South expected the war to end quickly, but the fighting dragged on. In 1862, President Lincoln announced the Emancipation Proclamation to weaken the South and broaden the war goals of the Union. By 1864, the greater resources of the North and Grant's plan of total war pushed the Union toward victory. In April 1865, Lee surrendered.

Chapter 19 Republicans in Congress disagreed with Presidents Lincoln and Johnson about how to reconstruct the South. After 1866, Congress took charge. It divided the South into military districts and gave black Americans the vote. Republican governments came to power in the South. They were opposed by white Conservatives, who worked to regain control. By 1877, Republican control had ended in the South.

★ **Unit Checkup** ★

Choose the word or phrase that best completes each of the following statements.

1. The issue of slavery in the Mexican Cession was settled by the
   (a) Missouri Compromise.
   (b) Compromise of 1850.
   (c) Kansas–Nebraska Act.

2. Lincoln's election led to
   (a) the Dred Scott decision.
   (b) a raid on Harpers Ferry.
   (c) creation of the Confederacy.

3. The Union won its first major battle at
   (a) Bull Run.
   (b) Antietam.
   (c) Shiloh.

4. A plan of total war to break the South's will to fight was devised by
   (a) Sherman.
   (b) Grant.
   (c) Lincoln.

5. Lincoln outlined his ideas about Reconstruction in the
   (a) Ten Percent Plan.
   (b) Wade–Davis Bill.
   (c) Gettysburg Address.

★ **Building American Citizenship** ★

1. Southerners called the Civil War the War for Southern Independence. Why did white Southerners feel that they had to leave the Union in order to protect their rights?

2. During the Civil War, Frederick Douglass said that once a black American put on an army uniform, "no power on earth . . . can deny that he has earned the right to citizenship in the United States." Why do you think Douglass believed that blacks would win more rights after they had served in the army? Do you think Douglass was right?

The cartoon at right was published during Reconstruction. Study the cartoon. Then answer the following questions.

1. Figure out what each person and thing in the cartoon stands for. (a) What does the woman stand for? (b) What does the carpetbag stand for? (c) Which President is pictured on top of the carpetbag?

2. (a) What is the woman in the cartoon walking on? (b) Why did the cartoonist show this?

3. (a) Why is the woman carrying the carpetbag? (b) Why are federal troops shown holding the carpetbag in place? (c) Why did the cartoonist show these things?

4. (a) What did the cartoonist think the North was doing to the South during Reconstruction? (b) Do you think the cartoonist was a Northerner or a Southerner?

5. Did the cartoonist exaggerate the facts in order to make a point? Explain.

History Writer's Handbook

Arranging Information In Time Order

Time order is arrangement of supporting information in order of occurrence. You often can use time order when the supporting information is events or steps in a process.

Look at the following topic sentence. *The Union gained control of the Mississippi through a series of military victories.* In writing detail sentences, you might arrange the supporting information in time order. For example: *In February 1862, Union troops captured Fort Henry and Fort Donelson. In early April, they seized Shiloh. In late April, Union gunboats took New Orleans and Memphis. In July 1863, Union troops captured Vicksburg, the last southern*

stronghold. Note that the dates show the time order.

You need not always give dates. You can use other *transitions*, or connecting words or phrases, to show time order. Some common transitions for time order include *after, afterward, at last, before, earlier, eventually, finally, first, formerly, last, later, meanwhile, next, now, previously, soon, then, ultimately, until,* and *while.*

Practice Rewrite each of the detail sentences above. Use transitions other than dates to show time order. For example: *First, Union troops captured Fort Henry and Fort Donelson.* Underline the transition in each sentence.

Unit 7

AMERICA IN A CHANGING TIME

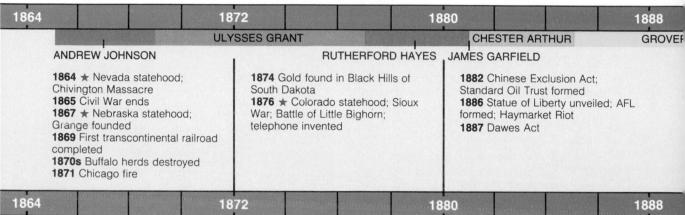

1864		1872		1880		1888

ULYSSES GRANT

CHESTER ARTHUR

GROVER

ANDREW JOHNSON

RUTHERFORD HAYES   JAMES GARFIELD

1864 ★ Nevada statehood; Chivington Massacre
1865 Civil War ends
1867 ★ Nebraska statehood; Grange founded
1869 First transcontinental railroad completed
1870s Buffalo herds destroyed
1871 Chicago fire

1874 Gold found in Black Hills of South Dakota
1876 ★ Colorado statehood; Sioux War; Battle of Little Bighorn; telephone invented

1882 Chinese Exclusion Act; Standard Oil Trust formed
1886 Statue of Liberty unveiled; AFL formed; Haymarket Riot
1887 Dawes Act

1864		1872		1880		1888

Late 1800s Alexander Graham Bell improved on his first telephone.

Late 1800s Railroads opened up the West to settlers from the East.

1800s Indians developed a culture well suited to life on the treeless plains. Here, Comanche women dry meat and prepare hides.

1888	1896	1904	1912

CLEVELAND · BENJAMIN HARRISON · GROVER CLEVELAND · WILLIAM MCKINLEY · THEODORE ROOSEVELT · WILLIAM TAFT

1889 ★ Montana, North Dakota, South Dakota, Washington become states
1890 ★ Idaho, Wyoming become states; Battle of Wounded Knee; Sherman Antitrust Act
1892 Carnegie Steel founded; Populist Party formed
1894 Pullman strike

1896 ★ Utah statehood; Populists support William Jennings Bryan for President
1900 ILGWU formed
1902 Macy's department store opens

1904 New York City subway opens
1907 ★ Oklahoma statehood
1912 ★ Arizona, New Mexico become states

1888	1896	1904	1912

1889 Land-hungry settlers raced to claim the best lands in Oklahoma.

Late 1800s Pioneer women like this one helped turn the Great Plains into working farms.

Early 1900s In *Cliff Dwellers*, George Bellows captured the crowded conditions in booming cities.

CHAPTER

20

Settling the West (1865–1914)

Chapter Outline

1 Riches of the West
2 Native Americans of the West
3 A Way of Life Ends
4 Cowboys and Sodbusters
5 Farmers Organize

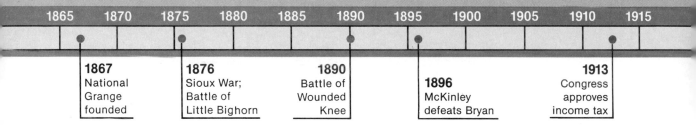

| 1865 | 1870 | 1875 | 1880 | 1885 | 1890 | 1895 | 1900 | 1905 | 1910 | 1915 |

1867
National
Grange
founded

1876
Sioux War;
Battle of
Little Bighorn

1890
Battle of
Wounded
Knee

1896
McKinley
defeats Bryan

1913
Congress
approves
income tax

About This Chapter

The country grew quickly after the Civil War. White Americans moved west and settled for the first time on the Great Plains east of the Rocky Mountains. The newcomers took over Indian hunting grounds. As a result, settlers and Indians were often at war in the late 1800s.

Many whites thought that the best way to end the wars was to force Indians to live as whites did. The government urged Indians to become farmers and send their children to white schools.

One group of Sioux children were taken from their homes in the Dakotas. They were sent to a Quaker school in Indiana. When the children arrived there, they were horrified to hear that the Quakers planned to cut their long hair. Among the Sioux, only cowards wore short hair.

One Indian girl, called Red Bird, hid from the teachers. But they found her and tied her to a chair. "I cried aloud," she later recalled, "shaking my head all the while I felt the cold blades of the scissors against my neck, and heard them gnaw off one of my thick braids. Then I lost my spirit."

Adopting white ways caused pain and hardship to Indians. Changes brought by the rapid settlement of the West had more tragic results for Native Americans. In this period, settlers, too, faced great hardships as they carved out a life on the plains.

Study the time line above. When did the Sioux War begin?

Cattle ranchers helped to open the West. Clara Williamson painted this picture of cowboys driving cattle north from Texas.

1 Riches of the West

Read to Learn

★ How did mining speed the development of the West?

★ How was the first cross-country railroad built?

★ What do these words mean: transcontinental railroad?

Settlers moving to California and Oregon in the 1840s and 1850s crossed over the Great Plains. The plains had few trees and received little rain.* Early pioneers thought that crops could not grow there. In fact, they called the Great Plains the Great American

---

*In Chapter 1, you read about the lands and climate of the Great Plains. See pages 23–24 and 28.

Desert. Pioneers also avoided settling in the rugged Rocky Mountains and Sierra Nevada.

The Mining Boom

Thousands of miners moved to California during the Gold Rush of 1849. From California, miners fanned out eastward. They hunted for gold in the Sierra Nevada and Rockies and in the Black Hills of the Dakota Territory.

The Comstock Lode. Among the many miners digging in the Sierra Nevada was Henry Comstock. Comstock found gold in 1859. Though the strike was rich, Comstock was unaware of its real value. He often complained

They spent the winter in small bands and gathered in large groups during the summer.

Indian bands. Indian bands of about 100 people lived together like a large family during the winter. Sometimes, a band included Indians from several nations, such as Cheyennes, Sioux, and Blackfeet. The band was open to all who worked for the common good. Indians in each band shared work and owned many things in common.

Bands also staged buffalo drives. During a drive, hunters built a *corral*, or enclosure, at the bottom of a steep hill. Then, hooting and waving colored robes, Indian riders drove a group of buffalo into the corral. There, they killed the trapped buffalo. Women cut up the buffalo meat and dried it out. The dried meat was called *jerky*.

Uses of the buffalo. The buffalo was extremely important to the Indians. Buffalo meat was rich in protein and made nourishing food. Indian women tanned buffalo hides to make leather. They also wove buffalo fur into a coarse, warm wool cloth. Buffalo horns and bones were carved into tools. Even the sinews of the buffalo had a use. Women used them as thread.

Women. Among the Plains Indians, women took charge of life in the village. Women were skilled in many crafts. They made clothing, tipis, tools—everything but weapons. In some bands, women also hunted with the men. A Blackfoot woman called Running Eagle led many raids herself. In other bands, when a woman was respected for her wisdom she had the final say in all decisions.

Sun Dance. In the summer, Indians from many bands met on the plains. They hunted together and kept many traditions alive. Bands of one nation, like the Sioux or Cheyenne, met in large councils. In the councils, Indians talked about problems. Indian doctors treated the sick. Most important, Indians celebrated the *Sun Dance*, a four-day ceremony.

This Kiowa Indian was named Two Hatchets. His headdress and elaborate shirt were worn only on special occasions. For centuries, the Kiowas lived on the southwestern plains. Like other Plains Indians, they hunted buffalo.

The Sun Dance took place in a lodge built of tree branches. The lodge had no roof, and a tall tree trunk stood in the middle. During the ceremony, members of the different bands danced together. Dancers looked up the tree trunk to the sky, where the Great Spirit dwelled. Plains Indians believed that the Great Spirit ruled the universe. They asked the Great Spirit to give them good fortune during the coming year.

■ SECTION REVIEW ■

1. **Define:** travois, tipi, corral, jerky.
2. How did the horse change the way of life of the Plains Indians?
3. Describe a buffalo drive.
4. What was the Sun Dance?
5. **What Do You Think?** Why do you think the buffalo was so important to the Plains Indians?

3 A Way of Life Ends

Read to Learn

★ Why did wars break out between settlers and Indians?
★ What battles took place on the plains?
★ How did the government end the wars?
★ What does this word mean: reservation?

In the 1860s, miners and railroad crews moved onto the plains. Indians saw that the newcomers threatened their way of life. As Chief Red Cloud told some railroad workers, "We don't want you here." But the railroads pushed on. Before long, wars spread across the plains as Indians fought to save their way of life.

Broken Promises

Conflicts between Plains Indians and settlers went back to the 1840s. Settlers and miners began to cross Indian hunting grounds at that time. Because of these conflicts, settlers and miners asked the federal government for protection.

Fort Laramie Treaty. In 1851, the government called a meeting of Indian nations near Fort Laramie in Wyoming. Federal officials wanted the Indians to settle in one place and give up following buffalo herds. They asked each nation to keep to a limited area. In return, they promised money, food, and other goods to Indians who accepted the government's plan. Officials told the Indians that the lands where they settled would be theirs forever.

Indian leaders agreed to the government's terms in the *Fort Laramie Treaty.* But settlers continued to trespass on Indian land. In 1859, miners struck gold at Pikes Peak in Colorado. The gold strike brought miners onto land that the government had promised to the Cheyennes and Arapahos.

The Chivington Massacre. In the 1860s, federal officials forced Indian leaders to sign a new treaty giving up the land around Pikes Peak. But young Indian men would not accept the agreement made by their chiefs. They attacked supply trains, burned homes, and killed miners and soldiers.

The army struck back. In 1864, Colonel John Chivington led his soldiers against a village of Cheyennes. These Cheyennes were not at war. In fact, the government had promised to protect them. When Chivington attacked, the Indians raised a white flag to show that they surrendered. Chivington ignored the flag. He ordered his men to destroy the village, saying he had come "to kill Indians." The soldiers slaughtered 450 men, women, and children in the *Chivington Massacre.*

The Chivington Massacre outraged Indians. Many fought back against the army. Across the plains, soldiers and Indians went to war.

Peace efforts. In 1867, federal officials set up a peace commission. The commission wanted to end the wars on the plains so that railroad builders and miners would be safe. It also wanted to force the Indians to "walk the white man's road." In other words, the commission urged Indians to settle down and live as white farmers did.

In 1868, the United States government signed a new treaty with the southern Plains Indians. The southern Plains Indians included the Kiowas, Comanches, and Arapahos. These nations promised to move to the Indian Territory in Oklahoma. Northern Plains Indians, the Sioux and Cheyennes, also signed a treaty. They agreed to live on reservations in the Black Hills of the Dakotas. A *reservation* is a limited area that is set aside for Indians.

Southern Plains Indians were unhappy with the new treaty. The soil in Oklahoma was poor. Also, most Indians were hunters, not farmers. Worst of all, white settlers ignored the treaty and moved onto Indian land. Because the treaty was broken, fighting continued.

Final Battles

The plight of the southern Plains Indians became worse during the 1870s. As you read, nearly all the Plains nations depended on buffalo. Buffalo were plentiful until railroad companies moved onto the plains. At first, railroads hired marksmen to kill buffalo for food. Then, in 1871, white hunters began shooting buffalo for their hide only. The meat was left to rot.

Buffalo herds destroyed. Millions of buffalo were killed each year in the early 1870s. The huge buffalo herds were nearly wiped out. Threatened with starvation, Indians fought back fiercely. In the end, however, the army forced the southern Plains Indians to settle on reservations.

The northern Plains Indians also faced extreme hardship. In 1874, pros-pectors found gold in the Black Hills of the Dakotas. Thousands of miners rushed onto land promised to the north-ern Plains Indians. Sioux and Chey-ennes fought back in the Sioux War of 1876. Led by Sitting Bull, a medicine man, and Crazy Horse, a Sioux chief, bands of Indians left the reservations.

Little Bighorn. The United States Army had orders to drive the Indians back to their reservations. In June 1876, Colonel George S. Custer led a column of soldiers into the Little Big-horn Valley. Custer's Indian scouts warned him that a large group of Sioux and Cheyennes were camped ahead. Although he was outnumbered, Custer did not wait for a second column of sol-diers to join him. Instead, he attacked with only 260 men.

Before Custer's attack, Sitting Bull had a vision. He told the Sioux that they would win a great victory. Inspired by this vision, Crazy Horse led his men against Custer. During the battle, Custer and his men were

Plains Indians got much of what they needed to live from the buffalo. But to travelers on the western railroads, a buffalo herd was often a nuisance. The title of this painting is *Held Up by Buffalo.* Herds of 20,000 buffalo took hours to cross railroad tracks. Sometimes, passengers shot the animals from their railroad cars. Hide hunters killed many more.

trapped. Unable to escape, the soldiers died to the last man.

The **Battle of Little Bighorn** was a victory for the Indians. "We all felt good about our victory," recalled a Sioux who fought there. "But our triumph was hollow. A winter or so later, more soldiers came to round us up on reservations. There were too many of them to fight now. We were split up into bands and no longer felt strong."

The Sioux and Cheyennes were forced onto reservations. A few Sioux leaders, including Sitting Bull and Crazy Horse, fled to Canada.

Death of a Dream

Some Indians still hoped to return to their old way of life. On Dakota reservations, the Sioux Indians turned to a new religious ceremony called the **Ghost Dance.** It celebrated the time when Indians ruled the plains.

The Ghost Dance frightened white settlers. They thought that the Indians were preparing for war. Whites convinced the government to outlaw the Ghost Dance. In 1890, police officers went onto the Sioux reservation. Sitting Bull, who had returned to his people from Canada, was leading the Ghost Dance. In the struggle to arrest Sitting Bull, he was shot and killed.

Angry Sioux groups gathered, ready to go to war. Army troops surrounded the Indians. Finally, the Sioux agreed to surrender. In December 1890, they began to give up their guns at Wounded Knee Creek in South Dakota. Soldiers stood by with weapons aimed at the Indians. Suddenly, a shot was fired. The army opened fire with rifles and machine guns. Nearly 200 Sioux men, women, and children were slaughtered. About 30 soldiers also died at the **Battle of Wounded Knee.**

Wounded Knee marked the end of the Indian wars. One Sioux leader said of the battle, "A people's dream died there." White settlers had taken over most of the West.

Chief Joseph

Chief Joseph was a leader of the Nez Percés. He tried to win better treatment for his people. "Whenever the white man treats the Indian as they treat each other," he said, "then we shall have no more wars." In 1879, Chief Joseph traveled to Washington. There, he persuaded President Hayes to let the Nez Percés return to their lands in Idaho.

The Nez Percés

In the Far West, other Indian nations tried to save their traditional culture. Among them were the Nez Percés. The Nez Percés lived in the beautiful Snake River valley where Oregon, Washington, and Idaho meet. Gold strikes in the 1860s brought miners and then settlers onto Indian land. The government ordered the Nez Percés to move from Oregon to a reservation in Idaho.

A leader of the Nez Percés, Chief Joseph, refused to move. In 1877, Chief Joseph and his people decided to flee

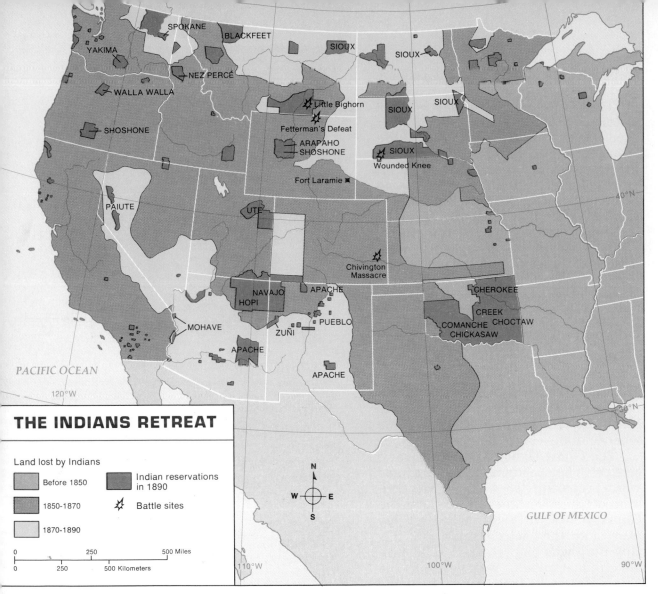

THE INDIANS RETREAT

Land lost by Indians

- Before 1850
- 1850-1870
- 1870-1890
- Indian reservations in 1890
- ✴ Battle sites

0   250   500 Miles

0   250   500 Kilometers

SPOKANE
BLACKFEET
YAKIMA
NEZ PERCÉ
SIOUX
SIOUX
WALLA WALLA
✴ Little Bighorn
✴ Fetterman's Defeat
SIOUX
SIOUX
SHOSHONE
ARAPAHO
SHOSHONE
✴ SIOUX
Wounded Knee
Fort Laramie ■
PAIUTE
UTE
✴ Chivington Massacre
NAVAJO
HOPI
APACHE
CHEROKEE
CREEK
MOHAVE
ZUÑI
PUEBLO
COMANCHE CHOCTAW
CHICKASAW
APACHE
PACIFIC OCEAN
APACHE
120°W
110°W
100°W
90°W
40°N
30°N
GULF OF MEXICO
N W E S

MAP SKILL In the 1800s, western Indians steadily lost their land to settlers from the United States. Wars between the army and the Indians raged for years. In the end, most Indians were forced onto reservations. What Indian nations had reservations in the same state as the Navajos?

north to Canada. Army troops pursued the fleeing Indians. Chief Joseph and his people suffered terrible hardships. As they fled through the Rocky Mountains toward Canada the Nez Percés had little time to find food or shelter. The frigid mountain weather killed dozens of Indians.

Soldiers finally caught the Nez Percés a short distance from the Canadian border. They forced Chief Joseph to surrender. "It is cold, and we have no blankets. The little children are freez-ing to death," said Chief Joseph as he gave up. "Hear me, my chiefs: I am tired. My heart is sick and sad. From where the sun now stands I will fight no more forever."

Attempts at Reform

During the late 1800s, the army forced more Indians onto reservations every year. On the reservations, many Indians depended on the federal government for food and other supplies.

But dishonest government workers often took goods meant for the Indians. Thousands of Indians died of starvation and of diseases brought by settlers.

Native Americans and white Americans spoke out against the tragedy taking place on the Great Plains. Susette La Flesche, daughter of an Omaha Indian chief, wrote articles and gave speeches about the destruction of the Indian way of life. Her work prompted others to speak out and work for Indian causes.

One reformer inspired by La Flesche was the poet Helen Hunt Jackson. In 1881, she published *A Century of Dishonor*. The book described the many treaties that the federal government had made with the Indians and then broken. Alice Fletcher also worked for Indian rights. She became an agent of the Indian Bureau, the government department that took care of Indian affairs.

Calls for reform led Congress to pass the **Dawes Act** in 1887. The act encouraged Indians to become farmers. Some Indian lands were divided up and given to individual families. Each family received 160 acres. The act also provided money to build schools for Indian children.

The Dawes Act did not work well, however. The Plains Indians did not have the same ideas about land that whites did. To the Indians, the land was an open place to ride and hunt—not something to divide into small plots. So few Indians cared much for their plots of land. Whites often tricked them into selling the land at a low price.

On the reservations, Indian culture changed. The government took away the power of Indian leaders. In their place, white government agents made most decisions. These agents believed that the Indians should give up their old ways, including their language, religion, and customs. Because Indians could no longer hunt buffalo, many depended on food and supplies from the government. Few Indians were content with life on the reservations.

SECTION REVIEW

1. **Locate:** Idaho, North Dakota, South Dakota, Oklahoma Territory, Wounded Knee.
2. **Define:** reservation.
3. How did settlers threaten the way of life of Plains Indians?
4. (a) What battles did the army and Indians fight on the plains? (b) Which side won in the end?
5. **What Do You Think?** Why do you think the government wanted the Plains Indians to settle down and become farmers?

4 Cowboys and Sodbusters

Read to Learn

★ How did cattle ranching become a big business?
★ How did farmers adapt to life on the plains?
★ Why did some black Americans move to the plains?
★ What do these words mean: longhorn, vaquero, sodbuster?

By the 1870s, the old residents of the Great Plains, the Indians, were growing fewer. New people and a new way of life pushed them aside. First, cowboys brought giant herds of cattle onto the plains. Later, pioneer farmers pushed out onto the plains to carve a living from the soil.

Cattle Drives

For many years, large herds of **longhorns,** or wild cattle, had roamed free in Texas. The herds had

hard time keeping the peace. Some cowboys spent wild nights drinking, dancing, and gambling.

The Cattle Kingdom

In the 1870s, ranching spread north from Texas. Cattle thrived on the grass of the plains. So ranchers grazed their herds from Kansas across the plains to Montana. They built a *Cattle Kingdom* in the West.

Ranching. Ranchers let their cattle run wild on the plains. Twice a year, they rounded up the animals and branded newborn calfs. A brand was a symbol that cowboys burned into the cattle's hide. Each ranch used a unique brand to identify its cattle.

Many black Americans became cowboys. Some had gone west as slaves. There, they worked to buy their freedom. After the Civil War, thousands more blacks headed west. They found that strength and skill meant more than skin color in the West.

At times, ranchers had problems with other people on the range. Water was scarce, and ranchers sometimes fought over water holes and streams. When sheep ranchers moved onto the plains, more trouble developed. Sheep nibbled the grass down so low that cattle could not eat it. As a result, cattle ranchers sometimes fought bitterly with sheep ranchers.

Farming. In the 1870s, farmers began moving onto the range, as the open plain was called. They fenced in their fields with barbed wire. Sharp barbs kept cattle from pushing over fences and trampling plowed fields. As more farmers strung barbed wire, the open range began to disappear.

End of the kingdom. Bad weather speeded the end of the Cattle Kingdom. The winter of 1885 was very harsh. The next summer was blistering hot and dry. In the bitter cold of the next winter, millions of cattle froze to death. By spring 1887, nine out of ten cattle on the northern plains had died.

The day of the Cattle Kingdom was over. Cattle ranchers began to buy land and fence it in. Soon, farmers and ranchers had divided the open range into a patchwork of large fenced plots.

Homesteaders and Exodusters

By 1900, half a million farmers had settled on the Great Plains. Many were attracted by the offer of free land. During the Civil War, Congress passed the *Homestead Act.* The act offered 160 acres free to anyone who worked the land for five years. Congress wanted to give poor people in the East a chance to own farms.

The Homestead Act was not a complete success. Big landowning companies took over large areas of land illegally. Also, even though the land was free, few poor city folk had enough money to move west and start a farm. Still, thousands of homesteaders settled on the Great Plains. They planted their 160 acres with wheat and corn.

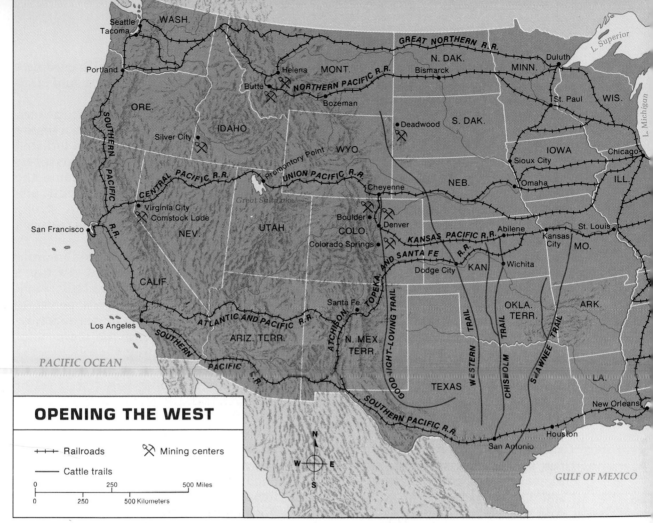

OPENING THE WEST

+++ Railroads   ⚒ Mining centers

—— Cattle trails

0   250   500 Miles

0   250   500 Kilometers

MAP SKILL Five railroads stretched across the continent by the 1890s. Two crossed the northern plains, ending in Washington and Oregon. The Central Pacific–Union Pacific line ran across the middle of the country to San Francisco. Where did the Goodnight–Loving Trail end?

Black Americans joined the rush for homestead land. The largest group of blacks moved west at the end of Reconstruction. Southern blacks had seen many of their hard-won freedoms slip away. In 1879, thousands of blacks decided to move to Kansas. They called themselves *Exodusters.**

Exodusters faced hardships long before they reached the plains. White Southerners dreaded losing the cheap labor supplied by blacks. So they stopped the boats that Exodusters used to travel up the Mississippi. An army general wrote to President Hayes, "Every river landing is blockaded by white enemies of the colored exodus; some of whom are armed and mounted, as if we are at war." Despite the danger, nearly 25,000 blacks moved to Kansas by 1900.

Hardships and Successes

The first farmers on the Great Plains staked out the best sites. They settled near water and trees. Later arrivals had to move onto the open plains. There, even the best farmers faced constant hardships.

---

* The name came from the second book of the Bible, Exodus, which tells about the Jews escaping slavery in Egypt.

Sod homes. The first problem for settlers was building a house. Because wood was scarce, farmers often built sod houses. First, they cut or burned off the grass. Since the matted grass roots held the soil, settlers could then cut the sod into long, flat bricks. Settlers usually used two rows of sod bricks for the walls of their homes. Thick walls kept the homes cool in summer and warm in winter.

Rain was a problem, however. One pioneer woman complained that her sod roof "leaked two days before a rain and for three days after." Sometimes, the only way to stay dry was to crawl under a table.

New farm methods. The soil of the plains is rich and fertile. But the first settlers on the plains had a hard time breaking through the thick sod that covered the soil. The sod often broke their wood or iron plows.

James Oliver of Indiana designed a special sodbusting plow that reached the market by 1877. The lightweight plow was made of strong steel. It helped *sodbusters,* as plains farmers were called, to cut through to the soil below. Seed drills also helped farmers by putting seeds deep into the earth. There, the seeds got the moisture they needed to grow. Farmers also used new reapers, threshing machines, and binders to harvest their crops.

Climate. The further west the sodbusters settled, the drier the climate was. Sometimes, too little rain fell, and farmers watched their crops shrivel up and die. With dry weather came the threat of fire. Even the bravest pioneers feared grass fires. In a strong wind, a grass fire traveled "as fast as a horse could run."

On the plains, water was often hundreds of feet below ground. To tap a deep water source, farmers built windmills. Windmills used wind power to pump water up to the surface. Strong winds whipping across the plains kept the windmills turning.

Fierce winters surprised the new settlers. The plains had few trees or hills to break the wind. As a result, icy gusts built up huge snowdrifts around barns and houses. Snow buried farm animals and trapped families inside their homes. Wise sodbusters kept enough food on hand to sit out a long blizzard.

Insects invade. Insects were another problem for settlers. At times, millions of grasshoppers swarmed over the plains. The clouds of grasshoppers

A plains family shows off its possessions in front of a soddie, or sod house. The roof of a soddie was often more than a foot thick. It was supported by wood taken from the family wagon. Most sodbusters lived in soddies only until they could buy lumber for a wooden house.

darkened the sky like a thunderstorm. "When they came down, they struck the ground so hard it sounded almost like hail," one settler recalled. Insects ate everything in sight. Sometimes, they piled up several inches thick on crops and trees.

Hard times on the plains discouraged many farmers. Some packed up their families and went back east. Others headed for the milder climates of the west coast. Empty sod houses reminded settlers that no one was sure of success.

Pioneer Women

Life on the plains was especially hard for women. They lived as colonial women had in the early days of the country. Because there were few stores on the plains, pioneer women made clothing, quilts, soap, candles, and other goods by hand. All the food needed through the long winter had to be cooked and preserved.

Families on the plains usually lived miles apart. As a result, families had to look after themselves. Women had many duties. They had to educate their children themselves. With no doctor nearby, women treated husbands and children who were sick or injured. Women helped with planting and harvesting and took care of sewing, cooking, washing, and housekeeping.

Pioneer women kept up their spirits. "Don't think that all of our time and thoughts were taken up with the problems of living," one woman wrote. "We were a social people." She explained that pioneer families relaxed by visiting with neighbors and gathering for church services. Picnics, weddings, and dances were special events.

The Frontier Closes

By the 1880s, few areas on the plains remained to be settled. Land-hungry pioneers pressured the federal government to open up Oklahoma to homesteaders. At the time, Oklahoma was home to Indians. Some had been moved there in the 1830s. (See pages 301–303.) The government had also sent Plains Indians to the area, as you have read. In 1885, the government bought back the western part of Oklahoma from the Indians.

Late in April 1889, 100,000 settlers lined up at the Oklahoma border. The government had announced that farmers could claim free homesteads in Oklahoma. But claims could not be staked until noon on April 22. That day, at the stroke of 12, a group of soldiers fired their guns. The "boomers" charged into Oklahoma on horses, buggies, wagons—even bicycles. They found others had got there first, however. The "sooners" had sneaked into Oklahoma and taken much of the best land.

The 1890 census* reported that, for the first time, the United States no longer had a frontier. The great West, which had absorbed immigrants, adventurers, and city folk for 100 years, at last was settled.

---

* Since 1790, the United States government has conducted a census every 10 years. A census is a count of the country's population. The census is used to figure out how many representatives in Congress each state is entitled to.

SECTION REVIEW

1. **Locate:** Texas, Kansas, Chisholm Trail, Abilene, Oklahoma.
2. **Define:** longhorn, vaquero, sodbuster.
3. What equipment did cowboys borrow from the Spanish vaqueros?
4. Describe a cattle drive.
5. (a) What encouraged settlers to move onto the plains? (b) How did the climate and geography of the plains create hardships for settlers?
6. **What Do You Think?** What do you think people in the East thought about life in the West?

5 Farmers Organize

Read to Learn
★ Why did farmers face hard times in the late 1800s?
★ How did farmers organize to help themselves?
★ Why did the Populist Party grow?
★ What do these words mean: cooperative, wholesale?

Despite hardships, farmers learned to survive on the plains. Many even did well after their first years of struggle. Soon, wheat and corn from the West was feeding people in the nation's growing cities. Some was also shipped to Europe. But before long, farmers faced serious economic problems.

Crisis for Farmers

Hundreds of thousands of acres on the plains were planted with wheat and corn. Farmers took huge amounts of grain to market. As a result, wheat prices fell. In 1881, a bushel of wheat sold for $1.19. By 1894, the price had plunged to 49 cents. One Kansas farmer said that even "with hundreds of hogs, scores of good horses and . . . 16,000 bushels of golden corn, we are poorer by many dollars than we were years ago."

Low grain prices hit small farmers the hardest. Many had borrowed money during good times to buy more land and machinery. When wheat prices fell, they could not repay their debts. In the South, cotton farmers faced the same problem. Falling cotton prices pushed sharecroppers and small farmers deep into debt.

The National Grange. As early as 1867, farmers tried to help each other by joining groups such as the *National Grange.* The Grange became even more important in the 1870s and 1880s. Grangers demanded that railroads lower the price they charged to ship grain.

Railroads often charged big farmers less to ship grain than they charged small farmers. Grangers thought that this was unfair.

Grangers also helped farmers to set up cooperatives. In a *cooperative,* a group of farmers put their money together to buy seed and tools wholesale. *Wholesale* means to buy or sell something in large quantities and at a lower price. Grangers built cooperative grain warehouses so farmers could store grain cheaply.

Grange leaders urged farmers to use their vote. In 1873, Grangers in the Midwest and South agreed to vote only for candidates who supported their goals. They elected some officials who understood their problems. Several states passed laws that put a limit on prices for grain shipment and storage.

In spite of the efforts of Grangers, life got worse for farmers. Crop prices continued to fall, and farmers went deeper into debt.

Farmers' Alliance. Another group, called the *Farmers' Alliance,* took up the fight to help farmers in the 1870s. Like the Grange, the Alliance set up cooperatives and warehouses. The Farmers' Alliance spread through the South and into the plains states. In the South, the Alliance brought black and white farmers together. Alliance leaders also tried to unite with factory workers who were angry about their treatment by big business.

Populist Party

Unhappiness among farmers led to the birth of a new political party. In 1891, farmers joined with members of labor unions to form the *Populist Party.* At their first convention, the Populists demanded an eight-hour workday, an income tax, a limit on immigration, and regulation of railroad rates.

One of the most important demands made by Populists was for free silver. They wanted all silver mined in the West to be coined, or made into money. Populists said that farm prices were going down because too little money was in circulation. Free silver would increase the supply of money. This would make it easier for farmers to pay back their debts, Populists argued.

Eastern bankers and factory owners opposed free silver. They said that increasing the money supply would cause inflation. (See page 406.) Business people feared that inflation would wreck the country's economy.

Still, many Americans supported Populist ideas. In 1892, the Populist candidate for President won one million votes. Two years later, Populists elected seven representatives and six senators. A severe depression in 1893 brought the Populists new support. They looked forward to bigger victories in the election of 1896.

Mary E. Lease was a Populist leader. She stirred audiences with her colorful speeches. Lease traveled around Kansas, urging farmers to support the Populist Party. The way to fight falling grain prices, Lease told Kansans, was to "raise less corn and more Hell."

William Jennings Bryan

In 1896, the Populists found a dynamic spokesman for their views. He was William Jennings Bryan, a Democratic congressman from Nebraska. Bryan agreed with the Populists on several issues. He believed that the nation needed to increase the supply of money. A gifted speaker, Bryan made many speeches on the benefits of free silver. He also spoke out for the farmer. Bryan won the Democratic nomination for President in 1896. After heated debate, the Populist Party also supported Bryan.

Bryan campaigned all over the country. Millions of people heard his electrifying speeches. Meanwhile, the Republican candidate, William McKinley, stayed at his Ohio home. McKinley knew that bankers and business people supported him. They were afraid that Bryan would ruin the economy.

In the election, Bryan carried the South and West. McKinley won the heavily populated states of the East. In the end, Bryan narrowly lost.

The Populist Party broke up after 1896. For one thing, the Democratic Party took up a number of Populist demands. Also, prosperity returned in the late 1890s. So people worried less about railroad rates and free silver. Even though the Populist Party died out, many of its ideas lived on. In the years ahead, the eight-hour workday became standard for American workers. In 1913, Congress imposed an income tax.

SECTION REVIEW

1. **Define:** cooperative, wholesale.
2. How did each of the following groups help farmers: (a) National Grange; (b) Farmers' Alliance?
3. (a) What did Populists mean by free silver? (b) How did they think free silver would help them?
4. **What Do You Think?** How do you think the Populists were ahead of their time?

Chapter 20 Review

★ Summary ★

After the Civil War, Americans moved into the West. They trespassed on Indian land and killed millions of buffalo. As a result, Indian wars raged on and off for years. By the 1880s, most Native Americans had been forced onto reservations.

Cattle ranchers took over the land once held by Indians. The Cattle Kingdom spread from Texas to the Dakotas. Farmers also moved onto the plains and began fencing in the open range.

Plains farmers produced too much grain, so prices fell. Falling prices hurt small farmers most of all. They joined factory workers to form the Populist Party. The party faded after William Jennings Bryan narrowly lost the race for President in 1896.

Test

 ## ★ Reviewing the Facts ★ *2 pts.*

Key Terms. Match each term in Column 1 with the correct definition in Column 2.

Column 1
1. sodbuster
2. vaquero
3. reservation
4. cooperative
5. wholesale

Column 2
a. farmers who put money together to buy seed and tools
b. limited area set aside for Native Americans
c. plains farmer
d. Spanish cowboy
e. to buy or sell in large quantities and at a lower price

Key People, Events, and Ideas. Identify each of the following.

1. Comstock Lode
2. Sun Dance
3. Chivington Massacre
4. Sitting Bull
5. George Custer
6. Battle of Little Bighorn
7. Chief Joseph
8. Susette La Flesche
9. Homestead Act
10. Exodusters
11. National Grange
12. Farmers' Alliance
13. Populist Party
14. William Jennings Bryan
15. William McKinley

 ## ★ Chapter Checkup ★ *4 pts.*

1. (a) What difficulties did builders of the transcontinental railroad face? (b) Why did the railroads rely on immigrant workers?

2. How did the railroads speed the growth of the West?

3. (a) How did the Fort Laramie Treaty try to end conflict between settlers and Indians? (b) Why did it fail to work?

4. (a) What did the Dawes Act encourage Indians to do? (b) Was it successful? Explain.

5. (a) Why did Congress pass the Homestead Act? (b) How did the act both succeed and fail?

6. (a) Why did some blacks leave the South after Reconstruction? (b) Why did whites try to keep them from leaving?

7. (a) Describe three hardships that plains farmers faced. (b) Describe two ways they adapted to life on the plains.

8. (a) Why did many farmers support the Populist Party? (b) Why did the Populist Party decline after 1896?

Thinking About History 5 pts.

1. **Taking a stand.** In the late 1800s, conflict between the Plains Indians and white settlers was unavoidable. Do you agree or disagree with this statement? Explain.

2. **Learning about citizenship.** Review the description of Plains Indian life on pages 442–444. What personal qualities did Indians need to live on the plains?

3. **Understanding geography.** (a) Why did few farmers settle on the Great Plains at first? (b) What new developments made it possible for farmers to grow crops on the plains?

4. **Relating past to present.** (a) Why did farmers in the late 1800s join together in cooperatives? (b) Describe ways that Americans today join together and cooperate.

5. **Understanding the economy.** (a) Why did some people in the late 1800s support free silver? (b) Why did others oppose it?

6. **Comparing.** (a) How did Indians make use of the buffalo? (b) How did whites make use of the buffalo? (c) How do the differences show a different attitude toward nature?

★ **Using Your Skills**

1. **Map reading.** Study the maps on pages 448 and 453. (a) Which Indian nations had several large reservations? (b) In which states did Indians give up nearly all their land by 1850? (c) Why do you think this happened?

2. **Placing events in time.** Study the time line on page 438. (a) When was the National Grange founded? (b) When was the Populist Party founded? (c) How many years passed between these two events? (d) Can you think of a connection between the events?

3. **Writing a summary.** A summary tells the most important ideas in as few words as possible. A summary can help you understand, remember, and review information. Read the section called "Hardships and Successes" on pages 453–455. (a) List the main idea of the section. (b) List three major facts of the section. (c) Write a one-paragraph summary of the section.

★ **More to Do**

1. **Researching.** Find out more about an Indian nation mentioned in this chapter. Write a report in which you describe where the people of this nation lived, how they survived, and their important customs.

2. **Drawing a picture.** Use an encyclopedia to learn more about how Indians made use of the buffalo. Then draw a buffalo. Label each part the Plains Indians used and explain how they used it.

3. **Exploring local history.** Study the map on page 448 to determine whether there was an Indian reservation in your state during the late 1800s. Find out whether there are reservations in your state today. If there are, when were they established?

4. **Drawing a cartoon.** Draw a cartoon showing how small farmers felt about railroads in the late 1880s.

CHAPTER

21

Industry Changes America (1865–1914)

Chapter Outline

1 Bridging the Nation
2 Big Business Surges Ahead
3 Magical Years of Invention
4 Workers in the Age of Industry

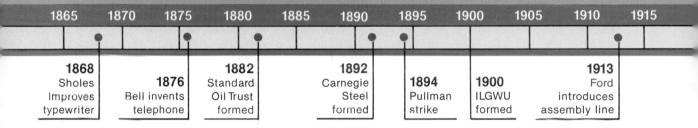

| 1865 | 1870 | 1875 | 1880 | 1885 | 1890 | 1895 | 1900 | 1905 | 1910 | 1915 |

1868 Sholes Improves typewriter

1876 Bell invents telephone

1882 Standard Oil Trust formed

1892 Carnegie Steel formed

1894 Pullman strike

1900 ILGWU formed

1913 Ford introduces assembly line

About This Chapter

American industry grew at a feverish pace after the Civil War. In 1876, Americans had a chance to show off their progress. That year, they celebrated the nation's 100th anniversary. A huge exhibition was held in Philadelphia. The Machine Hall at the Philadelphia Exhibition was the showcase for many American inventions.

Foreign visitors to Philadelphia were astonished at how quicky American industry was developing. One German praised "the diligence, energy, and inventive gift of the North Americans." He added, "In a short time, American industry has risen to a height of which those in Europe had no real idea and which filled with astonishment most of us." Visitors had good reason to marvel. In 1860, America had lagged far behind Europe in industry. But by 1900, American industry would produce more goods than any other nation in the world.

The growth of industry made America rich. It also created problems. Workers shared little of the wealth produced by industry. In the late 1800s, workers organized to win better wages and working conditions.

Study the time line above. How many new inventions does it show?

Hundreds of inventions helped American industry grow after the Civil War. Here, workers use a new method to make steel.

1 Bridging the Nation

Read to Learn
★ Why did railroads grow after the Civil War?
★ What impact did the railroads have?
★ What do these words mean: network, consolidate, rebate, pool?

The Civil War made politicians and business leaders realize how important railroads were. Railroads moved men and supplies quickly to battlefronts. They also carried raw materials to factories. After the war, railroads grew dramatically. Their expansion spurred other industries to grow as well.

The Railroad Boom

Thousands of miles of new rails knit the sprawling nation together after the Civil War. All over America, companies built new lines linking towns and cities.

Networks. As the railroads grew, they became more efficient. Companies standardized their track. In other words, all railroads laid rails of the same gauge, or width. The railroads then became a *network,* or system of connected lines. Trains from one line were able to run on the tracks of another.

In 1886, southern railroads decided to adopt the northern gauge. Some 13,000 miles of track had to be changed to a wider gauge. On May 30, 1886, railroads in the South stopped running so that work could begin. One company hired 8,000 men. Using crowbars and sledge hammers, they toiled from dawn to dusk to move the rails a few inches farther apart. Amazingly, they adjusted all 2,000 miles of the company's track in one day!

Companies improved service by adding sleeping and dining cars to trains. Travelers could make long trips quickly, comfortably, and safely. Going to San Francisco from New York City took only six days. Before the railroads, the trip took months.

Consolidation. Railroad companies also began to *consolidate,* or combine. Larger companies bought up smaller ones or forced them out of business. Hundreds of independent lines were taken over by a few large companies. The Pennsylvania Railroad, for example, consolidated 73 smaller companies into its system.

Consolidation was the work of hard-driving businesspeople known as railroad barons. The richest and most powerful railroad baron was Cornelius Vanderbilt. Vanderbilt was the owner of a steamship line. Early on, he realized the importance of railroads. In 1866, Vanderbilt bought up most of the track running between Buffalo and Chicago. He then tried to buy the New York Central, which connected Albany and Buffalo. The owners of the New York Central, however, refused to sell.

Vanderbilt tried another tactic. He refused to allow passengers from the New York Central to ride on his westbound trains. So travelers got stuck in Buffalo. Business on the New York Central dropped off sharply. Finally, the owners agreed to sell to Vanderbilt. In this way, Vanderbilt took control of the last section of a 4,500-mile (7,200 km) railroad network between New York City and Chicago.

Great Railroad Builders

Railroad building went on at a frantic pace. In the years after Leland Stanford drove the golden spike in 1869, Americans had built three more trans-

Business leaders like Cornelius Vanderbilt were as well known as Presidents of the United States. To admirers, they were "captains of industry." To critics, Vanderbilt and others were "robber barons." This 1879 cartoon shows Vanderbilt as a giant towering over his railroad kingdom.

continental railroads. James Hill, a Canadian, finished the last major cross-country line in 1893. (See the map on page 453.) His Great Northern wound from Duluth, Minnesota, to Seattle, Washington. Unlike other rail lines, the Great Northern was built without aid from Congress. As a result, Hill had to make sure that the railroad made a profit right from the start.

Hill encouraged ranchers and farmers to move to the Northwest and settle near his railroad. He gave seed to farmers and helped them buy equipment. He even imported a special breed of bull to help ranchers raise hardy cattle. Hill once said, "We consider ourselves and the people along our line as co-partners in the prosperity of the country we both occupy." Hill's policy was not only generous. It also made good business sense.

The hope of making big profits attracted other railroad builders. It also led to corruption. In the Southwest, Collis Huntington pushed ahead with his Southern Pacific Railroad. Once, another businessman tried to build a railroad near Huntington's Southern Pacific. Huntington bribed several congressmen to vote against a bill to give loans to his rival. "It cost money to fix things so that . . . his bill would not pass," Huntington later boasted.

Railroad Troubles

As a result of the railroad boom, many parts of the country ended up with too many rail lines. Between Atlanta and St. Louis, for example, 20 different railroads competed for business. There was not nearly enough rail traffic to keep all these lines busy.

Rate wars. In the West, especially, there were not yet enough people to make the railroads turn a profit. Instead, they began to lose money. Competition between railroads grew fiercer as a result. Rate wars became common as rival railroads slashed their fares to win customers. Usually, all the companies lost money.

Rebates. Big railroads secretly offered rebates to some customers. *Rebates,* or discounts, were given only to those who shipped big loads. By offering rebates, large railroads captured much of the grain traffic in the West and South. This in turn forced many small railroads out of business.

Pools. Railroad barons realized that cutthroat competition was ruining them. So they looked for ways to end it. One method was pooling. In a *pool,* several railroads agreed to divide up business in an area and then fix their prices at a high level.

Farmers in the South and West hated rebates and pools. Both practices kept shipping prices high for small farmers. As you read in Chapter 20, many farmers joined the Populist Party. It called for government regulation of railroad rates. Congress and several states passed laws regulating the railroads. But the laws did not end the problems. Railroad barons paid large bribes to officials to keep the laws from being enforced.

Railroads Change America

Despite their problems, railroads were the tinder that set American industry roaring after 1865. Just building now rail lines created thousands of jobs. Steel workers turned millions of tons of iron into steel for tracks and engines. Lumberjacks cut down whole forests to supply wood for railroad ties. Miners sweated in dusty mine shafts digging coal for railroad engines. The railroads themselves employed thousands of workers. They laid track, built trestles across rivers, and carved tunnels through mountains.

Railroads opened up every corner of the country to settlement and growth. They carried people all over, especially throughout the West. New businesses sprang up, and new towns grew where rail lines crossed and met. With rail lines in place, the United States was ready to grow into the greatest industrial nation in the world.

▬ SECTION REVIEW ▬

1. **Define:** network, consolidate, rebate, pool.
2. Why did railroads standardize their track?
3. (a) How did James Hill encourage people to settle the Northwest? (b) How did this help Hill's Great Northern Railroad?
4. **What Do You Think?** Why do you think the poet Walt Whitman called railroads the "pulse of the continent"?

2 Big Business Surges Ahead

Read to Learn

★ Why did steel become a big industry?
★ How did business leaders help build American industry?
★ Why did some people criticize big business?
★ What do these words mean: vertical integration, corporation, stock, dividend, trust, monopoly, free enterprise system?

Railroads opened the West to farmers, as this poster shows. Towns and cities grew up along railroad routes. They provided new markets for factories in the East and Midwest.

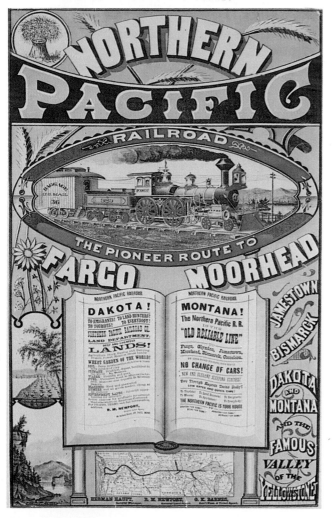

In the years after the Civil War, American industry surged ahead. The United States took its place as a world leader in industry. The growth of industry changed the way Americans did business.

King Steel

The steel industry got a big boost from the growth of railroads. Early railroads used iron rails. However, iron rails wore out quickly. Steel rails were much stronger and lasted many times longer. But steel was difficult and costly to make.

In the 1850s, inventors in both Great Britain and the United States discovered a new way to make steel. The British inventor, Henry Bessemer, gave his name to the new process. With the *Bessemer process,* steelmakers could produce strong steel at a lower cost. As a result, railroads began to lay steel rails. In time, steel replaced iron as the basic building material for industry.

Steel mills sprang up in cities throughout the Midwest. Pittsburgh became the steelmaking capital of the nation. Nearby coal mines and good transportation helped Pittsburgh's steel mills thrive.

Andrew Carnegie

The steel industry soon produced giants to match those of the railroad industry. Andrew Carnegie, a Scottish immigrant, became the king of steelmaking.

Carnegie's life was like a history of American industry. He was very poor when he arrived in New York in 1848. His first job was as a textile worker. Later, as telegraph wires were strung from city to city, Carnegie became a telegraph operator. When the railroad boom began, he found work as a railroad clerk. From this job, he quickly rose to become a division manager of the Pennsylvania Railroad.

On a trip to England in the 1870s, Carnegie saw the Bessemer process in use. When he returned home, Carnegie built a steel mill near Pittsburgh that used the Bessemer process. He hired the best technicians to run his mill. Because Carnegie was friendly with railroad owners, they agreed to buy steel from him.

Within a short time, Carnegie earned huge profits from his steel mill. He used the money to buy out rivals. He also bought up iron mines, railroad and steamship lines, and warehouses. Soon, Carnegie controlled all phases of the industry, from mining iron ore to shipping finished steel. Having control of an industry from raw materials to finished products is called *vertical integration.* In 1892, Carnegie combined all of his businesses into the giant *Carnegie Steel Company.*

Carnegie believed that the rich had a duty to improve society. He used $60 million to build public libraries in towns all around the country. Carnegie gave millions more to charities. In 1901, he sold Carnegie Steel and retired. From then on, he spent his time and money helping people.

Carnegie had a sense of humor. Once a critic demanded that Carnegie share his riches with the world. When Carnegie heard this, he added up his wealth and divided it by the world's population. Carnegie then sent the critic one share of his fortune: 16 cents.

Changes in Business

Just as railroads gave a boost to the steel industry, they also changed the way Americans did business. Before the railroad boom, nearly every American town had its own small factories. They produced goods such as soap, clothing, and shoes for people in the area. By the late 1800s, however, goods made in small local factories cost more than goods made in big factories. When railroads brought in cheaper goods from big factories, the demand for local goods fell. So many small factories closed.

Mail-order stores. As small companies closed, big factories increased their output. They developed new ways to sell products to the whole country. Stores such as Montgomery Ward and Sears, Roebuck, both based in Chicago, sold goods to western farmers by mail order.

The corporation. As factories expanded to meet demand, they needed more capital. Factory owners used capital to buy raw materials, pay workers, and cover shipping and advertising costs. To raise capital, Americans adopted new ways of organizing their businesses.

In the 1800s, many businesses that wanted to expand became corporations. A *corporation* is a business owned by many investors. The corporation sold *stocks,* or shares in the business, to investors. People who bought the stock became stockholders. The corporation could use the money invested by stockholders to buy new machines or build a new factory.

In return for their investment, stockholders received dividends. A *dividend* is a share of a corporation's profit. To protect the money they invested, stockholders chose a board of directors to run the corporation.

The rise of corporations helped American industry grow. Corporations could raise money more easily than individuals. Thousands of people bought stocks in corporations. Stockholders faced fewer risks than owners of private businesses. If a private business went bankrupt, the owner had to pay all its debts. But under the law, stockholders were not responsible for the debts of a bankrupt corporation.

People often have different views about what is good or bad for the economy. In the late 1800s, Americans debated how the great wealth of a few individuals affected the economy.

The selections below reflect differing views about the effects of great wealth. One selection was written by Rutherford B. Hayes, President of the United States from 1877 to 1881. The other was written by Andrew Carnegie, the multimillionaire steel baron.

Read both selections. Then answer the following questions.

1. **Decide what each selection says.** (a) Who wrote the first selection? (b) What does he say about great wealth? (c) Who wrote the second selection? (d) What does he say about great wealth?

2. **Identify each author's point of view.** Review Skill Lesson 5 (page 116). (a) What is Hayes' attitude toward wealth? (b) Give two examples of how he supports this point of view. (c) What is Carnegie's attitude toward wealth? (d) Give two examples of how he supports his point of view.

3. **Distinguish fact from opinion.** Review Skill Lesson 10 (page 232). (a) Is Hayes giving facts or opinions in his arguments? (b) How can you tell? (c) Is Carnegie giving facts or opinions in his arguments? (d) How can you tell?

4. **Compare the two points of view.** Decide how and why the two authors agree or disagree. (a) Do Hayes and Carnegie agree on any point? Explain. (b) On what points do they disagree? (c) Why do you think the two men had different points of view about wealth? (d) Which of the two do you think gives stronger arguments for his point of view? Explain.

Rutherford B. Hayes

It is time for the public to hear that the giant evil and danger in this country, the danger which goes beyond all others, is the vast wealth owned by a few persons. Money is power. In Congress, the state legislatures, in city councils, in the courts, in the political conventions, in the press, in the pulpit, in the circles of the educated and the talented its influence is growing greater and greater. Excessive wealth in the hands of the few means extreme poverty, ignorance, vice, and wretchedness as the lot of the many.

Andrew Carnegie

There remains, then, only one way of using great fortunes. . . . It is founded upon the present most intense individualism. . . . Under its sway we shall have an ideal state in which the surplus wealth of the few will become, in the best sense, the property of the many . . . and this wealth, passing through the hands of the few, can be made a much more powerful force for the elevation of our race than if it had been distributed in small sums to the people themselves. Even the poorest can be made to see this and agree that great sums gathered by some of their fellow citizens and spent for public purposes, from which the masses reap the principal benefit, are more valuable to them.

Banks and Industry

Americans invested huge amounts of capital in corporations after the Civil War. Average people put their savings into stocks. And banks lent millions of dollars to corporations. These loans helped American industry grow at an undreamed-of pace. The loans also made profits for the banks. In fact, bankers became leaders of business.

The most powerful banker of the late 1800s was J. Pierpont Morgan. Morgan, a New Yorker, thought of a way to become even more influential. By gaining control of a few major corporations, Morgan saw, he could dominate American industry. In hard times during the 1890s, Morgan and his friends bought many shares of stock in ailing corporations. As large stockholders, they won seats on the boards of directors. They then directed the companies in ways that avoided competition and made big profits.

Morgan gained control of most of the major rail lines between 1894 and 1898. Then, he moved to buy up steel companies and merge them into a single large corporation. By 1901, Morgan had become head of United States Steel Company. This giant corporation included Carnegie Steel and many other steel companies.

A Wealth of Natural Resources

The nation's rich supply of natural resources helped industry expand. Iron ore was plentiful, especially in the Mesabi Range of Minnesota. Large deposits of coal fueled the nation's steel mills. Coal sat beneath the soil of Pennsylvania, West Virginia, and the Rocky Mountain states. Minerals such as gold, silver, and copper were also found in the Rockies. (See the map on page 453.) And vast forests provided lumber for building.

Black gold. In 1859, Americans discovered a valuable new resource. That year, the nation's first oil strike was made near Titusville, Pennsylvania. Drillers stood dripping with oil as the Titusville gusher spurted skyward. Soon, an oil boom was under way in western Pennsylvania. Oil prospectors called the valuable liquid "black gold."

Most oil was refined, or purified, to make kerosene. Kerosene was used as a fuel in stoves and lamps. During the oil boom, hundreds of refineries sprouted up.

John D. Rockefeller. The booming new oil industry caught the notice of a young man from Ohio, John D. Rockefeller. Rockefeller came from humble beginnings. He was the son of a peddler in upstate New York. His family moved west to Cleveland, Ohio, when Rockefeller was 14 years old. At age 23, Rockefeller invested in his first oil refinery.

Rockefeller firmly believed that competition among oil companies was wasteful. So he used the profits from his refinery to buy up other oil companies. He then combined the companies into a single corporation, the *Standard Oil Company* of Ohio.

Standard Oil. Rockefeller was a shrewd businessman. He was always trying to improve the quality of his oil. And he did all he could to snuff out competition. Standard Oil slashed its prices to the bone in order to drive rivals out of business. It pressured its customers not to deal with any other oil company. And Standard Oil got rebates from railroads anxious to keep Rockefeller's business.

Rockefeller tightened his hold on the oil industry by forming the *Standard Oil Trust* in 1882. A *trust* is a group of corporations run by a single board of directors. Under Rockefeller's plan, stockholders in smaller oil companies turned over their stock to Standard Oil. In return, they got stock in the new trust. But they gave up their right to choose the board of directors. The board of Standard Oil then managed the business of all the companies, which before had been rivals.

John D. Rockefeller

John D. Rockefeller made millions in the oil business. He succeeded in part because he paid close attention to detail. Once, Rockefeller was watching workers seal full oil cans. He counted as the workers used 40 drops of solder, or melted metal, to seal each can. "Have you ever tried 38?" asked Rockefeller. With 38 drops, some of the cans leaked. However, 39 drops sealed them perfectly. By using one drop less on each can, Rockefeller saved thousands of dollars a year.

The Standard Oil trust ended competition in the oil industry. It created a monopoly. A *monopoly* is a company that controls all or nearly all the business of an industry. Through the Standard Oil trust, Rockefeller controlled 95 percent of all oil refining in the United States.

Other businesses followed the lead of Rockefeller. They set up trusts and tried to build monopolies. By the late 1890s, monopolies and trusts dominated some of the nation's most important industries.

Different Views of Big Business

Many Americans believed that trusts and monopolies threatened free enterprise. In a *free enterprise system,* businesses are owned by private citizens, not by the government. Owners decide what to make, how much to make, and what price to charge. Companies compete to win customers by making the best product at the lowest price.

Support for competition. Trusts and monopolies tended to end competition. Without competition, there was no reason for companies to keep their prices low. It was also hard for new companies to start up and compete against trusts. And workers often felt that they were treated badly by large corporations.

Critics worried about the political influence of trusts as well as their economic power. Carnegie and Rockefeller were richer than Americans had ever been before. When Carnegie sold his steel company in 1901, he received $250 million for it. With so much money, men like Carnegie could get favors from elected officials. The Chicago *Tribune* warned that "liberty and monopoly cannot live together."

Support for trusts. Carnegie and other business leaders defended trusts. Carnegie published articles arguing that competition ruined businesses and put people out of work. Supporters of trusts claimed that large corporations made goods cheaply and so helped the consumer.

The arguments for and against big business had little effect. Government did little to control the giant corporations. Under pressure from voters, Congress passed the *Sherman Antitrust Act* in 1890. The act banned the forma-

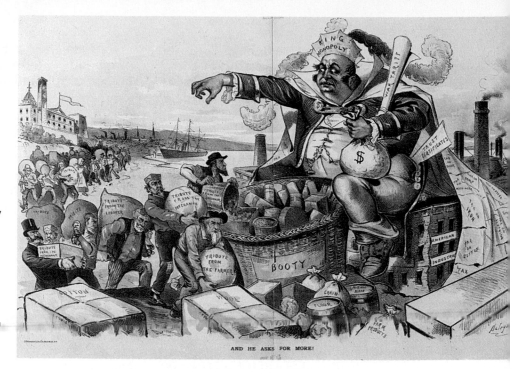

By the 1890s, trusts and monopolies controlled many industries. In this 1890 cartoon, King Monopoly takes hard-earned money from farmers, mechanics, and other working people. "And he asks for more!" reads the outraged caption.

AND HE ASKS FOR MORE!

tion of trusts and monopolies, but it was not effective.

=== SECTION REVIEW ===

1. **Define:** vertical integration, corporation, stock, dividend, trust, monopoly, free enterprise system.
2. How did the Bessemer process help the steel industry?
3. How did the growth of railroads affect small, local factories.
4. Explain what role each of the following played in the growth of American industry: (a) Andrew Carnegie; (b) J. Pierpont Morgan; (c) John D. Rockefeller.
5. **What Do You Think?** Why do you think some people felt that "liberty and monopoly cannot live together"?

3 Magical Years of Invention

Read to Learn

★ How was the telephone invented?
★ What discoveries did Thomas Alva Edison make?
★ How did Henry Ford create a new way to make cars?
★ What do these words mean: assembly line, mass production?

In the late 1800s, Americans created thousands of new inventions every year. The inventions helped industry to grow and become more efficient. They also made daily life easier for many Americans.

Talking Wires

Better communication was vital to growing American businesses. The telegraph, in use since 1844, helped people stay in touch with each other. But Americans still waited weeks for news from Europe to arrive by boat. In 1858, Cyrus Field tried to lay a telegraph cable across the Atlantic. After carrying only a few messages, the cable snapped. Field tried again in 1866. This time, he succeeded. The new transatlantic cable pulled Europe and America closer together.

The telegraph sent only dots and dashes over the wire. Several inventors were trying to transmit voices. Alexander Graham Bell, a teacher of the deaf, struggled to perfect his telephone. In March 1876, Bell was at last ready to test it.

Before the test began, Bell spilled battery acid on himself. His assistant, Thomas Watson, was in another room. Bell spoke into the machine, "Watson, come here, I want you!" Watson rushed to Bell's side. "Mr. Bell," he cried, "I heard every word you said, distinctly!" The telephone worked.

The telephone caught on slowly, however. Scientists praised Bell's invention, but most people looked on it as a toy. The Western Union Telegraph Company refused to buy the telephone when Bell offered to sell it for $100,000. In the end, the telephone earned him millions.

Bell formed the *Bell Telephone Company* in 1881. By 1885, over 300,000 phones had been sold, mostly to businesses. With the telephone, the pace of business speeded up even more.

People no longer had to go to a telegraph office to send messages. Businesses could find out about prices or supplies by picking up the telephone.

The Wizard of Menlo Park

Many inventions came from the laboratory of Thomas Alva Edison. Edison was born in Ohio in 1847. He spent very little time at school. Yet he earned worldwide fame as the greatest inventor of the age. The key to his success was hard work. "Genius," Edison said, "is one percent inspiration and ninety-nine percent perspiration."

In 1876, Edison set up a research laboratory in Menlo Park, New Jersey. The research laboratory was a new idea. Edison and other scientists spent their time trying to come up with useful new inventions. Their "invention factory" produced amazing results. Edison earned the nickname Wizard of Menlo Park for inventing the light bulb, phonograph, mimeograph machine, storage battery, and hundreds of other devices.

Thomas Edison believed that hard work was the key to success. This photo was taken after Edison had gone without sleep for three days while working on his phonograph. At last, Edison heard his own voice reciting "Mary had a little lamb." The first recordings were made on tubes such as those on the table.

A Time of Invention

Inventor	Date	Invention
Elisha Otis	1852	passenger elevator
Henry Bessemer	1856	perfected Bessemer process
Gordon McKay	1858	machine for sewing shoe soles onto uppers
George Pullman	1864	sleeping car
Thaddeus Lowe	1865	compression ice machine
George Westinghouse	1868	air brake
Thomas Alva Edison	1869	electric voting machine
Andrew S. Hallide	1871	cable streetcar
Stephen Dudley Field	1874	electric streetcar
Melville Bissell	1876	carpet sweeper
Alexander Graham Bell	1876	telephone
Thomas Alva Edison	1878	phonograph
Thomas Alva Edison	1879	first practical incandescent bulb
James Ritty	1879	cash register
Henry W. Seely	1882	electric iron
Lewis E. Waterman	1884	fountain pen
Elihu Thomas	1886	electric welding machine
King C. Gillette	1888	safety razor with throwaway blades
Singer Manufacturing Co.	1889	electric sewing machine
Charles and J. Frank Duryea	1893	gasoline-powered car
John Thurman	1899	motor-driven vacuum cleaner

CHART SKILL Major inventions, such as the telephone and the Bessemer process, had a dramatic effect on American industry. But lesser inventions also helped the economy grow. Which of these inventions might be found in a home today?

One of Edison's most important creations was the electric power plant. He built the first power plant in New York in 1882. It supplied electricity to homes and businesses. Soon, more power plants were built. Factories replaced steam-powered engines with safer, quieter electric engines. Electric energy powered streetcars in many cities. The modern age of electricity had begun.

A Rush of New Technology

Around the world, America was known as the land of invention. Almost every day, it seemed, new American inventions made business more efficient and life more pleasant.

Refrigeration. One such invention changed what Americans had for dinner In the late 1800s, Gustavus Swift brought refrigeration to the meat industry. Swift shipped cattle from western ranches to Chicago by train. There, the animals were slaughtered. Cut beef was loaded onto refrigerated railroad cars. Even in summer, Swift could send fresh meat from Chicago to eastern cities. As a result, Americans ate more meat.

Black inventors. Black Americans contributed to the flow of inventions. In 1872, Elijah McCoy created a special cup that oiled engines automatically. The device was widely used on railroad engines and in factories. The saying

Orville and Wilbur Wright owned a bicycle shop in Dayton, Ohio. During the 1890s, the two brothers read about Europeans who were experimenting with glider planes. The Wrights were soon caught up by the dream of flying.

The two brothers decided to try their own experiments. They built a wind tunnel next to their bike shop. There, they tested hundreds of wings in all different shapes. By 1903, they had learned enough from their tests to build a plane. Instead of making a glider, they built an airplane powered by a small gasoline engine.

The Wright brothers took their airplane to Kitty Hawk, North Carolina. On December 17, 1903, Orville Wright took off and flew the plane above the chilly beach. On its first flight, the plane stayed in the air for 12 seconds and flew 120 feet. Orville flew 3 more times that day. His longest flight lasted 59 seconds. The Wrights were not surprised at their success. They were confident that they had built an airplane that could fly.

★ Why do you think the Wright brothers decided to try their own experiments?

"the real McCoy" probably comes from customers who would buy only McCoy's invention, not a copy.

Granville Woods, another black inventor, found a way to send telegraph messages between moving railroad trains. Because of racial prejudice, many black inventors had trouble getting patents. Some never got credit for their inventions.

The typewriter and camera. Christopher Sholes perfected the typewriter in 1868. This invention changed office work. With the typewriter, business people could write letters, contracts, and reports much faster.

Some inventions, such as the camera, affected individuals more than businesses. George Eastman introduced the lightweight Kodak camera in 1888. Because the Kodak sold at a low price, taking pictures at the beach, on picnics, and at ball games became part of American life.

The Horseless Carriage

In the late 1890s, Americans perfected an invention that would change the nation—the automobile. The automobile was as exciting a breakthrough as the railroad had been 70 years earlier. The automobile, like the railroad, took a number of years to catch on.

No single person invented the automobile. Europeans produced motorized vehicles in the 1860s. By 1890, France led the world in automaking. Several Americans began building cars in the 1890s. But it was Henry Ford who revolutionized automaking.

The first cars were noisy and often gave horses a fright. Here, a rider walks his horse past an automobile. When cars broke down, drivers were greeted with the shout "Get a horse!"

Assembly line. In 1913, Ford in troduced the assembly line. On the *assembly line,* the frame of each car edged along on a moving belt. Workers on each side of the belt added parts to the frame. The assembly line cut the time needed to build a car. Soon other industries began to use it.

Ford's assembly line allowed mass production of cars. *Mass production* means making large quantities of a product quickly and cheaply. Because of it, Ford sold his cars at a lower price than other auto makers.

At first, most people laughed at cars. Some thought the "horseless carriage" was a nuisance. A backfiring car engine could scare a horse right off the road. Towns and villages across the country posted the sign "No horseless carriages allowed." In Tennessee, a person planning to drive a car had to advertise the fact a week ahead of time. This warning gave others time to prepare for the danger!

Slowly, the attitude of the public changed. More and more people bought cars. In 1900, only 8,000 Americans owned cars. By 1917, more than four and a half million autos were chugging along American roads.

====SECTION REVIEW====

1. **Define:** assembly line, mass production.
2. Describe two breakthroughs in communication in the late 1800s.
3. What inventions came from Edison's laboratory in Menlo Park?
4. How did Henry Ford's assembly line change automaking?
5. **What Do You Think?** Why do you think Americans came up with so many inventions in the late 1800s?

4 Workers in the Age of Industry

Read to Learn

★ How did factory work change in the 1880s?

★ How did workers try to improve their lives?

★ Why did violence break out between workers and owners?

★ What does this word mean: injunction?

America's growing factories needed workers just as much as they needed coal and iron. Workers built the factories and ran machines that produced goods. They drove trains, worked switchboards, and strung telephone wire. By the late 1800s, changes in industry forced workers to face harsh new conditions.

Changes in the Workplace

As large factories replaced smaller ones, they drew workers from different backgrounds. Most workers were native-born white men. Many left farms to take jobs in Pittsburgh, Chicago, and other cities. Millions of immigrants coming to America in the late 1800s also found jobs in factories. And some blacks left farms in the South to find work in the North. Women and children also worked in factories in growing numbers. Immigrants, women, blacks, and children always earned less than native-born white men.

Factory life. All these workers had to adjust to life in new factories. Before the Civil War, the boss of a workplace knew "every man in his shop; he called his men by name and inquired after their wives and babies," wrote one observer. "There had been a friendly relationship between employer and employee."

During the 1870s and 1880s, the friendly relationship between worker and boss ended. In giant factories, workers did not chat with their employer. More likely, they stood all day tending a machine in a large, crowded, noisy room.

Hazards on the job. Working conditions were often miserable in factories. Owners spent little on the safety and comfort of workers. Textile workers got lung diseases from breathing in dust and fiber all day. Steel workers risked injuries working close to red-hot vats of melted steel. In one year, 195 workers died in the steel mills of Pittsburgh alone. In mines, cave-ins buried miners alive. Others were killed by gas in mine shafts.

Child labor. Child labor was a growing issue in the late 1800s. Many Americans felt it was wrong for children to toil in factories. But as long as factory owners could hire children at low pay, they did so. The 1900 census showed close to 2 million children under age 15 at work throughout the country.

Children worked in many industries, often doing hazardous jobs. In coal mines, they picked stones out of the coal for 12 hours a day, 6 days a week. Other children toiled in textile mills, tobacco factories, and garment workshops. Working children could not go to school. So they had little hope of making a better life for themselves.

Knights of Labor

Since the early 1800s, workers had tried to organize unions to win better conditions. Most early efforts to form unions failed. Then, in 1869, workers formed a labor union called the ***Knights of Labor.***

At first, the Knights of Labor was open to skilled workers only. Workers held secret meetings and greeted each other with special handshakes. Secrecy was needed because employers fired workers who joined unions. In 1879, the Knights of Labor chose Terence Powderly as their president.

Terence Powderly. Powderly decided to end the secret meetings. To make the union stronger, he expanded it. Powderly let women, blacks, immigrants, and unskilled workers join. Powderly was an idealist. He wanted to make the world a better place for both workers and employers. Powderly did not believe in using strikes. Like earlier reformers, he tried to win public support by holding rallies and meetings. The goals of the Knights included an end to child labor, equal pay for men and women, and a shorter workday.

In 1885, some members of the union took part in a major strike against the railroads. The strikers won and got back pay. The Knights did not officially support strikes. But workers everywhere saw the railroad strike as a victory for the union. As a result, membership soared.

The Haymarket Riot. The next year, the fortunes of the Knights again changed. In 1886, workers at the McCormick reaper plant in Chicago went out on strike. The Knights did not endorse this strike either. On May 3, workers clashed with strikebreakers outside the factory. Chicago police opened fire, killing four workers.

The next day, thousands of workers gathered to protest the violence. As the protest was ending, a bomb exploded, killing a policeman. Police peppered the crowd with bullets. Ten more people died, and 50 were injured.

Eight men were arrested for their part in the *Haymarket Riot,* as the incident was called. No real evidence linked the men to the bombing, but four were tried, convicted, and hanged. A wave of antilabor feeling swept the nation. Membership in the Knights of Labor dropped off sharply.

Gompers and the AFL

In 1886, year of the Haymarket Riot, Samuel Gompers formed a new union in New York. The *American Federation of Labor,* or AFL, was a union for skilled workers only. Workers could not join the AFL directly. They had to belong to a trade union—for example, the cigarmakers or typesetters union. The trade union then joined the AFL. In effect, the AFL was a union made up of other unions.

The AFL was more practical than the Knights of Labor. It did not want to change the world. As one AFL member said, "We are fighting only for immediate objects—objects that can be realized in a few years." The AFL concentrated on getting higher wages, shorter hours, and improved working conditions for its members. And it used strikes as a tactic.

The AFL collected money from its member unions. Some of it went into a strike fund. When AFL members went out on strike, they got paid from the fund. In this way, striking workers could still feed their families. This helped to make the strike an effective weapon for the AFL.

The direct approach of the AFL worked. It soon became the most powerful union in the nation. In 1886, the

Terence Powderly dreamed of bringing all workers—skilled, unskilled, immigrant, women, and black—together in "one common brotherhood." Here, Frank Farrell, at left, introduces Powderly to cheering workers in Richmond, Virginia.

AFL claimed 150,000 members. By 1904, one million skilled workers swelled its ranks. However, because blacks, immigrants, and unskilled workers were barred from most trade unions, they could not join the AFL.

Women in Industry

Women made up the majority of workers in some industries. More women than men worked in the textile mills of New England and tobacco factories in the South. In New York City, women outnumbered men in the garment, or clothing, industry. By 1890, one million women had taken jobs in factories.

Efforts to organize. During the 1800s, women formed their own unions to work for better conditions. But none of these unions lasted. In 1900, men and women garment workers organized the *International Ladies' Garment Workers Union,* or ILGWU. In 1910, more than 20,000 women and men in the ILGWU struck. After several weeks, employers met their demands for better pay and shorter hours. This was a great victory for the union. The ILGWU became an important member of the AFL.

The Triangle Fire. A tragic event focused attention on the dangers faced by women workers. In 1911, fire swept through the Triangle Shirtwaist Company in New York City. The company always locked the doors to keep young women workers at their jobs. When fire broke out, the women were trapped in the factory high above the street. Many leaped to their deaths to escape the flames. Altogether, 146 young women died. The *Triangle Fire* shocked the public. Because of the fire, New York and other states approved new factory safety laws.

Mother Jones. Women took leading roles in the labor movement. Among the most famous was Mary Harris Jones, known as Mother Jones. Jones worked as a dressmaker in Chicago until the Chicago Fire of 1871

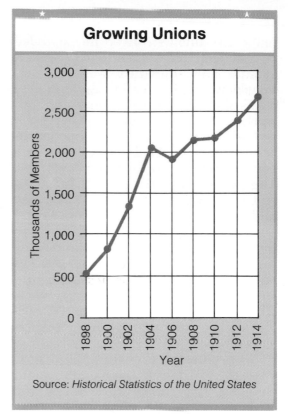

Growing Units

Thousands of Members (y-axis): 0, 500, 1,000, 1,500, 2,000, 2,500, 3,000

Year (x-axis): 1898, 1900, 1902, 1904, 1906, 1908, 1910, 1912, 1914

Source: *Historical Statistics of the United States*

GRAPH SKILL A growing number of workers joined unions in the late 1800s and early 1900s. By 1904, the AFL alone had one million members. What was the total number of union members in 1904?

destroyed her shop. In 1877, Jones helped striking railroad workers in Pittsburgh. Later, she traveled the country to organize coal miners and campaign for workers.

Mother Jones called attention to the hard lives of children working in textile mills. (See the photo on page 477.) By pointing out such abuses, Mother Jones paved the way for reform.

The ILGWU and other groups tried to help women workers. However, most women with factory jobs did not join unions. First, many of them were young and single. They expected to marry and stop working. Second, many unions refused to accept women members. Third, even unions that accepted women did little to organize them. They often held meetings in saloons, which women could not enter.

Hard Times for Unions

Between 1865 and 1914, violence plagued the struggle for better working conditions. Strikers often battled with strikebreakers, nonunion workers hired by factory owners.

Violent strikes. For workers, economic depressions caused hard times. During depressions, some workers faced pay cuts. Others lost their jobs. Often they had no money to pay rent or buy food.

In the mid-1870s, during a severe depression, railroad workers had to take several cuts in pay. Finally, in July 1877, workers struck, shutting down rail lines across the country. Riots erupted in many cities. In Pittsburgh, railroad companies hired an army of strikebreakers. A battle between workers and strikebreakers left 25 dead.

Strikers aroused little sympathy at first. Most Americans did not support unions. Many thought that unions were run by foreign-born radicals. Americans believed that individuals who worked hard would be rewarded. Because unions lacked popular support, owners were free to try to crush them.

Government response. During strikes, the federal government usually sided with factory owners. Several Presidents sent in federal troops to end strikes. Also, courts ruled against striking workers.

A Chicago court dealt a serious blow to unions in 1894. The year before, George Pullman cut the pay of workers at his Pullman rail car factory. But he refused to lower the rents that workers had to pay for company houses. So workers walked off the job.

A federal judge in Chicago issued an injunction against the strikers. An *injunction* is a legal order to do something. The judge ordered the Pullman workers to stop their strike.

Union setbacks. Leaders of the Pullman strike were jailed for violating the Sherman Antitrust Act. This act

In the late 1800s, many children worked in factories and mills. After seeing children in one mill, Mother Jones wrote, "Tiny babies of six years old with faces of sixty did an eight-hour shift for ten cents a day. If they fell asleep, cold water was dashed in their faces, and the voice of the manager yelled above the ceaseless racket of the machines."

was meant to keep trusts from limiting free trade. But a court said that the strikers were limiting free trade. This was a major setback for unions.

Workers staged thousands of strikes during the late 1800s. Skilled workers in the AFL won better conditions and higher pay. And overall, wages for workers rose slightly between 1870 and 1900. But progress was slow. In 1910, only one worker out of 20 belonged to a union. Thirty years would pass before unskilled workers joined unions in large numbers.

SECTION REVIEW

1. **Define:** injunction.
2. List three dangers workers faced on the job.
3. Explain the major goals of the following: (a) Knights of Labor; (b) AFL.
4. How did the Haymarket Riot affect public opinion?
5. **What Do You Think?** Why do you think workers gained so little from strikes in the late 1800s and early 1900s?

Chapter 21 Review

★ Summary ★

After the Civil War, expansion of the railroads fueled growth in many other industries. Large factories flourished as railroads opened up new markets.

Men like Vanderbilt, Carnegie, and Rockefeller created business empires. The corporation and the trust became impor-

tant ways to organize businesses. Countless inventions boosted industry and made life easier.

The workers who toiled in America's factories shared little of the wealth they helped to make. They joined unions to demand better wages and conditions.

★ Reviewing the Facts ★   *2 pts. each*

Key Terms. Match each term in Column 1 with the correct definition in Column 2.

Column 1	Column 2
1. consolidate	**a.** company that controls all the business in one industry
2. pool	**b.** business owned by many investors
3. corporation	**c.** combine small companies into a large one
4. monopoly	**d.** system in which a product is put together as it moves on a belt
5. assembly line	**e.** agreement among railroads to divide up business and keep prices high

Key People, Events, and Ideas. Identify each of the following.

1. Cornelius Vanderbilt
2. Andrew Carnegie
3. J. Pierpont Morgan
4. John D. Rockefeller
5. Standard Oil Trust
6. Sherman Antitrust Act
7. Alexander Graham Bell
8. Thomas Alva Edison
9. Elijah McCoy
10. Henry Ford
11. Knights of Labor
12. AFL
13. ILGWU
14. Triangle Fire
15. Mother Jones

★ Chapter Checkup ★   *4 pts. each*

1. What improvements were made in the nation's railroads after the Civil War?
2. (a) How did the growth of railroads spark the growth of industry? (b) How did railroads compete?
3. (a) What is a corporation? (b) What advantages did a corporation offer?
4. (a) What is free enterprise? (b) Why did some people think monopolies and trusts threatened free enterprise?
5. (a) What inventions helped industry in the late 1800s? (b) Which inventions

from this period are credited to black Americans?

6. Describe the changing conditions in factories in the late 1800s.
7. (a) What industries did women work in during the 1800s? (b) How did women try to improve working conditions?
8. How did each of the following try to limit the power of unions: (a) factory owners; (b) government?

★ Thinking About History ★

5 pts. each

1. **Understanding the economy.** After the Civil War, railroads consolidated as large railroad companies took over smaller ones. (a) What were the benefits of consolidation? (b) Why do you think railroads were more likely to consolidate than other businesses?

2. **Relating past to present.** (a) What were the goals of the Knights of Labor? (b) How many of these goals have workers achieved today?

3. **Learning about citizenship.** (a) How did business leaders like Andrew Carnegie use their money for the public good? (b) Why do you think they did so?

4. **Analyzing a quotation.** In the late 1800s, a manufacturer who had guard dogs at his factory compared the dogs to his human workers: "They never go on strike for higher wages, have no labor unions, never get intoxicated and disorderly, never absent themselves from work without good cause, obey orders without growling, and are very reliable." (a) What problems do you think the manufacturer had with his workers? (b) What does the quotation show about his attitude toward workers?

★ Using Your Skills ★

5 pts. each

1. **Using a poster as a primary source.** Like a cartoon, a poster can give you useful information about the past. A poster can tell you about political and economic developments in a time. Study the railroad poster on page 464. (a) What kind of people is the poster trying to attract? (b) How does the poster try to attract people? (c) Why did railroads want settlers to move west?

2. **Making a chart.** Make a chart with four columns and two rows. Title the columns Membership, Goals, Leaders, and Tactics. Title the rows Knights of Labor and AFL. Then fill in the chart. Which features of the AFL helped it to succeed?

3. **Identifying a point of view.** Jay Gould, a railroad baron, once said, "I can hire one half of the working class to kill the other half." (a) What do you think Gould's opinion of unions was? (b) How can you tell?

4. **Using a time line.** Review the time line on pages 436–437. (a) When was the first trust organized? (b) When was the Sherman Antitrust Act made law? (c) How are these two events related?

★ More to Do ★

1. **Exploring local history.** Research and prepare an oral report about the first railroad systems in your local area. Begin by studying the maps on pages 369 and 453.

2. **Making flash cards.** As a group project, make a set of flash cards for inventions devised between 1865 and 1914. On one side of each card, draw a sketch of the invention. On the other, tell who invented it, when it was invented, and its purpose. Then have the rest of the class try to identify each invention by looking at the sketch.

3. **Researching.** Read more about one of the business or labor leaders in this chapter. Write a brief biography of the person.

22

One Land, Many Peoples (1865–1914)

Chapter Outline

1 Fresh Start in America
2 Striving Upward
3 The World of the Cities
4 A Thriving Culture

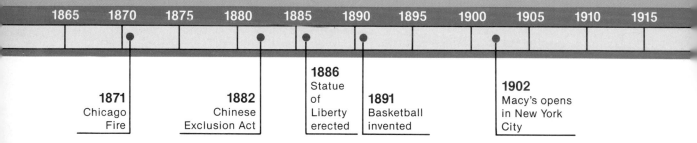

| 1865 | 1870 | 1875 | 1880 | 1885 | 1890 | 1895 | 1900 | 1905 | 1910 | 1915 |

1871
Chicago
Fire

1882
Chinese
Exclusion Act

1886
Statue
of
Liberty
erected

1891
Basketball
invented

1902
Macy's opens
in New York
City

About This Chapter

From the start, America has been a land of many peoples. First, Native Americans developed their own cultures here. Then, in the 1600s and 1700s, Spanish, French, Dutch, British, Swedish, Finnish, German, Irish, and Jewish settlers moved to America. Blacks, first brought as slaves, became an important part of American society. By the mid-1800s, more newcomers than ever before were arriving.

In 1886, the people of France gave the United States a gift, the Statue of Liberty. The statue was set up in New York harbor, where most immigrants landed. It stood as a symbol of the hope and freedom of America.

Emma Lazarus wrote a poem that was carved at the base of the statue. The poem offers a "world-wide welcome" to the new-comers. It ends with these words, addressed to the Old World:

Give me your tired, your poor,
Your huddled masses yearning to breathe
  free,
The wretched refuse of your teeming
  shore.
Send these, the homeless, tempest-
  tossed to me:
I lift my lamp beside the golden door!

In the late 1800s, immigrants flooded through America's golden door. They faced many struggles in the new land. Yet the many people who came helped build the nation.

Study the time line above. How many years after the Chicago Fire was the Statue of Liberty unveiled?

In the late 1800s, America's growing cities bustled with activity. This painting shows downtown Indianapolis at sunset.

1 Fresh Start in America

Read to Learn

★ Why did millions of people come to America?

★ How did newcomers make their way in America?

★ How did native-born Americans respond to immigrants?

★ What does this word mean: assimilation?

Millions of immigrants flooded into America after the Civil War. They came for many reasons, but above all, they came to find jobs. In Europe, they had little hope for the future. In America, they took part in building a better future for themselves and the nation.

Dreams of the New World

Over 25 million immigrants came to the United States between 1866 and 1915. Many of them were farmers. In Europe, farmers faced problems because there was not enough land for the growing population. Many poor farmers could barely grow enough to feed their families.

In Eastern Europe, many people also faced political and religious persecution. In Russia and elsewhere, people who criticized the government were jailed or sent into exile. Jews suffered from pogroms (poh GRAHMS), or organized massacres. A Jewish immigrant described pogroms in Russia. "Every

The photo at top shows immigrants aboard a ship arriving in New York. Immigrants often put up with bad food, foul water, and crowded quarters. The terrible voyage made seeing the Statue of Liberty in New York harbor all the more exciting. The painting below shows the celebration held when the statue was unveiled in 1886.

night," she said, "they were chasing after us, to kill everyone." After years of fear, her father said: "We're going to get out. . . . I want my family alive."

To poor farmers and oppressed people in Europe, the United States was a land of hope and freedom. They saw America as a place to improve their lives. Often, one bold family would leave a village and set off for America. Soon, the villagers would get letters from the family telling about the rich land across the Atlantic. The effect was amazing. In the late 1800s, one out of every ten Greeks left for America. One third of the people in Iceland headed for the New World. Millions of Irish came to the United States.

American industry welcomed the strong backs and skilled hands of European workers. Factory owners went to Europe and hired workers at low wages. Steamship companies offered low fares for the trip to America. Railroads posted notices in Europe advertising cheap land in the West.

Reaching America

Immigrants needed great courage to leave home and cross the Atlantic. The voyage was hard, sometimes miserable. Most immigrants took the cheapest berths in a ship. Shipowners sometimes jammed 2,000 people in the cheap rooms below deck. Because of overcrowding, disease often spread quickly among the immigrants.

One passenger remembered the awful trip on board the *Batvia,* an immigrant ship. "We left from Germany and we got water in the boat and all the children got measles. Some of them died and they threw them into the water like cattle. It was something I will never forget."

For many immigrants, the Atlantic crossing ended in New York City. There, after 1886, they saw the Statue of Liberty, which you read about on page 480. After the hardships of the crossing, immigrants faced one more hurdle, however. They had to pass through immigration before they could enter America.

After 1892, ships stopped at *Ellis Island.* There, government officials and doctors inspected the newcomers. Doctors watched as men, women, and children climbed a long flight of stairs. Anyone who had trouble climbing the stairs was examined. People who were sick had to stay on Ellis Island until they got well, or else they were sent back to Europe.

Immigration officials had just a few minutes to examine each newcomer. To save time, they often changed names that they found difficult to spell. Krzeznewski became Kramer, and Smargiasso ended up as Smarga.

A few lucky immigrants went straight from Ellis Island into the welcoming arms of friends and relatives. Most stepped into a terrifying new land whose language and customs they did not know.

Old and New Immigrants

Before 1885, most immigrants came from Northern and Western Europe. They included people from England, Ireland, Germany, and Scandinavia. They became known as the old immigrants.

Many old immigrants were Protestants. Those from Britain and Ireland spoke English. Some were skilled workers. Textile workers from England and coal miners from Germany found jobs in cities in the East and Midwest. Thousands of Norwegians, Swedes, and Germans built farms on the northern Great Plains. At first, the old immigrants faced some discrimination. But as the nation grew, they were drawn into American life.

After 1885, a new group of immigrants began arriving in the United States. They came from Southern and Eastern Europe, including Italy, Poland, Russia, Greece, and Hungary. Few spoke English. Many were Catholic, Eastern Orthodox, or Jewish. Their languages and religions set them apart from the old immigrants. As a result, new immigrants found it harder to make a place in America.

Life in the New World

New immigrants faced many problems. By the time they arrived, much of the good farmland in the West was taken. Also, newcomers often had less than $50 in their pockets. This was not enough to buy land. Therefore, newcomers often stayed in the cities where they landed. The slums of lower Manhattan became home to thousands of poor immigrants. By 1900, this area of New York City was the most crowded place in the world.

Neighborhoods. Many newcomers adjusted to life in the New World by

---

GRAPH SKILL By the 1880s, many immigrants came from Southern and Eastern Europe. Where did the third largest group of immigrants come from between 1880 and 1900?

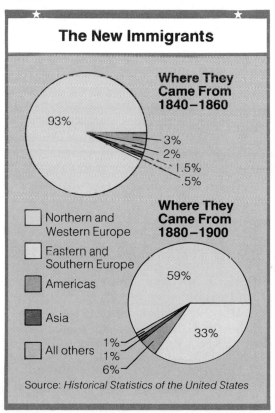

The New Immigrants

Where They Came From 1840–1860

93%

3%
2%
1.5%
.5%

☐ Northern and Western Europe
☐ Eastern and Southern Europe
☐ Americas
☐ Asia
☐ All others

Where They Came From 1880–1900

59%

33%

1%
1%
6%

Source: *Historical Statistics of the United States*

settling in neighborhoods among their own people. In cities across America, Italians lived in Little Italies. Poles settled in Little Warsaws. Cities were patchworks of Italian, Irish, Polish, Hungarian, German, Jewish, and Chinese neighborhoods. (See Skill Lesson 22 on page 485.)

In their neighborhoods, newcomers spoke their own language, celebrated special holidays, and bought foods from the old country. Italians joined social groups such as the Sons of Italy. Hungarians bought and read Hungarian newspapers. Sharing laughter and tears with their own people eased the loneliness of life in America.

Excitement and challenges. Despite their problems, many immigrants found the New World exciting. They saw skyscrapers and electric lights for the first time. They were amazed at the babble of languages, the variety of clothing, and the different foods.

After the newcomers were settled, they had to find jobs. European peasants had little need for money, but it took cash to live in America. Through friends and relatives, they found jobs. So people from one country often did the same kind of work. Many Italians became subway workers or grocers. Jewish immigrants from Eastern Europe took jobs in New York City's garment district. Jews with education and skills became teachers and merchants. Poles and Slavs labored in the coal mines and steel mills of the Midwest.

Becoming Americans

After finding a job, the next challenge for immigrants was to become American citizens. Newcomers were often torn between old and new ways of life. However, many eagerly rose to the challenge of learning English and becoming citizens. The process of becoming part of another culture is called *assimilation.*

Children helped immigrant families adjust to America. They wanted to be accepted as Americans. So they often gave up the customs their parents honored. Children learned English in school. They played American games and dressed like native-born Americans. Immigrant parents felt both pride and pain as they saw their children change.

Guidebooks for immigrants told them to adopt the customs of the new land. "Forget your past, your customs, and your ideals," one guide said. "Select a goal and pursue it with all your might. No matter what happens to you, hold on. You will experience a bad time, but sooner or later you will achieve your goal."

Life was difficult for the new immigrants. Most worked hard to escape from poverty. Many succeeded. They created a better life for themselves and their children.

Response to Newcomers

The flood of new immigrants worried many Americans. Even before the Civil War, nativist feeling ran strong. (See page 340.) By the 1880s, some native-born Americans felt that there were too many immigrants to be absorbed by American society. They worried about the many different languages, religions, and customs coming into America. Also, workers watched new immigrants take jobs for low pay. This meant that they, too, had to accept low pay if they wanted to work.

The American Protective Association. In 1887, nativists formed the American Protective Association. It soon had one million members. They led a drive for laws to restrict immigration. Congress responded by passing a bill that denied entry to people who could not read their own language. However, President Cleveland vetoed the bill. It was wrong, he said, to keep out peasants who had never gone to school in Europe. Congress passed the bill again and again, but three more Presidents vetoed it. In 1917, Congress

Road maps and local maps often have grids to help people find towns and roads. Grid maps have lines similar to lines of latitude and longitude. The evenly spaced lines make a grid, or network, of squares. You can locate a place easily if you know which square it is in.

The map at right shows Chicago about 1890. Each color on the map marks a neighborhood in which people of one *ethnic group,* or nationality, lived. By 1900, 80 percent of the people in Chicago were immigrants or the children of immigrants. Many ethnic groups other than the ones shown on the map lived in Chicago.

Use the grid map at right to answer the following questions.

1. **Locate the squares on the grid.** The map has lines running from north to south and from east to west. The lines divide the map into squares. Across the top of the map are numbers. Each number marks one column of squares. Along the side of the map are letters. Each letter marks one row of squares. (a) Which letter marks the square in which the Chicago River flows into Lake Michigan? (b) Which number marks the same square? (c) Which number marks the column of squares that is farthest to the west?

2. **Locate a place by identifying which square it is in.** To locate a place on the grid map, use the letter and the number of the square that the place is in. For example, the point where the Chicago River flows into Lake Michigan is in square C5. (a) What ethnic groups live in square D4? (b) What squares contain the largest Polish neighborhood on the map?

3. **Draw conclusions using the grid map.** Use the grid map and your reading of this chapter to answer the following questions. (a) Find a street or river that forms the border of an ethnic neighborhood. In what square or squares is the neighborhood? (b) Why do you think that a street or river forms the border of some neighborhoods? (c) Why did people of the same ethnic group live in the same neighborhood?

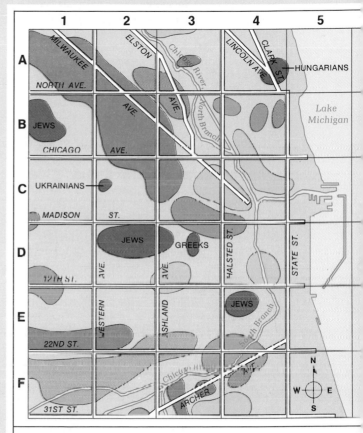

IMMIGRANT NEIGHBORHOODS IN CHICAGO, 1890

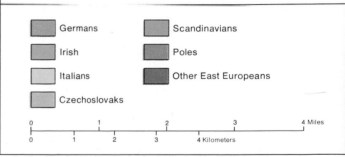

Germans   Scandinavians

Irish   Poles

Italians   Other East Europeans

Czechoslovaks

Many native-born Americans felt threatened by the wave of immigrants from Europe. In this nativist cartoon, Uncle Sam is a piper leading the "rats" of Europe to the United States. Nativists portrayed the newcomers as dangerous criminals. How does the cartoon show this?

overrode President Wilson's veto, and the bill became law.

Immigrants from China. Chinese immigrants faced special problems. In the 1860s, railroad builders brought over thousands of Chinese workers. After the railroads were finished, the Chinese looked for other jobs. They found many doors closed to them. Sometimes, they took jobs as strikebreakers, which made them unpopular with other workers.

The language, clothing, and customs of the Chinese set them apart. Some Chinese did not try to learn English and adopt American customs. They planned to stay in America for only a few years to make money. Then they expected to return home. But many other Chinese settled permanently on the west coast. Some opened restaurants and laundries. Others worked as shoemakers, tailors, and farmers. They helped to build up the economy of the West.

As the number of Chinese grew, violence broke out against them. Gangs attacked and sometimes killed Chinese during riots. In 1882, Congress responded to anti-Chinese feeling and passed the *Chinese Exclusion Act.* The act barred immigration from China for ten years. Congress renewed the law several times. It was finally repealed in 1943.

With the Chinese Exclusion Act, Congress limited immigration for the first time. But despite pressure from nativists, the country continued to welcome immigrants from Europe. What Emma Lazarus called America's "golden door" stayed open for most immigrants until 1917.

SECTION REVIEW

1. **Define:** assimilation.
2. **Locate:** Italy, Poland, Russia, Greece, China.
3. What conditions in Europe prompted many people to come to America?
4. (a) Where did most immigrants come from before 1885? (b) Where did most immigrants come from after 1885?
5. Describe two problems faced by immigrants.
6. **What Do You Think?** Why do you think immigration from China but not Europe was limited in the 1800s?

2 Striving Upward

Read to Learn

★ Why did American cities grow?
★ What different groups lived in cities?
★ How did people try to improve cities?
★ What do these words mean: settlement house?

By 1890, most of the lands of the West had been divided into farms and cattle ranches. As a result, fewer pioneers headed west to homestead. In fact, many people left their farms to move into cities.

A Growing Population

The population of American cities mushroomed in the late 1800s. In 1860, only one American in six lived in a city. By 1890, one out of every three Americans was a city dweller. By 1920, more than half of the American people lived in cities. Horace Greeley, a newspaper publisher, said, "We cannot all live in cities, yet nearly all seem determined to do so." For the first time in its history, the United States had cities as large as Paris and London. (See the maps below.)

The flood of immigrants from Europe was one reason cities grew so fast. Another reason was that many Americans gave up their farms to move to cities. A young man in a story by Hamlin

MAP SKILL These two maps show the growth of American cities from 1860 to 1900. How many cities appear on the 1860 map? On the 1900 map? How many cities had over 500,000 people by 1900?

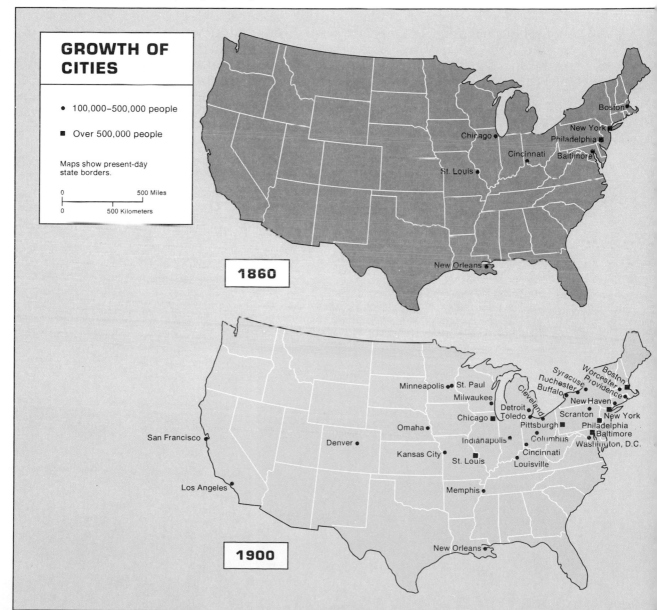

GROWTH OF CITIES

- ● 100,000–500,000 people
- ■ Over 500,000 people

Maps show present-day state borders.

0 — 500 Miles
0 — 500 Kilometers

1860

1860 map cities: Boston, New York, Philadelphia, Baltimore, Chicago, Cincinnati, St. Louis, New Orleans

1900

1900 map cities: San Francisco, Los Angeles, Denver, Minneapolis, St. Paul, Milwaukee, Omaha, Kansas City, St. Louis, Chicago, Detroit, Toledo, Cleveland, Indianapolis, Columbus, Cincinnati, Louisville, Memphis, Pittsburgh, Buffalo, Rochester, Syracuse, Scranton, New Haven, Worcester, Providence, Boston, New York, Philadelphia, Baltimore, Washington, D.C., New Orleans

Garland summed up the feelings of many farmers by saying, "I'm sick of farm life . . . it's nothing but fret, fret, and work the whole time, never going any place, never seeing anybody." In Chapter 20, you read about the hardships faced by many small farmers. (See pages 456–457.) Farmers, like immigrants, hoped to make a better life in the cities.

Cities attracted people because they offered jobs. Newcomers worked in steel mills, meat-packing plants, and garment factories. They took jobs as sales clerks, waiters, barbers, bank tellers, and secretaries. The bright lights and bustle of the city attracted people, too. Actors, singers, writers, and musicians found cities exciting places to live.

Life in the City

As cities grew in the late 1800s, many took on a similar shape. Poor people lived downtown, in the oldest section of the city. Farther out, the middle class lived in neat row houses or new apartment buildings. Beyond them lived the rich. They had fine homes with big lawns and plenty of trees. There were exceptions to this pattern, but most cities held to it.

Crowded slums. Poor families struggled to survive in crowded slums. Streets were jammed with people, horses, pushcarts, and trash. People lived in buildings packed side by side. Their apartments, called tenements, often had no windows, heat, or inside bathrooms. Sometimes, ten people slept together in one small room.

Outbreaks of typhoid and cholera were common in slums. Babies ran the greatest risk of dying from disease. In one Chicago slum, more than half of all babies died before they were one year old. In spite of the dangers, city slums became more and more crowded. Factories moved in to take advantage of low rents and cheap labor. They took over buildings and forced more people to live in fewer apartments.

The middle class. Just beyond the slums stood the well-kept houses of the middle class. The middle class included doctors, lawyers, office workers, and skilled crafts people. Middle class

American cities were home to the very rich and the very poor. At left, the Hatch family relaxes in the finely decorated living room of their home. At right, a poor family makes artificial flowers to sell. For the poor, a rundown apartment was often a workshop as well as a home. Children as young as age 4 worked all day. The seven workers in this picture made $3 a week.

homes often had a patch of lawn and a tree or two. In these neighborhoods, disease was kept under control.

Many middle class citizens joined clubs, bowling leagues, singing societies, and charity groups. These activities gave them a sense of community and purpose. One writer said that the clubs "bring together many people who are striving upward, trying to uplift themselves."

Life at the top. The very rich built mansions on "the cool green rim of the city." In Chicago, 200 millionaires lived along the exclusive lakefront by the 1880s. In New York, huge houses dotted Fifth Avenue, still on the city's outskirts. The rich lived like European royalty. They filled their mansions with priceless art works and gave lavish parties. Once, a man served the finest foods at a dinner for his friends' dogs. One couple gave a party that cost $369,000.

Improving City Life

People pouring into cities in the late 1800s created many problems. Cities did not have enough clean water for their booming populations. Crowded streets were littered with garbage. At night, unlighted streets became havens for pickpockets and thieves. Tenement buildings were death traps when fire broke out.

Cleaning up. In the 1880s, city dwellers campaigned to improve city life. They forced city governments to hire engineers and architects. These experts designed new water systems. New York City, for example, dug underground tunnels 100 miles north to the Catskill Mountains. The tunnels brought millions of gallons of pure water to the city every day.

Cities passed building codes. These codes required new buildings to have fire escapes and decent plumbing. Zoning laws passed in many cities put factories in different neighborhoods from apartment buildings. This cut down air pollution where people lived.

Cities hired workers to collect garbage and sweep the streets. They set up professional fire companies and trained police. Many cities improved public transportation as well.

A better life. Street lights were put up in many cities. The first street lights used gas. Later, electric lights lit city streets and avenues.

City planners like Frederick Law Olmstead found ways to get the most from open space in the city. Olmstead planned Central Park in New York City in the 1850s. Other cities followed this example. They set up zoos and gardens to give city people a taste of the country.

The largest cities created symphony orchestras, opera companies, and museums. Italians, Germans, Jews, and other immigrants made up most of the musicians and opera singers in America. Wealthy people like Andrew Carnegie gave money to build museums and concert halls.

Help for the Poor

Despite these improvements, many city people still faced hardships. For the poor, the only help came from charity. The Catholic Church responded to the needs of millions of poor Irish, Polish, and Italian immigrants. An Italian nun, Mother Cabrini, helped found more than 70 hospitals in North and South America. These hospitals treated poor people who could not afford to pay a doctor.

Protestant churches also set up charity programs for the poor. In 1878, a Methodist minister created the *Salvation Army* in London. A year later, the Salvation Army expanded to the United States. It offered food and shelter to the poor. The *YMCA* (Young Men's Christian Association) and *YWCA* (Young Women's Christian Association) were formed in this period.

Hull House offered many services to the poor of Chicago, most of whom were immigrants. Here, children and adults take part in a singing class. Singing songs helped the newcomers learn English.

Both taught classes, organized team sports, and held dances. These activities gave young people a chance to escape the drudgery of life in the slums.

Jane Addams and Hull House

Individuals like Jane Addams worked hard to help the poor. Although Addams came from a well-to-do family, she felt strong sympathy for poor people. After college, she devoted herself to improving life for the poor.

Addams moved into one of the poorest slums in Chicago. In 1889, she set up one of America's first settlement houses in an old mansion called Hull House. A *settlement house* is a center offering help to the poor. Other women volunteered to help Addams. These reformers cared for the children of mothers who worked outside the home. They organized sports and a theater for young people. They taught English to immigrants and showed people how to prevent disease.

Jane Addams and the other women at Hull House were called social workers. They worked as private citizens, but they felt that the government, too, should help the poor. Alice Hamilton, a doctor working in Hull House, campaigned for better health laws. Florence Kelley, also from Hull House, wanted to amend the Constitution to ban child labor. Despite Kelley's efforts, this was never done. But the success of Hull House inspired reformers to set up other settlement houses in cities around the country.

SECTION REVIEW
---

1. **Define:** settlement house.
2. Why did city populations boom in the late 1800s?
3. (a) Where did the poor usually live in cities? (b) Where did the rich live? (c) Where did the middle class live?
4. How did Jane Addams try to improve life for the poor?
5. **What Do You Think?** Why do you think so many people wanted to live in cities?

3 The World of the Cities

Read to Learn
★ How did cities change in the late 1800s?
★ What sports did Americans enjoy?
★ How did music influence American life?
★ What do these words mean: vaudeville, ragtime?

On a May evening in 1883, the New York sky sparkled with fireworks. The city was celebrating its newest wonder, the Brooklyn Bridge. It was the longest suspension bridge on earth. Its soaring arches were a monument to the bold new spirit of American cities.

The Building Boom

A tremendous building boom transformed America's cities in the late 1800s. Cities such as Chicago and New York grew so fast that there was hardly room to build in the downtown areas. As a result, planners and architects decided to build up instead of out.

Skyscrapers. The Chicago Fire of 1871 leveled the city's whole downtown. As the city was rebuilt, planners tried out many new building ideas. One was putting up tall buildings with many floors. New technology made these high-rise buildings possible. The high-rise had a skeleton of lightweight steel that held the weight of the building. Electric elevators zoomed office workers to upper floors.

The first high-rise was built in Chicago in 1885. It was ten stories tall. Soon, with better building methods, builders put up skyscrapers that towered over city streets. Skyscrapers got their name because their tops seemed to touch the sky.

Travel in cities. As skyscrapers went up, cities faced another problem, the traffic jam. Thousands of people worked in a small downtown area. At rush hour, streets were choked with horse-drawn buses, carriages, and carts.

To solve the traffic problem, New York built an elevated train, called the El. Steam engines pulled cars along tracks right past apartment buildings. One immigrant described her first trip on the El: "I was looking out the train window, and seeing what was going on. People had their windows open, and the train was going by. . . . I thought the train was going to go right through their rooms!" The El was fast. However, its steam engines showered soot and hot ashes onto streets and people below.

A great advance in city travel was the trolley, or streetcar. Trolleys ran on electricity carried by wires strung above the tracks. The first trolley was built in Richmond by Stephen Dudley Field, a friend of Thomas Edison's. Trolleys were fast, clean, and quiet. Their use soon spread throughout the country.

In 1897, Boston became the first American city to build a subway. A subway is an electric train that runs in tunnels under a city. In 1904, New York opened the first section of its subway system.

Department stores. The shopping areas of cities changed also in the late 1800s. Department stores offered shoppers everything they needed in one place. Earlier, people bought shoes in one store, socks in another, and dishes in a third.

In 1902, R. H. Macy's opened a nine-story building at Herald Square in New York. It had 33 elevators and a famous motto: "We sell goods cheaper than any house in the world." Other cities soon boasted large department stores like Macy's. They created a new form of entertainment—shopping. On Saturdays, customers spent hours going from floor to floor, looking at clothing, furniture, jewelry, cosmetics, and gifts.

In 1890, a new sensation swept the country, bicycling. That year, the safety bicycle went on the market. Earlier bicycles had a huge front wheel, so riders had to perch on a seat five feet off the ground. Safety bikes had wheels the same size. They got their name because their low seats made accidents far less likely.

Americans bought millions of safety bikes in the 1890s. Business people rode bikes to and from work. Whole families rode on Sunday outings. Many women were enthusiastic riders. Cycling gave them a new freedom. For middle class women, cycling was a way to get exercise and spend time outdoors.

The bicycle changed America. Because riders clamored for better roads, towns began paving roads for the first time. But the bicycle craze ended suddenly. After 1900, bike sales dropped off. Roads had been paved just in time for a new vehicle to enter the scene, the automobile. Many bike shops turned into auto repair shops after 1900.

★ Why do you think bicycle sales dropped off when people began to drive automobiles?

Sports in America

Most city dwellers worked in factories, stores, and offices. In their free time, they looked for ways to get outdoors. Sports gave them a chance to get outside and have a few hours of fun.

Baseball. Baseball became America's favorite sport. It was first played in New York in the 1840s. During the Civil War, soldiers from New York taught the sport to other Union troops. By the 1870s, the country had several professional teams and its first league.

Baseball was different in those days. Pitchers threw the ball underhand. Catchers caught it after the first bounce. Fielders did not wear gloves, so it was hard to catch the speeding hardball. As a result, scores were often high. One championship game ended with a score of 103 to 8.

Football. Another popular sport, football, grew out of soccer. Soccer had been played in America since colonial times. Some colleges had football teams even before the Civil War.

Early football called for lots of muscle and little skill. On every play, the two teams crashed together like fighting rams. The quarterback ran or jumped over the tangle of bodies. A European visitor described one football game as "a heap of 22 bodies tumbling on top of one another, like a knot of serpents with human heads."

Players did not wear helmets in the early days. They often were hurt. In one brutal season, 44 college players died from injuries. Some colleges banned the sport in response. Others drew up strict rules.

Basketball. In 1891, James Naismith invented a new sport called basketball. Naismith taught physical education at a YMCA in Springfield, Massachusetts. He wanted to create a sport that could be played indoors all winter.

At first, Naismith planned to use boxes, not hoops, as goals in the new game. But the janitor at the YMCA nailed two bushel baskets on the walls of the gym. Naismith had his players try to throw a soccer ball into the baskets. The game became very popular. It spread to other YMCAs and to schools and colleges around the country.

A Musical Nation

Sports was only one way people spent their leisure time. In the late 1800s, music was a popular pastime. Wealthy people attended the opera and the symphony. Many more people went to vaudeville shows or listened to ragtime music. *Vaudeville* (VAWD vihl) was a variety show that included comedians, song-and-dance routines, and acrobats. *Ragtime* was a new kind of music with a lively, rhythmic sound. Scott Joplin, son of a freed slave, helped make ragtime popular. His "Maple Leaf Rag," written in 1899, was a nationwide hit.

American songwriters produced many popular songs. Even though the radio had not yet been invented, songs such as "There'll Be a Hot Time in the Old Town Tonight" swept the nation in weeks. New songs were played in music halls and on vaudeville stages. Among the most popular were military marches written by John Philip Sousa. Sousa wrote more than 100 marches, including "The Stars and Stripes Forever." His marches became favorites at Fourth of July celebrations.

In the 1880s and 1890s, Edison's phonograph was steadily improved. Americans bought phonographs to listen to recordings of popular songs. By 1900, millions of records had been sold.

Music and other entertainments brought Americans together. People from different backgrounds enjoyed popular songs and stage shows. And it was not only city people who saw shows. The growing train system made it possible for stage shows, circuses, and wild west shows to tour the nation. Traveling shows brought the excitement and action of city life to small towns.

━━SECTION REVIEW━━

1. **Define:** vaudeville, ragtime.
2. Why did cities put up skyscrapers?
3. Describe two ways cities improved transportation.
4. What sports were popular in the late 1800s?
5. **What Do You Think?** Why do you think music was especially important in a nation of people from many different countries?

4 A Thriving Culture

Read to Learn

★ How did the country's education system improve?
★ What did Americans read?
★ What American painters won acclaim?
★ What do these words mean: yellow journalism, realist?

By the late 1800s, America was taking its place as a leading nation in the world. Its bustling cities were signs of a strong economy. American culture also thrived. Both native-born Americans and immigrants produced works of art, music, and literature.

Educating Americans

After the Civil War, American schools improved rapidly. In the South, the Freedmen's Bureau built thousands of grade schools for blacks and whites. In the North, most states passed laws that required children to attend school, usually through sixth grade. In cities such as Boston and New York, public schools taught young immigrants to speak English. Schoolchildren also learned about the duties and rights of American citizens.

Many cities and towns built public high schools after 1870. By 1900, the country had 6,000 high schools. Higher education improved as well. New private colleges opened. Many states built universities that offered free or low-cost college education to women and men. The number of private colleges for women also increased.

Gifts from Andrew Carnegie and other wealthy people helped many cities and towns build public libraries. Libraries were more than a place to find books and magazines. Often, speakers gave talks on topics such as archaeology and medicine. The growth of education through schools and libraries made Americans eager to learn new ideas.

Read All About It

As Americans became better educated, they read more of everything—newspapers, magazines, and books. Newspapers grew dramatically after 1880. By 1900, half the newspapers in the world were printed in the United States.

The need to know. The large number of newspapers reflected the growth of American cities. In towns and villages, people got news from friends and neighbors. But in the city, people had thousands of "neighbors." There was so much news every day that people needed newspapers to keep up with it.

Newspapers let people find out important news in a hurry. Papers featured short, colorful stories about local politics, business, fashion, and sports. Many immigrants learned English by spelling their way through a daily paper. At the same time, they learned about life in America.

Native-born Americans, in turn, learned about immigrants through the papers. Stories about the Greek, Slavic, Polish, and Italian communities helped people understand and accept their immigrant neighbors. In this way, newspapers helped tie together the different people who lived in cities. They also helped people develop a sense of being New Yorkers, Chicagoans, or Bostonians.

Pulitzer and Hearst. The first really modern paper was Joseph Pulitzer's New York *World*. Pulitzer was a Hungarian immigrant. When he bought the *World* in 1883, he wanted to make it bright, lively, and "truly democratic."

Pulitzer introduced sports pages and comic strips. The *World* was also the first paper to use pictures and bold headlines. They made news stories more exciting. The *World* covered crime stories and political scandals in a sensational way. These changes made the *World's* circulation skyrocket.

William Randolph Hearst, who came to New York City from San Francisco, soon challenged Pulitzer. Hearst bought the New York *Journal* and began to print more scandals, crime stories, and gossip than the *World*. Critics coined the term **yellow journalism** for the sensational style of the *World* and the *Journal*. They said that the papers offered less news and more scandal every day.

Women and the press. Newspapers included special sections for women. These sections covered fashion, social events, health, homemaking, and family matters. Papers rarely pushed for women's rights, however. Most were afraid to take bold positions that would lose readers.

Some women worked as reporters. Nellie Bly became a reporter for Pulitzer's *World*. Once, she pretended to be

Many new grade schools and high schools were built after the Civil War. In farm areas, however, one-room schoolhouses were still common. Winslow Homer painted this picture, called *The Country School*.

insane in order to find out about care in a New York mental hospital. Her articles exposed cruelty and led to reform in the care of the mentally ill.

The Reading Public

Newspapers flourished in part because more Americans were reading. The public turned to magazines and books as well as newspapers.

Magazines appealed to different readers. Middle class women enjoyed the *Ladies' Home Journal,* begun in the 1880s. It featured articles about famous people and stories by well-known authors. By 1900, it had one million readers. Older magazines, such as *Harper's Monthly* and the *Nation,* also won new readers. Their articles about politics and current events helped keep the public informed.

Dime novels. In the late 1800s, paperback books became popular. Among the best-selling books of the time were dime novels. These low-priced paperbacks featured adventure stories. Many told about the "Wild West." Young people read dime novels eagerly, even though parents often disapproved of the stories. One critic complained: "Stories for children used to begin, 'Once upon a time there lived— ' Now they begin, 'Vengeance, blood, death," shouted Rattlesnake Jim.' "

American writers. Many American writers became popular in the late 1800s. For the first time, Americans read more books by American authors than British authors.

Horatio Alger was a best-selling author of the time. He wrote over 100 books for children. Most told the story of a poor boy who becomes rich and respected through his hard work and honesty. These rags-to-riches stories were widely read. They gave many people the hope that even the poorest person could get rich in America.

In the 1880s, a new crop of writers appeared. Many had been newspaper

AMERICANS WHO DARED

Mark Twain

Mark Twain was the best-known American author of the late 1800s. This fame meant that newspapers and magazines were always ready to publish his opinions. At times, however, Twain's biting criticisms of America angered readers. He spared no one. In one article, Twain attacked the harsh rule of the Russian emperor. In another, he criticized Congress for passing the Chinese Exclusion Act. Yet Twain never lost his sense of humor. When newspapers wrote that he had died of a disease, Twain sent out this note: "Reports of my death are greatly exaggerated."

reporters. They had seen the poverty created by the Industrial Revolution. They were called realists. *Realists* wanted to show life just as it was. In reaction to writers like Alger, they told about people who had little hope.

Stephen Crane wrote one story about a young girl who is born and dies in a filthy slum. He is best known for his short novel about the Civil War, *The Red Badge of Courage*. Hamlin Garland, another author, wrote about the hardships faced by farmers in the 1890s. Jack London, born in California, told about the hard life of miners and sailors on the west coast.

One writer of the 1800s was almost unknown in her time. Emily Dickinson lived a quiet life in Amherst, Massachusetts. She wrote hundreds of poems, but only seven were printed while she lived. After her death, her sister collected the poems and published them. Today, Dickinson is counted among the most important American poets.

Mark Twain. The most popular American writer of the 1800s was Samuel Clemens. He was better known by his pen name, Mark Twain. Twain was born in Missouri. As a young man, he worked on a Mississippi steamboat. There, he heard the boatmen's cry "Mark Twain," meaning that the river was two "marks," or 12 feet, deep. He took it as his name.

Twain had an ear for how Americans talked in different parts of the country. He also had an American dislike of snobbery. He used down-home, gritty characters to make fun of people who acted important. His stories became so well known that people would quote them to win an argument.

Twain's two best-known works were *Tom Sawyer* and *Huckleberry Finn*. *Huckleberry Finn* takes place along the Mississippi River before the Civil War. Huck is a country boy who ends up helping an escaped slave named Jim. Huck and Jim share adventures and become good friends.

Though the novel is funny, Twain had a serious point to make. He wanted to show that friendship is more important to Huck than the laws that made Jim a slave. *Huckleberry Finn* soon became a classic. Even so, some schools and libraries refused to buy the book. They claimed that Huck was a rough character who would have a bad influence on children.

Mary Cassatt learned to paint by studying works of art in museums. This painting, *The Boating Party,* shows Cassatt's bold use of color and her favorite subjects, a mother and child.

American Art

In the late 1800s, American artists also developed a realist style. They painted everyday scenes rather than great events.

One realist artist was Winslow Homer. As a young man during the Civil War, Homer drew battle scenes for northern magazines. After the war, he painted views of New England. In 1883, he moved to Maine. There, he painted the ocean and the hardy fishing people of the coast. (See page 495.)

Another realist was Thomas Eakins. Eakins studied in Europe, but his style was uniquely American. He paid great attention to detail and produced works as precise as photographs. One of Eakins' students was the black painter Henry Tanner. Tanner won fame for pictures of black sharecroppers. Later, he moved to Paris to escape prejudice in America.

Several other fine American artists moved to Europe. James Whistler of Massachusetts lived in Paris and London. His work influenced young European painters. John Singer Sargent also lived abroad. His portraits of wealthy Europeans made him rich.

The work of Mary Cassatt (kuh SAT), on the other hand, won few admirers at first. She was born in Pennsylvania but settled in Paris. Cassatt painted bright, imaginative pictures. Today, she is considered a founder of modern art.

━━SECTION REVIEW━━

1. **Define:** yellow journalism, realist.
2. How did Joseph Pulitzer make newspapers more popular?
3. What kinds of books did the reading public enjoy?
4. **What Do You Think?** Why do you think realism was a popular style of writing and painting in America in the late 1800s?

Chapter 22 Review

★ Summary ★

Newcomers flooded America after the Civil War. By 1885, many were coming from Southern and Eastern Europe. Some native-born Americans tried to limit immigration. But America's golden door stayed open to most people until 1917.

Cities grew rapidly. To cope with their booming populations, cities made improvements in many areas. But for the poorest, the only relief came from charity.

In the new cities, people worked in skyscrapers, rode trolleys, and shopped in stores. They enjoyed sports and a variety of music. Newspapers kept city people informed, and American writers and artists won larger audiences.

★ Reviewing the Facts ★

2 pts.

Key Terms. Match each term in Column 1 with the correct definition in Column 2.

Column 1	Column 2
1. settlement house	a. show including comedy, song and dance, and acrobatics
2. vaudeville	b. lively, rhythmic music
3. ragtime	c. sensational style used by some newspapers
4. yellow journalism	d. center offering help to the poor
5. realist	e. writer or artist who shows life as it is

Key People, Events, and Ideas. Identify each of the following.

1. Ellis Island
2. Chinese Exclusion Act
3. Mother Cabrini
4. Jane Addams
5. John Philip Sousa
6. Scott Joplin
7. Joseph Pulitzer
8. William Randolph Hearst
9. Nellie Bly
10. Jack London
11. Emily Dickinson
12. Mark Twain
13. Winslow Homer
14. Henry Tanner
15. Mary Cassatt

★ Chapter Checkup ★

5 pts.

1. (a) Why did millions of immigrants come to the United States in the late 1800s? (b) How did American businesses encourage immigrants to come?

2. (a) Why did the new immigrants have a hard time making their way in America? (b) How did children help immigrant families adjust to America?

3. (a) Why did Chinese immigrants face special prejudice? (b) How did Congress respond to anti-Chinese feelings?

4. (a) What problems did cities face as their populations grew? (b) What steps did cities take to improve urban life?

5. How did cities change as they grew in the late 1800s?

6. (a) How did public schools improve after the Civil War? (b) In what ways did higher education expand?

7. How did newspapers help immigrants and native-born Americans understand each other better?

8. (a) What realist writers were popular in the late 1800s? (b) What did they write about?

10pts

1. **Understanding the economy.** What economic factors prompted European immigrants and American farmers to move to American cities?

2. **Analyzing a quotation.** Read the quotation from the guidebook for immigrants on page 484. Why does the book advise immigrants to forget their past?

3. **Learning about citizenship.** (a) How do you think cheering for the same base-ball team helped bring together people of different backgrounds? (b) How might baseball have helped people develop a feeling of loyalty to their city?

4. **Relating past to present.** (a) What did city dwellers in the 1800s do to escape the pressure of city life? (b) How do city people relax today?

★ **Using Your Skills** ★

1. **Writing a summary.** A summary tells the most important ideas in as few words as possible. It helps you understand, remember, and review information. A useful summary includes the main ideas and several major facts. Read "A Growing Population" on pages 487–488. (a) List the main idea of each paragraph. (b) List two major facts for each main idea. (c) Write a summary of the three paragraphs.

2. **Comparing.** Study the two pictures on page 488. (a) What does each picture show? (b) How are the homes in the pictures different? (c) How do you think the lives of the two families differed?

3. **Map reading.** Study the two maps on page 487. (a) What does each map show? (b) Which cities had populations over 500,000 in 1860? In 1900? (c) In what part of the country were most of the cities in 1900?

4. **Using a time line.** Study the time lines on pages 436–437 and 480. (a) How many years after the passage of the Chinese Exclusion Act was the Statue of Liberty unveiled? (b) How many years after Macy's opened its doors was the first subway opened in New York City?

★ **More to Do** ★

1. **Drawing a cartoon.** Draw a cartoon that tells immigrants in the late 1800s how to adjust to America.

2. **Exploring local history.** Use the library to find out more about a city in your area. Then write a report describing how the city's population grew, what its main industries were and are today, and what immigrant groups came in large numbers to the city.

3. **Writing an article.** Imagine that you are a sportswriter for a newspaper in the 1890s. Write a newspaper article describing a new sport sweeping the nation, basketball.

4. **Illustrating a story.** Read a short story by Mark Twain, Hamlin Garland, Stephen Crane, or Jack London. Then draw a picture illustrating a scene in the story. Did the author's realism help you visualize the picture?

Unit 7 Review

Chapter 20 As Americans moved west after the Civil War, they forced the Plains Indians onto reservations. Ranchers built a Cattle Kingdom in the 1870s, and homesteaders steadily carved the plains into farms. Because of low grain prices, farmers organized the Populist Party in the 1880s. Populism faded after William Jennings Bryan failed to become President in 1896.

Chapter 21 Industry grew rapidly after 1865. Railroad building fueled the growth of big business by opening up new markets. New ways to do business, such as the corporation and trust, flourished. At the same time, factory workers faced harsh conditions. Their efforts to win better conditions often led to violence.

Chapter 22 Newcomers poured into America after the Civil War. For the first time, many came from Southern and Eastern Europe. They swelled American cities. Skyscrapers, trolleys, subways, and huge stores were features of the growing cities. American culture also thrived and helped to bind together people from many different backgrounds.

★ **Unit Checkup** ★

Choose the phrase that best completes each of the following statements.

1. In the late 1800s, buffalo herds were nearly wiped out by
   (a) Sioux Indians.
   (b) disease.
   (c) white hunters.

2. Because of low grain prices in the 1880s, farmers supported
   (a) free silver.
   (b) high railroad rates.
   (c) the Homestead Act.

3. Critics of big business said that trusts and monopolies
   (a) made better products.
   (b) lowered prices for consumers.
   (c) ended competition.

4. Factory owners hired women and children because
   (a) women and children worked harder than men.
   (b) women and children could be paid less than men.
   (c) factory owners wanted to help women and children make a living.

5. To keep immigrants out of the United States, nativists formed the
   (a) American Protective Association.
   (b) Salvation Army.
   (c) Knights of Labor.

★ **Building American Citizenship** ★

1. (a) How did the lives of women homesteaders differ from those of women in the East? (b) Why do you think women on the plains were treated more as equals by men than women in the East were?

2. (a) Why did farmers form the Populist Party in 1891? (b) Why do political parties today take an interest in the economic problems of farmers?

3. How did each of the following help immigrants in the late 1800s to be assimilated: (a) public schools and libraries; (b) newspapers; (c) sporting events; (d) popular music?

The bar graph below shows the growth of four American cities between 1850 and 1900. Study the bar graph. Then answer the following questions.

1. Which city had the largest population in 1850? In 1880? In 1900?

2. (a) Which city had the smallest population in 1850? (b) Where did this city rank in population in 1880? (c) Where did it rank in 1900?

3. (a) Which cities are on the east coast? (b) Which cities are in the Midwest?

4. (a) Why do you think the population of Chicago was small in 1850? (b) Why do you think Chicago grew so rapidly?

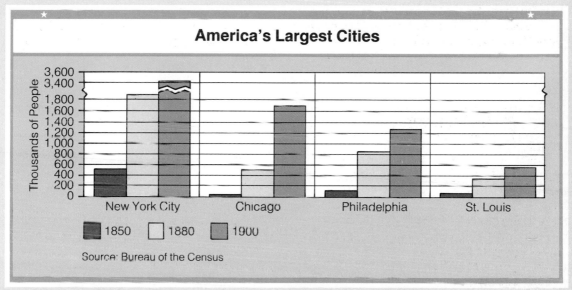

America's Largest Cities

Thousands of People

3,600 / 3,400 / 1,800 / 1,600 / 1,400 / 1,200 / 1,000 / 800 / 600 / 400 / 200 / 0

New York City   Chicago   Philadelphia   St. Louis

■ 1850   □ 1880   ▨ 1900

Source: Bureau of the Census

History Writer's Handbook

Arranging Information for Comparison

Comparison order is arrangement of supporting information according to similarities and differences. One way is to group the information by subject.

Look at the following topic sentence. *The new immigrants were different from the old immigrants.* The subjects being compared are the old and new immigrants. In the detail sentences, first present all the information about one subject. For example: *Most old immigrants came from Northern and Western Europe. Many spoke English. And many were Protestants.*

Then, using a transition, present all the information about the other subject. Put the information in the same order (area of origin, language, and religion).

Common transitions for differences include *but, however, in contrast, instead, on the contrary, on the other hand,* and *unlike.* Common transitions for similarities include *both, like, similarly,* and *similar to.*

Practice Using the instructions above, write detail sentences about the new immigrants to complete the comparison. (See page 483 for the information.)

Unit 8

BECOMING A WORLD POWER

1866		1875		1884		1893

ULYSSES GRANT

ANDREW JOHNSON · RUTHERFORD HAYES · CHESTER ARTHUR · BENJAMIN HARRISON

JAMES GARFIELD · GROVER CLEVELAND

1860s–70s Boss Tweed controls New York City politics
1867 ★ Nebraska statehood; Seward buys Alaska; Midway Island annexed
1869 National Woman Suffrage Association formed
1874 Women's Christian Temperance Union formed

1870s Cattle Kingdom spreads; Age of Imperialism begins
1876 ★ Colorado statehood; Battle of Little Bighorn
1877 Reconstruction ends
1882 Chinese Exclusion Act
1883 Civil Service Commission set up

1887 Interstate Commerce Commission set up
1889 ★ Montana, North Dakota, South Dakota, Washington become states; Pan-American Union
1890 ★ Idaho, Wyoming become states; Sherman Antitrust Act
1890s Great White Fleet built

1866		1875		1884		1893

1874 The Women's Christian Temperance Union worked to end the sale of alcohol.

Late 1800s Immigrants helped to build America's rapidly growing cities.

Late 1800s *Four-in-Hand* by Thoma Eakins shows a wealthy family out a ride in the country.

1893	1902	1911	1920

THEODORE ROOSEVELT   WILLIAM TAFT   WOODROW WILSON

GROVER CLEVELAND   WILLIAM MCKINLEY

1897–98 Alaska gold rush
1898 *Maine* explosion; Spanish–American War; Hawaii annexed
1899 Open Door Policy, Boxer Rebellion
1900s Progressive Movement wins reforms
1901 Platt Amendment gives United States naval base in Cuba

1904 Roosevelt Corollary; Supreme Court decides Northern Securities case
1905 United States intervenes in Dominican Republic
1906 Meat Inspection Act; Pure Food and Drug Act
1907 ★ Oklahoma statehood
1909 NAACP formed

1912 ★ New Mexico, Arizona become states; Bull Moose Party formed
1914 Panama Canal opens; Clayton Antitrust Act
1914–18 World War I
1915 *Lusitania* sunk
1917 Russian Revolution begins; United States enters World War I
1919 Versailles Treaty
1920 Women win suffrage

1893	1902	1911	1920

Late 1800s In *The Lost Bet* by Joseph Klir, a defeated candidate for office pulls his successful rival to city hall.

Early 1900s In this political cartoon, Theodore Roosevelt wears the Panama Canal as a crown.

I WANT YOU
FOR U.S. ARMY
NEAREST RECRUITING STATION

1917 Americans joined the armed services in response to recruiting posters such as this one.

Calls for Reform (1876–1914)

Chapter Outline

1 Reform Begins
2 The Progressive Spirit
3 Victories for Women
4 Progressives in the White House
5 The Struggle for Justice

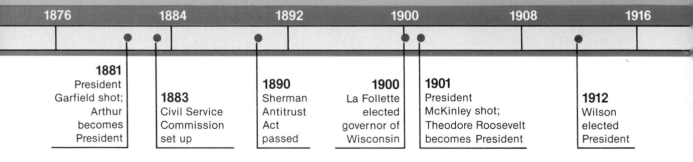

1876	1884	1892	1900	1908	1916

1881
President Garfield shot; Arthur becomes President

1883
Civil Service Commission set up

1890
Sherman Antitrust Act passed

1900
La Follette elected governor of Wisconsin

1901
President McKinley shot; Theodore Roosevelt becomes President

1912
Wilson elected President

About This Chapter

For many Americans, the early 1900s was a time of great hope. Prosperity had returned after hard times in the 1890s. People enjoyed luxuries their parents had never dreamed of, such as telephones, electric lights, and phonographs. On the eve of the year 1900, the New York *Times* wrote that the 1800s were "marked by greater progress in . . . the material wellbeing and enlightenment of mankind than all previous history." Most Americans hoped for even greater progress during the new century.

But the good times were not good for everybody. The rapid growth of American industry created problems as well as benefits. Many Americans worried about the political power wielded by trusts and monopolies.

The cities of America staggered under the burdens of overcrowding and corruption. In mines and factories, children still worked away their health and youth.

Beginning in the 1890s, Americans set out to correct the problems created by industrial growth. Reformers worked for a whole range of improvements. These reformers were united by their belief that in a great nation like the United States, life should be good for everyone. The reforms they achieved included four constitutional amendments. Their efforts helped to shape the society, government, and economy of the modern United States.

Study the time line above. Who became President after Garfield was shot?

In the late 1800s, many Americans worried that giant trusts had too much influence over Congress.

1 Reform Begins

Read to Learn

★ How did the government fight corruption in the late 1800s?

★ What steps did Congress take to regulate big business?

★ What do these words mean: civil service?

In the late 1800s, business rather than politics attracted the best minds of the day. Andrew Carnegie and John D. Rockefeller influenced American life more than President Cleveland or President Harrison. Yet important political issues did come up during these years. Among the most serious was corruption in government.

Efforts to End Corruption

Corruption in government was widespread during the late 1800s. One source of corruption was the spoils system. Another was the influence of big business in Congress.

Growth of the spoils system. Government had grown along with the country since the Age of Jackson. So, too, had the spoils system. Whenever a new President took over, hundreds of office seekers swarmed into Washington. Too often, officeholders used their positions for their own ends. A New York customs inspector or an Indian affairs agent in Oklahoma could steal money from those they were supposed to serve. Corrupt officials had little fear of being caught.

Reforming Presidents. Calls for reform in the spoils system slowly brought change. In 1877, Rutherford B. Hayes was elected President, in part because he was a reformer. Hayes took a first step toward ending the spoils system. He refused to appoint his own supporters to office unless they were qualified for the job.

James Garfield, a Republican, followed Hayes into the White House in 1881. He, too, tried to limit the spoils system. Garfield called for reform of the civil service. The *civil service* includes all federal jobs except for elected positions and those in the armed forces.

Garfield believed that people should get government jobs on the basis of merit instead of as rewards for political support. That way, he said, only the best-qualified people would work for the government.

Garfield had little chance to put his reform into practice. In July 1881, he was shot. His attacker was an angry office seeker who had not been given a government job. The public was outraged by the killing and demanded an end to the spoils system.

The Civil Service Commission. On Garfield's death, Vice President Chester A. Arthur became President. As a New York politician, Arthur had used the spoils system. But as President, he worked with Congress to curb it. In 1883, Congress set up the Civil Service Commission.

The *Civil Service Commission* was responsible for filling vacant jobs in the federal government. It was made up of both Democrats and Republicans. The commission gave exams to people seeking federal jobs. Those who did best on the exams got the jobs.

At first, only a few federal jobs were under the control of the Civil Service Commission. Under pressure from reformers, however, later Presidents added more jobs to the civil service list. By 1900, about 40 percent of all federal jobs were under the commission.

Controlling Big Business

By the late 1800s, big business had strong influence over politics. Often, business leaders wanted Congress to pass laws favorable to them. Railroad owners and other industrial giants offered bribes to congressmen. In return, congressmen voted for bills that would help these business leaders.

Ending bribes was not easy. However, the government did try to stop wrongdoing by railroad owners and other industrialists. President Grover Cleveland took the first steps. In 1887, he signed a bill creating the *Interstate Commerce Commission,* or ICC.

The ICC was set up to end abuses such as pools and rebates in the railroad industry. (See page 463.) At first, the commission was not very strong. Lawyers for the railroads won cases in court. Without support from the courts, the ICC had little power. Even so, the ICC showed that the government was trying to end the worst abuses by big business.

In 1888, President Cleveland lost his bid for reelection. Benjamin Harrison, grandson of President William Henry Harrison, became President. During Harrison's term, Congress passed the Sherman Antitrust Act. At first the act was used against unions, not trusts (see page 477.) As the reform spirit grew, however, courts began to use the Sherman Act to break up monopolies.

━━ SECTION REVIEW ━━

1. **Define:** civil service.
2. How did the following try to limit the spoils system: (a) Rutherford B. Hayes; (b) James Garfield; (c) Chester A. Arthur?
3. (a) Why did Congress create the ICC? (b) Why was the ICC weak at first?
4. **What Do You Think?** Why do you think President Garfield's death roused the public against the spoils system?

Jacob Riis:
How the Other Half Lives

Jacob Riis was born in Denmark and came to the United States when he was 21 years old. He learned English and became a police reporter for a New York City newspaper. Riis had a special concern for the poor. He worked with settlement house workers and other reformers to set up parks and playgrounds and to improve schools.

★ How do you think photographs like this one encouraged reform?

Riis did all he could to jolt the public into taking an interest in the poor. In a book on slum conditions called *How the Other Half Lives*, Riis beckoned to his readers: "Come over here. Step carefully over this baby—it is a baby, [in] spite of its rags and dirt." Riis was best known for his photographs of people living in New York's poorest slums.

2 The Progressive Spirit

Read to Learn

★ How did muckrakers change the mood of the public?
★ What was the Progressive Movement?
★ What do these words mean: muckraker, public interest, primary, initiative, referendum, recall?

While the President and Congress sought to reform national government, other calls for reform rang out. In cities across America, reformers tried to get rid of dishonest politicians. They also worked to give voters a greater role in government.

Newspapers Sound the Call

A spirit of reform swept America's cities in the late 1800s. Among the loudest voices for reform were those of city newspaper reporters. Reporters actually went into the worst slums. There, they saw the smoking ruins left by fires. They talked to mothers whose babies were dying of tuberculosis.

Jacob Riis, a New York reporter and photographer, wrote a book called *How the Other Half Lives*. In it, he took readers on a written tour of the city's slums. Riis and others reported on the terrible conditions there. They also exposed the corruption that prevented proper fire protection, medical care, and sanitation in the cities.

After reading these stories, many middle class city dwellers joined in the demand for reform. They were shocked to read of corrupt politicians who pocketed tax money and turned their backs on the problems of the cities.

Muckrakers

A New York politician, Theodore Roosevelt, made fun of one reporter who wrote about corruption. Roosevelt said the reporter was always sifting through the dirt, or muck. He called the reporter a *muckraker*. Roosevelt meant the name as an insult. But muckrakers proudly took up the title.

Lincoln Steffens was one muckraker. He made city corruption his target. In articles, he told how corrupt politicians ran cities such as St. Louis and Pittsburgh. He gave reformers the facts they needed to launch campaigns against corruption.

Muckrakers not only looked at city politics. They also studied big business. Ida Tarbell wrote a series of articles about unfair practices used by the Standard Oil Company. Her articles raised a clamor for tighter controls on business trusts. (See page 510.)

Even more shocking were the stories Upton Sinclair wrote. In a novel called *The Jungle,* Sinclair revealed gruesome details about the meatpacking industry in Chicago. Although *The Jungle* was fiction, it was based on true reports. For example, Sinclair told about rats in the meatpacking houses:

> These rats were nuisances, and the packers would put poisoned bread out for them: they would die, and then rats, bread, and meat would go into the hoppers together. This is no fairy story and no joke . . . there were things that went into the sausage in comparison with which a poisoned rat was a tidbit.

Sinclair wrote his novel to show the misery of workers in the meatpacking houses. But readers were much more outraged to learn about the rats and other filth that went into their breakfast sausages. The public outcry was so great that the federal government passed laws to ensure that meat was properly inspected. (See page 518.)

Muckrakers helped change the mood of the public. Before their stories were published, many people tolerated corruption and paid little attention to reformers. Once people saw how corrupt politicians and businesses threatened the nation, they joined with muckrakers to demand reform.

Battling Corrupt City Governments

In many cities, bribery and corruption were a way of life. Nothing could be done without paying off the city boss. Often, the boss did not even hold office. Instead, he worked behind the scenes to influence the mayor and other officials.

Big city bosses held power by taking advantage of immigrants and other poor city dwellers. Since the poor needed help badly, it was easy for bosses to win them over. Bosses gave the poor extra coal in winter and turkeys at Thanksgiving. They helped immigrants become citizens and find jobs. Bosses also threw big parties in parks or at beaches. In this way, bosses won the loyal support of the city poor.

In New York City during the 1860s and 1870s, Boss William Tweed carried corruption to new heights. Tweed fleeced New York out of $100 million. Reformers tried to put Tweed behind bars. The New York *Times* published stories about his wrongdoings. The *Times* also published cartoons by Thomas Nast attacking Tweed. (See page 509.)

Tweed disliked Nast's cartoons most of all. His followers might not be

Thomas Nast often attacked Boss Tweed in cartoons such as this. Tweed is the heavyset bearded man seated at left. He sits like a Roman emperor at the arena. The tiger stands for Tweed's political allies, who ran New York City. The tiger's victims represent voters, whose weapons—law and the ballot—lie useless on the ground.

able to read, Tweed admitted, but they could look at pictures. Tweed offered Nast $100,000 to go to Europe and "study art." Nast turned down the bribe and kept up his attacks. In the end, Tweed had to flee the country. Police in Spain arrested Tweed after recognizing him from one of Nast's cartoons. He died in a Manhattan jail in 1876. Thousands of poor New Yorkers mourned his death.

Reformers made city bosses like Tweed the target of their campaigns. Reform groups formed good government leagues. Their goal was to replace corrupt officials with honest leaders.

In many cities, reformers met with success. For example, the good government league in Minneapolis sent the corrupt mayor and his henchmen to prison. In Cleveland, reformers elected Tom Johnson as mayor. Johnson improved sewage systems and garbage collection in the city. He also set up ser-

vices to help the poor. To pay for these improvements, however, he had to raise taxes on business.

The Progressive Movement

By 1900, these efforts at reform in the cities were called the *Progressive Movement.* Both Republicans and Democrats were Progressives. Together, they worked to correct injustice in American society.

Progressives fought for many different causes. They were never united in a single party or group. Yet they held certain beliefs in common. They believed in the *public interest,* or the good of all the people. The public interest, they said, must not be sacrificed to the greed of a few huge trusts and city bosses.

The Wisconsin Idea. Progressives won their first great success in Wisconsin. There, voters elected Robert La

AMERICANS WHO DARED

Ida Tarbell

Ida Tarbell was a noted Progressive. She alarmed the public with a series of articles about John D. Rockefeller. For five years, Tarbell gathered facts about Rockefeller's business practices. She concluded that too often Rockefeller had "played with loaded dice, and it is doubtful if there has ever been a time since 1872 when he has run a race with a competitor and started fair."

Follette as governor in 1900. "Battling Bob" La Follette introduced a whole program of Progressive reforms. For this reason, people around the country spoke of the *Wisconsin Idea*.

La Follette relied on the advice of experts at the University of Wisconsin. Complicated problems, he claimed, needed experts to solve them. On the advice of experts, the governor lowered railroad rates. The result was increased rail traffic, which helped both railroads and customers.

Progressives from other states visited Wisconsin to learn about La Follette's system. Before long, voters in California, Indiana, Arkansas, Oregon, and New York had elected Progressive governors. They soon introduced far-reaching changes.

More power to voters. Progressive officials urged a number of reforms that gave voters more power. Among them were the primary, initiative, referendum, and recall.

Since Andrew Jackson's time, political parties held conventions to pick a candidate for President. But party leaders still picked candidates for local and state office. Progressives urged parties to hold primaries before the general election. In a *primary,* voters choose their party's candidate from among several people. Wisconsin was the first state to adopt the primary. By 1916, all but three states had done so.

Progressives did not like the fact that only members of a state legislature could introduce bills. They urged states to adopt the initiative. The *initiative* gave voters the right to introduce a law for the state legislature to vote on. All they had to do was get enough people to sign a petition in favor of the law.

The *referendum* went a step further by giving the voters themselves the power to make a bill become law. If enough voters signed a referendum petition, the people of the state voted on the bill on the next election day. If the voters approved it, the bill became state law.

Another Progressive measure was the recall. The *recall* allowed voters to remove an elected official from office. This gave voters a chance to remove corrupt officials.

Other Progressive Goals

Progressives had many other goals. Most wanted to lower the tariff on imported goods. They felt that American industry should compete against foreign imports. This competition would lower prices for consumers, Progressives argued.

Most Progressives also supported a graduated income tax. The tax would make up for money that the government lost by lowering the tariff. It required wealthy people to pay a higher percentage of their income as tax than poor and middle-class people.

In 1895, the Supreme Court ruled that an income tax was unconstitutional. As a result, Progressives called for an amendment to the Constitution. In 1909, Congress passed the *Sixteenth Amendment*. The amendment gave Congress the power to impose an income tax. It was ratified by three fourths of the states by 1913.

Progressives worked for another amendment. Since 1789, senators had been elected by state legislatures. Progressives believed that special inter- ests sometimes bribed legislators to vote for pro-business candidates. They wanted to end such abuses by having voters elect senators directly. In 1912 Congress approved the *Seventeenth Amendment*. By 1913, the amendment was ratified and became part of the Constitution.

SECTION REVIEW

1. **Define:** muckraker, public interest, primary, initiative, referendum, recall.
2. How did muckrakers help change the public attitude toward corruption?
3. (a) Who was Boss Tweed? (b) How did reformers attack Tweed's corrupt government?
4. (a) What was the Wisconsin Idea? (b) How did it influence reformers in other parts of the country?
5. **What Do You Think?** Why do you think Progressives wanted the voters to have more power?

3 Victories for Women

Read to Learn
★ How did women win the right to vote?
★ What other opportunities did women gain?
★ How did women try to ban the sale of alcohol?
★ What does this word mean: suffragist?

Women helped lead the Progressive Movement from the start. Jane Addams and other settlement house workers were among the best-known Progressives of the time.

Women and the Vote

The most important goal for many Progressive women was women's suffrage. With the vote, women could gain the political power to achieve other Progressive reforms.

A slow start. The struggle for women's suffrage went back many years. As you read, the Seneca Falls Convention in 1848 called for women's suffrage. After the Civil War, Elizabeth Cady Stanton and Susan B. Anthony took up the fight again. In 1869, they formed the National Woman Suffrage Association. The group worked to amend the Constitution to give women the vote.

Women in the West. Women faced an uphill battle. Few politicians supported their goal. However, in the late 1800s, women gained the right to vote in four western states: Wyoming, Utah, Colorado, and Idaho. Pioneer women had worked alongside men to build the farms and cities of the West. By giving women the right to vote, these states

Historians often try to identify trends, or developments that take place over time. They look at many facts over a period of years. From these facts, they learn about slow but important changes. In Skill Lessons 4 and 15, you used graphs to learn about trends. In this lesson, you will use three different pieces of evidence. Using this evidence, you will be able to identify changes that contributed to passage of the Nineteenth Amendment, which gave women the right to vote.

The map on page 513 shows when states gave women full suffrage. It also shows states that gave women partial suffrage—for example, the right to vote for state officials but not Presidents. The time chart shows important breakthroughs for women and facts about women working outside the home. The third piece of evidence is a quotation from a speech made by a suffragist in 1912. Study the three pieces of evidence on page 513. Then review the discussion of the suffrage movement on pages 511–514 of this chapter.

1. **Read different kinds of evidence.** Read the three pieces of evidence on page 513. (a) What does the map show? (b) What do the colors on the map stand for? (c) What do the dates on the map indicate? (d) What does the time chart show? (e) What is the subject of the quotation?

2. **Interpret the evidence.** Study the three pieces of evidence to find information about a historical trend. (a) According to the map, how many states gave women equal suffrage in 1890? In 1900? In 1918? (b) What region of the country first gave women equal suffrage? (c) What region of the country did not give statewide suffrage to women before 1919? (d) According to the chart, what breakthrough did a woman make in 1877? (e) How many states allowed women to practice law in 1869? In 1920? (f) How many women worked outside the home in 1890? In 1910? (g) What did Rose Schneiderman say to people who considered voting unladylike?

3. **Use the evidence to identify a historical trend.** Use the three pieces of evidence and your reading of this chapter to find a historical trend. (a) Did more women have the right to vote in 1900 or 1918? (b) Did women have more job and educational opportunities in 1870 or 1900? (c) How do you think that working outside the home encouraged women to demand the right to vote? (d) From your answers to these questions, describe a historical trend about the rights of women in the United States from the 1870s to 1920. (c) How do you think this trend helped the passage of the Nineteenth Amendment in 1919?

recognized how much women had contributed to the West.

When Wyoming applied for statehood in the 1880s, however, some members of Congress did not want to admit a state that let women vote. During the debate over the question, Wyoming wired Congress this message: "We may stay out of the Union for 100 years, but we will come in with our women."

Growing strength. By the early 1900s, the movement for women's suf-

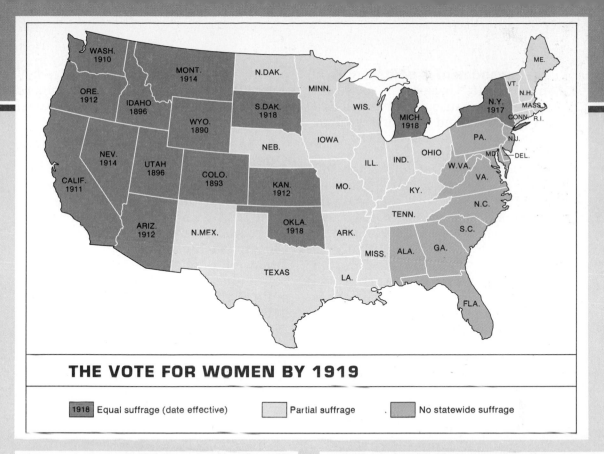

THE VOTE FOR WOMEN BY 1919

| 1918 Equal suffrage (date effective) | Partial suffrage | No statewide suffrage |

Time Chart

1869	Iowa is first state to let women practice law
1877	First American woman earns Ph.D.
1890	4 million women at work outside the home
1910	8 million women at work outside the home
1920	Women allowed to practice law in all states

Rose Schneiderman said:

Women in the laundries stand for 13 and 14 hours in the terrible steam and heat with their hands in hot starch. Surely these women won't lose any more of their beauty and charm by putting a ballot in the ballot box?

frage was growing in strength. More women than ever before were working outside the home. By earning wages, women gained a sense of power. Many demanded a say in making the laws that governed them. Jane Addams and other reformers realized that women needed the vote to work for social change. Slowly, more political leaders came to sympathize with the goals of *suffragists,* or women who campaigned for the right to vote.

The amendment is written. Carrie Chapman Catt became a powerful speaker for the cause. Catt worked as a school principal and a reporter. Later, she traveled across the country campaigning for suffrage.

The efforts of Catt and other suffragists slowly succeeded. Year by year, states in the West and Midwest gave women the vote. As they did, women pressed for an amendment to the Constitution. Some took extreme measures. Alice Paul organized women to picket the White House. Paul and others were arrested. In jail, they refused to eat. When prison officials force-fed them through tubes, there was an angry public outcry.

In 1919, Congress finally passed an amendment giving women the right to vote. The *Nineteenth Amendment* was approved by two thirds of the states by August 1920. As a result, the number of eligible voters in the United States doubled.

Opening New Doors

Women struggled to open doors to other opportunities. Most states refused to give women licenses to practice in professions such as law, medicine, or college teaching. For example, Myra Bradwell taught herself law, just as Abraham Lincoln had done. But the state of Illinois denied her a license in 1869 because she was a woman. In 1890, Illinois at last let Bradwell practice law. Later, she argued cases before the Supreme Court.

Despite obstacles, women managed to get the higher education that

Suffragists, like these women in New York City, marched to gain support for their cause. Women in the West won the vote in the late 1800s. Their example encouraged women in the East, where success came more slowly.

enabled them to enter the professions. In 1877, Boston University granted the first Ph.D. to a woman. In the next decades, women made important advances. By 1900, 1,000 women lawyers and about 7,000 women doctors were practicing around the country. Women entered the sciences, too. Mary Engle Pennington earned a degree in chemistry. She became the nation's top expert on preserving foods.

Millions more women worked at jobs that did not require professional training. By 1910, 8 million women had jobs outside their homes. Many worked as dressmakers, domestic servants, teachers, and farm hands.

Crusade Against Alcohol

Women reformers were the major force behind the temperance movement. Many were wives and mothers. They saw alcohol as a threat to their families. In 1874, women founded the Women's Christian Temperance Union, or WCTU. Frances Willard, leader of the WCTU, worked to educate people about the evils of alcohol. She urged states to pass laws banning the sale of liquor.

Another crusader against alcohol was Carrie Nation. Her husband died at an early age from heavy drinking. Afterwards, Nation dedicated her life to fighting "demon rum." She took her fight against alcohol right into the saloons. Swinging a hatchet, she stormed into taverns and hacked up beer kegs and liquor bottles. Nation also went on lecture tours across America and Europe.

The chief goal of the temperance movement was to amend the Constitution to prohibit the sale of liquor. During World War I, support for such an amendment grew. Temperance crusaders said that grain used to make liquor should go to feed American soldiers. Congress passed the *Eighteenth Amendment* in 1917. By 1919, three

Carrie Nation was famous for her bottle-smashing visits to saloons. Here, Nation is shown as a knight leading women on a crusade against alcohol. Many women in the temperance movement were deeply religious. How does their banner show this?

fourths of the states had ratified the amendment. It became illegal to sell alcoholic drinks anywhere in the United States.

■■■ SECTION REVIEW ■■■

1. **Define:** suffragist.
2. Which states first granted suffrage to women? Why?
3. How did working outside the home give women a sense of power?
4. What other opportunities did women gain in the late 1800s and early 1900s?
5. **What Do You Think?** Why do you think some women saw alcohol as a threat to their families?

4 Progressives in the White House

Read to Learn

★ How did Theodore Roosevelt become President?
★ What reforms did Roosevelt support?
★ What were Woodrow Wilson's policies as President?
★ What do these words mean: trustbuster, conservation?

The Progressive Movement had changed politics on the local and state levels. By the early 1900s, reformers won control of national politics. Between 1901 and 1914, three Progressive Presidents sat in the White House.

A New Kind of Politician

In 1896, voters elected William McKinley, a Republican, as President. McKinley was popular because American business surged ahead during his term in office. McKinley decided to run for reelection in 1900. He saw the Progressives gaining strength. So he looked for a running mate who stood for reform. At last, he chose a rising New York politician, Theodore Roosevelt.

Roosevelt's early years. Roosevelt, called Teddy by friends and foes alike, came from an old, wealthy New York family. As a child, Roosevelt was often sick. But he refused to accept weakness. He did exercises every day to build up his strength.

Roosevelt could have lived a life of ease and privilege in New York. Instead, he chose to enter politics after college. Roosevelt agreed with many Progressive goals. He despised corruption and firmly believed that the government should protect the public interest.

Roosevelt's friends laughed at his political ambitions. "They assured me that the men I met would be rough and brutal and unpleasant to deal with,"

Roosevelt later wrote. "I answered that I certainly would not quit until I . . . found out whether I was really too weak to hold my own in the rough and tumble."

A forceful politician. Roosevelt plunged into politics. But soon after he was elected to the New York State legislature, tragedy almost ended his political career. In 1884, his mother and his young wife died on the same day. Overcome by grief, Roosevelt moved to North Dakota. There, he worked as a cowboy on two cattle ranches he owned.

After a time, Roosevelt returned to the East and to politics. He served on the Civil Service Commission. Later, he became head of the New York City police department. Roosevelt fought in the Spanish–American War and won fame for his bravery. He returned to New York a hero and was elected governor in 1898.

Roosevelt proved to be a forceful governor. In fact, his independence made him a thorn in the side of the state's Republican bosses. They breathed a sigh of relief when Roosevelt ran with McKinley and won in November 1900.

Roosevelt and the Trusts

In September 1901, President McKinley was killed by an assassin. At 42, Roosevelt became the nation's youngest President.

Many business people were afraid of the Progressive ideas of the new President. Roosevelt assured them that he planned to stay with McKinley's pro-business policies. Roosevelt was a reformer, business leaders decided, but he was not dangerous.

The Northern Securities case. Roosevelt firmly supported the growth of industry. He was sure that the giant corporation was here to stay. But he believed that there were good trusts and bad trusts. Good trusts were efficient. The government should leave them alone, Roosevelt felt. Bad trusts cheated the public. The government had to control them or break them up. "Our aim is not to do away with corporations," Roosevelt said. "We draw the line against misconduct, not against wealth."

Roosevelt stood firm against the trusts when necessary. In 1902, he ordered his Attorney General* to bring a lawsuit against the Northern Securities Company. This giant trust had been put together by J. P. Morgan. Roosevelt said that Northern Securities violated the Sherman Antitrust Act by using unfair business practices.

Business leaders worry. The business world was shaken. Northern Securities operated the same way as other trusts. If it was illegal, so were they. J. P. Morgan rushed to the White House and asked if Roosevelt meant to attack other trusts. "Certainly not," said Roosevelt, "unless we find out that in any case they have done something we regard as wrong." The answer did not reassure business leaders.

Stock prices on Wall Street dipped sharply at news of the lawsuit. Business leaders feared that they had been right about Roosevelt after all. Yet ordinary people supported the President. "Wall Street is paralyzed at the thought that a President of the United States would sink so low as to try to enforce the law," one newspaper editor wrote.

The Court's decision. The case against Northern Securities went all the way to the Supreme Court. In 1904, the Court found Northern Securities guilty of violating the Sherman Antitrust Act. It ordered that the trust be

Some Progressives wanted to break up all trusts. As this cartoon shows, Roosevelt disagreed with them. He favored breaking up only bad trusts—those that fought against regulation. Here, good trusts are pictured as a bear on Roosevelt's leash. Bad trusts, however, lie dead under the President's foot.

broken up. The Court's decision showed how Progressives had influenced the country. In the 1890s, the Sherman Antitrust Act had been used to break up unions, not trusts.

The decision was a major victory for President Roosevelt. He ordered the Attorney General to file suit against other trusts that had broken the law. The government accused Standard Oil and the American Tobacco Company of blocking free trade. The courts eventually ordered both to be broken up.

Some business leaders called Roosevelt a *trustbuster* who wanted to end all trusts. But Roosevelt preferred to control trusts, not "bust" them. Only companies that fought government regulation were brought to court.

*The Attorney General is the chief lawyer for the United States government.

The coal strike. Roosevelt had another run-in with big business in 1902. That year, coal miners in Pennsylvania went on strike. They asked for better pay and a shorter day. Mine owners refused to talk to the miners' union.

As winter approached, schools and hospitals around the country ran out of coal. Roosevelt was angered by the stubbornness of the mine owners. At last, he threatened to send in troops to run the mines. In response, owners sat down with the union and reached an agreement.

Earlier Presidents had used federal troops to break strikes. Roosevelt used his power to force owners to deal with the union. Working people around the country cheered for Roosevelt.

The Square Deal

Roosevelt ran for President in 1904. During the campaign, he promised all Americans a *Square Deal.* By this, he meant that all people—rich and poor, native-born and immigrant—should have an equal opportunity to succeed. The promise of a Square Deal helped Roosevelt win an overwhelming victory in the election.

Railroad reform. Railroad abuses were one target of Roosevelt's Square Deal. He saw that the Interstate Commerce Act, passed in 1887, had done little to end rebates and other abuses. So he urged Congress to pass the Elkins Act in 1903. It ended rebates. In 1906, Congress passed the Hepburn Act. It gave the ICC greater power, including the right to set railroad rates.

Cleaner food. Like many Americans, Roosevelt was shocked by Upton Sinclair's *The Jungle.* After reading it, he wanted to send government inspectors into meatpacking houses. The meatpackers refused. So Roosevelt gave the newspapers copies of a government report that backed up Sinclair's picture of the meatpacking industry. The public was even more outraged. In 1906, Congress passed the Meat Inspection Act. It forced packers to open their doors to inspectors.

Roosevelt pushed for reforms in the food and drug industries. Muckrakers had reported that the food industry was adding dangerous chemicals to canned foods. Other reporters found that drug companies made untrue claims about their medicines. In 1906, Congress passed the *Pure Food and Drug Act.* The act required food and drug makers to list all ingredients on their packages. It tried to end false advertising and the use of impure ingredients.

Conservation. All his life, Roosevelt loved the outdoors. As President, he grew alarmed that the nation's untouched lands were being destroyed. To fuel America's growth, lumber companies were cutting down whole forests. Mining interests ripped iron and coal out of the earth at a frantic pace. Roosevelt objected to the thoughtless destruction of America's beautiful landscape. "The rights of the public to natural resources," he said, "outweigh private rights, and must be given first consideration."

Roosevelt believed that the outdoors could serve many purposes. Some forest and mountain areas should be kept as wilderness. But other forests could supply wood for lumber. If lumber companies replanted trees, Roosevelt believed, they could use the forests without destroying them. Mining, too, could go on as long as it was controlled. The protection of natural resources is called *conservation.*

Roosevelt made the first important steps toward conserving America's natural resources. He convinced Congress to ban lumbering in 150 million acres of government land. But he also supported a bill that opened up some government land to use by industry. Roosevelt created five natural wilderness areas and favored irrigation projects to make arid western lands suitable for farming.

Newspapers often showed President Roosevelt hunting, hiking, and fishing. The President knew a great deal about plants and animals. Once, in England, he amazed his host by correctly naming every bird he saw. This knowledge made Roosevelt a persuasive voice for conservation.

The Taft Years

As Roosevelt's term drew to an end in 1908, he threw his support behind William Howard Taft. Taft had served in Roosevelt's cabinet. Taft easily defeated his Democratic opponent and took office. Roosevelt went to Africa for a year to go hunting.

President Taft was very different from the rough-riding Roosevelt. Roosevelt was energetic and active. Taft was quiet and cautious. Still, Taft supported many Progressive causes. For example, he pushed ahead with trust-busting even more vigorously than Roosevelt had. Nevertheless, Taft lost Progressive support. For one thing, he signed a high tariff bill that Progressives opposed.

When Roosevelt returned from his trip to Africa, he was shocked to hear that Taft had betrayed reformers. Roosevelt decided to run against Taft for the Republican nomination in 1912.

The Bull Moose Party. At their convention, the Republicans chose to stick with Taft. Many business people in the party felt that Roosevelt could not be trusted. However, Progressive Republicans were angry about their party's choice for President. Some of them launched a new party, the Progressive Party. They chose Roosevelt to run for President. Roosevelt gladly accepted. He entered the battle with typical energy. "I feel as strong as a bull moose," he exclaimed. Many people began calling Roosevelt's supporters the *Bull Moose Party.*

Election of 1912. Democrats chose Woodrow Wilson as their Progressive candidate. Wilson was the governor of New Jersey. Before that, he had been president of Princeton University. He

Woodrow Wilson was a well-known scholar before he ran for office. Some Americans doubted whether a college professor would make a good President. But Wilson brought both high ideals and common sense to the White House.

was known as a brilliant scholar and a cautious reformer.

When the votes were counted, Wilson had won the election. Taft and Roosevelt together had more votes than Wilson. But they had split the Republicans and left Wilson the victor.

Wilson's New Freedom

Wilson called his program the *New Freedom.* Unlike Roosevelt, he did not want government to control large trusts. Wilson worried that the federal government would grow too large and powerful if it tried to control business. Instead, he wanted to break trusts up into smaller companies. By doing so, he hoped to restore the competition that had once existed in America.

When Wilson took office, however, he found it impossible to break up large corporations. Like Roosevelt, Wilson worked to control big business, not end it. He urged Congress to set up the *Federal Trade Commission.* This commission could investigate companies and order them to stop using unfair business practices.

In 1914, Congress passed the *Clayton Antitrust Act.* This act prohibited business practices that tried to destroy competition. The act stated that antitrust laws could not be used against unions. It also recognized the right of workers to form unions and strike. Samuel Gompers, chief of the AFL, hailed the Clayton Antitrust Act as a major victory for workers.

Wilson also pressured Congress to lower the tariff, which was raised while Taft was President. After a long struggle, Congress did as Wilson asked. At the same time that it lowered the tariff, Congress imposed a graduated tax on incomes. To regulate banking, Congress passed the *Federal Reserve Act* in 1913.

Despite Wilson's successes, the Progressive Movement slowed down by 1916. One reason for the slowdown was that the Progressives had achieved many of their goals. Another reason was the outbreak of war in Europe in 1914. Americans watched with concern as major industrial nations battled one another in Europe.

▬▬ SECTION REVIEW ▬▬

1. **Define:** trustbuster, conservation.
2. (a) What did the Supreme Court decide in the Northern Securities case? (b) Why did the ruling show that Progressives had influenced the country?
3. What actions did Roosevelt take in the area of natural resources?
4. (a) Why did Roosevelt decide to run against Taft in 1912? (b) What helped Wilson to win the election?
5. **What Do You Think?** In what ways do you think the Progressive Movement did achieve its goals?

5 The Struggle for Justice

Read to Learn

★ How did life for black Americans get worse in the 1890s?

★ How did black leaders fight discrimination?

★ What problems did black, Asian, Mexican, and Native Americans face?

The Progressive Movement won important victories against corruption and business abuses. Some groups, however, did not benefit from the reforms. For the most part, Progressives ignored the interests and needs of blacks, Asian Americans, Mexican Americans, and Native Americans.

Black Americans

After Reconstruction, black Americans in the South steadily lost their political rights. (See page 431.) Northern blacks also faced prejudice. They could not rent houses in white neighborhoods. Hotels and restaurants often refused to serve blacks. And as in the South, blacks had to accept the lowest-paying jobs.

Life got worse for black Americans in the 1890s. During the depression of 1893, many thousands of people were thrown out of work. In some areas, mainly in the South, unemployed whites took out their anger on blacks. In the 1890s, lynch mobs murdered one thousand blacks.

Booker T. Washington. How could blacks combat discrimination and violence? Booker T. Washington offered one answer. As a young man, he taught himself to read. Washington later founded Tuskegee Institute in Alabama. Tuskegee taught practical skills to black students.

Washington urged blacks to learn trades and earn money. Blacks, he said, had to improve their economic standing. Only then would they have the power to insist on political and social equality. In the meantime, Washington said, blacks had to accept segregation.

Washington became the foremost spokesman for blacks. White business leaders like Andrew Carnegie and John D. Rockefeller gave him money to build trade schools for blacks. Several Presidents of the United States asked his advice on racial issues.

Some black Americans disagreed with Washington, however. How could blacks save money when racism barred them from decent jobs? After all, blacks had been struggling to improve their economic standing for years.

W. E. B. Du Bois. W. E. B. Du Bois (doo BOIZ) took issue with Washington. Du Bois was an educator and a brilliant scholar. He was the first black to earn a Ph.D. at Harvard University. Du Bois agreed that "thrift, patience, and industrial training" were important. But he urged blacks to fight discrimination. "So far as Mr. Washington apologizes for injustice," Du Bois said, "we must firmly oppose him."

In 1909, Du Bois joined with Jane Addams and other reformers to form the *National Association for the Advancement of Colored People,* or NAACP. Blacks and whites in the NAACP worked together to gain equal rights for blacks.

Other Progressives showed little concern for the problems of black Americans. In 1913, black leaders met with President Wilson to protest segregation. Wilson told them that "segregation is not humiliating, but a benefit." Black Americans were deeply disappointed by Wilson's attitude.

Successes. Some blacks did succeed despite great obstacles. Sarah Walker was the first American woman, black or white, to become a millionaire. Orphaned at age six, Walker later became a laundry worker. In 1905, she created a line of cosmetics for black women. At first, she sold her products door to door. They were so popular that Walker's business expanded until she headed a major company.

Another success story was that of George Washington Carver. Carver was a black scientist who taught at Tuskegee Institute. Beginning in the 1890s, he found hundreds of new uses for crops grown in the South. For example, his research on the peanut led to the use of peanut butter, which became a favorite American food.

Other Minority Groups

As you read, anti-Chinese feelings led Congress to pass the Chinese Exclusion Act of 1882. This act kept Chinese from coming to America. However, the act caused a new wave of immigration from Asia.

Asian Americans. Business people in California wanted cheap labor. So they got around the Chinese Exclusion Act by helping thousands of Japanese come to America.

Many Japanese were excellent farmers. They settled on land that white farmers thought was useless. Through hard work and careful man-

All his life, Booker T. Washington urged blacks to learn skills and try to get good jobs. Like the students in this science class, Washington studied at Hampton Institute in Virginia. Hampton offered training in agriculture and trades. Tuskegee Institute, which Washington founded in 1881, also taught practical skills.

The Dawes Act encouraged Indians to take up farming. But the act struck at basic traditions. One result is shown in these photographs. At left is Tom Torlino in the traditional clothing of a young Navajo. At right, Torlino is shown after only a few months at a school run by whites. All trace of his Navajo heritage seems to have vanished from his appearance.

agement of resources, the Japanese made their farms profitable.

White farmers resented the success of the Japanese. They put pressure on President Roosevelt to limit immigration from Japan. In response, he made a *Gentlemen's Agreement* with Japan in 1907. Japan agreed to limit the number of workers coming to America.

Mexican Americans. For Mexican Americans, life in the United States was often difficult. A revolution began in Mexico in 1911. Thousands of Mexicans crossed the border into the American Southwest.

The wave of newcomers stirred up resentment among white Americans. Whites attacked both newcomers and Mexican Americans who had lived all their lives in the Southwest. So many Mexican Americans were lynched that in 1912 Mexico protested. To defend themselves, Mexican Americans formed mutualistas, or mutual aid groups. Members of mutualistas pooled money to buy insurance and pay for legal advice.

Native Americans. Like Mexican Americans, Indians faced discrimination and poverty. The Dawes Act, passed in 1887, had divided the land of Native Americans into plots of 160 acres. Congress had hoped that Indians would become farmers and be drawn into the mainstream of American life. Instead, Indians were swindled out of 90 million acres of land. Most lived on the fringe of American society.

=== SECTION REVIEW ===

1. (a) How did Booker T. Washington think blacks should respond to discrimination? (b) How did W. E. B. Du Bois disagree with Washington?

2. How did the Chinese Exclusion Act result in the immigration of Japanese to the United States?

3. (a) What problems did Mexican Americans face? (b) Why was life difficult for Native Americans?

4. **What Do You Think?** Why do you think many Progressives had little concern for problems faced by minorities?

Chapter 23 Review

★ Summary ★

In the late 1900s, Congress took steps to end the spoils system and stop unfair business practices. Public support for reform grew as reporters exposed many problems. Reformers who battled these problems were called Progressives.

Progressives wanted to control trusts, get rid of city bosses, give voters more power, and protect consumers. Women in the movement fought for suffrage, which they won in 1919. After 1900, Progressives elected three Presidents: Theodore Roosevelt, William Howard Taft, and Woodrow Wilson.

Some Americans were left out of the progress of the time. Blacks and other minorities faced prejudice and sometimes violence.

★ Reviewing the Facts   2 pts.   ★

Key Terms. Match each term in Column 1 with the correct definition in Column 2.

Column 1	Column 2
1. civil service	a. good of all the people
2. muckraker	b. power of voters to make a bill become law
3. public interest	c. election in which voters choose their party's candidates
4. primary	d. all federal jobs except elected and military ones
5. referendum	e. reporter who exposed corruption and other problems

Key People, Events, and Ideas. Identify each of the following.

1. James Garfield
2. Civil Service Commission
3. Jacob Riis
4. Theodore Roosevelt
5. Ida Tarbell
6. Upton Sinclair
7. Thomas Nast
8. Robert La Follette
9. Carrie Chapman Catt
10. William McKinley
11. William Howard Taft
12. Bull Moose Party
13. Woodrow Wilson
14. Booker T. Washington
15. W. E. B. Du Bois

★ Chapter Checkup   5 pts.   ★

1. How did the Civil Service Commission try to limit the spoils system?
2. (a) Who were the Progressives? (b) What beliefs did they hold in common?
3. How did the following give voters more power: (a) primary; (b) initiative; (c) direct election of senators?
4. Why did the women's suffrage movement gain strength in the early 1900s?
5. (a) What was Roosevelt's attitude toward trusts? (b) What did he do in the Northern Securities case?
6. What was the effect of each of the following reforms: (a) Elkins Act; (b) Hepburn Act; (c) Meat Inspection Act; (d) Pure Food and Drug Act?
7. What was the effect of each of the following reforms: (a) Federal Trade Commission; (b) Clayton Antitrust Act; (c) Federal Reserve Act?
8. What groups did not share in the advances made during the Progressive era? Why?

1. **Analyzing a quotation.** After Boss Tweed died, *The Nation* magazine wrote the following: "The bulk of the poorer voters of this city today revere his memory, and look on him as the victim of the rich men's malice; as, in short, a friend of the needy." (a) Why did the poor look on Tweed as a friend? (b) How do you think this made reform of city government more difficult?

2. **Learning about citizenship.** (a) How did the initiative and referendum increase the power of voters to create new laws? (b) How did these reforms reflect the spirit of the Progressive Movement?

3. **Relating past to present.** (a) What new opportunities did women gain in the early 1900s? (b) What new opportunities have women gained in recent years?

4. **Understanding the economy.** (a) How did Roosevelt and Wilson disagree about handling trusts? (b) Do you think the government regulates big business today?

★ **Using Your Skills**   ★

1. **Outlining.** Review the outlining skill you learned on page 31. Then prepare an outline of the material under "Muckrakers" on page 508. Using your outline, write a summary of what the muckrakers reported on and what they accomplished.

2. **Identifying point of view.** Reread Roosevelt's statement about natural resources on page 518. What was Roosevelt's point of view about the public interest? How does this show that Roosevelt was a Progressive?

3. **Making a review chart.** Make a chart with 4 rows and 3 columns. Title the rows Sixteenth, Seventeenth, Eighteenth, and Nineteenth amendment. Title the columns When Passed, When Ratified, and Effect. Then complete the chart.

4. **Comparing.** Study the discussion of the ideas of Booker T. Washington and W. E. B. Du Bois on page 521. (a) On what points did Washington and Du Bois agree? (b) On what points did they disagree? (c) With whom do you agree?

★ **More to Do**   ★

1. **Drawing a cartoon.** Draw a cartoon that shows the public response to the assassination of James Garfield by an office seeker.

2. **Exploring local history.** Look through a local newspaper for an article that you think could be called muckraking. Write a brief report explaining how the article is similar to muckraking reports at the turn of the century.

3. **Preparing a pamphlet.** Use the library to find examples of Thomas Nast's cartoons. Photocopy one cartoon and use it as a part of a two-page pamphlet urging city voters to do away with corrupt city officials.

4. **Organizing a debate.** As a group, organize a debate about women's suffrage. One side should present the point of view of people living in western states that allowed women to vote in the early 1900s. The other side should take the position of people from states that did not allow women's suffrage.

24
America Looks Overseas (1865–1916)

Chapter Outline

1 Across the Pacific
2 The Spanish–American War
3 The United States and Latin America

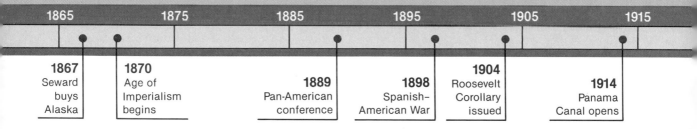

| 1865 | 1875 | 1885 | 1895 | 1905 | 1915 |

1867
Seward buys Alaska

1870
Age of Imperialism begins

1889
Pan-American conference

1898
Spanish–American War

1904
Roosevelt Corollary issued

1914
Panama Canal opens

About This Chapter

In July 1898, the United States was at war with Spain. A major battle of the war took place in Cuba. There, American troops fought a truly uphill battle to capture the heights above the city of Santiago. Atop the hills, Spanish rifles and artillery rained bullets and shells down on the advancing American troops.

"Our situation was desperate," wrote an American reporter. "Our troops could not retreat, as the trail for two miles behind them was wedged with men. They could not remain where they were for they were being shot to pieces. There was only one thing they could do—go forward and take the San Juan hills by assault."

Colonel Theodore Roosevelt charged up one of the hills. "He wore on his sombrero a blue polka-dot handkerchief. As he advanced, it floated out straight behind his head." Soldiers followed. "They walked to greet death at every step, many of them, as they advanced, sinking suddenly or pitching forward and disappearing in the high grass." Finally, the Americans captured the San Juan hills.

At home, Americans celebrated Roosevelt's brave actions. The war with Spain was popular in the United States. Yet the war marked a new era in American history. After years of expanding across the continent, Americans now looked to expand their interests overseas.

Study the time line above. During what century did the Spanish–American War take place?

During the Spanish–American War, Commodore George Dewey won a spectacular victory at Manila Bay. No American lives were lost in the battle.

1 Across the Pacific

Read to Learn

★ Why did some Americans call for expansion overseas in the late 1800s?

★ How did the United States gain Alaska?

★ How did the United States increase its influence in the Pacific?

★ What do these words mean: isolation, imperialism, sphere of influence?

For much of the 1800s, the United States had little to do with other nations. In the late 1800s, however, this policy changed. By then, many European nations were expanding their trade and influence around the world. Many Americans, too, wanted to compete for resources and new markets in other parts of the world.

Changing Views

Early American Presidents had warned against involvement with other nations. Washington urged the nation to "steer clear of permanent alliances with any portion of the foreign world." Jefferson advised the United States to avoid "entangling alliances."

This policy was called *isolation,* or having little to do with foreign nations. Isolation suited most Americans. They were busy settling the continent, building railroads, and setting up new industries. By the late 1800s, however, American business leaders looked beyond the nation's borders. They wanted new sources of raw materials and new markets in which to sell their goods. In

1890, Secretary of State James Blaine summed up the new view of the world: "Our great demand is expansion . . . of trade with countries where we can find profitable exchanges."

Some Americans supported expansion overseas to offset the closing of the western frontier. For years, people had moved to the West to get away from crowded cities in the East. By the late 1800s, the western lands had all been claimed. This meant that people could no longer move on and start again. Expansion overseas would open up new opportunities for restless Americans.

Climate of Imperialism

European nations such as Britain, France, and Germany were busily carving up the world. The period from about 1870 to 1914 has been called the Age of Imperialism. *Imperialism* is a policy by which one country takes control of the land and people of another country or region. For example, between 1870 and 1914, Europeans took control of almost the entire continent of Africa.

Causes. Imperialism had several causes. One was economic. The industrial nations of Europe wanted raw materials from Africa and Asia. They wanted the people of these regions to buy goods made in European factories.

A second cause was the belief that Europeans had a duty to spread their own ideas and culture to the rest of the world. A third cause was competition. One European nation might take over an area to keep a rival nation from gaining it.

Expanding trade. Many Americans entered into the competition for new markets. Captain Alfred Mahan of the United States Navy called on America to build up its merchant marine, the ships that carry trade goods. Then, Mahan urged the nation to strengthen its navy. A strong navy was needed to protect the merchant marine. The navy would need bases and refueling stations throughout the world, he said.

Even before Mahan's call, Congress had begun to expand and modernize the navy. New steam-powered warships with steel hulls were already being built. Mahan's writings encouraged the building of still more. By the late 1890s, a large and powerful navy was ready for action. Its ships were called the *Great White Fleet* because they were painted white.

Seward's Folly

An early supporter of American expansion was William Seward, Secretary of State under Presidents Lincoln and Johnson. Seward believed that the United States should expand into the Pacific. He saw Alaska as the base for that expansion.

The land and climate. Alaska is a land of ice-capped mountains and low-lying coastal areas. From time to time, earthquakes raise and lower the shore. It is rich in natural resources such as copper and timber.

Alaska has an arctic and subarctic climate. The lowlands of southern Alaska are suited to farming. In the summer, herds of caribou and flocks of birds feed on marshy plains of the interior. In the winter, they migrate in search of food.

The purchase. In the 1800s, however, Alaska was a Russian colony. One night in 1867, while playing cards, Seward received good news from the Russian ambassador. The Russian czar, Alexander II, was willing to sell Alaska to the United States for $7.2 million. Seward agreed to buy the land then and there. "But your Department is closed," said the Russian ambassador. "Never mind that," Seward replied. "Before midnight you will find me at the Department, which will be open and ready for business."

By the next morning, Seward had bought Alaska at a cost of two cents an

In 1898, word reached the United States of rich gold strikes in Alaska. Thousands of Americans rushed north to seek their fortunes. They traveled any way they could. Some, like the women at right, hauled their equipment by hand.

Miners in the Yukon heard of a gold strike near Nome, Alaska, which was 2,000 miles (3,200 km) to the west. The fastest route was by boat down the Yukon River. But in the winter, the river was frozen. A few hardy miners hitched up their dogsleds and set off down the frozen river.

One miner, Ed Jesson, had a better idea. He bought a bicycle for $150—much cheaper than a good sled dog that cost $350. He learned to ride on snow-covered ice. Jesson planned to pedal 50 miles a day down the frozen river and sleep at roadhouses along the way.

On the second day out, the temperature dropped to −48°F. "The rubber tires on my wheels were frozen hard," wrote Jesson in his diary. "My nose was freezing and I had to hold the handlebars with both hands, not being able to ride yet with one hand and rub my nose with the other." The one good thing about the bicycle was that "it didn't eat anything, and I didn't have to cook dogfeed for it."

Strong winds forced Jesson to give up the river route. He cut overland on his bike and pedaled into Nome about a month after leaving the Yukon. In Nome, he received a warm welcome. The town was cut off from the rest of the world in the winter. So people gathered around to hear Jesson read the latest newspapers from the United States.

★ Why do you think men and women were willing to risk any hardship to reach Alaska?

acre. The land he bought was larger than the southwestern lands of the Mexican Cession. (See the map on page 571.)

To many Americans, Seward's purchase of Alaska was an absurd act. They called the vast icy land Seward's Folly or Seward's Icebox. They would change their tune 30 years later when prospectors found gold in Alaska. In 1897, thousands of Americans risked their lives in a mad gold rush to Alaska. In the 1940s, "black gold"—oil—was found in great quantities in Alaska.*

*Alaska remained a territory for more than 90 years. In 1959, as you will read, it became the largest state in the United States.

Seward pressed for still more territory. In 1867, the United States annexed Midway Island in the Pacific. Seward then urged the United States to take control of the Hawaiian Islands. He also wanted to build a canal across Central America to link the Atlantic and Pacific oceans.

Perry Visits Japan

American interest in the Pacific did not begin with Seward. In the late 1700s and early 1800s, New England whaling ships sailed around Cape Horn into the Pacific. Other American ships traded with China. In the mid-1800s, American trade with China grew. But Japan, China's neighbor to the east, refused to trade with any nation.

In the 1600s, Japan had expelled all westerners* and ended its trade with foreigners. It imposed complete isolation on itself. Only one ship a year from the Dutch East India Company was

---

*To the Japanese, Westerners were white people from Europe and North America.

allowed to trade at the port of Nagasaki in Japan.

American merchants and sailors were eager to end Japan's isolation. They wanted the Japanese to agree to help shipwrecked American sailors who washed up on Japan's shores. Also, they wanted to set up refueling stations in Japan and open up Japan to trade.

President Millard Fillmore sent Commodore Matthew Perry to negotiate a treaty with Japan. In July 1853, Perry's four steam-propelled warships sailed into Tokyo Bay. Japanese officials ordered Perry to leave, but he stood firm. He presented a letter from President Fillmore to the Japanese. Before sailing away, he promised to return the next year for an answer.

Early in 1854, Perry returned with seven warships. The Japanese took note of this menacing display of force. In March, the emperor signed the *Treaty of Yokohama.* It granted American demands for kindly treatment of shipwrecked sailors and for refueling rights. It also opened up two Japanese ports to trade.

A Japanese artist painted this picture of Commodore Matthew Perry landing in Japan. Perry was determined to open Japan to trade with the United States. In 1854, Japan signed a treaty opening two ports to trade.

Perry's visit had far-reaching effects. First, it opened trade between Japan and the West. Second, it made the Japanese realize the power of the industrial nations of the West. As a result, Japanese leaders set their nation on a course to become a modern, industrial nation.

Americans Annex Hawaii

In the 1800s, Americans looked with interest at the Hawaiian Islands. Europeans and Americans first learned about the Hawaiian Islands in 1778. That year, a British captain, James Cook, visited the islands and traded with the Hawaiians.

The land and climate. Hawaii is made up of eight large islands and over 100 smaller islands. They are located in the Pacific Ocean, about 2,400 miles (3,800 km) southwest of California. The islands have rich soils, a warm climate, and plenty of rainfall. These conditions make it possible to grow crops all year.

The islands were first settled about 2,000 years ago by people from Polynesia, islands in the Central and South Pacific. In the early 1800s, Yankee whaling ships and merchant ships bound for China stopped at the Hawaiian Islands. A few American sailors and traders settled in Hawaii. In 1820, the first American missionaries arrived to convert the Hawaiians to Christianity.

The sugar industry grows. By the mid-1800s, Americans had set up many large sugar plantations. Planters brought in Chinese workers to join Hawaiians in the sugar cane fields.* As the sugar industry boomed, American sugar planters gained great influence over the government and economy of Hawaii. They used their influence to

Queen Liliuokalani, shown here, was a Hawaiian patriot. She wrote "Aloha Oe," a well-known Hawaiian song of farewell. As queen, she tried to preserve the islands' independence. In 1893, an American-backed revolution overthrew her.

force the Hawaiian king, Kalakaua, to accept a new constitution. It reduced the king's power and increased American influence.

In 1891, Kalakaua died. His sister Liliuokalani (lee lee oo oh kah LAH nee) took the throne. The new queen was a Hawaiian patriot. She deeply resented the control of American planters. She decided to throw out the new constitution and restore some of the ruler's former powers.

American sugar planters opposed any change that would reduce their power. In 1893, they led a bloodless revolt against Queen Liliuokalani. The queen had to give up her throne. The Americans set up a republic and asked to be annexed by the United States. In 1898, Congress finally granted their

---

*Chinese workers, called coolies, were shipped to Hawaii, South America, and the West Indies almost like slaves. Conditions on shipboard were similar to those on the Middle Passage.

request. In 1900, Hawaii became a United States territory. Finally, in 1959, Hawaii became the 50th state.

Rivalries in the Pacific

The United States was one of several nations competing for power in the Pacific. Two other industrial powers, Great Britain and Germany, also wanted trading and refueling rights there. In the late 1800s, the three nations competed for control of Samoa, a chain of islands. (See the map on page 532.) In the end, the United States and Germany divided control of Samoa.

Open Door Policy. Rivalry among industrial nations extended to China. China had once been the strongest, most advanced empire in the world. Marco Polo, you remember, was awed by the wealth of China in the 1270s.

But while European nations industrialized in the 1800s, China did not. So by the late 1800s, it was at a disadvantage in fighting western imperialism.

At a time when Chinese rulers were weak, Britain, France, Germany, Russia, and Japan carved up China. Each nation set up its own sphere of influence. A *sphere of influence* was an area, usually around a seaport, where a nation had special trading privileges. Each nation made laws for its own citizens in its own sphere.

Americans were afraid that other nations would prevent them from trading in China. In 1899, Secretary of State John Hay wrote a letter to all the nations that had spheres of influence in China. He urged them to follow an *Open Door Policy* in China. Under such a policy, all nations would have the right to trade in any other nation's

MAP SKILL In the late 1800s, the United States gained islands across the Pacific. American trading ships stopped at these islands to take on fuel and food on their way to China and Japan. What is the latitude and longitude of Wake Island?

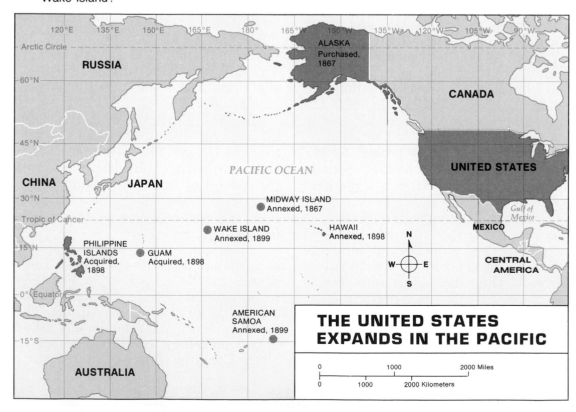

THE UNITED STATES EXPANDS IN THE PACIFIC

The battle cry of the Boxers was "Protect the country; destroy the foreigners." Christian missionaries were among the foreigners killed in the Boxer Rebellion. Here, troops of the international force attack the Boxers.

sphere of influence. In this way, the United States protected its own trading interests in China. Other nations reluctantly agreed to follow the Open Door Policy.

The Boxer Rebellion. Many Chinese resented the foreigners who were carving up their land. Some blamed foreigners for all of China's troubles. In 1899, a group of Chinese organized a secret society called the Righteous Fists of Harmony, or Boxers. The Boxers wanted to drive all foreigners out of China.

In 1900, the Boxers rebelled. They attacked foreigners all over China. In Peking, foreigners fled to safety in a walled area called the foreign compound. They were trapped there for many weeks.

Foreign governments were quick to respond to the *Boxer Rebellion.* They organized an international army that included 2,500 American soldiers. The army marched on Peking to rescue the trapped foreigners. Armed with more advanced weapons than the Chinese, the foreign army soon crushed the rebellion.

Several nations saw the Boxer Rebellion as an excuse to take more land in China. Once again, Secretary of State Hay stepped forward. He sent a second Open Door letter. It urged all nations to respect China's independence. In this letter, the United States protected the rights of nations to trade freely in any part of China, not just in foreign spheres of influence.

━━ SECTION REVIEW ━━

1. **Locate:** Alaska, Midway Island, Japan, Hawaii, Samoa, China.
2. **Define:** isolation, imperialism, sphere of influence.
3. How did the United States acquire each of the following: (a) Alaska; (b) Hawaii?
4. What did Commodore Perry achieve?
5. **What Do You Think?** How do you think the Open Door Policy helped the United States?

2 The Spanish–American War

Read to Learn
★ Why was Latin America important to the United States?
★ What were the causes of the Spanish–American War?
★ Why were Americans divided over the peace treaty?

During the Age of Imperialism, the United States carefully watched developments in Latin America. In the 1880s, European nations invested heavily in Latin America. These investments increased European influence in the Western Hemisphere. The United States resented this and took steps to protect its own interests in the region.

Protecting American Interests

As the United States industrialized, Latin America became more important to it. The United States saw Latin America as a source of raw materials and as a market for its goods. European nations eyed Latin America in the same way. They sold manufactured goods to Latin American nations and won markets that the United States wanted.

Enforcing the Monroe Doctrine. The United States tried to use the Monroe Doctrine to limit European influence in Latin America. For example, in 1878, a French company planned to build a canal across Panama to link the Atlantic and Pacific oceans. President Hayes objected. He claimed that the French plan interfered in the affairs of Latin America. The French company started building a canal anyway. In the end, poor planning, disease, and lack of money forced the company to give up the project.

At times, the United States interfered directly to protect its interests. In

1891, it took sides in a civil war in Chile. A few years later, it threatened to go to war against Britain over a border dispute in Venezuela.

An effort to improve relations. Many Latin American nations resented interference by the United States. As anti-American feeling grew, Secretary of State Blaine tried to improve relations between the United States and the nations of Latin America. In 1889, he invited Latin American nations to send delegates to a conference in Washington, D.C. He hoped to increase cooperation among the nations of the Western Hemisphere.

Many Latin American nations sent delegates to the conference. Still, they remained suspicious of the United States. The conference set up a group to work together to solve the problems of the hemisphere. In 1910, this group became known as the *Pan-American Union*.

Trouble in Cuba

In the late 1800s, the United States became more and more deeply involved in Latin America. The involvement brought the nation to the brink of war with Spain. At the center of the dispute were two Spanish colonies in the Caribbean: Cuba and Puerto Rico.

Rebellion against Spain. Spain called Cuba its Ever-Faithful Isle, because it did not rebel against Spanish rule in the early 1800s as other colonies had. Yet many Cubans and Puerto Ricans wanted independence. In 1868, Cubans did rebel, but they were defeated.

When revolutionaries were forced to leave their homeland, many fled to New York. In New York, patriots like Lola Rodríguez de Tió and José Martí kept up the battle for freedom. Born in Puerto Rico, Lola Rodríguez de Tió wrote patriotic poems in support of independence from Spain. Martí, a Cuban, told of the Cuban struggle for freedom in his newspaper, *Patria*.

In 1895, Cubans rebelled again. They won control of many rural areas. In response, Spain sent a new governor to Cuba, General Valeriano Weyler (WAY ee lair). General Weyler used harsh measures to regain control. He rounded up 500,000 Cubans and put them in detention camps. Conditions in these camps were so terrible that at least 200,000 people died.

American concern. In the United States, people watched the revolt in Cuba with growing concern. Cuba lay only 90 miles (144 km) south of Florida. Americans had invested about $50 million in Cuba. The money was invested in sugar and rice plantations, railroads, tobacco, and iron mines. Also, American trade with Cuba was worth about $100 million a year.

Opinion was split over whether the United States should intervene in Cuba. Many business leaders opposed intervention. They thought that it might hurt trade. Other Americans sympathized with the Cuban desire for freedom.

Remember the *Maine*

The press took a hand in the debate. It whipped up American sympathies for Cuba. Two New York newspapers, Joseph Pulitzer's *World* and William Randolph Hearst's *Journal,* competed with each other in printing grisly stories about Spanish cruelty. These newspapers used yellow journalism, or sensational stories, to play on the emotions of their readers. "Blood on the roadsides," one story cried, "blood in the fields, blood on the doorsteps, blood, blood, blood!" The press called the Spanish governor "Butcher" Weyler and showed him as a complete villain.

President Cleveland wanted to avoid war with Spain. He called the

AMERICANS WHO DARED

Lola Rodríguez de Tió

Lola Rodríguez de Tió took part in the Puerto Rican struggle for independence from Spain in the late 1800s. Forced to flee her homeland, she settled in Cuba and then in New York. She published several books of poems. In one poem, she spoke of freedom.

Freedom comes if you want it,
Be you called a man or woman,
If you can aspire to justice
If you can recognize duty.

war fever in the United States an "epidemic of insanity." When President McKinley took office in 1897, he, too, tried to keep the country neutral.

In 1898, fighting broke out in Havana, Cuba. President McKinley sent the American battleship *Maine* to Havana to protect American citizens and property. On the night of February 15, 1898, the *Maine* lay quietly at anchor. Just after the bugler sounded taps, an earsplitting explosion ripped

During the Spanish–American War, the all-black 10th Cavalry fought bravely. Black soldiers, shown here, helped capture San Juan Hill. Their commander was a white officer, John Pershing. He was nicknamed Black Jack.

In a letter to Roosevelt, John Hay, who was soon to become the Secretary of State, summed up American enthusiasm for the war. "It's been a splendid little war," he wrote. A malaria-ridden veteran of the war had a different view: "I was lucky—I survived."

Ruling an Empire

In December 1898, the United States and Spain signed a peace treaty. In it, Spain granted Cuba its freedom. Spain gave the United States two islands: Puerto Rico in the Caribbean and Guam in the Pacific. In return for a payment of $20 million, Spain also gave the Philippines to the United States. By the treaty, the United States won an empire.

Debate over the treaty. The treaty set off a heated debate in the United States. Many Americans objected to the treaty. They said that it made the United States into a colonial power. What right, they asked, did Americans have to take over these lands? Hadn't Americans fought their own revolution in 1776 to end colonial rule? Also, they feared that American expansion would involve the nation in new wars overseas.

Expansionists favored the treaty, however. They argued that the United States needed bases in the Caribbean and the Pacific for its ships. The new lands offered business opportunities to Americans. Also, some people felt that Americans had a duty to spread their ideas of democratic government and their culture to people in other parts of the world.

Cuba. Governing the new empire posed certain problems. When Congress declared war on Spain, it stated that the United States would "leave the government and control of [Cuba] to its people." However, after the war, the United States Army stayed on in Cuba while Congress debated what to do about the island nation. Many members of Congress believed that Cubans were not ready to run their own government. American business leaders wanted to protect their investments in Cuba. So they opposed complete independence.

Finally, in 1901, Cuba was allowed to write its own constitution. The United States then forced the Cubans to accept the *Platt Amendment.* It limited Cuba's right to make treaties or borrow money. The amendment gave the United States the right to intervene in Cuba to protect American life and property. The Platt Amendment also gave the United States control of the naval base at Guantanamo Bay. The amendment meant that Cuba was not really an independent nation.

Puerto Rico. The United States set up a new government for Puerto Rico by the *Foraker Act* of 1900. The act gave Puerto Ricans a limited say over their own affairs. In 1917, Puerto Ricans were made citizens of the United States. Americans set up schools, improved health care, and built roads on the island. Still, many Puerto Ricans wanted independence. They wanted to control their own government and be free of foreign rule.

The Philippine Islands. During the Spanish–American War, Filipinos had fought for their independence from Spain. When the United States annexed their land after the war, Filipinos felt betrayed. So they renewed their struggle for independence.

For almost three years, Emilio Aguinaldo led rebel forces against the United States. American troops imprisoned thousands of Filipino men, women, and children. The long, brutal war deeply divided American opinion. Expansionists believed that the United States must win control of the Philippines. Other Americans criticized the

GRAPH SKILL As American industry grew in the years after the Civil War, its foreign trade expanded. Expansionists like Alfred Mahan called for a large navy to defend the nation's trade. What was the value of foreign trade in 1865? in 1900? in 1915?

American Foreign Trade, 1865–1915

Source: *Historical Statistics of the United States*

harsh measures used to fight the Filipinos. When Aguinaldo was captured in 1901, the war finally ended.

In 1902, the United States set up a government in the Philippines similar to the one in Puerto Rico. But Filipinos were not made American citizens because the United States planned to give them independence. It was not until 1946, however, that the United States decided that the Filipinos were ready for self-government.

■ SECTION REVIEW ■

1. **Locate:** Cuba, Puerto Rico, Philippine Islands, Guam.
2. Give three reasons why Americans watched events in Cuba with interest.
3. What lands did the United States acquire as a result of the Spanish–American War?
4. **What Do You Think?** Why do you think many Americans opposed the idea of ruling an overseas empire?

3 The United States and Latin America

Read to Learn

★ How did the United States build the Panama Canal?

★ What policies toward Latin America did the United States follow?

★ Why did the United States invade Mexico in 1916?

★ What do these words mean: dollar diplomacy?

The Spanish–American War made the United States a world power.* With new lands to rule in the Caribbean and the Pacific, the United States felt an urgent need for a canal linking the Atlantic and Pacific oceans. A canal would let the navy move quickly to defend America's new possessions. It would cut 7,000 miles (11,200 km) off the trip between the Atlantic and the Pacific. And it would help trade.

Revolution in Panama

Ever since Balboa crossed the narrow Isthmus of Panama in 1517, people dreamed of digging a canal between the Atlantic and Pacific oceans. The isthmus is only about 50 miles (80 km) wide. But there were many obstacles to making the dream of a canal come true. Mosquitoes carrying yellow fever and malaria thrived in the hot climate of Panama. Steep mountains had to be cut through. Also, since the 1800s, Panama belonged to Colombia. (See the map on page 541.)

Talks with Colombia. When Theodore Roosevelt became President, he was determined to see a canal built. Roosevelt favored direct action. He often quoted an African proverb: "Speak softly and carry a big stick, and you will go far." Roosevelt's policy toward Latin America reflected his faith in this saying.

Roosevelt asked Secretary of State John Hay to talk to Colombia about building a canal across Panama. In 1903, Hay offered Colombia $10 million in cash and $250,000 each year in rent for the rights to a strip of land across Panama. Colombian officials turned down the offer. They hoped to get a better price.

President Roosevelt stormed at the delay. American newspapers talked of encouraging the people of Panama to revolt. Roosevelt favored this idea. Many people in Panama were eager for the canal. They hoped that it would make their land a crossroads for world

---

*The United States gained land in other ways. For example, in 1917, it bought the Virgin Islands from Denmark.

trade. Besides, they had been trying to break away from Colombia for more than 50 years.

Panama wins independence. On November 2, 1903, the American warship *Nashville* sailed into the port of Colón, Panama. The next day, the people of Panama rebelled against Colombia. American forces stopped Colombian troops from crushing the revolt. On November 4, Panama declared itself an independent republic.

Word soon reached the White House that the revolt had succeeded. The United States at once recognized the new nation. Panama then agreed to let the United States build the canal on terms similar to those it had offered to Colombia.

Roosevelt's high-handed action in Panama angered many Latin American nations. But the President was proud of his achievement. "I took the Canal Zone," he said later, "and let Congress debate. And while the debate goes on, the canal does also."

Building the Panama Canal

Building the Panama Canal was more difficult than winning the right to build it. The canal builders faced great hazards. First, they had to rid the Canal Zone of mosquitoes that carried yellow fever and malaria. They used knowledge gained by United States Army doctors in Cuba.

Beating disease. During the Spanish–American War, thousands of American soldiers had contracted yellow fever in Cuba. Walter Reed, an army doctor, searched for the cause of yellow fever. A major breakthrough came when a Cuban doctor, Carlos Juan Finlay, discovered that the disease was transmitted by a certain kind of mosquito.

With this information, another young army doctor, William Gorgas, set out to destroy the insect's breeding grounds. Within a year, the number of

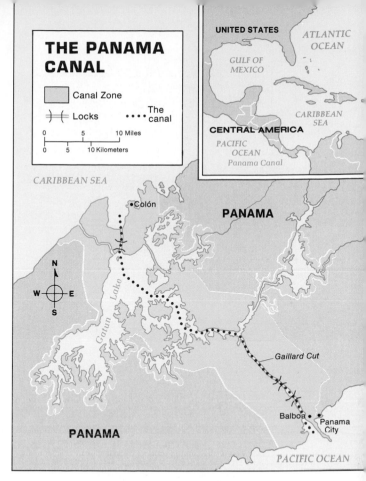

MAP SKILL The Panama Canal linked the Atlantic and Pacific oceans. The canal took about 43,000 workers almost 10 years to finish. A series of locks raised and lowered the water level so that ships could move through the canal. In what direction did ships travel from Colón to Balboa?

new cases of yellow fever dropped off sharply.

In 1904, the United States government sent Gorgas to fight yellow fever in Panama. There, Gorgas drained swamps and destroyed the breeding grounds of disease-bearing mosquitoes. This work almost wiped out yellow fever and malaria in Panama.

Engineering problems. Second, builders faced many engineering problems. They had to cut through solid rock, dam rivers, and remove more than 200 million cubic yards of earth. The Army Corps of Engineers, under Colonel George Goethals, supervised

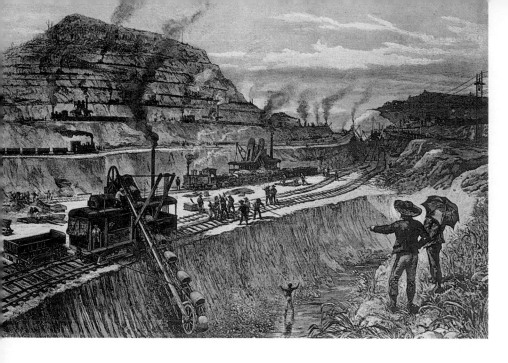

The building of the Panama Canal was an engineering marvel. Perhaps the hardest job was digging the Gaillard, or Culebra, Cut, at left. When President Roosevelt visited the Culebra Cut, he wrote to his son, "They are eating steadily into the mountain, cutting it down and down."

the building of the Big Ditch, as the canal was called. More than 40,000 workers struggled to complete the project. They blasted a path through the mountains. Then, they built canal locks and a railroad. Finally, in 1914, the first ocean-going steamship traveled through the *Panama Canal.*

The United States benefited most from the canal. However, the new waterway helped the trade of many nations. Despite the advantages of the canal, many Latin American nations remained bitter about the way the United States had won it.

The Big Stick

The United States was anxious to protect the Panama Canal. So it became more heavily involved in Latin America than ever before. In the early 1900s, President Roosevelt viewed the growing European interest in Latin America with concern. When Britain, Germany, and Italy threatened to use force to make Latin American nations such as Venezuela pay their debts, Roosevelt took action.

The Roosevelt Corollary. In 1904, Roosevelt announced a new policy. It was known as the Roosevelt Corollary. The *Roosevelt Corollary* was an expansion of the Monroe Doctrine. In it, Roosevelt claimed the right of the United States to intervene in Latin America to preserve law and order. By exercising this "international police power," the United States planned to make Latin American nations pay their debts to foreign nations.

The President soon put his policy to work. When the Dominican Republic could not pay its debts in 1905, the United States Navy collected customs taxes there. It then paid off the country's debts. Over the next 20 years, several American Presidents used this police power.

Dollar diplomacy. Like Roosevelt, President Taft favored a strong American role in Latin America. Taft encouraged American bankers and business leaders to invest in Latin America. He wanted to "substitute dollars for bullets." Economic ties, he said, were the best way to expand American influence. This policy became known as *dollar diplomacy.*

American bankers and business leaders responded eagerly. They invested even more in Latin America.

They helped build roads, railroads, and ports. These improvements, in turn, benefited Americans and local governments. The new railroads, for example, brought minerals and other resources to ports. From there, they were shipped all over the world.

However, dollar diplomacy led to military involvement. When a revolution broke out in Nicaragua, where Americans had invested in land and businesses, the United States sent in marines to restore order. Later, American troops occupied the Dominican Republic, Haiti, and Honduras. The United States claimed that its troops were protecting American lives and property. However, many Latin American nations bitterly resented these invasions.

Relations With Mexico

Dollar diplomacy affected relations between the United States and Mexico. Since the 1870s, Americans had invested heavily in Mexico. By 1912, Americans had about $1 billion invested there. The money was used to develop mines, oil wells, railroads, and ranches. Despite these investments, most Mexicans were poor.

Most Mexicans were peasants who owned little land. They worked on the land owned by a few wealthy families. But peasants got little in return for their labor. These conditions led to widespread discontent.

The Mexican Revolution. In 1911, Mexico was plunged into a violent revolution. The fighting lasted until 1917. Several Mexican leaders battled for power. For a time, President Woodrow Wilson followed a policy of "watchful waiting." He hoped that Mexico would develop a democratic government. And he refused to recognize any Mexican government that did not meet his approval.

In 1914, a minor incident led Wilson to intervene in Mexico. A Mexican official in Tampico arrested several American sailors. The sailors were soon released, and the Mexican government apologized to the United States. But the incident angered Wilson. He ordered the United States Navy to occupy the Mexican port of Veracruz.

Pershing invades. Troubles continued to plague the two nations. In March 1916, General Francisco "Pancho" Villa, a rebel leader, crossed the border into New Mexico. He raided the town of Columbus, New Mexico, killing

Cartoonists often drew Teddy Roosevelt holding a "big stick." Here, he is shown as a policeman, restoring order around the world. Early in his career, Roosevelt served as police commissioner of New York City.

Sometime this year, you may be writing research reports. To write a report, you need to choose a topic, research and take notes on it, then organize your notes. Finally, you need to outline and write the report.

Imagine that your report is on the Panama Canal. Write down several questions about the topic. The questions give you a framework for research and note taking. Use the card catalog, encyclopedias, and magazines to find information. Take notes on note cards such as the ones below.

1. **Set up a note-taking system.** Fill out one note card for each question about your topic and for each book or article you use. In the upper right corner, write the question your notes cover. In the upper left corner, write the title and author of the book or article you are using. For articles, include the title and date of the magazine. (a) What question does the information on Card A answer? (b) From what book do the notes on Card A come?

2. **Set quotations off from your own words.** Put quotation marks around a direct quotation and include the page number where you found it. For facts or information in your own words, you do not need quotation marks. Always include the page number where you found the information. (a) Which card has information that is a direct quotation? (b) On what page was it found?

3. **Organize your note cards.** When you are ready to write your report, put all cards that cover the same question together. (a) Which of the cards below belong together? (b) What question do they answer?

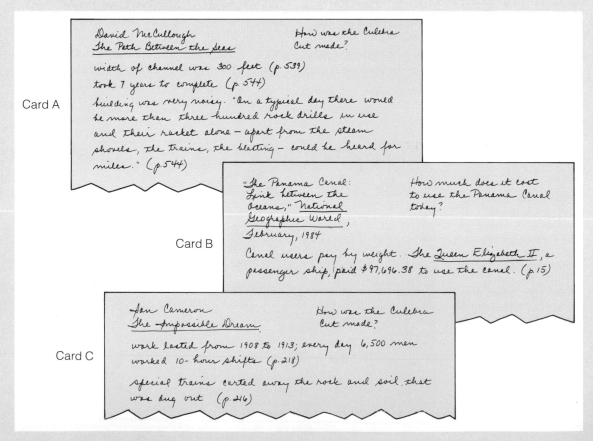

Card A

David McCullough
The Path Between the Seas

How was the Culebra Cut made?

width of channel was 300 feet (p. 539)
took 7 years to complete (p. 544)
building was very noisy. "On a typical day there would be more than three hundred rock drills in use and their racket alone — apart from the steam shovels, the trains, the blasting — could be heard for miles." (p. 544)

Card B

"The Panama Canal: Link between the Oceans," National Geographic World, February, 1984

How much does it cost to use the Panama Canal today?

Canal users pay by weight. The Queen Elizabeth II, a passenger ship, paid $97,696.38 to use the canal. (p. 15)

Card C

Ian Cameron
The Impossible Dream

How was the Culebra Cut made?

work lasted from 1908 to 1913; every day 6,500 men worked 10-hour shifts (p. 218)
special trains carted away the rock and soil that was dug out (p. 216)

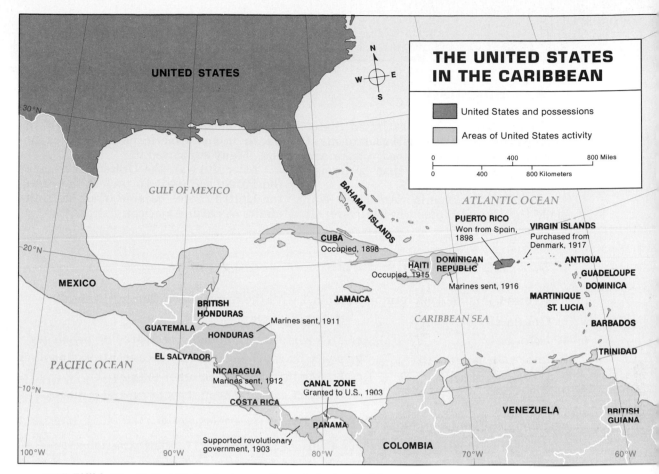

THE UNITED STATES IN THE CARIBBEAN

United States and possessions

Areas of United States activity

| 0 | 400 | 800 Miles |
| 0 | 400 | 800 Kilometers |

UNITED STATES

GULF OF MEXICO

BAHAMA ISLANDS

ATLANTIC OCEAN

PUERTO RICO
Won from Spain, 1898

VIRGIN ISLANDS
Purchased from Denmark, 1917

CUBA
Occupied, 1898

ANTIGUA

GUADELOUPE

DOMINICA

HAITI
Occupied, 1915

DOMINICAN REPUBLIC
Marines sent, 1916

MARTINIQUE
ST. LUCIA

MEXICO

BRITISH HONDURAS

JAMAICA

CARIBBEAN SEA

BARBADOS

GUATEMALA

HONDURAS
Marines sent, 1911

EL SALVADOR

TRINIDAD

PACIFIC OCEAN

NICARAGUA
Marines sent, 1912

CANAL ZONE
Granted to U.S., 1903

VENEZUELA

BRITISH GUIANA

COSTA RICA

PANAMA
Supported revolutionary government, 1903

COLOMBIA

MAP SKILL The United States took an active role in the Caribbean after 1890. In the early 1900s, President Taft used the Roosevelt Corollary to justify sending troops to Nicaragua and Honduras. What areas in the Caribbean did the United States control outright?

19 Americans. President Carranza of Mexico agreed to let the United States send a few troops into Mexico to pursue Villa.*

Wilson appointed General John J. Pershing to command the American force. When the force grew to 6,000 soldiers, Carranza protested what he called the American invasion. The crisis deepened. In the end, Wilson withdrew the American troops. By then, a larger war demanded his attention. As you will read in Chapter 25, the United States was being drawn into a world war that had been raging since 1914.

━━ SECTION REVIEW ━━

1. **Locate:** Colombia, Panama, Panama Canal, Venezuela, Dominican Republic, Haiti, Honduras, Mexico.

2. **Define:** dollar diplomacy.

3. List three problems that faced the builders of the Panama Canal.

4. How did the Roosevelt Corollary expand American power in the Western Hemisphere?

5. **What Do You Think?** Why do you think many Latin American nations criticized the United States in the early 1900s?

---

*Villa was angry at the United States for supporting a rival government in Mexico headed by Venustiano Carranza.

Chapter 24 Review

★ Summary ★

In the late 1800s, the United States changed from a policy of isolation to one of expansion. The nation gained Alaska and Hawaii and opened up Japan to foreign trade.

In 1898, the Spanish–American War made the United States a world power. It gained lands in the Caribbean and the Pacific. Some Americans opposed expansion. Many supported it.

After the war, the United States built the Panama Canal. To protect the canal, the United States became involved in the affairs of Latin American nations.

★ Reviewing the Facts ★

2 pts.

Key Terms. Match each term in Column 1 with the correct definition in Column 2.

Column 1
1. isolation
2. imperialism
3. sphere of influence
4. dollar diplomacy

Column 2
a. area where a nation had special trading privileges
b. policy by which one country takes control of another
c. having little to do with other nations
d. policy of using economic ties to expand influence

Key People, Events, and Ideas. Identify each of the following.

1. Treaty of Yokohama
2. Liliuokalani
3. Open Door Policy
4. Boxer Rebellion
5. John Hay
6. Lola Rodríguez de Tió
7. "Butcher" Weyler
8. Rough Riders
9. Emilio Aguinaldo
10. Battle of San Juan Hill
11. Platt Amendment
12. Foraker Act
13. Roosevelt Corollary
14. Francisco "Pancho" Villa
15. John J. Pershing

★ Chapter Checkup ★

5 pts. each

1. Give three reasons why the United States turned to a policy of expansion in the late 1800s.
2. How did each of the following help the United States expand: (a) William Seward; (b) Matthew Perry; (c) Theodore Roosevelt?
3. How did the United States acquire the Hawaiian Islands?
4. Why did the United States want other nations to accept the Open Door Policy?
5. (a) Why did Cubans revolt in 1895? (b) What role did the *Maine* play in the Spanish–American War?
6. Explain why some Americans objected to the peace treaty that ended the Spanish–American War.
7. (a) Why did Roosevelt recognize the independence of Panama so quickly? (b) How did the Panama Canal involve the United States more deeply than before in Latin America?
8. (a) Why were peasants unhappy with conditions in Mexico? (b) How was the United States drawn into the Mexican Revolution?

★ Thinking About History ★

8 pts. each

1. Understanding the economy. (a) How did expansion overseas in the late 1800s and early 1900s help the American economy? (b) Why do you think Americans had more interest in overseas markets in the late 1800s than in the early 1800s?

2. Relating past to present. (a) Why was Alaska called Seward's Folly? (b) Do you think people today would say Seward made a mistake when he bought Alaska? Explain.

3. Analyzing a quotation. (a) Why do you think John Hay called the Spanish–American War "a splendid little war"? (b) What other Americans would agree with him?

4. Understanding geography. (a) Describe three ways in which geography affected the building of the Panama Canal in the early 1900s. (b) Explain why each was important.

★ Using Your Skills ★

1. Identifying a point of view. Senator Albert Beveridge of Indiana claimed: "American factories are making more than the American people can use. American soil is producing more than they can consume. Fate has written our policy for us. The trade of the world must and shall be ours." (a) What does Beveridge say about the American economy? (b) What do you think Beveridge's point of view was toward overseas expansion?

2. Understanding cause and effect. Review pages 534–540 on the Spanish–American War. (a) List two causes of the war. (b) List two effects of the war. (c) Show how one cause and effect of the war are related.

3. Map reading. Study the maps on pages 541 and 545. (a) Is Panama north or south of Colombia? (b) In what direction does a ship go when it sails through the Panama Canal from the Pacific to the Atlantic? (c) What is the latitude of the Panama Canal?

4. Analyzing a political cartoon. Study the cartoon on page 543. (a) What is the subject of the cartoon? (b) What title would you give this cartoon? Explain.

5. Making a generalization. List three facts about the relationship between the United States and the nations of Latin America in the early 1900s. Then make a generalization based on these facts.

★ More to Do ★

1. Presenting a scene. As a group project, present a scene in which Commodore Perry meets Japanese officials for the first time and gives them a letter from President Fillmore.

2. Making a model. Make a model of the Battle of San Juan Hill showing Spanish defenders and American attackers.

3. Organizing a debate. Organize a debate on this question: Was President Roosevelt right to help the people of Panama revolt against Colombia?

4. Exploring local history. Locate local newspapers dating from 1865 to 1914. Report on how your community felt about American involvement overseas.

25

World War I (1914–1919)

Chapter Outline

1 War in Europe
2 From Neutrality to War
3 The United States at War
4 Making the Peace

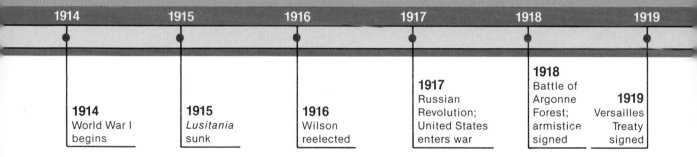

| 1914 | 1915 | 1916 | 1917 | 1918 | 1919 |

1914
World War I
begins

1915
Lusitania
sunk

1916
Wilson
reelected

1917
Russian
Revolution;
United States
enters war

1918
Battle of
Argonne
Forest;
armistice
signed

1919
Versailles
Treaty
signed

About This Chapter

In August 1914, a major war broke out in Europe. The United States quickly declared its neutrality. A song called "I Didn't Raise My Boy to Be a Soldier" became popular in 1915. The song reflected American feelings about the war in Europe.

I didn't raise my boy to be a soldier,
I brought him up to be my pride and joy,
Who dares to place a musket on his
    shoulder,
To shoot some other mother's darling
    boy?

In Europe, millions of "mothers' darling boys" were dying on the battlefield. But Americans wanted no part of this foreign war.

In the next two years, American feelings underwent a change. By 1917, a new song was popular. It was called "America, Here's My Boy."

America, I raised a boy for you,
America, you'll find him staunch and
    true,
Place a gun upon his shoulder,
He is ready to die or do.

By 1917, Americans no longer saw their nation far removed from the great war in Europe. They were now eager to join the battle to "make the world safe for democracy."

Study the time line above. When did the United States enter the war?

Soldiers went into World War I with thoughts of fighting glorious battles. Real life meant months in the trenches under heavy bombardment.

1 War in Europe

Read to Learn

★ What tensions existed among European nations in 1914?

★ How did the murder of Archduke Francis Ferdinand lead to war?

★ How did Americans feel about the war?

★ What do these words mean: militarism, kaiser, trench warfare, propaganda?

In the spring of 1914, Europe stood on the brink of war. An American diplomat in Europe wrote to President Wilson: "Everybody's nerves are tense. It only requires a spark to set the whole thing off." All too soon, the spark came. And Europe exploded into war.

Rivalries Among Nations

Why did Europe stand on the brink of war in 1914? For years, the nations of Europe were locked in rivalries that led to great tension.

Sources of tension. Nationalism was one source of tension. During the 1800s, nationalism helped to unite people with a common language and culture. It also set countries against one another.

In Europe, nationalism created deep mistrust and even hatred between nations. France and Germany were bitter rivals. In 1871, Germany seized

Alsace–Lorraine, an area rich in iron ore, from France. Austria–Hungary and Russia were rivals in Eastern Europe. Russia encouraged Slavs in Austria–Hungary to rebel against their rulers. Slavs included peoples of Eastern Europe such as Poles, Czechoslovaks, and Serbs.

Imperialism was another source of tension. In the late 1800s and early 1900s, Britain, France, Germany, Italy, and Russia scrambled for colonies in Africa and Asia. Each nation wanted to profit from new markets and raw materials. Often, two or more nations competed for power in the same area. This competition sometimes led to wars in places far from Europe.

Militarism was a third source of tension. *Militarism* is the policy of building up strong armed forces to prepare for war. European nations prepared for war by expanding their armies and navies. The military build-up led to new tension. When Germany expanded its navy, Great Britain felt that its naval power was threatened. So it built more ships. This naval race heightened tensions between these two nations.

The alliance system. To protect themselves, major European powers formed two rival alliances. One was the *Triple Alliance.* It included Austria–Hungary, Germany, and Italy. The other was the *Triple Entente* (ahn TAHNT). It included Great Britain, France, and Russia. Members of each alliance promised to support one another in case of attack. The alliance system increased tension because any crisis involving one member of an alliance affected that nation's allies. It also meant that a fairly minor incident could lead to a general war.

The Powder Keg Explodes

In fact, the spark that set off war in Europe seemed at first to be a minor incident. On June 28, 1914, the streets of Sarajevo in Bosnia were hung with flags. Archduke Francis Ferdinand, heir to the throne of Austria–Hungary, was visiting Bosnia, a part of the empire ruled by Austria–Hungary. Crowds thronged the parade route.

Murder in Sarajevo. Along the route were several determined young men. They were Serbian nationalists. Serbia was an independent nation that wanted Bosnia to break away from Austria–Hungary and join it.

As the archduke's open car passed by, one of the men hurled a bomb into it. The archduke quickly flicked the bomb out of the car before it exploded. The driver speeded up. Then, he stopped because he realized he had gone the wrong way. At that point, Gavrilo Princip stepped from the curb and fatally shot both the archduke and his wife.

The road to war. Austria–Hungary accused its neighbor Serbia of hatching the plot against the archduke and threatened war. Russia moved to protect Serbia. Diplomats tried hard to ease the crisis, but with no success. The alliance system came into play. When Germany moved to support its ally, Austria–Hungary, France prepared to help its ally, Russia.

On July 28, Austria–Hungary declared war on Serbia. The next day, Russia ordered its forces to prepare for war. Germany called on Russia to stop readying for war. When Russia did not reply, Germany declared war on Russia on August 1. Two days later, Germany declared war on Russia's ally, France. It wanted to win a quick victory in the west before fighting Russia in the east. When German armies invaded Belgium on their way into France, Great Britain entered the war.

What began on June 28 as a local crisis in Bosnia grew into a major war. For years, people had expected war. When it came, many nations welcomed the chance to prove their power and strength. Others, however, feared what war might bring.

On the Battlefronts

When war broke out in August 1914, both sides thought that it would end soon. "You will be home before the leaves have fallen from the trees," the *kaiser,* or German emperor, told his troops as they marched off to fight. But both sides were mistaken. The war dragged on for four years and was fought all over the globe. At the time, the war was called the Great War. Later, it became known as World War I.

On one side were the *Central Powers:* Germany, Austria–Hungary, and the Ottoman Empire. Although Italy had been a member of the Triple Alliance, it decided to remain neutral. On the other side were the *Allied Powers:* Britain, France, and Russia. In the end, 20 other nations joined the Allies in World War I.

The western front. When the war began, armies clashed on the western front. (See the map below.) German troops in their steel-gray uniforms poured into Brussels, the Belgian capital. As one witness wrote, they were "a force of nature like a tidal wave, an avalanche, or a river flooding its banks." The tiny Belgian army fought bravely but was soon overcome.

MAP SKILL In August 1914, war broke out in Europe. The war was fought on several fronts. The Allies clashed with the Central Powers in France, Belgium, Russia, Italy, and Turkey. Find Sarajevo on the map. In what country is it located? What country is directly west of Sarajevo?

Poison gas was one of the horrible new weapons used in World War I. This picture is called *Blinded by Gas*. It shows Allied soldiers on the western front waiting for medical treatment. Later, soldiers were given gas masks.

German armies swept on into France. By September, the Germans were advancing on Paris. The German offensive was slowed, however, when French and British troops took a stand along the Marne River. The *Battle of the Marne* ended the German hope for a quick victory in the west.

War in the trenches. By November 1914, it was clear that neither side could win a final victory. So both sides dug trenches protected by mines and barbed wire. For the next three years, there was almost no change in the position of either side.

In the maze of trenches, a new way of life emerged. Thousands of soldiers spent weeks at a time in muddy, rat-infested ditches. Some trenches were simple shelters. Others were elaborate tunnels that served as headquarters and first-aid stations. Between the front-line trenches of each side lay "no-man's land." This area was a wasteland of barbed wire and deadly land mines.

Trench warfare consisted of days of shelling the enemy. Then, troops would be ordered "over the top." They crawled out of the trenches to race across "no-man's-land" and attack the enemy. Most offensives resulted in huge losses. They gained little territory. The Battle of Verdun in 1916 lasted for six months. In it, the Germans lost 330,000 men trying to overrun French lines. The French lost just as many men defending their position.

The eastern front. On the eastern front, the fighting ended up in trench warfare, too. The armies of Germany and Austria–Hungary faced Russian and Serbian troops across endless lines of trenches. Both sides suffered heavy losses. By mid-1916, the Russians had lost over one million soldiers. Yet neither side won a decisive victory.

America Remains Neutral

When war broke out in Europe, Americans wanted no part of it. President Woodrow Wilson called on Americans to "be neutral in fact as well as in name." Officially, the United States was neutral. But many Americans supported the Allies. After all, they had ties to Britain. The British and Americans spoke the same language and had many traditions in common. Also, France had been America's first ally.

Still, millions of German Americans favored the Central Powers. Many Irish Americans hated the British. So they sympathized with the Central Powers. Also, American Jews often sided with Germany against Russia. Many of them had fled persecution in Russia.

The war in Europe had several effects on America. First, it brought an economic boom to the United States. The Allies badly needed food, arms, oil, steel, and other goods. American farmers and manufacturers rushed to fill orders from Europe. By 1917, trade with the Allies had grown seven times in value. However, this trade meant that the United States was not strictly neutral.

Second, both the Allies and the Central Powers used propaganda to win support in the United States. *Propaganda* is the spreading of ideas or beliefs that help a particular cause and hurt an opposing cause. The Allies pictured the Germans as savage beasts who committed horrible acts. The Germans painted the Allies in similar ways. (See Skill Lesson 25 on page 556.)

German Submarine Warfare

The propaganda war fed a growing anti-German feeling in America. That feeling increased when Germany began attacking American ships. Early in the war, Britain used its navy to blockade German ports. They wanted to cut off supplies to Germany and force it to surrender. Germany replied by setting up a blockade around Britain. Germany used a powerful new weapon in this sea war, its fleet of submarines. U-boats, or undersea boats, attacked ships as they entered or left British ports.

The use of submarines against neutral shipping raised a storm of protest. Under international law, a country at war could stop and search a neutral ship suspected of carrying war goods. However, submarines were not equipped to do this. Instead, they simply sank shipping on sight, with great loss of life.

The Germans warned neutral nations such as the United States that they would attack any ship entering the blockade zone. President Wilson refused to accept this limit on neutral shipping. He said that he would hold Germany responsible if American lives or property were lost because of German submarine warfare.

Germany ignored Wilson's threat. On May 7, 1915, a German submarine torpedoed the British passenger ship *Lusitania* off the coast of Ireland. Nearly 1,200 people were lost, including 128 Americans. (See page 555.)

The sinking of the *Lusitania* set off a wave of anti-German feeling in the United States. President Wilson threatened to break off diplomatic relations with Germany if it did not stop sinking passenger ships. Germany did not want to risk war with the United States. So it agreed to the American demand.

1. **Locate:** Great Britain, France, Germany, Alsace, Lorraine, Italy, Russia, Austria–Hungary, Sarajevo, Central Powers, Allied Powers.
2. **Define:** militarism, kaiser, trench warfare, propaganda.
3. Give two reasons why tensions were high in Europe in 1914.
4. (a) What position on the war did the United States take in 1914? (b) How did the United States benefit from the war?
5. **What Do You Think?** How do you think the alliance system helped cause the war?

2 From Neutrality to War

Read to Learn
★ Why did the United States declare war on Germany?
★ How did Americans support the war effort?
★ What does this word mean: pacifist?

As the war dragged on in Europe, pressure for war mounted in the United States. Former President Theodore Roosevelt called people who wanted neutrality "flubdubs, mollycoddles, and flapdoodle pacifists." Still, President Wilson stood firm. "There is such a thing," he said, "as a nation being so right that it does not need to convince others by force. There is such a thing as a man being too proud to fight."

Election of 1916

In the election of 1916, Wilson ran on the slogan "He kept us out of war." However, by 1916, the President saw the need to be prepared for war. So he pledged to strengthen American armed forces. The Republicans chose Charles Evans Hughes to run against Wilson. Hughes was a Supreme Court Justice and former governor of New York. Like Wilson, Hughes supported American neutrality.

The race was close. On election night, Hughes went to bed believing he had won. Shortly after midnight, a newspaper reporter phoned him. "The President cannot be disturbed," a Hughes friend told the reporter. "Well, when he wakes up," said the reporter, "just tell him he isn't President." Returns from California had come in. They showed that Wilson had won that state and, with it, the election.

Since the early days of the war, President Wilson had taken on the role of peacemaker. More than once, he asked the warring powers to stop fighting and meet at the peace table. He urged both sides to accept "peace without victory."

Decision for War

Wilson's peace moves failed, however. By late 1916, the British blockade of Germany was causing severe shortages in Germany. A desperate Germany decided to fight back. On February 1, 1917, the German government announced that its submarines would sink any ship approaching Britain.

The Germans knew that this policy would probably bring the United States into the war. But they hoped to defeat the Allies before American troops could get to Europe. Wilson protested this move by breaking off diplomatic relations with Germany. Still, the President hoped for peace.

Zimmermann telegram. A few weeks later, the United States moved closer to war when it learned of the

The New York Times.

"All the News That's Fit to Print"

EXTRA
5:30 A.M.

LUSITANIA SUNK BY A SUBMARINE, PROBABLY 1,260 DEAD;
TWICE TORPEDOED OFF IRISH COAST; SINKS IN 15 MINUTES;
CAPT. TURNER SAVED, FROHMAN AND VANDERBILT MISSING;
WASHINGTON BELIEVES THAT A GRAVE CRISIS IS AT HAND

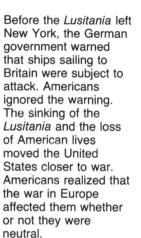

Before the *Lusitania* left New York, the German government warned that ships sailing to Britain were subject to attack. Americans ignored the warning. The sinking of the *Lusitania* and the loss of American lives moved the United States closer to war. Americans realized that the war in Europe affected them whether or not they were neutral.

Zimmermann telegram. This secret telegram was sent by the German foreign secretary, Arthur Zimmermann, to his minister in Mexico. It told the German minister to urge Mexico to attack the United States if the United States declared war on Germany. In return, Germany promised to help Mexico win back its "lost provinces" in the American Southwest.* When Americans learned of this secret telegram, a new wave of anti-German feeling swept the nation.

In March 1917, two events moved the country still closer to war. First, German submarines sank several American merchant ships. Second, a revolution in Russia forced Czar Nicholas II from his throne.

The Russian Revolution. The Russian Revolution, which began in 1917, was one of the most important events of

this century. For hundreds of years, czars, or emperors, had ruled Russia with absolute power. Several times in the 1800s and early 1900s, Russians had revolted. Each effort ended in failure and even more harsh rule.

When World War I began, the Russians at first united behind the war effort. As conditions at home and on the front grew worse, many supported revolutionaries who wanted to overthrow the czar. In March 1917, bread riots turned into a revolution. The czar was forced to give up power. Revolutionaries set up the Provisional Government and called for democratic freedoms. The new government promised to bring about social and political reforms.

President Wilson was pleased with events in Russia. He was a firm believer in democracy. He had not liked the idea of fighting on the same side as the czar. With the new government in power, Wilson believed that the Allied cause would be stronger.

*As you read in Chapter 14, the United States gained this land in the Mexican Cession.

During World War I, both the Allies and the Central Powers used propaganda. Propaganda is a deliberate attempt to spread ideas that help a certain cause or hurt an opposing cause. Propaganda is used to shape public opinion.

Propaganda has been used throughout history. It is important to be able to recognize propaganda in order to understand historical events. During World War I, newspapers and governments on both sides used propaganda to win public support for the war effort. For example, both Britain and Germany used propaganda to convince Americans to enter the war on their side.

1. **Identify the facts.** Propaganda such as drawings or posters present facts and opinions in a visual way. Remember that facts can be shown to be true. Opinions are the beliefs or ideas of a person or group. They are not necessarily true. (a) What facts are shown in this drawing? (b) How do you know that these are facts? (c) What opinions are shown?

2. **Identify the propaganda technique.** Propaganda can shape public opinion through many different techniques. One technique is presenting half-truths. For example, a picture, newspaper article, or chart can show facts that are correct, but only show some of the facts.

A second propaganda technique is name-calling. One side might call the other side barbarians. A third technique is identifying a cause with a famous person or noble idea. A fourth is using symbols or pictures that show the other side in the worst possible light.

Study the drawing at left. (a) What symbol is used to represent Germany? (b) How are the Allies shown? (c) Which of the propaganda techniques listed above does this drawing use? (d) Do you think this drawing is an effective piece of propaganda? Why?

3. **Draw conclusions based on the evidence.** Study the drawing to figure out why it was used in the United States. (a) Which side do you think would have wanted this drawing published in the United States? Why? (b) Describe two ways in which this drawing might have affected public opinion in the United States.

4. **Make a generalization.** Based on your reading in this chapter, why do you think propaganda is often used in wartime?

Declaration of war. On April 2, the President asked Congress for a declaration of war. "The world must be made safe for democracy," he declared. "It is a fearful thing to lead this great peaceful people into war, into the most terrible and disastrous of all wars. . . . But the right is more precious than the peace."

Congress voted for war 511 to 56. On April 6, the President signed the document. It thrust Americans into the deadliest war the world had yet seen.

Organizing for War

The day after war was declared, George M. Cohan wrote a song that quickly caught on across the country. It began:

> Over there, over there, send the word,
> send the word, over there,
> That the Yanks are coming, the Yanks are
> coming . . .

The song ended on this confident note:

> We'll be over, we're coming over, and we
> won't come back till it's over over
> there.

Declaring war and singing a catchy tune were just the beginning. In April 1917, the country had to organize for war—and do it quickly. The Allies were short of everything from food to arms. Britain had only a few weeks' supply of food. In France, war-weary soldiers were near to collapse. In Russia, soldiers were leaving the front to join the revolution.

The armed forces. The United States moved quickly to raise a large army. On May 18, Congress passed the *Selective Service Act.* The act was a draft law. It called for all young men between the ages of 21 and 30 to register for the draft. In the next 18 months, 4 million men and women joined the armed forces. Young men marched off to training camps. Because of a lack of weapons, many trained using broomsticks for guns. Women served in the army and navy as radio operators, clerks, and stenographers.

At first, black Americans were not allowed to fight for their country. Then, the Selective Service Act opened the doors. Blacks joined the armed forces in large numbers. They were not allowed into regular units. Instead, they were organized into segregated "black-only" units. These units were commanded by white officers.

Despite discrimination, more than 2 million blacks registered for the armed services. Nearly 400,000 were accepted for duty. Black units were among the first to reach France. There, they fought bravely and were among the most highly decorated in the war.

Soldiers from every ethnic group fought. About 20,000 Puerto Ricans served in the armed forces. Many Native Americans, too, responded to the nation's call to arms.

Resources for war. The United States channeled its entire economy into producing the food, arms, and other goods needed to win the war. President Wilson set up government agencies to oversee the war effort.

Herbert Hoover headed the Food Administration. His job was to boost food production. The nation needed to feed its soldiers and help the Allies. "Food Will Win the War," said Food Administration posters.

Farmers planted more crops. Families set up "victory gardens" in their backyards to grow their own food. Americans were asked to go without wheat on Mondays and meat on Tuesdays. Patriotic Americans gladly agreed to "wheatless Mondays" and "meatless Tuesdays" to help their boys "over there."

Another government agency, the War Industries Board, told factories what to produce. It also divided up limited resources. The War Labor Board settled disputes over working hours and wages. Its job was to prevent strikes that would slow down the war effort. In fact, the AFL was able to win better pay and working conditions during the war. The main reason for this was the shortage of workers.

The Home Front

Americans on the home front united behind the war effort. Well-known movie stars like Charlie Chaplin, Mary Pickford, and Douglas Fairbanks did their part. They traveled across the country and urged people to buy *Liberty Bonds.* By buying bonds, people were lending money to the government to pay for the war. The government raised $21 billion through the sale of Liberty Bonds.

The President sent out speakers to rally support for the war. They were called Four-Minute Men because their speeches lasted four minutes. The speakers addressed crowds in movie theaters, clubhouses, and convention halls. They called on patriotic Americans to sacrifice their own wants to the war effort. They carried the message that the war was being fought for freedom and democracy.

Support for the war effort. As men joined the armed forces, women stepped in to take on their jobs. Millions of women took jobs outside the home for the first time. The idea that "a woman's place is in the home" was replaced with the idea that "a woman's place is in the war."

Women drove trolley cars and delivered mail. Some served as police officers. Others worked in factories, making weapons and uniforms. By working in jobs once thought to be for men only, women changed the view that they could do only certain kinds of jobs.

During the war, thousands of black Americans moved from farms in the South to factories in the North. They took jobs in war plants, making goods needed by American and Allied armies.

Blacks left the South because of bad economic and social conditions there. Many were sharecroppers or day laborers. They got almost nothing for their work. Also, they suffered from frequent violence. When blacks saw the chance to make a decent wage and escape harsh conditions in the South, they left in waves.

Silencing protests. A small number of Americans opposed the war. Among them were some labor groups and *pacifists,* people who refuse to fight in any war. These people as well as many German Americans were suspected of being disloyal. They suffered from hate campaigns in the newspapers. Some were even attacked on the streets.

The government tried to stop people from speaking out against the war. Congress passed laws making it a

Posters urged Americans to support the war effort by growing their own food. How does this poster mock, or make fun of, Germany?

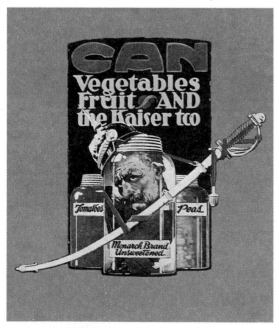

During World War I, many women worked in factories for the first time. Here, women have replaced men in a Detroit tire factory.

crime to criticize the government or interfere with the war effort. Nearly 1,600 men and women were arrested for breaking these laws.

Antiwar feeling ran high among socialists* and radical labor groups. Eugene V. Debs, Socialist candidate for President four times, was jailed. So, too, was William "Big Bill" Haywood, head of the Industrial Workers of the World. A few people questioned the silencing of protests. They said it violated the Constitution, which guarantees freedom of speech. Most, however, felt that Americans had to make sacrifices for the war effort.

SECTION REVIEW

1. **Define:** pacifist.
2. Give two reasons why the United States declared war on Germany.
3. (a) Name three government agencies that helped organize the war effort. (b) What did each agency do?
4. How did women help the war effort?
5. **What Do You Think?** Why do you think the government tried to stop people from criticizing the war?

---

*Socialists believed that the means of producing goods—such as banks and factories—should be publicly owned. They thought all people should share in the work and in the goods produced.

3 The United States at War

Read to Learn

★ Why were the Allies in a desperate condition in 1917?
★ How did Americans help in the final battles of the war?
★ What were the costs of World War I?
★ What does this word mean: armistice?

MAP SKILL During World War I, armies battled back and forth across the western front. Tens of thousands of soldiers fell in costly assaults on enemy positions. Early in 1918, fresh American troops gave the Allies new strength. Name three rivers that were near major battle sites.

THE WESTERN FRONT

— Farthest German advance, 1914
---- Armistice line 1918
← Allied offensive 1918
✩ Major battles

NORTH SEA
NETHERLANDS
Ypres
Brussels
BELGIUM
GERMANY
Meuse R.
Rhine R.
Somme
Amiens
LUXEMBOURG
Moselle R.
Oise R.
Aisne R.
Belleau Wood
Reims
Argonne Forest
Verdun
LORRAINE
Saar R.
Paris
Chateau-Thierry
Marne R.
ALSACE
FRANCE
Seine R.
SWITZ.

0   50   100 Miles
0   50   100 Kilometers

On June 26, 1917, the first American troops reached France. On July 4th, they paraded through Paris. The French showered the Yanks with flowers and cries of "Vive l'Amerique," or "Long live America!" Within a few days, the soldiers marched off to the front.

Some Americans felt that they were repaying France for its help during the Revolution. A captain in one American unit visited the tomb of Lafayette, the French noble who fought in the American Revolution. The captain stood before the tomb and called out, "Lafayette, we are here!"

A Desperate Moment

Only a few American troops landed in France in 1917. They did not reach full strength until the spring of 1918. By that time, the Allies were in a desperate position. During the war, the British and French lost huge numbers of soldiers. At the front, some exhausted troops refused to obey orders to go "over the top."

Russia makes peace. Even more serious, the Russians pulled out of the war. In November 1917, a second revolution took place in Russia. The *Bolsheviks* seized power from the Provisional Government. The Bolsheviks had their own far-reaching program for changing Russia. Led by V. I. Lenin, the Bolsheviks wanted to bring a communist revolution to Russia.

Lenin had read the writings of Karl Marx, a German thinker of the 1800s. Marx had predicted that workers around the world would unite to overthrow the ruling class. Their revolution would end private property and set up a classless society. Lenin thought he could bring about such a revolution in Russia.

Once in power, Lenin asked Germany for peace. To him, peace was needed so that the communists could bring about their revolution. In the *Treaty of Brest–Litovsk,* signed in March 1918, Russia gave up large amounts of land to Germany.

The treaty was a terrible blow to the Allies. It gave Germany coal mines and other resources in Russia. More important, it let Germany move its armies from the eastern front to the western front. In the spring of 1918, Germany used these troops in an all-out offensive against the Allies.

German peace offensive. The Germans called this attack their "peace offensive." They hoped that it would end the war—in their favor. The offensive began on March 20 near Amiens. (See the map on page 560.) Dozens of German divisions massed up against a small British force. Late at night, 6,000 German cannons opened fire on the British. Despite the heavy bombing, the British held on to Amiens. The battle lasted until April 5, when the Germans gave up the attack. They did not give up their offensive, however.

By late May, the Germans had smashed through Allied lines along the Aisne River. On June 3, they reached the Marne River, just east of Chateau-Thierry (sha TOH tee AIR ree). By then, they were only 50 miles (80 km) from Paris.

Americans in Battle

The American Expeditionary Force was commanded by General John J. Pershing. Early in his career, Pershing earned the nickname Black Jack because he commanded an all-black unit.* By 1916, Pershing was well known in the United States for leading

---

*General Pershing had led the famous black 10th Cavalry in the Battle of San Juan Hill during the Spanish American War.

AMERICANS WHO DARED

Alvin York

Alvin York won fame for his brave deeds in World War I. York grew up on a backcountry farm in Tennessee. At first, he opposed World War I for religious reasons. Later, he enlisted in the army. In October 1918, York, armed only with a rifle, cleared out a nest of German machine gunners. His brave work opened up the way for advancing American troops. When his ammunition ran out, he grabbed a captured pistol. He then rounded up 132 German prisoners. Both the United States and France honored Sergeant York with their highest medals.

an American army into Mexico to hunt for Francisco "Pancho" Villa in Mexico. (See page 545.)

General Pershing was a man of few words but a will of iron. When the Americans reached France, the Allies

By the time the United States entered World War I, a new kind of battle had developed—the battle in the air. Armed with machine guns and bombs, planes tangled in the skies in deadly combat.

As volunteers in the French Flying Corps, many American pilots were already well trained in air warfare. They and the new arrivals from the United States took to the skies with daring and courage.

Far above the soldiers in the trenches, American "knights of the air" clashed with the enemy in dramatic dogfights. Swooping and weaving, they maneuvered for the best position to fire at enemy planes.

At evening mess, pilots sang as they toasted comrades, country, and cause. The mess hall echoed with their chorus: "Tails up and flying, any weather, where e'er the call may be."

Pilots became aces when they downed five enemy planes. By the end of the war, the United States boasted 66 aces. Eddie Rickenbacker, shown here with his plane, won the title Ace of Aces for downing more planes than any other American pilot.

★ What special qualities did American pilots have?

wanted the fresh troops to reinforce their own war-weary soldiers. Pershing wanted his troops to operate as a separate unit. In the end, Pershing agreed to let some Americans fight with the British and French. At the same time, he insisted on having his own part of the western front to defend.

We dig no trenches. In June 1918, American troops plunged into their first major battle in Belleau (BEHL loh) Wood. A French general sent General James Harbord of the United States a message: "Have your men prepare entrenchments some hundreds of yards to the rear in case of need." Harbord replied: "We dig no trenches to fall back on. The marines will hold where they stand."

The **Battle of Belleau Wood** raged on for three weeks. Finally, on June 25, General Harbord passed along the good news: "Wood now exclusively U.S. Marine Corps."

In mid-July, the Germans made another desperate attempt to take Paris. The Americans stubbornly fought back. Within three days, the Allies "turned the tide of the war," Pershing wrote. Even the Germans "knew all was lost" as their troops were driven into retreat.

Final battles. The Allies took the offensive. The commander of the Allied forces was a Frenchman, Marshal Ferdinand Foch (fohsh). He wanted to attack German forces along a line stretching from Verdun to the North Sea. Foch agreed to let Pershing and the Americans attack the area between the Meuse River and the Argonne Forest. (See the map on page 560.) The land was a crazy quilt of hills and ridges—perfect for the Germans to defend.

The *Battle of the Argonne Forest* was one of the bloodiest of the war. On September 26, over one million Americans pushed into the forest. At first, they fought well despite heavy German fire. Then, rains and the difficult woods bogged down their advance. Small units drove forward to capture deadly German positions. Finally, after 47 days, the Americans broke through the German defense.

British, French, and Belgian forces smashed through the German lines in their areas, too. By November, German forces on the western front were in retreat. The end of this "war to end all wars" was in sight.

The Armistice

On October 6, Prince Max of Baden, head of the German cabinet, secretly cabled President Wilson: "To avoid further bloodshed, the German government requests the President to arrange the immediate conclusion of an armistice on land, by sea, and in the air." An *armistice* is an agreement to stop fighting. Wilson made two demands before an armistice could be signed. First, Germany must accept his plan for peace. Second, the German emperor must give up his power.

While leaders in Germany discussed what to do, conditions there grew worse. German sailors rebelled. Revolutions simmered in several German cities. On the battlefront, German armies lost ground daily.

On November 9, the German emperor resigned and fled to Holland. Germany became a republic. The new German leaders agreed to the armistice terms. On November 11, 1918, at 11:00 A.M.—the eleventh hour of the eleventh day of the eleventh month—the guns fell silent. World War I ended.

The costs of the war were huge. Battle deaths numbered between 10 and 13 million. Germany, alone, lost about 2 million men. More than 4 million

The fighting on the western front turned northern France and Belgium into a barren wasteland. An American soldier who fought in the trenches recalled, "The men slept in mud, washed in mud, ate mud, and dreamed mud." Here, American soldiers cross the mud on wooden planks.

Costs of the War for the Allies

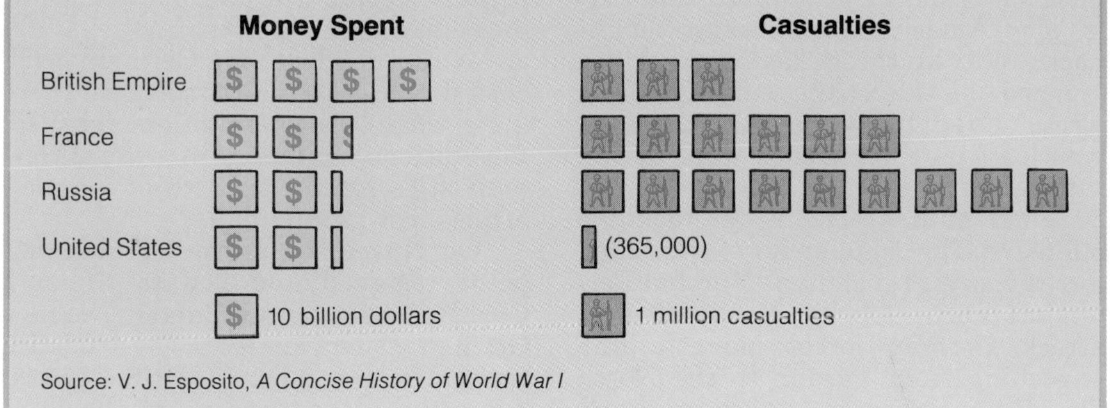

	Money Spent	Casualties
British Empire	$ $ $ $	👤 👤 👤
France	$ $ $	👤 👤 👤 👤 👤
Russia	$ $	👤 👤 👤 👤 👤 👤 👤 👤 👤
United States	$ $	(365,000)

$ = 10 billion dollars   👤 = 1 million casualties

Source: V. J. Esposito, *A Concise History of World War I*

GRAPH SKILL During World War I, there were millions of casualties, that is, dead or wounded people. The graph above is called a picture graph because it shows statistics in picture form. How many casualties did the Russians have? How much did the United States spend on the war?

Russian, French, and British soldiers were killed. During 6 months of heavy fighting, the United States lost over 50,000 men. Many more people died of disease. More than 20 million soldiers on both sides were wounded.

Much of northern France was destroyed. Millions of Germans were near starvation. In 1918, another disaster struck. All over the world, people suffered from a terrible influenza epidemic. Between 1918 and 1919, more than 500,000 Americans died in the epidemic. The death toll in other countries numbered in the millions.

SECTION REVIEW

1. **Locate:** Amiens, Marne River, Chateau-Thierry, Paris, Belleau Wood, Meuse River, Argonne.
2. **Define:** armistice.
3. (a) What was the Treaty of Brest–Litovsk? (b) How did it affect the Allies?
4. Describe two battles in which Americans fought.
5. **What Do You Think?** Why do you think President Wilson refused to sign an armistice unless the German emperor gave up power?

4 Making the Peace

Read to Learn

★ What were the Fourteen Points?
★ How did the Allies differ on goals for the peace?
★ Why did some Americans object to the Versailles Treaty?
★ What do these words mean: self-determination, reparations?

During the war, President Wilson often stated his goals for the peace. "The world must be made safe for democracy," he declared. When the guns fell silent in France, Wilson crossed the Atlantic. He went to France, hoping to set up a just and lasting peace.

Wilson's Fourteen Points

In December 1918, Wilson sailed to Paris, France, to take part in the peace conference. He was the first American President to visit Europe while in office. In Paris and later in London, Milan, and Rome, cheering crowds welcomed the American leader. People showered him with flowers and cried with joy as he rode by in his car. Wilson believed that this support would help him achieve his goals for the peace.

Almost a year earlier, in January 1918, Wilson had given a speech outlining the *Fourteen Points,* his goals for the peace. The Fourteen Points were meant to prevent international problems such as those that had caused World War I from causing another war. Wilson called for an end to secret agreements such as those that created the rival alliances in 1914. He wanted freedom of the seas, free trade, and a limit on arms. Also, he urged peaceful settlement of conflicts over colonies.

In other points, Wilson explained his goal of *self-determination.* By this, he meant that national groups had the right to their own territory and forms of government. Wilson's last point called for the creation of a "general association of nations." The purpose of this association, or *League of Nations,* would be to protect the independence of both large and small nations.

Wilson persuaded the Allies to accept the Fourteen Points as the basis for the peace. When talks began, however, Wilson realized that the Allies were more concerned with their own interests than with the Fourteen Points.

The Peace Conference

More than 30 nations met in Paris and Versailles (vuhr sī), where the peace talks were held. The main work was done by the Big Four—Woodrow Wilson of the United States, David Lloyd George of Britain, Georges Clemenceau (KLEHM uhn soh) of France, and Vittorio Orlando of Italy.

Goals for peace. At the Paris Peace Conference, each leader had his own goals. Wilson favored "peace without victory." He wanted the Allies to set up a just peace rather than punish Germany and the other Central Powers. But Wilson stood alone. The Allies ached for revenge. They demanded *reparations,* or payments for the losses they had suffered during the war. They wanted to take over German colonies and make Germany admit its guilt for the war.

During months of haggling, Wilson was forced to compromise on his Fourteen Points. By June 1919, the *Versailles Treaty* was ready. None of the Allies was wholly satisfied with the results. Germany had not even been allowed to send delegates. It was horrified at the treaty. Still, it had no choice but to sign. The treaty made Germany take full responsibility for the war. Germany was completely disarmed. It was forced to pay huge reparations to the Allies. German colonies were put under the control of other nations.

New nations. Wilson had his way on a few issues. In Eastern Europe, several new nations were created based on self-determination. The new nations included Poland, Czechoslovakia, and Yugoslavia. They were created out of lands once ruled by Germany, Russia, and Austria–Hungary. (See the map on page 567.)

For Wilson, the greatest success was including a League of Nations in the peace treaty. The President fought hard for the League. He believed that it would keep the peace in the future. Exhausted, the President returned to the United States. There, he faced the biggest battle of his life. He had to convince two thirds of the Senate to approve the Versailles Treaty.

Battle Over the League

Wilson arrived home to find that many Americans opposed the peace treaty. Some said that the treaty was too soft on the defeated powers. Many

German Americans felt that the treaty was too harsh. Isolationists, or people who wanted the United States to keep out of world affairs, did not want to join the League of Nations under the terms of the treaty.

Lodge fights the treaty. People who opposed the treaty found a leader in Henry Cabot Lodge of Massachusetts. Lodge, a Republican, was chairman of the Senate Foreign Relations Committee. He objected to Article 10 of the treaty. This article said that League members would act together to put down any threats to peace.

Senator Lodge accepted the idea of the League. But he insisted that changes be made in it. He argued that Article 10 could involve the United States in future European wars. He wanted to make sure that the United States remained independent of the League. He also wanted Congress to decide whether the United States would follow League policy.

Wilson responds. Wilson refused to compromise with Lodge. Instead, the President took his case to the American people. In early September 1919, Wilson set out on a national speaking tour.

The treaty that ended World War I was signed in the palace of Versailles, near Paris. Here, President Wilson holds the treaty in his hand. The German delegates, facing him, had not seen the treaty until they were told to sign it. Later, the United States Senate rejected the treaty because of Article 10 and the League of Nations.

EUROPE AFTER WORLD WAR I

New nations

0   300   600 Miles

0   300   600 Kilometers

ICELAND

ATLANTIC OCEAN

NORWAY

SWEDEN

FINLAND

ESTONIA

LATVIA

LITHUANIA

NORTH SEA

BALTIC SEA

Moscow

IRELAND

GREAT BRITAIN

London

DENMARK

GER.

RUSSIA

NETH.

Berlin

BELG.

GERMANY

POLAND

Paris

LUX.

Versailles

CZECHOSLOVAKIA

FRANCE

Vienna

SWITZ.

AUSTRIA   HUNGARY

ROMANIA

PORTUGAL

Madrid

SPAIN

ITALY

YUGOSLAVIA

Sarajevo

BLACK SEA

BULGARIA

Constantinople

Rome

ALBANIA

MEDITERRANEAN SEA

GREECE

TURKEY

SP. MOROCCO

MAP SKILL The treaties that ended World War I created several new nations. Urged on by President Wilson, the Allies recognized the right of self-determination. Compare this map to the one on page 551. What three countries had to give up land to the new nations?

As his train crisscrossed the country, he made 37 speeches praising the treaty in 29 cities. He urged people to let their senators know that they supported the treaty.

Wilson kept up a killing pace. On September 25, the exhausted President complained of a headache. His doctors canceled the rest of the trip. Wilson returned to Washington. A week later, Wilson suffered a severe stroke that left him bedridden.

In November 1919, the Senate voted to reject the Versailles Treaty. In doing so, the United States also rejected the League of Nations that Wilson had fought so hard to establish. The United States did not sign a peace treaty with Germany until 1921. By then, many nations had joined the League of Nations. Without the United States, however, the League had limited power and influence.

SECTION REVIEW

1. **Define:** self-determination, reparations.
2. What were the Fourteen Points?
3. (a) Who were the Big Four? (b) What country did each represent?
4. **What Do You Think?** Why do you think some Americans disliked the idea of the League of Nations?

Chapter 25 Review

★ Summary ★

Years of tension in Europe exploded into war in 1914. When the war began, both the Allied and Central Powers thought that it would end quickly. Instead, it dragged on for four years. President Wilson tried to keep the United States neutral. But the United States was drawn into the war.

When the United States entered the war, the Allies were in a desperate posi-tion. American troops helped stop the final German offensive and turn the tide in favor of the Allies.

In 1919, President Wilson attended the Paris Peace Conference. Wilson wanted a peace treaty based on his Fourteen Points. But other Allies had their own goals. In the end, the Senate rejected the Versailles Treaty.

★ Reviewing the Facts ★

 2pts.

Key Terms. Match each term in Column 1 with the correct definition in Column 2.

Column 1
1. militarism
2. propaganda
3. pacifist
4. armistice
5. reparations

Column 2
a. person who refuses to fight in any war
b. policy of building up strong military forces to prepare for war
c. payment for loss
d. spreading of ideas that help a cause and hurt an opposing cause
e. agreement to stop fighting

Key People, Events, and Ideas. Identify each of the following.
1. Francis Ferdinand
2. Central Powers
3. Allied Powers
4. *Lusitania*
5. Zimmermann telegram
6. Selective Service Act
7. Liberty Bonds
8. Treaty of Brest–Litovsk
9. John J. Pershing
10. Ferdinand Foch
11. Battle of the Argonne Forest
12. Fourteen Points
13. League of Nations
14. Versailles Treaty
15. Henry Cabot Lodge

★ Chapter Checkup ★

 5pts

1. How did each of the following contribute to tension in Europe: (a) nationalism; (b) imperialism; (c) militarism?
2. Describe trench warfare during World War I.
3. (a) What was the official American posi-tion on the war in 1914? (b) Why did some Americans favor the Central Pow-ers? (c) Why did some Americans favor the Allied Powers?
4. (a) Why did anti-German feeling in-crease in the United States? (b) What events led the United States to declare war on Germany?
5. Explain three ways Americans helped organize for the war.
6. (a) Why was American help needed so badly in 1917? (b) Describe how Ameri-cans helped defeat Germany.
7. (a) Why did President Wilson propose his Fourteen Points? (b) Why did he have to compromise on some of them?
8. Why did Lodge and others object to the Versailles Treaty?

★ Thinking About History

1 and 4 only 10 pts. ★

1. **Understanding the economy.** During World War I, the United States government set up agencies to regulate different parts of the economy. (a) How did these agencies step in to regulate the free enterprise system? (b) Why do you think Americans let the government have so much power?

2. **Learning about citizenship.** During World War I, the government and individual people tried to stop anyone from criticizing the war. Do you agree with their view that protesters were dangerous to the war effort? Explain.

3. **Relating past to present.** Before and after World War I, many Americans were isolationists. Review what you have learned about American foreign policy since 1789. (a) When did the tradition of isolation begin? (b) How did this position change in the late 1800s? (c) What position does the United States take today?

4. **Taking a stand.** Do you think Woodrow Wilson should have agreed to compromise with Senator Lodge on the League of Nations issue? Explain.

★ Using Your Skills

Extra Credit #2 - 5 pts ★

1. **Understanding cause and effect.** Decide whether each of the following was a cause of the murder of Archduke Francis Ferdinand or an effect of the murder: (a) nationalism grows among the Slavs; (b) Austria–Hungary declares war on Serbia; (c) Germany invades Belgium.

2. **Ranking.** List four reasons why the United States was drawn into World War I. Then rank them according to which you think had most influence on the United States.

3. **Recognizing propaganda.** Study the poster on page 558. (a) What does it show? (b) What message does it carry?

(c) Would you call it propaganda? Why or why not?

4. **Map reading.** Study the map on page 567. (a) Name three new nations created after World War I. (b) In what part of Europe were most of these nations? (c) Which nation or nations were set up on the border of Russia? (d) What new nation was north of Austria?

5. **Writing a summary.** Review pages 561–567 on Making the Peace. Then write a summary that shows President Wilson's goals for the peace, the goals of other Allies, and the outcome of the peace talks.

★ More to Do

1. **Building a model.** Make a model of trenches on the western front. Study pictures and research in books about World War I to find out about trench warfare.

2. **Listening to music.** Listen to tapes or records of songs from World War I. Then prepare a report on what the songs tell about World War I.

3. **Exploring local history.** Report on how local industries or farms were affected

by European demand for supplies in the first years of the war.

4. **Writing a skit.** As a group project, prepare a skit on the peace talks in Paris. Have people take the roles of each of the Big Four. Others can take the roles of smaller countries or advisers. Negotiate among yourselves on one of the issues of the peace.

Unit 8 Review

Chapter 23 In the late 1800s and early 1900s, a reform movement swept the country. Progressives worked to end corruption at all levels of government. Women demanded suffrage. Other reformers urged city governments to respond to the needs of the poor. As President, Theodore Roosevelt supported many Progressive ideas. He curbed the power of trusts.

Chapter 24 The United States followed a course of expansion in the late 1800s. After the Spanish–American War, the United States acquired the Philippines and Puerto Rico. Ruling an overseas empire brought problems as well as economic ben-

efits. Presidents Roosevelt and Taft extended American influence in Latin America. In 1904, the United States started work on the Panama Canal. It was opened in 1914.

Chapter 25 When World War I broke out in Europe, the United States chose to remain neutral. German submarine warfare and Allied propaganda helped bring the nation into the war in 1917. American troops blunted the final German offensive and helped win the war. President Wilson negotiated the Versailles Treaty. But the Senate rejected the treaty.

★ **Unit Checkup**

Choose the word or phrase that best completes each of the following statements.

1. To end the spoils system, Congress created the
   (a) Civil Service Commission.
   (b) Interstate Commerce Commission.
   (c) Northern Securities Company.

2. Tuskegee Institute was set up by
   (a) Carrie Chapman Catt.
   (b) W. E. B. Du Bois.
   (c) Booker T. Washington.

3. The United States supported the revolution in Panama to
   (a) punish Francisco "Pancho" Villa.
   (b) end the Spanish–American War.
   (c) win the right to build a canal.

4. Commodore Perry opened up trade with
   (a) Hawaii.
   (b) Japan.
   (c) China.

5. One cause of World War I was the
   (a) Boxer Rebellion.
   (b) European alliance system.
   (c) Russian Revolution.

★ **Building American Citizenship**

1. During the Progressive era, writers published stories of corruption in America. (a) Give two examples of problems that were brought to the public's attention. (b) Find a recent article that points out a problem in your area. (c) What is being done to solve the problem?

2. After the Spanish–American War, Americans debated whether the country should take on an overseas empire. (a) What other reasons do you think Americans had for wanting an overseas empire? (b) How did America's role in the world change after the Spanish–American War?

The map at right shows Alaska, which Secretary of State William Seward bought in 1867. Study the map. Then answer the following questions.

1. What nation borders Alaska to the east? To the west?

2. Name two physical features of Alaska.

3. What city on the map is the farthest north?

4. About how far is it from Nome to Anchorage?

5. What is the latitude and longitude of Fort Yukon?

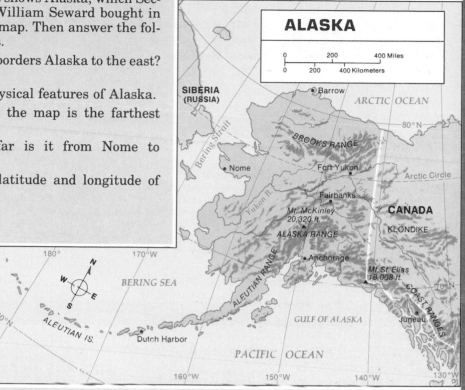

History Writer's Handbook

Arranging Information in Order of Importance

Order of importance is arrangement of supporting information from most important to least important, or vice versa. You often will need to use your own judgment in ranking the information.

Look at the following topic sentence. *The Treaty of Yokohama helped American trade.* In the detail sentences, you might begin with the treaty term that benefited trade the least and end with the term that benefited trade the most. For example: *First, it provided for kindly treatment of shipwrecked sailors. Second, it gave refueling rights to ships. Most important, it opened up two Japanese ports to trade.* Note that the transitions *first, second,* and *most important* show the order of importance of the treaty terms.

Transitions for order of importance include *also, even more serious, finally, first, for one reason, furthermore, more important, moreover, most important, one, perhaps the greatest reason,* and *second.*

Practice Look at the following topic sentence. *The Allies were in a desperate condition by the spring of 1918 for three reasons.* Using order of importance, write detail sentences. (See pages 560–561 for the information.)

Unit 9

A TROUBLED TIME

1920	1924	1928	1932

WILSON | WARREN HARDING | CALVIN COOLIDGE | HERBERT HOOVER

1920 Prohibition begins; women get the vote
1920s Harlem Renaissance
1921 United States signs peace treaties with defeated Central Powers; Emergency Quota Act; Washington Conference
1922 First radio station set up
1923 Teapot Dome Scandal

1925 Scopes trial
1926 Marines sent to Nicaragua
1927 Lindbergh flies across Atlantic Ocean alone; first talking movie; Sacco and Vanzetti executed

1928 Kellogg–Briand Pact; bull market on Wall Street
1929 Stock market crash
1929–41 Great Depression
1930 Jobless total reaches 5 million people

1920	1924	1928	1932

1920s The flapper, left, and the farm couple, right, show different ways of life in the Roaring Twenties.

1930s During the Great Depression, millions of Americans faced the hopeless task of finding work.

1932			1936			1940			1944

FRANKLIN ROOSEVELT

1932 Jobless total reaches 12 million people; Bonus Army
1933 New Deal begins; drought on Great Plains
1935 WPA set up; Wagner Act; Social Security Act; First Neutrality Act; Mussolini invades Ethiopia

1936 Hitler moves into Rhineland
1937 Japan invades China
1938 Pure Food and Drug Act extended; *War of the Worlds* broadcast; Hitler annexes Austria; Munich Conference
1939 Hitler seizes Czechoslovakia; Nazi–Soviet Pact; World War II begins

1940 Germany overruns Western Europe; Roosevelt elected to third term
1941 Hitler invades USSR; Lend–Lease Act; Atlantic Charter; Japan attacks Pearl Harbor
1942 Battles of Coral Sea, Midway, El Alamein; Allied invasion of Italy
1944 D–Day; Roosevelt elected to fourth term

1932			1936			1940			1944

1932 Americans elected Franklin Roosevelt to lead the nation out of the Great Depression.

1930s As part of the New Deal, President Roosevelt put millions of Americans back to work building projects such as this giant dam.

1940s Late in World War II, Americans pushed deep into German-occupied Europe, while Allied leaders, below, mot to discuss postwar plans.

CHAPTER

26

The Roaring Twenties (1919–1929)

Chapter Outline

1 Return to Normalcy
2 Business Booms
3 Changing Ways of Life
4 The Jazz Age
5 Clouds on the Horizon

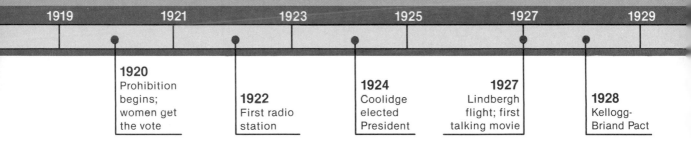

| 1919 | 1921 | 1923 | 1925 | 1927 | 1929 |

1920
Prohibition begins; women get the vote

1922
First radio station

1924
Coolidge elected President

1927
Lindbergh flight; first talking movie

1928
Kellogg-Briand Pact

About This Chapter

On May 20, 1927, Captain Charles A. Lindbergh set out on a bold adventure. He planned to fly his single-engine airplane, *The Spirit of St. Louis,* alone from New York to Paris, France. Lindbergh piloted the tiny plane through fog, rain, and sleet over the stormy Atlantic. Finally, he reached the coast of France and landed outside Paris.

"I flew low over the field once, then circled around into the wind and landed," he wrote later. Thousands of people raced toward the plane. "I cut the switch to keep the propeller from killing someone. . . . When parts of the ship began to crack from the pressure of the [crowd], I decided to climb out of the cockpit in order to draw the crowd away." The cheering French pulled Lindbergh from the plane and carried him like a hero across the field.

Back home in America, headlines announced LINDY DOES IT—TO PARIS IN 33½ HOURS. Overnight, Lindbergh won the hearts of Americans. Huge crowds welcomed him when he returned home. A popular song, "Lucky Lindy," celebrated his flight. The Lindy hop became a new dance.

Why did Lindbergh become such a hero? In the 1920s, people needed a hero. World War I and the years after the war brought great changes to America. Many people welcomed the changes. To them, Lindbergh's flight pointed to a new age. Many others looked back on the past with longing. To them, Lindbergh was a confident, courageous hero like those of the past.

Study the time line above. What other event happened in the year of Lindbergh's flight?

In this painting, *Boom Town,* Thomas Hart Benton shows how industry, movies, automobiles, and the telephone were changing America.

1 Return to Normalcy

By 1920, the American people were tired of crusades. The guns of war were silent, and the battle over the peace treaty was over. People longed for calm after an era of reform and war. They found a leader who promised a return to a more normal life. That leader was Warren G. Harding.

Harding's Landslide Victory

In the election of 1920, both candidates were from Ohio. Republicans put up Senator Warren G. Harding to run against Ohio Governor James Cox, a Democrat. During the campaign, Harding coined a new phrase. He pledged a "return to normalcy." By this, he meant a return to life as it had been before the war. In the election, Harding swamped Cox in a landslide victory.

The cabinet. Harding named the best minds of his party to top cabinet jobs. He made Charles Evans Hughes Secretary of State. For Secretary of the Treasury, he chose Andrew Mellon, the

Cheering crowds welcomed Charles Lindbergh home after his solo Atlantic flight. This parade in New York City was the biggest in the city's history. One newspaper praised Lindbergh for performing "the greatest deed of a solitary man in the records of the human race."

millionaire aluminum king of Pittsburgh. Mellon put the nation on a balanced budget. Herbert Hoover became Secretary of Commerce. During the war, Hoover earned the nickname the Great Humanitarian for arranging food supplies for millions of starving people in Belgium.

The President was an honest, hardworking man. But he once told a friend, "I knew that this job would be too much for me." To escape the burdens of office, Harding surrounded himself with political friends known as the Ohio Gang. When these friends asked for jobs, Harding could not say no.

Scandals at the top. Harding's friends involved the White House in financial scandals. Harding had made Charles Forbes head of the Veterans Bureau. Early in 1923, Forbes was con-victed of pocketing millions of dollars of the bureau's money.

The President was shocked by Forbes's betrayal. He was even more upset when rumors of new scandals surfaced. In August 1923, Harding became seriously ill and died. His death was blamed on pneumonia and a blood clot. Many believed that the scandals involving his friends helped him into the grave.

In the next months, new scandals unfolded. The *Teapot Dome Scandal* involved Secretary of the Interior Albert Fall. Fall had secretly leased government lands in Elk Hills, California, and Teapot Dome, Wyoming, to two oil companies. In exchange for the leases, Fall had accepted large bribes. Fall was tried and found guilty. He was the first cabinet officer ever to be jailed.

Coolidge Takes Office

Vice President Calvin Coolidge was on his father's farm in Vermont when he learned of Harding's death. Coolidge's father was a justice of the peace. So he gave the oath of office to his son. They used the old family Bible. News of the simple ceremony reassured the American people.

The new President was nothing like the friendly Harding. Coolidge came from an old New England family. He was known for being tight with both money and words. A young woman once told Coolidge she had bet a friend that she could get the President to say more than three words. "You lose," replied Coolidge.

Silent Cal, as he was known, helped to clean up the scandals in the government. He forced officials involved in the scandals to resign. In the 1924 election, Coolidge ran against Democrat John Davis and Progressive Robert La Follette. Voters chose to "Keep Cool with Coolidge" and returned the cautious New Englander to office.

America and World Affairs

In foreign affairs, both Harding and Coolidge wanted to preserve the hard-won peace. At the same time, they did not want to involve the United States in the burdens of world peace keeping. Most Americans strongly supported this isolationist policy. In 1921, Harding signed peace treaties with Germany, Austria, and Hungary, the powers defeated in World War I. The United States sent observers to the League of Nations. But it would not be bound by any league decisions.

American aid. The United States refused to recognize Lenin's communist government in the Soviet Union.* Yet in 1921, when famine threatened millions of Russians, Congress voted $20 million in aid. American aid may have saved as many as 10 million Russians from starvation. Although Americans disapproved of the Soviet government, they were still willing to help the Russian people.

Preserving the peace. In the 1920s, the United States worked for peace through disarmament. *Disarmament* means reducing a nation's armed forces or weapons of war. At the Washington Conference of 1921, the United States, Britain, and Japan agreed to limit the size of their navies.

Political scandals were not new to Americans. However, the scandals among President Harding's officials rocked the nation. This cartoon points a finger at both Republicans and Democrats. What does the big campaign contributor get from the "General Store"? What does the little man get?

---

*After the Bolshevik Revolution, Russia was officially renamed the Union of Soviet Socialist Republics (USSR), or Soviet Union.

In 1928, the United States joined 61 other countries in signing the ***Kellogg-Briand Pact.*** This pact, or treaty, summed up the world's hopes for peace by outlawing war. However, it did not set up any means of enforcing the peace. So one nation could use force against another without fear of punishment.

Latin America. The United States kept a careful watch on Latin America. In Nicaragua, it followed a policy of intervening to protect American investments. So when a revolution broke out there in 1926, American marines were sent in to oversee new elections.

With Mexico, however, the United States chose to negotiate rather than intervene. In 1927, Mexico announced plans to take over foreign-owned oil and mining companies. American investors called on President Coolidge to send in troops. Instead, Coolidge sent a diplomat, Dwight Morrow, to Mexico. After much hard bargaining, Morrow worked out a compromise with the government of Mexico.

━━ **SECTION REVIEW** ━━

1. **Define:** disarmament.
2. What did Harding mean by a "return to normalcy"?
3. What was the Teapot Dome Scandal?
4. Why was Coolidge known as Silent Cal?
5. **What Do You Think?** Why do you think Americans were willing to help the Russian people in 1921?

2 Business Booms

Read to Learn
★ Why did business boom in the 1920s?
★ What new business methods were developed?
★ What do these words mean: installment buying, bull market?

When World War I ended, more than 2 million soldiers returned home to look for jobs. As the economy changed back to meeting peacetime needs, the nation suffered from hard times. After 1921, however, the economy grew steadily.

Coolidge Prosperity

The 1920s brought prosperity, or economic good times, to most Americans. People called it the Coolidge prosperity. In the 1920s, the quantity of goods produced by industry almost doubled. More important to most Americans, their incomes rose. As a result, people were able to buy more goods. This in turn increased the demand for goods, which fueled still more growth.

Changes in the economy. World War I helped the economy. During the war, industry developed many new materials such as nylon, rayon, and plastics. More efficient ways of making goods and the use of mass production helped business. Americans produced and sold large quantities of goods more cheaply than foreign competitors.

As the economy grew, millions of Americans moved from the country to cities and suburbs. For the first time, more Americans lived in cities than in the country. City people needed apartments and houses in which to live. As a result, the housing industry boomed.

Growth of big business. During the Coolidge years, big business expanded. Coolidge believed that prosperity for all Americans depended on business prosperity. "The chief business of the American people," said Coolidge, "is business."

In the 1920s, promoters offered people many ways to "get rich quick." One way was buying land in Florida. Prices of Florida real estate soared in the mid-1920s. As this cover of *Life* magazine shows, however, sometimes people found they had bought worthless swampland.

Competition gave way to consolidation, or the combining of many companies. In 1928, for example, the Colgate Company merged with Palmolive–Peet to form Colgate–Palmolive. Other large companies did the same. Most people did not see these changes taking place. What they did see was the progress of chain stores in replacing small local stores. Chain stores like A&P, Safeway, and Piggly-Wiggly opened around the country.

The Automobile Industry

The economic boom was fueled by the rapid growth of the automobile industry. In the early 1900s, only the rich could afford to buy cars. In the 1920s, one out of every five Americans had a car.

Increased efficiency contributed to the boom in the auto industry. In 1914, you will remember, Henry Ford introduced the assembly line in his factory. (See page 473.) This new method of production reduced the time it took to make a Model T from 14 hours to 93 minutes. Increased efficiency also led to lower prices. By 1924, the cost of a Model T had dropped from $850 to $290.

Other companies copied Ford's success. By 1927, General Motors had passed Ford as the top auto producer. General Motors offered buyers a variety of models and colors. Ford had once boasted that people could have the Model T in "any color they want as long as it's black." Faced with the success of General Motors, Ford changed his tune. He introduced the Model A in different colors.

The growing auto industry affected other parts of the economy. For example, more paved roads, or highways, were built. Highways were soon clogged with travelers. So gas stations, tourist cabins, and restaurants sprang up to provide all the services that travelers needed.

By 1929, about 4 million Americans owed their jobs to the automobile or related industries. Thousands of people worked in steel mills, producing metal sheets for auto bodies. Others had jobs in tire, paint, or glass plants. The oil industry expanded to meet the demand for gasoline.

Buy Now, Pay Later

The automobile was one of many new products that flooded onto the market in the 1920s. Radios, electric refrigerators, vacuum cleaners, and many other appliances took their place in American homes. More and more people signed up for telephone service. (Silent Cal, however, refused to have a phone on his White House desk.)

A new business method, known as ***installment buying,*** or buying on credit, helped Americans buy these new goods. Installment buying allowed a person to make a small down payment on an item. The down payment was only a fraction of the cost of the item. A buyer would put down a few dollars toward an electric refrigerator, take it home, and use it. The buyer paid off the rest in monthly installments.

The practice of "buy now, pay later" helped people get many goods they wanted even if they did not have enough money saved to pay for them. Installment buying also increased the demand for goods.

Businesses used advertising to attract new customers. Advertisements often showed a world of happy young couples surrounded by the products and services that businesses supplied. Advertisements encouraged people to think that they would be happy if they bought the new products.

Bull Market on Wall Street

While many Americans bought consumer goods such as cars, radios, and refrigerators, millions also invested in the stock market. As you read in Chapter 21, corporations sold stocks, or shares of ownership, to investors.

During the 1920s, more people invested in the stock market than ever before. In the late 1920s, stock prices rose so fast that some people made fortunes by buying and selling stocks. Stories of waiters and other ordinary people becoming instant millionaires by investing in the stock market made others hope for similar success.

GRAPH SKILL In the 1920s, more Americans could afford to buy cars than ever before. Many different companies competed for a share of this rapidly growing market. In which year were the most cars sold?

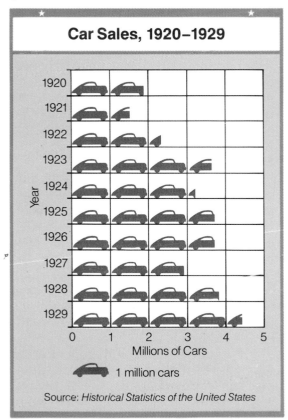

Car Sales, 1920–1929

Millions of Cars

🚗 = 1 million cars

Source: *Historical Statistics of the United States*

Confidence

Wonderful driving simplicity of the Baker and Rauch & Lang Electric inspires utmost confidence on the part of the occupants at all times.

The mother finds comfort in knowing that the safety and pleasure of her little ones are enhanced because of this driving simplicity—this independence from mechanical obtrusion and confusion.

And in full keeping with this is the rich coach work—genuine coach work—the best that can come of over sixty years' leadership in fashionable coach building.

Baker Electrics

Confidence all 'round—in the knowledge that your Baker and Rauch & Lang represents the best, and that it insures the utmost in safety.

The Baker R. & L. Company
Cleveland, Ohio

See our latest models at the New York Show, Dec. 31—Jan. 8

Rauch & Lang Electric

"The Social Necessity"

Auto makers and other manufacturers used advertising to encourage people to buy their products. Both the picture and the words in this automobile ad were meant to encourage women to buy this electric car.

The rising stock market, called a *bull market,* caused great interest. People bought stocks on margin, a practice similar to installment buying. A person could buy a stock for as little as 10 percent down. The buyer would hold onto the stock until the price rose, then sell it at a profit.

In 1928 and 1929, however, the prices of many stocks rose faster than the value of the companies themselves. This was an unhealthy sign. A few experts warned that the bull market would end. But most people ignored the warnings. They wanted to believe that the bull market would last forever.

SECTION REVIEW

1. **Define:** installment buying, bull market.
2. Give two reasons for the business boom in the 1920s.
3. How did the growth of the automobile industry affect other industries?
4. **What Do You Think?** Why do you think people kept on investing in the stock market despite warnings?

3 Changing Ways of Life

Read to Learn

★ What was Prohibition?
★ How did women's lives change in the 1920s?
★ How did Americans spend their leisure time?
★ What do these words mean: bootlegger, speakeasy?

World War I changed the way many Americans lived. In the 1920s, new products and new ideas speeded up the changes. Many Americans wanted to preserve older traditions. As a result, the 1920s were a time when traditions of the past mingled with new ways.

America Goes Dry

During the 1920s, the nation set out on what some people called a "noble experiment." The experiment was *Prohibition.* It was made into law when the Eighteenth Amendment was ratified in 1919. (See page 515.) The law took effect in 1920. Under the new law, it was illegal to make or sell liquor anywhere in the United States.

Prohibition had some positive effects. Alcoholism and diseases of the liver caused by drinking declined sharply. But in the end, Prohibition did not work.

The first Prohibition commissioner believed that his job would be easy. "This law will be obeyed," he declared, "and where it is not obeyed, it will be enforced." Yet Ben Shahn's painting, *Prohibition Alley,* shows that many people broke the law, including bootleggers and those who bought illegal liquor from them. By 1924, almost half of all federal arrests were for violations of Prohibition.

The speakeasy. From the start, people found ways to get around the law. They made their own alcohol. Smugglers, called *bootleggers,* brought millions of gallons of illegal liquor from Canada and the Caribbean. The *speakeasy,* or illegal bar, opened its doors in most towns and cities. Bars were once considered places for men only. With Prohibition and the opening of speakeasies, women were now welcomed to drink in public bars.

Organized crime. Prohibition resulted in the growth of organized crime. Gangsters and hoodlums took over the manufacture and sale of illegal liquor. They made it into a huge business. Gangsters divided up cities and forced speakeasy owners to buy from them. On occasion, they gunned down rivals in battles for control of different parts of town.

Newspapers played up stories of the violence. They showed how gangsters broke the law and got away with it. With their illegal profits, gangsters bribed poorly paid policemen, federal officials, and judges.

Many Americans came to think that Prohibition was a mistake. It did not stop drinking. It undermined respect for the law. Every day millions of Americans broke the law to buy drinks in speakeasies. In 1933, the Twenty-First Amendment repealed the Eighteenth Amendment.

New Horizons for Women

Another amendment to the Constitution had a different impact on American life. The Nineteenth Amendment, ratified in 1920, gave women the right to vote. Women went to the polls for the first time in November 1920. Their votes helped elect President Harding. However, the election results showed that women did not vote as a group, as some people had feared. Like men, some women voted for Republicans, some for Democrats. And some did not vote at all.

When women in the United States won the right to vote, women in Puerto Rico asked if the new law applied to them.* They were told it did not. Led by Ana Roqué de Duprey, an educator and writer, Puerto Rican women crusaded for suffrage. In 1929, their crusade finally succeeded.

Goals for equal rights. Leaders of the suffrage movement in the United States celebrated the Nineteenth Amendment. But they continued to work for other goals. In 1919, Carrie Chapman Catt, head of the National Woman Suffrage Association, organized the League of Women Voters. The league worked to educate voters. It is still active today.

Alice Paul, an outspoken leader of the suffrage movement, began to work for an equal rights amendment in 1923. The proposed amendment called for men and women to have equal rights throughout the United States. The amendment was not adopted in the 1920s. Paul kept working for it until her death in 1977.

At home and in the work place. The 1920s were a time when women won greater freedom of choice. During World War I, thousands of women worked outside the home for the first time. They worked in offices and factories. They filled the jobs of men who had gone off to war. After the war, women were forced to give these jobs up to returning soldiers. Still, many women stayed in the work force.

In general, women were paid less than men for doing the same job. Yet earning wages gave women a sense of independence. Most women needed jobs to support their families or themselves. Despite discrimination, a few women entered professions such as law and medicine. Some owned and operated successful businesses.

Daily life became easier for women in the 1920s. They bought ready-made clothes instead of sewing for the whole family as in the past. New appliances such as refrigerators, clothes washers, electric irons, and vacuum cleaners

Since the 1800s, women who had worked for suffrage heard cries of "Go home and wash the dishes!" Yet the work of American women during World War I helped convince lawmakers to support suffrage. Here, a voter, Maud Powell, casts a ballot for the first time in 1920.

---

*In 1917, you will remember, Puerto Ricans were made citizens of the United States. (See page 539.)

made housework simpler. With more free time, women at home took an active role in community projects.

The Silver Screen

Millions of Americans found new ways to spend their leisure time. In the late 1800s, Thomas Edison and George Eastman helped develop the technology needed to make movies. In the 1920s, the movie industry came of age. Hollywood became the movie capital of the world. (See page 585.)

Each week, millions flocked to the movies, giving a boost to the new industry. Comedies, romances, adventures, and westerns flashed across the screens in over 20,000 movie theaters across the country. Some theaters were simple rooms with hard chairs. Others were huge palaces with red velvet seats.

Hollywood movie studios created the big-name stars that people flocked to see each week. In the movies, heroes and villains battled across the "wild west" and danced at glittering balls. In real life, Hollywood stars seemed to live in an equally glamorous world. Perhaps the most popular star of the 1920s was Rudolph Valentino. In a famous movie, *The Sheik,* Valentino rode across the desert on a magnificent white horse. To millions of women, he was the hero of their dreams.

During the 1920s, movies benefited from technical change. The first movies had no sound tracks. In these silent movies, posters printed with the dialogue appeared on the screen. Usually, a theater hired a pianist who played music to go along with the action. In 1927, *The Jazz Singer* caused a sensation. It was a "talkie," a movie with a sound track. Soon, all movies were talkies.

New Images of America

Movies created a new image of glamor. People copied the way their

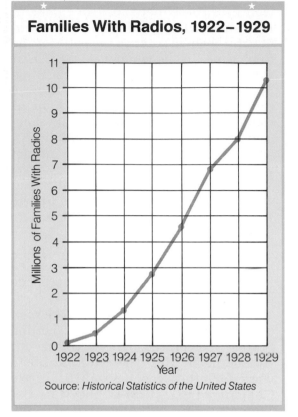

Families With Radios, 1922–1929

Millions of Families With Radios (vertical axis, 0 to 11)

Year (horizontal axis: 1922 1923 1924 1925 1926 1927 1928 1929)

Source: *Historical Statistics of the United States*

GRAPH SKILL The 1920s could be called the age of radio. Millions of American families bought radios and listened to popular radio shows. Between 1927 and 1928, about how many families bought radios?

favorite stars walked, talked, and dressed. Movie studios carefully groomed the image of leading stars. Douglas Fairbanks appeared as the swashbuckling hero. Mary Pickford was "America's sweetheart." Gloria Swanson was seen as the perfect society woman. Fan magazines printed photographs and stories about these and other Hollywood stars.

Like the movies, radio programs were very popular. The first radio station began broadcasting in Pittsburgh in 1922. By the late 1920s, millions of Americans owned radios. They tuned in each night to radio shows such as "Ma Perkins" and "Just Plain Bill." To

From the 1920s on, millions of Americans went to the movies. In the early days, movies were simple and very short. They lasted only about 15 minutes. *The Great Train Robbery,* the first western, included three short scenes—a train robbery, a horse-and-rider chase, and a sudden ending when the villain pointed his gun at the screen and fired.

In the early 1900s, New York City and New Jersey were centers of the movie industry. They were close to Broadway, where many actors and producers lived and worked. Most movies were made out of doors because indoor lights were not strong enough for filming. Naturally, production stopped on rainy days and in the winter.

Moviemakers then found that the sunny, warm climate of southern California let them film all year. In 1911, the Nestor Film Studio set up shop in Hollywood. By the end of the year, 15 other movie companies had opened in Hollywood.

In the 1920s, Hollywood grew from a small town into the bustling center of a major industry. Actors like Charlie Chaplin and Clara Bow who had once earned a few dollars a day now earned $10,000 a week. Directors made longer movies that told more complicated stories. As movies won ever larger audiences, Hollywood became known worldwide. Before long, the name Hollywood came to stand for movies and the rich, glamorous people who starred in them.

★ How did climate influence the growth of Hollywood?

many, these programs pictured the real America of ordinary people. Yet they were entertainment. Radio listeners enjoyed comedies, westerns, and mysteries.

The automobile changed the image of America, too. Cars influenced life in the city and in the country. Many city dwellers wanted to escape crowded conditions. So they moved to nearby towns in the country, which soon grew into suburbs.

With cars, suburban families could drive to the city many miles away. They could also drive to stores, schools, or work. No longer did people have to live where they could walk or take a trolley to work.

In the country, having a car meant driving to towns, shops, or the movies. In the past, trips like these took several hours by horse and buggy. In the 1920s, people traveled to more places and moved more quickly than ever before.

SECTION REVIEW

1. **Define:** bootlegger, speakeasy.
2. (a) Describe one benefit of Prohibition. (b) Describe one disadvantage of it.
3. How did the Nineteenth Amendment affect women?
4. Describe how cars changed the way Americans lived.
5. **What Do You Think?** Why do you think millions of Americans attended movies in the 1920s?

4 The Jazz Age

Read to Learn
★ What was the Harlem Renaissance?
★ What sports were popular in the 1920s?
★ Why did some writers criticize American society?
★ What do these words mean: fad, flapper?

The decade of the 1920s has many nicknames. It has been called the Roaring Twenties because of the boom in everything from business to bootlegging. It has been called the Jazz Age because of a new kind of music that became popular. It has also been called the Era of Wonderful Nonsense because of the silly games and songs that came into fashion.

Fads and Flappers

During the Era of Wonderful Nonsense, many fads became very popular, then quickly disappeared. A *fad* is a style or fashion that becomes popular for a short time. Flagpole sitting was one fad. Another was swallowing live goldfish. Mah-jongg, a Chinese tile game, was another fad of the 1920s.

Among those who adopted the new fads were the flappers. *Flapper* was a nickname given to a young woman who declared her independence from traditional rules. Flappers symbolized the rebellion of young people against older ways. Flappers bobbed their hair, or cut it short. They wore short dresses with hemlines above the knee. Flappers shocked their parents by wearing rouge and bright red lipsticks.

A flapper's behavior shocked people even more than her clothes. Flappers smoked in public and drank in speakeasies. Only a few young women were flappers. But they set a style for others. Slowly, older women adopted the new fashions. They bobbed their hair and wore shorter skirts and makeup. For many women, the new fashions symbolized a new freedom.

Sounds of Jazz

Another symbol of the 1920s was jazz. Jazz was a new form of music that mixed several musical traditions. Black musicians in New Orleans and Chicago created jazz out of ragtime and blues. Jazz combined African rhythms and European harmonies. It became popular with all American groups and spread around the world. Some people considered jazz America's greatest contribution to music.

With jazz came new styles of dancing. Dance floors shook to the bouncy steps of the Charleston and Black Bottom. At big city nightclubs, people heard popular jazz bands and danced the night away.

Louis Armstrong, a trumpet player, was one of the jazz greats. Millions thrilled to the sounds of his trumpet. Armstrong had the ability to take a simple melody and show listeners many sides of it, as if he were taking a plain stone and turning it into a rare gem.

Jazz continued to grow after the 1920s. It influenced other popular music. For example, the rock 'n' roll music of the 1950s and the rock music of today grew out of the sounds of the Jazz Age.

The Harlem Renaissance

The home for many black jazz musicians was Harlem in New York City. Thousands of black Americans moved to Harlem during and after World War I. In the 1920s, black artists, writers, and musicians gathered there. They contributed to the *Harlem Renaissance,* or rebirth of black culture.

Black writers like Countee Cullen and Claude McKay told of the experiences of black Americans. A graduate of New York University and Harvard, Cullen taught in public schools. In the 1920s, he won prizes for his books of poetry. McKay came to the United States from Jamaica. In his poem "If

AMERICANS WHO DARED

Bessie Smith

Bessie Smith was known as Empress of the Blues in the 1920s. The blues were songs developed by black musicians and closely tied to jazz. As a child in Chattanooga, Tennessee, Smith was very poor. Through her singing, she earned worldwide fame. An admirer once summed up Smith's talents. "Her blues could be funny and boisterous and gentle and angry and bleak, but underneath all of them ran . . . raw bitterness." Smith's songs were especially popular among black Americans who bought millions of her records.

We Must Die," he protested lynchings and mob violence that black Americans suffered after World War I.

Among the best-known poets of the Harlem Renaissance was Langston Hughes. His first published poem, "The

Negro Speaks of Rivers," was written soon after he graduated from high school. Like McKay, he protested violence against blacks. Hughes wrote proudly about being black:

The night is beautiful,
So the faces of my people.

The stars are beautiful,
So the eyes of my people.

Beautiful, also, is the sun.
Beautiful, also, are the souls
    of my people.

Among the women writers of the Harlem Renaissance was Zora Neale Hurston. A talented writer, she published novels, essays, and short stories. In *Mules and Men,* she collected folk tales, songs, games, and prayers of black Southerners.

Heroes of Sport

Newspapers, radios, and movies created many heroes and heroines in the 1920s. As you read on page 574, Charles Lindbergh became a popular hero for his solo flight. Five years after Lindbergh's flight, Amelia Earhart won fame for her solo flight across the Atlantic.

Among the greatest heroes of the day were athletes. Every sport had its own heroes. Bobby Jones won almost every golf championship. Bill Tilden and Helen Wills ruled the tennis courts. Gertrude Ederle awed the world when she became the first woman to swim the English Channel.

Football. College football rose to new heights of popularity. Many Americans who had never been to college rooted for college teams. People living near colleges attended Saturday afternoon games. Flappers and their dates paraded into the stands wearing the latest fashion—thick, warm raccoon coats.

The Fighting Irish of the University of Notre Dame and their great coach Knute Rockne had a devoted following.

Red Grange, known as the Galloping Ghost, played for the University of Illinois.

Baseball. Americans loved football, but they saved their true passion for baseball. The greatest baseball player of the 1920s was Babe Ruth. Ruth became a legend in his own time. He had all the makings of an American hero. He was an orphan and often in trouble as a child. He worked hard and succeeded.

Ruth changed the way baseball was played by increasing game scores. He was a home-run hitter for the New York Yankees. Fans flocked to games to see "the Babe" hit home runs. He made the record books by hitting 60 home runs in one season. Ruth's home-run record stood for 34 years.

Literature of the Twenties

American writers produced many outstanding works. Some criticized American society. They attacked what they saw as shallow goals and an emphasis on money and material things. Some became so unhappy with life in America that they moved to Europe.

Among the best-known writers was Ernest Hemingway. A teenager during World War I, he went to Europe to drive an ambulance on the Italian front. In a bestselling novel, *A Farewell to Arms,* Hemingway told of a young man's war experiences.

Another writer, Sinclair Lewis, angered some Americans with his view of small-town life. Lewis grew up in a small town in Minnesota. In his novel *Main Street,* he wrote about Gopher Prairie, a small town where the people were dull, greedy, and narrow-minded. Yet Lewis admired the courage of small-town Americans.

A third popular novelist was F. Scott Fitzgerald. In *The Great Gatsby,* he captured the spirit of the Roaring

Babe Ruth wore the pin-striped uniform of the New York Yankees and was called the Sultan of Swat for his home-run hitting. In one year, Ruth's salary was $80,000—an enormous sum in the 1920s. When a sportswriter once pointed out that Ruth was paid more than the President, Ruth replied, "I had a better year than he did."

Twenties. The novel described the hollow lives of wealthy people who attended endless parties but could not find happiness.

Among poets, Edna St. Vincent Millay seemed to speak of the frantic pace of the 1920s:

My candle burns at both ends;
It will not last the night;
But ah, my foes, and oh, my friends—
It gives a lovely light.

SECTION REVIEW

1. **Define:** fad, flapper.
2. Describe three fads of the 1920s.
3. What musical traditions gave rise to jazz?
4. What did writers of the Harlem Renaissance speak of in their works?
5. **What Do You Think?** How do you think Millay's line "My candle burns at both ends" reflects the spirit of the Roaring Twenties?

5 Clouds on the Horizon

Read to Learn

★ What groups of Americans did not share in the Coolidge prosperity?
★ Why did many Americans want to limit immigration?
★ What problems did black Americans face after the war?
★ What do these words mean: anarchist, quota system?

On the surface, the 1920s presented a glamorous image. However, many Americans faced serious problems. Not everyone benefited from the Coolidge prosperity. While some industries flourished, others did not.

Uneven Prosperity

Despite the business boom, many Americans did not share in the nation's wealth. Also, many industries went through hard times in the 1920s. The clothing industry, for example, was hurt by changes in women's fashions. Shorter skirts meant that dresses needed much less cloth. Also, synthetic fabrics, such as rayon, cut into the market for cotton and other natural fibers. Coal miners had a hard time. Oil took the place of coal as the major source of energy. Then, too, railroads, a major coal consumer, lost much business to cars and trucks.

Problems for farmers. Worst hit by economic hardships were farmers. In 1919, farm income stood at $10 billion. By 1921, it had plunged to $4 billion. It remained low for the rest of the decade.

Several factors contributed to farmers' problems. During World War I, demand for farm products in Europe soared. So farm prices rose. Farmers borrowed heavily to buy more land and farm machines. They planned to pay off these loans with profits from increased production.

When the war ended, however, farmers in Canada, Australia, and France began producing more. This increase created an oversupply on the world market. Prices for farm products fell sharply. As a result, farmers were unable to pay their debts.

Other events made matters worse for the farmer. As automobiles replaced horses, the demand for farm products such as hay and oats fell. Taxes increased. So, too, did the price of tools,

GRAPH SKILL Farm families did not share in the Coolidge prosperity. On average, farmers earned less than most other workers. As a result, they could not buy many of the new goods on the market. How much were the yearly wages of farmers in 1920? 1922? 1924? 1929?

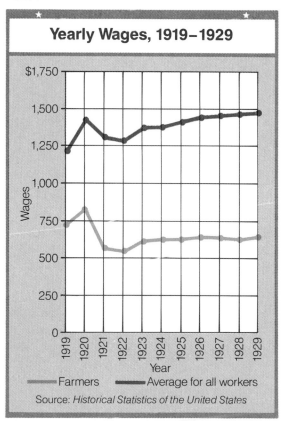

Yearly Wages, 1919–1929

Source: *Historical Statistics of the United States*

machines, and clothing. Finally, farmers were just too efficient for their own good. They produced too much. Farm surpluses made prices drop.

Problems for labor. Labor discontent surfaced at the end of the war. Wages had not kept up with rising prices during the war. So workers demanded pay increases. When employers turned them down, labor unions went on strike.

Often, employers tried to stop workers from joining unions. For example, in September 1919, the city of Boston fired 19 police officers who tried to join the AFL. This action led to a protest strike by the Boston police. Many Americans were deeply shocked at the sight of police walking the picket lines. They saw such a strike as a threat to law and order. They blamed labor unrest on radical foreign influences.

In 1919, coal miners and steel workers went on strike. When these strikes failed, unions lost much of their support among workers.

The Red Scare

During and after the war, fear of foreigners grew in America. The Bolshevik Revolution in Russia added to this fear. As you read, Russia fought on the side of the Allies until the Bolsheviks took power in 1917. The Bolsheviks, called Reds, set up a communist government under Vladimir Lenin.

Communists called on workers around the world to rise up against their governments. Lenin boasted that a worldwide communist revolution would soon take place. Many Americans feared that strikes and labor problems were the start of a communist revolution.

The actions of *anarchists,* people opposed to organized government, added to this sense of danger. A group of anarchists plotted to kill well-known people like John D. Rockefeller and Attorney General A. Mitchell Palmer.

Because anarchists were often foreign-born, these attacks led to an outcry against all foreign-born radicals.

In 1919 and 1920, Attorney General Palmer responded to demands for government action against radicals. Thousands of people were arrested and jailed during the *Red Scare.* When the government failed to uncover any plot, the panic died down. Yet suspicion of foreigners remained. So in the 1920s, the government faced new demands to limit immigration.

Limits on Immigration

The move to limit immigration began in the 1800s. In part, it showed a prejudice against recent arrivals from Southern and Eastern Europe. Also, the closing of the western frontier left the feeling that America could no longer absorb so many newcomers.

Closing the door. After World War I, millions of Europeans hoped to escape economic problems at home by moving to the United States. American workers feared that the new arrivals would force wages down. Nativists campaigned for the government to close the door to immigrants.

In 1921, Congress responded to this pressure by passing the Emergency Quota Act. The act limited the number of immigrants to 350,000 a year. It also set up a *quota system* that allowed only a certain number of people to immigrate from each country. The quota system favored immigration from Northern Europe, especially from Britain. Later, Congress passed new laws to slow immigration even more, especially from Asia and Eastern Europe.

The only group not included in the quota system was Mexicans. Large farms and factories in the Southwest depended on Mexican workers. Owners of these businesses argued against any limits on Mexican immigrants. Nativists protested, but business interests won.

The changes taking place in America disturbed many people. They looked back on a time when the nation was mostly rural. In *Stone City, Iowa,* the artist, Grant Wood, captured the peaceful scene of a country farm. Compare this painting to the one on page 575. How do you think the lives of rural Americans were different from those of city dwellers?

Sacco and Vanzetti trial. Antiforeign feeling remained high in the 1920s. When two Italian immigrants in Massachusetts were accused of robbery and murder, their trial attracted national attention. Nicola Sacco (SAK oh) and Bartolomeo Vanzetti (van SEHT ee) were anarchists and atheists, or people who did not believe in God. A jury convicted them of murdering two men during the robbery of a shoe factory. The two men were then sentenced to death.

The *Sacco and Vanzetti trial* created a heated debate. The evidence against the two men was limited. The judge was openly prejudiced against the two immigrants. Many Americans thought that Sacco and Vanzetti were convicted because of their beliefs and not because of the evidence. A long court fight to overturn the convictions failed. In 1927, Sacco and Vanzetti were executed. The issue of whether they received a fair trial has been debated ever since.

Tensions Between Old and New

In the 1920s, more and more people were moving to cities. Cities encouraged more modern styles of living. In the country, older traditions remained strong. Rural Americans saw city people with their modern ideas as a threat.

In 1925, this tension between old and new ways of life made front page headlines during the Scopes trial. John Scopes was a young biology teacher in Dayton, Tennessee. He challenged a Tennessee law that forbid the teaching of Charles Darwin's theory of evolution. This theory claimed that all life had evolved, or developed, from simpler forms of life.

Darwin's theory of evolution aroused strong opposition from some churches that thought it denied the teachings of the Bible. In some areas, church members urged state lawmakers to ban the teaching of evolution in schools. Tennessee, Mississippi, and Arkansas passed laws like this.

The trial of John Scopes pitted older traditions and beliefs against new ideas of science. William Jennings Bryan, once the Populist candidate for President, led the prosecution. A well-known Chicago lawyer, Clarence Darrow, defended Scopes.

Newspaper reporters swarmed into Dayton to record the courtroom battle between these two men. "Scopes isn't on trial," thundered Darrow at one point, "civilization is on trial."

Darrow even called Bryan to the witness stand and showed how little Bryan knew about modern science. Despite Darrow's defense, Scopes was convicted and fined. The law against teaching about Darwin's theory remained on the books.

Rebirth of the KKK

Another cloud on the horizon in the 1920s was the Ku Klux Klan. The Klan reappeared in the South in 1915, where it attacked blacks. After the war, its membership grew in the Midwest, Southwest, and West.

The Klan allowed only white, native-born Protestants to join. The Klan believed that certain racial and religious groups did not belong in America. It wanted to deny these groups the basic rights guaranteed to all Americans under the Constitution. In public statements, Klan leaders explained

In the 1920s, the Ku Klux Klan claimed that it had 5 million members. They preached hatred and violence against many Americans. By 1930, however, Klan membership had fallen to less than 10,000. Here, Klansmen parade near the Capitol in Washington, D.C.

When you do research for a report, you often will use secondary sources. **Secondary sources** are different from primary sources because they are not firsthand accounts. Instead, they are accounts based on the writings or evidence of others. Secondary sources include biographies and textbooks.

1. **Identify the parts of the book.** At the front, most books have a title page, copyright page, and table of contents. The **title page** lists the title, author, and publisher of the book. The **copyright page** is found right after the title page. It tells when the book was published. The **table of contents** is found near the beginning of a book. It includes a list of chapter titles and sometimes a list of maps or photographs in a book. Find a book on the 1920s. (a) List the full title, author's full name, and publisher of the book. (b) When was the book first published? (c) How many chapters are in the book?

2. **Study the table of contents.** By studying the table of contents, you can see at a glance the major subjects covered in the book. At right, is the table of contents of *Boom and Bust* by Ernest R. May. (a) How many chapters are in this book? (b) List three kinds of information the table of contents gives. (c) According to the table of contents, what is the book about?

3. **Practice using an index.** Most history books include an index at the end of the book. An **index** is an alphabetical list of the main subjects in a book. An index lets you find out if the book has information on a certain subject. Practice using the index at the back of this textbook. Notice that the index breaks some subjects down into subtopics. See the note at the beginning of the index. (a) Does the book have

CONTENTS

information on the Jazz Age? On Bessie Smith? (b) Besides listing subjects, what other information does the index give? (c) Where would you look in the index to find out if the book discusses the Sacco and Vanzetti trial?

4. **Practice skimming a chapter.** Another way to find information in a book is to skim a chapter. Skimming is a way of looking quickly at a chapter to see if it has information that you might find useful. To skim a chapter, read through the first paragraph. Then look at the first and last sentences of each paragraph. Using the book you selected for step 1, skim Chapter 2. (a) What does the first paragraph of Chapter 2 tell you about the chapter? (b) What are the main subjects covered in the chapter?

that their mission was to frighten and drive out groups they opposed.

Klan members attacked immigrants, Jews, Catholics, and blacks. They burned crosses outside peoples' homes, sent hate letters, and used lynchings and other methods to terrorize these groups. Often, they put pressure on employers to fire black or foreign-born workers.

Because of its large membership, the Klan gained political influence. However, in the mid–1920s, scandals surfaced that involved the misuse of Klan money. Klan membership declined. But the remaining Klan members kept up the violence.

Unfulfilled Hopes

Attacks by Klan members were only one of several problems faced by black Americans. Racial prejudice was widespread in the 1920s. During World War I, 400,000 black soldiers fought to make the world safe for democracy. Black Americans hoped that their efforts in the war would lead to better treatment after the war. But black soldiers came home to the same prejudice and discrimination as before. Often, conditions were even worse. When black veterans spoke out against these conditions, they were threatened, attacked, and sometimes lynched.

During the war, many blacks moved to northern cities such as Chicago, Detroit, and Philadelphia. There, they took jobs in industry. At work, they faced discrimination. They were usually allowed to take only the lowest-paying jobs. In housing, they also faced problems. Many landlords refused to rent to blacks or else charged high rents for poor housing.

Many white workers in the North felt threatened by the arrival of so many blacks. After the war, racial tension grew. In 1919, race riots broke out in several northern cities. The worst race riot took place in Chicago and left 38 dead.

A popular black leader, Marcus Garvey, organized the Universal Negro Improvement Association. His goal was to promote unity and pride among blacks. He urged black Americans to seek their roots in Africa. Hundreds of thousands of black Americans supported Garvey's "back to Africa" movement. Although few black Americans actually went to Africa, the movement helped to build black pride.

Victory for Herbert Hoover

Despite problems, life seemed calm on the surface. As the election of 1928 drew near, President Coolidge declared, "I do not choose to run for President." Herbert Hoover easily won the Republican nomination. The Democrats chose Governor Al Smith of New York.

The two candidates came from different backgrounds. Hoover was a midwesterner and a self-made millionaire. He won strong support from rural America and from big business. Smith was a New Yorker. He was also the first Catholic chosen by a major party for President.

The campaign centered on Smith's religion and his stand against Prohibition. These issues showed the split between rural and urban America. In the election, Hoover won easily. The Republican victory was helped by the Coolidge prosperity. Still, Democrats carried the 12 largest cities, a trend that would grow in the 1930s.

═══ SECTION REVIEW ═══

1. **Define:** anarchist, quota system.
2. What problems did farmers have after World War I?
3. Why did the Red Scare lead to demands to limit immigration?
4. How were the hopes of black Americans disappointed after the war?
5. **What Do You Think?** How do you think the Coolidge prosperity helped Hoover win the election?

Chapter 26 Review

★ Summary ★

After World War I, Americans voted for a return to normalcy under President Harding. Despite scandals, Harding was a popular President. When he died in office, Coolidge succeeded him.

During the Coolidge years, businesses boomed. The automobile changed American life as did new business methods such as installment buying. Women benefited from new freedom and the right to vote. Movies and radio brought popular entertainment to millions of Americans. Movie stars and sports heroes won the hearts of Americans.

Despite the glamorous image of the 1920s, problems existed. Farmers fell deeply into debt. Antiforeign and antiblack feelings were widespread.

★ Reviewing the Facts ★

 2 pts.

Key Terms. Match each term in Column 1 with the correct definition in Column 2.

Column 1	Column 2
1. installment buying	a. woman who bobbed her hair and wore short skirts
2. bull market	b. smuggler of illegal liquor
3. bootlegger	c. buying on credit
4. flapper	d. rising stock market
5. anarchist	e. person opposed to organized government

Key People, Events, and Ideas. Identify each of the following.

1. Teapot Dome Scandal
2. Kellogg-Briand Pact
3. Prohibition
4. Alice Paul
5. Ana Roqué de Duprey
6. Carrie Chapman Catt
7. *The Jazz Singer*
8. Louis Armstrong
9. Harlem Renaissance
10. Babe Ruth
11. Ernest Hemingway
12. Red Scare
13. Sacco and Vanzetti trial
14. Marcus Garvey
15. Herbert Hoover

★ Chapter Checkup ★

4 pts.

1. Describe three ways American Presidents worked for peace in the 1920s.
2. How did each of the following contribute to the Coolidge prosperity: (a) mass production; (b) growth of cities?
3. (a) Why did more people buy cars in the 1920s than ever before? (b) What other industries were helped by the auto industry?
4. (a) How did installment buying help increase the demand for consumer goods? (b) How did radio and movies affect American life?
5. Give two reasons why many Americans finally decided that Prohibition was a mistake.
6. Describe three ways in which women's lives were changing in the 1920s.
7. How did each of the following contribute to the literature of the 1920s: (a) Langston Hughes; (b) Sinclair Lewis?
8. (a) Name three groups of people in America who faced problems in the 1920s. (b) Explain why each group faced hard times.

1. **Understanding the economy.** (a) What areas of the economy boomed in the 1920s? (b) What areas did not prosper? (c) Why do you think some areas prospered while others did not?

2. **Analyzing a quotation.** Harding once complained: "I listen to one side and they seem right . . . I talk to the other side and they seem just as right, and here I am where I started." What does this statement tell about the problems faced by a President?

3. **Applying information.** (a) Why was Prohibition called the "noble experiment"? (b) Did the experiment succeed or fail? Explain.

4. **Learning about citizenship.** (a) How did the Nineteenth Amendment make the United States more democratic? (b) Why do you think this was an important step?

5. **Taking a stand.** Groups like the KKK have a right to exist under the Constitution. Defend or criticize this statement.

6. **Relating past to present.** (a) Describe three ways in which American life was changing in the 1920s. (b) How did these changes make America more like it is today?

★ **Using Your Skills** ★

1. **Placing events in time.** Use the time lines on pages 572–573 and 574 to answer the questions below. (a) Who was President when the first radio station was set up? (b) Who was President when Lindbergh flew across the Atlantic? (c) Who became President after Coolidge?

2. **Graph reading.** Study the graph on page 580. (a) How many autos were sold in 1920? In 1923? In 1929? (b) Does this graph show an upward or downward trend in auto sales?

3. **Reading for the main idea.** Review "Clouds on the Horizon" on pages 590–595. (a) What are the main ideas of this section? (b) Give one example to support each main idea.

4. **Using visual evidence.** Study the photograph on page 593. (a) What does the photograph show? (b) What symbols did the Ku Klux Klan use? (c) Why do you think Klan members carried the American flag?

★ **More to Do** ★

1. **Writing advertisements.** Write advertisements for three new products of the 1920s. In each ad, include a complete description of the product.

2. **Exploring local history.** Create a bulletin board comparing pictures of your local area taken during the 1920s with those taken today.

3. **Researching a report.** Find out more about Hollywood movies in the 1920s.

Then write a report about the stars, producers, and movies of that period.

4. **Using music.** Listen to tapes or records of jazz music of the 1920s. Give an oral report about the development of jazz in that decade.

5. **Preparing a sportscast.** Choose a sports figure of the 1920s. Prepare a sportscast in which you report on the greatest victory in that person's life.

CHAPTER

27

The Great Depression (1929–1941)

Chapter Outline

1 The Great Depression Begins
2 The Promise of a New Deal
3 Responses to the New Deal
4 Years of Struggle

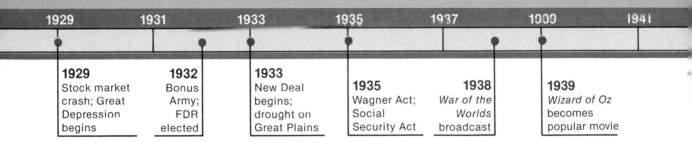

1929	1931	1933	1935	1937	1939	1941

1929
Stock market
crash; Great
Depression
begins

1932
Bonus
Army;
FDR
elected

1933
New Deal
begins;
drought on
Great Plains

1935
Wagner Act;
Social
Security Act

1938
*War of the
Worlds*
broadcast

1939
Wizard of Oz
becomes
popular movie

About This Chapter

The boom of the Roaring Twenties ended suddenly in 1929. During the 1930s, the nation plunged into the Great Depression. Millions of Americans lost their jobs. One popular song spoke very clearly about the hard times. In "Brother, Can You Spare a Dime?" two songwriters, E. Y. Harburg and Jay Gorney, captured the hopelessness and despair felt by many during the Great Depression.

> They used to tell me I was building a
>   dream
> And so I followed the mob.
> When there was earth to plow, or guns to
>   bear
> I was always there
> Right on the job.
>
> Once I built a railroad, I made it run,
> Made it race against time.

> Once I built a railroad,
> Now it's done.
> Brother, can you spare a dime?
>
> Once I built a tower up to the sun,
> Brick and rivet and lime.
> Once I built a tower,
> Now it's done.
> Brother, can you spare a dime?

In the 1930s, people who had plowed the earth, fought in America's wars, and built its railroads were suddenly jobless. The phrase "Brother, can you spare a dime?" became a familiar one. To struggle out of the depression, Americans turned to Franklin Delano Roosevelt. As President, he began many new programs to lift the nation out of the economic crisis.

Study the time line above. In what decade did the Great Depression begin?

During the Great Depression, the government hired jobless artists to paint murals such as this one of life in San Francisco.

1 The Great Depression Begins

Read to Learn

★ What were the causes of the Great Depression?

★ How did Hoover respond to the depression?

★ What do these words mean: consumer, relief, public works program, bonus?

When Herbert Hoover became President in March 1929, he firmly believed that the nation would continue to prosper. "I have no fears for the future of our country," he declared. "It is bright with hope." Before the year ended, however, the United States plunged into the worst economic depression in its history.

Warning Signals

During the election campaign, Hoover declared, "We in America are nearer to the final triumph over poverty than ever before in the history of any land." To Hoover and other leaders, the economy seemed to be growing at a rapid pace. But as you have read, many people, especially farmers, did not share in this prosperity.

The President realized that farmers needed help. So he persuaded Congress to create the Federal Farm Board. The Farm Board helped farmers market their products and keep prices stable—neither rising too high nor dropping too low. However, farmers did not cut back on production. So prices for farm products stayed low.

Low farm prices were only one warning signal of economic problems. The economy was slowing down. Fewer new homes and buildings were started. And *consumers,* or people spending money on goods and services, were buying less. No one noticed the slowdown because in the 1920s the government did not keep detailed statistics.

The Stock Market Crash

In the summer of 1929, a few cautious investors worried that the stock market boom might end. They began selling their stock. In September and early October 1929, more people decided to sell. As a result, stock prices began to fall.

The President tried to reassure investors. "The business of the country," he declared, "is on a sound and prosperous basis." Despite the President's words, a flood of orders to sell stock reached the New York Stock Exchange. Prices tumbled.

Many investors, you remember, had bought stock on margin. (See page 581.) Brokers asked investors to put up the money they still owed for the stock. But investors could not pay. Instead, they tried to sell their stock. This caused prices to drop even more. Between October 24 and October 29, millions of shares of stock were sold each day.

When the stock market opened on Tuesday, October 29, a wild stampede of selling began. On *Black Tuesday,* prices crashed until there were no buyers for the stock. Tens of thousands of people who could not sell their stock now held worthless paper. In a matter of hours, people who had been millionaires became poor.

Causes of the Great Depression

The *Great Depression* was the period from 1929 to 1941 in which Ameri-cans faced economic hard times. The stock market crash did not cause the Great Depression. But it did cause many people to lose confidence in American business. People who had invested their savings in stocks suddenly had nothing left.

As the depression set in, Americans asked again and again: How could the nation that was so prosperous in the 1920s be plunged into such a severe crisis in the 1930s?

Overproduction. Among the chief causes of the depression was overproduction. American farms and factories produced more goods than people could buy. Wages did not rise as much as prices in the 1920s. So workers could not afford to buy many goods. And farm families often could not afford cars and other goods. As orders for goods fell, factories closed down.

Bank failures. Another cause of the depression was the weakness of the banking system. During the 1920s, banks loaned large sums of money to investors. When the stock market crashed, the investors could not repay their loans. Without the repayments, banks could not give depositors their money. As a result, many banks were forced to close.

Almost 5,000 banks closed between 1929 and 1932. With each closing, hundreds of people lost the money they had deposited in banks. Often the savings of a lifetime disappeared almost overnight.

The downward trend. After the stock market crash, the economy slid downhill at a fast pace. One disaster triggered another. The stock market crash, for example, ruined investors. Without their money, or capital, businesses could no longer grow and expand.

When many banks closed, businesses found it hard to borrow money. So factories cut back on production. Such cutbacks meant wage cuts and layoffs for employees. Unemployed workers, in turn, had little money to spend. So they bought less, and the demand for cloth-

Long lines of hungry people were a common sight in American towns and cities during the Great Depression. Here, people in a rural area wait to get food from a soup kitchen. Most early efforts to help the poor and jobless were organized by charities or local governments. However, the number of needy became so huge that these local efforts were not enough.

ing, cars, and other goods fell. Many businesses went bankrupt.

Effects of the Depression

In the 1920s, the United States loaned large sums to European nations. When American banks stopped making loans in 1930 and 1931, the effects were soon felt in Europe. By 1931, European banks, too, began to fail. The Great Depression spread from one nation to another, leading to a worldwide economic collapse. You will read more about the effects of the depression on other countries in Chapter 28.

The Great Depression lasted longer and was more severe in the United States than elsewhere. The nation had suffered other economic depressions. None was as bad as this one.

The jobless. Between 1930 and 1932, the number of people without jobs rose from 4 million to 12 million. Millions more worked shortened hours for low pay. Many of the jobless lost their

homes and were forced onto the street. The chance of finding a job was small. On an average day, one New York job agency had 5,000 people looking for work. There were jobs for only about 300 of them. In another city, police had to keep order as 15,000 women pushed and shoved to apply for 6 jobs cleaning offices.

Some of the jobless shined shoes on street corners. Others set up sidewalk stands and sold apples. Sometimes, the apple seller was someone who had been rich before the depression began.

Families suffer. During the depression, families suffered. Hungry parents and children searched through city dumps or restaurant garbage cans. The pressure of hard times caused some families to split up. Fathers and even children, some as young as 13 or 14, left home to hunt for work. Their leaving meant the family had fewer mouths to feed.

Many of the homeless and jobless moved from town to town looking for

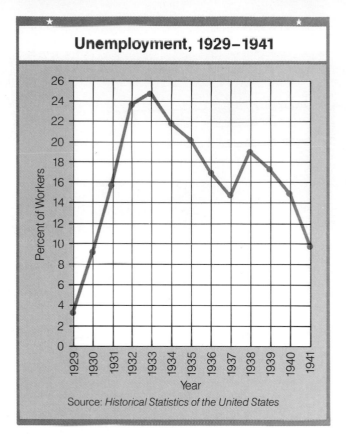

Unemployment, 1929–1941

Percent of Workers / Year

Source: *Historical Statistics of the United States*

GRAPH SKILL Millions of Americans had no work and no way to earn a living during the Great Depression. According to this graph, in what year was unemployment the highest? Why do you think many people feared a new depression in 1938?

work. Some "rode the rails." They lived in railroad cars and hitched rides on freight trains. In cities around the country, the homeless built shacks out of wooden crates and scraps of metal. These shack villages were called *Hoovervilles* because people blamed President Hoover for the Great Depression.

Hoover Responds

President Hoover was deeply concerned about the millions of jobless. He firmly believed that he must restore confidence in the economy. But he did not believe the government should interfere with business or set up relief programs. *Relief* means giving help to the needy. Instead, he called on busi-

ness leaders to keep workers on the job. And he urged private charities to help the needy.

Public works programs. As the hard times grew worse, Hoover took another approach. He set up *public works programs.* The government hired workers to put up new schools and courthouses, build dams, and pave highways. By providing jobs, the government programs helped people earn money. People could then spend their earnings on goods. The increased demand for goods, it was hoped, would make businesses expand and set the nation on the road to recovery.

Hoover asked Congress to approve the *Reconstruction Finance Corporation,* or RFC. The RFC loaned money to railroads, banks, and insurance companies to keep them in business. If these businesses were saved, Hoover believed, jobs would be saved.

The depression deepens. Hoover's efforts did not lift the country out of the depression. In 1931, as the third winter of the depression approached, more people filled the ranks of the hungry and homeless. "Men are sitting in the parks all day long and all night long, hundreds and thousands . . . out of work, seeking work," wrote one man in Detroit.

Hoover was widely blamed for not doing enough. People spoke of "Hoover blankets," the newspapers used by the homeless to keep warm when they slept outside. An empty pocket turned inside out was a "Hoover flag." A cardboard patch that covered a hole in a shoe was called "Hoover leather." In cities, charities set up soup kitchens to feed the hungry. Men, women, and children lined up for "Hoover stew," as the thin soup was called.

The Bonus Army

While people waited for the government to help, one group of Americans took action. After World War I, Con-

The Bonus Army included about 17,000 veterans from all over the country. Here, veterans from Sioux City, Iowa, stand outside the "Hotel Bonus." After they were driven out of Washington, D.C., "army" members told people back home how the government had treated them.

gress voted to give veterans a *bonus,* or sum of money, to be paid in 1945. In 1932, jobless veterans from all over the country marched on Washington to demand the bonus right away. For many veterans, the bonus was their only hope.

The marchers called themselves the Bonus Expeditionary Force. For two months, the *Bonus Army* camped in shacks and tents near the Potomac River. The House of Representatives voted to give the veterans the bonus at once, but the Senate rejected the bill. Some discouraged veterans packed up and went home. Thousands of others refused to leave. They vowed to stay until 1945 if necessary.

When the Washington, D.C., police tried to force the former soldiers to leave, the veterans fought back. Four people were killed in the battle. The President then ordered General Douglas MacArthur to clear out the veter-

ans. Using cavalry, tanks, machine guns, and tear gas, MacArthur moved into the camp and burned it to the ground.

Most Americans sympathized with the veterans. They were shocked at Hoover's action. The forced breakup of the Bonus Army hurt the President in the next election.

SECTION REVIEW

1. **Define:** consumer, relief, public works program, bonus.
2. What economic problems existed before the Great Depression?
3. What happened to stock prices during the stock market crash?
4. (a) List two causes of the Great Depression. (b) How did cutbacks in production make the depression worse?
5. **What Do You Think?** Why do you think the depression caused some families to break up?

2 The Promise of a New Deal

Read to Learn

★ Why did Roosevelt win the election of 1932?

★ How did FDR handle the banking crisis?

★ What were the major programs of the New Deal?

★ What do these words mean: fireside chat?

By 1932, the nation had suffered through three years of depression. Many Americans looked for a new leader. That year they turned to a man who promised "direct and vigorous action."

Election of 1932

In 1932, the Republicans chose Hoover to run for President again even though they knew he had little chance of winning. When the Democrats nominated Franklin Delano Roosevelt as their candidate, they felt sure he would win. Roosevelt was a distant cousin of Theodore Roosevelt, the 26th President. So the Roosevelt name was well known to the voters. Franklin Roosevelt was also a successful governor of New York.

Early in the campaign, Roosevelt, or FDR as he was called, sounded a hopeful note. "I pledge myself," he declared, "to a new deal for the American people." He did not spell out what the "new deal" would be. But he did promise to fight for the jobless, poor farmers, and the elderly.

Voters responded to FDR's confident manner and personal charm. On election day, Roosevelt won a landslide victory. Democrats also gained many seats in Congress.

After his inaugural speech, Roosevelt called on the public to show courage. "The only thing we have to fear," he said, "is fear itself." He promised to bring change. "The nation asks for action and action now. We must act and act quickly." These words offered hope to the American people.

Franklin Roosevelt was a cheerful, outgoing man. He wore heavy leg braces because he had suffered from polio as a young man. In one election campaign, FDR's theme was "Happy Days Are Here Again." The message was one that Americans wanted to hear.

FDR: A Man of Action

To many Americans, the new President seemed like a man of action. Although Roosevelt came from a privileged background, he had learned at an early age to help people in need. After graduating from law school, he married Eleanor Roosevelt, a distant cousin and niece of the then President Theodore Roosevelt.

Early career. FDR first entered politics in New York State. During World War I, he served as Assistant Secretary of the Navy. Then in the summer of 1921, Roosevelt was stricken with polio. The disease left his legs paralyzed.

Urged on by his wife, FDR worked hard to rebuild his strength. The long struggle taught Roosevelt patience and courage. After a person spends two years just trying to wiggle his small toe, Roosevelt once joked, everything else seems pretty easy. In the end, he was able to walk with the help of heavy leg braces. Roosevelt returned to politics. In 1928, he was elected governor of New York.

The Brain Trust. Before taking office as President, Roosevelt sought advice on how to fight the depression. He organized a group of college professors who were experts on many subjects. This group, called the *Brain Trust,* helped him plan new programs. Members of the Brain Trust included Raymond Moley and Rexford Tugwell.

Once in office, President Roosevelt chose able advisers. Among them was Harold Ickes, who was Secretary of the Interior. Ickes was a progressive Republican and leader of reform politics in Chicago. FDR chose Frances Perkins as Secretary of Labor. Perkins was the first woman cabinet member.

As Secretary of Labor, Frances Perkins was a strong supporter of FDR's programs. The American Federation of Labor had opposed her nomination because she had never been a trade union official. However, her firm stand on the rights of workers soon won her the AFL's approval and respect. Here, Perkins greets a group of workers.

The Banking Crisis

The first challenge facing the new President was the near collapse of the nation's banking system. Many banks had failed. Fearful depositors withdrew their savings. They hid their money in mattresses or buried it in their yards.

Right after taking office, the President declared a "bank holiday" and closed every bank in the nation. The President then asked Congress to pass the *Emergency Banking Relief Act.* The act let the government decide which banks could reopen. Healthy banks were allowed to reopen. Banks that were failing had to stay closed.

President Roosevelt then explained the new act on radio to the American public. Under the new law, the President told the people, "it is safer to keep your money in a reopened bank than under your mattress." The radio broadcast worked. Depositors returned their money to banks, and the banking system grew stronger.

During his years in office, FDR gave 30 radio speeches. He called them *fireside chats* because he spoke from a chair near a fireplace in the White House. Families gathered around their radios to listen to the President. As he spoke, they felt he understood the problems they faced every day.

New Deal Programs

Between March 9 and June 16, Roosevelt sent many bills to Congress. Congress passed a number of them during the *Hundred Days,* as this period was called. The bills covered a range of programs from job relief to planning for economic recovery. Together, the programs made up Roosevelt's *New Deal.* The New Deal had three main goals— relief for the unemployed, plans for recovery, and reforms to prevent another depression.

Help for the jobless. By 1933, more than 13 million Americans were out of work. As one way to provide help for the jobless, the President asked Congress to set up the *Civilian Conservation Corps* (CCC).* The CCC provided jobs and helped conserve natural resources. Unemployed single men between the ages of 18 and 25 enlisted in the CCC. They were paid $30 a month to plant trees, build bridges, work on flood control projects, and set up new parks.

During the New Deal, the President pushed for a number of other programs to help the jobless. Under some programs, such as the Federal Emergency Relief Administration (FERA), the government gave money to state and local agencies. These agencies in turn gave

---

*In the 1930s, people often called New Deal programs by their initial letters.

This young man is learning to survey in the Civilian Conservation Corps. During the depression, the CCC provided jobs for many young Americans. The work was demanding. A typical day began at 6 A.M. Young people volunteered for the CCC so that they could learn new skills and earn $30 a month to help their families.

New Deal Programs

Program	Initials	Begun	Purpose
Civilian Conservation Corps	CCC	1933	Provided jobs to young men to plant trees, build bridges and parks, and set up flood control projects
Tennessee Valley Authority	TVA	1933	Built dams to provide cheap electric power to seven southern states; set up schools and health centers
Federal Emergency Relief Administration	FERA	1933	Gave relief to unemployed and needy
Agricultural Adjustment Administration	AAA	1933	Paid farmers not to grow certain crops
National Recovery Administration	NRA	1933	Enforced codes that regulated wages, prices, and working conditions
Public Works Administration	PWA	1933	Built ports, schools, and aircraft carriers
Federal Deposit Insurance Corporation	FDIC	1933	Insured savings accounts in banks approved by government
Rural Electrification Project	REA	1935	Loaned money to extend electricity to rural farmers
Works Progress Administration	WPA	1935	Employed men and women to build hospitals, schools, parks, and airports; employed artists, writers, and musicians
Social Security Act	SSA	1935	Set up a system of pensions for elderly, unemployed, and handicapped

CHART SKILL Congress passed dozens of new laws as part of FDR's New Deal. Ten of Roosevelt's major programs are listed in the chart above. Which programs provided jobs for the unemployed?

the money to the needy. Other programs put the jobless to work.

In 1935, the Emergency Relief Appropriations Act set up the Works Progress Administration (WPA). The WPA employed men and women to build hospitals, schools, parks, playgrounds, and airports. WPA workers included artists, photographers, actors, writers, and composers. Artists painted murals on public buildings. Writers prepared hundreds of reports. Some writers interviewed black Americans who had been slaves until 1863. These "slave narratives" provided a firsthand view of slave life.

Through other New Deal programs, college and high school students were able to get part-time work. Although the pay was low, the jobs helped students stay in school.

Help for farmers. To bring about recovery, the President and his advisers tried to help American farmers. As you have read, the problem for farmers was that they produced too much. Farm surpluses sent prices down and lowered farmers' income.

In 1933, the President asked Congress to pass the *Agricultural Adjustment Act* (AAA). Under the act, the government paid farmers not to grow certain crops. If fewer crops were grown, prices would rise. Americans were shocked to learn that crops and livestock were being destroyed when people in the cities were going hungry. Yet, the plan seemed necessary to help the farmers.

Despite New Deal programs, farmers continued to suffer from hard times. Roosevelt kept trying new programs to help them. Among the most popular was the Rural Electrification Administration (REA). The REA loaned money to extend electric lines to rural farms. In the early 1930s, only one out of ten farms had electricity. With REA loans and WPA labor, the number rose to four out of ten by 1941.

Help for Industry

A major New Deal goal was to help industry recover from the depression. To achieve this goal, the President supported the National Industrial Recovery Act (NIRA). The act set up groups in each industry to write codes. These codes set up rules for production, wages, prices, and working conditions. The act tried to end price cutting and worker layoffs.

The *National Recovery Administration* (NRA) was set up to enforce the codes. Companies that cooperated with the NRA codes stamped a blue eagle on their products. People were encouraged to do business only with companies displaying the NRA eagle. The NRA quickly ran into trouble, however. Many companies ignored the codes. Small businesses felt that the codes favored the biggest firms.

The NIRA also set up the Public Works Administration (PWA). The PWA built 34,000 small and large projects. They included the Grand Coulee Dam in Washington, a deep-water port in Brownsville, Texas, public schools in Los Angeles, and two aircraft carriers for the navy.

Efforts at Reform

The third major New Deal goal was to make reforms to prevent another depression. During the Hundred Days, Roosevelt asked Congress to pass laws regulating the stock market and reforming the banking system. The Truth-in-Securities Act was passed to end the kind of wild speculation that led to the stock market crash.

MAP SKILL The TVA helped millions of people in at least eight states. Review what you learned about using a grid map on page 485. Give the letter and number of the square or squares where most of the TVA dams were built.

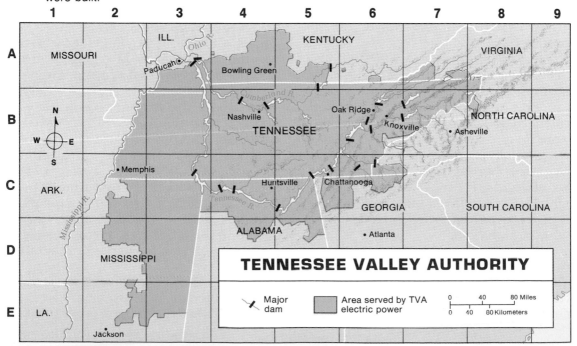

TENNESSEE VALLEY AUTHORITY

Another law, the Glass-Steagall Banking Act, set up the *Federal Deposit Insurance Corporation* (FDIC). The FDIC insured savings accounts in banks approved by the government. If an FDIC-insured bank failed, the government would make sure depositors received their savings.

Later, the New Deal brought about other kinds of reforms. The government passed laws to regulate gas and electric companies. It set up a program to provide new housing. In 1938, a new law extended the Pure Food and Drug Act of 1906. The new law protected consumers by requiring manufacturers to list ingredients of certain products. It also made sure that new medicines passed strict tests before they were put on the market.

An Ambitious Program: TVA

Perhaps the most ambitious program of the Hundred Days was the *Tennessee Valley Authority* (TVA). The program set out to remake the Tennessee River valley. In 1933, this area was a poor farming region. Because the farmland was so poor, more than half the families were on relief.

The TVA was a huge project. It built a string of 40 dams along the Tennessee River. (See the map on page 608.) The dams stopped flooding in the area and produced cheap electric power. The TVA deepened river channels for shipping. It planted new forests for soil conservation and developed fertilizers for improving farmland. It also set up schools and health centers in the regions.

At the time, the TVA sparked a heated debate. Critics argued that the government did not have the right to interfere in the economy of the region. Supporters applauded the TVA. They said it showed how the government could use its resources to help private enterprise.

━━━SECTION REVIEW━━━

1. **Locate:** Tennessee River.
2. **Define:** fireside chat.
3. How did Roosevelt deal with the banking crisis?
4. (a) List the goals of the New Deal. (b) Describe one law that met each goal.
5. **What Do You Think?** Do you think that FDR was a man of action? Explain your answer.

3 Responses to the New Deal

Read to Learn
★ Why did some people criticize the New Deal?
★ How did the New Deal help workers and older Americans?
★ What do these words mean: collective bargaining, sitdown strike, deficit spending?

During the Hundred Days, the President set up the framework of the New Deal. In the years ahead, he expanded his programs for relief, recovery, and reform. By 1935, the nation had recovered somewhat from the worst of the depression. Yet the President's programs did not succeed in ending the depression. At the same time, critics voiced their dissatisfaction with the New Deal.

Critics Speak Up

Some critics of the New Deal were people who had supported the President in 1932. The most outspoken of

In 1936, the Olympics offered a brief escape from the hardships of the Great Depression. That year, the Olympics were held in Berlin, Germany. In the track and field events, Americans pinned their hopes on a young black athlete named Jesse Owens.

The German leader, Adolf Hitler, sneered at the black American athlete. To Hitler, members of the white race were superior to people of any other race. He expected the Berlin Olympics to show that whites were the best athletes. But Owens proved Hitler wrong by winning one event after another. In all, he chalked up four gold medals. Hitler stormed out of the stadium rather than watch Owens accept the medals he won.

Not all Germans wanted Owens to fail, however. During the qualifying heat for the broad jump, Owens was nervous. On his first attempt, he started his jump beyond the take-off point. His second jump was too short to qualify. With only one jump left, the pressure mounted.

At that moment, Lutz Long walked over to Owens. Long, a German athlete, was competing against Owens in the broad jump. But he wanted Owens to qualify. Relax, Long told the American, do the best you can. Owens did. In the finals of the broad jump, Owens broke the world record held by Long.

On his return to the United States, Owens was greeted as a hero. Yet he found he could not make a living as an athlete. After he retired from running, Owens helped young people get started in sports.

★ How do you think Owens' success helped other black Americans?

these was Senator Huey Long of Louisiana. Long, nicknamed the Kingfish, attacked FDR's programs. He wanted a heavy tax on the rich. The new tax money, he said, should be used to provide every American family with a house, a car, and a fair income. "Share our wealth" was his motto. Millions of people, especially the poor, supported Long's idea.

Francis E. Townsend, a retired California doctor, said the government had not done enough to help older citizens. He wanted the government to give anyone over 60 a pension of $200 a month. People receiving the pension would have to retire—thereby opening up jobs. They would have to spend the money at once to boost the economy.

Another critic was Father Charles E. Coughlin (KAWG lihn), a Catholic priest. Known as the radio priest, Father Coughlin spoke each week to almost 10 million radio listeners. He criticized Roosevelt for not taking strong action against banking and money interests that he believed controlled the country.

Business and political leaders criticized the President's programs. They believed that the New Deal interfered too much with business and peoples' lives. The government, they warned, was taking away some of their basic freedoms.

The Supreme Court Acts

Roosevelt answered critics by saying that the depression was a national emergency just like a war. Therefore, he argued, the government had to increase its powers just as it had during World War I. The Supreme Court disagreed with this view. In 1935, it ruled the National Industrial Recovery Act unconstitutional. A year later, it struck down the Agricultural Adjustment Act.

The Court struck down other New Deal programs. In all, it declared 11 laws unconstitutional in a little over a year. In its 140-year history, the Court had overturned only 60 laws.

The President responds. Roosevelt was afraid that the Supreme Court would undo other New Deal programs. But he waited until after the 1936 election to take action. That year, FDR won by a large margin.

To Roosevelt, the election showed that Americans favored his programs. FDR's second term began on January 20, 1937.* Soon after, the President asked Congress to redesign the federal

courts. He suggested raising the number of justices on the Supreme Court from 9 to 15. The President then could choose six new justices who would support his programs.

A loss and a win. The President's move raised a loud outcry. Supporters and critics of the New Deal accused him of trying to pack the Court with his own appointees. They saw his move as a threat to the separation of powers so carefully set up by the Constitution. For six months, the President tried to push his ideas forward. In the end, he had to give up in defeat.

At the same time, the President won on another front. One justice who had voted against many New Deal laws changed his views. Another justice opposed to the New Deal retired. The President then appointed a new justice favorable to his programs. During his years in office, FDR had the chance to appoint nine new justices—the most any President had chosen since George Washington.

Benefits for Workers

Roosevelt's plans also included programs to help workers. In 1935, Congress passed the National Labor Relations Act, or *Wagner Act* as it was often called. The act protected workers from unfair management practices such as being fired if they joined a union. It also guaranteed workers the right to collective bargaining. *Collective bargaining* is the process whereby a union representing a group of workers negotiates with management for a contract. Workers had been fighting for this right since the late 1800s.

The Wagner Act led to a surge in union organizing. In the 1930s, union membership grew from 3 million to 9 million. Unions gained more economic and political power than ever before. The American Federation of Labor increased its size and bargaining power. John L. Lewis, head of the United Mine Workers, and other labor leaders

---

*The date was changed from March 4 by the Twentieth Amendment.

The Great Depression affected Americans across the nation. You can learn about its impact on people in your local area by studying primary sources of the 1930s.

Your library is one of several valuable resources. Besides books on local history, it may have county and city newspapers on microfilm. Local historians and historical societies can show you letters, diaries, and pictures. Senior citizens can tell you their own experiences. Even the buildings, roads, and parks around you may themselves be evidence.

Shown below is a letter that appeared in a New Jersey county newspaper during the Great Depression. It reveals how local events affected an ordinary citizen.

1. **Determine basic information about the letter.** (a) Who wrote the letter? (b) To whom is it addressed? (c) What is the date of the letter? (d) What is the writer's purpose?

2. **Analyze the contents of the letter.** (a) What general problem does the writer discuss in the second paragraph? (b) What specific problem does the writer refer to in the third paragraph?

3. **Identify the writer's point of view.** (a) Has the writer personally experienced these problems? How can you tell? (b) What solution does the writer suggest? (c) Why does the writer feel that the solution would be fair?

4. **Draw conclusions about the effect of the depression in the county.** (a) How did the county government try to deal with its economic problems? (b) What hardships did people face as a result? (c) Did the New Deal later help these people? Explain.

 Letter to an Editor

Editor, Bergen Evening Record:

Will you please print this letter about unemployment and economy? Being one of the people, I am speaking for the people.

During this depression, many people have lost their jobs through the reduction of staffs in places where they earned a wage that provided them a home, food, clothes, and other necessaries of life. When these are taken away by economy reductions in country and city, what will become of them?

I have read that the "taxpayers are grateful for the reduction." But these jobs were a Godsend to people who have to work. So I don't think Mr. Kulken will receive the glad hand from any of the 77 working men who recently have lost their livelihood, and other men besides who have been out of work for a year or more.

What will become of us who have to live now on the bounty of friends and neighbors? What will become of the county when we all become beggars? Mr. Kulken should have cut the wages of the men higher up to less than half, because their pockets are already well lined, and given the men who have to work a living wage.

Grace Cross

Hackensack, New Jersey
January 21, 1933

formed the Congress of Industrial Organizations (CIO). The CIO represented unions in whole industries such as steel, automobiles, and textiles.

Despite the Wagner Act, employers tried to stop workers from joining unions. Workers used sitdown strikes to force employers to recognize their unions. In a *sitdown strike,* workers stopped all machines and refused to leave the factory until they won recognition for their union.

Roosevelt persuaded Congress to help nonunion workers, too. The Fair Labor Standards Act of 1938 set a minimum wage of 40 cents an hour. The act set maximum hours—44 a week—in a number of industries. Also, it ended child labor under the age of 16 in these industries.

Help for Older Americans

The depression struck older Americans with great force. Many retired people lost their savings when the banks closed. Secretary of Labor Frances Perkins made a program for old age and unemployment insurance her top priority.*

In September 1935, Congress passed the *Social Security Act.* The act set up a system of pensions for the elderly. Payments from employers and employees supported this system. The act also set up state-run programs to provide unemployment benefits to workers who lost their jobs. Finally, it gave states money to support the handicapped and dependent children.

Some critics of the Social Security Act argued that the law did not provide enough for the elderly and unemployed. Also, people like farm workers and the self-employed were not covered by the system. Other critics said this program was another example of government moving into people's lives.

Despite the criticism, the Social Security system survived. It has been enlarged over the years. Today, it provides medical benefits to older Americans as well as pensions and unemployment insurance.

Ongoing Debate

Since the 1930s, the New Deal has created much debate. A major concern has been the increased power of government. Another has been the fact that the government spent more than it took in from taxes. This practice is called *deficit spending.* It meant a large increase in the national debt.

In the 1930s, business leaders warned that the New Deal was making labor unions too powerful. They also pointed out that FDR's programs were not bringing recovery. In fact, full recovery did not come until 1941. By then, the country was producing goods for nations fighting in World War II.

Defenders of the New Deal believed that the government must meet the needs of all citizens. Programs like Social Security, they said, were necessary for the public good. Further, they argued, the government had to regulate industries such as banking to prevent another depression. Americans slowly came to accept the expanded role of government. Their fears that regulation would destroy the free enterprise system faded.

═══ **SECTION REVIEW** ═══

1. **Define:** collective bargaining, sitdown strike, deficit spending.
2. Give three reasons why people criticized the New Deal.
3. (a) What programs did the Supreme Court strike down? (b) How did FDR respond to the Court's actions?
4. How did the Wagner Act help workers?
5. **What Do You Think?** How do you think the depression made many Americans willing to support the Social Security Act?

---

*In the 1930s, the United States was the only major industrial nation that did not have an old age pension system.

4 Years of Struggle

Read to Learn
★ What caused the Dust Bowl?
★ How did the depression affect women?
★ How did FDR reach out to help minorities?
★ What does this word mean: migrant

The 1930s were a time of struggle. New Deal programs helped some Americans but not all. During Roosevelt's years in office, the economy went through ups and downs, but the effects of the depression lingered.

The Dust Bowl

During the depression, a long drought brought hardships to people on the Great Plains. Between 1933 and 1936, little rain fell on states from Texas to the Dakotas. The topsoil dried out. High winds then carried the soil away, creating huge dust storms. In the 1930s, much of the Great Plains became the *Dust Bowl.*

Black blizzards. The dust storms, called black blizzards, were often worse than snowstorms. Windblown soil buried farmhouses. On roads, drivers had to turn on their headlights in the daytime. People put shutters over doors and windows. But still the dust sifted through, piling up on floors and sills.

Black blizzards were widespread. One storm blew dust from Oklahoma to Albany, New York, and out into the Atlantic Ocean. A Kansas farmer sadly

MAP SKILL The Dust Bowl stretched across the Great Plains from Texas to North Dakota. In the 1930s, high winds carried off tons of soil, creating huge dust storms. Look at the average yearly precipitation, or rain- and snowfall. Which part of the United States had an average of less than 20 inches of precipitation each year?

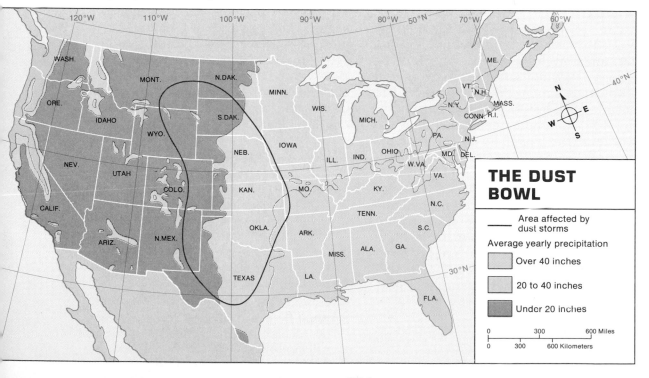

THE DUST BOWL

—— Area affected by dust storms

Average yearly precipitation

Over 40 inches

20 to 40 inches

Under 20 inches

For Okies and Arkies, the journey west was a tragic time. They left their homes and family friends. The trip across the country often proved too much for old cars loaded with belongings. In this photograph by Dorothea Lange, the family car has stalled on a highway in New Mexico.

reported that he sat by his window counting the farms going by.

What caused the Dust Bowl? Years of overgrazing by cattle and plowing by farmers destroyed the grasses that held the soil in place. The drought of the 1930s and high winds did the rest. A reporter described his uncle's farm in South Dakota. "It was a farm until he plowed it. Then it blew away."

Moving west. The drought and dust storms hurt poor farmers in Oklahoma and Arkansas the hardest. Many Okies and Arkies, as these people were called, packed their belongings into cars and trucks and headed west. They became *migrants,* or people who move about the country to find work. They hoped to find work in orchards and farms along the West Coast.

Once they reached California, Oregon, or Washington, the migrants found a new disaster—they were not wanted. In some areas, local citizens blocked the highways and sent the migrants away. Those who did find work were paid very little. They lived in tents and cardboard shacks without water or electricity.

Women in the Depression

For women, as for men, the depression brought great hardships. But many women faced a different set of problems. If jobs were available, employers hired men over women. Many companies and even the federal government refused to hire a woman if her husband had a job.

Eleanor Roosevelt admired women "whose hearts were somehow so touched by the misery of human beings that they wanted to give their lives to relieve it." She herself was such a woman. Here, she ladles out food in a soup kitchen. As the "eyes and ears" of the President, she traveled the country and reported back to him on what she learned.

Despite limits on hiring, many women worked outside the home. Most were from minority groups such as blacks and Hispanics. They earned very little, but their wages were desperately needed.

Strike for better pay. Sometimes, women workers struck for better pay. For example, at least 80 percent of the pecan shellers in San Antonio, Texas, were Mexican American women. A 20-year-old woman, Emma Tenayuca, helped organize the pecan shellers. When employers lowered their pay, workers walked off the job. Tenayuca said later, "I had a basic underlying faith in the American idea of freedom and fairness. I felt something had to be done."

The First Lady speaks out. Eleanor Roosevelt was the wife of the President. She took the most active role of any First Lady in history. As the "eyes and ears" of the President, she toured the nation. She visited coal mines and talked to people on unemployment lines. She went into the homes of poor families. On her return to Washington, she told the President what she had seen and heard.

Eleanor Roosevelt also kept up her own career. She wrote a newspaper column. She also had her own radio program. As a reformer, she called on Americans to live up to the goals of equality and justice.

In speaking out on social issues, Eleanor Roosevelt angered some people who thought a President's wife should not be such a public figure. Many other Americans admired the First Lady for her stands.

Minorities Look for Justice

FDR reached out to many groups who were once excluded from American life. In doing so, he won their support for the Democratic Party.

Black Americans. During the depression, black workers were the first to lose their jobs. Often, they were denied food and public work jobs because of their color. At relief centers, young black men were threatened or beaten when they went to sign up for work. Even some charities refused to serve blacks in the soup lines. Eleanor Roosevelt and others close to the President tried to help blacks get food and relief payments when private and public agencies refused to aid them.

The President invited black leaders to advise him in the White House. Roosevelt's unofficial **Black Cabinet** included a Harvard-educated economist, Robert C. Weaver, and Mary McLeod Bethune, a well-known educator. Both held high-level jobs in the government.

Many black leaders realized that all blacks had to unite to press for justice. By using their votes, winning higher-level government jobs, and presenting demands for equal treatment, they slowly moved a few steps forward. The struggle for equality, however, would take many more years.

Mexican Americans. During the depression, Mexican Americans had jobs in many industries and lived in cities around the country. A large number, however, were farm workers in the Southwest and West. There, they faced discrimination in education, jobs, and at the polls. Mexican American children were forced to attend poorly equipped "Mexican schools." Local school boards admitted that if these children were well educated, farmers would lose a good supply of cheap labor.

Since the late 1800s, employers had encouraged Mexicans to work in factories or on farms in the United States. When bad times hit in the 1930s, Americans pressured the government to force Mexican workers to leave the country. More than 400,000 people were rounded up and sent back to Mexico. Some were American-born and therefore citizens of the United States. But the government ignored their rights.

The Indian New Deal. The 1930s brought changes in policies toward Native Americans. FDR called on Congress to pass a series of reforms that have often been called the Indian New

AMERICANS WHO DARED

Mary McLeod Bethune

Mary McLeod Bethune was the daughter of former slaves. A bright girl, she won scholarships to college. After graduating, she set up a school for black women in Florida. Bethune went on to become a well-respected educator and adviser to both President Coolidge and President Roosevelt. She once told FDR, "I speak, Mr. President, not as Mrs. Bethune, but as the voice of 14 million Americans who seek to achieve full citizenship." In 1936, Roosevelt appointed her head of the National Youth Administration's Division of Negro Affairs. She was the first black American to head a government agency.

Deal. The President chose John Collier to head up the Bureau of Indian Affairs. Collier ended the government policy of breaking up Indian land holdings. In 1934, Congress passed the

Indian Reorganization Act. It protected and even expanded land holdings of Indian reservations.

The government also ended its policy of destroying Indian religions. It supported the right of Indians to live according to their own traditions.

To provide jobs during the depression, the government set up the Indian Emergency Conservation Work group. It employed Native Americans on land conservation projects. In 1935, Congress set up the Indian Arts and Craft Board. By promoting sales of Indian art, it encouraged talented Native Americans to create new works.

Escape From Hard Times

During the 1930s, many Americans looked for ways to escape from the hard times. They found an escape in radio and movies.

Radio. Millions of Americans listened to radio for two or three hours each night. Comedians like George Burns and Gracie Allen made people laugh and forget their troubles for a time. Programs of classical music were also popular. Through radio, Americans were able to enjoy music that they could not have heard otherwise.

Daytime shows were popular because so many people were out of work. People listened to serials, or programs that told a story over weeks or months. Serials were often called soap operas because they carried advertisements for soap companies.

Perhaps the most famous broadcast took place on Halloween eve, 1938. That night, an actor named Orson Welles gave a make-believe newscast based on *The War of the Worlds*. Welles grimly reported the landing of invaders from the planet Mars. People who tuned in late missed the reminder that the show was not real. They panicked at the thought of an actual invasion of Martians.

Movies. During the depression, movie makers tried to restore people's faith in America. Movies told stories about happy families in comfortable neighborhoods. Child actors like Shirley Temple and Mickey Rooney starred in hugely successful movies.

Among the most popular movies was Walt Disney's *Snow White and the Seven Dwarfs. Snow White* was the first full-length animated film. In 1939, Judy Garland won American hearts in *The Wizard of Oz*. The movie told of a girl's escape from a bleak life in depression Kansas to the colorful land of Oz.

The longest, most expensive, and most profitable movie of the 1930s was *Gone With the Wind*. It was based on a novel by Margaret Mitchell. The movie showed the Civil War in a romantic light. For over three hours, Americans forgot their own worries as they watched the story of love and loss amid the battlefields of the South.

Vivid Images

Writers, painters, and photographers recorded images of depression life. In the 1930s, many writers showed the hard times Americans faced in villages, mines, and factories across the country. In *The Grapes of Wrath,* John Steinbeck traced the heartbreaking story of a family of Okies who migrated to California. Steinbeck's book shocked and angered some people because it showed the despair and injustice that the homeless met in America.

Black writers of the Harlem Renaissance continued to create new works. In *Black Boy,* Richard Wright told of his childhood in the South during the 1920s.

Many painters in the 1930s turned to themes that tied ordinary Americans together. In a huge mural, Thomas Hart Benton brought to life the history of frontier America. Another artist, Grant Wood, is best known for a paint-

Americans adored young Judy Garland in *The Wizard of Oz*. Her song "Over the Rainbow" gave hope of a better future—a hope desperately needed in the Great Depression. Here, Garland in the role of Dorothy dries the tears of the Cowardly Lion (Bert Lahr) as the Tin Woodman (Jack Haley) and the Scarecrow (Ray Bolger) look on.

ing called *American Gothic*. In it, Wood shows an Iowa farm couple who look strong enough to survive any hardship.

Photographers captured painful images of depression life. Dorothea Lange took hundreds of unforgettable pictures of the Dust Bowl farms and families. (See page 615.) Margaret Bourke–White took photographs of poor tenant farmers in the South. Through the work of photographers, people today can get a sense of American life during the Great Depression.

SECTION REVIEW

1. **Define:** migrant.
2. Describe problems faced by people living in the Dust Bowl.
3. What group of Americans did each of the following try to help: (a) Emma Tenayuca; (b) Eleanor Roosevelt; (c) John Collier?
4. How did Americans find an escape from the hardships of the depression?
5. **What Do You Think?** Why do you think Mexican Americans and blacks suffered even greater discrimination during the depression than during good times?

Chapter 27 Review

★ Summary ★

In 1929, the stock market crash spelled an end to the prosperity of the 1920s. By 1930, the nation was sinking into the worst economic depression in its history.

In 1932, voters chose Franklin Roosevelt as President. FDR promised a new deal for Americans. In the years ahead, he tried out many programs. Together, they were called the New Deal.

During the Great Depression, the Dust Bowl spread across the Great Plains. Thousands of Americans were forced off their farms. The depression brought hard times to minority groups like blacks and Mexican Americans. Under the New Deal, however, Indians benefited from new government policies.

★ Reviewing the Facts ★

 2 pts

Key Terms. Match each term in Column 1 with the correct definition in Column 2.

Column 1
1. consumer
2. public works program
3. fireside chat
4. collective bargaining
5. deficit spending

Column 2
a. government project to provide jobs
b. government spends more than it collects in taxes
c. person spending money on goods and services
d. radio speech of FDR
e. talks between union and management for a contract

Key People, Events, and Ideas. Identify each of the following.

1. Herbert Hoover
2. Bonus Army
3. Frances Perkins
4. Mary McLeod Bethune
5. Emergency Banking Relief Act
6. CCC
7. AAA
8. NRA
9. TVA
10. Huey Long
11. Wagner Act
12. Social Security Act
13. Dust Bowl
14. Eleanor Roosevelt
15. Richard Wright

★ Chapter Checkup ★

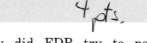 4 pts.

1. (a) Describe the stock market crash. (b) How did the crash help cause the Great Depression? (c) Explain at least one other cause of the Great Depression.
2. Describe the problems faced by many Americans during the depression.
3. (a) What different groups of Americans did the New Deal try to help? (b) How did the WPA help people?
4. How did the TVA improve conditions in the Tennessee Valley?
5. (a) Why did FDR try to pack the Supreme Court? (b) Did he succeed? Explain.
6. (a) What caused the Dust Bowl? (b) What areas were affected most by the black blizzards? (c) Why did Okies and Arkies move west?
7. What was the Indian New Deal?
8. (a) Why were radio shows popular during the depression? (b) Name two successful movies of the 1930s.

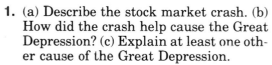

★ Thinking About History   *8 pts.*   ★

1. **Understanding the economy.** American farmers produced too much for their own good. (a) Explain how this statement was true. (b) Why do you think farmers were not willing to cut back on production unless the government paid them to do so? (c) Why do you think other Americans were angry about government payments to farmers?

2. **Analyzing a quotation.** During the 1932 campaign, FDR said, "It is common to take a method and try it. If it fails, admit it frankly and try another. But above all, try something." How did FDR's programs under the New Deal reflect this view?

3. **Relating past to present.** (a) Who did President Hoover think should help the unemployed? (b) How did FDR's ideas differ from Hoover's? (c) Do most Americans today expect the government to follow programs like Hoover's or FDR's? Explain.

4. **Taking a stand.** As a result of the New Deal, the government acquired too much power over people's lives. Do you agree or disagree with this statement? Explain your stand.

5. **Evaluating.** (a) What goals did FDR set for the New Deal? (b) Do you think FDR achieved these goals? Explain.

★ Using Your Skills   ★

1. **Understanding cause and effect.** Make a list of the causes of the Great Depression. Next to each cause, describe at least one effect.

2. **Graph reading.** Study the graph on page 602. (a) About how many Americans were unemployed in 1932? In 1934? In 1938? (b) In what year was unemployment the highest? (c) Why do you think unemployment fell in the 1940s?

3. **Making a review chart.** Make a chart with five rows and two columns. Title the rows Jobless, Farmers, Workers,

Older Americans, Native Americans. Title the columns New Deal Program, How Program Helped. Complete the chart. (a) What New Deal program helped Native Americans? (b) How did the New Deal try to help older Americans? (c) Using the chart, make one generalization about the New Deal.

4. **Reading for the main idea.** Reread pages 614–615 to find the main idea. (a) What is the main idea of the first paragraph under "Moving west"? (b) What is the main idea of "The Dust Bowl"?

★ More to Do   ★

1. **Researching.** Find out what kinds of statistics the government keeps on the economy today. Then describe how keeping these statistics might help prevent another depression.

2. **Writing a diary.** Imagine that you are a woman whose family lives in the Dust Bowl. Write several entries in your diary to describe your life, a dust storm, and

how you are going to survive the next few years.

3. **Exploring local history.** Find someone in your area who remembers the Great Depression. Draw up a series of questions before you go to interview him or her. Use a tape recorder to get an oral history of what the person remembers about life during the depression.

World War II (1935–1945)

Chapter Outline

1 Threats to the Peace
2 The World at War
3 The War Effort at Home
4 Allied Drive to Victory
5 Winning the Peace

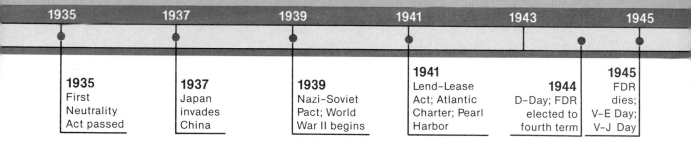

1935	1937	1939	1941	1943	1945

1935
First
Neutrality
Act passed

1937
Japan
invades
China

1939
Nazi–Soviet
Pact; World
War II begins

1941
Lend–Lease
Act; Atlantic
Charter; Pearl
Harbor

1944
D–Day; FDR
elected to
fourth term

1945
FDR
dies;
V–E Day;
V–J Day

About This Chapter

In 1939, Americans tried to steer clear of the war that broke out in Europe. In December 1941, however, the war struck home with shattering results.

December 7, 1941, was a sleepy Sunday at Pearl Harbor, Hawaii. On board ships in the harbor, many sailors were still in bed at 7:55 A.M. Suddenly, Japanese planes came roaring over the harbor. Tourists on an American luxury liner watched the planes, thinking they were about to see an air raid drill. When the planes started bombing the harbor, Seaman Robert Osborne remarked to a friend, "Boy, is somebody going to catch it for putting live bombs on those planes."

On the battleship *Nevada,* a military band was getting ready to play "The Star-Spangled Banner" as they did each morning. They saw the first wave of planes fly over and heard the bombs explode. The ship next to theirs, the *Arizona,* took a direct hit. The hit sent the *Arizona* and 1,100 men to the bottom. A Japanese tail gunner sprayed the *Nevada's* deck with bullets. Fortunately, no one in the band was hit. The band finished the national anthem before taking cover.

The Japanese attack on Pearl Harbor damaged or destroyed 19 ships and killed about 2,400 people. It brought Americans into the war to fight alongside people from many other nations.

Study the time line above. How long had World War II been going on before Japan attacked Pearl Harbor?

On June 6, 1944, Allied troops invaded France. "The free men of the world are marching together to victory," declared General Eisenhower.

1 Threats to the Peace

Read to Learn

★ How did dictators gain power in Italy and Germany?
★ What events led to the outbreak of World War II?
★ What do these words mean: dictator, totalitarian state, collective farm, aggression, appeasement?

During the 1930s, the Great Depression brought hardships to every country in the world. Nations responded to the hard times in different ways. In the United States, President Roosevelt introduced major democratic reforms. Elsewhere, democratic governments crumbled under the pressure of hard times.

American Foreign Policy

During the depression, Americans were more concerned with economic troubles at home than with events overseas. A strong isolationist mood gripped the country. When European nations again moved toward war in the late 1930s, many Americans felt strongly that they must stay out of another conflict.

Victory for isolationists. In 1935, isolationists pushed Congress to pass the first of the *Neutrality Acts.* These laws banned arms sales or loans to countries at war. They stopped Americans from traveling on ships of countries at war. By limiting economic ties with nations at war, the United States meant to stay out of any foreign war.

Good Neighbor Policy. While the United States tried to avoid conflicts overseas, it made new efforts to improve relations with the nations of Latin America. In 1930, President Hoover announced that the United States no longer claimed the right to intervene in the affairs of Latin American nations.

When President Roosevelt took office, he promised that the United States would follow "the policy of the good neighbor." FDR put the *Good Neighbor Policy* to work. He withdrew American troops from Nicaragua and Haiti. Then he lifted the Platt Amendment, which had limited the independence of Cuba.

In 1936, President Roosevelt visited Argentina. He urged close ties among the nations of the Western Hemisphere. As war clouds loomed in other parts of the world, the United States was eager to build friendly relations with the nations of Latin America.

Rise of Dictators

In the 1930s, the rise of dictators threatened the peace of the world. A *dictator* is a ruler who has complete power over a country. Economic troubles, anger over the Versailles Treaty, and appeals to extreme nationalism helped dictators win popular support in Italy and Germany.

Benito Mussolini. Italy was disappointed with the outcome of World War I. It did not receive all the lands it wanted in the peace treaties. Also, economic problems led to riots and fears of revolution. In 1919, Benito Mussolini organized the *Fascist Party*. He called on Italians to unite behind him and restore the country to the grandeur of ancient Rome. By 1922, Mussolini was strong enough to seize power in Italy.

In the next few years, Mussolini tightened his control. He outlawed all political parties except his own. He controlled the press and banned criticism of the government. In schools, children recited the motto "Mussolini is always right." They learned discipline and total obedience to Mussolini.

Ethiopia invaded. When the Great Depression struck, Mussolini tried to distract Italians from the economic crisis by starting a foreign war. In 1935, he sent his army into Ethiopia in North Africa. The Ethiopians fought bravely. But their cavalry and old-fashioned rifles were no match for the modern Italian tanks and airplanes.

Emperor Haile Selassie (HI lee suh LAS ee) of Ethiopia asked the League of Nations for help. The league took little action. Nations such as Britain and France were distracted by their own economic problems. Also, they did not want to anger Mussolini. So the world stood by as Italy took over Ethiopia.

Adolf Hitler. Another dictator, Adolf Hitler, watched Mussolini's actions with interest. Like Mussolini, Hitler won power in Germany by organizing his own political party—the National Socialist Workers Party, or *Nazis*.

Hitler believed Germans belonged to a superior "Aryan" race. He preached hatred of Jews and blamed them for Germany's troubles. He savagely attacked the Versailles Treaty as unfair to Germany. Germany, he claimed, had not even lost the war. Rather, Jews and traitors had "stabbed Germany in the back" in 1918.

In the 1920s, Hitler built up Nazi strength. He was a powerful speaker and skillful leader. Many Germans came to believe in his ideas. When the Great Depression brought hard times to Germans, they turned to him as a strong leader.

Nazis in power. Hitler became chancellor of Germany in 1933. In the next two years, he ended democratic government and created a totalitarian state. In a *totalitarian state*, a single party controls the government and every aspect of the lives of the people. Citizens must obey the government without question. The government silences any critics.

Under Hitler, the Nazis controlled the press, schools, and religion. Nazis passed laws against Jews. In 1938, thousands of Jews were sent to concentration, or prison, camps. Persecution of Jews would increase in the years ahead.

Hitler built up the German armed forces and claimed that Germany had the right to expand to the east. The League of Nations condemned Hitler's actions. Hitler ignored the league and moved ahead with his plans to expand Germany.

The Soviet Union Under Stalin

Hitler's plans worried Joseph Stalin, the dictator who ruled the Soviet Union after Lenin died. To strengthen the Soviet economy, Stalin launched a series of five-year plans. These plans were economic programs to build up industry and farming.

To meet his goals, Stalin used all the weapons of the totalitarian state. He urged the Russian people to make superhuman efforts to produce more goods. If people resisted the government, they were punished harshly. For example, the government ordered all peasants to give up their land and farm animals and join *collective farms*, or government-run farms. When farmers resisted this change, millions were executed or sent to forced-labor camps.

Despite the harsh conditions under which most Russians lived, the Soviet economy expanded. Steel and oil production increased sharply. These materials, as Stalin knew, would be needed to fight any German aggression. *Aggression* is any warlike act by one country against another without just cause.

Japanese Aggression

Japan was hard hit by the Great Depression. The economic crisis cut deep into Japanese trade. It also ruined many businesses. Many Japanese grew

In 1936, Hitler, at right, and Mussolini, at left, signed an agreement creating the Rome–Berlin Axis. Both dictators won popular support by staging huge parades. Each wanted to conquer new lands.

impatient with their democratic government that seemed unable to solve the crisis.

In the early 1930s, military leaders took power in Japan. They wanted Japan to expand into Asia. Because Japan was a small island nation, it lacked many important resources, such as coal and oil. In 1931, the Japanese army seized Manchuria, part of northeastern China. By taking over Manchuria, Japan gained rich supplies of coal and iron. Japan created a state called *Manchukuo* in the area.

China called on the League of Nations to help. The league condemned Japanese aggression but did little else. The United States refused to recognize Manchukuo but took no other action against Japan.

The military continued its program of expansion. In 1937, Japan launched a full-scale war against China. Japanese planes bombed Peking, Shanghai, and other Chinese cities. Japanese troops defeated Chinese armies and occupied northern and central China.

The United States watched events in China with concern. Japanese aggression undermined the Open Door Policy. Also, Japanese expansion threatened the Philippines, which the United States controlled. In spite of these threats to peace, most Americans wanted to avoid war at almost any cost.

Road to War

By the mid-1930s, Italy had conquered Ethiopia, and Japan had seized Manchuria. In 1936, Hitler moved his army into the Rhineland near the border of France and Belgium. As Hitler expected, neither France nor Britain did anything to stop him. In 1938, Hitler peacefully annexed Austria to Germany.

Next, he claimed the Sudetenland, or the western part of Czechoslovakia. Britain and France had signed treaties to protect Czechoslovakia. At the *Munich Conference* in 1938, however, they gave in to Hitler's demand in order to preserve the peace. This practice became known as *appeasement*. At Mu-

MAP SKILL In the late 1930s, Hitler and Mussolini threatened the peace of Europe. Hitler took over neighboring lands and had even more ambitious plans. In 1939, Italy, which had already conquered Ethiopia in Africa, seized Albania. What country bordered Germany in the east?

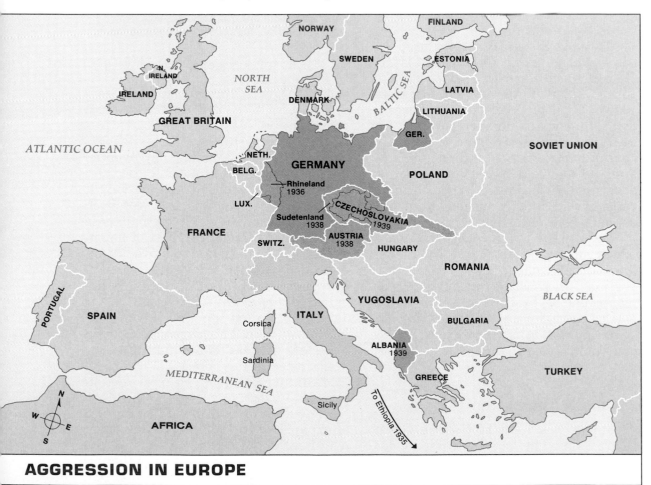

AGGRESSION IN EUROPE

Areas taken over by Germany by September 1, 1939

Areas taken over by Italy by September 1, 1939

nich, Hitler said that he wanted no more territory. But then in March 1939, he took over the rest of Czechoslovakia.

Britain and France saw that Hitler's ambitions must be stopped. Britain tried to form an alliance with the Soviet Union. Stalin thought that the western democracies, such as Britain and France, lacked the will to fight. So instead, he signed the *Nazi–Soviet Pact* on August 23, 1939. In this treaty, Hitler and Stalin agreed not to attack each other. Secretly, the two nations agreed to divide up Poland and other parts of Eastern Europe.

The Nazi–Soviet Pact freed Hitler to attack Poland without fear of fighting Russia. On September 1, 1939, German armies marched into Poland. Two days later, Britain and France declared war on Germany. World War II had begun.

━━ SECTION REVIEW ━━

1. **Locate:** Italy, Germany, Soviet Union, Japan, Manchuria, China, Czechoslovakia, Poland.
2. **Define:** dictator, totalitarian state, collective farm, aggression, appeasement.
3. What foreign policy did the United States follow in the 1930s?
4. Describe one way that each of the following leaders threatened the peace: (a) Mussolini; (b) Japan's military leaders; (c) Hitler.
5. **What Do You Think?** How do you think the Great Depression helped dictators rise to power?

2 The World at War

Read to Learn

★ What did the United States do when World War II began?
★ How did the United States help the Allies?
★ What happened at Pearl Harbor?

The war that broke out in Europe in 1939 soon spread around the world. On one side were the major *Axis* powers, Germany, Italy, and Japan. On the other side were the *Allies*. Before the war was over, the Allies included Britain, France, the Soviet Union, the United States, China, and 41 other nations.

Hitler Conquers Europe

In September 1939, German troops stormed into Poland. The Poles resisted fiercely but were soon forced to surrender. Meanwhile, the Soviet Union invaded eastern Poland. It also invaded Finland and later annexed Estonia, Latvia, and Lithuania. Stalin took these steps, he claimed, to strengthen Russian defenses. He expected that Hitler would eventually attack the Soviet Union, in spite of their treaty.

The fall of France. In April 1940, Hitler's armies turned toward the west. They overpowered Denmark and Norway. The next month, they occupied Holland and Belgium and pushed into France. Britain sent troops to help the French fight the Germans.

By May, however, the Germans had trapped the Allies at Dunkirk on the English Channel. The British sent every available warship, merchant ship, and even fishing and pleasure boats to rescue the trapped soldiers. They carried 338,000 English and French soldiers to safety in England. German armies then marched on to Paris. And on June 22, 1940, France surrendered.

Battle of Britain. Britain now stood alone. The new British prime minister, Winston Churchill, warned the people

WORLD WAR II IN EUROPE AND NORTH AFRICA

Main Axis powers 1942	
Greatest extent of Axis control, 1942	
Neutral nations, 1942	
Allied territory, 1942	
← Allied advances	
✯ Major battles	

0   300   600 Miles
0   300   600 Kilometers

MAP SKILL Early in the war, the Axis powers overran most of Europe. In 1943, however, the tide turned as the Allies went on the offensive. When did the Allies first invade Italy? France? Germany?

to prepare for an attack. Ahead, he told them, he could offer only "blood, toil, tears, and sweat." His courage inspired the British people. "We shall defend our island," he promised, "whatever the cost may be. . . . We shall never surrender."

German planes pounded London and other English cities during the **Battle of Britain.** British fighter pilots used radar, a new invention, to detect the approach of enemy planes. They then took to the air, shooting down thousands of German planes. By late 1940, Hitler had to give up his plans to invade Britain. Still, his armies occupied most of Europe.

America Stays Neutral

When the war broke out in Europe, Americans sympathized with the Poles, Finns, French, and British. Although most Americans supported the Allies, few wanted to be drawn into the war. In September 1939, Roosevelt issued a statement proclaiming American neutrality.

Cash-and-carry arms sales. At the same time, the President pushed for changes in the Neutrality Acts. He tried to get Congress to repeal the law that banned the sale of arms to warring nations. Isolationists defeated the move. In the end, a cash-and-carry compromise was worked out. Under it, the United States could sell arms to the Allies. The Allies had to pay cash for the goods and carry the arms in their own ships.

By 1940, German submarines were sinking tons of British shipping. Churchill asked the United States for ships to help Britain. President Roosevelt convinced Congress to trade 50 old American destroyers to Britain. In exchange, Britain gave the United States 99-year leases on military bases in Newfoundland and the Caribbean.

The nation rearms. As Hitler's war machine swept through Europe, Americans came to believe they had to be ready for war. Congress increased spending for the army and navy. In September 1940, it set up the first peacetime draft in American history.

Isolationists criticized the President and Congress for aiding Britain and building up American defenses. Many other Americans supported the President. They believed that the United States must help Britain defend democracy against totalitarian states.

FDR Wins a Third Term

Because of the war in Europe, FDR decided to run for a third term in 1940. His decision broke the precedent set by George Washington of serving only two terms as President. The Republicans nominated Wendell Willkie. Willkie agreed with Roosevelt on many issues. He favored sending aid to Britain. But he forced FDR to pledge that Americans would not be sent to fight in foreign wars. He also played up the third-term issue.

Even some Democrats were upset that FDR was running again. Roosevelt answered all critics with Abraham Lincoln's slogan in the 1864 campaign—"Don't change horses in midstream." In 1940, voters chose to stay with an experienced leader. They reelected FDR.

Arsenal of democracy. After the election, Roosevelt increased aid to Britain. By late 1940, however, Britain had little money left to pay for arms and supplies. Roosevelt wanted to lend Britain the supplies it needed. But many Americans opposed making loans to Britain.

Roosevelt argued that if your neighbors' house was on fire and they needed to borrow your garden hose, you would not waste time talking about how much the hose cost. FDR's comparison helped people see the need to make loans to Britain.

In March 1941, Congress passed the *Lend–Lease Act*. The act allowed FDR to sell or lend war materials to "any country whose defense the President deems vital to the defense of the United States." Under the Lend–Lease Act, the President said, America would become the "arsenal of democracy." Roosevelt spoke of the Four Freedoms the nation wanted to defend—freedom of speech and worship as well as freedom from want and fear.

Lend–Lease extended. In 1941, America sent airplanes, tanks, guns, and ammunition to the British. In June of that year, Hitler launched a surprise invasion of the Soviet Union. German armies drove deep into the Russian heartland. Although Roosevelt condemned Stalin's totalitarian rule, he decided to extend the Lend–Lease Act to the Soviet Union. Roosevelt and Churchill agreed that the destruction of Hitler outweighed everything else.

Under the Lend–Lease Act, the United States sent supplies across the Atlantic on British merchant ships. To safeguard these supplies, Roosevelt sent American warships to accompany the ships as far as Iceland. When German submarines began to attack American destroyers, Roosevelt issued a shoot-on-sight order. American warships in United States waters could now fire on German or Italian ships.

The Atlantic Charter. In August 1941, President Roosevelt and Prime Minister Churchill issued the *Atlantic Charter*. The charter set up goals for the postwar world. In it, the two leaders agreed to seek no territorial gain. They pledged to support "the right of all peoples to choose the form of government under which they will live." The charter also called for a "permanent system of general security."

War in Asia

By 1941, Roosevelt was not only worried about Hitler's advance through Europe. He was also concerned about Japan's conquests in Asia. When Germany defeated Holland and France in 1940, Japan moved to take over their colonies in Southeast Asia. In September 1940, Japan had signed an alliance with Germany and Italy and continued to expand. (See the map on page 636.)

Worsening relations. The United States tried to stop Japanese aggression by cutting off the sale of oil and scrap metal to Japan. These moves angered the Japanese because they badly needed the oil and metal.

In November 1941, Japanese and American officials tried to settle their differences. Japan wanted the United States to lift the embargo on oil and scrap metal. The United States wanted Japan to withdraw its armies from China and Southeast Asia. Neither side would compromise. So the talks broke off. Meanwhile, Japan planned a secret attack on the United States.

Attack on Pearl Harbor. At 7:55 A.M. on Sunday, December 7, 1941, Japanese planes appeared in the sky over *Pearl Harbor,* Hawaii. The United States Pacific fleet sat peacefully in the harbor below. In less than two hours, Japanese bombs sank or seriously damaged 19 American ships, destroyed 150 American planes, and killed about 2,400 people. Fortunately for the United States, all three aircraft carriers of its Pacific fleet were at sea.

Americans were stunned by the attack on Pearl Harbor. (See page 622.)

In August 1941, President Roosevelt and Prime Minister Churchill met on board the HMS *Prince of Wales* off the Newfoundland coast. Churchill wanted more aid from the United States. Roosevelt wanted an agreement on principles for the postwar world. Together, they wrote the Atlantic Charter, which stated their hopes for peace.

This drawing by Griffith Baily Coale shows the Japanese attack on Pearl Harbor. In the front, the minelayer *Ogalala* sinks. At left, the *Nevada,* the only battleship to escape, steams out of the harbor amid exploding bombs. The Japanese hoped to knock out the entire American Pacific fleet in the attack. However, several of the damaged ships were repaired and returned to action.

The day after the bombing, Roosevelt appeared before a joint session of Congress. Grimly, he described December 7 as "a date which will live in infamy." He then asked Congress to declare war on Japan. Three days later, Germany and Italy declared war on the United States.

World War II was already two years old when the United States joined the Allies. The forces of democracy faced dark days ahead. But even most Americans who had defended isolationism now joined the fight for freedom.

◾ SECTION REVIEW ◾

1. **Locate:** Poland, Denmark, Norway, Holland, Belgium, France, Britain, Pearl Harbor.
2. What lands did Hitler conquer early in the war?
3. How did the Lend–Lease Act help the Allies?
4. What were the main points in the Atlantic Charter?
5. **What Do You Think?** Why do you think Roosevelt called December 7 "a date which will live in infamy"?

3 The War Effort at Home

Read to Learn

★ How did Americans organize for war?
★ Why were women urged to take paying jobs?
★ How did the war affect different ethnic groups in America?

In December 1941, the United States faced a tremendous task. It had to build up its armed forces and change its economy into making goods for war. The war would be fought in many distant places. Yet victory depended on the war effort at home.

Organizing for War

The attack on Pearl Harbor united Americans behind the war. Millions of men and women volunteered to serve their country in the armed forces. Many of those who stayed home worked in war industries. They produced guns, tanks, aircraft, and other supplies needed to win the war.

The armed forces. During World War II, 10 million men were drafted. Another 6 million men and women enlisted. At first, the chief military task was to train the fighting forces. The army, navy, and air force set up bases across the country. There, recruits trained to fight in the jungles of the Pacific, the desert of North Africa, or the towns and farmlands of Europe.

Women joined all the armed services. They took over office jobs once filled by servicemen. In the air force, they ferried bombers and other planes from one base to another. Although women did not take part in combat, many served near the front lines.

The wartime economy. To organize for war, the government played a larger role in the economy than ever before. It set up agencies to control prices, negotiate with labor unions, and ration scarce goods. The War Production Board, for example, helped factories shift from making consumer goods to war goods. Auto makers shifted from turning out cars to producing tanks and trucks.

The war quickly ended the Great Depression. With the demand for war goods, millions of jobs opened up in factories. During the war, wages rose. Farmers prospered, too, and prices for farm goods doubled. Relief programs such as the CCC and WPA were no longer needed, and they passed into history.

Production grows. A Nazi leader, Hermann Goering, scoffed at American efforts to increase production. "Americans can't build planes," he said, "only electric iceboxes and razor blades." Goering was dead wrong. During the war, Americans met the demand for increased production. FDR set staggering goals for 1942, including 60,000 aircraft and 8 million tons of shipping. Americans then topped these goals.

Consumers suffered some shortages because industries were making war goods. After February 1942, no new cars were made. Tires were scarce because most new tires were used on military vehicles. If people asked for scarce items, they heard the reply, "Don't you know there's a war on?"

Jobs for Women

During the war, women were encouraged to take jobs outside the home. "If you can drive a car," women were told, "you can run a machine." As men left for the front, women filled their places. They worked in offices and in factories. Some ran huge cranes, welded, and tended blast furnaces. Others became bus drivers, police officers, and gas station attendants.

Because women were needed in industry, they were able to gain better pay and working conditions. The government agreed that women and men should get the same pay for the same job. Many employers, however, found ways to avoid equal pay.

The war changed fashions for women. Instead of wearing skirts, many women dressed in trousers. On the job, they wore overalls and tied scarves around their hair. More important, war work gave women a steady income.

Defending Freedom

Every ethnic and racial group in America contributed to the war effort. Many of the men and women in the armed forces were recent immigrants or the children of immigrants. A higher proportion of Native Americans served in World War II than any other group. More than one out of three able-bodied Indian men were in uniform.

Black Americans. The war helped end some of the worst discrimination against black Americans. Yet the struggle for equality was not easy. When the war began, "No Help Wanted" signs were replaced by "Help Wanted, White" signs. A. Philip Ran-

The artist Norman Rockwell created "Rosie the Riveter," at right. Rosie quickly became the symbol of American women working in war industries. At first, employers were doubtful that women could perform jobs traditionally held by men. Women, like the welders at left, proved them wrong. They put on overalls and hammered, riveted, and operated cranes as well as any men. By the end of the war, women made up one third of the work force.

dolph, head of the Brotherhood of Sleeping Car Porters, threatened a mass protest by black Americans unless FDR moved to end such discrimination. In 1941, the President ordered employers doing business with the government to support racial equality in hiring.

More than a million blacks enlisted or were drafted. Still, they had to serve in segregated, or all-black, units commanded by white officers. Despite such prejudice, blacks served heroically. Armed only with machine guns, fighter planes from an all-black air force squadron, for example, destroyed seven German ships. The courage and brav-

ery of black fighting units finally convinced President Truman to end segregation in the armed forces in 1948.

Hispanics. Thousands of Puerto Ricans and Mexican Americans fought for the United States during the war. These and other *Hispanics,* or Spanish-speaking Americans, won many awards for bravery. A Marine Corps private, Guy Gabaldon, won a Silver Star for capturing 1,000 Japanese. Many years later, the movie *From Hell to Eternity* told the story of Gabaldon's heroism.

Despite the contribution of Mexican Americans to the war, they felt the sting of racial prejudice. During the early 1940s, young Mexican Americans in Los Angeles dressed in showy "zoot" suits. Their clothing and language set them apart from white sailors on shore leave. In June 1943, bands of sailors attacked the young zoot-suiters, beating and clubbing them on the streets.

Newspapers blamed the violence on the zoot-suiters. However, Eleanor Roosevelt, wife of the President, disagreed. In her column, she noted that the riots were the result of "longstanding discrimination against the Mexicans in the Southwest."

Tragedy for Japanese Americans

The worst discrimination, however, was felt by Japanese Americans. Most Japanese Americans lived on the West Coast. Many were successful farmers and business people. For years, they had faced racial prejudice in part because of their success.

After the attack on Pearl Harbor, many white Americans distrusted Japanese Americans. They warned that Japanese Americans on the West Coast could act as spies and help Japan invade the United States. The President agreed to an order to move Japanese Americans away from the coast to "relocation" camps farther inland. Over 100,000 Japanese Americans on the West Coast were ordered to sell their homes, land, and belongings.

In relocation camps, Japanese Americans had to live behind barbed wire. Housing was poor. The people did not understand why they, as American citizens, were singled out. Americans of German and Italian backgrounds were not sent to camps. In 1944, the Supreme Court ruled that the camps were a necessary wartime measure. Only when an Allied victory seemed certain were Japanese Americans allowed to return to their homes.

At first, Japanese Americans were barred from serving in the military. Later, this policy was changed. More than 10,000 Japanese Americans vol-

In February 1942, a Japanese American schoolgirl recalled coming home to find FBI agents searching her family's farm. One man was reading her diary. Others were looking for flashlights or radios that they suspected might be used to help the enemy. Her family, like the one above, were tagged and sent to a "relocation camp" in the desert. Of the 117,000 Japanese Americans interned during the war, 71,000 were native-born Americans.

unteered for service. Many were cited for their bravery. One unit of Japanese Americans used the slogan "Go for broke!" It became a popular rallying cry across the nation.

SECTION REVIEW

1. Describe two ways the war affected the economy.
2. (a) List three kinds of jobs women held during the war. (b) How did the war help women get better pay?
3. Explain one way the war affected each of the following groups: (a) Native Americans; (b) black Americans; (c) Hispanics.
4. **What Do You Think?** Why do you think Japanese Americans were the only group forced to live in relocation camps?

4 Allied Drive to Victory

Read to Learn
★ What setbacks did the Allies face in 1942?
★ What were the major turning points in the war?
★ What was V–E Day?

By December 1941, the Allies had suffered many defeats. Axis armies occupied almost all of Western Europe and much of North Africa. After Pearl Harbor, Japan won a string of victories in the Pacific. As 1942 began, the Allies faced the darkest days of the war.

Dark Days

When the United States entered the war, the Allies were fighting the Axis powers on three fronts—the Pacific, North Africa, and Europe. Even before Pearl Harbor, American and British planners had agreed that the Allies must defeat Germany and Italy first. Then they would turn their full attention toward defeating Japan.

Early in 1942, Germany seemed almost unbeatable. Most of Europe was in German hands. German armies were threatening Moscow, Leningrad, and Stalingrad in the Soviet Union. They were pushing southeast to seize Soviet oil fields and farmlands.

The Russians fought back fiercely. They burned crops and destroyed farm equipment so that the advancing Germans would find only useless land. In Leningrad and elsewhere, the people suffered terrible hardships. More than one million Russian men, women, and children died during the siege of Leningrad.

In the Pacific, Japan, too, seemed unbeatable. After Pearl Harbor, Japanese armies overran Guam, Wake Island, Hong Kong, and Singapore. (See the map on page 636.) General Douglas MacArthur, commander of the United States forces in the Pacific, faced an impossible task. With few troops, he had to defend a huge area.

General MacArthur led the defense of the Philippines. American and Filipino troops fought bravely against enormous odds. In the end, MacArthur was forced to withdraw. "I shall return," he promised the people of the Philippines. The Japanese pressed on, taking the Dutch East Indies, Malaya, and Burma.

Turning Points

By mid-1942, the Allies were reeling from the Japanese and German advances. German submarines were sinking ships faster than the Allies could replace them. Despite setbacks, the Allies began to turn the tide.

Battles in the Pacific. In May 1942, American and Australian naval forces held the Japanese at bay in the *Battle of the Coral Sea*. A month later at the *Battle of Midway,* American planes sank four Japanese aircraft carriers. This battle crippled the Japanese offensive. Also, it protected Hawaii from further Japanese attacks.

In August, United States Marines landed on Guadalcanal (gwah d'l kuh NAL) in the Solomon Islands. In a long, hard-fought battle, the marines finally won control of the island. Guadalcanal gave the marines a base from which to counterattack.

Success in North Africa. In North Africa, British and American forces were turning the tide. In October 1942, the British won an important victory at El Alamein in Egypt. German forces under General Erwin Rommel, known as the Desert Fox, were driven west into Tunisia.

Meanwhile, an American army under General Dwight D. Eisenhower was marching east through Morocco and Algeria. The Allied armies trapped

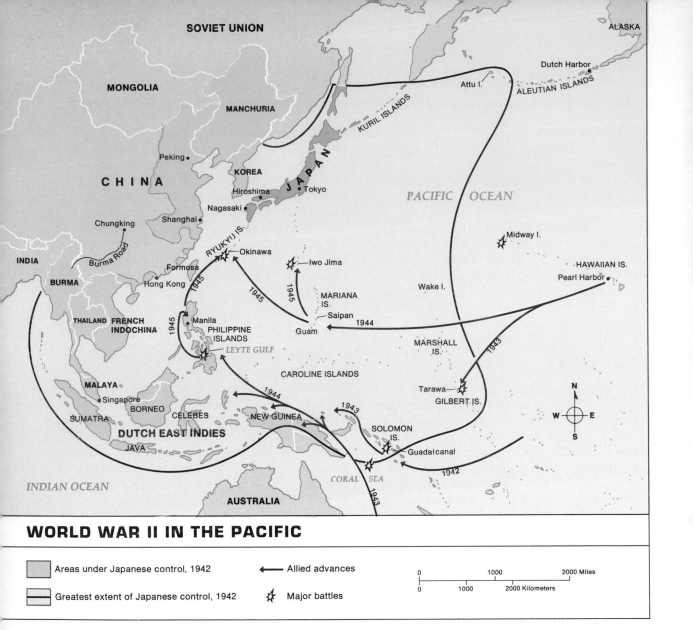

WORLD WAR II IN THE PACIFIC

Areas under Japanese control, 1942

Greatest extent of Japanese control, 1942

← Allied advances

☆ Major battles

0   1000   2000 Miles

0   1000   2000 Kilometers

MAP SKILL In 1942, Japan controlled much of China, Southeast Asia, and the Pacific. After the Battle of Midway, however, the United States took the offensive. By island hopping across the Pacific, the United States gained bases for invading Japan. Fierce Japanese resistance showed the Allies how tough a battle they faced. What island or islands is southeast of Midway?

Rommel's forces in Tunisia. In May 1942, his army had to surrender. With this success, the Allies cleared North Africa of Axis troops.

Invasion of Italy. From bases in North Africa, the Allies leaped across the Mediterranean to invade Italy. They used paratroopers, or airborne troops, and soldiers brought in by sea.

The combined forces captured Sicily in 38 days. In early September 1943, the Allies crossed from Sicily to the Italian mainland.

Meanwhile, the Italians overthrew Mussolini. The new Italian government joined forces with the Allies. Peace did not come to Italy, however, because the Germans still occupied

Skill Lesson 28   Writing a Research Paper

In earlier Skill Lessons, you learned how to collect the information for a research paper. Before you begin to write the paper, you need to organize your notes and ideas.

1. **Focus the paper on a single topic.** To write a good research paper, focus on a single topic. Pick a topic that is narrow or broad enough to be covered in your paper. Look at the sample topics below. (a) Which topic is the broadest? (b) Which topic or topics is the narrowest? (c) If you were writing a short paper, which topic or topics would be the easiest to cover in just a few pages?

2. **Prepare an outline for the paper.** An outline lets you organize information in a logical way. Review the outlining steps you learned on page 31. Then study the sample outline below for a research paper on the Battle of Midway. The Roman numeral is the major topic. The letters are subtopics.

Copy the outline into your notebook. Then complete the outline with the appropriate information. (a) What major topic did you put for II.? (b) What subtopics fit under II. A. and II. B.? (c) What major topic did you put for III? Why?

3. **Use the outline to write the paper.** Begin your paper with an introduction. In an introduction, you set out the main ideas of the paper. In the body of the paper, each paragraph should begin with a topic sentence. Use facts to support the topic sentence. End the paper with a conclusion. In the conclusion, you summarize the main points that you have made in the paper.

Read the writing sample below. (a) Is it from an introduction or a conclusion? How can you tell? (b) What is the main idea of the paragraph? (c) From reading the paragraph, what can you tell about the topic of the paper?

Sample topics
World War II
Battle of Midway
General Douglas MacArthur
The War at Sea

Writing sample
In 1943, Americans celebrated the news of these victories. They knew the final defeat of Japan was still a long way off. Yet they also knew that they had finally stopped Japan in its advance across the Pacific.

Sample outline
Paper topic: The Battle of Midway

I. Background to the battle
   A. Location of Midway
   B. U.S. island-hopping strategy
II. _____   Japanese fight back
   A. _____   Results of battle
   B. _____   A long, hard struggle
III. _____   American victory
   A. _____   Americans attack
   B. _____   Japanese losses

much of it. So the Allies had to fight their way up the Italian peninsula in tough, bloody battles. On June 4, 1944, Allied troops marched into Rome. It was the first capital city in Europe to be freed from Nazi control.

Gains in the east. Allied fortunes also improved on the Russian front. By early 1943, the Soviet army ended the 17-month siege of Leningrad. At Stalingrad, after months of fierce house-to-house fighting, the Russians forced the German army to surrender. Slowly, the Soviet army forced the Germans out of Russia. As the Russians pushed the Germans back through Eastern Europe, Allied armies opened up a long-awaited second front in Western Europe.

Invasion of France

Since 1941, Stalin had called on the Allies to open a second front by sending armies across the English Channel into France. Such an invasion took time and careful planning, however. In December 1943, Churchill and Roosevelt agreed to a cross-channel invasion. The code name for the attack was *Operation Overlord.* General Eisenhower was giv-

en the job of commanding the Allied forces in Europe.

Planning. The Allies faced huge problems. They had to assemble a vast army, get it across the English Channel, and provide it with ammunition, food, and other supplies. Eisenhower expertly smoothed out differences among the many officers. By June 1944, more than 2,886,000 troops were ready for Operation Overlord.

The Germans knew an attack was coming. They did not know when or where. They had built a strong "Atlantic wall" to stop an Allied landing. They had mined beaches, strung barbed wire, dug ditches, built antitank concrete walls and pillboxes armed with machine guns.

D–Day. On June 6, 1944, called *D–Day,* a fleet of 4,000 Allied ships launched the great invasion. Allied troops scrambled ashore at Normandy, on the French coast. There, they met withering German gunfire. On some beaches, American forces took heavy losses.

Yet the Allied forces pushed on. Every day, more soldiers crossed the channel to reinforce the advance. On

After landing at Normandy, the Allies fought their way inland. Thousands died in battles across France. Here, a Frenchman offers flowers and prayers beside a dead American soldier.

August 25, 1944, the Allies entered Paris. After four years under Nazi rule, French men, women, and children greeted their liberators with joy.

Advance on Germany

By September, the Allies were moving east toward Germany. Yet the Allied advance was slowed by a supply bottleneck. Germany still held many French ports. So the Allies had trouble getting supplies to their advancing troops.

On December 16, 1944, the Germans launched a fierce counterattack. It put a big bulge in the Allied forward lines. The *Battle of the Bulge* slowed the Allies but failed to stop them. During the battle, an American unit commanded by General Anthony McAuliffe was surrounded. When the Germans called on him to surrender, he replied, "Nuts!" and fought on to victory.

While Allied armies advanced on the ground, their planes bombed German industries and cities. At night, British planes dropped tons of bombs on German cities. By day, American planes applied precision bombing of factories and oil refineries. The bombing caused severe fuel shortages. But it did not break German morale or slow war production.

Election of 1944. In the autumn of 1944, the Allied advance shared headlines in American newspapers with the upcoming election. Voters had to choose between giving Franklin Roosevelt a fourth term or electing Thomas E. Dewey, the Republican candidate. As governor of New York, Dewey had earned respect as a crime buster.

By 1944, Roosevelt was tired and ill. "All that is within me cries to go back to my home on the Hudson," FDR told reporters early in 1944. Still, he and his running mate, Senator Harry S. Truman of Missouri, campaigned strongly. In November, their efforts paid off. Roosevelt won more than 54 percent of the vote.

AMERICANS WHO DARED

George S. Patton

In 1944, General George S. Patton was named to head the United States Third Army in Europe. Patton was a logical choice for the job. He had led American forces in North Africa and the Seventh Army when it landed in Sicily. Patton was an outspoken man. His blunt language and tough manner often created controversy. He wore twin ivory-handled revolvers on his belt. And he loved the challenge of war. Under Patton, the Third Army advanced across Europe so rapidly that new maps and fuel had to be parachuted to his troops.

Five months later, while vacationing in Warm Springs, Georgia, Roosevelt suffered a stroke. He died on April 12, 1945. FDR was mourned the world over. His death shattered Americans. Many could hardly remember anyone else as their leader.

V–E Day. Vice President Harry S. Truman was suddenly thrust into the highest office in the country. Eleanor

Roosevelt gave Truman the news: "Harry, the President is dead." Truman asked her, "Is there anything I can do for you?" "Is there anything we can do for *you*?" she replied. "For you are the one in trouble now."

By April 1945, however, Truman knew that the war in Europe was almost over. Germany was collapsing. American troops approached Berlin from the west. Soviet troops moved in from the east. On April 25, American and Soviet troops met at Torgau, just 60 miles (96 km) south of Berlin.

In Berlin, Hitler hid in his underground bunker as Allied air raids pounded the city. Unwilling to accept the certain defeat of Germany, he committed suicide on April 30. A week later, on May 7, 1945, Germany surrendered to the Allies. On May 8, the Allies celebrated *V–E Day,* Victory in Europe.

SECTION REVIEW

1. **Locate:** Soviet Union, Stalingrad, Philippines, Midway, El Alamein, Sicily, Italy, English Channel, Normandy, France, Germany.
2. (a) List two Allied setbacks in 1942. (b) Describe two Allied victories in 1942.
3. (a) What was Operation Overlord? (b) Who commanded the Allied forces in Europe?
4. Describe the final Allied drive to victory in Europe.
5. **What Do You Think?** Why do you think FDR decided to run again in 1944?

5 Winning the Peace

Read to Learn
★ What was the American plan of attack in the Pacific?
★ How did the United States use its secret weapon?
★ What were the costs of World War II?
★ What do these words mean: island hopping?

With Hitler's defeat in Europe, the Allies turned their full attention to the war against Japan. In the Pacific, Southeast Asia, and China, Allied forces went on the offensive.

Campaign in the Pacific

After Midway, the United States had two main goals. It wanted to win back the Philippines and invade Japan. American leaders worked out an island-hopping plan to achieve this goal. *Island hopping* meant capturing some Japanese-held islands and going around others. The islands won by Americans could be used as stepping stones for the invasion of Japan.

Island hopping was a deadly routine. First, American ships shelled a Japanese-held island. Next, troops waded ashore under heavy gunfire. In hand-to-hand fighting, Americans overcame fierce Japanese resistance.

In October 1944, American forces under General MacArthur finally returned to the Philippines. By February 1945, he had freed Manila, the capital. In hard-fought battles, the Americans captured the islands of Iwo Jima (EE woh JEE muh) and Okinawa (oh kuh NAH wuh), just 350 miles (563 km) from the Japanese home islands.

At Okinawa and elsewhere, the Japanese fought back with fanatic zeal. Japanese pilots carried out kamikaze (kah mih KAH zee) attacks. They loaded old planes with bombs. They then deliberately crashed their planes in suicide missions into Allied ships.

By the spring of 1945, American bombers were pounding the Japanese home islands. American ships bombarded the coast and destroyed ship-

During World War II, sending messages in code was standard practice. Both sides spent a lot of time and effort deciphering each other's codes. In the Pacific, Americans were able to shoot down Admiral Yamamoto's plane because they had broken the Japanese code and knew his flight plan. The Americans used one code the Japanese were never able to break. The code was not a typical one. It was based on the Navajo language.

When the war began, many Navajos volunteered for service. Some joined the Marine Corps. The marines soon discovered the advantages of the Navajo language. Few parts of the Navajo language had ever been written. It was hard to learn and was not like any European or Asian language. So it made a perfect code.

A group of Navajos volunteered to become code talkers. After careful training, they were sent to the Pacific. Each man was assigned to a separate unit. They used portable telephones and two-way radios. One Navajo would send a message to a second Navajo. He would then translate the message back into English. The code talkers gave the names of birds, fish, and other animals to different military terms. They then used these terms to call in air strikes or artillery fire.

The Navajo code talkers left the Japanese baffled. The enemy intercepted many radio messages, but they never realized that the code was a real language. In the end, more than 350 Navajos worked as code talkers in the Pacific. Others performed the same service in Italy.

★ Why do you think Navajo was such a little-known language?

---

ping. The Japanese people were starving. Yet Japanese leaders still talked of winning a glorious victory over the Allies. President Truman made plans for invading Japan in the autumn. His military advisers warned him that the invasion would cost over a million casualties.

Defeat of Japan

In late July 1945, Truman met with Churchill and Stalin at Potsdam, outside Berlin. While there, Truman learned that a secret new weapon—the atomic bomb—had been successfully tested in the New Mexico desert. The new weapon was so powerful that it could destroy an entire city. Some scientists warned against using this terrible new weapon.

From Potsdam, the Allied leaders sent a message to Japan. In the *Potsdam Declaration,* they told Japan to surrender or face "utter and prompt destruction." Japanese military leaders did not know about the atomic bomb. So they ignored the Allied message.

On August 6, 1945, the *Enola Gay,* an American bomber, dropped an atomic bomb on *Hiroshima,* Japan. The blast killed at least 70,000 people and injured an equal number. It destroyed at least 80 percent of the city. Two days later, the Soviet Union declared war on Japan, as it had promised earlier. Still, Japan said nothing. The next day, August 9, the United States dropped a second atomic bomb—this time on *Nagasaki.* There, 40,000 were killed. Later, many more people in both cities would die from the effects of radiation.

Unit 9 Review

Chapter 26 For much of the 1920s, the economy prospered. Business grew rapidly. More and more people bought automobiles and other consumer goods. During this period, the nation tried Prohibition, and women voted for the first time. Even though many people prospered, there were underlying economic and social problems.

Chapter 27 The stock market crash of 1929 sent the nation into the Great Depression. Banks failed. Businesses closed. And millions of Americans lost their jobs. Franklin Roosevelt won the election of 1932 with the promise of a New Deal. FDR's New Deal did not end the Great Depression. It did, however, help some Americans, like unemployed older Americans and Indians.

Chapter 28 By 1939, dictators in Europe and Asia had plunged the world into a new war. When World War II began, the United States remained neutral. After the Japanese bombed Pearl Harbor, however, the United States joined the Allies. Slowly, Allied forces turned the tide of war. Yet the drive to victory was long and costly. By May 1945, the Allies had defeated Germany. Japan was forced to surrender after the United States dropped atomic bombs on Hiroshima and Nagasaki.

★   **Unit Checkup**   ★

Choose the word or phrase that best completes each of the following statements.

1. Another name for the 1920s is the
  (a) Jazz Age.
  (b) Great Depression.
  (c) Hundred Days.

2. The United States limited immigration by passing the
  (a) Neutrality Acts.
  (b) Emergency Quota Act.
  (c) Wagner Act.

3. A New Deal program that provided jobs for the unemployed was the
  (a) Civilian Conservation Corp.
  (b) Bonus Army.
  (c) Emergency Banking Relief Act.

4. The Great Depression ended when
  (a) the New Deal was passed.
  (b) Herbert Hoover was elected President.
  (c) World War II opened up new jobs.

5. During World War II, Allied troops in Europe were commanded by
  (a) Winston Churchill.
  (b) Erwin Rommel.
  (c) Dwight D. Eisenhower.

★   **Building American Citizenship**   ★

1. (a) Which amendments to the Constitution were passed between 1919 and 1945? (Review pages 827–829.) (b) What did each amendment say? (c) Why do you think each passed when it did?

2. (a) Why did President Roosevelt want to appoint six new justices to the Supreme Court? (b) Do you think that a President should consider a person's economic views before appointing him or her to the Supreme Court? Explain.

3. (a) Give two examples of how the government's role in the economy increased in the 1930s and 1940s. (b) Describe two benefits and two disadvantages of government regulation.

Study the two circle graphs at right. Based on your reading in this unit and Unit 8, answer the following questions.

1. What does each circle graph show?

2. What percentage of immigrants came from Northern and Western Europe in the period 1900–1920? 1920–1940?

3. From what area did the percentage of immigrants increase most in the periods shown?

4. How did the immigration laws of the 1920s affect immigrants from Eastern and Southern Europe?

5. Why do you think immigration from Asia remained about the same?

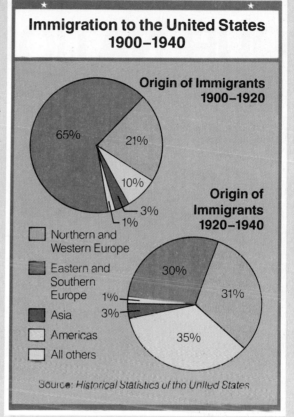

Immigration to the United States 1900–1940

Origin of Immigrants 1900–1920

65% 21% 10% 3% 1%

Origin of Immigrants 1920–1940

30% 31% 35% 1% 3%

☐ Northern and Western Europe
☐ Eastern and Southern Europe
■ Asia
☐ Americas
☐ All others

Source: *Historical Statistics of the United States*

History Writer's Handbook

Arranging Information to Show Cause and Effect

A *cause* is an event that produces an *effect,* another event. Often that effect becomes a cause. It produces still another event. To show this chain reaction, you would arrange supporting information in order of cause and effect.

Look at the following topic sentence. *During World War II, many Japanese Americans were put in relocation camps.* You might arrange the events leading to relocation in cause-and-effect order. The following diagram of events shows the chain reaction of cause and effect.

(first event) Japanese attack on Pearl Harbor
(causes) ↓

(second event) Fear of Japanese Americans
(causes) ↓

(third event) Government decision

Transitions to show cause and effect include *as a result, because, consequently, therefore, thus,* and *so.*

Practice Use the diagram to write detail sentences that support the topic sentence above. (See page 634 for information.)

Unit 10

OUR NATION TODAY

1944		1952		1960		1968

HARRY TRUMAN   DWIGHT EISENHOWER   LYNDON JOHNSON

JOHN KENNEDY

1944 D–Day; FDR elected to fourth term
1945 V–E Day; atomic bombs dropped on Hiroshima and Nagasaki; World War II ends
1947 Truman Doctrine; Marshall Plan
1949 NATO formed
1950 Korean War begins; Rosenbergs arrested

1953 Cease-fire in Korea
1954 McCarthy–Army hearings; *Brown* v. *Board of Education of Topeka*
1955 Warsaw Pact formed; Rosa Parks arrested in Montgomery, Alabama
1957 Eisenhower sends troops to Little Rock Central High School
1959 ★ Alaska, Hawaii become states

1961 Bay of Pigs invasion; Berlin Wall built; Alan Shepard becomes first American in space
1962 Cuban missile crisis
1963 March on Washington; John Kennedy killed
1965 Voting Rights Act; Watts riots; marines land in Dominican Republic

1944		1952		1960		1968

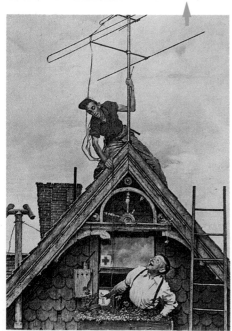

1950s After World War II, antennas on rooftops became a common sight as large numbers of Americans bought television sets.

1950s–60s Campaign buttons were used by Dwight Eisenhower and John Kennedy.

1960s *Varoom,* by Roy Lichtenstein, is an example of the Pop Art of this period.

UNIT OUTLINE

1968	1976	1984	1992
RICHARD NIXON	JIMMY CARTER	RONALD REAGAN	GEORGE BUSH

GERALD FORD

1968 Martin Luther King, Jr., and Robert Kennedy shot; Soviet Union invades Czechoslovakia
1969 Neil Armstrong lands on moon
1972 Nixon visits China; SALT Agreement
1973 Watergate hearings; Arab oil embargo
1975 Vietnam War ends; Helsinki Agreement

1976 Bicentennial celebrated
1978 Camp David Agreement
1979 Americans held hostage in Iran; Soviet invasion of Afghanistan; Three Mile Island accident
1981 *Voyager I* photographs Jupiter; first space shuttle; Sandra Day O'Connor appointed to Supreme Court
1983 Marines join peace-keeping force in Lebanon

1984 Geraldine Ferraro runs for Vice President
1985 Reagan begins second term
1986 Immigration Reform and Control Act passed; Tax Reform Act passed
1987 INF Treaty signed
1988 George Bush elected President
1992 500th anniversary of Columbus' voyage

1968	1976	1984	1992

960s–70s Some youthful protesters nged to return to the simple, rural ay of life of earlier Americans.

1976 With flags flying proudly, Americans wished the nation a Happy 200th Birthday on July 4th.

1986 This picture of the Statue of Liberty was created on a computer. The statue was restored for its 100th birthday.

29

America in the Fifties (1945–1960)

Chapter Outline

1 The Cold War Begins
2 The Cold War Heats Up
3 Challenges at Home
4 Changing Ways of Life

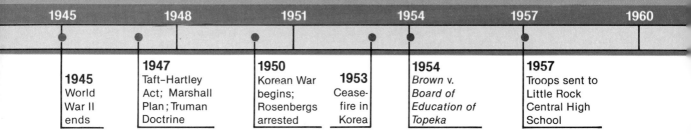

1945	1948	1951	1954	1957	1960

1945
World War II ends

1947
Taft–Hartley Act; Marshall Plan; Truman Doctrine

1950
Korean War begins; Rosenbergs arrested

1953
Cease-fire in Korea

1954
Brown v. Board of Education of Topeka

1957
Troops sent to Little Rock Central High School

About This Chapter

Even before World War II ended, differences arose among the wartime Allies. By 1945, armies of the Soviet Union occupied most of Eastern Europe. The former prime minister of Britain, Winston Churchill, warned that Stalin was setting up harsh Soviet-style governments in Eastern Europe. On March 5, 1946, Churchill spoke to students at Westminster College in Fulton, Missouri, about the Soviet threat.

From Stettin in the Baltic to Trieste in the Adriatic, an iron curtain has descended across the Continent. Behind that line lie all the capitals of the ancient states of Central and Eastern Europe. Warsaw, Berlin, Prague, Vienna, Budapest, Belgrade, Bucharest, and Sofia, all these famous cities and populations around them lie in what I must call the Soviet sphere, and all are subject in one form or another . . . to a very high and, in many cases, increasing measure of control from Moscow.

To Churchill, the iron curtain was an uncrossable line cutting off Eastern Europe from the rest of the world. In Eastern Europe, people were not allowed to travel freely. Books, newspapers, and radio broadcasts were censored. Citizens who opposed the government were imprisoned or killed. In this "Iron Curtain Speech," Churchill pleaded for Americans to stand firm against Stalin.

During the postwar period, tension grew between the United States and the Soviet Union. In the late 1940s, the United States led the struggle to preserve freedom and democratic governments around the world.

Study the time line above. What war was fought in the 1950s?

During the 1950s, millions of Americans moved to the suburbs. From the suburbs, men and women went by train to jobs in the cities.

1 The Cold War Begins

Read to Learn

★ What were the goals of the UN?

★ What was the Cold War?

★ What do these words mean: cold war, satellite?

A few months before World War II ended, delegates from 50 nations met in San Francisco. There, they agreed to set up an international peace-keeping organization. The United States took a leading role in the new organization.

The United Nations

Even before the war ended, the Allies made plans for the peace. In April 1945, delegates at the San Francisco Conference created the *United Nations* (UN). Its goal was to help solve conflicts between nations. President Roosevelt avoided the mistake Woodrow Wilson made after World War I. He won the support of Congress for the UN.

Under the United Nations Charter, member nations agreed to bring disputes before the UN.* The UN would then look for peaceful ways to settle disputes. Members also agreed to work together to solve problems such as disease and hunger around the world. By solving these problems, the UN hoped to make the world a safer place for all people.

---

*The number of UN members has more than tripled since 1945. Today, the UN has 159 member nations.

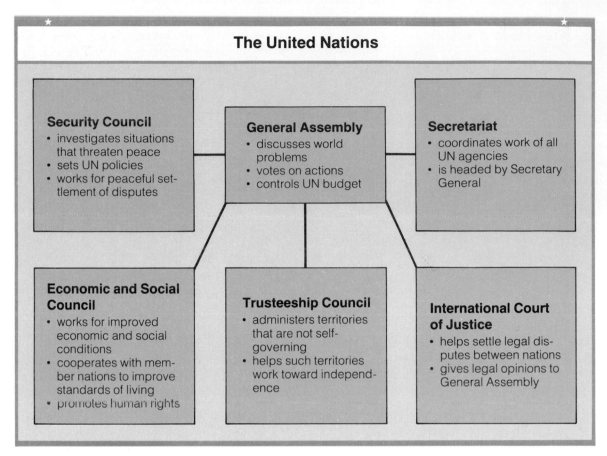

The United Nations

Security Council
- investigates situations that threaten peace
- sets UN policies
- works for peaceful settlement of disputes

General Assembly
- discusses world problems
- votes on actions
- controls UN budget

Secretariat
- coordinates work of all UN agencies
- is headed by Secretary General

Economic and Social Council
- works for improved economic and social conditions
- cooperates with member nations to improve standards of living
- promotes human rights

Trusteeship Council
- administers territories that are not self-governing
- helps such territories work toward independence

International Court of Justice
- helps settle legal disputes between nations
- gives legal opinions to General Assembly

DIAGRAM SKILL Since the UN was set up in 1945, its peace-keeping forces have served in many parts of the world. The UN has also served as a place where nations can try to solve international problems. This diagram shows the six major bodies of the UN. Which body controls the UN budget?

Organization. The United Nations has six major bodies. (See the diagram above.) Every member nation sends delegates to the General Assembly. It discusses problems brought before it and recommends action.

The Security Council has fifteen members. Ten members serve for two-year terms. The five permanent members are the United States, Great Britain, the Soviet Union, China, and France. The Security Council investigates conflicts between nations. It decides what action the UN should take. However, it has no power to enforce its decisions.

Aid programs. The UN's greatest successes have been in fighting hunger and disease and improving education. UN health officers have vaccinated millions of children. They have helped to wipe out smallpox and reduce malaria. Through relief programs, the UN has provided tons of food, clothing, and medicine to victims of disasters. It has trained more than a half million teachers and provided school children with books and desks. The UN has also saved many cultural treasures, such as ancient Egyptian temples.

Since 1945, the UN has achieved mixed results. Sometimes, nations have refused to go along with its decisions. Yet in other cases, the UN has kept crises from blowing up into full-scale wars.

Soviet Expansion

During World War II, the Allies worked together to defeat the Axis powers. Yet the United States and Britain deeply distrusted the Soviet Union. When the war ended, this distrust grew.

Eastern Europe. An early crisis arose over Eastern Europe. During the war, Soviet armies drove the Nazis out of Bulgaria, Rumania, Hungary, Poland, and Czechoslovakia. In February 1945, Roosevelt, Churchill, and Stalin had met at Yalta in southern Russia. There, Stalin agreed to hold "free elections as soon as possible" in Poland and other Eastern European nations. After the war, however, Stalin stepped back from his promise. "A freely elected government in any of the Eastern European countries would be anti-Soviet," he said, "and that we cannot allow."

As tension over Eastern Europe grew, the British statesman Winston Churchill made his famous Iron Curtain Speech. (See page 650.) At first, some people thought Churchill exaggerated the danger of Soviet expansion. By late 1947, however, many saw that the wartime friendship among the Allies was over. In its place, a cold war developed. A *cold war* is a state of tension between nations without actual fighting.

By 1948, the government of every Eastern European country was under communist control. The nations of Eastern Europe were called Soviet *satellites* because like small planets, they were held in orbit by the Soviet Union.

Communist influence spreads. Communist parties supported by the Soviet Union were active in Western Europe, too. After the war, the Italian Communist Party won 104 out of 556 seats in the Italian Parliament. At the same time, the Soviet Union expanded its influence in the Middle East and Asia.

By early 1947, the Soviet Union posed a threat to Greece and Turkey. In Greece, communist rebels fought a civil war to overthrow the king. The rebels were supported by Yugoslavia, a communist nation on the northern border of Greece. The Turkish government felt Soviet pressure when Stalin cancelled a treaty of friendship between the two nations.

The United States Responds

President Truman grew more and more concerned about Soviet expansion. Like Churchill, he saw the danger of letting communist governments take power in other countries. He decided that only a show of strength would stop Soviet expansion.

In March 1947, he asked Congress for $400 million in military and economic aid for Greece and Turkey. In a statement to Congress, later called the

During the Cold War, Stalin used name-calling propaganda to attack the United States. This cartoon shows the Soviet leader criticizing the United States for aggression. Who controlled the countries Stalin is standing on?

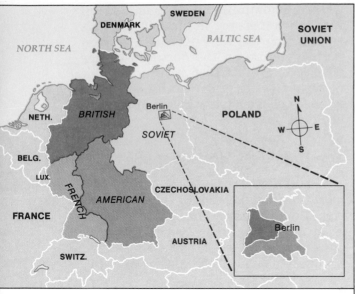

GERMANY DIVIDED

- American zone
- British zone
- French zone
- Soviet zone

| 0 | 100 | 200 | 300 | 400 | 500 Miles |
| 0 | 100 | 200 | 300 | 400 | 500 Kilometers |

MAP SKILL Germany was divided among the Allies after World War II. So, too, was the city of Berlin. In 1948, the Soviet Union set up a blockade to keep the other Allies from moving in and out of Berlin. What nation or nations controlled the western part of Germany? Who controlled the eastern part of Berlin?

Truman Doctrine, the President declared:

> The free peoples of the world look to us for support in maintaining their freedoms. If we falter in our leadership, we may endanger the peace of the world—and we shall surely endanger the welfare of our own nation.

Under the Truman Doctrine, the United States sent aid to Greece and Turkey. With this aid, both governments put down revolts and restored order.

Greece and Turkey were not the only countries that needed aid. Much of Europe was in ruins after the war.

Homes, roads, and factories had been destroyed. Truman's Secretary of State, George Marshall, toured Europe in 1947. There, he saw many people were struggling just to find food to eat.

Marshall feared that people in these nations might support a communist revolution. So in June 1947, he urged the United States to help European nations rebuild their economies.

President Truman agreed to the *Marshall Plan.* Between 1948 and 1952, the United States gave $12 billion in aid to Western Europe. By helping these nations recover, the Marshall Plan lessened the danger of communist revolutions in Western Europe. The United States also offered aid to the nations of Eastern Europe, but they turned it down.

Crisis Over Berlin

In 1948, a new crisis developed in the Cold War. This time, it was over Berlin. This city was once the capital of Nazi Germany. During the war, Allied leaders agreed to divide Germany into four zones. In 1945, American, British, French, and Soviet troops each occupied one zone. The city of Berlin was also divided among the four Allies. But the city itself lay deep inside the Soviet zone.

The division of Germany was meant to be only for a short time. By 1948, the United States, Britain, and France wanted to reunite Germany into one country. Stalin was determined to stop Germany from becoming a strong nation that might again threaten the Soviet Union. Also, he wanted to keep Soviet influence in the eastern part of Germany.

Blockade. In June 1948, the United States, Britain, and France joined their zones into the German Federal Republic, or West Germany. In response, Stalin closed all the roads, railway lines, and river routes leading into West Berlin. The blockade cut the city of West Berlin off from the rest of the world.

Truman was in a difficult position. He did not want to let West Berlin fall into Soviet hands. Yet if he ordered American troops to open a path to West Berlin through the Soviet-occupied zone, he risked a new war. In the end, Truman set up a huge airlift.

The airlift. Day after day, planes flew in food, fuel, and other supplies to 2 million West Berliners. At the height of the *Berlin Airlift,* over 5,000 tons of supplies arrived each day. One plane landed or took off every three minutes. Stalin saw that the western powers were determined to keep Berlin open. Finally, in May 1949, he ended the blockade.

Germany and Berlin remained divided, however. With aid from the United States, West Germany rebuilt its economy. The Soviet zone became the German Democratic Republic, or East Germany.

Opposing Alliances

The Berlin crisis showed that Europe was split into two camps. On one side was the Soviet Union and its satellites in Eastern Europe. The Soviet camp promoted communism around the world. On the other side were the western powers led by the United States. The western powers supported democratic government and the free enterprise system.

In 1949, the United States and other western powers formed the North Atlantic Treaty Organization, or *NATO.* (See the map on page 656.) Each member of NATO agreed to help any other if it was attacked by an outsider. By joining NATO, the United States showed that it would defend the

All through the winter of 1948, cargo planes roared across the skies into Berlin. Here, Berliners standing on top of a ruined building watch a plane fly in. Three years after World War II ended, much of Berlin was still in rubble.

THE COLD WAR IN EUROPE

■ NATO, 1955	□ Nonaligned nations	
□ Warsaw Pact, 1955	■ Areas added to the Soviet Union after World War II	

0   250   500 Miles
0   250   500 Kilometers

MAP SKILL By 1955, the United States, Canada, and ten Western European nations belonged to NATO. That year, the Soviet Union and seven Eastern European nations formed the Warsaw Pact. The growth of two rival alliances increased Cold War tensions in Europe. Which NATO nations had borders with Warsaw Pact nations?

nations of Western Europe against Soviet aggression.

In 1955, the Soviet Union formed its own military alliance, called the *Warsaw Pact.* The Soviet Union demanded the loyal backing of its Warsaw Pact neighbors. In 1956, Hungary tried to follow its own independent course. The Soviet Union responded by sending in the Red Army to crush the revolution. To many Americans, the Soviet invasion of Hungary proved the danger from that communist nation.

SECTION REVIEW

1. **Locate:** Greece, Turkey, Germany, Berlin, NATO, Warsaw Pact.

2. **Define:** cold war, satellite.

3. (a) What is the purpose of the UN? (b) What are the six major bodies of the UN?

4. Describe the purpose of each of the following: (a) Truman Doctrine; (b) Marshall Plan; (c) Berlin Airlift.

5. **What Do You Think?** Why do you think the wartime friendship among the Allies fell apart in the late 1940s?

2 The Cold War Heats Up

Read to Learn

★ What was the result of the civil war in China?

★ Why did the United States become involved in the Korean War?

★ What do these words mean: demilitarized zone?

During the late 1940s, President Truman faced crises in Asia as well as Europe. Violent struggles took place in China, India, and much of Southeast Asia. The United States watched events in Asia with concern. When the Soviet Union extended its influence in Asia, the United States stepped in to stop the spread of communism in that area.

Road to Independence

At the end of World War II, nationalist groups in many parts of Asia fought for independence. In 1934, the United States had promised independence to the Philippines. After World War II, the United States lived up to its promise. On July 4, 1946, Filipinos celebrated their independence. A constitution set up the basis for democratic government.

Unrest in the Philippines. Several years after independence, unrest developed in the Philippines. Many Filipinos wanted reforms, especially land reform. A small percentage of rich Filipinos owned most of the land. Reformers wanted to divide the land more equally among the peasant farmers.

When the government moved too slowly toward making changes, fighting broke out. Some of the rebels were communists. By 1954, the government had defeated the communist rebels. It also made some needed land reforms.

After Ferdinand Marcos became President in 1965, however, the government became less democratic. In the years that followed, communists as well as noncommunists continued to push for greater reforms.

The United States supported Marcos even though he was unpopular with many Filipinos. First, he was strongly anticommunist. Second, he allowed the United States to have naval bases in the Philippines. The bases were important to American defense of the Pacific region. However, the United States did put pressure on Marcos to return to democratic government.

Other developments. In 1947, India won independence from Britain. But the land was divided into two nations: India and Pakistan. India and Pakistan became independent at a time when the Cold War divided the world. Both the United States and the Soviet Union tried to win the support of these nations. India remained neutral. Pakistan, however, became an ally of the United States.

In Southeast Asia, Indonesia won freedom from the Netherlands. Burma, Malaysia, and Singapore became independent from Britain. In Indochina,* nationalists fought for independence from France. Fighting there would last for almost 30 years. Before it ended, it would involve the United States in a long war, as you will read later.

Civil War in China

In the late 1940s, American attention was focused on China. Chiang Kai-shek (chiang kī SHEHK) was the ruler of China. For years, he had battled the Chinese Communists led by Mao Zedong (MOW dzuh doong). By 1945, Mao's forces occupied northern China. Chiang's armies held the south.

---

*Indochina included the present-day countries of Laos, Cambodia, and Vietnam.

The United States gave Chiang millions of dollars in aid. But Chiang Kai-shek's government was corrupt, and he lost popular support. In 1949, the battle for the Chinese mainland ended with a communist victory. Mao set up the People's Republic of China. Chiang Kai-shek and his forces retreated to Taiwan, an island about 100 miles (160 km) off the coast of China.

Mao Zedong's victory meant that the largest nation in Asia had become communist. The Chinese Communists did not always agree with the Soviet Union. Yet between them, these two communist nations controlled over a quarter of the earth's surface. Many Americans worried that communist forces would soon take over all of Asia.

War in Korea

The fear of communist expansion became real when war broke out in Korea in 1950. From 1911 to 1945, Korea had been a Japanese colony. After World War II, Korea was divided at the 38th parallel. The Soviet Union supported a communist government in North Korea. The United States backed a noncommunist government in South Korea.

In June 1950, North Korean soldiers invaded South Korea. President Truman acted quickly. He asked the United Nations to send armed forces to Korea to stop the invasion.* The Security Council agreed to set up a UN force. Its commander would be a general chosen by President Truman. The President chose General Douglas MacArthur for the job.

MacArthur went at once to Korea. His job was to push the North Koreans out of South Korea. About 80 percent of the UN forces were Americans. They

*The Soviet Union could have vetoed this request in the Security Council. But at the time, it was boycotting council meetings because the UN refused to recognize Mao Zedong's government in China.

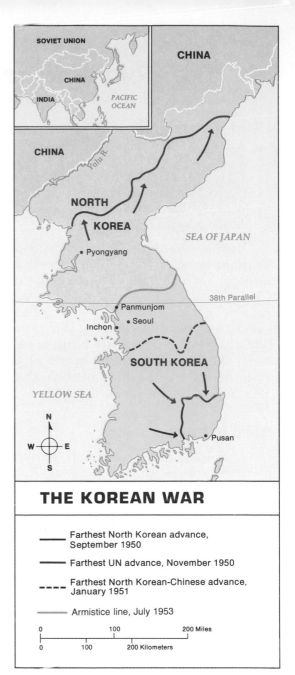

THE KOREAN WAR

——— Farthest North Korean advance, September 1950

——— Farthest UN advance, November 1950

- - - - Farthest North Korean-Chinese advance, January 1951

——— Armistice line, July 1953

0   100   200 Miles
0   100   200 Kilometers

MAP SKILL The Korean War began when North Korean troops invaded South Korea. UN forces fought back. Which side controlled Seoul in September 1950? In November 1950? At the end of the war?

were rushed to Korea from bases in Japan. Most of the rest were South Koreans.

The UN forces were outnumbered and poorly armed. The North Koreans had huge new Soviet tanks. American soldiers had only World War II weapons that were useless against the new tanks. The UN forces fought bravely but were soon driven to retreat.

By August 1950, the North Koreans controlled almost all of South Korea. Then, MacArthur launched a daring counterattack. He landed by sea at Inchon behind North Korean lines. From there, his forces swept eastward. Another UN force pushed up from the south. Together, they pushed the North Koreans back across the 38th parallel. (See the map at left.)

New Goals for the War

Under MacArthur's original orders, he was to drive the North Koreans out of South Korea. However, Truman and his advisers wanted to punish North Korea for its aggression. They also wanted to unite the two Koreas. So they won UN approval for MacArthur to cross into North Korea.

MacArthur met success as he pushed northward. The Chinese communists warned that they would not "stand idly by" if the United States invaded North Korea. When UN forces neared the Chinese border, thousands of Chinese crossed the Yalu River into North Korea. They helped the North Koreans turn the tide. Once again, UN troops were forced to retreat deep into South Korea.

A public disagreement. General MacArthur fought back. He regained control of South Korea by March 1951. By then, he believed that the United States could win in Korea only if it attacked China. So he called publicly for the bombing of supply bases in China.

President Truman was more cautious. He wanted to limit the war and restore the boundary between North and South Korea at the 38th parallel. An American attack on China, he believed, might start a new world war. Truman warned MacArthur against making further public statements.

MacArthur continued to complain that he could not win the war because of politicians in Washington. Truman was furious and fired MacArthur. The firing angered many Americans, however. They gave the general a hero's welcome when he returned to the United States.

Truman strongly defended his stand. The President felt that MacArthur's statements undercut attempts to reach a peace settlement. Under the Constitution, the President is commander in chief. As the chief elected leader, it was Truman—not any military officer—who had power to make the key decisions about war and peace.

Peace talks. Peace talks began in 1951. At first, they made little progress. In 1952, the popular World War II general, Dwight D. Eisenhower, was elected President. During the cam-

In December 1952, the President-elect Dwight Eisenhower visited Korea. By then, talks between the two sides had been going on for 17 months. It would take many more months, however, before an armistice was signed.

paign, Eisenhower promised to go to Korea to get the peace talks moving. After his election he went to Korea.

In July 1953, the two sides finally signed a cease-fire. They agreed to set the border between North and South Korea at the 38th parallel. The cease-fire called for a demilitarized zone along the border. A *demilitarized zone* is an area where no troops are allowed.

In Korea, the Cold War had heated up and led to actual fighting. With the cease-fire, the battles ended. However, tensions between North and South Korea continued. From time to time, crises have developed between the two nations. So far, none has led to a new war.

More than 54,000 Americans lost their lives during the Korean War. Thousands of soldiers from other nations also were killed. By fighting in the Korean War, the United States showed that it was ready to fight communist expansion into noncommunist nations.

SECTION REVIEW

1. **Locate:** India, Pakistan, Philippines, China, North Korea, South Korea, Inchon, 38th parallel, Yalu River.
2. **Define:** demilitarized zone.
3. (a) What two groups fought in the civil war in China? (b) Which group won?
4. (a) What was the cause of the Korean War? (b) Why did the Chinese join the fighting? (c) How did the war end?
5. **What Do You Think?** Why do you think the Constitution makes the President the commander in chief of the military?

3 Challenges at Home

Read to Learn

★ What economic problems did the nation face after the war?
★ How did the Cold War affect Americans at home?
★ What do these words mean: demobilize, closed shop?

At the end of World War II, Americans faced a number of urgent decisions. How would the nation return to a peacetime economy? Did people want to keep the New Deal programs of Franklin Roosevelt? Or had the time come to turn away from these programs?

Economic Troubles

During the war, millions of Americans were employed in making goods for the military. When peace came, defense plants closed. In 1945, soldiers and sailors were *demobilized,* or released from military service. As a result, the nation faced a serious problem—how to change back to a peacetime economy.

In 1944, even before the war ended, Congress had passed the Serviceman's Readjustment Act. The act was better known as the *GI Bill of Rights.** Under it, the government spent billions of dollars to help veterans set up farms and businesses. Many GIs received loans to go to college. Also, the act gave veterans up to a year of unemployment insurance.

Another postwar problem was inflation. During the war, the government had controlled the price of food and other goods as well as wages. When the war ended, Truman lifted the wage

---

*GI stands for "government issue." During World War II, GI came to mean any member of the United States armed forces.

and price controls. The price of food, clothing, and other goods soared.

Workers whose wages had not risen during the war now demanded more pay. When employers refused worker demands, unions went on strike. Steelworkers walked off the job. So did meatpackers, auto workers, and coal miners. When railroad workers struck, President Truman was angry. "What decent American would pull a strike at a time like this?" he asked.

Truman threatened to draft railroad workers and order them back to work. Truman's threat brought a settlement of the strike. Still, many Americans asked whether the President had the right to use the draft in this way.

Political Struggles

In 1946, strikes and soaring prices helped Republicans who were running for Congress. "Had enough?" one slogan read. "Vote Republican!" Many Americans did. For the first time in years, they gave Republicans a majority in both the House and the Senate.

The election victory gave Republicans the power to cancel many New Deal programs. When Truman asked for funds for public housing and education, the Republican majority in Congress turned him down.

In 1947, Congress passed the *Taft–Hartley Act* over the President's veto. The act was meant to stop another wave of strikes. It let the government get a court order to delay a strike for 80 days, if the strike threatened public safety or health. Under the act, unions could not contribute to political campaigns. Also, the act banned the *closed shop,* a business that agreed to hire only union members.

Election of 1948

In 1948, polls showed that Truman's popularity was at an all-time low. Republicans nominated Thomas Dewey as their candidate for President. They felt confident he would win easily. Truman fought back. He crossed the country by train. At every stop, he made forceful speeches warning that

Baseball was still America's most popular sport after World War II. However, before 1947, no black players were allowed into the major leagues. That year, the Brooklyn Dodgers hired Jackie Robinson, at right, to play second base. Robinson had an outstanding career and was elected to baseball's Hall of Fame.

Republicans were "just a bunch of old mossbacks all set to do a hatchet job on the New Deal." Crowds warmed to his scrappy style. "Pour it on 'em, Harry!" they yelled.

On election night, people still expected a Dewey victory. In fact, the Chicago *Tribune* printed its first edition with the headline "DEWEY DEFEATS TRUMAN." When all the votes were counted, however, Truman squeaked past Dewey to victory.

When Truman took office, he declared that "every individual has the right to expect from his government a fair deal." Truman's ***Fair Deal*** was a program to extend the reforms of the New Deal.

Congress passed some of his Fair Deal programs. Under the National Housing Act of 1949, poorer Americans could get loans to buy low-cost houses. Congress raised the minimum wage from 40 cents an hour to 75 cents. It also expanded Social Security to cover more people. However, Congress defeated Truman's efforts to end racial discrimination.

Fear of Communists at Home

The Cold War that split the world divided Americans at home. Several spy trials made many Americans fear that communists were at work within the government. In 1950, Ethel and Julius Rosenberg were accused of giving atomic secrets to Soviet agents. A jury found them guilty of spying. They were executed in 1953.

Early in 1950, Senator Joseph McCarthy of Wisconsin said that he had a list of 205 State Department employees who were communists. This claim was never proven. But McCarthy won national attention. During the next four years, McCarthy made many more charges about communists in the government. Thousands of government employees had to undergo questioning. Little evidence of communists was found.

During the Army–McCarthy hearings, Americans heard Senator McCarthy make many charges about communists in the government. Here, McCarthy stands before a large map of the United States. On it, he has shown places that he said were centers of the Communist Party. At left, Joseph Welch holds his head. Welch was the chief Army lawyer. Welch strongly objected to McCarthy's "cruelly reckless" attacks on the reputations of respectable Americans.

McCarthy's campaign spread fear and suspicion around the country. Businesses, colleges, and even movie studios questioned employees. Some respectable people lost their jobs even though they were loyal citizens.

In 1954, the Senate televised hearings on McCarthy's charges that there were communists in the army. Millions of Americans watched as McCarthy made wild charges without any proof. As a result of the McCarthy–Army hearings, the Wisconsin senator lost influence. In December 1954, the Senate passed a resolution that condemned McCarthy for his conduct.

The Road Down the Middle

In 1952, President Truman announced that he would not run for reelection. Democrats nominated Adlai Stevenson, the governor of Illinois. Republicans rallied behind General Dwight Eisenhower, nicknamed Ike. GOP campaign buttons that said "I like Ike" seemed to reflect the mood of the country. Eisenhower won a landslide victory. After 20 years of Democratic Presidents, a Republican returned to the White House.

Like most Republicans, Eisenhower believed that the federal government should limit its control over the economy. Still, he kept some New Deal programs, such as Social Security. The new President summed up his goals when he said, "The great problem of America today is to take that straight road down the middle."

The Eisenhower years were prosperous ones for many Americans. In 1956, Eisenhower won reelection easily. In 1957, however, the nation suffered an economic slowdown. As unemployment rose, some Democrats called for more New Deal-style programs. Eisenhower resisted. By 1959, the economy had improved. So the President felt that his middle-of-the-road course had worked.

In 1959, the United States reached another landmark. That year, it grew to include 50 states when Alaska and Hawaii entered the Union.

SECTION REVIEW

1. **Define:** demobilize, closed shop.
2. (a) Why did many workers go on strike after the war? (b) What was the Taft–Hartley Act?
3. How did McCarthy win national attention?
4. **What Do You Think?** How do you think Eisenhower's success in World War II helped make him a popular President?

4 Changing Ways of Life

Read to Learn

★ How were the baby boom and building boom linked?
★ How did television become important in the 1950s?
★ What victories did blacks win in the struggle toward equal rights?
★ What do these words mean: baby boom, civil disobedience?

The Eisenhower years brought few dramatic changes in politics. Even so, the 1950s were a time of important social change.

A Growing Nation

In the 1930s and early 1940s, the population of the United States did not grow very fast. During the depression, hard times made it difficult to support large families. Also, couples who married during World War II waited until after the war to have children.

This photograph of Levittown, Long Island, was taken from an airplane. In the 1950s, developers built rows and rows of identical houses. The houses were inexpensive so that many Americans could afford to buy them.

The baby boom. In the late 1940s and 1950s, the birth rate, or number of children being born, soared. Population experts talked about the *baby boom*. In the 1950s, the population grew by 29 million compared to 19 million in the 1940s and 9 million in the 1930s.

Improvements in health and medical care helped the baby boom. Fewer children died from childhood diseases than in the past. For example, in 1953, Dr. Jonas Salk announced a vaccine against polio, a virus that killed or crippled both adults and children. Better care for pregnant women and newborn infants also meant that more babies lived.

The baby boom had a major effect on the economy. Growing families needed homes. The demand for housing led to a building boom. Factories increased production to keep up with the demand for building materials and furniture. As the number of children grew, the need for schools increased. Towns and cities put up thousands of new schools, further helping the building boom.

Move to the suburbs. The government encouraged the building boom by offering low-interest loans to veterans. Such loans let many Americans achieve their dream—owning a house. Most new houses were built in the suburbs. During the 1950s, suburbs grew faster than any other part of America. Federal, state, and local governments encouraged the move to the suburbs by building thousands of miles of highways. New roads let people commute from homes in the suburbs to jobs in the cities.

In the 1950s, William Levitt pioneered a new way of building houses in the suburbs. He bought land in large amounts. Then he subdivided the land. On each small piece of land, he built the same size and style of house. (See the picture above.) These houses were mass produced. So they could be put up much more cheaply than custom-built houses.

The Constitution of the United States calls for a census, or population count, to be made every ten years. The chief purpose of the census is to find out how many people live in each state so that the number of representatives in the House of Representatives can be divided up correctly.

Today, the Census Bureau collects many kinds of information about the population of the United States. Census information includes the number of people, age, ethnic background, number of children in families, education level, and income. It does not use people's names, however.

The Census Bureau also collects information about businesses. For example, it publishes statistics showing the number of employees, average wages, and union membership in different industries. Census information is useful to government and private businesses. By studying where people live, they can decide where new highways, schools, hospitals, or airports need to be built. Businesses use census data to decide where to open new stores or whether to expand.

1. **Study a census table to see what it shows.** Like all other tables, graphs, and charts, a census table has a title. Each column is also labeled. (a) What is the title of the table at left? (b) What does the first column show? The second column? (c) How many American homes had TV sets in 1948? In 1956? In 1960?

2. **Practice reading a population pyramid.** Census data is shown in many different ways. Below is a population pyramid. A *population pyramid* is a useful way to show both age and sex of the population. It generally uses five-year age groups.

The pyramid has bars that represent age groups going up from youngest to oldest. Bars for males are on the left side of the vertical axis. Bars for females are on the right side. The number of males or females in a particular age group is shown by the length of the bars. (a) In 1950, were there more boys or more girls under age 5? (b) In 1950, what percent of the American population over the age of 75 was female?

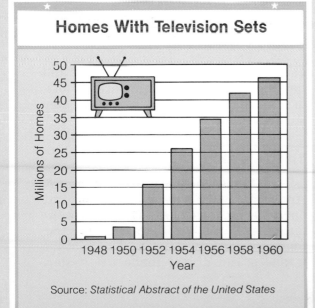

Homes With Television Sets

Millions of Homes / Year

1948 1950 1952 1954 1956 1958 1960

Source: *Statistical Abstract of the United States*

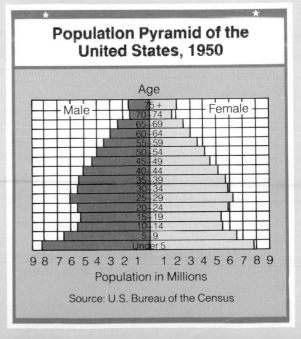

Population Pyramid of the United States, 1950

Age

Male — Female

75+, 70-74, 65-69, 60-64, 55-59, 50-54, 45-49, 40-44, 35-39, 30-34, 25-29, 20-24, 15-19, 10-14, 5-9, Under 5

9 8 7 6 5 4 3 2 1   1 2 3 4 5 6 7 8 9
Population in Millions

Source: U.S. Bureau of the Census

The 1950s brought in a new era of popular music—rock 'n' roll. Rock 'n' roll was a blend of black rhythm-and-blues and country music. Many early rock 'n' roll songs were written and performed by black artists like Chuck Berry, Little Richard, and the Shirelles. White singers like Buddy Holly and Jerry Lee Lewis were also popular. Their songs had roots in country music played in the South.

The most popular rock 'n' roll singer was Elvis Presley, shown at left. Millions of teenagers bought records such as "Hound Dog" and "Don't Be Cruel." Many adults, however, disliked the music and style of Presley. They were shocked at the way he shook his hips and pounded his guitar. One Chicago radio station smashed Presley records on the air. When Presley sang on Ed Sullivan's television show, cameras focused on his upper body. The network was afraid to show the popular singer swinging his hips.

Despite outrage, rock 'n' roll became a big business. Record companies made huge profits from the songs of Presley and other rock 'n' roll stars. Radio stations saw their ratings soar when they played rock 'n' roll.

Critics in the 1950s said that rock 'n' roll was just a passing fad. One early rock group answered by singing, "I don't care what people say, rock 'n' roll is here to stay." Rock music has remained popular. In the 1980s, the audience for rock 'n' roll includes people of all ages from around the world.

★ Describe one economic effect of rock 'n' roll.

Levitt's first big project was on Long Island, outside New York City. There, he put up 17,000 homes. Each house had the same plan. Teams of carpenters, plumbers, and electricians moved from house to house. When they worked on schedule, a new house was finished every 16 minutes! Levitt called the project **Levittown**. Later, he built other Levittowns in New Jersey and Pennsylvania.

Shopping centers sprang up near suburban housing developments. In the 1950s, shopping centers were a brand new sight. They had large parking lots, department stores, and sparkling new supermarkets.

The Television Age Begins

As the economy prospered, many Americans were able to buy goods that once were considered luxuries. Appliances such as refrigerators, electric toasters and irons, as well as clothes washers and dryers made life easier.

New products and comfortable houses gave Americans the highest standard of living of any nation.

The product that probably had the greatest effect on American life was television. In 1946, only about 17,000 television sets existed in the country. By 1949, Americans were buying almost 250,000 sets a month. In the 1950s, TV sales rose to almost 7 million a year.

Television visually brought news, sports, and entertainment into people's homes every day. In 1952 and 1956, millions of Americans watched political conventions on TV for the first time. They saw political leaders in action. Politicians, in turn, became aware of the power of the television camera.

Television brought to life a new set of personalities. Every week, 20 million teenagers tuned in to Dick Clark's "American Bandstand." On the program, they saw and heard rock 'n' roll stars sing their latest hits. Children enjoyed "Howdy Doody."

Their parents watched Ed Sullivan, Arthur Godfrey, and Milton Berle. Edward R. Murrow conducted interviews with well-known people. Lucille Ball starred in the family comedy series, "I Love Lucy." As more and more families bought TVs, the influence of television—for good or bad—became a topic of debate.

A Segregated Nation

During the 1950s, black Americans kept up their struggle to win equal rights. In both the North and South, blacks faced segregation in jobs, housing, and education. In the North, qualified blacks were not hired for many jobs. Blacks were often forced to live in segregated neighborhoods. In the South, many states had "Jim Crow" laws. These laws kept blacks out of public places such as restaurants, hotels, movie theaters, and laundromats.

All black Americans—whether rich or poor—felt the effects of segregation. In the 1930s, Charles Drew, a black doctor, discovered a way to preserve blood. When World War II began, Drew set up blood banks that helped save the lives of many fighting men. In 1950, Drew was injured in an accident. He died because the segregated hospital to which he was taken did not have blood that might have saved his life.

During and after the war, black groups such as the NAACP worked for change. In 1948, President Truman finally ordered the armed forces to stop segregating blacks into separate units. During the Korean War, black and white soldiers fought together in integrated, or mixed, units. As part of the Fair Deal, Truman asked Congress for a law making poll taxes illegal. But Congress refused to pass the bill.

The Supreme Court Acts

Despite setbacks, black leaders pressed on. Their efforts became known as the civil rights movement. They made segregated schools a major issue.

In 1896, the Supreme Court had decided in *Plessy* v. *Ferguson* that "separate but equal" facilities for blacks and whites were constitutional. (See page 431.) In the 1940s, the NAACP challenged this idea with some success. In 1954, however, laws in 21 states and the District of Columbia still allowed segregated public schools.

Brown's appeal. Oliver Brown of Topeka, Kansas, challenged this law. He asked the local school board to let his daughter, Linda, attend the all-white school near his home rather than a distant black school. The school board turned down his request. With the help of the NAACP, Brown then took his case to court. In 1954, the case of *Brown* v. *Board of Education of Topeka* reached the Supreme Court.

AMERICANS WHO DARED

Rosa Parks

On December 1, 1955, Rosa Parks boarded a nearly empty bus in downtown Montgomery, Alabama. After paying the fare, she sat in the first empty seat. Under a local law, seats in the front of the bus were reserved for whites. As the bus filled up, the driver called out, "Niggers move back." Several black riders moved to the back of the bus. But Mrs. Parks kept her seat. "I don't know why I wouldn't move," she said later. "There was no plot or plan at all. I was just tired from shopping. My feet hurt." The driver stopped the bus and called the police. Rosa Parks was arrested. News of her arrest led blacks to boycott the bus system. In the end, the Supreme Court ruled the Montgomery law unconstitutional.

Brown's lawyer, Thurgood Marshall,* argued that the "separate but equal" ruling was not fair. Segregated schools, he said, could never provide equal education. Therefore, segregated schools violated the Fourteenth Amendment, which gave "equal protection" to all citizens.

The Supreme Court justices agreed with Marshall. As Chief Justice Earl Warren wrote, segregation affected the "hearts and minds" of black students "in a way unlikely ever to be undone." He ordered the schools to be desegregated "with all deliberate speed."

Integration begins. In some areas, schools were integrated fairly quickly. Elsewhere, problems arose. In Little Rock, Arkansas, Governor Orville Faubus opposed integration. He called out the National Guard to keep black students from attending Little Rock Central High School in 1957. President Eisenhower stepped in because the Arkansas governor was defying a federal law. Eisenhower sent troops to Little Rock to protect the black students while they went to school.

Nonviolent Protests

In the 1950s, blacks challenged other segregation laws. When Rosa Parks of Montgomery, Alabama, refused to give up her bus seat to a white rider, she was arrested. Her arrest in December 1955 set off a yearlong boycott of the bus system by blacks. (See the picture at left.)

A minister at the local Baptist church, the Reverend Martin Luther King, Jr., led the boycott. King believed in *civil disobedience,* or nonviolent protests against unjust laws. He told his followers: "We must use the

---

*In 1967, Thurgood Marshall was appointed to the Supreme Court. He thus became the first black justice on the nation's highest court.

In 1957, President Eisenhower had to use federal troops to enforce the Supreme Court order to end segregation in public schools. Here, troops guard nine black students entering Central High School in Little Rock, Arkansas.

weapon of love. We must have compassion and understanding for those who hate us."

The boycott in Montgomery attracted national attention. In 1956, the Supreme Court ruled that segregation on buses was unconstitutional. The Montgomery bus company agreed to integrate the buses and hire black bus drivers.

King's nonviolent protests spread. In 1960, several black college students in Greensboro, North Carolina, led a "sit-in" at a lunch counter. The students refused to leave their seats even though no one would serve them. Thousands of blacks and whites conducted sit-ins at restaurants and theaters in the South. These nonviolent protests brought results. Many public places were integrated for the first time. Still, segregation remained widespread.

━━ SECTION REVIEW ━━

1. **Define:** baby boom, civil disobedience.
2. Describe three changes that were taking place in American life in the 1950s.
3. List three ways that segregation affected black Americans.
4. **What Do You Think?** Why do you think the Supreme Court ruled that segregated schools were unconstitutional?

Chapter 29 Review

★ Summary ★

After World War II, Soviet expansion in Eastern Europe and elsewhere led to the Cold War. Each side in the Cold War formed its own military alliances. In 1950, American soldiers fought in Korea against communist forces from North Korea.

In the late 1940s, President Truman tried to continue the programs of the New Deal with limited success. In the 1950s, Eisenhower chose a middle-of-the-road course.

During the 1950s, the population grew rapidly. Many Americans moved to houses in the suburbs. In an age of prosperity, they enjoyed the highest standard of living of any nation.

★ Reviewing the Facts ★

Key Terms. Match each term in Column 1 with the correct definition in Column 2.

Column 1	Column 2
1. civil disobedience	a. release from service
2. cold war	b. nonviolent protest against unjust laws
3. satellite	c. state of tension without actual warfare
4. demobilize	d. nation closely tied to a more powerful country
5. closed shop	e. business that could hire only union workers

Key People, Events, and Ideas. Identify each of the following.

1. United Nations
2. Truman Doctrine
3. Marshall Plan
4. NATO
5. Ferdinand Marcos
6. Douglas MacArthur
7. GI Bill of Rights
8. Taft–Hartley Act
9. Fair Deal
10. Joseph McCarthy
11. Jonas Salk
12. William Levitt
13. Charles Drew
14. Thurgood Marshall
15. Martin Luther King, Jr.

★ Chapter Checkup ★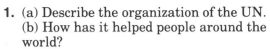

1. (a) Describe the organization of the UN. (b) How has it helped people around the world?

2. (a) Why did the United States object to Soviet expansion? (b) How did the United States respond to the Berlin blockade?

3. (a) Who was fighting for control of China in the 1940s? (b) Which side won?

4. (a) What was the immediate cause of the Korean War? (b) How did the United States get involved in the war? (c) Describe one result of the war.

5. Why was the result of the election of 1948 a surprise to many Americans?

6. How did McCarthy's charges affect Americans?

7. How did each of the following change American life in the 1950s: (a) baby boom; (b) move to the suburbs; (c) television?

8. (a) How did segregation affect black Americans in the 1950s? (b) Describe one result of the Supreme Court's decision in *Brown* v. *Board of Education of Topeka?*

★ Thinking About History ★

1. **Analyzing a quotation.** When Truman fired MacArthur, he said, "By this act, MacArthur left me no choice—I could no longer tolerate his insubordination [disobedience]." Why do you think Truman felt he had no choice?

2. **Understanding the economy.** Political and social events or developments often have economic results. (a) What problems with the economy did the return to peace after World War II cause? (b) How did the baby boom of the 1950s affect the economy? (c) Explain how a current political event or social development might affect the American economy today.

3. **Relating past to present.** Compare the Supreme Court decision in *Plessy* v. *Ferguson* on page 431 to its decision in *Brown* v. *Board of Education of Topeka*. (a) What issue was brought up in both cases? (b) What decision did the Supreme Court make in each case? (c) Why do you think the 1890 decision differed from the 1954 decision?

4. **Learning about citizenship.** Led by Martin Luther King, Jr., nonviolent protestors risked arrest by breaking segregation laws. (a) Why do you think King felt that breaking certain laws was necessary? (b) Do you agree with his position? Explain your answer.

★ Using Your Skills ★

1. **Using a diagram.** Study the diagram on page 652. (a) What are the six major bodies of the UN? (b) Which body is in charge of legal disputes? (c) Which body is central to the other five?

2. **Analyzing a political cartoon.** Study the cartoon on page 653. (a) What is Stalin standing on in this cartoon? (b) What is he reading? (c) Why do you think he is accusing the United States of aggres-sion? (d) Is this cartoon for or against Stalin? Explain.

3. **Map reading.** Study the map on page 658. Then find Korea on the world map on pages 758–759. (a) What nations lie to the north and east of Korea? (b) How many times did North Korea advance into South Korea? (c) In 1950 when MacArthur landed at Inchon, was he in North Korea or South Korea?

★ More to Do ★

1. **Exploring local history.** Report on how your state voted in the presidential election of 1948. Locate old newspaper articles and editorials and decide why your state voted the way it did.

2. **Writing a skit.** As a group project, prepare a skit on the McCarthy–Army hearings in the Senate. Before you begin, find out more about these hearings. Then, have one person take the part of Senator McCarthy. Others can take the parts of senators and different army officers who were questioned during the hearings.

3. **Listening to music.** Listen to a record or tape of a rock 'n' roll song from the 1950s. Describe what the song is about and compare it with the popular music of today.

4. **Writing a speech.** Prepare a speech to be given to a group of parents in the 1950s in which you support or criticize television.

30

Years of Protest and Change (1960–Present)

Chapter Outline

1 New Goals for the Nation
2 Politics and the White House
3 Freedom Now!
4 Other Banners of Reform

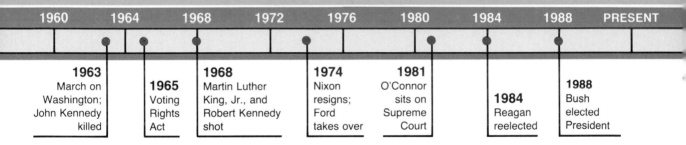

| 1960 | 1964 | 1968 | 1972 | 1976 | 1980 | 1984 | 1988 | PRESENT |

1963
March on
Washington;
John Kennedy
killed

1965
Voting
Rights
Act

1968
Martin Luther
King, Jr., and
Robert Kennedy
shot

1974
Nixon
resigns;
Ford
takes over

1981
O'Connor
sits on
Supreme
Court

1984
Reagan
reelected

1988
Bush
elected
President

About This Chapter

Friday, January 20, 1961, dawned bright but very cold in Washington, D.C. Snow had fallen on the capital the night before. In the morning, workers cleared Pennsylvania Avenue for the inauguration. They used flame throwers to melt frozen drifts around the reviewing stand in front of the Capitol.

A few minutes after noon, the President-elect, John F. Kennedy, stepped out onto the platform. The cold did not seem to affect him. He was hatless and wore no overcoat. Robert Frost, a New England poet, recited from "The Gift Outright": "The land was ours before we were the land's." Chief Justice Earl Warren administered the oath of office to Kennedy.

Then, the new President gave his inaugural speech. "Let the word go forth from this time and place," he proclaimed, "that the torch has been passed to a new generation of Americans." He asked for renewed commitment to America's role as leader of the free world. He ended with words that are still repeated today: "And so, my fellow Americans, ask not what your country can do for you—ask what you can do for your country."

John Kennedy was the youngest President ever elected. His youthful ideals were echoed by others during the 1960s. Yet ahead lay the tragic deaths of several American leaders and years of turmoil as Americans tried to fulfill the hopes and goals they had set for the nation.

Study the time line above. Name two events that took place in the decade of the 1960s.

The nation celebrated its 200th birthday in 1976. A bald eagle, symbol of the United States, is the subject of this float in Washington, D.C.

1 New Goals for the Nation

Read to Learn

★ What was the New Frontier?
★ What goals did the Great Society achieve?
★ What do these words mean: poverty line?

In the 1950s, President Eisenhower led the nation through a period of relative calm. In the 1960s, his successors in the White House faced more turbulent times. At the same time, they set new goals toward improving the life of all Americans.

Kennedy's New Frontier

In 1960, the Republicans chose Vice President Richard Nixon to run for President. Democrats chose John F. Kennedy. Kennedy came from a wealthy Irish American family in Boston. During World War II, young Kennedy commanded a torpedo boat in the Pacific. After the war, he served in the House and Senate.

In the campaign, Kennedy's youthful appearance, wit, and charm appealed to many Americans. Nixon's image was more earnest. The two candidates met in the first televised debates ever held. Nixon seemed an awkward and unsure debater, while Kennedy came across as a confident leader. Still, the election was close. At age 43, Kennedy was the youngest person to be elected President of the United States.

Social and economic programs.

During the campaign, Kennedy promised to lead Americans "to the edge of a New Frontier." The *New Frontier* had several goals. Kennedy hoped to end poverty, fight disease, and ensure social justice for all Americans.

Kennedy wanted Congress to pass laws to help the poor in city slums and in rural areas. In his travels as President, he was shocked to find hungry families in America.* After visiting poor coal-mining areas in West Virginia, the President exclaimed, "Just imagine, kids who never drink milk!"

Kennedy called on Congress to pass other programs. They included medical care for the aged, aid to education, and civil rights laws. The President could not get Congress to support his poverty programs. However, it did approve funds to explore the "new frontier" of space. It also funded two new foreign aid programs: the Alliance for Progress

---

*In the 1960s, it was estimated that 36 million Americans were living in poverty.

President Kennedy called on Americans to achieve the goals set down for the nation by its founders. His youthful manner and style held special appeal for young Americans.

and the Peace Corps, which you will read about later.

Tragedy in Dallas.

Despite setbacks in Congress, the President was a popular figure. On November 22, 1963, Kennedy flew to Dallas, Texas. He rode in an open car from the airport to the center of the city. Crowds waved and cheered along the way. Suddenly, shots rang out. The President fell forward, fatally wounded. He was rushed to a nearby hospital but died soon after. That afternoon, Vice President Lyndon Johnson was sworn in as President.

The nation and the world were stunned by the news of Kennedy's death. Dallas police arrested Lee Harvey Oswald and charged him with the murder. Two days later, Oswald was under a police escort when Jack Ruby shot him to death. The incident horrified millions of Americans who saw it on television.

The tragic death of the President raised many questions. Did Oswald act alone? How was Ruby able to shoot him? The Chief Justice of the Supreme Court, Earl Warren, held hearings. In the end, the *Warren Commission* concluded that Oswald had acted alone. However, many questions about Kennedy's death remain unanswered to this day.

The Johnson Years

Lyndon Johnson took office as the nation mourned. The new President assured Americans that he would carry on Kennedy's programs. In November 1964, a year after the tragedy in Dallas, voters sent Johnson back to the White House. During the 1964 election, Johnson ran against Senator Barry Goldwater of Arizona.

Background.

Lyndon Johnson had grown up on a farm in southwestern Texas. He lived through the hard times of the 1920s and 1930s. "When I was young," Johnson recalled later, "poverty was so common that we didn't know it had a name."

Here, Lyndon Johnson is sworn in as President. Jacqueline Kennedy, at right, looks on as Judge Sarah Hughes administers the oath of office. The ceremony took place on the plane that was carrying the coffin of John Kennedy from Dallas to Washington.

The tall Texan was first elected to Congress in 1937. From the start, he was a strong supporter of Franklin Roosevelt's New Deal. During his years in Congress, Johnson learned the art of persuading lawmakers to do what he wanted.

The Great Society. Johnson called his program the *Great Society.* It was an ambitious program to improve the standard of living of all Americans. As Johnson explained, the Great Society "asks not only how much, but how good; not only how to create wealth, but how to use it; not only how fast we are going, but where we are headed." Johnson's experience helped him push programs through Congress. During his first two years in office, he got Congress to pass more than 50 laws to carry out the Great Society.

Perhaps the most important program was *Medicare.* Under this plan, the government helped pay the hospital bills of citizens over age 65. Another program, *Medicaid,* gave money to states to help poor people of all ages with their medical bills. These two programs were a first step toward making sure that all Americans would have a minimum level of health care.

War on poverty. To achieve the Great Society, Johnson declared a "war on poverty." His goal was to help Americans who lived below the *poverty line.* This line was the minimum income the government said people needed to live. In 1964, Congress passed the *Economic Opportunity Act.* It gave loans to poor farmers and to businesses in poor sections of cities. The act set up job-training programs for the poor.

The government also set up programs to build more housing for low income and middle income families. To carry out these programs, Johnson created the Department of Housing and Urban Development, or HUD. Robert Weaver was named to head the department. He became the first black to be appointed to a cabinet position.

In 1964, President Johnson visited Appalachia, an area where poverty was widespread. Here, Johnson talks to Thomas Fletcher, who had been out of work for almost two years. Fletcher had been able to earn only $400 to support his wife and eight children.

Tens of thousands of young Americans protested the Vietnam War. This march took place in San Francisco. The protests that began while Johnson was in office continued through the Nixon years.

Urged on by the President, Congress passed important civil rights legislation. You will read about the Civil Rights Act of 1964 and the Voting Rights Act of 1965 later in this chapter.

Protests Against the Vietnam War

By 1965, much of Johnson's Great Society was in place. In foreign policy, however, the President ran into trouble. You will read in Chapter 31 how the United States became involved in the Vietnam War. Criticism of the war grew in the late 1960s. The most outspoken critics were college students.

Upheavals and violence. By 1968, antiwar protests disrupted college campuses around the country. Students burned draft cards. Some even burned American flags to show their anger at the President's policy. Thousands of Americans marched on Washington, D.C. As protests grew louder, Johnson announced that he would not seek reelection in the fall. His decision, however, did not bring calm to the nation.

Several Democrats sought the party's nomination. They included Senator Robert Kennedy of New York, brother of the late President, Senator Eugene McCarthy of Minnesota, and Vice President Hubert Humphrey. In June 1968, Senator Kennedy was shot and killed by Sirhan Sirhan. The gunman was a Palestinian (see page 708) who opposed Kennedy's support for Israel. The assassination again shocked the nation. To many, violence and death were a dark cloud hanging over American political life.

Election of 1968. In the summer, the Democrats chose Vice President Humphrey to carry their banner. However, during the convention in Chicago, police clashed in violent battles with antiwar demonstrators.

Republicans chose Richard Nixon to run against Humphrey. Nixon was helped by divisions in the Democratic Party. He promised to end the turmoil at home and bring "peace with honor" in Vietnam. Nixon narrowly won the election of 1968.

■ SECTION REVIEW

1. **Define:** poverty line.
2. List three goals of the New Frontier.
3. Describe two Great Society programs that became law.
4. How did the Vietnam War help Richard Nixon win the election of 1968?
5. **What Do You Think?** How do you think the social programs of Kennedy and Johnson were changing America?

2 Politics and the White House

Read to Learn

★ Why did Nixon resign from office?
★ What troubles did Carter face?
★ What were Reagan's major goals?
★ What do these words mean: bicentennial, balanced budget?

During the 1968 campaign, Richard Nixon promised a return to law and order. The "silent majority," he said, wanted an end to the crime and chaos in the streets. Yet Nixon's years in office proved to be just as turbulent as those of President Johnson's.

Nixon in Office

In foreign policy, President Nixon worked slowly toward ending American involvement in Vietnam. At home, he tried to carry out his law-and-order program. He used federal funds to help local police departments. He ordered the Justice Department to arrest protestors who broke the law. More important, he had the chance to name four justices to the Supreme Court. The new justices were more conservative than the ones who retired.

Nixon thought that some programs of the Great Society were too ambitious and too costly. Together with the Vietnam War, they contributed to rapid inflation. As a result, Nixon backed off from the reforms of the Johnson years. He cut federal funds for job training, low income housing, and education.

Voters approved of Nixon's policies. In 1972, Nixon ran for reelection against Senator George McGovern of South Dakota. McGovern was a leader of the antiwar movement. In November, Nixon won by a landslide.

The Watergate break-in. Nixon's victory at the polls came apart early in his second term. The cause was a burglary that took place before the elec- tion. On June 17, 1972, police in Washington, D.C., caught five men breaking into Democratic Party headquarters in the Watergate apartment building. Evidence suggested that the burglars were linked to a committee that was organizing Nixon's reelection. The President denied that anyone in the White House was involved in the *Watergate Affair.*

Early in 1973, however, new evidence linked the burglars to the White House. Advisers close to the President were accused of trying to cover up the truth about the break-in. Some were fired. Others resigned.

In May 1973, a Senate committee, headed by Samuel Ervin of North Carolina, began public hearings. The committee learned that the President had secretly recorded all conversations in

Day after day, Americans watched the Watergate hearings. They heard Senators Samuel Ervin, at right, and Howard Baker, at left, question White House officials. The hearings revealed much about the Nixon White House. They also showed that the American system of checks and balances worked.

his office. In the end, these tapes showed that Nixon himself had been involved in the Watergate cover-up.

The President resigns. During the Watergate affair, Nixon faced another scandal. Vice President Spiro Agnew was accused of accepting bribes and was forced to resign. Under the Twenty-fifth Amendment, the President had to choose a new Vice President.* Nixon chose Representative Gerald Ford of Michigan as his Vice President. Congress quickly approved the appointment.

The Watergate crisis continued into 1974. In July, a committee of the House of Representatives passed three articles of impeachment against the President. The charges included obstructing, or blocking, justice. Nixon realized that he had lost the support of Congress and the public. In August 1974, Nixon became the first American President to resign from office.

---

*The amendment, ratified in 1967, was passed in part because Lyndon Johnson had no Vice President after Kennedy's death. (See page 674.)

Ford Takes Over

When Nixon stepped down, Vice President Gerald Ford took over the reins of government. The new President knew the ways of Washington. He had served in Congress for 25 years. As President, he pledged to be open and honest. Watergate had shaken the nation, but Ford offered comfort. "The Constitution works," he said. "Our long national nightmare is over."

Ford chose Governor Nelson Rockefeller of New York to be Vice President. He then granted Nixon a "full, free and absolute pardon." To those who felt that Nixon should have stood trial, Ford replied that he wanted to spare the country from prolonging the Watergate agony.

In July 1976, the nation proudly celebrated its *bicentennial,* or 200th anniversary. That summer, Ford won the Republican nomination for President. The Democrats chose Jimmy Carter, a former governor of Georgia. Carter had no experience in Washington. During the campaign, he turned this to

President Nixon, at far right, chose Gerald Ford, center, to replace Spiro Agnew, who had resigned as Vice President. Here, Betty Ford, wife of the new Vice President, holds a Bible as Chief Justice Warren Burger administers the oath of office.

his own advantage. He offered Americans a change from Washington politicians. In the election, Carter narrowly defeated Ford.

Carter's Goals

In his campaign and as President, Carter had an informal style. Like Thomas Jefferson, he avoided pomp and ceremony when he took office. Carter walked down Pennsylvania Avenue to the White House instead of riding in a limousine. He chose to be called Jimmy Carter instead of the more formal James Carter.

Troubles in office. The Carter years began with hope for a fresh new approach. During his first year, the President sent Congress more than ten major bills. They included changes in the Social Security system, tax reform, and a plan to encourage oil and coal companies to look for new sources of energy. Yet he achieved few of his goals because he could not win the support of Congress.

Another problem Carter faced was runaway inflation. In the late 1970s, it averaged 10 percent a year. The government tried to slow inflation, but with little success. When people went to shop, they found that prices were always rising. Many families had a hard time paying for such basic needs as food, clothing, and rent.

Human rights. President Carter did win praise for arranging a peace treaty between Egypt and Israel. (See page 710.) He also took a firm stand on human rights. In 1975, the United States joined many other nations in signing the *Helsinki Agreement.* In it, they promised to respect basic human rights such as freedom of religion and freedom of thought. President Carter took this promise seriously. He believed that the United States should refuse to give aid to countries that violated human rights.

Jimmy Carter's open and informal style helped him win the election of 1976. Here, the new President walks down Pennsylvania Avenue after taking office. Carter often appeared in public wearing casual clothes. His down-home style showed Americans that the President was one of the people.

Some people criticized Carter's stand on human rights. They felt that the United States had no right to meddle in the affairs of other countries. Yet many other Americans approved of Carter's human rights policy. They believed that the United States should condemn any country—even an ally—that imprisoned, tortured, or killed its citizens for political reasons.

In 1980, Carter won the Democratic nomination. In the election, however, he was soundly beaten by the Republican candidate, Ronald Reagan.

Reagan Takes Charge

In 1980, Ronald Reagan was a well-known name in the United States. His early career was as a movie actor. From 1966 to 1975, he was governor of California. Reagan's experience before the cameras helped him when he spoke on television. Many Americans felt that he truly cared about the problems of the nation. His skill at presenting his ideas to the public won him the name "the great communicator."

GRAPH SKILL The budget deficit increased sharply during the 1980s. According to this graph, what was the budget deficit in 1980? In 1985?

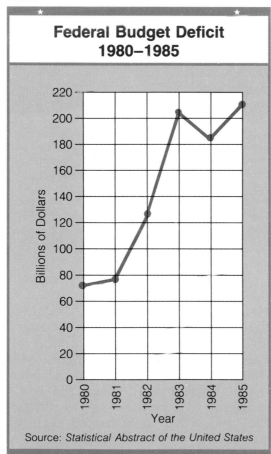

Federal Budget Deficit 1980–1985

Billions of Dollars

Year

Source: *Statistical Abstract of the United States*

New goals. Reagan pledged to lead the nation in a more conservative direction. He believed that the federal government had grown too big. State and local governments, he said, should take on a larger role.

Soon after Reagan took office in 1981, he was shot by a would-be assassin. The President recovered quickly and pressed forward with his program to reduce taxes and federal spending. At his urging, Congress agreed to cut taxes and to cut back funds for many social programs. Critics charged that many of these program cuts hurt the poor and the elderly.

As he had promised, Reagan brought down inflation. At first, the President's economic program led to high unemployment. But by the mid–1980s, the economy was booming.

One of Reagan's goals—balancing the federal budget—proved more difficult to achieve. With a *balanced budget,* the government does not spend more than its income. Reagan, however, wanted to increase military spending. He believed that the nation must be in a strong military position to face the Soviet Union.

Increased military spending and a promised tax cut meant that the President could not have the balanced budget he so badly wanted. In fact, the budget deficit soared. (A deficit, you will recall, was the amount the government spent over its income.) By 1985, the deficit had reached an all-time high of $212 billion.

Election of 1984. Despite the growing deficit, many Americans had confidence in the President. In the election of 1984, Reagan ran against Senator Walter Mondale of Minnesota. Mondale made history when he chose Geraldine Ferraro as his running mate. She was the first woman to run for Vice President on a major party ticket. In November 1984, voters gave Reagan a sweeping victory.

In the 1984 election, much attention was focused on the Democratic candidate for Vice President, Geraldine Ferraro. However, Walter Mondale and Geraldine Ferraro, at left, lost to Ronald Reagan and George Bush. At right, Reagan is sworn in for a second term, as his wife, Nancy Reagan, looks on.

Reagan's Second Term

The President began his second term with three major goals. tax reform, arms control, and a balanced budget. He made great strides toward achieving the first two goals. At his urging, Congress passed the Tax Reform Act of 1986. The act lowered tax rates for individual Americans. And in 1987, Reagan negotiated an arms treaty with the Soviet Union. (See page 703.)

Although both the President and Congress talked of a balanced budget, the deficit continued to soar. The two sides could not agree on where to cut spending. By 1988, the nation's deficit was double what it had been in 1980. A sharp drop in stock prices in October 1987 increased public concern about the economy.

The Iran–Contra deal. Late in 1986, a secret deal came to light. Members of the President's staff had sold arms to Iran. In return, Iran used its influence to gain the release of some American hostages in Lebanon. Americans were shocked that arms had been traded for hostages. The President had vowed not to bargain with kidnappers and other terrorists.

Later, Americans learned more disturbing news about the deal. Money from the arms sales was to be used to secretly aid the Contras in Nicaragua. The Contras were fighting against the socialist government of the country. (See page 717.) At the time, Congress had banned Contra aid. So many people saw this part of the deal as illegal. In the end, the President was cleared of any wrongdoing in the Iran–Contra deal. But his image was shaken.

Despite problems during his second term, Ronald Reagan remained a popular leader. Many Americans felt that he had done much to restore traditional values and to boost confidence in the nation.

In a country with a democratic form of government, public opinion—or what people think on different issues—is important. Since the 1930s, Americans have read or heard the results of **public opinion polls.** These polls are surveys that measure the opinions, attitudes, or beliefs of large numbers of people.

Polls are taken by newspapers, radios, politicians, and private groups whose main job is surveying public opinion. They are taken on issues such as who will win the next election or how well people think the President's economic policy is working.

At right is a table about the most important problems Americans thought the country faced. The table is based on Gallup Polls.

1. **Identify the subject of the poll.** When polls are taken, pollsters choose a sample group of people. They then ask these individuals one or more questions to determine their opinions. (a) What question does the table answer? (b) What time period is covered by the table?

2. **Practice reading the data.** The table at right shows the five issues that concerned Americans most at different times. Study the data in the table to see what you can learn. (a) According to the table, what foreign policy issue worried Americans in 1963? In 1969? In 1987? (b) What economic worry did Americans have in each year shown in the table?

3. **Evaluate the information.** Use the table and your reading in this chapter to answer the following questions. (a) Why do you think race relations were a concern in the 1960s and 1970s? (b) Why were college demonstrations a concern in 1969? (c) What do you think are the five most important issues facing the nation today?

Public Opinion Polls

Question: "What do you think is the most important problem facing this country today?"

Year	Problem	%
1963	Cuba, Castro	24%
	Other international problems	39%
	Unemployment	11%
	Racial problems	4%
	High cost of living	4%
1969	Vietnam War	69%
	Crime and lawlessness	17%
	Race relations	16%
	Inflation	9%
	College demonstrations	8%
1973	High cost of living	59%
	Drugs	20%
	Crime and lawlessness	17%
	Race relations	16%
	Unemployment	16%
1981	Inflation, high cost of living	52%
	Unemployment	17%
	Budget cuts	6%
	High government spending	4%
	International problems	4%
1987	Economic problems	47%
	Fear of war	23%
	Drug abuse	11%
	Dissatisfaction with government	5%
	Moral and religious decline	5%

Source: The Gallup Poll

George Bush won the hearts and minds of many Americans at the Republican convention in New Orleans. Critics and supporters alike hailed his acceptance speech as the "speech of his life." Here, he responds to the applause of convention delegates.

Election of 1988

In the summer of 1988, the Republican and Democratic parties each chose their candidate for President. Vice-President Bush was the clear favorite of the Republicans. After a primary battle with black leader Jesse Jackson, Governor Michael Dukakis of Massachusetts emerged as the choice of the Democrats.

Bush argued that the Republicans had brought peace and prosperity to the nation. Under his leadership, he promised, Americans could be sure of more of the same. No increase in taxes, strong military defense, and American values such as patriotism and family life would continue as major concerns in his administration.

Dukakis, on the other hand, attacked the Republican record. He pointed to the budget deficit and the Iran-Contra deal as proof that the nation needed a new brand of leadership. He promised strong management of the economy, more jobs for more Americans, new education programs, and a strong antidrug campaign.

On November 8, George Bush was elected 41st President of the United States. The Republicans continued to dominate the White House.

SECTION REVIEW

1. **Define:** bicentennial, balanced budget.
2. Why did Nixon cut back on some programs of the Great Society?
3. Why did Carter achieve so few of his goals?
4. Describe Reagan's economic program.
5. **What Do You Think?** Do you think President Ford did the right thing when he pardoned Richard Nixon? Explain.

3 Freedom Now!

Read to Learn
★ What new laws ensured equal rights for all Americans?
★ Who put forward the idea of black power?
★ Why did violence break out in American cities in the 1960s?
★ What does this word mean: ghetto?

In 1984 and again in 1988, Jesse Jackson, a black leader, sought the presidential nomination of the Democratic Party. The nation had come a long way since the 1960s. At that time, the slogan of the civil rights movement was "Freedom Now!" Black Americans felt that they had waited long enough for equality.

Push for Change

During the 1960s, civil rights groups moved ahead on several fronts. The Southern Christian Leadership Conference, or SCLC, was led by Martin Luther King, Jr. It joined with other groups, such as the Congress of Racial Equality and NAACP. They used the courts to fight cases of discrimination. Sit-ins and boycotts also brought results. In towns and cities, black citizens let store owners and employers know that they would use their economic power to end segregation.

Dangers. Peaceful protests took much courage. Police sometimes used high-pressure water hoses, attack dogs, and electric cattle prods to break up protest marches. Several civil rights workers, white and black, were killed.

In 1963, more than 200,000 blacks and whites marched on Washington, D.C. Their purpose was to let Congress know that they wanted laws to end discrimination and help the poor in America. At the huge rally, Martin Luther King, Jr., made his moving "I Have a Dream" speech. (See page 685.)

Housing was one area where blacks faced much discrimination. Often, they were not allowed to buy houses or rent apartments in certain areas. These protesters are demonstrating for the right to rent apartments in a housing project.

On August 28, 1963, more than 200,000 people marched peacefully to the Lincoln Memorial in Washington, D.C. The marchers included black and white Americans, young and old. Their march was a call to end discrimination and poverty in America. Among the speakers that day was the Reverend Martin Luther King, Jr. King, a Baptist pastor, had been active in the civil rights movement since the 1950s. Part of King's speech is printed below:

I say to you today, my friends, that in spite of the difficulties and frustrations of the moment I still have a dream. It is a dream deeply rooted in the American dream.

I have a dream that one day this nation will rise up and live out the true meaning of its creed: "We hold these truths to be self-evident, that all men are created equal."

I have a dream that my four little children will one day live in a nation where they will not be judged by the color of their skin but by the content of their character.

When we let freedom ring, when we let it ring from every village and every hamlet, from every state and every city, we will be able to speed up that day when all of God's children, black men and white men, Jews and Gentiles, Protestants and Cath-olics, will be able to join hands and sing in the words of the old Negro spiritual, "Free at last! Free at last! Thank God Almighty, we are free at last!"

★ What was the main point of King's speech?

New laws. Soon after the March on Washington, President Kennedy sent Congress a strong civil rights bill. "This nation," he said, "for all its hopes and all its boasts, will not be fully free until all its citizens are free." After Kennedy's death, Lyndon Johnson saw the bill through Congress. The *Civil Rights Act of 1964* protected the right of all citizens to vote. It outlawed discrimination in hiring and ended segregation in public places.

Other laws followed. In 1964, the Twenty-fourth Amendment was ratified. It prohibited poll taxes, which had been used to keep blacks from voting. In 1965, Johnson signed into law the *Voting Rights Act.* It allowed federal officials to register voters in states where local officials practiced discrimination. The new law also ended literacy tests. Taken together, the new laws helped tens of thousands of black Americans to vote for the first time.

Black Power Movement

Some blacks felt that laws and non-violent protests would never bring equality. They pointed to the *ghettos* (geht OHS), or rundown areas of cities, where millions of poor blacks lived. Many people in the ghettos were unemployed or held very low-paying jobs.

Black leaders disagreed over how to change these conditions. Some, like the *Black Muslims,* believed that blacks could succeed only if they separated from white society. Others, like Angela Davis and Stokely Carmichael, urged a new approach—black power.

Differing views. Black Americans interpreted the idea of black power in different ways. Carmichael talked about blacks "taking over." Radical groups, such as the *Black Panthers,* urged blacks to arm themselves and fight for their rights when necessary.

Moderate blacks emphasized more peaceful aspects of black power. They urged blacks to rely on themselves and to start their own businesses. During the 1960s, black Americans began studying more about their past and the many African cultures from which they came. In a best-selling book, called *Roots,* Alex Haley traced his own family back to Africa. James Brown, a black singer, composed a popular song that summed up what many blacks felt: "Say It Loud—I'm Black and I'm Proud."

Violence in the cities. In crowded ghettos, young blacks took up the call to violence of the more radical leaders. Anger over poverty, lack of jobs, and discrimination led to riots. Among the most violent was the revolt in Watts, a black ghetto of Los Angeles. For six days in August 1965, rioters roamed the streets. They set fire to buildings and looted stores. Before the rioting ended, 4,000 people had been arrested, 34 killed, and 1,000 injured.

In 1966 and 1967, rioting broke out in other cities. Newark, Cincinnati, and Atlanta each suffered. In Detroit, over 4,000 fires left large sections of the city in ruins. Army tanks patrolled the streets to keep the peace.

A man of peace dies. During the riots, Martin Luther King, Jr., remained committed to nonviolence. In April 1968, he went to Memphis, Tennessee, to support black sanitation workers who were on strike. When he stepped outside his motel room, a white gunman shot and killed him. News of King's death set off another wave of violence in the cities.

King was buried in Atlanta, Georgia. These words were written on his gravestone: "Free at last, free at last, thank God Almighty I'm free at last." Despite his violent death, King's life continued to inspire people to work for peaceful change. By the 1980s, Americans honored Martin Luther King, Jr., with a national holiday each year.

Progress and Problems

In 1968, President Johnson appointed a commission to study the causes of the riots. The commission warned that America "is moving toward two societies, one black, one white—separate and unequal." It urged a national commitment to ensure equal rights for all.

Gains for blacks. Since the 1960s, black Americans have made important gains. In politics, blacks won office in small towns and large cities. Atlanta, Cleveland, Chicago, Newark, Philadelphia, and Los Angeles all have had black mayors.

Blacks gained places in the federal government. In 1966, Edward Brooke was elected to the Senate from Massachusetts. He became the first black senator since Reconstruction. A year later, President Johnson appointed Thurgood Marshall to the Supreme Court. Jesse Jackson's campaigns for the Democratic nomination for President showed

The peaceful protests of the early 1960s won some important rights for blacks. However, many blacks in poor city neighborhoods saw little improvement. Their frustration with lack of jobs and poverty led to a series of riots. In Detroit and elsewhere, the National Guard was called in to restore the peace.

that blacks were committed to an active role in American politics.

The civil rights movement helped blacks gain places in universities and businesses, often through affirmative action programs. These programs were set up to hire and promote minorities, women, and others who had experienced discrimination in the past. In the late 1960s and 1970s, more blacks entered professions such as medicine and law. The black middle class grew. Despite progress, many blacks faced discrimination in winning promotion and advancement.

In the 1980s, official support for affirmative action declined. Critics said that such programs discriminated against people who were not members of minority groups. Rising costs of education and reduced financial aid also limited the number of black students in universities.

Poverty and unemployment. By the 1980s, middle class blacks had made progress. Yet the number of poor blacks had increased. In the 1980s, one out of every four black families lived below the poverty line—20 percent more than in 1970. Unemployment among young blacks soared. Many of them had dropped out of school. So they lacked the skills and training to find jobs.

To balance the budget, President Reagan cut back on job training and

Despite a growing number of poor blacks, the black middle class expanded in the 1980s. Armed with education and skills, these blacks gained executive jobs in businesses and corporations.

welfare programs. He urged state and local governments to do more to solve the problem of jobless youth. In the meantime, many black and white leaders warned that an "underclass" of poorly educated, jobless blacks was growing. Finding ways to promote education and skills and to limit other problems of poverty remained a challenge for the 1990s.

═══SECTION REVIEW═══

1. **Define:** ghetto.
2. (a) What peaceful means did blacks use to win equal rights? (b) What dangers did civil rights workers face?
3. Describe one law that helped end segregation.
4. (a) What did radical black leaders mean by black power? (b) What did moderates mean by this idea?
5. **What Do You Think?** Do you think America is still "moving toward two societies" as it was in 1968? Explain your answer.

4 Other Banners of Reform

Read to Learn

★ How did the people of Puerto Rico gain more control over their government?
★ What conditions did Native Americans protest?
★ What were the goals of the women's rights movement?
★ How did Americans with disabilities win changes?
★ What do these words mean: braceros, women's rights movement?

In the 1960s and 1970s, other ethnic groups and women struggled for equality. They used boycotts, sit-ins, and protest marches to achieve their goals. In the 1980s, civil rights groups and Americans with disabilities sought to protect hard-won gains.

Hispanics

Hispanics formed the second largest—and fastest growing—minority in the United States. By 1988, they numbered about 19 million. Hispanics included Spanish-speaking people from different countries. Among the most numerous groups were Puerto Ricans, Cubans, and Mexican Americans.

Puerto Rico becomes a commonwealth. In 1952, Puerto Ricans adopted a new constitution. Under it, the island became a self-governing commonwealth. This meant that the people gained more say over their own affairs. Many Puerto Ricans wanted to remain a commonwealth. Others demanded independence for the island.

In the 1950s, thousands of Puerto Ricans traveled to the United States to find work. Many took jobs in the garment factories of New York City, New Jersey, Connecticut, and Pennsylvania. Others settled in major cities such as Boston, Chicago, and San Francisco. Puerto Ricans in the United States did not have an easy time. Many faced discrimination in housing and jobs.

In response, Puerto Ricans formed groups to help their communities. In the 1960s and 1970s, these groups worked to end discrimination. Their efforts together with those of other groups brought results. For example, the *Voting Rights Act of 1975* created bilingual* elections. This made it easier for all Hispanics to vote. Puerto Ricans as well as other Hispanics also gained more representation in state and local government.

Cuban immigration. More than 200,000 Cubans fled to the United States after Fidel Castro set up a communist government there. (See page 698.) Most of the newcomers settled in south Florida. Many were well educated, and they adapted to life in the United States.

In 1980, a new wave of Cubans arrived when Castro allowed 125,000 people to leave the island. Again, many settled in south Florida. The new refugees were unskilled workers. They found it hard to make a living and support their families. Cuban American groups as well as state and federal agencies tried to help the newcomers find homes and jobs.

By the 1980s, Cuban culture influenced the life of south Florida. Cuban-owned businesses flourished. Cubans operated newspapers, Spanish-language radio stations, and a television station in Miami.

---

*Bilingual (bi LIN gwuhl) means in two languages. Under the act, in areas with large numbers of Spanish-speaking or Asian voters, election information has to be in more than one language.

AMERICANS WHO DARED

Henry Cisneros

Henry Cisneros has served four terms as mayor of San Antonio, Texas. When he won office in 1981, he became the first Mexican American mayor of the city since 1842 —before Texas joined the Union. In 1987, Cisneros shocked supporters. He refused the chance to run for governor of Texas in order to care for his sick son. Many praised his decision to put his family first. His decision did not mean that he closed the door forever to a political career.

A New Future for Mexican Americans

By the late 1980s, there were more than 11 million Mexican Americans in all parts of the United States. For Mexican Americans, as for other groups, the struggle for equality was long and hard.

Need for reform. Many Mexican Americans were migrant farm workers. They planted, weeded, or harvested crops wherever they were needed. The pay was low, and working conditions were poor. If they tried to bargain for better pay, employers brought in Mexican farm workers, known as *braceros* (brah SAIR ohs), to harvest crops. The braceros program kept wages low.

Besides low pay, migrant farm workers had little chance to get an education. Since parents moved often, children could not go to school easily. Also, most schools did not have programs to teach Spanish-speaking children. Mexican Americans often met with prejudice. Even well-trained doctors and lawyers found it difficult to get jobs outside their own communities.

César Chávez. During the 1960s, many Mexican Americans campaigned for a better future. For example, César Chávez (SAY zahr CHAH vehz) tried to help migrant farm workers by forming a union. Organizing farm workers was difficult because workers were spread out over a wide area. Also, farm owners strongly opposed unions.

In 1962, Chávez formed the *National Farm Workers Association.* Later, it became known as the United Farm Workers of America (UFW). He traveled 300,000 miles in 6 months to sign up members. When farmers refused to negotiate with the union, Chávez used nonviolent tactics like those of Martin Luther King, Jr. He called for nationwide boycotts of certain products. Slowly, the boycotts worked. Farm owners had to recognize the union, and workers won higher wages.

Ethnic pride. Like blacks, Mexican Americans took pride in their history and culture. Some Mexican Americans called themselves *Chicanos.* They actively supported the civil rights movement. Chicano groups helped to register voters. They made sure that voting laws were enforced. As a result, voters elected more Hispanic officials to represent their interests. In 1987, there were 332 Hispanic mayors and state legislators in the United States. With an increased role in government, Mexican Americans continued to press for better education and job training.

Native Americans

As you have read, the United States government made and broke many treaties with Native American nations. By the 1970s, several Native American groups were working to improve conditions. Some, such as the National Congress of American Indians, wanted more control over their own affairs. They also wanted the government to honor treaties that had been broken in the past.

Other groups, such as the Native American Rights Fund, focused on legal struggles. They worked to regain title to Indian lands as well as mineral and fishing rights. In some cases, the courts awarded Indians money for lands that had been taken illegally.

César Chávez was a firm believer in nonviolence. He led the struggle for better conditions for migrant farm workers. For more than 15 years, Chávez tried to get farmowners to accept the union he organized for farm workers. He used only peaceful methods such as boycotts and protest marches.

Native American leaders have urged companies to open plants on reservations. Here, a Navajo woman makes missile parts at a General Dynamics plant on a reservation.

The Women's Rights Movement

Like other groups in America, women struggled to achieve equal rights. Women faced discrimination in jobs, pay, and schooling. In the 1950s, many employers refused to hire women for certain jobs even though the women were qualified. When men and women held the same job, women were often paid less. Also, they were seldom promoted as fast as men. Women students were often turned down by medical and law schools in favor of men.

In 1966, Betty Friedan helped to set up the *National Organization for Women*, or NOW. Its goal was to work for equal rights for women in jobs, pay, and education. Since the 1960s, this struggle for equality has become known as the *women's rights movement*.

In 1969, a group of Native Americans, called Indians of All Tribes, made a dramatic protest to call attention to Indian problems. It took over Alcatraz Island in San Francisco. The group offered to buy Alcatraz for $24 "in glass beads and red cloth"—the price Peter Minuit had paid for Manhattan Island in 1626.

Another group, the *American Indian Movement*, or AIM, took an active role in protesting treatment of Indians. In 1973, AIM members occupied Wounded Knee, South Dakota, for several weeks. In 1890, you will recall, the United States Army had massacred 200 Indians at Wounded Knee. By occupying the site, AIM wanted to remind people of the government's failure to keep its treaties.

Protests and court cases have won sympathy for Indian causes. Today, Native Americans have more freedom of choice than in the past. Some have proudly claimed their traditions and heritage. Others have chosen to live and work outside the reservation.

GRAPH SKILL The number of women working outside the home has risen steadily in the past 35 years. About what percentage of women were working outside the home in 1960? In 1970? In 1980?

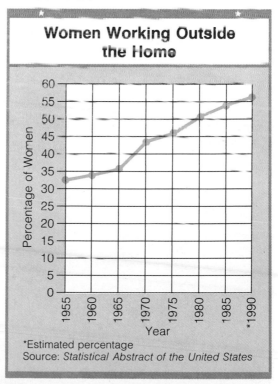

Women Working Outside the Home

*Estimated percentage
Source: *Statistical Abstract of the United States*

New laws. Women made some gains through new laws. Under the Equal Pay Act of 1963, workers had to get equal pay for equal work. The Civil Rights Act of 1964 outlawed discrimination in hiring not only based on race but also on sex. Yet some employers ignored these laws. They continued to deny women equal opportunities. As a result, women brought their cases to the courts and often won.

An effort to add an equal rights amendment to the Constitution failed. Many Americans supported the idea. But opponents, led by Phyllis Schlafly, argued that the amendment was not needed. Also, they said, it threatened American traditions.

Ongoing struggles. The women's rights movement gave women new opportunities. More women became lawyers, doctors, engineers, and business executives than ever before. In 1983, for example, Sally Ride became the first woman astronaut in space. Prodded by affirmative action programs, businesses made efforts to hire and promote qualified women.

During the 1970s and 1980s, the number of women elected to political office rose. In 1981, Ronald Reagan named Sandra Day O'Connor the first woman justice of the Supreme Court. As you read, Geraldine Ferraro made history when the Democratic Party chose her to run for Vice President in 1984. The gains were impressive when compared to the past. However, women still held only a tiny percentage of elected offices.

The women's rights movement helped open new jobs to women. However, many women continued to find satisfaction in the roles of wife and mother. At top, a research scientist works in her laboratory. Below, a woman and her young son prepare a meal.

In the 1970s and 1980s, women's income rose but not as fast as men's. Because some jobs were seen as "women's work," they paid less well than jobs usually held by men. Women's groups called for "equivalent pay." They wanted the pay for each job to be based on the skills it required.

By the 1980s, more than half of all women worked outside the home. The two-job family became typical. At the same time, the number of households headed by single women increased. These families were often poor, in part because women earned less than men. More than half the children in families headed by women lived below the poverty line. To solve this problem, women's groups have proposed better child care arrangements and more job training.

The women's rights movement opened new fields to women. But many women chose to work at home in traditional roles as wives and mothers. As in the past, they volunteered their time for important social and political causes.

Lowering the Barriers

Americans with handicaps numbered some 37 million by the late 1980s. Like other minority groups, people with disabilities faced discrimination in education, jobs, and housing. In the past two decades, however, they have organized. Backed by 250,000 disabled Vietnam veterans, the movement pushed ahead on many fronts.

People with handicaps used their power as consumers and voters. They pressured stores to remove barriers such as aisles too narrow for wheelchairs to pass. A bumper sticker, "Disabled but Able to Vote," proclaimed their strength in numbers. The disabled lobbied states and cities. They won laws requiring ramped curbs, parking spaces for the handicapped, and wheelchair lifts on buses.

In recent years, some businesses have met the needs of people with handicaps. Here, a low bank teller machine enables a person in a wheelchair to do his banking easily.

New laws protected children with disabilities. In 1975, Congress passed the Education for All Handicapped Children Act. The act required public schools to provide a suitable education for children with disabilities. Handicapped children were to attend classes with nonhandicapped students.

Much still remained to be done. Activists pointed to social prejudices against people with disabilities. In 1988, people with handicaps joined with civil rights and women's groups. Together, they pressured Congress to pass the Civil Rights Restoration Act. The act required colleges and universities that receive federal aid to end discrimination in all activities.

SECTION REVIEW

1. **Define:** braceros, women's rights movement.

2. How did César Chávez try to help farm workers?

3. Why did Native Americans occupy Wounded Knee?

4. **What Do You Think?** How do you think the successes of women like O'Connor and Ride helped other women?

Chapter 30 Review

In the 1960s, Presidents Kennedy and Johnson pushed for new civil rights laws and social programs. By 1968, protests against the Vietnam War led to turmoil. That year, Nixon won the election.

Nixon's second term was marred by the Watergate affair. In 1974, he resigned, and Ford took over. When Jimmy Carter became President in 1976, he was unable to achieve most of his goals. In the 1980s, President Reagan brought a conservative approach to government.

In the 1960s, various groups pressed for equal rights. Black Americans, Hispanics, Native Americans, women, and the disabled showed the need for new laws to protect all Americans. By the 1980s, the civil rights movement had made important gains. But much remained to be done.

★ Reviewing the Facts ★

Key Terms. Match each term in Column 1 with the correct definition in Column 2.

Column 1	Column 2
1. poverty line	**a.** 200th anniversary
2. bicentennial	**b.** rundown area of a city where poor people live
3. balanced budget	**c.** minimum income the government said people needed to live
4. ghetto	**d.** Mexican farm workers brought in to harvest crops
5. braceros	**e.** government spending equals its income

Key People, Events, and Ideas. Identify each of the following.

1. New Frontier
2. Great Society
3. Medicare
4. Watergate affair
5. Helsinki Agreement
6. Geraldine Ferraro
7. Civil Rights Act of 1964
8. Black Panthers
9. Edward Brooke
10. Jesse Jackson
11. Voting Rights Act of 1975
12. César Chávez
13. Chicano
14. AIM
15. Betty Friedan

★ Chapter Checkup ★

1. What social programs did Kennedy and Johnson want?

2. (a) List three major political events of 1968. (b) How was each significant?

3. (a) What changes did Reagan promise to make as President? (b) What goals did he achieve in his second term?

4. Explain the importance of each of the following in the civil rights movement: (a) Voting Rights Act of 1965; (b) Martin Luther King, Jr.

5. (a) What are the three largest groups of Hispanics in the United States? (b) How have Puerto Ricans fought discrimination?

6. What were some of the goals of Native Americans in the past few decades?

7. (a) What changes did the women's rights movement want? (b) What gains have women made since the 1950s?

8. What victories have people with handicaps achieved?

★ Thinking About History ★

1. **Relating past to present.** Compare the New Frontier and Great Society programs of the 1960s to the New Deal programs of the 1930s. (a) How were they similar? (b) How were they different?

2. **Learning about citizenship.** Dr. Antonia Pantoja, a Puerto Rican educator, set up the Puerto Rican Forum to help Puerto Ricans work for improvement. She also founded the Universidad Boricua, a Puerto Rican-centered university in Washington, D.C. How do you think the work of individuals and groups helped minorities in America?

3. **Looking into the future.** (a) Why do you think jobs usually held by women, such as nursing, pay less than jobs usually held by men, such as driving a city bus? (b) How do you think "equivalent pay" would affect the economy?

★ Using Your Skills ★

1. **Recognizing a point of view.** Review the words from Kennedy's inaugural speech on page 672. (a) What do Kennedy's words tell you about his attitude toward change? (b) What feelings does he appeal to in his speech?

2. **Outlining.** Prepare an outline of the section "Politics and the White House" on pages 677–683. Then write a brief summary of the major problems facing the nation between 1968 and 1984.

3. **Making a generalization.** Review the description of the "Black Power Movement" on page 686. Make a generalization about black power. Then give two facts to support your generalization.

4. **Understanding cause and effect.** Review pages 689–690 on Mexican Americans. List two reasons why Mexican Americans were willing to form a union such as the National Farmworkers Association. Then describe one effect of the union.

5. **Making a review chart.** Make a large chart with three headings across the top: Group, Goals, and Achievements. Fill in the chart for the different groups who worked for equal rights in the 1960s and 1970s. Then write a brief summary in which you compare the goals and achievements of two of the groups on your chart.

★ More to Do ★

1. **Exploring local history.** Make a poster showing front page headlines of local newspapers dated April 5, 1968, the day after Martin Luther King, Jr., was assassinated.

2. **Drawing a cartoon.** Draw a political cartoon to illustrate an event in the Watergate affair.

3. **Listening to music.** Find a record or tape recording of protest songs of the 1960s and 1970s. Play the songs for the class. Explain what each song was protesting and who wrote and sang it.

4. **Giving an oral report.** Choose one of the Presidents you read about in this chapter. Find out more about his background, education, and early career. Then give an oral report in which you describe why he was a strong candidate to lead the American nation.

5. **Writing an editorial.** Prepare an editorial for your local newspaper on a major issue you think the nation is facing today. In your editorial, explain your position on the issue and support it with specific examples.

CHAPTER

31

Challenges to Peace (1960–Present)

Chapter Outline

1 Rivalry Between the Superpowers

2 War in Southeast Asia

3 Search for Peace in the Middle East

4 America's Neighbors

1960	1964	1968	1972	1976	1980	1984	1988	PRESENT

1961
Bay of Pigs;
Berlin Wall;
Alliance for
Progress

1965
Marines
land in
Dominican
Republic

1969
Bombing
of
Cambodia
begins

1975
Vietnam
War
ends;
Cambodia
falls

1979
Afghanistan
invaded;
hostages
seized in
Iran

1987
INF Treaty
signed

About This Chapter

In 1975, Yang Choeun and his family lived in a village in Cambodia in Southeast Asia. They owned a house, some land, and a few farm animals. Then, war came to Cambodia. Pol Pot, a Cambodian communist, took over the government. He forced people to leave their homes. Yang and his family were separated. Later, he learned his parents and sisters died of hunger.

Eventually, Yang and a few relatives escaped from Cambodia. In 1984, an American church helped them to come to the United States. Church members gave them a place to live, food, and clothing. Yang found a job and hoped to save enough money so that he could be on his own. Like other immigrants, Yang found life in his new home very

different. Yet, he was glad to have escaped the miseries of war-torn Cambodia.

Since 1960, war and revolutions have disrupted the lives of millions of people around the world. Often, these conflicts have been tied to the Cold War.

The United States and the Soviet Union have faced each other as suspicious and often hostile powers in different parts of the globe. In one crisis after another, the United States has given military and economic aid to one side while the Soviet Union has helped the other. Both nations recognize the danger of this rivalry, however. From time to time, they have tried to improve relations.

Study the time line above. What event or events took place in 1975?

In 1972, President Nixon went to the People's Republic of China. His visit opened the way for trade between the two nations.

1 Rivalry Between the Superpowers

Read to Learn

★ What crises in the Cold War came up in the 1960s?

★ How did the superpowers move toward détente?

★ How did relations between the United States and China change in the 1970s?

★ What do these words mean: superpower, exile, stockpile, détente?

During the 1960s and 1970s, the two superpowers—the United States and the Soviet Union—faced each other around the world. A *superpower* is a powerful nation that competes with another powerful nation for worldwide influence. At times, the tense relations between the superpowers eased. But basic differences remained.

Tensions Over Cuba

When President Kennedy took office in 1960, he had to make some hard decisions about Cuba. In 1959, Fidel Castro had led a successful revolution in Cuba. Soon after, he announced that he was a communist and that he planned to make Cuba a socialist state.* Castro then began to take over American-owned businesses in Cuba. He strongly criticized the role played by the United States in Latin America. At the same time, he built close ties with the Soviet Union.

Castro's actions worried American leaders. After all, Cuba was just 90

*In a socialist state, the government owns the factories, railroads, and other major industries.

miles (145 km) off the coast of the United States. Also, Castro encouraged rebels in other parts of Latin America to overthrow their governments.

Many Cubans, especially those from the middle and upper classes, did not like Castro's government. Thousands fled to the United States. Cuban exiles told how Castro had seized their property and taken away many freedoms. An *exile* is a person forced to leave his or her own country.

Bay of Pigs invasion. In 1961, President Kennedy approved a plan to overthrow Castro. The plan used Cuban exiles. They were secretly trained by the Central Intelligence Agency, or CIA, of the United States. On April 21, 1961, about 2,000 exiles landed at the *Bay of Pigs* on the southern coast of Cuba. They hoped other Cubans who opposed Castro would join them.

The invasion was badly planned. Also, the United States hesitated to give air support. As a result, Castro easily defeated the exiles. In the end, the Bay of Pigs invasion failed. It made Castro more popular in Cuba and embarrassed the United States.

Cuban missile crisis. The invasion also led the Soviet Union to give more weapons to Cuba. In October 1962, President Kennedy learned that the Soviet Union was secretly building missile bases in Cuba. The President knew that the bases could be used to launch missiles against the United States. Kennedy asked the Soviet leader, Nikita Khrushchev (KROOS chehv), to stop work on the bases. Khrushchev refused.

The President then announced that the United States Navy would blockade Cuba. American warships would stop any Soviet ship from bringing missiles to Cuba.

A tense week followed as Soviet ships steamed toward Cuba. American armed forces were put on the alert during the *Cuban missile crisis.* Across the country, Americans wondered what would happen if the Soviet ships did not turn back. At the last minute, they did. "We were eyeball to eyeball," said Secretary of State Dean Rusk, "and I think the other fellow just blinked."

President Kennedy's strong stand forced Khrushchev to compromise. The

Tensions between the United States and the Soviet Union reached a peak during the Cuban missile crisis in 1962. Here, an American navy plane flys over a Soviet freighter. The canvas-covered cargo on its deck may have been missiles.

Before the Berlin Wall was built, East Berliners, such as the soldier at left, made dramatic escapes to freedom in West Berlin. In 1963, President Kennedy, at right, visited West Berlin. He promised American support for the people of that city.

Soviet leader agreed to take the missiles out of Cuba. In turn, the United States agreed not to invade the island.

Cold War Crises in Europe

During the 1960s, Cold War tensions flared up again in Europe. Berlin was a focus of attention because of its location within East Germany. Between 1949 and 1961, thousands of East Germans fled to West Berlin. From there, they flew to West Germany. The flight of so many people embarrassed the communist governments of East Germany and the Soviet Union.

The Berlin Wall. In August 1961, the East German government built a wall along the border between East and West Berlin. Barbed wire, concrete blocks, and guard towers cut off East Berliners from their neighbors in the west. The *Berlin Wall* created a new crisis between the two superpowers. President Kennedy called up army reserves in case West Germany was attacked.

In the end, the crisis passed. But the Berlin Wall remained as a symbol of a divided Germany and a divided Europe.

Invasion of Czechoslovakia. Other crises developed in Eastern Europe. In 1968, Alexander Dubček (DOOB chehk) became the leader of Czechoslovakia. He introduced reforms to give the Czech people more freedom. People were allowed to express their opinions more freely and openly.

The Soviet Union was alarmed by Dubček's ideas. Soviet leaders worried that Czechoslovakia was growing too independent. They were afraid, too, that Dubček's ideas would spread to other Eastern European countries. To stop this, thousands of Soviet troops invaded Czechoslovakia in August 1968. They occupied Prague, the capital, and ended the new freedoms. The United States condemned the Soviet invasion but took no direct action.

Efforts at Détente

During the Cold War, the United States and the Soviet Union spent huge sums of money to develop deadly new weapons. Each side *stockpiled,* or stored up for use, many nuclear weapons. The superpowers said that nuclear weapons were needed to keep the peace. Many people feared that this arms race would lead to a nuclear war. In a nuclear war, they said, all human life might be destroyed.

In the early 1970s, American leaders looked for ways to ease tensions between the superpowers. The United States and the Soviet Union moved toward *détente* (day TAHNT), or an easing of tensions. In the 1960s, a "hot line," or direct telephone line, linked Washington and Moscow. With the hot line, Soviet and American leaders could talk with each other directly in case of a crisis.

The superpowers also took steps to slow the arms race. In May 1972, President Nixon traveled to Moscow. He was the first American President to visit the Soviet Union since World War II. In Moscow, Nixon signed the *SALT Agreement.* SALT stands for Strategic Arms Limitations Talks. Under the agreement, each country pledged to limit the number of nuclear warheads and missiles that it would keep.

Détente continued under President Gerald Ford. Trade between the two nations increased. The United States sold tons of wheat to the Soviet Union. In 1975, Soviet and American astronauts met in outer space and linked up their capsules.

A New China Policy

In the 1970s, the United States also sought better relations with another communist country, the People's Republic of China. In 1949, you will remember, Mao Zedong won control of China. The United States refused to recognize Mao's communist government in mainland China. Instead, it recognized the government of Chiang Kai-shek on the island of Taiwan.

For years, the United States and the People's Republic eyed each other with suspicion. The United States gave arms and aid to Taiwan. Mao Zedong, however, insisted that Taiwan was part of China.

Many people were surprised when President Nixon visited the People's Republic of China in February 1972. Nixon met with Mao Zedong and announced the start of a new era. "What we have done," said Nixon, "is simply opened the door, opened the door for travel, opened the door for trade." After more than 20 years of hostility, the United States and China agreed to set up normal diplomatic relations.

Other American Presidents have visited China since 1972. In 1984, President Reagan received a warm welcome when he met with Chinese leaders. The two countries agreed to new trade agreements. Some Americans felt that by improving relations with China, the United States was betraying its old ally, Taiwan. However, the United States continued to aid Taiwan.

An End to Détente

Hopes for détente ended in the late 1970s. In June 1979, President Carter met with the Soviet leader, Leonid Brezhnev (BREHZH nehf). They discussed ways to slow the arms race and signed the *SALT II Treaty.* The new treaty ran into trouble in the Senate, however. Some senators argued that the Soviet Union had more nuclear weapons than the United States. By

After President Nixon's trip to China, the United States and China renewed trade and cultural exchanges. Thousands of American tourists have visited China since. Here, an American visiter shows her camera to two Chinese women.

accepting the new SALT limits, they said, the United States would give the Soviets the lead in the arms race.

Invasion of Afghanistan. While the SALT treaty was stalled in the Senate, relations with the Soviet Union took a turn for the worse. On December 27, 1979, Soviet troops invaded Afghanistan, a country bordering the Soviet Union. Soviet troops seized control of the major cities. They backed a government friendly to the USSR. In the countryside, however, Afghan rebels fiercely resisted the Soviet army.

The invasion of Afghanistan shocked Americans. It reminded them of the invasion of Czechoslovakia ten years earlier. "The Soviet Union must pay a price for its aggression," President Carter announced. He withdrew the SALT II Treaty from the Senate and ended grain sales to the Soviet Union. He then announced that the United States would protest the inva-

sion in another way. American athletes would not compete in the 1980 summer Olympic Games in Moscow.

A tough stand. When President Reagan took office in January 1981, he took a tough stand toward the Soviet Union. "Détente," he said, "has been a one-way street." Reagan believed that the United States was serious about détente. However, he felt that the Soviet Union used détente to achieve its own goals.

A new setback to détente came in Poland. In December 1981, the Polish government cracked down on Solidarity, an independent labor union. The Polish government outlawed Solidarity. It then put the country under martial law, or military rule.

President Reagan believed that Polish leaders had acted under pressure from the Soviet Union. The United States protested the arrest of Solidarity leaders. It also put economic pressure on Poland to end martial law.

Skill Lesson 31 Analyzing Newspaper Editorials

In a free society, newspapers play an important role. They print news articles. Most also print unsigned articles, called editorials. An **editorial** is an article that gives a newspaper's opinion on an issue.

Editorials are different from news articles. They mix both facts and opinions. Editorials have at least four different purposes: to criticize, persuade, explain, or praise. Often, editorials criticize a decision or action. Some try to persuade or encourage people to follow a certain course of action. Others explain or interpret an issue or event. Still others praise a person or organization for doing a good job.

1. **Identify the subject of the editorial.** Read the editorials reprinted below to decide what each is about. When you read Editorial A, keep in mind the fact that the white-controlled government of South Africa follows a policy of apartheid (uh PAHRT hayt). That is, it rigidly separates each racial group.

Nonwhites have very little freedom and few political rights. (a) What is the subject of Editorial A? Editorial B? (b) In what newspaper did each appear? (c) When was each printed?

2. **Decide what position or opinion each editorial takes.** Review Skill Lesson 10 (page 232). (a) List two facts included in Editorial A. (b) Does Editorial A approve or disapprove of South Africa's policy? Explain. (c) What opinion does Editorial B express about the arms talks?

3. **Analyze how editorials might influence public opinion.** Newspapers have a large number of readers. Many readers want to know what the editors of the paper think about an issue or event. (a) Which of the four purposes described above do you think Editorial A has? Editorial B? (b) Which editorial do you find most convincing? Why?

 Editorial A

When President Reagan meets today with South African Bishop Desmond Tutu, he should heed the example of 25 congressional Republicans. . . .

In a letter this week to South Africa's ambassador to the United States, the congressmen expressed exasperation with apartheid policies that exclude South African blacks from civil rights and political power. "The reality of apartheid and the violence used to keep it in place," their letter said, undermine the good relations that this country seeks with South Africa's government. Reagan should make the same point. . . .

Minneapolis Star and Tribune, December 7, 1984
Minneapolis, Minnesota

 Editorial B

Moscow and Washington have announced that Secretary of State Shultz and Soviet Foreign Minister Gromyko will meet in Geneva on Jan. 7 and 8. According to the White House statement, they will "enter the new negotiations with the objective of reaching mutually acceptable agreements on the whole range of questions concerning nuclear and other space arms."

So, these are nothing more than talks about talks. They haven't even set the agenda yet for actual arms control. National Security Adviser McFarlane, with nice diplomatic understatement, says, "I would not say that this is a milestone of conclusion but, rather, an opening of a process that will be difficult and sustained over time."

The Dallas Morning News, November 24, 1984
Dallas, Texas

Star Wars. President Reagan wanted to negotiate with the Soviets from a position of strength. He convinced Congress to approve an increase in military spending. His defense program included *Star Wars,* the development of anti-missile weapons for use in space.

Star Wars stirred heated debate. Some scientists argued that this new defense system would be costly and impractical. Many people opposed the spread of nuclear weapons to space. Still others protested that testing of the new system violated a 1972 arms treaty with the Soviet Union.

A Renewal of Détente

Relations between the superpowers improved in 1985. That year, Mikhail Gorbachev (mihk HĪ uhl gor buh CHAWF) became the new Soviet leader. Gorbachev spoke out against the United States on many issues, including *Star Wars.* But at the same time, he was eager to renew détente. His goals for the Soviet Union included easing tight controls over the people and rebuilding the economy. Arms control, he thought, would allow the Soviets to focus on these goals.

Reagan and Gorbachev met face to face at Geneva, Switzerland, in 1985. Then in 1986 at Reykjavik (RAY kyah VEEK), Iceland, the two leaders met again. They discussed arms control and other issues. The talks ended without an agreement. But they paved the way for a third meeting in the United States.

Reducing nuclear arms. Americans gave Gorbachev a warm welcome when he arrived in Washington, D.C., in 1987. This time, Reagan and Gorbachev put aside their differences and signed an arms agreement, called the INF Treaty. In the treaty, the two leaders agreed to get rid of short-range and medium-range missiles. To prevent cheating, each side had the right to inspect the other side's missile sites.

President Reagan, left, and Soviet leader Mikhail Gorbachev, right, met in Washington, D.C., in December 1987. Besides signing the INF Treaty, they agreed to work toward a meeting in Moscow in 1988.

After the Washington meeting, Secretary of State George Schultz held further talks with Soviet Foreign Minister Eduard Shevardnadze (sheh vahrd NAHD zee). They discussed START, a plan to cut in half the number of long-range missiles. Other topics included *Star Wars,* Soviet withdrawal from Afghanistan, and human rights in the Soviet Union. Many Americans were pleased. They saw the talks as signs that détente would continue.

■■■ SECTION REVIEW ■■■

1. **Locate:** Cuba, Berlin, Czechoslovakia, Moscow, China, Taiwan, Afghanistan, Poland.

2. **Define:** superpower, exile, stockpile, détente.

3. What was the Cuban missile crisis?

4. Describe two setbacks to détente in 1979 and 1981.

5. **What Do You Think?** Why do you think the arms race worried many people?

2 War in Southeast Asia

Read to Learn
★ How did the United States get involved in the Vietnam War?
★ Why did many Americans oppose the Vietnam War?
★ What do these words mean: guerrilla, domino theory, escalate?

During the 1960s and 1970s, American attention was focused on Southeast Asia. To fight the spread of communism, American forces were sent to a land they knew little about—Vietnam. American involvement in Southeast Asia sparked fierce debates at home.

Vietnam—A Divided Country

After World War II, the nations of Southeast Asia wanted independence. In Vietnam, Ho Chi Minh (hoh chee mihn) led the fight for independence from France. Because Ho was a communist who had Soviet backing, the United States backed the French with military aid and money. In May 1954, Ho's forces defeated the French.

At a peace conference in Geneva, Vietnam was divided at the 17th parallel. The communists, under Ho Chi Minh, controlled North Vietnam. A noncommunist government backed by the United States ruled South Vietnam. Both sides agreed to hold elections in 1956 to reunite the country.

By 1956, however, Ngo Dinh Diem (noh din ZEE em) had become president of South Vietnam. Diem refused to hold elections. He was afraid that Ho Chi Minh would win. Many Vietnamese admired Ho for leading them to independence.

Growing American involvement. In South Vietnam, Diem refused to take steps to improve the lives of ordinary people. Most Vietnamese were peasants, but the land was owned by a wealthy few. Some peasants joined the *Vietcong,* communist guerrillas supported by North Vietnam. A *guerrilla* (guh RIL uh) is a fighter who uses hit-and-run attacks. Guerrillas do not wear uniforms or fight in large forces.

The success of the Vietcong worried American leaders. They were afraid that South Vietnam would become a communist nation. If South Vietnam fell, they believed, other countries in Southeast Asia would become communist. They argued that other nations would fall to communism like a row of falling dominoes. This idea became known as the *domino theory.*

President Kennedy believed in the domino theory. To help Diem fight the Vietcong, he sent military advisers to Vietnam in 1961. During the 1960s, American involvement grew. After Kennedy's death, President Johnson continued his policies. By 1968, more than 500,000 American troops were fighting alongside the South Vietnamese army. By then, the war had spread to North Vietnam as well.

Bombing of North Vietnam. In July 1964, North Vietnamese torpedo boats attacked two American destroyers in the Gulf of Tonkin. (See the map on page 706.) North Vietnam claimed that the American ships were inside their waters. President Johnson denied the charge.

Congress then passed the *Gulf of Tonkin Resolution.* It allowed the President "to take all necessary measures to repel any armed attack or to prevent further aggression." Johnson used the resolution to order the bombing of North Vietnam.

Antiwar protests. As the fighting *escalated,* or built up, more Americans called for an end to the war. Many believed that the bombing of towns and cities in North Vietnam was wrong.

Thousands of Americans fought and died in Vietnam. On missions like this one, soldiers searched villages and fields where they thought the Vietcong were hiding. Sometimes, they destroyed villages they thought were Vietcong hideouts. Although Americans were trying to help the South Vietnamese government, they often did not have the support of the Vietnamese people.

American planes also bombed targets in South Vietnam. Every night, Americans saw television news programs that showed the horrors of the war. They watched villages burn and saw wounded soldiers, children, and old people. Reporters announced the daily body count—or number of dead—on both sides.

On college campuses, antiwar protests grew louder. Protesters joined in huge marches on Washington. They argued that the United States was wasting lives and money on an unjust war. The South Vietnamese government, they said, was no better than the Vietcong or the North Vietnamese. They pointed out that American bombs were destroying the country they wanted to save.

An end to American involvement. When Richard Nixon was elected President in 1968, he promised to withdraw American troops from Vietnam. But

During the Vietnam War, thousands of Americans were captured as POWs, or prisoners of war. The 1973 cease-fire agreement called for all POWs to be released. Here, Colonel Robert Strim is greeted by his family after many years as a POW.

During and after the 1973 war, President Nixon sent Henry Kissinger, his Secretary of State, back and forth between Israel and the Arab countries. Kissinger's peace efforts became known as *shuttle diplomacy.* He arranged a cease-fire in 1973. But Arab leaders refused to recognize Israel.

Camp David Agreement. In 1977, a major step toward peace occurred. President Anwar el-Sadat of Egypt visited Israel. He met with Israeli Prime Minister Menachem Begin (mehn AHK ehm BAY gihn). Sadat was the first Arab head of state to visit Israel.

When peace talks threatened to break down, President Carter stepped in. He invited Sadat and Begin to Camp David, the President's retreat in Maryland. For two weeks in 1978, the three leaders talked and argued about a framework for a peace settlement.

The *Camp David Agreement* set up a timetable for Israel to return the Sinai Peninsula to Egypt. The two

nations pledged to work toward a solution to the Palestinian refugee problem. In 1979, Sadat and Begin signed a peace treaty in Washington. It was the first agreement between an Arab nation and Israel.

Stumbling blocks to peace. Despite the Camp David Agreement, stumbling blocks to peace remained in the 1980s. Other Arab nations still refused to recognize Israel. After Sadat's assassination, the drive for peace lacked leadership. Israel continued to rule and settle in the occupied lands of the West Bank and the Gaza Strip. And efforts to solve the Palestinian refugee problem came to a halt.

Today, there are more than 3.5 million Palestinians. Most live in refugee camps outside Israel and in the occupied lands. They want to return to their homeland. Many support the *Palestine Liberation Organization,* or PLO. It has waged a guerrilla war against Israel from bases in Lebanon and elsewhere.

In 1988, many Palestinians in the occupied lands took to the streets to protest Israeli rule. The riots called attention to the need for solutions to Arab–Israeli problems. The United States renewed efforts to help bring peace to the area. But many obstacles remained.

Crisis in Iran

In the 1970s, the United States faced another crisis in the Middle East. Iran, an ally of the United States, was shaken by revolution. Iran produces much of the world's oil. It also commands important sea routes through the Persian Gulf. (See the map on page 709.)

Revolution. Since World War II, the United States had supported the shah, or ruler, of Iran in part because he was anticommunist. The shah used money from oil sales to modernize Iran. He built schools, roads, and factories. And he gave women the right to vote.

As a result of their meeting at Camp David, President Sadat of Egypt, left, and Prime Minister Begin of Israel, right, signed a peace treaty. President Carter, center, helped bring about the peace talks. The historic treaty ended a state of war that had existed between the two nations for 30 years.

Many Muslim religious leaders opposed the shah's plans to make Iran like western countries. Others criticized the shah's undemocratic rule. To silence his opponents, the shah used his secret police. The police arrested and tortured critics of the shah.

In 1979, a revolution forced the shah to flee Iran. A Muslim religious leader, the Ayatollah* Khomeini (ī ah TOH luh koh MAY nee) took command. The new ruler forced Iranians to return to the strict traditions of Islam. Khomeini fiercely disliked the United States, which had supported the shah and his efforts to modernize Iran.

Hostages seized. In November 1979, President Carter let the exiled shah enter the United States for medical treatment. This angered the Iranian revolutionaries. A few days later, some young Iranians seized the American embassy in Teheran, the capital of Iran. They took 53 American citizens as hostages. The hostages would be freed, they said, only if the United States sent the shah back to Iran for trial.

President Carter refused this demand. For months, he looked for ways to free the hostages. The crisis dragged on through the election campaign of 1980. The Iranians finally released the hostages on January 21, 1981, minutes after Ronald Reagan was sworn into office as President.

War with Iraq. The freeing of the hostages did not end American worries about Iran. The Ayatollah was anticommunist. Yet the United States feared growing Soviet influence in the Persian Gulf region.

Also, by the 1980s, Iran and its neighbor Iraq were locked in a bloody border war. During the fighting, both countries attacked ships carrying oil through the Persian Gulf. In 1987, President Reagan took steps to protect oil shipments. He reflagged foreign oil tankers as American vessels. And he

Here, Iranian students in Teheran show off one of the 53 Americans they seized in November 1979. For 14 months, President Carter tried to win the release of the hostages in Iran. Freedom finally came in January 1981.

sent American warships to escort the tankers through the gulf.

War-torn Lebanon

Another Middle Eastern trouble spot was Lebanon. This country lies between Israel and Syria. Its population includes different groups of Christians and Muslims. In 1975, civil war broke out among different religious groups.

During the war, Syria invaded Lebanon. Meanwhile, PLO fighters attacked Israel from bases in Lebanon. In 1982, Israel invaded Lebanon to drive out the PLO. Israeli troops swept north to Beirut, the capital of Lebanon.

The United States worked through the United Nations to restore order in Lebanon. In 1982, President Reagan sent United States Marines to Beirut as part of an international peacekeeping force. France, Great Britain, and Italy also sent troops.

---

*Ayatollah means "reflection of Allah [God]." It is a title given to religious leaders in Iran.

In 1982, United States Marines joined an international peace-keeping force in Lebanon. They set up positions like this one near Beirut, the capital. The peace-keeping troops were withdrawn after hundreds were killed by a truck bomb driven into their barracks.

Despite the presence of these troops, the fighting continued. Almost every day, bombs exploded in Beirut. In April 1983, 50 people died when a bomb destroyed the American embassy. Then, on October 23, a truck loaded with explosives drove into the American marines' barracks. More than 230 marines were killed.

The killing led to protests in the United States against American involvement in Lebanon. At the urging of Congress, President Reagan withdrew American troops in 1984. He later advised American civilians to get out of Lebanon to avoid kidnappings and other acts of terrorism.

The United States has continued to play a role in Lebanon. It worked to get Israel to withdraw most of its troops. And it has supported other efforts to restore peace.

===SECTION REVIEW===

1. **Locate:** Israel, Jordan, Lebanon, Syria, Egypt, Sinai Peninsula, Beirut, Iran, Persian Gulf, Teheran, Iraq.
2. **Define:** shuttle diplomacy.
3. How did the 1973 Arab–Israeli war affect the United States?
4. Why did Iranian revolutionaries hold American citizens as hostages?
5. **What Do You Think?** Why do you think the United States wanted to keep peace in the Middle East?

4 America's Neighbors

Read to Learn

★ How has the United States aided nations in Latin America?
★ What are the goals of American policy in Latin America?
★ Why have some American policies caused debate?

A major goal of American foreign policy has been keeping good relations with its neighbors. The United States and Canada have cooperated to solve problems. However, relations with other neighbors in the Western Hemisphere have sometimes been strained.

Relations With Canada

The United States and Canada share a border that is more than 4,000 miles (6,400 km) long. In general, relations between the two countries have been friendly. In the 1950s, the United States and Canada cooperated on building the *St. Lawrence Seaway.* The huge project called for building dams for electric power and deepening the river channel. The seaway opened in 1959. It let ocean-going ships travel as far west as the Great Lakes.

The two countries have cooperated in other ways. They have set up joint defense programs for North America. Canada is also a member of NATO.

The United States and Canada look forward to improved trade relations. In 1987, President Reagan and Prime Minister Mulroney signed a free-trade agreement. It provided for an end to tariffs and other trade barriers between the countries within ten years.

Aid to Latin America

Latin America is made up of more than 40 nations. Each nation has its own government and economy. Some have democratic governments. Many have not. Almost all face severe social and economic problems. Among the most serious problems is the population explosion. Between 1950 and 1980, the population of some countries doubled. Some countries in Latin America cannot produce enough food for their growing populations. There are too few jobs, houses, schools, and hospitals.

Poverty is widespread in Latin America. Many poor people move to the cities looking for jobs and a better life. There, they crowd into tin or cardboard shacks with no heat, light, or water. In these crowded conditions, disease spreads rapidly. Poverty and other problems have led to unrest and violent revolutions in some countries.

Alliance for Progress. The United States has helped Latin American na-

AMERICANS WHO DARED

James Grant

A "silent emergency," warned James Grant, is taking the lives of almost 15 million children each year. Grant is executive director of the United Nations Children's Fund, or UNICEF. An American who was born in China, Grant has a long career in the field of helping developing nations. In a recent UNICEF report, Grant predicted that the agency could bring about a "child survival revolution." A worldwide program to vaccinate and give health care to children would cut the death rate by half. The question Grant asks is "Have we the will to do it?"

tions that were friendly to it. President Kennedy made aid to Latin America a top priority. In 1961, he joined Latin American nations in setting up the *Alliance for Progress.* The aim of the alliance was to improve the lives of millions of people through major social and economic reform.

The United States agreed to contribute $1.3 billion every year for ten

Since 1945, the United States has given billions of dollars in foreign aid to other nations. Much of the aid has gone to developing nations that are working to industrialize. Another form of foreign aid has been the hard work of thousands of Peace Corps volunteers.

During the 1960 Presidential campaign, John Kennedy promoted the idea of a "peace army" dedicated to helping the poor of the world. In March 1961, Congress set up the Peace Corps. The new program sought to build friendships between Americans and the people of other nations. It also wanted to encourage economic growth in developing nations.

Within weeks after the Peace Corps was set up, thousands of Americans, young and old, had volunteered for service. They spent several months learning the language, history, and culture of the countries where they would serve. Then, for two years, they contributed their skills and labor. They worked in cities, towns, and villages of many nations.

Volunteers helped set up health clinics and schools. Farm experts experimented with better ways to grow foods. The Peace Corps volunteer at right taught in a school in Sierra Leone, a country in Africa. Peace Corps volunteers have served in countries in Africa,

Asia, and Latin America. They brought enthusiasm and hope to people who were struggling to improve their standards of living.

★ Why do you think many Americans volunteered for the Peace Corps?

years. Private investors and other countries were to provide additional funds. The alliance planned to use the money to build schools, hospitals, and housing, improve farming, and bring about major economic and social reforms.

OAS. The alliance did not live up to its goals. Yet some progress was made. The United States has given billions of dollars of aid to Latin America through other programs. For example,

it is a major supporter of the *Organization of American States,* or OAS. Through the OAS, it has helped economic progress by investing in transportation and industry.

Despite its aid, the United States is resented by Latin Americans. Over the years, the United States has sent troops into different countries to protect American interests. It has often supported military dictators because they were strongly anticommunist. Also,

American businesses have made large profits from their investments in Latin America.

Danger of Revolution

In Latin America, many poor and even some middle-class people have been attracted to communism. They see it as a way to bring major changes to their countries. The United States has stood firmly against the spread of communism in the Western Hemisphere.

As you have read, Castro made Cuba into a communist nation in 1959. Since then, Cuba has supplied military aid and trained revolutionaries to fight throughout Latin America. The United States called on OAS members to stop trading with Cuba. From 1964 to 1975, the OAS kept up this trade embargo.

Dominican Republic. The United States has used other methods to fight the spread of communism. In 1965, President Johnson sent American marines to the Dominican Republic. Fighting was going on there between the military rulers of the country and Juan Bosch, who supported a democratic government. President Johnson said that the marines were needed to protect Americans living in the Dominican Republic. He was also afraid that Bosch might let communists take over. American troops helped the military rulers stay in power.

Bosch was bitter. "This was a democratic revolution smashed by the leading democracy in the world." Many Americans agreed with Bosch. The United States, they argued, should not help dictators and military rulers stay in power. Others disagreed. They felt that revolutions in Latin America were often supported by communists. The United States, they said, should support noncommunist governments even if they are run by dictators.

Grenada. More recently, President Reagan grew worried about Cuban influence in Grenada. This tiny island nation is located in the Caribbean. Extremists seized power there in October 1983. They were fiercely anti-American and received aid from Cuba.

President Reagan believed that Americans living in Grenada were in

GRAPH SKILL The United States has spent billions of dollars in foreign military and economic aid. By the 1980s, the United States was giving $5 billion a year in economic aid to countries around the world. What part of the world was receiving the most economic aid?

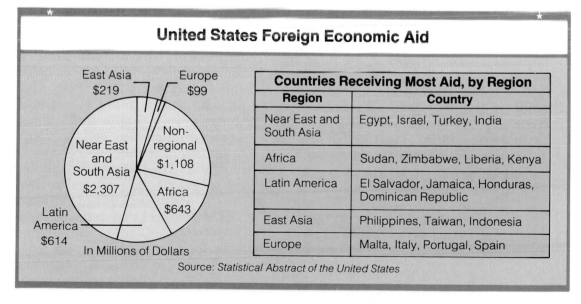

United States Foreign Economic Aid

Pie chart (In Millions of Dollars):
East Asia $219, Europe $99, Non-regional $1,108, Near East and South Asia $2,307, Africa $643, Latin America $614

Countries Receiving Most Aid, by Region	
Region	Country
Near East and South Asia	Egypt, Israel, Turkey, India
Africa	Sudan, Zimbabwe, Liberia, Kenya
Latin America	El Salvador, Jamaica, Honduras, Dominican Republic
East Asia	Philippines, Taiwan, Indonesia
Europe	Malta, Italy, Portugal, Spain

Source: *Statistical Abstract of the United States*

Chapter 31 Review

★ Summary ★

For decades, the United States and the Soviet Union have been rivals for world power. The rivalry has led to an arms race. In the 1970s, the superpowers moved toward détente. They signed agreements to limit the arms race. But by the 1980s, the Cold War seemed to have returned. The superpowers renewed détente in 1985 and signed a new arms treaty.

During this time, wars and revolutions broke out around the world. From the 1960s to 1975, the United States was involved in the Vietnam War. In the Middle East, the United States has tried to bring about peace between Israel and its Arab neighbors. In Latin America, it has worked to improve economic conditions and prevent communist revolutions.

★ Reviewing the Facts ★

Key Terms. Match each item in Column 1 with the correct definition in Column 2.

Column 1
1. détente
2. exile
3. guerrilla
4. domino theory
5. shuttle diplomacy

Column 2
a. person forced to leave his or her own country
b. back-and-forth travel to bring about peace
c. belief that communism would spread from one country to another
d. easing of tensions
e. fighter who uses hit-and-run attacks

Key People, Events, and Ideas. Identify each of the following.
1. Fidel Castro
2. Cuban missile crisis
3. Berlin Wall
4. SALT Agreement
5. Ho Chi Minh
6. Vietcong
7. Gulf of Tonkin Resolution
8. PLO
9. Camp David Agreement
10. Ayatollah Khomeini
11. St. Lawrence Seaway
12. Alliance for Progress
13. OAS
14. Sandinistas
15. Contras

★ Chapter Checkup ★

1. (a) Why did Castro's revolution in Cuba worry the United States? (b) What was the Bay of Pigs invasion?
2. (a) What efforts at détente were made in the 1970s? (b) Why did détente end?
3. (a) How did the United States get involved in Vietnam? (b) Why did it start bombing North Vietnam?
4. (a) How did the fighting spread to Cambodia? (b) What happened to that country after 1975?
5. (a) When was Israel set up? (b) What countries refused to recognize it?
6. Describe the hostage crisis in Iran.
7. Explain how the United States has tried to help the nations of Latin America.
8. (a) Why did the United States help the Contras in Nicaragua? (b) How did this action create debate?

★ Thinking About History ★

1. **Taking a stand.** Do you think President Carter was right to withdraw the SALT II Treaty after the Soviet Union invaded Afghanistan? Explain your stand.

2. **Understanding geography.** On a world map, find Czechoslovakia, Poland, and Afghanistan. (a) Describe their location with respect to the Soviet Union. (b) Why do you think it would be hard for these nations to break free of Soviet control?

3. **Applying information.** Despite massive amounts of aid from the United States, South Vietnam was unable to defeat the Vietcong and North Vietnamese. (a) Why do you think South Vietnam could not stop the Vietcong and the North Vietnamese? (b) How do you think antiwar protests forced the United States to change its policy in Vietnam?

4. **Evaluating.** (a) How has the United States tried to help bring peace to the Middle East? (b) To what extent has it been successful?

5. **Relating past to present.** Compare relations between the United States and Latin America in recent years to relations in the 1890s and early 1900s. (See pages 540–545.) (a) How are they similar? (b) How are they different?

★ Using Your Skills ★

1. **Skimming a chapter.** Practice the skill on skimming a chapter that you learned on page 239. (a) What are the main topics covered in this chapter? (b) What is the general idea of "Rivalry Between the Superpowers" (pages 697–703)?

2. **Map reading.** Study the map on page 706. (a) What countries border Vietnam? (b) Through what countries did the Ho Chi Minh Trail run? (c) What major rivers run through Vietnam?

3. **Graph reading.** Study the graph on page 715. (a) What was the total value of United States foreign economic aid? (b) Did Africa or Latin America receive more aid? (c) What African nation received the most aid? (d) Suggest one reason why Europe received little aid.

4. **Outlining.** Review the outlining skill you learned on page 31. Then prepare an outline of the last two sections of this chapter on pages 708–717. Using your outline, write a summary of the major foreign policy crises the United States has faced in the Middle East and in Latin America.

★ More to Do ★

1. **Exploring local history.** Find two people in your local area who remember the Cuban missile crisis. Interview them about the crisis. Did they approve of President Kennedy's handling of the crisis? Were they frightened by the crisis? How did they feel when it was over?

2. **Organizing a debate.** As a group project, prepare a debate on the following topic: The United States should go ahead with plans to develop nuclear weapons for use in space. You will need to do research on the topic before the debate.

3. **Writing a newspaper editorial.** Review "Search for Peace in the Middle East" (pages 708–712). Then write an editorial for your local newspaper explaining why the United States should not depend on oil from the Middle East.

32

Pioneers of Today and Tomorrow (1960–Present)

Chapter Outline

1 Moving Ahead in Science
2 New Directions in the Economy
3 The New Pioneers

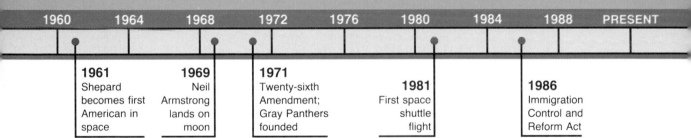

1960	1964	1968	1972	1976	1980	1984	1988	PRESENT

1961
Shepard becomes first American in space

1969
Neil Armstrong lands on moon

1971
Twenty-sixth Amendment; Gray Panthers founded

1981
First space shuttle flight

1986
Immigration Control and Reform Act

About This Chapter

On May 5, 1961, a Redstone rocket blasted off from Cape Canaveral in Florida. Squeezed into a small capsule atop the rocket was Commander Alan Shepard of the United States Navy. The capsule was called *Freedom 7*. It was so tiny that Shepard could hardly move. For 15 minutes after blastoff, the rocket raced into space. When it reached a height of 115 miles (190 km), *Freedom 7* separated from the rocket. With Shepard at the controls, it then parachuted into the Atlantic Ocean.

Millions of Americans watched on television as Shepard became the first American in space. Shepard's flight boosted the confidence Americans felt in their space program. Four years earlier, the Soviet Union had launched *Sputnik,* the first artificial satellite to orbit the earth. A month before *Freedom 7*

went aloft, Yuri Gagarin, a Soviet pilot, had become the first human in space.

Shepard's flight was soon followed by others. Designers built more powerful rockets and larger capsules. In the 1960s, American astronauts trained for missions to the moon. Before the decade ended, Americans landed on the moon.

The moon landing was only one sign that Americans were still pioneering in new fields. For years, the United States has led the world in inventions. Recently, Americans have pioneered in such areas of research as computers, lasers, and advanced medical treatment. Successful breakthroughs in these areas have changed the way people live around the world.

Study the time line above. What event occurred 20 years after Shepard's flight?

In 1975, an American and Soviet satellite joined up in space. This painting shows the Apollo-Soyuz linkup.

1 Moving Ahead in Science

Read to Learn

★ What are some achievements of the American space program?

★ How are computers used in businesses?

★ How have advances in medicine affected Americans?

★ What do these words mean: computer, computer literacy, software, vaccine, antibiotic?

Americans have pioneered in scientific research. They have also made many practical inventions. In the mid-1700s, you will remember, Benjamin Franklin earned fame as an inventor. Thomas Jefferson, second President of the United States, experimented in science and invented many new devices. In the late 1800s, Americans produced hundreds of new machines. Their inventions spurred the growth of American industry.

Today, the nation is a leader in science and technology, or applied science. Dozens of Americans have captured Nobel Prizes in the sciences. American successes have been due in part to the money put into research. Yet in large part, they are due to the pioneer spirit. This spirit has led Americans to explore the world around them.

Exploring Space

In October 1957, many Americans were shocked when the Soviet Union launched *Sputnik,* the first satellite.

—721—

They wondered whether the United States had fallen behind in exploring space. Within a year, however, the United States sent its own satellite, *Explorer 1,* into orbit.

Mission to the moon. In 1960, President Kennedy set high goals for the American space program. "I want you to start on the moon program," he told his space advisers. "I'm going to ask Congress for the money. I'm going to tell them you're going to put a man on the moon by 1970."

Kennedy's request was a tall order. But the *National Aeronautics and Space Administration*, or NASA, went to work. In 1962, astronaut John Glenn orbited the earth three times. By 1968, NASA astronauts had circled the moon in an Apollo spacecraft. Then in 1969, astronauts Neil Armstrong and Buzz Aldrin piloted the *Eagle,* a small lunar landing craft, onto the moon's surface.

With millions of people all over the world watching, Armstrong became the first person to walk on the moon. "That's one small step for a man, one giant leap for mankind," he radioed back to earth. In five more Apollo missions, other American astronauts visited the moon.

Deeper into space. Landing on the moon was one of many space programs. NASA sent unpiloted spacecraft far past the moon. Their goal was to explore other planets. For example, Viking spacecraft sent back detailed pictures of Mars before landing on its surface. In 1981, *Voyager 1* photographed Jupiter and Saturn. It then headed out of the solar system.

Meanwhile, *Voyager 2* explored distant planets with its cameras. It looped around Saturn before heading toward Uranus. From there, it beamed back images to earth. Scientists will spend years analyzing these photos.

Plans for the next century include launching an unmanned spacecraft that will flash through space at 250,000 miles per hour. This spacecraft will travel far beyond the solar system.

Americans have seen amazing photographs from space. At left, astronaut Buzz Aldrin walks on the moon. At right, astronaut Kathryn Sullivan studies the earth as she orbits in the space shuttle *Challenger.*

The Space Shuttle

The space shuttle program was developed for experiments closer to earth. Most spacecraft were made for a single flight. The space shuttle was designed to be reused. The first shuttle, *Columbia,* took off in April 1981. After it returned to earth, mechanics and technicians got it ready to fly again. By 1985, *Challenger* and *Discovery* had joined the shuttle fleet.

On one shuttle flight, scientists produced medicines that could not be made on earth. On another flight, astronaut Sally Ride became the first American woman in space. She used a mechanical arm to catch a wobbling satellite. It was taken on board for repairs back on earth. On still another flight, scientists Kathryn Sullivan and David Leestma put on spacesuits for work outside the shuttle. They tested ways to refuel satellites in space.

A tragic accident altered NASA's plans for a monthly shuttle mission. In January 1986, just seconds after liftoff, the *Challenger* exploded. All seven passengers died, including Christa McAuliffe, a New Hampshire social studies teacher. Investigators uncovered a design problem in the shuttle rocket. Scientists are testing new designs to ensure the safety of future astronauts.

Useful Discoveries

The space program has developed products and gathered useful information. For example, research for space travel has led to the development of freeze-dried foods. Today, people can buy freeze-dried goods in grocery stores. Scientists have developed new fabrics for spacesuits and new ways of insulating spacecraft. Businesses have then produced these materials in forms anyone can use.

Every day, satellites send back information for weather reports. Photographs from spacecraft let mapmakers draw detailed maps of the earth. Satellite photographs have helped locate water in deserts and stores of natural resources. As you read in Chapter 2, satellite photos revealed traces of ancient Maya fields in Guatemala.

The moon missions and probes into outer space also provide useful data. They have helped scientists learn more about the chemical makeup of other planets. With this information, scientists are trying to discover if life as we know it exists on another planet.

The Computer Revolution

The success of the space program has depended in part on computers. *Computers* are machines that process information at lightning-fast speed. In space, computers track and control each step of a flight. On-board computers send information to computers at mission control centers on the ground.

The first computers were built in the 1940s. They were enormous. The Mark I, an early computer, was 8 feet high, 8 feet deep, and 51 feet long. A huge glass frame held together a tangle of switches, vacuum tubes, and relays.

In the 1960s, a big breakthrough in computers came with development of silicon chips. Chips are small units often just the size of a fingernail. Each chip, however, controls electric currents that make the computer work. With chips, scientists could develop small computers that worked very fast.

Business uses. These changes made computers smaller and less expensive. A machine that cost millions of dollars in the 1950s was replaced in the 1980s by one that cost only $10,000. And the new computer was much more powerful.

By the 1980s, the computer revolution was in full swing. Businesses both large and small used computers for payrolls and many other tasks.

Computers took on major roles in routing telephone calls and directing air traffic. They stored large amounts of information for government and corporations. Researchers used computers to design new products and solve complex problems.

Personal computers. Many Americans bought computers for use in their homes. People used them to figure their taxes and plan budgets. They played video games on computers. Children learned spelling, math, reading, and typing on home computers.

Many schools bought computers. *Computer literacy,* or the ability to use computers, was added to the goals of education. Students used different kinds of software. *Software* is the program that tells a computer what to do. Some educational programs had games or quizzes to practice skills.

Questions about computers. As the use of computers spread, many peo-

Today, many American schools have computers in the classroom. Students learn to use computers at an early age.

ple feared its effects. They worried, for example, about the large amount of personal information stored in computers. Could this information be used to violate a person's right to privacy? Also, people wondered about top-secret information in Defense Department computers. Could an enemy find some way to get at this information? Also, breakdowns could occur. Such breakdowns would cause problems in industries that depend on computers.

Computer experts have tried to find ways to ensure that none of these fears come true. Despite worries, computers continue to gain a greater place in people's lives than ever before.

Advances in Medicine

Computers have brought about changes in medicine, too. They help medical researchers by storing and sorting large amounts of information. Doctors can consult computers to find out about the latest research on a disease. A computerized machine called a *CAT-scanner* helps doctors diagnose illnesses. (CAT stands for Computerized Axial Tomography.)

Vaccines and antibiotics. Other advances have taken place in medicine in the past few decades. Among them are vaccines and antibiotics. *Vaccines* are substances that cause a mild form of a disease. They help the body to build up the ability to fight off disease. The use of vaccines has wiped out smallpox and has slowed the spread of other diseases around the world.

Other advances have also increased life expectancy, or how long a person is likely to live. (See the graph on page 725.) During World War II, scientists developed *antibiotics,* substances that kill harmful bacteria. Since then, many new antibiotics have been developed.

Medical technology. Research has led to many other major developments. Through the use of thin glass fibers, called fiber optics, light can be sent around curves and along twisting paths. Doctors can use fiber optics to examine the stomach and bladder.

Powerful microscopes help doctors perform surgery that was once impossible. Surgeons can repair tiny blood vessels or nerves. Sometimes specially trained doctors reattach a hand or arm severed in an accident. This kind of operation is called microsurgery.

Advances in open heart surgery and organ transplants have given many people a second chance at life. Pioneer efforts with artificial hearts have also prolonged the lives of some people.

Superconductors

Recently, scientists have been excited by a new development in physics. After years of work, researchers have made major breakthroughs in superconductors. These materials allow elec-

Computers have many different uses in medicine. Here, a CAT-scanner is used to help with a medical diagnosis. It provides clear pictures of tissues inside the body.

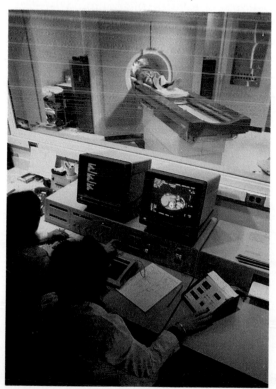

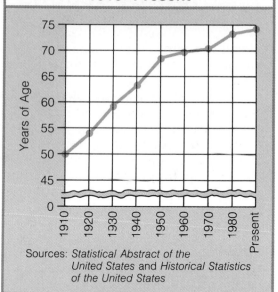

Changes in Life Expectancy 1910–Present

Sources: *Statistical Abstract of the United States* and *Historical Statistics of the United States*

GRAPH SKILL Better medical care is changing life expectancy in the United States. What was the life expectancy of someone in 1910? In 1950? In which ten-year period did life expectancy increase the most?

trical current to flow without any loss of energy.

Scientists hope to use superconductors in practical devices. This technology could have as great an impact on society as the lightbulb. In the next century, the world may see powerful electric cars, trains cruising as fast as planes between many cities, and tremendous savings in energy costs.

SECTION REVIEW

1. **Define:** computer, computer literacy, software, vaccine, antibiotic.
2. (a) How was the space shuttle different from earlier spacecraft? (b) List three useful discoveries of the space program.
3. How has the computer changed people's lives?
4. Describe one breakthrough in medicine.
5. **What Do You Think?** Do you think computers will continue to play an important role in people's lives? Explain.

2 New Directions in the Economy

Read to Learn

★ How does the price of oil affect the American economy?

★ What different sources of energy are available to Americans?

★ What economic problems did the United States face in the 1970s and 1980s?

★ What do these words mean: Petrochemical, solar energy, environmentalist, recession, high technology?

When wagon trains headed west, the vast land seemed endless. To the early settlers, America was a land full of riches, with more than enough for everyone. In the 1970s, this view began to change. True, the land was rich. But its riches were not endless. Many people came to believe that America's resources had to be used carefully.

The Energy Crunch

After World War II, petroleum, or oil, replaced coal as the main source of power for American industry. Oil was cleaner to burn and easier to ship.

Petroleum was refined into gasoline. Gas powered trucks, cars, and buses. Fuel oil ran factory engines and heated buildings. Many chemicals were also made from petroleum. *Petrochemicals,* as they are called, were used to make plastics, fertilizers, and hundreds of other items, from nail polish to phonograph records.

Oil shortages. By the 1960s, Americans imported about one third of the oil they used. Much of the imported oil came from the Arab nations of the Middle East. As a result, the 1973 Arab oil embargo (see page 708) quickly affected the United States. Many gas stations ran out of fuel. Some schools and factories closed because of heating oil shortages.

Effects on Americans. In the 1970s and early 1980s, the oil shortages and price rise contributed to inflation. During a period of inflation, prices rise and the value of money falls. (See page 730.)

During the Arab oil embargo in 1973, long lines such as this one formed at many gas stations. Prices of gas also climbed.

Because oil was used so widely, consumers had to pay the increased cost of gasoline, heating oil, plastics, and fertilizers. Businesses had to charge more for the goods they made.

Americans looked for ways to save energy and use less oil. Congress reduced the speed limit on highways to 55 miles an hour. At this speed, cars used millions of gallons less gasoline. Auto companies made cars that used less fuel. People insulated their homes better to reduce the amount of fuel needed for heating or cooling. Large companies and factories also found ways to conserve, or save, energy.

Between 1973 and 1981, the price of a barrel of oil rose from $4 to $35. But efforts to conserve energy paid off. A decrease in demand for oil, as well as overproduction of oil, led to a glut, or excess, by the mid-1980s. The price of a barrel of oil dropped 50 percent or more. In 1987, Congress allowed certain states to raise the speed limits on some highways.

Other Sources of Energy

The energy crisis taught Americans an important lesson. To ensure the security of the nation, they had to develop other sources of energy.

Coal. The most available substitute for oil was coal. In the 1970s, some industries returned to using coal. But burning coal sends harmful gases into the air. Some companies put "scrubbers" on their smokestacks to filter the smoke. However, scrubbers raised the price of using coal.

Faced with a challenge, engineers have recently developed a new, clean way to burn even low-quality coal. This technology could help reduce acid rain, which results when rain combines with pollution in the air.

The United States has 25 percent of the world's coal reserves. These reserves could provide the energy the nation needs for another 300 years.

Nuclear power. Another source of energy is nuclear power. In the 1950s, the United States began to build nuclear power plants to make cheap electrical power. By 1978, there were more than 70 of these plants.

Some people opposed nuclear power plants. They were concerned about radioactive wastes and possible accidents. In 1979, equipment failed at the *Three Mile Island* nuclear power plant

This photograph of Three Mile Island was taken from an airplane. It shows the huge towers that are part of the cooling system of the nuclear power plant. A failure in the plant's cooling system in 1979 made people aware of problems with nuclear power plants.

near Harrisburg, Pennsylvania. In 1986, an explosion occurred at the Chernobyl (cher NOH buhl) nuclear power plant in the Soviet Union. These incidents increased worries about the safety of nuclear power plants.

Solar energy. Scientists still hope to find low-cost ways to use *solar energy,* or power from the sun. They continue to work on technology for changing energy from the sun into useable power. In the future, people may ride in cars powered by sunlight.

Protecting the American Land

The energy crisis focused attention on the issue of conservation. Citizen groups such as the Friends of the Earth and the Sierra Club pointed out that wastes from factories were polluting the air, land, and water. Factory smokestacks, for example, sent harmful fumes into the air. Some rivers and lakes were so polluted that fish and plant life died. Oil leaks from tankers killed wildlife and ruined beaches.

Many Americans shared the concerns of *environmentalists,* people who work to control pollution and protect the land. In 1970, they joined together to celebrate *Earth Day.* That day, millions of people discussed issues that affected the environment.

Pollution laws. Congress responded to the concerns of citizens. In 1970, it passed the Clean Air Act. The act set stricter standards for factory smokestacks. Other laws were passed to clean up rivers and lower pollution from automobiles. In 1970, Congress also created the *Environmental Protection Agency,* or EPA. The agency's job was to enforce the new laws.

Laws to protect the environment raised serious questions. Who would pay the cost of cleanup—the government or private industry? Some factory owners complained that the new laws made it too costly to stay in business. Where would workers find jobs if factories were forced to close? Should the government interfere in private business by making these laws?

Earth Day was held on April 22, 1970. Many Americans made special efforts to let fellow citizens know about the problems of pollution. These Boston University students have collected a pile of rubbish that had "polluted" their city's streets.

Disposal of trash is a growing concern of many communities. A "garbage barge" in New York, shown above, waited for months before it could find a place to unload. Recycling projects, such as the one shown at right, can help limit trash.

Tons of trash. Concern for the environment raised other issues. The Clean Air Act ended the burning of trash by most communities. Instead, they deposited trash in landfills, or dumps. But the size and wealth of the United States has allowed Americans to have a carefree attitude toward garbage. Americans produce more trash per person than any other society. Experts predict that most landfills will be full by the late 1990s.

Efforts are already being made to limit the problem. More and more communities require residents and businesses to separate items that can be recycled, or reused. Paper, aluminum cans, newspapers, and glass are among these products.

Communities are once more looking at incineration, or burning, as a means of getting rid of their trash. Improved incinerators have solved many earlier pollution problems. Also, the heat from these new incinerators is used to produce steam and electricity. Another byproduct of incineration is tons of reusable scrap metal.

Economic Challenges

The United States economy has produced a higher standard of living for more people than that of any other

An Wang

A leading name in the field of advanced electronics is a Chinese-born inventor, An Wang. Wang left China in 1945 to study physics in the United States. By age 28, he had earned a Ph.D. and had taken out a patent for a device that stored memory in computers. This was the first of many ideas that made his fortune. In 1951, Wang sold his patent to IBM and started his own company. Since then, he has invented such electronic gadgets as the first digital scoreboard for a sports stadium. In the 1970s, he pioneered word processors for offices. By the 1980s, he was selling Wang office systems to countries around the world.

major industrial nation. The growth of the economy has continued despite some periods of recession. A *recession* is a mild depression. During a recession, business slows down temporarily and some workers lose their jobs.

Inflation and recovery. During the Carter years, Americans faced rapid inflation as well as a recession. The inflation had several causes. In the 1960s, the government spent billions on the Vietnam War. Social programs such as the Great Society were also costly. Government spending fueled inflation.

The Arab oil embargo pushed prices up still further. Even food prices rose because the cost of gasoline for tractors, fertilizers, and heating oil for food-processing plants went up.

Every President from Richard Nixon to Ronald Reagan worked to end inflation. During his first term, President Reagan reduced government spending and cut taxes in an effort to spur the economy. (See page 680.) But the economy continued to stall. Unemployment rose to more than 10 percent—the worst jobless rate since the Great Depression. At the same time, however, inflation fell from 13 percent to less than 5 percent.

By 1985, the economy had recovered. Businesses expanded, and unemployment began to fall. By 1987, it had dropped below 6 percent.

Foreign competition. During the recession of the 1980s, Americans saw that the economy faced other problems. Among them were foreign competition and outdated factories. Today, large corporations sell in a world marketplace. The United States must compete with other nations, such as Japan, Germany, South Korea, and Taiwan.

Recently, American companies have invented many new products, such as advanced computers or medical equipment. Foreign competitors have found ways to make the same goods more cheaply. Often, they pay their workers less than American workers. So it costs them less to make the goods.

Since the 1960s, competition from Japan has hurt American companies.

Americans have bought billions of dollars' worth of cameras, automobiles, radios, and tape recorders from Japan. Many Japanese factories are newer and more efficient than American factories. So they have been able to produce goods such as steel more cheaply than American companies.

Trade deficit. A trade deficit occurs when a nation buys more goods from foreign countries than it can sell to them. The United States has faced a trade deficit recently. To help solve the problem, American companies have begun to modernize their factories to make them more efficient. In the meantime, companies have asked the government to limit foreign imports.

Some people argue that Americans should let older industries lose out to foreign competition. Instead, they say, Americans should concentrate on *high technology*, or advanced electronic industries.

In universities and company headquarters, scientists and researchers have developed new high-technology products for Americans to sell worldwide. For example, companies such as IBM, Wang, and Digital have sold their computer products around the globe. Some experts think that the development of superconductors could give the United States an important edge in foreign trade.

A changing work force. Competition from other industrial nations has led to a decline in manufacturing jobs in the United States. Growth in the American economy has shifted to the service industries. A service industry is any industry that does not produce goods. Service industries include banking, research, and health care. At present, the service industries are expanding rapidly. Nine out of ten new job openings are in these areas.

The move from heavy manufacturing to service industries offers new opportunities for the future. People will learn to program, monitor, and repair manufacturing systems. New technology will allow factories to produce goods more efficiently.

■ SECTION REVIEW ■

1. **Define:** petrochemical, solar energy, environmentalist, recession, high technology.
2. How did oil shortages in the 1970s affect Americans?
3. (a) List two sources of energy besides oil. (b) What problems does each have?
4. Why has Japan been able to compete strongly with American companies?
5. **What Do You Think?** Do you think the federal government should help pay for the cleanup of the environment? Explain your stand.

---

3 The New Pioneers

Read to Learn
★ How have new technologies provided new popular pastimes?
★ How is the American population changing?
★ What recent changes have been made in immigration law?
★ What do these words mean: laser, illegal alien?

The new technologies developed by Americans have fascinated people around the world. Popular American movies such as *Star Wars* and *Starman* showed the influence of space-age technology. In *Star Wars,* robots played alongside humans in a movie full of amazing special effects. In *Starman,* a visitor from another galaxy reaches earth. The visitor has come to earth after hearing a broadcast by a Voyager spacecraft.

Popular Pastimes

In the 1980s, "high tech" invaded the daily life of millions of Americans. People cooked in microwave ovens. They watched movies at home on video cassette recorders, or VCRs.

Many young people spent their free time playing video games. Games such as Pac-Man and Space Invaders used computer technology to keep track of winning scores. Other technology, such as lasers, affected popular pastimes. *Lasers* are devices that send out very strong, narrow beams of light. At first, they were used in industry and medicine. Today, rock groups such as Pink Floyd and YES also use lasers to create dazzling images while they sing.

Music for the times. In 1983, the first compact disk player was sold. It was the latest system for playing music. Instead of using a phonograph needle as in the past, the new machine used lasers to "read" disks. The disks were far sturdier than records. They did not scratch or wear out.

Popular music has changed with the times, too. In the 1960s, folk singers like Bob Dylan and Arlo Guthrie wrote protest songs calling for peace and justice. Groups such as the Beatles poked fun at society.

Popular music drew on many traditions. Many black singers of the 1960s had their roots in the gospel-singing tradition. Detroit's "Motown" sounds led the way. Singers like the Supremes, the Temptations, and Stevie Wonder attracted a wide audience.

In the 1970s, amplified rock took over. The "disco" music of this period drew on Latin traditions. By the 1980s, popular music took on a new form— music videos. These were short films for TV showing rock music groups performing in scenes of fantasy.

Fads and fancies. Every decade has its fads and fancies. In the 1950s, young people twirled hula hoops around their waists. In the 1970s, roller skaters whirled along the streets. They moved to the beat of popular music playing on their headsets. Disco dancing was popular, too. In the early 1980s, young break dancers awed audiences with their fast acrobatic movements. And the sound of rap music filled the airwaves.

Classical art forms. Many Americans preferred classical music to popular sounds. By the 1980s, the United States had more symphony orchestras than any other nation. In cities from Minneapolis to Houston and from Boston to Atlanta, audiences heard the finest musicians play. Ballet and modern dance companies sprang up in many cities. The all-black Dance Theatre of Harlem toured the country. Companies such as Ballet Hispanico explored ethnic dance traditions.

Sports and Fitness

Since the 1950s, Americans have had more leisure time than ever before. Workdays were shorter and vacations were longer than in the past. With more free time, interest in sports grew tremendously. During the 1970s, professional baseball, football, hockey, and basketball all added teams to their leagues.

New technology affected sports. Some cities built huge domed stadiums such as the Astrodome in Houston. This meant teams could play in any weather. Artificial grass also changed the games. Millions of sports fans watched games on TV. They enjoyed the benefits of such new techniques as instant replay to cover the games. Spectacular events such as the Olympic Games were beamed by satellite around the world.

A major change in sports was the increased role of women. In 1970, only

Americans can choose from a rich variety of cultural activities. At left, graceful dancers of the Boston Ballet perform in *The Nutcracker*. At right, Michael Jackson dazzles audiences with his energetic music.

about 7 percent of high school athletes were women. By 1980, that figure had jumped to 35 percent. Tennis stars like Billie Jean King and Chris Evert showed that women could play world-class tennis and attract large audiences. Women also set new records in track and field, golf, and other sports.

Americans were more than spectators when it came to sports. They looked for ways to stay physically fit. People jogged on country roads and along busy city streets. Health spas became a booming business. More people paid attention to their diets. Many Americans chose natural foods that were low in fats. Fast-food restaurants picked up on the nation's health kick and added salad bars to their menus.

Concern for fitness was often tied in to an interest in the outdoors. Families camped in national parks. They backpacked on mountain trails. New technology helped by providing lightweight packs and tents.

The Changing Population

In recent decades, the American population has changed, too. The baby boomers of the 1950s became young adults during the turbulent 1960s. Many of them marched for civil rights and protested against the Vietnam War.

Voting age lowered. Young Americans had a strong influence on politics in the 1960s and 1970s. Many of them worked to change the voting age. In most states, only people over age 21 could vote. Young people wanted to have the voting age lowered to age 18. If 18-year-olds could be drafted to fight in Vietnam, they argued, they should be allowed to vote. In 1971, the *Twenty-sixth Amendment* was ratified. This amendment gave the vote to all citizens over age 18.

By the 1980s, the baby boomers had become adults. Many had gone to college. So they were the best-educated generation in American history. Some chose to live in cities, not in the suburbs as their parents had.

Smaller families. The baby boomer generation tended to marry at a later age than their parents. Often, both husband and wife had careers. With two incomes, these families enjoyed a high standard of living. They could afford luxuries such as two cars, stereos, home computers, and vacation travel.

In the 1970s and 1980s, however, families tended to have one or two children instead of three or more. As the birthrate fell in the 1980s, less than 30 percent of the American population was under age 20. America has always been a country with a large population of young people. Today, this trend is changing.

Older Americans. Change is evident in other ways. Today, a larger percentage of Americans are over age 65 than ever before. Thanks to better medical care, people live longer.

Older Americans have contributed to progress in many ways. Some, like Captain Grace Hopper of the United States Navy, continued to work. Hopper was an early pioneer in computers. Up to her 70s, she remained on active duty. Other older Americans put their knowledge and experience to good use in the arts, sciences, and education. President Reagan, for example, was 72 when he was reelected in 1984.

In 1971, Margaret Kuhn founded the *Gray Panthers.* It is an organization made up of people of all ages that works to end discrimination against

Older Americans have organized groups like the Gray Panthers to stand up for their rights. Here, older Americans hold a rally in Sacramento, California. They are demonstrating for a better system of national health insurance.

No one knows exactly what will happen in the future. However, people often make forecasts, or predictions, based on trends that are already evident today.

Long-term planners in business and government make forecasts in order to predict what goods and services will be needed in the future. They make their forecasts for 5, 10, 20, or even 50 years ahead.

The graphs at right show forecasts for the American population.

1. **Identifying a trend.** As you learned in Skill Lesson 4 (page 81), a trend can be an upward or downward movement over time. Review the population trends discussed in this chapter. Then study the graphs at right. Median means in the middle. In Graph 2, half the population is above and half is below the median age. (a) Describe two trends shown in Graph 1. (b) Describe one trend shown in Graph 2.

2. **Decide how trends affect long-term planning.** (a) According to Graph 1, will population growth ever slow down? Explain. (b) How might a slowdown in population growth affect planning for the future? (c) How will the expected rise in the median age of the population affect planning?

3. **Forecast possible future developments.** Choose one of the trends discussed in this chapter or shown on the graphs at right. Research the trend in current magazines, newspapers, or census reports. Then write a paper in which you describe possible future developments in this trend. Decide which of the possible developments is most likely to happen. Explain your conclusion in your paper.

GRAPH 1

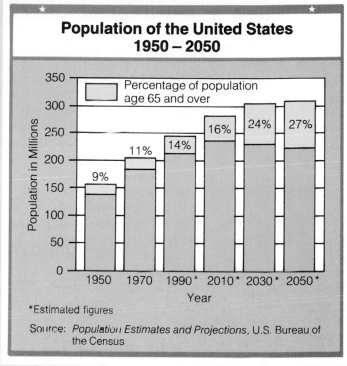

Population of the United States 1950 – 2050

*Estimated figures

Source: *Population Estimates and Projections*, U.S. Bureau of the Census

GRAPH 2

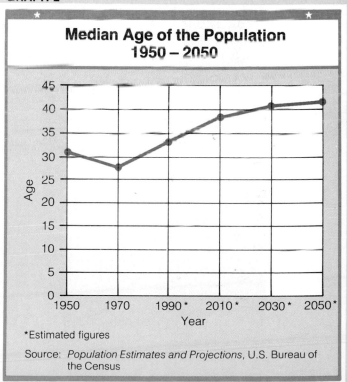

Median Age of the Population 1950 – 2050

*Estimated figures

Source: *Population Estimates and Projections*, U.S. Bureau of the Census

older Americans. The Gray Panthers have called for an end to laws that make people retire at a certain age.

Concerns. Millions of older Americans enjoy the benefits of retirement. However, they worry about the effects of rising prices, especially for medical care. In the early 1960s, a patient paid about $35 a day for a hospital bed. By the 1980s, the cost had jumped to about $250 a day. Medicare, the government health insurance program, pays some costs. Yet individuals have to pay the rest.

Another concern of older Americans has been the Social Security system. As you have read, this system pays benefits to retired workers. However, Social Security benefits have not always kept up with rising prices. To older people who have no other income, this has posed great hardship.

In 1935 when the Social Security system was set up, 42 people paid in to the system for every person who collected benefits. But today, the percentage of young people in the population is dropping. As a result, only 3 people pay in for every person who collects. The Social Security system will face even more strain when the baby boomers reach retirement.

Congress passed a law in 1983 reforming the Social Security system. The act delayed certain payments and raised social security taxes. The government continues to search for ways to ensure Social Security benefits for future generations.

Social Issues

In the past 30 years, Americans have adjusted to a changing world. The civil rights movement expanded people's idea of equality. The Vietnam War tested America's role in world affairs. Charges of corruption focused attention on honesty in government and business. The existence of hunger and poverty showed the need for people to help one another.

Traditional values. Many young adults of the 1960s and 1970s became involved in these issues. In their view, society and its leaders had lost direction. It was up to their own generation, they felt, to set new standards. Among the causes they supported were the struggle for civil rights and demonstrations for peace.

By the late 1970s, young people had different concerns. They turned away from social and political causes. Instead, they looked to their own well-being. New cars, stylish clothes, and vacations were seen as needs rather than luxuries. Some Americans now

Many American families look forward to spending time together. Here, family members study travel information to plan a vacation.

It was a tired group of people who got off the chartered bus in New York City. They were not in front of a major hotel in a classy midtown neighborhood. Instead, these Habitat for Humanity volunteers were looking for the rooms they would share in a rundown part of town. Armed with hammers and nails, they would soon wage war against poverty and homelessness.

Habitat for Humanity is a Christian organization that renovates or builds homes in poor neighborhoods. Volunteers have worked on Habitat projects in 141 cities in the United States.

Among the workers are people whose own homes have been built by Habitat. One such worker was Jessica Wallace, who devoted time to a Habitat project in Chicago after she received a home in New York. The skills she learned on the job encouraged her to become a carpenter's apprentice.

Habitat dwellings are sold at no profit to low-income people. The residents receive interest-free loans, which they have 20 years to repay. In return, they give their labor for other projects. According to one volunteer carpenter, former President Jimmy Carter, "The entire project is designed in accordance with biblical teachings. . . . It has a strong connotation of human rights, justice, car-

ing for people who are poor, and a willingness to share blessings with those who are needy."

The organization has provided hope and pride for people who otherwise might not have a chance for a decent home. As stated by Habitat's founder, Millard Fuller, "The idea of Habitat involves more than just building homes. We're trying to build the Kingdom of God on Earth. We believe that God does not want people living like rats."

★ How has Habitat for Humanity improved the lives of people?

worried that young people were selfish and uncaring.

Leaders of the 1980s blamed national problems on a loss of traditional values. They called for a return to patriotism, honesty, and concern for others. Some people thought that government should take an active role in promoting values. Others disagreed. They felt that values were personal matters and should be left to churches and the family.

Caught in the midst of a changing society was the family. Many mothers worked outside the home. Children were tended by day-care workers or babysitters. Americans sought to strengthen family life to preserve an important source of children's moral education.

Education. The Soviet launch of *Sputnik* in 1957 drew attention to American schools. Critics called for more mathematics and science education. In the 1960s, the federal government supported special programs. One program, Head Start, aimed to prepare needy preschoolers for elementary school. At the same time, educators experimented with new courses to capture student interest.

During the 1980s, there was a new wave of interest in educational reform. Many studies recommended tougher standards and more schoolwork. Since then, many states have increased requirements for high school graduation. "Back to basics" became the key word for reform.

Education will continue to be a concern. As a democracy, the United States depends on educated voters to choose leaders and make decisions. Now that technology is more and more important to the economy, the nation also needs an educated work force.

Public health. Health care has become a large part of federal and state budgets. For this and other reasons, issues of public health are important to everyone.

One health concern is the use of illegal drugs. Drug use increases the number of days workers are absent. It also affects the progress of students. Powerful drugs such as heroin and crack can lead to disability or death.

The sharing of needles by drug users is tied to the spread of AIDS (acquired immune deficiency syndrome). Victims of AIDS require long-term health care. Either through medical insurance or government aid, society will have to pay the cost of this deadly disease.

Recently, the link between smoking and heart and lung disease has sparked public debate. Local laws ban smoking in public buildings and in work areas. They also require nonsmoking sections in restaurants and theaters. Federal law has limited smoking in airplanes. Smokers claim that these laws violate their rights. Nonsmokers argue that they should not have to inhale someone else's smoke.

The widespread use of crack, a highly addictive drug, has increased concern about drug abuse. The message in this poster is a simple, but powerful, warning of the dangers of crack.

Americans on the Move

Many older Americans move to the Sunbelt when they retire. The *Sunbelt* is the band of states from Florida to California that have mild climates. The migration of older people to the Sunbelt is part of a larger population shift. Today, as in the past, Americans are on the move. High heating costs have spurred industries to shift to the Sunbelt. People have followed the jobs.

The Sunbelt and the Frostbelt. As the map on this page shows, the shift to the Sunbelt continues the tradition of Americans moving westward. In 1960, only two of the ten largest American cities were in the South or West. By 1980, five of the top ten were Los Angeles, Houston, Dallas, Phoenix, and San Diego.

In the decade from 1970 to 1980, the population in the West grew by nearly 24 percent. The population in the Northeast and Midwest, an area sometimes called the Frostbelt, grew by only 2 percent. However, changing economic conditions have helped the Northeast.

MAP SKILL In the 1970s, many Americans moved to the Sunbelt. As this map shows, the population of states in the Sunbelt increased. Name two states whose population grew by more than 30 percent. In what squares on the grid map is each of these states located?

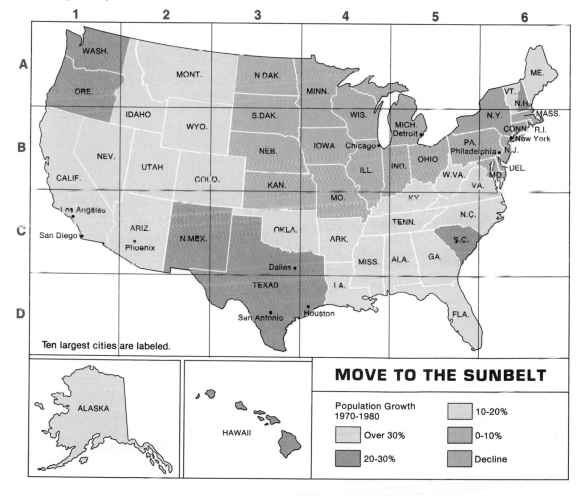

Ten largest cities are labeled.

MOVE TO THE SUNBELT

Population Growth 1970–1980

Over 30%

20–30%

10–20%

0–10%

Decline

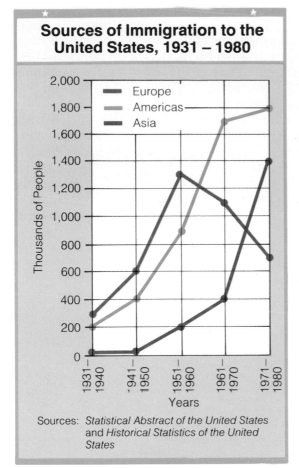

Sources of Immigration to the United States, 1931 – 1980

Thousands of People (y-axis: 0, 200, 400, 600, 800, 1,000, 1,200, 1,400, 1,600, 1,800, 2,000)

Legend:
- Europe
- Americas
- Asia

Years (x-axis: 1931–1940, 1941–1950, 1951–1960, 1961–1970, 1971–1980)

Sources: *Statistical Abstract of the United States* and *Historical Statistics of the United States*

GRAPH SKILL The United States is often called a nation of immigrants. Ever since the first Americans crossed the Bering Sea 70,000 years ago, newcomers have been settling this land. In recent years, the patterns of immigration have changed. Between 1971 and 1980, where did the largest number of immigrants come from?

The area around Boston has become a center for high-tech industries. And international trade has spurred the economy of New York.

The new immigration. By the mid-1980s, there were more than 236 million Americans. As in the past, America's population was growing in part because of a tide of newcomers. They flocked to America hoping to share in its dream of a better life. However, the pattern of immigration has changed in recent years.

From the 1920s to the early 1950s, immigration laws sharply limited the number of newcomers to America. In 1965, Congress changed these laws to let more people enter the United States. The new immigration laws made it easier for non-Europeans to enter the country. Between 1965 and 1984, almost a half million immigrants entered the country legally each year. During the 1970s, many came from Asia, especially from Vietnam. The largest group of immigrants, however, came from Latin America.

Immigration reform. In recent years, millions of people have entered the United States without legal permission. Most of the *illegal aliens* have fled poverty or harsh governments at home. Some cross the border from Mexico or Canada. Others come to the United States as tourists and then simply remain in the country. In 1983, for example, more than one million people were caught trying to enter the country illegally. By 1985, at least 6 million illegal aliens lived in the United States.

For years, Congress debated what to do about the rising number of illegal aliens. In 1986, Congress took action. It passed the Immigration Reform and Control Act. The act allowed illegal aliens who lived in the United States before January 1, 1982, to remain and apply for citizenship. But to discourage further illegal immigration, the act imposed heavy fines on businesses that hired illegal aliens.

Many Hispanics opposed the act. They claimed that employers might refuse to hire anyone who appeared to be a foreigner. But since the act was passed, the government has tried to educate the public about the terms of the law.

Challenges of the future. Today, as in the past, newcomers have contributed to the growth and strength of

Each year, thousands of immigrants become citizens of the United States. Many are sworn in at large ceremonies such as this one in Miami, Florida. At the Orange Bowl Stadium there, almost 10,000 people took the oath of allegiance to the United States in September 1984.

America. Some immigrants have met prejudice. Like immigrants in other times, they have often lived in ethnic neighborhoods. However, as newcomers learned English, they and their children have moved into the mainstream of American life.

Today, Americans face many challenges as they head into the 21st century. Young and old, newcomers and long-settled citizens try to meet these challenges.

In this book, you have read about the events and developments that have shaped the American nation. In 1992, people throughout the Western Hemisphere will celebrate the 500th anniversary of the voyage of Columbus. The

pioneering spirit that sent sailors across the Atlantic continues to launch Americans into new ventures. New generations build on past traditions and become the pioneers of the future.

SECTION REVIEW

1. **Define:** laser, illegal alien.
2. Describe two ways that new technology affected daily life.
3. How have sports changed in recent years?
4. What are two concerns shared by older Americans?
5. **What Do You Think?** Why do you think it is hard to stop illegal aliens from entering the country?

Chapter 32 Review

★ Summary ★

In recent years, Americans have continued to pioneer in many areas. The space program has contributed useful inventions to daily life. The widespread use of the computer has changed the way Americans live.

In the 1970s, the energy crisis was one of a series of economic problems that Americans faced. Among them were recession, inflation, and foreign competition. President Reagan brought inflation under control.

The American population, too, is changing. The baby boomers of the 1950s have grown up. The number of older Americans has also increased. At the same time, newcomers have entered this country from all over the world.

★ Reviewing the Facts ★

Key Terms. Match each term in Column 1 with the correct definition in Column 2.

Column 1	Column 2
1. computer	a. chemical product made from petroleum
2. software	b. machine that processes information very fast
3. vaccine	c. mild depression
4. petrochemical	d. program that tells a computer what to do
5. recession	e. substance that causes a mild form of a disease

Key People, Events, and Ideas. Identify each of the following.

1. Alan Shepard
2. NASA
3. Neil Armstrong
4. *Voyager 1*
5. *Columbia*
6. Sally Ride
7. CAT-scanner
8. Three Mile Island
9. Earth Day
10. EPA
11. Billie Jean King
12. Twenty-sixth Amendment
13. Gray Panthers
14. Sunbelt
15. Frostbelt

★ Chapter Checkup ★

1. Describe the successes in the American space program.
2. (a) When were the first computers built? (b) How have they changed over time?
3. (a) How have vaccines and antibiotics affected people's lives? (b) What new instruments help surgeons?
4. (a) Why did Americans seek new sources of energy in the 1970s? (b) How did they try to conserve energy?
5. (a) Why did many Americans become concerned about the environment in the 1960s and 1970s? (b) What was done to help clean up the environment?
6. (a) List two causes of the inflation of the later 1970s. (b) How did President Reagan try to end the inflation?
7. (a) What changes were made in education in the 1960s? (b) What reforms were recommended in the 1980s?
8. (a) Why have many Americans chosen to live in the Sunbelt? (b) How has the move to the Sunbelt affected cities in the South and West?

★ Thinking About History ★

1. **Evaluating.** Do you think the benefits of the space program outweigh its huge costs? Explain your position by evaluating both sides of the issue.

2. **Understanding the economy.** (a) How has foreign competition hurt American businesses? (b) How would raising tariffs on imports help American businesses? (c) How might raising tariffs hurt American businesses?

3. **Relating past to present.** (a) How is the move to the Sunbelt today similar to the westward movement of early settlers? (b) How is it different?

4. **Learning about citizenship.** (a) Why do you think Americans today and in the past have sometimes resented newcomers? (b) How do you think newcomers contribute to the growth of America?

★ Using Your Skills ★

1. **Placing events in time.** Study the time lines on page 720 and on pages 648–649. (a) During which decade did Americans first land on the moon? (b) Name one event that happened in the same decade in which you were born. (c) Choose one event on the time line and explain its long-term effects.

2. **Graph reading.** Study the graph on page 725. (a) What is the subject of the graph? (b) Describe the trend in life expectancy since 1910.

3. **Ranking.** List four events or developments in science and technology that you have read about in this chapter. Then rank them according to which ones you think are the most important. Explain your ranking.

4. **Making a generalization.** Based on your study of American history this year, make three generalizations about trends in American life since the 1600s. For each generalization, list three or four facts to support it.

★ More to Do ★

1. **Working with a computer.** On a computer at school or home, write a short program on some aspect of American history. Then present your program to the class.

2. **Researching.** Find out more about one of the recent advances in medicine. Then write a report about the advance and how it affects people's lives.

3. **Making posters.** Choose the ten events you think are most important in American history. Then make a series of posters to illustrate those events. Each poster should show why you think the event is important.

4. **Writing a diary.** Imagine that George Washington or Martha Washington returned to the United States today. Write a series of diary entries that show what one of them might think of the country in the 1980s.

5. **Exploring local history.** Obtain information from the Chamber of Commerce about the people, industries, schools, hospitals, and recreation programs in your city or town. Prepare an illustrated pamphlet about these features that could be used to attract new residents and businesses.

Unit 10 Review

Chapter 29 After World War II, a cold war developed between the United States and the Soviet Union. At home, the country returned to a peacetime economy. As the population boomed, many American families moved to the suburbs.

Chapter 30 In the 1960s, Kennedy and Johnson introduced programs to end poverty and protect the civil rights of all Americans. The 1970s and 1980s saw the Watergate affair, Carter's human rights policy, and Reagan's conservative approach to government. In this period, many different groups pressed for equal rights.

Chapter 31 Since the 1960s, the Cold War influenced American foreign policy. In the 1970s, the policy of détente eased tensions for a short time. The Vietnam War created bitter debate at home and abroad. In the 1980s, the superpowers renewed détente.

Chapter 32 Inventions such as the computer have changed the way Americans live. In the 1970s and 1980s, Americans faced inflation and unemployment. However, new industries are today helping the economy grow. The American population is changing with more people living longer.

★ **Unit Checkup**

Choose the word or phrase that best completes each of the following statements.

1. The organization set up to solve world conflicts is the
   (a) PLO.
   (b) Alliance for Progress.
   (c) United Nations.

2. Johnson's poverty program was the
   (a) New Frontier.
   (b) Great Society.
   (c) Fair Deal.

3. In 1973, Wounded Knee was occupied by the
   (a) Sandinistas.
   (b) Contras.
   (c) AIM.

4. President Carter brought Egypt and Israel together in the
   (a) Camp David Agreement.
   (b) Helsinki Agreement.
   (c) Gulf of Tonkin Resolution.

5. Congress passed an immigration reform bill in 1986 that
   (a) allowed some illegal aliens to apply for citizenship.
   (b) encouraged businesses to hire illegal aliens.
   (c) increased quotas for immigrants.

★ **Building American Citizenship**

1. In the 1970s, President Carter cut off aid to some countries in Latin America that violated the human rights of their citizens. His actions were criticized because these countries were supporters of the United States. What policy do you think the United States should take toward an ally that violates the human rights of its citizens?

2. In the 1980s, President Reagan called for the government to reduce its role in the lives of American citizens, cut back on spending for social programs, and increase spending on military defense. Choose one of these goals and find out more about why he supported it. Then decide whether you agree or disagree with his goal. Explain your position.

Read the excerpt from the editorial in the *Orlando Sentinel*. Then answer the questions below.

1. What is the subject of the editorial?

2. List two statements of fact in the editorial.

3. List two statements that express an opinion.

4. Does the editorial criticize or praise the President?

5. What do you think is the point of view of the editors of this newspaper with regard to arms control? Give evidence to support your answer.

The Orlando Sentinel,
February 27, 1983
Orlando, Florida

Those urging President Reagan to be more flexible in his approach to nuclear arms negotiation must be encouraged by his Monday speech to the United Nations.

It contained strong indications that as the United States prepares to deploy a new generation of nuclear weapons in Western Europe, an agreement limiting those arms might yet be struck in Geneva. Certainly the general tone of his speech, coupled with three arms offers, allows us to be far more optimistic in our hopes for an agreement.

History Writer's Handbook

Writing a One-Paragraph Answer

You may use the following checklist to prepare and write a one-paragraph answer. Refer to earlier lessons if you need help with any of the steps.

1. Analyze the question. Find the key word and other clues in the question. Determine what the key word is telling you to do. Take note of the topic limits set by the other clues.

2. Write a topic sentence that states the main idea of the answer. Try to reword the question as a topic sentence.

3. Select information that supports the main idea. Keep in mind the key word and the limits of the topic while making your selection. You might make a list of possible supporting information and then cross out items that you cannot use. Make sure you have enough information.

4. Arrange the supporting information in a logical order. Consider time order, comparison order, order of importance, or cause-and-effect order. If you cannot use one of these orders, the topic sentence or the supporting information might suggest a logical order.

5. Write detail sentences to present the supporting information. Use transitions to show the order you are using.

6. Check your answer. If necessary, lengthen or shorten sentences for smoothness. Correct any mistakes in grammar and spelling.

Practice Using the checklist, write a one-paragraph answer for the following question. *Compare the two opposing camps in Europe after World War II.* (See page 655 for information.)

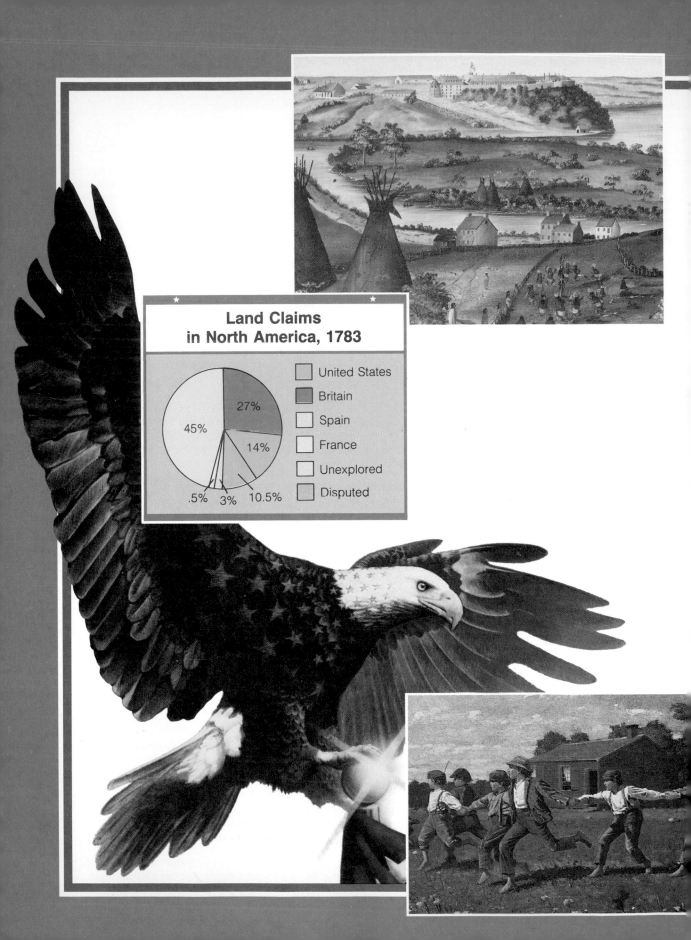

Land Claims
in North America, 1783

- United States
- Britain
- Spain
- France
- Unexplored
- Disputed

45%

27%

14%

.5%   3%   10.5%

REFERENCE SECTION

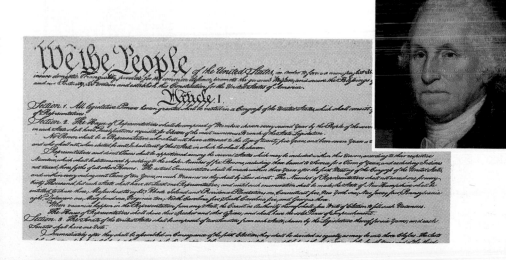

North America Before 1500

The first Americans discovered a land of endless diversity when they traveled across North America. The land itself ranges from lush coastal plains to high rugged mountain peaks, from deep forest to barren desert. As the earliest Americans spread across the two continents, they learned to use the land and what it offered. Hundreds of different cultures developed. The map at right shows some of these cultures. Study the map, chart, and illustrations. Then answer these questions:

1. Which Indian nations were part of the Southwest cultural group?

2. Which illustrations represent Indian nations found in the Middle America cultural group?

3. Why would the spirit of the sun be important to the Bella Coola in the winter?

4. What geographic characteristics of the Eastern Woodlands are shown in the picture of the Algonquin village?

5. Review what you learned about Native American cultures in Chapter 2. Then study the chart at right. Which pictures show the influence of climate or geography on the culture of the groups shown on the map?

Mayan women were skilled weavers. Here, one end of a loom is attached to the woman's waist and the other to a tree.

Environment of Early American Cultures

Culture Group	Environment
Far North	Very short summers; long cold winters
Northwest Coast	Mild, rainy; dense forests
California-Intermountain	Mild and rainy along coast; dry and hot in deserts; cold winters in mountains
Southwest	Very hot and dry in desert
Great Plains	Hot summers; cold winters; little rainfall
Eastern Woodlands	Hot summers; cold winters; dense forests
Southeast	Humid summers; mild winters

This ancient bowl was found on the Hopi Mesa. The ring around the edge is called a lifeline. The Anasazi woman making the bowl left an opening in the ring because her life was not yet complete.

Although from the 1800s, this painting shows some ways of life on the Plains that had changed little. Note the hides used for the tipi.

The Bella Coola used this wooden mask of the sun spirit during winter religious ceremonies.

This scene of an Algonquin village, painted in 1585, shows life much as it was before Europeans arrived.

TLINGIT
ESKIMO
FAR NORTH
BEAVER
CREE
BELLA COOLA
NORTHWEST COAST
CHIPPEWA
BLACKFEET
ALGONQUIN
HURON
PACIFIC OCEAN
COOS
NEZ PERCÉ
CROW
MANDAN
IROQUOIS
EASTERN WOODLANDS
POMO
CALIFORNIA-INTERMOUNTAIN
CHEYENNE
GREAT PLAINS
MIAMI
DELAWARE
ATLANTIC OCEAN
SHOSHONE
ARAPAHO
SHAWNEE
HOPI
NAVAJO
PUEBLO
OSAGE
CHEROKEE
SOUTHWEST
COMANCHE
SOUTHEAST
NATCHEZ
APACHE
SEMINOLE
GULF OF MEXICO

NATIVE AMERICAN CULTURES

Present-day state boundaries

0   500   1000 Miles
0   500   1000 Kilometers

MIDDLE AMERICA
MAYA
AZTEC

Daring explorers sought adventure, wealth, and glory in North America as early as the late 1400s. Settlers soon followed. Some came in search of a better life. Many came looking for religious freedom. By 1753, English colonies flourished along the Atlantic coast. The Spanish had set up missions and towns in the Southwest. French forts lined the Mississippi River in Louisiana and the Great Lakes in New France. The map at right shows European land claims in 1753. Competition for land in North America led to war between England and France the following year, in 1754. Study the map, graph, and pictures. Then answer these questions:

1. Which nation claimed land along the Mississippi in 1753?

2. How did geographic location make conflict between France and England likely?

3. Based on the pictures, which European settlers were probably the greatest threat to Native Americans? Why?

4. Compare the map with the one on page 156. How would the wedges in the circle graph change between 1753 and 1763?

This Spanish mission at El Paso was founded in 1659. It became a gateway for Spanish settlers in the Southwest.

Settlers in Pennsylvania turned dense forests into productive farmland. This prosperous farm grew up during the mid-1750s.

Land Claims in North America, 1753

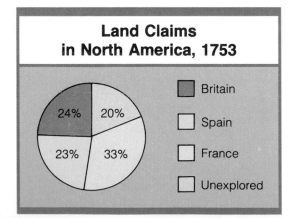

24% | 20%
23% | 33%

- ▨ Britain
- ☐ Spain
- ☐ France
- ☐ Unexplored

French trappers traveled far along roaring rivers. Their fur trade with Indian nations was the basis of French claims in North America.

New York was a thriving colonial port town in the mid-1750s.

The New England Primer was used in schools and homes in the English colonies. It illustrates the strong influence of religion among colonists.

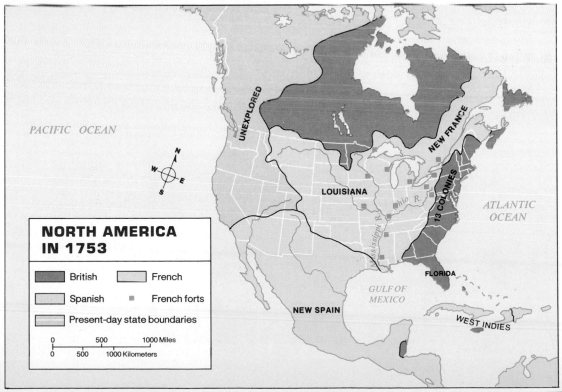

NORTH AMERICA IN 1753

- British
- Spanish
- Present-day state boundaries
- French
- French forts

0   500   1000 Miles
0   500   1000 Kilometers

PACIFIC OCEAN

UNEXPLORED

NEW FRANCE

LOUISIANA

Ohio R.

13 COLONIES

ATLANTIC OCEAN

Mississippi R.

FLORIDA

GULF OF MEXICO

NEW SPAIN

WEST INDIES

North America in 1783

A new nation was born when the American colonists defeated Britain in the American Revolution. The United States had begun as 13 colonies wedged between the Appalachian Mountains and the Atlantic coast. In 1783, it stretched west to the Mississippi, north to Canada and the Great Lakes, and south to Florida. As settlers moved west across the Appalachians, they took along the ideals of liberty that had given birth to the country.

The French had lost their claims to land in North America during the French and Indian War. But most of the continent was still claimed by the Spanish and the British. Study the map, graph, and pictures. Then answer the questions below.

1. What nation claimed the land west of the United States in 1783?

2. Which nation claimed the largest portion of North America in 1783?

3. (a) Based on the map, which European nations might have been a threat to settlers near Fort Snelling? (b) What other groups did settlers probably consider a threat? Why?

4. What do you think American settlers would do when they reached the Mississippi River? Why?

Paul Revere made this silver bowl in 1768 at the beginning of the American colonists' struggle for liberty.

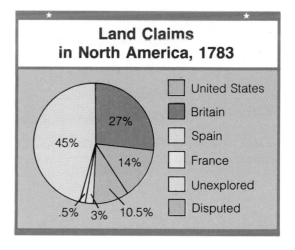

Land Claims in North America, 1783

- United States
- Britain
- Spain
- France
- Unexplored
- Disputed

45%
27%
14%
.5% 3% 10.5%

Although most of North America was claimed by the United States or European nations, Native Americans lived throughout the land. In northern areas, such as Canada, snowshoes helped hunters move easily on snow.

Settlers used flatboats to move goods along the rivers of the western part of the new nation, as this painting from the 1800s shows.

After 1783, American settlers moved west in a steady stream. The army built forts to protect them. Fort Snelling, shown here, was built on the northwest frontier on the Mississippi River.

To the west of the new nation, Spanish settlers were building thriving towns and rancheros, or ranches.

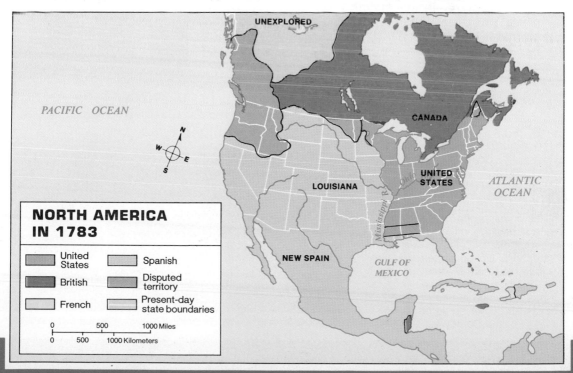

NORTH AMERICA IN 1783

- United States
- British
- French
- Spanish
- Disputed territory
- Present-day state boundaries

PACIFIC OCEAN

UNEXPLORED

CANADA

LOUISIANA

UNITED STATES

ATLANTIC OCEAN

NEW SPAIN

GULF OF MEXICO

Mississippi R.

0 500 1000 Miles

0 500 1000 Kilometers

Growth of the United States to 1853

By 1853, the United States stretched from sea to sea. The nation acquired huge tracts of land through purchase, treaty, and war. This land, far from being empty, was home to many different peoples. They included Native Americans who had lived there long before Europeans arrived. Many Mexicans also had found themselves in a foreign land after the Mexican War. Plus, adventurers from all over the world had come in search of gold. The expansion of the country was to offer great opportunities and difficult challenges in the years ahead. Territorial expansion is shown on the map at right. Study the map, the graph, and the pictures. Then answer these questions:

1. (a) When did the Oregon Country become part of the United States? (b) Which picture best illustrates the trip to Oregon?

2. (a) What was the last addition to the United States shown on the map? (b) What cultural heritage was probably strongest in that area?

3. (a) Based on the graph, during which period was the most land added to the United States? (b) Which pictures help you understand the geography and culture of those areas?

Settlers began moving toward Oregon in the early 1800s. At first, they traveled by covered wagons. Later, railroads would crisscross the country.

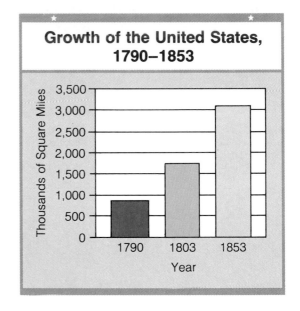

Growth of the United States, 1790–1853

(Bar graph. Y-axis: Thousands of Square Miles, 0 to 3,500. X-axis: Year — 1790, 1803, 1853. 1790 ≈ 850; 1803 ≈ 1,750; 1853 ≈ 3,100.)

This painting of a horse race shows the influence of Mexican culture in areas the United States acquired from Mexico. This cultural influence has remained strong in Texas and other areas of the Southwest.

These Sioux are playing lacrosse, a game that settlers learned from Indians. As settlers moved onto the Plains, the lives of Indians changed forever.

The discovery of gold in California attracted people from all over the world. Miners such as these spread out in search of priceless treasure.

In the early 1800s, canals, such as the Erie Canal, became part of a vast system of transportation.

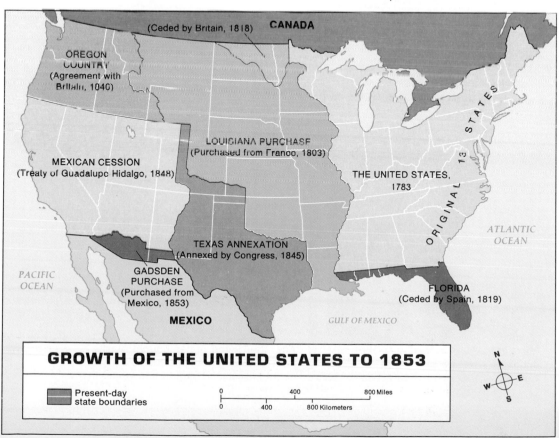

(Ceded by Britain, 1818) CANADA

OREGON COUNTRY (Agreement with Britain, 1846)

LOUISIANA PURCHASE (Purchased from France, 1803)

MEXICAN CESSION (Treaty of Guadalupe Hidalgo, 1848)

THE UNITED STATES, 1783

ORIGINAL 13 STATES

MEXICAN CESSION

TEXAS ANNEXATION (Annexed by Congress, 1845)

GADSDEN PURCHASE (Purchased from Mexico, 1853)

FLORIDA (Ceded by Spain, 1819)

PACIFIC OCEAN

ATLANTIC OCEAN

MEXICO

GULF OF MEXICO

GROWTH OF THE UNITED STATES TO 1853

Present-day state boundaries

0   400   800 Miles
0   400   800 Kilometers

N W E S

American Expansion in the Late 1800s

Historical Atlas

The United States burst upon the world scene as a major power late in the 1800s. With its thriving industrial economy, it competed with European nations for trade and colonies. Some Americans argued that once the country had spread to the Pacific, it should expand overseas. During the late 1800s, the United States acquired territory in the Caribbean and in the Pacific. Trade with Asian nations also expanded dramatically. With its victory in the Spanish-American War, the country became an imperial power, as the map at right shows. Study the map, graph, and pictures. Then answer the following questions:

1. When did the United States annex Hawaii? Wake Island?

2. Review what you read in Chapter 24. Which territories shown on this map did the United States win in the Spanish-American War?

3. Study the two cartoons. Do you think the cartoonists were critical of American expansion? Explain.

4. How do the map and graph help explain the connection between growing trade and acquiring territory?

The Battle of Manila Bay, shown here, was a major victory for the United States in the Spanish-American War.

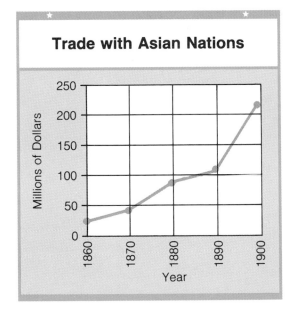

Trade with Asian Nations

(Graph: x-axis "Year" 1860, 1870, 1880, 1890, 1900; y-axis "Millions of Dollars" 0, 50, 100, 150, 200, 250)

After the United States bought Alaska from Russia in 1867, cartoonists joked about politicians trying to find voters there.

The island of Oahu looked like this when the first American missionaries arrived in Hawaii in the early 1820s.

In this cartoon, the American eagle has spread its wings from Puerto Rico to the Philippines.

Commodoro Perry opened Japan to American trade in 1854. A Japanese artist painted this portrait of Perry.

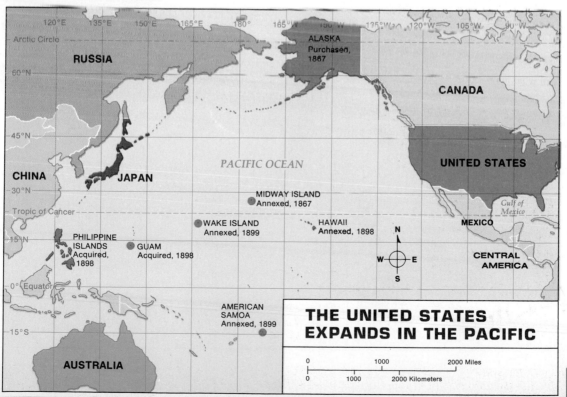

THE UNITED STATES EXPANDS IN THE PACIFIC

RUSSIA

ALASKA
Purchased,
1867

CANADA

CHINA

JAPAN

PACIFIC OCEAN

UNITED STATES

MIDWAY ISLAND
Annexed, 1867

Tropic of Cancer

PHILIPPINE
ISLANDS
Acquired,
1898

WAKE ISLAND
Annexed, 1899

GUAM
Acquired, 1898

HAWAII
Annexed, 1898

MEXICO

Gulf of
Mexico

CENTRAL
AMERICA

AMERICAN
SAMOA
Annexed, 1899

AUSTRALIA

0   1000   2000 Miles
0   1000   2000 Kilometers

ARCT

ALASKA
(U.S.)

GREENLAND
(Denmark)

Svalbard Is.
(Norway)

Reykjavik★   ICELAND

NORWAY

FINLAND

Helsinki★

SWEDEN   Len

Mo

EUROPE
(see inset map)

FRANCE

Ki

CANADA

NORTH
AMERICA

Montreal
Ottawa★
Chicago★

San Francisco★

UNITED STATES

New York★
★Washington, D.C.

Houston★   ★New Orleans

MEXICO

Havana★

Mexico City★

CUBA

THE
BAHAMAS

DOMINICAN
REPUBLIC

Port-au-Prince★
GUATEMALA BELIZE JAMAICA HAITI
Guatemala★ HONDURAS Santo
EL SALVADOR San Salvador★ ★Tegucigalpa Domingo
Managua★ ★NICARAGUA ST. LUCIA

Azores
(Port.)

SPAIN

ITALY

Algiers★ ★Tunis

Rabat★
MOROCCO

TUNISIA

NORTH

ATLANTIC OCEAN

BERMUDA
(U.K.)

Canary Is.
(Spain)
W. SAHARA
(Morocco)

ALGERIA

LIBYA

MIDD
EAST
(see inset m
EGYPT

Puerto Rico (U.S.)
ST. CHRISTOPHER AND NEVIS
ANTIGUA & BARBUDA
DOMINICA

San José★
COSTA RICA
PANAMA

Panamá★

GRENADA

BARBADOS
ST. VINCENT & THE GRENADINES
TRINIDAD
& TOBAGO

CAPE VERDE

MAURITANIA

SENEGAL ★Nouakchott

Dakar★

GAMBIA
GUINEA-BISSAU

MALI

BURKINA

Bamako★

GUINEA
Conakry★
Freetown★
SIERRA LEONE

NIGER

Niamey★

NIGERIA

N'Djamena★
CHAD

C. AFR.
REP.

SUDAN

AFRICA

Caracas★
VENEZUELA

Bogotá★
COLOMBIA

GUYANA

Georgetown★ ★Paramaribo
SURINAME
FR. GUIANA
(France)

IVORY
COAST
Abidjan★

TOGO BENIN
Lomé Lagos
Accra★ Porto
Novo
Monrovia★ ★Yaoundé★
LIBERIA
GHANA EQ. GUINEA
Libreville★

CAMEROON

Bangui★

UGANDA
Kampala★

Galapagos Is
(Ecuador)

Equator

ECUADOR
Quito★

SOUTH

AMERICA

BRAZIL

PERU

Lima★

SÃO TOMÉ AND PRÍNCIPE

GABON CONGO

Brazzaville★ ★Kinshasa
CABINDA
(Angola)

Luanda★

RWANDA Nairo
ZAIRE
BURUNDI TANZ

BOLIVIA
La Paz★
★Sucre

Brasília★

SOUTH
PACIFIC OCEAN

SÃO Francisco

ANGOLA

ZAMBIA
Lusaka★

MALAWI
Lilongwe★

ZIMBABWE

São Paulo★
Rio de Janeiro★

PARAGUAY
Asunción★

SOUTH

ATLANTIC OCEAN

NAMIBIA
Windhoek★
WALVIS BAY
(S. Africa)

Pretoria★

MOZAM

BOTSWANA
Gaborone★

SWA
LESO

CHILE
Santiago★

URUGUAY
★Montevideo

Maseru★
SOUTH
AFRICA

Cape Town★

Buenos Aires★
ARGENTINA

Falkland Is.
(U.K.)

S. Georgia
(Falkland Is.)

N
W ─⊕─ E
S

ANTARCTICA

EUROPE

0   250 Miles
0   250 Kilometers

NORWAY
Oslo★

N.
IRELAND
Dublin★
IRELAND

UNITED
KINGDOM

London★

Stockholm★
SWEDEN
DENMARK
Copenhagen★

Amsterdam
NETH. Berlin★
BELGIUM
Brussels★ ★Bonn E. GERMANY
LUX. W.
GER. ★Prague
LIECH. CZECHOSLOVAKIA
AUS. Vienna★
Budapest★
HUNGARY
ROMANIA

POLAND
★Warsaw

U.S.S.R.
(SOVIET
UNION)

Paris★
FRANCE
Bern★
SWITZ.
ITALY
SAN
MARINO
Rome★

ANDORRA
MONACO

PORT.
Lisbon★

SPAIN
★Madrid

Belgrade★
YUGOSLAVIA

★Bucharest

BULGARIA
Sofia★

ALBANIA
Tirane★

GREECE
Athens★

TURKEY

MEDITERRANEAN
SEA

MALTA

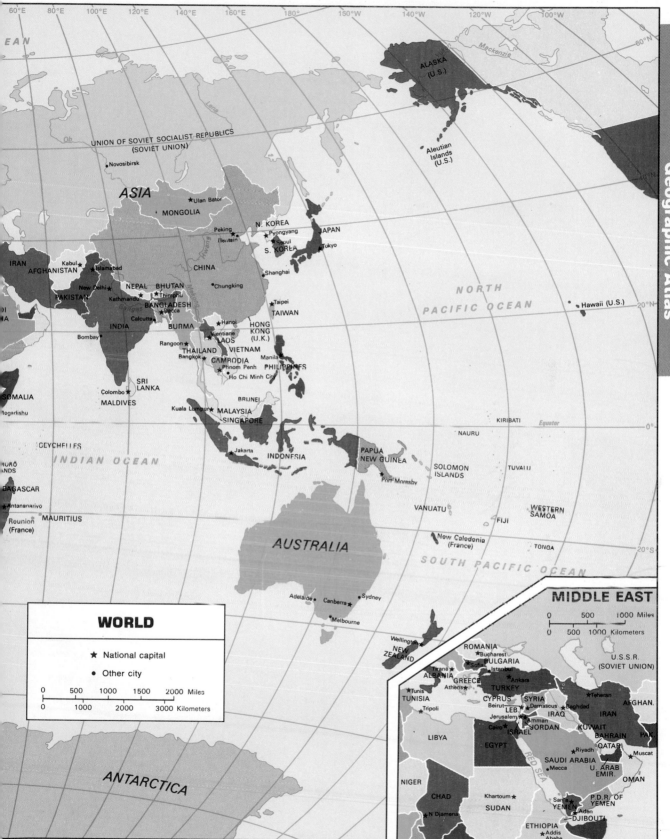

60°E 80°E 100°E 120°E 140°E 160°E 180° 160°W 140°W 120°W 100°W

60°N

EAN

ALASKA
(U.S.)

Mackenzie

UNION OF SOVIET SOCIALIST REPUBLICS
(SOVIET UNION)

Ob

Lena

40°N

Novosibirsk

Aleutian
Islands
(U.S.)

ASIA

★ Ulan Bator

MONGOLIA

N. KOREA
Peking ★Pyongyang
Tientsin ★Seoul
S. KOREA

JAPAN

★Tokyo

IRAN

Kabul★

Islamabad

AFGHANISTAN

CHINA

Chungking

NORTH

PACIFIC OCEAN

20°N

New Delhi★

PAKISTAN

NEPAL BHUTAN

Kathmandu★ ★Thimphu
BANGLADESH
Calcutta● ●Dacca

Shanghai

★Taipei

TAIWAN

Hawaii (U.S.)

Bombay●

INDIA

BURMA

★Hanoi

HONG
KONG
(U.K.)

●Chungking

MA

Rangoon●

★Vientiane
LAOS

Bangkok★ CAMBODIA

VIETNAM
Manila

THAILAND

★Phnom Penh

PHILIPPINES

SRI
LANKA

Ho Chi Minh City

SOMALIA

Colombo★

BRUNEI

ogadishu

MALDIVES

Kuala Lumpur★ ★MALAYSIA
SINGAPORE

KIRIBATI

Equator

SEYCHELLES

NAURU

0°

INDIAN OCEAN

Jakarta●

INDONESIA

PAPUA
NEW GUINEA

SOLOMON
ISLANDS

TUVALU

URO
NDS

DAGASCAR

Antananarivo

MAURITIUS

Réunion
(France)

VANUATU

★Port Moresby

FIJI

New Caledonia
(France)

WESTERN
SAMOA

TONGA

AUSTRALIA

SOUTH PACIFIC OCEAN

20°S

Adelaide● Canberra★

●Sydney

Melbourne●

WORLD

★ National capital

● Other city

0   500   1000   1500   2000 Miles

0   1000   2000   3000 Kilometers

ANTARCTICA

Wellington●
NEW
ZEALAND

ROMANIA
★Bucharest
BULGARIA
★Sofia
Istanbul●

Tirane★
ALBANIA GREECE
Athens★

Ankara★
TURKEY

★Tunis
TUNISIA

Tripoli★

CYPRUS
Beirut●
LEB.★
Jerusalem★
ISRAEL

Cairo●

SYRIA
★Damascus ★Baghdad
IRAQ

Amman★
JORDAN

MIDDLE EAST

0   500   1000 Miles

0   500   1000 Kilometers

U.S.S.R.
(SOVIET UNION)

★Teheran

IRAN

AFGHAN.

KUWAIT

BAHRAIN

QATAR

PAK.

Muscat●

LIBYA

EGYPT

NIGER

CHAD

SUDAN

N'Djamena●

Khartoum★

RED SEA

★Riyadh

Mecca●

SAUDI ARABIA

U. ARAB
EMIR.

San'a
YEMEN

Aden●

DJIBOUTI

P.D.R. OF
YEMEN

OMAN

ETHIOPIA

Addis
Ababa●

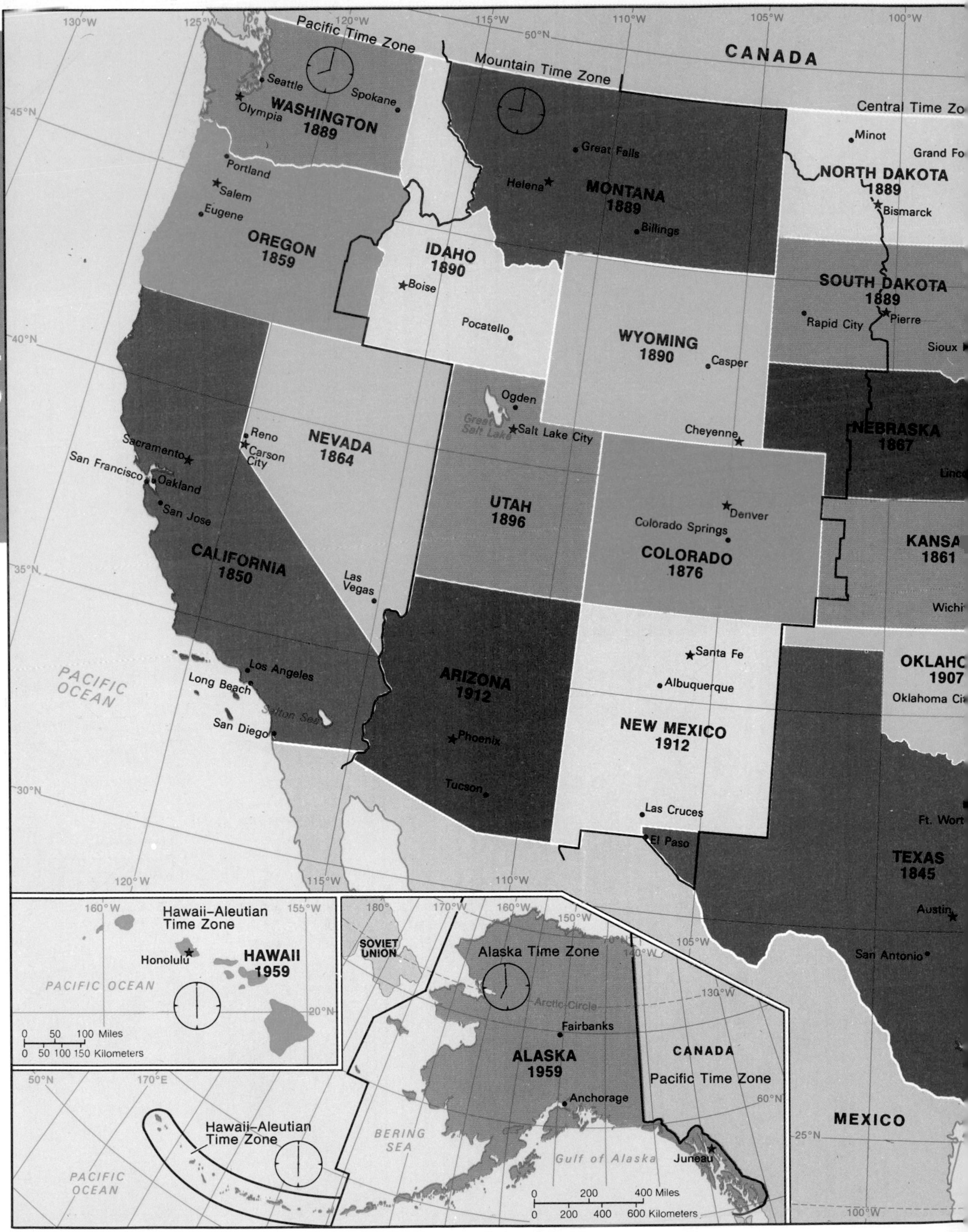

Pacific Time Zone

Mountain Time Zone

CANADA

Central Time Zone

WASHINGTON 1889

Seattle

Spokane

Olympia

Portland

Salem

Eugene

OREGON 1859

Great Falls

Helena

MONTANA 1889

Billings

IDAHO 1890

Boise

Pocatello

NORTH DAKOTA 1889

Minot

Grand Fo

Bismarck

SOUTH DAKOTA 1889

Rapid City

Pierre

Sioux

WYOMING 1890

Casper

Ogden

Great Salt Lake

Salt Lake City

Cheyenne

NEBRASKA 1867

Linco

Reno

Carson City

NEVADA 1864

Sacramento

San Francisco

Oakland

San Jose

CALIFORNIA 1850

Las Vegas

UTAH 1896

Denver

Colorado Springs

COLORADO 1876

KANSAS 1861

Wichit

Los Angeles

Long Beach

Salton Sea

San Diego

PACIFIC OCEAN

ARIZONA 1912

Phoenix

Tucson

Santa Fe

Albuquerque

NEW MEXICO 1912

Las Cruces

El Paso

OKLAHOMA 1907

Oklahoma Cit

TEXAS 1845

Ft. Wort

Austin

San Antonio

Hawaii–Aleutian Time Zone

HAWAII 1959

Honolulu

PACIFIC OCEAN

0 50 100 Miles
0 50 100 150 Kilometers

SOVIET UNION

Alaska Time Zone

Arctic Circle

Fairbanks

ALASKA 1959

Anchorage

CANADA

Pacific Time Zone

Juneau

MEXICO

BERING SEA

Gulf of Alaska

Hawaii–Aleutian Time Zone

PACIFIC OCEAN

0 200 400 Miles
0 200 400 600 Kilometers

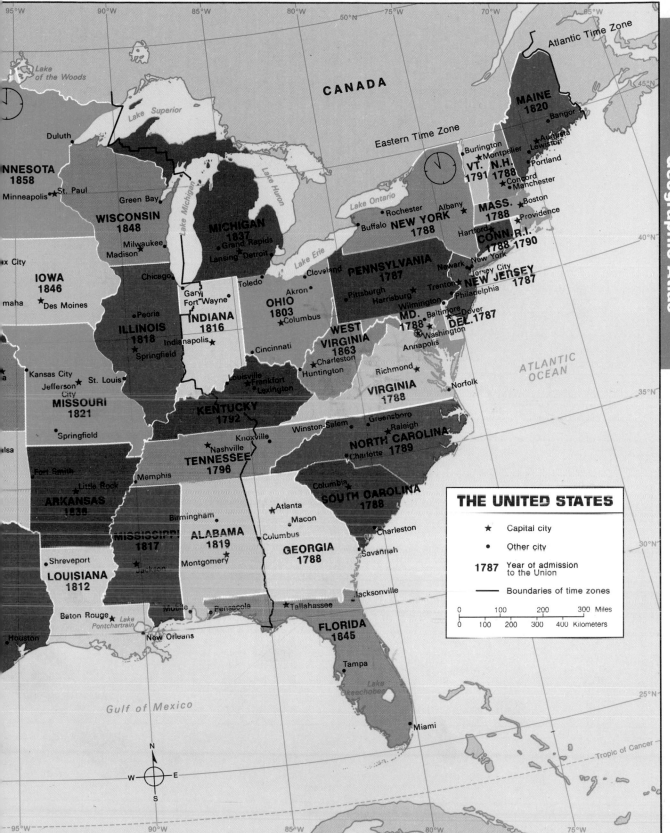

THE UNITED STATES

★ Capital city

• Other city

1787 Year of admission to the Union

— Boundaries of time zones

0   100   200   300 Miles
0   100   200   300   400 Kilometers

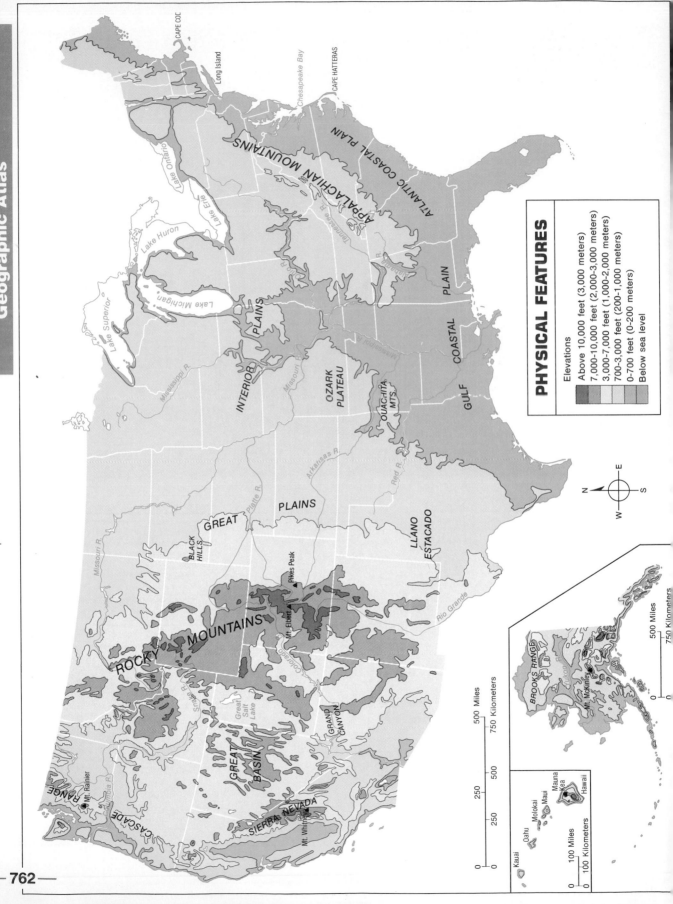

PHYSICAL FEATURES

Elevations

Above 10,000 feet (3,000 meters)
7,000-10,000 feet (2,000-3,000 meters)
3,000-7,000 feet (1,000-2,000 meters)
700-3,000 feet (200-1,000 meters)
0-700 feet (0-200 meters)
Below sea level

CAPE COD
Long Island
Chesapeake Bay
CAPE HATTERAS

Lake Ontario
Lake Erie
Lake Huron
Lake Michigan
Lake Superior

APPALACHIAN MOUNTAINS
ATLANTIC COASTAL PLAIN

PLAIN

COASTAL

GULF

INTERIOR

PLAINS

OZARK
PLATEAU

OUACHITA
MTS.

Mississippi R.
Missouri R.
Tennessee R.
Ohio R.
Arkansas R.
Red R.

GREAT

PLAINS

BLACK
HILLS

Pikes Peak
Mt. Elbert

LLANO
ESTACADO

Platte R.
Rio Grande
Colorado R.

ROCKY MOUNTAINS

Missouri R.

GREAT
SALT
Great Salt
Lake

BASIN

GRAND
CANYON

Snake R.

Columbia R.

CASCADE RANGE
Mt. Rainier

SIERRA NEVADA
Mt. Whitney

N
W   E
S

0   250   500 Miles
0   250   500   750 Kilometers

BROOKS RANGE
Yukon R.
Mt. McKinley

0   500 Miles
0   750 Kilometers

Kauai
Oahu
Molokai
Maui
Mauna Kea
Hawaii

0   100 Miles
0   100 Kilometers

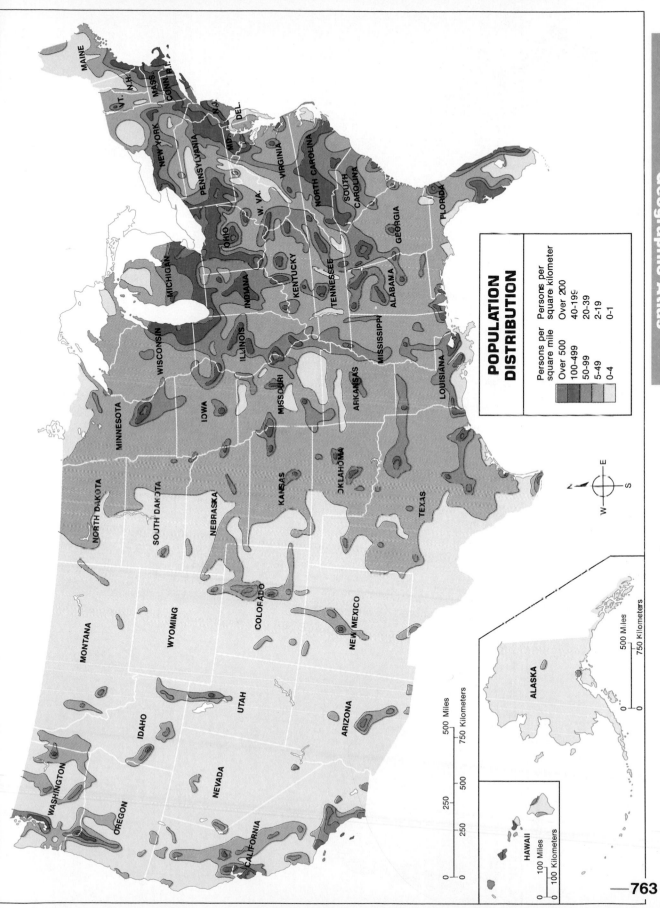

POPULATION DISTRIBUTION

Persons per square mile	Persons per square kilometer
Over 500	Over 200
100-499	40-199
50-99	20-39
5-49	2-19
0-4	0-1

MAINE
N.H.
VT.
MASS.
CONN. R.I.
N.J.
DEL.
NEW YORK
PENNSYLVANIA
MD.
W. VA.
VIRGINIA
OHIO
KENTUCKY
NORTH CAROLINA
SOUTH CAROLINA
TENNESSEE
GEORGIA
FLORIDA
ALABAMA
MISSISSIPPI
LOUISIANA
ARKANSAS
MICHIGAN
INDIANA
ILLINOIS
WISCONSIN
MINNESOTA
IOWA
MISSOURI
OKLAHOMA
KANSAS
TEXAS
NORTH DAKOTA
SOUTH DAKOTA
NEBRASKA
COLORADO
NEW MEXICO
MONTANA
WYOMING
UTAH
ARIZONA
IDAHO
NEVADA
WASHINGTON
OREGON
CALIFORNIA

N
E
S
W

500 Miles
750 Kilometers
0 250 500
0 250 500 750

ALASKA

0 500 Miles
0 750 Kilometers

HAWAII

0 100 Miles
0 100 Kilometers

763

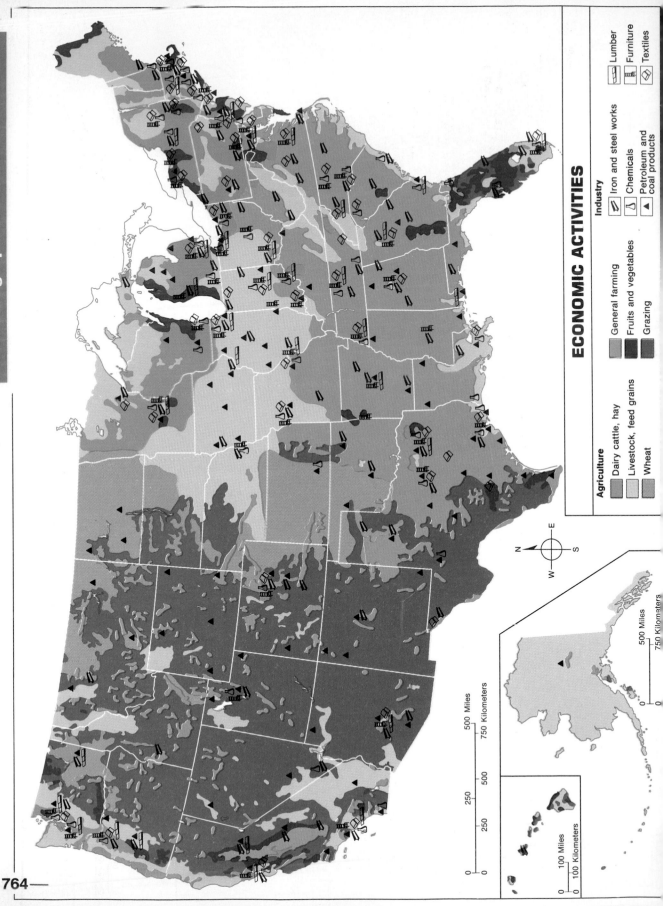

ECONOMIC ACTIVITIES

Agriculture

- Dairy cattle, hay
- Livestock, feed grains
- Wheat
- General farming
- Fruits and vegetables
- Grazing

Industry

- Iron and steel works
- Chemicals
- Petroleum and coal products
- Lumber
- Furniture
- Textiles

100 Miles

100 Kilometers

0   250   500 Miles

0   250   500   750 Kilometers

500 Miles

750 Kilometers

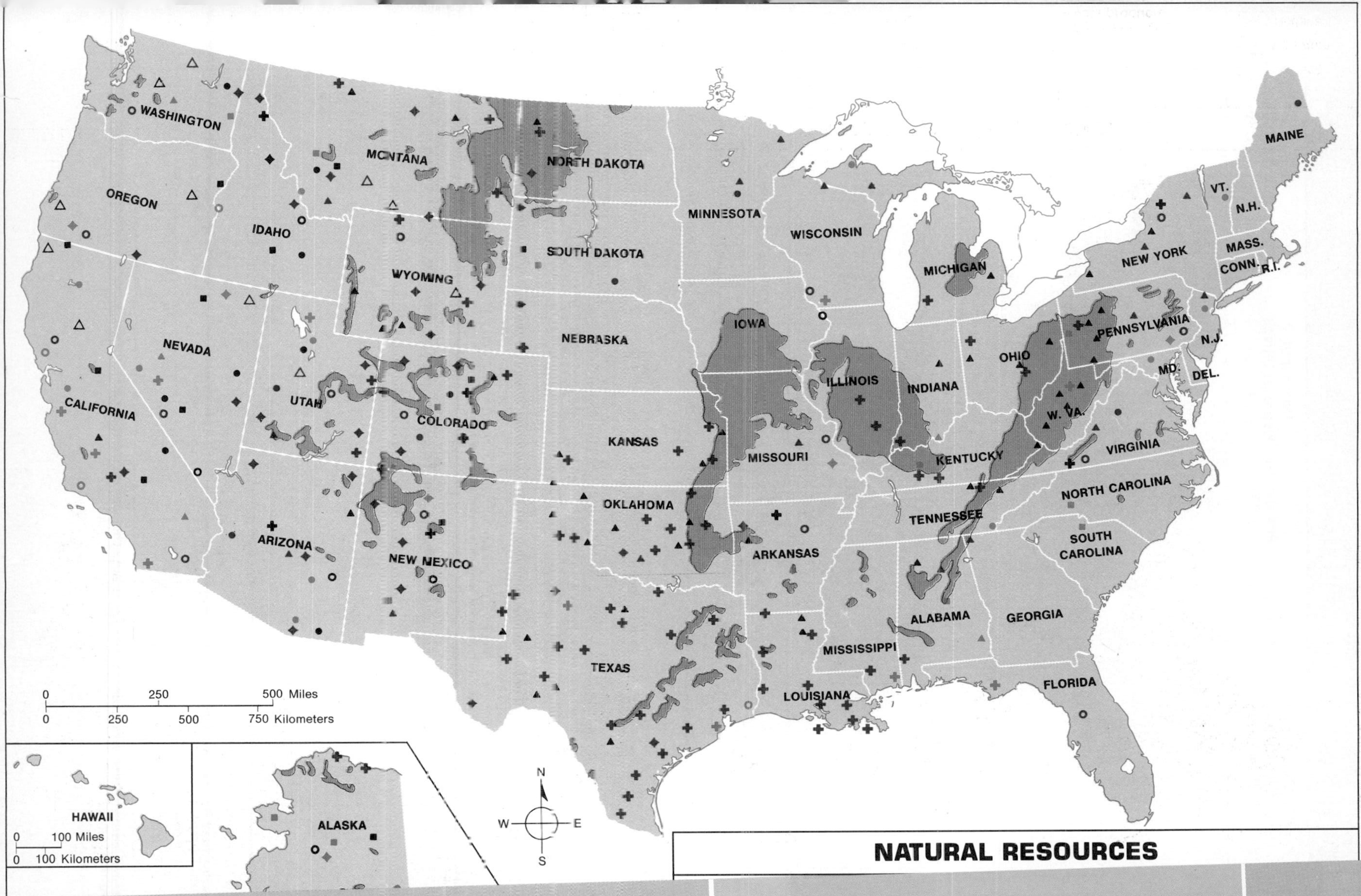

NATURAL RESOURCES

The Fifty States

The Fifty States

State	Date of Entry to Union (Order of Entry)		Area in Square Miles	Population (1985)	Number of Representatives in House	Capital	Largest City
Alabama	1819	(22)	51,705	4,004,435	7	Montgomery	Birmingham
Alaska	1959	(49)	591,004	514,819	1	Juneau	Anchorage
Arizona	1912	(48)	114,000	3,086,827	5	Phoenix	Phoenix
Arkansas	1836	(25)	53,187	2,345,431	4	Little Rock	Little Rock
California	1850	(31)	158,706	25,816,590	45	Sacramento	Los Angeles
Colorado	1876	(38)	104,091	3,253,425	6	Denver	Denver
Connecticut	1788	(5)	5,018	3,160,280	6	Hartford	Bridgeport
Delaware	1787	(1)	2,044	605,711	1	Dover	Wilmington
Florida	1845	(27)	58,664	11,071,358	19	Tallahassee	Jacksonville
Georgia	1788	(4)	58,910	5,878,225	10	Atlanta	Atlanta
Hawaii	1959	(50)	6,471	1,050,270	2	Honolulu	Honolulu
Idaho	1890	(43)	83,564	1,004,071	2	Boise	Boise
Illinois	1818	(21)	56,345	11,502,433	22	Springfield	Chicago
Indiana	1816	(19)	36,185	5,489,287	10	Indianapolis	Indianapolis
Iowa	1846	(29)	56,275	2,894,273	6	Des Moines	Des Moines
Kansas	1861	(34)	82,277	2,453,581	5	Topeka	Wichita
Kentucky	1792	(15)	40,409	3,747,769	7	Frankfort	Louisville
Louisiana	1812	(18)	47,751	4,553,903	8	Baton Rouge	New Orleans
Maine	1820	(23)	33,265	1,158,539	2	Augusta	Portland
Maryland	1788	(7)	10,460	4,342,562	8	Annapolis	Baltimore
Massachusetts	1788	(6)	8,284	5,764,125	11	Boston	Boston
Michigan	1837	(26)	58,527	8,992,766	18	Lansing	Detroit
Minnesota	1858	(32)	84,402	4,199,749	8	St. Paul	Minneapolis
Mississippi	1817	(20)	47,689	2,623,069	5	Jackson	Jackson
Missouri	1821	(24)	69,697	5,004,162	9	Jefferson City	St. Louis
Montana	1889	(41)	147,046	826,933	2	Helena	Billings
Nebraska	1867	(37)	77,355	1,606,779	3	Lincoln	Omaha
Nevada	1864	(36)	110,561	933,451	2	Carson City	Las Vegas
New Hampshire	1788	(9)	9,279	980,841	2	Concord	Manchester
New Jersey	1787	(3)	7,787	7,509,625	14	Trenton	Newark
New Mexico	1912	(47)	121,593	1,446,347	3	Santa Fe	Albuquerque
New York	1788	(11)	49,108	17,676,828	34	Albany	New York
North Carolina	1789	(12)	52,669	6,178,329	11	Raleigh	Charlotte
North Dakota	1889	(39)	70,703	692,027	1	Bismarck	Fargo
Ohio	1803	(17)	41,330	10,763,309	21	Columbus	Cleveland
Oklahoma	1907	(46)	69,956	3,427,371	6	Oklahoma City	Oklahoma City
Oregon	1859	(33)	97,073	2,680,087	5	Salem	Portland
Pennsylvania	1787	(2)	45,308	11,895,301	23	Harrisburg	Philadelphia
Rhode Island	1790	(13)	1,212	958,151	2	Providence	Providence
South Carolina	1788	(8)	31,113	3,321,520	6	Columbia	Columbia
South Dakota	1889	(40)	77,116	705,027	1	Pierre	Sioux Falls
Tennessee	1796	(16)	42,144	4,723,332	9	Nashville	Memphis
Texas	1845	(28)	266,807	16,384,800	27	Austin	Houston
Utah	1896	(45)	84,899	1,684,942	3	Salt Lake City	Salt Lake City
Vermont	1791	(14)	9,614	529,396	1	Montpelier	Burlington
Virginia	1788	(10)	40,767	5,642,183	10	Richmond	Norfolk
Washington	1889	(42)	68,138	4,366,248	8	Olympia	Seattle
West Virginia	1863	(35)	24,231	1,968,989	4	Charleston	Charleston
Wisconsin	1848	(30)	56,153	4,792,115	9	Madison	Milwaukee
Wyoming	1890	(44)	97,809	534,744	1	Cheyenne	Casper
District of Columbia			69	621,251	1 (nonvoting)		

Self-Governing Areas, Possessions, and Dependencies	Area in Square Miles	Population (1980)	Capital
Puerto Rico	3,515	3,196,520	San Juan
Guam	209	105,821	Agana
U.S. Virgin Islands	132	95,591	Charlotte Amalie
American Samoa	77	32,395	Pago Pago

Gazetteer of American History

This gazetteer, or geographical dictionary, lists places of importance to American history. The approximate latitude and longitude is given for cities, towns, and other specific locations. See Skill Lesson 3 (page 56), Using Latitude and Longitude. After the description of each place, there are usually two numbers in parentheses. The first number refers to the text page where you can find out more about the place. The second number is *italicized* and refers to a map (*m*) where the place is shown.

A

Abilene (39°N/97°W) Former cow town in Kansas. Grew in 1860s as the railhead at the end of the Chisholm Trail. (p. 450, *m453*)

Afghanistan Land-locked country in south-central Asia. Invaded by the Soviet Union in 1979. (p. 701, *m758–59*)

Alabama 22nd state. Nicknamed the Heart of Dixie or the Cotton State. (p. 766, *m760–61*)

Alamo (29°N/99°W) Spanish mission and fort in San Antonio, Texas. After Texans defending the fort were killed by Mexican soldiers in 1836, "Remember the Alamo" became the battle cry of Texans in their struggle for independence. (p. 316, *m317*)

Alaska 49th state. Largest in size but the least populated of the 50 states. (p. 766, *m760–61*)

Albany (43°N/74°W) Capital of New York State. Called Fort Orange by the Dutch of New Netherland. (p. 47, *m760–61*)

Alsace-Lorraine (48°N/7°E) Area seized by Germany from France in 1871. Returned to France after World War I. (p. 550, *m560*)

Amiens (50°N/2°E) World War I battle site in northeastern France. (p. 561, *m560*)

Andes Rugged mountain chain in South America. (p. 26, *m45*)

Antietam (39°N/78°W) Creek in Maryland. Site of a Union victory in 1862. (p. 399, *m399*)

Appalachian Mountains Stretch from Georgia to Maine and Canada. Heavily forested and a barrier to colonial expansion. (p. 23, *m136*)

Appomattox Courthouse (37°N/79°W) Small town in Virginia where Lee surrendered to Grant on April 9, 1865. (p. 412, *m411*)

Argonne Forest (49°N/6°E) World War I battle site in northeastern France. (p. 563, *m560*)

Arizona 48th state. Nicknamed the Grand Canyon State. (p. 766, *m760–61*)

Arkansas 25th state. Nicknamed the Land of Opportunity. (p. 766, *m760–61*)

Atlanta (34°N/84°W) Capital and largest city of Georgia. Burned by Sherman in 1864 before his "march to the sea." (p. 411, *m411*)

Atlantic Ocean World's second largest ocean. (p. 22, *m21*)

Atlantic Plain Part of the coastal plain in the eastern United States. (p. 25, *m24*)

Austria-Hungary One of the Central Powers in World War I. Divided up into several countries after 1918. (p. 550, *m551*)

B

Badlands Dry region of South Dakota. (p. 25)

Baltimore (39°N/77°W) Port city in Maryland. (p. 99, *m112*)

Bataan (13°N/124°E) Peninsula at the entrance to Manila Bay in the Philippines. Scene of the Bataan Death March in 1942. (p. 642)

Bay of Pigs (22°N/81°W) Located in southern Cuba. Site of an unsuccessful invasion to overthrow Fidel Castro. (p. 698, *m716*)

Beirut (34°N/36°E) Capital of Lebanon. (p. 711, *m709*)

Belgium Small country in northwestern Europe. (p. 260, *m758–59*)

Belleau Wood (49°N/3°E) World War I battle site in northeastern France. (p. 562, *m560*)

Bering Sea Narrow sea between Asia and North America. Scientists think a land bridge existed here during the last ice age. (p. 20, *m21*)

Berlin (53°N/13°E) City in East Germany. Capital of Nazi Germany. Divided after World War II into East and West Berlin. (p. 640, *m654*)

Boston (42°N/71°W) Seaport and industrial city in Massachusetts. U.S.S. *Constitution*, retired in 1897, can be seen in the Boston Navy Yard. (p. 100, *m102*)

Brazil Largest country in South America. Became independent in 1822. (p. 27, *m758–59*)

Breed's Hill (42°N/71°W) Overlooks Boston Harbor. Site of fighting during the Battle of Bunker Hill. (p. 174, *m175*)

Breuckelen (41°N/74°W) Dutch settlement in New Netherland. Now called Brooklyn. Located in New York. (p. 87, *m87*)

Buena Vista (26°N/101°W) Site of an American victory in the Mexican War. (p. 323, *m324*)

Buffalo (43°N/79°W) Industrial city in New York State on Lake Erie. Free Soil Party was founded there in 1848. (p. 375, *m760–61*)

Bull Run (39°N/78°W) Small stream in Virginia. Site of Confederate victories in 1861 and 1862. (p. 398, *m399*)

Bunker Hill (42°N/71°W) Overlooks Boston Harbor. Was fortified by Americans, then abandoned in favor of nearby Breed's Hill in 1775. Site of an early battle during the Revolution. (p. 173, *m175*)

C

Cahokia (39°N/90°W) Fur-trading post in southwestern Illinois in the 1700s. Captured by George Rogers Clark in 1778 during the Revolution. (p. 187, *m186*)

California 31st state. Nicknamed the Golden State. Ceded to the United States by Mexico in 1848. (p. 766, *m 760–61*)

Cambodia Nation in Southeast Asia. Also known as Kampuchea. (p. 706, *m706*)

Canada Northern neighbor of the United States. Made up of 10 provinces: Ontario, Quebec, Nova Scotia, New Brunswick, Alberta, British Columbia, Manitoba, Newfoundland and Labrador, Prince Edward Island, and Saskatchewan. (p. 150, *m758–59*)

Cape Bojador (26°N/16°W) Located at the bulge of West Africa. (p. 56, *m57*)

Gazetteer

Cape Cod (42°N/70°W) Located on the coast of Massachusetts. Pilgrims on the *Mayflower* landed here. (p. 94, *m94*)

Cape Horn (56°S/67°W) Southern tip of South America. Magellan rounded this cape in 1520. (p. 60, *m61*)

Cape of Good Hope (34°S/18°E) Southern tip of Africa. Dias rounded this cape in 1488. (p. 55, *m57*)

Caribbean Sea Tropical sea in the Western Hemisphere. Dotted with islands of the West Indies. Since 1823, United States has tried to exclude foreign powers from the region. (p. 22, *m58, m758–59*)

Central America Part of North America that lies between Mexico and South America. (p. 27, *m758–59*)

Central Plains Eastern part of the Interior Plains. Once covered with tall prairie grasses. Now a productive farming region with many cities. (p. 24, *m24*)

Chancellorsville (38°N/78°W) Site of a Confederate victory in 1863. (p. 409, *m411*)

Charleston (33°N/80°W) City in South Carolina. Spelled Charles Town in colonial days. (p. 110, *m112*)

Chateau-Thierry (49°N/3°E) World War I battle site in northeastern France. (p. 561, *m560*)

Chesapeake Bay Large inlet of the Atlantic Ocean in Virginia and Maryland. (p. 90, *m94*)

Chicago (42°N/88°W) Second largest city in the United States. Developed as a railroad and meatpacking center in the late 1800s. (p. 24, *m760–61*)

China Country in East Asia. Visited by Marco Polo in the 1200s. Now the world's most populous country. (p. 48, *m758–59*)

Chisholm Trail Cattle trail from Texas to the railroad at Abilene, Kansas. Opened in 1865. (p. 450, *m453*)

Colombia Country in South America. (p. 280, *m758–59*)

Colorado 38th state. Nicknamed the Centennial State. (p. 766, *m760–61*)

Columbia River Chief river of the Pacific Northwest. (p. 247, *m247*)

Comstock Lode (39°N/120°W) Rich silver deposit near Virginia City, Nevada. (p. 440, *m453*)

Concord (43°N/71°W) Village near Boston, Massachusetts. Site of the first battle of the American Revolution in April 1775. (p. 163, *m169*)

Connecticut One of the 13 original states. Nicknamed the Constitution State or the Nutmeg State (p. 766, *m760–61*)

Coral Sea (14°S/150°E) Arm of the Pacific Ocean near Australia. Site of a victory by American and Australian naval forces over Japanese in World War II. (p. 635, *m636*)

Costa Rica Country in Central America. Won independence from Spain in 1821. (p. 281, *m758–59*)

Cotton Kingdom In the 1850s, many plantations worked by slaves produced cotton in this region. Stretched from South Carolina to Georgia and Texas. (p. 342, *m342*)

Cowpens (35°N/82°W) Located in South Carolina. Site of a decisive American victory in 1781 during the Revolution. (p. 191, *m191*)

Croatoan Island Place where Roanoke settlers may have moved between 1587 and 1590. (p. 89, *m94*)

Cuba (22°N/79°W) Island nation in the Caribbean. Gained independence from Spain in 1898. Strongly influenced by the United States until Fidel Castro established communist control in 1959. (p. 79, *m537*)

Cumberland Gap (37°N/84°W) Pass in the Appalachian Mountains near the border of Virginia, Kentucky, and Tennessee. (p. 271, *m272*)

Cuzco (14°S/72°W) Inca capital located high in the Andes Mountains of Peru. (p. 44, *m45*)

Czechoslovakia Country in Eastern Europe. Created after World War I. Seized by Hitler in 1939. Under communist control since 1945. (p. 626, *m567*)

D _____

Dallas (33°N/97°W) City in Texas. Located on the Interior Plains. (p. 24, *m760–61*)

Delaware One of the 13 original states. Nicknamed the First State and the Diamond State. (p. 766, *m760–61*)

Delaware River Flows into the Atlantic Ocean through Delaware Bay. (p. 105, *m94*)

Denmark Small country in northern Europe. Part of Scandinavia. (p. 627, *m628*)

Detroit (42°N/83°W) Largest city in Michigan. (p. 257, *m258*)

District of Columbia Located on the Potomac River. Seat of the federal government of the United States. (p. 766, *m760–61*)

Dominican Republic Country in the Caribbean. Shares the island of Hispaniola with Haiti. Invaded by the United States in 1905, 1916, and 1965. (p. 57, *m545*)

Dust Bowl Drought-stricken farming region in the 1930s. Stretched across the Great Plains from Texas to North Dakota. (p. 614, *m614*)

E _____

East Indies Islands in Southeast Asia. Now part of Indonesia. Source of cloves and spices in the 1500s and 1600s. (p. 51, *m758–59*)

Ecuador Country in South America. (p. 82, *m758–59*)

Egypt Country in the Middle East. Borders Israel. Controls the Suez Canal. (p. 54, *m706*)

El Alamein (31°N/29°E) Located on the north coast of Egypt. Site of a decisive British victory over the German army in World War II. (p. 635, *m628*)

Ellis Island (41°N/74°W) Island in New York Harbor. Chief port of entry for immigrants arriving between 1892 and 1943. (p. 483)

El Paso (32°N/106°W) City on the Rio Grande in Texas. Settled by Spanish. (p. 83, *m760–61*)

El Salvador Country in Central America. Won independence from Spain in 1821. Torn by civil war in recent years. (p. 716, *m716*)

England Part of Great Britain. (p. 53, *m758–59*)

English Channel (50°N/3°W) Narrow body of water separating Britain from the European mainland. Site of Operation Overlord and D-Day crossing of Allies into France in World War II. (p. 638, *m628*)

Equator Line of latitude labeled 0°. Separates the Northern and Southern hemispheres. (p. 27, *m57*)

Erie Canal Linked the Mohawk River with Buffalo and Lake Erie. Built between 1817 and 1825. (p. 275, *m275*)

Europe Smallest continent except for Australia. (p. 48, *m758–59*)

F _____

Florida 27th state. Nicknamed the Sunshine State. (p. 766, *m760–61*)

Fort McHenry (39°N/77°W) Located in Baltimore Harbor. British bombardment there in 1814 inspired Francis Scott Key to write "The Star-Spangled Banner." (p. 261)

Fort Orange (43°N/74°W) Dutch name for Albany, New York. (p. 86, *m87*)

Fort Oswego (44°N/76°W) British fort and fur-trading post. Located on Lake Ontario. (p. 153, *m182*)

Fort Pitt (40°N/80°W) British name for Fort Duquesne after its capture from the French in 1758. (p. 154, *m186*)

Fort Sumter (33°N/80°W) Guarded the entrance to Charleston Harbor in South Carolina. Confederates fired the first shots of the Civil War there in 1861. (p. 393, *m411*)

Fort Ticonderoga (44°N/74°W) French, then British, fort at the south end of Lake Champlain. Captured by Ethan Allen and his Green Mountain Boys in 1775. (p. 173, *m176*)

France Country in Western Europe. First ally of the United States. Scene of heavy fighting in both World War I and II. (p. 53, *m758–59*)

Fredericksburg (38°N/78°W) Located in eastern Virginia. Site of a Confederate victory in 1862. Now part of Fredericksburg and Spotsylvania County Battlefields Memorial National Military Park. (p. 409, *m411*)

G

Gadsden Purchase Land purchased from Mexico in 1853. Now part of Arizona and New Mexico. (p. 324, *m320*)

Georgia One of the 13 original states. Nicknamed the Peach State or the Empire State of the South. (p. 766, *m760–61*)

Germany Country in central Europe. Divided since World War II into East and West Germany. (p. 52, *m758–59*)

Gettysburg (40°N/77°W) Small town in southern Pennsylvania. Site of a Union victory in 1863 and Lincoln's famous Gettysburg Address. (p. 410, *m411*)

Goliad (29°N/97°W) City in Texas near San Antonio. After Mexicans executed 300 Texans there in 1836, "Remember Goliad" became a battle cry during the Texan war for independence. (p. 317, *m317*)

Gonzalez (97°N/30°W) City in Texas near San Antonio. Site of the first Texan victory over Mexico in 1835. Called "the Lexington of Texas." (p. 316, *m317*)

Great Britain Island nation of Western Europe. Includes England, Scotland, Wales, and Northern Ireland. (p. 151, *m758–59*)

Great Lakes Group of five freshwater lakes in the heart of the United States. (p. 26, *m24*)

Great Plains Western part of the Interior Plains. Once grazed by large herds of buffalo. Now an important wheat-growing and ranching region. (p. 24, *m24*)

Great Salt Lake Vast salt lake in Utah. (p. 23, *m760–61*)

Great Wagon Road Early pioneer route across the Appalachians to Pittsburgh and the Ohio Valley. (p. 128, *m130*)

Greece Country in southeastern Europe. Member of NATO since 1952. (p. 482, *m656*)

Greenland World's largest island. Colonized by Vikings in the 10th century. (p. 48, *m758–59*)

Grenada (12°N/61°W) Island nation in the Caribbean. Invaded by the United States in 1983 to end the threat of communist influence. (p. 715, *m716*)

Guam (14°N/143°E) Island in the Pacific Ocean. Territory of the United States. Acquired from Spain in 1898. (p. 766, *m758–759*)

Guatemala Country in Central America. Gained independence from Spain in 1821. Mayas built an advanced civilization there over 3,000 years ago. (p. 27, *m760–61*)

Gulf of Mexico Body of water along the southern coast of the United States. (p. 25, *m24*)

Gulf of Tonkin (20°N/108°E) Located off the coast of North Vietnam. Attack on American destroyers there in 1964 led to a widening of the Vietnam War. (p. 704, *m706*)

Gulf Plain Part of the coastal plain lowland that lies along the Gulf of Mexico. (p. 25, *m24*)

H

Haiti Country in the West Indies. Won independence from France in the early 1800s. Occupied by United States troops from 1915 to 1934. (p. 57, *m716*)

Harpers Ferry (39°N/78°W) Town in West Virginia. Abolitionist John Brown raided the arsenal there in 1859. (p. 385, *m399*)

Hawaii Newest of the 50 states. Nicknamed the Aloha State. (p. 766, *m760–61*)

Hiroshima (34°N/133°E) City in southern Japan. Largely destroyed by an atomic bomb dropped there on August 6, 1945. (p. 642, *m636*)

Hispaniola (18°N/73°W) Island in the Caribbean that Columbus visited on his first voyage. Occupied today by the Dominican Republic and Haiti. (p. 57, *m58*)

Ho Chi Minh Trail Overland route from North Vietnam to South Vietnam to supply the Vietcong. Passed through Cambodia. (p. 706, *m706*)

Holland Name for the Netherlands, a country in northwestern Europe. (p. 627, *m628*)

Honduras Nation in Central America. Invaded by the United States in 1912 and 1919 to protect American lives and property. (p. 281, *m716*)

Hudson Bay Large inlet of the Arctic Ocean. Named for the explorer Henry Hudson. (p. 68, *m66*)

Hudson River Largest river in New York State. Explored by Henry Hudson in 1609. (p. 67, *m87*)

I

Iceland (65°N/20°W) Island nation in the north Atlantic Ocean. Settled by Vikings in the ninth century. (p. 49, *m758–59*)

Idaho 43rd state. Nicknamed the Gem State. Acquired by the United States as part of Oregon Country. (p. 766, *m760–61*)

Illinois 21st state. Nicknamed the Inland Empire. Settled as part of the Northwest Territory. (p. 766, *m760–61*)

Inchon (37°N/127°E) Port city in South Korea. Site of heavy fighting during the Korean War. (p. 659, *m658*)

Independence (37°N/96°W) City in western Missouri. Starting point of the Oregon Trail in the 1840s. (p. 312, *m320*)

India Country in South Asia. World's second most populated country after China. Gained independence from Britain in 1947. (p. 657, *m758–59*)

Indiana 19th state. Nicknamed the Hoosier State. Settled as part of the Northwest Territory. (p. 766, *m760–61*)

Indian Ocean Separates Africa from India. (p. 55, *m57*)

Interior Plains Region of the central United States that stretches from the Rockies to the Appalachians. (p. 23, *m24*)

Intermountain Region Rugged and mostly dry region from the Rocky Mountains to the Sierra Nevada and coastal mountains of the western United States. (p. 23, *m24*)

Gazetteer

Iowa 29th state. Nicknamed the Hawkeye State. Acquired by the United States as part of the Louisiana Purchase. (p. 766, *m760–61*)

Iran Oil-producing country in the Middle East. Commands sea routes through the Persian Gulf. (p. 710, *m709*)

Iraq Oil-producing country in the Middle East. At war with neighboring Iran since 1980. (p. 711, *m709*)

Israel Country in the Middle East. Set up as a Jewish homeland in 1948. (p. 708, *m709*)

Isthmus of Panama Narrow strip of land joining North and South America. (p. 22, *m61*)

Italy Country in southern Europe. Fought with the Allies in World War I and with the Axis Powers in World War II. (p. 51, *m758–59*)

Iwo Jima (25°N/141°E) Small island south of Japan's main islands. Site of a hard-won American victory in World War II. (p. 640, *m636*)

J

Jackson (32°N/90°W) City in western Mississippi. Captured by Grant in 1863. (p. 400, *m411*)

Jamestown (37°N/77°W) First successful English colony in North America. (p. 76, *m112*)

Japan Densely populated industrial nation in East Asia. Opened up to trade with the West by Commodore Matthew Perry. One of the Axis Powers in World War II. (p. 530, *m532*)

Jordan Arab country in the Middle East. (p. 708, *m709*)

K

Kansas 34th state. Nicknamed the Sunflower State. Acquired by the United States as part of the Louisiana Purchase. (p. 766, *m760–61*)

Kaskaskia (38°N/90°W) French, then British, fur-trading post on an island in the Mississippi River. Captured by George Rogers Clark in 1778. First state capital of Illinois. (p. 187, *m186*)

Kentucky 15th state. Nicknamed the Bluegrass State. Was the first area west of the Appalachians to be settled by early pioneers. (p. 766, *m760–61*)

L

Lake Champlain (45°N/73°W) Borders New York and Vermont. Part of the water route connecting the Hudson and St. Lawrence rivers.

Fort Ticonderoga is at the southern end. (p. 173, *m175*)

Lake Erie One of the five Great Lakes. Shared by the United States and Canada. (p. 26, *m24*)

Lake Huron One of the five Great Lakes. Shared by the United States and Canada. (p. 26, *m24*)

Lake Michigan Only one of the Great Lakes located wholly within the United States. (p. 26, *m24*)

Lake Ontario One of the five Great Lakes. Shared by the United States and Canada. (p. 26, *m24*)

Lake Superior Highest and farthest inland of the five Great Lakes. Shared by the United States and Canada. (p. 26, *m24*)

Latin America Name for those parts of the Western Hemisphere where Latin languages such as Spanish, French, and Portuguese are spoken. Includes Mexico, Central and South America, and the West Indies. (p. 282, *m282*)

Lebanon Country in the Middle East. Home to many Palestinian refugees. Torn by civil war since 1975. (p. 708, *m709*)

Lexington (42°N/71°W) Site of the first clash between minutemen and British troops in 1775. Now a suburb of Boston. (p. 169, *m169*)

Line of Demarcation Line drawn by the Pope in 1494. Divided the non-Christian world between Spain and Portugal. (p. 60, *m61*)

Little Bighorn Site of a Sioux and Cheyenne victory over Colonel George S. Custer in 1876. (p. 447, *m448*)

Lone Star Republic Another name for the Republic of Texas (1836–1845). (p. 317, *m317*)

Louisbourg (46°N/60°W) Fort built by France on Cape Breton Island in eastern Canada. Changed hands several times between France and Britain. (p. 154, *m154*)

Louisiana 18th state. Nicknamed the Pelican State. First state created out of the Louisiana Purchase. (p. 766, *m760–61*)

Louisiana Purchase Region between the Mississippi River and the Rocky Mountains purchased from France in 1803. (p. 245, *m247*)

M

Maine 23rd state. Nicknamed the Pine Tree State. Originally part of Massachusetts. Maine gained separate statehood in 1820 under the terms of the Missouri Compromise. (p. 766, *m760–61*)

Manchuria (48°N/125°E) Industrialized region of northeastern China. Seized by Japan in the 1930s. Returned to China after World War II. (p. 625, *m636*)

Marne River (48°N/4°E) Located in northeastern France. Site of heavy fighting in World War I. (p. 552, *m560*)

Maryland One of the 13 original states. Nicknamed the Old Line State or the Free State. (p. 766, *m760–61*)

Massachusetts One of the 13 original states. Nicknamed the Bay State or the Old Colony. (p. 766, *m760–61*)

Massachusetts Bay Colony Founded and settled by Puritans in the 1630s. (p. 100, *m102*)

Meuse River (51°N/5°E) Crosses France, Belgium, and the Netherlands. Battleground in World War I. (p. 563, *m560*)

Mexican Cession Lands acquired by the United States from Mexico under the Treaty of Guadalupe Hidalgo in 1848. (p. 324, *m326*)

Mexico Southern neighbor of the United States. Gained independence from Spain in 1821. (p. 23, *m758–59*)

Mexico City (19°N/99°W) Capital of Mexico. Was the capital of New Spain. Site of the ancient Aztec city of Tenochtitlan. (p. 82, *m78*)

Michigan 26th state. Nicknamed the Great Lake State or the Wolverine State. Settled as part of Northwest Territory. (p. 766, *m760–61*)

Midway Island (28°N/179°W) Annexed by the United States in 1867. American victory here was a turning point in World War II. (p. 530, *m532*)

Minnesota 32nd state. Nicknamed the Gopher State. Most of it was acquired by the United States as part of the Louisiana Purchase. (p. 766, *m760–61*)

Mississippi 20th state. Nicknamed the Magnolia State. (p. 766, *m760–61*)

Mississippi River Second longest river in the United States. Links the Great Lakes with the Gulf of Mexico. (p. 25, *m24*)

Missouri 24th state. Nicknamed the Show Me State. Acquired by the United States as part of the Louisiana Purchase. (p. 766, *m760–61*)

Missouri Compromise line Line drawn across the Louisiana Purchase at latitude 36°36'N to divide free states from slave states. (p. 374, *m380*)

Missouri River Longest river in the United States. Rises in the northern Rocky Mountains and joins the Mississippi River near St. Louis. (p. 20, *m24*)

Montana 41st state. Nicknamed the Treasure State. Acquired in part by the United States through the Louisiana Purchase. (p. 766, *m760–61*)

Montreal (46°N/74°W) Major city in Canada. Located on the St. Lawrence River. Settled by the French. (p. 155, *m154*)

Moscow (56°N/38°E) Capital of the Soviet Union. (p. 635, *m628*)

N

Nagasaki (33°N/130°E) Japanese port city. Largely destroyed by the atomic bomb dropped there on August 9, 1945. (p. 530, *m636*)

National Road Early road to the Old West. Now part of U.S. Highway 40. (p. 272, *m272*)

NATO North Atlantic Treaty Organization. Alliance formed in 1949 by the United States and other Western powers. (p. 655, *m656*)

Nebraska 37th state. Nicknamed the Cornhusker State. Acquired by the United States as part of the Louisiana Purchase. (p. 766, *m760–61*)

Nevada 36th state. Nicknamed the Sagebrush State or the Battle Born State. Acquired by the United States at the end of the Mexican War. (p. 766, *m760–61*)

New Amsterdam (41°N/74°W) Settlement founded by the Dutch on Manhattan Island. Now called New York City. (p. 86, *m87*)

New England Name for the region that today includes the states from Maine to Connecticut. (p. 98, *m102*)

Newfoundland (48°N/57°W) Island at the mouth of the St. Lawrence River. Part of Canada. (p. 66, *m66*)

New France Colony established by France in North America. (p. 84, *m85*)

New Hampshire One of the 13 original states. Nicknamed the Granite State. (p. 766, *m760–61*)

New Jersey One of the 13 original states. Nicknamed the Garden State. (p. 766, *m760–61*)

New Mexico 47th state. Nicknamed the Land of Enchantment. Acquired by the United States at the end of the Mexican War. (p. 766, *m760–61*)

New Netherland Dutch colony on the Hudson River. Conquered by the English and renamed New York in 1664. (p. 83, *m87*)

New Orleans (30°N/90°W) Port city in Louisiana near the mouth of the Mississippi River. Settled by the French in the 1600s. Site of a battle between American and British forces in 1815. (p. 84, *m85*)

New Spain Area ruled by Spain for 300 years. Included Spanish colonies in West Indies, Central America, and North America. (p. 77, *m78*)

New Sweden Swedish colony on the Delaware River. Founded about 1640. Taken over by the Dutch in 1655, then by the English in 1664. Now part of Pennsylvania, New Jersey, and Delaware. (p. 87, *m87*)

New York One of the 13 original states. Nicknamed the Empire State. (p. 766, *m760–61*)

New York City (41°N/74°W) Port city at the mouth of the Hudson River. Founded by the Dutch as New Amsterdam. First capital of the United States. (p. 126, *m127*)

Nicaragua Country in Central America. Won independence from Spain in 1821. Ruled by the Sandanistas since 1979. (p. 281, *m716*)

Normandy (49°N/0°) Region of northern France. Allies landed there on D-Day in World War II. (p. 638, *m628*)

North America World's third largest continent. Separated from South America by the Isthmus of Panama. (p. 20, *m760–61*)

North Carolina One of the 13 original states. Nicknamed the Tar Heel State or the Old North State. (p. 766, *m760–61*)

North Dakota 39th state. Nicknamed the Sioux State or the Flickertail State. Acquired by the United States as part of the Louisiana Purchase. (p. 766, *m760–61*)

North Korea Country in East Asia. Divided at the 38th parallel from South Korea. (p. 658, *m658*)

Northwest Territory Name for lands north of the Ohio River and east of the Mississippi River. Acquired by the United States by the Treaty of Paris in 1783. (p. 200, *m201*)

Nova Scotia Province of eastern Canada. Early French, then British colony. (p. 83, *m85*)

Nueces River Claimed by Mexico as the southern border of Texas in the Mexican War. (p. 322, *m324*)

O

Ohio 17th state. Nicknamed the Buckeye State. Settled as part of the Northwest Territory. (p. 766, *m760–61*)

Ohio River Important transportation route. Begins at Pittsburgh and joins the Mississippi River at Cairo. (p. 20, *m24*)

Okinawa (27°N/129°E) Small island southwest of Japan. Captured by Americans at the end of World War II. (p. 640, *m636*)

Oklahoma 46th state. Nicknamed the Sooner State. Acquired by the United States as part of the Louisiana Purchase. (p. 766, *m760–61*)

Oregon 33rd state. Nicknamed the Beaver State. Acquired by the United States as part of Oregon Country. (p. 766, *m760–61*)

Oregon Country Located in the Pacific Northwest. Claimed by the United States, Britain, Spain, and Russia. (p. 309, *m326*)

Oregon Trail Overland route from Independence on the Missouri River to the Columbia River valley. (p. 309, *m310*)

P

Pacific Northwest Stretches from Alaska to northern California along the west coast of North America. (p. 27)

Pacific Ocean World's largest ocean. (p. 22, *m21*)

Pakistan Country in South Asia. Gained independence from Britain in 1947. (p. 657, *m758–59*)

Panama Country on the isthmus separating North and South America. Gained independence from Colombia in 1903. (p. 281, *m537*)

Panama Canal (9°N/80°W) Located on the Isthmus of Panama. Links the Atlantic and Pacific oceans. (p. 540, *m541*)

Paris (49°N/2°E) Capital of France. (p. 184, *m758–59*)

Pearl Harbor (21°N/158°W) American naval base near Honolulu, Hawaii. Bombed by Japan on December 7, 1941. (p. 622, *m636*)

Pennsylvania One of the 13 original states. Nicknamed the Keystone State. (p. 766, *m760–61*)

Persian Gulf (28°N/51°E) Major sea route for ships carrying Middle Eastern oil exports. (p. 710, *m709*)

Peru Country in South America. Gained independence from Spain in 1821. (p. 27, *m758–59*)

Philadelphia (40°N/75°W) Major port and chief city in Pennsylvania. Second capital of the United States. (p. 108, *m107*)

Philippine Islands (14°N/125°E) Group of islands in the Pacific Ocean off the east coast of Asia. Magellan was killed there. Acquired by the United States in 1898. Won independence in 1946. (p. 61, *m532*)

Pikes Peak (39°N/105°W) Located in the Rocky Mountains of central Colorado. Named for Zebulon Pike, who reached it in 1806. (p. 249, *m247*)

Plymouth (42°N/71°W) New England colony founded in 1620 by Pilgrims. Absorbed by the Massachusetts Bay Colony in 1691. (p. 76, *m102*)

Poland Country in Eastern Europe. Became a Soviet satellite after World War II. (p. 193, *m656*)

Portugal Country in western Europe. In the 1400s, sailors set out from there to explore the coast of Africa. (p. 53, *m758–59*)

Potomac River Forms part of the Maryland-Virginia border. Flows through Washington, D.C., and into Chesapeake Bay. (p. 90, *m94*)

Prime Meridian Line of longitude labeled 0°. (p. 56, *m57*)

Princeton (40°N/75°W) Located in New Jersey. Site of an American victory during the Revolution. (p. 182, *m182*)

Promontory Point (42°N/112°W) Located just north of the Great Salt Lake. Place where the Central Pacific and Union Pacific were joined on May 10, 1869, to form the first transcontinental railroad. (p. 441, *m453*)

Puerto Rico (18°N/67°W) Island in the Caribbean Sea. Acquired from Spain after the Spanish-American War. Now a self-governing commonwealth of the United States. (p. 58, *m758–59*)

Q

Quebec City (47°N/71°W) Located in eastern Canada on the St. Lawrence River. Founded in 1608 by the French explorer Samuel de Champlain. Captured by the British in 1759. (p. 83, *m85*)

R

Republic of Texas Independent nation set up by American settlers in Texas. Lasted from 1836 to 1845. (p. 316, *m317*)

Rhode Island One of the 13 original states. Nicknamed the Little Rhody or the Ocean State. (p. 766, *m760–61*)

Richmond (38°N/78°W) Located on the James River. Capital of the Confederacy. (p. 397, *m191*)

Rio Grande Forms the border between the United States and Mexico. (p. 26, *m317*)

Roanoke Island (36°N/76°W) Located off the coast of North Carolina. Site of the "lost colony" founded in 1587. (p. 88, *m94*)

Rocky Mountains Stretches from Alaska to New Mexico through the western United States. Barrier to travel in pioneer days. (p. 23, *m24*)

Russia Name for the country that became the Union of Soviet Socialist Republics in 1922. (p. 481, *m551*)

S

Sacramento (39°N/122°W) Capital of California. Developed as a Gold Rush boom town. (p. 327, *m760–61*)

Sagres (37°N/9°W) Town facing the Atlantic at the tip of Portugal. In the 1400s, Prince Henry the Navigator set up an informal school for sailors there. (p. 53, *m57*)

St. Augustine (30°N/81°W) City in Florida. Founded by Spain in 1565. Oldest European settlement in the United States. (p. 83, *m78*)

St. Lawrence River Waterway leading from the Great Lakes to the Atlantic Ocean. Forms part of the border between the United States and Canada. (p. 26, *m85*)

St. Lawrence Seaway (45°N/75°W) System of canals, locks, and dams on the St. Lawrence River. Built to let ocean-going ships travel as far west as the Great Lakes. Opened in 1959. (p. 713)

Salt Lake City (41°N/112°W) Largest city in Utah. Founded in 1847 by Mormons. (p. 23, *m760–61*)

Samoa (15°S/171°W) Group of Pacific Islands. Now divided into American Samoa and the independent nation of Western Samoa. (p. 532, *m532*)

San Antonio (29°N/99°W) City in southern Texas. Chief Texas settlement in Spanish and Mexican days. Site of the Alamo. (p. 83, *m317*)

San Diego (33°N/117°W) City in southern California. Founded as a Spanish mission. (p. 320, *m320*)

San Francisco (38°N/122°W) City in northern California. Boom town of the 1848 California Gold Rush. (p. 23, *m320*)

San Jacinto River Flows across southeastern Texas into Galveston Bay. Site of a Texan victory in 1836. (p. 317, *m317*)

Santa Fe (35°N/106°W) Capital of New Mexico. First settled by the Spanish. (p. 83, *m320*)

Santa Fe Trail Overland trail from Independence to Santa Fe. Opened in 1821 after Mexico gained independence from Spain. (p. 319, *m320*)

Sarajevo (43°N/18°E) City in southeastern Europe where Archduke Francis Ferdinand was assassinated on June 28, 1914. (p. 550, *m551*)

Saratoga (43°N/75°W) City in eastern New York. Also called Saratoga Springs. The American victory there in 1777 was a turning point in the Revolution. (p. 181, *m182*)

Savannah (32°N/81°W) Oldest city in Georgia. Founded in 1733. (p. 112, *m132*)

Shiloh (35°N/88°W) Site of a Union victory in 1862. Located on the Tennessee River. (p. 399, *m411*)

Sicily (38°N/14°E) Island in the Mediterranean that is part of Italy. Invaded by the Allies in World War II. (p. 636, *m628*)

Sierra Nevada Mountain range mostly in California. (p. 23, *m24*)

Sinai Peninsula (29°N/33°E) Desert region in northeastern Egypt. Captured by Israel in 1967. Returned to Egypt under the terms of the Camp David Agreement. (p. 708, *m709*)

Songhai Ancient West African kingdom. (p. 54, *m57*)

South America World's fourth largest continent. Part of the Western Hemisphere. (p. 22, *m758–59*)

South Carolina One of the 13 original states. Nicknamed the Palmetto State. (p. 766, *m760–61*)

South Dakota 40th state. Nicknamed the Coyote State or the Sunshine State. Acquired by the United States as part of the Louisiana Purchase. (p. 766, *m760–61*)

South Korea Country in East Asia. Divided at the 38th parallel from North Korea. (p. 658, *m658*)

Soviet Union Short name for the Union of Soviet Socialist Republics. Known as Russia before 1922. (p. 577, *m628*)

Spain Country in southwestern Europe. Columbus sailed from Spain in 1492. (p. 53, *m758–59*)

Gazetteer

Spanish Florida Part of New Spain. Purchased by the United States in 1821. (p. 112, *m85*)

Stalingrad (49°N/42°E) City in the Soviet Union. Withstood a siege by Nazis in World War II. Renamed Volgograd in 1961. (p. 635, *m628*)

Strait of Magellan (53°S/69°W) Narrow water route at the tip of South America. (p. 22, *m61*)

Syria Arab country in the Middle East. (p. 708, *m709*)

T

Taiwan (24°N/122°E) Island off the coast of China. Chiang Kai-shek retreated there in 1949 after the Communist Chinese took over mainland China. (p. 658, *m758–59*)

Teheran (36°N/52°E) Capital of Iran. American hostages were held there from November 1979 to January 1981. (p. 711, *m709*)

Tennessee 16th state. Nicknamed the Volunteer State. Gained statehood after North Carolina ceded its western lands to the United States. (p. 766, *m760–61*)

Tennessee River (35°N/88°W) Tributary of the Ohio River. Used to flood often. Brought under control in 1930s by the Tennessee Valley Authority. Dams provide cheap electricity to the surrounding region. (p. 25, *m608*)

Tenochtitlan (19°N/99°W) Capital of the Aztec empire. Now part of Mexico City. (p. 42, *m45*)

Texas 28th state. Nicknamed the Lone Star State. Proclaimed independence from Mexico in 1836. Was a separate republic until 1845. (p. 766, *m760–61*)

Thames River Flows southwest across Ontario into the Great Lakes near Detroit. Site of battle during the War of 1812. (p. 258, *m258*)

Tikal (17°N/90°W) Ancient Maya city. (p. 42, *m45*)

Timbuktu (17°N/3°W) City on the southern edge of the Sahara Desert.

Flourished as a center of trade and learning. (p. 54, *m57*)

Turkey Country in the Middle East. Member of NATO since 1952. (p. 653, *m656*)

U

Utah 45th state. Nicknamed the Beehive State. Settled by Mormons. (p. 766, *m760–61*)

V

Valley Forge (40°N/76°W) Winter headquarters for the Continental Army in 1777–78. Located near Philadelphia. (p. 183, *m182*)

Venezuela Oil-rich country in South America. Part of the Republic of Great Colombia from 1819 to 1831. (p. 281, *m758–59*)

Veracruz (19°N/96°W) Port city in Mexico on the Gulf of Mexico. (p. 323, *m324*)

Vermont 14th state. Nicknamed the Green Mountain State. First new state to join the Union after the Revolution. (p. 766, *m760–61*)

Vicksburg (42°N/86°W) Located on a high cliff overlooking the Mississippi River. Site of a Union victory in 1863. (p. 400, *m411*)

Vietnam Country in Southeast Asia. Divided into North and South Vietnam in 1954. Remained divided until North Vietnam defeated South Vietnam in a long war. (p. 657, *m706*)

Vincennes (39°N/88°W) City in Indiana. Settled by the French. British fort there was captured by George Rogers Clark in 1779. (p. 187, *m186*)

Virginia One of the 13 original states. Nicknamed the Old Dominion. (p. 766, *m760–61*)

Virgin Islands (18°N/64°W) Territory of the United States. Purchased from Denmark in 1917. (p. 766)

W

Warsaw Pact Military alliance formed by the Soviet Union in 1955. Includes nations of Eastern Europe. (p. 656, *m656*)

Washington 42nd state. Nicknamed the Evergreen State. (p. 766, *m760–61*)

Washington, D.C. (39°N/83°W) Capital of the United States since 1800. Called Federal City until it was renamed for George Washington in 1799. (p. 234, *m258*)

Washington-on-the-Brazos (30°N/96°W) Town in Texas near Houston. Texans signed their declaration of independence from Mexico there in 1836. (p. 316, *m317*)

Western Hemisphere Western half of the world. Includes North and South America. (p. 22)

West Indies Islands in the Caribbean Sea. Explored by Columbus in 1492. (p. 47, *m758–59*)

West Virginia 35th state. Nicknamed the Mountain State. Separated from Virginia early in the Civil War. (p. 766, *m760–61*)

Willamette River Flows across fertile farmlands in northern Oregon to join the Columbia River. (p. 310, *m310*)

Wisconsin 30th state. Nicknamed the Badger State. Settled as part of the Northwest Territory. (p. 766, *m760–61*)

Wounded Knee (43°N/102°W) Site of a massacre of Indians in 1890. Located in what is now South Dakota. (p. 447, *m448*)

Wyoming 44th state. Nicknamed the Equality State. (p. 766, *m760–61*)

Y

Yalu River (41°N/127°E) Forms part of the border between North Korea and China. (p. 659, *m658*)

Yorktown (37°N/76°W) Town in Virginia near the York River. Site of a decisive American victory in 1781. (p. 189, *m191*)

Gazetteer

A Chronology of American History

This chronology includes some of the most important events and developments in American history. It can be used to trace developments in the areas of government and citizenship, exploration and invention, American life, and the world of ideas. The number after each entry refers to the chapter where the event or development is discussed in the text.

	Government and Citizenship	Explorers and Inventors
Prehistory–1499	Mayas, Aztecs, Incas build empires in Americas 2 Crusades for Holy Land begin 3 Rulers build strong nations in Europe 3	Mayas develop accurate calendar 2 Incas use quinine to treat malaria 2 Columbus sails to America 3 Vasco da Gama reaches India 3
1500–1599	Cortés defeats Aztecs 3 Pizarro captures Inca capital 3 Spanish pass Laws of the Indies 4 English colony set up at Roanoke 4	Spanish explore North America 3 Magellan's expedition circles globe 3 Cartier sails up St. Lawrence River 3 Drake sails around world 3
1600–1649	House of Burgesses set up in Virginia 4 Mayflower Compact signed 4 Massachusetts Bay Colony founded 5 Fundamental Orders of Connecticut written 5	Joint stock companies finance English settlements in North America 4 Champlain founds Quebec 4 West Indian tobacco brought to Virginia 4
1650–1699	France claims Louisiana 4 Glorious Revolution in England 5 Town meetings held in New England 6	Marquette and Joliet explore Mississippi River 4 La Salle reaches Mississippi delta 4
1700–1749	Georgia founded 5 Carolinas divided into two colonies 5 English settlers move into Ohio Valley 7	Indigo developed as cash crop 6 Benjamin Franklin invents Franklin stove 6
1750–1799	French and Indian War 7 Intolerable Acts passed 7 Declaration of Independence signed 8 American Revolution 8 Constitution ratified 9	Fitch launches first steam-powered boat 12 Slater sets up textile mills in New England 12 Eli Whitney invents cotton gin 12

Changes in American Life	The World of Ideas	
Agriculture develops in Americas 2 Great Serpent Mound built 2 Trade between Europe and Asia expands 3	Mayas develop system of writing 2 Aztecs build Tenochtitlan 2 Renaissance begins in Europe 3	**Prehistory–1499**
Native American population of Spanish America declines 4 French develop fishing and fur trading in North America 4	Spanish convert Native Americans to Christianity 4 Universities open in Spanish America 4 John White paints in North America 4	1500–1599
Spanish, French, Dutch, and English colonists adapt to life in New World 5 John Smith helps Jamestown survive 5 Slavery introduced in Virginia 5	Religious toleration granted in Maryland 5 Harvard College founded 6 First public schools set up in Massachusetts 6	1600–1649
Navigation Acts passed 5 New England becomes trade and shipbuilding center 6	Quakers seek religious freedom in Pennsylvania 5 College of William and Mary founded 6	1650–1699
Triangular trade flourishes 6 Plantations expand in South 6 Growth of port cities 6	Yale College founded 6 *Poor Richard's Almanac* published 6 Great Awakening begins in colonies 6	1700–1749
Proclamation of 1763 7 Parliament passes Sugar, Quartering, Stamp, and Townshend acts 7 Colonies boycott British goods 7 Northwest Ordinance takes effect 9	Thomas Paine writes *Common Sense* 8 Phillis Wheatley publishes poetry 8 Northern states ban slave trade 9 National capital designed and built 10	1750–1799

	Government and Citizenship	Explorers and Inventors
1800–1824	Louisiana Purchase 11 War of 1812 11 Missouri Compromise passed 17 Monroe Doctrine 12	Lewis and Clark expedition 11 Steamboats improved 12 Eli Whitney develops interchangeable parts 12
1825–1849	Age of Jackson 13 Indian Removal Act passed 13 Texas wins independence 14 Oregon divided along 49th parallel 14	Erie Canal opened 12 Mechanical reaper, steel plow, and telegraph developed 15 Railroads expand 15
1850–1874	Compromise of 1850 17 Civil War 18 Emancipation Proclamation 18 Indian wars on Great Plains 20	Passenger elevator, sleeping car, and air brake invented 21 Bessemer process developed 21 Transcontinental railroad completed 21
1875–1899	Battle of Little Bighorn 20 Populist Party formed 20 Sherman Antitrust Act passed 21 Spanish–American War 24	Refrigeration developed 21 Telephone, phonograph, and incandescent light bulb invented 21 First skyscraper built 22
1900–1924	Progressive Movement 23 Roosevelt Corollary 24 World War I 25 Fourteen Points 25 United States rejects Treaty of Versailles 25	Panama Canal built 24 Airplane invented 21 Assembly line introduced 21 Electric appliances become widespread 26
1925–1949	New Deal 27 World War II 28 Truman Doctrine and Marshall Plan 29 NATO created 29	Lindbergh flies across Atlantic 27 Antibiotics developed 32 Atomic bomb developed 28 First computers invented 32
1950–1974	Korean War 29 Civil Rights Act passed 30 Watergate affair 30 Vietnam War 31	*Explorer 1* launched into orbit 32 American astronauts land on moon 32 Nuclear power plants built 32 Vaccines increase life expectancy 32
1975–Present	Camp David Agreement on Middle East 31 Sandra Day O'Connor appointed to Supreme Court 30	Computers and microsurgery advance medicine 32 Space shuttle flights 32 *Voyager 1* passes Saturn 32

Chronology

Connections With American Literature

TOPIC	AUTHOR	WORK	GENRE
UNIT 1 THE WORLD OF THE AMERICAS			
Peoples of the Desert, pages 34–35	Zuñi Indians	The Girl Who Hunted Rabbits	myth
Peoples of North America, pages 36–41	Tewa Indians	Song of the Sky Loom	myth
Peoples of North America, pages 36–41	Ella E. Clark	The Origin of Fire	myth
Spain Joins the Search, pages 55–57	Joaquin Miller	Columbus	poem
UNIT 2 SETTLING THE NEW WORLD			
Fur Trappers and Traders, pages 83–84	James Fenimore Cooper	The Deerslayer The Pathfinder	novels
New Netherland, pages 105–106	Washington Irving	Rip Van Winkle	tale
The New England Way of Life, pages 121–125	Henry Wadsworth Longfellow	The Village Blacksmith	poem
Benjamin Franklin, pages 136–137	Benjamin Franklin	Poor Richard's Almanac	book
UNIT 3 THE STRUGGLE FOR INDEPENDENCE			
Paul Revere's Ride, page 168	Henry Wadsworth Longfellow	Paul Revere's Ride	poem
Fighting Begins, pages 173–177	Esther Forbes	Johnny Tremain	novel
The Voice of Common Sense, pages 177–178	Thomas Paine	Common Sense	pamphlet
Women in the Revolution, pages 188–189	Phillis Wheatley	To the Right Honourable William, Earl of Dartmouth	letter
UNIT 4 STRENGTHENING THE NEW NATION			
Washington's Farewell Address, page 229	George Washington	Farewell Address	speech
Election of 1800, page 237	Edward Everett Hale	The Man Without a Country	short story
Benjamin Banneker, page 237	Benjamin Banneker	Letter to Thomas Jefferson	letter
The Nation Doubles in Size, pages 244–249	Carl Sandburg	Paul Bunyan of the North Woods	folk tale
UNIT 5 A GROWING NATION			
The Lone Star Republic, pages 315–319	Adrien Stoutenburg	Davy Crockett	folk tale
The Underground Railroad, page 353	Ann Petry	Harriet Tubman: Guide to Freedom	biography
Sojourner Truth, pages 355–356	Sojourner Truth	Ain't I a Woman?	speech
Emerson and His Circle, pages 362–363	Ralph Waldo Emerson	Concord Hymn	poem

Connections With Literature

Presidents of the United States

1. **George Washington** (1732–1799)
   Years in office: 1789–1797
   No political party
   Elected from: Virginia
   Vice Pres.: John Adams

2. **John Adams** (1735–1826)
   Years in office: 1797–1801
   Federalist Party
   Elected from: Massachusetts
   Vice Pres.: Thomas Jefferson

3. **Thomas Jefferson** (1743–1826)
   Years in office: 1801–1809
   Democratic Republican Party
   Elected from: Virginia
   Vice Pres.: Aaron Burr, George Clinton

4. **James Madison** (1751–1836)
   Years in office: 1809–1817
   Democratic Republican Party
   Elected from: Virginia
   Vice Pres.: George Clinton,
             Elbridge Gerry

5. **James Monroe** (1758–1831)
   Years in office: 1817–1825
   Democratic Republican Party
   Elected from: Virginia
   Vice Pres.: Daniel Tompkins

6. **John Quincy Adams** (1767–1848)
   Years in office: 1825–1829
   National Republican Party
   Elected from: Massachusetts
   Vice Pres.: John Calhoun

7. **Andrew Jackson** (1767–1845)
   Years in office: 1829–1837
   Democratic Party
   Elected from: Tennessee
   Vice Pres.: John Calhoun,
             Martin Van Buren

8. **Martin Van Buren** (1782–1862)
   Years in office: 1837–1841
   Democratic Party
   Elected from: New York
   Vice Pres.: Richard Johnson

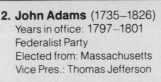

Presidents

9

10

9. William Henry Harrison* (1773–1841)
Years in office: 1841
Whig Party
Elected from: Ohio
Vice Pres.: John Tyler

10. John Tyler (1790–1862)
Years in office: 1841–1845
Whig Party
Elected from: Virginia
Vice Pres.: none

11. James K. Polk (1795–1849)
Years in office: 1845–1849
Democratic Party
Elected from: Tennessee
Vice Pres.: George Dallas

12. Zachary Taylor* (1784–1850)
Years in office: 1849–1850
Whig Party
Elected from: Louisiana
Vice Pres.: Millard Fillmore

13. Millard Fillmore (1800–1874)
Years in office: 1850–1853
Whig Party
Elected from: New York
Vice Pres.: none

14. Franklin Pierce (1804–1869)
Years in office: 1853–1857
Democratic Party
Elected from: New Hampshire
Vice Pres.: William King

15. James Buchanan (1791–1868)
Years in office: 1857–1861
Democratic Party
Elected from: Pennsylvania
Vice Pres.: John Breckinridge

16. Abraham Lincoln** (1809–1865)
Years in office: 1861–1865
Republican Party
Elected from: Illinois
Vice Pres.: Hannibal Hamlin,
　　　　　Andrew Johnson

11

12

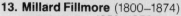

13

14

15

16

Presidents

*Died in office　　**Assassinated　　***Resigned

17

18

17. **Andrew Johnson** (1808–1875)
Years in office: 1865–1869
Republican Party
Elected from: Tennessee
Vice Pres.: none

18. **Ulysses S. Grant** (1822–1885)
Years in office: 1869–1877
Republican Party
Elected from: Illinois
Vice Pres.: Schuyler Colfax, Henry Wilson

19. **Rutherford B. Hayes** (1822–1893)
Years in office: 1877–1881
Republican Party
Elected from: Ohio
Vice Pres.: William Wheeler

20. **James A. Garfield**** (1831–1881)
Years in office: 1881
Republican Party
Elected from: Ohio
Vice Pres.: Chester A. Arthur

21. **Chester A. Arthur** (1830–1886)
Years in office: 1881–1885
Republican Party
Elected from: New York
Vice Pres.: none

22. **Grover Cleveland** (1837–1908)
Years in office: 1885–1889
Democratic Party
Elected from: New York
Vice Pres.: Thomas Hendricks

23. **Benjamin Harrison** (1833–1901)
Years in office: 1889–1893
Republican Party
Elected from: Indiana
Vice Pres.: Levi Morton

24. **Grover Cleveland** (1837–1908)
Years in office: 1893–1897
Democratic Party
Elected from: New York
Vice Pres.: Adlai Stevenson

20

22

23

24

Presidents

25

26

25. Willam McKinley** (1843–1901)
Years in office: 1897–1901
Republican Party
Elected from: Ohio
Vice Pres.: Garret Hobart,
Theodore Roosevelt

26. Theodore Roosevelt (1858–1919)
Years in office: 1901–1909
Republican Party
Elected from: New York
Vice Pres.: Charles Fairbanks

27. William Howard Taft (1857–1930)
Years in office: 1909–1913
Republican Party
Elected from: Ohio
Vice Pres.: James Sherman

28. Woodrow Wilson (1856–1924)
Years in office: 1913–1921
Democratic Party
Elected from: New Jersey
Vice Pres.: Thomas Marshall

29. Warren G. Harding* (1865–1923)
Years in office: 1921–1923
Republican Party
Elected from: Ohio
Vice Pres.: Calvin Coolidge

30. Calvin Coolidge (1872–1933)
Years in office: 1923–1929
Republican Party
Elected from: Massachusetts
Vice Pres.: Charles Dawes

31. Herbert C. Hoover (1874–1964)
Years in office: 1929–1933
Republican Party
Elected from: California
Vice Pres.: Charles Curtis

32. Franklin D. Roosevelt* (1882–1945)
Years in office: 1933–1945
Democratic Party
Elected from: New York
Vice Pres.: John Garner, Henry Wallace,
Harry S. Truman

27

28

30

31

32

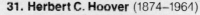
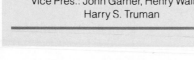
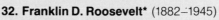

Presidents

*Died in office   **Assassinated   ***Resigned

33.

34.

35.

36.

37.

38.

39.

40.

41.

Presidents

33. Harry S. Truman (1884–1972)
Years in office: 1945–1953
Democratic Party
Elected from: Missouri
Vice Pres.: Alben Barkley

34. Dwight D. Eisenhower (1890–1969)
Years in office: 1953–1961
Republican Party
Elected from: New York
Vice Pres.: Richard M. Nixon

35. John F. Kennedy** (1917–1963)
Years in office: 1961–1963
Democratic Party
Elected from: Massachusetts
Vice Pres.: Lyndon B. Johnson

36. Lyndon B. Johnson (1908–1973)
Years in office: 1963–1969
Democratic Party
Elected from: Texas
Vice Pres.: Hubert Humphrey

37. Richard M. Nixon*** (1913–   )
Years in office: 1969–1974
Republican Party
Elected from: New York
Vice Pres.: Spiro Agnew, Gerald R. Ford

38. Gerald R. Ford (1913–   )
Years in office: 1974–1977
Republican Party
Elected from: Michigan
Vice Pres.: Nelson Rockefeller

39. Jimmy Carter (1924–   )
Years in office: 1977–1981
Democratic Party
Elected from: Georgia
Vice Pres.: Walter Mondale

40. Ronald W. Reagan (1911–   )
Years in office: 1981–1989
Republican Party
Elected from: California
Vice Pres.: George Bush

41. George Bush (1924–   )
Years in office: 1989–
Republican Party
Elected from: Texas
Vice Pres.: Dan Quayle

*Died in office   **Assassinated   ***Resigned

This glossary defines all vocabulary words and many important historical terms and phrases. These words and terms appear in dark slanted type the first time they are used in the text. The page number after each definition refers to the page on which the word or phrase is first discussed in the text. For other references, see the Index.

Pronunciation Key

When difficult names or terms first appear in the text, they are respelled to aid pronunciation. A syllable in SMALL CAPITAL LETTERS receives the most stress. The key below lists the letters used for respelling. It includes examples of words using each sound and showing how they would be respelled.

Symbol	Example	Respelling
a	hat	(hat)
ay	pay, late	(pay), (layt)
ah	star, hot	(stahr), (haht)
ai	air, dare	(air), (dair)
aw	law, all	(law), (awl)
eh	met	(meht)
ee	bee, eat	(bee), (eet)
er	learn, sir, fur	(lern), (ser), (fer)
ih	fit	(fiht)
ī	mile	(mīl)
ir	ear	(ir)
oh	no	(noh)
oi	soil, boy	(soil), (boi)
oo	root, rule	(root), (rool)
or	born, door	(born), (dor)
ow	plow, out	(plow), (owt)

Symbol	Example	Respelling
u	put, book	(put), (buk)
uh	fun	(fuhn)
yoo	few, use	(fyoo), (yooz)
ch	chill, reach	(chihl), (reech)
g	go, dig	(goh), (dihg)
j	jet, gently, bridge	(jeht), (JEHNT lee), (brihj)
k	kite, cup	(kīt), (kuhp)
ks	mix	(mihks)
kw	quick	(kwihk)
ng	bring	(brihng)
s	say, cent	(say), (sehnt)
sh	she, crash	(shee), (krash)
th	three	(three)
y	yet, onion	(yeht), (UHN yuhn)
z	zip, always	(zihp), (AWL wayz)
zh	treasure	(TREH zher)

A

abolition act of ending something completely. (p. 352)

Act of Toleration (1649) law that gave religious freedom to all Christians in Maryland. (p. 110)

Adams–Onís Treaty agreement by which Spain gave Florida to the United States in return for $5 million. (p. 282)

adobe sun-dried clay brick. (p. 34)

aggression warlike act by one country against another without just cause. (p. 625)

alien foreigner. (p. 236)

Alien Act (1798) law that allowed the President to expel foreigners thought to be dangerous to the country. (p. 236)

Alliance for Progress organization set up in 1961 to bring about social and economic reform in Latin America. Included the United States and Latin American nations. (p. 713)

Allied Powers nations that fought Germany and its allies in World War I and World War II. Included Britain, France, Russia, and the United States. (p. 551)

almanac book containing calendars and other useful information. (p. 136)

amend change. (p. 213)

American Colonization Society group founded in 1817 that wanted to set up a colony for free blacks in Africa. (p. 352)

American System plan offered by Henry Clay for internal improvements. (p. 279)

anarchist person opposed to organized government. (p. 591)

annex add on, such as territory. (p. 318)

antibiotic substance that kills harmful bacteria. (p. 724)

Antifederalist person opposed to the Constitution during the ratification debate in 1787. (p. 211)

appeasement practice of giving in to an aggressor nation's demands in order to preserve the peace. (p. 626)

apprentice person who learns a trade or craft from a master craftsman. (p. 135)

archaeologist scientist who studies evidence left by early people. (p. 33)

armistice agreement to stop fighting. (p. 563)

arsenal gun warehouse. (p. 385)

Articles of Confederation first American constitution. (p. 198)

assembly line method of production where workers add parts to a product that moves along a belt. Introduced by Henry Ford in 1913. (p. 473)

assimilation process of becoming part of another culture. (p. 484)

astrolabe instrument used by sailors to figure out their latitude at sea. (p. 54)

Atlantic Charter (1941) agreement between the United States and Britain that set goals for the postwar world. (p. 630)

Axis Powers nations that fought the Allies in World War II. Included Germany, Italy, and Japan. (p. 627)

B

baby boom increased birth rate in the United States during the late 1940s and 1950s. (p. 664)

backcountry area in western Maryland and Virginia along the Appalachian Mountains. (p. 128)

balanced budget spending plan in which the government cannot spend more than its income. (p. 680)

Bear Flag Republic country set up in 1845 by Americans in California. (p. 323)

Berlin Airlift program to fly food, fuel, and other supplies to West Berlin after the Soviet Union blockaded the city. (p. 655)

Bessemer process way of making strong steel at a low cost. (p. 464)

bicentennial 200th anniversary. (p. 678)

bill proposed law. (p. 208)

Bill of Rights first ten amendments to the Constitution of the United States of America. Ratified in 1791. (p. 213)

black code set of laws that limited the rights of freedmen. Passed by southern legislatures after the Civil War. (p. 421)

blockade shutting off a port to keep people or supplies from moving in or out. (p. 177)

bond certificate that promises to pay the holder a sum of money plus interest on a certain date. (p. 223)

bonus sum of money. (p. 603)

bootlegger person who smuggled liquor into the United States during Prohibition. (p. 582)

Boston Associates group of capitalists who built textile factories in Massachusetts. (p. 267)

Boston Massacre shooting of five Bostonians by British soldiers on March 5, 1770. (p. 163)

Boston Tea Party protest by a group of Bostonians who dressed as Indians and threw tea into Boston Harbor. (p. 166)

bounty payment. Given to men who joined the Union army. (p. 404)

boycott refuse to buy certain goods or services. (p. 159)

bracero Mexican farm worker brought to the United States to harvest crops. (p. 690)

Breadbasket Colonies name for the Middle Colonies because they exported so much grain. (p. 126)

bull market rising stock market. (p. 581)

burgess representative to the colonial assembly of Virginia. (p. 92)

C

cabinet group of officials who head government departments and advise the President. (p. 222)

canal channel dug and filled with water to allow ships to cross a stretch of land. (p. 275)

capital money raised for a business venture. (p. 90)

capitalist person with money to invest in business to make a profit. (p. 266)

caravel ship with a steering rudder and triangular sails. (p. 54)

carpetbagger name for a Northerner who went to the South during Reconstruction. (p. 425)

cash crop surplus of food that is sold for money on the world market. (p. 126)

CAT-scanner computer that helps doctors diagnose illnesses. (p. 724)

caucus private meeting of political party leaders. (p. 295)

cavalry troops on horseback. (p. 184)

cede give up. (p. 324)

Central Powers European nations that fought the Allies in World War I. Included Germany, Austria–Hungary, and the Ottoman Empire. (p. 551)

century 100-year period. (p. 167)

charter document giving certain rights to a person or company. (p. 89)

checks and balances system set up by the Constitution in which each branch of the federal government has the power to check, or limit, the actions of other branches. (p. 208)

Chicano name for Mexican Americans. Used by Mexican Americans to show pride in their history and heritage. (p. 690)

civil disobedience nonviolent protest against unjust laws. (p. 668)

civilian person not in the military. (p. 407)

civil service all government jobs except for elected positions or those in the armed forces. (p. 506)

civil war war between people of the same country. (p. 376)

climate average weather of a location over a period of 20 or 30 years. (p. 26)

clipper ship fastest sailing ship of the 1840s and 1850s. (p. 335)

closed shop business that agrees to hire only union members. (p. 661)

cold war state of tension between nations without actual warfare. (p. 653)

collective bargaining process whereby a union negotiates with management for a contract. (p. 611)

collective farm farm in the Soviet Union run by the government. (p. 625)

colony group of people settled in a distant land who are ruled by the government of their native land. (p. 58)

committee of correspondence group of colonists who wrote letters and pamphlets protesting British rule. (p. 163)

compromise settlement in which each side gives up some of its demands in order to reach an agreement. (p. 204)

Compromise of 1850 agreement over slavery that admitted California to the Union as a free state, allowed popular sovereignty in New Mexico and Utah, banned slave trade in Washington, D.C., and passed a strict fugitive slave law. (p. 377)

computer machine that processes information at lightning-fast speed. (p. 723)

computer literacy ability to use computers. (p. 724)

Confederate States of America nation formed by the states that seceded from the Union in 1860 and 1861. (p. 388)

conquistador Spanish word for conqueror. (p. 62)

consolidate combine, such as businesses. (p. 462)

constitution document that sets out the laws and principles of government. (p. 197)

Constitutional Convention meeting of delegates from 12 states who wrote a constitution for the United States in 1787. (p. 202)

consumer person who spends money on goods and services. (p. 600)

continental divide mountain ridge that separates river systems. (p. 248)

cooperative group of farmers who put their money together to buy seeds and tools at lower prices. (p. 456)

Copperhead Northerner who opposed fighting to keep the South in the Union. (p. 404)

corduroy road log road. (p. 272)

corporation business owned by many investors. Raises money by selling stocks, or shares, to investors. (p. 465)

corral enclosure used for catching and holding large numbers of animals. (p. 444)

cotton gin invention of Eli Whitney's that speeded up the cleaning of cotton fibers. (p. 266)

coureur de bois (koo RUHR duh BWAH) French phrase meaning runner of the woods. (p. 83)

creole descendant of Spanish settlers who was born in the Americas. (p. 79)

Crusades series of wars fought by Christians to conquer the Holy Land. (p. 51)

Cuban missile crisis tense situation caused by the Soviet effort to build missile bases in Cuba. (p. 698)

culture way of life of a given people. (p. 33)

D

Daughters of Liberty group of colonial women who joined together to protest the Stamp Act and protect colonial liberties. (p. 160)

decade 10-year period. (p. 167)

Declaration of Independence (1776) document that stated the colonies had become a free and independent nation. (p. 178)

Declaratory Act (1766) British law that allowed Parliament to tax the colonists. (p. 159)

deficit spending government practice of spending more than it takes in from taxes. (p. 613)

demilitarized zone area where no troops are allowed. (p. 660)

demobilize release people from military service. (p. 660)

democratic ensuring that all people have the same rights. (p. 242)

democratic government type of government in which people hold the ruling power. (p. 242)

détente easing of tensions. (p. 700)

dictator ruler who has complete power. (p. 624)

disarmament reduction of a nation's armed forces or weapons of war. (p. 577)

discrimination policy or attitude that denies equal rights to certain people. (p. 303)

dividend payment to stockholders from a corporation's profit. (p. 465)

dollar diplomacy President Taft's policy of encouraging Americans to invest in Latin America. (p. 542)

domino theory belief that if South Vietnam became communist, other countries in Southeast Asia would become communist. (p. 704)

draft law requiring men of a certain age to serve in the military. (p. 404)

Dred Scott decision Supreme Court decision in 1857. Stated that slaves were property, not citizens. (p. 382)

drought long dry spell. (p. 35)

due process right of every citizen to the same fair rules in all cases brought to trial. (p. 213)

dumping selling goods in another country at very low prices. (p. 278)

E

economic depression period when business activity slows, prices and wages fall, and unemployment rises. (p. 201)

electoral college group of electors from each state that meets every four years to vote for the President and Vice President. (p. 208)

elevation height. (p. 22)

emancipate set free. (p. 401)

Emancipation Proclamation (1863) declaration issued by Lincoln that freed slaves in the Confederacy. (p. 401)

embargo ban on trade with another country. (p. 253)

emigrate leave one's own country and settle elsewhere. (p. 100)

encomienda (ehn koh mee EHN dah) right to demand taxes or labor from Native Americans living in the Spanish colonies. (p. 79)

enumerated article any of the goods that Parliament said colonists could sell only to England. (p. 113)

environmentalist person who works to control pollution and protect the land. (p. 728)

escalate build up. (p. 704)

execute carry out. (p. 198)

executive branch part of a government that carries out the laws. (p. 203)

exile person forced to leave his or her own country. (p. 698)

export trade good sold outside a country. (p. 113)

extended family close-knit family group that includes grandparents, parents, children, aunts, uncles, and cousins. (p. 346)

F

fact something that actually happened and can be proved. (p. 232)

factory system method of producing goods that brings workers and machines together in one place. (p. 266)

fad style or fashion that becomes popular for a short time. (p. 586)

famine severe shortage of food. (p. 339)

Farewell Address George Washington's advice to his fellow citizens when he left office in 1796. (p. 229)

federalism sharing of power between the states and the national government. (p. 206)

Federalist supporter of the Constitution in the ratification debate in 1787. Favored a strong national government. (pp. 211, 231)

feudalism system of rule by lords who owed loyalty to their king. (p. 50)

Fifteenth Amendment constitutional amendment that gave black Americans the right to vote in all states. (p. 424)

fireside chat radio speech given by President Franklin Roosevelt. (p. 606)

First Continental Congress meeting of delegates from 12 colonies in September 1774. (p. 166)

flapper nickname for a young woman in the 1920s who declared her independence from traditional rules. (p. 586)

forty-niner person who went to California during the Gold Rush in 1849. (p. 327)

Fourteen Points President Wilson's goals for peace after World War I. (p. 565)

Fourteenth Amendment constitutional amendment that granted citizenship to all persons born in the United States. Encouraged states to allow blacks to vote. (p. 423)

Frame of Government document that set up the government of the Pennsylvania colony. (p. 107)

freedman freed slave. (p. 418)

Freedmen's Bureau government agency that helped freed slaves. (p. 418)

free enterprise system economic system in which businesses are owned by private citizens, not by the government. (p. 468)

Free Soil Party political party founded in 1848 by antislavery Whigs and Democrats. (p. 375)

French and Indian War conflict between the French and British in North America. Fought from 1754 to 1763. (p. 151)

fugitive runaway, such as an escaped slave in the 1800s. (p. 376)

Fugitive Slave Law of 1850 law that required citizens to help catch runaway slaves. (p. 377)

Fundamental Orders of Connecticut system of laws in the colony of Connecticut that limited the powers of the government. (p. 101)

G

General Court representative assembly in the Massachusetts Bay Colony. (p. 101)

gentry highest social class in the colonies. (p. 135)

geography physical features, climate, plants, animals, and resources of a region. (p. 19)

Gettysburg Address speech given by Lincoln in 1863 at this Civil War battle site in Pennsylvania. (p. 410)

ghetto rundown area of a city where poor people live. (p. 686)

glacier thick sheet of ice. (p. 19)

Good Neighbor Policy President Franklin Roosevelt's policy toward the nations of Latin America. Intended to strengthen friendly relations. (p. 624)

grandfather clause law passed by southern states after the Civil War. Excused a voter from a poll tax or literacy test if his father or grandfather had voted in 1867. Kept most blacks from voting. (p. 431)

Great Awakening religious movement in the colonies in the 1730s and 1740s. (p. 137)

Great Compromise Roger Sherman's plan at the Constitutional Convention for a two-house legislature. Settled differences between large and small states. (p. 204)

Great Depression period of economic hard times from 1929 to 1941. (p. 600)

Great Migration movement of thousands of English settlers to the Massachusetts Bay Colony. (p. 100)

Green Mountain Boys group of patriots from Vermont. Led by Ethan Allen. Captured Fort Ticonderoga in 1775. (p. 174)

guerrilla fighter who uses hit-and-run attacks. (p. 704)

H

habeas corpus right to have charges filed or a trial before being jailed. (p. 406)

Hartford Convention meeting of New Englanders who opposed the War of 1812. (p. 260)

high technology advanced electronics industries. (p. 731)

hill raised part of the earth's surface. Less steep than a mountain. (p. 22)

Hispanic Spanish-speaking American. (p. 633)

hogan Navajo house built of mud plaster and supported by wooden poles. (p. 39)

House of Burgesses representative assembly in colonial Virginia. (p. 92)

House of Representatives lower house of Congress. Each state is represented according to the size of its population. (p. 204)

Hudson River School group of artists who painted Hudson River and Catskill Mountains landscapes. (p. 365)

I

igloo Eskimo house made of snow and ice. (p. 36)

illegal alien person who has entered the country without legal permission. (p. 740)

immigrant person who comes from his or her own homeland to settle in another country. (p. 339)

impeach bring charges against an official such as the President. (p. 210)

imperialism policy by which one country takes control of the land and people of another country or region. (p. 528)

import trade good brought into a country. (p. 113)

impressment act of seizing men from a ship or village and forcing them to serve in the navy. Practiced by the British in the 1700s and 1800s. (p. 251)

indentured servant person who signed a contract to work for a certain length of time in exchange for passage to the colonies. (p. 117)

Indian Removal Act (1830) law that forced Native Americans to move west of the Mississippi. (p. 301)

Industrial Revolution process whereby machines replaced hand tools, and new sources of power, such as steam and electricity, replaced human and animal power. Caused a shift from farming to manufacturing. (p. 265)

inflation economic cycle in which the value of money falls and the prices of goods rise. (p. 406)

initiative procedure that allows voters to introduce a bill by collecting signatures on a petition. (p. 510)

injunction legal order to do something. (p. 477)

installment buying method of buying on credit. (p. 580)

interchangeable parts identical parts of a tool or instrument that are made by machine. Such parts can be easily assembled or replaced. (p. 268)

Intolerable Acts laws passed by Parliament in 1774 to punish colonists in Massachusetts for the Boston Tea Party. (p. 166)

irrigate bring water to an area such as farmland. (p. 27)

island hopping Allied military plan to capture some Japanese-held islands and go around others. Used in the Pacific during World War II. (p. 640)

isolation policy of having little to do with foreign nations. (p. 527)

isthmus narrow strip of land. (p. 22)

J

Jay's Treaty (1795) agreement to stop British attacks on American merchant ships and settle other differences between the two nations. (p. 227)

jerky dried meat. (p. 444)

joint stock company private company that sold shares to investors to finance trading voyages. (p. 90)

judicial branch part of a government that decides if laws are carried out fairly. (p. 203)

judicial review right of the Supreme Court to review laws passed by Congress and declare them unconstitutional. (p. 244)

Judiciary Act (1789) law that organized the federal court system into district and circuit courts. (p. 222)

K

kaiser name for the German emperor. (p. 551)

Kansas–Nebraska Act (1854) law that divided Nebraska into two territories. Provided that the question of slavery in the territories would be decided by popular sovereignty. (p. 379)

Kentucky and Virginia Resolutions (1798, 1799) declarations that states had the right to declare a law unconstitutional. (p. 236)

King Philip's War conflict between English settlers and Indians in Massachusetts in 1675. (p. 105)

kitchen cabinet group of unofficial advisers to President Andrew Jackson. (p. 297)

Know-Nothing Party political party organized by nativists in the 1850s. (p. 340)

Ku Klux Klan secret group first set up in the South after the Civil War. Members terrorized blacks and other groups they hated. (p. 427)

L

laissez faire French term meaning let alone. Referred to the idea that government should not interfere in people's lives. (p. 243)

Land Ordinance of 1785 law that set up a system for settling the Northwest Territory. (p. 200)

laser device that sends out very strong, narrow beams of light. (p. 732)

Laws of the Indies laws that governed Spanish colonies in the New World. (p. 78)

League of Nations association of nations to protect the independence of member nations. Proposed by Woodrow Wilson in his Fourteen Points. (p. 565)

League of the Iroquois council of the five nations of the Iroquois. (p. 41)

legislative branch part of a government that passes laws. (p. 203)

legislature group of people with power to make laws for a country or colony. (p. 115)

Lincoln–Douglas Debates series of political debates between Abraham Lincoln and Stephen Douglas in 1858. (p. 384)

literacy test examination to see if a person can read and write. (p. 431)

longhorn wild cattle that once roamed free in Texas. (p. 449)

long house Iroquois dwelling. (p. 40)

Loyalist colonist who stayed loyal to Great Britain during the American Revolution. (p. 179)

M

Magna Carta document that guaranteed rights to English nobles in 1215. (p. 92)

magnetic compass Chinese invention brought to Europe by the Arabs. Showed which direction was north. (p. 54)

Manifest Destiny belief of many Americans in the 1840s that the United States should own all the land between the Atlantic and Pacific oceans. (p. 321)

manor part of a lord's holding in the Middle Ages. Included a village or several villages and the surrounding lands. (p. 50)

Marshall Plan American plan to help European nations rebuild their economies after World War II. (p. 654)

martial law rule by the military. (p. 394)

mass production rapid manufacture of large numbers of a product. (p. 473)

Mayflower Compact agreement signed by Pilgrims before landing at Plymouth. (p. 94)

mercantilism economic theory that a nation's strength came from building up its gold supplies and expanding its trade. (p. 113)

mestizo person in the Spanish colonies of mixed Spanish and Indian background. (p. 79)

Mexican War conflict between the United States and Mexico over Texas. Lasted from 1846 to 1848. (p. 323)

Middle Ages period in Europe from about 500 to 1350. (p. 50)

Middle Passage ocean trip from Africa to the Americas in which thousands of slaves died. (p. 131)

migrant person who moves from place to place to find work. (p. 615)

militarism policy of building up strong military forces to prepare for war. (p. 550)

militia army of citizens who serve as soldiers in an emergency. (p. 169)

minuteman volunteer who trained to fight the British in 1775. (p. 168)

mission religious settlement. Run by Catholic priests and friars in the Spanish colonies. (p. 78)

Missouri Compromise (1820) plan proposed by Henry Clay to keep the number of slave and free states equal. Admitted Missouri as a slave state and Maine as a free state. (p. 374)

monopoly company that completely controls the market of a certain industry. (p. 468)

Monroe Doctrine policy statement of President James Monroe in 1823. Warned European nations not to interfere with the newly independent nations of Latin America. (p. 283)

Mormon member of the Church of Jesus Christ of Latter Day Saints. (p. 325)

Mound Builders group of Native Americans who built thousands of huge earth mounds from eastern Oklahoma to the Atlantic. (p. 34)

mountain high, rugged land usually at least 5,000 feet above sea level. (p. 22)

Mountain Men trappers who followed Indian trails across the Rockies into Oregon in the early 1800s. (p. 310)

muckraker person who reports on corrupt politicians and other problems of the cities. (p. 508)

N

national debt money a government owes. (p. 223)

nationalism pride in or devotion to one's country. (p. 254)

Native American descendant of people who reached America thousands of years ago. (p. 36)

nativist person who wanted to limit immigration and preserve the United States for native-born white Americans. (p. 340)

navigation practice of plotting a course at sea. (p. 53)

Navigation Acts series of laws passed in the 1600s that governed trade between England and its colonies. (p. 113)

Nazi member of the German National Socialist Workers Party, organized by Adolph Hitler. (p. 624)

network system of connected railroad lines. (p. 461)

neutral choosing not to fight on either side in a war. (p. 186)

Neutrality Proclamation (1793) Washington's statement that the United States would remain neutral in the war between France and other European nations. (p. 227)

New Deal name for the programs of President Franklin Roosevelt. (p. 606)

New England Anti-Slavery Society group organized by William Lloyd Garrison to end slavery. (p. 353)

New Jersey Plan William Paterson's plan for the new government presented to the Constitutional Convention. (p. 204)

Nineteenth Amendment (1919) constitutional amendment that gave women the right to vote. (p. 514)

nominating convention meeting at which a political party selects its candidate for President. (p. 295)

nonimportation agreement promise of colonial merchants and planters to stop importing goods taxed by the Townshend Acts. (p. 160)

Northwest Ordinance (1787) law that set up a government for the Northwest Territory. Set up a way for new states to be admitted to the United States. (p. 200)

nullification idea of declaring a federal law illegal. (p. 299)

Nullification Crisis tense situation created by South Carolina when it declared the tariffs of 1828 and 1832 illegal. (p. 301)

nullify cancel, such as a law. (p. 236)

O

Olive Branch Petition letter sent to King George III by the Continental Congress asking him to repeal the Intolerable Acts. (p. 174)

Open Door Policy (1899) policy toward China set out by Secretary of State John Hay. Allowed any nation to trade in any other nation's sphere of influence. (p. 532)

Organization of American States (OAS) group of North and South American countries that has promoted peace and economic progress. (p. 714)

override overrule. Congress can override a President's veto if two thirds of both houses vote to do so. (p. 210)

P

pacifist person who refuses to fight in a war. (p. 558)

Glossary

Panic of 1837 economic crisis in which hundreds of banks failed. (p. 304)

Patriot colonist who supported the American Revolution. (p. 179)

patroon rich landowner in the Dutch colonies. (p. 105)

peninsular person sent from Spain to rule the Spanish colonies. (p.78)

pet bank state bank used by President Jackson and Roger Taney for government money. (p. 299)

petrochemical chemical made from petroleum. (p. 726)

Pickett's Charge Confederate attack led by General George Pickett at the Battle of Gettysburg. (p. 410)

pictograph picture that represents an object. (p. 42)

Pilgrims group of English people who went to the New World in search of religious freedom. (p. 92)

Pinckney Treaty (1795) agreement between the United States and Spain to keep the port of New Orleans open. (p. 245)

plain broad area of fairly level land. (p. 22)

Plan of Union Benjamin Franklin's plan to unite the colonies in 1754. (p. 153)

plantation large estate farmed by many workers. (p. 79)

plateau area of mostly high, level land usually at least 2,000 feet (600m) above sea level. (p. 22)

poll tax fee paid by a voter in order to vote. (p. 431)

pool method of ending competition used by railroads in the late 1800s. Railroads divided up business in an area and fixed prices at a high level. (p. 463)

popular sovereignty practice of allowing each territory to vote whether to allow slavery. (p. 374)

population number of people living in a place. (p. 153)

Populist Party political party formed by farmers and members of labor unions.in 1892. (p. 456)

potlatch ceremonial dinner among some Native Americans of the Northwest Coast. (p. 37)

poverty line minimum income the government says that people need to live. (p. 675)

precedent act or decision that sets an example for others to follow. (p. 221)

prejudice unfavorable opinion about people who are of different religion, race, or nationality. (p. 340)

presidio fort that housed soldiers in the Spanish colonies. (p. 78)

primary election held before a general election in which voters choose their party's candidate for office. (p. 510)

primary source firsthand information about people or events of the past. (p. 43)

Proclamation of 1763 British law that forbade colonists to settle west of a line along the Appalachian Mountains. (p. 157)

profiteer person who takes advantage of an emergency to make money. (p. 406)

Progressive Movement reform movement that worked to correct abuses in American society. Included both Republicans and Democrats. (p. 509)

Prohibition period from 1920 to 1933 when the making and sale of liquor was illegal in the United States. (p. 581)

propaganda spreading of ideas or beliefs that help a particular cause and hurt an opposing cause. (p. 553)

proprietary colony English colony in which the king gave land to one or more proprietors in exchange for a yearly payment. (p. 106)

protective tariff tax placed on goods from another country. (p. 279)

Protestant Reformation movement in the 1500s to reform the Catholic Church. (p. 68)

public interest the good of all the people. (p. 509)

public school school supported by taxes. (p. 134)

public works program government program that hires workers for projects such as building schools, courthouses, dams, and highways. (p. 602)

pueblo Spanish word for village or town. (p. 35)

Pueblos group of Native Americans who lived in the Southwest. (p. 38)

Puritans group of English Protestants who wanted to purify the practices of the Church of England. Settled in Massachusetts. (p. 100)

Q

Quakers Protestant group founded by George Fox. Settled in Pennsylvania. (p. 107)

Quartering Act (1766) law that required colonists to pay for the housing of British soldiers. (p. 161)

Quebec Act (1774) law that set up a government for Canada and protected the rights of French Catholics. (p. 166)

quota system limit on immigration that allowed only a certain number of people to immigrate to the United States from each country. (p. 591)

R

racism belief that one race is superior to another. (p. 130)

Radical Reconstruction period after the Civil War when Republicans controlled Congress and passed harsh laws affecting the South. (p. 422)

Radical Republicans group of Republicans in Congress who wanted to protect the rights of freedmen in the South and keep rich southern planters out of power. (p. 421)

ragtime popular music in the late 1800s that had a lively, rhythmic sound. (p. 493)

ratify approve. (p. 192)

realist writer or artist who shows life as it really is. (p. 496)

rebate discount on services or merchandise. (p. 463)

recall special election that allows voters to remove an elected official from office. (p. 510)

recession mild depression. (p. 730)

referendum process by which people can vote directly on a bill. (p. 510)

relief government program that gives help to the needy. (p. 602)

relief on a map, differences in height of land. Shown by using special colors. (p. 21)

Renaissance period from 1350 to 1600 in which Europeans made great advances. (p. 52)

rendezvous French word for a get-together. Annual meeting of Mountain Men where they traded furs for supplies. (p. 311)

reparations payments for losses that a nation has suffered during a war. (p. 565)

repeal cancel. (p. 159)

representative government system of government in which voters elect representatives to make laws for them. (p. 92)

republic nation in which voters choose representatives to govern them. (p. 205)

Republican Party political party formed in 1854 by a group of Free Soilers, northern Democrats, and antislavery Whigs. (p. 383)

reservation limited area set aside for Indians by the United States government. (p. 445)

Roosevelt Corollary (1904) expansion of the Monroe Doctrine announced by President Theodore Roosevelt. Claimed the right of the United States to intervene in Latin America to preserve law and order. (p. 542)

royal colony English colony directly under the king's control. (p. 107)

Rush–Bagot Agreement (1817) agreement between the United States and Britain that forbade warships on the Great Lakes. (p. 261)

S

satellite nation closely tied to a more powerful country. (p. 653)

scalawag white Southerner who supported Radical Republicans. (p. 425)

secede withdraw. (p. 300)

sectionalism strong sense of loyalty to a state or section instead of to the whole country. (p. 374)

sedition stirring up of rebellion against government. (p. 236)

Sedition Act (1798) law that allowed citizens to be fined or jailed for criticizing public officials. (p. 236)

segregation separation of people of different races. (p. 431)

self-determination right of national groups to their own territory and forms of government. (p. 565)

Seminole War conflict between the Seminole Indians and the United States Army. Lasted from 1835 to 1842. (p. 303)

Senate upper house of Congress. Each state is represented by two senators. (p. 204)

Seneca Falls Convention meeting at which leaders of the women's rights movement voted on a plan for achieving equality. (p. 356)

separation of powers system in which each branch of government has its own powers. (p. 207)

serf peasant who had to stay on the manor where he or she was born. (p. 50)

settlement house center offering help to the poor. (p. 490)

sharecropper farmer who works land owned by another and gives the landowner part of the harvest. (p. 428)

Shays' Rebellion (1786) revolt of Massachusetts farmers whose farms were being seized for debt. (p. 201)

shuttle diplomacy efforts of Secretary of State Henry Kissinger to restore peace in the Middle East. (p. 710)

sitdown strike work stoppage when workers shut down all machines and refuse to leave a factory until their demands are met. (p. 613)

skilled worker person with a trade, such as a carpenter, a printer, or a shoemaker. (p. 338)

slave code series of laws that controlled behavior of slaves and denied them basic rights. (p. 130)

sodbuster plains farmer. (p. 454)

software program that tells a computer what to do. (p. 724)

solar energy power from the sun. (p. 728)

Sons of Liberty group of colonial men who joined together to protest the Stamp Act and protect colonial liberties. (p. 160)

Spanish Armada large fleet sent by Spain against England in 1558. (p. 69)

speakeasy illegal bar that operated during prohibition (p. 582)

speculator person who invests in a risky business venture in hopes of making a large profit. (p. 224)

sphere of influence area in China where a foreign nation had special trading privileges and made laws for its own citizens. (p. 532)

spinning jenny invention that let a person spin several threads at once. (p. 266)

spoils system practice of giving government jobs to loyal supporters. Used by the winning political party after an election. (p. 296)

Stamp Act (1765) law passed by Parliament that taxed legal documents, newspapers, almanacs, playing cards, and dice. (p. 159)

states' rights idea that individual states had the right to limit the power of the federal government. (p. 299)

statistics facts in number form. (p. 81)

stock share in a corporation (p. 465)

stockade high fence made of wooden posts. Built by colonists to protect settlements from Indian attacks. (p. 92)

stockpile store up for use. (p. 700)

stocks wooden frames with holes for the arms and legs. Used to punish people found guilty of crimes. (p. 123)

strike organized work stoppage by union workers in order to win better pay or working conditions. (p. 338)

subsistence farmer person who grew enough for his or her own needs (p. 121)

suffrage right to vote. (p. 293)

suffragist person who campaigned for women's right to vote. (p. 513)

Sugar Act (1764) law passed by Parliament that taxed molasses. (p. 158)

superpower powerful nation that competes with another powerful nation for influence over other countries. (p. 697)

surplus extra, such as food. (p. 121)

Swamp Fox nickname for the Patriot Francis Marion of South Carolina. (p. 190)

T

tariff tax. Placed on goods brought into a country. (p. 225)

Tariff of Abominations name given by Southerners to the Tariff of 1828. (p. 299)

tax-in-kind tax paid with goods rather than money. (p. 406)

Tea Act (1773) law passed by Parliament that let the British East India Company sell tea directly to colonists. (p. 164)

telegraph machine that sends electrical signals along a wire. Invented by Samuel F. B. Morse in 1840. (p. 334)

temperance movement campaign against the sale or drinking of alcohol. (p. 360)

tenant farmer person who works land owned by another. Tenant pays rent to the landowner. (p. 127)

Ten Percent Plan Lincoln's plan for Reconstruction whereby southern states could be readmitted to the Union. (p. 418)

Thanksgiving day set aside by the Pilgrims to give thanks to God for a good harvest. (p. 95)

Thirteenth Amendment constitutional amendment that banned slavery in the United States. (p. 419)

Three Fifths Compromise agreement of delegates to the Constitutional Convention that three fifths of the slaves in any state be counted in that state's population. (p. 204)

tidewater coastal plain such as the Atlantic coast of the Southeast. (p. 130)

time line chart showing the relationship between events with dates marked on a line. (p. 167)

toleration willingness to let others have their own beliefs. (p. 102)

totalitarian state country where a single party controls the government and every aspect of the lives of the people. (p. 624)

Townshend Acts (1767) laws passed by Parliament that taxed goods such as glass, paper, silk, lead, and tea. (p. 160)

trade union association of workers formed to win better wages and working conditions. (p. 338)

Trail of Tears forced march of the Cherokee Indians to lands west of the Mississippi. (p. 302)

traitor person who betrays his or her country. (p. 178)

transcontinental railroad railroad that stretches across the continent from coast to coast. (p. 440)

travois type of sled. Used by Plains Indians to carry goods. (p. 443)

Treaty of Ghent (1814) peace treaty between the United States and Britain that ended the War of 1812. (p. 260)

Treaty of Greenville (1795) treaty between the United States and 12 Indian nations of the Northwest Territory (p. 229)

Treaty of Paris (1763) agreement between the British and French that ended the French and Indian War. (p. 155)

trench warfare type of fighting during World War I in which both sides dug trenches protected by mines and barbed wire. (p. 552)

triangular trade series of colonial trade routes between New England, the West Indies, Europe, and Africa. (p. 139)

tributary branch of a river. (p. 25)

Truman Doctrine statement of President Truman that promised military and economic support to nations threatened by communism. (p. 654)

trust group of corporations run by a single board of directors. (p. 467)

trustbuster person who wanted to end all trusts. (p. 517)

turnpike road built by a private company. Charged tolls to those using it. (p. 272)

U

unconstitutional not permitted by the constitution of a nation. (p. 236)

underground railroad secret network of people who helped runaway slaves reach freedom in the North or Canada. (p. 353)

United Nations international organization formed in 1945 to help solve conflicts between nations. (p. 651)

unskilled worker person who does a job that requires little special training. (p. 339)

V

vaccine substance that causes a mild form of a disease. Injected into a

healthy person to cause the body to build up the ability to fight off the disease. (p. 724)

vaquero Spanish cowboy. (p. 450)

vaudeville variety show that included comedians, song-and-dance routines, and acrobats. (p. 493)

V–E Day (May 8, 1945) Marked the end of World War II in Europe. Stands for Victory in Europe. (p. 640)

vertical integration method of controlling an industry from raw materials to finished products. (p. 465)

veto reject. Under the Constitution, the President can veto a bill passed by Congress. (p. 210)

viceroy official who rules an area in the name of a king or queen. (p. 77)

vigilante person who deals out punishments without holding a trial. Formed in western mining camps to reduce crime. (p. 328)

Vikings seagoing people from Scandinavia. (p. 49)

Virginia Company joint stock company that received a charter from King James I to start a colony. (p. 89)

Virginia Plan plan of government presented by Edmund Randolph and James Madison to the Constitutional Convention. (p. 203)

V–J Day (August 14, 1945) Marked the end of World War II in the Pacific. Stands for Victory over Japan. (p. 642)

W

Wade–Davis Bill Reconstruction plan passed by Republicans in Congress in July 1864. Vetoed by Lincoln. (p. 418)

War Hawks members of Congress who wanted war with Britain in 1812. (p. 254)

Watergate affair political scandal that led to the resignation of President Nixon. Began when burglars broke into Democratic Party Headquarters in the Watergate apartment building in Washington, D.C. (p. 677)

weather condition of the air at any given time and place. (p. 26)

Whiskey Rebellion (1794) revolt of farmers to protest the tax on whiskey. (p. 225)

wholesale goods bought or sold in large quantities at low prices. (p. 456)

Wilmot Proviso proposed law of Congressman David Wilmot to outlaw slavery in any land won from Mexico. (p. 374)

women's rights movement the struggle of women for equality. (p. 691)

writ of assistance legal document that let a British customs officer inspect a ship's cargo without giving any reason for the search. (p. 160)

X

XYZ Affair (1797) incident when French agents asked American ambassadors in Paris for a bribe. (p. 235)

Y

Yankee name for New England merchant who won a reputation for always getting a good buy. (p. 139)

yellow journalism sensational style of reporting used by some newspapers in the late 1800s. (p. 495)

The Declaration of Independence

On June 7, 1776, the Continental Congress approved the resolution that "these United Colonies are, and of right ought to be, free and independent States." Congress then appointed a committee to write a declaration of independence. The committee members were John Adams, Benjamin Franklin, Robert Livingston, Roger Sherman, and Thomas Jefferson.

Jefferson actually wrote the Declaration, but he got advice from the others. On July 2, Congress discussed the Declaration and made some changes. On July 4, 1776, it adopted the Declaration of Independence in its final form.

The Declaration is printed in black. The headings have been added to show the parts of the Declaration. They are not part of the original text. Annotations, or explanations, are on the tan side of the page. Page numbers in the annotations show where a subject is discussed in the text. Hard words are defined in the annotations.

When in the course of human events it becomes necessary for one people to dissolve the political bands which have connected them with another and to assume, among the powers of the earth, the separate and equal station to which the laws of nature and of nature's God entitle them, a decent respect to the opinions of mankind requires that they should declare the causes which impel them to the separation.

dissolve: break **powers of the earth:** other nations **station:** place **impel:** force

The colonists feel that they must explain to the world the reasons why they are breaking away from England

The Purpose of Government Is to Protect Basic Rights

We hold these truths to be self-evident, that all men are created equal; that they are endowed by their Creator with certain unalienable rights; that among these are life, liberty, and the pursuit of happiness. That, to secure these rights, governments are instituted among men, deriving their just powers from the consent of the governed; that, whenever any form of government becomes destructive of these ends, it is the right of the people to alter or to abolish it, and to institute a new government, laying its foundation on such principles, and organizing its powers in such form, as to them shall seem most likely to effect their safety and happiness. Prudence, indeed, will dictate that governments long established should not be changed for light and transient causes; and, accordingly, all experience hath shown that mankind are more disposed to suffer, while evils are sufferable, than to right themselves by abolishing the forms to which they are accustomed. But when a long train of abuses and usurpations, pursuing invariably the same object, evinces a design to reduce them under absolute despotism, it is their right, it is their duty, to throw off such government and to provide new guards for their future security. Such has been the patient sufferance of these colonies, and such is now the necessity which constrains

endowed: given **unalienable rights:** so basic that they cannot be taken away **secure:** protect **instituted:** set up **deriving:** getting **alter:** change **effect:** bring about

People set up governments to protect their basic rights. Governments get their power from the consent of the governed. If a government takes away the basic rights of the people, the people have the right to change the government.

prudence: wisdom **transient:** temporary, passing **disposed:** likely **usurpations:** taking and using powers that do not belong to a person **invariably:** always **evinces a design to reduce them under absolute despotism:** makes a clear plan to put them under complete and unjust control **sufferance:** endurance **constrains:** forces **absolute tyranny:** harsh and unjust government **candid:** honest

People do not change governments for slight reason. But they are forced to do so when a government becomes tyrannical. King George III has a long record of abusing his power.

assent: approval relinquish: give up
inestimable: too great a value to be
measured formidable: causing fear

This part of the Declaration spells out three
sets of wrongs that led the colonists to break
with Britain.

The first set of wrongs is the king's unjust use
of power. The king has refused to approve laws
that are needed. He has tried to control the
colonial legislatures.

depository: central storehouse
fatiguing: tiring out compliance:
giving in dissolved: broken up
annihilation: total destruction
convulsions: disturbances

The king has tried to force colonial legislatures
into doing his will by wearing them out. He has
dissolved legislatures (such as those of New
York and Massachusetts. See pages 162, 166).

endeavored: tried obstructing:
blocking naturalization: process of
becoming a citizen migration:
moving hither: here appropriations:
grants obstructed the administration
of justice: prevented justice from being
done judiciary powers: system of law
courts tenure: term (of office) erected:
set up multitude: large number swarms:
huge crowds harass: cause trouble
render: make

Among other wrongs, he has refused to let
settlers move west to take up new land. He has
prevented justice from being done. Also, he
has sent large numbers of customs officials to
cause problems for the colonists.

jurisdiction: authority quartering: housing mock: false

The king has joined with others, meaning Parliament, to make laws for the colonies. The Declaration then lists the second set of wrongs—
unjust acts of Parliament.

them to alter their former systems of government. The
history of the present King of Great Britain is a history
of repeated injuries and usurpations, all having, in direct object, the establishment of an absolute tyranny over
these States. To prove this, let facts be submitted to a
candid world:

Wrongs Done by the King

He has refused his assent to laws the most wholesome and
necessary for the public good.

He has forbidden his governors to pass laws of immediate
and pressing importance, unless suspended in their operation till his assent should be obtained; and, when so suspended, he has utterly neglected to attend to them.

He has refused to pass other laws for the accommodation
of the large districts of people, unless those people would
relinquish the right of representation in the legislature: a
right inestimable to them and formidable to tyrants only.

He has called together legislative bodies at places unusual, uncomfortable, and distant from the depository of
their public records, for the sole purpose of fatiguing them
into compliance with his measures.

He has dissolved representative houses, repeatedly for
opposing, with manly firmness, his invasions on the rights
of the people.

He has refused, for a long time after such dissolutions, to
cause others to be elected: whereby the legislative powers,
incapable of annihilation, have returned to the people at
large for their exercise; the state remaining, in the meantime, exposed to all the danger of invasion from without
and convulsions within.

He has endeavored to prevent the population of these
States; for that purpose, obstructing the laws for naturalization of foreigners, refusing to pass others to encourage their migration hither, and raising the conditions of
new appropriations of lands.

He has obstructed the administration of justice by refusing his assent to laws for establishing judiciary powers.

He has made judges dependent on his will alone for the
tenure of their offices and the amount and payment of
their salaries.

He has erected a multitude of new offices and sent hither
swarms of officers to harass our people and eat out their
substance.

He has kept among us, in time of peace, standing armies,
without the consent of our legislatures.

He has affected to render the military independent of,
and superior to, the civil power.

He has combined with others to subject us to a jurisdiction foreign to our Constitution and unacknowledged
by our laws, giving his assent to their acts of pretended
legislation—

For quartering large bodies of armed troops among us;

For protecting them by a mock trial from punishment for

any murders which they should commit on the inhabitants of these States;

For cutting off our trade with all parts of the world;

For imposing taxes on us without our consent;

For depriving us, in many cases, of the benefit of trial by jury;

For transporting us beyond seas to be tried for pretended offences;

For abolishing the free system of English laws in a neighboring province, establishing therein an arbitrary government, and enlarging its boundaries, so as to render it at once an example and fit instrument for introducing the same absolute rule into these colonies;

For taking away our charters, abolishing our most valuable laws, and altering, fundamentally, the powers of our governments;

For suspending our own legislatures and declaring themselves invested with power to legislate for us in all cases whatsoever.

He has abdicated government here by declaring us out of his protection and waging war against us.

He has plundered our seas, ravaged our coasts, burnt our towns, and destroyed the lives of our people.

He is, at this time, transporting large armies of foreign mercenaries to complete the works of death, desolation, and tyranny already begun with circumstances of cruelty and perfidy scarcely paralleled in the most barbarous ages, and totally unworthy, the head of a civilized nation.

He has constrained our fellow citizens, taken captive on the high seas, to bear arms against their country, to become the executioners of their friends and brethren, or to fall themselves by their hands.

He has excited domestic insurrections amongst us and has endeavored to bring on the inhabitants of our frontiers, the merciless Indian savages, whose known rule of warfare is an undistinguished destruction of all ages, sexes, and conditions.

In every stage of these oppressions, we have petitioned for redress in the most humble terms; our repeated petitions have been answered only by repeated injury. A prince whose character is thus marked by every act which may define a tyrant is unfit to be the ruler of a free people.

Nor have we been wanting in attention to our British brethren. We have warned them, from time to time, of attempts made by their legislature to extend an unwarrantable jurisdiction over us. We have reminded them of the circumstances of our emigration and settlement here. We have appealed to their native justice and magnanimity, and we have conjured them, by the ties of our common kindred, to disavow these usurpations, which would inevitably interrupt our connections and correspondence. They, too, have been deaf to the voice of justice and consanguinity. We must, therefore, acquiesce in the necessity which denounces our separation, and hold them, as we hold the rest of mankind, enemies in war, in peace, friends.

imposing: forcing **depriving:** taking away **transporting us beyond the seas:** sending colonists to England for trial **neighboring province:** Quebec **arbitrary government:** unjust rule **fit instrument:** suitable tool **invested with power:** having the power

During the years leading up to 1776, the colonists claimed that Parliament had no right to make laws for them because they were not represented in it. Here, the colonists object to recent laws of Parliament such as the Quartering Act (page 166) and the blockade of colonial ports (page 177) that cut off their trade. They also object to Parliament's claim that it had the right to tax them without their consent.

abdicated: given up **plundered:** robbed **ravaged:** attacked **mercenaries:** hired soldiers **desolation:** misery **perfidy:** falseness **barbarous:** uncivilized **constrained:** forced **brethren:** brothers **domestic insurrections:** internal revolts

Here, the Declaration lists the third set of wrongs—warlike acts of the king. Instead of listening to the colonists, the king has made war on them. He has hired soldiers to fight in America (page 177).

oppressions: harsh rule **petitioned:** asked **redress:** relief **unwarrantable jurisdiction over:** unfair authority **magnanimity:** generosity **conjured:** called upon **common kindred:** relatives **disavow:** turn away from **consanguinity:** blood relationships, kinship **acquiesce** agree **denounces:** speaks out against

During this time, colonists have repeatedly asked for relief. But their requests have brought only more suffering. They have appealed to the British people but received no help. So they are forced to separate.

Colonies Declare Independence

As the representatives of the United States, they declare that the colonies are free and independent states.

The states need no longer be loyal to the British king. They are an independent nation that can make war and sign treaties.

Relying on Divine Providence, the signers of the Declaration promise their lives, money, and honor to fight for independence.

We, therefore, the representatives of the United States of America, in general Congress assembled, appealing to the Supreme Judge of the world for the rectitude of our intentions, do, in the name and by the authority of the good people of these colonies, solemnly publish and declare, that these united colonies are, and of right ought to be, free and independent states: that they are absolved from all allegiance to the British Crown, and that all political connection between them and the state of Great Britain is, and ought to be, totally dissolved; and that, as free and independent states, they have full power to levy war, conclude peace, contract alliances, establish commerce, and to do all other acts and things which independent states may of right do. And, for the support of this declaration, with a firm reliance on the protection of Divine Providence, we mutually pledge to each other our lives, our fortunes, and our sacred honor.

Signers of the Declaration of Independence

John Hancock, President   **Charles Thomson,** Secretary

New Hampshire
Josiah Bartlett
William Whipple
Matthew Thornton

Massachusetts
Samuel Adams
John Adams
Robert Treat Paine
Elbridge Gerry

Rhode Island
Stephen Hopkins
William Ellery

Connecticut
Roger Sherman
Samuel Huntington
William Williams
Oliver Wolcott

New York
William Floyd
Philip Livingston
Francis Lewis
Lewis Morris

New Jersey
Richard Stockton
John Witherspoon
Francis Hopkinson
John Hart
Abraham Clark

Delaware
Caesar Rodney
George Read
Thomas McKean

Pennsylvania
Robert Morris
Benjamin Rush
Benjamin Franklin
John Morton
George Clymer
James Smith
George Taylor
James Wilson
George Ross

Maryland
Samuel Chase
William Paca
Thomas Stone
Charles Carroll

Virginia
George Wythe
Richard Henry Lee
Thomas Jefferson
Benjamin Harrison
Thomas Nelson, Jr.
Francis Lightfoot Lee
Carter Braxton

North Carolina
William Hooper
Joseph Hewes
John Penn

South Carolina
Edward Rutledge
Thomas Heyward, Jr.
Thomas Lynch, Jr.
Arthur Middleton

Georgia
Button Gwinnett
Lyman Hall
George Walton

Declaration of Independence

You and the Constitution

★   ★

To appreciate how the Constitution of the United States affects you, imagine for a moment that it never existed. The United States might still be the loose confederation of highly independent, squabbling states it was in 1787. Some of the states might even have broken away and declared themselves separate nations.

Suppose that you plan to visit a friend in a neighboring state. Without the Constitution, you might need a passport to enter the state. Or the state might deny you entry because of your race or religion.

Now suppose that you send a letter to your local newspaper strongly criticizing your governor. Without the Constitution, the newspaper might reject your letter because it only prints articles that the state government approves. The governor might order your arrest and imprisonment without the benefit of a trial.

The Constitution affects you personally. It protects your freedom to express your opinions and criticize your leaders. It defends your choice of religion and guarantees you equal opportunity under the law, whatever your race, sex, or national background. Most important of all, it allows you to make your own choices about how you will live your life.

The 200th anniversary of the Constitution in 1987 was cause for joyous celebrations. But it also led Americans to reflect on the meaning and importance of the Constitution. Having existed for two centuries, with only 26 formal changes, the Constitution was sometimes taken for granted.

Contents of the Constitution

★   ★

Exploring Our Constitution

Impact of the Constitution on You

How much do you know about the Constitution and its impact on your life? Do you know that you

★ are protected from working under the age of 14?

★ are guaranteed a minimum wage when you do work?

★ are entitled to hear criminal charges brought against you and have a lawyer represent you?

★ have a right to a hearing if you are suspended from school?

★ can have your purse or locker searched if school officials have a reasonable suspicion that you have done something wrong?

★ are allowed to pursue a peaceful political protest in school?

★ have greater freedom of speech and press outside school than inside school?

CHART SKILL The Constitution affects your life in many ways. Name two ways that it impacts on your working rights. Name one way that it impacts on your rights at school.

The Constitution was the first attempt in history to design a national government on paper. More important, the document contained ideas that were considered revolutionary at the time. For example, it held that a society could exist without being divided into nobles and common people. It also held that a stable government could be based on elections, not heredity.

To some people, this new experiment in government was bold and reckless. Yet, the Constitution has remained the framework of our government for over 200 years. And it has become the basis of the constitutions of more than 160 other nations.

The Constitution is a success because it is flexible. That is, it can be adapted to changing conditions. The framers knew that they had not produced a perfect document. They also realized that the nation would grow. So they provided the means to change the Constitution. The framers did not make it easy to make changes, but they did make it possible. You will learn more about changing the Constitution on page 808.

Five Principles of the Constitution

You know that you must obey the law. But do you know that the President must also? There are no exceptions to that rule under the Constitution. It applies to every person and to every group. This is so because the Constitution has guaranteed that the nation is dedicated to the rule of law.

In the pages that follow, you will look at five principles basic to the Constitution: popular sovereignty, limited government, federalism, separation of powers, and checks and balances. See the chart on page 799.

As you can see from the contents of the Constitution on page 797, the Constitution includes a preamble, or opening statement, 7 articles, and 26 amendments. Because the Constitution is only a framework, it does not spell out in detail how to apply the basic principles of government. Since 1787, therefore, Americans have debated about the principles as well as how the government should work. As you look at the basic principles of the Constitution, think about how they help protect your way of life.

Principles of the Constitution

Principle	Definition
Popular sovereignty	Principle of government in which the people hold the final authority or power
Limited government	Principle that the government is not all powerful but can do only what the people say it can do
Federalism	Division of power between the national government and the state governments
Separation of powers	Division of the operations of the national government into three branches, each with its own powers and responsibilities
Checks and balances	Means by which each branch of the national government is able to check, or control, the power of the other two branches

CHART SKILL The Constitution is based on five principles. According to the principle of popular sovereignty, who holds the final power in government? Which principle calls for dividing power between the national government and the state governments?

Popular Sovereignty Means the People Rule

Popular sovereignty is a term that means that the people hold the final authority, or ruling power. The framers of the Constitution believed in this principle. They also held that a contract exists between the people and the government. The government receives the power to rule from the people. In return, the government provides certain guarantees for the people.

We, the people. The Preamble of the Constitution contains both ideas—popular sovereignty and a contract between the government and its people. "We, the people," it begins. The "people" then list the purposes of the government they are establishing. These include "to form a more perfect Union, establish justice, insure domestic tranquillity, provide for the common defense, promote the general welfare, and secure the blessings of liberty to ourselves and our posterity."

The rest of the Constitution spells out the powers that the people give to the government to carry out its purposes. The Constitution also limits the power of government. It says what the government may not do.

The people vote. The Constitution guarantees the people a democratic government. But the people exercise their ruling power indirectly. They do not make the laws themselves. Instead, they elect representatives to make laws. At the same time, they hold these representatives responsible for the acts of government.

Americans today have the right to vote for members of the House of Representatives (Article 1, Section 2) and for members of the Senate (Amendment 17). The people also elect the members of the electoral college. The electors, in turn, choose the President (Article 2, Section 1).

When the Constitution was ratified, or approved, only white men over age 21 who owned property could vote.

As the chart below shows, other Americans have won the right to vote since then. Today, if you are a citizen, you are eligible to vote at age 18.

★ How do the American people carry out their right to rule themselves?

ISSUES FOR TODAY

Every election day, the polls are open from early morning until late evening. But often, fewer than one half of the eligible voters show up to vote. Many people offer the excuse that they are not registered. That is, they have not signed up in advance of the election as required by state law.

States have the right under the Constitution to set voting requirements. They require voter registration to prevent people from voting more than once in the same election. In the past, some people used another person's name in order to vote a second time.

Voters have to register only once unless they move or fail to vote for a long period. Yet, many Americans think registration is a bother. Some reformers want to end registration entirely. Others want to make it easier. They propose registration by mail or at the polls on election day. Or perhaps, they suggest, officials could make home visits to register citizens.

★ Do you think registration reform would increase the number of people who vote? Explain.

CHART SKILL The right to vote has expanded since the Constitution first went into effect. Who could vote in 1789? In 1971? Which amendment granted women the right to vote?

The Right to Vote

Year	People Allowed to Vote
1789	White men over age 21 who meet property requirements (state laws)
Early 1800s–1850s	All white men over age 21 (state laws)
1870	Black men (Amendment 15)
1920	Women (Amendment 19)
1961	People in the District of Columbia in presidential elections (Amendment 23)
1971	People over age 18 (Amendment 26)

The Government's Power Should Be Limited

The authors of the Constitution remembered well what life had been like under British rule. They knew that most Americans feared a strong government because of their experiences with the British king.

No one wanted to give up the rights gained by fighting the American Revolution. Yet, the failures of the Articles of Confederation made it clear that the new government had to be powerful. How could the framers achieve a balance between guaranteed rights and a strong government? The answer was limited government, or a government by law.

Limits on power. As the law of the land, the Constitution limits the powers of government to those granted by the people. It clearly states the powers of Congress and the President and describes the role of the judiciary. In this way, you and every other citizen know exactly what powers the federal government has. In addition, the Constitution spells out the powers denied to the national government and to the state governments.

The most important limits on government are set out in the Bill of Rights. In these amendments, the Constitution guarantees the individual freedoms of the people. One of these amendments also gives the states or the people any powers not specifically granted to the national government.

As you have read, the principle of popular sovereignty limits the government. As you read about the other principles of government, you will see that they help limit any part of the government from gaining too much power.

━━ISSUES FOR TODAY━━

Recently, the growing federal debt has gained nationwide attention. Legislators and the President have struggled to find a solution.

According to the Constitution, only Congress can authorize spending. In 1985, Congress passed a law requiring itself to limit spending. But some people urge a stronger measure. They want an amendment requiring a balanced budget. A balanced-budget amendment would forbid the government from spending more money than it takes in.

Supporters of the amendment think that it would force the government to face the issue of the national debt and make budget cuts. For them, ending the debt is important to the future of the country.

Opponents of the amendment fear that it will limit the ability of the government to deal with economic crises. During a slowdown in the economy, the government's income drops. But at the same time, more people are out of work and need aid. If the budget must be balanced, Congress would have to cut

spending just when the nation might need it most.

★ How would a balanced-budget amendment limit the government?

Federalism Results in a Sharing of Power

When the 13 colonies became the 13 states, they did not want to give much power to the central government. As a result, the government under the Articles of Confederation was weak. It took Shays' Rebellion to convince some people that they needed a stronger government. (See page 201.)

Framers choose federalism. The framers of the Constitution were faced with a real problem. They had to balance the need for a stronger central government with the stubborn resistance of many people to such a measure. Their solution was to base the new government on the principle of federalism.

Federalism is a system of government in which power is divided between the national government and the state governments. This system set up a strong national authority to deal with national issues. At the same time, it gave the states the authority to govern their own citizens.

The Constitution delegates, or assigns, some powers to the national, or federal, government. Other powers are reserved to the states. Still other powers, sometimes called concurrent powers, are shared by the national and state governments. The chart on page 802 shows how powers are divided under federalism.

The national government. The powers of the national government include those given specifically to Congress or to the President. The power to tax, to coin money, and to declare war are among the powers granted to Congress in Article 1, Section 8. Amend-

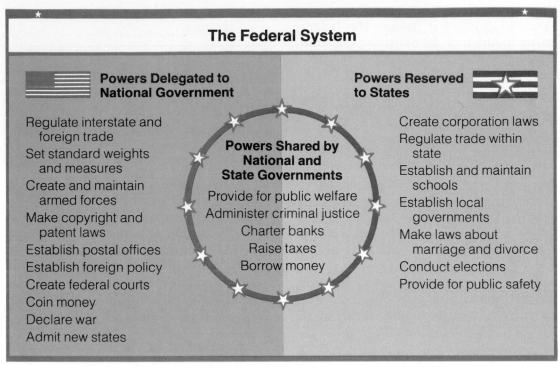

The Federal System

Powers Delegated to National Government

Regulate interstate and foreign trade

Set standard weights and measures

Create and maintain armed forces

Make copyright and patent laws

Establish postal offices

Establish foreign policy

Create federal courts

Coin money

Declare war

Admit new states

Powers Shared by National and State Governments

Provide for public welfare

Administer criminal justice

Charter banks

Raise taxes

Borrow money

Powers Reserved to States

Create corporation laws

Regulate trade within state

Establish and maintain schools

Establish local governments

Make laws about marriage and divorce

Conduct elections

Provide for public safety

CHART SKILL The system of federalism divides power between the national government and the state governments. Name two powers reserved to the states. Who has the power to raise taxes?

ment 16 adds the power to impose an income tax. Article 2, Section 2, describes the powers of the President. These include being commander in chief of the army and navy, granting reprieves and pardons, and making treaties with the advice and consent of the Senate.

The framers knew that they could not foresee what life would be like in the future. So Article 1, Section 8, Clause 18, gives Congress the power "to make all laws which shall be necessary and proper" to carry out its functions. This so-called "elastic clause" has allowed Congress to deal with changing conditions. For example, Congress has passed laws regulating the airline industry, television, and genetic engineering.

Protection of the states. The Constitution protects the rights of the states. In addition to having all powers not specifically granted to the national government, the states are guaranteed other rights. All states must be treated equally. And each state must respect the laws of the others.

If a dispute should arise between the national government and a state, however, there is no doubt where the final authority lies. The Constitution is the "supreme law of the land." The federal courts settle disputes between the states and the national government.

★ The age at which a person can legally marry is different in New York and Louisiana. But a person legally married in Louisiana is considered legally married in New York. Why?

ISSUES FOR TODAY

How well does the principle of federalism work? In general, the state governments and the federal government

—802—

cooperate. But clashes can occur. In the 1970s, there was a severe oil shortage. To help solve the problem, the federal government passed a law reducing the speed limit on interstate highways to 55 miles (80 km) per hour. Reduced speeds, Congress claimed, would save millions of gallons of gas as well as thousands of lives.

Many states followed suit. They reduced speed limits on state and local highways, which they alone control. But some states, mainly in the West, resisted the change. They argued that travel over the huge distances in their states would take too long at the slower speeds and therefore would increase the costs of moving goods.

The federal government tried to force the states to reduce their speed limits. It threatened to cut off federal dollars for building and repairing highways. Before long, the states gave in. But the federal government's threats to cut budgets in order to get its way caused bitterness.

★ Do you think the federal government should be able to cut funds to force states to follow national policy? Explain.

Separation of Powers Further Limits the Government

Separation of powers is the division of the national government into three branches, each with its own powers and responsibilities. When the framers set up the government this way, it was a novel experiment. At the time, nearly every government in Europe was a monarchy. The king or queen made the laws, enforced the laws, and appointed the judges to interpret the laws. This system was efficient, but it was also dangerous.

Three branches. The Constitution prevents one person or agency from having all the power. The first three articles set up three branches of government. See the chart below. The leg-

CHART SKILL The Constitution set up three branches of government. Each branch has its own powers. Who heads the executive branch? What is the role of the legislative branch?

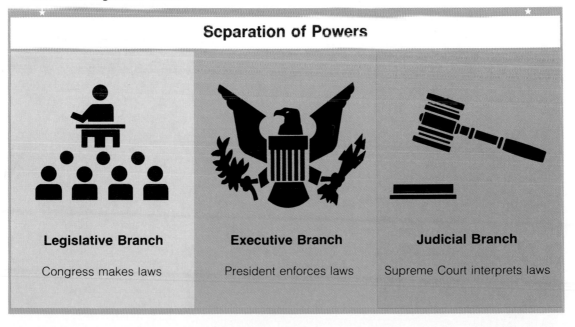

Separation of Powers

Legislative Branch	Executive Branch	Judicial Branch
Congress makes laws	President enforces laws	Supreme Court interprets laws

islative branch (Article 1) makes the laws. The executive branch (Article 2) enforces the laws. And the judicial branch (Article 3) interprets and explains the laws of the United States.

The House of Representatives and the Senate make up the legislative branch, called Congress. The President heads the executive branch and appoints advisers and other officials to oversee the operations of the government. The Supreme Court and other federal courts make up the judicial branch.

More safeguards. The framers did not fear only the concentration of power. They also distrusted the judgment of the masses. Suppose the people were swayed to vote for tyrants worse than any monarch? Separation of powers was an added safeguard. It made it difficult, if not impossible, for any one group to control all three branches of government.

Little was left to chance. For example, you probably have seen advertisements for candidates on television. Have you ever wondered who can be a candidate? The Constitution includes specific requirements about who can run for office. It also details the selection process for members of each branch of government. (See the chart below.)

★ How do you think European history affected the framers' decision to set up a separation of powers?

CHART SKILL The Constitution details the number, length of term, method of selection, and requirements of officeholders in the three branches of government. What are the requirements for the President? A senator? Which officeholders are elected directly by the voters?

Federal Officeholders

Office	Number	Term	Selection	Requirements
Representative	At least 1 per state; based on state population	2 years	Elected by voters of congressional district	Age 25 or over Citizen for 7 years Resident of state in which elected
Senator	2 per state	6 years	Original Constitution—elected by state legislature Amendment 17—elected by voters	Age 30 or over Citizen for 9 years Resident of state in which elected
President and Vice-President	1	4 years	Elected by electoral college	Age 35 or over Natural-born citizen Resident of U.S. for 14 years
Supreme Court judge	9	Life	Appointed by President	No requirements in Constitution

No one can seriously claim that separation of powers is an efficient way to run a government. In fact, one historian, James MacGregor Burns, calls the separation of powers "a deadlock of democracy." By that, he refers to the standstill that occurs when the President and Congress disagree on what should be done.

For example, in the 1980s, both the President and Congress saw the need to balance the federal budget. Both agreed that spending had to be cut. They disagreed, however, on where to make cuts. While they argued, the huge government debt ballooned. It threatened the nation's economy.

In today's fast-changing world, the government must make difficult decisions. Failure of the President and Congress to act can pose a real danger. But some people argue that the bargaining that goes on between the President and Congress is important to democratic government. It prevents any one branch from becoming too powerful.

★ Do you think that the benefits of a separation of powers outweigh the need for immediate action? Explain your answer.

Checks and Balances Protect Against Tyranny

Federalism and separation of powers are only two of the ways the Constitution limits the government. The framers went a step further and gave each branch of government the means to check, or control, the power of the other two branches. They hoped that this system of checks and balances would keep any one branch from gaining too much power.

Examples. How does the system of checks and balances work? The chart on page 806 shows some of the checks the President, the Congress, and the Supreme Court have on each other. For example, the President can check Congress by vetoing a bill, or proposed law. The Supreme Court, in turn, can check the President and Congress by declaring a law unconstitutional.

Judicial review, or the right of the Supreme Court to decide if a law is constitutional, is not stated directly in the Constitution. It is implied, however, in Article 3, Section 2. In the case of *Marbury* v. *Madison,* an early Supreme Court decision interpreted that clause to give the Supreme Court the right of judicial review (see page 244).

As the chart shows, Congress has several checks on the power of the President. For example, the Senate must approve many of the President's appointments. It must also approve treaties signed by the President. In addition, Congress can override a presidential veto so that a bill can become a law without the President's signature.

Need for compromise. The system of checks and balances often requires the President and Congress to reach compromises. This is especially true when the President and the majority of the members of Congress are from different political parties. If the President threatens to veto a bill in Congress, the lawmakers might decide to change parts of the bill to make it more acceptable. In the same way, the President might choose a person for a cabinet position or judgeship whom the Senate is likely to approve.

★ What might result if the President could not veto bills or Congress could not override a veto?

Do the nine black-robed justices on the Supreme Court hold too much power? Your answer to that question will probably depend on whether you agree with the decisions the Court has made.

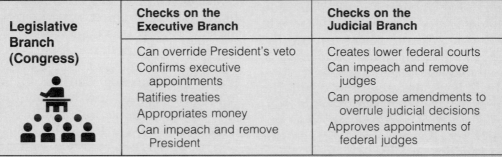

System of Checks and Balances

Executive Branch (President)	Checks on the Legislative Branch	Checks on the Judicial Branch
	Can propose laws Can veto laws Can call special sessions of Congress Makes appointments Negotiates foreign treaties	Appoints federal judges Can grant pardons to federal offenders

Legislative Branch (Congress)	Checks on the Executive Branch	Checks on the Judicial Branch
	Can override President's veto Confirms executive appointments Ratifies treaties Appropriates money Can impeach and remove President	Creates lower federal courts Can impeach and remove judges Can propose amendments to overrule judicial decisions Approves appointments of federal judges

Judicial Branch (Supreme Court)	Check on the Executive Branch	Check on the Legislative Branch
	Can declare executive actions unconstitutional	Can declare acts of Congress unconstitutional

CHART SKILL Through the system of checks and balances, each branch of government has checks, or controls, on the power of the other branches. Name one check that the President has on Congress. How can the Supreme Court check Congress?

In recent years, the Supreme Court has dealt with many troubling legal issues. For example, it has ruled on cases involving busing to desegregate schools, the rights of people under age 18 to freedom of speech, and the death penalty.

Supreme Court justices vow to uphold the Constitution. But their interpretations can, and do, vary. A Supreme Court decision requires a majority vote of the nine justices. In a 5–4 decision, the opinion of only one justice affects the outcome of the case.

Various groups have called for changes in the way the Supreme Court operates. For example, some argue that it should take more than five justices to declare a law unconstitutional.

★ Do you think declaring a law unconstitutional should require the vote of at least six justices? Explain.

Protection of Individual Liberties

What does the Constitution mean to most Americans? First and foremost, it is the document that protects their individual, or civil, rights and liberties. These include freedom of religion, speech, press, assembly, and petition. Protection of rights is central to the Constitution. As you have read, the principles of the Constitution came out of the framers' personal experiences. They had seen injustice done, and they sought to prevent it.

Guarantees of liberty. The framers wanted to create a government that would protect the rights and freedoms of the people. Thomas Jefferson had stated the following in the Declaration of Independence:

> We hold these truths to be self-evident, that all men are created equal, and that they are endowed by their Creator with certain inalienable Rights, that among these are Life, Liberty, and the pursuit of Happiness.

The new government was designed to fulfill all these promises of equality and liberty.

The original Constitution safeguarded some rights by forbidding or limiting government actions that might affect those rights. Article 6, Section 3, for example, says that "no religious test shall ever be required as a qualification to any office or public trust under the United States."

Some people, however, did not think that the Constitution provided enough protection for their individual rights. Several states refused to approve the Constitution until they were promised that a bill of rights would be added. See page 797 for the amendments in the Bill of Rights.

Ideas of liberty grow. Individual liberties are not limited to those specifically named in the Constitution. Amendment 9 states that the people have rights beyond those discussed in the Constitution. Today, Americans believe that individual liberties include the right to free, quality education, to safe working conditions, and to equal job opportunities.

Until this century, many Americans were denied the protections of the Constitution. Even though Amendment 13 (1865) ended slavery and Amendment 14 (1868) defined the rights of citizens, black Americans faced discrimination. Only after years of struggle have blacks won equal protection under the law. Women and other minority groups also have struggled to gain equal protection and equal rights.

CHART SKILL Amendment 1 of the Constitution guarantees some basic individual liberties. Name two freedoms it protects. Which freedom allows you to hold and attend meetings?

Liberties Protected by the First Amendment

Freedom of the Press

Freedom of Religion

Freedom of Petition

Freedom of Assembly

Freedom of Speech

Since the 1960s, federal courts have interpreted Amendment 14 to mean that state and local governments must abide by the guarantees of the Bill of Rights. For example, a state cannot deny a person a speedy trial or impose cruel and unusual punishments. Applying the guarantees of the Bill of Rights to state governments has been a giant step toward protection of individual liberties.

★ How has the protection of individual liberties expanded since the signing of the original Constitution?

▬ISSUES FOR TODAY▬

"I can say whatever I want," argues a citizen. "I have rights." Right? Wrong. The constitutional guarantees of individual liberties are not absolute. That is, even though you have the right to freedom of speech, you do not have the right to say anything at any time. For example, you do not have the right to deliberately lie about a person. Similarly, even though you have religious freedom, you cannot commit a crime in the name of religion.

People often turn to the courts when their rights come into conflict with the rights of others. Again and again, the Supreme Court has been called on to interpret and apply the Constitution.

Consider the case of *Hazelwood School District* v. *Kuhlmeier et al.* The principal of Hazelwood East refused to allow the school newspaper to publish an article. He said that the article violated the right to privacy of certain families. The school journalists claimed that the principal's decision violated their rights to freedom of speech and press. Lawyers for the school district argued that the newspaper was a school activity and, therefore, could be regulated by the principal.

In 1988, the Supreme Court agreed that the issue was not freedom of speech but the right of the school to control education. The school, it ruled, could censor the newspaper.

★ How would you interpret this statement: Your right to swing your fist ends where my nose begins?

Changing the Constitution

★   ★

The framers of the Constitution wanted to set up a lasting government, and they succeeded. They wrote a constitution that we recognize today as a living document. That is, its basic principles have survived for over 200 years. At the same time, it has adapted to tremendous change.

The amendment process. The framers provided formal methods to amend, or change, the Constitution. Article 5 describes two ways to propose amendments and two ways to ratify amendments. See the chart on page 809.

The amendment process guarantees that changes will not be made

lightly. Since 1789, more than 9,000 amendments have been proposed in Congress. Only 26 have made it through the ratifying process. Of those, 10 were in the Bill of Rights passed in 1791.

Informal changes. The Constitution has stayed up to date through many informal changes. The framers outlined the structure of the government. But they left it to future generations to fill in the details. Informal changes have been made by laws passed in Congress (see page 685), treaties (see page 246), court decisions (see page 667), customs and practices of political parties (see page 295), and

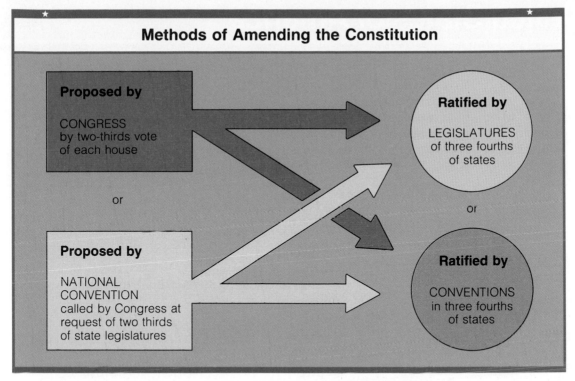

Methods of Amending the Constitution

Proposed by

CONGRESS
by two-thirds vote
of each house

or

Proposed by

NATIONAL
CONVENTION
called by Congress at
request of two thirds
of state legislatures

Ratified by

LEGISLATURES
of three fourths
of states

or

Ratified by

CONVENTIONS
in three fourths
of states

CHART SKILL The amendment process requires proposal and ratification. Name one way to propose an amendment. Name one way to ratify an amendment.

rules of government agencies (see page 728).

"I do not think we are more inspired, have more wisdom, or possess more virtue than those who will come after us," said George Washington. Believing this, the framers of the Constitution kept the document brief and kept their language general. In this way, the Constitution has been able to adapt to the challenges of an ever-changing world.

★ Why do you think only 26 amendments have been ratified?

◼ISSUES FOR TODAY◼

Many Americans are unhappy with the workings of the political process. They suggest changing the Constitution to make the government more democratic and efficient. Some proposals for amendments to the Constitution are listed below. Read the proposals and think about which principle of the Constitution is involved.

The Constitution should be amended to:

● Allow for a direct national vote on a major issue.
● Limit the amount of money candidates can spend on political campaigns.
● Abolish the electoral college and let citizens vote directly for the President.
● Give the President one six-year term.
● Repeal the two-term limit on the President.
● Give members of the House of Representatives longer terms.
★ Choose one of the proposals and explain why you would or would not support an amendment.

The Constitution of the United States of America

The Constitution is printed in black. The titles of articles, sections, and clauses are not part of the original document. They have been added to help you find information in the Constitution. Some words or lines are crossed out because they have been changed by amendments or no longer apply. Annotations, or explanations, are on the tan side of the page. Page numbers in the annotations show where a subject is discussed in the text. Hard words are defined in the annotations.

Preamble

The Preamble describes the purpose of the government set up by the Constitution. Americans expect their government to defend justice and liberty and provide peace and safety from foreign enemies.

We, the people of the United States, in order to form a more perfect Union, establish justice, insure domestic tranquillity, provide for the common defense, promote the general welfare, and secure the blessings of liberty to ourselves and our posterity, do ordain and establish this Constitution for the United States of America.

Article 1. The Legislative Branch

Section 1.   A Two-House Legislature

The Constitution gives Congress the power to make laws. Congress is divided into the Senate and House of Representatives.

All legislative powers herein granted shall be vested in a Congress of the United States, which shall consist of a Senate and House of Representatives.

Section 2.   House of Representatives

1. Election of Members   The House of Representatives shall be composed of members chosen every second year by the people of the several states, and the electors in each state shall have the qualifications requisite for electors of the most numerous branch of the state legislature.

Clause 1 *Electors* refers to voters. Members of the House of Representatives are elected every two years. Any citizen allowed to vote for members of the larger house of the state legislature can also vote for members of the House.

2. Qualifications   No person shall be a Representative who shall not have attained to the age of twenty-five years, and been seven years a citizen of the United States, and who shall not, when elected, be an inhabitant of that state in which he shall be chosen.

Clause 2   A member of the House of Representatives must be at least 25 years old, an American citizen for 7 years, and a resident of the state he or she represents.

Clause 3   The number of representatives each state elects is based on its population. An *enumeration,* or census, must be taken every ten years to determine population. Today, the number of representatives in the House is fixed at 435.

  This is the famous Three Fifths Compromise worked out at the Constitutional Convention (page 204). *Persons bound to service* meant indentured servants. *All other persons* meant slaves. All free people in a state were counted. However, only three fifths of the slaves were included in the population count. This three fifths clause became meaningless when slaves were freed by the Thirteenth Amendment.

3. Determining Representation   Representatives ~~and direct taxes~~ shall be apportioned among the several states which may be included within this Union, according to their respective num-~~bers which shall be determined by adding to the whole number of free persons, including those bound to service for a term of years, and excluding Indians not taxed, three-fifths of all other persons.~~ The actual enumeration shall be made within three years after the first meeting of the Congress of the United States, and within every subsequent term of ten years, in such manner as they shall by law direct. The number of Representatives shall not exceed one for every 30,000, but each state shall have at least one Representative; ~~and until such enumeration shall be made, the state of New Hampshire shall be entitled to choose three; Massachusetts, eight; Rhode Island and Providence Plantations, one; Connecticut, five; New York, six; New Jersey, four; Pennsylvania, eight;~~

The Constitution

Delaware, one; Maryland, six; Virginia, ten; North Carolina, five; South Carolina, five; and Georgia, three.

4. Filling Vacancies When vacancies happen in the representation from any state, the executive authority thereof shall issue writs of election to fill such vacancies.

5. Selection of Officers; Power of Impeachment The House of Representatives shall choose their Speaker and other officers; and shall have the sole power of impeachment.

Section 3. The Senate

1. Selection of Members The Senate of the United States shall be composed of two Senators from each state chosen by the legislature thereof, for six years, and each Senator shall have one vote.

2. Alternating Terms; Filling Vacancies Immediately after they shall be assembled in consequence of the first election, they shall be divided as equally as may be into three classes. The seats of the Senators of the first class shall be vacated at the expiration of the second year, of the second class at the expiration of the fourth year, and of the third class at the expiration of the sixth year, so that one-third may be chosen every second year; and if vacancies happen by resignation, or otherwise, during the recess of the legislature of any state, the executive thereof may make temporary appointments until the next meeting of the legislature, which shall then fill such vacancies.

3. Qualifications No person shall be a Senator who shall not have attained to the age of thirty years, and been nine years a citizen of the United States, and who shall not, when elected, be an inhabitant of that state for which he shall be chosen.

4. President of the Senate The Vice-President of the United States shall be president of the Senate, but shall have no vote, unless they be equally divided.

5. Election of Senate Officers The Senate shall choose their other officers, and also a president *pro tempore,* in the absence of the Vice-President, or when he shall exercise the office of the President of the United States.

6. Impeachment Trials The Senate shall have the sole power to try all impeachments. When sitting for that purpose, they shall be on oath or affirmation. When the President of the United States is tried, the Chief Justice shall preside; and no person shall be convicted without the concurrence of two-thirds of the members present.

7. Penalties Upon Conviction Judgment in cases of impeachment shall not extend further than to removal from office, and disqualification to hold and enjoy any office of honor, trust, or

Clause 4 *Executive authority* means the governor of a state. If a member of the House leaves office before his or her term ends, the governor must call a special election to fill the seat.

Clause 5 The House elects a speaker. Today, the speaker is usually chosen by the party that has a majority in the House. Also, only the House has the power to *impeach,* or accuse, a federal official of wrongdoing.

Clause 1 Each state has two senators. Senators serve for six-year terms. The Seventeenth Amendment changed the way senators were elected.

Clause 2 Every two years, one third of the senators run for reelection. Thus, the makeup of the Senate is never totally changed by any one election. The Seventeenth Amendment changed the way of filling *vacancies,* or empty seats. Today, the governor of a state chooses a senator to fill a vacancy that occurs between elections.

Clause 3 A senator must be at least 30 years old, an American citizen for 9 years, and a resident of the state he or she represents.

Clause 4 The Vice President presides over Senate meetings, but he or she can only vote to break a tie.

Clause 5 *Pro tempore* means temporary. The Senate chooses one of its members to serve as president pro tempore when the Vice President is absent.

Clause 6 The Senate acts as a jury if the House impeaches a federal official. The Chief Justice of the Supreme Court presides if the President is on trial. Two thirds of all senators present must vote for *conviction,* or finding the accused guilty. No President has ever been convicted. The House impeached President Andrew Johnson in 1868, but the Senate acquitted him of the charges (page 424). In 1974, President Richard Nixon resigned before he could be impeached.

Clause 7 If an official is found guilty by the Senate, he or she can be removed from office and barred from holding federal office in the future. These are the only punishments the Senate can impose. However, the convicted official can still be tried in criminal court.

Clause 1 Each state legislature can decide when and how congressional elections take place, but Congress can overrule these decisions. In 1842, Congress required each state to set up congressional districts with one representative elected from each district. In 1872, Congress decided that congressional elections must be held in every state on the same date in even-numbered years.

Clause 2 Congress must meet at least once a year. The Twentieth Amendment moved the opening date of Congress to January 3.

Clause 1 Each house decides if a member has the qualifications for office set by the Constitution. A *quorum* is the smallest number of members who must be present for business to be conducted. Each house can set its own rules about absent members.

Clause 2 Each house can make rules for the conduct of members. It can only expel a member by a two-thirds vote.

Clause 3 Each house keeps a record of its meetings. The *Congressional Record* is published every day with excerpts from speeches made in each house. It also records the votes of each member.

Clause 4 Neither house can *adjourn,* or stop meeting, for more than three days unless the other house approves. Both houses of Congress must meet in the same city.

Clause 1 *Compensation* means salary. Congress decides the salary for its members. While Congress is in session, a member is free from arrest in civil cases and cannot be sued for anything he or she says on the floor of Congress. This allows for freedom of debate. However, a member can be arrested for a criminal offense.

Clause 2 *Emolument* also means salary. A member of Congress cannot hold another federal office during his or her term. A former member of Congress cannot hold an office created while he or she was in Congress. An official in another branch of government cannot serve at the same time in Congress. This strengthens the separation of powers.

profit under the United States; but the party convicted shall nevertheless be liable and subject to indictment, trial, judgment, and punishment, according to law.

Section 4. Elections and Meetings

1. Election of Congress   The times, places, and manner of holding elections for Senators and Representatives shall be prescribed in each state by the legislature thereof; but the Congress may at any time by law make or alter such regulations, except as to the places of choosing Senators.

2. Annual Sessions   The Congress shall assemble at least once in every year, and such meeting shall be on the first Monday in December, unless they shall by law appoint a different day.

Section 5. Rules for the Conduct of Business

1. Organization   Each house shall be the judge of the elections, returns, and qualifications of its own members, and a majority of each shall constitute a quorum to do business; but a smaller number may adjourn from day to day, and may be authorized to compel the attendance of absent members, in such manner, and under such penalties, as each house may provide.

2. Procedures   Each house may determine the rules of its proceedings, punish its members for disorderly behavior, and with the concurrence of two-thirds, expel a member.

3. A Written Record   Each house shall keep a journal of its proceedings, and from time to time publish the same, excepting such parts as may in their judgment require secrecy; and the yeas and nays of the members of either house on any question shall, at the desire of one-fifth of those present, be entered on the journal.

4. Rules for Adjournment   Neither house, during the session of Congress, shall, without the consent of the other, adjourn for more than three days, nor to any other place than that in which the two houses shall be sitting.

Section 6. Privileges and Restrictions

1. Salaries and Immunities   The Senators and Representatives shall receive a compensation for their services, to be ascertained by law and paid out of the Treasury of the United States. They shall in all cases, except treason, felony, and breach of the peace, be privileged from arrest during their attendance at the session of their respective houses, and in going to and returning from the same; and for any speech or debate in either house, they shall not be questioned in any other place.

2. Restrictions on Other Employment   No Senator or Representative shall, during the time for which he was elected, be appointed to any civil office under the authority of the United States, which shall have been created, or the emoluments whereof shall have been increased, during such time; and no person holding any office under the United States shall be a member of either house during his continuance in office.

Section 7. Law-Making Process

1. Tax Bills   All bills for raising revenue shall originate in the House of Representatives; but the Senate may propose or concur with amendments as on other bills.

2. How a Bill Becomes a Law   Every bill which shall have passed the House of Representatives and the Senate shall, before it become a law, be presented to the President of the United States; if he approve, he shall sign it, but if not, he shall return it, with his objections, to that house in which it shall have originated, who shall enter the objections at large on their journal, and proceed to reconsider it. If after such reconsideration two-thirds of that house shall agree to pass the bill, it shall be sent, together with the objections, to the other house, by which it shall likewise be reconsidered, and, if approved by two-thirds of that house, it shall become a law. But in all such cases the votes of both houses shall be determined by yeas and nays, and the names of the persons voting for and against the bill shall be entered on the journal of each house respectively. If any bill shall not be returned by the President within ten days (Sundays excepted) after it shall have been presented to him, the same bill shall be a law, in like manner as if he had signed it, unless the Congress by their adjournment prevent its return, in which case it shall not be a law.

3. Resolutions Passed by Congress   Every order, resolution, or vote to which the concurrence of the Senate and House of Representatives may be necessary (except on a question of adjournment) shall be presented to the President of the United States; and before the same shall take effect, shall be approved by him, or being disapproved by him, shall be repassed by two-thirds of the Senate and House of Representatives, according to the rules and limitations prescribed in the case of a bill.

Section 8. Powers Delegated to Congress

The Congress shall have power

1. Taxes   To lay and collect taxes, duties, imposts, and excises, to pay the debts and provide for the common defense and general welfare of the United States; but all duties, imposts, and excises shall be uniform throughout the United States;

2. Borrowing   To borrow money on the credit of the United States;

3. Commerce   To regulate commerce with foreign nations, and among the several states, and with the Indian tribes;

Clause 1   *Revenue* is money raised by the government through taxes. Tax bills must be introduced in the House. The Senate, however, can make changes in tax bills. This clause protects the principle that people can be taxed only with their consent.

Clause 2   A *bill,* or proposed law, that is passed by a majority of the House and Senate is sent to the President. If the President signs the bill, it becomes law.

A bill can also become law without the President's signature. The President can refuse to act on a bill. If Congress is in session at the time, the bill becomes law ten days after the President receives it.

The President can *veto,* or reject, a bill by sending it back to the house where it was introduced. Or if the President refuses to act on a bill and Congress adjourns within ten days, then the bill dies. This way of killing a bill without taking action is called the *pocket veto.*

Congress can override the President's veto if each house of Congress passes the bill again by a two-thirds vote. This clause is an important part of the system of checks and balances (pages 208–210).

Clause 3   Congress can pass resolutions or orders that have the same force as laws. Any such resolution or order must be signed by the President (except on questions of adjournment). Thus, this clause prevents Congress from bypassing the President simply by calling a bill by another name.

Clause 1   *Duties* are tariffs. *Imposts* are taxes in general. *Excises* are taxes on the production or sale of certain goods. Congress has the power to tax and spend tax money. Taxes must be the same in all parts of the country.

Clause 2   Congress can borrow money for the United States. The government often borrows money by selling *bonds,* or certificates that promise to pay the holder a certain sum of money on a certain date (page 223).

Clause 3   Only Congress has the power to regulate foreign and *interstate trade,* or trade between states. Disagreements over interstate trade was a major problem with the Articles of Confederation (pages 199–200).

Clause 4 *Naturalization* is the process whereby a foreigner becomes a citizen. *Bankruptcy* is the condition in which a person or business cannot pay its debts. Congress has the power to pass laws on these two issues. The laws must be the same in all parts of the country.

Clause 5 Congress has the power to coin money and set its value. Congress has set up the National Bureau of Standards to regulate weights and measures.

Clause 6 *Counterfeiting* is the making of imitation money. *Securities* are bonds. Congress can make laws to punish counterfeiters.

Clause 7 Congress has the power to set up and control the delivery of mail.

Clause 8 Congress may pass copyright and patent laws. A *copyright* protects an author. A *patent* makes an inventor the sole owner of his or her work for a limited time.

Clause 9 Congress has the power to set up *inferior,* or lower, federal courts under the Supreme Court.

Clause 10 Congress can punish *piracy,* or the robbing of ships at sea.

Clause 11 Only Congress can declare war. Declarations of war are granted at the request of the President. *Letters of marque and reprisal* were documents issued by a government allowing merchant ships to arm themselves and attack ships of an enemy nation. They are no longer issued.

Clauses 12, 13, 14 These clauses place the army and navy under the control of Congress. Congress decides on the size of the armed forces and the amount of money to spend on the army and navy. It also has the power to write rules governing the armed forces.

Clauses 15, 16 The *militia* is a body of citizen soldiers. Congress can call up the militia to put down rebellions or fight foreign invaders. Each state has its own militia, today called the National Guard. Normally, the militia is under the command of a state's governor. However, it can be placed under the command of the President.

Clause 17 Congress controls the district around the national capital. In 1790, Congress made Washington, D.C., the nation's capital (page 234). In 1973, it gave residents of the district the right to elect local officials.

4. Naturalization; Bankruptcy To establish a uniform rule of naturalization, and uniform laws on the subject of bankruptcies throughout the United States;

5. Coins; Weights; Measures To coin money, regulate the value thereof, and of foreign coin, and fix the standard of weights and measures;

6. Counterfeiting To provide for the punishment of counterfeiting the securities and current coin of the United States;

7. Post Offices To establish post offices and post roads;

8. Copyrights; Patents To promote the progress of science and useful arts by securing for limited times to authors and inventors the exclusive right to their respective writings and discoveries;

9. Federal Courts To constitute tribunals inferior to the Supreme Court;

10. Piracy To define and punish piracies and felonies committed on the high seas and offenses against the law of nations;

11. Declarations of War To declare war, ~~grant letters of marque and reprisal~~, and make rules concerning captures on land and water;

12. Army To raise and support armies, but no appropriation of money to that use shall be for a longer term than two years;

13. Navy To provide and maintain a navy;

14. Rules for the Military To make rules for the government and regulation of the land and naval forces;

15. Militia To provide for calling forth the militia to execute the laws of the Union, suppress insurrections, and repel invasions;

16. Rules for the Militia To provide for organizing, arming, and disciplining the militia, and for governing such part of them as may be employed in the service of the United States, reserving to the states, respectively, the appointment of the officers, and the authority of training the militia according to the discipline prescribed by Congress;

17. National Capital To exercise exclusive legislation in all cases whatsoever, over such district (not exceeding ten miles square) as may, by cession of particular states, and the acceptance of Congress, become the seat of government of the United States, and to exercise like authority over all places purchased by the consent of the legislature of the state in which the same shall be, for the erection of forts, magazines, arsenals, dock-yards, and other needful buildings;—and

18. Necessary Laws To make all laws which shall be necessary and proper for carrying into execution the foregoing powers, and all other powers vested by this Constitution in the government of the United States, or in any department or officer thereof.

Section 9. Powers Denied to the Federal Government

1. The Slave Trade ~~The migration or importation of such persons as any of the states now existing shall think proper to admit shall not be prohibited by the Congress prior to the year 1808; but a tax or duty may be imposed on such importation, not exceeding $10 for each person.~~

2. Writ of Habeas Corpus The privilege of the writ of *habeas corpus* shall not be suspended, unless when in cases of rebellion or invasion the public safety may require it.

3. Bills of Attainder and Ex Post Facto Laws No bill of attainder or *ex post facto* law shall be passed.

4. Apportionment of Direct Taxes ~~No capitation or other direct tax shall be laid, unless in proportion to the census or enumeration herein before directed to be taken.~~

5. Taxes on Exports No tax or duty shall be laid on articles exported from any state.

6. Special Preference for Trade No preference shall be given any regulation of commerce or revenue to the ports of one state over those of another; nor shall vessels bound to, or from, one state, be obliged to enter, clear, or pay duties in another.

7. Spending No money shall be drawn from the Treasury, but in consequence of appropriations made by law; and a regular statement and account of the receipts and expenditures of all public money shall be published from time to time.

Clause 18 Clauses 1–17 list the powers delegated to Congress. The writers of the Constitution added Clause 18 so that Congress could deal with the changing needs of the nation. It gives Congress the power to make laws as needed to carry out the first 17 clauses. Clause 18 is sometimes called the elastic clause because it lets Congress stretch the meaning of its power.

Clause 1 *Such persons* means slaves. This clause resulted from a compromise between the supporters and the opponents of the slave trade (pages 204–205). In 1808, as soon as Congress was permitted to abolish the slave trade, it did so. The $10 import tax was never imposed.

Clause 2 A *writ of habeas corpus* is a court order requiring government officials to bring a prisoner to court and explain why he or she is being held. A writ of habeas corpus protects people from unlawful imprisonment. The government cannot suspend this right except in times of rebellion or invasion.

Clause 3 A *bill of attainder* is a law declaring that a person is guilty of a particular crime. An *ex post facto law* punishes an act which was not illegal when it was committed. Congress cannot pass a bill of attainder and ex post facto laws.

Clause 4 A *capitation tax* is a tax placed directly on each person. *Direct taxes* are taxes on people or on land. They can only be passed if they are divided among the states according to population. The Sixteenth Amendment allowed Congress to tax income without regard to the population of the states.

Clause 5 This clause forbids Congress to tax exports. In 1787, Southerners insisted on this clause because their economy depended on exports.

Clause 6 Congress cannot make laws that favor one state over another in trade and commerce. Also, states cannot place tariffs on interstate trade.

Clause 7 The federal government cannot spend money unless Congress *appropriates* it, or passes a law allowing it. This clause gives Congress an important check on the President by controlling the money he or she can spend. The government must publish a statement showing how it spends public funds.

The Constitution

Clause 8 The government cannot award titles of nobility such as Duke or Duchess. American citizens cannot accept titles of nobility from foreign governments without the consent of Congress.

Clause 1 The writers of the Constitution did not want the states to act like separate nations. So they prohibited states from making treaties or coining money. Some powers denied to the federal government are also denied to the states. For example, states cannot pass ex post facto laws.

Clauses 2, 3 Powers listed here are forbidden to the states, but Congress can lift these prohibitions by passing laws that give these powers to the states.

Clause 2 forbids states from taxing imports and exports without the consent of Congress. States may charge inspection fees on goods entering the states. Any profit from these fees must be turned over to the United States Treasury.

Clause 3 forbids states from keeping an army or navy without the consent of Congress. States cannot make treaties or make war unless an enemy invades or is about to invade.

Clause 1 The President is responsible for *executing*, or carrying out, laws passed by Congress.

Clauses 2, 3 Some of the writers of the Constitution feared allowing the people to elect the President directly (pages 207–208). Therefore, the Constitutional Convention set up the electoral college. Clause 2 directs each state to choose electors, or delegates to the electoral college, to vote for President. A state's electoral vote is equal to the combined number of senators and representatives. Each state may decide how to choose its electors. Members of Congress and federal officeholders may not serve as electors. This much of the original electoral college system is still in effect.

Clause 3 called upon each elector to vote for two candidates. The candidate who received a majority of the electoral votes would become President. The runner-up would become Vice President. If no candidate won a majority, the House would choose the President. The Senate would choose the Vice President.

The election of 1800 showed a problem with the original electoral college system (page

8. Creation of Titles of Nobility No title of nobility shall be granted by the United States; and no person holding any office of profit or trust under them, shall, without the consent of the Congress, accept of any present, emolument, office, or title, of any kind whatever, from any king, prince, or foreign state.

Section 10. Powers Denied to the States

1. Unconditional Prohibitions No state shall enter into any treaty, alliance, or confederation; grant letters of marque and reprisals; coin money; emit bills of credit; make anything but gold and silver coin a tender in payment of debts; pass any bill of attainder, *ex post facto* law, or law impairing the obligation of contracts, or grant any title of nobility.

2. Powers Conditionally Denied No state shall, without the consent of the Congress, lay any imposts or duties on imports or exports, except what may be absolutely necessary for executing its inspection laws; and the net produce of all duties and imposts, laid by any state on imports or exports, shall be for the use of the Treasury of the United States; and all such laws shall be subject to the revision and control of the Congress.

3. Other Denied Powers No state shall, without the consent of Congress, lay any duty of tonnage, keep troops, or ships of war in time of peace, enter into any agreement or compact with another state, or with a foreign power, or engage in war, unless actually invaded, or in such imminent danger as will not admit of delay.

Article 2. The Executive Branch

Section 1. President and Vice-President

1. Chief Executive The executive power shall be vested in a President of the United States of America. He shall hold his office during the term of four years, and together with the Vice-President, chosen for the same term, be elected as follows:

2. Selection of Electors Each state shall appoint, in such manner as the legislature thereof may direct, a number of electors, equal to the whole number of Senators and Representatives to which the state may be entitled in the Congress; but no Senator or Representative, or person holding an office or trust or profit under the United States, shall be appointed an elector.

3. Electoral College Procedures ~~The electors shall meet in their respective states, and vote by ballot for two persons, of whom one at least shall not be an inhabitant of the same state with themselves. And they shall make a list of all the persons voted for, and of the number of votes for each; which list they shall sign and certify, and transmit sealed to the seat of the government of the United States, directed to the president of the Senate. The president of the Senate shall, in the presence of the Senate and House of Representatives, open all the certificates, and the votes shall then be counted. The person having the greatest number of votes shall be the President, if such number be a majority of the whole number of electors appointed; and if there be more than one who have such majority, and have an equa~~

number of votes, then the House of Representatives shall immediately choose by ballot one of them for President; and if no person have a majority, then from the five highest on the list the said House shall in like manner choose the President. But in choosing the President the votes shall be taken by states, the representation from each state having one vote. A quorum for this purpose shall consist of a member or members from two-thirds of the states, and a majority of all the states shall be necessary to a choice. In every case, after the choice of the President, the person having the greatest number of votes of the electors shall be the Vice-President. But if there should remain two or more who have equal votes, the Senate shall choose from them by ballot the Vice-President.

237). Thomas Jefferson was the Republican candidate for President, and Aaron Burr was the Republican candidate for Vice President. In the electoral college, the vote ended in a tie. The election was finally decided in the House, where Jefferson was chosen President. The Twelfth Amendment changed the electoral college system so that this could not happen again.

4. Time of Elections   The Congress may determine the time of choosing the electors, and the day on which they shall give their votes; which day shall be the same throughout the United States.

Clause 4   Under a law passed in 1792, electors are chosen on the Tuesday following the first Monday of November every four years. Electors from each state meet to vote in December.

Today, voters in each state choose **slates,** or groups, of electors who are pledged to a candidate for President. The candidate for President who wins the popular vote in each state wins that state's electoral vote.

5. Qualifications for President   No person except a natural-born citizen or a citizen of the United States, at the time of the adoption of this Constitution, shall be eligible to the office of the President; neither shall any person be eligible to that office who shall not have attained to the age of thirty-five years, and been fourteen years a resident within the United States

Clause 5   The President must be a citizen of the United States from birth, at least 35 years old, and a resident of the country for 14 years. The first seven Presidents of the United States were born under British rule, but they were allowed to hold office because they were citizens at the time the Constitution was adopted.

6. Presidential Succession   In case of the removal of the President from office, or of his death, resignation, or inability to discharge the powers and duties of the said office, the same shall devolve on the Vice-President, and the Congress may by law provide for the case of removal, death, resignation, or inability, both of the President and Vice-President, declaring what officer shall then act as President, and such officer shall act accordingly, until the disability be removed, or a President shall be elected.

Clause 6   The powers of the President pass to the Vice President if the President leaves office or cannot discharge his or her duties. The wording of this clause caused confusion the first time a President died in office. When President William Henry Harrison died, it was uncertain whether Vice President John Tyler should remain Vice President and act as President. Or should he be sworn in as President? Tyler persuaded a federal judge to swear him in. So he set the precedent that the Vice President assumes the office of President when it becomes vacant. The Twenty-fifth Amendment replaced this clause.

7. Salary   The President shall, at stated times, receive for his services, a compensation, which shall neither be increased nor diminished during the period for which he shall have been elected, and he shall not receive within that period any other emolument from the United States, or any of them.

Clause 7   The President is paid a salary. It cannot be raised or lowered during his or her term of office. The President is not allowed to hold any other federal or state position while in office. Today, the President's salary is $200,000 a year.

8. Oath of Office   Before he enter on the execution of his office, he shall take the following oath or affirmation:—"I do solemnly swear (or affirm) that I will faithfully execute the office of President of the United States, and will to the best of my ability, preserve, protect, and defend the Constitution of the United States."

Clause 8   Before taking office, the President must promise to protect and defend the Constitution. Usually, the Chief Justice of the Supreme Court administers the oath of office to the President.

Clause 1 The President is head of the armed forces and the state militias when they are called into national service. So the military is under **civilian,** or nonmilitary, control.

The President can get advice from the heads of executive departments. In most cases, the President has the power to grant a reprieve or pardon. A **reprieve** suspends punishment ordered by law. A **pardon** prevents prosecution for a crime or overrides the judgment of the court.

Clause 2 The President has the power to make treaties with other nations. Under the system of checks and balances, all treaties must be approved by two thirds of the Senate. Today, the President also makes agreements with foreign governments. These executive agreements do not need Senate approval.

The President has the power to appoint ambassadors to foreign countries and other high officials. The Senate must **confirm**, or approve, these appointments.

Clause 3 If the Senate is in **recess,** or not meeting, the President may fill vacant government posts by making temporary appointments.

The President must give Congress a report on the condition of the nation every year. This report is now called the State of the Union Address. Since 1913, the President has given this speech in person each January.

The President can call a special session of Congress and can adjourn Congress if necessary. The President has the power to receive, or recognize, foreign ambassadors.

The President must carry out the laws. Today, many government agencies oversee the execution of laws.

Civil officers include federal judges and members of the cabinet. **High crimes** are major crimes. **Misdemeanors** are lesser crimes. The President, Vice President, and others can be forced out of office if impeached and found guilty of certain crimes. Andrew Johnson is the only President to have been impeached.

Judicial power means the right of the courts to decide legal cases. The Constitution creates the Supreme Court but lets Congress decide on the size of the Supreme Court. Congress

Section 2. Powers of the President

1. Commander in Chief of the Armed Forces The President shall be Commander in Chief of the Army and Navy of the United States, and of the militia of the several states, when called into the actual service of the United States; he may require the option, in writing, of the principal officer in each of the executive departments, upon any subject relating to the duties of their respective offices, and he shall have power to grant reprieves and pardons for offenses against the United States, except in cases of impeachment.

2. Making Treaties and Nominations He shall have power, by and with the advice and consent of the Senate, to make treaties, provided two-thirds of the Senators present concur; and he shall nominate, and by and with the advice and consent of the Senate, shall appoint ambassadors, other public ministers and consuls, judges of the Supreme Court, and all other officers of the United States, whose appointments are not herein otherwise provided for, and which shall be established by law; but the Congress may by law vest the appointment of such inferior officers, as they think proper, in the President alone, in the courts of law, or in the heads of departments.

3. Temporary Appointments The President shall have power to fill up all vacancies that may happen during the recess of the Senate, by granting commissions which shall expire at the end of their next session.

Section 3. Duties

He shall from time to time give to the Congress information of the state of the Union, and recommend to their consideration such measures as he shall judge necessary and expedient; he may, on extraordinary occasions, convene both houses, or either of them, and in case of disagreement between them, with respect to the time of adjournment, he may adjourn them to such time as he shall think proper; he shall receive ambassadors and other public ministers; he shall take care that the laws be faithfully executed, and shall commission all the officers of the United States.

Section 4. Impeachment and Removal From Office

The President, Vice-President, and all civil officers of the United States, shall be removed from office on impeachment for, and conviction of, treason, bribery, or other high crimes and misdemeanors.

Article 3. The Judicial Branch

Section 1. Federal Courts

The judicial power of the United States shall be vested in one Supreme Court, and in such inferior courts as the Congress may from time to time ordain and establish. The judges, both of the Supreme and inferior courts, shall hold their offices during good behavior, and shall, at stated times, receive for their services a compensation, which shall not be diminished during their continuance in office.

Section 2.   Jurisdiction of Federal Courts

1. Scope of Judicial Power   The judicial power shall extend to all cases, in law and equity, arising under this Constitution, the laws of the United States, and treaties made or which shall be made, under their authority; to all cases affecting ambassadors, other public ministers and consuls; to all cases of admiralty and maritime jurisdiction; to controversies to which the United States shall be a party; to controversies between two or more states; between a state and citizens of another state; between citizens of the same state claiming lands under grants of different states, and between a state or the citizens thereof, and foreign states, citizens, or subjects.

2. The Supreme Court   In all cases affecting ambassadors, other public ministers and consuls, and those in which a state shall be a party, the Supreme Court shall have original jurisdiction. In all the other cases before mentioned, the Supreme Court shall have appellate jurisdiction, both as to law and fact, with such exceptions, and under such regulations as the Congress shall make.

3. Trial by Jury   The trial of all crimes, except in cases of impeachment, shall be by jury; and such trial shall be held in the state where the said crimes shall have been committed; but when not committed within any state, the trial shall be at such place or places as the Congress may by law have directed.

Section 3.   Treason

1. Definition   Treason against the United States shall consist only in levying war against them, or in adhering to their enemies, giving them aid and comfort. No person shall be convicted of treason unless on the testimony of two witnesses to the same overt act, or on confession in open court.

2. Punishment   The Congress shall have power to declare the punishment of treason, but no attainder of treason shall work corruption of blood or forfeiture except during the life of the person attainted.

Article 4. Relations Among the States

Section 1.   Official Records and Acts

Full faith and credit shall be given in each state to the public acts, records, and judicial proceedings of every other state. And the Congress may by general laws prescribe the manner in which such acts, records, and proceedings shall be proved, and the effect thereof.

has the power to set up inferior, or lower, courts. The Judiciary Act of 1789 (pages 222–223) set up a system of district and circuit courts, or courts of appeal. Today, there are 95 district courts and 11 courts of appeals. All federal judges serve for life.

Clause 1   *Jurisdiction* refers to the right of a court to hear a case. Federal courts have jurisdiction over cases that involve the Constitution, federal laws, treaties, foreign ambassadors and diplomats, naval and maritime laws, disagreements between states or between citizens from different states, and disputes between a state or citizen and a foreign state or citizen.
     In *Marbury* v. *Madison* (pages 243–244), the Supreme Court established the right to judge whether a law is constitutional.

Clause 2   *Original jurisdiction* means the power of a court to hear a case where it first arises. The Supreme Court has original jurisdiction over only a few cases, such as those involving foreign diplomats. More often, the Supreme Court acts as an appellate court. An **appellate court** does not decide guilt. It decides whether the lower court trial was properly conducted and reviews the lower court's decision.

Clause 3   This clause guarantees the right to a jury trial for anyone accused of a federal crime. The only exceptions are impeachment cases. The trial must be held in the state where the crime was committed.

Clause 1   Treason is clearly defined. An **overt act** is an actual action. A person cannot be convicted of treason for what he or she thinks. A person can only be convicted of treason if he or she confesses or two witnesses testify to it.

Clause 2   Congress has the power to set the punishment for traitors. Congress may not punish the children of convicted traitors by taking away their civil rights or property.

Each state must recognize the official acts and records of any other state. For example, each state must recognize marriage certificates issued by another state. Congress can pass laws to ensure this.

Clause 1 All states must treat citizens of another state in the same way it treats its own citizens. However, the courts have allowed states to give residents certain privileges, such as lower tuition rates.

Clause 2 *Extradition* means the act of returning a suspected criminal or escaped prisoner to a state where he or she is wanted. State governors must return a suspect to another state. However, the Supreme Court has ruled that a governor cannot be forced to do so if he or she feels that justice will not be done.

Clause 3 *Persons held to service or labor* refers to slaves or indentured servants. This clause required states to return runaway slaves to their owners. The Thirteenth Amendment replaces this clause.

Clause 1 Congress has the power to admit new states to the Union. Existing states cannot be split up or joined together to form new states unless both Congress and the state legislatures approve. New states are equal to all other states.

Clause 2 Congress can make rules for managing and governing land owned by the United States. This includes territories not organized into states, such as Puerto Rico and Guam, and federal lands within a state.

In a *republic,* voters choose representatives to govern them. The federal government must protect the states from foreign invasion and from *domestic,* or internal, disorder, if asked to do so by a state.

The Constitution can be *amended,* or changed, if necessary. An amendment can be proposed by (1) a two-thirds vote of both houses of Congress or (2) a national convention called by Congress at the request of two thirds of the state legislatures. (This second method has never been used.) An amendment must be *ratified,* or approved, by (1) three fourths of the state legislatures or (2) special conventions in three fourths of the states. Congress decides which method will be used.

Section 2. Privileges of Citizens

1. Privileges The citizens of each state shall be entitled to all privileges and immunities of citizens in the several states.

2. Extradition A person charged in any state with treason, felony, or other crime, who shall flee from justice, and be found in another state, shall on demand of the executive authority of the state from which he fled, be delivered up, to be removed to the state having jurisdiction of the crime.

3. Return of Fugitive Slaves No person held to service or labor in one state, under the laws thereof, escaping into another, shall in consequence of any law or regulation therein, be discharged from such service or labor, but shall be delivered up on claim of the party to whom such service or labor may be due.

Section 3. New States and Territories

1. New States New states may be admitted by the Congress into this Union; but no new state shall be formed or erected within the jurisdiction of any other state; nor any state be formed by the junction of two or more states, or parts of states, without the consent of the legislatures of the states concerned as well as of the Congress.

2. Federal Lands The Congress shall have power to dispose of and make all needful rules and regulations respecting the territory or other property belonging to the United States; and nothing in this Constitution shall be so construed as to prejudice any claims of the United States, or of any particular state.

Section 4. Guarantees to the States

The United States shall guarantee to every state in this Union a republican form of government, and shall protect each of them against invasion; and on application of the legislature, or of the executive (when the legislature cannot be convened) against domestic violence.

Article 5. Amending the Constitution

The Congress, whenever two-thirds of both houses shall deem it necessary, shall propose amendments to this Constitution, or, on the application of the legislatures of two-thirds of the several states, shall call a convention for proposing amendments, which, in either case, shall be valid to all intents and purposes, as part of this Constitution, when ratified by the legislatures of three-fourths of the several states, or by conventions in three-fourths thereof, as the one or the other mode of ratification may be proposed by the Congress; provided that no amendments which may be made prior to the year 1808 shall in any manner affect the first and fourth clauses in the Ninth Section of the First Article; and that no state, without its consent, shall be deprived of its equal suffrage in the Senate.

Article 6. National Supremacy

Section 1. Prior Public Debts

All debts contracted and engagements entered into, before the adoption of this Constitution, shall be as valid against the United States under this Constitution, as under the Confederation.

The United States government promised to pay all debts and honor all agreements made under the Articles of Confederation.

Section 2. Supreme Law of the Land

This Constitution, and the laws of the United States which shall be made in pursuance thereof, and all treaties made, or which shall be made, under the authority of the United States, shall be the supreme law of the land; and the judges in every state shall be bound thereby, anything in the constitution or laws of any state to the contrary notwithstanding.

The Constitution, federal laws, and treaties that the Senate has ratified are the supreme, or highest, law of the land. Thus, they outweigh state laws. A state judge must overturn a state law that conflicts with the Constitution or with a federal law.

Section 3. Oaths of Office

The Senators and Representatives before mentioned, and the members of the several state legislatures, and all executive and judicial officers, both of the United States and of the several states, shall be bound by oath or affirmation, to support this Constitution; but no religious test shall ever be required as a qualification to any office or public trust under the United States.

State and federal officeholders take an oath, or solemn promise, to support the Constitution. However, this clause forbids the use of religious tests for officeholders. During the colonial period, every colony except Rhode Island required a religious test for officeholders.

Article 7. Ratification

The ratification of the convention of nine states shall be sufficient for the establishment of the Constitution between the states so ratifying the same

During 1787 and 1788, states held special conventions. By October 1788, the required nine states had ratified the Constitution.

Done in Convention, by the unanimous consent of the states present, the seventeenth day of September, in the year of our Lord one thousand seven hundred and eighty-seven, and of the independence of the United States of America the twelfth. *In Witness* whereof, we have hereunto subscribed our names.

Attest: **William Jackson** **George Washington**
Secretary President and Deputy from Virginia

New Hampshire
John Langdon
Nicholas Gilman

Massachusetts
Nathaniel Gorham
Rufus King

Connecticut
William Samuel Johnson
Roger Sherman

New York
Alexander Hamilton

New Jersey
William Livingston
David Brearley
William Paterson
Jonathan Dayton

Pennsylvania
Benjamin Franklin
Thomas Mifflin
Robert Morris
George Clymer
Thomas Fitzsimons
Jared Ingersoll
James Wilson
Gouverneur Morris

Delaware
George Read
Gunning Bedford, Jr.
John Dickinson
Richard Bassett
Jacob Broom

Maryland
James McHenry
Dan of St. Thomas Jennifer
Daniel Carroll

Virginia
John Blair
James Madison, Jr.

North Carolina
William Blount
Richard Dobbs Spaight
Hugh Williamson

South Carolina
John Rutledge
Charles Cotesworth Pinckney
Charles Pinckney
Pierce Butler

Georgia
William Few
Abraham Baldwin

The Constitution

Amendments to the Constitution

The first ten amendments, which were added to the Constitution in 1791, are called the Bill of Rights. Originally, the Bill of Rights applied only to actions of the federal government. However, the Supreme Court has used the due process clause of the Fourteenth Amendment to extend many of the rights to protect individuals against action by the states.

Amendment 1
Freedoms of Religion, Speech, Press, Assembly, and Petition

Congress shall make no law respecting an establishment of religion, or prohibiting the free exercise thereof; or abridging the freedom of speech, or of the press; or the right of the people peaceably to assemble, and to petition the government for a redress of grievances.

The First Amendment protects five basic rights: freedom of religion, speech, the press, assembly, and petition. Congress cannot set up an established, or official, church or religion for the nation. During the colonial period, most colonies had established churches. However, the authors of the First Amendment wanted to keep government and religion separate.

Congress may not **abridge,** or limit, the freedom to speak and write freely. The government may not censor, or review, books and newspapers before they are printed. This amendment also protects the right to assemble, or hold public meetings. **Petition** means ask. **Redress** means to correct. **Grievances** are wrongs. The people have the right to ask the government for wrongs to be corrected.

Amendment 2
Right to Bear Arms

A well-regulated militia, being necessary to the security of a free state, the right of the people to keep and bear arms shall not be infringed.

State militia, such as the National Guard, have the right to bear arms, or keep weapons. Courts have generally ruled that the government can regulate the ownership of guns by private citizens.

Amendment 3
Lodging Troops in Private Homes

No soldier shall, in time of peace, be quartered in any house, without the consent of the owner; nor in time of war, but in a manner to be prescribed by law.

During the colonial period, the British quartered, or housed, soldiers in private homes without the permission of the owners (page 166). This amendment limits the government's right to use private homes to house soldiers.

Amendment 4
Search and Seizure

The right of the people to be secure in their persons, houses, papers, and effects, against unreasonable searches and seizures, shall not be violated; and no warrants shall issue but upon probable cause, supported by oath or affirmation, and particularly describing the place to be searched, and the persons or things to be seized.

This amendment protects Americans from unreasonable searches and seizures. Search and seizure are permitted only if a judge has issued a **warrant,** or written court order. A warrant is issued only if there is probable cause. This means an officer must show that it is prob-

Amendment 5
Rights of the Accused

No person shall be held to answer for a capital, or otherwise infamous, crime, unless on a presentment or indictment of a grand jury, except in cases arising in the land or naval forces, or in the militia, when in actual service in time of war or public danger; nor shall any person be subject for the same offense to be twice put in jeopardy of life and limb; nor shall be compelled, in any criminal case, to be a witness against himself; nor be deprived of life, liberty, or property, without due process of law; nor shall private property be taken for public use, without just compensation.

Amendment 6
Right to Speedy Trial by Jury

In all criminal prosecutions, the accused shall enjoy the right to a speedy and public trial, by an impartial jury of the state and district wherein the crime shall have been committed, which district shall have been previously ascertained by law, and to be informed of the nature and cause of the accusation; to be confronted with the witnesses against him; to have compulsory process for obtaining witnesses in his favor, and to have the assistance of counsel for his defense.

Amendment 7
Jury Trial in Civil Cases

In suits at common law, where the value in controversy shall exceed $20, the right of trial by jury shall be preserved, and no fact tried by a jury shall be otherwise re-examined in any court of the United States than according to the rules of the common law.

able, or likely, that the search will produce evidence of a crime. A search warrant must name the exact place to be searched and the things to be seized.

In some cases, courts have ruled that searches can take place without a warrant. For example, police may search a person who is under arrest. However, evidence found during an unlawful search cannot be used in a trial.

This amendment protects the rights of the accused. **Capital crimes** are those which can be punished with death. **Infamous crimes** are those which can be punished with prison or loss of rights. The federal government must obtain an **indictment,** or formal accusation, from a grand jury to prosecute anyone for such crimes. A **grand jury** is a panel of between 12 to 23 citizens who decide if the government has enough evidence to justify a trial. This procedure prevents the government from prosecuting people with little or no evidence of guilt. (Soldiers and members of the militia in wartime are not covered by this rule.)

Double jeopardy is forbidden by this amendment. This means that a person cannot be tried twice for the same crime. However, if a court sets aside a conviction because of a legal error, the accused can be tried again. A person on trial cannot be forced to testify, or give evidence, against himself or herself. A person accused of a crime is entitled to **due process of law,** or a fair hearing or trial.

Finally, the government cannot seize private property for public use without paying the owner a fair price for it.

In criminal cases, the jury must be **impartial,** or not favor either side. The accused is guaranteed the right to a trial by jury. The trial must be speedy. If the government purposely postpones the trial so that it becomes hard for the person to get a fair hearing, the charge may be dismissed. The accused must be told the charges against him or her and is allowed to question prosecution witnesses. Witnesses who can help the accused can be ordered to appear in court.

The accused must be allowed a lawyer. Since 1942, the federal government has been required to provide a lawyer if the accused cannot afford one. In 1963, the Supreme Court decided that states must also provide lawyers for a defendant too poor to pay for one.

Common law refers to rules of law established by judges in past cases. This amendment guarantees the right to a jury trial in lawsuits where the sum of money at stake is more than $20. An appeals court cannot change a verdict because it disagrees with the decision of the jury. It can only set aside a verdict if legal errors made the trial unfair.

Bail is money the accused leaves with the court as a pledge that he or she will appear for trial. If the accused does not appear for trial, the court keeps the money. **Excessive** means too high. This amendment forbids courts to set unreasonably high bail. The amount of bail usually depends on the seriousness of the charge and whether the accused is likely to appear for the trial. The amendment also forbids cruel and unusual punishments such as mental and physical abuse.

The people have rights that are not listed in the Constitution. This amendment was added because some people feared that the Bill of Rights would be used to limit rights to those actually listed.

This amendment limits the power of the federal government. Powers not given to the federal government belong to the states. The powers reserved to the states are not listed in the Constitution.

This amendment changed part of Article 3, Section 2, Clause 1. As a result, a private citizen from one state cannot sue the government of another state in federal court. However, a citizen can sue a state government in a state court.

This amendment changed the way the electoral college voted. Before the amendment was adopted, each elector simply voted for two people. The candidate with the most votes became President. The runner-up became Vice President. In the election of 1800, however, a tie vote resulted between Thomas Jefferson and Aaron Burr (page 237).

In such a case, the Constitution required the House of Representatives to elect the President. Federalists had a majority in the House. They tried to keep Jefferson out of office by voting for Burr. It took 35 ballots in the House before Jefferson was elected President.

Amendment 8
Bail and Punishment

Excessive bail shall not be required, nor excessive fines imposed, nor cruel and unusual punishments inflicted.

Amendment 9
Powers Reserved to the People

The enumeration in the Constitution, of certain rights, shall not be construed to deny or disparage others retained by the people.

Amendment 10
Powers Reserved to the States

The powers not delegated to the United States by the Constitution, nor prohibited by it to the states, are reserved to the states respectively, or to the people.

Amendment 11
Suits Against States

Passed by Congress on March 4, 1794. Ratified on January 23, 1795.

The judicial power of the United States shall not be construed to extend to any suit in law or equity, commenced or prosecuted against one of the United States, by citizens of another state, or by citizens or subjects of any foreign state.

Amendment 12
Election of President and Vice-President

Passed by Congress on December 9, 1803. Ratified on June 15, 1804.

The electors shall meet in their respective states, and vote by ballot for President and Vice-President, one of whom, at least, shall not be an inhabitant of the same state with themselves; they shall name in their ballots the person voted for as President, and in distinct ballots the person voted for as Vice-President, and they shall make distinct lists of all persons voted for as President, and of all persons voted for as Vice-President, and of the number of votes for each, which lists they shall sign and certify, and transmit, sealed, to the seat of government of the United States, directed to the President of the Senate; the President of the Senate shall, in the presence of the Senate and House of Representatives, open all the certificates and the votes shall then be counted; the person having the greatest number of votes for President shall be the President, if such number be a majority of the whole number of electors appointed; and if no person have such majority, then from the persons having the highest numbers not exceeding three on the list of those voted for as President, the House of Representatives shall choose immediately, by ballot, the President. But in choosing the President, the votes shall be taken by states, the representation from each state having one vote; a quorum for this purpose shall consist of a member or members from two-thirds of the states, and a majority of all the states shall be necessary to a choice. And if the House of Representatives shall not choose a President whenever the right of choice shall devolve upon them, before the fourth day of March next following, then the Vice-President shall act as President, as in the case of the death or other constitutional disability of the President. The person having the greatest number of votes as Vice-President, shall be the Vice-President, if such number be a majority of the whole number of electors appointed, and if no person have a majority, then, from the two highest numbers on the list, the Senate shall choose the Vice-President; a quorum for the purpose shall consist of two-thirds of the whole number of Senators, and a majority of the whole number shall be necessary to a choice. But no person constitutionally ineligible to the office of President shall be eligible to that of Vice-President of the United States.

To keep this from happening again, the Twelfth Amendment was passed and ratified in time for the election of 1804.

This amendment provides that each elector choose one candidate for President and one candidate for Vice President. If no candidate for President receives a majority of electoral votes, the House of Representatives chooses the President. If no candidate for Vice President receives a majority, the Senate elects the Vice President. The Vice President must be a person who is eligible to be President.

This system is still in use today. However, it is possible for a candidate to win the popular vote and lose in the electoral college. This happened in 1876 (pages 430–431).

Amendment 13
Abolition of Slavery

Passed by Congress on January 31, 1865. Ratified on December 6, 1865.

Section 1. Neither slavery nor involuntary servitude, except as a punishment for crime whereof the party shall have been duly convicted, shall exist within the United States, or any place subject to their jurisdiction.

Section 2. Congress shall have power to enforce this article by appropriate legislation.

The Emancipation Proclamation (1863) only freed slaves in areas controlled by the Confederacy (pages 401–402). This amendment freed all slaves. It also forbids **involuntary servitude**, or labor done against one's will. However, it does not prevent prison wardens from making prisoners work.

Congress can pass laws to carry out this amendment.

Amendment 14
Rights of Citizens

Passed by Congress on June 13, 1866. Ratified on July 9, 1868.

Section 1. Citizenship All persons born or naturalized in the United States and subject to the jurisdiction thereof, are citizens of the United States and of the state wherein they reside. No state shall make or enforce any law which shall abridge the privileges or immunities of citizens of the United States; nor shall any state deprive any person of life, liberty, or property, without due process of law; nor deny to any person within its jurisdiction the equal protection of the laws.

This section defines citizenship for the first time in the Constitution, and it extends citizenship to blacks. It also prohibits states from denying the rights and privileges of citizenship to any citizen. This section also forbids states to deny due process of law.

Section 1 guarantees all citizens "equal protection under the law." For a long time, however, the Fourteenth Amendment did not protect blacks from discrimination. After Reconstruction, separate facilities for blacks and whites sprang up (page 431). In 1954, the Supreme Court ruled that separate facilities for blacks and whites were by their nature unequal. This ruling, in the case of *Brown* v. *Board of Education*, made school segregation illegal.

This section replaced the three fifths clause. It provides that representation in the House of Representatives is decided on the basis of the number of people in the state. It also provides that states which deny the vote to male citizens over age 21 will be punished by losing part of their representation in the House. This provision has never been enforced.

Despite this clause, black citizens were often prevented from voting. In the 1960s, federal laws were passed to end voting discrimination.

This section prohibited people who had been federal or state officials before the Civil War and who had joined the Confederate cause from serving again as government officials. In 1872, Congress restored the rights of former Confederate officials.

This section recognized that the United States must repay its debts from the Civil War. However, it forbade the repayment of debts of the Confederacy. This meant that people who had loaned money to the Confederacy would not be repaid. Also, states were not allowed to pay former slave owners for the loss of slaves.

Congress can pass laws to carry out this amendment.

Previous condition of servitude refers to slavery. This amendment gave blacks, both former slaves and free blacks, the right to vote. In the late 1800s, southern states used grandfather clauses, literacy tests, and poll taxes to keep blacks from voting (page 431).

Congress can pass laws to carry out this amendment. The Twenty-fourth Amendment barred the use of poll taxes in national elections. The Voting Rights Act of 1965 gave federal officials the power to register voters in places where voting discrimination was found.

Section 2. Apportionment of Representatives Representatives shall be apportioned among the several states according to their respective numbers, counting the whole number of persons in each state, excluding Indians not taxed. But when the right to vote at any election for the choice of electors for President and Vice-President of the United States, Representatives in Congress, the executive and judicial officers of a state, or the members of the legislature thereof, is denied to any of the male inhabitants of such state, being twenty-one years of age and citizens of the United States, or in any way abridged, except for participation in rebellion, or other crime, the basis of representation therein shall be reduced in the proportion which the number of such male citizens shall bear to the whole number of male citizens twenty-one years of age in such state.

Section 3. Former Confederate Officials   No person shall be a Senator or Representative in Congress or elector of President and Vice-President, or hold any office, civil or military, under the United States, or under any state, who, having previously taken an oath, as a member of Congress, or as an officer of the United States, or as a member of any state legislature, or as an executive or judicial officer of any state, to support the Constitution of the United States, shall have engaged in insurrection or rebellion against the same, or given aid or comfort to the enemies thereof. But Congress may, by vote of two-thirds of each house, remove such disability.

Section 4. Government Debt   The validity of the public debt of the United States, authorized by law, including debts incurred for payment of pensions and bounties for services in suppressing insurrection or rebellion, shall not be questioned. But neither the United States nor any state shall assume or pay any debt or obligation incurred in aid of insurrection or rebellion against the United States or any claim for the loss or emancipation of any slave; but all such debts, obligations, and claims shall be held illegal and void.

Section 5. Enforcement   The Congress shall have power to enforce, by appropriate legislation, the provisions of this article.

Amendment 15
Voting Rights

Passed by Congress on February 26, 1869. Ratified on February 2, 1870.

Section 1. Extending the Right to Vote   The right of citizens of the United States to vote shall not be denied or abridged by the United States or any state on account of race, color, or previous condition of servitude.

Section 2. Enforcement The Congress shall have power to enforce this article by appropriate legislation.

Amendment 16
The Income Tax

Passed by Congress on July 12, 1909. Ratified on February 3, 1913.

The Congress shall have power to lay and collect taxes on incomes, from whatever source derived, without apportionment among the several states, and without regard to any census or enumeration.

Congress has the power to collect taxes on people's income. An income tax can be collected without regard to a state's population. This amendment changed Article 1, Section 9, Clause 4.

Amendment 17
Direct Election of Senators

Passed by Congress on May 13, 1912. Ratified on April 8, 1913.

Section 1. Method of Election The Senate of the United States shall be composed of two Senators from each state, elected by the people thereof, for six years; and each Senator shall have one vote. The electors in each state shall have the qualifications requisite for electors of the most numerous branch of the state legislatures.

This amendment replaced Article 1, Section 2, Clause 1. Before it was adopted, state legislatures chose senators. This amendment provides that senators are directly elected by the people of each state.

Section 2. Vacancies When vacancies happen in the representation of any state in the Senate, the executive authority of such state shall issue writs of election to fill such vacancies: *Provided* that the legislature of any state may empower the executive thereof to make temporary appointments until the people fill the vacancies by election as the legislature may direct.

When a Senate seat becomes vacant, the governor of the state must order an election to fill the seat. The state legislature can give the governor power to fill the seat until an election is held.

Section 3. Exception This amendment shall not be so construed as to affect the election or term of any Senator chosen before it becomes valid as part of the Constitution.

Senators who had already been elected by the state legislatures were not affected by this amendment.

Amendment 18
Prohibition of Alcoholic Beverages

Passed by Congress on December 18, 1917. Ratified on January 16, 1919.

Section 1. Ban on Alcohol After one year from the ratification of this article the manufacture, sale, or transportation of intoxicating liquors within, the importation thereof into, or the exportation thereof from, the United States and all territory subject to the jurisdiction thereof for beverage purposes is hereby prohibited.

This amendment, known as **Prohibition,** banned the making, selling, or transporting of alcoholic beverages in the United States. Later, the Twenty-first Amendment **repealed,** or canceled, this amendment.

Section 2. Enforcement The Congress and the several states shall have concurrent power to enforce this article by appropriate legislation.

Both the states and the federal government had the power to pass laws to enforce the amendment.

Section 3. Method of Ratification This article shall be inoperative unless it shall have been ratified as an amendment to the Constitution by the legislatures of the several states, as provided in the Constitution, within seven years from the date of the submission hereof to the states by the Congress.

The amendment had to be approved within seven years. The Eighteenth Amendment was the first amendment to include a time limit for ratification.

Amendment 19
Women's Suffrage

Passed by Congress on June 4, 1919, Ratified on August 18, 1920.

Section 1. The Right to Vote The right of citizens of the United States to vote shall not be denied or abridged by the United States or by any state on account of sex.

Neither the federal government nor state governments can deny the right to vote on account of sex. Thus, women won **suffrage,** or the right to vote. Before 1920, some states had allowed women to vote in state elections.

Section 2. Enforcement Congress shall have power to enforce this article by appropriate legislation.

Congress can pass laws to carry out the amendment.

Amendment 20
Presidential Terms; Sessions of Congress

Passed by Congress on March 2, 1932. Ratified on Janurary 23, 1933.

Section 1. Beginning of Term The terms of the President and Vice-President shall end at noon on the 20th day of January, and the terms of Senators and Representatives at noon on the 3rd day of January, of the years in which such terms would have ended if this article had not been ratified; and the terms of their successor shall then begin.

The date for the President and Vice President to take office is January 20. Members of Congress begin their terms of office on January 3. Before this amendment was adopted, these terms of office began on March 4.

Section 2. Congressional Sessions The Congress shall assemble at least once in every year, and such meeting shall begin at noon on the 3rd day of January, unless they shall by law appoint a different day.

Congress must meet at least once a year. The new session of Congress begins on January 3. Before this amendment, members of Congress who had been defeated in November continued to hold office until the following March. Such members were known as **lame ducks.**

Section 3. Presidential Succession If at the time fixed for the beginning of the term of the President, the President-elect shall have died, the Vice-President-elect shall become President. If a President shall not have been chosen before the time fixed for the beginning of his term, or if the President-elect shall have failed to qualify, then the Vice-President-elect shall act as President until a President shall have qualified; and the Congress may by law provide for the case wherein neither a President-elect nor a Vice-President-elect shall have qualified, declaring who shall then act as President, or the manner in which one who is to act shall be selected, and such person shall act accordingly until a President or Vice-President shall have qualified.

If the President-elect dies before taking office, the Vice President-elect becomes President. If no President has been chosen by January 20 or if the elected candidate fails to qualify for office, the Vice President-elect acts as President, but only until a qualified President is chosen.
    Finally, Congress has the power to choose a person to act as President if neither the President-elect or Vice President-elect has qualified to take office.

Section 4. Elections Decided by Congress The Congress may by law provide for the case of the death of any of the persons from whom the House of Representatives may choose a President whenever the right of choice shall have devolved upon them, and for the case of the death of any of the persons from whom the Senate may choose a Vice-President whenever the right of choice shall have devolved upon them.

Congress can pass laws in cases where a Presidential candidate dies while an election is being decided in the House. Congress has similar power in cases where a candidate for Vice President dies while an election is being decided in the Senate.

Section 5. Date of Implementation Sections 1 and 2 shall take effect on the 15th day of October following the ratification of this article.

Section 5 sets the date for the amendment to become effective.

Section 6. Ratification Period This article shall be inoperative unless it shall have been ratified as an amendment to the Constitution by the legislatures of three-fourths of the several states within seven years from the date of its submission.

Section 6 sets a time limit for ratification.

Amendment 21
Repeal of Prohibition

Passed by Congress on February 20, 1933. Ratified on December 5, 1933.

Section 1. Repeal of National Prohibition The eighteenth article of amendment to the Constitution of the United States is hereby repealed.

The Eighteenth Amendment is repealed, making it legal to make and sell alcoholic beverages. Prohibition ended December 5, 1933.

Section 2. State Laws The transportation or importation into any state, territory, or possession of the United States for delivery or use therein of intoxicating liquors, in violation of the laws thereof, is hereby prohibited.

Each state was free to ban the making and selling of alcoholic drink within its borders. This section makes bringing liquor into a "dry" state a federal offense.

Section 3. Ratification Period This article shall be inoperative unless it shall have been ratified as an amendment to the Constitution by conventions in the several states, as provided in the Constitution, within seven years from the date of the submission hereof to the states by the Congress.

Special state conventions were called to ratify this amendment. This is the only time an amendment was ratified by state conventions rather than state legislatures.

Amendment 22
Limit on Number of President's Terms

Passed by Congress on March 12, 1947. Ratified on March 1, 1951.

Section 1. Two-Term Limit No person shall be elected to the office of the President more than twice, and no person who has held the office of President, or acted as President, for more than two years of a term to which some other person was elected President shall be elected to the office of the President more than once. But this Article shall not apply to any person holding the office of President when this Article was proposed by the Congress, and shall not prevent any person who may be holding the office of President, or acting as President, during the term within which this Article becomes operative from holding the office of President or acting as President during the remainder of such term.

Before Franklin Roosevelt became President, no President served more than two terms in office. Roosevelt broke with this custom and was elected to four terms. This amendment provides that no President may serve more than two terms. A President who has already served more than half of someone else's term can only serve one more full term. However, the amendment did not apply to Harry Truman, who had become President after Franklin Roosevelt's death in 1944.

A seven-year time limit is set for ratification.

Section 2. Ratification Period ~~This Article shall be inoperative unless it shall have been ratified as an amendment to the Constitution by the legislatures of three-fourths of the several states within seven years from the date of its submission to the states by the Congress.~~

Amendment 23
Presidential Electors for District of Columbia

Passed by Congress on June 16, 1960. Ratified on April 3, 1961.

This amendment gives residents of Washington, D.C., the right to vote in Presidential elections. Until this amendment was adopted, people living in Washington, D.C., could not vote for President because the Constitution had made no provision for choosing electors from the nation's capital. Washington, D.C., has three electoral votes.

Section 1. Determining the Number of Electors The District constituting the seat of Government of the United States shall appoint in such manner as the Congress may direct:

A number of electors of President and Vice-President equal to the whole number of Senators and Representatives in Congress to which the District would be entitled if it were a State, but in no event more than the least populous State; they shall be in addition to those appointed by the States, but they shall be considered, for the purposes of the election of President and Vice-President, to be electors appointed by a State; and they shall meet in the District and perform such duties as provided by the twelfth article of amendment.

Congress can pass laws to carry out the amendment.

Section 2. Enforcement The Congress shall have the power to enforce this article by appropriate legislation.

Amendment 24
Abolition of Poll Tax in National Elections

Passed by Congress on August 27, 1962. Ratified on January 23, 1964.

A *poll tax* is a tax on voters. This amendment bans poll taxes in national elections. Some states used poll taxes to keep blacks from voting. In 1966, the Supreme Court struck down poll taxes in state elections, also.

Section 1. Poll Tax Banned The right of citizens of the United States to vote in any primary or other election for President or Vice-President, for electors for President or Vice-President, or for Senator or Representative in Congress, shall not be denied or abridged by the United States or any state by reason of failure to pay any poll tax or other tax.

Congress can pass laws to carry out the amendment.

Section 2. Enforcement The Congress shall have power to enforce this article by appropriate legislation.

Amendment 25
Presidential Succession and Disability

Passed by Congress on July 6, 1965. Ratified on February 11, 1967.

If the President dies or resigns, the Vice President becomes President. This section clarifies Article 2, Section 1, Clause 6.

Section 1. President's Death or Resignation In case of the removal of the President from office or his death or resignation, the Vice-President shall become President.

Section 2. Vacancies in Vice-Presidency Whenever there is a vacancy in the office of the Vice-President, the President shall nominate a Vice-President who shall take the office upon confirmation by a majority vote of both houses of Congress.

When a Vice President takes over the office of President, he or she appoints a Vice President who must be approved by a majority vote of both houses of Congress. This section was applied after Vice President Spiro Agnew resigned in 1973. President Richard Nixon appointed Gerald Ford as Vice President. After President Nixon resigned in 1974, President Gerald Ford appointed Nelson Rockefeller as Vice President.

Section 3. Disability of the President Whenever the President transmits to the President pro tempore of the Senate and the Speaker of the House of Representatives his written declaration that he is unable to discharge the powers and duties of his office, and until he transmits to them a written declaration to the contrary, such powers and duties shall be discharged by the Vice-President as Acting President.

If the President declares in writing that he or she is unable to perform the duties of office, the Vice President serves as Acting President until the President recovers.

Section 4. Whenever the Vice-President and a majority of either the principal officers of the executive departments or of such other body as Congress may by law provide, transmit to the President pro tempore of the Senate and the Speaker of the House of Representatives their written declaration that the President is unable to discharge the powers and duties of his office, the Vice-President shall immediately assume the powers and duties of the office as Acting President.

Thereafter, when the President transmits to the President pro tempore of the Senate and the Speaker of the House of Representatives his written declaration that no inability exists, he shall resume the powers and duties of his office unless the Vice-President and a majority of either the principal officers of the executive department or of such other body as Congress may by law provide, transmit within four days to the President pro tempore of the Senate and the Speaker of the House of Representatives their written declaration that the President is unable to discharge the powers and duties of his office. Thereupon Congress shall decide the issue, assembling within 48 hours for that purpose if not in session. If the Congress, within 21 days after receipt of the latter written declaration, or, if Congress is not in session, within 21 days after Congress is required to assemble, determines by two-thirds vote of both houses that the President is unable to discharge the powers and duties of his office, the Vice-President shall continue to discharge the same as Acting President; otherwise, the President shall assume the powers and duties of his office.

Two Presidents, Woodrow Wilson and Dwight Eisenhower, have fallen gravely ill while in office. The Constitution contained no provision for this kind of emergency.

Section 3 provided that the President can inform Congress that he or she is too sick to perform the duties of office. However, if the President is unconscious or refuses to admit to a disabling illness, Section 4 provides that the Vice President and cabinet may declare the President disabled. The Vice President becomes Acting President until the President can return to the duties of office. In case of a disagreement between the President and the Vice President and cabinet over the President's ability to perform the duties of office, Congress must decide the issue. A two-thirds vote of both houses is needed to find the President is disabled or unable to fulfill the duties of office.

Amendment 26
Voting Age

Passed by Congress on March 23, 1971. Ratified on July 1, 1971.

Section 1. Lowering of Voting Age The right of citizens of the United States, who are 18 years of age or older, to vote shall not be denied or abridged by the United States or any state on account of age.

In 1970, Congress passed a law allowing 18-year-olds to vote in state and federal elections. However, the Supreme Court decided that Congress could not set a minimum age for state elections. So this amendment was passed and ratified, giving the right to vote to citizens age 18 or older.

Section 2. Enforcement The Congress shall have the power to enforce this article by appropriate legislation.

Congress can pass laws to carry out the amendment.

Index

Page numbers that are *italicized* refer to illustrations. An *m*, *c*, or *p* before a page number refers to a map (*m*), chart (*c*), or picture (*p*) on that page. An *n* after a page number refers to a footnote. Black dots are next to names of people.

A

Abilene, Kansas, 450, *m453*
Abolition movement, 352–54, 374, 384, 420; John Brown and, 381, 384–85; Kansas and, 380, 381; political parties and, 375, 383; religious influences in, 352, 353; responses of North and South, 354. *See also* Antislavery movement; Slavery.
Acid rain, 727
Acquired immune deficiency syndrome (AIDS), 738
Act of Toleration, 110
• Adams, Abigail, 180, *p233*, 234, 291
• Adams, John, 161, 166, 174, 180, 192, 227, 242, 291, *p780;* Boston Massacre, 163; Declaration of Independence, 178, *p179;* as President, 233–36, 243, 244; as Vice President, 213, 220
• Adams, John Quincy, 260, 294, *p780;* election in 1824, 291–92; in election of 1828, 293; as President, 292, *p292;* as Secretary of State, 282–83
• Adams, Samuel, 161, 163, 165, 174
Adams-Onís Treaty, 282
• Addams, Jane, 490, 511, 513, 521
Adobe, 34
Afghanistan, 701–03
Africa, *m51, m61;* European imperialism and, 528, 550; European trade and exploration, 53, 54–55, *m57;* return of blacks to, 352
Aggression, 625
Agricultural Adjustment Act (AAA), 607, *c607*, 611
• Aguinaldo, Emilio, 537, 539, 540
Airplanes: in World War I, 562; Wright brothers, 472, *p472*
Aisne River, France, *m560*, 561
Alabama, 271, *m272*, 521, *m760–61*, 766
Alamo, 316–17, *m317, p318*
Alaska, 20, 23, *m24, m532, m571;* gold in, 529; land and climate, 27, *m28*, 528; purchase of, 528–29, *p756;* statehood, *529n*, 663, *m760–61*, 766
Albany, N.Y., 67, 86, *m127*, 153, *m154*, 271, *m272;* in American Revolution, *m182, 183*
• Aldrin, Buzz, 722, *p722*
• Alger, Horatio, 495, 496
Algonquins, *m38, p74*, 87, 150, 186
Alien Act, 236, 237, 242, 243
Aliens, 236; illegal, 740
• Allen, Ethan, 173–74, *m175*
Alliance for Progress, 674, 713–14
Allied Powers: in World War I, 551–

63, *m551*, 565, *m567;* in World War II, 627–43, *m628;* plans for peace, 651. *See also* World War I, World War II.
Almanacs, 136
Alsace–Lorraine, 550, *m560*
Amendments, constitutional, 213. *See also* specific amendments.
American Colonization Society, 352
American Expeditionary Force, 561
American Federation of Labor (AFL), 475–77, *c476*, 520, 558, 611
American Indian Movement (AIM), 691
American Indians, *See* Native Americans.
American Protective Association, 484
American Revolution, 172–81, 192, 280, 295, 327; blacks in, 187–88, 193, *p205;* events leading to, 156–69; France and, 184; in Middle Colonies, 181–85; money borrowed during, 223, 224; money printed in, 199–200, 211; Native Americans and, 186–87; peace treaty, 191–92; at sea, 187; in South, 189–91; in West, 186–87; women in, 184, 188–89, 193
American System, 279
• Amherst, Jeffrey, 154, 157
Anarchists, 591, 592
Anasazis, 34–35, 38, *p748*
• Anderson, Robert, 389
Andes Mountains, 26, 29, *p32,* 44, *m45*, 281, 282
• Anthony, Susan B., 356, 511
Antibiotics, 724
Antietam, Battle of, 399, *m399*, 402, *p405*, 408
Antifederalists, 211, 212, 232
Antislavery movement, 350, 351–54, 362; women in, 355. *See also* Abolition movement; Slavery.
Apaches, *m38*, 315, 319, *m448*
Apartheid, 702
Apollo missions, *p721*, 722
Appalachian Mountains, 23–25, 84, 128, *m136*, 157, *m186*; crossing, 270, 271, *m272*
Appeasement, 626
Appomattox Courthouse, *m311;* surrender at, 413
Apprentice, 135
Arabs: Crusades, 51; Israel and, 708–10; war with Spain, 53, 55
Arapaho, *m38*, 445, *m448*
Archaeologists, 33–34
Arctic climate, 28, *m28*
Argentina, 29, 624; independence, 281, *m282, m758–59*
Argonne Forest, Battle of, *m560*, 563
Arizona, 27, 35, 149, 319, 324, *m760–61*, 766
Arkansas, *m760–61*, 766; Civil War, 397; dust storms, 615; secession, 394; statehood, 375
• Arkwright, Richard, 266
Armistice, 563
Arms race, 700–01, 703
Arms treaty, 681, 703
• Armstrong, Louis, 587
• Armstrong, Neil, 722
• Arnold, Benedict, *m175*, 177, *m182*, 183, 184, 190

Arsenal, 385
Art: African, *p55;* American, 361, 363, 365; Aztec, *p63;* Civil War photography, 405; colonial, 82; in Great Depression, 618–19; late 1800s, 497; Native American, *p39, p43;* 1920s, 584–89, *p592;* 1950s, 666, 667; 1980s, 732. *See also* Culture.
• Arthur, Chester A., 506, *p782*
Articles of Confederation, 196, 198–202, 203, 204, 800, 801
Artists: American, 1820–1860, 361, 363, 365; in Great Depression, *p599*, 607. *See also* specific artists.
Asia, 591; imperialism and, 550; immigrants from, 521, 522–23, *c740;* land bridge between North America and, 20, *m21;* sea route to, 53–59, 60–61, 65–68; Soviet influence in, 653; trade with, *c756;* after World War II, 657–60; in World War II, 625–26, 630, 640–43, *m758–59*
Asian Americans, 521, 522–23, *c740*. *See also* specific nationalities.
Assemblies, colonial, 101, 107, 110, 115, 117
Assembly line, 473, 579
Assimilation, 484
• Astor, John Jacob, 310
Astrolabe, 54
Astronauts, 720, 722–23, *p722*
Atlanta, Ga., 686; in Civil War, 411, *m411*, 412, 417
Atlantic Charter, 630, *p630*
Atlantic Ocean, *m21*, 22, 25, *m58*, *m61, m66;* Columbus and, 55–57
Atlantic Plain, *m24*, 25
Atomic bomb, 641, 642, *p642*
Attorney General, 222, 517, *517n*
• Attucks, Crispus, 162–63
Auschwitz, 643
• Austin, Moses, 315
• Austin, Stephen, 315, *p316*
Australia, 635, *m636, m758–59*
Austria, 282, *m567, m758–59;* peace treaty with, 577; war with France, 227; in World War II, 626
Austria–Hungary: World War I, 550, 551, 553, 565
Automobile, effects on America, 586, 590; Henry Ford and, 472–73, *p473;* growth in 1920s, 579–80, *c580, p581*
Axis powers, 627, *m628*, 635–43, *c643*, 652
Aztecs, *m38*, 42, 44, *p44, m45*, 82; fall of, 62, 63

B

Baby boom, 664, 733–34, 736
Backcountry: in Middle Colonies, 128, 129; southern, 130, 133–34
Bacon's Rebellion, 110
Badlands, 24, 25
Balanced budget, 680, 681, 687, 801
• Balboa, Vasco Núñez de, 60, *m61*, 63
Baltimore, *p99, m112, m127, m130*, 133, *m136*, 141, 335; in Civil War, 394; in War of 1812, *m258*, 259, 261
• Baltimore, Lord, 109, 110, *p110*

Index

Index

Index

Index

Index

Index

Index

recto.; **50** Pierpont Morgan Library; **52** EPA/Scala; **54** National Maritime Museum, London; **55** Museum of Primitive Art, Lee Boltin; **59** MMA; **62** NYPL; **63** Vatican Library; **66** Arizona Department of Library, Archives and Public Records © David Barr 1982 (detail); **67** British Museum; **69** Bettmann Archive; **73** Bibliothèque Publique, Universite de Genève.

UNIT 2 **Pages 74–75** *l to r* American Numismatic Society; British Museum; Virginia Historical Association; Courtesy of Glenbow Museum, Calgary, Alberta; Connecticut Historical Society; *t* Corning Museum of Glass, Corning, NY; *b* Yale; **77** NYHS; **80** Hispanic Society of America; **82** Laurie Winfrey (detail); **86** Bettmann Archive; **88** NYPL; **89** NYPL (detail); **91** National Portrait Gallery, SI; **93** Collection of Mr. and Mrs. Paul Mellon, Upperville, VA; **95** Architect of the Capitol; **99** Maryland Historical Society, Baltimore; **100, 101** Bettmann Archive; **103** The Granger Collection; **104, 106** NYHS; **108** Thomas Gilcrease Institute of American History and Art, Tulsa, OK; **110** Enoch Pratt Free Library, Baltimore, MD; **111** Courtesy, Henry Francis duPont Winterthur Museum; **114** City of Bristol, Museum and Art Gallery; **121** MMA, Gift of Edgar William and Bernice Chrysler Garbisch, 1963; **123** The Granger Collection; **124** Bettmann Archive; **125** Culver Pictures; **126** MFA; **128** NG; **131** National Maritime Museum, Greenwich, England; **132** Colonial Williamsburg Foundation; **135** Free Library of Philadelphia; **137** Harry T. Peters Collection, MCNY; **139** LC.

UNIT 3 **Pages 146–147** *l to r* Anne S.K. Brown Military Collection, Brown University Library; *t* LC; *b* Colonial Williamsburg Foundation; NYSHA; The Granger Collection; **149** Kirby Collection of Historical Paintings, Lafayette College; **151** Public Archives of Canada; **152** *l* NYHS, *r* LC; **155** Royal Ontario Museum, Canadian Gallery; **157** Historical Pictures Service, Chicago; **158** NYPL; **160** John Carter Brown Library, Brown University; **161** Patrick Henry Memorial Foundation; **162** LC; **164** Rhode Island Historical Society; **165** LC; **169** NYPL, Stokes Collection; **173** Yale; **176** Joseph Dixon Crucible Collection; **179** Yale; **183, 185** Valley Forge Historical Society; **187** American Antiquarian Society; **188** Yale, Bequest of Mrs. Katherine Rankin Wolcott Verplanck (detail); **189** LC; **190** The Granger Collection; **192** Abby Aldrich Rockefeller Folk Art Collection, Williamsburg, VA; **193** US Postal Service; **197** Independence National Historical Park; **198** The Granger Collection; **200** Abby Aldrich Rockefeller Folk Art Collection; **203** The Granger Collection; **205** Historical Society of Pennsylvania; **211** Metropolitan Museum of Art, Gift of Mrs. A. Wordsworth Thompson, 1899; **212** Courtesy of Kennedy Galleries, Inc., NY.

UNIT 4 **Pages 218–219** *l to r* NYSHA; Washington University Gallery of Art, St. Louis, MO; The Granger Collection; Irving S. Olds Collection; MMA, Rogers Fund, 1942; **221** Mr. and Mrs. John Harney; **222** Brooklyn Museum; **223** *t* NYPL, *b* City Art Commission of New York; **225** MMA, Gift of Edgar William and Bernice Chrysler Garbisch; **226** Bibliothèque Nationale; **228** Courtesy, Henry Francis duPont Winterthur Museum; **229** NA; **233** *l and r* Massachusetts Historical Society; **234** LC; **235** The Granger Collection; **237** NYHS; **241** Courtesy United States Naval Academy Museum; **242** *l* Edwin S. Roseberry, Thomas Jefferson Memorial Foundation; *r* Independence National Historical Park; **243** Library of the Boston Athenauem; **245** The Granger Collection; **248** Thomas Gilcrease Institute of American History and Art, Tulsa, OK; **251** Courtesy of the Mariners Museum, Newport News, VA; **252** The Granger Collection; **253** British Museum; **256** *l* Field Museum of Natural History; *r* NMAA, SI, Gift of Mrs. Joseph Harrison, Jr. (detail); **259** NYHS; **260** New Orleans Museum of Art; **261** NYPL, I.N. Phelps Stokes Collection of Historical Prints; **264** Maryland Historical Society, Baltimore; **267** SI; **268** Yale, Mabel Brady Garvan Collection; **269** NYSHA; **271** Filson Club; **273** MFA; **276** NYSHA; **277** Dartmouth College Museum and Galleries; **281** Caribbean Tourism Association; **283** Courtesy of the Essex Institute, Salem, MA.

UNIT 5 **Pages 288–289** *l to r* SI, Lee Boltin for American Heritage; Memphis Brooks Museum of Art; Texas Memorial Museum; The Rockwell Museum; National Portrait Gallery, SI; **291** St. Louis Art Museum; **292** MMA, Gift of I.N. Phelps Stokes, Edward S. Hawes, Alice Mary Hawes, Marion Augusta Hawes, 1937 (37.14.34); **294** LC; **296** Chicago Historical Society; **297** Boston Public Library; **298** The Granger Collection; **300** National Portrait Gallery, SI; **301** The Granger Collection; **303** Michal Heron; **305** NYHS; **309** Corcoran Gallery of Art; **311** State Historical Society of Colorado; **312** Culver Pictures; **314** Thomas Gilcrease Institute of American History and Art, Tulsa, OK; **316** Texas State Capitol, Austin, TX; **318** State of Texas, Governor's Mansion; **321** Thomas Gilcrease Institute of American History and Art, Tulsa, OK; **327** Church of Jesus Christ of the Latter Day Saints; **329** California State Library; **333** Louisiana State Museum; **336** The Whaling Museum, New Bedford, MA; **338** Yale; **339** The Granger Collection; **341** State of North Carolina, Department of Cultural Resources, Division of Archives and History, Raleigh; **343** Yale, Gift of George Hoadley, B.A. 1801; **347** *l* Missouri Historical Society, *r* LC; **351** MMA, Gift of Christian A. Zabriskie, 1950; **353** LC; **354** Cincinnati Art Museum, purchased from the Webber Estate by a popular subscription fund (detail); **355** NYHS; **356** Bettmann Archive; **357** The Granger Collection; **358** Bettmann Archive; **359** By permission of the Houghton Library, Harvard University; **360** Yale, Mabel Brady Garvan Collection; **361** NYPL, Astor, Lenox, Tilden Foundation; **365** MMA, Morris K. Jesup Fund, 1933.

UNIT 6 **Pages 370–371** *l to r* Musée de Pau; NYPL; Missouri Historical Society; N.S. Meyer, Inc.; NYHS; The Granger Collection; **373** Brooklyn Museum, Gift of Miss Gwendolyn O.L. Conkling; **374** Bancroft Library; **376** The Granger Collection; **378** NYHS; **381** The Granger Collection; **382** The Granger Collection; **384** Illinois State Historical Library, Old State Capitol; **385** Pennsylvania Academy of Fine Arts; **388** National Portrait Gallery; **389** Harry T. Peters Collection, MCNY; **393** The Granger Collection; **400** Corcoran Gallery of Art; **402, 404, 405** *t and b* LC; **407** Kean Archives; **408** The Granger Collection; **409** *l* NA, *r* LC; **410** LC; **413** West Point Museum; **417** LC; **419** Anne S.K. Brown Military Collection, Brown University Library; **420** The Granger Collection; **424** LC; **426** Chicago Historical Society; **427** Alabama Department of Archives and History; **428** LC; **429** State of North Carolina, Division of Archives and History; **435** NYPL.

UNIT 7 Pages 436–437 *l to r* NMAA, SI (detail); Harry T. Peters Collection, MCNY; SI; US Department of the Interior (detail); City Library of De Smet, SD (detail); Los Angeles Museum of Art: Los Angeles County Funds (detail); 439 Wichita Art Museum; 441 The Granger Collection; 442 Thomas Gilcrease Institute of American History and Art, Tulsa, OK; 443 Newberry Library; 444, 446 SI; 447, 452 The Granger Collection; 454 Nebraska State Historical Society, Solomon D. Butcher Collection; 457 Kansas State Historical Society, Topeka; 461 Bethlehem Steel Co.; 462 LC; 464 Chicago Historical Society; 468 Bettmann Archive; 469 NYHS; 470 Edison National Historic Site, US Department of the Interior; 472 North Carolina State Division of Archives and History; 473 Ford Archives/Henry Ford Museum, Dearborn, MI; 475 The Granger Collection; 477 International Museum of Photography, George Eastman House; 481 Indianapolis Museum of Art, Gift of a Couple of Old Hoosiers; 482 *t* LC, *b* Katherine Hellman; 488 *l* MMA, Gift of Frederick H. Hatch, 1926; *r* MCNY; 490 International Museum of Photography, George Eastman House; 492 The Granger Collection; 495 St. Louis Art Museum; 496 Trustees of the Estate of Samuel L. Clemens; 497 NG, Chester Dale Collection, 1962.

UNIT 8 Pages 502–503 *l to r* MCNY; Philadelphia Museum of Art, Given by William Alexander Dick; Chicago Historical Society; NYPL; LC; 505 Newberry Library; 507 MCNY, Photograph by Jacob A. Riis, Jacob A. Riis Collection; 509 Harper's Weekly; 510 The Granger Collection; 514 Bettmann Archive; 515 The Granger Collection; 517, 519 Theodore Roosevelt Collection, Harvard College Library; 520 National Portrait Gallery; 522 LC; 523 *l and r* SI; 527, 529 LC; 530 Milt and Joan Mann, Cameramann International; 531, 533 LC; 535 Institute of Puerto Rican Culture; 536 Chicago Historical Society; 538 LC; 542 The Granger Collection; 543 LC; 549 The Granger Collection; 552 Imperial War Museum, London; 555 AP/WW; 556 LC; 558 West Point Museum; 559 Keystone View Co.; 561, 562 NA; 563, 566 Imperial War Museum, London.

UNIT 9 Pages 572–573 *l to r* LC; Art Institute of Chicago; Collection of the Whitney Museum of American Art; FDR Library; National Collection of Fine Art, SI; *t* Civic Center Department, City of Detroit; *b* US Army Photo; 575 Memorial Art Gallery of the University of Rochester, Marion Stratton Gould Fund; 576 Culver Pictures; 577, 579, 581 LC; 582 MCNY; 583 Culver Pictures; 585 *l* The Granger Collection, *r* Judith Katten; 587 Brown Brothers; 589 Culver Pictures; 592 Joslyn Art Museum; 593 LC; 599 Coit Tower, San Francisco; 601, 603 LC; 604 UPI/Bettmann Newsphotos; 605 LC; 606, 610 NA; 615 LC; 616 AP/WW; 617 National Portrait Gallery; 619 Culver Pictures; 623 US Navy, Combat Art Section; 625 The Granger Collection; 630 FDR Library; 631 US Navy, Combat Art Section; 633 *l* LC, *r* Curtis Publishing Company; 634 LC; 638 US Army Photo; 639 Brown Brothers; 642 US Army Photo; 643 FDR Library.

UNIT 10 Pages 648–649 *l to r* Curtis Publishing Company; *t and b* J. Doyle Dewitt Collection; John and Kimiko Powers; Dennis Stock, Magnum Photos, Inc.; Wally McNamee, Woodfin Camp and Assoc.; Howard Sochurek, Woodfin Camp and Assoc.; 651 Curtis Publishing Company; 653 LC; 655 Fenno Jacobs/Black Star; 659, 661 Culver Pictures; 662, 664 UPI/Bettmann Newsphotos; 666 Courtesy LIFE Picture Service, Photo by Don Wright; 668, 669 UPI/Bettmann Newsphotos; 673 Wally McNamee, Woodfin Camp and Assoc.; 674 UPI/Bettmann Newsphotos; 675 *t and b* AP/WW; 676 Shostal Associates; 677 Owen Franken, Stock Boston; 678 Wally McNamee, Woodfin Camp and Assoc.; 679 Gamma—Liaison/Naython; 681 *l* Larry Downing, Woodfin Camp and Assoc.; *r* John Ficara, Woodfin Camp and Assoc.; 683 © John Ficara 1988, Woodfin Camp and Assoc.; 684 NA; 685 Bob Adelman, Magnum Photos, Inc.; 686 AP/WW; 688 Gabe Palmer/The Stock Market; 689 Michal Heron; 690 Christopher Brown, Stock Boston; 689 Kim Newton/Woodfin Camp & Assoc.; 692 *t and b* Michal Heron; 693 James Wilson/Woodfin Camp & Assoc.; 697 John Dominis, *LIFE Magazine;* 698 AP/WW; 699 *l* AP/WW; *r* LC; 701 Ira Kirschenbaum, Stock Boston; 703 J.L. Atlan/Sygma; 705 *t* Pentagon, *b* AP/WW; 707 Patricia Fisher, Folio Inc.; 710 Wally McNamee, Woodfin Camp and Assoc.; 711 AP/WW; 712 Bill Foley, Woodfin Camp and Assoc.; 713 UN Photo, Milton Grant; 714 ACTION Photograph by Carolyn Redenius; 717 *l and r* Bob Nicklesberg, Woodfin Camp and Assoc.; 721, 722 *l and r* NASA; 724 Michal Heron; 725 Don Carstens, Folio Inc.; 726 Patricia Hollander Gross, Stock Boston; 727 Marvin Ickow, Folio Inc.; 728 Jeff Albertson, Stock Boston; 729 *t* Dennis Capolong/Black Star; *b* Courtesy of AL-COA; 730 Wang Laboratories; 731 *l* Herb Snitzer, Stock Boston; *r Kansas Star-Times,* Woodfin Camp and Assoc.; 734 Elizabeth Crews, Stock Boston; 736 Michal Heron/Woodfin Camp & Assoc.; 737 D. Goldberg/Sygma; 738 A. Tannenbaum/Sygma; 741 AP/WW.

REFERENCE SECTION Page 746 *t* Minneapolis Institute of Arts, Julia B. Bigelow, Fund by John Bigelow; *b* MMA, Gift of Christian A. Zabriskie; 747 *l* Granger Collection; *r* National Portrait Gallery, SI; 748 *t* Laurie Platt Winfrey, Inc.; *b* Laurie Platt Winfrey, Inc.; 749 *tl* Thomas Gilcrease Institute, Tulsa, OK; *bl* American Museum of Natural History; *r* The Granger Collection; 750 *t* BBC Hulton/Bettmann Archive; *b* Prints Collection/NYPL, Miriam & Ira D. Wallach Division of Art, Prints & I. Noual MEZL+Photographs, Astor, Lenox & Tilden Foundations; 751 *t* Museum of Fine Arts, Boston, M. & M. Karolik Collection; *bl* NYHS; *br* Rare Book Div./NYPL, Astor, Lenox & Tilden Foundations; 752 *t* Museum of Fine Arts, Gift by Subscription & Francis Bartlett Fund; *b* Dept. of Ethnology, Royal Ontario Museum, Toronto, Canada; 753 *l* Minneapolis Institute of Arts, Julia B. Bigelow, Fund by John Bigelow; *tr* Daniel J. Terra Collection, Terra Museum of American Art; *br* Oakland Museum, Gift of Kahn Foundation; 754 *t* Nelson-Atkins Museum of Art (Nelson Fund); *b* Oakland Museum, Gift of Mrs. Leon Bocqueraz; 755 *t* Gift of William Wilson Corcoran, Corcoran Gallery of Art; *bl* Laurie Platt Winfrey, Inc.; *br* Laurie Platt Winfrey, Inc.; 756 *t and b* The Granger Collection; 757 *t* Peabody Museum of Salem; *bl* Honolulu Academy of Arts; *br* The Granger Collection; 774 *l* Independence National Historical Park; *r* Thomas Gilcrease Institute of American History and Art, Tulsa, OK; 775 *l* The Granger Collection; *r* MMA, Gift of Christian A. Zabriskie; 776 *l* Wally McNamee, Woodfin Camp and Assoc.; *r* NASA; 777 *l* Curtis Publishing Company, *r* John and Kimiko Powers; 780–784 portrait nos. 1,2,4,5–7,9,10,12–18,20,21,25–27 National Portrait Gallery, SI; portrait nos. 3,8,11,19,22–24,28–40, White House Historical Association, Photos by National Geographic Society; portrait no. 41, © Larry Downing, Woodfin Camp and Assoc.